John Erickson was educated at St John's College,
Cambridge, and served in British Army Intelligence
from 1946 to 1949. He has been Fellow in Soviet
military affairs of St Anthony's College, Oxford, and
Lecturer at the University of St Andrew's and the
University of Manchester. He has been Visiting
Professor at Indiana University, Yale University,
Texas A & M University, and the US Army Russian
Institute. He was latterly Professor and Director
of the Centre for Defence Studies at the University
of Edinburgh.

John Erickson was the author of numerous books and
articles about the Soviet Army. He contributed
biographies of Soviet commanders to *The Warlords*
(edited by Field Marshal Lord Carver) and *Stalin's
Generals* (edited by Harold Shukman). *The Road to
Stalingrad*, the first volume in his authoritative
history of the Soviet-German war, is also available as
a Cassell Military Paperback.

THE ROAD TO BERLIN

STALIN'S WAR WITH GERMANY
VOLUME TWO

JOHN ERICKSON

CASSELL

Cassell Military Paperbacks

Cassell
Wellington House, 125 Strand
London WC2R 0BB

Copyright © John Erickson 1983

First published by Weidenfeld & Nicolson 1983
This Cassell Military Paperbacks edition 2003
Reprinted 2003, 2004

British Library Cataloguing-in-Publication Data
A catalogue record for this book is available from the
British Library

ISBN 0-304-36540-8

Printed and bound in Great Britain by
Cox & Wyman Ltd., Reading, Berks.

Contents

Maps

Note on abbreviations

The following abbreviations have been used in the maps. For the Soviet side: A = Army, ShA = Shock Army, TA = Tank Army, GA = Guards Army, GTA = Guards Tank Army, AA = Air Army, PolA = Polish Army, RA = Rumanian Army, CavMechGp = Cavalry Mechanized Group, MechC = Mechanized Corps.

On the German side, roman numerals in bold type have been used for the Armies. Thus, for example, **IX A** = Ninth Army, **II PzA** = Second *Panzer* Army, etc.

To my late father Harry who gave his utmost and my father-in-law Branko who gave his life, fighting for the cause of all good men:

Smrt fašizmu, sloboda narodu.

Preface

Not very long ago a Soviet colleague, remarking on *The Road to Stalingrad* which preceded this present study, wagged an admonitory finger in my direction, deploring and disparaging any talk of 'Stalin's war with Germany'. The 'Great Patriotic War', which lasted from 22 June 1941 to 9 May 1945 and spanned 1,418 days, could not and should not, he said, be so personalized. On the contrary, it was the saga of the Soviet people and a fiery vindication of the resilience of the Soviet state, a record of sacrifice and achievement (coupled with the exertions of the Communist Party) whereby the burden of this, the most gruelling of all wars, was carried through to a triumphant end. The record speaks for itself. In the course of 1,320 days of active military operations (93 per cent of the entire wartime period) the Red Army destroyed or disabled 506.5 German divisions in the east, while Germany's sullen satellites lost a further 100 divisions as the price of participating in the war against the Soviet Union. Out of the grand total of Germany's losses of 13,600,000 killed, wounded, missing and made prisoner, Soviet military statisticians reckon that no less than 10,000,000 men met a grim fate on the Eastern Front.

The horrendous carnage was also accompanied by a mighty clash of war machines, the Red Army claiming the battlefield destruction of 48,000 enemy tanks, 167,000 guns and almost 77,000 aircraft, while Soviet war industry, having carried through the greatest enforced industrial migration in history, furnished the battlefronts with no less than 78,000 tanks and 16,000 self-propelled guns, 108,028 combat aircraft, 12 million rifles and carbines, 6 million sub-machineguns, almost 98,000 field guns and 110,000 lorries. By these demonstrations, whatever the scale of measurement, the decisive role in defeating the 'Fascist bloc' was played by the Soviet Union. Superiority over the enemy was finally attained but this was no mere matter of numbers, for true superiority lay in Soviet economic performance, in the Soviet political system and in the ideology of socialist society, with the Communist Party playing its vital role as 'leader, organizer and inspirer'. So runs the Soviet argument.

None can gainsay the gigantic effort by Soviet society nor gloss over the grievous hurts inflicted upon it, that numbing catalogue of bestiality, devastation, hardship and illimitable private griefs. Yet in these seemingly bloodless recapitulations of what was the bloodiest of conflicts, the name of Stalin is used sparingly, if at all. Ironically, the suppression of one form of personalization, 'Stalin's war', was largely engineered and exploited to pander to other vanities and to bolster other pretensions, producing 'Khrushchev's war' followed in turn by 'Brezhnev's war', hence the thriving trade in manufactured memoirs and dubious adjustments to historical narratives. With the demise of Leonid Brezhnev, we might expect yet more versions, though 'Andropov's war' would appear to be somewhat improbable.

The doctoring of history notwithstanding, the significance of Stalin as a war leader cannot be so easily erased from any appraisal of the Great Patriotic War or even the Second World War as a whole. His is perforce the ghost at any feast of retrospective reputations, whether it is the Party preening itself as the focus of national unity—when Stalin himself acknowledged almost at the outset that the Russian people were not fighting 'for us', only for Mother Russia—or the military first salvaging, then embellishing, its honour or indeed any individual usurpation of status. That any evaluation of Stalin as war leader must inevitably involve either panegyric or apologia has been brilliantly belied by Averell Harriman in a recent publication, *Stalinism*, edited by G.R. Urban; here is historical reality, which shuns melodrama and makes no recourse to pseudo-psychological explanation.

I do not see that formal recognition of Stalin's role as war leader must necessarily diminish any collective achievement or repudiate any individual sacrifice. On the contrary, the very singularity of Stalin's style in operating the system (one largely fashioned at his own behest) tends rather to magnify many aspects of Soviet performance at the front and in the rear alike. Not least, the overall 'command and control' of the entire war machine as well as the particular resolution of strategic issues was frequently degraded or distorted as a result of those chillingly brusque, characteristically brute interventions by Stalin, generated by what Professor Leonard Schapiro has called an 'inordinate suspiciousness', be it of persons, plans or proposals. Yet action was forthcoming, even to the point of near impossible achievement in the field or in the workshops, when Stalin sent out signals of such terrifying import: 'I demand more. This is my last warning.' 'More' usually materialized.

It is this problem, the properties of the man and the performance of the system—both operating under maximum stress—which I have tried to approach in this volume. Obviously the operational narrative must take precedence, though I trust that such priority has not totally obscured other features of the wartime scene, what might be called the social dimension (presently attracting more of the attention of Soviet historians—one could conjecture that this has some relevance to 'post-attack recovery', to use the language of modern strategic studies). Here paradoxes certainly abound, one of the most taxing being the relationship between centralized (indeed super-centralized) control and the role of improvisation, again both in the field and in the war industry. In many respects the operational command system was improvised, through a process of desperate trial and serious error, a lesson not lost on present-day Soviet military planners preoccupied with the problem of combining centralized strategic direction with decentralized battle management. Nor can the factor of 'style', the distinctiveness for good or ill of the Soviet style of war, be excluded from these quite urgent explorations and discussions, which also in their own way turn on the relationship between the man (or the men) and the system.

Such a concatenation of the past with the present, together with the multiplicity of versions tailored to the times, virtually impelled me to compile two books, one a military–political narrative, the other (subsumed under References and Sources) more in the nature of a commentary on materials. Under that latter rubric, comprising compilation with commentary, I have attempted to span both past and present, using the categories of *non-Soviet works, captured German military documents* (supplemented by printed war diaries), *Soviet publications,* and finally, *East European* contributions where relevant. In particular, with respect to Soviet sources, I was anxious not merely to identify a specific page reference but also to delineate the context of, say, an entire chapter, the structure of an article or the wider discussion of a theme or topic. In yet another vein, though one no less important to me, I had it in mind to convey for readers not wholly familiar with Soviet publications either for reasons of language or accessibility the several flavours, not a few of which are tinged with wormwood, diffused throughout these pages. Nevertheless, the intimidating mass of Soviet publication, with more than 15,000 volumes devoted to the Great Patriotic War, rules out any claim to comprehensive coverage. What I have assembled by way of formal bibliography can only be avowedly and admittedly selective.

At the risk of being overly cumbersome in explanation I should mention those problems associated with 'weights and measures', registration of time (or timings) and treatment of proper names. There seemed to be no easy escape from an ungainly and inconvenient admixture of miles with kilometres, or yards with metres, and so on; this was no laxity or oversight on my part, for it stems in the first instance from extreme reluctance to interfere with the substance of documentation. While the translations are mine, I have kept the original metric measurement if that was used and *vice versa*. In any event, to go for one or the other would have meant altering the records of inter-Allied exchanges, where each side tended to use its own measurement terms, hence my leaving them as they were uttered (or recorded). As for the registration of time and timing, where Soviet military documents, reports and narratives state timings in terms of the 24-hour clock (as in 0630 hours and the like), this I have also retained, otherwise reverting to the conventional and conversational mode. Proper names present difficulties all their own, causing me to infringe my own pedantic rule over documents, to the further vexation of the purist. For example, my own rule in translating Soviet documents would render Šubašić or Beneš as 'Shubashich' and 'Benesh', or Winston Churchill as 'Uinston Cherchill'' (complete with soft sign); indeed, the convention of diacritic points is not always observed and I therefore proposed the compromise of confining the full notation of proper names to the index. Like all compromises, an imperfect solution.

As the time taken first to write and then perforce to rewrite substantial portions of this book expanded, so did the catalogue of my indebtedness both to individuals and to institutions grow proportionately. It is all too plain to see what guidance and insight I have gained from previous publications on the war in the east, primarily the splendid writings of Professor Earl F. Ziemke, in particular his *Stalingrad to Berlin: The German Defeat in the East,* Colonel Albert Seaton's comprehensive analysis in *The Russo-German War 1941–1945* and his study of Stalin as a war leader, the work on Soviet partisans in World War II edited by Professor John A. Armstrong (published by the University of Wisconsin Press), together with the revised edition of Professor A. Dallin's monumental and quite invaluable monograph, *German Rule in Russia.* It was from Professor Dallin that I first learned how to work my way into and through the captured German records, a tutorial experience supplemented by lessons in the kind of rigour necessary in dealing with German materials exemplified in David Irving's *Hitler's War.* Nor can I omit mention of the benevolent and beneficial instruction in the modes of wartime diplomacy I derived from Sir Llewellyn Woodward's peerless five-volume history of British foreign policy, published by H.M. Stationery Office. In approaching that most distressing and anguished issue, the Polish question, I owe much to Professor Edward J. Rozek and his study, *Allied Wartime Diplomacy: A Pattern in Poland,* as well as to his personal elaboration of key documents.

I count myself singularly fortunate in having been able to work with the late Alexander Werth and the late Cornelius Ryan, thus bringing me into contact not only with fine writers but also their voluminous holdings. Helping to edit Alexander Werth's own book *Russia at War* was a unique experience and taught me much of wartime Russia as seen by a highly gifted observer, an advantage further supplemented by the unselfish generosity of the lady who made a complete collection of *Soviet War News* available to me. For the further illumination of the printed page and the formality of documents I can only record the extensive and unstinted assistance of senior Soviet commanders, Soviet military historians and Soviet soldiers, none of whom were sparing with their time or patience in appraising those wide variations in memoir literature or evaluating documentary evidence. Here none, I think, can quarrel with a tribute to the major contributions of Academician A.M. Samsonov, of the Soviet Academy of Sciences, author and editor of works which no historian, Soviet or non-Soviet, can afford to neglect.

Help has also flowed in liberally from many other quarters. For example, David Fisher and Anthony Read freely discussed the nature of their quest for 'Lucy' and the implications of their findings. Michael Parrish, Indiana University, author of a massive bibliographical work on the Soviet Union at war, kept me through our mutual exchanges abreast of important publications, while the business of my obtaining these same sources owes so much to Mme Kira A. Caiafa, for whose advice and expertise I am deeply grateful. Obtaining books is but one aspect of producing a book and here I have been in the extremely capable hands of Susan Loden, Dr Robert Baldock and Benjamin Buchan of Weidenfeld and Nicolson (Publishers), deftly combining the mechanisms of publishing with the balm of psychology. The most gruelling task, however, fell to Miss K.U. Brown of Defence Studies in the University of Edinburgh, who took charge of the manuscript at every stage in highly skilful fashion, so that her secretarial expertise and managerial competence have been an indispensable element in completing this work.

These past few years have been largely taken up with traversing these two roads, the one to Stalingrad, the other to Berlin. It has been both an academic and a personal trek, shared by my wife Ljubica who first pointed me in this direction and who has endured so many of the pains and penalties involved in journeys of this kind. But, in the last resort, all and any responsibility for mistaking the route, for misreading the signs and even for inadvertently misconstruing or misunderstanding the actions and motives of all those—high or low—who mapped or traversed these gruesome highways, must remain mine.

John Erickson
University of Edinburgh
1982

1

'Surrender is Ruled Out': The End at Stalingrad

In a matter of only days, from 19 to 23 November 1942, the impossible, the unthinkable and the unimaginable happened on the Eastern Front. The formidable German Sixth Army commanded by General Friedrich von Paulus was caught in a giant Soviet encirclement west of Stalingrad.

Two powerful Soviet armoured thrusts, striking from Kletskaya to the north of the city and from the 'Beketovka bell' to the south, hurled aside the flimsy Rumanian divisions covering the German flanks and raced to link up near Sovetskii, a dozen or so miles south-east of Kalach, on 22 November. The shock of the Soviet counter-offensive seemed to numb the *Führer*, who evinced great nervousness and whose headquarters gave no firm lead or instruction; at best there was only confusion or contradiction, with Col.-Gen. von Weichs, commander-in-chief of Army Group B, first receiving permission to act independently and then having it rescinded almost at once. For von Paulus, the extent of the disaster became all too plain at midday on 21 November, when Soviet tanks burst through not many miles from Sixth Army's own HQ at Golubinskaya and the headquarters had to be hurriedly transferred to the railway station at Gumrak, west of Stalingrad.

As events took a nightmarish turn on 21 November, von Paulus at his temporary command post at the mouth of the river Chir contacted Army Group B and proposed pulling the seriously endangered Sixth Army back to the block of territory between the rivers Don and Chir, a move to which von Weichs apparently assented. However, the *Führer's* own radio message in the evening ordered Stalingrad and the Volga front to be held at all costs, requiring von Paulus and his staff to return to the Stalingrad area and Sixth Army to set up a circular defence. 'Further instructions' would follow. But time was running out for von Paulus, and on 22 November the shape of the *Kessel*—the trap—became clearer. Soviet tank columns had already covered almost 150 miles from their initial positions at Kletskaya and Beketovka; no less than seven Soviet rifle armies with up to sixty divisions piling up behind them were closing on Sixth Army, whose land communications were practically severed, hemming in the German divisions west and south of Stalingrad.

The *Kessel*, the Stalingrad 'cauldron', stretched for about thirty-five miles from the east at Stalingrad to the west and some twenty miles from north to south, the encirclement line assuming the sinister and gruesomely symbolic shape of a flattened skull with its 'nose' protruding to the south-west. Five German corps headquarters (4th, 8th, 11th, 51st, and XIV *Panzer* Corps) stood on the bare steppe, isolated like their component twenty German divisions (and elements of two Rumanian divisions) from the main body of the German army and sliced away from their nearest neighbour, General Hoth's Fourth *Panzer* Army whose units had also been sundered by the Soviet southern thrust. As von Paulus hurried to his Gumrak HQ, battle-fatigued German divisions dug in where they could along the perimeter line. Inside the shattered and fire-blackened ruination of Stalingrad six German battle groups defied blinding weariness to hold cellars, rooms, sections of skeletal factories won after weeks of the gruelling hand-to-hand fighting which raged by day and night. In round figures, some 240,000 men—though not the 400,000 first feared by the German High Command—with over 100 tanks, 1,800 guns and 10,000 assorted vehicles, were presently trapped, battered but maintaining good order, with the hard-bitten among them mocking their predicament of being 'the mice in the mousetrap' and impatient for release or relief, defiantly recalling that this was by no means the first *Kessel* to appear in the east.

At two o'clock on the afternoon of 22 November, von Paulus and his Chief of Staff, Maj.-Gen. Schmidt, flew into the 'pocket' and to their new HQ at Gumrak, alongside 51st Corps HQ. Encirclement appeared to be imminent, and in the evening von Paulus confirmed it. Though Sixth Army had to be saved from being chopped to pieces and the greater danger of being taken in the rear, von Paulus and his five corps commanders agreed on the need for an early break-out, with 51st Corps commander, General von Seydlitz-Kurzbach taking the lead in pressing this course, a break-out to the south-west. At 1800 hours (22 November), von Paulus summed up his position in a radio message to Army Group B: encirclement was now an accomplished fact, with Sixth Army attempting to build defensive lines; but fuel was fast running out, ammunition seriously depleted and rations sufficient only for six more days; the Sixth Army would strive to hold the area between the Volga and the Don though this must be contingent on plugging the gap ripped through the Rumanians to the south and on Sixth Army receiving supplies by air. Failing this, Sixth Army must perforce abandon Stalingrad itself and the northern sector, attack in full strength on the southern front in order to link up once more with Fourth *Panzer* Army. To attack westwards could only invite disaster.

Von Paulus waited, brooded and pondered. Von Seydlitz-Kurzbach acted, determined to force the issue while time still remained. On his personal orders, elements of 51st Corps in the course of 23 November blew up or burned everything not needed for a break-out operation and began to pull back for about five miles on the Yersovka sector towards the northern edge of Stalingrad.

Accompanied by spectacular, flaring explosions German units abandoned their deep-dug winter bunkers only to be caught on open ground where Chuikov's 62nd Army, manning their own positions in Stalingrad, decimated the German 94th Infantry Division with a mass attack. The few survivors of the 94th finally wound up with the 16th and 24th *Panzer* divisions, but the sacrifice of an entire division failed to start that south-westerly push which von Seydlitz believed to be the sole salvation of Sixth Army.

The gravity of the situation, together with further pleas from von Paulus for freedom of action, had by now fully impressed itself on von Weichs at Army Group B. In a lengthy signal sent on the evening of 23 November to the German high command, von Weichs fully supported plans for a break-out by Sixth Army, which could not be supplied effectively by air—only one-tenth of the essential items could be delivered in view of weather conditions and the lack of transport aircraft—while any attempt to break in to Sixth Army from outside the encircling ring must entail considerable delay, by which time Sixth Army would have run out of food and ammunition. Whatever the cost in weapons and equipment, Sixth Army must forthwith attempt to break out to the south-west: the alternative was for the army to starve to death. With the express permission of von Weichs, Paulus transmitted his own signal to the *Führer,* stressing that the gaps to the west and south-west could not be closed, that fuel and ammunition were running desperately low, and guns had fired off their remaining shells—Sixth Army faced being wiped out in a short time unless it fought its way out to the south-west, a move fully supported by all the corps commanders in Sixth Army.

Hitler arrived in his East Prussian *'Wolfsschanze'* HQ on 23 November, having left Obersalzberg the previous evening. For all the frantic chatter of the teleprinters and the buzz of radio signals, no decision had as yet been taken to determine the fortunes of Sixth Army, even as heavier fighting developed on the northern and southern sectors of the 'pocket'. During the course of the evening conference at the *Wolfsschanze* it seemed at this stage that General Zeitzler, Army Chief of Staff, had persuaded the *Führer* of the logic and the overweening necessity of authorizing Sixth Army's break-out; Zeitzler even alerted Army Group B that the relevant orders would soon be forthcoming. However, a hint of Hitler's obduracy and his deepest instinct to hold Stalingrad at all costs and to pinion Sixth Army came with his reaction to news of von Seydlitz's unauthorized withdrawal: ironically and fantastically, von Paulus became suspect as less than steadfast, whereupon Hitler detached 51st Corps from Sixth Army and put von Seydlitz in command of the north-east sector, personally responsible to the *Führer.* This hardly settled the fate of Sixth Army but the decisions of the morning of 24 November and the intervention of *Reichsmarschall* Göring, guaranteeing the supply of the encircled army—by air—tipped the scales decisively. *Festung Stalingrad* would hold and stand fast.

Göring's undertaking, which directly contradicted the advice of his own air commanders, was given 'frivolously', in the words of von Manstein, who was now summoned by Hitler to take command of the newly created Army Group Don comprising Sixth Army, Fourth *Panzer* Army and two Rumanian armies. The new army group would halt the Soviet advance westwards and mount a counter-blow, which would also accomplish the relief of Stalingrad. To sustain itself Sixth Army radioed that it required a daily delivery of 750 metric tons (380 tons of food, 250 tons of ammunition and 120 of fuel); the Luftwaffe transport command considered 350 tons to be a feasible daily target, though one dependent on the availability of aircraft, adequate ground organization outside the *Kessel* and four landing fields inside it. In spite of the fact that Luftflotte IV could muster only 298 aircraft—little more than half needed for the full lift— Göring nevertheless promised a daily delivery of 500 tons, apparently reckoning on the possibility of whisking transport planes from other theatres. Of the Russian winter and the vigorous presence of the Soviet air force, he took no account.

Keyed up to expect orders to break out, the men of the Sixth Army received the *Führer*'s order of 24 November to stand fast within their 'temporary encirclement' with a mixture of resignation, complacency and stoicism. Hitler's order to von Paulus not only stipulated that Sixth Army should remain on the Volga but also pinpointed the precise geographical area which the encircled divisions should hold; supplies would be delivered and in due course the relief of the entire army. With the break-out plans scrapped, divisions regrouped and redeployed within the *Kessel* with all possible speed, with 24th and 16th *Panzer* Divisions holding the northern front closest to the Volga; the 113th Infantry Division and 60th Motorized to their left; three divisions (76th, 384th and 44th) clinging to the north-western sector; the 3rd Motorized Division stationed in the south-western 'nose'; and the southern sector manned by rhe 29th Motorized Division, 297th and 371st Divisions (plus the remnants of the 20th Rumanian Division). Two divisions, 14th *Panzer* and 9th Anti-Aircraft (Flak) Divisions, formed a mobile reserve; the German 71st, 295th, 100th, 79th, 305th and 389th Divisions held the eastern sector and positions in Stalingrad itself. The nearest German units were by now twenty-five miles away.

On 25 November, *Luftwaffe* transport aircraft took off for Pitomnik, fighting the deteriorating weather and steadily increasing forces of Soviet fighters. The loads delivered at once fell far short of the barest needs of Sixth Army. Inside the ring German troops attacked the frozen ground, grimly attentive to the task of hacking out weapon pits and blasting trenches, in many cases entrenchments to replace stout bunkers not occupied by Russians. Far away in distant East Prussia, the *Führer* remained unaffected, being on 25 November 'confident about the position of Sixth Army'—'Der Führer ist hinsichtlich der Lage der 6. *Armee* zuversichtlich'. Thus were the first nails of procrastination and self-delusion driven into what was soon to become the coffin of the German Sixth Army.

*   *   *

If Hitler's confidence was dangerously premature and grievously misplaced, Stalin could sensibly anticipate growing and grandiose gains. Operation *Uranus*, the encirclement of enemy forces on 'the Stalingrad axis', was only one phase in the constellation of Soviet operations aimed at the entire southern wing of the German armies in the east. *Uranus* was to be followed in rapid succession by *Saturn*, a mammoth outer sweep aimed directly at Rostov-on-Don and designed to seal off the German Army Group A fighting in the Caucasus. With the German southern wing smashed in, the prospects were dazzling indeed and loaded with intimations of decisive strategic success. The road to the Dnieper would be opened, and with it access once more to the coalmines and power stations of the Donbas and the eastern Ukraine.

The Soviet war industry urgently needed more coal and increased supplies of power. Although a new industrial base had been expanded in Siberia and the Urals, these plants were also suffering from serious shortages of fuel, power and metals: total fuel resources presently available were only half of what they had been in 1941, a sombre point emphasized by Voznesenskii in his report to the Central Committee in November 1942. In particular, the vital Chelyabinsk tank factories were critically short of fuel, power and raw materials. With the liberation of the north Caucasus, at least a portion of the grain lands would be won back and oil resources also supplemented. Nor was Stalin's attention directed exclusively to the southern theatre. In Leningrad, suffering its own agonies in the fearful siege, Govorov had submitted plans for two offensive operations at Schlusselburg and Uritsk, designed to 'raise the blockade of Leningrad in order to secure rail traffic along the Ladoga canal and thus establish normal traffic between Leningrad and the rest of the country'. These plans went to the *Stavka* between 17 and 22 November; not much later, on 2 December, the Leningrad and Volkhov Front commands received orders to breach the German blockade with the 'Schlusselburg operation', timed for 1 January 1943 and codenamed *Iskra* ('Spark').

As soon as *Uranus* reached its final stage, Vasilevskii raced north on Stalin's express instruction to complete the operational planning for *Saturn* with the Voronezh and South-Western Front commands. Before leaving Serafimovich, Vasilevskii had held a series of preliminary conversations with Vatutin on the role of the South-Western Front in the forthcoming offensive. On 25 November with the hazards of the journey behind them, the *Stavka* officers left Golikov's HQ on the Voronezh Front and went by truck to the area of 6th Army which was under the command of Kharitonov. Like Volskii, Kharitonov was another of Vasilevskii's *protégés*; as 9th Army commander in May 1942, Kharitonov had been closely involved in the bloody disaster of the Kharkov offensive, after which Stalin had relieved him of his command and wanted him tried by court-martial, or rather the special tribunals which formally degraded the luckless and the scapegoats. On Vasilevskii's intervention Stalin waived the retribution and gave Kharitonov another chance, this time with 6th Army.

After examining the terrain and investigating enemy dispositions facing Lt.-Gen. Kharitonov's 6th Army, the *Stavka* officers left for a further conference on 26 November with Vatutin. The next day they conducted a final survey of the operational area. That night Vasilevskii submitted his proposals to Stalin for launching *Saturn:*

To facilitate the administration of the forces of the South-Western Front for the forthcoming operation, it is suggested that as expeditiously as possible the troops of 1st Guards Army, which at the moment are included in Lieutenant-General V.I. Kuznetsov's operational group, be reorganized into the 1st Guards Army, Kuznetsov be appointed commander and an administration be set up for him. The remaining formations of 1st Guards Army, operating on the line river Don, Drivaya and Chir as far as Chernyshevskaya, be split off into an independent [army]—3rd Guards under Lieutenant-General D.D. Lelyushenko (who is at present in command of these troops). The front from Chernyshevskaya to the mouth of the river Chir, that is, as far as the junction with the Stalingrad Front, be assigned primarily to the troops of 5th Tank Army.

Most immediate aim of the operation to be the destruction of the 8th Italian Army and Operational Group 'Hollidt', for which South-Western Front to establish two assault groupings: one on the right flank with 1st Guards Army (six rifle divisions, one tank corps, and reinforcements) to attack from bridgehead south of Verkhnyi Mamon in a southerly direction towards Millerovo; second [grouping]—on 3rd Guards Army front to the east of Bokovskaya (five rifle divisions and one mechanized corps) to attack simultaneously from east to west also on Millerovo to tighten encirclement ring. Further, after destruction of 8th Italian Army, after the exit of mobile forces at the Northern Donets and seizure of crossings in the area of Likhaya, to establish favourable positions for a renewal of the offensive against Rostov.

To secure the operation from the north-west and west a shock group of 6th Army Voronezh Front (five rifle divisions and two tank corps) must attack from south-west of Verkhnyi Mamon in direction of Kantemirovka–Voloshino.

Readiness of troops for operations—10 December. By that time it is necessary to complete movement of reinforcements assigned by the *Stavka* to South-Western Front, five rifle divisions, three tank corps, one mechanized corps, six independent tank regiments, 16 artillery and mortar regiments: and for 6th Army Voronezh Front—three rifle divisions, one tank corps, seven artillery and mortar regiments.

5th Tank Army must be committed in the immediate future to the destruction of enemy forces in the area of Chernyshevskaya–Tormosin–Morozovsk to obtain a more definite isolation in the south-west of enemy forces encircled in Stalingrad, with a view to developing its offensive further towards Tatsinskaya in order to exit on the line of the Northern Donets. [*VIZ*, 1966 (1), p. 19.]

Stalin raised no objection to these proposals. Vatutin and Golikov were now to get down to detailed operational planning, so that all plans could be submitted, scrutinized and approved by early December. The reinforcements would be forthcoming, and the General Staff would report separately on the movement of these units. To free Vatutin for *Saturn*, Chistyakov's 21st Army with 26th and

4th Tank Corps, would be handed over to the Don Front for operations along the inner encirclement. Even more important, Vasilevskii would be free to devote his full attention to reducing 'the ring'—on this, Stalin was emphatic:

> Enemy forces encircled at Stalingrad must be liquidated. . . . That is an extremely important matter. . . . Mikhailov [Vasilevskii] must concentrate on that task alone. As for the preparations for operation *Saturn*, let Vatutin and Kuznetsov get busy with that. Moscow will help them. [*IVOVSS*, 3, p. 43.]

At this point Stalin nursed the highest hopes of decisive strategic success against the whole southern wing of the German armies, but everything depended on a rapid reduction of the encircled Sixth Army in order to free Soviet troops for the new offensive operations. Time and time again Stalin urged rapid 'liquidation' on the *Stavka* officers and Front commanders, and early in December he became utterly demanding in this matter. He had meanwhile built up a special and extremely powerful reserve which he apparently intended to loose against Rostov when the situation turned in his favour—the 2nd Guards Army, formed from the 1st Reserve Army in the Tambov-Morshansk area under the *Stavka* order of 23 October. This new formation was one of the most formidable in the Red Army, and now received orders to move to the Stalingrad area at top speed; Malinovskii, formerly a deputy commander of the Voronezh Front, took over the army command from Kreizer (who remained as deputy commander). Biryuzov had been summoned at two hours' notice from 48th Army to take over as chief of staff. But very shortly 2nd Guards was at the centre of a major Soviet dilemma, whom to strike down first—Paulus in his huge, bristling 'hedgehog', or Manstein who was leading the de-blockading force?

On 21 November Manstein had been ordered south from Vitebsk to take over 'Army Group Don', which would include Fourth *Panzer* Army, Sixth Army and 3rd and 4th Rumanian Armies; Army Group B comprised 8th Italian, 2nd Hungarian and Second German Armies. When at the end of the month Army Group Don, standing now between Army Group B and A, took over the Don-Volga area, the situation looked bleak, though at the time of Manstein's assumption of his new command a moment of relative calm had settled. The situation between the Don and the Chir had been momentarily stabilized and the line presently held by *Armeeabteilung Hollidt*, formed from units scratched up on the Chir. Out of the wave of men swept down by the first Soviet attacks, Colonel of *Panzertruppen* Wenck had formed 'screens' made up of motley units assembled from the roadsides and headquarters. Manstein used the Wenck-Hollidt group to bar the way on the Don-Chir front against any Soviet attack against Rostov. He also proposed to use General Hollidt's *Armeeabteilung* in an attack on Kalach to burst into the Stalingrad 'ring'; while from the south *Armeegruppe Hoth* (with XLVII *Panzer* Corps) would attack from Kotelnikovo in the direction of the Stalingrad 'ring', to roll up the western or southern Soviet encirclement. In the event, Operation *Wintergewitter* ('Winter Tempest') was mounted by *Armeegruppe*

Hoth from the south with 232 tanks; *Armeeabteilung Hollidt* was also to have struck out for Stalingrad, but remained pinned down by ceaseless Soviet attacks. On 2 December, Manstein and Hoth considered the final plan for the break-in from the south, an attack west of the railway line running from Kotelni-kov–Shutovo–Abganerovo after taking the line of the river Aksai; after the elimination of Soviet forces between the Aksai and the Myshovka, they were to advance north-eastwards in order to make contact with Sixth Army south-west of Tundotov railway station. The attack was provisionally fixed for 8 December, but the *Panzer* divisions had still not reached their positions and at this time rain made the going difficult. Col.-Gen. Hoth nevertheless finally decided to attack on 12 December, irrespective of whether or not 17th *Panzer* Division had arrived to fill out XLVII *Panzer* Corps.

At the beginning of December, the German command had managed to establish a strong circular defence for the encircled Sixth Army and had momentarily halted Soviet troops on the outer encirclement; more than half the available Soviet strength was tied down on the inner encirclement holding Sixth Army. The liquidation of Sixth Army had been assigned primarily to the Don Front and to 62nd, 64th and 57th Armies of the Stalingrad Front; on 27 November, 21st Army and its supporting tank corps was assigned to the Don Front, and Col.-Gen. Vasilevskii ordered by Stalin to supervise the elimination of 'the pocket'. On 30 November Vasilevskii issued a revised version of his earlier orders for operations against Sixth Army's 'hedgehog'—the Don and Stalingrad Fronts were to attack from the south, west and north-east, once again with the object of splitting the pocket and joining up in Gumrak; the main attack would be delivered from west to east. The Don Front would attack with 21st, 6th and 24th Armies along the river Rossoshka-Borodin line on 2 December, to link up at Alekseyevka; the Stalingrad Front would secure the operation from the south, thus splitting the main enemy force in the Marinovka–Karpovka–Bolshaya Rossoshka–Gumrak area. Yeremenko selected Alekseyevka as the axis of his main attack to be launched by 62nd and 64th Armies. He duly attacked on 2 December and Rokossovskii attacked two days later, but five days of bloody fighting brought no sign of the pocket being cracked open and split. Stalin, along with the *Stavka* officers, only now realized the extent and resilience of the force trapped in the Stalingrad pocket, which would have to be broken up by sledgehammer blows—such as 2nd Guards could provide.

From Don Front HQ at Zavarykin, Col.-Gen. Vasilevskii had already reported to Stalin on 4 December that the inner encirclement needed drastic reinforcement before it could reduce Sixth Army in its positions. Stalin thereupon ordered Vasilevskii, Rokossovskii and Yeremenko to prepare a fresh offensive operation that must be ready not later than 18 December. To strengthen the assault, Malinovskii's 2nd Guards would be released to the Don Front, while the junction of the Stalingrad and South-Western Fronts would be strengthened by setting up a new army, 5th Shock, to be introduced between 5th Tank and 51st Armies.

Lt.-Gen. M.M. Popov, one of Yeremenko's deputy commanders, would take command of 5th Shock Army, established from 10th Reserve Army and made up from 7th Tank Corps (from *Stavka* reserve), 300th, 315th, 87th Rifle Divisions and 4th Mechanized Corps (from Yeremenko's front), 4th Guards, and 258th Rifle Division plus 3rd Guards Cavalry Corps (from Vatutin's front). Malinovskii's 2nd Guards was especially powerful: three corps (1st Guards, 13th Guards Rifle Corps, 2nd Guards Mechanized Corps), three divisions in the rifle corps, three mechanized brigades in the mobile corps, manned largely by experienced Guards troops. Malinovskii and his staff flew from the rear areas to the Don Front, while the men and equipment of 2nd Guards followed in 165 trains due to unload north-west of Stalingrad. The first units began arriving on 10 December and made for the concentration area of Vertyachii–Peskatovka, the tough Siberians and well-trained units of the Far Eastern command now all welded into the 2nd Guards. Both Yeremenko and Rokossovskii had been told in telephone messages from Vasilevskii during the night of 4–5 December of the arrival of fresh forces for the inner encirclement front, and both Front commanders had specific orders to work out new attack plans incorporating 2nd Guards. Malinovskii himself took part in the meeting of the Don Front Military Soviet which assembled on 8 December to decide on the employment of the new formation, and the next day Stalin had the revised plans submitted for his inspection.

This new plan envisaged a three-stage operation to split up and then to annihilate Sixth Army: the first stage would use Don Front troops—basically 2nd Guards—to destroy the four German infantry divisions west of the river Rossosh; the second stage would use Don Front troops in an operation aimed south-eastwards on Voroponovo, for which the 64th Army of the Stalingrad Front would also strike (isolating and destroying the southern sector of the pocket); the third stage would be a general assault by all the armies of the Don and the Stalingrad Fronts committed to the inner encirclement, aimed at Gumrak. These proposals were submitted on the morning of 9 December to the *Stavka*, after which Vasilevskii left for an inspection of 5th Tank and 51st Army lines at the outer encirclement, where a critical situation was building up as more and more reports filtered in of German concentrations obviously gathering for a breakthrough operation to relieve Sixth Army. As for the plan to reduce the pocket, Operation *Koltso* ('Ring'), Stalin insisted on only marginal alterations, mainly to telescope the first two stages, a modification stipulated in his signal of 11 December to Vasilevskii (*VIZ*, 1966 (1), p. 25):

Comrade Mikhailov   *Strictly Personal*

1. Operation Koltso will proceed in two stages.
2. First stage—break-in to area Basargino, Voroponovo and liquidation of western and southern groupings of the enemy.
3. Second stage—general assault by all armies of both fronts for liquidation of main body of enemy troops to west and north-west of Stalingrad.

4. Operations in the first stage to begin no later than that date fixed in telephone conversation between Vasiliev [Stalin] and Mikhailov [Vasilevskii].

5. Operations in the first stage to finish no later than 23 December.

11 December 1942, 0020 hours   VASILIEV [Stalin]

But events precipitated by Manstein's breakthrough attack overtook this plan, and both *Koltso* and *Saturn* underwent major revision once *Armeegruppe Hoth* went over to the attack at Kotelnikovo as the darkness gathered on 12 December.

Both German and Soviet commanders raced the clock. On the Soviet side, although the attack plans for Operation *Saturn* had been submitted by Golikov and Vatutin by the end of November and approved by the *Stavka* on 2 December, Col.-Gen. Voronov (who acted as *Stavka* 'co-ordinator' of these two fronts for the operation aimed at Rostov) was forced to seek a postponement of the attack due to open on 10 December. To allow time for final preparations and troop movements, *Saturn* would now unroll on 16 December. While this was the first significant departure from the 'timetable' set up in the Stalin-Vasilevskii conversation of 7 November, the second was the failure of Romanenko's 5th Tank Army to clear German forces from the lower Chir (the German salient which jutted towards Stalingrad and reduced the distance between the Soviet inner and outer encirclement to a mere twenty miles). The capture of Tormosin and Mozorovsk was intended as a prelude to *Saturn* to isolate Paulus fully from the south-east and to establish good jumping-off positions for an advance on Tatsinskaya, Likhaya—and then Rostov. Once in Likhaya, the Red Army would have a stranglehold on a vital rail communications centre for Army Group Don; at Rostov, the trap would close over the million men of Army Group A stranded in the Caucasus. Wiping out the German troops in the Chir salient would also affect the inner encirclement, since the 'isolation' of Paulus would then be fully secured, at least by the reckoning of the Soviet command.

Romanenko had opened his attack on 30 November along a front of some thirty miles on the Oblivskaya–Rychkovskii sector, with 50,000 men, 900 guns and mortars and 72 tanks. His objective was a line running from Mozorovsk to Loznoi (twenty-five miles south-east of Mozorovsk), to be reached by 5 December. To reinforce 5th Tank Army, four rifle divisions had already been stripped from the inner encirclement (from 21st and 65th Armies); along the attack sector Romanenko deployed six rifle divisions, two cavalry corps, one tank corps, a tank brigade and eight artillery regiments. On the morning of 2 December, 5th Tank Army attacked after a thirty-minute artillery barrage. This was the prelude to a full week of very heavy fighting that precipitated a severe crisis for Manstein, aware that the lower Chir had to be held at almost any cost and with it the one bridge over the Don at Verkhne-Chirskaya. There was nothing for it but to use XLVIII *Panzer* Corps to hold this front.

The Soviet response to stiffening resistance on the Chir front was to form the 5th Shock Army to bolster 5th Tank; Popov's shock army, its divisions drawn from the South-Western and Stalingrad Fronts (plus 7th Tank Corps under Maj.-Gen. Rotmistrov from the *Stavka* reserve), numbered 71,000 men, 252 tanks and 814 guns (in all, five rifle divisions, one tank, one mechanized and one cavalry corps). On the edge of Yeremenko's outer encirclement was 51st Army, 34,000 men with 77 tanks, three rifle divisions (302nd, 96th, 126th), 13th Tank Corps, 4th Cavalry Corps and 76th UR 'garrison troops'. (To the south lay 28th Army with 44,000 men, 40 tanks, and 707 guns and mortars.) What Vasilevskii sought to establish at once after his inspection of the junction between South-Western and Stalingrad Fronts was the whereabouts of the divisions earmarked for 5th Shock Army (87th, 300th and 315th Rifle Divisions), as well as those of 7th Tank Corps. The whole of the next day, 10 December, he spent with 51st, 5th Shock and left-flank units of 5th Tank Army, estimating Soviet effectiveness and gathering intelligence of German strength and movements. Army Group Don's strength was set at thirty divisions, seventeen of which faced the South-Western Front, 13th, 5th Shock and 51st Armies of Stalingrad Front; in front of 5th Shock were units of XLVIII *Panzer* Corps (and prisoner interrogation indicated that 17th *Panzer* Division was in reserve at Tormosin), while ten divisions (six of them Rumanian) were ahead of 51st Army.

While Col.-Gen. Vasilevskii probed the German build-up at Tormosin, Col.-Gen. Yeremenko suspected that there was a big German armoured claw at Kotelnikovo; he had advanced two cavalry divisions from 4th Corps towards Kotelnikovo at the end of November, and both were severely mauled early in December. But at least he had discovered that 6th *Panzer* Division was moving into the area, its armour unloading at Morozovsk. All these ominous signs were duly reported to Stalin, from whom Yeremenko requested armoured reinforcement. Stalin replied that, 'circumstances permitting', the reinforcement would be sent (a sign to Yeremenko that Stalin was hedging against a German attack from the Tormosin area). Vasilevskii, still on the outer encirclement line, held a special conference on 11 December at Rotmistrov's command centre (7th Tank Corps) with Popov of 5th Shock and Pliev, commander of 3rd Guards Cavalry Corps. The commanders decided on a fresh attack designed to split the 'Kotelnikovo' and 'Nozhne-Chirskaya' enemy groups, using 7th Tank with two rifle divisions in a surprise attack on the German bridgehead at Rychkovskii. Yeremenko, after consultation with his chief of staff Varennikov and his intelligence officers, decided to pull 4th and 13th Mechanized Corps into reserve, at the same time issuing orders to Tolbukhin at 58th Army to hold his positions on the inner encirclement, in the event of a breakout by Sixth Army to meet any relief force. Trufanov's 51st Army covered Kotelnikovo, though both Yeremenko and Vasilevskii knew it was a relatively weak and scattered formation.

On the morning of 12 December, after a short artillery bombardment, LVII *Panzer* Corps of *Armeegruppe Hoth* opened its attack from the Kotelnikovo area, aimed north-eastwards to cover the sixty miles and so to burst through the Soviet encirclement to link up with Sixth Army. General Rauss's 6th *Panzer* Division, transhipped from France, made a highly successful start: 23rd *Panzer* Division took a bridgehead on the southern bank of the Aksai. To stiffen the punch of this armoured fist was a battalion of the new Tiger-I 56-ton tanks equipped with an 88mm gun, a few of which had already been tested on the Eastern Front. Hitler entertained great hopes for his Tigers. Yeremenko feared at once for the rear of 57th Army which could quickly be exposed by Hoth's armoured thrust. Once it was confirmed that here was a major German attack, Yeremenko telephoned Stalin to outline the position and to underline the dangers. Stalin's response was terse enough—'Hold on, we will be sending you reinforcements'—but meanwhile Yeremenko had to do something fast with the forces he had on the spot and what he could move out of reserve. His first response was to put General Zakharov (his deputy commander) in charge of an improvised battle group out on the steppe, moving up 13th Tank Corps to 51st Army to block 23rd *Panzer* and 4th Mechanized Corps from 5th Shock Army to check 6th *Panzer* which was already astride the Aksai. During the night of 12–13 December, Volskii's 4th Mechanized, reduced now to 5,600 men with 70 tanks (32 T-34s and 38 T-70s), took up its main positions north of the Aksai at Verkhne–Kumskii. Vasilevskii had been on the Aksai during the first day of the German attack, hurrying there from 57th Army HQ at Verkhne-Tsartsynskii with Khrushchev of the Stalingrad Front Military Soviet; from the Aksai Vasilevskii raced back to Don Front HQ, having first informed Rokossovskii and Malinovskii of the situation produced by Hoth's attack. In particular, he advised Malinovskii to start organizing a move to the Stalingrad Front, using Tolbukhin's 57th Army HQ as a forward base from which to operate—but unable to contact Stalin, Vasilevskii had no authority to order 2nd Guards to move. All these were precautionary moves.

Finally, late on 12 December, Vasilevskii was in radio contact with Stalin. He requested permission to move 2nd Guards under Stalingrad Front command and suggested that Operation *Koltso* be postponed (which was inevitable if Malinovskii moved). Stalin was furious. Stalin laced into Vasilevskii, accusing him of 'extortion' in bringing reserves from the *Stavka,* above all to a sector for which Vasilevskii was personally responsible. (Since Stalin had on the night of 27 November specifically charged Vasilevskii with responsibility for the inner encirclement, his present accusations were extremely wild.) Over the proposal to swing 2nd Guards to block Manstein, Stalin refused any immediate reply. All the satisfaction Vasilevskii obtained was that the question would have to be thrashed out in a session of the State Defence Committee (*GKO*), of which Stalin himself was chairman.

That night, when Vasilevskii at Zavarykin sweated out the hours to Stalin's eventual reply and while the rain swept down out in the steppe on Soviet and German tankmen, each concentrating their efforts on the high ground to the north of the Aksai, Soviet plans for the next stage of the Stalingrad–Rostov operations passed through the storm stirred by Hoth's attack to relieve Sixth Army—thirty-six hours of reformulating strategic plans which vitally affected both *Koltso* and *Saturn*. At 5 am on the morning of 13 December Stalin passed Vasilevskii an authorization to move 2nd Guards from the Don to the Stalingrad Front, effective as from 15 December, when Vasilevskii himself would assume the direction of operations on 'the Kotelnikovo axis'. An operational plan was to be submitted to the *Stavka* without delay. The formal order on the postponement of *Koltso* duly went out to Yeremenko and Rokossovskii at 2250 hours on 14 December:

Dontsov [Rokossovskii] and Ivanov [Yeremenko] are ordered to continue the systematic harassment of the encircled enemy troops by air and ground attacks, denying the enemy any breathing space by night or by day, pulling the encirclement ring ever tighter and nipping off any attempt by the encircled troops to break out of the ring. . . . The main task of our southern forces is to defeat the enemy group at Kotelnikovo, using the troops of Trufanov [51st Army] and Yakovlev [Malinovskii and 2nd Guards], to capture Kotelnikovo in the immediate future and to dig in there. [*VIZ*, 1966 (3), pp. 28–9.]

Trufanov had already been ordered to hold Hoth's advance with his rifle divisions while the armour went for the flanks; 5th Shock Army was straightway to attack the German bridgehead at Nizhne-Chirskaya, and on the morning of 14 December Rotmistrov's 7th Tank Corps opened this assault. The next day German troops were finally forced out of this vital bridgehead and fell back, blowing up the bridge over the Don behind them.

During the night of 14 December, the Voronezh and South-Western Front commanders, Golikov and Vatutin (under the control of *Stavka* 'co-ordinator' Voronov), had received Stalin's new orders relating to *Saturn:* by shifting the direction of the attack south-eastwards rather than southwards, *Bol'shoi Saturn* ('Big Saturn') was transformed into *Malyi Saturn* ('Small Saturn'), aimed at the rear of Manstein's forces trying to fight their way into Stalingrad. The new directive (dated 13 December) laid out the basis of the revised decision (*VIZ*, 1966 (3), pp. 29–30):

[To: Comrades Voronov, Golikov and Vatutin.]

First: Operation 'Saturn' aimed at Kamensk–Rostov was conceived when the overall situation was in our favour, when the Germans had no more reserves in the Bokovsk–Morozovsk–Nizhne Chirskaya area, when the tank army [5th Tank] had made successful attacks in the direction of Morozovsk and when it appeared that an attack from the north would be supported at the same time by an offensive from the east aimed at Likhaya. Under these circumstances it was proposed that 2nd Guards Army should be swung into the area of Kalach and used to develop a successful advance in the direction of Rostov–Taganrog.

Second: Recently, however, the situation has not developed in our favour. Romanenko [5th Tank] and Lelyushenko [3rd Guards Army] are on the defensive and cannot advance, from the west a number of infantry divisions and tank formations, which are containing the Soviet forces. Consequently, an attack from the north would not meet with direct support from the east by Romanenko, as a consequence of which an offensive in the direction of Kamensk–Rostov would meet with no success. I have to say that 2nd Guards Army can no longer be used for Operation 'Saturn' since it is operating on another front.

Third: In view of all this, it is essential to revise Operation 'Saturn'. The revision lies in the fact that the main blow will be aimed not at the south, but towards the south-east in the direction of Nizhnyi Astakhov, to exit at Morozovsk in order to take the enemy grouping at Bokovsk–Morozovsk in a pincer movement, to break into his rear and to destroy these forces with a simultaneous blow from the east with the forces of Romanenko and Lelyushenko and from the north-west with the forces of Kuznetsov and mobile formations subordinated to his command. Filippov [Golikov: Voronezh Front] has as his assignment to help Kuznetsov to liquidate the Italians [8th Army], get to the river Boguchat in the area of Kramenkov to set up a major covering force against possible enemy attacks from the west.

Fourth: The breakthrough will proceed in those sectors which were projected under Operation 'Saturn'. After the breakthrough, the blow will be turned to the south-east in the direction of Nizhnii Astaskhov–Mozorovsk, breaking into the rear of the enemy forces facing Romanenko and Lelyushenko. The operation will begin December 16. The operation has the codename 'Small Saturn'.

Fifth: You must now operate without 6 Mechanized Corps, meanwhile tank regiments are on their way to you. This is because the 6th Mechanized Corps has been handed to the Stalingrad Front for use against the Kotelnikovo enemy concentration. In place of 6th Mechanized Corps you can get a tank corps from Filippov, 25th or 17th [Tank Corps].

                                                                    VASILIEV [Stalin]

Golikov accepted these new orders without argument. Vatutin of the South-Western Front refused to take them lying down and tried every argument to save 'Big Saturn'—the drive to the sea of Azov. Vatutin insisted that 6th Army should attack towards Markovka–Chetkova as he expected, and 17th Tank Corps should go for Voloshino to the west of Millerovo; Vatutin therefore pressed for the subordination of 17th Tank to his Front command. During the night of 14 December, Voronov, Golikov and Vatutin met to try and get an agreed course of operations, but Vatutin stuck out for the bigger drive. Throughout that day, 14 December, the two staffs fired signals at each other, whereupon the General Staff intervened and 'in the name of the *Stavka'* ordered compliance with the orders for 'Small Saturn'.

As these arguments raged over the projected attack on the junction between Army Groups B and Don, Malinovskii's 2nd Guards (of which 1st Guards Rifle Corps was fully assembled) began its movement to the Stalingrad Front, 125 miles to be covered in forced marches of up to thirty miles a day down through the steppe amidst raging blizzards, in the van riflemen with anti-tank rifles on their shoulders ready to go straight into action. But that left a full four days before 2nd Guards could be pulled in behind the Myshkova, the last barrier before Stalingrad. Although the 4th Mechanized and 13th Tank Corps put in furious counter-attacks near Kumskii, Yeremenko was gravely concerned over the outlook beyond the Aksai as Hoth's *blitz* column—and behind it lorries piled with fuel and ammunition, buses for wounded and tractors, all to supply the armoured striking force which was to burst out from Sixth Army itself—crunched forward past the half-way mark. Yeremenko's telegram to the *Stavka* on the morning of 15 December heavily underscored the danger:

. . . since all Front reserves (300, 315, 87 RDs [rifle divisions]), despatched earlier to the south-west and concentrated in the area of Plodovitoe, Zety, received different assignments . . . it is considered impossible to guarantee in any effective sense the axis running along the Kotelnikovo–Abganerovo railway. It follows that this must be reinforced. [Yeremenko, *Stalingrad*, p. 403.]

Since Front reserves had already been committed, the situation was critical:

East of the line Ivanovka [on the Myshkova]–Aksai there is not a single man. If the enemy unleashed a blow along the railway line to Abganerovo and from the Tsybenko area to Zety, that will put the forces of the Front in a severely critical situation. [*Ibid.*]

Both armoured formations (4th Mechanized and 13th Tank Corps) had inflicted, but also suffered, heavy losses; 4th Cavalry Corps was badly battered. For forty-eight hours Volskii's 4th Mechanized and VI *Panzer* Corps grappled in the biting frost and snow. The modernized Soviet 57mm and 76mm anti-tank guns proved extremely effective, while 65th *Panzer* Battalion deployed the new German weapon, the Tiger-1 tanks. Both sides raced for the Myshkova river line. On 17 December 17th *Panzer* Division succeeded at last in reaching the battle area and was engaged the next day, but two rifle divisions and 2nd Guards Mechanized Corps of 2nd Guards Army (its forward HQ at Kolpachki) had also reached the Myshkova. At 2400 hours, 17 December, Yeremenko subordinated 87th Rifle Division, 4th Cavalry and 4th Mechanized Corps to Malinovskii's command, and set the boundaries between 2nd Guards, 51st and 5th Shock Armies.

Slowly, in the midst of its own sweat, the Soviet command pulled itself out of the highly dangerous situation south-west of Stalingrad; but the race with time was not yet fully run. On 19 December, 6th *Panzer* succeeded in forcing its way up to (and, by night, across) the Myshkova, to just under fifty kilometres from the line held by Paulus's Sixth Army. In theory, on receipt of codeword *Donnerschlag*, Sixth Army was to make its own fighting break-out. The critical 96-hour phase now set in. As 2nd Guards Army deployed its units for action behind the Myshkova straight off the march, Vasilevskii despatched as instructed a new operational plan that reached Moscow at 1530 hours on 18 December (*VIZ*, 1966 (3), pp. 32–3):

Report Nos. 42–47: Yakovlev's [Malinovskii, 2nd Guards] army continues to concentrate in the area of Verkhne Tsarinskii–Bratskiisovkhoz (farms), Krep, Yurkin and Zety. From 24 hours 17.XII Volskii's corps [4th Mechanized], 300 and 87 RDs and 4 Cav. Corps, covering the deployment of the army, transferred from Trufanov and subordinated to Yakovlev.

Concentration of Yakovlev's army with the exception of one RD, three independent tank regiments and reserve units to be completed during the night of 21.XII.

Request you confirm the following plan for further operational planning and operations by Yakovlev. During night of 21 and 22 [December] to deploy Guards rifle corps of Yakovlev's army on river Myshkova on the Nizhne Kumskii–Kapkinskii front and to concentrate 2nd Guards Mechanized Corps in area Peregruznyii, Aksai, Shelestov, and from morning of 22.XII to go over to active operations.

22.XII—Guards rifle corps, making main attack in the direction of Gromoslavka, Shestakov and further along the *railway [line]* to Kotelnikovo, together with Volskii's corps to effect final destruction of enemy in the Verkhne-Kumskii area, clear nor[thern] bank of the river Aksai and exit on southern bank of the Aksai and dig in.

2 Gds. Mech. Corps from the Aksai area to operate against enemy flank and rear through Darganov and by the evening of 22.XII must, having taken Kotelnikovo with powerful forward elements, bring its main force into the area Pimen–Cherchen, Gremyschii, and thus straddle the rear of enemy grouping operation north of Kotelnikovo.

23.XII—Liquidation of enemy to nor[th]-east of Kotelnikovo with powerful covering force from 2 Gds. Mech. Corps in the direction of Dubovskoe and with the movement of the Gds. rifle corps by the evening to the line Verkhne–Yablochnyi, Pimen–Cherni, Darganov.

24.XII—Movement of Gds. rifle corps to line Maiorskii, Kotelnikovo, Poperchernyi, to advance 2 Gds. Mech. Corps and Volskii's corps to river Sal, cutting railway line.

Securing of these operations by Yakovlev from the east assigned to Trufanov's army with 38, 302, 126 and 91 RDs, two tank brigades and additionally to Cav. Corps Shapkin [4th Cavalry], which in immediate future to move into area Plodovitoe.

Popov [5th Shock Army] instructed 20.XII to attack from north-west to take Nizhne–Chirskaya and then to co-ordinate operations with Romanenko [5th Tank Army] towards Tormosin and by evening of 24.XII to be on river Tsymla.

Of two tank corps recently moved up I consider it urgent to subordinate one to Popov, the other and the Mech. Corps (should Yakovlev's operations go well) to use for the final destruction of enemy forces encircled at Stalingrad.

Request your authorisation.

MIKHAILOW [Vasilevskii]

At 0530 hours on 19 December Stalin returned a reply (*ibid.*):

SPECIALLY URGENT: Comrade Mikhailov. Your operational plan No. 42, confirmed by Supreme Commander's *Stavka*.

VASILIEV [Stalin]

From their forward positions in the Myshkova bridgehead, the tankmen of VI *Panzer* could at this very moment see the flares fired on the Stalingrad perimeter, the city itself shining in the cold, clear night.

Three days earlier, however, the Voronezh and South-Western Fronts had launched 'Small Saturn' on the upper reaches of the Don against the northern flank of Army Group Don and the right flank of Army Group B; 'Small Saturn' was aimed specifically at the rear of the de-blockading forces trying to break into Stalingrad. Under the revised plan that Vatutin was finally obliged to accept, the main task of his South-Western Front was to use his 1st Guards and 3rd Guards Armies in co-operation with the Voronezh Front to encircle and destroy the 8th Italian Army and then to attack through Nizhne–Astakhov on to Morozovsk. V. I. Kuznetsov's 1st Guards Army with five rifle divisions and three tank corps would attack through Mankovo–Kalitvenskaya, Degtevo, Tatsinskaya, Morozovsk to destroy 8th Italian Army and Group *Hollidt* (rifle formations to reach the line Markovka–Nikolskaya–Chertkovo, tank corps to reach Tatsin-skaya–Morozovsk); while Lelyushenko's 3rd Guards was to breach the enemy defences at Bokovskaya and attack along the lines Bokovskaya–Verkhne Chirskaya and Bokovskaya–Nizhne Astakhov–Kashara to link up with 1st Guards Army. Romanenko's 5th Tank Army would destroy enemy forces in the Nizhne–Chirskaya and Tormosin area, and 'under no circumstances' permit any break-out from here towards other encricled groups. Kharitonov's 6th Army (Voronezh Front) was assigned the attack on Kantemirovka after breaking through the defences at Novaya Kalitve–Derezovka, to reach the line Golubaya–Krinitsa–Pasyukov–Klenovy–Nikoslaya by the fifth day of its operations. Three tanks corps would be committed on the first day of the Voronezh–South-Western Front operations; on the second day rifle units of 1st and 3rd Guards Armies were to encircle the main force of the 8th Italian Army, to complete its destruction by the evening of the fourth day, and by the sixth day to advance the main forces to a line running from Valentinovka–Markovka–Chertkovo–Ilinka–Tatsinskaya–Moro-zovsk–Chernyshkovskii. As reinforcement, the *Stavka* had released three rifle divisions (267th, 172nd and 350th), a rifle brigade (106th), 17th Tank Corps and seven artillery regiments to 6th Army, as well as four Guards rifle divisions (35th, 41st, 38th, and 54th), the 159th Rifle Division, three tank corps (18th, 24th and 25th), one mechanized corps (1st Guards), six independent tank regiments and sixteen artillery regiments; but armour and artillery had still to reach Vatutin's Front. By 12 December, the main body of reserve formations had nevertheless moved up, and both Fronts were regrouping. Engineers built their six-ton, sixteen-ton, forty-ton and sixty-ton capacity bridges over the Don, and during the night of 16 December the tanks moved up to their start lines, some three to five miles from the front line. Along a front running from Novaya, Kalitva in the north (6th Army) to Nizhne–Chirskaya (5th Tank Army), a little over 200 miles, 36 rifle divisions, 425,476 men, 1,030 tanks, almost 5,000 guns and mortars (81mm and upwards in calibre) waited out the night of 16 December.

'Small Saturn' opened in the thick morning mist of 16 December at 0800 hours, when Soviet artillery opened fire. On some sectors, however, visibility was too poor for a punctual start and Soviet planes were grounded on the forward airfields. Kuznetsov's 1st Guards and Kharitonov's 6th Army crossed the ice of the Don, the prelude to some savage fighting in the forward positions. Shortly before noon Vatutin ordered the tank corps—25th and 18th in the lead, 17th following—to move out only to have the lead units blunder into unreconnoitred minefields, disorganizing the attack and bringing losses at once. Similarly Lel-yushenko with 3rd Guards Army enjoyed no success on the first day. During the night Soviet forces regrouped, moved up the artillery and cleared lanes through the minefields. On 17 December the offensive was renewed, and all four tank corps—25th, 18th, 17th and 24th—moved on in two echelons, tank brigades in the lead followed by motorized infantry. Lelyushenko's 3rd Guards, short of fuel and ammunition when its first attack opened, brought up supplies and resumed its attack on the following day.

After seventy-two hours, when the Italians had taken to their heels and the German batteries were silenced, 1st Guards and 6th Army had ripped a thirty-mile gap in the front to a depth of twenty miles and Lelyushenko had penetrated ten miles. On the evening of 19 December the *Stavka* subordinated 6th Army to Vatutin's command and agreed to Vatutin's suggestion to expand 'Small Saturn' as the South-Western Front turned to a general pursuit. All armoured formations—17th, 18th, 24th, 25th Tank Corps and 1st Guards Mechanized Corps—were turned loose in a south-easterly direction with orders to reach Tatsinskaya by 23 December (24th Corps), Morozovsk by 22 December (25th Corps and 1st Guards); 17th and 18th Tank Corps were to take Millerovo by the evening of 24 December.

Maj.-Gen. P.P. Poluboyarov's 17th Tank Corps raced into Kantemirovka (an important traffic junction between Voronezh and Rostov-on-Don) at noon on 19 December, to find trains loaded with ammunition and supplies, and the streets strewn with blazing vehicles and abandoned guns. Poluboyarov's success secured the right flank of 1st Guards Army and secured 6th Army also; 17th Tank Corps swung south on Voloshino while Maj.-Gen. Badanov's 24th Tank Corps pushed south through the shattered Italian divisions. The main body of 6th Army also turned south-east, as did 1st and 3rd Guards Armies with two tank corps (24th and 25th) on their outer flank and two (18th Tank and 1st Guards Mechanized) on their inner flank operating with rifle formations, chopping up the remnants of the Italians and breaking Group *Hollidt* apart.

At Army Group Don, Manstein was aware that a situation of the utmost gravity, yet one of baffling obscurity, was developing by 20 December, when a message was sent to *OKH* emphasizing that decisive Soviet action following the destruction of the Italian divisions could lead to a massive threat to Rostov (and hence to Army Group A). That dire forecast received confirmation almost within hours, when German intelligence officers interrogated Maj.-Gen. Krupennikov, deputy commander of 3rd Guards Army who had taken over 3rd Guards while Lelyushenko had fallen ill; I.P. Krupennikov was, in fact, chief of staff and was captured on 20 December (to be succeeded in his post by Maj.-Gen. Khetagurov). From Krupennikov, German officers learned the attack assignments of 6th, 1st Guards and 3rd Guards Armies and concluded from the interrogation that Rostov was the objective of the Soviet offensive. Two days later, Maj.-Gen. P.P. Privalov (commander of 15th Rifle Corps) and his artillery commander Colonel Lyubinov were taken prisoner on the Kantemirovka–Smyaglevsk road. Privalov, forty-four years old, married and with children (their fate unknown since they lived in the Carpathian region), had commanded a shock group at Tikhvin in 1941–2; after attending a staff course, he had been interviewed by Ryumantsev of the Cadres Administration and assigned to 15th Corps. Now, with grenade splinters in his head, he was a prisoner and from him German intelligence officers derived more information about the operations of his own corps, 6th Army and the Voronezh Front. (One item that Privalov also vouchsafed to his interrogators, who had a detailed picture of his corps, was that shoulder-boards were to be reintroduced as rank markings into the Red Army from 1 January—a move Privalov thought should have been made a year ago to stiffen discipline.) And to their information derived from interrogation, German intelligence added the data produced by air reconnaissance and radio monitoring (which had identified 3rd Guards Army well before it attacked).

The front on the Lower Chir still held against the attacks launched on 22 December by 5th Tank Army, although this engulfed XLVIII *Panzer* Corps in such fighting that none of its strength could be used for the relief of Stalingrad. Badanov's 24th Tank Corps was meanwhile launched on its 120-mile raid deep into the German rear: on 22 December, 24th Tank was fighting in the Bolshinka–Ilinka area and pressed on for Tatsinskaya, one of the main German air bases for flying transports into Stalingrad and, as a vital junction on the Likhaya–Stalingrad railway, stuffed with supplies and weapons. More than 150 miles now separated Badanov from his supply base; 24th Tank Corps had run low on fuel and ammunition when its forward units bypassed Skosyrskaya to the north of Tatsinskaya. Screened by thick fog on the morning of 24 December, Badanov's 130th, 54th and 4th Guards Tank Brigades took up positions for the attack on the railway station, village and airfield at Tatsinskaya. At 0730 hours one salvo from the rocket-launchers signalled the beginning of the assault that rolled on the station and towards the airfield, where German planes tried desperately to take off as the advancing T-34s came on firing. A Soviet tank and a taxiing Ju-52 both collided, disappearing in one sheet of flame in the roaring explosion. With the airfield shot to pieces, with aircraft, weapons and supplies destroyed on the railway trucks at the junction, Badanov at 1830 hours radioed Front and 1st Guards Army HQ that he had carried out his orders. But behind 24th Corps, German troops took up positions north of the Tatsinskaya and Morozovsk stations, thereby holding any further advance by South-Western Front and sealing off Badanov.

The fortunes of 24th Tank Corps, and the mounting concern about it on both the Soviet and German side, are traced in its signals. On Christmas Day 1942, Badanov reported that he had 58 tanks left (39 T-34s and 19 T-70s), with the corps woefully short of fuel and ammunition. At 0500 hours on 26 December a column of five tankers and six lorries with ammunition, escorted by five T-34s, reached the forward brigades, and an hour later 24th Motorized Rifle Brigade moved up to Tatsinskaya, but behind the tankers and the lorried infantry the few routes—in or out—snapped shut with German troops. On the morning when the tankers arrived, Badanov learned an hour later by radio that 24th Tank was now 2nd Guards Tank Corps and he, himself, the first recipient of a new decoration, the Order of Suvorov. In the afternoon the corps came under heavy attack, and Badanov signalled to Vatutin and Kuznetsov (Samsonov, *Stalingrad. bitva*, p. 483):

Corps suffering serious shortage of ammunition. Substitute for diesel fuel exhausted. Request you cover corps operations from the air and speed up movement of army units [assigned] to secure operations of corps units. Request aircraft to drop ammunition.

Badanov

During the night of 27 December German units closed in on 24th Tank Corps and attacked all through the day. At 1800 hours Badanov radioed Vatutin urgently (*ibid.*):

Situation serious. No shells. No tanks. Heavy losses in personnel. Can no longer hold Tatsinskaya. Request permission to break out of encirclement. Enemy aircraft on aerodrome destroyed.

Badanov

Vatutin had ordered Badanov to hold Tatsinskaya, but 'if the worst came to the worst' he could use his discretion and attempt to break out. At 2200 hours Badanov had decided to hold on and an hour later Soviet planes air-dropped ammunition over his lines. At this point Stalin took a hand. During the course of his report to the Supreme Commander, Vatutin outlined the situation:

Badanov sent me today eight signals. At the moment he is fighting in Tatsinskaya having taken up a circular defence. The corps has 39 T-34 tanks and 15 T-70 tanks. Right now our night aircraft are operating in the Tatsinskaya area, and with the morning all Front aviation will destroy the enemy in the Tatsinskaya–Skosyrskaya area. I ordered Badanov to hold on at Tatsinskaya, but I also informed him that if the worst comes to the worst he may take the other decision. [*IVOVSS*, 3, p. 49.]

Vatutin also transmitted a lengthy appreciation of his Front's progress and an estimate of enemy intentions:

All the forces which were earlier facing the Front, i.e. about 17 divisions, can now be said to have been completely destroyed and their dumps captured by us. More than 60,000 men have been taken prisoner, no less a number killed, so that the sorry remnants of these former formations offer almost no resistance except in rare cases. Ahead of Front forces the enemy continues to offer stubborn resistance along the Oblivskaya–Verkhne Chirskaya front. In the area of Morozovsk prisoners were taken today from 11th *Panzer* Division and 8th Air Luftwaffe Field Division which were previously facing Romanenko's army. The stiffest resistance to Lelyushenko's army and our mobile troops is coming from enemy units which moved up to the Chernyshkovskii–Skosirskaya–Tatsınskaya. These enemy troops are trying to hold a line in order to prevent the further offensive operation of our mobile formations and thus secure for themselves the possibility of pulling their own troops back, but perhaps the enemy, under favourable conditions for himself, will make the attempt to hang on to the whole of the salient in order later to try to rescue the encircled forces through it. However he will not succeed in this. All forces will be committed to eliminate that salient. [Zhukov, *Vosp.* (2), pp. 124–5.]

The German defence, Vatutin reported, would be on the Northern Donets:

Aerial reconnaissance produced daily reports of the movement of enemy forces into the following regions: Rossosh, Starobelsk, Voroshilovgrad, Chebotovka, Kamensk, Likhaya, Zverevo. It is difficult to judge enemy intentions, but apparently he is setting up his basic defence line on the Northern Donets. In the first place the enemy must seal off the breach made by our troops and which is 350 kilometres wide. It would be excellent to go on defeating the enemy without any special pause but for that it would be necessary to send reinforcements since the forces we have on the spot are taken up with completing *Small Saturn*, but for *Big Saturn* we need extra forces. [*Ibid.*]

Both Zhukov and Stalin studied Vatutin's messages, and sent him immediate instructions:

Your first task is not to allow Badanov to be destroyed and to despatch with all speed Pavlov and Russiyanov to help him. You took the correct decision when you gave Badanov permission to abandon Tatsinskaya if the worst came to the worst. Your link-up thrust on Tormosin with the 8th Cavalry Corps could well be reinforced with any infantry units to hand. As regards 3rd Guards Cavalry Corps and a rifle division driving through Suvorovskii on Tormosin, that is a very timely move. Over transforming *Small Saturn* into *Big Saturn* we have already sent you 2nd and 23rd Tank Corps. In the course of the next week you will get two more tanks corps and three to four rifle divisions.

We have some doubts about 18th Tank Corps which you wish to push in the direction of Skosirskaya: better to leave it in the area of Millerovo–Verkhne Tarasovskii, together with 17th Tank Corps. In general you must bear in mind that it is better to push tank corps along extended advances in pairs, rather than singly, so as not to get into Badanov's position. [*Ibid.*, p. 125.]

But where was 18th Tank Corps at the moment? Zhukov quizzed Vatutin immediately about the location of the corps. Vatutin replied that 18th Tank was due east of Millerovo and 'will not be isolated'. In closing, Stalin repeated to Vatutin:

Remember Badanov, do not forget Badanov, get him out at any cost.

Vatutin promised:

We will take absolutely every possible measure and we will get Badanov out. [*Ibid.*, p. 126.]

At 0130 hours on 29 December Vatutin sent Badanov orders for an 'independent break-out' from encirclement. No other decision was possible. Maj.-Gen. Pavlov's 25th Tank Corps and Lt.-Gen. I.N. Russiyanov's 1st Guards Mechanized Corps were fighting to Badanov's left in the Tatsinskaya–Mozorovsk area, but they could not make contact with Badanov's 24th Tank Corps. Half an hour later Badanov issued his own orders for the break-out. The critical fuel shortage was partly remedied by mixing German fuel-oil and aviation octane, pre-heating the fuel oil in tin cans, and pouring the final mixture into the fuel tanks of the remaining T-34s and T-70s. The corps formed itself into 'a spike' to pierce the German units holding the encirclement line. Under cover of darkness 24th Tank Corps suddenly burst out, hammering a gap in the German positions and then swinging out to left and right, making for the corps 'base' at Ilinka. Those tanks still with ammunition were used to provide covering fire for the staffs, kitchens, wheeled vehicles and the wounded to pull back first to the village of Nadezhevka and then on to Ilinka. German aircraft tried to destroy the Soviet tank units and a German column opened fire at extended range, but once in the area of Nadezhevka–Mikhailovka Badanov's tanks were free of the encirclement. Badanov ordered Colonel Gavrilov, chief of the corps rear service, to ammunition the tanks from the supplies at Ilinka and the chief of staff to search for all corps units. Throughout 29 December, Soviet and German tank-gunners fought a prolonged duel along the Nadezhevka–Mikhailovka line; only in the evening did the German tanks move back on Tatsinskaya, where the supply-dumps at the railway station— set on fire as the Russians pulled out—continued to burn. On 30 December, in the area of Kostino, Badanov made contact with 25th and 1st Guards Corps, and on Zheltov's orders he took command of a 'tank group' comprising all three mobile formations. The raid—which accounted for nearly 12,000 German casualties, pulled in 4,769 prisoners and destroyed 84 tanks, 106 guns and 431 aircraft—was over.

On the afternoon of 23 December, Manstein could no longer ignore the crucial situation which had built up on his left, where three Soviet tank formations roamed almost at will: on the lower Chir, 3rd Rumanian Army was directed to release 11th *Panzer* Division (which went after Badanov), while 6th *Panzer* was pulled out of Hoth's assault force to bolster up the lower Chir. During the night of 23–24 December, Hoth appealed for the rescinding of the order about 6th *Panzer* Division—one final desperate push and LVII *Panzer* Corps would be close enough to the Stalingrad perimeter for Paulus to make his break-out; Army Group Don had taken its decision to strip Hoth of a vital division at a point when Sixth Army could no longer break out--Operation *Donnerschlag*—in time. Operation *Wintergewitter* (Winter Storm) and *Donnerschlag* (Thunderclap) re-mained dead letters. The whole structure was beginning to tumble in ruins as Soviet armies tore away miles and miles of front between Army Group B and

Don, as well as piling up mobile formations behind the Myshkova. On the 'Kotelnikovo axis' where Hoth was engaged, Soviet formations now totalled nineteen and a half divisions (149,000 men), 635 tanks and more than 1,500 guns. Vasilevskii's plan presented to Stalin on 18 December had envisaged offensive operations beginning in four days (22 December) but on that date the requisite regrouping was by no means complete. Rotmistrov's 7th Tank Corps was still engaged with 5th Shock Army and Bogdanov's 6th Mechanized Corps had not yet arrived from *Stavka* reserve, while Volskii's 4th Mechanized (awarded Guards status on 18 December as 3rd Guards Mechanized) had been drawn into reserve for replenishment in men and machines. Vasilevskii reported the delay to Stalin, but without recommending any basic change in plans (though reinforcement in armoured formations supplied several possibilities). The Guards rifle corps would attack with right-flank elements of 51st Army to destroy enemy units between the Myshkova and the Aksai, with the main attack being mounted by 1st Guards Rifle and 7th Tank Corps on the right between Chernomorov and Gromoslavka; while by the evening of 24 December, 2nd Guards Mechanized and 6th Mechanized Corps would reach the Aksai–Peregruznyi area to strike at the Rumanian units covering the flank of LVII *Panzer* Corps.

During the course of 23 December, Vasilevskii, Yeremenko and Malinovskii met at Verkhne-Tsaritsynskii to complete the attack plans. The next morning, at 0800 hours, ten minutes of Soviet artillery fire signalled the opening of the Soviet attack on the Myshkova, and by noon Malinovskii estimated that he could go for the flanks of 17th and 23rd *Panzer* Divisions by introducing 7th Tank and 2nd Guards Mechanized Corps straight away. That afternoon Lt.-Gen. G.F. Zakharov wrote a letter of congratulations to Volskii of 3rd Guards (Samsonov, *Ot Volgi do Baltiki,* p. 92):

Vasilii Timofeyevich [Volskii]

It has now become clear how much 3rd Guards Mechanized Corps has accomplished:

1. 2nd Guards Army—fully concentrated.
2. Today, 24 December 1942, it went over to the general offensive and just now, at 1620 hours, its forward elements have taken Verkhne-Kumskii, Height 146.9.
3. 6th Infantry and 23rd Panzer Divisions destroyed. The Party and the country will not forget the history of all this. . . . I am honoured that at a critical hour for our native land, for 4th Mechanized Corps, I was up with you. I am convinced—3rd GMK [Guards Mechanized Corps] will get to the Northern Caucasus.

Yours, *G. Zakharov*

Within seventy-two hours, 3rd Guards Mechanized and 13th Tank Corps with 51st Army had smashed up the flimsy Rumanian positions after striking from the Sadovoe–Umantsevo area and had threatened a deep outflanking movement of the entire German 'Kotelnikovo concentration' from the south. *Armeegruppe Hoth* was forced back to the south-west, pressed back relentlessly out of range of Sixth Army which was now left, alone and beleaguered, without hope of relief. Whatever hope there had been vanished on Christmas Eve 1942, though with the initiative east and west of the Don now firmly in Soviet hands the fate of nearly 300,000 men trapped in the Stalingrad pocket paled in comparison with the development of an enormous threat to Army Groups A, B and Don. Manstein might prejudice one army group in order to rescue Sixth Army, but not three.

Not that Stalin allowed Sixth Army to slip from his horizon. On the morning of 19 December he had telephoned Col.-Gen. Voronov, the Stavka 'co-ordinator' with the South-Western and Voronezh Fronts, which were only beginning to exploit their initial successes against the Italian formations on the middle Don, and opened as enigmatically as ever with his standard first question—'*Kakova obstanovke na fronte?*' ('What is the situation on the front?'), at which Voronov duly presented his report. What followed, however, was something Voronov had not anticipated. Stalin asked him if he could not wind up his work on the South-Western Front and return to the inner encirclement, a proposal which reduced Voronov to silence and thereby promoted Stalin's displeasure:

You make no reply to the question I put. It seems to me that you do not wish to go. . . . Apparently you, like some other people, underestimate how important it is to us to liquidate the encircled German troops. You had better give this some serious thought. [*VIZ*, 1962 (5), p. 74.]

Such thought as Voronov did give the question—and it was no light matter to drop his 'co-ordination' at a crucial stage in Vatutin's and Golikov's operations—was rudely shattered on his receipt of formal *Stavka* orders (copies to Vasilevskii, Vatutin, Rokossovskii and Yeremenko):

(1) The Supreme Commander's *Stavka* considers that comrade Voronov has in a thoroughly satisfactory manner carried out his assignment of co-ordinating the operations of the South-Western and the Voronezh Fronts, and moreover, since 6th Army (Voronezh Front) has been subordinated to the command of South-Western Front, comrade Voronov's mission may be considered to have come to an end.

(2) Comrade Voronov is assigned to the area of the Don and Stalingrad Fronts in the capacity as deputy to comrade Vasilevskii for duties connected with the liquidation of the encircled enemy troops.

(3) Comrade Voronov as a *Stavka* representative and deputy to comrade Vasilevskii is instructed to present not later than 21.12.42 to the *Stavka* an operational plan for the liquidation of enemy troops in the space of five-six days. [*Ibid.*, note to p. 74.]

The next day, 20 December, with two senior artillery generals (Velikov and Sivkov) and three officers, Voronov flew down to Zavarykin, 'residence' of the Don Front commander Rokossovskii. With less than two days in which to work out a new operational plan there was no time to lose, though time enough for a brief consultation with Vasilevskii before he left to supervise the preparations for the attack on the Myshkova that was scheduled for 22 December.

The first job was to size up the opposition before settling on any plan. Colonel Vinogradov, intelligence officer on the Don Front, presented a report, estimating the strength of the encircled forces at 'between 80–90,000 men'; asked to 'be specific', he settled for 86,000—five infantry divisions, two motorized divisions, three *Panzer* divisions and three 'battle groups'. Front intelligence considered that rear-service units could make up for losses sustained by Sixth Army in its Stalingrad fighting, but this would not comprise appreciable reinforcement. Meanwhile transport aircraft brought in supplies and took out wounded or staff officers. (In its early stages, the air-lift had caused the Soviet command little concern, but early in December Stalin had ordered an 'aerial blockade' with a proper system of ground observation of aircraft movements and regular fighter interception; Colonel Podgornyi's 235th Fighter Division was detailed for interceptor duties specifically against the German transports, though the weather wrought more havoc than fighters and AA guns.) Stalingrad was to be stormed a second time, but only slowly did it filter through the Soviet command what a formidable force had been walled in by the Soviet armies. One German transport plane forced down behind Soviet lines on its outward flight carried some 1,200 letters from German soldiers. On looking through them and checking names against formations, Voronov finally saw for himself that the 'guard units' mentioned by Front intelligence were in fact nothing less than full-scale German infantry divisions.

Voronov, Rokossovskii and Malinin were unanimous in their opinion that the Don Front should carry the main attack. Voronov himself was all for the Soviet forces on the perimeter being unified into one force under Don Front command and he was aware that the *Stavka* would not object overmuch to this. At the same time, the stipulated 'five–six days' in which to wipe out Sixth Army now appeared wholly unreasonable, after an inspection of the defensive positions (built earlier for the Red Army and now manned by German infantry) and an examination of the strengths of Soviet divisions. Plan *Koltso*, which was ready by 27 December, proposed one main attack from west to east designed to split the pocket in two: 65th, 21st and 24th Armies of the Don Front would attack along an axis running through Baburkin to the workers' settlement at Krasnyi Oktyabr–Gumrak–Alekseyevka. With Soviet divisions down to less than half-strength, Voronov planned to make massive use of artillery to blast passages for the infantry. Once drafted, Plan *Koltso* was put on an aircraft for Moscow on 27 December. As Voronov sat back to wait, the chance of serious revision of the plan seemed to him remote since the General Staff had generally confirmed the ideas in a series of exchanges over the telephone.

However, Voronov's plan came in for some rough handling by the *Stavka*, which the signal of 28 December made plain:

Comrade Voronov:

The main shortcoming of the plan you presented for *Koltso* lies in the fact that the main and the supporting attacks diverge from each other and doubtful outcomes which might prejudice success are nowhere eliminated.

In the *Stavka*'s view, your main task in the first stage of the operation must be the splitting up and annihilation of the western grouping of encircled enemy troops in the Kravtsov–Baburkin–Marinovka–Karpovka area in order to turn the main attack by our troops south from the Dmitrovka–Baburkin area into the Karpovka railway station district, and to direct a supporting attack by 57th Army from the Kravtsov–Sklyarov area into linking up with the main attack, so that both join at Karpovsk railway station.

In line with this should be organized an attack by 66th Army through Orlovka towards *Krasnyi-Oktyabr* and to meet this—an attack mounted by 62nd Army so that both attacks would link up and thus cut off the factory district from the main enemy forces.

The *Stavka* instructs you to revise your plan on the basis of these foregoing suggestions. The *Stavka* confirms the date for opening operations [6 January 1943] as presented by you in your first plan. The first phase of the operation will terminate 5–6 days after its commencement. The plan for the second stage of operations will be presented through the General Staff on January 9, utilizing the first results of the first stage. [*VIZ*, 1962 (5), note to p. 77.]

Nevertheless, Voronov gained something: the *Stavka* agreed to a unified command, decided on reinforcing the artillery needed for the operation and despatched 20,000 men as an infantry component. On 1 January 1943, 62nd, 64th and 57th Armies were subordinated to the Don Front, giving Voronov and Rokossovskii a force of thirty-nine rifle divisions, ten rifle brigades, thirty-eight High Command Artillery Reserve regiments, ten Guards Mortar (Katyusha) regiments, five tank brigades, thirteen tank regiments, three armoured trains, seventeen AA regiments, six 'fortified garrisons' and fourteen flame-thrower companies. The entire force on the inner encirclement comprised forty-seven divisions (218,000 men), 5,610 guns and mortars, 169 tanks and 300 planes. It was little wonder that Stalin wanted this force freed for other operations as speedily as possible.

On the morning of 3 January, Voronov, Rokossovskii and Malinin met to review the state of the preparations for the attack in three days' time. There was little to encourage optimism. The reinforcements and supplies lagged behind on the railways, although Voronov had pressed Khrulev to speed things up. To attack on time was a risk; to ask for a postponement meant running foul of Stalin. There was nothing for it, however, in view of the delays with men and ammunitions, but to seek four more days, reasons for which Voronov set out in his letter to the *Stavka*:

To proceed with the execution of *Koltso* at the time authorized by you does not seem possible owing to the 4–5 day delay in the arrival of reinforcement units, trains with reinforcement drafts and ammunition trains.

To speed up their movement we agreed to unloading many trains and transport columns at a considerable distance from the points agreed in the plans for detraining and unloading. That measure involved the loss of a great deal of time in then shifting units, reinforcements and ammunition up to the front.

Our correctly proportioned plan was then thrown out of gear by the unscheduled movement of trains and transports to comrade Vatutin's left wing. Comrade Rokossovskii requests that the opening of operations be changed to plus four. I have personally checked all calculations.

All this impels a request for you to authorize commencement of *Koltso* at plus four. [*VIZ*, 1962 (5), p. 81.]

Stalin telephoned at once to find out what Voronov meant by 'plus four'. The rebuke was stinging when it came:

You'll sit it out so long down there that the Germans will take you [Voronov] and Rokossovskii prisoner. You don't think about what can be done, only about what can't be done. We need to be finished as quickly as possible there and you deliberately hold things up. [*Ibid.*]

Grudgingly Stalin gave Voronov 'plus four'. *Koltso* was now to open on 10 January.

Faced with the problem of relating requisite strength to maximum speed, there was some justification for Stalin's fierce impatience with Voronov. During the last ten days of December 1942 the *Stavka* had worked feverishly to finish the planning for the massive counter-offensive designed to roll over the German southern wing to engulf Army Groups A, Don and B. At the northern end of the Soviet–German front, the Leningrad and Volkhov Front command received confirmation of orders despatched on 8 December to proceed with the de-blockading of Leningrad. The freeing of Leningrad, the destruction of Sixth Army at Stalingrad, a Soviet offensive into the eastern Donbas, an attack in the direction of Kursk and Kharkov, and the trapping of Army Group A in the Caucasus would signal the general expulsion of German forces from Soviet territory, and the destruction of the entire southern wing of the German army would offer a decisive strategic success. At the end of 1942 the Soviet command reckoned that twenty-five per cent of German strength on the southern wing had been eliminated: Sixth Army, one of the most powerful in the *Wehrmacht*, was encircled and the force sent out to its relief defeated; Fourth *Panzer* had been severely mauled; 3rd and 4th Rumanian Armies had been battered to pieces; and 8th Italian Army for all practical purposes shattered. With the distance between inner and outer encirclement now some sixty-five miles, Paulus and his men were doomed. The Soviet outer encirclement ran from Novaya Kalitva in the north (Voronezh Front) through Millerovo, west of Tormosin and east of Zimovniki. The time had come for a concerted attack on the three German army groups in the south.

In the early hours of 22 December, Golikov, commander of the Voronezh Front, attended a *Stavka* session which discussed the operational plans for a second strike on the middle reaches of the Don, aimed this time at the 2nd Hungarian Army and the remnants of 8th Italian Army. This attack would clear enemy forces from the Ostrogorzhsk–Kamenka–Rossosh area (between Kante-mirovka and Voronezh), an indispensable prelude to developing a Soviet offensive in the direction of Kursk and Kharkov. The South-Western Front would at the same time attack in the direction of Voroshilovgrad. Golikov's new offensive would bring his forces into the south-western sector of the Voronezh *oblast* between the Don and the Oskol, the shortest route to Kursk and Kharkov, and a key railway network. In Stalin's plans to liberate the Kharkov industrial region, the Donbas and the northern Caucasus, the rail links had a key role to play; both the Voronezh and South-Western Fronts were severely restricted by lack of rail facilities. (The storming of Stalingrad would also reopen direct rail links with the north Caucasus.) Golikov's orders were precise enough: to attack on his centre and on his left, to eliminate enemy forces between Voronezh and Kantemirovka, and to seize the Liskaya–Kantemirovka rail link (upon which both the Voronezh and South-Western Fronts could then be based for future offensive operations aimed at Kharkov and the Donbas). To secure Voronezh Front operations from the south, Vatutin was to use his 6th Army in an attack 'in the general direction of Pokrovskoe'. General Zhukov and Col.-Gen. Vasilevskii would 'co-ordinate' the offensive, which was timed for mid-January.

On the Trans-Caucasus Front, Tyulenev had submitted his own plan for an offensive designed to liberate Maikop: his front consisted of two elements, the right wing holding the Kayasula–Mozdok–Bakhan line and the left running along the coast, the 'Black Sea Group' under Petrov. The left wing held First *Panzer* Army; the right, 17th Army. In November Tyulenev had been ordered to strengthen Petrov's group with troops and artillery, movement which involved the Front command in vast construction work to build roads and erect bridges. At the same time, Tyulenev held back a considerable body of troops—10th Guards Rifle Corps, 3rd Rifle Corps and two rifle divisions—on his right wing, the 'Northern Group', in spite of the *Stavka*'s insistence that they should go to Petrov.

On 29 December Tyulenev was told to scrap his plans for an attack on Maikop and to prepare an entirely new operation. The encirclement of Army Group A was to be accomplished now by two Soviet drives, one by the 'Black Sea Group' (Trans-Caucasus Front) attacking towards Krasnodar-Tikhoretsk and a second by the Southern Front (the new designation of the Stalingrad Front from 1 January 1943), using 51st and 28th Armies to advance on Salsk-Tikhoretsk, followed by a joint advance on Rostov. In addition, the Black Sea Group would attack right-flank units of Seventeenth Army in the Novorossiisk area and seize the Taman peninsula, the German escape route to the Crimea. Neither Petrov nor Tyulenev were exactly enamoured of the *Stavka* plan for the Trans-Caucasus

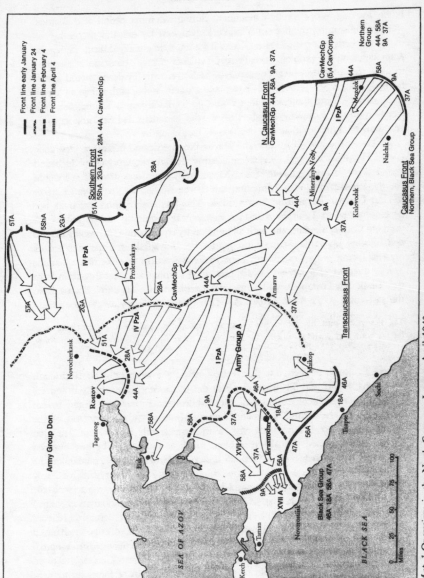

Map 1 Operations in the North Caucasus, January–April 1943

Front. Moving troops through mountains during the worst period of the winter weather, or shifting them from Vladikavkaz to Poti by rail and thence by sea to the northerly sections of Petrov's coastal forces, were equally difficult prospects. After debating the problem with Petrov, Tyulenev telephoned Stalin in an effort to have the 'Maikop operation' restored. Stalin refused: Tyulenev would attack from the Black Sea Group, the 'Krasnodar variant' stood, and to cut off Army Group A the Trans-Caucasus Front would go for Bataisk and Tikhoretsk to cut escape routes at Rostov and Eisk. Petrov, who had defended Sevastopol, wryly admitted to Tyulenev that this one was a 'tough nut'.

To crack 'the nut', Tyulenev and Petrov proposed two operations, Operation *Gory* ('Heights') to break Seventeenth Army defences at Goryschii Kluch and then a drive to the river Kuban and Krasnograd; Operation *More* ('Sea') would use the left flank of 47th Army and a seaborne landing at Yuzhnaya Ozereika to clear German forces from Novorossiisk. This met with Stalin's approval, but he emphasized to Tyulenev that First *Panzer* was beginning to pull out of the northern Caucasus—shipping back all unnecessary equipment, demolishing dumps and blowing up roads. Petrov must get to the Tikhoretsk area and stop enemy material being moved westwards. The main assignment was formalized in the *Stavka* directive of 4 January, which prescribed forming a powerful column from the 'Black Sea Group' to strike towards Bataisk–Azov, 'slip into' Rostov from the east and cut off Army Group A. Stalin himself gave Tyulenev his orders:

Tell Petrov to start his movement on time, without holding back for anything even for an hour and without waiting for reserves to move up. [Tyulenev, *Cherez tri voiny*, p. 250.]

When Tyulenev pointed out that Petrov had no experience in breakthrough operations, Stalin told Tyulenev to go to the Black Sea Group himself and see that these orders were carried out. Meanwhile First *Panzer* had begun to fall back towards the Kuma, a situation which Maslennikov in command of the 'Northern Group' (44th, 58th, 9th, 37th Armies, 4th Kuban and 5th Don Cavalry Corps) failed dismally to exploit, much as in October he had bungled the defence. Still in fear of a German attack on Groznyi and Dzaudzhikai, he had closed up on his left and centre, thus depriving the right flank of badly needed strength. With signals completely disorganized he lost touch with the formation trying to attack First *Panzer* Army. Vasilevskii on 7 January was obliged to intervene in the interests of speeding the attack; on his orders, 4th Kuban, 5th Don Cavalry Corps and tank units were assembled into a 'cavalry-mechanized group' under Lt.-Gen. N.Ya. Kirichenko and given instructions to strike north-westwards for Armavir or Nevinnomysska in an effort to trap German forces on that axis. Maslennikov was told to leave only a minimum of forces on his left; while Kirichenko's mobile force moved on Armavir, 44th Army would attack in the direction of Stavropol. Petrov meanwhile had to report to the *Stavka* on 7 January that 'full concentration of forces assigned primarily [to me] is impossible'.

The winter gales seriously interfered with supply by sea and since 5 January rainstorms had washed away roads and brought floods which swept down bridges; heavy artillery was stuck in the mountain passes. Petrov's operation was postponed for four days, until 16 January.

Trapping First *Panzer* Army depended on close co-ordination between the Southern Front and the two groups of the Trans-Caucasus Front, the Northern and Black Sea Group. While Petrov struggled to build up his Black Sea Group for its attack on Krasnodar and thence Tikhoretsk, the Southern Front received orders to attack in two directions, with its right wing along the lower reaches of the Don towards Rostov and with its left towards Salsk and Tikhoretsk. The Soviet armoured formations had already taken a heavy battering in the Kotelnikovo fighting; now, ploughing through snow and moving every hour away from their supply bases, 3rd Guards and 13th Mechanized Corps needed more tanks and fresh supplies. The Front command asked for 300 new tanks. The *Stavka* on 4 January promised 150 and suggested that the remainder be made up from machines repaired on the spot. Trufanov's 51st and Gerasimenko's 28th Armies ran into stiff opposition at Zimovniki, which was finally cleared on 7 January; this left an open flank, which was closed by moving 2nd Guards Army armoured formations to the Zimovniki area to operate between the Don and the Sal. On the right wing of the Southern Front, Popov's 5th Shock Army and part of 2nd Guards, under its deputy commander Kreizer, pressed on to the Kagalnik. By 11 January, Malinovskii's 2nd Guards and Trufanov's 51st Armies had reached the river Manych between its mouth and the railway station of Proletarskaya; Rotmistrov (whose 7th Tank Corps was now 3rd Guards) was in command of a 'mechanized group' consisting of his own corps (3rd Guards), 2nd and 6th Mechanized Corps and 98th Rifle Division—a force Malinovskii hoped to use in seizing Rostov and Bataisk by a very rapid drive. Malinovskii issued orders for Rotmistrov to seize crossing bridgeheads on the southern bank of the Manych by the morning of 17 January, and then to go for Bataisk and Rostov.

For all this pressure south of the Don, and for all Popov's attacks with 5th Shock Army along the lower Don through Konstantinovskii, Rostov would not be so speedily closed off. Nor could the Southern Front, for all its exertions, break through to Tikhoretsk. After the middle of January, First *Panzer* Army, having speeded up its withdrawal very considerably, had established 'operational co-operation' with Fourth *Panzer*. Rostov must now be held to secure lines of communication, though the survival of First *Panzer* was scarcely at risk. Meanwhile, Petrov's offensive with his Black Sea Group, aimed at Krasnodar-Tikhoretsk, slowly but surely ground to an inevitable halt. Struggling with floods and winter mud, Petrov could only attack in stages; on 11 January, Lt.-Gen. Leselidze's 4th Army and Maj.-Gen. Ryzhkov's 18th Army began their diversionary attacks aimed at Maikop and Belorechenskaya, but within twenty-four hours pouring rain flecked with light snow brought havoc to transport columns. Ryzhkov's troops fighting in the mountains floundered in snow drifts. The diversionary attack on the left flank, mounted by Maj.-Gen. Kamkov's 47th Army—the main instrument of Operation 'Heights'—began its operations on 16 January in much the same appalling conditions in the wooded, mountainous terrain. With roads awash and streams turned into miniature rivers, with artillery bogged down despite the feverish manhandling of guns and with aircraft the only means of supply on his left, Grechko made only painful progress towards Krasnodar. On 20 January Petrov reported to Vasilevskii that any movement of armour was out of the question. Four days later Grechko was glued to the ground on the southern approaches to Krasnodar, and the prospect of the drive on Tikhoretsk vanished completely.

On 24 January, when to the north-east of Rostov Vatutin's South-Western Front and 5th Shock Army on the northern wing of Southern Front had reached the rivers Aidar and Northern Donets, and while to the east and south-east the Soviet line of advance ran along the lower reaches of the Don and the Manych, and on to Belaya Glina, Armavir and Labinskaya, the *Stavka* decided upon a rapid change of plan to sever the German escape routes. The three armies of the Southern Front (2nd Guards, 51st and 28th Armies) operating south of the Don were to operate with the right-flank armies of the Northern Group of the Trans-Caucasus Front (44th and 58th Armies plus the 'cavalry-mechanized group'), in an attack on Baṭaisk, shutting off Rostov from the south and then moving along the coast of the sea of Azov. The capture of Bataisk would halt the movement of German forces through Rostov· into the Donbas (and would thus hinder the build-up of a new German front). In order to trap Seventeenth Army, the left-flank armies of the Northern Group (9th and 37th Armies) were to operate with Petrov's Black Sea Group; Petrov was to concentrate his main forces north-east of Novorossiisk in order to break through at Krimskaya and thereby prevent any escape into the Taman peninsula. Finally, the Northern Group of Tyulenev's command was established as an independent front, the North Caucasus Front. On the same day, Hitler finally decided to bring all of First *Panzer,* whose southern wing was still at Armavir, back through Rostov; Fourth *Panzer* would, therefore, have to hold south of the Don.

Manstein's grip on the lower Don, however, was made totally precarious by the calamities precipitated on the upper Don by Golikov's attack launched on 12 January against the 2nd Hungarian Army—the Ostrogorzhsk–Rossosh operation. This had ripped a huge and gaping hole in the German front from south of Voronezh to Voroshilovgrad, and dangerously loosened the German hold on the Donbas by opening the way to the Donets and on to the Dnieper crossings or the sea of Azov. Golikov's operational plan called for three simultaneous strikes by his Front command, a method selected to ensure surprise and to inhibit enemy reserves. The 'northern group' (Maj.-Gen. Moskalenko's 40th Army), was to aim for Alekseyevka, where it would link up with the 'southern group' (Maj.-Gen. Rybalko's 3rd Tank Army) moving out from north-west of Kantemirovka; meanwhile the 'central group' (Maj.-Gen. Zykov's 18th Independent Rifle Corps) would move west, south-west and south. For immediate security of the operations to the south, Maj.-Gen. Sokolov's 7th Cavalry Corps would attack towards Valuiki, while to the north 4th Tank Corps would secure Moskalenko's external flank (a guard against possible German attack from the Voronezh–Kastornoe direction). For the forthcoming operations the *Stavka* had substantially reinforced the Voronezh Front: Rybalko's 3rd Tank Army (its HQ in the Tula area) was moved in with its two tank corps, 12th and 15th, four rifle divisions (48th, 184th, 180th and 111th), one independent rifle brigade (87th) and two artillery components. With a second burst of reinforcement, Golikov was assigned three more rifle divisions, one tank brigade and a ski brigade.

Moskalenko's planning was finished by 25 December (40th Army had prepared a contingency plan even before 21 December), but the planning of the Front operation was supervised by General Zhukov, joined by Col.-Gen. Vasilevskii and with the participation of Maj.-Gen. V.D. Ivanov from the Operations Section of the General Staff. Peresypkin, head of Red Army Signals, was also present during the planning and preparation. From 3 January 1943, Front preparations came under the immediate control of Zhukov and Vasilevskii as *Stavka* representatives, and not without Zhukov laying about him a little. It was, nevertheless, an offensive planned with minute attention to detail, bearing many of the marks of Zhukov's close, unbending scrutiny: he was furious at a suspected breach of security (though none had in fact occurred and the offensive enjoyed its advantage of surprise). Enemy air reconnaissance failed to reveal the preparations, and the Hungarian commanders reported nothing untoward. Soviet units moved at night, though snow-bound roads made movement far from easy; at the 'northern group', 4th Tank Corps was behind schedule and finally Golikov was obliged to seek Stalin's permission for a postponement, to 14 January. Stalin agreed.

Two days earlier, on 12 January, Moskalenko had begun a reconnaissance in force. On the following day the 7th Hungarian Division took to its heels and Moskalenko decided to commit his main force, breaking through the enemy defensive zone to a depth of some three miles. Rybalko's 3rd Tank Army attacked on 14 January in thick mist; by the evening, with two tanks corps in action, Rybalko was twelve miles into the enemy positions and Maj.-Gen. Koptsov's 15th Tank Corps had overrun the HQ of XXIV *Panzer* Corps. Soviet cavalry struck out very successfully for Valuiki and under the pale winter sun on 19 January the horsemen in black capes and flying hoods charged down the hapless Italians, killing and wounding more than a thousand before this brief resistance by the fleeing, hungry and frostbitten men of the 5th Italian Infantry Division ended. By that time thirteen divisions had been trapped, 56,000 men made prisoner (and approximately the same number killed by Soviet reckoning), and 1,700 tanks, 2,800 machine-guns, 55,000 rifles, and lorries and horses by the thousand, as well as whole ammunition dumps, had been captured. A few days later in Budapest the rumours flew round the streets that 'the Hungarians have perished to a man'. The final elimination of the encircled divisions lasted until the end of the month, by which time the tally of prisoners rose to 86,900; in his letter to Hitler, Admiral Horthy subsequently listed the loss of 80,000 officers and men killed, with 63,000 wounded. The 2nd Hungarian Army, remnants of the 8th Italian Army, the Italian Alpine Corps and XXIV *Panzer* Corps were rubbed out of the German order of battle. Between Voronezh and Kantemirovka a 120-mile breach gaped in the German line.

On the evening of 18 January, when the Soviet pincers first closed on the Hungarians and Italians, Vasilevskii, who had supervised the execution of the present operation, presented Stalin with proposals for the next attack. This was to unroll on the German Second Army and thereby eliminate Army Group B completely: the 'Voronezh–Kastornoe operation' was directed at the exposed northern and southern flanks of Second Army, which was now trapped in a salient, with the Bryansk Front to the north and the Voronezh Front to the south. Wiping out this twelve-division force (125,000-men strong) would establish ideal conditions for an attack on Kursk (and also release more north-south railway lines). Two Soviet fronts, Bryansk and Voronezh, would co-operate to accomplish the Voronezh–Kastornoe encirclement. On Lt.-Gen. Max Reiter's Bryansk Front, Maj.-Gen. N.P. Pukhov's 13th Army—that disastrously unlucky army of 1941—would attack from the north to Kastornoe, and, from Golikov's right and centre, Moskalenko's 40th, Maj.-Gen. Chernyakhovskii's 60th and Lt.-Gen. Chibisov's 38th Army would attack from the south-east (40th and 60th) and the north-west (38th). The *Stavka* permitted the use of Reiter's left flank, but could make no other reinforcement available. The provisional date was fixed at 24–26 January. On 24 January Moskalenko attacked in the worst of wintry conditions—fog, a blizzard which blew from dawn onwards, and the temperature down to minus twenty degrees; shortly after noon, the tanks of Kravchenko's 4th Tank Corps (recently at Stalingrad) moved up, using up great quantities of fuel by slithering off the roads and in towing stranded machines. By night Soviet U-2s dropped them drums of diesel oil. German troops had already started to pull back from Voronezh and the Don, but three Soviet armies, 60th, 38th and finally Pukhov's 13th, now joined the attack. On the morning of 28 January, armoured units of the Bryansk Front moving from the north and west, and those of the Voronezh Front advancing from the south and east, closed on Kastornoe, where the fighting lasted until the early hours of 29 January.

Although the trap had not closed entirely on Second Army, two of its three corps had been encircled. Army Group B had been sliced away from Army Group Don and destroyed as an effective command. Along a 150-mile sector running along the railway line from Kursk–Kastornoe and south to Kupyansk (South-Western Front) only five German divisions were holding the line, with only three in operational reserve at Kharkov. On this calculation, the quicker Soviet armies struck out for Kursk and Kharkov the better, before German reserves concentrated at Kharkov. Vasilevskii and Golikov pressed this argument upon Stalin on 21 January in a survey of the possibilities presented by the breakthrough on the upper Don. Once the Voronezh–Kastornoe operation was completed, the Voronezh Front would concentrate its striking forces on the line of the river Oskol on a sector running from Stary Oskol to Urazovo, and from there launch a three-pronged attack on Kharkov. This idea Stalin approved in principle, and Golikov was ordered to prepare this offensive which would be opened no later than 1–2 February, an operation which received the codename *Zvezda* ('Star'). On the eve of the Kastornoe operation, Golikov let Chernyakhovskii and Chibisov in on the course of future operations, 'promising' the Kharkov operation to the army which first liberated Kastornoe. As Soviet armour moved in on this important rail junction on 28 January, Golikov issued the first orders connected with the Kursk–Kharkov attack—Second Army was to be fully eliminated as right-flank armies moved up to the Tim and Oskol river-lines, from which the Kursk–Kharkov attack would be launched. Voronezh Front operations, however, were themselves only part of a much greater undertaking, the strategic counter-offensive on the southern wing, also involving the South-Western and Southern Fronts, to liberate the Ukraine, the Donbas and to drive along the shore of the sea of Azov. The *Stavka* directives, which were being prepared and which would within days be on their way to Front commanders, set the terminal line for the Soviet advance before the spring thaw at Chernigov–Kherson. In the Stalingrad ring, where Operation *Koltso* had opened on 10 January with an enormous barrage followed at 0900 hours by the first tank and infantry attacks, Paulus had surrendered himself at his HQ in the *Univermag* building on 31 January. Behind the humiliation of one man lay the appalling agonies and grievous suffering of thousands of men in Sixth Army, the army which had done much to fell the Low Countries, Yugoslavia, Greece and the Ukraine. Before the opening of the attack, Voronov on 4–5 January had conceived the idea of sending an ultimatum to Sixth Army to surrender or be destroyed. The *Stavka* approved the text submitted by Voronov, and on 7 January radio contact was established with Sixth Army HQ to arrange the passage of emissaries, Major Smyslov and Captain Dyatlenko. The first attempt to hand over the ultimatum failed. The *Stavka* was all for calling off the attempt, but on the morning of 9 January the two Soviet officers, blindfolded (with bandages they carried already prepared in their own pockets), were taken to a German command post. Paulus refused to meet the emissaries, who were informed that Sixth Army's commander already knew the contents of the message from Soviet radio transmission.

At the German refusal to accept surrender terms, the *Stavka* inquired of Voronov: 'What do you propose to do next?' Voronov signalled that *Koltso* would open as planned on 'plus four'. Just after dawn on the morning of 10 January, Rokossovskii and Voronov took their stations at Batov's command post with 65th Army. At 0805 hours with the signal rockets flickering along the perimeters, massed Soviet artillery—more than 7,000 guns, howitzers and heavy mortars mounting the heaviest Soviet barrage so far in the war—opened fire through the swirling winter fog, a fierce bombardment that ranged over the German defences as the prelude to the attack from the west, the north-west, the north-east and the south, along the fifty miles of the inner encirclement. During the night, bombers of the 16th Air Army raided German positions on the perimeter and in the depth of the pocket; while the barrage was fired off in the morning, more bombers and ground-attack planes with fighter escorts pounded the positions again, paying close attention to the aerodromes. Soviet artillery spotters correcting the fire through the mist watched 'a sea of flame' and columns of smoke rising from the German positions. After fifty-five minutes of this battering, a salvo of rockets signalled the infantry attack: Soviet riflemen riding on tanks followed by more infantry moved through the thick snow into the smoke-covered German lines, a bludgeoned ruin of bodies, smashed guns and tumbled pillboxes. The fierceness of the Soviet assault appalled the Germans (who had expected the attack somewhat later), and the tenacity of the Germans troubled the Russians. On the perimeter, for all the short, savage counter-attacks, the Soviet tanks rolled on to gun-pits and dugouts flattening guns which fired off their meagre ammunition. On the first day Soviet troops had advanced as far as five miles on some sectors. Voronov began the first of his daily reports to the *Stavka* on the course of the operations.

After three days of very heavy fighting, the western tip of the pocket, the 'Marinovka nose', was reduced on 12 January at the cost to the Don Front of 26,000 casualties and the loss of 135 tanks (by the evening of 12 January only 122 of the original tank force of 257 remained). Four days later the south-eastern area (Tsybenko–Elkhi–Peschanki–Alekseyevka) was occupied, while 65th and 21st Armies drove forward into the middle pocket. The main supply airfield, Pitomnik, had fallen to the Russians; along the road to Pitomnik lay the ghastliest human wreckage, the wounded who in their thousands had hauled themselves in their infinity of agonies towards the German transport aircraft. As the Russians closed in, maddened men fought to board the JU-52s, behind them great clumps of dead frozen to a brittle stiffness. Elsewhere, batteries and battalions fought down to the last rounds, and in the closing act divisional and corps commanders with their staff officers took up posts as the last, despairing riflemen of their formations. The withdrawal eastwards pressed more and more ragged, starving men into the terrible ruins of the city as supplies and ammunition finally dribbled away without even the minuscule scraps of the past weeks.

The bitter and unyielding German resistance baffled Voronov on two counts: why was there no surrender, and where did this strength spring from? One answer was provided by the capture of German orders forbidding surrender, while the interrogation of prisoners showed that German officers were stiffening garrisons, however minute, wherever possible. The real shock came with the interrogation of the quarter-master of Sixth Army, Colonel von Kulowsky. The Soviet command now learned that up to 22 November, 250,000 German troops had been encircled, of which 215,000 remained by 10 January: losses to that date had been 10,000 killed and 25,000 wounded (10,000 wounded being taken out by transport

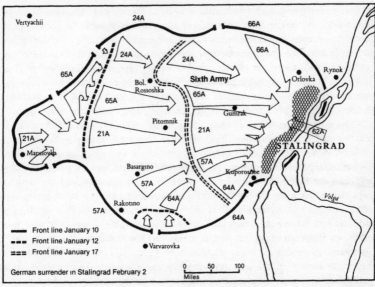

Map 2 Operation *Koltso*, Stalingrad, January–February 1943

planes). Since the Soviet attack began, only 1,200 casualties had been evacuated by air; no reinforcements had been flown in save for 500 men returning from leave. The German troops were now living off their horses and had already consumed 39,000 of them.

On the morning of 17 January, Soviet army commanders met at a command conference at which Voronov and Rokossovskii were late in arriving. The commanders wanted a break in operations, two or three days' pause, in which to regroup; the low tally of prisoners taken by the Red Army—6,896—as well as Soviet casualties was proof enough of the savagery of the fighting. The offensive continued, however, without 'the pause' suggested by the formation commanders. From Gumrak, the only airfield left to the defenders apart from one air-strip, the transports flew out the last of the wounded. Four aircraft had landed at Gumrak on 18 January, but this small runway, covered with the debris of scattered stores and smashed machines, could render only minute aid to the Stalingrad 'fortress', which had shrunk in depth and width to a mere ten miles by five. On 22 January Soviet troops began the final reduction of the German divisions now bereft of two-thirds of their strength. Gumrak fell that day after heavy fighting, and the Soviet tanks moved eastwards along the railway line. On the same day, forward elements of 21st Army made contact at Krasnyi Oktyabr with Rodmitsev's 13th Guards from Chuikov's 62nd Army. Having halved the pocket, Soviet troops had finally split it in two. Throughout the seven hours of winter daylight, Soviet guns were ranged as rapidly as possible on their targets; the tanks churned over section after section, wiping out weapon-pits and dugouts or simply grinding the defenders into their holes in the ground. Outside in the high wind and under the endless bombardment survivors of divisions, privates and generals alike, assembled to fight the last battle to the last round; below ground were the horrendous cellars, the largest in the centre of the city, cavernous clammy morgues filled with the dead, the dying and even more wounded.

During the night of 31 January, units of the 38th Motorized Rifle Brigade and 329th Engineer Battalion blockaded the *Univermag* building, headquarters of Sixth Army. All telephone lines were cut. In the morning, senior lieutenants Il'chenko and Mezhirko with a few tommy-gunners went into the ruined building and into the basement to present a formal Soviet ultimatum and demand for capitulation. At noon, Field-Marshal Paulus was driven off in a car to Shumilov's HQ and thence to Zavarykin, Don Front command centre, where Voronov and Rokossovskii waited to interrogate him. Although a general surrender now took place, in the northern sector the German garrison continued to resist. On 1 February, concentrating many thousands of guns (300 to one kilometre, five times the density of the opening barrage), Soviet gunners poured shells on to this group in a fifteen-minute pulverisation bombardment. At 1600 hours on 2 February 1943, operations formally ceased at Stalingrad.

It remained only to round up the prisoners and bury the dead. The Soviet tally was twenty-two divisions destroyed, plus 160 support and reinforcement units. The list of captured equipment from the Don Front rolled on—5,762 guns, 1,312 mortars, 156,987 rifles, 10,722 automatic weapons, 10,679 motorcycles, 240 tractors, 3,569 bicycles, 933 telephone sets, 397 kilometres of signals cable. . . . On 4 February Voronov and Rokossovskii flew to Moscow. The Don Front was wound up, and its forces, organized into the Central Front, were on their way to deployment between the Voronezh and Bryansk Fronts, facing Kursk. During his stay in Moscow, Rokossovskii learned that he would command the new Front and that its assignment was to carry out a deep outflanking blow in the direction of Gomel–Moghilev–Orsha and Smolensk, a great scything attack into the flank and rear of Army Group Centre.

A new glittering Red Army, laden with decorations, loaded with honours and stiffened with braid, rose swiftly out of the blood and grime of the Stalingrad victory. First came the new marshals, among whom Stalin himself was to figure very shortly. On 18 January 1943, the day on which the Leningrad blockade was pierced by the junction of the Leningrad and Volkhov Fronts and the day after the Soviet communiqué on the breaking of the German defences at Stalingrad, General Zhukov publicly received his appointment as Marshal of the Soviet Union; Col.-Gen. Voronov also became a Marshal of Artillery (the Supreme

Soviet having two days earlier formalized the wholly new appointments of 'Marshal of Artillery', 'Marshal of the Armoured Forces' and 'Marshal of Aviation' for the Soviet armed forces). Novikov, who had commanded the air forces at Stalingrad, and Fedorenko both became colonel-generals. Within two months, Novikov, the iron man of the Red air force who had pulled this arm out of the shattering chaos of 1941, became the first Marshal of Aviation (and went on to become chief Marshal of Aviation). Vasilevskii was promoted to full general on 18 January and a month later, with the fall of Kharkov, was appointed a Marshal of the Soviet Union, a meteoric rise which had taken him from major-general to marshal in just under twenty months. The field commanders received their share of promotion, but none as yet attained the Marshal's gold star: Rokossovskii became a colonel-general (and was by April a full general); Govorov in Leningrad became a colonel-general. The formation commanders each received higher notches of rank. Important also were the decorations, a whole array of which had been introduced in all their evocative distinctiveness, like the Order of Suvorov (with three classes) of which Badanov at 25th Tank Crops had been, for his raid, the first recipient.

Stalin moved swiftly and adroitly into this newly constituted military elite. Up till now he had enjoyed the title of 'Supreme Commander', *Verkhovnyi*, though without formal military rank as such; after the capture of Kharkov in mid-February, and the first Red Army Day (23 January) with a real scent of triumph about it, Stalin himself assumed the title of Marshal of the Soviet Union, a 'concession' to the collective appeal of the *Politburo*. There was, however, more to it than the Marshal's star with its gold and jewels and mere adhesion to the powerful cult of the army. Stalin's assumption of rank came at a time which he himself identified in his Order of the Day on 23 February as 'the decisive moment of the war'; simultaneously, and for the first time, Soviet operations were publicly identified with 'Stalinist strategy' and a 'Stalinist military school of thought' (the very first hint of which had appeared exactly a year before in the Order of the Day No. 55 which put the five 'permanently operating factors'—*postoyanno deistvuyushchii faktory,* the solidity of the rear, the morale of the army, the quantity and quality of divisions, weaponing, and the capability of the command staff—above 'transitory' aspects such as 'surprise attack'). The great and subsequently grotesque rationalization of early defeat was the myth of 'planned withdrawal', though this great exculpation of Stalin had yet to be formulated into a set of ritual phrases.

Stalin had also announced the transformation of the Red Army into a regular, professional force, a cadre army upon which was conferred all the outward signs of military professionalism—promotion, decoration and now badges of rank with the introduction of the shoulder-boards, the *pogon,* which in 1917 soldiers had torn off the shoulders of officers of the Imperial Russian Army. When new rank marks were being debated, Marshal Budenny reminded the officers discussing the problem of the revolutionary slogan *'Doloi zolotopogonnikov!'* ('Down with the golden shoulder-boards!'). The question of formal rank insignia (instead of the collar badges with their geometrical rhomboids and diamonds) came to the fore early in 1942, over the need to distinguish the Guards regiments and divisions: men in Guards units wore their distinctive sign, *Gvardiya*, and it was proposed to give them special Guards uniforms and the *pogon*. But to give shoulder-boards to elite formations and to ignore the rest meant, as a number of officers pointed out, 'making two armies'. Three times Stalin refused to take any binding decision although he was shown all the designs for uniforms and shoulder-boards for 'soldiers, sergeants, officers and generals'. Then in October 1942 Stalin decided—the *pogon* for each man in the Red Army. Front and formation commanders were all for the idea, to distinguish 'officers from men', and to increase 'the authority of the commanders'.

Early in October Zhukov and Vasilevskii were consulted by Stalin at the close of a *Stavka* session (dealing with the Stalingrad offensive) over the question of the *pogon*. Stalin told them that the State Defence Committee had decided to go ahead in the interests of 'strengthening discipline', in which the first step would be the elimination of 'dual command' and the institution of *edinonachalie*— duly enacted on 9 October—and then the formalization of ranks in the Soviet armed forces. Khrulev then showed Zhukov and Vasilevskii the proposed new uniforms and shoulder-boards. At the final meeting at the Kremlin, all those present voted in favour of the *pogon*—including Shchadenko, head of the Main Administration for Forming New Units, hitherto a bitter opponent of the *pogon* but who now raised both his hands in agreement, to the astonishment of the assembled officers. At the beginning of January Khrulev approached Stalin for a final decision on the *pogon*, much to Stalin's annoyance, who jumped at him for 'going on about it'; but in a few minutes Col.-Gen. Drachev, chief supply officer, was summoned to the Kremlin, where Stalin, Kalinin and Khrulev were looking at the designs. Kalinin was full of approval; Stalin joked about Khrulev's 'suggesting that we bring back the old regime'. On 6 January 1943 the Supreme Soviet issued its decree on the introduction of the *pogon*, which would be put up in the first half of February. (A special factory in Moscow had to run out the new emblems; a Soviet order to Britain for gold braid angered British officials, incensed at shipping what to them were mere fripperies. But this was no mere ornament, for it marked, physically and visibly, a major transition in the Red Army.)

The final, and irrevocable, transition to military orthodoxy meant more than gold braid. A few months later, on 24 July 1943, ranks from corporal to lieutenant-colonel were formalized, and if the *pogon* associated the Red Army with the traditions of the Imperial officer corps, the rehabilitation of what had been once one of the most hated words and which had endured as a rigid class taboo—'officer', *ofitser*—closed the circle completely. Side by side with the privileges, however, went the penalties; during the autumn of 1942 penal-battalions, the *strafbats* (with special officer penal-battalions) were introduced into the Red Army.

Discipline was screwed tighter and tighter; the commissars were militarized; the less the obligation to 'socialism', the greater the duty to sheer professionalism and strict military orthodoxy. At the same time, the party organs within the armed forces were restructured to compensate for the loss of direct influence: the battalion party organization became the fundamental unit of party activity (previously it had been at regimental level), with the object of bringing the widest range of 'officers, sergeants and men' into the circle of party influence. The Central Committee pronouncement of 24 May assigned to the battalion party organization the position of 'primary party organization'. There was also a defensive as well as a compensating aspect to this reorganization, for the officers were now inclined to press their military advantages to the full and already by February 1943 some of the previous army–party tension had begun to reassert itself. One of the chief targets of discontent within the military was the 'military soviet' system (with its separate representation for the political apparatus), which senior officers sought to displace.

Far-reaching though this face-lift was, the crucial change had come with the stabilization of the very highest level of the Soviet command, within the compass of Supreme Commander–Deputy Supreme Commander–*Stavka*. In August 1942 Zhukov had taken over as Stalin's 'deputy', a post formalized as Deputy to the Supreme Commander, and Vasilevskii had only just taken over the General Staff. Almost at once, Vasilevskii spent a great deal of time away from Moscow, involved as he was with the planning of the Stalingrad operations. This, in turn, threw an immense strain on the General Staff, in particular upon the head of the Operations Section, where there was a rapid turnover in officers. A.I. Bodin held this post in June–July 1942 (he was later killed on the Trans-Caucasus Front), then came A.N. Bogolyubov, V.D. Ivanov (who in January 1943 was severely wounded on the Voronezh Front), as well as P.G. Tikhomirov, P.P. Vechnyi, and Sh.N. Geniatulin. At one point even the commissar attached to the General Staff, Maj.-Gen. F.E. Bokov, took over the duties of chief, a post far beyond his capabilities for all his amiableness and his career as a party official. While at the front, Vasilevskii kept in contact with Front commanders through the General Staff signals units that followed him on his travels. At noon he reported to Stalin on developments which had taken place during the previous night, and at 21–2200 hours he reported on the day's events. Urgent matters were signalled at once. Vasilevskii's report was based on information received from Operations Section, where each officer responsible for a 'sector' or 'axis'—the *napravlentsy*—compiled the data. While out of Moscow, Vasilevskii confined his basic report to the operations he was presently 'co-ordinating', though he found it 'a rare day' when Stalin had no question about the other fronts or raised no query about the movement of reserves. The *Stavka* was a personal staff which served Stalin as Supreme Commander, and the General Staff in turn served the *Stavka* as an operational planning group. For this reason, the head of the Operations Section, as well as the other administrations of the General Staff (transport, signals, intelligence) and the Defence Commissariat, had a key role. The Chief of Operations and the heads of administrations kept their *nachalniki napravlenii*, specialists for given theatres and fronts, always on call; these officers assembled in what they called 'the dressing room', working or resting, ready to answer a summons from Stalin at a *Stavka* session in the Kremlin war-room. Either they supplied the requisite information to their chiefs or else they attended the *Stavka* session in person to present detailed situation reports.

The news in December 1942 that Lt.-Gen. A.I. Antonov, chief of staff to the Trans-Caucasus Front, was to become Chief of Operations raised a few sceptical eyebrows and prompted remarks that he would probably last as long as the others—after two or three 'journeys' to the *Stavka*, they were marched out for good on Stalin's orders, hence the rapid turnover in personnel. Forty-six years of age, Antonov had emerged from the pre-war staff courses generally recognized as a very talented staff officer. In June 1941 he was chief of staff in the Kiev military district, served as chief of staff to the Southern Front (August 1941) and then in the Caucasus. His reputation with Stalin and the senior officer 'permanent members' of the *Stavka* was already high when in December 1942 Vasilevskii recommended him as Chief of Operations with the General Staff. Unlike his predecessors, Antonov did not rush to put in an appearance at a *Stavka* session; he worked for a full week, familiarizing himself with the overall situation before presenting himself to a summons. The critics and sceptics, sure that it would be a case as before of 'a few visits and then—out', were confounded. The first encounters with the *Stavka* passed off very smoothly and Antonov quickly put an end to the vigils in the 'dressing room' where so many officers had previously kicked their heels.

So well did Antonov acquit himself that within a month Stalin despatched him as *Stavka* representative to the Voronezh Front, where he arrived on 10 January, first to assist Vasilevskii and second to prepare recommendations for the *Stavka* on future operations. None of this impinged in the slightest on Stalin's methods of command control, which demanded absolute obedience and ruthless punishment if caught in any infringement of 'the rules'. During the liquidation of the Stalingrad pocket, Voronov was not allowed to begin the second stage of his operations since Karpovka had to be taken first; in fact, Voronov had launched the second phase but Stalin demanded that Voronov report 'specially' on the capture of Karpovka. Earlier, during the critical Kotelnikovo fighting, Stalin had refused to accept Vasilevskii's recommendations about switching 2nd Guards Army from the inner encirclement. If Stalin was not better informed, he was at least now better advised; under Antonov's new regime he usually asked for 'the General Staff evaluation' while weighing the reports of the Front commanders. Antonov presented his materials for Stalin in three sets of files, red for urgent matters (draft directives and orders), blue for matters of lower priority, and finally the green (which needed careful choice about the moment to present them), covering promotions and appointments.

On the fronts, Stalin had two sets of representatives, those from the *Stavka* and his civilian supervisors who joined military soviets as the political member (in addition to the commander and the chief of staff). For critically important operations, the top officers were on hand as *Stavka* representatives, either to supervise preparation or 'co-ordinate' execution (or both). Marshal Zhukov had supervised the preparations for the Voronezh Front attack on the middle Don, after which he moved to the north-west even though Marshal Voroshilov had been sent to the Leningrad area by Stalin as *Stavka* representative. Marshal Timoshenko had also taken over the North-Western Front but this did not preclude the 'co-ordination' of Marshals Zhukov and Voronov. Vasilevskii, joined by Antonov, remained with the Voronezh and Bryansk Fronts as the focus of attention shifted from the south itself into the northern Ukraine. From the *Politburo* or the State Defence Committee (*GKO*) Stalin also sent out his representatives; Malenkov of the *GKO* had already held a watching brief at Stalingrad during the critical days of the defence. Mekhlis, reduced since May 1942 in rank to corps commissar (lieutenant-general), returned to the front as a member of the Volkov Front military soviet; Lt.-Gen. Bulganin joined the military soviet of the Bryansk Front, and Zhdanov (a lieutenant-general at the beginning of 1943 but well ahead in the prestige race as a colonel-general by the end of it) formally sat on Govorov's Leningrad Front military soviet as the third member. Lt.-Gen. Khrushchev soldiered on as the political member of the Southern Front.

Victory at Stalingrad was immediately and perceptibly decisive in terms of the survivability of the Soviet Union. Hitler had proclaimed that 'a decision' was mandatory on the Eastern Front in 1942 and he had invited his allies to join in this 'crushing blow'. But the blow was spent and still the decision eluded him— for ever, as it transpired. Militarily, the results of the Russian triumph were impressive in scale—the amputation of a crack army from the *Wehrmacht*, the destruction of a whole segment of the *Ostheer*, the damage inflicted on the *Luftwaffe*, and the annihilation of large bodies of Axis satellite troops, Italians, Hungarians and Rumanians (who had not always served Germany so badly)— though not with such catastrophic short-term effect upon German arms as the Soviet command tended to believe. Politically, Stalingrad was a victory full of long-term potency, a slow-burning fuse which worked its way through the subsequent history of the war both on the Eastern Front and at large. If the battle of Poltava in 1709 turned Russia into a European power, then Stalingrad set the Soviet Union on the road to being a world power. In Germany, Stalingrad wrought immense psychological havoc as a harbinger of defeat. Mussolini quaked immediately. In 1943, Germany presented Japan with a plain *démarche* at the transfer of Soviet troops to the European theatre without any hint of Japanese 'threat', still less an aggressive move. Turkey had now to reckon on the Soviet Union as a potential victor.

In one of the most nightmarish battles of modern war, its duration matched by its ferocity, the Red Army had ground down a crack German army to unparalleled defeat. It was now Stalin's turn to capitalize upon disaster, to seek decisive strategic success. Exuberance there was certainly over Stalingrad, in abundance and at all levels—German intelligence reports underlined the movement of *kampflustig* Soviet formations to the front—but the Soviet command did not as yet draw definite distinctions between confidence, overconfidence and miscalculation. At the end of January, vastly overrating the present capabilities of the Red Army and seriously underestimating the ability of the *Wehrmacht* to recover itself, Stalin prepared for the transition to a massive, multi-front counter-offensive aimed along three strategic axes: south-western, western and north-western. One year ago, in the winter battles of early 1942, he had tried a simultaneous assault on all three German army groups only to fail. Now he was about to repeat the strategy and, with it, the blunder (as costly as ever to the Red Army) of failing to concentrate decisively on clearly prescribed objectives—either the destruction of enemy forces in the field or the recapture of territory (with vital fuel supplies, sources of power and raw materials). Stalin wanted both. Therefore the 'main blow', the *glavnyi udar,* would unroll in staggered offensives across the entire face of the Eastern Front.

2

The Duel in the South:
February–March 1943

With the German line from Voronezh to the foothills of the Caucasus ripped apart, and confident that the strategic initiative rested with the Red Army, the Soviet command planned to entomb an estimated seventy-five German divisions in the Ukraine. The *Stavka* assigned the liberation of the second greatest political unit in the USSR after the Russian Federal Republic (RSFSR) itself, the Ukraine, to three fronts, the Voronezh, South-Western and Southern. The Voronezh Front would seize north-eastern Ukraine, including Kharkov, its left-flank armies (40th, 69th and 3rd Tank) aimed at Kharkov itself, the right flank (60th and 38th Armies) pointed at Kursk and Oboyan respectively; the final objective was the line running from Rylsk to Lebedin to Poltava. The eastern Ukraine including the Donbas would be liberated by the South-Western and Southern Fronts. Vatutin's South-Western command would play the principal part, using 6th and 1st Guards Armies with 'mobile groups' to strike out from Starobelsk through Slavyansk and on to Mariupol, outflanking German forces in the Donbas from the west and pinning them to the sea of Azov, while the Southern Front would advance westwards along the coast also in the direction of Mariupol. Next would come the turn of Army Group Centre, whose destruction was also planned at the end of January as five more Soviet fronts were alerted for large-scale offensive operations. The basic idea was to use the Bryansk Front and the left wing of the Western Front to destroy Second *Panzer* Army in the Orel area. Once the Central Front (formed out of Rokossovskii's divisions pulled away from Stalingrad) attacked, fresh Soviet armies, stiffened with new reserve formations, would drive through Bryansk and on to Smolensk to break into the German rear, whereupon the Kalinin and Western Fronts would first encircle and then destroy the main forces of Army Group Centre. Meanwhile to the north the armies of the North-Western Front would wipe out German troops in the Demyansk area and ensure the passage of powerful mobile formations into the rear of German troops operating against the Leningrad and Volkhov Fronts. At the beginning of February 1943 the Front commanders were already in possession of the main outlines of this plan and their orders instructed them to begin operational preparations.

Operations in the south were conceived as pursuit, designed to bring the armies of the Voronezh, South-Western and Southern Fronts to the Dnieper on a front reaching from Chernigov to Kherson by the time the spring thaw came. The *Stavka* directive of 6 February 1943 set the strategic objective of the Voronezh Front as the line Lgov–Glukhov–Chernigov (right wing) and Poltava–Kremenchug (left wing): this instructed Vatutin 'to prevent an enemy withdrawal on Dnepropetrovsk and Zaporozhe' and at the same time to 'drive the Donets group of enemy forces into the Crimea, seal off the approaches at Perekop and the Sivash, and thus isolate the [enemy] Donets forces from the remainder of enemy forces in the Ukraine'. After the Donbas had been cleared, the South-Western Front would make for the Dnieper on a front running from Kremenchug to Nikopol, while Southern Front forces would invest the lower reaches of the river. Southwards, the 'Rostov gap', which the Germans were fighting fiercely to hold open, was slowly but surely closing. First *Panzer* Army was nevertheless well within sight of safety and coming under Don Army Group, while Army Group A fell back on the Kuban and into the Taman peninsula, all of 400,000 (with the two *Panzer* divisions, 50th and 13th, deflected in this direction) isolated from the main course of operations, though presenting some threat to the Soviet rear and also securing the defence of the Crimea. For these reasons, the Soviet command at the end of January prepared to assault Novorossiisk and to attack Krasnodar, operations timed to begin very early in February.

Vatutin's South-Western command and Golikov's Voronezh Front forces opened their major offensive operations within days of each other; Vatutin opened on 29 January, Golikov on 2 February 1943. The South-Western Front, embarked on the Donbas operations and a deep outflanking of Army Group Don from the west, comprised four armies (north to south: 6th, 1st Guards, 3rd Guards, 5th Tank), one air army (17th, with some 300 aircraft), a 'Front mobile group' under Lt.-Gen. M.M. Popov (four tank corps, three rifle divisions, two independent tank brigades and ski units, a total tank strength of 137 machines)—twenty-nine rifle divisions, six tanks, one mechanized and one cavalry corps, three independent tank brigades. On the morning of 29 January Kharitonov's 6th Army jumped off north-west of Starobelsk aiming for Balakleya: the next day Lelyushenko's 1st Guards struck from the south-west in the direction of Krasnyi Liman, and within a few hours Popov's mobile formations were introduced between 1st Guards and 6th Armies, to drive south-westwards on an outward sweep aimed at Krasnoarmiesk–Volnovakha–Mariupol to slice the German escape route from the Donbas. V.I. Kuznetsov's 3rd Guards Army on 2 February was over the Donets east of Voroshilovgrad. On that day also, in the great hole in the German line that gaped between Voronezh and Voroshilovgrad, at 0600 hours Golikov's left-flank armies (40th, 69th and 3rd Tank Armies) attacked in the first phase of Operation *Zvezda* aimed at Kursk–Belgorod–Kharkov. 40th Army would attack in the general direction of Belgorod–Kharkov, outflanking Kharkov from the north-west, 69th was to strike directly at the city through

Volchansk and 3rd Tank (on whose left was Kharitonov's 6th Army) would outflank Kharkov from the south-west. One new army had been raised on this front, on the basis of the 18th Independent Rifle Corps; the new formation, 69th Army, was assigned to M.I. Kazakov, with Maj.-Gen. Zykov (18th Corps commander) as his deputy. Like all the Soviet units, it was feeling the effect of the previous month's strain, the troops far from fresh, with ranks depleted by 'significant losses' and with ammunition and supplies running low.

As Golikov's left wing and centre attacked on the Staryi Oskol–Valyuiki sector towards Kharkov, Maj.-Gen. I.D. Chernyakhovskii's 60th Army on the left drove along the Kastornoe–Kursk railway line with Kursk as its objective. Chernyakhovskii had divided his army into two assault formations, one with two rifle divisions and a tank brigade to outflank Kursk from the north, the other with a single rifle division to outflank from the south. Moskalenko's 40th Army was under orders to be ready by 1 February to attack Belgorod and to drive on Kharkov, but by the morning of 3 Feburary only elements of the first echelon were at their start lines; the remaining units and formations, including the 4th Tank Corps, were still regrouping. Chernyakhovskii was well on the way to Kursk by 5 February. At 0900 hours on the morning of 3 February Moskalenko had committed the divisions he had assembled, but Kravchenko's 4th Tank Corps was tangled up with encircled German units on the line of its movement, and was even further slowed as tanks ran out of fuel and ammunition. On the left, where Golikov had concentrated the main weight of his attack, and where Vasilevskii was supervising the co-ordination of the offensive against Kharkov, Rybalko's lead tanks had reached the northern Donets by 4 February, though the presence of the *SS Panzer* division *Adolf Hitler* ruled out a crossing straight off the march. Rybalko would have to force a crossing in the Pechengi–Chuguev sector, with the high western bank firmly in German hands. Frontal attacks merely brought heavy losses in men and tanks, as well as fruitless expenditure of the limited quantities of ammunition. Not until 10 February did Rybalko manage to smash the resistance on his centre when Maj.-Gen. Kopstov's 15th Tank Corps and Maj.-Gen. Zenkovich's 12th Tank Corps took Pechengi and Chuguev, though a serious threat to Kharkov had already developed with Soviet outflanking movements to the north-east and south-west. Moskalenko's 40th Army reached Belgorod on the ninth, when Kazakov's 69th was through Volchansk; they then stormed across the ice of the northern Donets and within twenty-four hours were on the inner defensive line covering Kharkov, while away to the south-west the cavalry formations on Rybalko's flank had swung through Andreyevka and were approaching Merefa.

Kharkov was a major prize, the second city of the Ukraine and the fourth largest in the Soviet Union, and Soviet troops were closing in on it at speed, putting the *SS Panzer* Corps and *Armee-Abteilung Lanz* at risk and bringing an even greater threat in their wake, tearing this time another great gap in the German 'line' between the southern formations and Army Group Centre. By noon on 15 February, Soviet units closed on Kharkov from three sides, west, north and south-east. That night they were fighting inside the city. The *SS Panzer* Corps, right in the face of Lanz's veto, pulled out of Kharkov and the danger of immediate encirclement, and on 16 February Kharkov was in Soviet hands, with a 100-mile breach torn open between what had been Army Groups B and Don (the latter redesignated Army Group South, taking over from the liquidated Army Group B and thus becoming immediate neighbour to Army Group Centre).

Throughout the first half of February, Vatutin had been steadily widening the scope of the operations of his right wing, moving across the Lisichansk–Slavyansk line and fanning out west and south, aiming at the Dnieper crossings. In two weeks, striking from the Starobelsk area, the right-flank formations—6th Army, 1st Guards and Popov's armour (fourteen rifle divisions, two rifle brigades, four tank corps and three tank brigades)—were approaching Dnepropetrovsk and the Krasnoarmeisk area. The left wing (3rd Guards and 5th Tank Army) was fighting west of Voroshilovgrad (along the Nizhne Gorskoe–Astakhovo sector). To the south the Southern Front had finally closed the 'Rostov gap' by taking Rostov-on-Don and was now pursuing *Armee-Abteilung Hollidt* as it fell back on the river Mius line. On the Soviet order-of-battle maps, the bulk of the 18 divisions of Army Group Don were identified on a line running from Slavyansk to Taganrog (that is, committed against Vatutin's left flank and against Southern Front), but from Zmiev (south of Kharkov) to Slavyansk there gaped a mighty, 200-mile hole between *Abteilung Lanz* and First *Panzer* Army, with only the thinnest screen to hold it.

The prospect of amputating the German southern wing by closing off the Dnieper crossings looked dazzling. Northwards, at Kharkov, Golikov on 17 February issued formal orders for an advance on Poltava with Rybalko's 3rd Tank Army in the lead. The General Staff had put Golikov 'in the picture' about developments with his 'left neighbour' (Vatutin) whose objective was now Dnepropetrovsk and asked Golikov what aid he could render. Golikov replied that the Voronezh Front would contribute support by striking at Poltava and Kremenchug with all speed. As for Vatutin, he decided to pile on the power of his offensive through 6th Army which would go first for Zaporozhe and then for Melitopol. Kharitonov's 6th Army at this time consisted of two rifle corps (15th and 4th Guards), to which was attached a 'mobile group' formed up at Lozovaya out of two tank corps (1st Guards and 25th Corps) with one cavalry corps (1st Guards Cavalry)—in all, 150 tanks. Popov's 'Front mobile group' with its four corps (4th Guards, 18th, 3rd and 10th Tank Corps) was now down to 13,000 men and 53 tanks fit for battle. Half the entire tank strength of the South-Western Front was out of action owing to battle damage or loss, and the tank units of Front reserve had exactly 267 operational machines between them. Now Popov's 'mobile group', which had just lost almost 90 tanks in two days, was to attack in two directions—first towards Stalino and then on to Mariupol. Kuznetsov's 1st Guards would meanwhile transfer part of its strength

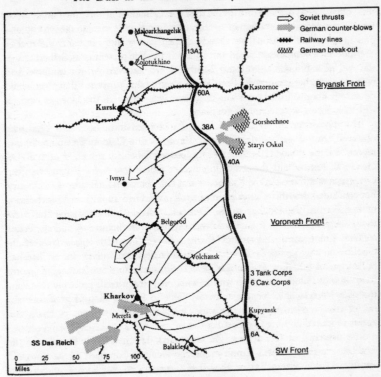

Map 3 The Soviet drive on Kharkov, February 1943

to Kharitonov and Popov, holding the Slavyansk–Nizhne Gorskoe line with the remaining divisions; 3rd Guards and 5th Tank Army would press forwards to the west on Stalino, which troops of the Southern Front would also attack from the south-east. The race against time, against the weather, against depleted strength and stiffening German resistance was on, a furious fling to sew up the Donbas bag and to tie it off on the Dnieper.

Vatutin had decided on this 'broadening' of his offensive on 12 February. Golikov had also set his sights on the Dnieper, even though his senior commanders, their divisions down to 1,000 men, a handful of guns and perhaps 50 mortars, pleaded for a pause. Both the Voronezh and the South-Western Fronts had done some prodigious fighting and covered great stretches of ground, following nothing less than a train of destruction as retreating German units blew up bridges, buildings and airfields, tangled railway lines and damaged the few roads as much as possible. Both Vatutin and Golikov, however, embarked on an expansion of their offensives as a result of three factors: overestimation of their own capabilities, wholly erroneous interpretation of the intelligence of German movement and *Stavka* approval. Vatutin had already dipped deeply into his reserves. Golikov overrode his commanders when they pointed to their present drastic shortages—the two tank brigades (88th and 113th) of 3rd Tank Army, for example, had only six tanks between them. Both Front commanders supposed that they would be mainly conducting the pursuit of a retreating enemy to the Dnieper, and for this their forces were certainly adequate.

The movement of German tanks and motorized formations had been duly observed, but it gave little cause for alarm. South-Western Front intelligence reports for the period 10–26 February, countersigned by the chief of staff Lt.-Gen. S.P. Ivanov and the senior intelligence officer Maj.-Gen. Rogov, recorded German concentration in the Krasnodar and Krasnoarmeisk area after 17 February, but concluded that this was an attempt to clear the German lines for 'a withdrawal of troops from the Donbas to the Dnieper'. Vatutin himself shared this view, though when he used it to justify further extensions of offensive operations, Popov (deputy Front commander) and Kuznetsov (1st Guards) objected forcefully. Golikov on the Voronezh Front was similarly beguiled; enemy forces that had pulled out of Kharkov and which were also concentrated at Krasnograd, to the south-east of Poltava, must be withdrawing on Poltava itself, probably to defend the river Vorskla line. No major enemy force in Poltava showed itself, nor any rail or road movement from the west. Intelligence reports from partisans and agents produced nothing to contradict this picture. On 21 February, Stalin ordered the deputy chief of Operations (General Staff), Lt.-Gen. A.N. Bogolyubov, to establish exactly what was happening in the Donbas. The staffs of the Voronezh and the South-Western Fronts, as well as General Staff Intelligence, all presently shared the same view (because they shared the same information) that German troops were pulling back to the Dnieper. From Maj.-Gen. Varennikov, chief of staff to the Southern Front, Bogolyubov learned that, 'according to precise information, yesterday [20 February] solid enemy columns were pulling out of the Donbas'.

All three Soviet fronts had substantial intelligence of German movement. On the afternoon of 19 February and at dawn on 20 February Soviet reconnaissance planes reported large concentrations of German armour in the Krasnograd area, troop movements on Dnepropetrovsk and what looked like armour regrouping to the south-east of Krasnoarmeisk. These concentrations—lying slap across the path of Vatutin's right wing—were immediately interpreted at Front HQs as German tank cover for the withdrawal of the main body of German forces from Donbas. At 1600 hours on 20 February, Lt.-Gen. S.P. Ivanov, Vatutin's chief of staff, signed an operational appreciation which affirmed that German armoured movements—the tank columns of divisions from XLVIII *Panzer* Corps observed by Soviet reconnaissance planes on the 70-mile sector between Pokrovskoe and Stalino—were proof positive of *continued withdrawal* from the Donbas on

Zaporozhe. The wish was father to the thought. For this reason, Kharitonov's orders to advance remained unchanged on 20 February, while the day before Vatutin had expressly ordered Popov and his 'Front mobile group' to press on with all speed, though Popov's tank strength was dwindling daily and he had little in the way of supplies.

The German tank columns were certainly moving, but not to cover any withdrawal. Plans for a German counter-stroke had been finalized on 19 February and the *Panzer* divisions were deploying for attack, timed for the following day. The crisis was clearly of the first magnitude as Soviet formations appeared to be hacking the German southern wing to pieces; but now Manstein's counter-stroke proposed to chop off the Soviet advance to the Dnieper crossings, to restore the situation between the Dnieper and the Donets, and then—depending on circumstances—to deal with the situation at Kharkov. Manstein had already moved HQ Fourth *Panzer* Army on to Dnepropetrovsk, thereby 'centring' the gap between *Armee-Abteilung Kempf* (formerly under Lanz) and First *Panzer* ; Fourth *Panzer* was split into two assault groups, one near Krasnograd formed out of the SS *Panzer* Corps, the other from two divisions of XLVIII *Panzer* Corps west of Krasnoarmeisk, with First *Panzer* concentrating 40th Corps to the south. Meanwhile the Mius river line, which had already been pierced in three places, had to be held as tenaciously as possible.

On the morning of 20 February, Manstein's armoured shears went into action. From Krasnograd, SS *Panzer* troops struck at the right flank of Kharitonov's 6th Army, while XL *Panzer* Corps attacked northwards to hit Popov's 'mobile group'. This 'mobile group', which Vatutin had ordered to be attached to Kharitonov's 6th Army, was still concentrating when it was hit by German bombers in the Pavlograd area. Popov found himself in dire straits when the *Panzer* corps jumped him; the three tank corps of the 'Front mobile group' could muster only twenty-five tanks between them. During the night of 21 February Popov urgently requested permission from Vatutin to pull back to the north of Krasnoarmeisk, to a line some twenty miles away—a decision Vatutin refused to countenance as being 'counter to the assignments given to the [mobile] group and to the situation as it stands, when the enemy is doing everything he can to speed the withdrawal of his forces from the Donbas to the Dnieper'. Vatutin categorically forbade withdrawal and insisted upon the fulfilment of the 'offensive assignment' to cut enemy escape routes to the west. Kharitonov, with SS divisions biting into his right flank, was scarcely better off, but his orders were to force the river Dnieper some fifteen miles north-west of Dneprodzerzhinsk during the night of 21–22 February, to take both this town and Dnepropetrovsk and to hold a bridgehead; at the same time, mobile formations were to go for Zaporozhe and to prepare to strike down to Melitopol. During the night of 21 February these orders were again confirmed in an exchange between Kharitonov and Vatutin. Kharitonov duly attempted to carry out his orders but his lead divisions only plunged on to their doom. A division of 25th Tank Corps pushed on to Zaporozhe, only to lie stranded for lack of fuel within ten miles of the town, while the main force of 25th Corps was itself stranded fifty miles from the body of 6th Army and running desperately short on fuel and ammunition, even as XLVIII *Panzer* Corps, moving on Pavlograd from the east, was slicing through its slender line of communication.

The implications of the situation failed to impress themselves on the higher Soviet command. Vatutin literally hurled his troops forward in one final offensive thrust, though they were fast running out of power and were speeding into acute danger. On 21 February Bogolyubov at the General Staff ordered Malinovskii on the Southern Front to get a move on—'Vatutin's troops are speeding on at extraordinary pace: his right flank is beyond Pavlograd and the hold-up on his left is due to the absence of active operations on the part of your Front'—though 3rd Guards Mechanized Corps had broken over the Mius only to find itself in a grievous position at Matveyev Kurgan, and were finally encircled. When 48th *Panzer* Corps joined battle on 22 February, attacking from the region some twenty-five miles west of Krasnoarmeisk in the direction of Pavlograd, the crisis on Vatutin's right wing had become dangerous. Some of Kharitonov's units, like 106th Rifle Brigade and 267th Rifle Division, were already fighting in encirclement. Four of Kharitonov's corps were enmeshed in this trap; 1st Guards Tank and 4th Guards Rifle Corps were pulling back eastwards, and 25th Tank Corps was splayed out along the road to Zaporozhe. Popov with his mobile group was fighting to hold off XL *Panzer* Corps and was falling back northwestwards, the remnants of the 'Front mobile group' struggling now to bar the way to Barvenkovo.

On his own initiative Golikov during the night of 21 February ordered Kazakov's 69th and Rybalko's 3rd Tank Army, presently engaged on their own westerly drive to the Dnieper, to prepare a turn to the south to bring them into the flank of the German *Panzer* formations operating against Kharitonov south of Kharkov; Kazakov's 69th Army would attack from south of Bogodukhova towards Krasnograd, which Rybalko would also aim for by attacking through the area west of Merefa. The divisions of both Soviet armies duly turned south, moving on parallel tracks but only very slowly, the infantry without any armoured support, short of ammunition and stiffened, not with trained soldiers, but with local conscripts—raw recruits still in their peasant gear. Within forty-eight hours, as Kazakov and Rylbalko rolled into the regiments of SS *Gross Deutschland*, the Soviet counter-thrust came to a halt, and Golikov issued orders for a renewal of the westerly thrust, which now caused Manstein little concern since he had already stopped the most dangerous Soviet drive. During the night of 23–24 February, Vatutin's report to the *Stavka* admitted that a serious situation had developed on his right flank—three German division with 400 tanks were loose in attacks on Pavlograd and from the Krasnograd area, where the German objective seemed to be Lozovaya. Nevertheless, Vatutin still mentioned 'the withdrawal in columns of the Donbas group of enemy forces' on the central sector of the front. The front had already been committed in building up assault formations for the final phase of the offensive, but now, entirely lacking general reserves of anti-tank forces, Vatutin was obliged to order Kuznetsov of 1st Guards to move 6th Guards Rifle Corps from Slavyansk to the Barvenkovo–Lozovaya sector in order to bar the German advance.

With each successive day the outlook worsened. On 24 February several units of Kharitonov's 6th Army were fighting in encirclement but only 25th Tank Corps—largely immobilized for lack of fuel—received orders to pull back northwards. Popov's Front group was falling back on Barvenkovo, joining two divisions of 6th Guards Rifle Corps (1st Guards Army) holding the Lozovaya–Slavyansk line; Popov's 'mobile group', even with its recent reinforcement, was a shadow of its former self—a mere 35 T-34s and 15 T-70 light tanks. All hope for the offensive had long gone, but only on 25 February did Vatutin order his right flank over to the defensive and submit a report to the *Stavka* that revealed the true state of affairs. The need for reinforcement consequent upon heavy losses made confession to the *Stavka* imperative and unavoidable. In particular, the tank forces urgently needed increased repair facilities; all Front repair units were up with the tank corps, so that the armour in the rear went completely untended, partly because the two mobile tank repair workshops promised to the Front had not arrived.

At Barvenkovo, a motley assortment of Soviet units, the wreckage of the right flank, tried to halt XL *Panzer* Corps striking north-westwards to the northern Donets; the remnants of Popov's group and a severely weakened 1st Guards Army—13th Guards Tank Brigade and 4th Guards Tank Corps (with fifty tanks between them, most stuck fast for lack of fuel), the remnants of 10th and 18th Tank Corps, two brigades of 3rd Tank Corps, units of three rifle divisions and a couple of ski battalions—held on until the afternoon of 28 February, when German tanks broke through to the Donets. That same evening the *Stavka* detached Rybalko's 3rd Tank Army from Golikov's left wing and subordinated it to Vatutin for a counter-attack aimed at the German armour ripping into 6th Army. It was a plan that miscarried and misfired almost from the start. German bombers and tanks caught Rybalko as he tried to form up for the attack, inflicting heavy damage on the already weakened 3rd Tank. By the evening of 2 March the attack formations were themselves encircled, only 6th Guards Cavalry Corps managing to break out, though at the cost of heavy losses. With only about fifty tanks left, Rybalko's tank army was itself almost wholly encircled by 4 March. They tried desperately to break out towards the south-west of Kharkov, but in falling back 3rd Tank was uncovering the flank of 69th Army. All this time 6th Army and 1st Guards Army, continually battered by German attacks, fell back on the Donets between Andreyevka (north-west of Izyum) and Krasnyi Liman (to the south-east), the frozen river allowing Soviet units to slip back into comparative safety even if the tally of losses was high—6th Army severely mauled, 1st Guards seriously weakened, four tank corps practically obliterated (25th, 3rd,

10th and 4th Guards) and several armoured brigades and rifle formations badly damaged in manpower and equipment.

The second phase of the German counter-stroke, the northerly drive into Golikov's left flank and on to Kharkov, was now proceeding at full speed, racing the Russians and the thaw. On 7 March Fourth *Panzer* attacked northwards from the Krasnograd area and by 8–9 March it had driven a twenty-mile gap between 69th and 3rd Tank Army, whose rifle divisions fought fiercely to hold off the German advance. Attached to Rybalko's army was the 1st Czechoslovak Independent Battalion, 979 men strong, raised in February 1942 at Buzuluk in Orenburg *oblast* and under the command of Ludvik Svoboda. Svoboda's men slid into position south-west of Kharkov between the Soviet 62nd and 25th Guards Rifle Divisions. *SS Totenkopf* and *Adolf Hitler,* out to avenge their earlier defeat at Kharkov, aimed to batter their way into the city from the south, the direct route. West of Kharkov, however, on to Akhtyrka and Poltava—the road to Kiev—lay Soviet divisions over-extended in their offensive, divisions Manstein hoped to trap, though on 2 March Golikov had already reined them in to draw them back eastwards. By 10 March German units were in the northern suburbs of Kharkov, the *SS Panzer* Corps had been swung to the east of the city, straddling the escape route to the Donets. The capture of Rogan on 12 March effectively cut off 3rd Tank, while *Gross Deutschland* units, moving through the thirty-mile breach between 69th and 3rd Tank Armies, raced north-eastwards for Belgorod, thereby putting Kursk at risk and creating the danger of a German breakthrough into the rear of the Central Front, or the encirclement of Soviet troops west of Kursk in the event of German forces in the Orel area also striking out.

The German drive on Belgorod made the reinforcement of the Voronezh Front a very urgent matter. Rokossovskii on the Central Front was ordered 'not later than March 13th' to move 21st Army south of Kursk; 64th Army was ordered to move from the Stalingrad area and Katukov's 1st Tank Army received orders to block the German thrust. For the moment, Kazakov's 69th had to hold off the SS troops who threatened to split 69th Army from Moskalenko's 40th. Not that Kazakov could do much with divisions ground down to less than 1,000 men each and one (340th Rifle) with only 275 men left; 69th had no tanks and less than 100 guns. To hold the junction between 69th and 40th, Golikov brought up two tank corps, 3rd and 2nd Guards, the latter with more than 170 tanks moving into 69th's areas. Under cover of darkness, Kazakov's men quit Belgorod on 18 March, but to Kazakov's disgust the command of 2nd Guards did not seize their chance to attack the SS tank units in the flank; HQ 2nd Guards remained on the eastern bank of the Donets directing their brigades by radio but failing to follow up their chance. With 69th back over the Donets, 21st Army moved to the north of Belgorod, 1st Tank concentrated at Oboyan, and 64th Army moved on to the line of the Donets; thus Kursk was secured from the south (to form the southern face of the 'Kursk salient'). Within a week, the line stabilized on the Donets from Belgorod to Chuguev, and on the South-Western Front further down the Donets to the Mius.

The race for the survival or the destruction of the entire southern group of German armies had been run terribly close. From Manstein's point of view, the Soviet thrusts to the Dnieper crossings were chopped off in the nick of time, for with these crossings in Soviet hands his whole army group would have died swiftly enough from fuel starvation. From the Soviet side, to attempt to clear the Donbas and to force the Dnieper with formations already worn with heavy fighting was a high risk turned into a brush with calamity when reconnaissance reports were so persistently misinterpreted after mid-February; Golikov and Vatutin pounded west and south-west without pause. Late in February, even with the German attacks on Kharitonov and Popov, Golikov signalled to Kazakov of the 69th: 'There are 200–230 miles to the Dnieper, and to the spring *rasputitsa* [mud] there are 30–35 days. Draw your own conclusions and make your own reckoning from this.' Kazakov drew the same conclusion as ever, that there should have been a pause in operations after the capture of Kharkov. Even more fundamental was the redeployment of the Soviet troops liberated for fresh action once the German forces in Stalingrad had been eliminated; Rokossovskii's Don Front forces were to be transported north-west of Voronezh to form the basis of the Central Front (interposed between the Voronezh and Bryansk Fronts), while the insertion of this strength between Golikov's and Vatutin's fronts would have poured enormous power into the Soviet drive for the Dnieper, an operation borne largely by Vatutin's right-flank strength.

In terms of the map, the Germans had regained the Donets–Mius line by March 1943 but the situation had undergone a major, if not a profound transformation. Five armies, four German-allied and one the formidable Sixth, had been swept clean off the German order-of-battle map. The wound was very deep. As Kazakov, Rybalko, Kharitonov, Popov and Kuznetsov finally fought their way through the German attacks in late March, the front stabilized itself on the Donets and the Mius, over which Soviet troops held a few bridgeheads and, in Golikov's area, the southern face of what finally became the Kursk salient. Here the armies were held fast in the mud of the spring thaw.

'The real struggle is only beginning. . . .': with this cautionary phrase Stalin in his 23 February Red Army Day order introduced a note of reservation into otherwise effusive praise for the Soviet winter offensive, which—on Stalin's tally— had inflicted almost a million casualties on German and German-allied troops and brought staggering losses in equipment. The Red Army was now a cadre formation, its troops skilled and experienced in battle, its commanders masters of 'modern operating art'. The *Wehrmacht,* torn by the terrible battles of the Eastern Front, had lost much of its pristine 1941 quality, though it was by no means finished. Much as the enemy had been battered, however, his grip on

Soviet territory would have to be prised open, for the German armies would not relinquish their gains without a struggle.

Nevertheless, with Soviet armies striking westwards and penetrating for more than 150 miles, the 'mass expulsion of the enemy'—*izgnanie vraga*—had now definitely begun. From the rear, Soviet factories were now pumping equipment and ammunition to the field armies in vast quantities. But of Allied aid—or Allied achievement in the Western Desert and North Africa—there was not a word. On the contrary, Stalin threw out the blunt statement that the Soviet Union alone carried the weight of the war-waging. Not all of this was the mere flush of victory at Stalingrad. In December 1942 Stalin had again returned to the question of the Second Front, which he now pressed to be opened in 'the spring of 1943'. The decisions of the Casablanca conference, communicated to Stalin on 26 January 1943, certainly did not come within his specification of a 'second front in Europe', which meant unambiguously a full-scale sea-borne invasion launched across the Channel against northern France. All that Stalin got in this 26 January signal by way of commitment was that powerful forces, already being assembled, would 're-enter the continent of Europe as soon as practicable'. In his own message of 30 January to the British Prime Minister and the American President, Stalin now asked for information on 'the concrete operations planned and of their timing', announcing at the same time that the Soviet armed forces would 'finish our winter campaign, circumstances permitting, in the first half of February'—though orders had just gone out for a massive activation of the Soviet offensive as from the middle of the month. On 9 February, Winston Churchill sent Stalin an answer about 'the concrete operations'—eastern Tunisia, Sicily, further operations in the eastern Mediterranean and preparations 'for a cross-Channel operation in August'. Stalin's reply a week later (16 February), though smoothly phrased, had a ring of reproof and a sting of complaint about it—'for some reason' Anglo-American operations in Tunisia were 'suspended' at the end of December, since when twenty-seven German divisions (five of them armoured) had been moved on to the Eastern Front; 'in other words, instead of the Soviet Union being aided . . . what we get is relief for Hitler, who, because of the slackening in Anglo-American operations in Tunisia, was able to move additional troops against the Russians.' And that signal Stalin could end with a flourish, with the announcement of a considerable Russian triumph: 'This morning our troops have taken Kharkov.'

For all of Stalin's disclaimers about continuing the offensive, five Soviet fronts—the North-Western, Kalinin, Western, Bryansk and Central—were about to embark on a huge new round of operations, for which the directives were being prepared and orders issued even as Stalin phrased his message. The objectives were hugely ambitious in what was essentially a repetition of the 1942 offensive pattern: the destruction of Second *Panzer* Army in the Orel area; the encirclement of Army Group Centre; the destruction of German troops at Demyansk; and the introduction of a powerful mobile force into the rear of Army Group North.

While the Voronezh Front struck south-westwards to Kursk and Kharkov and the Bryansk Front towards Orel, the gap between the flanks of the two fronts would be sealed by the deployment of the Central Front under Rokossovskii, who immediately after the German capitulation at Stalingrad had flown to Moscow to receive instructions about the movement and operations of the new front. The Central Front, organized on the basis of the old Don Front, would include the 21st, 65th Army and 16th Air Army (Don Front formations) plus 70th Army and 2nd Tank Army from the *Stavka* reserve. Lt.-Gen. A.G. Rodin's 2nd Tank Army was brand new; established by *Stavka* orders of 15 January 1943, it comprised two tank corps (16th under Maj.-Gen. Pavelkin and 11th under Maj.-Gen. Lazarev) with supporting units. Rokossovskii's troops were to be ready to attack on 15 February, to carry out their deep outflanking operations against Second *Panzer* in the direction of Gomel–Smolensk; but the ten days or so allotted for moving up all the formations proved to be woefully inadequate, with only one road and one railway line in service. The shortage of lorries and horses meant that Soviet infantrymen carried their heavy machine-guns, anti-tank weapons and even mortars on their own backs, while more often than not ammunition was shifted from village to village by the porterage of the local civilians. Guns and men went their separate ways; tractors and gun-tows were separated from the guns, and in the Stalingrad area more than 150 supply or rear service units waited for trains which came only slowly, and which could move only as far as Shchigry in the Front area. Rodin's 2nd Tank had a 150-mile approach march ahead of it before reaching its deployment area at Fatezh; to keep control over the movement of the columns driving on through snow drifts and blizzards, Rodin organized an aerial watch with the small U-2 planes and directed the progress of his tanks in this fashion himself. By the evening of 12 February the lead tanks were moving out to the Front area, but not until 24 February were 65th Army, 2nd Tank Army and 2nd Guards Cavalry Corps fully concentrated; 21st and 70th Armies were even then still on the move.

Reiter's Bryansk Front had already jumped off on 12 February with 13th and 48th Armies, left-wing formations seeking to outflank Orel from the south and south-east. After twelve days of difficult fighting, these two armies had penetrated some fifteen miles to reach the line Novosil–Maloarkhangelsk–Rozhdestvennoe, thereby turning the offensive front in a northerly direction, by which time also Bagramyan's 16th Army from the Western Front under the command of Col.-Gen. Sokolovskii had already begun its attacks from the north. This northerly attack in the Orel–Bryansk operation by Bagramyan's units made precious little progress after breaking through the first German defence line; all too soon 16th Army, having advanced some seven miles, was brought to a halt when it bumped into two German divisions. The blame for this outcome Bagramyan subsequently laid squarely at the door of Sokolovskii himself who had failed to provide the requisite forces for the operation. Reiter's Bryansk Front striking from the south had so far managed only fifteen miles and had already come up against the

German reinforcements brought down from Vyazma and Rzhev to Orel; by Soviet calculation, some seven German divisions had been newly deployed to the south of Orel.

At this juncture Rokossovskii with elements of his Central Front was making ready to attack, deploying as fast as possible to the north of Kursk. The original timetable had called for Rokossovskii to take the offensive on 15 February; that had now been revised to 25 February. The original plan had assumed that the Central Front would drive for Smolensk through Bryansk and then, in co-operation with the Western and Kalinin Fronts, destroy the bulk of an encircled Army Group Centre. On Stalin's instructions, the Bryansk Front was now relieved of the assignment to take Bryansk (which devolved on the Central Front): Reiter was to concentrate on freeing Orel and destroying the flank formations of Second *Panzer*. On the morning of 26 February Rokossovskii's 65th and 2nd Tank Armies, together with a 'cavalry-rifle group' (under Maj.-Gen. V.V. Kryukov and consisting basically of 2nd Guards Cavalry Corps), attacked in the direction of Bryansk. Rodin's tank army—reinforced with three rifle divisions and a rifle brigade—was to break the German defences on the river Svap, push armoured units into the breach between the 'central' and the 'Orel' German forces and then go for Pochep–Unech (south-west of Bryansk) to encircle German troops at Orel in co-operation with Western Front forces coming from the north. Batov's 65th, with its six divisions, would attack to the right. Neighbour to Batov was the newly formed 70th Army under Maj.-Gen. Tarasov, a young and inexperienced officer whose new army had been formed largely out of former frontier guards. This army had been having a hard time before it reached the line, for it lacked ammunition and food supplies. The men in its regiments had gone hungry for some time now, and Tarasov came over to Batov's HQ to ask 65th to help out as best it could. Tarasov received orders to attack at 0800 hours on 26 February. Rokossovskii also had some bad news for Batov: owing to the German counter-stroke to the south, 21st Army had been diverted and would not now follow Batov in the attack. To bolster up the Voronezh and South-Western Fronts, a large part of the Central Front air force was similarly ordered south. As Rokossovskii remarked, 'they are flinging "the Don boys" about all over the place'.

Rokossovskii's offensive unrolled very successfully at first on the left, where Colonel Sankovskii's brigade penetrated the German defences. First the motorized infantry and cavalry, and finally the bulk of Rodin's 2nd Tank Army passed through this gap and raced ahead for some thirty miles. Rodin and Kryukov had exploited one unreinforced German sector, but within a few days German resistance stiffened visibly as fresh units moved in; on 7 March 2nd Tank received orders to shift the axis of its advance with right-flank units to the north-east, in the direction of Karachev (south-west of Bryansk), at a time when the tanks were beginning to run out of ammunition and fuel as well as to need overhaul badly. Within forty-eight hours, Rodin's tanks were heavily engaged with two German divisions, 45th and 72nd Infantry. Kryukov with his mobile group pressed on north-westwards, reaching the river Desna in the Novgorod–Severskii area by 10 March, a deep penetration of 60 miles, making a considerable Soviet salient. But what the Soviet command hoped for did not happen; German units did not pull back from Orel. On the contrary, strong German forces, up to six divisions on Soviet reckoning, now assailed Kryukov's force.

Elsewhere the situation had deteriorated in an ugly fashion. *Stavka* instructions to Rokossovskii now envisaged the Central Front attacking Orel in co-operation with left flank of the Bryansk Front (once Rokossovskii had made it plain that his front could not carry out the vast advance implied in its original orders), but the formation assigned to the new Orel attack—21st Army—was now hurriedly switched to Oboyan and put under the command of the Voronezh Front. On 12 March the *Stavka*, in an effort to centralize the control of operations in the Orel–Bryansk area, compressed the Bryansk Front, subordinating most of its formations to Rokossovskii except for 61st Army which went to the Western Front. It was, however, all too late. Under heavy attack, Kryukov and Sankovskii's brigade, struck from north and south, were forced to pull back to the river Sev, where Kryukov himself moved to the eastern bank with the last of the Soviet rearguards. Kryukov lamented his running out of fuel, ammunition and forage; Sankovskii was angry at the dispersal of his brigade, scattering in battalions over a broad front. The military soviet of 2nd Tank Army investigated the reasons for the withdrawal from the Desna—'voluntary retirement' by Kryukov and Sankovskii. Since the latter were operationally subordinated to Batov at 65th, the matter had to be investigated by commission representing the Front Military Soviet and the court of inquiry was duly held, its findings being that the withdrawal was unavoidable. This Rokossovskii supported and wrote on the report: 'Conclusions agreed. No basis for turning matter over to field tribunal'. By 21 March the Central Front had turned over to the defensive along its entire front running from Mtsensk through Novosil and on to Bryantsevo, Sevsk and Rylsk—the northern face of the 'Kursk salient'.

Late in February Gehlen completed a major intelligence survey of the Eastern Front—*Beurteilung der Feindabsichten vor der deutschen Ostfront im Grossen* (Fremde Heere Ost: IIa)—which set present Russian objectives as the destruction of 17th Army (the Kuban), First *Panzer* and *Armee-Abteilung Hollidt* (the Donbas), as well as the winning of operational freedom south of lake Ladoga. The development of a major offensive against Army Group Centre was certainly part of Russian intentions, but there was now no hope of a general breakthrough on both German wings. Already the attempt to splinter the German centre had failed to produce any decisive breakthrough, though the persistent attacks in the Orel–Bryansk area, in addition to holding Second *Panzer* from any co-ordinated action with Fourth *Panzer*, had also forced the German command to bring down reinforcement from the Vyazma–Rzhev *place d'armes,* that dagger which had hitherto been pointed straight at the heart of the Soviet Union. Sixteen German divisions were shipped out of Vyazma–Rzhev for Orel and Kharkov. On 27 February to forestall the danger of being outflanked from the south and to minimize the risk of encirclement, the German Ninth Army received orders to pull out westwards, pursued now by troops of the Kalinin and Western Fronts. On 3 March Soviet troops took Rzhev, and found it torn to shreds by battle and by ruthless German demolitions; in their wake, German troops left a horrible debris of destruction, mass killing and slave-labour deportation. Villages were burned to the ground, buildings blown up, rail tracks systematically ripped away with special rail-wrecking equipment. For three weeks Soviet troops traversed the oozing mud, through devastated zones and over obstacles that had been piled wherever possible to impede the advance; on 12 March, Vyazma, one more ghastly ruin, was liberated. Ten days later the line 'stabilized' at Ribshevo (thirty miles north of Smolensk)—Safonovo (twenty miles east of Yartsevo)—Milyatino (thirty miles south-west of Yukhnov). The front had sprung fifty miles westwards in the direction of Smolensk and was now shortened by well over a hundred miles, which enabled the Soviet command to take two armies and a mechanized corps into immediate reserve as well as using spare divisions to build up second echelons on the Western and Kalinin Fronts.

To the north the situation had also eased considerably. Operation *Iskra,* piercing the Leningrad blockade, was finally successful when the Leningrad and Volkhov Fronts linked up, forging a seven-mile 'corridor' through the German investment. At 0930 hours on 12 January 1943, Maj.-Gen. M.P. Dukhanov's 67th Army began its attack from inside the ring, attacking from west to east; after forcing the Neva, 67th Army was to break the German defences in the Moskovskaya Dubrovskaya–Schlusselburg sector and then strike eastwards to link up with Lt.-Gen. V.Z. Romanovskii's 2nd Shock Army attacking westwards from the Volkhov Front. Dukhanov's 67th had trained furiously throughout the latter half of December (1942) for the formidable job of launching itself across the ice of the Neva straight into the German fixed defences. On 25 December, a meeting of commanders—attended by Zhdanov, Govorov (Leningrad Front commander) and Marshal Voroshilov (*Stavka* 'co-ordinator')—looked into questions raised by the assault exercise. Until well into the first week in January 1943, regiments underwent special training on the Toksovskii grounds to learn how to move through 'fire walls' put up by Soviet artillery. The 67th had no combat experience behind it in tackling the storming of heavily fortified positions; for this reason, training was essential. During the night of 11 January the assault units changed positions with 11th Rifle Brigade and took up their posts on their start lines; during the night of 12 January the remainder of the first echelon of 67th Army moved into position and at 0800 hours, the assault group was lined up ready to go. At 0930 hours 286 guns opened fire, sustaining the bombardment for 140 minutes; at 1150 hours, after a salvo from the Guards *Katyusha* rocket launchers, Dukhanov's assault groups were launched on to the ice. That same cold, clear morning, Romanovskii's 2nd Shock Army to the east attacked on the Volkhov Front.

Six days later, after heavy fighting amidst the German strong-points immured in the frozen bog and snow-covered woods, Soviet troops finally drove through their 'corridor' between the two fronts. South-east of Schlusselburg, units of 123rd Rifle Brigade of the Leningrad Front made contact to the east of Settlement No. 1 with forward elements of 372nd Rifle Division (Volkhov Front) at 0930 hours on 18 January. A little to the south, at Settlement No. 5, Leningrad and Volkhov Front forces also linked up; Schlusselburg was also cleared of German troops on the eighteenth, and by the evening the southern shore of lake Ladoga swept clean of German units. Leningrad had established direct overland communication with the rest of the country. Work began at once on building a railway line some eighteen miles long through the 'corridor' from Schlusselburg to Polyany. The first train steamed along it on 6 February, though with German guns still within range of the 'corridor' it proved to be a hazardous route, full of death-traps. With the first trains came coal, and coal meant more power for the factories and more electricity. The Ladoga 'ice road' (augmented by a fuel pipeline), for all the German bombing and mine-dropping, continued to carry essential supplies, but with the new railway greater bulk could be handled. The grip of the 'bony hand of hunger', which had crushed the life out of so many Leningraders, men, women, old people and children alike, was now a little loosened, but the attempt to snap it completely—by taking Mga and thereby opening the Leningrad–Volkhov line—failed as German reserves clustered in the Sinyavino area. The 'corridor' just south of lake Ladoga would have to do, and Soviet troops set about fortifying villages and exposed sectors to hold off any German attempt to re-impose total blockade.

Southwards, below lake Ilmen and to the north of Smolensk, lay the 'Demyansk salient', sticking into the North-Western Front (presently under the command of Marshal Timoshenko). The German forces encircled at Demyansk had been marked down for the kill in 1942, but that plan misfired; the 'Ramushevo corridor' had been blasted through to join the encircled Demyansk garrisons with the main body of the German forces. Once again the divisions of Sixteenth Army in the Demyansk salient were marked down for annihilation. The *Stavka* plan envisaged shutting off the 'Ramushevo corridor' with the 27th and 1st Shock Armies, then using 11th, 34th and 53rd Armies to reduce the pocket; at the same time, a new combat group under Lt.-Gen. Khozin (including the reformed 1st Tank Army and 68th Army) was to concentrate at the end of January in the Ostashkov area, from which it would pass through the gap blown by 1st Shock Army to turn to Soltsy and drive north-westwards to Luga into the flank and rear of the Eighteenth Army investing Leningrad. Timoshenko's offensive was due to begin in mid-February, but the main assault mounted by 27th and 1st Shock Armies was seriously delayed, though 11th and 53rd Armies opened the attack on 15 February. Kurochkin's Kalinin Front, which in January had cleared Velikie Luki, now attacked northwards with the 3rd Shock Army.

Two days after the Soviet attacks at Demyansk began, the twelve German divisions in the salient began to draw themselves out, with the inevitable result that considerable strength gathered at 'the neck' of the salient, the very place 1st Shock and 27th Armies hoped to pierce. Only on 23 February did 27th Army begin its attacks, followed by 1st Shock three days later, by which time German units were draining out of the salient; within two days (28 February) Soviet troops reached the river Lovat and the salient was erased. The idea of the sweep into the rear of Eighteenth Army had to be abandoned. All of Marshal Zhukov's thunder had been in vain. During the planning of the offensive, together with Marshal Voronov he had, in his capacity as '*Stavka* representative', visited his particular wrath on the formation commanders; half a year they had sat down in front of Demyansk and still they did not know the terrain, nor apparently was much known about German dispositions except perhaps for what they read in the newspapers, 'A captured NCO reported. . . .' Staffs were much too far from their formations and units; no contact had been maintained with partisan HQ in Dno and consequently no information exchanged; commanders had their eyes glued to the rear (where in truth great confusion and shortage did prevail, the tank army especially suffering critical shortage). The tanks of Khozin's 'special group', Katukov's 1st Tank Army, once they got up to their positions, made almost no progress as they sank up to the turret in the snowy slush of the bogs. In the midst of sending up for tractors to pull the tanks out, Katukov received orders to abandon his attack and within the hour received further orders to turn his armour to the railhead. Early in March, at all the stations between Ostashkov and Andreapol, Katukov's brigades were loading their tanks on to flat-cars, destination unknown, with instructions enjoining great urgency. Katukov's 1st Tank was in fact being speeded to Kursk. North-Western Front meanwhile received revised assignments—to capture Staraya Russa and to break through to the river Polist; on 4 March the abortive offensive was renewed, bogging down finally on the evening of 17 March when Soviet troops reached the river Redya after moving forward some eight miles.

With March came the mud and the end of the Soviet winter offensive for 1942–3. The entire Soviet–German front from the Baltic to the Black Sea now wore a much foreshortened look: it was more of a straight line, though bent back in the north on Leningrad and in the south on the Donets–Mius line. The most striking feature was the massive Soviet salient at Kursk, which jutted out westwards. German troops had abandoned their Gzhatsk–Vyazma–Rzhev *place d'armes:* the Demyansk salient was now emptied. The Soviet armies had not unhinged the German southern wing, though they came within an ace of it. If Rokossovskii's Don Front had been committed alongside Vatutin, the outcome might have been the decisive success Stalin was so determinedly seeking. The results over four months were nevertheless very impressive: the great strike force in the Stalingrad area had been blotted out; the encirclement and destruction of the German Sixth Army and elements of Fourth *Panzer*, 3rd and 4th Rumanian with the 8th Italian Armies, had transformed the scene on the southern wing; Army Group A in the Caucasus had been badly mauled and Army Group B, assaulted by three Soviet fronts (Bryansk, Voronezh and South-Western), had been pounded to pieces; Second *Panzer* had taken heavy punishment in the Orel area. The Soviet tally of damage inflicted on enemy forces ran to over 100 divisions (43 per cent of the strength committed on the Eastern Front): 68 German divisions, along with 19 Rumanian, 10 Hungarian and 10 Italian divisions, were completely wrecked. German losses in senior commanders climbed steeply, with more than a score of generals taken prisoner at Stalingrad (with one field-marshal at their head) and seventeen others killed. The Italians had lost 185,000 men, the Hungarians some 140,000, the Rumanians over a quarter of a million in killed, wounded, prisoners and missing. The Russians claim to have put over one million men out of action between November 1942 and March 1943; on 1 March 1943 German estimates of *Ostfront* strength set it short of 470,000 men. In the north Leningrad had been linked once more with 'the country'; in the south, the main rail and waterway communications with the centre had been re-established. Full of the exhilaration of Stalingrad, the Red Army rushed headlong into an enormous offensive. The great mistake of 1942, the dispersal of effort, had been repeated (and certainly cost the Soviet command the Donbas), but for all the over-straining of Soviet resources, the *Wehrmacht* and its allies had taken a bludgeoning the like of which they had never before experienced.

In mid-February, at the very height of the crisis facing the southern wing of the German armies, Manstein on the occasion of the *Führer's* visit to his headquarters had drawn attention not only to the problems of immediate military rescue but also to some of the implications of a summer campaign in the east. These talks began on 17 February at Zaporozhe and lasted until 19 February, the day on which lead tanks of the Soviet 25th Tank Crops, driving for the Dnieper, were less than fifty miles away. That afternoon Hitler flew out, to Manstein's relief. In considering future operations, Manstein and his officers had already submitted a 'tentative plan' to Hitler covering German offensive action, which might either pre-empt or take advantage of a Russian offensive. In anticipating a Russian attack on the Donbas from north and south, Manstein preferred to see German forces pulled back to the Dnieper while strong armoured forces assembled west of Kharhov to destroy Soviet forces in that area, and then to lunge into the flank of Soviet formations on the move to the Dnieper. This backhand chop would slice up Soviet troops and pin them down for destruction on the sea of Azov. Since it smacked too much of 'withdrawal', Hitler rejected this variant. The second solution centred on the Russian salient at Kursk, which presented the Red Army with favourable positions from which to strike into the flanks of both Army Group Centre and Army Group South. A rapid attack in the wake of the thaw would catch the Russians on the wrong foot, slice away the salient and engulf Soviet armoured forces in the process of refitting. The massed attack on the Kursk salient finally took shape as *Zitadelle,* Operation 'Citadel'.

Much as Manstein wished it, the elimination of the salient by extension of the Kharkov counter-stroke in March, breaking into the rear of the Voronezh and Central Fronts to accomplish what Stalin subsequently called 'a German Stalingrad', proved impossible; Army Group Centre declared itself unable to 'co-operate' in any extensive operation on the northern face. In the second half of March, the Voronezh and Central Fronts had gone over to the defensive to hold the German thrusts at Belgorod and south-east of Kharkov. Fresh from the bogs of Demyansk, Katukov's 1st Tank Army was concentrating in the Oboyan area: 64th Army, rushed up from the *Stavka* reserve, was lining the northern Donets: 21st Army was in position some fifteen miles north of Belgorod. Further south, three groups from Rybalko's 3rd Tank Army had broken through German encirclement south-east of Kharkov to reach the eastern bank of the northern Donets not far from Chuguev by 17 March; here the remnants of 3rd Tank were incorporated into the South-Western Front. As German tanks ploughed through the mud, the Soviet defence settled on the Belgorod–Volchansk–Chuguev sector.

The huge salient (about half the size of England) presented both dangers and opportunities. While Soviet troops were positioned to strike north and south, the presence of German *place d'armes* to the north (the Orel salient) and the south (the Kharkov–Belgorod salient) put the Voronezh and Central Fronts themselves at risk. Soviet intelligence data at the end of March emphasized the risk; by these calculations, the German command had in the Orel, Belgorod and Kharkov areas up to 40 infantry divisions, up to 20 *Panzer* divisions, one motorized and one cavalry division, with a powerful shock group in the Kharkov area—*SS* divisions *Gross Deutschland, Adolf Hitler, Totenkopf* and *Das Reich.* The distribution of these German forces—15–17 infantry, 7–8 *Panzer* divisions facing the Central Front, 12–13 infantry and 4 *Panzer* divisions at Belgorod facing the Voronezh Front, 7–9 infantry and 9 *Panzer* divisions (six of them *SS* formations) facing the South-Western Front—meant by Soviet reading of the signs a definite offensive intention. Stalin had already conceived a grand plan for the Central and Voronezh Fronts; his first idea was to use these fronts in an attack towards Gomel and Kharkov, to force the Dnieper and thereby lay the foundations for the recapture of both the Donbas and Belorussia. With such formidable force, however, building up on either side of the salient, this plan was unworkable in such simple form. At the beginning of April, Stalin, the *Stavka,* the General Staff and the Front commanders had to work out new plans to deal with a disquieting and potentially very dangerous situation.

The vital decision was to let the German offensive lead off. Though Stalin evidently wanted and went on wanting to pre-empt, he was dissuaded from this dangerous predilection, and here the views very forcefully propounded by Vatutin seemed to have triumphed (and to have been especially influential). Soviet operational planning at Kursk, and in the complex of operations connected with Kursk, proceeded from three premises:

1. An offensive to spoil the German attack would be pointless.
2. The Central and Voronezh Fronts would remain strictly on the defensive, and would grind down the enemy in defensive battles, but the moment the assault lost its power they would go over to a decisive counter-offensive.
3. The Bryansk and Western Fronts would prepare an offensive aimed at Orel.

There was much upon which Stalin had to brood. While the top-level agent 'Lucy' supplied him through the spring of 1943 with nothing less than the day-to-day decisions of the *OKW* ('the Centre' acknowledged its indebtedness for information in January on the Caucasus and for detailed items on the movement of German divisions eastwards from Europe), during the winter of 1942 Soviet intelligence had also dispatched a 'special group' of highly trained, regular intelligence officers to enemy-occupied areas in southern Russia. Among these Soviet officers was N.I. Kuznetsov, who operated as *Oberleutnant* Kurt Ziebert. In this capacity, he was a party to the secrets of the infamous Koch, *Reichskommissar* of the Ukraine, with his headquarters in Rovno; Kuznetsov certainly transmitted information on 'Citadel' (and a little later he stumbled on the details of a German plan to kill 'the Big Three', Stalin among them, when they met in Teheran at the end of the year).

Although after March the longest 'lull' in the whole war set in, both sides worked feverishly to prepare for a decisive encounter. Step by step, the Soviet plan took shape, each item of information fitting into the gigantic jigsaw. The *Stavka* was persuaded that the Red Army could indeed take the field first, but this time the Soviet intention was to absorb the German blow before going over to a Soviet offensive. The strategic objective for the summer–autumn offensive was fixed at pushing German forces back to a line running from Smolensk to the river Sozh and the middle and lower reaches of the Dnieper, to smash in the German defensive system of the 'Eastern Wall' and also to wipe out German forces in the Kuban; the main Soviet thrust would be in a south-westerly direction to liberate the eastern Ukraine and the industrial region of the Donbas. A second offensive would be aimed due west, to liberate eastern Belorussia and to destroy Army Group Centre. Already as a result of field intelligence data, certain assumptions could be made about impending German operations; the concentration of crack *Panzer* divisions was almost certainly a sign of an offensive intention, and when the blow came it would be mounted this time not on a broad front but 'as a limited blow on a single axis'. Kursk was the axis, and Kursk it had to be. With a major offensive towards the south-west scheduled after the outcome of the defensive battle, there was every reason to build up Soviet forces in this area; within a short time almost half (40 per cent) of the rifle formations of the Red

Army, together with *Stavka* reserves, augmented by every existing Soviet tank army, had been jammed into the reaches of the salient. A year before the General Staff had pleaded for a strategic defensive; Stalin accepted in principle but exploded it in practice. Now, as *Stavka* directives for the most rigid defence went out to the Voronezh and Central Fronts, the die was irretrievably cast, and men, machines, ammunition, aircraft, guns, tanks, SP (self-propelled) guns and army engineers, rolled steadily into the salient. The fortifications, when they were finished, stretched in their various configurations the equivalent distance of Moscow to Irkutsk. At the beginning of April, both the Voronezh and Central Fronts had received the first batch of reinforcements: Voronezh Front formations were brought up to strength, the Front itself being stiffened with four rifle divisions and 1st Tank Army, while Central Front acquired one tank corps (2nd Tank Army being taken into reserve) and six rifle divisions. On 1 April 1943 both fronts mustered a combined strength of 1,200 tanks. Two months later this had tripled. With the output of Soviet tanks and SP guns running at some 2,000 per month—and aircraft at 2,500—the Russians stood fair to win the war of the production-shop. It was as Manstein had warned Hitler—to delay with *Citadel* would mean no less than sixty newly-equipped Soviet armoured brigades at the front.

Early in April, Marshal Zhukov made both an extensive tour and a minute inspection of the Voronezh Front, where Vatutin had been installed. One immediate result was to stiffen 52nd Guards Division, which Zhukov felt to be particularly vulnerable, but a much vaster enterprise was afoot, a major ground and air reconnaissance effort mounted by the Central, Voronezh and South-Western Fronts to register enemy strength and to estimate enemy reserves. Marshal Vasilevskii and the General Staff assumed responsibility for seeing this through, and on 8 April Zhukov considered the information acquired adequate enough to submit a major strategic appreciation to Stalin, a key document in the planning process on the Soviet side (Zhukov, *Vosp.* (2), pp. 139–41):

To: Comrade Vasil'ev [Stalin]
    0530 hrs. 8 April 1943.

I herewith submit my view on possible enemy operations in the spring and summer of 1943 and my estimates of our defensive operations in the immediate future:

    1. The enemy, having suffered heavy losses in the winter campaign of 1942/3, cannot apparently establish by the spring large reserves in order once more to renew his offensive operations to seize the Caucasus and break through to the Volga with the object of deeply outflanking Moscow.

    In view of the limitation of his major reserves the enemy will be forced in the spring and in the first half of the summer of 1943 to develop his offensive operations on a much narrower front and to solve his problems stringently by stages, having as the basic aim of the 1943 campaign—the capture of Moscow.

    Considering the deployment of enemy forces at the present moment against our *Central, Voronezh and South-Western Fronts,* I am of the opinion that the main enemy offensive will develop against these three fronts in order to destroy our forces on this axis and thereby gain freedom of manoeuvre for the outflanking of Moscow on the shortest line of advance.

2. Apparently, in the first stage, the enemy, having assembled his maximum forces, which will include up to 13–15 tank divisions, supported by large numbers of aircraft, will direct a blow with his Orel–Kromy concentration to outflank Kursk from the north-east and with his Belgorod–Kharkov concentration will attack to outflank Kursk from the south-east.

A supporting attack, designed to split our front, can be expected from the west from the area of Vorozhba, between the Psel and Seim rivers, to drive on Kursk from the south-west. With this attack the enemy will attempt to destroy and encircle our 13, 70, 65, 60, 38, 40 and 21 Armies.

The terminal stage of this phase of the operations must be to bring enemy forces on to the line of the river Korocha, Koracha, Tim and the river Tim, Droskovy.

3. In the second stage the enemy will try to break into the flank and rear of the South-Western Front, in the general line of advance through Baluiki–Urazovo.

To meet this attack the enemy can launch an attack from the Lisichansk area along a northern axis towards Svatovo, Urazovo.

In the remaining sectors the enemy will try to reach the line Livny, Kastornoe, Stary and Novy Oskol.

4. In the third stage, after regrouping, the enemy very possibly will try to reach a front running from Liska to Voronezh and Yelets and, covering himself to the south-east, can organize a blow to outflank Moscow from the south-east through Ranenburg, Ryazhsk, Ryazan.

5. It is to be anticipated that this year the enemy will put the chief burden for offensive operation on his armoured divisions and his air force, since at the present moment his infantry is much less ready for offensive operations than in the previous year.

At the present time the enemy deploys in front of the Central and Voronezh Fronts up to 12 tank divisions, and by drawing off 3–4 tank divisions from other sectors, the enemy could commit against our forces at Kursk up to 15–16 tank divisions with a strength of some 2,500 tanks.

6. *So that the enemy should smash himself to pieces against our defences, in addition to the measures to strengthen the anti-tank (PTO) defence of the Central and Voronezh Fronts, we must as speedily as possible draw off from passive sectors* and concentrate in *Stavka* reserve for use on heavily threatened axes 30 regiments of anti-tank artillery, concentrate all self-propelled gun regiments on the Livny–Kastornoe–Stary Oskol sector, part of the regiments if so desired being given at once to reinforce Rokossovskii and Vatutin, and concentrate as many aircraft as possible in *Stavka* reserve, so that massed air attacks in co-operation with armour and rifle formations can smash enemy attacks and thus frustrate his offensive plan.

I am unfamiliar with the latest disposition of our operational reserves, but I consider it right to suggest their deployment in the area of Yefremov, Livny, Kastornoe, Novy Oskol, Valuiki, Rossosh, Liska, Voronezh and Yelets.

This would put the main body of the reserves in the area of Yelets, Voronezh. The deep reserves would be at Ryazhsk, Ranenburg, Michurinsk, Tambov.

In the area of Tula, Stalinogorsk, it is essential to have one reserve army.

An offensive on the part of our troops in the near future aimed at forestalling the enemy I consider to be pointless. It would be better if we grind down the enemy in our defences, break up his tank forces, and then, introducing fresh reserves, go over to a general offensive to pulverize once and for all his main concentrations.

KONSTANTINOV [Zhukov]

Shortly afterwards Marshal Vasilevskii arrived at Voronezh Front HQ and here the two marshals worked out a draft *Stavka* directive on reserves and the establishment of the new Steppe Front.

On the evening of 11 April Marshal Zhukov arrived in Moscow to attend the *Stavka* conference scheduled for the evening of 12 April, for which Stalin ordered all operational maps, calculations and proposals for future operations to be prepared. From early morning onwards on 12 April Marshal Zhukov, Marshal Vasilevskii and General Antonov worked furiously to prepare all the documents and maps Stalin had called for. The Front commanders had also submitted estimated and operational plans, Central Front (Lt.-Gen. Malinin's report) on 10 April, Voronezh Front on 12 April itself. These estimates of German intentions conformed very largely to Marshal Zhukov's first appreciation, but in Moscow the three senior Soviet officers worked out a final appreciation for Stalin himself. Zhukov and Vasilevskii took the view that German forces would attack on one of the main strategic axes and that the most dangerous area was at Kursk. The German command was prepared to break through 'at any price' in order to restore the strategic balance in favour of the German Army: destroying the Central and Voronezh Fronts would do just this. The German attack at Kursk would be concentric, one attack reaching out from south of Orel, the other from the Belgorod area. Elsewhere on the Soviet–German front German troops would go on the defensive, for by General Staff calculations the *Ostheer* no longer disposed of sufficient strength for multiple offensive operations.

Stalin duly met his commanders late in the evening of April 12. To the reports and the appreciations he listened 'as never before'. He agreed that the main German striking forces were clustered around the Kursk salient, but his overriding concern remained for 'the Moscow axis'. To cover all eventualities it was agreed to begin the construction of deeply echeloned defence systems on all the 'main axes', but to give priority to Kursk. On the basis of this decision, Front commanders were given preliminary orders and the General Staff set about a systematic movement of *Stavka* reserves to bring them up to the areas under threat. By mid-April the decision for a planned defensive action by Soviet troops, to be followed by a carefully timed offensive, had begun to take on fairly solid shape. The Front commanders Vatutin and Rokossovskii also submitted their wider appreciations, and both plumped for the defensive. General Vatutin in his report (12 April) set out his view of German intentions:

The enemy is preparing to attack and will mount concentric blows from the area of Belgorod-Borisovka to the north-east and from the area of Orel to the south-east, with the aim of encircling our forces deployed west of a line running from Belgorod to Kursk. By way of development, the enemy may seek either to repeat his offensive to the south-east into the rear of the South-Western Front with a subsequent sweep northwards or this year he may refrain from an attack to the south-east and adopt a different plan, namely, after concentric blows from the Belgorod and Orel areas he will aim his attack to the north-east to outflank Moscow. [*IVOVSS*, 3, p. 246.]

The enemy would rely heavily on massed air and tank attacks, so it would be advisable to plan offensive air actions to deal with German airfields and to deploy Soviet ground forces to deal with massed tank blows. Once the enemy had been worn down in the defensive fighting, the Soviet forces 'at a favourable moment' should go over to a counter-offensive 'aimed at the final destruction of the German forces', a drive to destroy enemy forces in the Ukraine, thereby putting out of action 'the most active section of the German Army'. Rokossovskii in his *sluzhebnaya zapiska* set out similar views from the Central Front—German attacks would materialize from the Belgorod-Kharkov and the Orel concentration areas, and substantial German success would pose a grave threat to the rear of the Soviet fronts, the Central and Voronezh. The primary role of Soviet troops must for the present be a carefully prepared defensive action; in order to give the defence effective operational depth, a powerful reserve—two or three armies at the very least—must be set up east of Kursk.

As April drew to a close, the Central and Voronezh Fronts completed their basic deployment for a defensive battle, following their first *Stavka* instructions. Stalin, however, remained at heart unconvinced and even gloomy about the outcome of a major defensive battle. Stalin sent out the strictest orders, embodied in the *Stavka* directive of 8 May, to Central, Voronezh and South-Western Front commands to maintain a state of full readiness to meet a German attack, but he toyed with the idea of a Soviet spoiling attack. General Vatutin, while still insisting on the need for more defensive effort, suggested in a report to Stalin that the Voronezh Front might stage a spoiling attack on German concentrations in the Belgorod–Kharkov area: Marshal Zhukov, Marshal Vasilevskii and General Antonov promptly squashed this idea in the joint opinion they submitted to Stalin. But for all this no one succeeded in stilling Stalin's doubts, whose mind apparently dwelt on the disastrous defensive operations of 1941 and 1942.

Meanwhile, as Stalin wavered, Soviet troops dug in. On the Central Front, Rokossovskii submitted that the greatest danger would come on his right wing with the German attack unfolding along the Orel–Kursk axis, running south or south-east. An attack on any other sector would not present any particular threat since enough troops were available to counter it and to hold the ground in sufficient strength; the worst that might happen would be that some forces would be cut off, but they would not be destroyed. Since the main threat must come from the right, from the direction of Ponyr–Zolotukhino–Kursk, Rokossovskii proposed to deploy his main strength here along a fifty-mile front, with three armies—48th, 13th and 70th—in the first echelon. Pukhov's 13th Army (with

48th on its right and 70th on its left) held a sixteen-mile front, with two rifle corps (29th and 15th) in its first echelon and four rifle divisions (15th, 81st, 148th and 8th) advanced as the first echelon of the corps, and with two divisions (307th and 74th) in the second. Second echelon of 13th Army consisted of two Guards rifle corps (17th and 18th), six rifle divisions and a tank regiment. The neighbouring armies, 48th and 70th, were similarly deployed in two echelons, while Rokossovskii held Rodin's 2nd Tank Army at Fatezh as reserve echelon. For the 100 miles of the remainder of the Central Front (on the front bulge of the salient) there were two armies, 65th and 60th: the Front reserve consisted of 18th Guards Rifle Corps, two tank corps (9th and 19th), and anti-tank artillery regiments. For air support the *Stavka* had supplied 16th Air Army.

Vatutin on the Voronezh Front reported three sectors as being those most likely to be attacked: from the area west of Belgorod to Oboyan, or to Korocha or yet again from the area west of Volchansk to Novy Oskol. For this reason, the main strength of the Front was deployed at the centre and on the left, a sixty-mile stretch of front occupied by two Guards armies, 6th and 7th. Chistyakov's 6th Guards Army (the old 21st of the Don Front) covered Oboyan, its front running some thirty miles, with four rifle divisions in the first echelon (71st, 67th, 52nd Guards and 375th Rifle Division) reinforced with a tank brigade and two tank regiments; the second echelon had three Guards Rifle Divisions (90th, 51st and 89th) with a tank brigade. To the left was another Stalingrad army, Shumilov's 7th Guards (formerly 64th), on a 25-mile front with four Guards divisions (81st, 78th, 72nd and 36th) with a tank regiment in the first echelon and three rifle divisions in the second (73rd, 15th Guards, 213th Rifle Division) with two tank brigades and two tank regiments. Drawn up behind 6th and 7th Guards was Katukov's 1st Tank Army (31st, 6th Tank Corps, 3rd Mechanized Corps) covering the Oboyan–Kursk approach, with 69th Army covering the Belgorod–Korocha and the Volchansk–Novy Oskol reaches. The remaining two armies, 40th and 38th, held the Front face and the right wing. Both Katukov's 1st Tank (with three corps) and 69th Army (five divisions) formed the second echelon: the Front reserve consisted of three corps, 35th Guards Rifle (with three divisions), and 5th Guards Tank Corps. Of the thirty-five divisions finally available to Vatutin, eighteen were assigned to the Front second echelon or to army and Front reserve. And behind the Central and Voronezh Fronts, on the lines of Rokossovskii's suggestion, a powerful strategic reserve was assembled; the Steppe Military District, which already existed on 15 April, was to be converted in some six weeks to the Steppe Front, whose first commander was Popov, the 'mobile group' commander of the south-west. Col.-Gen. Koniev subsequently took over this Front command, at a time when its power was enormous and still growing, to comprise finally five rifle armies including 4th Guards and 5th Guards, one tank army (Rotmistrov's 5th Guards), one air army (5th) and six reserve corps—4th Guards and 10th Tank Corps, 1st Guards Mechanized Corps, 5th Guards and 7th, 3rd Cavalry Corps. This was the most powerful strategic reserve assembled by the *Stavka* at any time during the war.

On *Stavka* orders, the artillery poured into the salient. Within eight weeks, more than 20,000 guns and mortars were at the disposal of the Central and Voronezh Fronts and more than 6,000 anti-tank guns, with 920 *Katyusha* M-13 rocket-batteries in position. The actual reinforcement amounted to just under 10,000 guns and mortars, as 92 High Command Artillery Reserve regiments moved up. Pukhov's 13th Army, covering the Orel–Kursk railway line, received a massive addition of fire-power with the assignment to it of 4th Artillery Breakthrough Corps (700 guns) and half the artillery reserve regiments despatched to the Central Front. For AA defence, 9 Anti-Aircraft Artillery Divisions, 40 regiments, 17 battalions and 5 batteries were deployed throughout the salient, with heavy machine-guns distributed throughout the defensive zones for firing at aerial targets. On the ground, Red Army engineers set about laying 40,000 mines. In the air, the three Soviet Air Armies were able to deploy some 3,500 aircraft (2,000 fighters, 800 ground-attack planes and 700 bombers, some from 'strategic aviation'); in Central Front area alone, 110 airfields were built, and by the beginning of May the reinforced squadrons of Rudenko's 16th Air Army moved up at dusk to their forward deployment, while 40 dummy fields and bases worked all in the glare of enemy reconnaissance. The fighter squadrons moved forward in small groups, flying low at some 300 feet under cover of early darkness; only the day bombers were kept back on airfields dispersed in the rear.

The lull on the ground persisted, but the war in the air began to hot up very quickly and by mid-May German planes were making their massed flights over Kursk, Yelets, Shchigry, Kastornoe and other rail junctions. Penetrating much deeper eastwards, German bombers put the Moscow defences on the alert and induced the same tremors of attack at Gorkii. To counter German raids in the front-line areas, the Soviet air armies scrambled as many fighters as possible; 16th Air Army responsible for Kursk itself was kept at full stretch, though the Russians were both gratified and relieved to see heavy bombloads delivered on the dummy airfields scattered about the salient. The defensive and reconnaissance air operations of the salient, however, were only one part of Soviet Air Force activity during the early spring of 1943; on *Stavka* orders, the several Soviet air armies were to engage in a battle for air superiority, a struggle which was opened by the two air armies (4th and 5th) of the North Caucasus Front, where the Soviet command planned to wipe out the Kuban residue of German forces and to reduce the Taman bridgehead. For the preliminary aerial offensive the *Stavka* released Maj.-Gen. Ushakov's 2nd Bomber corps; Maj.-Gen. Tupikov's 6th Long-Range Bomber Corps (*ADD*) also added its strength to the coming air offensive, which opened towards the end of April. The Soviet squadrons had a certain number of American planes (Bostons and Airocobras) and a few Spitfires but the bulk of the strength was Soviet including the new *Yak-7b* and *La-5* fighters. The co-ordination of the operations covering several fronts was entrusted to Novikov (*Stavka* representative for air operations in the south and now a Marshal of Aviation). On both sides, upwards of 1,000 aircraft were involved, and step by step the tempo of the air war was increased. Over the Kuban on 28 April, 300 Soviet fighters were in action against German bombers attacking Soviet ground troops and targets, and heavy air fighting continued until 10 May.

In the Kursk salient the civilian population was mobilized to build the mass of defence works that all commanders considered indispensable; in April, 105,000 workers were digging, a few weeks later, 300,000. At the end of March, Soviet troops had thrown up hurried field-works as the *Panzer* units drove into them, but in April the fortification of the salient was reorganized and developed in highly systematic fashion. The civilian population presented a major problem— should it be evacuated from what would obviously soon become a major battle area? The Kursk *oblast* party committee suggested to Rokossovskii that civilians should be evacuated and anything of value which was also movable should be shipped out; the Military Soviet of the Central Front decided against evacuation, if only because such a move might have a depressing effect on morale among the troops. The civilians stayed put, many to work on the trenches and gun-pits (though troops were used to build the main system of fortification). Each rifle army in the salient established three defensive zones, two of them ('main' and 'second-line') constituting the tactical defensive zone with a depth of up to ten miles, and a third being the 'army defensive field'. The basis of this defensive system was trenching and communication passages. Each front in turn built up three defensive lines, 'Front positions', which gave the defences a depth of up to thirty miles and on selected axes up to fifty miles. In addition to the Central and Voronezh Front fortifications, Steppe Front troops, assisted by the local population, constructed two more rear lines. Altogether in the salient there were finally eight defence lines, echeloned in depth to a distance of 100 miles. The strongest fortification went on the main defence lines, which had a depth of some three miles, with two or three positions connected by a system of trenches in turn connected by communication passages also fitted out with firing points.

Forward of the main line were wire obstacles, mines, explosive charges and anti-tank ditches; on critical sectors 1,500 anti-tank and 1,700 anti-personnel mines were laid to each kilometre. Battalion fire and support positions were laid out in circular fashion, with special attention to securing junctions of units. The anit-tank defence, based on 'anti-tank resistance points' (*protivotankovye opornye punkty: PTOP*), was laid out chessboard-style over each half-mile or so of the salient; the *PTOP*s included up to five guns, up to five anti-tank rifles, a section of sappers and a squad of tommy-gunners, with tanks or SP guns in one or two places. 'Anti-tank areas' were in a few cases organized by consolidating *PTOP*s with regimental sectors. The whole anti-tank defence was supported by 'mobile blocking squads' formed from anything up to a battalion of Red Army engineers supported by tommy-gunners, the whole squad motorized and ready to be deployed along the axis of any tank movement. The thickening of defensive installations on certain sectors depended on the operational planning of the Front commands.

Rokossovskii had selected three 'variants' (assumptions about the areas of projected enemy attacks); Vatutin, four. The movement of troops, the deployment of artillery and the scope of air operations were all planned within the terms of the Front 'variants'. (Rokossovskii fought the first stage of the Central Front defensive battle under 'No. 2 Variant'—the main German blow along the axis Glazunovka–Ponyr–Kursk, well enough known to the rifle formation commanders, because Lt.-Gen. P.L. Romanenko, 48th Army, Lt.-Gen. N.P. Pukhov, 13th Army, and Lt.-Gen. I.V. Galanin, 70th Army, helped to work out the general defensive plan.)

While the field-works went up, the officers and men of the reinforced divisions were put through an extensive training programme, more than half of which was devoted to night operations; staffs at all levels went through their drills. Infantrymen and gunners were given some instruction on the characteristics of the new German Tiger tanks; each formation built a practice range to train gunners in firing at tanks. Units in the 'main defence fields' were pulled out by rota for training on identical terrain in the rear. Rifle divisions held command briefings to review the entire defensive deployment, briefings organized by the Front Military Soviets and usually attended by the army commander with his staff. While this training programme went on, more labour was expended on bringing the rear into good order. Both the Central and Voronezh Fronts depended to a high degree on the Voronezh–Kastornoe–Kursk and Kursk–Yelets railway lines, both of which had been extensively damaged during the German retreat; bridges, not least that over the Don, had been blown and repair installations wrecked. Since half a million railway trucks were used to bring up men and supplies to the salient, the lines were put back in working order but they had to be secured against further damage by air attack. AA batteries were deployed by the bridges, 'duty brigades' with spare rail and equipment stood by at likely spots, while 'mobile AA ambushes' were sprinkled along the line to discourage the bombers.

The wealth of new equipment was not, however, offset by any similar largesse with men. Much of the reinforcement coming into the salient consisted of men locally conscripted and therefore in urgent need of training; Rokossovskii's divisions numbered on average between 5–6,000 men, and only one corps (17th Guards) had 7,000-man divisions. Troops fit for operations were now combed out of the Front and army hospitals in order to stiffen the divisions. The defence in the tactical zones was assigned to the rifle corps deployed in two echelons (two rifle divisions in the 'main field', one division in the 'second field'), but through deficiencies in the war establishment of the corps they could not be fully deployed. In only a few cases was it possible to provide rifle armies with tank and anti-tank artillery reserves, though independent tank brigades and regiments of SP guns were split up among the rifle divisions to provide either support or a tactical reserve. This worked out at an average density of 5–7 tanks per kilometre of front. The main tank formations were themselves fitting out or training, absorbing

the new models of the T-34, the heavy KV-85 and the SP guns, SU-122s and
SU-152s.

To fight the battle of Kursk, Stalin was assembling not only quantity but
quality. The 'Stavka representatives' for the operations were the Marshals Zhukov
and Vasilevskii: Malenkov acted as the State Defence Committee (GKO) 'representative', his duties and responsibilities connected with the non-operational side
though nonetheless important for mobilizing resources. Most of the rifle armies
in the Kursk salient were veteran formations, many from Stalingrad, like the
commanders—Batov, Chistyakov, Shumilov, Zhadov. Vatutin, who was enormously experienced, had taken over Golikov's command at the Voronezh Front;
for the moment, Col.-Gen. Popov was in charge of the 'Reserve Front', but in
May he was transferred to the Bryansk Front (to take over from Col.-Gen. Reiter)
and Col.-Gen. Koniev finally assumed command of the Steppe Front (the 'Reserve
Front'), which became fully operational in June. Koniev received explicit instructions
from the Stavka to ensure that his army, corps and divisional commanders had
not only a deal of war experience behind them but also some practice in peacetime
troop training. As long as the lull lasted, the Steppe Front trained, as Stalin
intended that it should; Lt.-Gen. Rotmistrov (in his pre-war days one of the
lecturers at the Stalin Academy of Mechanization and Motorization), now with
5th Guards Tank Army under him, was responsible for training the armoured
forces assigned to Koniev. The battle of Kursk (and the related complex of
operations) in 1943 did in fact represent the ultimate graduation of the 'class of
"36" ', the first intake in the autumn of 1936 to the new General Staff Academy:
the first graduates included Vasilevskii, Antonov, M.V. Zakharov, Vatutin,
Bagramyan. And taking men out was as important as putting them in; two
changes for the better were the removal of Rumyantsev from the Cadres (Personnel)
Administration in the Defence Commissariat and the removal of Shchadenko
from the Training Administration, both disastrous appointments which had done
no small amount of damage.

At this time also the General Staff 'stabilized' its position, owing to the regime
imposed by Antonov at the turn of the year. Stalin himself organized the work
of the General Staff on a 24-hour basis; Antonov was relieved from duty from
0600 to 1200 hours, Shtemenko (head of Operations) from 1400 to 1800 hours
each day. Three times a day the General Staff reported to Stalin, in his presence
or by telephone; the first report went in at 10–1100 hours, usually by telephone
and from Shtemenko, and Antonov delivered the evening report at 16–1700
hours. The night report, accompanied by a map presentation on a 1:200,000
scale map for each front with positions down to division (in some cases down
to regiment), was made by Antonov, accompanied by Shtemenko, who made
their way after a summons by telephone either to the Stavka, the Kremlin war-
room, or to Stalin's dacha (some little drive out of Moscow). Once in the Kremlin,
the officers made their way to Stalin's own quarters, to which they were admitted

by Poskrebyshev, Stalin's secretary, after passing the small personal guard:

In the left part of [Stalin's] *kabinet* a small way from the wall stood a long, rectangular table. We spread out the maps on it and delivered a report on each Front separately, beginning with those where the main events were taking place. We made no preliminary notes, since we knew the situation from memory and it was outlined on the map. Behind the table, in the corner, a large globe of the world stood on the floor. [Shtemenko, *Soviet General Staff*, pp. 120–21.]

This was the scene that met Antonov and Shtemenko so often; usually in attendance at these sessions, which ended round about 3 am, were Marshal Voronov, Fedorenko (armoured forces commander), Yakovlev (head of the Main Artillery Administration), Khrulev (chief of Rear Services) and Novikov (for the air force), as well as members of the *Politburo*.

The next item after the report was drafting the *Stavka* directives. Stalin's practice was to refer to all fronts, armies, tank and mechanized corps by the names of their commanders, to divisions by their designation only; once back at the General Staff, the whole thing had to be sorted out into formal language. Stalin would dictate the *Stavka* directives himself, with Shtemenko noting them down; they would then be read back, corrected on the spot and finally transmitted by a signals unit situated only yards away.

Over the projected attack on the German bulge at Orel, Stalin was inclined to jump the gun. In April, Reiter's Bryansk Front command received instructions to prepare an offensive operation against Orel, the *Stavka* itself suggesting a three-Front attack—concentric blows by the Western, Bryansk and Central Fronts, with the Bryansk Front playing the principal part. The Western Front would use its left-flank 11th Guards Army (Bagramyan's old 16th), Rokossovskii his right-flank formations. A plan was duly worked out, but it was rapidly overtaken by events and, even as late as June, by the personal intervention of Col.-Gen. Fedorenko, who examined the proposals to use Rybalko's 3rd Tank Army for the attack. This army was still not fully reconstituted after the battering it received south of Kharkov in March—its tank crews were newly arrived and still arriving, and the three corps (12th and 15th Tank, 2nd Mechanized) were still reforming. Fedorenko advised a change of plan and recommended this to the *Stavka*, adding that as such it would be accepted. Meanwhile Col.-Gen. M.M. Popov took over the Bryansk Front; Fedyuninskii, who had been wounded in the leg in the Volkhov Front operations in January, was now posted south as his deputy commander. Mekhlis—apparently much chastened after his folly at Kerch—was the political member of the Military Soviet. Popov found the Front 'gone stale in defence . . . it has dug itself into the ground'. But none of the commanders were 'hopeless cases', as Popov chose to call them.

On the left flank of Sokolovskii's Western Front, Bagramyan was unhappy about the attack plans for 11th Guards, now a formidable force with twelve rifle divisions (three corps), two tank corps, four tank brigades, four High

Command Reserve artillery divisions plus AA and engineer units. Bagramyan was sure that, as it stood, the plan meant that 11th Guards would hit empty air; the Orel bulge should be cut into a circle, but this meant more formations for the job. Upon none of his seniors, however, did his views prevail. Early in May, Sokolovskii, Reiter, Bagramyan and 61st Army commander were summoned to the *Stavka*, where Antonov submitted the operational plan for the Orel attack. With no objections raised, and after a few perfunctory questions from Stalin, the latter was about to close the briefing when Bagramyan seized the opportunity to raise his objections. Stalin instructed him to proceed with a presentation. To his own astonishment, Bagramyan's 'variant' was accepted as a valid basis for revised operational planning and he received fresh instructions from Sokolovskii, with twenty days in which to make 11th Guards ready to attack. On 24 May, Bagramyan reported in the evening that 11th Guards was ready. The proposed attack was, however, postponed as Stalin now waited to follow through the strategy of wearing down a German offensive before launching on his own. The counter-offensive design had become, through its interlinking with the Kursk defensive battle, even more vast; two groups of fronts would operate in two directions, the left flank of the Western Front, the Bryansk Front and the Central Front against Orel, the Steppe and Voronezh Fronts against Belgorod–Kharkov. Vasilevskii and Voronov 'co-ordinated' the plans for the first, Zhukov those for the second.

Throughout the month of May, during the pleasant spring days, the plans and 'co-ordination' were increasingly advanced; in the Kursk salient itself the troops, between attending their frequent tactical exercises, shovelled alongside the civilians in the trenches, fire positions and bunkers; the infantry commanders reconnoitred the ground for their several 'variants'; the tank officers rehearsed their movement; and the gunners and engineers laboured on all their variously complicated installations. Early in May the tension suddenly increased. On 2 May Stalin sent out an alert about the forthcoming German offensive and ordered a full state of readiness. But the attack did not materialize at this moment (although the German plan timetabled it for the first half of May). More time was needed on the German side to fit out their *Panzer* divisions with more Tiger-2 68-ton tanks—Tiger battalions had already fought with SS-*Leibstandarte Adolf Hitler* and *Gross Deutschland* at Kharkov—as well as the Panther medium tank and Ferdinand 88mm SP guns. Massed both in and behind the salient were the T-34s, the new KV-85s (the immediate counter to the Tiger-1s), growing numbers of SP guns, the SU-76, the SU-122 and the SU-152, the *samokhodnyi ustanovki (SU)* to provide mobile medium and heavy-gun support. When it came, and as both sides reached their fighting peak, Kursk provided for many ghastly days the greatest clash of armour ever seen, a monsterish confrontation which consumed men and machines in one appalling, fiery nightmare. On the eve of it, the Russians in the salient were under no illusions over what was about to hit them.

*   *   *

Entering now on its third year, though it had lost none of its terror and agonies, the war had finally ceased to be a matter of the rawest improvisation or of Stalin's broad lunges for a speedy kill, two of which had already failed to come off. In his February and May Day statements Stalin emphasized that triumph was on its way, but while measuring off present gains—not without the standard exaggeration of enemy losses—he made it plain enough that the expulsion of the Germans would mean more very heavy fighting. With the battle of Kursk looming over them, the Russians needed little reminder of what they were presently facing. On the eve of Kursk the Red Army mustered 6,442,000 officers and men; 93,500 trained officers were in reserve. In equipment, the Soviet forces could field 103,085 guns and mortars, 9,918 tanks and SP guns and 8,357 combat aircraft—although more than half the guns and mortars were of 76mm and 82mm calibre only, and a third of the tank force consisted of light tanks. An enormous effort was now going into turning out a massive increase, less in manpower than in firepower and mobility—a struggle to win the battle of quality as well as quantity. The scientific and technological war in which the Russians engaged was dictated by the nature of their battlefield commitments: unlike the British military–scientific effort, which was directed to compensating for lack of manpower through advanced machines, the Russian activity aimed to augment rather than to displace purely physical resources.

The Soviet Academy of Sciences had been mobilized for war work on the second day of the war; in July 1941 the Presidium at its plenary session announced that the transition to war work was already 'basically successful'. The Seismological Institute under corresponding member P.M. Nikiforov, was engaged entirely upon 'defence work', which included participation in the huge surveying operation in the Urals for new sources of energy and raw materials, research on the anti-aircraft defence of Moscow and the construction of bomb shelters, as well as developing 'military technology', particularly aircraft. Individual scientists were sent out to plants to advise on special projects. Academician Grebenshchikov supervised the construction of a factory for optical glass and visited all evacuated optical–mechanical factories to supervise their operation; the Physics, Chemical and Technical Institutes of the Academy advised on the demolition of factories and on the reorganization in the east. Institute work was now done in the plants themselves, much as the General and Inorganic Chemistry Institute's analytical laboratory worked in one factory on new methods of producing aluminium. In the autumn of 1941 a great enterprise was launched—Komarov's 'commission for the mobilization of the Urals resources for defence purposes'. The State Defence Committee set up a 'Scientific–Technical Soviet' under the chairmanship of S.V. Kaftanov to deal with the problems of the chemical industry, part of which was also handled by the All-Union Scientific Chemical Society. In the east, in the heart of the new and the recently evacuated plants, Soviet scientists worked on a whole range of 'military–technological problems'; in Magnitogorsk, K.I. Burtsev and his engineers were engaged in improving the armour plate for tanks, while out in the field the geologists expanded their surveys, not the least successful of which was Trofimuk's discovery of large oil deposits in Bashkir. From 1942 Soviet designers were engaged on constant modification to existing weapons and the design of new models. Ya.I. Baran and A.I. Shlaikter improved the T-34 tank (which in 1943 was up-gunned with an 85mm weapon), Engineer Kipgart worked on new light tanks, E.V. Sinilshchikov on producing the SU-122 self-propelled gun on the basis of a T-34 tank chassis, N.N. Kuznetsov on a more powerful M-30 *'Katyusha'* rocket-launcher. Gone were the days when German infantrymen enjoyed their terrifying monopoly in light automatic weapons. Shpagin had produced the Soviet *PPSh*, the machine-pistol liberally distributed among Soviet infantrymen, so that both the veterans (the tough *frontovniki*) and the fresh riflemen were their own walking arsenals. Degtyarev and Tokarev continued to turn out improved models of first-class infantry weapons.

In spite of the increase in aircraft production in the second half of 1942, still more aircraft were needed, and their performance needed to be improved. Lavochkin's LA-5 fighter was modified and its weight reduced; in 1943 the M-28-FN (FN—*forsirovanie neposredstvennim,* 'boosted engine') was fitted to the LA-5 to improve its performance, the modified machine going into service as the LA-5 FN. Large numbers of these fought at Kursk. The LA-5 FN led in turn to the development of the LA-7 with three 20mm cannon and a speed in excess of 400 mph. Yakovlev's Yak-7 fighter (the modified Yak-1) also underwent drastic and very rapid modification in 1942, but now the State Defence Committee demanded a fighter aircraft capable of mounting the heavy 37mm aerial cannon. In record-breaking time a new fighter, the Yak-9, was in quantity production by May 1943; the Yak-9 was also produced as a long-range escort fighter (the Yak-9D, minus the heavy cannon) and, as a 'tank-buster', the Yak-9T. Petlyakov, who was killed in an air crash in 1942, had already produced his twin-engined bomber, the Pe-2, though the first models could not be used in dive-bombing roles; in the second half of 1943 the aircraft was modified and its speed increased, and it went into quantity production. The Tu-2, Tupolev's twin-engined bomber, with a bomb-load of some two tons and a range of 800 miles, also went into production after modification to the prototypes. On the orders of the State Defence Committee, Ilyushin set about improving the Il-2, the famous ground-attack plane, which in February 1943 was fitted with an AM-38f engine and equipped with a 37mm cannon. Soviet aero-engine designers were bringing their power plants up to the 2,000hp mark (and after 1943 they surpassed this, achieving the boost in half the time expended elsewhere on similar efforts). Yakovlev's fighters rolled in growing quantities from Factory No. 153 under V.N. Lisitsyn, Ilyushin's 'tank-busters' from Belyanskii's Factory No. 18, the Yakovlev, Ilyushin and Lavochkin designs marking great strides towards technical superiority.

On the ground lay the challenge of the Tiger and Panther tanks. In Soviet tank factories (as in the aircraft plants) mass line production swelled output; in the Kirov Tank Factory at Chelyabinsk, with its sixty-four production lines, turrets for T-34s were pressed from the metal instead of being cast. The T-34 was undergoing modernization, but meanwhile Kotin's tank design team was working on a new heavy tank, the IS (*Iosip Vissarionovich*), the 'Joseph Stalin', which made its appearance in September 1943. In October 1942 Uralmashzavod received orders to build a prototype self-propelled gun within one month; in January 1943 the first batch of these guns (the SU-122 was delivered to the front, after the State Defence Committee had decided in favour of quantity production in December 1942. Two regiments of SP guns were tested on the Volkhov Front in January, part of the process of forming thirty SP-gun regiments. The Korov Factory was allowed twenty-five days in which to build its SU-152, which in February went into production. Altogether, twenty-one new tank and SP-gun designs were produced in 1943, of which six (including the Joseph Stalin heavy tank) were accepted for production. As the battle for Kursk opened, the Red Army had 500 self-propelled guns organized in its new regiments (and treble that number by the end of that year), weapons that were more akin to the turretless tank than the self-propelled gun, the most orthodox of which was the SU-76, a 76.2mm gun on a T-70 tank chassis.

It was in the summer of 1942 that the State Defence Committee, issuing orders for new aircraft, tanks and guns, took one enormous new decision whose consequence ultimately far overshadowed all others. Soviet scientists would proceed to develop an A-bomb. The great dispersal of Soviet scientists and scientific institutes had thrown fundamental research for the moment out of gear; Professor Joffe's own Radium Institute where research had previously been concentrated, was packed off from Leningrad to distant Kazan. The wartime research programme gave first priority to radar, followed by anti-mine protection for ships, and only then to 'the uranium bomb'. In December 1941 Georgi N. Flerov travelled to Kazan in search of Professor Kurchatov, hoping to persuade him to renew the nuclear experimental programme at the evacuated institute, but as Kurchatov was not there (he was at that time ill), Flerov left notes for a possible experimental programme, and pursued the matter through talks with the Soviet physicists Joffe and Peter Kapitsa. Kurchatov had meanwhile left Kazan for Murmansk to continue work on mines for the Soviet Navy; even if he had wished to embark on an 'experimental programme', Kazan presented major difficulties for such an undertaking, the outcome of which would be highly problematical. Meanwhile news had filtered through to Moscow of German and American work on a 'super-weapon'; Academicians Joffe, Kapitsa, Vernadskii and Khlopin were called to Moscow to discuss the question of the new weapon, while in June 1942 Flerov had written to the State Defence Committee about the urgency of embarking on a programme to build a 'uranium bomb'. Flerov was ordered to report to Kaftanov, the science controller on the State Defence Committee; the Academicians were meanwhile called upon to nominate a director for the Soviet bomb programme, a choice that fell upon Kurchatov. Kurchatov, understandably, was awed at the magnitude of the task and by no means convinced of its utility; vast resources would be consumed at a time when the front required anything and everything to hand.

The work began under the very worst conditions. Flerov started up the experiments with uranium in Kazan, while Leningrad was ransacked for its special equipment and for uranium. At a time when German troops were on the offensive against Stalingrad, there were some who saw no point in this highly recondite work, but at the close of 1942 Kurchatov was appointed director of atomic research and ordered to start operations in Moscow, his association with anti-mine defence and armour plate now ended. The project was given top priority and Kurchatov full powers; the men he wanted were brought back from the front or from the factories, the State Defence Committee supplying a small taskforce to bring the project into existence. In the Seismological Institute, Kurchatov's scientists and engineers started on the design of a new cyclotron, and eventually overflowed into the Institute of Inorganic Chemistry. Once Kharkov was fully and finally liberated, in July 1943 (after Kursk), Soviet scientists set up 'Laboratory No. 1' in the city, while in Moscow Kurchatov sought a site for a completely new 'Laboratory No. 2'. In spite of the grievous difficulties, not least having to organize research amidst the rubble and destruction of recent enemy occupation, the 'bomb project' went ahead into 1943–4—Sinelnikov in his Kharkov laboratory, Kurchatov in Moscow, with Kapitsa and Kurchatov holding main seminars in Moscow, including a secret seminar on nuclear fission and chain reaction.

While the scientists struggled for their long-term results, the soldiers had to master the priorities of the battlefield. By the summer of 1943 the Red Army was in the throes of a major reorganization. The Soviet infantryman had become a walking arsenal, equipped as no other for anti-tank fighting; by June 1943 there were 1,450,000 anti-tank rifles, with 21,000 small-calibre anti-tank weapons distributed among the infantry units (double the amount at the end of 1942). The new *RPG-43* anti-tank grenade was capable of knocking out a medium tank. The High Command artillery reserve regiments—over 200 of them—were equipped largely with 76mm guns. Soviet anti-tank guns enjoyed a good reputation—even Rommel had used captured Soviet anti-tank guns to great effect in the Western Desert. The 45mm and 57mm guns were now modernized and added to the anti-tank resources. At this time also the Goryunov heavy machine-gun replaced the old Maxim system, the trolleyed weapon that had been so prominent earlier in the war.

The structure of both the infantry and the artillery also underwent drastic revision. Among rifle troops, brigades were formed into divisions (with revised establishments) and the corps system was more widely adopted in order to facilitate mass offensive operations. In the artillery, anti-tank regiments were brigaded: for breakthrough operations, howitzer regiments (with the new 152mm and 203mm weapons) were also brigaded, and from the twenty-six artillery divisions raised late in 1942 sixteen were established as 'artillery breakthrough divisions' (with

356 guns as opposed to 168). In April 1943 'artillery breakthrough corps' were introduced. 'Guards mortar brigades', handling the *Katyusha* rocket-launchers, were set up in November 1942; by the end of the year there were four *Katyusha* divisions, each division firing 3,840 projectiles with a weight of 230 tons. In July 1943 the State Defence Committee ordered the rifle armies to take on an artillery component of three artillery regiments and one mortar regiment.

In the offensive operations of 1942–3 the Red Army had been severely inhibited by the lack of lorries. Here Lend-Lease supplies, which pumped in 183,000 lorries and jeeps by mid-1943 (and a grand total of 430,000 by 1944), certainly relieved some of the Red Army's chronic lorry starvation. Every operation, both in preparation and execution, had been impeded by the shortage of lorries; every armoured formation needed more lorries than it could muster. Because of the lack of lorries, the rail links were exploited to a fantastic degree, even to running small trains (a few wagons at the most) for the most diverse purposes. Horse-drawn columns were also used extensively. 'Supplies' of necessity consisted of basic items—ammunition, fuel and food, in that order. The 'Rear Administration', which had first been organized in August 1941, was now reorganized under Order No. 0379 issued by the Defence Commissariat on 12 June 1943, which was essentially a consolidation of all rear services (including the Red Army medical services) under the aegis of the 'chief of the rear', *Nachalnik tyla Krasnoi Armii,* a post Khrulev already held and which he continued to occupy.

In the course of 1943, Stalin added new 'main administrations' to Khrulev's empire—the Main Motor Administration (*Glavnoe Avtomobilnoe Upravlenie*) and the Main Administration for Military Roads (*Glavnoe Dorozhnoe Upravlenie*), responsible for maintaining supply roads and for shifting supplies by road. The Motor Administration supplied and serviced lorries. This reorganization gave Khrulev's 'Rear Administration' a rail unit (Transport), road transportation units (Motors and Military Roads), its supply echelon (Quartermaster or Intendance, for food and clothing), Fuels and Lubricants, and finally Medical and Veterinary Administrations. At Front and army level, the administrative chain was maintained by officers operating as 'chief of the rear' and running similar organizations, with the operational function of relating supplies to Front and army assignments. Khrulev's men supplied and shifted everything except ammunition, weapons and special military equipment. Ammunition, infantry weapons and artillery came under Yakovlev's Main Artillery Administration, whose organization ran right through the artillery command-chain down to battalion: Fedorenko's Armoured Forces Administration similarly controlled the supply (and maintenance) of armoured fighting vehicles; Peresypkin's Signals Administration, the supply of signals equipment; and so on through each 'administration'. The air forces relied on their technical and supply administrations for everything but food, which, like the shipping of air force supplies in general, came within Khrulev's competence.

The Soviet 'tail' from 1943 absorbed just under one-fifth of the manpower of the field strength; by the late summer of 1943 the number of troops assigned to the Main Military Roads Administration amounted to 125,000 men servicing 86,000 kilometres of 'military highway', with 'technical servicing points' over-hauling some 185,000 lorries. The number of railway troops had meanwhile doubled. At Stalingrad, during the preparation of the counter-offensive, fixed 'norms' for supply and daily consumptions in ammunition and fuel were first laid down, all of which subsequently became standard practice; rifle-division ammunition was calculated in 'issues' *(boekomplekty)*, fuel for the armoured formations in 'fills' *(zapravki)* of diesel oil and petrol. These 'norms' could not always be met: Rokossovskii learned this as he prepared his Central Front offensive in February, when the trains failed to show up, when the rear unloading points were far from the concentration areas, when his infantrymen carried their heavy weapons on their backs for long marches and could carry no more. As often as not the Soviet rifleman, weighted with his own weapons and ammunition, would also lug artillery ammunition into the forward areas while horse-drawn columns dashed back into the unloading areas for the divisional supplies. There were never enough lorries, the railways never stretched far enough, but for all the enormous difficulties of terrain, distance, damaged and defective communications, Soviet supply troops shifted some staggering loads, not least as the great multiple offensives were unleashed after the summer of 1943. At Kursk, great quantities of weapons and ammunition were piled up to beat off the German attacks.

Meanwhile the Soviet tank arm, which in 1941–2 had undergone a baptism of fire that almost consumed it, made its massed, dramatic re-entry. Large tank formations had appeared once again in the summer of 1942, only to be ground to pieces in the enormous battles in the south. Their fate then hung in the balance, but it was the practice rather than the principle that was wrong; after November 1942 the large formations had come to stay and to grow. One great handicap, the paucity of equipment, was now being overcome and permitted real development in the tank forces. Lack of tank radios (with no individual radio communications at company level, save for the company commander himself) had made battle control a nightmare, lack of lorries had severely inhibited the tank divisions, and in the 'mechanized' formations the tanks could not synchronize their operations with 'motorized infantry' that lacked transport. The devotees of the tank may have been dispirited, but they were by no means discouraged, and they found an ally in Fedorenko, for all his previous reservations. As chief of the Main Administration for Armoured Forces, Fedorenko started in 1942 upon a major overhaul of the Red Army's tank component after the disasters of the summer, operations that he had commanded in person at one stage. The sudden introduction of large armoured formations (corps) then had meant calling on infantry officers (and officers from other arms) to handle them, an improvisation that had disastrous consequences. One of Fedorenko's first 'reforms' was Order No. 305 of 16 October 1942, laying down firm principles for the conduct of armoured operations, instructions that served the Red Army until the introduction of the combat regulations on armoured and mechanized troops in 1944. By the autumn of 1942 experienced armoured corps commanders like Rotmistrov were convinced that the 'mixed' (tank and infantry) establishment was utterly wrong and that new, wholly armoured, unities must be built up. This was not a view Fedorenko shared, but he became persuaded of its validity. In turn, Fedorenko was able to persuade Stalin and the State Defence Committee at the end of 1942 of the need to form 'tank armies' made up of tanks alone (one–two tank corps, one mechanized corps)—unlike Romanenko's 5th Tank Army, which was an infantry army with tanks attached to it. The 'Front mobile groups' such as Popov's were more like true armoured concentrations. Romanenko's 'tank army' had consisted of two tank corps, six rifle divisions, one cavalry corps, an independent tank brigade, a motorcycle regiment and artillery. Stalin was persuaded. At the beginning of 1943 five 'tank armies', new armoured shock forces, formed up—Katukov's 1st, Rodin's 2nd, Rybalko's 3rd, Badanov's 4th and Rotmistrov's 5th, at a time when the Front commands disposed of 8,500 tanks (as of January 1943), the *Stavka* reserve 400, and non-operational commands and districts 4,300.

The T-34 medium tank, a machine of such basic excellence in design and performance that it lasted the war without major modification (and whose features were incorporated into new marks of German tanks, German engineers having discovered that making a straight copy of the T-34 would not pay off), was basic equipment for the tank armies. Now the new heavy tanks were coming into service. Since the autumn of 1942 the KV-1 had been produced as the KV-1S (thicker armour, a 76mm gun and three machine-guns), and by the summer of 1943 the KV-1S acquired yet more armour and an 85mm gun, emerging as the KV-85. Mounting a 152mm howitzer, the KV-1S chassis was used to produce the SU-152, a self-propelled gun nicknamed 'the hunter'. The KV-85 had squared up to the Tiger-I, but the new heavy battle tank was the IS-1, the 'Joseph Stalin-1', utilizing the KV chassis but with modifications to the hull front and a larger turret, an 85mm gun and a weight of 44 tons. The IS-2 soon eclipsed the IS-1; with a 122mm gun, three machine-guns and a heavy-calibre AA machine-gun, strong armour, low profile and a weight of 45 tons, the IS-2 combined speed, protection, hitting power and relatively low weight. Only 102 IS-2s were produced in 1943, but in 1944 2,250 rolled out of the factories. Meanwhile the Soviet command proceeded to build up special tank formations. Already at Stalingrad 'Guards special tank breakthrough regiments' had appeared, and in 1943, as newer machines became available, no less than eighteen 'High Command reserve independent heavy tank breakthrough regiments' had been quickly brought into existence.

In 1943 the Armoured Forces Administration complained to Mikoyan that they were receiving 'no great quantity' of tanks from Lend-Lease, and that among present deliveries the percentage of medium tanks fell constantly, so that light tanks predominated. By 1942 more than 2,000 American tanks and upwards of 2,500 British machines had been delivered to Russia: for the whole period from June 1941 to April 1944 the Red Army was sent 3,734 American tanks, 4,292 British tanks and a further 1,400 tanks from Canada. The Soviet command was not overly impressed with the performance of these machines, the British tanks in particular coming in for some harsh remarks. For their battle equipment, the Russians relied mainly on the products of their own factories. In 1942 Stalin himself had said that he wanted lorries before tanks. Lorries and jeeps did flood the Russians and were eagerly snapped up. Food and petroleum products were delivered in massive bulk and provided support for Soviet stamina. By mid-1943 the Americans had shipped in over 900,000 tons of steel, 1.5 million tons of food, 138,000 trucks and jeeps, boots, industrial equipment, raw materials— in all a highly variegated military–industrial shopping list which included 12,000 tons of butter sent for Soviet troops convalescing in military hospitals, shipped specifically at Russian request. It was not for the tanks or even the aircraft that Stalin pressed so furiously over interruption of delivery, but for the food and industrial supplies—metals (aluminium, steel billets, steel sheets, steel strip and tubing, copper and zinc), chemicals and machine-tools ($150 million worth of which were sent to the Soviet Union by mid-1943).

Innovation and modernization in organization and weapons, proof that Soviet commanders had learned much and were not inclined merely to copy, whetted several appetites for very drastic change. In effect, two armies were emerging in the Soviet establishment, the army of 'quality', the élite tank arm, the Guards and the crack formations, behind which the army of 'quantity' formed up in its solid ranks. The tank arm had finally liberated itself from the shackle of infantry-support roles. The new tank armies, bulging with modern tanks, were to become both the shock-force and the spearhead of the Red Army, whatever the doctrine about 'harmonious development', which itself was mainly a rationalization of binding fast, mobile formations to slower-moving rifle troops. There were other shackles, however, that irked the senior commanders, who were now enjoying the freedom of *edinonachalie* and the prestige of victory, a prestige with which Stalin was carefully aligning himself. The army had forced concessions, major ones like 'unitary command', subtle ones like having security officers wear standard uniform and military insignia. But there were limits. Stalin wanted his army 'run by the book'—*golye prikazy*, 'straight orders'—and this was now being done. There were senior officers, among them Gordov, who began to read these signs of the times very literally, judging that now was the moment to shove the party political apparatus aside and the political officers along with it. In June 1943 General Gordov (then commanding 33rd Army) wrote to Stalin and Zhukov suggesting that 'the Military Soviet of Armies should be liquidated, as an organ which had outlived its usefulness and which brought no advantage'; the political sections should be incorporated into the military staff, their right of contact with political organs in higher echelons eliminated and the local army newspapers produced by the military staff. Such a suggestion probably did not rub Stalin too much the wrong way; he had already pushed the Party out of the way himself, brutally if it suited his purposes, and he showed very consistently that the kind of 'control' he preferred was that exercised by the *NKVD* mechanism rather than through the Party agencies. In 1941, when all seemed lost, he used the *NKVD* to move in behind the military commissars as the real controlling agency and he kept the secret police at it, whether to keep a persistent eye on commanders or on the armed forces at large. The military soviet at army level (comprising the commander, chief of staff and the 'political member') was not formally abolished as Gordov suggested, though, as a captured Soviet lieutenant-general explained to his German interrogators, the operation of the military soviet turned increasingly on the personality of the commander himself. The system looked as clumsy as ever, but if not actually discarded it became less unwieldy as the authority of the officers continued to grow. Gordov's letter of June 1943 nevertheless remains an enigmatic document with only the tip of the iceberg showing. Though it had no immediate sequel, in 1946 Gordov was abruptly removed from his command. Either in 1943 or subsequently, he had gone further with his 'suggestions', advocating not merely kicking the Party out of the army but even the elimination of the communist imprint itself, by establishing a 'national', explicitly 'Russian' army—a move Stalin would never have countenanced.

The Red Army was presently being geared for massive offensive operations. Marshal Vasilevskii put it succinctly to Tolbukhin and Biryuzov at the end of May: it was plain that Germany was weakened, that Soviet troops overshadowed the enemy 'in quality and in quantity', that the Soviet command had 'solid experience' of waging offensive operations on a grand scale, that discipline had been strengthened, order instituted and that *organizovannost* ('being lined up') prevailed. The slump that all authority, military governmental and party political, had suffered was a thing of the past. Basically Vasilevskii was right, if a little over-sanguine. From its atom-bomb project to the roaring factories of the east, or the frantic work to put the liberated areas to rights, the country was economically enormously stretched, but it was turning out the weapons and bringing up the supplies. The cost was appalling and continued to rise, an enormous toll of men, machines and resources; one part of the country wrecked by a fearsome and greedy enemy occupation, the other stripped by its own authorities for war. The old, the women and the youngsters took over from the men who had vanished, on the land (where ninety per cent of the lorries and a third of the tractors were 'mobilized' for transportation and gun-towing) and in the factories, where even children worked a few hours a day on uncomplicated jobs, for which their meagre rations were fractionally increased.

In the early summer of 1943 a point of balance was reached, which each side hoped to tip decisively in its favour. The Russians could not now lose the war, but the Germans could scarcely count on winning. For all the relative quietness of the front, as both sides massed their men and concentrated their most modern weapons, moments of profound significance were passing. Finally, on 16 June, Hitler decided that *Citadel,* the attack on Kursk that was to bring a victory 'to shine like a beacon round the world', the momentous offensive which the *Führer* confessed to Guderian made his 'stomach turn over', was to open early in July.

3

Breaking the Equilibrium:
Kursk and its Aftermath

On Friday, 4 June 1943, Stalin learned officially of 'certain decisions on strategic matters' taken by the American President and the British Prime Minister. The cross-Channel invasion, proposed for August–September 1943, was now postponed until the spring of 1944. It was a decision which, as Stalin underlined in his reply of 11 June, created 'exceptional difficulties for the Soviet Union . . . and leaves the Soviet Army, which is fighting not only for its country, but also for its allies, to do the job alone, almost single-handed . . .'; the postponement would produce 'a dishearteningly negative impression' among the Soviet people and in the army. The message, mild enough in its phrasing, was nevertheless laden with the gravest implications, a point Stalin himself underscored in his final sentence; from Moscow the British ambassador, Sir Archibald Clark Kerr, warned his government not to mistake this mildness for anything but badly shaken confidence in the coalition. The subsequent exchange between Stalin and Churchill was certainly tart. Prime Minister Churchill in his communication of 19 June reminded Stalin that he would not be a party to a 'useless massacre' which would scarcely aid the Soviet armies; the 'Mediterranean strategy' with German defeat in North Africa and 'the consequent threat to Southern Europe', was itself bringing results, having already delayed Hitler's plans for a major attack in Russia. Stalin had complained that he had not been consulted over these decisions: this was the outcome of the failure to meet earlier with Churchill and Roosevelt, though all understood that Stalin could not abstract himself—'even for a week'—from the direction of an 'immense and victorious campaign'. But now there must be a 'Big Three' meeting. Five days later Stalin replied, opening in legalistic style with a list of Anglo-American 'undertakings' (including the *aide-mémoire* of June 1942) to attack across the Channel; Stalin was not asking for the slaughter of 'a hundred thousand men in a disastrous cross-Channel attack', because he understood that an Anglo-American force 'exceeding one million men at the very start of the operation' would be involved. This was not mere 'disappointment', but the issue of preserving Soviet confidence in its Allies, a confidence 'being subjected to severe stress'. Lives in occupied Europe and Russia must be saved, the 'enormous sacrifices of the Soviet armies'—compared to which Anglo-American losses were 'insignificant'—must be reduced.

These were reproaches that left Churchill, on his own declaration in the 27 June message, 'unmoved'; everything that could be done had been done, there was still only one American division in England, landing craft were in short supply and war with Japan made additional demands. Stalin himself had described the 'Mediterranean strategy' as 'militarily correct'. So far, no major German attack in Russia had materialized and it was already deep into June; should it not materialize at all, this would demonstrate that 'the Mediterranean strategy' was not only 'correct' but in essence decisive. Here, for the moment, the Churchill-Stalin exchange rested, though the tussle continued through other events interlinked with the correspondence—Soviet recognition of General de Gaulle's French National Committee of Liberation (which the British and Americans would not recognize), and one issue of far wider significance and even greater sensitivity, the problem of Poland, which Stalin now seemed determined to solve in his own fashion. In the early spring of 1943 a separate Polish national–political organization (separate, that is, from the 'London Poles') had been set up in Moscow; this *SPP*, 'Union of Polish Patriots', then 'suggested' to the Soviet government that a formation of Polish fighting troops be organized on Soviet soil, an 'initiative' that the Soviet government found admirable and was prepared to support, according to a decision made public on 9 May. The Soviet government bore all costs, and assigned a military camp near Ryazan for the forming and equipping of the First Kościuszko Division, trained by Soviet officer–instructors and manned by Polish volunteers. On 13 May, the first six men of the Polish division arrived at the Ryazan camp: the next day the commander-designate, Colonel Berling (promoted colonel the day of the Soviet governmental announcement), arrived, followed within the month by 10,000 men, who on 15 July took the military oath. The Kościuszko Division was formed, the military core of the 'new Poland' which the *SPP* itself foreshadowed.

The Germans had already inserted themselves with some skill into the trip-wires of what was a very delicate Anglo–Russian–Polish relationship. At 9:15 pm on the evening of 13 April 1943, Berlin radio announced the discovery near Smolensk—at Kosogory, part of Katyn wood—of 'a great pit . . . 28 metres long and 16 metres wide, filled with 12 layers of bodies of Polish officers, numbering about 3,000' mummified bodies 'clad in full military uniform . . . many of them had their hands tied, all of them had wounds in the back of their necks caused by pistol shots'. New layers were being found under those already exhumed: the total figure of the murdered officers 'is estimated at about 10,000, which would more or less correspond to the entire number of Polish officers taken as prisoners of war by the Bolsheviks'. Goebbels was overjoyed at the success of this propaganda *coup* (though on 8 May he confided to his diary that 'German ammunition has been found in the graves at Katyn', one item of information to be kept 'a top secret', else 'the whole Katyn affair would have to be dropped'). The Soviet press vehemently (if somewhat confusedly) denied that there was evidence of a Soviet crime: relations between the Soviet government and the London Polish government underwent an 'interruption', while at the end of April (the twenty-eighth) Wanda Wassilevska forecast in *Izvestiya* a new Polish army, raised on Soviet soil and independent of the London government. Ten days later that became an accomplished fact. Stalin's message of 4 May explained 'the Soviet government's view of Soviet–Polish relations' to the British Prime Minister. Sikorski, 'helpless and browbeaten', could not keep the 'vast pro-Hitler following' of the London government in order, the German version that 'a new Polish government' was being formed in the Soviet Union was a 'fabrication' which scarcely needed a denial, but nevertheless the time had come 'to improve the composition' of the present Polish government—'the sooner this is done, the better'. Three days later in a talk with the British ambassador in Moscow Stalin made this point once again, that the Polish government would have to be 'reconstructed'.

Wherever possible, Stalin applied pressure on his allies, though he was careful to strike some cordial notes, most of which coincided with Soviet successes. The Allies came in for some praise for their North Africa operations at the time of the Soviet victory at Stalingrad; with the Germans on the rampage at Kharkov, Stalin in his February order of the day passed over the Western Allies in silence; after an ugly incident when the American ambassador in March complained of Russian denigration of Lend-Lease help, public tribute was paid forthwith. The acrid correspondence between Churchill and Stalin in May and June followed this pattern consistently, for Stalin knew that he was facing another major German attack. At the same time, a new (or rather a refurbished) theme entered the exchanges—that Russia was a 'second-class ally', whose interests were considered only at second-hand. From the Russian side, the picture was not vastly encouraging, in spite of all the organized *bonhomie* in the press about Western contributions. The convoys through 'the northern route' were again suspended; the 'aerial second front', which was formally opened with the United States Air Force daylight raids into the Ruhr in January 1943, scarcely held up the supply of new weapons to the German armies in the east. The cross-Channel invasion was postponed yet again when by Soviet estimates only twenty-five German divisions, many of them withdrawn from the east where they had been battered on the Russian front and were therefore in the process of re-fitting, held northern France, Belgium and Holland (about which Stalin could gain first-hand information from Soviet intelligence operating in western Europe through an 'arrangement' with SOE— (Special Operations Executive). In spite of Churchill's efforts to convince him, Stalin was reluctant to admit much merit in the 'Mediterranean strategy' (which he had earlier endorsed): he had complained that for 'unexplained reasons' Allied operations in North Africa seemed to have stalled, and he then turned on *Husky* (the proposed invasion of Sicily) as a wholly unacceptable substitute for operations across the Channel. The British Prime Minister piled on the detail about the

massive bomber offensive against Germany, which again failed to evince much
of a response from Stalin (though Soviet airmen felt the effects of German fighter
strength drawn westwards as the Soviet air offensive opened in the spring of
1943).

Stalin pounded on obstinately, arguing that out of present circumstance and
previous commitment the Americans and British should disregard all else in
favour of priority for the second front in northern France, an invasion before the
end of the summer of 1943. His 16 March message to President Roosevelt put
this at its bluntest: '. . . I consider it my duty to state that the early opening
of a second front in France is the most important thing [and] it is . . . particularly
essential for us that the blow from the West be no longer delayed, that it be
delivered this spring or in early summer.' In May Joseph E. Davies, former
ambassador to the Soviet Union during the period of the great purges and author
of *Mission to Moscow,* which had so favourably mirrored those purges, arrived
in Moscow bearing a private message from the President suggesting 'an informal
and completely simple visit for a few days between you [Stalin] and me [Roosevelt],
possibly on the American or Russian sides of the Bering Straits'. The President
hoped for a 'meeting of minds'. By way of intelligence, President Roosevelt added
that 'our estimates' were that 'Germany will deliver an all-out attack on you this
summer', which American officers indicated would fall 'against the middle of
your line'. In his reply (26 May), Stalin referred straightway to the military
situation: '. . . this summer—possibly as early as June—we should expect the
Hitlerites to launch a new major offensive. . . . Hitler has already concentrated
about 200 German divisions and up to 30 divisions of his allies. . . . We are
getting ready to repel the new German offensive and to launch counter-attacks,
but we are short of aircraft and aircraft fuel.' For that reason, since 'the summer
months will be exceedingly trying for the Soviet armies', Stalin could not commit
himself to leave Moscow in June but he would plan it for July or August. The
degree of Stalin's concern over the forthcoming German attack was constant; his
pressure upon his Allies to win from them a major re-ordering of priorities reached
its peak late in June, though by that time his hopes for any solution along these
lines must have been faint indeed. From this point his concern was preparation
for the high-level meetings which were already clearly foreshadowed, though
Stalin lost not a single opportunity to remind his allies of their 'obligation' and
of his own 'difficulties'.

In spite of the sense of dislocation and the exchange of recriminations, the
coalition was not coming apart at the seams. The very real acrimony of the
Stalin–Churchill exchange in May and June led the British Prime Minister to
wonder if the Russians might be contemplating 'a change of policy'—negotiating
their way out of the war—but the Foreign Office, though aware of one 'peace-
feeler' waved vaguely about in neutral circles, dismissed this as a most unlikely
eventuality. Moreover, Stalin fixed to his public standards in no uncertain fashion
both 'unconditional surrender' and going on to victory in the company of his

allies; in his May Day order Stalin referred to the 'peace-feelers' as a mere German trap, while the real prize was victory, the rout of Nazi Germany and its allies, accomplished by the Red Army *together with the Allied armies*. This public proclamation also served another purpose, as an indirect warning to these allies by Stalin not to dicker too deviously behind his back.

There had been one bout of abortive negotiation between the United States and Finland; the Russians were inevitably curious about rumours of the Rumanians considering surrender to the 'Anglo-American command', a situation that became seriously contorted when Antonescu visited Mussolini in Rome in June 1943, just before the fall of Mussolini, and the ensuing negotiations for an armistice with Italy. In North Africa, Stalin had already opened a passage for his presence, even by proxy, by recognizing the French National Committee of Liberation in Algiers and by 'legitimizing' de Gaulle. On 26 June Stalin informed Churchill that 'the Soviet government had no information that could support the British government's present attitude [witholding recognition]' and had none in the respect concerning General de Gaulle, but 'the Soviet Government' would meet the British Government 'half-way' if 'the Soviet interest in French affairs' was recognized and if 'timely information' on these events was not denied to 'the Soviet Government'. Information of a kind the Soviet government did indeed possess: on 11 May 1943 Ambassador Bogomolov in London (accredited to the Allied governments in exile and to the Free French) had listened to General de Gaulle's list of difficulties and reservations, the latter directed towards General Giraud:

I [Bogomolov] said that I completely understood the difficulties in the situation of the National Committee, which the Soviet Union looked upon with a sympathetic attitude, sympathy which might well find its expression in a formula of recognition of the National Committee by the Soviet government. On the other hand, the policy of the Soviet Union comprised support or encouragement for all those anti-Hitlerite forces which, whatever their shape or form, took an active part in the struggle against Hitlerite Germany.

At this, which apparently did not please de Gaulle, de Gaulle reaffirmed his view, that if Giraud acquired full power in his own hands and influence in France, then France would become a weapon in the hands of reactionary American circles and the people of Vichy inside France itself, which outcome would not be favourable for Russia.

. . . Further, I asked de Gaulle how he appraised the present situation in Africa. De Gaulle outlined the successes of the English and the Americans in moderate terms and in reproachful tone said that neither England nor America, nor anybody else for that matter, had mentioned the part of his troops in the Tunis operation. I asked de Gaulle how many Frenchmen had taken part in the operation. He said that there had been about 50,000 of Giraud's men and about 30,000 of his troops.

To my question as to how he placed himself in present conditions in the matter of the Soviet–Polish conflict, de Gaulle made this reply: on the one hand, France was concerned that a free and independent Poland should exist, yet, on the other hand, France was also concerned that Russia should have a most favourable strategic frontier to the west and, of course, on the Baltic. In this connection de Gaulle added that should he come to power, then France, without reservation, would support Russia over the question of the frontiers in the spirit of the Curzon Line. [*Sov./Frantsuzskie Otnosheniya*, no. 55, pp. 132–3.]

From both sides, Soviet and Free French, this was a skillfully angled conversation.

On the same day that Stalin sent his soothing reply to Churchill on de Gaulle (26 June), he followed up his concession with an immediate request, that Bogomolov be allowed to proceed to North Africa to 'report on the situation'. This produced Anglo-American objections, which in turn met with a furious intervention by Molotov on 2 July, demanding of the American ambassador in Moscow that 'the Soviet government' be allowed some first-hand representation in North Africa. While the invasion of Sicily went forward, Soviet pressure for representation in North Africa was relaxed, but in August, when the Italian armistice negotiations were afoot, Stalin intervened personally to complain once more of 'not being kept informed of the Anglo-American negotiations', with delays in the transmission of highly important matters which Stalin found hard to understand. The time had come to set up a tripartite military–political commission to deal with 'various governments falling away from Germany': 'To date it has been like this: the USA and Britain reach agreement between themselves while USSR is informed of the agreement between the two Powers as a third party looking passively on.'

Viewed in their collectivity, these events and *démarches* did not suggest that Stalin was embarking on any new major policy initiatives, but he was certainly establishing bridgeheads, enlisting lesser allies within the alliance and clearing the ground for action against a number of eventualities. To the consternation of the rigidly orthodox, he did away with the *Komintern,* which gave him a double advantage—it had the air of a concession to the West, and it rid him of a wholly obsolete political organization, the 'grocer's shop', the *lavochka,* which had for so long been a symbol in East and West of a virulent, menacing communism. (If anything, the Stalinist techniques of 1943–4 were strongly reminiscent of Civil War days, with separate national 'liberation committees' and the widespread agitation in the prisoner-of-war camps, out of which now came a German committee and a 'prisoner-of-war congress' quite on the lines of its famous ancestor held in Samara in 1918.) While Stalin set about brow-beating the London Poles, he was careful to handle the Czech government in London with great care and punctiliousness. Benes himself in May propounded plans to discuss Soviet–Czech relations with Stalin, though in June Eden raised objections with Benes over any move to formalize agreement, since a treaty at this stage might impinge damagingly on Soviet–Polish relations. After hearing further from Molotov early in July, Eden persisted in his objection since any Soviet–Czech treaty would contribute to the isolation of Poland. That point certainly did not escape Stalin's attention.

Late in July Stalin evoked another minor sensation with the revelation of the 'Free German Movement', the National Committee for a Free Germany (*Nationales*

Komitee für ein Freies Deutschland: NKD), whose 'preparatory committee' included Walter Ulbricht, Erich Weinert and Lieutenant Count Heinrich von Einsiedel (a prisoner of war and Bismarck's great-grandson). On 12–13 July 1943 a special conference at Krasnogorsk, not far from Moscow, brought the *NKD* officially into existence: Weinert became president, Count von Einsiedel and Major Karl Hetz vice-presidents. The newsheet of this body was *Freies Deutschland*— flamboyantly and evocatively 'national' with the Imperial German colours of black–white–red emblazoned across; and if this was not something to set the teeth of the exiled German Communists on edge, then there were the six broadcasts each day going out on twelve wave-lengths, all preceded by the patriotic song of the first 'Liberation War' of 1813, *'Der Gott, der Eisen wachsen liess . . .'*. But the *NKD*, for all the special fanfare, cut little ice with senior German officers in Russian captivity; *Institute 205* (successor to the *Komintern*, so ostentatiously 'dissolved') deliberately stressed the 'national' line, but the captured German generals were largely unmoved by this. Another 'special committee' set about organizing a new body, the *Bund Deutscher Offiziere (BDO)*, the 'League of German Officers'; in July Generals Seydlitz, Lattmann and Korfes were transferred to a special camp at Lyunovo, also near Moscow, and though at first unwilling to participate in activities smelling of a 'stab in the back', on being persuaded on 11 September 1943 of the existence of a 'reasonable' Soviet policy in the event of the war in the East ending through the German military's action against Hitler, the generals agreed to the *BDO*. The *BDO* subsequently 'merged' with the *NKD*.

During the summer of 1943 also the campaign against the captured Soviet general Vlasov, engaged in forming the 'Russian Liberation Army' *(ROA)*, hotted up—the *Anti-Wlassow Aktion*, with its highly organized and carefully differentiated propaganda programme, considered methods of infiltrating the 'Vlasov movement' and even of killing Vlasov himself. It was not just Vlasov however. Before the Kursk offensive, the Germans had begun a large-scale propaganda campaign designed to restore the confidence and to excite the allegiance of the population in the occupied districts, at the same time aiming to recruit former Soviet citizens for military or para-military service on the German side and to incite Red Army troops to desert. Vlasov was a name to exploit, and it was exploited in the *Smolensker Aufruf*, the 'Smolensk manifesto', of early 1943. A real change in German policy, a definite shift from the barbarities and inhuman excesses which had worked automatically to alienate the population, had serious implications for the further development of the Soviet partisan movement. If the Vlasov movement was to be a catalyst of important changes on the German side, then it was doubly dangerous: in an interrogation of Captain Boris Rusanov, who had served on the staff of Col.-Gen. Strokach (chief of staff to the Soviet partisan movement in the Ukraine), the Germans learned that the Soviet leadership had seen considerable menace in this new German 'initiative'. Stalin himself had apparently commented on Vlasov that he was 'at the very least a large obstacle on the road to victory over the German Fascists'. General Strokach repeated that as Stalin's own words. Because it was in the German-occupied areas that 'the Vlasov movement' had become very well known in a relatively short period, it was here that Soviet counter-effort first made its real appearance.

Through printed propaganda the Soviet authorities made a widespread and systematic effort to blacken Vlasov as a traitor and as a tool of the Germans, in addition to attacking the *ROA* and exposing the fraudulence of the political programme, the 'thirteen points.' This open and official blast was accompanied by a more subtle 'whispering campaign' aimed at those who were 'patriotic' even if they were not 'loyal to the regime'. 'Collaborators' were downright 'anti-Soviet', but there were other dispositions, inclinations open to persuasion. None of the lines of demarcation were exact, a condition produced partly by German policy itself; units collaborating with the Germans—like the Kaminsky Brigade in its anti-partisan operations or the '*SS Druzhina*', an extraordinary unit under Gill-Rodionov (ex-Major Gill of the Red Army, defector, using Rodionov as his *nom de guerre*) which changed sides in a highly complicated pattern—were scattered over wide areas and different regions, increasingly infiltrated after 1942 by Soviet intelligence agents and partisans or partisan sympathizers with orders to arrange the re-defection of the unit or to kill the renegade commanders (or both). German policy itself, with stiff Nazi resistance to the idea of using the *Untermensch* to fight in the line, added other peculiarities. German anti-partisan forces by 1943 nevertheless had a strong component of 'defector–collaborationist units' (the powerful Kaminsky Brigade being most prominent), usually organized along battalion lines. But much as there was a significant degree of Red Army 'defection–collaboration', what was equally distinctive was the incidence of 're-defection'. In July 1943, the Soviet campaign to induce 're-defection', in order to discredit German propaganda and to penetrate the Vlasov movement, was in full swing; the convening of a trial at Krasnodar at this time to sentence to death Russians who had collaborated with *Gestapo*, an occasion attended by the dissemination of much appalling material on German atrocities, followed the next day by the announcement of *Freies Deutschland*, was evidently part of a systematic and sustained psychological and propaganda offensive. There was 'defection' too on the German side.

The Soviet Major Kapustin was assigned (presumably with others) a singular role in the *Anti-Wlassow Aktion* (the files of which contain his interrogation report): recruited by the *NKVD* from a Soviet penal institution, Kapustin could purchase his rehabilitation at the price of infiltrating the Vlasov movement. In May, Kapustin duly 'deserted' to the Germans in order to get into the Vlasov circle with the aim of encouraging re-defection and finally of killing Vlasov himself. To encourage this re-defection, Kapustin with Moscow's special authorization was allowed to propagate a political programme shrewdly conceived to appeal to collaborator patriotism and self-interest:

–the German aim was the enslaving of Russia; the *ROA* was a German tool;

–the Soviet system had already conceded a number of popular demands (the recognition of the Church, the displacement of the commissars);

–Soviet leadership had now decided that only the Great Russians had passed the test of war; the post-war 'Soviet Union' would merge the separate republics under Great Russian rule;

–the post-war political system would be drastically modified, with the republics dismantled, with the Communist Party turned into a people's party with a broad educational mission, with Stalin himself removed in favour of Andreyev and with the collective farms also disbanded. (See GMD, T-78/R491, 6477824-26/827-31.)

This had lavish patriotic appeal and a chauvinistic twist to Russian feelings—Russia for the Russians, minus Stalin and stripped of its collectivization. Of immediate interest in the 'Kapustin programme' was the offer of amnesty for men who turned away from collaboration, and finally a flourish at the end over Russians settling Russian problems without the Germans coming in as interlopers. This was shrewd stuff, with its broad patriotic appeal and its man-to-man admission that things were by no means perfect but that they would get better, plus the artful but very positive displacement of the Germans. Elsewhere throughout occupied Russia, and especially in partisan-controlled areas, the notion grew up and was widely spread that 'the people' were themselves under arms, that Stalin's leadership, though very necessary to beat the Germans, was only 'temporary'; once the war was won, who knows what the future would bring. This popular myth, if not actually cultivated by the Soviet authorities, was certainly exploited to the full and proved to have many positive benefits and attractions.

For the poor Soviet prisoners of war caught between two masters, sacrificed on the battlefield only to be hurled into a terrible hell of starvation, extermination or slave labour, all on an appalling scale, with both sides attracted by this pool of manpower, the struggle over 'collaboration' only made their situation worse. Gill-Rodionov's record was a prime illustration. 'I betrayed my country not from political motives, but to save my skin': that was Gill-Rodionov's own explanation. Chief of staff to the 29th Rifle Division, Gill-Rodionov was made prisoner in July 1941, taken to Berlin, trained in a *Gestapo* institution and then sent back to Suwalki PW (prisoner-of-war) camp to set up 'national units'—the *druzhina*, which in October 1942 was moved up, 500 men strong, to Moghilev to operate against Nichiporovich's Soviet partisans. Six months later Gill-Rodionov took another *druzhina*, formed by Blazhevich, into his command and formed under German auspices the '1st Russian *SS* National Regiment', 1,200 men strong. In the summer of 1943, Gill-Rodionov set about organizing a brigade of the *ROA*, well equipped and operating with regular *SS* formations. The brigade was assigned to anti-partisan operations, though it was evidently penetrated by partisan agents who reported on the decline in morale among Gill's men. The time for a 're-defection' operation was ripe.

At the end of July the Belorussian Staff of the Partisan Movement authorized the Soviet partisan brigade *Zheleznyak* to open negotiations with the *ROA* brigade. Gill-Rodionov nominated Bogdanov, brigade counter-intelligence officer and a man with close *Gestapo* connections, as his representative. Bogdanov systematically sabotaged the talks, and with his own neck at stake he had little option. The second round of negotiations were conducted with Gill-Rodionov himself and the deal was done—Gill-Rodionov and his own men were to 'wipe out their treason' by fighting the Germans; the *ROA* brigade was to come over to the Soviet side fully armed; Bogdanov and *SS* commander Count Mirsky were to be handed over to the partisans; the rest of the Germans were to be dealt with as Gill-Rodionov saw fit. On 13 August 1943 the *ROA* brigade, already standing to, attacked the Germans in its midst, carried off Bogdanov and Mirsky and passed over to the Soviet side, where it was formally organized as the '1st Anti-Fascist Brigade' under Gill-Rodionov, who finally carried out all the terms of the bargain—he was killed in action and his brigade was decimated. The 're-defection' of this brigade was a signal success for the Russians, and passing back to the Soviet side became widespread; late in 1943 the Germans began pulling these PW para-military formations into the west, to France, the Low Countries and Italy, away from occupied Russia. There remained a collaborationist core of militia men and lowly officials which melted more slowly, but after Kursk the writing was on the wall for them. The main Soviet objective was attained, the paralysis of the *Wlassow-Aktion* to obtain military manpower and civilian allegiance, pitting Russians against Russians, though the Nazi leadership itself inflicted the heaviest blows by refusing to allow any concession that might have given the *Wlassow-Aktion* some political reality.

Military defeat, cracking the armour of German invincibility, coupled with hideous manias which mutilated any realistic policies, automatically doomed the collaborators. Vlasov himself during his Smolensk 'tour' strenuously resisted the idea that he was being used as a German 'dupe'; his aim, by his own definition, was to school Russians in resistance to Stalin, to train a politically intelligent and discriminating group. The Germans came a good second in all this, they were even a means to an end. But it was a sadder, sombre Vlasov who went about his 'tours', conducted by courtesy of the Germans in the occupied districts. The Nazis meant to throttle him and Soviet counter-propaganda steadily cut the ground from under his feet.

At home, on both sides of the line, and also abroad, the nationalist line with its strong chauvinist overtones pursued by Stalin paid handsome dividends. At home, the vague, wafted promises of improvement linked with the stimulus to patriotic fervour, the recognition of the Patriarchate or the dissolution of the *Komintern* (which appeased his Western allies) were construed by Russians and foreigners alike as signs of real respectability now emerging through the deep murk of war. Yet, as his compatriots and allies were to discover (if they did not already guess), for Stalin respectability and tractability had virtually no connection at all.

Having already postponed Operation *Citadel* once, on 18 June Hitler decided in his famous 'irrevocable' style to proceed with the attack, although he weighed a proposal by *OKW* to cancel *Citadel* in favour of building up a strong central reserve. On 1 July at his headquarters in East Prussia Hitler harangued his commanders about the need to demonstrate German superiority and the necessity to open the way to final victory; this would be done at Kursk, where the German offensive would open on July 5. In spite of the pleas of senior officers to change tactics, the plan prepared by Zeitzler, chief of the Army General Staff, was a repeat performance of methods used so often; the Kursk salient would be eliminated by a double envelopment, with Model's Ninth Army (seven infantry, eight *Panzer* and *Panzer-Grenadier* divisions) concentrated west of Maloarkhangelsk on the northern face, and on the southern face in the Belgorod area *Armee-Abteilung Kempf* and Hoth's Fourth *Panzer* Army (seven infantry, eleven *Panzer* divisions, three assault-gun brigades), with two air fleets (*Luftflotten* 4 and 6) in support. It was certainly a formidable demonstration of German strength—2,700 tanks and assault-guns (more than half fielded by Hoth and Kempf in the south), 1,800 aircraft, two-thirds of the infantry divisions brought up to a strength of 12,500 officers and men, the *Panzer* divisions with 16,000 men and up to 209 tanks and assault guns in each, the *SS Panzer* formations packed with tanks.

At this point 'Lucy' served Stalin superbly. Hitler held his battle conference on 1 July: the next day Stalin sent out an urgent signal to the commanders of the Central, Voronezh and Steppe Fronts:

According to information at our disposal, the Germans may go over to the offensive on our front between 3–6 July.

The *Stavka* of the Supreme Commander orders:

1. intensification of reconnaissance and observation of the enemy in order to ensure timely discovery of his intentions;
2. ground troops and aircraft to be at readiness to repel possible enemy blow.

Soviet troops were at once deployed in their defensive lines, though the Front commands were baffled by the totally unexpected stillness that descended in the German concentration areas west of Belgorod and south of Orel; even night-time movements of troops and equipment ceased. Heavy traffic was reported far to the south of Kharkov on roads into the Donbas—tanks, trucks and lorries, which suggested German movement away from the salient. The German radio gave much deliberate coverage to Field-Marshal von Manstein's visit to Bucharest to award Antonescu his gold cross; on the evening of 3 July, however, Manstein was back in his HQ, while Model moved to his forward command centre. German air attacks delivered by day and night had intensified during late

June; one German bomb load in a night raid hit Rokossovskii's HQ, and Rokossovskii escaped only because on a whim he had decided to set up his signals group in the officers' mess. After that, Central Front HQ went underground in a bunker in the garden of a former monastery. While German bombers massed for their heavy raids and flew by day with heavy fighter protection, aiming for the rail links and airfields in the Kursk salient, Soviet aircraft—fulfilling Stalin's order that 'attacks on railway traffic, strikes at road transport columns are the prime assignments of our aviation'—hammered away at the German concentration areas. Both sides went for each other's aerodromes: the dummy airfields in the salient—the brain-children of Major Lukyanov of the 2nd Air Army, who lavished infinite care on them—were heavily pounded. Soviet fighters were now ordered to keep German reconnaissance planes away from Soviet defences, while at the beginning of July Vatutin learned from the pilot of a shot-down He-111 that fresh squadrons were moving up to Kharkov from the Crimea.

All the signs indicated a German attack, and although the *Stavka* signal confirmed this, Rokossovskii and Vatutin were severely exercised to know just when and where. In the late afternoon of 4 July one hundred German planes coming out of the clouds bombed and strafed Soviet forward positions northwest of Belgorod; artillery fire and tank attacks followed the aerial bombardment, which was renewed for several hours. The evening when it came was clear and starlit, lit by occasional flares, with wisps of smoke drifting over the ground; in the Soviet lines the riflemen and machine-gunners stood to, while the food was brought up. There had been no action along the perimeter of the Central Front on 4 July; the fighting had died down on the Voronezh Front section but the sound of tank engines could be heard. On the Central Front, before which Model's assault divisions were taking up their positions, there was nothing at all to be heard. At 2200 hours a Soviet patrol came across a group of seventeen German sappers clearing passages in the Soviet minefields south of Tagino; one German was taken prisoner, and from him Rokossovskii learned that a German attack was due at 0200 hours (European time) on the morning of 5 July. Aviation and tank commanders were called to Vatutin's HQ at midnight, where the prisoners under interrogation had also indicated that an attack was imminent. Vatutin decided that the *Stavka* instructions were fully confirmed and issued orders to make operational 'Variant No. 1'—a main German attack directed at Oboyan, with Chistyakov's 6th Guards taking the brunt and Shumilov's 7th Guards absorbing the supporting attack.

At 2230 hours on the evening of 4 July, with rockets and flares soaring along the Soviet perimeter between Belgorod and Tomarovka, 600 guns and mortars in the two army areas (6th and 7th Guards) loosed off the first artillery *kontrpodgotovka*, disruptive fire aimed at German troops moving into their jumping-off positions. At Central HQ, Rokossovskii had to decide quickly, on the basis of prisoner interrogation, what orders to give his own artillery—no light decision, because the *kontrpodgotovka* meant firing off more than half the ammunition *boekomplekt*. It was 2 am before the Front Military Soviet got the full interrogation report, and with only twenty minutes left there was no time for an involved exchange of signals with the *Stavka*: the artillery and infantry commanders knew that if they blundered now, 'he'—and all of them knew who was meant by 'he'—would make them pay dearly. Rokossovskii finally decided to open fire and to bring 'Variant No. 2'—envisaging the main German thrust in the Glazunovka–Ponyr–Kursk direction—into effect. At 0220 hours on the morning of 5 July Central Front guns in 13th Army area opened fire. An hour later on Vatutin's front 6th Guards fired off a second *kontrpodgotovka* with the Front commander's special permission. Soviet commanders now sweated out the remaining hour or so to dawn.

'*Nachalos*': 'It's begun'. At 0430 hours German guns opened fire against the Central Front, while on the Voronezh Front German guns and aircraft were in action even before first light. Under cover of the darkness, four German battalions with tank support were already attacking Soviet forward positions. Shortly after 5 am both Soviet Fronts reported tank and infantry attacks in great strength, aimed at 13th Army on the Central Front and 6th Guards on the Voronezh Front. Fourth *Panzer's* massive tank fist of 700 machines was aimed at Chistyakov's 6th Guards; first came the Tigers, followed by the Panthers and assault guns, the infantry in armoured personnel carriers or riding on the tanks, four *Panzer* and two infantry divisions—3,000 men, over 40 tanks and 50 assault guns to the kilometre, on some sectors up to 100 massed tanks. The attack on 6th Guards was mounted north-west of Belgorod: to the south-east, where Shumilov's 7th was deployed on the eastern bank of the northern Donets, eight battalions of German infantry were across to the Soviet side, investing the Mikhailovka bridgehead, which had been heavily shelled during the *kontrpodgotovka*. The Soviet bombardment played havoc with the work of the German engineers shifting the bridges into position for 19th *Panzer* Division's 60-ton Tigers. Further south, two German bridges were in position just before noon and German armour began rolling over the Donets, ready to strike east and north-east. From the Mikhailovka bridgehead German tanks and infantry ran straight into the dense minefields laid down in 81st Guards Rifle Division positions.

At 0510 hours German bombers appeared over the forward positions of Lt.-Gen. Pukhov's 13th Army on the northern face: on the half hour German tanks and infantry attacked along the 25-mile sector from Krasnaya Slobodka to Izmailovo, falling on 13th Army and the right flank of the 70th. For this first attack, Model had concentrated nine infantry divisions and a *Panzer* division, using his Tiger tanks and Ferdinand assault guns in small but powerful battalions—a deployment governed by his view of the Soviet defensive system, which Model intended to break by constantly feeding in new units to grind down the defenders. His main thrust narrowed down to a ten-mile sector with six infantry divisions and a *Panzer* division, supported all the while by Tiger and Ferdinand units whose job it was to smash through the Soviet defences. The infantry came on in open order or with the tanks, or in their armoured carriers; behind the massive Tigers came the light and medium tanks, overhead German planes operating in groups of 50–100 machines. This was the *Wehrmacht,* biting into the Soviet defences, more grimly formidable than it had ever been seen. Soviet gunners and infantrymen fought like madmen, even bringing 45mm guns into action to fire at the tracks of the monster tanks. Firing over open sights, Soviet guns were left with only one or two men alive, while the 'anti-tank squads' went in with their explosive charges and petrol bottles. After its fifth battering, the junction of 15th and 81st Rifle Divisions (13th Army) began to give way; fifteen Tigers were on the Oka, firing on the move at Soviet troops, with clumps of medium tanks up to fifty strong sweeping into the first line of Soviet positions. At noon Rokossovskii decided that he had discerned the German plan; the attack was not coming down the railway line for Ponyr but was aiming to the west of it in the direction of Olkhovatka (which meant altering 'Variant No. 2'): here Rokossosvkii planned to put in a counter-blow with 2nd Tank Army, while moving up 17th Guards Rifle Corps, with two anti-tank and a mortar brigade to reinforce 13th Army. The original plan had been for the 13th Army to hold on and 2nd Tank first to concentrate in the rear of the defensive field, stiffening 13th Army, and on the second day of operations to counter-attack to destroy German forces at Ponyr. Now the tank and infantry corps had to re-deploy rapidly—3rd Tank Corps to the south of Ponyr, 16th Tank to the north-west of Olkhovatka and 19th Tank to the west of it, 17th Guards Rifle Corps to the rear of 13th Army's defensive zone and 18th Guards Rifle Corps to Maloarkhangelsk to prevent the Germans widening the breakthrough on the flank. Towards the close of the first day, 5 July, Model's tanks and infantry had penetrated four miles into the Soviet defences. Rokossovskii assumed—correctly—that not all the German divisions had been committed (two *Panzer* divisions and two motorized divisions were waiting south of Orel to exploit success), and he anticipated heavier attacks.

At midnight Rokossovskii reported to Stalin, who promised 27th Army under Lt. Gen. Trofimenko from the *Stavka* reserve as reinforcement, relief which Stalin within a few hours had to withdraw since the situation on the Voronezh Front on the Oboyan axis had become very serious. Trofimenko was now going there with his troops, Rokossovskii would have to make do, and would also be responsible for the defence of Kursk itself in the event of a German breakthrough from the south. Vatutin had decided on the morning of 5 July that Oboyan was the main German objective, while the attacks against Shumilov aimed at Korocha were designed to draw off Soviet front-line reserves. During the morning and afternoon, the full weight of Hoth's *SS Panzer* formations and 11th *Panzer* Division crashed down on the Cherkasskoe–Korovino sector held by rifle troops of Chistyakov's 6th Guards: under a gleaming sky, where Soviet fighters were making their maximum effort, German dive-bombers and ground-attack planes laid down a roadway of high explosive, a lane of fire in the narrow sector between Cherkasskoe and Korovino, down which more than 200 German tanks with infantry now began to push. To hold Cherkasskoe, Chistyakov rushed in two regiments of anti-tank guns, which fought side by side with units of 67th Guards Rifle Division defending the village. In the afternoon the Tigers came and Cherkasskoe was half-encircled, outside it a litter of smashed and mined tanks and a trail of pulverized Soviet guns. A Soviet rearguard of fifteen Guardsmen, all of them finally wiped out, covered the withdrawal from Cherkasskoe. At 1640 hours Vatutin personally ordered Katukov of 1st Tank Army to move two corps (6th Tank, 3rd Mechanized) to cover Oboyan, and to prepare a counter-attack towards Tomarovka for dawn on 6 July; two more reserve tank formations, 5th Guards and 2nd Guards Tank Corps, were to concentrate to the east of Luchki to attack in the direction of Belgorod. To strengthen Shumilov fighting off the tanks and infantry of *Armee-Abteilung Kempf*, Vatutin at 1940 hours brought three rifle divisions of 35th Guards Rifle Corps to reinforce 7th Guards Army and to cover the Korocha axis. Shumilov was ordered to clean up the Germans who had broken over the northern Donets.

Within twelve hours both sides were furiously stoking the great glowing furnace of the battle for Kursk. The armour continued to mass and move on a scale unlike anything seen anywhere else in the war. Both commands watched this fiery escalation with grim, numbed fascination: German officers had never seen so many Soviet aircraft, while Soviet commanders—who had seen a lot—had never before seen such formidable massing of German tanks, all blotched in their green and yellow camouflage. These were tank armadas on the move, coming on in great squadrons of 100 and 200 machines or more, a score of Tigers and Ferdinand assault guns in the first echelon, groups of 50–60 medium tanks in the second and then the infantry screened by the armour. Now that Soviet tank armies were moving up into the main defensive fields, almost 4,000 Soviet tanks and nearly 3,000 German tanks and assault guns were being steadily drawn into this gigantic battle, which roared on hour after hour leaving ever-greater heaps of the dead and the dying, clumps of blazing or disabled armour, shattered personnel carriers and lorries, and thickening columns of smoke coiling over the steppe. With each hour also, the traffic in mangled, twisted men brought to steaming, blood-soaked forward dressing stations continued to swell. The Russian *svodka,* the communiqué on the first day's fighting, revealed the scale of operations in its mammoth total of reported German tank losses: 'During the course of the day [5 July], 586 tanks were destroyed or put out of action.'

On Rokossovskii's Central Front, the dawn counter-attack on 6 July enjoyed a moment's success, only to be rolled back by a force of 250 German tanks with infantry in their wake; the three right-flank divisions of Pukhov's 13th Army also counter-attacked and were also rolled back by tanks. The main German tank force, reinforced by 2nd and 9th *Panzer* Divisions, was now concentrated on a sector running from Ponyr-1 to Soborovka (to the west of Ponyr itself and the railway line), six miles holding more than 3,000 guns and mortars, 5,000 machine-guns and over 1,000 tanks. To stiffen his reserve, Rokossovskii now

drew troops from sectors that were momentarily inactive: Lt.-Gen. Chernyakhovskii's 60th Army would have to take the place of the 27th Army, promised
by Stalin but now re-directed to the Voronezh Front. One division was taken
from Chernyakhovskii, and men, weapons and supplies moved by lorry to 13th
Army area; Batov's 65th Army had to give up two tank regiments. Throughout
6 July Model's and Rokossovskii's men were literally locked in face-to-face combat.
Rodin's 2nd Tank Army had not made much gain by its counter-blow, but
German troops attacking on the left and centre had made only a quarter of the
progress they had managed the first day, for now they were right in Pukhov's
main defensive zone. Rokossovskii ordered his tank formations over to the defensive,
the tanks to be dug in with only the turrets showing at ground level, tank
counter-attacks to be made only against light tanks and German infantry. So far
Pukhov and Rodin's tank-men were holding six German infantry and three
Panzer divisions, attacking in great strength on a narrow sector; for the morrow,
the German command held a fresh *Panzer* division (the 18th) with over 200
tanks ready to attack, plus 4th *Panzer* approaching the battlefield and three
divisions south of Orel (12th *Panzer*, 10th and 36th Motorized) at a further
state of readiness.

On the morning of 7 July the German offensive rolled on: 18th and 9th
Panzer attacked on a narrow sector west of the railway line towards Olkhovatka,
2nd and 20th *Panzer* further west towards Samodurovka–Molotych, and a
powerful assault group making for Ponyr, a major junction on the Orel–Kursk
line against which Soviet troops were now leaning their backs. Ten infantry
divisions and four *Panzer* divisions, all with massed tank forces, were now in
action as Model bit through the Soviet defences. The main German thrust was
now developing towards the vitally important high ground near Olkhovatka,
control of which would command the eastern, southern and western area. From
here, the Germans would look out to Kursk. Rokossovskii proceeded to strengthen
the defences at the approaches to the Olkhovatka heights and at Ponyr, by
moving up more artillery, mortars and heavy guns including howitzers. Soviet
commanders reckoned that the heavy German attack on Ponyr was designed to
distract their attention from Olkhovatka; while savage fighting for Ponyr raged
as more massed German tank attacks ran into Soviet minefields, artillery barrages,
buried tanks and the squads of 'tank-busters', there was momentary pause in
German attacks on Olkhovatka, which were nevertheless resumed when 4th
Panzer moved up. Up to 300 German tanks now broke through to Kashara
and Samodurovka: at Ponyr the tank and infantry fighting continued, with the
junction changing hands several times, and only the school and the western tip
was in German possession on the morning of 8 July. That morning at 0800
hours, after an initial bombardment, 18th, 9th, 2nd, and 4th *Panzer* Divisions
with the 6th German Infantry Division renewed their attack along the sector
running from Ponyr-2 to Samodurovka towards Olkhovatka. Putting in thirteen
attacks by noon, German tanks and tommy-gunners had to crunch their way on

towards the south and south-west. North-west of Olkhovatka, one Soviet anti-tank brigade, the 3rd, under Colonel Rukosuyev, faced a massed tank attack, with one battery taking the full shock. At a little over 700 yards the Soviet anti-tank guns opened fire; in a little while, the battery was left with one gun and three men alive, who managed to knock out two more tanks. This remaining gun was destroyed along with its crew by a direct hit from a bomb, and the battery was totally wiped out. Just before noon Lieutenant Gerasimov's battery, with its remaining anti-tank-gun—its shield blown away and the trail shattered— propped up on ammunition boxes and aimed by the barrel, was also pounded to pieces. The brigade commander finally signalled Rokossovskii: 'Brigade under attack by up to 300 tanks. No. 1 and No. 7 batteries wiped out, bringing last reserve, No. 2 battery, into action. Request ammunition. I either hold on or will be wiped out. *Rukosuyev*.' The 3rd Brigade did both: it held but it was destroyed almost to a man. For forty-eight hours the fighting raged on, with the German formations bumping up against the prepared positions on the Sredne–Russki heights, the high ground some twelve miles inside the northern face of the salient which the German command knew it could not assault frontally.

On the southern face under Vatutin's control the situation had begun to look dangerous. During the first day of the offensive, Hoth's massive tank blows had driven into the defensive field covering Oboyan. By the evening Vatutin was drawing on his second echelon (Katukov's 1st Tank Army) and Front reserves, ordering Katukov into 6th Guards Army area, reinforcing with two more tank corps (5th Guards and 2nd Guards), bringing a division of 35th Guards Rifle Corps to Prokhorovka and four divisions into the Korocha area covered by 7th Guards. The next day Hoth moved up two fresh *Panzer* divisions for his breakthrough attempt towards Oboyan: Vatutin had planned a large-scale counter-attack for dawn on 6 July, but Katukov managed to persuade the Front commander of the wisdom of putting the tank formations on the defensive. The counter-attack was called off and, as on the Central Front, the tanks were dug in, the anti-tank guns deployed in camouflaged positions. Towards evening the *SS Panzer* troops had carved their way into Chistyakov's main defensive field; further south, Shumilov's 7th Guards Army was pushed back and on the right flank German assault units were in the second defensive field, where at 1700 hours up to 100 German tanks were pushing eastwards.

That night Vatutin reported to Stalin, who had already shifted 27th Army to the south of the salient. Underlining the intensity of the fighting, Vatutin submitted that 'as a result of a day's fierce engagement, 332 enemy tanks, 80 aircraft had been destroyed, large numbers of officers and men killed. In the sectors of 7th Guards Army alone twelve attacks were beaten off and more than 10,000 enemy troops killed.' Stalin approved Vatutin's request for further reinforcement, but repeated his orders that the front was to fight attrition battles and to hold the enemy on the prepared defence lines until 'such time as our offensive operations begin on the Western, the Bryansk and other fronts'. Marshal

Vasilevskii, who with Marshal Zhukov was co-ordinating operations on the
southern face, now proposed to move up two fresh tank corps, 2nd and 10th,
to reinforce the Voronezh Front in the Prokhorovka area; at the same time,
Rotmistrov's 5th Guards Tank Army (part of Koniev's Steppe Front) was put
under *Stavka* contol and ordered to begin moving from Ostrogorzhsk to Stary
Oskol. This was utilization of the 'strategic reserve', taking it apart piece by
piece, whereupon Koniev protested very forcefully to Stalin and the *Stavka*,
suggesting that the entire Steppe Front should be committed as a unity in the
defensive battle, a proposal which the *Stavka* turned down flat, though the Steppe
Front was finally 'turned' on to the Belgorod–Kharkov axis forty-eight hours
later.

On 7 July the summer heat suddenly faded. The night was cold and fighting
went on in the mist. When daylight came the *SS Panzer* corps—*Adolf Hitler,
Das Reich* divisions, the flank secured by *Totenkopf*—fought their way along the
motor-road towards Oboyan. Shortly after 4 am 400 tanks, with motorized
infantry and artillery support, fell on Katukov's 1st Tank Army on the Syrtsevo–Yakovlevo sector and Katukov called up Soviet dive-bombers which came
down on the massed German columns. To the north-west of Syrtsevo, Katukov
and Chistyakov moved in tank units, a rifle division (67th Guards) and more
artillery to block the German advance. 7 July was a grim day for the 1st Tank
Army: the front held by 51st Guards Rifle Division was shattered at its centre,
and the tanks lacked a firm front across the line of the motor-road. Fourth *Panzer*
Army had begun to bite deeply into 6th Guards Army's defensive field. Vatutin
now issued orders for a Soviet counter-blow at the flanks of the German units
striking on Oboyan, where the defences were also to be put at immediate readiness.
Vatutin planned two blows, one north-west of Tomarovka, the other on the
Kursk–Belgorod railway line, to the north of Shopino, where *Abteilung Kempf*
was attacking. The orders, issued at 2300 hours on 7 July and going also to
Moskalenko's 40th Army, were to prepare an attack: a few hours later Moskalenko
received revised instructions to transfer most of his tanks and artillery, with one
entire division, to 6th Guards and 1st Tank. At 1000 hours on 8 July 40th
Army made little more than a 'demonstration attack'; on the Oboyan axis, Col.-
Gen Hoth had won a few hours' margin, and at 1100 hours 500 of his tanks,
straddling a four-mile sector astride the motor-road, pressed their own attack
towards Oboyan, three *Panzer* divisions in the lead with Tigers and Ferdinands
to the fore. By noon a force of 100 tanks had smashed the junction between
3rd Mechanized and 31st Tank Corps and was moving on Sukho–Solotino. At
this juncture Marshal Vasilevskii promised *Stavka* reinforcement and Katukov
duly received 10th Tank Corps, plus five tank and artillery regiments.

On the Verkhopene–Sukho/Solotino–Kochetovka sector, Fourth *Panzer* now
concentrated five *Panzer* Divisions (*Gross Deutschland, Adolf Hitler, Totenkopf,*
3rd and 11th *Panzer*) with four infantry divisions covering the flanks: 11th *Panzer*
would fight directly up the motor-road to Oboyan, the other armoured formations

to the east and west of it, in one final, flailing drive through the last Soviet defensive belt before Oboyan–Kursk. Tank fists of 60 machines and 200 machines, with assault infantry, dive-bombers and heavy artillery fire, battered their way forward on 9 July against Katukov's tanks and Chistyakov's riflemen. German tanks drew up to Kochetovka, Chistyakov's HQ at 6th Guards; Chistyakov moved his main HQ to 1st Tank Army area, but his chief of staff Maj.-Gen. V.A. Penkovskii remained at Kochetovka with a forward battle headquarters to maintain contact with the rifle units of 6th Guards. By the evening Chistyakov had established a new defensive area for his army, but the *Waffen-SS* had crashed on—by Soviet reckoning, at the cost of 11,000 men, 230 tanks and assault guns—to within a dozen miles of the small town of Oboyan, no great prize in itself, but a foundation stone of the Soviet defence covering Kursk from the south. Deep though German tanks were into the defences of 6th Guards, the going had been agonizing and it now dragged to a halt. The axis of the German assault was about to be changed, from the frontal attack to the north-west along the motor-road to the north-east, towards the small town of Prokhorovka and its high ground which commanded the surrounding area. This would outflank Oboyan from the east and open another route for the German advance on Kursk.

Massing the main strength of Fourth *Panzer* Army on a narrow four-to-five-mile sector west of Prokhorovka would surely guarantee smashing in the Soviet defences; to the south, *Armee-Abteilung Kempf* would strike upwards to the north and north-west on Prokhorovka from the bulge pushed in the positions of 69th and 7th Guards Armies. To divert the attention of the Soviet command, the pressure on the motor-road to Oboyan would be renewed. Success would mean the encirclement and destruction of the two main groups of Soviet forces, and the route to Kursk would be open. To exploit any major success, XXIV *Panzer* Corps (with *SS Wiking* and 10th *Panzer* Division) would be used when available. On the evening of 10 July these fresh divisions were moving up to Kharkov from the Donbas, with orders to continue moving on to Belgorod and further north. At the northern face of the salient, opposite Rokossovskii, eight *Panzer* and motorized divisions, with eight infantry divisions, supported by Tigers and Ferdinands, would renew the attempt to crack these Soviet defences; six *Panzer*, two motorized and three infantry divisions would make the main effort, their flanks secured by five infantry divisions.

Between 10 and 11 July, as the Central and Voronezh Fronts submitted hourly situation reports to Stalin, the Germany Army Groups Centre and South were re-grouping. The climax was near. Great chunks of armour and infantry were being moved on the Soviet side into blocking positions on the Voronezh Front. Rotmistrov's 5th Guards Tank Army was now directly subordinated to Vatutin and had been ordered on the evening of 9 July to concentrate north-west of Prokhorovka. Col.-Gen. Zhadov's infantry, 5th Guards Army, also one of the

components of the Steppe Front, received orders on 8 July placing it under
Vatutin's command. Moving by night, 5th Guards Army would advance itself
some seventy miles up to the river Psel, take up positions on a twenty-mile sector
running from Oboyan to Prokhorovka and be at full readiness on this line on
the morning of 11 July. In addition to the two Guards armies, Trofimenko's
27th Army with 4th Guards Tank Corps would move to Kursk and 53rd Army
with 4th Mechanized Corps to the south-east of the city. Throughout Saturday,
10 July, though German attacks were pressed in the direction of Oboyan, Vatutin's
staff were aware that the German forces were re-grouping and reinforcing, with
the likelihood of the attack swinging in the direction of Prokhorovka. During
the night of 10–11 July Vatutin reported to Stalin on the imminence of the new
German attacks on Prokhorovka; having failed to break through towards Oboyan
(though the penetration was almost twenty miles deep), Army Group South
would now apply the greatest pressure against Prokhorovka, attacking in this
direction from the south and from the south-west. In six days of fighting, the
enemy had suffered enormous losses and had expended his reserves. To mount
this new attack, German units would have to be taken from the flank to feed
the assault, which gave the Voronezh command opportunity to prepare an attack
to encircle German forces operating against Oboyan and Prokhorovka. Within
a short time, Stalin and the *Stavka* approved Vatutin's plan to attack, a series
of concentric blows from the east, north-east, north, north-west and west aimed
at Yakovlevo and Bykovka. The two newly arrived Guards armies would be
committed against the mass of the SS tank formations in the Prokhorovka area.
Rotmistrov's 5th Guards Tank Army would attack southwards from Prokhorovka
to the Pokrovka–Yakovlevo–Bykovka line, Zhadov's 5th Guards Infantry Army
(in co-operation with Rotmistrov's tanks) also to the south and south-west, 6th
Guards and 1st Tank Army from the west and north-west would drive south-
eastwards for Yakovlevo, and Shumilov's 7th Guards would attack due west.
This would lop off the top of the German bulge driven into the Voronezh Front,
and with their flanks so caved in, the German assault formations would be
encircled. Rotmistrov's tank army (18th, 29th Tank, 5th Guards Mechanized
Corps) was filled out with two more armoured corps, 2nd Tank and 2nd Guards
Tank Corps, making altogether 850 tanks, 500 of them in the first echelon
(though half only light machines) and with only 35 heavy tanks or self-propelled
guns in the entire army.

At dawn on Sunday (11 July), with the regrouping complete, Army Group
South's new attacks thudded into the Voronezh Front. *Abteilung Kempf* jumped
off first, 6th, 7th, 19th *Panzer* divisions with three infantry divisions striking for
Prokhorovka from the south; at 0900 hours, 3rd and 11th *Panzer* and *Gross
Deutschland* divisions attacked towards Oboyan and thirty minutes later came
the main, battering attack from the north-east, *SS Totenkopf, Adolf Hitler* and
Das Reich on the march for Prokhorovka itself. The weather matched the stormy
battle on the land, with high, driving winds and great bouts of rain, through

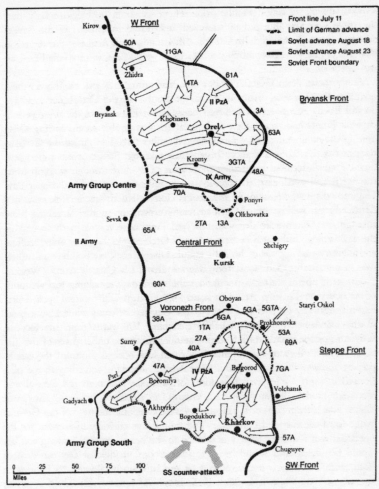

Map 4 Kursk, July–August 1943

which German and Soviet planes fought each other or the ground troops. Shortly after noon, 100 German tanks were moving along the road to Prokhorovka; late in the afternoon a powerful tank force was on the outskirts and at Storozhevoe (to the south-west) more *SS* tanks had broken through to present a danger to the rear of the 5th Guards Tank Army, itself preparing to attack. Towards the end of this murderous day, the *SS* attacks were slowed and halted, with German armour jabbing all round Prokhorovka. There had been no breakthrough, but the triple German attacks had squeezed and boxed in almost all the Soviet armies—1st Tank, 6th and 7th Guards, 5th Guards Tank Armies—due to attack at dawn on 12 July. Rotmistrov's 5th Guards would have to carry the brunt of this operation.

At the hour when German troops had first jumped off on 11 July in their drive for Prokhorovka, many miles to the north—in the Orel bulge held by Second *Panzer* Army—reinforced reconnaissance battalions from the Western and Bryansk Fronts had begun their probing of the German defences covering Orel. During the night, Golovanov's long-range bomber force had raided the German rear; before the Soviet battalions began their probing, Soviet dive-bombers laid down smoke-screens to cover their movement. This movement in strength from the north and north-east, the prelude to the offensive timed for the next day, had immediate repercussions on the struggle for the Kursk salient; Rokossovskii's Central Front, well aware of German reinforcement for another smashing blow through the Olkhovatka defences, observed German columns in the course of the day turning northwards in the direction of Orel—tanks, engineer units, artillery and infantry moving out of Model's assault groups, back on Bolkhov and Orel. The reconnaissance battalions from Bagramyan's 11th Guards Army (Western Front) kept up their attacks throughout the entire day, remaining forward until 0300 hours on 12 July. At 0320 hours, 3,000 guns and mortars opened fire, hammering away for over two hours at the German defences while assault units of the first echelon of 11th Guards, crouching 100 yards from the forward German position, made their final preparations to attack under cover of the 'fire zones'. The artillery of the Bryansk Front had also opened fire from the east to prepare the way for 61st, 3rd and 63rd Armies, attacking according to the plan devised in April, when the fixed focus of attention had been the Central and Voronezh Fronts. Bagramyan's 11th Guards, an extremely powerful army, was due to attack from the north; rifle armies were attacking the nose of the German bulge from the east and north-east. The timing was critically important, for the operation was conceived wholly in relation to the Kursk battles. Striking too late would be useless and would bring Russian troops up against German armour both refitted and even rested, or at least not sufficiently blunted by fighting in the salient. The Western–Bryansk Front blow was certainly loosed off at a very sensitive moment, though possibly fractionally late; Bagramyan's rate of advance, however, took the *Stavka* completely by surprise and there were no resources to exploit the successes of what was conceived initially as a localized relieving attack. The *Stavka* began rushing the 4th Tank Army to the Western Front, but it was already too late.

Stalin had become seriously concerned at the fairly deep penetration of the Voronezh Front. The splintering of the 6th Guards Army Front, where a deep incision had been made, was due basically to the fact that Vatutin (unlike Rokossovskii) had spread his forces more thinly over greater distances; local

German superiority soon made itself felt very painfully. The defence of the Prokhorovka area had now been handed over to the two *Stavka* representatives, Marshal Zhukov and Marshal Vasilevskii, who had assumed the general supervision of operations here after 11 July. Marshal Vasilevskii had supported Vatutin in his submission of the counter-attack plans due to be executed on 12 July, though the severe crisis at Prokhorovka itself, with two masses of German armour driving on it from the west and the south, gravely hampered the preparations for an attack. Marshal Zhukov had assembled ten regiments of artillery into 'tank fists', clenched in the area of Prokhorovka, to assist in holding off the German columns, while Rotmistrov of 5th Guards Tank Army and Zhadov's 5th Guards fought heavy defensive actions and made their units ready for the counter-blow. Zhadov's divisions, directed to the Oboyan–Prokhorovka line, had gone into action off the march. His anti-tank artillery had been taken away to strengthen the general defences; his left-flank formations were due to attack along with Rotmistrov, but 5th Guards Army badly needed more infantry support tanks.

The night of 12 July, when the Soviet relief attack opened a long way north against the Orel bulge, was a very tense one in the Prokhorovka area. Few men slept in the two Guards armies. The day broke with overcast skies and intermittent, scudding rain. The battle area itself was a comparatively narrow sector, bounded on one side by the river Psel, on the other by the railway cutting. Ahead of Prokhorovka itself lay the steppe, dotted with small cultivated plots and gardens; in the cornland round about, Soviet anti-tank batteries and tank units lay hidden in their camouflage. Up on the high ground Rotmistrov had established his forward command post, affording him good observation of the entire area.

With the advance of 6th and 7th *Panzer* Divisions, striking northwards to Rydinka and Rzhavets and thus to within some seven miles of the SS *Panzer* corps operating against Prokhorovka from the west, a highly dangerous situation was building up by dawn on 12 July. Rotmistrov's flank formations were ordered down to block this movement at all costs, while the prospect of another heavy German attack on Prokhorovka—and with it a doubling of the danger—had to be forestalled by speeding up the planned Soviet attack by two hours. Thus in the area of Prokhorovka two great bodies of armour, Soviet and German, rushed into a huge, swirling tank battle with well over a thousand tanks in action. The two groups of German armour, one west, the other south of Prokhorovka, mustered some 600 and 300 tanks respectively; Rotmistrov's 5th Guards just under 900 tanks—approximate parity, except that the German forces were fielding about 100 Tigers. Both Soviet and German planes massed at Prokhorovka, pounding away at the area of the heaviest tank fighting which ran roughly three miles in length by four in depth. At 0830 hours, after a short artillery bombardment and a salvo from the *Katyushas,* four masses of Soviet tanks attacked on the sector running from Petrovka to the station at Belenikhino (a line facing west of Prokhorovka); west of Prokhorovka, along the line of the Psel, XVIII *Panzer* Corps was attacking at the same time. The Soviet tanks tore into the first German echelon, and by closing the range the T-34s deprived the Tigers of the advantage of their heavier armament. The tanks fought it out practically at point-blank range as the Soviet T-34s and a few KVs raced into the German formation, whose Tigers stood immobile to deliver their fire: once at close range, with scores of machines churning about in individual engagements, front and side armour was more easily penetrated, when the tank ammunition would explode, hurling turrets yards away from the shattered hulls or sending up great spurts of fire as burning Soviet tanks rammed the Tigers. Driving along the road and railway line to the south-east of Prokhorovka, 29th Tank Corps (with 9th Guards Parachute Division in support) plunged into some of the heaviest fighting of the day as it collided with SS Totenkopf and Adolf Hitler; 2nd Guards and 2nd Tank Corps by the early afternoon had managed to break into the woods west of Belenikhino and the farms east of the village of Kalinin, but at 1500 hours tanks from SS Adolf Hitler and Das Reich were themselves attacking. The fighting in the Kalinin–Belenikhino–Storozhovoe area went on far into the darkness.

South and south-east of Prokhorovka, where Abteilung Kempf was attacking 69th Army and part of 7th Guards, the situation had taken a dangerous turn during the early hours of 12 July; at 0400 hours Rotmistrov received orders from Vatutin to move an armoured brigade into 69th Army area, followed by two mechanized brigades and artillery regiments which were to be moved up a few hours later from Rotmistrov's second echelon on the orders of Vatutin and Vasilevskii. Attacking straight off the march, the fresh brigades operating under the command of General Trufanov pushed German units back over the northern Donets and out of the village of Rydinka. With units of 7th Guards, the tanks of 5th Guards Army also pushed 6th and 7th Panzer Divisions out of the villages of Kuzminka and Aleksandrovka. The attack from the south towards Prokhorovka was temporarily localized by mid-afternoon when Rotmistrov had to look suddenly to the west of Prokhorovka, to the area of 18th Tank Corps round about Andreyevka and to the security of his right flank. At this point Rotmistrov poured the last of 5th Guards into the battle, 10th Guards Mechanized and 24th Guards Tank Brigade, the last of his second echelon. Along some axes, the tanks of 5th Guards were fighting offensive actions; along others they were pursuing tense defensive battles, setting up tank ambushes or putting in short, jabbing counterstrokes. The whole of this 'giant tangle of tanks', rolling about and locked with each other between Prokhorovka and Rzhavets to the south, wound and re-wound itself over full eighteen hours.

With the coming of the deep night, when thunderclouds piled over the battlefield, the gunfire slackened and the tanks slewed to a halt. Silence fell on the tanks, the guns and the dead, over which the lightning flickered and the rain began to rustle. The Prokhorovskoe poboishche, the 'slaughter at Prokhorovka', was momentarily done, with more than 300 German tanks (among them 70 Tigers), 88 guns and 300 lorries lying wrecked on the steppe; more than half the Soviet 5th Guards Tank Army lay shattered in the same area. Both sides

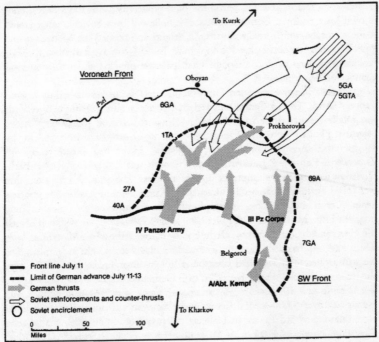

Map 5 The Prokhorovka tank battle, July 1943

had taken and delivered fearful punishment. The German attack, from the west and the south, however, had been held. At Oboyan the attack had been halted. On the broad slopes of the Sredne-Russki heights on Rokossovskii's Central Front the attack on Kursk from the north had also been halted, and Rokossovskii had considerable reserves in hand.

For three more days, from 13 to 15 July, German troops stabbed at the Soviet defences in the Prokhorovka area. While Rotmistrov's headquarters was analysing the results of the Prokhorovka tank-battle and assessing what had happened at Rzhavets, Zhadov's infantrymen from 5th Guards were still involved in very heavy fighting north-west of Prokhorovka. Two divisions of 5th Guards (95th and 52nd Guards Rifle Divisions) had been fighting for long hours to contain the SS bridgehead on the right bank of the Psel to the east of Krasnyi Oktyabr. Rotmistrov had had to throw in his tanks to ward off a threat to his flank and rear, a commitment that scarcely sweetened relations between Rotmistrov and Zhadov. During the night of 12–13 July SS troops continued to hammer at the Soviet infantry between Veselyi and Polezhaev; at 1000 hours on 13 July Zhadov's

Guards counter-attacked and seized the high ground between the villages, only to be thrown off by a German tank attack, followed by a Soviet counter-attack in the afternoon which finally cleared the heights and pushed the SS back to the Psel, flattening the bridgehead completely. The SS could get neither through Prokhorovka nor round it, although Fourth *Panzer* prowled about making local gains here and there.

As a major offensive operation, *Zitadelle* (Citadel) had been smashed up beyond recovery. Army Group Centre reported that Model's Ninth Army in the north was totally blocked and Army Group had now to fight off the Orel offensive. Manstein pleaded for more time to finish off Soviet armoured reserves, but by 19 July this attempt sputtered out completely. Hitler had already called off *Zitadelle* and after 13 July Army Group South was slowly easing itself back. Guderian recognized the failure as 'a decisive defeat'; the armoured divisions that had rolled against the Soviet breakwaters at Kursk were now, through grievous losses in men and machines, 'unemployable for a long time to come'. Coming from the inspector-general of the Germany army's *Panzertruppen,* who had nursed the Tigers and the Panthers through the boiling battles—the whole *Materialschlacht* which had now recoiled upon the *Wehrmacht*—this was no light judgement. The Russian artillery especially had contributed to this mangling of the *Panzer* arm; the Russians claimed that at Kursk 70,000 German officers and men were killed, 2,952 tanks and 195 assault guns destroyed, along with 844 field guns, 1,392 planes and over 5,000 lorries. Certainly the losses in individual *Panzer* divisions were calamitous; 3rd *Panzer* had 30 tanks left out of almost 300, 17th *Panzer* after Prokhorovka was left with 60 tanks, *Panzer* General Schmidt's 19th had 17 patched-up machines left to it. The infantry divisions were torn to tatters with companies down to 40 men and regiments not much stronger, even including wounded. On the southern face, the Germans reckoned that 10 Soviet armoured formations had been smashed up, no less than 1,800 tanks crippled, more than 1,000 anti-tank guns destroyed and 24,000 prisoners captured. Immediately after Prokhorovka, Soviet tank strength was certainly down to half what it had been eight days before; the losses in anti-tank guns were heavy indeed, and battle casualties high. The *Ostfront* had more than once seen some appalling fighting, but German infantrymen insisted that there had never been anything like this. Ponyr in the north had been the site of one of these savage, blood-soaked grapples; in the south at the Belgorod blood-bath, *'die Blutmühle von Belgorod',* the arrogant, merciless ideological shock-troops of Nazi Germany, whose very emblem was so often their automatic death-warrant once they were prisoners in Soviet hands, had been impaled on the stakes of Oboyank and Prokhorovka. When the Russians came to excavate the Prokhorovka battlefield, they reported coming upon 400 shattered tank-hulls. In the small outlying woods they found the tank workshops, and though in previous battles the time won by covering troops had always been used to tow off damaged machines, this time the Tigers stood mostly where they had been knocked out, some straddling Soviet trenches, others inert in firing positions, the crews splayed out beside them or interred within these steel tombs, mainly fragments of men in a horrifying litter of limbs, frying-pans, shell-cases, playing-cards and stale bread.

On the evening of 14 July the right-flank formations of Rokossovskii's Central Front, holding the northern face of the Kursk salient, prepared to attack the following day; Pukhov's 13th Army would drive into the Orel bulge from the south, aiming for Kroma. *Panzer* and motorized units from Model's Ninth Army were already moving north to stiffen Second *Panzer* Army, whose lines Bagramyan's 11th Guards had already pierced to a depth of more than ten miles; to reinforce Bagramyan a second army, the 11th Army under Fedyuninskii (deputy commander of the Bryansk Front, well known for his operations on the Volkhov Front) was moving into 11th Guards area and the *Stavka* was rushing Badanov's 4th Tank Army up to the scene. The Germans nevertheless won the race to the gap, and by 17 July Bagramyan's advance was greatly slowed down. The Soviet air force could not check the flow of German reinforcement. The *Stavka* had already handed Rybalko's 3rd Guards Tank Army over to Popov to use in the drive on Orel, though the 3rd and 63rd Armies of the Bryansk Front were making but slow progress. On the evening of 18 July Bagramyan's forward units were only a dozen miles from Khotinets and Karachev (north-west of Orel) on a sector that the Germans had not reinforced; but Bagramyan had no striking force to exploit this—although if Col.-Gen. Fedorenko's suggestions had been adopted when the Orel operation was planned, he would now have had 3rd Guards Tank Army ready to push in. It was Popov who had the tank army, and he now proposed to commit it on 19 July; Rybalko was to crash through to the river Oka, cut off German units to the east and outflank Orel from the south, while 11th Guards and 63rd Army came on from the north and north-east. Rybalko's tank formations were well supplied with bridging units and even had tanks fitted for an underwater crossing of the Oka. At noon on 18 July Antonov telephoned from the General Staff; to help Rokossovskii's right wing, the tanks were to be switched to an attack on Stanovoi-Kolodez and Kromy on Stalin's orders. Sandalov, Popov's chief of staff, protested that the front was just about to launch the operation to encircle German forces in the Mtsensk and Bolkhov area; Antonov replied that 3rd Tank would still attack Stanovoi-Kolodez, since Bagramyan was now getting 4th Tank Army from Narofominsk and 2nd Guards Cavalry Corps from Medyn as well as 11th Army. On the morning of 19 July, its path previously bombarded by Golovanov's long-range bomber group, Rybalko's 3rd Guards Tank Army went into action, turning south-west on Stanovoi-Kolodez only to collide with two *Panzer* formations.

Col.-Gen. Popov telephoned Stalin at noon on 20 July to report that Rybalko was practically stalled and suffering heavy losses in tanks. The *Stavka* agreed to turn Rybalko's tanks north-east and that evening they broke out to the Orel–Mtsensk highway, managing in company with 3rd Army troops to get to the river Oka, but 3rd Guards tanks did not manage to rush a crossing. While Gorbatov's 3rd Army prepared to force the Oka, Rybalko was again shunted back by the *Stavka* to the south-west. In the early hours of 22 July Stalin telephoned Popov, but the Front commander was not in his HQ; the Bryansk Front chief of staff Sandalov took the call, noting each word down in his notebook. Stalin made no bones about it: 'Why has Rybalko not yet taken Stanovoi-Kolodez? Tell the commander that I am not pleased with the handling of the tank army.' Within fifteen minutes Stalin had traced Popov, who straightway dictated fresh orders to Rybalko: '*Khozyain* [the boss] has ordered capture of Stanovoi-Kolodez 22.7. Once again I require you to commit I.P. Korchagin [mechanized corps] through Mokhovoe on Stanovoi-Kolodez, to mount combined attack with M.I. Zinkovich [12th Tank Corps] to destroy enemy holding out there. *Popov*. 1.20 22.7' Both Popov and Sandalov knew that they were throwing Rybalko's tanks against a well-fortified line which it would be folly to rush. But there was no going against a direct order from Stalin, and this was a direct order. After a few bloody days bereft of any success, Rybalko's tank formations had to be pulled out of the line into reserve and were finally sent to Rokossovskii's front.

During the night of 20 July Marshals Zhukov and Vasilevskii had examined the situation on the front circling Orel; in the north, 11th Guards had cut its way forty miles through the German defences; to the east the Bryansk Front was making a frontal attack, with Rokossovskii's divisions coming in from the south-west, an additional drive strengthened when Romanenko's units attacked towards Zmievka on the morning of 21 July. The partisan attacks on German rail communications, the Bryansk–Huro Mikhailovskii line especially (linking German forces at Orel and in the Belgorod–Kharkov area), were meant as definite co-ordination with the military operations; an enormous intensification of partisan activity against German lines of communication in late July—the Russians record 10,000 separate demolitions of track—was a major effort (save for the Yelnaya Dorogobuzh area, where the partisans had been flattened as an effective force). Where the Soviet command knew it could not call on more than token activity, the Soviet air force was called in for interdiction duties. The *relsovaya voina*, 'the war on the rail track', had been carefully planned as part of the Soviet break-out after the end of the defensive fighting at Kursk: the Central Staff of the Partisan Movement had issued specific orders (Directive No. 006 of 17 July) which assigned particular partisan detachments to the destruction of set sections of track (with details of how much track was to be blown), the entire operation to be set in motion on a given signal from the Central Staff. The main operational aim was to pin Second *Panzer* and Ninth Army well forward in the Orel bulge, to maroon them by destroying their rearward links. The *relsovaya voina* was nothing less than a full-scale partisan offensive launched in the German rear in direct and immediate support of Red Army front-line operations. To ensure success, large quantities of explosives were flown in to the partisans before their assault on the rail links began. But for all the mass-mining and the demolitions, the railway lines upon which the *Ostheer* depended were not completely severed. The partisan effort may have been widespread but it was also dispersed, and in spite of the original orders of the Central Staff about a sustained 'follow-through', this failed to materialize. Thousands of charges did go off, but too many exploded against less vital secondary lines and the few massive demolitions on the trunk routes failed to close them.

While the partisan offensive continued well into August, the Soviet pincers dug deeper into the bulge. After 20 July, however, the four *Panzer* divisions rushed into the Orel bulge succeeded in blocking the several Soviet moves. The Germans dug in their tanks and hid their assault guns in the high wheatfields. Lt.-Gen. Badanov's 4th Tank Army had now closed up with Bagramyan, but on explicit *Stavka* orders it was to be used in the Bolkhov fighting and not drive into the German rear through Khotinets. Badanov had more than 500 brand-new tanks with his army. Bagramyan was furious at the *Stavka* orders; he was also none too pleased with Badanov, whose earlier success in the Donbas had— according to Bagramyan—'completely gone to his head'. Bagramyan warned that this kind of breakthrough operation was not easy and that the tank-men should have some rapid training. Badanov hotly contested this and emphasized that his tank army could break through anything. Sokolovskii came out on Badanov's side and at 1100 hours on 26 July two of Badanov's corps (11th Tank and 6th Guards Mechanized) put in a ragged attack towards Bolkhov. For the next few hours, under the very gaze of Bagramyan and Badanov, both corps were heavily battered by the concealed German tanks and assault guns; the next day the 30th Volunteer Urals Tank Corps pushed in with a fierce attack, but the tank army covered only about one mile in all. The German units now began pulling out of the Bolkhov pocket and Belov's 61st Army moved up; Bagramyan, Fedyuninskii, Badanov and Kryukov (with his 'operational group') now came under the direct command of Popov, who moved his forward HQ to Mtsensk and now set the 3rd and 63rd Armies in motion right up against Orel. At dawn on 5 August, after slogging through the German defences and crossing the Oka, the main body of these two armies closed on Orel, which was already being cleared of German troops.

While fighting in the Orel bulge drained German strength away from the Kursk salient towards the north, to the south a powerful Soviet attack on the 'Mius Front', launched by the Southern Front, opened on 17 July. Fedor Ivanovich Tolbukhin, promoted colonel-general in April 1943, had that same month returned on *Stavka* orders from the North-Western Front, where he had been involved in the Demyansk operations, to a Front command in the south. The constant postings depressed Tolbukhin, but he was reassured by his new assignment to a full Front command. At Southern Front HQ in Novoshakhtinsk he took over from Malinovskii, who went to the South-Western Front. Tolbukhin had a considerable force at his disposal—five infantry armies (twenty-eight rifle divisions), an air army, two mechanized corps, three tank brigades and a cavalry corps: Zakharov's 51st Army on the right, Tsvetayev's 5th Shock Army to its left, Gerasimenko's 28th Army at the centre, Khomenko's 44th on the left flank and Kreizer's 2nd Guards Army as second echelon. Kryukin commanded the 8th Air Army. A few days after the opening of the German attack on Kursk, Tolbukhin received orders to prepare an attack on the heavily fortified German 'Mius line', to strike for the river Krunka and thence to Stalino. The German defences on the Mius ran for some twenty-five miles and were manned by the Sixth Army, a new Sixth raised from *Armee-Abteilung Hollidt* to replace the Sixth Army which had perished at Stalingrad. Tolbukhin planned to break the German defences with 5th Shock and 28th Armies operating on a twelve-mile sector, with 2nd Guards ready to exploit the initial successes.

Once Tolbukhin's units had forced the Mius, German armour began to move to the southern wing of Army Group South, first to contain the Soviet bridgehead and then at the end of July to put in a formidable counter-blow with four *Panzer* divisions, a *Panzer Grenadier* division and two infantry divisions. On the evening of 1 August, after reporting on the situation to the *Stavka,* Tolbukhin—much downcast at what he considered his own considerable failure—ordered his front to pull back to their old positions. Stalin, however, was far from displeased; Marshal Vasilevskii arrived at Tolbukhin's HQ to inform the Front commander that the Southern Front attacks had fulfilled their role perfectly—the German command could not move divisions up to Kursk and had even brought armour down from the north to bolster up the Donbas, first-class divisions which would have made their presence felt on the 'Belgorod–Kharkov axis'. For all this reassurance, Tolbukhin knew that he had blundered, principally by introducing 2nd Guards too early and with too much of a rush.

While *Panzer* units moved to the southern wing of Army Group South, Soviet troops—much to the astonishment of the German command—had already struck on the northern wing. Manstein and his staff had thought the Soviet formations in the southern part of the Kursk salient too badly mauled to leap into a counter-blow. On 16 July, Fourth *Panzer* and *Abteilung Kempf,* screened by powerful rearguards, had begun to pull back to their original positions. Vatutin ordered 6th Guards and 1st Tank Army to push down the Oboyan–Belgorod motorway. The *Stavka* had issued orders on 16 July for Koniev's Steppe Front to become fully operational and at 2300 hours on 18 July the rump of what ten days before had been a massive strategic reserve but was now reduced to three fresh armies (53rd, 47th and 4th Guards) and two battered armies (7th Guards and 69th) handed over from the Voronezh Front moved up with Vatutin's men. Within five days both Koniev and Vatutin were drawing up to the lines from which Army Group South had jumped off against Kursk on 5 July; here the two Soviet fronts halted until 3 August, when an enormous Soviet attack unrolled against the Belgorod–Kharkov *place d'armes,* the significance of which was not lost on either the German or Soviet commands. By Soviet reckoning there were eighteen German divisions (including four *Panzer*), or some 300,000 men with 600 tanks and more than 3,000 guns, to hold positions that had been ringed with defence lines. Kharkov was covered with seven lines of defences to the north, three to the east. As Koniev reported, the significance of Kharkov for the whole German defence in the eastern Ukraine and the presence of strong armoured forces made a bitter struggle inevitable. Belgorod was also heavily protected by defence lines, the suburbs fortified with timbered fire-points and the bigger buildings fitted out as strong points.

By 24 July the bulk of the Voronezh and Steppe Fronts had clustered to the north of Belgorod. At this juncture the Soviet command waited to see if a German counter-attack would eventually materialize; Malinovskii had attacked across the Donets south-east of Izyum, digging into First *Panzer* area, while Tolbukhin was already trying to break away from the Mius, but after a week neither Soviet attack had made much progress. Nevertheless, German armour was moving *into* the Donbas and not, as the Soviet commanders first feared, out of it. And there was the frantic labour to supply the forthcoming Soviet offensive. Koniev had no rear organization at all, a shortcoming corrected on the evening of 18 July when Stalin ordered Khrulev to set up 'the necessary rear organizations' in the Steppe Front. The Bryansk Front was stripped of four full artillery divisions to build up artillery strength in the south; enough ammunition for twelve to fifteen days of continuous operations, food supplies for a week and fuel for ten to twelve days was stockpiled with the Voronezh and Steppe Fronts. Day by day, Soviet tank strength crept up, making good the losses incurred during *Citadel* at a rate far surpassing the calculations of the German command; but tanks and crews had to be scraped up from every corner. Katukov's 1st Tank (recommended for distinction as a 'Guards army') had lost half its tanks and many of its crews by 25 July, yet Vatutin warned Katukov that the *Stavka* ordered not a single reinforcement—'not a man, not a machine'. For more tanks, Katukov had to rely on battlefield salvage and workshop repair; for more crews, on the field hospitals and the rear hospitals (the latter the most likely reservoir, for tank crews had only a small proportion of lightly wounded). In the evacuation hospitals tank-men were kept in one group because their wounds usually required special treatment, but their tags—the *kartochka peredovo rayona,* the transit tag on wounded—did not identify their function, driver-mechanic, turret-gunner or crew commanders. Slowly the crews were re-assembled.

At the end of July, German radio intercepts and air reconnaissance detected signs of a major Soviet build-up, and on 2 August Army Group South signalled its expectation of an immediate Soviet offensive west of Belgorod and south-east of Kharkov, the latter thrust to pin German forces in the city and also to prise open the way to the Dnieper. The final decision to proceed with 'the Belgorod–Kharkov operation' had actually been taken by Stalin on 22 June 1943, as the Voronezh and Steppe Fronts drew up to the original line of 5 July and as the northern wing of Army Group South was now bereft of six *Panzer* divisions and an infantry division. Marshal Zhukov had the management of this major offensive operation, a great deal of which bore a typical Zhukov 'look'. The operations would be mounted across a very large front, with a rapid breakthrough aimed in considerable depth and to be accomplished by powerful assault groupings: the two tank armies (1st and 5th Guards) were concentrated in the area of 5th Guards Army and would operate in dense formation of up to 70 tanks to the kilometre; the artillery was similarly concentrated to bring up to 230 guns to the kilometre on the axes of the main attacks. Zhukov ruled out any protracted regrouping; the Voronezh and Steppe Fronts would attack with their flanks mixed, striking from north and north-west of Belgorod in a south-westerly direction to outflank Kharkov from the west. For this operation, 6th Guards, 5th Guards, 53rd Armies and 48th Rifle Corps of 69th Army would deploy on a line running from the village of Gertsovka up to the northern Donets (to the east of Gostishchevo): 1st and 5th Guards Tank Armies would be ready to exploit the success of this shock force. To the right, 40th and 27th Armies would produce a supporting attack in the direction of Akhtyrka. On Koniev's Steppe Front, Shumilov's 7th Guards operating with 69th Army would encircle the German forces at Belgorod, then attack along the eastern bank of the northern Donets and reach Kharkov. The recapture of Kharkov involved three fronts, Voronezh, Steppe and South-Western. Vatutin was to outflank the city from the west and cut off the main body of German troops, Koniev would attack Kharkov from the north and as Koniev approached the city Malinovskii on the South-Western Front would unleash the 57th Army in a westerly attack towards Merefa to outflank Kharkov from the south.

Zhukov aimed the offensive at the junction of Fourth *Panzer* and *Abteilung Kempf*; Vatutin would press Fourth *Panzer* westwards, attacking towards Bogodukhov, and Koniev would push *Abteilung Kempf* away in his southerly drive. Zhukov rejected a proposal from Moskalenko at 40th Army to slant the main attack; the Voronezh Front would strike straight into Fourth *Panzer*. The artillery preparation would have to be carefully planned and not 'the routine stuff' about which Zhukov had already protested vigorously during the planning of the attack on the Orel bulge—the artillery would provide supporting fire through a 'fire wall' reaching 1,500 metres, the whole depth of the first German defence line. Air operations were planned to engage fifty-five per cent of the sorties planned against enemy troops in the battle zone, each tank army being assigned up to one corps of ground-attack planes (with appropriate fighter cover, though this was not always forthcoming). What was not adequately provided for, as subsequent events showed, was battlefield interdiction; only ten per cent of the planned sorties covered air action against the movement of enemy reserves.

On 1 August Zhukov held the pre-attack review of plans and preparations, the last phase to check on the readiness of the fronts and the grasp by army commanders of their assignments. Throughout the discussions, the greatest care and most intense scrutiny was lavished on the plans to commit the tank armies, about their role on the first day of offensive operations. Soviet experience in introducing powerful mobile formations into breakthrough operations of this type was at this time not only limited but also barren of real results; the gains from committing three tank armies—4th, 3rd and 2nd—into the battle for the Orel bulge had been extremely disappointing. This time Zhukov and his armoured commanders meant to get it right. The Red Army at Kursk had shown that it could stop massed tank attacks supported by aircraft, if not in their tracks then at least by pulling them up short; now there was a premium on Soviet expertise in mobile warfare, for though the *Panzertruppen* had been savaged at Kursk they were by no means done. Zhukov now concentrated armour against the northern flank of Army Group South and intended to use it in order to slice very deeply into the whole German southern wing.

Tolbukhin and Malinovskii had also received revised orders to prepare offensive operations, timed for mid-August and aimed at the liberation of the Donbas: the South-Western Front was to reach Zaporozhe, the Southern Front to strike through the northern Tauride on to the lower reaches of the Dnieper and the approaches to the Crimea, thus erasing First *Panzer* and Sixth Army across the Donets–Mius Front. As Tolbukhin reminded his senior officers, twice they had failed to break the Mius Front, but this third time they must succeed: there was no other way for them through the Donbas. The first stage of the operation would take them to Taganrog; the front would then swing north-west to liberate Stalino and to co-operate with the left flank of Malinovskii's front in destroying German forces in the Artemovka–Krasnyi Luch–Gorlovka area, after which the Southern Front would swing south-west and south to the Dnieper reaches.

During the night of 3 August, Voronezh and Steppe Front assault formations moved up to their start lines. At 0500 hours on 3 August, Soviet artillery fired the first five-minute barrage; after that there was silence until 0535 hours when the guns began firing at selected targets. One hour later exactly, all the artillery and mortars of the assault armies opened fire and at 0745 hours every *Katyusha* launched its rocket salvoes, at which the gunfire pounded over the foremost German defences, while Soviet aircraft carried out their first attacks on German positions and reserves. When the guns laid down their 'fire lanes' at 0800 hours, the infantry and tanks moved forward into the attack. Within three hours Chistyakov's 6th Guards and Zhadov's 5th Guards assault units were through the main German positions; Rotmistrov's great worry—how quickly Zhadov's men could break in—was dissolved. Precisely at 1100 hours, Zhukov loosed 1st and 5th Guards Tanks Armies; at 1130 hours, 49th Tank Brigade. Ten minutes later, 200th Tank Brigade of Katukov's 1st Tank had overhauled Zhadov's riflemen and the full weight of 1st Tank Army burst after them. By 1 pm Rotmistrov's 18th and 29th Tank Corps were also driving on at full speed. On the Steppe Front, 53rd Army and 48th Corps, for all the destruction wrought by the artillery fire, were caught up in some heavy fighting, and though Soviet troops drove some nine miles into the German defences, the pace was slackening.

Koniev made ready to deploy the 1st Mechanized Corps in 53rd Army area.

During the morning of 5 August, as further north Soviet troops cleared Orel of German rearguards, Koniev's Steppe Front closed in on Belgorod: 69th Army moved in from the north, units of 7th Guards forced the northern Donets south of Belgorod, while 1st Mechanized Corps raced to the west past Belgorod to cut the road and rail links leading to Kharkov. The German garrison was encircled by noon; the furious street fighting that cleared the town left over 3,000 German dead in the ruins of Belgorod. Now Koniev could strike for Kharkov, though intelligence reported the presence of SS Das Reich, Totenkopf, Wiking and 3rd Panzer Divisions which had been moved back from the Izyum–Barvenkovo area: SS Gross Deutschland was moving into the Kharkov area from Orel. (Manstein had urgently requested the return of III Panzer Corps with its SS formations and 3rd Panzer Division from the Donets area and also the armour earlier moved up to Army Group Centre.) Vatutin's Voronezh Front attack had meanwhile struck deep into the German positions; as Koniev's men stormed Belgorod, the two tank armies were moving on to the south-west, their penetration already thirty miles deep. To widen the breach, Marshal Zhukov ordered Moskalenko and Trofimenko with 40th and 27th Armies to attack on a fifteen-mile front. This thrust from the north cut in for some eight miles, providing a right pincer arm and threatening to trap three German infantry and two Panzer divisions between Soviet rifle and tank armies at Borisovka. A 25-mile gap had been opened between Fourth Panzer and Abteilung Kempf (soon to become the Eighth Army). With 27th Army driving on Graivorona and Katukov closing from the south-west, the German divisions had to pull out fast down the one road to Golovchino open to them. As the German columns took to the road, German fighters carried out a series of mock dive-bombing attacks on their own men in an effort to mislead Russian forward observation that these were Red Army units under Luftwaffe attack. The ruse failed and Lt.-Gen. Varentsov, Voronezh Front artillery commander, ordered Trofimenko to bring all his artillery to bear on the columns; in the artillery fire, supplemented by Soviet air attacks, about fifty tanks were knocked out and Lt.-Gen. Schmidt, commander of 19th Panzer, was killed. To head off the German columns, 13th Guards Rifle Division rushed up a tank-supported battalion to Golovchino; twenty-four hours later the German units were hammered to death as 6th Guards drove into Borisovka and 13th Guards Division drew up to fight it out at Golovchino.

By 8 August Fourth Panzer and Abteilung Kempf had been thrust almost forty miles apart. Vatutin's right wing pushed on to the south-west: Koniev's formations were moving towards the outer defences of Kharkov. To augment this assault, Koniev acquired Lt.-Gen. Gagen's 57th Army (South-Western Front) and Rot-mistrov's 5th Guards Tank Army, which operated within the area of Lt.-Gen. Managarov's 53rd Army moving on Kharkov from the north-west; 53rd and 5th Guards Tank Army would outflank Kharkov from the north-west, 57th Army from the south-east, with 69th and 7th Guards Army coming straight on to the German perimeter from the north-east. Koniev issued the formal attack directive on 10 August, on which morning Vatutin received *Stavka* orders instructing him to effect the isolation of Kharkov by cutting the road and rail links with Poltava, Krasnograd and Lozovaya; Katukov would therefore swing on to Balki and Rotmistrov's units would aim for Merefa.

On the morning of 11 August, driving south from Bogodukhov, 1st Guards Brigade (1st Tank Army) cut the Kharkov–Poltava railway line. At this stage Fourth *Panzer* pressure on Katukov's and Chistyakov's western flank was steadily increasing; German counter-attacks were aimed at Bogodukhov and came from the south and south-east, while to the north-west, at Akhtyrka, German armour in some strength was assembling for another attack on Bogodukhov. South-east of Bogodukhov, on a line from Kadnista to Aleksandrovka, SS tank troops were aiming for the other flank of 1st Tank Army and for Zhadov's 5th Guards. To counter, this, Vatutin moved up two corps from Rotmistrov's tank army. The German attempt to chop off the Soviet spearheads failed for all the heavy fighting of 12–13 August. The main threat, however, still loomed at Akhtyrka; Vatutin now proposed to attack the flank and rear of the German forces by using 38th, 40th and 47th Armies, 2nd, 10th Tank Corps and 3rd Guards Mechanized Corps driving westwards, and 27th Army to advance to the south of Akhtyrka. When 47th and 27th Armies linked up, the German divisions in the Akhtyrka area would be encircled.

Koniev was meanwhile fighting the fourth and final battle of Kharkov, the city Hitler had determined to hold to the end. After 19 August Managarov's 53rd was clear of the dense woods west and northwest of the city outskirts; Rotmistrov's tank army, now down to about 150 tanks, held off German tank counter-attacks, while Gagen's 57th got round to the south and right-flank units of 69th Army moved in from the west and north-west. During the afternoon of 22 August Soviet air reconnaissance reported small columns of German vehicles pulling out of Kharkov to the south-west. In the evening reconnaissance troops signalled larger withdrawals, with fires raging in the city and dumps being blown up. The escape route along the road and railway line to the south-west was covered by the guns and mortars of 53rd and 5th Guards Tank Armies as well as being under air attack. Koniev's dilemma—whether to bottle the enemy up in the city or trap him while withdrawing—was resolved for him. Kharkov would be stormed at night. By dawn on 23 August two Soviet divisions, 183rd and 89th Guards, had reached the city centre; 89th Guards hoisted its red banner over the *Gosprom* building and by 11 am the city was clear of German troops. At noon Kharkov was officially liberated.

Towards the end of August the Red Army's summer offensive, mounted on a vast front running from Velikie Luki in the north to the shores of the Black Sea, now roared into top gear. On the western axis, facing the Soviet Kalinin, Western and Bryansk Fronts, Army Group Centre fielded three armies (Third *Panzer*, Fourth and Ninth Armies) with fifty-five divisions and one brigade on the south-western axis, opposite the Central, Voronezh, Steppe, South-Western and Southern Fronts, Army Group Centre deployed 35th Corps (Ninth Army) and Second Army, while Army Group South had Fourth *Panzer,* Eighth Army, First *Panzer* and Sixth Army, in all some sixty-eight divisions. On the Taman peninsula and in the Crimea was Seventeenth Army (and the Crimea operational group), a force of twenty-one divisions. Of the 226 German divisions and eleven brigades on the Eastern Front, 157 divisions and one brigade were on the Velikie Luki–Black Sea line with only insignificant reserves. Yet for all the numerical superiority suggested by the mass of Soviet divisions on the order-of-battle tables, these formations and units, especially in the south-west, had taken a tremendous hammering in the past seven weeks. The strongest Soviet tank army on 25 August was the 2nd with 265 tanks and SP guns, with Katukov's down to 162 tanks and Rotmistrov's reduced to 153. At the beginning of September, even though they were badly needed on the battle-fronts, the tank armies and individual tank corps had to be brought into reserve to rearm and refit. The Red Army had also just about consumed all the stocks of fuel and ammunition built up on the eve of the Kursk battles. Although in July–August the fronts received 26,619,000 shells and mines, they had fired off no less than 42,105,000 rounds and the dumps were running low. Nor could the railways, for all their fantastic shuttles and rapid short-hauls, cope with the traffic needed to shift supplies; traffic fell off disastrously in the area adjacent to the front where German wrecking and systematic demolition not only severed but actually tore the rail and the sleepers into little pieces.

Stalin's immediate objective was to hurl the Soviet armies to the Dnieper on a broad front. This would recover the important industrial regions of the Donbas and the eastern Ukraine breadlands; Soviet troops were to advance westwards before the German command could in any way 'stabilize' the situation. (Hitler on 11 August had decided in principle for the *Ostwall,* the fortified barrier running from Kerch, along the Molochnaya and Dnieper rivers, along the upper reaches of the great barrier of the Dnieper on to Gomel and east of Orsha; here the German armies in the east would rest their backs, holding the western Ukraine and Belorussia secure for the *Reich.*) To operate on the 'south-western axis', where Stalin intended that the main blow should presently fall, the Soviet command had assembled and was maintaining, in spite of the severe logistical strains, a sizable force: 2,633,000 men on five fronts (Central, Voronezh, Steppe, South-Western and Southern), 51,200 guns and mortars, 2,400 tanks and assault guns supported by 2,850 aircraft—superior to the German forces, reckoned at one million men and 2,000 tanks, but not overwhelmingly so. The breakdown in supplies delayed the unrolling of the offensive—Rokossovskii's was postponed for a week—but the armies of the south-west were to be driven with all speed to the Dnieper. In his correspondence with his allies, Stalin displayed a note of caution (9 August), but he hid the most gigantic plans behind this facade. Now he began to lay on all the trappings of his being the *generalissimo*—'I am obliged to be with the troops'; he must visit this or that sector of the front 'more often than usual'; and a little later, in discussing his participation in a Big Three meeting, the date of the *rendez-vous* must depend on 'the situation on the Soviet-German Front', where 'more than 500 divisions are engaged on both sides' and where 'the supervision of the Supreme Command of the USSR is required almost daily'. For a man who scarcely visited any front or any unit, and whose regulation of his command was minute, strict and all-pervading, the word 'almost' was a master-stroke in its disingenuousness.

If Stalin's strategy had become militarily more realistic, it remained still highly ambitious, if not dangerously over-ambitious, as he escalated the scale and scope of the Soviet summer–autumn offensive between the end of August and the first week in October. This time Stalin sought decisive success in the Ukraine and in Belorussia. The orders for the great south-western sweep had gone out as the battle for Kharkov was beginning. The destruction of German forces on the southern wing would be accomplished in the Donbas, in the eastern Ukraine, while the North Caucasus Front would destroy German forces on the Taman peninsula and eliminate the German Seventeenth Army in the northern Kuban. Vatutin and Koniev received their orders on 12 August; the Voronezh Front would destroy German forces in the Kharkov area and then advance in the direction of Poltava–Kremenchug, break out to the Dnieper and establish bridgeheads on the western bank; the Steppe Front, its operations co-ordinated with the Voronezh Front, was to move on Krasnograd–Verkhne Dneprovsk, make for the Dnieper in the Dnepropetrovsk area and also establish bridgeheads. Rokossovskii received his orders on 12 August; his Central Front would strike on Sevsk–Khutor Mikhailovskii, reach a line running from Rylsk to Glukhov to Novgorod Severskii by 1–3 September, then drive south-west in the general direction of Konotop–Nezhin–Kiev, and, if the operational situation was favourable, force the Desna so as to drive on Chernigov along its western bank. The South-Western and Southern Fronts, their offensive already detailed by the *Stavka,* would aim for the lower reaches of the Dnieper.

The partisans had a specific part to play in the operational plans drawn up by the *Stavka.* Strokach at the head of the Ukrainian Partisan Movement staff attached himself with fourteen officers of his staff group to Vatutin's Front staff. Strokach's Ukrainian Partisan staff was in many respects a singular organization, enjoying the special attention and favours of the top command group, the Central Staff of the Soviet Partisan movement. Strokach and his staff had their top headquarters in Moscow, with an operational command group (a miniature of the Moscow staff organization) deployed in Voroshilovgrad. Strokach pressed on with his main assignment, building up partisan activity in the western Ukraine particularly, a difficult undertaking managed by 'seeding' the lands west of the Dnieper with groups or bands moving in from southern Belorussia; Kovpak with his considerable guerrilla force had moved into this westerly region during the winter of 1942 and in the spring and summer of 1943 began great, sweeping raids with Naumov's band into 'right-bank Ukraine'. The guerrillas suffered heavy losses, but Kovpak, Naumov, Fyodorov and Saburov regrouped and reorganized the partisan units, out of which a new guerrilla strike force was assembled, the force Strokach was currently co-ordinating and mobilizing from Vatutin's HQ. (The Ukrainian partisans operated under the immediate auspices of the Red Army and during the winter passed under direct Red Army control.) These August plans envisaged twenty partisan groups (about 17,000 men) operating in the western Ukraine, their main mission being another partisan offensive against the German lines of communication deep in the rear to prevent the movement of reserves on Kiev, Kremenchug and Dnepropetrovsk.

Delayed for a week by shortage of fuel and ammunition, Rokossovskii launched his Central Front attack on 26 August in the direction of Sevsk–Novgorod Severskii with three armies. The next day he ordered in 2nd Tank Army (now under Lt.-Gen. S.I. Bogdanov since Rodin had been taken ill during the fighting for Kursk), but Bogdanov's tanks only crashed into German reserves hurriedly moved up from other less exposed sectors. Bogdanov's tank army took a heavy battering and the assault armies made only slow, painful progress. But not so Chernyakhovskii's 60th Army (with Rudchenko's 9th Tank Corps in support), operating south of Sevsk; 60th Army had put in a supporting attack which now began to roll faster and faster to the south-west, and on into the northern Ukraine. Rokossovskii swung all available divisions from his right to his left flank: the *Stavka* ordered Popov to transfer 13th Army to the Central Front and moved up four additional corps including 7th Guards Mechanized (2nd Tank Army) which had been taken into reserve. Within a week Rokossovskii's left-flank formations had reached the Desna on a broad front, tearing away a fifty-mile gap between Army Group Centre and South. This south-westerly sweep on Rokossovskii's left now menaced the rear of German units holding out against the right-wing thrusts of the Voronezh Front. Fearing eventual encirclement, German armour had already pulled out of the Akhtyrka positions; Vatutin's right-wing and centre armies pushed on westwards, aiming for Romny and Poltava. Malinovskii's South-Western Front had attacked on 13 August, Tolbukhin's Southern Front five days later; Malinovskii's first attacks rolled along the eastern bank of the northern Donets (covering Koniev's assault on Kharkov), while Tolbukhin began to smash in the Mius Front once and for all, pouring the fire of 5,000 guns and mortars on the German defensive positions. At the end of the month the Mius line had been shattered, Tolbukhin's armies had taken Taganrog; rushing eastwards to Vinnitsa from his East Prussian headquarters, Hitler finally authorized Sixth Army—'if necessary'—to pull back to the river Kalmius, and First *Panzer's* right wing to retire westwards.

During the night of 2 September, 3rd Guards Army on Malinovskii's front forced the northern Donets: regrouping on his left, Malinovskii aimed to drive south-west and south, but the *Stavka* on the eve of these operations ordered him to transfer two corps (one rifle, one cavalry) and five divisions to *Stavka* reserve,

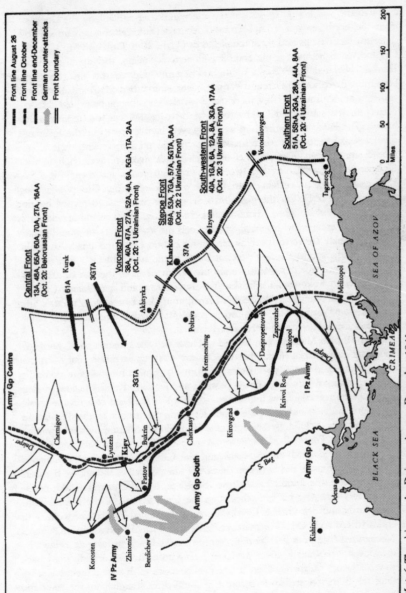

Central Front
13A, 48A, 65A, 60A, 70A, 27A, 16AA
(Oct. 20: Belorussian Front)

Voronezh Front
38A, 40A, 47A, 27A, 52A, 4A, 6A, 5GA, 1TA, 2AA
(Oct. 20: 1 Ukrainian Front)

Steppe Front
69A, 53A, 7GA, 57A, 5GTA, 5AA
(Oct. 20: 2 Ukrainian Front)

South-western Front
40A, 1GA, 6A, 12A, 8A, 3GA, 17AA
(Oct. 20: 3 Ukrainian Front)

Southern Front
51A, 5ShA, 2GA, 28A, 44A, 8AA
(Oct. 20: 4 Ukrainian Front)

Front line August 26
Front line October
Front line end-December
German counter-attacks
Front boundary

Kursk
61A
3GTA
Akhtyrka
3GTA
Kharkov
37A
Izyum
Poltava
Kremenchug
Dnepropetrovsk
Zaporozhe
Nikopol
Krivoi Rog
1 Pz Army
Kirovgrad
Cherkassy
Butrin
Fastov
Kiev
Lyutezh
Chernigov
Dnieper
Korosten
Zhitomir
IV Pz Army
Berdichev
Kishinev
Odessa
S. Bug
Army Gp A
Army Gp South
Army Gp Centre
Voroshilovgrad
Taganrog
Melitopol
Dnieper
CRIMEA
SEA OF AZOV
BLACK SEA
Miles
0   50   100   150   200

Map 6 The drive to the Dnieper, August–December 1943

although this was bound to weaken the attack aimed at outflanking the Donbas from the north. It was Tolbukhin who received reinforcement, amounting to thirteen rifle divisions and three mobile corps (11th, 20th Tank and 5th Guards Cavalry); on 8 September the Southern Front took Stalino, the capital town of Donbas, liberated by Svetayev's 5th Shock Army. During this first week in September Rokossovskii's left and Vatutin's right wing rushed on towards Konotop and Romny; Shumilov's 7th Guards Army on Koniev's Steppe Front had cleared Merefa to the south of Kharkov, but the drive on Poltava was momentarily halted. The Poltava–Kremenchug axis, however, had ceased to be the focus of the *Stavka*'s attention as Rokossovskii and Vatutin pressed on with their Konotop–Romny sweep. The prospect of developing a major breakthrough to the Dnieper at the junction of the two German army groups and then racing for Kiev—simultaneously driving into the deep flank of Army Group South—beckoned irresistibly. On the night of 6 September Stalin issued revised orders to the fronts and realigned frontal boundaries: Central Front would attack with its left on Chernigov, with its right on Gomel; the Voronezh Front would strike toward Pereslav (to force the Dnieper in the Bukrin bend and finally outflank Kiev from the south); Koniev's Steppe Front would now aim for Kremenchug. As reinforcement for this intensification of the Soviet drive, the *Stavka* assigned 61st Army to Rokossovskii, 3rd Guards Tank Army and 1st Guards Cavalry Corps to Vatutin and, to Koniev, 37th Army from *Stavka* reserve, Zhadov's 5th Guards from Vatutin and 46th Army from Malinovskii. The Southern Front had also acquired quite hefty reinforcement.

Field-Marshal Manstein emphasized to Hitler that the situation on his northern wing was deteriorating fast. Marshal Zhukov was out to break Fourth *Panzer* Army and would brook no dilatoriness from his own commanders in doing it; he urged Katukov forward as fast as possible, and Lt.-Gen. Kulik, the downgraded marshal who reappeared in the summer of 1943 at the head of a reserve army, got short shrift—Zhukov berated him for using the tactics of the 1920s and finally sent him packing. By 14 September Manstein's northern wing was beginning to break up as Fourth *Panzer* split into three parts. The road to Kiev was rapidly being uncovered. Both the Russians and the Germans raced for the Dnieper, though lack of tanks and lorries on the Soviet side (as well as shortage of bombers in the air divisions) blunted and slowed Soviet probings. Chernyakhovskii nevertheless was enlarging his bridgeheads on the western bank of the Desna, while 61st Army and 7th Guards Cavalry Corps were pushed forward between 65th and 13th Armies. On 15 September, 60th and 13th Armies with 7th Guards Mechanized Corps reached Nezhin; Vatutin's right wing, outflanking Poltava by its wide north-westerly drive, was pushing up to eight German divisions back towards Kanev on the Dnieper. If Chernyakhovskii's 60th now turned due south (and the 60th consisted of four corps), it could drive straight into the flank and rear of these German formations as well as cutting off the escape route for no less than thirteen German divisions. Rokossovskii now put this proposal to Marshal

Zhukov, *Stavka* representative at Voronezh Front HQ—60th Army should swing to link up with 38th Army on Vatutin's right. Zhukov, for reasons as yet unexplained, turned down this plan; under orders issued on 18 September 38th Army would drive on the Dnieper in the area south of Kiev. But three days later the 38th had to be swung north as the frontal boundaries between Rokossovskii and Vatutin were also shifted northwards. On 21 September, 38th Army received orders to regroup so as to bring it into Central Front territory, force the Desna north of Pukhovka—although 60th Army had already crossed the Desna—then force the Dnieper in order to establish a bridgehead not later than 27 September to the north of Kiev. Thereafter, 38th Army in co-operation with Moskalenko's 40th would encircle the enemy in the area of Kiev and take the city itself. The net result was to shift 60th Army from its sites on the Dnieper further to the north, while only small detachments of 38th Army made it over the Dnieper on 26 September.

At the beginning of the last week in September more and more Soviet armies, driving over 150 miles to the west, drew up at the river Dnieper. Rokossovskii's left forced the Desna south of Chernigov and reached the Dnieper on 21 September (the entire Central Front advancing to Sozh and Dnieper by the end of the month). Vatutin aimed the main body of his Front at the Rzhintsev–Kanev crossings and on the night of 22 September forward units of 3rd Guards Tank Army improvized a rapid crossing. First across from Koniev's Steppe Front was Shumilov's 7th Guards, whose forward elements went over during the night of 25 September south-west of Kremenchug. Malinovskii's South-Western Front reached the Dnieper on 26 September when detachments of 6th Army seized two small bridgeheads south of Dnepropetrovsk. Within a week, as Soviet troops improvized rafts or used little boats hidden by partisans, or hacked timber to build the first bridges, twenty-three bridgeheads, ranging in depth from a thousand yards to twenty miles, dotted the western bank of the mighty Dnieper. While these men heaved their way over the river and clung on as best they might on the far bank, the Soviet command flung in three airborne brigades to hold and to expand the Bukrin bridgehead, which a mechanized brigade had widened to some ten miles by 24 September. Aerial reconnaissance showed at that time only a weak German defence with no reserves, though much of the situation remained obscure. The airborne drop, directed by the Airborne Forces commander Maj.-Gen. A.G. Kapitokhin with the corps (1st, 3rd and 5th Airborne Brigades) under his deputy, Maj.-Gen. Zatevakhin, received Marshal Zhukov's full approval: 3rd and 5th Brigades would go in during the night of 26 September, 1st would be held in reserve to be dropped during the second or third night. Golovanov's ADD, the long-range bomber force, would provide 50 PS-84 bomber-transports and 150 Il-4 and B-25 night-bombers; the Airborne air force, 10 glider-tugs, 13 Il-4s for dropping weapons by parachute, 35 A-7 and G-11 gliders. The transports were scheduled to carry twenty paratroops but the pilots pointed out that the planes would at best take only fifteen to eighteen men: fewer transport planes arrived at the forward airfields than had been planned and planes were late owing to the bad weather.

During the night of 26 September, 3rd Airborne Brigade flew out westwards; 296 aircraft sorties dropped 4,575 men but none of their 45mm guns, 13 planes turned back unable to find the dropping zone (DZ), 2 dropped their paratroops too deep in the rear, one plane unloaded its paratroopers in the Dnieper and one dropped the men on Soviet positions; 5th Brigade had only 48 of an expected 65 transports, and the 4 tankers could not refuel all the machines on time. Nor was there enough fuel at Bogodukhov airfield to supply all the transports, so that planes took off singly as and when they were fuelled. Two battalions—some thousand men—got down, but lack of fuel caused the cancellation of further flights. German AA guns now forced the remaining transport planes up, the men and canisters going out at between 2,000 and 3,000 feet. With transports speeding over the dropping zones, the paratroops fell in widely scattered groups. As radio operators were separated from their few (about half a dozen) sets or sets were separated from their batteries, the brigades were practically bereft of communications with Front HQ. The three signals groups dropped during the night of 28 September never linked up, and a PO-2 plane sent in with powerful equipment that same day was shot down.

Towards the end of September, forty-three independent groups, 2,300 men under the officers of 3rd and 5th Brigades, operated in the German rear; about 600 men under Colonel Sidorchuk concentrated in the woods near Kanev. The Soviet paratroopers landed in a hornet's nest, with three German divisions in the area of the drop and two on the move towards it, information actually in the possession of Vatutin's HQ but not passed on to the airborne commanders. Nor did the airborne corps have any mission other than to 'hold ground' until 40th Army moved up, but Front HQ was none too confident that 40th Army could close up. Assembling a corps staff had been done pell-mell, an over-rapid improvization in which the worst weakness was the lack of unified command over the actual aircraft designated for the operation. Throughout October Sidorchuk's 'Kanev group' grew to about 1,000 men as other detachments linked up with him or sabotage squads joined the beleaguered paratroopers. From the woods near Kanev the brigade moved into hiding at Tagancha, also heavily wooded; flushed out of there, Sidorchuk's men slipped through to the Cherkassy woods, twenty miles east of Korsun, where they came within the operational area of 52nd Army. During the night of 14 November, 52nd Army began its assault crossing of the Dnieper, and at long last the Soviet paratroopers linked up with their own line.

In their race for the Dnieper the Soviet fronts and armies all too often outran their supplies and resources. The rush towards the great river line became one great frontal pursuit, though slowed by lack of powerful mobile formations and weakened as fuel or ammunition (or both) petered out. The decision of 6 September on the part of the *Stavka* to regroup and reinforce had come very late, given that it needed almost a fortnight for the formations to shuttle around: 3rd Guards Tank Army and 37th Army arrived on the scene when German troops were already speedily falling back to the Dnieper. The first Soviet divisions to show up on the Dnieper had rushed far ahead of their rear units with heavy bridging equipment (much of which was immobilized anyway through shortage of fuel); the two divisions of 37th Army (62nd and 92nd) set about their assault crossing 'off the march' with eight N2P pontoons and six A-3 light boats supplied by the two engineer battalions that had moved along with them. Soldiers and partisans elsewhere scoured the banks for barges sunk by the Germans, raised them and shipped tanks across on these or on platforms lashed to pontoons. As skiffs and light craft used for fishing were collected at the water's edge, squads of soldier-axemen chopped out hundreds of rafts or assembled piers, causeways and timber trestles to shore up shattered bridges. Ahead, in some places 3,500 yards away across the deep Dnieper water, lay the high western bank humped with hills, ridges and crests, obscured by day with smoke screens and lit by gun-flashes or exploding shells at night. The *Stavka* early in September had underlined the vital importance of forcing rivers 'off the march' in its directive to Front and Army Military Soviets: the directive ('On the rapid and decisive assault crossing of rivers and the award of decorations to Soviet army personnel . . .', issued on 9 September) prescribed that for forcing the Desna to the north and other rivers 'presenting a comparable hazard' army commanders would receive the Order of Kutuzov 1st Class, corps down to brigade commanders would receive the Kutuzov Order 2nd Class and regimental commanders the 3rd Class: for forcing the Dnieper at Smolensk and lower down its reaches (and for rivers of comparable difficulty), the prize was the decoration Hero of the Soviet Union. With assault units paddling and ferrying themselves over the Dnieper, with tanks plugged up with putty or pulled across on barges, the bridgeheads north of Kiev and between Kremenchug and Dnepropetrovsk swelled by the hour. Those who lived could claim their hard-won decorations. Meanwhile the Soviet command regrouped its forces and planned for the battle of the Dnieper line, upon the success of which so much turned.

In late August, when the Central and Bryansk Fronts rolled on Bryansk, as the Voronezh and Steppe Fronts were locked in the slogging fighting for Kharkov, the Western Front (under Sokolovskii) and the Kalinin Front (under Yeremenko) made their final preparations for the second stage of the operations aimed at the liberation of Smolensk, the assault on Army Group Centre—Third *Panzer,* Fourth Army and elements of Second *Panzer* (by Russian estimates some forty divisions in all). The first stage of the Western Front offensive was aimed at Yelnaya–Spas Demensk to open the road to Roslavl, while the right wing co-operated with the Kalinin Front to capture Yartsevo–Dorogobuzh and then on to Smolensk; Yeremenko's left wing would attack Dorogobuzh, operating with Sokolovskii's right in the offensive aimed on Smolensk after which both fronts would drive on deep into Belorussia. Marshal of Artillery Voronov acted as 'Stavka co-ordinator' for the Smolensk operations. When the Western Front offensive opened on the morning of 7 August, German troops were ready and waiting within their systems of fortification; east of Spas Demensk the Western Front assault force—5th Army under Lt.-Gen. V.S. Polenov, 10th Guards under Trubnikov and 33rd Army under Gordov—moved only slowly into the German defences. To reinforce the attack Sokolovskii ordered Lt.-Gen. Zhuravlev's 68th Army from the second echelon into action, but it was Lt.-Gen. V.S. Popov's 10th Army attacking north of Kirov that was really making progress away to the south. Sokolovskii now ordered 5th Tank Corps to move ahead of 10th Army, to cut the Warsaw motorway and to hold it until the rifle units drew up, after which 5th Corps would advance into the wooded area west of Spas Demensk and cut the railway line leading to Yelnaya. Equipped largely with British-built Valentine tanks, 5th Corps ran into tough German opposition; caught with its AA defences badly disorganized, the corps took a terrible beating from the air and a pounding on the ground as its light tanks were shot to pieces under it. The deflection of German units to the south-west nevertheless had its effect in the Spas Demensk bulge and Spas Demensk itself fell on 13 August, the day on which Yeremenko on the Kalinin Front ordered Lt.-Gen. A.I. Zygin with 39th Army and Lt.-Gen. K.D. Golubev with 43rd Army to begin their attacks aimed at Dukhovshchina, the capture of which Yeremenko had earmarked for the second day of the offensive. But five days of fighting in this boggy ground brought the Kalinin Front, its way barred by repeated German counter-attacks, only two miles forward into the German defences. The Stavka called a halt.

The revised plan for the Smolensk operation received Stavka approval on 22 August. The Western Front would now direct its main effort in the direction of Yelnaya rather than Roslavl, and for the next five days Sokolovskii regrouped to bring Trubnikov's 10th Guards and Krylov's 21st Army on to their new lines, their sector set at eighteen miles with the breakthrough planned along the length of a ten-mile front. Yeremenko had meanwhile brought up Front reserves and attacked again on 23 August, only to have more than a fortnight of battering German defences bring little result. Early in September the Stavka once more intervened to call a halt. With heavy ground and air bombardment, Sokolovskii renewed his offensive on 28 August and by the end of the month Yelnaya was in Soviet hands. With Soviet troops over the Dnieper, Dorogobuzh fell on 1 September, but ahead lay a well-prepared German defence line upon which German reserves including 1st SS Brigade were already closing. Sokolovskii halted again to organize the third stage of the Smolensk attack; the centre would attack Smolensk directly, the left was to aim for the Desna and Roslavl, the right to co-operate with the Kalinin Front and destroy German forces in the Yartsevo area.

The final attack opened on 15 September. The next day Yartsevo fell, in a welter of bloody fighting. On the left Popov's 10th Army was over the Desna and aiming for Roslavl. Berzarin took over control of the left-flank operations of the Kalinin Front directed against Rudnya–Vitebsk. In support of the left-flank operations of the Western Front, Popov of the Bryansk Front, whose armies had already reached the Desna, pressed on for Bryansk and Bezhitsa, which fell on 17 September to Bagramyan's 11th Guards. The *Stavka* now ordered Popov to move as rapidly as possible to the river Sozh, which in any event he must reach by 2–3 October, whereupon the Bryansk Front was to strike into the flank of Army Group Centre. One by one the German bastions were toppled in late September—Bryansk, Roslavl and Smolensk, the latter being finally cleared of German troops on the morning of 25 September, the ancient city having been set to the torch as the Germans pulled out. The fighting here, at the centre of the whole Soviet–German front, had been heavy and costly for both sides; Sokolovskii's first attacks, preparations for which had been carefully monitored by *Luftwaffe* reconnaissance, had inevitably met powerful and well-organized German resistance. The Soviet command, however, reckoned that these attacks at the centre held down fifty-five German divisions and kept any reinforcement away from the southern wing which the Red Army was intent upon annihilating.

For a few days early in October the briefest lull settled over the length of the front, a moment of short-lived calm before Stalin unleashed his autumn storm designed to burst over two regional capitals, Minsk in Belorussia and Kiev in the Ukraine. Orders for the attack on Kiev had already gone out, and those for the very ambitious undertaking of the liberation of Belorussia were on their way. Taking on the simultaneous re-conquest of 'right-bank [western] Ukraine' and Belorussia was a mammoth requirement, one that once more overestimated the capabilities of the Red Army and in particular oversimplified the problems of supplying it. Certainly the summer campaign had done serious damage to the north–south interlinking of the three German army groups, and it had also inhibited—permanently, as events proved—their capacity for combined manoeuvring. If Stalin had not devised present operations in conjunction with the winter offensives as the decisive campaign of the war, there were compelling reasons for it, not the least being the need to ensure the full co-operation of his western allies. That became plain in the course of the Moscow conference of foreign ministers held in Moscow later in October, the clearing ground for the projected meeting of the 'Big Three', the 'Cairo Three' who were to meet towards the end of the year in Teheran. Press as they might, Molotov and Voroshilov could obtain only 'the spring of 1944' as the date of the cross-Channel invasion; Anthony Eden and Cordell Hull reaffirmed the validity of the Quebec Conference decisions, but the British Prime Minister asked that Stalin be warned of a possible stretching of the term 'spring' even into July. On the evening of 29 October Stalin asked Mr Eden, who had the Prime Minister's signals to hand, whether delays with *Overlord* might run to one or two months; it was a question the British Foreign

Secretary could scarcely answer, but Stalin showed no great dissatisfaction. That he meant to soldier on with the coalition Stalin signalled in no uncertain fashion at the dinner held on the following evening; here he told Cordell Hull that, not only was the Soviet Union bent upon the destruction of Nazi Germany, but she would then participate with her allies in the defeat of Japan. (At this time, almost exactly, the *Führer* lashed out at his Japanese partners to keep alive the 'military threat' to Russia from the east.)

The simmering ill feeling and the half-smothered row over the Arctic convoy question now began to fade. In September Molotov directed a blunt message on the urgent need to resume sailings to the British, a missive to which the Prime Minister took strong exception. Nevertheless, on 1 October he informed Stalin that the convoys would sail again, the first coming in November. Within the week Stalin summoned Admiral Golovko, Northern Fleet commander, to Moscow, where he questioned him very closely on recent mishaps in the Kara Sea and demanded details of naval deployment to protect Allied convoys moving into the Northern Fleet's operational zone. For instance, would the Fleet be ready to receive an Allied convoy in November? The land-lubber members of the *Politburo* who joined in the discussion obviously had no idea what the Kara Sea was like; Golovko understandably lost his temper, whereupon Stalin rebuked him sharply, but he agreed to supply anti-submarine aircraft and promised naval reinforcement of 'various types'.

At the end of the month Stalin had reasonable cause for satisfaction. He had a firm undertaking about *Overlord* even if the date hovered somewhat uncertainly between spring and summer; he had implanted himself deeply in the coalition on advantageous terms with his offer of eventual aid in the Pacific war; and he was on the way to correcting what he himself had called 'that catastrophic diminution' in war supplies now that the convoys were set sailing once more. In his talk with Golovko he had been singularly confident: 'Be prepared to meet the convoys. No matter how the allies might delay—Churchill especially—they will have to resume the convoys.'

The Soviet autumn offensive was, therefore, a 'war-shortening' move undertaken in line with proposals to 'shorten the duration of the war in Europe' (the cross-Channel attack, the entry of Turkey into the war and the use of Swedish air bases for the air offensive against Germany) which Molotov presented to the Moscow Conference. For their autumn strikes the Soviet fronts in the south-west came out decked in new designations, the 1st Ukrainian (Voronezh), the 2nd Ukrainian (Steppe) and the 3rd and 4th Ukrainian (South-Western and Southern) Fronts. Vatutin's 1st Ukrainian would mass its main force on 'the Kiev axis' and build up a strategic bridgehead here. Koniev's 2nd Ukrainian Front with Malinovskii's 3rd was to destroy enemy forces on the Kirovgrad–Krivoi Rog axis and build a second strategic bridgehead south-west of Kremenchug; Koniev was to attack south-westwards, while Malinovskii would destroy the German bridgehead at Zaporozhe on the eastern bank and then move westwards. Tolbukhin's 4th

Front would advance from the river Molochnaya to the lower reaches of the Dnieper from the northern Tauride. Both the Soviet and German commands had their eyes fixed on the Kiev axis, the northern wing of Army Group South; a collapse here would imperil the entire Army Group and sweep the Red Army forward to the approaches to Poland and the Carpathians. That line of march emerged in the *Stavka* directive (29 September) to Vatutin, whose Voronezh (1st Ukrainian) Front was to co-operate with the left wing of the Central (Belorussian) Front in driving on Kiev, moving to the line Stavishche–Fastov–Belaya Tserkov and thereafter toward Berdichev–Zhmerinka–Moghilev Podolskii. Vatutin's first operational plan proposed to launch the Front shock group (40th, 27th and 3rd Guards Tank Army) from the Bukrin bridgehead to outflank Kiev from the south-west and to cut the German escape route westwards; a supporting attack would come from the Lyutezh bridgehead to the north of the city, with 38th Army and 5th Guards Tank Corps outflanking the city from the north-west. It was a plan that failed to survive the tests of actual execution and was finally consummated in reverse, the main attack coming from the Lyutezh bridgehead after 3rd Guards Tank Army and the bulk of artillery moved the hundred miles northward into 38th Army area, for at Bukrin Soviet troops were hemmed in by ten German divisions. Moskalenko with 38th Army, Lt.-Gen. A.G. Kravchenko with 5th Guards Tank Corps, Chernyakhovskii's 60th, Rybalko's 3rd Guards Tank Army and Baranov's 1st Guards Cavalry Corps were all massed at the end of October north of Kiev and about to fall on Fourth *Panzer*.

The *Stavka* had simultaneously issued revised instructions for the conduct of operations at the centre of the front, on the sector running from Vitebsk to Gomel, where a three-sided assault would be launched on Army Group Centre, from the north, the east and the south. During the first week in October the Bryansk Front was wound up, formally disappearing from the Soviet order of battle on 8 October; 50th, 3rd, 63rd and 11th Armies moved under Rokossovskii's command on the Central Front (shortly redesignated the Belorussian Front), the remaining formations going further north. Rokossovskii's new offensive, coming from the south, was aimed at Gomel–Bobruisk, *Stavka* instructions requiring him to align his assault armies in the direction of Zhlobin–Bobruisk–Minsk, to capture Minsk itself and then to move on the Minsk–Slutsk–river Sluch line. From the east Sokolovskii with the Western Front would drive on Orsha–Moghilev, both of which had been uncovered by the recapture of Smolensk and Roslavl. In the north Yeremenko on the Kalinin Front (redesignated 1st Baltic) would aim his offensive in the direction of Vitebsk. Yeremenko had already in early October set his attacks in motion, using two left-flank armies (43rd and 49th) to distract attention from his main blow with 3rd and 4th Shock Armies against Third *Panzer*, directed at the junction between Army Groups Centre and North in the Nevel area. This was no great territorial adjustment, but success here was of immense significance in putting the Red Army astride the routes leading to the rear of Army Group North and also for cutting through a vital tendon—

the Dno–Novosokolniki–Nevel railway circuit—whose severance would leave the whole German left wing without its internal connection and flapping all too loosely. Wider success would also put the Red Army along the shortest routes to Poland and East Prussia.

The non-stop Soviet offensive was now running into its fourth month, and into all the autumnal clogging brought by rain and soft, slithery ground. Soviet divisions, outrunning their supply columns and with their bases a hundred miles behind them, were moving into areas specially carved and cut with the demolitions brought on by retreating German troops, meant as more than mere harassment and designed to gouge out the economic vitals of the country as the *Wehrmacht* abandoned it. None of this eased supply and transportation problems. In the north lay the German strongholds, and though Nevel had gone in October, Vitebsk became another fortress. Between Orsha and Vitebsk lay a powerful German line covering the gap between the Dvina and the Dnieper. Down to Rogachev and Zhlobin, nature provided the barriers, with massive swamps and minor rivers by the score, behind them the Berezina and the Drut. Behind these lines improvized by men or established by nature were hard, tough, battle-tested German infantry divisions, veterans of the *Ostfront* and all its nightmares. The *Ostwall* as a great fortified rampart might have been a comforting figment of Hitler's imagination, but the fixed lines in the north were real enough. To the south lay the one great natural barrier, the Dnieper, less fitted out with fortification, but formidable in its own span. There was, therefore, every reason for a great surge of Russian confidence as in October division after division crossed over, though the battle for the whole 'Dnieper line' was to be protracted. For Soviet and German armies alike, the *Schwerpunkt* remained anchored in the southern wing.

Soviet successes since Kursk had been on an impressive scale, not only in the forward sweep but in cracking the structure of the German Eastern Front, that great dispersal of German forces which Stalin had claimed in October was the very essence of his 'war-shortening' strategy. Whatever the guise in which he presented it, Stalin's strategy was basically an admixture of attrition and offensiveness, much of the latter ill-judged and even reckless, though just for once—in the critical period before the battle for Kursk—Stalin had been prevailed upon to exercise restraint, patience and confidence in his own troops. That decision had now begun to make a handsome pay-off and Stalin was gaining ground diplomatically, militarily and politically. There was to be a 'Big Three' conference, the preparation for which had been set in train in Moscow; in military and political terms he now held the initiative in the struggle on the Eastern Front. With the 'Free German movement' he held a valuable bargaining card. The *Bund Deutscher Offiziere*, the *BDO*, had from the outset refused to be identified with the seditious propaganda—particularly the incitement to German soldiers to desert—which emanated from the *NKD*, but early in September the generals Seydlitz, Lattmann and Korfes had been persuaded by General Melnikov, an emissary of the Soviet government and an officer of the *NKVD*, that in the event of a collapse of the *Ostfront* owing to the *Wehrmacht* intervening against Hitler, then the Soviet government would 'guarantee' Germany its 1938 frontiers, the continued existence of the *Wehrmacht* and no 'Bolshevization' of Germany. This, coupled with the *NKD*'s agreement not to subvert German soldiers in the field, swung the German generals into the *BDO*, and finally into a 'merger' of the *BDO* and the *NKD*. In the late summer Stalin may have overestimated the effect of the disaster at Kursk on Germany, but with his captive soldier 'committees' he did at least have a faint 'shadow' German authority representing 'the army' and 'the people', at least in name, a propaganda pincer to nip the native army and the nation as he chose, and a possible counter-weight to any Anglo-American 'deal' with Hitler—an 'anti-Bolshevik Germany' against which Stalin could respond with his own 'pro-Bolshevik Germany'.

The ominous implications for Nazi Germany, not merely in the field but across the whole military–political board, were underlined by General Gehlen, himself chief of *Fremde Heere Ost*, in a chilling chart, the extrapolation of which he submitted in mid-October under the toneless title of *Bisherige Entwicklung der deutsch-sowjetrussischen Kräfteverhältnisse seit Kriegsbeginn und seine mögliche Weiterentwicklung bis Ende 1943*, a comparative survey of Soviet and German strength and performance in great detail, hung with maps and charts. From these data, from the *Gesamtbild,* General Gehlen drew only the most sombre conclusion: '. . . so in the future will the Soviet-Russian enemy surpass Germany in terms of manpower, equipment and in the field of propaganda' (T-78/R466, 644031-45: 17.10.43). To think, or to hope, that the Russians would now lie back was the gravest self-deception; the Soviet Union would surely—*'mit Sicherheit'*—unleash a powerful winter offensive. Gehlen was not guessing and indeed he was proved right. Plans were afoot for that massive winter attack which would bring the Soviet armies to the line from which they would be able to launch the truly decisive blows. Equally, as Gehlen predicted, the Red Army swelled with men and machines: 78 reformed rifle divisions (from what had been hitherto brigades), 126 rifle corps, an array of 5 tank armies, 24 tank corps, 13 mechanized corps, 80 independent tank brigades, 106 tank regiments and 43 regiments of self-propelled guns, 6 artillery corps, 26 artillery divisions, 7 *Katyusha* rocket-launcher divisions, plus a score of artillery brigades.

Within twelve months of unleashing the counter-offensive at Stalingrad, the situation had taken a profound turn in favour of the Russians. Stalingrad itself brought premonitions of disaster to the Germans, but the killing-ground at Kursk, the miles of fire that consumed the *Panzer* divisions and burned out the infantry, brought the full reality of vast destruction. After the frenzied mechanized jousting on the battlefields in the salient at Kursk, the *Ostheer,* fearfully mangled at the hands of the Red Army, now began to wither. The last offensive and the last victories of the German Army in Russia had come and gone forever.

4

The Drive to the Western Frontiers: October 1943–March 1944

The autumn of 1943 once more brought low-hung cloud, fogbanks and rain to the battlefields. By day the sun, if it appeared, shone pale and fitful and at night autumnal frosts crackled on the surface of the mud and the ooze. Winter was only weeks away, but for the Red Army the coming winter was to prove very different from the two previous winter campaigns, fought much further east amidst the frost, ice and snow. Since storming the ice-bound Don and Donets, Soviet troops had moved many hundreds of miles to the west where conditions were markedly different; only in the north, on the Leningrad and Volkhov Fronts, could there be any parallel with the past. In the south-west winter conditions were very fickle, with the lower Dnieper and the southern Bug freezing over at different times and for different periods; at the centre of the Soviet–German front winter also assumed a milder form. The Soviet command did take these climatic vagaries and fluctuations into its general calculations, but it could scarcely foresee that not only would the winter of 1943–4 prove to be different but would also turn out to be enormously capricious.

At the end of October, what Manstein calls 'the decisive struggle' for the Dnieper line was already well advanced, as the Red Army piled on the pressure in four sectors: the Zaporozhe bridgehead, the two Dnieper sectors and the bridgehead to the north of Kiev (the left flank of Fourth *Panzer*). To hold this Dnieper Front, all 440 miles of it, Manstein mustered thirty-seven infantry and seventeen *Panzer/Panzergrenadier* divisions, the bulk of them mauled and mangled; the hopes of safety behind the high western bank of the Dnieper were to prove both temporary and illusory. For the moment the main Soviet effort appeared to be directed in the Dnieper bend itself, where Koniev's 2nd Ukrainian and Malinovskii's 3rd Ukrainian Fronts, facing in turn First *Panzer* and Eighth Army, were hacking out a giant emplacement on the western bank from Cherkassy to Zaporozhe, a bridgehead fifty miles deep and over two hundred miles in length. General Koniev's left wing had pushed itself into a relatively shallow but extended bridgehead south of Kremenchug, four armies (5th Guards, 37th, 7th Guards and 57th) in all, behind which followed Rotmistrov's 5th Guards Tank Army, newly released from *Stavka* reserve. On 7 October Koniev submitted his attack plans to the *Stavka*: he proposed to strike from his bridgehead with his main attack directed at Pyatikhatka–Krivoi Rog, after which he suggested a drive on Apostolovo in order to cut off the German escape route for units holding Dnepropetrovsk against Malinovskii. The *Stavka* duly approved.

For his main attack Koniev intended to use his four bridgehead armies, with 37th and 5th Guards opening the German defences whereupon Rotmistrov's tanks would go in. Zhadov's 5th Guards Army had a fifty-mile march ahead of it to redeploy, Rotmistrov's 5th Guards Tank Army (the bulk of it still refitting at Poltava on 10 October) a 100-mile approach march. With his Guards armour and infantry finally in position, Koniev attacked on the morning of 15 October out of the bridgehead. That afternoon Rotmistrov's tanks were introduced and manoeuvred through the autumn mud. Within three days Soviet units had taken Derievka and on 19 October Pyatikhatka, another important rail junction. Four days later Rotmistrov's lead tanks were on the outskirts of Krivoi Rog, with another tank force driving on Mitrofanovka (fifteen miles to the east of Kirovograd). With riflemen riding atop their tanks, 18th Tank Corps (5th Guards Tank Army) broke into Krivoi Rog on the morning of 24 October, but 11th *Panzer* Division managed to hold up 37th Army advancing to support 18th Corps. That evening, running short of ammunition, 18th Corps tanks began pulling back, having both to find and to fight their way through unfamiliar streets increasingly engulfed in darkness.

Though momentarily checked at Krivoi Rog, Koniev's attack threatened the left flank of the German units holding Dnepropetrovsk. This was Malinovskii's target. In the first half of the month Malinovskii's 3rd Ukrainian Front had been engaged in the reduction of the heavily fortified German bridgehead on the eastern bank of the Dnieper, Zaporozhe—which Hitler insisted must be held at all costs and which the *Stavka* demanded categorically must be swept away. The first attempt to rush the defences of Zaporozhe failed. Malinovskii resolved to lay his hand on a sledgehammer, Lt.-Gen. V.I. Chuikov's 8th Guards Army (the old 62nd, the defenders of Stalingrad), a formation drawn into *Stavka* reserve from 3rd Ukrainian strength. Contacting Stalin, because Stalin's permission was required, Malinovskii found inordinately difficult, but having asked for 8th Guards he got it, at the price of giving his word to Stalin that Zaporozhe would be taken 'in two days'. Three infantry armies—8th and 3rd Guards and 12th Armies—and two armoured corps (1st Guards Mechanized and 23rd Tank), with 270 tanks and 17th Air Army in support, would storm Zaporozhe. Malinovskii's decision to attack at night brought a deal of misgiving from his Military Soviet, but Chuikov strongly supported the Front commander.

At 2200 hours on the night of 13 October Chuikov's Guards with 1st Guards Mechanized and 23rd Tanks Corps launched the main assault: 12th Army attacked from the north and 3rd Guards from the south. German armour and infantry abandoned Zaporozhe, blowing up the road along the dam and the Dnieper railway bridge behind them. Malinovskii's 3rd Ukrainian Front could now broaden its bridgehead in the Dnepropetrovsk bend, an operation that was co-ordinated with Koniev's 2nd Ukrainian drive on Krivoi Rog. The objective was to trap First *Panzer* in the eastern reaches of the Dnieper bend, a danger to which Manstein was very much alive. Koniev's operations secured Malinovskii's right flank: as Rotmistrov's tanks drove on Krivoi Rog, two of Malinovskii's formations, 8th Guards and 46th Armies, developed concentric attacks designed to trap German units in Dnepropetrovsk and Dneprodzerzhinsk, the site of the huge hydroelectric power stations—*Dneproges*—that the Germans were intent on blowing up, tucking aerial bombs round the turbines. Glagolev's units (46th Army) raced into Dnepropetrovsk on 25 October and caught the 'torch-bearers' (the German demolition crews) about to light their fires of destruction. But not all the demolitions could be prevented; the aerial bombs and dynamite blew many of the *dneproges* installations to pieces. Dnepropetrovsk was finally taken by 39th Guards Divisions (8th Guards Army).

The fusion of Koniev's left and Malinovskii's right at this time produced the consolidation of the two fronts' bridgehead holdings into the single 'Kremenchug–Dnepropetrovsk bridgehead'. For the moment, First *Panzer* was saved as Koniev's units were held off from Krivoi Rog and pushed behind the river Ingulets; Koniev had been halted for the moment, but it was only the Ingulets, not the Dnieper, behind which his forward units had been shunted. And now, from another direction, further dangers loomed over First *Panzer*. Tolbukhin's 4th Ukrainian Front to the south had smashed into the Sixth Army on a front running from the Dnieper to the sea of Azov. Tolbukhin was under orders to destroy German forces at Melitopol, seize the Dnieper crossings and a bridgehead on the western bank, then shut off the German Seventeenth Army in the Crimea by seizing the Perekop isthmus. Striking out from the river Molochnaya, Tolbukhin's first attacks with 5th Shock, 44th and 2nd Guards Armies in the lead had made little progress by 9 October, but on 24 October Kreizer's 51st Army had finally ground its way into Melitopol, whereupon the German Sixth Army fell back on the heavily fortified Nikopol bridgehead, a massive defensive position fitted out with great skill and much care, utilizing the reach of the river and the swamplands that stretched beside it. With the Sixth Army shovelled out of the northern Tauride and withdrawn behind the lower Dnieper, the German Seventeenth Army in the Crimea was in a precarious position, on the point of being marooned. When Sixth Army fell back beyond Perekop, Seventeenth Army—which Hitler refused permission to evacuate, demanding that the Crimea be held at all costs to deny the Russians bomber-bases from which to launch attacks on the Rumanian oilfields—was well and truly isolated. Early in November Tolbukhin's troops had established bridgeheads on the Sivash lagoons, while on the Kerch peninsula General Petrov's North Caucasus Front, having cleared Taman, landed more troops. Putting down units of the 56th and 18th Armies from ships of the Black Sea Fleet and the Azov Flotilla at Kerch incurred all the hazards of the amphibious operation launched in December 1941, but this time, once ashore, the Soviet troops were there to stay.

This crisis in the south, however, could not match the real danger now building up in the area of Fourth *Panzer*, the northern wing of Army Group South, which remained 'operationally decisive', a view shared by Marshal Zhukov and Manstein alike. Twice Vatutin's 1st Ukrainian Front formations had tried to charge out of the Bukrin bridgehead (south of Kiev) to lunge deeply into the western Ukraine and reach the Berdichev–Zhmerinka–Moghilev Podolskii line laid down by *Stavka* orders on 29 September. The attacks out of Bukrin failed: shortages of men and ammunition, lack of heavy artillery, the terrain itself—and ten German divisions—brought Soviet attempts to nought. Vatutin came, therefore, to examine the possibilities of the Lyutezh bridgehead north of Kiev (presently held by Chibisov's 38th Army) with a much heightened interest. The Military Soviet of the 1st Ukrainian Front had already made a suggestion on these lines to the *Stavka* on 18 October:

At the present time in the bridgehead 20–30 kilometres directly north of Kiev Chibisov's 38th Army has crushed enemy opposition and is pursuing the enemy. The complete possibility does exist of developing this success in a south-westerly direction; however, we lack reserves to do this. There is also a possibility of developing success from the bridgehead held by 60th Army [Chernyakhovskii] but here also we are lacking forces. [A.A. Grechko, *VIZ*, 1963 (11), p. 5.]

Vatutin himself put the matter plainly: one infantry army and one tank army would be needed to exploit any northerly attack. In a week (by 24 October), the *Stavka* signalled its permission for Vatutin to work out attack plans utilizing the Lyutezh bridgehead. This revised plan for 1st Ukrainian Front finally called for a northerly attack, with the Bukrin bridgehead mounting a diversion; the main assault force (38th, 60th, 3rd Guards Tank Army, 1st Guards Cavalry Corps) would attack on 1–2 November, supported by Krasovskii's 2nd Air Army. In the Bukrin bend, 40th and 27th Armies, supported by two tank corps would hold German strength south of Kiev by attacking two days earlier. The immediate task of 1st Ukrainian Front was the destruction of Fourth *Panzer* and the liberation of Kiev, after which the offensive would unroll west and south-west: on the fourth day of operations infantry formations were to be on the Korosten–Zhitomir–Berdichev–Rakitno line, armour at Khmelnik–Vinnitsa–Zhmerinka.

Vatutin had now to empty the Bukrin bend of much of its armour, artillery and support units. In pouring rain and amidst the mud the 3rd Guards Tank Army, 7th Artillery Breakthrough Corps, 23rd Rifle Corps and clusters of other units drew over to the eastern bank of the Dnieper and then took four routes for their hundred-mile journey to the north into the Lyutezh bridgehead. As the tanks, guns, lorries and mortars toiled northwards, 38th and 60th Armies lapped up the reinforcements detached to them from 13th Army. Red Army engineers worked like madmen to repair or erect bridges over the Dnieper for Rybalko's 3rd Guards armour. At Svaroma (directly opposite Lyutezh on the eastern bank of the Dnieper) German dive-bombers and artillery brought the last remaining bridge under continuous bombardment, blasting it piece by piece into the river. The rain of bombs and shells had also blown nearby buildings to pieces, loosing logs and planking which Russian bridge-building units seized to rebuild the bridge. At the end of October, for all the bombardment, the heavy tanks had recrossed the Dnieper and were moving on to Lyutezh. In the Bukrin bend 3rd Guards Tank HQ and radio units stayed put until 0500 hours on 28 October, surrounded by dummy tanks as the real ones trundled north. If the rain hampered Soviet movement, it also helped to hide it.

Three days before the Kiev attack began, Vatutin himself moved into the Lyutezh bridgehead, setting up his HQ in the cellar of a half-ruined house in Novo Petrovtsy; here he briefed his army and corps commanders. Front forward HQ also moved into the bridgehead. To the south, Lt.-Gen. F.F. Zmachenko's 40th and Trofimenko's 27th Armies had opened their attack in the Bukrin bend on 1 November. The northern attack was now timed for 3 November and on the eve of the offensive Vatutin received a specific directive from the *Stavka* to operate with the maximum speed—'the operation which is to open on the right flank of the Front must not be dragged out, since each day lost only contributes to the enemy's advantage, permitting him to concentrate his forces in this area using his good roads while our movement is delayed or hampered by roads damaged by enemy action'. Kiev must fall within forty-eight hours, no later than 5–6 November; the directive emphasized that the 'Kiev bridgehead' was the most important of any on the western bank of the Dnieper, a key position from which to eject German troops from the western Ukraine.

Speed the *Stavka* demanded, and speed it got. In the greatest artillery barrage so far seen anywhere on the Eastern Front, 2,000 guns and mortars with 50 *Katyushas*, 480 guns to the mile—one-third of the entire artillery strength of 1st Ukrainian Front—Moskalenko (who had taken over 38th Army) and Chernyakhovskii (the brilliant and energetic commander of 60th Army who had earlier pleaded with Rokossovskii for the 'Kiev axis' to be his) burst out from the Lyutezh bridgehead on the morning of 3 November. During the afternoon of 4 November, as the rain came down in a steady, unpleasant drizzle, Vatutin committed Rybalko's 3rd Guards armour and Baranov's 1st Guards cavalry, ordering them to move through 38th Army and then to drive south-westwards for Fastov, Belaya Tserkov and Grebenka. Passing through the Soviet infantry, Rybalko's tanks were four miles deep in the German positions by the evening. With sirens wailing and headlamps blazing, the tanks fought through the night and by morning reached Svyatoshino (west of Kiev), cutting the Kiev–Zhitomir road. Moskalenko's units were by now already fighting in the outskirts of Kiev, with Chernyakhovskii's 60th swinging south-west on the right flank. Fighting alongside Moskalenko's 38th were the men of the 1st Czechoslovak Independent

Brigade, encouraged by Colonel Svoboda to fight for Kiev as they would fight
for 'Prague and Bratislava'. The Czechs fought in exemplary fashion, capturing
the railway station by the evening of 5 November. Moskalenko's two corps (50th
and 51st) were at this juncture right inside the city along with the lead tanks
of Kravchenko's 5th Guards Tank Corps. The rattle and crack of the street
fighting was drowned by the roar of demolitions, but the German 7th Corps
began to pull back as the Soviet encirclement tightened. At 0400 hours on 6
November, 38th Army reported that 'the mother of Russian cities', ancient Kiev,
ripped and torn by bombardment and demolition, a city that had taken savage
punishment from its occupiers, was cleared of enemy troops. One hour later the
Military Soviet of the 1st Ukrainian Front radioed to the *Stavka* that Kiev had
been liberated: 'With unbounded joy we report to you that the assignment under
orders from you of capturing our fair city of Kiev, the capital of the Ukraine,
has been carried out by the troops of the 1st Ukrainian Front. The city of Kiev
has been completely cleared of its Fascist occupiers' (G.K. Zhukov, *Vospominaniya*
. . . , vol. 2, p. 203). It was a handsome contribution by Vatutin and his men
to the forthcoming anniversary celebrations of the October Revolution, and was
handsomely acknowledged in turn by the victory salutes fired off by the Moscow
gun batteries.

During the next ten days Vatutin's front raced to fill out the 'Kiev bridgehead'
until it became a sizeable strategic holding: 3rd Guards Tanks and 38th Army
moved south-west and west beyond Kiev, the right-flank formations (60th and
13th Armies) advancing north-west and west. Rybalko's tanks took the important
rail junction of Fastov. Zhitomir fell on 12 November: five days later Chernyakhovskii's 60th took Korosten, and on the following day (18 November)
Pukhov's 13th Army was in possession of Ovruch to the north-west. The capture
of Zhitomir and Korosten severed the main rail links between the German Army
Groups South and Centre: the loss of Fastov also appreciably complicated Army
Group South's internal movement. Fourth *Panzer* was being steadily chopped
into three pieces. With each day the outlook on Manstein's northern wing became
gloomier, the most dangerous threat emanating from Rybalko's south-westerly
armoured drive. Heavy German counter-attacks at Tripole (south of Kiev) and
at Fastov on 8 November had caused Vatutin to order 40th and 27th Armies
from the Bukrin bridgehead to regroup, so that they might operate more effectively
with 38th Army units in the Fastov area in countering German movements along
the Dnieper. Soviet units driving to the west of Fastov gave Manstein less cause
for alarm—provided they did not swing south; Manstein even derived a certain
comfort from the diversity of the Soviet thrusts to the west and south-west. West
of Fastov, Soviet units in the Zhitomir and Chernyakov areas splayed themselves
out on an ever-widening front, a dispersion that could become dangerous as Army
Group South moved up divisions to strike back. The *Stavka* also saw some of
the danger. Vatutin received orders to rein in his formations moving westwards
at the centre, to reinforce 38th Army to block any German thrust for Kiev, after

which offensive operations were to be resumed in the direction of Kazatin, south-west of Kiev. Though his left and centre went over to the defensive, Vatutin's right wing (60th and 13th Armies) nevertheless continued to drive on.

With fresh armoured divisions moving up, Manstein launched his counter-blow in mid-November. In the first bout of heavy fighting, which lasted until the end of the month, Zhitomir was recaptured and 49th Corps took Korosten, thus reopening the rail link with Army Group Centre. Vatutin's formations fell back on a line running east of Korosten, on to Radmyshl, east of Brusilov and west of Fastov. The German attack developed along both sides of the main Kiev–Zhitomir highway and aimed at Kiev, but for all the severity of the fighting German units came to grief in the mud and in Vatutin's 'defensive zones'. On 28 November the *Stavka* ordered Vatutin to go over to the defensive, 'wear down' the enemy and prepare a counter-offensive as strategic reserves moved up. Col.-Gen. A.A. Grechko's 1st Guards Army took station in the gap between 38th and 60th Armies, holding off one danger, while Vatutin mobilized all his reserves. At the beginning of December, Marshal Zhukov as *Stavka* 'representative' worked over the new plans for an offensive with Vatutin and the 1st Ukrainian Front Military Soviet, of which Lt.-Gen. A.N. Bogolyubov was chief of staff and Lt.-Gen. N.S. Khrushchev and Maj.-Gen. K.V. Krainyukov the 'political' members. The Zhukov–Vatutin plan envisaged the destruction of the main enemy force in the Berdichev–Kazatin area, to bring the main body of the front to a line running from Lyubar to Khmelnik and the southern Bug (on the Khmel-nik–Vinnitsa sector), and thence to Tetiev–Volodarka: mobile formation would strike for Zhmerinka. Right-wing armies must wipe out German forces at Korosten: the left flank would eliminate enemy forces at Belaya Tserkva. Reinforcement was meanwhile massive. Grechko's 1st Guards, Leselidze's 18th Army, the 1st Tank Army, 25th Tank and 4th Guards Tank Corps and enormous quantities of artillery piled up on the 1st Ukrainian Front in early December, finally giving Vatutin a strength of 452,000 men, 1,100 tanks (most of them reconditioned and repaired), 750 aircraft, almost 6,000 guns and mortars—66 rifle divisions, 3 cavalry divisions, 8 armoured or mechanized corps: 7 infantry armies, 2 tank armies and one air army made up Vatutin's strength in November, his target that convergence of the road and rail links connecting Manstein with his deep rear. Kazatin was again the main target, with a south-westerly drive from Fastov into the 'black earth' area and the sugarbeet factories.

Zhukov proposed to smash in the northern wing of Army Group South, and to do Fourth *Panzer* to death. In late November Manstein had momentarily shored up the Fourth's position (though Hitler undermined its command by precipitate removal of Col.-Gen. Hoth, for three full years a *Panzer* commander on the Eatern Front). The fate of Army Groups South and A depended on holding Fourth *Panzer* together, keeping this 'lid' battened down as tightly as possible, but Manstein's appreciation of 20 November was sombre. Even if the present German counter-blow attained substantial success, this could not of itself eliminate Soviet forces from their giant assembly areas west of the Dnieper, in which case Army Group dare not contemplate transferring divisions from the northern to the southern wing to fight the battle of the Dnieper bend. And even assuming that both battles—on the northern and southern wings—did result in success for Army Group, nothing in the situation had altered fundamentally; Army Group South, weakened by losses and utterly bereft of reserves, would be still 'completely at the enemy's mercy'.

The second battle for the Dnieper bend had just opened. On 14 November Koniev resumed his attack in the direction of Kirovograd and Krivoi Rog, but the mud swallowed up his men and machines. New success, however, was in the offing as Lt.-Gen. K.A. Koroteyev's 52nd Army (on Koniev's right flank) forced the Dnieper at Cherkassy; Soviet troops had their foothold by 13 November, though the German Eighth Army managed to get hold of two mobile formations from First and Fourth *Panzer* and clung to Cherkassy until halfway through December. Finally, Galanin's 4th Guards Army fought its way along the western bank of the Dnieper and linked up with Koroteyev's 52nd. Koniev worked throughout November and December at enlarging his bridgehead west and south of Kremenchug–Dnepropetrovsk and in the Cherkassy area, stabbing into the German defensive system with short blows. In December came the frosts, which enabled Rotmistrov to move once more, and on 9 December, 5th Guards Tank, operating with the riflemen of Zhadov's 5th Guards Army, took Znamenka. Rotmistrov's tank columns prepared to strike for Kirovograd, while at Cherkassy Galanin's and Koroteyev's had made contact and sealed off the German 'hedgehog'. After four days of heavy house-to-house fighting, Cherkassy was in Soviet hands and a new route on the Dnieper opened. The 2nd Ukrainian Front was now emplaced to mount offensive operations of strategic significance. Malinovskii continued to push his bridgehead out to the west of Zaporozhe, while to the south the German Seventeenth Army lay trapped in the Crimea.

The 'Dnieper line', now cracked and crumpled, still held by early winter, but the *Stavka* had plans to smash it in completely when four Soviet fronts would crash down in a great avalanche of men and tanks on Army Group South, clearing the western Ukraine completely. Meanwhile the October operations designed to clear Belorussia and to destroy the central group of German armies between Vitebsk and Gomel had produced impressive, though by no means decisive, results. The capture of Nevel had been a major success, shearing the junction between Army Groups North and Centre: Vitebsk now became the focus of Soviet and German attentions. Here strong German fortifications amplified all the hazards of the terrain, the patchwork of small lakes and thick forest to the north of the Dvina and the marshes of the Luchesa in the south. Next in the chain of forts came Orsha. To close off the gap between the Dvina and the Dnieper, German troops had fortified the area between Orsha and Vitebsk, while south of Orsha, towards Rogachev and Zhlobin on the upper reaches of the Dnieper, swamps and numerous river barriers provided abundant natural hazards.

Unfrozen, the little lakes and marshy land could be defended with relative ease. And unfrozen they remained to the north of Vitebsk, for December brought only a glancing frost instead of the normal 'freeze-up'. Intermittent thaw produced slush, mud and sleet.

Throughout November and December, the 1st Baltic, 2nd Baltic and Western Fronts fought their wet, wintry actions for Vitebsk, outflanking the town from the north-west and making a direct approach from the east—a hard, slogging operation which finally gave the Russians Gorodok to the north, but left Bagramyan to push into the swampland in the Dvina bend. Sokolovskii's Western Front, while approaching Vitebsk from the south, attacked simultaneously in the Orsha–Moghilev direction. Rokossovskii's Belorussian Front was aimed at Gomel–Bobruisk, with Minsk as its main objective; Rokossovskii's left-flank armies had already forced the Dnieper south of Loev in mid-October, making a drive to outflank Gomel quite feasible. After little more than a month, on 26 November, Gomel fell after being approached on three sides and Soviet troops cleared the town in a fierce burst of street fighting. In late November Rokossovskii's right flank was on the Dnieper all the way from Novy Bykhov to Gadilovich; the left-flank armies had already crossed the Berezina. To hold the Zhlobin–Rogachev–Bobruisk 'triangle', the German command moved up five infantry divisions. Having pressed Army Group Centre back from the river Sozh, Rokossovskii's operations halted on a line running from Petukhovka in the north, through Novy Bykhov, on to the east of Zhlobin and Mozyr. Bagramyan, Sokolovskii and Rokossovskii each suffered from the abnormal weather, which kept swamps soft and streams wet and dangerous. Part of eastern Belorussia had been freed, Vitebsk was threatened but by no means subdued; but by the end of 1943 the 'Smolensk gate', the highway pressed out by nature between Orsha and Vitebsk leading to the west, had still not been lifted off its hinges.

At the end of the first week in December 1943 the General Staff completed the final schedules and attack timetables (*Plan operatsii*) for the winter offensive proper, designed to unroll 'without pause' in the wake of the autumnal battles waged in thick, clogging mud and under dismal skies laden with rain or mist. Front commands had already received specific directives or were submitting their final operational proposals. The forthcoming strategic offensive, the winter campaign proper, envisaged four main actions: the destruction of German forces in the Leningrad area, in Belorussia, in the western Ukraine and in the Crimea. The main Soviet striking forces would gather on the outer flanks, in the Leningrad area (aimed at Army Group North) and in the western Ukraine (facing Army Groups South and A). The main attack would be mounted in the south-western theatre in order to recover the substantial industrial resources and raw materials still in German hands, as well as to bring Soviet troops most speedily to the 1941 frontiers of the Soviet Union.

By Soviet calculation the *Wehrmacht* at this time deployed more than sixty per cent of its total strength, and more than fifty per cent of all its armour, on the Eastern Front: 236 divisions, including 25 *Panzer* and 18 motorized divisions, 4,906,000 men (706,000 of them from Germany's allies), 5,400 tanks and assault guns, over 54,000 guns and mortars, supported by 3,000 aircraft. The Soviet Union fielded a gigantic army at this juncture: 5,568,000 men served with the field armies (419,000 in reserve), 480 divisions (19 in *Stavka* reserve) with an average strength fluctuating between 6,000 and 7,000 men, 35 armoured and mechanized corps (12 in reserve), 46 tank brigades (4 in reserve), 80 artillery and mortar divisions (4 in reserve), 5,628 tanks (271 in reserve) and 8,818 aircraft (312 in reserve). Four types of army made up this enormous force: the infantry army ('all-arms'—*obshchevoiskovyi*), the Guard armies ('all-arms' and armoured), the shock armies for assault operations and the tank army: infantry and Guards infantry armies comprised usually three to four corps with an artillery brigade, anti-tank, mortar and AA regiments; the Guards army incorporated somewhat heavier firepower; the *udarniya armiya*, the 'shock armies', included tough and experienced units with heavy artillery support to crack open fixed defences; the tank army combined two tank corps with a mechanized corps. At the end of 1943 the Red Army fielded some sixty 'all-arms' armies, five shock armies and five tank armies (increased to six when the *Stavka* on 20 January 1944 raised the 6th Tank Army from 5th Guards Tank and 5th Mechanized Corps and put it under the command of Lt.-Gen. Kravchenko).

Three rifle regiments made up a rifle division; between two and four rifle divisions, a rifle corps. The basic tactical unity in the armoured forces was the tank brigade, with a shade over 1,000 men and three tank battalions, twenty-one tanks to a battalion. The tank corps consisted of three tank brigades, the mechanized corps of three mechanized brigades (this brigade consisting of three motorized rifle battalions with tank, artillery and mortar support) and a tank brigade. It was in artillery, however, that the Red Army showed its enormous power. The artillery reorganization in 1941 under Voronov probably did more than anything else to save the Red Army from total annihilation: the trend towards greater concentration of artillery continued throughout 1942, so that by 1943 divisional artillery had shrunk to a mere score of guns and a dozen howitzers. The Artillery Reserve of the High Command went on forming its own artillery regiments, divisions and corps, deploying them at will and by design for particular operations; the artillery division usually numbered some 200 guns and howitzers, with an additional 100 heavy mortars.

On the eve of the 1943–4 winter campaign, the *Stavka*, mindful of earlier disasters, set about amassing considerable reserves, taking into '*Stavka* reserve' five infantry armies, two tank armies and nine armoured corps. These formations (save for the 20th and 70th Armies, which existed only as HQ administrations) were already earmarked for use on the flanks both north and south, a decision that took little account of the difficulties facing Soviet troops at the centre—the 'western theatre'—and which in no way affected the process of setting the targets for the central fronts (1st Baltic, the Western and the Belorussian), with the result that ends and means here remained dangerously lopsided.

Stalin intended the main Soviet blow to fall in the south-west, in the 'southern theatre', running from the Pripet to the Black Sea. This southern drive involved four fronts—1st, 2nd, 3rd and 4th Ukrainian—and was to unfold in two stages, the first to crush enemy opposition on the Dnieper and bring Soviet troops to the line of the southern Bug, the second to shatter the German strategic grouping throughout the south by destroying the individual German armies and moving the Red Army to a line running from Rovno to Moghilev Podolskii and the Dniester. In effect, the German Army Group South was to be crushed between the Dnieper and the Dniester, while Tolbukhin's 4th Ukrainian Front and the Independent Coastal Army received orders to prepare themselves for the recapture of the Crimea.

The second great drive was also to be on an outer flank, in the north-west, where the Leningrad, Volkhov and 2nd Baltic Fronts must destroy Army Group North and in the process free Leningrad completely, clearing the Leningrad and Kalinin *oblasts,* after which Soviet troops must push on to a line running through Pskov–Narva–Balka and the river Velikaya, thus positioning themselves for an advance into the Baltic republics. At the centre, the operation tasks needed little additional definition; the Western and 1st Baltic Fronts received orders to destroy German forces in the Orsha–Vitebsk area, to be followed by an advance on Polotsk–Moghilev–Lepel. Rokossovskii's first target on the Belorussian Front was Bobruisk and his terminal point Minsk, those two names that had figured in *Stavka* directives dating back some time.

These Soviet plans accorded a special place to partisan operations, which were to be integrated as far as possible with those of the regular formations in the field. An important change in the direction of partisan activities was in the offing, for on 13 January 1944 the General Staff of the Partisan Movement was wound up on orders from the State Defence Committee. The Central Committee of the various Soviet republics, the *oblast* committees and individual partisan staffs, now assumed direction of the partisan movement, bringing Soviet power back into the partisan areas. Moscow's long reach was now no longer necessary or desirable: control had to be exercised from closer range. Front Military Soviets assumed responsibility for supplying arms to partisan units; Front commands worked out integration through the partisan staffs. There was a massive movement up to the front. In Belorussia, the Belorussian Party Central Committee moved the Belorussian Partisan Staff from Moscow to newly liberated Gomel; in the north-west the Leningrad and Kalinin *obkoms* (the Party's *oblast* committees) directed the partisan movement at close range, as did the Crimean *obkom* in the Crimea.

Stalin had set his sights on success in the south where the fruits of victory would be both substantial and immediate—the complete restoration of the Ukrainian political unit to Soviet possession, the restitution of the metallurgical resources of Krivoi Rog and Kerch, the manganese of Nikopol, the grain lands, the Black Sea ports and the enormous population. The bulk of the Red Army's present striking power was going to the outer flanks, with the Ukrainian Fronts receiving the lion's share. Though the *Stavka* had assigned the 'western theatre' an enormous task, nothing less than a westerly advance of up to one hundred miles to reach the line running from Polotsk through Minsk and to the river Ptich would have to be accomplished without reinforcement. (Over the next three months 1st Baltic, Western and the Belorussian Fronts received only nineteen per cent of the available infantry reinforcements, twenty-five percent of the artillery and four percent of the reserve armour.) On the eve of the winter offensive in the south, the Red Army mustered 169 rifle and 9 cavalry divisions (divisional strength wavering at this time between 2,600 and 6,500 men), slightly more than 2,000 tanks and self-propelled guns, and 2,360 aircraft for operations in the western Ukraine. Soviet intelligence set the strength of Army Groups South and A at 103 divisions and 2 brigades, with 93 divisions (18 *Panzer* and 4 motorized)—2,200 tanks and 1,460 aircraft—in the western Ukraine itself. Almost half of the entire German strength on the Eastern Front lay on the southern wing, which also disposed of just under three-quarters of all German armoured forces in the east.

These equations Stalin proposed to solve irreversibly in his own favour on ground suitably adapted for large-scale manoeuvre by powerful mobile formations, the very ground where in 1941 the *Panzer* divisions had wounded the Soviet Union so terribly. The reconquest of the western Ukraine, in addition to all its internal benefits, would station the Red Army on the Soviet Union's south-western frontiers, poised there for an advance through Rumania into the Balkans or on to Poland and into the flank and rear of Army Group Centre. Operations in the 'south-western theatre' involved not only Front offensives but the co-ordination of several fronts on a line running from Ovruch in the north to Kahkovka on the lower Dnieper: Vatutin (1st Ukrainian), while striking westwards for Lutsk, would develop his main offensive in a south-westerly direction on Vinnitsa–Moghilev Podolskii; Koniev (2nd Ukrainian) was to attack towards Kirovgrad–Pervomaisk with an additional drive aimed at Khristonovka (a point of aim for Vatutin also); while Malinovskii (3rd Ukrainian) and Tolbukhin (4th Ukrainian) developed concentric attacks to destroy German forces in the Nikopol–Krivoi Rog area, after which both fronts would advance on Nikolayev and Odessa. The first phase of the destruction of the German armies on the southern wing was to take place in the easterly reaches of 'right-bank Ukraine' (the western Ukraine), the clearing of all enemy forces from the Dnieper and then a Soviet advance to a line running from the southern Bug to Pervomaisk, on to Shirokoe and the river Ingulets. The second phase involved a Soviet advance to a line running from Lutsk, north-west of Rovno, to Moghilev–Podolskii, south-west to Vinnitsa, thence to the Dniester—by which time the Crimea was to be cleared.

As autumn gave way to winter in 1943, Stalin positioned fifty-eight armies across the whole length of the Eastern Front, from the Arctic to the Black Sea.

Far to the north, from the Barents Sea to the Gulf of Finland, where the Front ran from the west of Murmansk through Belomorsk on to the river Svir and the southern shore of lake Ladoga, German, Finnish and Soviet troops had not budged since the autumn of 1941; the Soviet Karelian Front deployed four armies of its own plus men from the 7th Independent Army, with the 23rd Army of the Leningrad Front holding the Karelian isthmus. From the Gulf of Finland to Nevel, the front ran south of Leningrad, east of Chudov, Novgorod and Staraya Russa and on to the west of Velikie Luki—three Soviet fronts (Leningrad, Volkhov and 2nd Baltic) with eleven armies facing the forty-four divisions of Army Group North. The 'western theatre', from Nevel to Mozyr, came within the area of the 1st Baltic, Western and Belorussian Fronts with a combined strength of fifteen armies operating against the sixty-three divisions of Army Group Centre along a line that ran to the east of Orsha and Vitebsk and to the west of Gomel. From Mozyr to the Black Sea lay the tier of Ukrainian Fronts, 1st, 2nd, 3rd and 4th, fielding twenty-one 'all-arms' armies and three tank armies; south of Kanev and on to the Black Sea the front more or less followed the Dnieper held by Army Groups South and A with ninety-three divisions. Though the Crimea was still in German hands, Seventeenth Army was trapped; 51st Army (4th Ukrainian Front) was at Perekop and on the Sivash, while Petrov's Independent Coastal Army was ashore at Kerch.

The scale of these forthcoming offensive operations, the results anticipated and the probable outcome—indeed, the whole turn of events on the Eastern Front since the late summer of 1943 (*korennoi perelom*, 'the fundamental turning point')—imparted both urgency and singular relevance to Stalin's participation in the 'Big Three' meeting held at Teheran towards the end of November. The decisive year was almost over. In the east Germany had neither won success nor achieved its nearest equivalent, a stalemate. In a future well within Stalin's immediate grasp Soviet divisions would once more be on the 1941 frontier lines and in many places across them, thus enabling Stalin to promote his widest strategic enterprises with none of that premature ambition he had displayed in the bitter spring of 1942. Teheran was the opportunity for which he had stubbornly and determinedly pressed, for which he had manoeuvred, blustered and bullied. With his pocket full of plans and his mind implanted with his own notion of 'co-ordination', it was an opportunity to exploit to the full.

In all probability, Stalin travelled to Teheran forewarned by Soviet intelligence that a special German commando was bent on killing him, along with the two other members of the 'Big Three'. The actual details known to Stalin remain unclear, but well before he reached Teheran the Soviet leader took care to preserve himself from the whims of fate as well as the machinations of man. He travelled by train to Baku, where he arrived early in the morning, and by 8 am he was at the airfield where a cluster of SI-47s stood about, with Novikov (Air Force commander) and Golovanov (commander of the Long-Range Air Force) waiting to report. Novikov informed Stalin that two machines were ready, one to be flown by Col.-Gen. Golovanov, the other by Colonel Grachov, with two more aircraft to be flown off in half an hour carrying Ministry of Foreign Affairs personnel. Novikov invited Stalin to board the aircraft to be piloted by Golovanov. Stalin had other views: 'Colonel-generals don't often pilot aircraft—we'd better go with the Colonel', at which Stalin's entourage clambered into Grachov's plane. Once Stalin's plane took off, fighter escorts covered it from above and flew on either side.

Teheran had been largely Stalin's choice of venue. The Foreign Ministers conference that had met in October had assembled in Moscow at Stalin's insistence, a concession he had been determined to extract, and for the 'Big Three' meeting he steadily resisted the Prime Minister's suggestion of Egypt, Cyprus or Khartoum. Relaxing inch by inch, Stalin finally proposed Iran, 'where all three countries are represented' (thus having legations), and Teheran it had to be, itself no great distance from the Soviet border. In effect, and the effect was deliberately contrived, the British Prime Minister and the President of the United States were both journeying to meet Stalin, who increased the scope of this indebtedness in his own style: once in Teheran, and to thwart would-be assassins, President Roosevelt was persuaded to move into the heavily guarded Soviet compound, rather than risk travelling from the outlying American Legation. The British Legation stood not far from the Soviet Embassy buildings where the conference itself was to take place. Thus were these diplomatic outposts for a brief time transformed into 'the centre of the world', where the three Allied leaders, masters between them of more than twenty million fighting men, sat down to confer in unison for the first time. Within an hour of President Roosevelt being installed within his own villa inside the Soviet perimeters on Sunday afternoon (28 November), Stalin paid a call upon him and the talk began.

With the President immured within the Soviet compound, and assuming that these premises were wired for every sound, the Russians were well placed to do some prime eavesdropping, which may have been the motive for all the flurry about a threat to the lives of the Allied leaders. In his talks with Ambassador Harriman, Molotov never referred in any specific terms to a 'plot', though he delivered a warning couched in strong terms about the presence of numerous German agents: precautions were being taken out of *fear* of a plot, not from certain knowledge that one existed and was about to be implemented.

Molotov was being either realistic or massively discreet about what Soviet intelligence had learned and how it had come by the information. Subsequent Soviet revelations of intelligence operations related to the Teheran 'plot' pinpointed two sources, both involved in penetrating the higher levels of the German command. The first was Ilya Svetlov, and the second was *'Oberleutnant* Ziebert', supposedly from Königsberg but in reality Nikolai Ivanovich Kuznetsov, the Soviet intelligence officer who had already delivered valuable information about

Citadel as a result of his penetration of the German command in the Ukraine.

Ilya Svetlov's story dates back into the 1920s and even the Russian Civil War, where it becomes intertwined with that of Friedrich Schultz, son of Otto Schultz, a German immigrant in Russia. The Svetlov family lived and worked on a farm near Baku, no great distance from the Persian border, and close to the farm settlement of Helenendorf with its contingent of German immigrants where German was freely and widely spoken. Here Ilya Svetlov and Friedrich Schultz grew up, sharing not only the settlement but finally the same house, when the fathers of both boys were killed fighting for the Bolsheviks in Azerbaijan during the Civil War. As a young man, Ilya Svetlov left the farm and moved to Baku where he worked as an organizer with the *Komsomol:* in this capacity he came to the notice of the *OGPU,* the Soviet intelligence service, which selected the young Svetlov for further training and an education in law.

In 1928 Ilya Svetlov went home on leave to Helenendorf. Friedrich Schultz still lived there, although his fortunes had just taken a surprising turn: his father's brother Hans Schultz, presently living in Munich and an early supporter of the Nazi Party, had not long before lost both his wife and his daughter, bereavements which prompted him to write to his brother's son in Russia and invite him to take his place within the now sadly depleted Schultz family. The prospect of this return to a distant family bosom did not, however, arouse Friedrich's enthusiasm, fully diverted as this was in the direction of his Russian fiancée. Ilya persuaded him to delay replying to his uncle and meanwhile took the news of this development with him on his return to the *OGPU* in Baku.

Within a month Ilya's superiors produced their solution. Hans Schultz's offer was to be accepted, except that Ilya Svetlov and Friedrich Schultz would change places. The genuine Friedrich could marry his fiancée, assume her maiden name and move away to distant Novosibirsk, while the *OGPU* fashioned a new 'Friedrich Schultz' out of Ilya Svetlov. Not that the changes were drastic; Ilya spoke excellent German, he had lived with the real Friedrich; and, in addition to his personal qualities, the *OGPU* gave him a rigorous intelligence training, explaining that he would be on his own after his move to Germany until such time as he found himself in a position to furnish useful information.

In February 1930 Svetlov met his 'uncle' Hans Schultz at the railway station in Munich, a scene discreetly observed by another Soviet agent. From this point forward it was Hans Schultz who took charge of 'Friedrich's' fortunes, using his money and his influence to obliterate every trace of the Russian background of his nephew (whose father had died fighting for the Bolsheviks) and providing yet another identity for Ilya Svetlov by giving him the name of Walter Schultz (a younger scion of the Schultz family in Hamburg whose suicide had been hushed up by the family), transferring himself to Berlin and letting 'Friedrich' vanish into obscurity by putting it about that his nephew had, in fact, never arrived from Russia. The re-born Walter Schultz took up a course of Oriental studies in the University of Berlin; he also prevailed upon his 'uncle' to get him into the Nazi Party, which the elder Schultz managed with a recommendation emanating from no less a person than Hess himself.

Schultz–Svetlov advanced quickly. He graduated, became engaged to the daughter of a senior official of the German Foreign Office and joined the Storm Troopers. Once a graduate, Schultz–Svetlov found his 'uncle's' connections with Admiral Canaris admirably suited to having him placed in the eastern section of the *Abwehr;* his marriage, however, did not materialize, a painful episode from a personal point of view but an advantage for his ultimate concealment. And in due course came Ilya Svetlov's first operational assignment for the *Abwehr,* orders that sent him early in 1941 to Iran with instructions to penetrate the Iranian transport system and to prepare for sabotage action that would block any Soviet incursion into Iran. In Iran he was to operate under the auspices of a Swiss textile firm whose representative he ostensibly was (and preparations for which he had already made through his stay in Switzerland). Schultz–Svetlov travelled to Iran through Poland and the Soviet Union, where on a Soviet train he shared his compartment with another 'foreign passenger', English-speaking and also in transit through the Soviet Union, who proved to be the same Soviet intelligence officer who had first dispatched him to Germany in 1930. Once in Baku, Svetlov travelled on to Teheran from which he made frequent tours north in pursuit of his textile business and also to set up the sabotage network manned by anti-Soviet elements, simultaneously passing full details of the men involved and the locations of their explosive dumps to the Soviet command. He managed to discreetly bungle the actual sabotage when Soviet troops prepared to move into Iran in the autumn of 1941; ahead of the Soviet columns came Soviet squads who rounded up the saboteurs and disposed of their explosives.

Though he had 'failed' in Iran, Schultz–Svetlov resumed work in the eastern section of the *Abwehr* when he returned to Germany, and it was from this post that he was again plucked, in 1943, to operate in Iran, with Schellenberg himself supplying the details of the mission—Operation *Long Jump,* the plan to disrupt the Teheran conference, kill the Prime Minister and Stalin, and carry off President Roosevelt. A German commando group would be flown to Iran, dropped by parachute, conducted to Teheran and hidden there; they would then burst into the city and kill the Allied leaders before the local security forces realized what was happening. Schellenberg had his man in the city itself, a reliable agent named Alexander Gluszek (supposedly a Polish refugee)—what he wanted from Schultz was a contact in the frontier area who could assist the landing operation. Schultz mentioned his earlier dealings with a local leader who was avowedly pro-German, which satisfied Schellenberg for the moment. The next day the conversation was resumed, and Schultz was informed that he was 'in' on the operation; he was to go back to Iran under his earlier Swiss cover, to prepare the secret landing-sites and to conduct the commandos to Teheran, where Gluszek would conceal them. This time, however, Schultz–Svetlov was to be accompanied by his 'wife', a German woman agent acting as radio operator. Schellenberg ordered Schultz not to report back to the *Abwehr* but to consider himself—along with all other participants in the operation—sealed off in total quarantine from the outside world, since any 'leak' would be fatal to the undertaking.

Major Ilya Svetlov (alias Major Walter Schultz) evidently managed to inform Soviet intelligence in Moscow of what was brewing: Maj.-Gen. Vasili Ivanovich Pankov and Colonel Avdeyev picked up his message and at once made for Teheran, breaking their air journey at Baku. Here the local intelligence command handed over more information about *Long Jump,* emanating this time from '*Oberleutnant* Ziebert' who was operating behind the German lines in the Ukraine: Ziebert (Nikolai Kuznetsov) also garnered his information from the German command, in this case *Obersturmbannführer* von Ortel, though Soviet accounts of how this was managed vary. One version (compiled by Alexander Lukin, himself a Soviet officer operating in the German rear) intimates that a Ukrainian girl, Maya Mikota, engaged on 'softening up' von Ortel, was promised 'Persian carpets' after a particular mission was finished, a tip that she passed on to 'Ziebert', who then got more details by loading von Ortel with drink: in the account of Schultz–Svetlov's activity, it was the local partisan commander who reported that 'Ziebert' had been recruited to take part in the operation in Teheran by von Ortel, but that the *Oberleutnant* never finished reporting in full on the German plans because he had vanished into thin air. This was the report Pankov and Avdeyev read in Baku, and they concluded that the 'disappearance' was connected with the isolation Schellenberg ordered for all participants and which Schultz–Svetlov had reported. (The inference, nevertheless, is that Soviet intelligence received some kind of corroboration relating to Schultz–Svetlov's signal and that Kuznetsov was either involved or had learned something at a high level.)

In Teheran Pankov and Avdeyev set another Soviet officer, Oleg Smirnov, to watch Gluszek; Schultz–Svetlov, with his radio operator 'wife', also reached Teheran and then set out for the frontier area to set up the dropping zones (Svetlov having already contacted Pankov and Avdeyev). With the dropping zones organized, local reception arrangements made and an illegal crossing point into Turkey established, as well as suitable houses overlooking the allied diplomatic buildings in Teheran rented, Schultz signalled Berlin that preparations were complete and gave the co-ordinates for the airdrop, which would be carried out by aircraft coming in from the Turkish side. He himself would wait at the dropping zone and then take the German commandos into Teheran to their hiding-places.

But at this point the coincidences that had so often served Schultz–Svetlov in fantastic fashion, turned against him. His 'wife' grew suspicious of his trips inside Teheran, and now a German SS officer, Ressler, who had earlier stumbled on the trail of the false 'Friedrich' (only to be removed by the influential uncle), suddenly arrived to take part in *Long Jump.* Together, Schultz's 'wife' and Ressler proposed to radio Berlin that Schultz–Svetlov was a major suspect. But Svetlov struck first; he put the radio out of action and alerted Pankov about the incoming German transport aircraft.

Racing back to Teheran from the smashed transmitter, Schultz's 'wife' tried to throw off the pursuing Russian cars, only to crash to her death into a bridge. Maj.-Gen. Pankov meanwhile kept in contact with a Soviet fighter squadron, which reported a Ju-52—without national markings—crossing into Iranian territory from the direction of Turkey: intercepted, the transport plane seemed to accept directions to land and then it suddenly swung off towards the Turkish frontier. 'Fire warning shots': the fighter pilots reported that the aircraft still held its course, at which Pankov ordered the fighters to shoot down the Ju-52. 'The aircraft is burning and has exploded', came the report from the Soviet flight commander. Pankov ordered an immediate move to the scene of the crash, where the wreckage was scattered over a thousand yards or more; no papers were picked up but the ground was littered with bits of small arms, automatic weapons and mortars, among which ammunition continued to explode. Pankov returned to Teheran; Smirnov went to the frontier area to arrest German sympathizers and hand them over to the Soviet garrison at Kazvin. Only then did Pankov inform his officers that President Roosevelt would now move into the Soviet compound in Teheran. One assassination attempt had been foiled on the eve of the conference (the actual date has never been specified), and Pankov, in giving orders to reinforce all guards, emphasized the danger of 'the second variant' which could follow once the first one had been frustrated. But this 'first variant', the mission initially entrusted to Otto Skorzeny (who abandoned it after a brief study), was all there was to the German plan; there was no 'second variant', and Molotov was possibly only relaying Pankov's fears and relying on the circumstantial evidence of that crashed Ju-52—inconclusive, perhaps, but it helped to give Stalin what he wanted.

It was Stalin who came both to dominate and to domineer at the Teheran conference, his opportunity magnified by the lack of prior agreement between the British and Americans on strategic policy and his occasion provided by President Roosevelt's attempt at a Soviet–American bilateralism. The October conference of Foreign Ministers had already taken most of the sting out of the thoroughly unpleasant situation that had built up in the summer of 1943 when Stalin's ire reached its climax; Stalin had signified his willingness to soldier on with the coalition but not his readiness to take any place he considered subordinate. On the contrary, his position was hardening, and his success strengthened his hand—Soviet troops were less than a hundred miles from the former frontiers. Early in June Maiskii confidently pointed out the implications of a Soviet advance in a talk with R.A. Butler: Soviet troops would soon be on the 1941 frontiers, they would perforce stay on them, and now was the time to talk terms. Then there was the whisper of Soviet–German negotiation: in September Japanese proposals for 'mediation' between Germany and the Soviet Union were brushed aside in Moscow, and the fact of the Soviet rejection registered in Washington. Stalin had every reason to take 'war-shortening' measures seriously; remaining in the coalition was one, but again not at the price of a Russia so physically debilitated and so fearfully bled as to be incapable of participation in the post-war settlements. Any and every pressure had to be exerted for the 'Second Front', which Stalin understood at the end of October would take place in the spring of 1944. Almost on the eve of the Teheran conference, Stalin jabbed the conscience of his allies, complaining on 6 November that German divisions from Italy and the Balkans— adding France to the list ten days later—were moving to the Eastern Front. This pot had to be kept constantly on the boil.

From the moment of his first private meeting with the President, who prided himself on his ability to deal with the Soviet leader and win him for the cause of peace and democracy, Stalin could discern disparities between the British and American positions over the waging of the war and the winning of the peace. Stalin took upon himself the onus for the delay in meeting the President, but explained that 'the front' called; somewhat gloomily, he sketched out events there—the fall of Zhitomir, the threat to Korosten, the *Wehrmacht* moving up fresh divisions. The President responded by stating that this was the purpose of the present meeting, to take thirty to forty German divisions off the Red Army's back. In a rapid, verbal tour of the world, President Roosevelt touched on many items—merchant ships for Russia, France, the Far East: in his denigration of de Gaulle and his ill-concealed contempt for the Chinese Army, Stalin seemed bent on reducing the world to its 'Big Three' proportions, suffering no other contenders, ruling out France through defeatism and China through incompetence. Over the colonial areas, India in particular—a topic the President warned Stalin to leave alone in his dealings with the Prime Minister—this computation was reduced almost to a 'Big Two' progressivism. The meetings drew to a close shortly before 4 pm, when the first plenary session of the Teheran conference was due to begin.

At the express wish of Stalin and the Prime Minister, President Roosevelt took the chair. After an exchange of compliments, he launched into a Western view of the war, reviewing the Pacific and European theatres and emphasizing the strain that the war against Japan had put on operations in Europe. Shortage of ships and landing-craft had ruled out a cross-Channel attack in 1943 but the Quebec conference had decided upon *Overlord* for 1944. In the event of a major operation in the Mediterranean, *Overlord* would not be feasible, and would have to be delayed for anything up to three months for a lesser attack. None wished to see *Overlord* delayed, but on the question of a further Mediterranean operation before the invasion the President and the Prime Minister were anxious to have Soviet advice on the optimum strategy for drawing the greatest weight off the Red Army: Italy, the Balkans, the Aegean, the enlistment of Turkey—a number of variants had been discussed, as well as landing in southern France.

Stalin then spoke of the Soviet Union. He directed his opening remarks with unerring accuracy, commending Allied successes in the Pacific, excusing the Soviet forces from immediate participation but promising their speedy entry against Japan once Germany was defeated; the Soviet Far Eastern forces would be tripled for the attack in which the Soviet Union would join the 'common effort'. The Soviet Far Eastern Front did not meanwhile go untended; for more than eighteen months it had provided vital reinforcements to the European front, all the while maintaining its level of strength by local mobilization. In 1942 the *Stavka* ordered the establishment of a new post, Deputy Chief of the General Staff (Far East). Senior officers from divisional level upwards rotated for periods of duty on the European front to acquire experience of modern warfare. At Kursk General Anapasenko, Far Eastern Front commander doing his 'tour'—*na stazhirovku*—on the European front, was killed by a shell-burst. His place in the Soviet Far East had been taken by General Purkayev, an experienced 'shock army' commander who later took over the Kalinin Front. In the autumn of 1943 the Soviet Air Force also took stock of the reports on the state of Soviet air strength in the Far East and set about modernizing it.

The Soviet announcement about eventual participation in the war against Japan was not new, for an assurance on these lines was delivered at the October conference; but coming as this did from Stalin himself, and directed as it was to the President, it meant a formal guarantee. In return for the Western powers bringing the heaviest weight against Germany, the Soviet Union would contribute to the elimination of Japan, taking on the Kwantung Army in Manchuria and providing bases for bombers in the air assault on Japan itself. By its very place in the proceedings at Teheran, Stalin's undertaking was not merely an announcement but also a pre-emptive bid, tugging at American desires and fears—the desire to strike hard and deep into Europe, the fear of being burdened with a prolonged war in the Far East. Stalin offered a way out in return for a quick kill in Europe. The picture he now went on to present of the war on the Soviet–German front was by no means sombre: though the Germans had anticipated the Soviet offensive in July, the Red Army's considerable successes had surprised Stalin himself, who had surmised German strength to be greater. Soviet offensive operations had slowed or halted for the moment, and the Germans had recovered the initiative west and south of Kiev—they were in fact bent on retaking Kiev—but the wider initiative remained with the Russians. Both Russian and Western estimates of German strength on the Eastern Front more or less tallied, but it was news indeed that the Red Army had 330 divisions in the field; more information than ever before on Soviet operations was forthcoming at Teheran, though the disclosures were enormously discreet, not least because the Red Army had well over 450 divisions in action and a margin of strength therefore greater than Stalin acknowledged.

Without denigrating the Italian campaign, Stalin dismissed it as a staging area for an invasion of Germany, if only because of the Alps, which Field-Marshal

Suvorov in his time had found a formidable barrier. Turkey was better, but still a long way from Germany. The direct route lay through France, and it was here that the Anglo-American armies should attack. Stalin wanted *Overlord*, without the trimmings and within the shortest possible space of time. Although in October the Russians had urged greater effort upon their allies to bring Turkey into the war, now Stalin showed less enthusiasm for the Balkan theatre; and here he came into direct collision with the Prime Minister, who set out 'the British position' in the wake of Stalin's remarks. Mr Churchill stressed that what had been done by the Western allies up till now had been secondary, but it represented all that could be done, given the resources. *Overlord* was a definite commitment for the late spring or summer of 1944—leaving a full six months, time which ought not to slip away in passivity but which should be geared to operations utilizing the resources within the Mediterranean without causing any delay with the cross-Channel attack. Once Rome fell to the Allied armies, it should prove possible to open a 'Third Front' 'in conformity with, but not in substitution for, *Overlord'*— a landing in southern France, or an attack into the German flank from a bridgehead high up on the Adriatic; greater activity in the Balkans and increased support for Tito; the enlistment of Turkey in war and thereby the opening of the Dardanelles, leading to a direct supply route into Soviet Black Sea ports and inducing 'a political landslide' among Germany's tottering allies; and finally (as a reminder from the President) a thrust north-eastwards from an Adriatic foothold.

Stalin straightaway went about dissecting the Prime Minister's arguments, sticking to numbers—the strength of the forces earmarked for *Overlord*, the number of divisions left in the Mediterranean, the number of men involved in any attack on southern France and what manpower might be drawn off in the event of Turkey entering the war. The Prime Minister duly presented the military statistics, promised proof of them, and stuck by his case that there would be no great offsetting in strength for *Overlord;* on the contrary, here was a sensible and profitable use of available manpower. At this, Stalin shoved the arithmetic aside and came out bluntly against any division of forces between Turkey and southern France. *Overlord,* he insisted, was basic to 1944: once Rome had been captured, troops in Italy could be landed in southern France, from which they could link up with the invasion force launched from the north. Turkey was a non-starter.

The Prime Minister returned to the problem of time, six months of operational idleness between the fall of Rome and the onset of *Overlord*. Stalin closed this gap abruptly by suggesting the abandonment of the attempt to take Rome, closing down the Italian front and putting the men down in southern France two months before *Overlord*. The Prime Minister protested with full vigour, and the President interceded with remarks related to the timing of the operations— he opposed any delay with *Overlord* but proposed an examination of the suggestion to put men ashore in southern France two months before *Overlord,* subject to the cross-Channel attack being held on schedule. It was eventually decided that the whole question would be turned over to the staffs for their consideration on

Monday morning. Stalin did not exactly leap at this but he agreed to allow Marshal Voroshilov to take part in these military conversations. Churchill made one last effort on behalf of his design for Turkey, and once again Stalin demonstrated his almost total lack of interest. Stalin had shifted his ground swiftly and shrewdly, from hot complaint that not enough was being done to detach German divisions from the east, to proposing the closing down of an Allied front and virtual inactivity elsewhere. The Prime Minister pushed, in rather hectic fashion, for an Eastern presence: Stalin steadily pushed the Anglo-American armies to the west. Watching his performance, assisted as it was by American disinclination for any Eastern *imbroglio,* General Brooke confessed to watching 'a military brain of the very highest calibre' in action. At least Stalin had his sums right.

'A bloody lot has gone wrong.' The Prime Minister had cause for irritation if not gloom at the end of the first session and he gave his feelings pungent expression. Three and a half hours of discussion ended without any real decision save for Stalin shunting his allies westwards, away from his southern flank. And whatever his political motives, there was every reason for Stalin to struggle against the 'dispersal' he foresaw in any effort in the eastern Mediterranean, a point that fell on ready American ears made more receptive as Stalin talked pointedly about warring on Japan. Over and after dinner, at which President Roosevelt played host, Stalin went on to explore the minds of his allies on two questions central to him and crucial to the alliance, the treatment of Germany and the place of Poland. To the President and Prime Minister alike he was gloomy, frank and brutal over Germany, questioning the wisdom of 'unconditional surrender' without any statement of terms, predicting in alarmist fashion the eventual recovery of Germany from the present war only to embark on a fresh one, hinting also that the political dismemberment of Germany was insufficient without gouging out the substance of Germanism. The attitude of German workers in the service of Hitler obviously enraged him: those German prisoners of war whom he taunted with this under interrogation he had shot when they answered that they served out of sheer obedience. Over Poland both parties trod warily at first; Stalin fell in very readily (and understandably) with the plan to lift Poland bodily to the west, setting her western frontiers on the Oder, but for the moment he was silent over the eastern frontier. With the aid of three match-sticks the Prime Minister demonstrated how this hopscotch amidst the frontiers would work, and Poland was already half sold out, for all the brave words. Stalin smiled and was visibly pleased.

The Monday morning staff talks brought in Marshal Voroshilov, who pounded away at General Brooke about *Overlord* as the prime operation to be executed as from 1 May 1944. None of General Brooke's arguments about actually releasing German strength by foreclosing Mediterranean operations made any dent in Voroshilov: the Channel was wide, that Voroshilov conceded, but so were the many rivers which the Red Army had crossed because it wanted to. Voroshilov taxed General Brooke directly on his own belief in *Overlord:* did he hold to it as strongly as General Marshall? *Overlord* must take absolute precedence, Voroshilov insisted; anything else in any other theatre was secondary. General Brooke signified full agreement with this order of priorities, but argued as always that a lesser operation could assist and must assist the accomplishment of the major one. The argument spilled over into the second plenary session held on the afternoon of 29 November, a meeting preceded by the President and Stalin conferring alone on possible Soviet–American arrangements covering the Far Eastern theatre and on the President's view of policing the post-war world, when Stalin deferred any commitment about operational matters in the Far East and narrowed down his concept of 'policing' to standing astride Germany and Japan.

The second plenary session opened with a bang. After the report on the morning's staff talks, Stalin lashed out at once: 'Who will command *Overlord*?' The President informed Stalin that as yet this had not been decided, whereupon Stalin retorted that without a man to prepare *Overlord* nothing would come of it. Stalin was not stopped by the information that General Morgan presently supervised preparations: there had to be a commander. He more or less brushed aside the Prime Minister's explanation of Anglo-American niceties in apportioning command, asking only for the selection of a man both to prepare and to command. The Prime Minister then set out once more to stamp the coalition strategy with his own imprint, lunging at the German flank, opening the Aegean, 'stretching' the enemy in the Balkan theatre, bringing Turkey into the war. Stalin shoved Turkey, the Aegean, Rumania, Rome and Yugoslavia aside with one stroke: in view of the urgency of rendering aid to the Red Army, *Overlord* must have precedence; the date must be fixed—no later than May 1944—there must be no postponement, and a supreme commander must be appointed. A descent on southern France would contribute directly to *Overlord*: anything in Italy or the Balkans was mere 'diversion'. Any argument leading to the commitment of forces in the Balkans Stalin axed down at once; by his reckoning, the thirty German divisions in the Balkans that the Prime Minister wished to entrap simply did not exist. After a further bout of argument between Stalin and Churchill, the latter made his final plea for Turkey and urged that questions of the timing and scale of operations be turned over to the Technical Military Committee. Stalin refused to consider this: the date of *Overlord*, the nomination of a supreme commander and the role of a support operation in southern France could be decided here and now. 'How long is this conference going to last?'—Stalin had to be away by 2 December at the latest. The President suggested a simple and direct instruction for the Chiefs of Staff, that *Overlord* was paramount for 1944, that any subsidiary operation must be considered in the light of any delaying effect on the cross-Channel attack. Stalin now attempted to nail down *Overlord* completely; he had tried the tactic of applying pressure for a commander, now he demanded a date so that the Red Army could co-ordinate its offensive from the east. His parting shot was aimed directly at the Prime Minister: did the British really believe in *Overlord*, or did they merely talk about it to 'keep the Russians quiet?'—*shtoby uspokoit Russkikh?* With complete malice aforethought, Stalin was bent on exposing the Prime Minister's isolation from the President and the prevalent 'Soviet–American' view.

At the first dinner Stalin had related how he taunted those prisoners whom he finally consigned to their doom. At the second dinner, on the evening of the twenty-ninth, Stalin set about baiting the Prime Minister. He had earlier observed to the President that he thought Mr Churchill too lenient in the matter of Germany. Now he warmed to his subject, suggesting that 50,000 Germans, the core of the 'German General Staff', be shot out of hand when the war was finished. In a surge of disgust the Prime Minister left the dinner, only to be wooed back by an affable Stalin dismissing it all as a joke. On the following day, 30 November, Stalin had cause for greater satisfaction. In the morning the Prime Minister—walled off as he was from the President—paid a call on Stalin to clarify the British attitude. Stalin gave little away: he was pleased that the commander for *Overlord* might be appointed almost at once, but hinted darkly that without *Overload* occurring in May 1944 the Red Army might falter, the Russians succumb to 'war-weariness'. If he knew *Overlord* would proceed on time, there would be no need 'to take steps' to circumvent feelings of 'isolation' in the Red Army and he could actually plan a simultaneous Soviet offensive for May–June. The definite date for *Overlord,* which Stalin did not extract from the Prime Minister in the morning, he obtained at the lunch attended by the three Allied leaders. Stalin got his prize at long last: *Overlord* timed for May 1944, enjoined as an Anglo-American decision. The political karate that Stalin practised at Teheran, numbing the President and jolting the Prime Minister, had paid off. Over lunch, with the discord submerged in high-sounding phrases and the rivalry smothered with talk of responsibilities, Stalin felt out the ground about territorial concessions. At no time did he enunciate any Soviet policy, and he had earlier explicitly refused to talk terms—'. . . When the time comes, we will speak'. Warm-water ports he was promised: in the Far East the President held out Dairen and a hint that expansive Soviet claims might be met, even though Stalin quite realistically pointed out that the Chinese would have a say in this.

The third plenary session that afternoon pulled the compact over *Overlord* into shape: the Anglo–American armies would attack in May, whereupon Stalin committed the Red Army to offensive operations in the east also timed for May. In the evening the Prime Minister played host at dinner where amiability appeared to rule once more. Stalin, having got the date for *Overlord,* now worried about the man and was assured by the Prime Minister that the commander would almost certainly be General Marshall. That reassured Stalin for the moment, and he turned next to the attitude of General Brooke who seemed no friend of the Russians. During the toasts and speeches Stalin put his opinion to the company, capping the President's compliments with the charge that General Brooke failed properly to appreciate the Red Army, an attack the intended victim managed to turn neatly enough.

The final day of the Teheran conference passed in a rapid shuffle of arguments and schemes about frontiers, those of friend and foe alike. The Prime Minister's plans for Turkey were steadily whittled away. After a break for lunch, Poland came up for discussion and this time Stalin had no time for toying with matchsticks. Slicing into the Prime Minister's exposition, he argued that now 'governments' were under discussion and one government he refused to treat with was that of the 'London Poles'. As for frontiers, Stalin stuck out for the 1939 demarcation which Molotov at once passed off as the 'Curzon line'. Both the 'Curzon line' and the 'Oder line' were scrutinized in great detail; the main discussion moved for the moment on to Finland, and here Stalin allowed himself to be talked into relative magnanimity, though forbearance was in any event the best investment for Soviet policy. On Germany, after chiding the Prime Minister for his faint-heartedness over real dismemberment, Stalin went on to support the President's plan for splitting Germany into five units since it came nearest to his own aim of partition: Germans were Germans and should be sundered one from another. Neither the President nor Stalin was inclined to give southern Germany the benefit of any doubt. Stalin tossed out the idea of a Danubian confederation in any form, insisting specifically on Germany and Hungary being kept at arm's length. Reverting to Poland, the Prime Minister finally extracted Stalin's agreement to his 'Curzon–Oder' line formula, to which Stalin tacked on Königsberg as the price of his accession to the idea. Stalin thus rewarded himself for having 'agreed' to a proposal that gave him what he wanted in the first place.

The Teheran conference dispersed, a common decision apparently agreed but in reality the basic divisiveness glowing like a hot coal through it all. Stalin had cause for self-congratulation, as his objective was fully attained: the contradictions within the capitalist camp had served him admirably. He had anchored *Overlord* irremovably in the late spring of 1944; he left open—and public—the option of 'dealing' with Soviet 'war-weariness'; he had kept rival armies away from his southern flank; he had splintered Poland and kept the Baltic states in his clutch with almost no effort, not to mention the claim staked out provisionally in the Far East. For all this Stalin could and did argue that the Russians had paid with a torrent of blood. His need for a decision governing *Overlord* was imperative, else the *perelom* would sag and even engulf him, or worse, bleed Russia still further into immobility. Whatever his political motives, his strategy of insisting on the decisive frontal attack was sound and his mistrust of Mr Churchill's 'diversions' was real enough. German intelligence, nevertheless, was 'sixty per cent' sure that the Prime Minister had been steered away from the Balkans at Teheran and was correspondingly pleased. President Roosevelt, who had taken some of Stalin's hectoring, remained convinced that he had established a personal, useful and durable relationship with Stalin. The British Prime Minister withdrew from Teheran in good order but a prey to foreboding: at the end of the second session his gloom deepened (and his health deteriorated). After his duels with Stalin public amiability gave way to private storms. Once in Cairo, Churchill fretted to be off to Italy, feverishly anxious to consult General Alexander and to 'do something with these bloody Russians'.

Some measure of Stalin's gratification showed in the enthusiastic, even exuberant, Soviet press reaction. The Red Army got its psychological boost and the promise that a second great pincer would soon reach into Germany. From Cairo the Prime Minister and the President sent Stalin confirmation of additional decisions to scale down the Bay of Bengal operation in order to release landing-craft for southern France, to step up production of amphibious craft for *Overlord* and also to divert them from the Pacific. Yet within little more than a month the same Soviet press that conveyed Stalin's momentary satisfaction also helped to communicate his continuing aggravation, which evidently centred on Churchill's reservations about *Overlord* and the welling 'Polish problem'. On 17 January 1944 *Pravda* published a story from its Cairo correspondent mentioning separate peace negotiations between Britain and Germany—'two leading British personalities and Ribbentrop' had met somewhere in the Iberian peninsula to talk terms. It was a story that Stalin himself disavowed not much later: the purpose, therefore, was less to report hot news than either to prod the British or to pre-empt possible stories of German–Soviet dickering. Shortly after the Teheran conference, the Japanese Legation in Stockholm handed yet another German 'peace-feeler' to the Russians, Berlin's proposals including autonomy for the Ukraine and Soviet aid in raw materials and supplies to keep Germany in the fight against the Western powers. This somewhat preposterous programme got short shrift, though it did not prevent yet another Japanese initiative in late January 1944, when the Japanese tried at the same time to induce a certain realism in the Germans, not least by abandoning wild plans for the Ukraine. Meanwhile *Pravda* fired off more warning shots, aimed this time in the direction of the Baltic states, Finland, Poland, even the Balkans— here was a Soviet preserve, in the case of the Baltic states walled off from any 'interference' by nothing less than 'the Soviet constitution itself'. As for the 'Cairo report' on German–British contacts (the Americans were conspicuously deleted from this cabal), Stalin parried the Prime Minister's protest by advising him that 'its significance should not be overrated'.

But Poland, over which a major row began to rumble in January, was altogether different. Stalin pushed his own preparations with gathering speed. During the night of 1 January the *Krajowa Rada Narodowa,* the 'National Council of the Homeland', the 'supreme underground organ of democratic elements [in Poland]', with Bierut on its council, suddenly sprang into existence. At once the *KRN* set about building up its own armed forces, the *Armija Ludowa,* which had centralized partisan detachments under its own control within a few weeks, weeks in which Soviet regular troops drew closer and closer to the old Polish frontier and Soviet partisan brigades operated more extensively in eastern Poland, backed by Soviet agents hard at work undermining the authority of 'the London government'. Perhaps the 'Cairo report' was of little real significance, as Stalin himself said, but in 'the Polish question' nothing was insignificant.

On Christmas Eve the Red Army resumed its offensive operations. Massed artillery on the Fastov sector south-west of Kiev fired off a fifty-minute barrage in the morning, battering a passage for Vatutin's 1st Ukrainian Front assault divisions—three infantry armies (1st and 3rd Guards). Vatutin planned to split the German front, to sweep away German tanks and infantry from Kiev once and for all and then to move his Front into position to co-operate with Koniev's 2nd Ukrainian Front, both fronts then driving deep into the German rear. To mask the Fastov attack Vatutin instructed Chernyakhovskii (60th Army) and Pukhov (13th Army) on the right flank to 'demonstrate' vigorous offensive preparations, as if to show that the main Soviet attack would develop in the Korosten area. Korosten was certainly one of Vatutin's objectives, but his present intention was to drive along the Zhitomir highway and the Fastov–Kazatin railway line. By the evening of 24 December the tank divisions of the assault force had driven up to twenty miles into the German defence, 3rd Guards Tank passing through 18th Army and 1st Tank through 38th Army, the T-34s finding passable going in the thin snow and shallow mud. That night the going was still good when the tracks took on a coating of frost, but the next day the rain came and the artillery had to provide the real weight behind the attack, which expanded as 40th Army joined in to operate with the motorized infantry of 38th Army. On 26 December Chernyakhovskii's 60th on the right attacked at noon; both right and left flanks of 1st Ukrainian Front were now engaged. Rybalko's 3rd Guards tank units pushed on for Korostyshev, a large village on the Zhitomir highway, where Russian artillery finally broke up a German armoured counter-attack.

In the last hours of 1943 the northern wing of Army Group South slithered nearer disaster. Zhitomir was almost encircled. On 29 December Chernyakhovskii's 60th had taken Korosten and outflanked Zhitomir from the north-west, severing the Zhitomir–Novograd Volynsk road and rail links. The next day Kazatin, the rail junction with lines leading to Kiev, into Poland and south to Odessa, fell to Soviet troops; Poluboyarov's 4th Guards Tank and 18th Army were moving from the south-east cutting the road and rail links between Zhitomir and Berdichev; 1st Guards outflanked Zhitomir to the east. On 31 December Zhitomir was cleared, the units involved receiving 'Zhitomir' as a battle honour. With the fall of Kazatin, the fate of Berdichev was sealed. Two Soviet battalions had already broken into the town, but 1st Tank Army and 18th Army could not follow through, and not until 5 January did Soviet units link up with the beleaguered battalions, clearing Berdichev completely.

Vatutin's infantry and tank armies broke out to a depth of fifty miles on a 150-mile front. The shortest road and rail communications linking Army Group South with Germany were now cut. On 2 January, Vatutin submitted fresh plans to the *Stavka:* 13th, 60th, 1st Guards and 18th Armies would drive on to the Rokitno–Goroditsa–Novograd Volynsk–Lyubarkhmelnik line in the next five days; 3rd Guards Tank Army would strike for Zhmerinka after eliminating enemy forces in the Berdichev area; and the left-flank armies (38th, 40th and 1st Tank

Armies) would advance south and south-west on Yanov, Vinnitsa, Ilintsa and Zhaskov. Katukov's 1st Tank Army was assigned a special role, to strike towards Khristinovka, there to link up with Koniev's 2nd Ukrainian Front, thus fusing the flanks of 1st and 2nd Ukrainian Fronts.

By 5 January both Belaya Tserkov and Berdichev were cleared by the infantry of 18th and 38th Armies and Katukov's tanks. That morning, in mist and low cloud, Koniev's 2nd Ukrainian Front suddenly attacked near Kirovograd. On 20 December the *Stavka* had ordered Koniev's front over to the defensive, using the breathing space to move up 300 tanks and 100 SP guns; the Front command worked on its plans for an offensive designed to bring it into the rear of German forces holding Nikopol, the destruction of which would be accomplished in co-operation with the 3rd and 4th Ukrainian Fronts. Towards the close of December, however, Stalin had suddenly changed this plan: in view of Vatutin's success, General Koniev received fresh instructions on 29 December to launch his main attack in the direction of Kirovograd–Pervomaisk, with a secondary operation aimed at Shpola–Kristinovka designed to encircle German forces in the Kanev–Zvenigorodka–Uman area (a joint operation with Vatutin). Koniev assigned 52nd and 53rd Armies to the supporting operation; his main striking force he split into two, Zhadov's 5th Guards and Katkov's 7th Mechanized Corps to outflank Kirovograd from the north-west, Shumilov's 7th Guards and Rotmistrov's 5th Guards Tank Army to move to the south-west. Koniev regrouped in great secrecy, forbidding all but verbal orders, banning radio transmission and issuing categorical instructions against telephone messages involving the offensive. The weather also lent its aid—light snow and light frost facilitated cross-country movement— though the overcast skies grounded Soviet aircraft.

The attack on Kirovograd got off to a flying start. Smashing down heavy German counter-attacks, the fiercest directed against Shumilov's 7th Guards, Soviet infantry opened up paths for the tanks; during the cold, clear night of 7 January Kirichenko's 29th Tank Corps (5th Guards Tank Army) broke into the southern suburbs of Kirovograd, with two rifle divisions following behind. At 0900 hours that morning Soviet columns had moved to the north-west cutting the Kirovograd–Novo Ukrainka road and railway line, while 18th Tank Corps swept round to the south. Kirovograd was cleared by 8 January and Soviet units pressed on some ten miles to the west of the town. Koniev's swift and incisive movement caused Vatutin to submit an adjustment of his own plans to the *Stavka* on 9 January: on his right wing, he proposed to move up to the river Goryn, on to Slutsk, Dubrovitsa and Sarny; at the centre and on the left, to eliminate German concentrations in the Zhmerinka and Uman area, and to take Vinnitsa, Zhmerinka and Uman. The *Stavka* approved but could provide nothing in the way of reinforcement.

On his northern wing Vatutin pushed Pukhov's 13th Army on to Sarny; forward elements reached the rivers Goryn and Styr by 12 January. Chernyak-hovskii's 60th made for Shepetovka, but both the 13th and 60th were running into stiffer resistance. On *Stavka* instructions Vatutin brought these two formations to a halt. Moving across a very broad front, Vatutin's armies were spread over some 300 miles; though the left wing was moving rapidly, gaps opened between the several armies. At Zhmerinka 8th Guards Mechanized Corps (1st Tank Army) was cut off by a German counter-thrust. Fuel and ammunition were running low in all the armies of 1st Ukrainian Front. On 12 January the *Stavka* issued orders to Koniev and Vatutin alike to wipe out the German salient at Zvenigorod–Mironovka by locking 1st Ukrainian and 2nd Ukrainian Front flanks at Shpola. This would secure the junction of the two fronts and position Soviet units for an advance to the southern Bug.

Neither Koniev nor Vatutin could push in the German salient which jutted between their fronts as far as Kanev on the Dnieper, the 'Korsun–Shevchenkovskii' salient, hilly country well suited for defence and held by twelve German divisions from First *Panzer* and Eighth Army. In mid-January, with the 'Zhitomir offensive' brought to a highly successful conclusion, 1st Ukrainian Front on *Stavka* orders went over to the defensive, to regroup, to reinforce and to allow supply lines to catch up; 47th Army (three divisions), 2nd Tank Army (two tank corps), 67th Rifle Corps, 6th Guards Cavalry Corps and 5th Mechanized Corps moved under Vatutin's command. For the assault on the Korsun salient, Vatutin assembled a force on his left flank from 40th, 27th and 6th Tank Armies (the last, Kravchenko's newly raised armoured army); Koniev assigned 4th Guards and 53rd Army, with Rotmistrov's 5th Guards Tank Army held ready to exploit the breakthrough. Between them, 1st and 2nd Ukrainian Fronts lined up twenty-seven rifle divisions, four tank corps and one mechanized corps, almost 4,000 guns and mortars with 370 tanks, to crush the Korsun salient.

After twenty-two days of operations, Vatutin's front began to slow up, outrunning its supplies and struggling in the mud, for the winter failed to come to the south. The 'Zhitomir attack' had been a conspicuous success, but the command decision to spread the Front armies amidst objectives running from Sarny to Vinnitsa and Zhmerinka has come in for certain criticism. These orders went out when the Front had spent its reserves: 1st Ukrainian could not reach the southern Bug, capture Vinnitsa and Zhmerinka and encircle German troops at Zvenigorodka. After the fall of Zhitomir, concentrating on the left flank—and closing with Koniev—might have been more productive. Vatutin's mobile columns had swept down on Voronovitsy and Nemirov, outflanking Vinnitsa from the south, and were now moving on Kristinovka in the direction of Uman. Here Soviet armour bumped into the reserves Manstein gathered to cover Vinnitsa and Uman, whereupon Vatutin drew back temporarily to the Samgorodok–Pogrebische–Zhaskov line.

On the lower Dnieper, Malinovskii's 3rd Ukrainian and Tolbukhin's 4th Ukrainian Front had tried to rush both Nikopol and Krivoi Rog in December. The attempt failed, whereupon the *Stavka* issued formal orders at the beginning of 1944 for these two strong-points to be taken, hinges that had to be lifted before the German defence, well entrenched and secured both by rivers and ravines, could be toppled. Malinovskii faced the fortified river line of the Kamenka; Tolbukhin, the Dnieper. The 4th Ukrainian Front had already come to grief before Nikopol: in the first attempt to rush the town the 44th Army under Khomenko, an *NKVD* officer who had made good as a commander, was badly mauled. Khomenko and his artillery commander, S.A. Bobkov, driving to a forward HQ, took the one road that ran through German positions, coming under murderous fire: Bobkov was killed in the first salvo, and Khomenko sustained fatal wounds. The German radio announced the desertion of two senior Soviet officers. In a rage Stalin ordered the disbanding of 44th Army, its units to be distributed to other commands. Only later in 1944, on the interrogation of a German prisoner, did the truth come out. The remains of the two officers, interred as they were in packing cases used for weapons, were brought to Melitopol.

On 10 January 1944 3rd Ukrainian Front attacked in the direction of Apostolovo, the 4th Ukrainian two days later directly against the Nikopol bridgehead. Malinovskii's assault suffered from lack of ammunition and a shortage of tanks. On Tolbukhin's front, Lelyushenko's 3rd Guards Army could not break into Nikopol. After one week of fruitless fighting the offensive was called off. At a session of the Military Soviet of 3rd Ukrainian Front, Marshal Vasilevskii, *Stavka* 'co-ordinator' for 3rd and 4th Ukrainian Fronts, worked out a new plan of attack which was forthwith submitted to Stalin. Vasilevskii also required reinforcements from the *Stavka* for Malinovskii's front, which carried the main weight of the assault. Malinovskii speedily acquired 37th Army from Koniev's command, 4th Guards Mechanized Corps from Tolbukhin, 31st Guards Rifle Corps from *Stavka* reserve—also 64 KV and T-34 tanks, fuel and ammunition. The revised plan called for the main attack on Malinovskii's front to be made by Glagolev's 46th Army, Chuikov's 8th Guards, and Tanaschishina's 4th Guards Mechanized Corps in the direction of Apostolovo–Kamenka, to break to the Dnieper and to co-operate with Tolbukhin in the reduction of Nikopol. Tolbukhin assigned Lelyushenko's 3rd Guards, Tsvetayev's 5th Shock Army and Grechkin's 28th Army (with Sviridov's 2nd Guards Mechanized Corps operating in Tsvetayev's area) to his attack on Nikopol.

On the morning of 30 January Lt.-Gen. M.N. Sharokhin's 37th Army and Lt.-Gen. I.T. Shlemin's 6th Army (3rd Ukrainian Front) opened the main and supporting attacks. At 0800 hours on 31 January three of Tolbukhin's armies, 3rd Guards, 5th Shock and 28th Armies, started their offensive. Further north the massive Soviet attack on the Korsun-Shevchenkovskii salient was already a week old: at dawn on 24 January 'hundreds of guns' had opened fire, the prelude to Koniev's savage attack, joined two days later by three armies of Vatutin's left flank. On Vatutin's right, 13th and 60th Armies were loosed on 27 January on a new operation to clear German forces from the Lutsk–Rovno–Shepetovka area, preparation for a further drive to the west and to the south.

North-west, south-east and south of Kiev, where Marshal Zhukov acted as *Stavka* 'co-ordinator' for the 1st and 2nd Ukrainian Fronts, operations of mounting strategic significance were building up by the end of January 1944. At this juncture a great deal hung on the fate of the Korsun salient, the great wedge stuck between the junction of 1st and 2nd Ukrainian Fronts, akin to a cork stoppering the Soviet offensive, a position which the German command planned to hold in a bid to rupture the Soviet timetable and thereby frustrate the development of a massed offensive in the southern theatre. Since the salient jutted right back to the Dnieper, Hitler could feed his imagination on thoughts of reconquest; the reality was much grimmer and was to involve the fate of many thousands of men held in this ransom to time and space. For the moment, however, Soviet armoured thrusts in the direction of Uman and Vinnitsa were held, though to the north-west, on the left flank of Army Group South, Soviet columns of light tanks and lorried infantry of Vatutin's right-wing armies had already pushed across the old (1939) Polish frontier, a deep and potentially very dangerous outflanking move directed by Pukhov and Chernyakhovskii in the Lutsk–Rovno operation. Much further south the second Soviet offensive, directed against the German Sixth Army entrenched in the Dnieper bend, was already beginning to bite deeper into the heavily fortified arc fitted out between Nikopol and Krivoi Rog.

As Soviet and German troops began fighting what became the appalling battle for the Korsun salient, amidst the mud and sleet of a winter already on the wane in the southern theatre, Soviet operations at the other end of the front, in the north, were already reaching their first critical phase.

The Leningrad battlefront, with its entrenchments, wire, fortification, fixed defences, emplacements and all the gear of positional warfare, looked like something from the First World War. German long-range and medium guns, seventy batteries north of Krasnoe Selo and another seventy in the 'Mga group', kept the city under steady bombardment, hurting Leningrad day by day. The trams scuttled out of the firing zone as best they could, and shells smashed into buildings or cascaded into the Neva as German and Soviet gunners waged the longest artillery duel in history. In 1943 the 3rd Leningrad Counter-Battery Artillery Corps, 195 guns including the 356mm naval guns, brought all five Soviet artillery concentrations under its control. Sound-detectors, aerial reconnaissance, ground-spotters, balloons, mobile railway guns, deeply emplaced heavy guns—all made their contribution of pinpointing and hitting German batteries. Life had become less nightmarish since the piercing of the tight blockade in January 1943, but it remained dangerous, cramped and hard—900 days of sudden or lingering death, unbroken privation and unending work. An oil pipeline had been laid into the city; the railway line opened in 1943 and running along its narrow corridor raked by German guns brought in fuel and essential supplies along the southern shore of lake Ladoga;

more factories started up production and fewer people dropped dead from hunger.

Field-Marshal Küchler's Army Group North clamped the blockade on Leningrad, the Eighteenth Army holding the ring round the city and a line running south to lake Ilmen, while southwards the Sixteenth Army held a line running along the river Lovat. The German northern group also kept the lid on the Baltic states, helped to hold Finland in the German orbit and trusted to its extensive fixed defences. The German command had steadily thinned the army group, drawing off men and equipment for other fronts and replacing first-line divisions with units of lower calibre and *Luftwaffe* field divisions. Two other defence lines covered a third defensive zone, which in turn protected a rear defence line; the 'Panther line' ran from Pskov to Ostrov. On the centre and left of the Soviet Volkhov Front, German troops set up defence lines on the western bank of the river Volkhov (where Soviet troops had a small bridgehead); lake Ilmen covered Novgorod on the right flank. The grip of winter was much fiercer here, but once again in 1943–4 the climate played tricks—the autumn dragged on, December was rainy. Milder temperatures brought sudden thaws, the ice on rivers and lakes could take the weight of lorries and light guns but not tanks. The marshes of the Volkhov failed to freeze solid.

After a burst of fierce fighting in September 1943 to take the Sinyavino heights, the Leningrad command set about preparing plans to lift the blockade completely, submitting a general outline of its assessment to the *Stavka:*

In connection with the general situation, the Military Soviet of the Leningrad Front considers it timely to raise the question of the destruction of 18 Army, the basic force on the northern wing of the Eastern Front, and not only to free Leningrad completely but also to capture the Luga bridgehead with an advance to the line of the river Luga from the mouth of the river to the town of Luga, a prerequisite for further operations in the Baltic area. [S.P. Platonov, *Bitva za Leningrad,* 1964, p. 300.]

The Leningrad command considered the Eighteenth Army to be on the brink of disaster, deprived as it was of operational reserves. At the end of September, at a session of the full Leningrad command, Lt.-Gen. D.N. Gusev (chief of staff, Leningrad Front) laid out the new attack plan: a concentric attack was to be made from the Oranienbaum bridgehead and from the Pulkovo heights to trap the German forces in the Peterhof–Strelna area, the two Soviet forces linking up at Ropsha, after which the Soviet offensive would develop towards Kingisepp and Krasnogvardeisk. The larger offensive design envisaged a northern attack on the Leningrad–Krasnogvardeisk–Kingisepp axis and an attack from the south-east towards Chudovo–Novgorod–Luga to cut the communications of Army Group North. The change in plans, compared with previous break-out attempts, was a radical one; previously all attacks had been made in an easterly direction from the left flank of the Leningrad Front against the Schlusselburg–Sinyavino group of Eighteenth Army. The weight of the new attack would come on the right flank from Oranienbaum–Pulkovo, with the thrust going south to link up with the Volkhov and 2nd Baltic Fronts.

The *Stavka* indicated its general approval for these plans but advised Govorov in Leningrad and Meretskov on the Volkhov to hold themselves ready for a possible German withdrawal. Govorov at his September staff conference had made the same point, that Army Group North might pull back from Leningrad and Novgorod; Front intelligence had learned of extensive German construction work on all the river lines—Mshaga, Plius, Narva, Velikaya—mainly field fortifications and minefields, with all approach bridges destroyed. For this contingency—a German withdrawal—Govorov drew up the operational plan *Neva 1*, and for a breakout operation, *Neva 2*. The *Stavka* meanwhile issued orders that no front must attempt a breakout without permission. And one very significant change it did institute in Govorov's attack plan, ordering 2nd Shock Army to move into the Oranienbaum bridgehead. This bridgehead was a narrow strip of coast, some twenty miles long and twelve deep, which was a remnant of the disastrous days of 1941 and the grim days of Eighth Army: the bridgehead was cut off from Leningrad but lay within range and under the protection of Soviet long-range guns at Kronstadt. Three divisions and three brigades of the Coastal Operational Group (*POG: Primorskaya Operativnaya Gruppa*) held Oranienbaum, in which the Germans had been largely disinterested. Now Govorov planned to bring one hook out of the bridgehead, the other from the southern outskirts of Leningrad, where Col.-Gen. Maslennikov's 42nd Army would attack. Planning proceeded on the basis of *Neva 2,* a break-out; as a result of the *Stavka*'s instruction, a fantastic amount of work had to be put in hand to shift 2nd Shock Army from Sinyavino in the east right round to the western Oranienbaum bridgehead.

The overall Soviet offensive involved three fronts, Leningrad, Volkhov and 2nd Baltic, now under the command of General M.M. Popov. After crushing in the flanks of Eighteenth Army, Soviet thrusts on Luga would trap the main German force and bring the Leningrad and Volkhov Fronts to a junction at Luga and on to the line of the river Luga. Having knocked out the Eighteenth, the Leningrad, Volkhov and 2nd Baltic Fronts would eliminate the German Sixteenth Army by striking for Narva, Pskov and Idritsa, thus freeing the whole of the Leningrad *oblast* as well as positioning themselves for a general offensive against the Baltic states. On the Leningrad Front Govorov planned a main and a subsidiary attack; the 2nd Shock Army, moving out of the Oranienbaum bridgehead, and 42nd Army, striking from inside the Leningrad perimeter at Pulkovo, would link up at Ropsha, eliminate the German forces in the Peterhof area and then advance on Kingisepp and Krasnogvardeisk; to the east, 67th Army would mount a supporting attack in the direction of Mga. Meretskov on the Volkhov Front, the scene of so much frustration, agony and heartbreak in the past, proposed to use the Soviet bridgehead on the western bank of the Volkhov and 59th Army for the main attack north and south of Novgorod: on the left flank two armies (8th and 54th) would attack in the direction of Tosno–Lyuban–Chudovo to pin down German troops that might otherwise move up to Novgorod. Once the Novgorod group had been encircled, Volkhov Front units would make for Luga, advance to the Luga–Utorgosh line and cut the German escape route to Pskov. General Popov on the 2nd Baltic Front intended to attack on his left to seize the Pustoshka–Idritsa area followed by a drive on Opochka–Sebezh.

Throughout November Soviet commanders began to mass their artillery, the instrument they would need most of all against the German defences. Dumps filled with ammunition, fuel, lubricants and food. On the Pulkovo Heights Govorov ordered a major concentration of artillery in 42nd Army area. In the autumn of 1941, when the German attack had been beaten off here, there had been eight guns per kilometre and never enough ammunition; now the attack plan called for 140 guns per kilometre. Elsewhere the terrain demanded as much engineering equipment as possible. Shifting 2nd Shock Army into the bridgehead at Oranienbaum, however, presented problems of great magnitude and complexity. It fell to the Baltic Fleet to get the men and equipment out of Leningrad by ship and ashore to the west, including two rifle corps, a tank brigade, artillery and all the assorted supplies. On 7 November a forward HQ party from 2nd Shock Army was landed on the bridgehead and took over from the Coastal Operational Group. For the rest of the month, motorized barges, small steamers and tugs towing barges and minesweepers with a covey of small craft steamed to the bridgehead under cover of darkness, speeding as best they could to remove every trace of barges, men and equipment from enemy sight by dawn. When the ice came to the gulf of Finland, the little ships gave way to fleet minesweepers and ice-breakers.

The miniature fleet sailed from the Neva bight, the Leningrad Naval Base command under Rear-Admiral I.D. Kuleshov and from Lisii Nos, a headland round the coast which came under the Kronstadt Naval Defence Zone (Rear-Admiral G.I. Levchenko). The tanks, self-propelled guns and heavy equipment loaded off the 300-yard piers built at Lisii Nos, though ice began to interfere with the later stages of this operation. Towards the end of December when the ice thickened, the second stage of the bridgehead build-up continued, with transport aircraft flying in corps staff and some artillery. The Russians did all they could to foster the idea that they were evacuating the bridgehead, but by January five rifle divisions (11th, 43rd, 90th, 131st and 196th)—44,000 men— with 600 guns of thirteen artillery regiments, a tank brigade with T-34 tanks, one tank regiment, two self-propelled gun regiments, 700 wagon-loads of ammunition and an assortment of supplies had been put down in thousands of nightly journeys. Towards the end of December, Fedyuninskii, hitherto in Rokossovskii's command though an old 'northern' commander, arrived by minelayer on the bridgehead, *Malaya zemlya*', the 'little land', where he took over 2nd Shock Army from a bitterly disappointed Romanovskii.

Between them the Leningrad and Volkhov Fronts mustered some 375,000 men, upwards of 1,200 tanks and self-propelled guns, 718 aircraft for tactical support as well as 192 aircraft from the Baltic Fleet and 330 bombers of Long Range Aviation. Govorov had 33 rifle divisions, 3 rifle brigades and Rybalchenko's 13th Air Army; Meretskov, 22 rifle divisions, 6 rifle brigades, 4 tank brigades and Zhuravlev's 14th Air Army. Popov's 2nd Baltic Front facing the Sixteenth Army numbered no less than 45 rifle divisions, 3 rifle and 4 tank brigades with 355 aircraft of Naumenko's 15th Air Army for tactical support. On 11 January 1944 Govorov and Zhdanov held a final review of plans and preparations at a full session of the Front Military Soviet, attended by formation and arms commanders: Fedyuninskii's attack from Oranienbaum was timed for 14 January, Maslennikov's from Pulkovo for the following day.

During the night of 13–14 January heavy bombers of Long Range Aviation attacked the German artillery concentrations at Bezzabotny: only 109 bombers flew their sorties, bad weather grounding most of the eight bomber corps and one bomber division assigned to these attacks. With the dawn, the mist rolled more densely round Leningrad. On the Oranienbaum bridgehead nothing broke the stillness along the forward line. Fedyuninskii in his forward command post, 300 yards behind the assault units, was nevertheless astounded to hear a cock crow in a spot miles from any farm or village. The bird belonged to Colonel Yashchenko, 90th Rifle Division commander: if the cock crowed loudly, the riflemen said, it signalled a good day ahead. At 0935 hours a salvo of rockets opened the artillery preparation for the attack, 2nd Shock Army guns being joined by the long-range guns from the Kronstadt forts and the warships of the Baltic Fleet, 100,000 rounds loosed off in a 65-minute bombardment. As the bombardment ended, the first echelon of 2nd Shock Army moved forward in attack order; the regimental band of 286th Regiment, 90th Rifle Division, played its men into action. That first day, under a cloudy sky, in weather at first unseasonally warm and with slush underfoot, 2nd Shock Army ground its way forward for 3,000 yards on a five-mile front; 90th Division reached the second German defence line.

Only the sappers clearing mines in front of 42nd Army were happy with the mist that closed on Leningrad. To confuse the German command about the direction of the Soviet attack, the guns of 42nd and 67th Armies had joined the first bombardment. Govorov, who had flown into the bridgehead earlier, now insisted on flying back to Leningrad even though the weather had closed down; after much hazardous circling over an airfield, he finally landed. On Fedyuninskii's front snow had begun to fall, while under cover of darkness Maslennikov's assault divisions took up their final positions. When daylight came, fog hung everywhere, shrouding the army engineers up front but hampering the gunners. Nevertheless, promptly at 0920 hours on 15 January 3,000 guns and heavy mortars opened a massive bombardment of the German positions, firing off over 200,000 rounds in one hundred minutes. A good half of the heavier-

calibre guns fired at the German defences in the breakthrough sector were assigned
to Maj.-Gen. Simonyak's 30th Guards Corps (42nd Army). It was Simonyak's
Corps that made the best progress that first day, driving over 4,000 yards into
the German trenches and pill-boxes. Fedyuninskii had resumed his attack at
11 am, but progress was so slow that Lt.-Gen. Gusev, Govorov's chief of staff,
flew out to the bridgehead to investigate; the infantry were having to fight it
out at German strong-points without support from heavy weapons, the tanks
having strayed into unreconnoitred minefields or become stuck in the snow.
Maslennikov's flank corps had meanwhile been badly knocked about and had
made little progress.

On 17 January came the crisis as Fedyuninskii and Maslennikov chopped and
hacked their way through the German defences, the infantry locked in hundreds
of separate engagements, the tanks churning about in deep snow or labouring
on narrow roads. German units pulled back out of the trap, blowing up the
bridges on the Duderhof and the dam, flooding the area near Krasnoe Selo. Both
Fedyuninskii and Maslennikov committed their second-echelon troops, and on
the evening of 19 January forward armoured units of 2nd Shock and 42nd
Armies linked up south-east of Ropsha. With the fall of Strelna, Russian troops
captured the heavy gun batteries which only hours before had been shelling
Leningrad—almost a hundred siege guns, pieces up to 400mm calibre, were
taken. The cost, however, was great; regiments in 42nd Army dropped to two-
battalion strength, battalions to two companies. The sapper battalions of the
'assault-engineer sapper brigades', fighting their close-range David and Goliath
contests with the concrete forts, suffered dreadful losses. The entire situation,
however, was transformed almost by the hour as 2nd Shock and 42nd Armies
clubbed in the left flank of Eighteenth Army; 67th Army made ready to strike
out on the Mga sector and Meretskov's Volkhov Front armies lunged forward.
Govorov now aligned 2nd Shock Army on Kingisepp, 42nd on Krasnogvardeisk
and 67th on Ulyanov–Tosno. Lt.-Gen. Sviridov, 67th Army commander, was
not to allow German units to pull back unmolested, but when on the night of
20–21 January the German withdrawal from Mga began, he let his chance slip.
Govorov upbraided him fiercely, demanding that 67th catch up and pin the
enemy.

Meretskov's Volkhov Front had also gone over to the attack on 14 January,
when Lt.-Gen. I.T. Korovnikov's 59th Army tried to break through the German
defences to the north of Novgorod. That first day the northerly attack made
only 1,000 yards, but to the south of Novgorod the 'southern group' under
Maj.-Gen. Sviklin crossed lake Ilmen screened by the dark and a driving snow-
storm, seized a bridgehead on the western bank of the Volkhov and by the
evening was deep into the German defences. North and south of Novgorod
Korovnikov committed more rifle divisions, strengthening the southern outflanking
drive. While this heavy fighting continued amidst ice and deep snow, Meretskov
ordered 54th Army on his right flank to attack towards Lyuban to prevent

German reinforcements being drawn off to Novgorod. Fresh German units had moved up from Mga, but by 18 January the threat of Soviet encirclement was very real. German troops were now pulling back from Novgorod to Batetskaya junction and Lyubolyada, though 59th Army had the one road to the west already within artillery range. Sviklin's 'southern group' meanwhile cut the Novgorod–Shimsk road and the railway line. North of Novgorod 14th Rifle Corps stopped dead on 19 January, making preparations that evening to storm the city at first light, but bad reconnaissance and faulty intelligence failed to disclose that the enemy facing 14th Corps had melted away; when rifle units of 14th and 7th Corps entered Novgorod at 0930 on 20 January, except for a demolition squad left to blow the bridge over the Volkhov the city was bare of German troops.

Circling and harassing the retreating Germans were numerous partisan groups, whose activity had intensified as far back as November 1943, when their chief function was reconnaissance in the German rear. Partisan units blew up railway lines, attacked railway stations, fought their own local actions with German garrisons and liberated small townships or villages, holding them until the Red Army arrived on the scene. The 11th Partisan Brigade operated against German lines of communication in the Kingisepp sector, the 9th at Gdov—thirteen partisan brigades with a combined strength of 35,000 men were in action in January 1944. In view of the heavy losses the partisan movement and the underground at large had suffered in 1943 this was no small achievement. While a brigade normally mustered some hundreds of partisans, one or two—like Karitskii's 5th Brigade—had a strength of 6,000. The main strength of the partisan movement was gathered in the Pskov area—at Gdov, at Luga and in the Novgorod region—where not long before German punitive detachments burned villages and shot local inhabitants in an effort to stamp out partisan activity. No less important in partisan operations was the rescue of civilians rounded up for deportation, lodged in some improvized concentration camp or even loaded on to trains.

By 20 January the double breakthrough was an accomplished fact. As 67th, 8th and 54th Armies were finally committed, the Soviet offensive was unfolding across a front running from the Gulf of Finland to lake Ilmen. As the first phase of the offensive drew to a close, Front commanders faced two problems: the first, to clear their operational plans for the next phase with the *Stavka;* the second, to eradicate the tactical deficiencies which slowed up progress and to shake up army and corps commanders who persisted with frontal attacks and used infantry for almost everything, leaving their armour or supporting artillery to idle on some road or track and too often failing to make adequate reconnaissance. On 22 January the *Stavka* approved Govorov's fresh directives, to set 2nd Shock on the march to Volosovo–Kingisepp and to take the river Luga line (from the mouth to Kingisepp) by the end of the month, to swing 42nd south-west on to the Luga after the capure of Gatchina, to move 67th Army south and west on Pushkino–Slutsk and Ulyanov–Tosno. Luga was the great prize, the vital junction in the rear of Eighteenth Army: to seize it would put the Red Army astride the escape route to the south-west. Meretskov had already submitted his proposals to the *Stavka* for committing 59th Army in a drive for Luga: 8th Army would clear the railway line between Tosno and Ushako, while 54th was to capture Lyuban. The *Stavka* authorized this plan and set 29–30 January as the date for the capture of Luga, 23–24 January for the clearing of Lyuban.

Divisions of the German Eighteenth Army no longer held a firm front; defensive actions centred on junctions, small towns, heights and the roads. Strong, skilful German rearguards deflected the Soviet advance wherever possible, a fighting retreat simplified by Soviet tactics. Fedyuninskii raged at his corps commanders in an order of 23 January for 'marking time'—*toptatsya na meste*—in front of 'insignificant enemy forces' which covered the German withdrawal south and south-west. Maslennikov issued similar orders, complaining that corps commanders used neither their fire-power nor their reserves, that artillery and mortars were not even deployed, much less used. Govorov in his orders demanded the end of 'linear tactics', more manoeuvre and more fire-power. On Meretskov's front, German rearguards, regiments covered by battalions, battalions by companies, fought in isolation or with the *Kampfgruppen* to hold up the Soviet drive to Luga and to keep escape routes open. From west to Novgorod 59th Army fought its way forward to Luga while Maj.-Gen. Roginskii's 54th Army stormed Lyuban and blockaded the remaining German units in Chudovo, thereby relieving the pressure on 59th Army's flank and clearing a whole stretch of the main Leningrad–Moscow railway. Like Govorov, Meretskov issued categorical instructions for energetic action—to outflank, to get into the German rear, if necessary to fight on inverted fronts, to keep corps and divisional HQs well forward. On the right flank of 59th Army, 112th Corps struggled along the Novgorod–Batetskaya railway line, a battleground of bog where Soviet riflemen fought up to their knees in icy slush, manhandling guns when the artillery units failed to find a track or road. Korovnikov's front widened continually; keeping four corps under control proved too difficult, whereupon Meretskov moved 8th Army HQ on to the right flank and gave it two corps from 59th, 7th and 14th. Both armies, 8th and 59th, were to co-operate in outflanking and capturing Luga.

Though the great encirclement failed to materialize, Leningrad was free on 26 January when the Moscow–Leningrad railway was cleared. The next day, with Stalin's permission, the Leningrad Front Military Soviet issued an order of the day formally announcing the end of the blockade and that same evening Leningrad's artillery—on ship and shore—fired off twenty-four salvoes in a victory salute. There was nothing grandiose in Leningrad saluting itself: it bought the right with its dead families, shattered buildings and emaciated survivors. Yet in the midst of jubilation, Eighteenth Army was fighting its way steadily out of the Soviet trap. On 29 January Stalin sent Meretskov an urgent signal, promising a reinforcement of 12,000–15,000 men and 130 tanks but demanding the capture of Luga: 'Don't get tied down in fighting for Shimsk and Soltsy; this is not the main thing, merely screen yourself on this axis. The main thing is to take the town of Luga at all possible speed. After capturing Luga, deploy in two columns and go for Pskov' (S.P. Platonov, *op. cit.,* p. 379). Luga, however, did not fall on time. With troops pulled back from the Mga salient, from Novgorod, from Lyuban and with 12th *Panzer* Division moved up from Army Group Centre, Army Group North hung on to cover the Luga–Pskov road and railway line; the battle for Luga dragged on, ending only when Govorov swung 42nd and 67th Armies down from the north to threaten the German rear. On 12 February, 67th Army finally took Luga, and German units fell back to the south-west, towards Pskov, clinging grimly to the Luga–Pskov railway line. Fedyuninskii's 2nd Shock Army had reached the river Narva north and south of Narva itself at the beginning of February: in the middle of the month the *Stavka* informed Govorov that 'military and political requirements' made the capture of Narva by 17 February mandatory, but the 2nd Shock Army now felt the impact of its losses, the effect of poor command at divisional and company level—a fact Fedyuninskii stressed in his report to the Front Military Soviet—and the limitations imposed by shortage of ammunition, especially for the heavier guns.

With the capture of Luga, the *Stavka* disbanded the Volkhov Front with its directive of 13 February; 59th, 8th and 54th Armies with the Front reserve (two divisions) came under Govorov's command and 1st Shock Army, 'loaned' to Meretskov for operations against Staraya Russa, reverted to Popov's 2nd Baltic Front. Throughout January, in God-forsaken country, 10th Guards and 22nd Army on Popov's front struggled to capture the rail junction at Novosokolniki, but the pressure here on Sixteenth Army was never great enough to prevent Army Group North moving units northwards to block Meretskov. Towards the middle of February, as Govorov struck out for Narva and Pskov, the *Stavka* proposed to use 2nd Baltic Front in operations aimed at Ostrov, with Popov's left flank—two armies, 'a minimum of twenty divisions'—committed in the direction of Rezekne (Rezhitsa)–Karsave, orders for which were issued on 17 February. The danger to Sixteenth Army was growing, from Govorov in the north and from Popov in the south-east, two outflanking moves which the German command could no longer ignore. To escape Govorov's flanking move in the north, German units at Staraya Russa began to pull back, a withdrawal that 1st Shock Army failed to discover for a couple of days. This blunder called down the wrath of the all-powerful State Defence Committee (the *GKO*) on Popov: so unsatisfactory was the performance of 2nd Baltic command deemed that the *GKO* issued its own special reprimand, more significant since Bulganin was the current third 'political' member of Popov's Military Soviet and Mekhlis had been his immediate predecessor. Somewhat tardily 1st Shock Army set out in pursuit, advancing towards Dno and Dedovichi.

One by one the German bastions toppled, the scene of fierce fighting in the past—Staraya Russa, Kholm, Shimsk. But the fall of Narva, Pskov and Ostrov proved for the moment, in spite of *Stavka* orders, beyond the Soviet troops. The Soviet offensive had nevertheless achieved its first objective, the elimination of Eighteenth Army south of lake Ladoga and on the eastern sector of the gulf of Finland. Leningrad was free, most of the Leningrad and Kalinin *oblasts* had been completely cleared, and Soviet troops were across the Estonian frontier. Behind them lay a trail of smashed towns, burned and blackened villages, and broken bridges; in front of them, the 'Panther line' upon which they were now closing. Ambitious plans for a rapid thrust into Estonia proved at this juncture too optimistic, a not-infrequent feature of *Stavka* directives, yet the Soviet victory was already bringing its political fall-out. With the left flank of Army Group North torn to shreds and the German hold on the northern theatre substantially, if not fatally, weakened, the warning lights began to flash for Finland. Pressure on Finland was no doubt part of the 'political requirement' brought to Govorov's attention by the *Stavka* directive on the need to take Narva quickly. Nothing was lost upon the Finns, who had already begun to probe the Soviet attitude in contacts carefully picked out in Stockholm.

On the southerly face of the Korsun-Shevchenkovskii salient, with its blunt nose pressed up to the Dnieper, the flash and roar of a massive artillery barrage fired off at dawn on 24 January signalled the opening of the Soviet attack. General Koniev's 2nd Ukrainian Front took the lead. By the evening of the first day, forward battalions of 4th Guards and 53rd Armies made, in places, up to three miles into the German positions: at dawn the next day the main body of the two infantry armies followed and at noon Rotmistrov's 5th Guards Tank Army, a crack armoured formation, moved into the attack, surging forward towards Shpola–Lebedin on the 'base' of the salient. Fighting towards the tanks and infantry of 2nd Ukrainian Front came the extreme left-flank armies of Vatutin's 1st Ukrainian, 27th, 40th and 6th Tank, developing their attack in the direction of Zvenigorodka.

Vatutin's offensive began on 26 January with forty minutes of artillery fire, but it developed only slowly. The tank army in the lead was brand-new, Lt.-Gen. Kravchenko's 6th, literally only a few days old; it was rushed at top speed into the battle for the Korsun salient, 160 tanks and 50 SP guns, 2 corps (5th Guards Tank and 5th Mechanized), up to strength in men but well below the mark in trained crews. Marshal Zhukov and General Vatutin demanded speed above all things from Kravchenko, and when 27th Army broke through a little to the north, Vatutin ordered 6th Tank to move a mobile group into 27th Army area, outflank Vinograd and drive on Zvenigorodka. Maj.-Gen. Savelev, deputy commander of 5th Mechanized Corps, took command of this 'mobile group', 233rd Tank brigade, with some 50 tanks and 200 tommy-gunners. Savelev's combat group cleared Lysanka late at night on 27 January and by the morning, in a burst of heavy fighting, worked its way into the north-western outskirts of

Zvenigorodka. German artillery fire in these actions killed Lt.-Gen. Shtevnev, 1st Ukrainian Front Armoured Forces commander, who with a group of officers from his 'operational group' followed in Savelev's wake. Pushing on Zvenigorodka, Savelev's tanks linked up with 20th Tank Corps from the 2nd Ukrainian Front. A thin outer encircling screen had been laid down and the internal encirclement solidified, shutting up the German divisions in Korsun; the outer encirclement was entrusted to 5th Guards and 6th Tank Army with their front facing south. From the inner front, Soviet units fought their way into the 'pocket', cutting and slicing it away. On the outer front the tank armies—reinforced with rifle divisions—had to hold off the clumps of *Panzer* divisions of General Hube's relief force trying to batter their way in to free the trapped divisions. The snow blizzards came, mixed with rain and sleet. Short of lorries, Soviet infantry marched in the tracks of the tank columns. In the Korsun area, with seven infantry divisions, an *SS Panzer* division, a Belgian *SS* formation and a varied collection of auxiliary units compressed into a space at no point wider than twenty miles, the German defence was hurriedly and painfully improvized. Against the belea- guered Germans, General Koniev unleashed a savage, remorseless attack, bombing, shelling, hacking the defences to pieces. The 'Free German Committee' moved captured German generals down to fire off a propaganda barrage of its own, inciting desertion and appealing for surrender. The effort was quite futile.

The hills, ravines and forests—even the marshy reaches of the Olshanka river— furnished some natural defences for the Korsun 'pocket', but inside the ring food and ammunition were in short supply from the first day of the encirclement. As long as German troops held the airfields, transport planes flew supplies in and officers out; General Wohler left in this fashion, as did senior *SS* officers. General Stemmermann stayed to meet the final storm. To smash in the Korsun ring, Koniev employed thirteen rifle divisions and three cavalry divisions with 2,000 guns and 138 tanks from 27th, 52nd and 4th Guards Armies. The first attacks fell south of Korsun to clear German units from the Olshanka and to 'thicken' the belt between them and German tank divisions trying to crash through the external front at Zvenigorodka–Shpola; attacks in the north steadily converged on Korsun. On 8 February General Stemmermann was offered but refused surrender terms; hope, in the shape of a relief force of *Panzer* divisions, flickered on the horizon. From Rizino four German armoured divisions blasted a hole in the Soviet outer encirclement and aimed for Lysyanka. Vatutin rushed up 2nd Tank Army to seal off the breach. By 10 February Koniev's assault divisions were closing in on Korsun, crushing the German 'pocket' to six miles by seven. When Korsun itself fell, the remnants of Stemmermann's divisions clustered in Shanderovka and Steblev.

The crisis came in full force after 12 February. Four German *Panzer* divisions had chopped their way into 6th Tank positions; the trapped German divisions tried desperately to fight their way south-west from Steblev out to Lysyanka, there to link up with the relief force. Stalin was much displeased and demanded a better performance from the ground troops and from the air force in blocking the German drive for Lysyanka, which in his view presented by far the greater danger. He recalled Khudyakov (*Stavka* 'representative' for air force matters) to Moscow and sent Marshal Novikov, the Soviet Air Force commander, himself. A special *Stavka* signal to Front commanders severely criticized the mistakes that allowed the Germans to break out in the Shanderovka–Stablev area, a minute salient which must now be speedily liquidated. Koniev got control of 27th Army, while 5th Air Army was assigned to support Vatutin's operations on the outer encirclement front and 2nd Air Army committed to preventing any German supply or support for the encircled divisions. Koniev determined at once to drive the Germans out of the shelter of Shanderovka into the open snow-swept fields, but the blizzards into which he intended to thrust the Germans also grounded his bombers. By dint of using volunteer crews and light aircraft from 392nd Aviation Regiment, Koniev finally got his air strike. The rain of incendiaries fell on Shanderovka, lighting up the target for the Russian guns, which rapidly ranged on the village from their positions not more than 5,000 yards away.

With their shelter burned about their ears, General Stemmermann and his remaining units determined on a final break-out, to march in two columns on Komarovka (only a few miles north-east of Lysyanka), *SS* units in the lead. At 0200 hours on 17 February, with a fierce snow-storm sweeping about them, Stemmermann's German troops finished their last supplies and consumed what *schnapps* was left. General Stemmermann issued his last orders; his men set about destroying guns, lorries, even personal equipment. There was no place in the columns for the wounded; according to Soviet accounts, they were killed where they lay, shot in the head. One hour later the two columns moved off.

Across the path of the marching Germans lay two Soviet armies, 27th and 4th Guards, with lines of infantry, tanks and Cossack cavalrymen, the artillery massed in the woods. Only when the German columns emerged from the ravines into a stretch of open country, with the German troops whooping their delight at having escaped, did the waiting Russians attack. Under the yellow sky of early morning and over ground covered with wet snow Soviet tanks made straight for the thick of the column, ploughing up and down, killing and crushing with their tracks. Almost simultaneously massed Cossack cavalry wheeled away from the tanks to hunt down and massacre men fleeing for the refuge of the hills: hands held high in surrender the Cossacks sliced off with their sabres. The killing in this human hunt went on for several hours and a new round opened on the banks of the river Gniloy Tikich, where the survivors of the first collision of the German column with Soviet troops dragged and fought their way. Soviet artillery fire caught more German troops on the river bank as Soviet tanks charged from the flanks and rear, a flailing, maddened battle where men flung themselves headlong into the Tikich to break away at any cost to Lysyanka. Prisoners came low down on the list of Russian priorities. Koniev set out to kill, and he killed with a hardened single-mindedness. The battle with the column cost 20,000

German dead; 8,000 prisoners were herded together or dragged out of their hiding places. The final Russian tally for the Korsun encirclement—another flick of the Stalingrad whip—rested at 55,000 dead and wounded, plus 18,200 prisoners (contested by the Germans, who insisted that 30,000 men made their way out of the Russian trap). For the Soviet commanders came high reward: Rotmistrov earned his Marshal's star, to make him the first 'Marshal of Armoured Forces' in Red Army history, and General Koniev also acquired his appointment to Marshal of the Soviet Union for his part in these Ukrainian battles. General Stemmermann lay dead from his wounds and was tidily coffined by his conquerors; for the rank and file there were only mass graves.

Further south, Malinovskii and Tolbukhin finally stove in the elaborate German defence system covering Nikopol and Krivoi Rog. On 5 February two Soviet divisions from 46th Army stormed Apostolovo junction, a thirty-mile advance which well-nigh outflanked both Nikopol and Krivoi Rog, and delivered the contents of a German supply base—Sixth Army's base—to the Red Army, effectively cutting Sixth Army in two. From Apostolovo 46th Army and 8th Guards turned west towards the river Ingulets. Tolbukhin meanwhile launched his front once more against Nikopol, first driving German troops out of their bridgehead on the Dnieper opposite the town. Soviet bombers and ground-attack planes bombed the German pontoon bridges south of Nikopol and the wooden bridge at Ushkalka; the bridge was blown, but a squad of assault engineers had to deal with the pontoons. On the morning of 8 February the bridgehead was cleared and that night the Soviet 6th Army (4th Ukrainian Front) broke into Nikopol from the north. After a night of heavy street fighting, Nikopol was also cleared. Malinovskii's attack from the north had reached Novo Vorontsovka, shutting off the German escape to the west. The attack on the pontoon bridges blocked the escape route for men in the eastern bridgehead; the units in Nikopol could only pull back along a narrow corridor to the west through swampland lying between the Dnieper and Novo Vorontsovka, but this meant bursting through 8th Guards Army. In this hazardous operation Sixth Army succeeded in holding the swamp and the sole road to safety—that leading down the Dnieper from Nikopol to Dudchino—until 5th Shock Army finally severed it late in February.

Malinovskii now turned his attention to Krivoi Rog, a tough nut protected by its outer layer of fortifications almost twenty miles across and by three rivers, the Ingulets, the Visun and the Ingul. Krivoi Rog also attracted Stalin's attention, who required of Malinovskii in a special signal sent on 22 February that the town must be in Soviet hands that same day. If only to prevent German demolition of the major electric power stations, speed was an urgent consideration. Already 37th Army command had formed a special squad under Colonel Shurupov to get behind the German lines and frustrate the blowing up of the Krivoi Rog power stations as well as the installations on the river Saksagan. Shurupov's men did succeed in saving the Saksagan installations, fighting in the German rear, while Sharokhin's 37th Army, repulsed like 6th and 46th Armies in a frontal attack, also crossed the Saksagan and broke into Krivoi Rog from the north-west. At 1600 hours on the day nominated by Stalin, Krivoi Rog was cleared. Now the barrier of the Ingulets was broken; 37th Army had a bridgehead on the western bank west of Krivoi Rog, 8th Guards on 6 February had broken through to the Ingulets at Shirokoe, and to the north 46th Army was over. By the end of February the bend in the lower Dnieper had been swept clean of German troops, the tangle of fortifications flattened, the precious iron-ore region back in Soviet hands and the German Sixth Army the poorer by 40,000 men. Without the Nikopol bridgehead to menace its rear, 4th Ukrainian Front could launch a full-scale attack on the Crimea, while Malinovskii's 3rd Ukrainian Front stood poised to strike at Nikolaevsk–Odessa.

Late in February most Soviet armies for all practical purposes had drawn to a halt. In the 'northern theatre', Govorov drew up to the Pskov–Ostrov defence line and was held there. In the centre, the 'western theatre', Rokossovskii, under-gunned and under-manned as his front was, could claw no further through the slime and the German defences. In the south, battered though Army Groups South and A were, they held a line bereft of the bulges and indentations that had engulfed so many divisions and which ran slanting from north to south more or less midway between the Dnieper and the Bug. But appearances were deceptive (and scarcely failed to deceive the German command). The bloody sacrifice at Korsun had delayed but not frustrated a massive Soviet general offensive in the south, designed to roll across vast areas of mud and to crash more major river barriers. Behind their present lines Soviet fronts and armies regrouped feverishly, taking in *Stavka* reserves, moving up reinforcements, stocking ammunition, fuel and food. The day after the Korsun battle brought catastrophe to the German columns, on 18 February, Stalin signed the formal *Stavka* directive for the new offensive timed for early March; simultaneously a new front, the 2nd Belorussian under the command of Col.-Gen. Kurochkin, was established at the junction of 1st Ukrainian and the Belorussian Fronts (redesignated 1st Belorussian).

The German high command was almost persuaded that the Russian *Ansturm*, the great onrush of early February threatening the northern and southern flanks, must now sink inexorably into the great morass of mud, to be renewed only when the ground became drier. Field-Marshal Manstein entertained fewer illusions: the greatest likelihood was that the Red Army would attack once more, this time in great strength, to sever the Lvov–Odessa railway running behind his northern flank. But what Stalin proposed for the March operations in southern Russia went far beyond German imagining, for he was intent on the complete destruction of the German armies in southern Russia, to be accomplished across a gigantic front running from the Pripet to the Black Sea and involving four fronts, 2nd Belorussian and 1st, 2nd and 3rd Ukrainian; Tolbukhin's 4th Ukrainian Front was presently handing over most of its armies to Malinovskii before being detached for its attack on the Crimea.

Vatutin's right wing was transformed into 2nd Belorussian Front, which became operational on 24 February, taking over 61st Army from Rokossovskii, a right-flank corps of 13th Army (77th Corps) and two armies from *Stavka* reserve, 47th and 70th, with 6th Air Army in support. Kurochkin received orders to attack Kovel and to aim at Brest (thus bringing him into the rear of Army Group Centre), an exploitation of the earlier Soviet success at Kovno and Lutsk. Vatutin's orders for 1st Ukrainian Front stipulated an attack from the Dubno–Shepetovka–Lyubar front towards Chortkov and Chernovitsy, a southerly sweep to cut off Army Group South's line of retreat north of the Dniester: Marshal Koniev's 2nd Ukrainian would drive from its present positions (the flattened Korsun salient, Zvenigorodka) through Uman on to Jassy: Malinovskii's 3rd Ukrainian was to strike from its bridgeheads over the Ingulets towards Nikolaev and Odessa. Stalin confirmed the operational orders on 18 February for 1st and 2nd Ukrainian, ten days later for 3rd Ukrainian Front. The three Ukrainian fronts would attack with a piston-like momentum, 1st Ukrainian opening on 4 March, 2nd Ukrainian on 5 March and 3rd Ukrainian on 6 March, a violent but co-ordinated motion.

The *Stavka* proposed to commit all six Soviet tank armies in the Ukraine. Badanov's 4th Tank Army moved out of *Stavka* reserve to Vatutin's front, which handed over 40th Army and 2nd and 6th Tank Army to Marshal Koniev, who in turn handed over 57th Army to Malinovskii at 3rd Ukrainian, already the recipient of 5th Shock Army and 28th Army from Tolbukhin. Vatutin and Koniev disposed of equal infantry strength, 56 rifle divisions, both deployed three tank armies (1st, 3rd Guards and 4th Tank on 1st Ukrainian, 2nd, 6th and 5th Guards on 2nd Ukrainian), Vatutin had five 'all-arms' armies (1st Guards, 13th, 18th, 38th and 60th), Koniev seven (4th, 5th and 7th Guards, 27th, 40th, 52nd and 53rd). Vatutin faced 26 divisions (none of them *Panzer* or motorized divisions) of Fourth and First *Panzer*, Koniev 21 divisions (erroneously estimated at 28 by Front intelligence) including four *Panzer* divisions of Eighth Army and elements of Sixth Army. Malinovskii enjoyed substantial reinforcement, bringing his strength to seven 'all-arms' armies (8th Guards, 5th Shock, 6th, 28th, 37th, 46th and 57th Army) and 57 rifle divisions with one tank and two mechanized corps in support, out of which Malinovskii formed a 'cavalry-mechanized group' (4th Guards Cavalry and 4th Mechanized Corps) under Lt.-Gen. Pliev, a raiding force to operate in the German rear. This final reinforcement and regrouping invested the Red Army with a general superiority of two to one in infantry and rather more than two to one in armour.

Moving into the Kovel–Lutsk area on the Volhynia proper, the Red Army also drove into the midst of another battlefield where German troops, Soviet partisans and Ukrainian nationalist guerrilla armies fought their appallingly brutal, multi-sided war. Soviet partisan brigades drifting south had turned the north-western Ukraine into a sizeable base, but in Polesia and northern Volhynia the Ukrainian nationalists, men of the *UPA*, the 'Ukrainian Insurgent Army' (*Ukrainska povstanska armiia*), had their guerrilla strongholds. The *UPA* at first helped to clear out communist partisans, but on being denied a separate 'state' by the Germans turned to fighting them also. In the struggle between the nationalist factions (the *OUN-B* and the *OUN-M*, representing the Bandera and Melnyk groups), a fresh force, the 'Ukrainian National-Revolutionary Army', *UNRA* (*Ukrainska Narodna-Revoliutsiina Armiia*), was organized to distinguish it from the *UPA*, which the Bandera group was bent on controlling. But by late 1943 *OUN-B* came out on top in this dog-fight and the *UPA* gathered fresh strength in Volhynia. East of Rovno the guerrillas were strong enough to set up their own administration, keeping the Germans confined to the towns.

The guerrillas fought both the German and Soviet authorities, but fighting it out with the Red Army was impossible. To maintain their struggle the *UPA* turned to attacking Soviet lines of communication and *NKVD* units, though in one action, however, they inflicted deep hurt on the Red Army. To complete preparations for the March offensive General Vatutin had arrived in Rovno on 29 February (after stopping at Pukhov's 13th Army HQ); his small convoy of three light cars then set out for Slavuta, Chernyakhovskii's 60th Army command post. Branching off the Rovno highway, the road ran through dips and hollows, out of which a burst of fire suddenly ripped into Vatutin's car, setting it alight. Another burst sent a second truck with Vatutin's escort up in flames. From the snow-covered fields a force of a hundred guerrillas closed in on the burning vehicles, but machine-gun fire from the dozen men in the escort party drove them back. Vatutin categorically ordered a staff officer to withdraw, taking the operational orders and one machine-gunner with him for protection. Vatutin himself refused to leave. At sunset the General's party set about disengaging, when Vatutin was severely wounded. The least badly damaged truck, punctured by bullets, refused to start. Under covering fire Maj.-Gen. Krainyukov and a staff officer carried Vatutin along the road, lighting finally upon a peasant with two horses; the officers put Vatutin, heavily soaked in blood, into a sledge and drove for the Rovno highway, where in a wayside hut a regimental doctor supplied emergency dressings for the General's mangled right leg. Though transferred to Kiev, Vatutin never recovered from his wounds; on 15 April at the age of forty-two he died, following his brothers Afanasii and Semyen who had been killed in action the month before.

Marshal Zhukov from 1 March assumed full command of the 1st Ukrainian Front.

At 0800 hours on the morning of 4 March, as massed artillery battered the German defences, Marshal Zhukov launched the Guards armies of the 1st Ukrainian Front upon their major offensive. Exercising direct command in place of Vatutin, Zhukov made few alterations in the operational plan for the front. Late in February armour and infantry moved up steadily from the left flank towards the right, 3rd Guards Tank on to Shimsk, 1st Guards and 60th Army almost entirely redeployed, 4th Tank Army to the west of Kiev. Chernyakhovskii's 60th covered the final deployment of 3rd Guards and 4th Tank Army. On the eve of the attack, fuel stocks for the armoured formations dropped alarmingly to less than two days' supply, but Zhukov ordered operations to begin on time, arguing that by the third day of operations the tanks would get their fuel (as indeed they did).

Chernyakhovskii, as professional and as nimble as any German commander facing him, took the lead; the moment 60th Army broke into the German defences Zhukov hurled 4th Tank and 3rd Guards Tank Armies into action, and within forty-eight hours Soviet tank and infantry armies had broken through on a 100-mile front to a depth of twenty-five miles, a wide front running from Ostrog in the west to the river Slutch in the east, with Shepetovka and the railway line to Tarnopol providing the central axis. Zhukov exerted formidable pressure at the centre, throwing in his tank armies and motorized infantry, their mobility much impeded but never eliminated by the mud over which the broad-tracked tanks and Studebaker trucks ploughed and gouged their way. The large bodies of Soviet riflemen did fall behind, marching stolidly through the mud, manhandling equipment amidst the ooze and fighting repeated infantry actions against German troops trapped in the soft squelching country lanes or immobilized in the glutinous fields. But by the evening of 7 March three Soviet armies—60th, 3rd Guards Tank and 4th Tank—were closing on the Tarnopol–Chernyi Ostrov line, while 1st Guards Army moved up to Staro Konstantinov (covering the approaches to Proskurov). With the capture of Volochisk, midway between Tarnopol and Chernyi Ostrov, Soviet tank columns had already cut the Lvov–Odessa trunk railway line, while the full force of Zhukov's blow fell on the junction of Fourth and First *Panzer* Armies. In this first Soviet onrush, three *Panzer* and eight infantry divisions had taken a fierce battering, but more German divisions now moved up to hold the Tarnopol–Proskurov sector and to push Soviet troops away from the trunk railway. As German resistance stiffened, the Soviet advance slowed down, but Marshal Zhukov ordered the outflanking of Tarnopol from the south and an extension of the offensive eastwards, in the direction of Proskurov.

Between 11 and 13 March the *Stavka* confirmed Marshal Zhukov's operational intention to sweep southwards on to and over the Dniester, with Chernovitsy as the main objective; this deep lancing of the German front would cut off First *Panzer* and slice into the remaining communications between German forces in Poland and those in southern Russia; Zhukov's left flank would strike out for Kamenets–Podolskii, the Dniester and the Soviet frontier, with 1st Tank Army moving towards Chortkov–Chernovitsy, and 4th Tank towards Kamenets–Podolskii. Two rifle armies, 18th and 38th, received fresh orders to take Vinnitsa and Zhmetinka and then to move on Kamenets–Podolskii. To extend the offensive in a westerly direction, Pukhov at 13th Army on the right flank had orders to advance to the Berestechka–Brody–Zalozhtsy line.

The prospect for this massive axe-blow to split the entire German southern grouping into two—one part pressed into Galicia and southern Poland, the other pushed into Moldavia and on to the Danube—was vastly increased by Marshal Koniev's own 'mud offensive' with the 2nd Ukrainian Front. Koniev's attack began on 5 March at dawn; yet another huge barrage followed at 0750 hours by tank and infantry attacks. Forward elements of 2nd Guards and 5th Guards Tank Army went in with the rifle divisions, the full strength of the two tank armies being committed that same day, and were even augmented with the introduction of 6th Tank Army. On the Gornyi Tikich, Rotmistrov's tanks smashed up the German defences and swung towards the great base of Uman along a path littered with abandoned German equipment—200 Tiger and Panther tanks, 600 guns and 12,000 lorries. At the junction of Potash Soviet troops came upon more heavy weapons and supplies in abundance, but Uman itself— taken in one swoop on 10 March by 2nd and 5th Guards Tank Army with 52nd Army—yielded even greater booty: dumps crammed with supplies, outlying districts strewn with German tanks, armed and fuelled but awash to their track-guards in the mud. The *Panzer* divisions so recently involved in the break-in attempts at Korsun were moving back westwards when they were engulfed by Koniev's sweep on Uman, and with the loss of Uman German hopes of holding off Koniev from the southern Bug slumped. Forward units of the tank armies forced the southern Bug off the march; Koniev ordered everything on to tracks, the artillery following in the wake of the tanks. Mobile groups of tanks, artillery, infantry and engineers made all speed for the southern Bug, where a lead brigade of 16th Tank Corps (2nd Tank Army) took the Dzhulinka crossing on the evening of 11 March, followed by 29th Tank Corps (6th Tank Army) at Gaivoron, with only hours between them. Within forty-eight hours Soviet units were across the river, having used all manner of boats and rafts, on a fifty-mile front.

At noon on 15 March the lead tanks of 16th Corps, with 156th Tank Regiment (6th Tank Army) in support, burst into Vapnyarka, a major junction on the Zhmerinka–Odessa railway line and not more than thirty miles from the Dniester. Maj.-Gen. Dubovoi's 16th Corps pressed on towards Yampol and closer to the Dnieper, while on the left Rotmistrov's 5th Guards raced on from the Bug to the Dniester. At 1300 hours on 17 March Lt.-Gen. Kirichenko's 29th Corps (5th Guards Tank) reached the Dniester a little to the east of Soroki and at once put a rifle regiment across. One after another Koniev's armies drew up to the Dniester—2nd and 5th Guards Tank, 4th Guards and 52nd Army fighting for the bridgeheads at Yampol–Soroki and further north at Moghilev–Podolskii. On the morning of 19 March a tank regiment from 5th Mechanized Corps (6th Tank Army) fought its way into the outskirts of Moghilev–Podolskii; that same evening the town was cleared and the main body of 5th Mechanized Corps moved up. The crossing of the Dniester began during the night of 20 March and shortly after noon on 21 March the entire corps was established on the western bank. The German front, running from Moghilev–Podolskii to Soroki, had been split, First *Panzer's* right flank had been pushed back to the north-west and Eighth Army's left to the south.

With Marshal Koniev over the Dniester, Marshal Zhukov loosed off his powerful drive to the south, to Chernovitsy. Both marshals co-ordinated their operations tactically and strategically, fighting tactically significant actions to clear Vinnitsa and Zhmerinka (on Zhukov's extreme left flank) as Koniev's columns cleared Bratslav on the southern Bug. The clearing of Podolia, however, paled somewhat in significance beside the giant sweep southwards planned on a major strategic scale.

Malinovskii on 3rd Ukrainian Front had meanwhile developed his own offensive, which opened on 6 March, forcing in turn the Ingulets, the Visun and the Ingul; Pliev's mobile group attacked Novy Bug off the march shortly after dawn on 8 March, clearing it completely in three hours. Cutting the Dolinskaya–Nikolayev railway line, Pliev's columns drove on southwards, while on the Dnieper 28th Army took Berislav and closed in on Kherson, clearing it by 13 March. The last stretch of the Dnieper had been cleared of German troops. Pliev's mobile columns moved out from Novy Bug on a deep out-flanking drive, while seven German divisions lay trapped in the Bereznegovatoe–Snigiriveka area between the Ingulets and the Ingul. Nikolayev, lying between the lower Ingul and the estuary of the Bug, held out almost until the end of March, but higher up the river Malinovskii's armies pulled up to the southern Bug by 22 March. The road to Odessa lay open and on 11 March, in the fresh set of *Stavka* directives designed to increase the co-ordination of the three Ukrainian fronts, Malinovskii had received instructions to speed up his pursuit, to cut the German escape route to the southern Bug, seize river crossings on the Konstantinovka–Voznesensk–Novaya Odessa and Tiraspol, with his ultimate objective the Prut and the Danube—the Soviet frontier.

In between urging greater speed on Malinovskii, Stalin also issued fresh personal instructions to Marshal Koniev; with Koniev over the Dniester in some strength, Stalin proposed that part of 2nd Ukrainian Front forces turn south to move along both banks of the river, while the remainder drive west and south-west for the Soviet frontier. The southerly drive Stalin aimed at the line of retreat of two German armies (Sixth and Eighth) and one Rumanian army (the 3rd), trapping them between Koniev and Malinovskii. Koniev therefore set 40th, 27th and 52nd Armies on southern and south-western courses, using one rifle corps (51st) of 40th Army to attack towards Khotin and thus collaborate with Zhukov's left flank in encircling German forces at Kamenets–Podolskii.

Koniev's columns set out in this last phase of the Soviet offensive and by the evening of 25 March had reached the Prut, the Soviet frontier with Rumania; during the next twenty-four hours the main body of 27th and 52nd Armies drew up to the river along a forty-mile front from Lopatkina (south-east of Lipkany) to Sklyana (a few miles north of Jassy). Marshal Zhukov had meanwhile loosed his best armoured formations and crack Guards armies to the south along the valley of the Zbruch, the tanks roaring across the mud through Trembovla,

Gusiatino, Chortkov and on to the Dniester crossing at Zaleshchiki. German resistance between the Zbruch and the Seret was flattened, and by 27 March Zhukov's armoured columns were only a few miles from Chernovitsy. Koniev's right-flank army, 40th, duly struck out for Khotin, having forced the Dniester north-west of Moghilev–Podolskii; by 28 March 163rd Rifle Division, 240th Rifle Division and 4th Guards Airborne Division had closed off Khotin and blocked the way to the Prut. First *Panzer* was now trapped, locked into the Cheremovtsy–Dunaevtsy–Studenitsa–Kamenets–Podolskii rectangle by six Soviet armies—3rd Guards Tank and 4th Tank Army, 1st Guards, 18th, 38th and elements of 40th Rifle Armies.

Two Marshals of the Soviet Union seemed to have a *Panzer* army at their mercy. But the trap had not shut tight. On the encirclement front a ten-mile gap stared out between 1st Guards and 4th Tank Army, the latter worn down to a mere sixty tanks. Both 4th Tank Army and 30th Rifle Corps (put under tank army command) had run very low on fuel and ammunition. Three other Soviet armies, 13th, 60th and 1st Tank Army, held the external encirclement, keeping Fourth *Panzer* at bay. On 18th Guards Corps, subordinated to 60th Army, fell the full responsibility for holding the 75-mile sector from Zalozhitsy to along the Dniester as far as Mariampol; further south this task fell to 1st Tank Army, charged with the Stanislav–Storozhnitsa sector. As Soviet armies steadily compressed First *Panzer*'s area north-east of Kamenets–Podolskii, Marshal Zhukov prepared to meet the *Panzer* army break-out—convinced that it would come towards the south, aimed across the Dniester and into Rumania. Soviet radio intelligence reports seemed to confirm this. At 1400 hours on 28 March radio intelligence reported First *Panzer* HQ installations, III *Panzer* Corps and at least two *Panzer* divisions operating behind the Dniester at Khotin. Other reconnaissance reported the preparation of crossing points on the Dniester. During the night of 29 March Marshal Zhukov transmitted warning orders that the 'Dunaevtsy group' was trying to force its way through Kamenets–Podolskii and on Skala–Zaleshchiki from the Lyantskorum–Gumentsy sector; all Soviet formations must proceed with the elimination of the trapped enemy forces and complete it by 31 March.

Within twenty-four hours it became unmistakably plain that First *Panzer* was breaking out to the west, not the south. From Stanislav to a point south-west of Tarnopol (where the encircled German garrison hung on so doggedly that the town had to be stormed), Manstein had built a new front from which he launched a powerful tank attack—with forces undetected by Soviet intelligence—on the external encirclement front which encased First *Panzer*. On 4 April two SS *Panzer* divisions fell right on 18th Guards Corps in the area of Podgaitsy. Soviet troops fell back on Buchach, where three days later the de-blockading *Panzer* divisions met up with the men of First *Panzer* fighting their way out westwards. North of Buchach the fighting went on until mid-April; Zhukov swung his two available tank armies, 1st and 4th, onto a westerly course to charge into the German relief force and to meet heavy German attacks in the Stanislav area, but First *Panzer* inched its way out of the trap. Further north at Tarnopol, *SS Panzer* units tried to smash their way into the beleaguered garrison, but this rescue attempt failed: by 12 April only the centre remained in German hands, but five days of fierce street fighting followed before Tarnopol was finally cleared.

If First *Panzer* escaped, even though badly mauled, the redesignation of Army Group South as Army Group North Ukraine and Army Group A as Southern Ukraine, effective from 5 April, reflected the damage wrought by Zhukov's great cleaving blow. But for all the designation, little of the Ukraine remained in German hands. Zhukov's right flank at Kovel and Vladimir Volynsk rested on Galicia, and to his left Soviet units moved south of Chernovtsy deeper into the Bukovina, with advance guards reaching out to the borders of sub-Carpathian Ruthenia, the doorstep to Czechoslovakia. Marshal Koniev's centre and right-flank armies had forced the Prut on a broad front and were pressing on Jassy; left-flank formations were now deep in Bessarabia on a line runing from Skulyany on to Orgeyev and Dubossari (north-west of Kishinev). Malinovskii's 3rd Ukrainian Front had taken Nikolayev on 28 March; after trapping several German and Rumanian divisions at Razdelnaya, where the German Sixth Army was split down the middle, Malinovskii's centre and left made straight for Odessa. On the evening of 9 April, 8th Guards, 5th Shock and 6th Army prepared to storm the city which was finally liberated on the morning of 10 April. Having freed the principal Black Sea ports—Nikolayev, Odessa and Ochakov—Malinovskii's mobile columns and assault armies drew up to the lower Dniester on a broad front, positioning themselves for a further drive into Moldavia and an advance deep into Rumania, locking their flanks with 2nd Ukrainian Front in the Dubossari–Grigoriopol area.

The great military earthquake that came boiling out of the seas of mud in the south sent violent shocks through Rumania, of which 'greater Rumania' was already being lopped into pieces by Soviet armies. 'Transnistria' carved out for the Rumanians between the Dniester and the southern Bug, sagged to the point of collapse, and the Bukovina, Bessarabia and Moldavia were being rapidly penetrated by Russian troops. The Crimea, in which the Rumanians had a last, lingering but by no means insignificant interest, was under major Russian attack by the first week in April, when Tolbukhin's 4th Ukrainian Front launched its assault in the north against the Perekop and through the Sivash lagoons, the spreading net of salt lakes and stagnant marshes, a livid, inland 'sea'. As the roof began to fall in on 'Greater Rumania', Marshal Antonescu took himself off on 22 March on a visit to Hitler, a step that General Maitland Wilson (British commander in chief, Middle East, with whom Antonescu had already been in contact over a possible 'Western response' to the Soviet advance into Rumania) did not advise. But Antonescu had already left for Berlin, to press for the evacuation or the rescue of Rumanian troops in the Crimea and to seek the concentration of Rumanian forces in Moldavia–Bessarabia, where the last Rumanian divisions, 4th Army, were being called out to man these lines. At Hitler's HQ it was agreed that north of the line Ploesti–Bucharest the newly designated *Heeresgruppe Süd-Ukraine* should take control, while the German command worked on plans for the military investment of Rumania, Operation *Margarethe-II* ('Margarethe'). Hitler had already closed in on Hungary; on 19 March German troops marched into Hungary from Austria, Slovakia and Croatia, meeting no resistance. Premier Kallay fled into the Turkish legation, the enemies of Germany were rounded up and General Szotaj took over the new government. In Bulgaria, communist-led and organized guerrilla activity was growing—the 'Fatherland Front'—but it remained small and militarily ineffectual, while the Bulgarian government still clung to Germany. But the shackles were being fastened on *Festung Europa* on whose easterly marshes Germany must be defended and kept immune from attack by land.

Meanwhile Moscow sounded out the Rumanians, initiating contact in Stockholm in January between the Rumanian minister, Nano and the Soviet *chargé;* Russian diplomats were out to learn what, or if, Antonescu could deliver. These dealings flickered on and off, while in Cairo, all in the presence of the Soviet ambassador, talks opened with representatives of the Rumanian opposition, the future 'Democratic Bloc'. Late in March as Soviet armies crashed into Bessarabia, these talks began to gather momentum. Early in April Molotov publicly asserted Soviet claims to Bessarabia and the northern Bukovina but disclaimed any Soviet intention of either annexing 'Rumanian territory' or 'changing the existing social order', though policy toward Rumania was apparently a cause of dissent and division between Russian officialdom and the Rumanian Communists, the *émigré* group in the USSR or the 'External Bureau' led by Ana Pauker and Vasile Luca. In Rumania, Gheorghiu-Dej and his associates languished in prison. Out of the Stalingrad prison camps, the *émigré* Communists built up the specially indoctrinated pro-communist Rumanian military units, formed into the 'Tudor Vladimirescu Division', one tangible achievement. Pauker and Luca strained hard to thwart a Soviet acceptance of any voluntary Rumanian surrender, preferring straight Red Army occupation, in the wake of which would come ready-made communist government and the indoctrinated ex-prisoner divisions to operate as the security arm. The Rumanian 'problem' had still some way to run.

The Soviet command could look with real satisfaction on the damage it had inflicted on the *Ostheer*'s southern wing, now visibly crumpled; ten German divisions destroyed, eight disbanded owing to losses, sixty divisions halved in strength and eight left with only a remnant of their men. The two super-soldiers Manstein and Kleist, who had for so long cast immense shadows in the east, suddenly vanished in a Hitlerian storm-cloud of dismissals. Marshal Zhukov had won his protracted encounter with Field-Marshal von Manstein.

Elsewhere the Soviet winter offensive had only partly lived up to expectations; in the nothern theatre, though Leningrad was freed, Soviet armies did not break right into the Baltic states; in the 'western theatre', for all the brief, promising start in late February when Rokossovskii attacked towards Rogachev and took it, the marsh and swamp of the Drut—wet as ever in the persistent thaw—dragged the Soviet advance to a halt. Only in the south, where Soviet war industry pumped in almost 5,000 guns and 4,600 tanks to the three Ukrainian fronts between January and March, were *Stavka* expectations not only fulfilled but surpassed. The German sacrifice at Korsun did not prevent the massed Russian attack. The very obliteration of that salient put Koniev in a position to crash through from the Dnieper to the Dniester in less than a fortnight, which in turn triggered off Zhukov's great slicing blow to the south.

Even as the German southern wing was being thus divided into one force covering southern Poland, the other pressed back into southern Moldavia and backing on the Danube, Stalin, the *Stavka* and the General Staff with select Front commanders began hammering out the shape of the next phase of Red Army operations. Simultaneously *Generalmajor* Gehlen at *Fremde Heere Ost* also examined Russian operational intentions in a sombre and alarming document, '*Zusammenfassende Beurteilung der Feindlage vor deutschen Ostfront . . .*', a summary of evidence and intelligence data compiled into an estimate dated 30 March. Gehlen, insisting upon a strictly limited circulation for this document, argued that the Russians would press through the Balkans, the *Generalgouvernement* (occupied Poland) and the Baltic states; breaking into *Mitteleuropa* and moving upon the 'easterly frontier areas of the *Reich*'. The Russians would aim above all else at shattering the remainder of organized German force and could be expected to utilize every fold of geography to assist this. For those who anticipated a 'pause', Gehlen pointed to previous experience—dating all the way back to Stalingrad—which amply proved that the Russians could sustain extended offensive operations (not least by extraordinary exploitation of railway networks); for others, Hitler included, who waited weekly for Russian 'exhaustion', Gehlen trundled out a sinister set of statistics on the state of Russian reserves. In sum, Gehlen took a very serious view indeed of developments on the Eastern Front now that the southern zone had virtually ceased to exist as a strategic entity. There could be 'no doubt' that the Soviet command would aim a very powerful blow through the great gap ripped out between the Dniester and the Pripet, attacking before the German Army could build a defensive front of any kind; any failure to counter this Soviet westerly north-westerly assault on the Lvov–Kovel axis meant jeopardizing the deep southern flank of Army Group Centre from which 'the gravest consequences' (*krisenhafte Entwicklung*) must ensue.

Col.-Gen. Kurochkin's 2nd Belorussian Front had already tried to develop an offensive in the direction of Kovel. The German garrison at Kovel had been encircled, but German tank attacks drove in a corridor to free the trapped men; Kovel remained in German hands and Soviet troops fell back to the outskirts of the town. On 5 April the 2nd Belorussian Front was disbanded. Marshal

Zhukov meanwhile proposed a deep outflanking move on Lvov in an operational plan he submitted to Stalin at the end of March: Zhukov envisaged the final destruction of German forces in the Kamenets–Podolskii area, the full investment of the Chernovitsy region, to be followed by an offensive against Lvov, bringing his right flank to Vladimir–Volynsk, the centre to Lvov and the left flank to Drogobych. Marshal Zhukov selected Peremysl as his terminal point, but the outflanking move on Lvov remained his prime thought. Lack of forces prevented the immediate implementation of this plan, but other factors also intruded, not least that Stalin had only just embarked on his great appraisal of the strategic situation. Front commanders received instructions to present their views on future operational commitments, whereupon Stalin conducted his long-distance telephonic interrogations, poking, probing and piling question on question, concentrating on Rokossovskii's Belorussian Front. The General Staff carried out a systematic survey of every Soviet front, beginning with Karelia in the north. While *Stavka* co-ordinators closeted themselves with Front Military Soviets, the General Staff put its first proposal in mid-April to the *Stavka*—a temporary turn to the defensive. Stalin refused to consider the idea at first: *'produmaem eshche'* ('Let's think this over'), which meant mulling over his own ideas for further Front offensives. On 16 April, however, Stalin permitted the north-western and western 'theatres' to go on to the defensive; all other fronts would also consolidate, but no commander was to 'rush on to the defensive'. All orders for the defensive must be read as 'preparatory moves for an offensive' and to make sure of no immediate slackening Stalin delayed the formal *Stavka* directive to the southern fronts until early May, though authorizing the requisite orders for the north and west between 17 and 19 April.

At the end of April, the General Staff completed the master plan for the summer offensive, the full scope of which was known only to Stalin and five Soviet officers—the Deputy Supreme Commander (Zhukov), the Chief of the General Staff (Vasilevskii) and his deputy (Antonov), the Chief of the Operations Section (Shtemenko) and his deputy. The new *Plan operatsii* embodied the main features of what was designed as the Red Army's decisive campaign—to feint on the flanks in the north-west and the south, with the massive core of the offensive aimed at the centre, in Belorussia, to wipe out the last great concentration of German strength, Army Group Centre, and thus blast a path into Germany itself.

5

Breaking the Back
of the *Wehrmacht*:
April–August 1944

General Antonov, deputy chief of the Soviet General Staff, received Anglo-American notification of 31 May (with a small margin on either side to allow for weather conditions) as the date for *Overlord,* the cross-Channel attack, at the end of the first week in April 1944. The information reached him direct from Maj.-Gen. Deane and Lt.-Gen. Burrows, heads of the American and British Military Missions in Moscow, who feared that the Russians might be so overstretched by their successes in the southern theatre that they would not be able to regroup in time to launch their offensive promised to synchronize with *Overlord.* It was wiser, therefore, to give the Soviet command as much warning time as possible. In the middle of the month the Prime Minister and the President sent their own signal to Stalin, intimating that the Channel invasion would be launched 'around "R" date,' which the British and American officers had already communicated to the Soviet General Staff, a signal that went out amidst growing Anglo-Soviet strain over the Polish question. At the end of March, Stalin turned on the Prime Minister with another denunciation of the Polish *émigré* government in London, coupled with a protest at the methods of 'intimidation and defamation' and a repudiation of the 'gratuitous insult' to the Soviet Union in suggesting Soviet–Polish hostility. Nor was it entirely fortuitous that Stalin linked his attack on the 'London Poles' with a lunge in the direction of the 'Yugoslav *émigré* Government', 'which is akin to it [the London Polish government]', and even more pointedly stressing the similarity between 'certain generals' of the Polish government in exile and the Serb General Mihajlovic, the latter a declared and discovered collaborator with the Germans.

At this juncture, Stalin, the *Stavka,* the State Defence Committee (*GKO*) and the General Staff were still involved in the preliminaries to planning the summer campaign of 1944, a campaign intended to inflict decisive defeat on the remaining German armies lodged on Soviet soil. The damage inflicted by Soviet forces in the 'southern theatre' had been both unexpected and immense: the winter campaign by Soviet reckoning had inflicted almost a million casualties on the German and

German-allied armies, the brunt of the losses being borne by German formations
(unlike the Stalingrad débâcle). One German army vanished at Stalingrad; in
1943-4 no less than four—the Sixth, Eighth, Sixteenth and Eighteenth—were
bludgeoned into military wreckage and a fifth army, the Seventeenth in the
Crimea, was near annihilation. Two army groups, North and South, had been
splintered, three *Panzer* armies had been severely mauled, leaving only one (Third
Panzer with Army Group Centre) relatively unscathed. At the end of 1943 the
German order of battle in the east paraded thirteen armies, four of them *Panzer*
armies; now only ten showed up on German strength, with only one full *Panzer*
army in being and one undergoing refitting in Galicia. 'Satellite armies' made a
sudden reappearance, first a Hungarian army and then two German-Rumanian
armies. The defence of what was left of the 'southern theatre' posed well-nigh
unmanageable problems for the German command since the unity of the area
was irreparably shattered. The deep Russian penetration into the Bukovina isolated
Galicia from the 'Rumanian zone' and communications between them could be
maintained only by the roundabout route through Hungary. Hungarian divisions
now in Galicia passed under General Model's command. Rumanian divisions
with German stiffening or under German command for the moment held on to
western Moldavia, but in Transylvania Hungarian and Rumanian troops eyed
each other in mutual hostility in territory bitterly disputed between them.

The Soviet–German front still ran its 2,000 miles from north to south, forming
two huge bulges: north of the Pripet marshes Army Group Centre anchored in
Belorussia and based on Minsk jutted into the Soviet lines, while south of Pripet
Soviet armies protruded deep into the German southern flank. Here in the south
the Red Army massed up to forty per cent of its infantry armies and eighty per
cent of its tank strength, with only one-third of its total fighting complement
lodged on the 'central sector' north of the Pripet marshes. The present limit of
the Soviet advance brought the front in the north-west to east of Narva, east of
lake Peipus and Pskov; in the west, the line ran from east of Vitebsk, Orsha,
Moghilev on to west of Mozyr; in the south-west Soviet armies drew up west
of Kovel, Lutsk and Tarnopol; in the south-east, west of Suchavi, north of Jassy
and along the line of the Dniester to the Black Sea. For the moment, and with
only a reluctant assent from Stalin, Soviet armies were turning to the defensive,
first in the north-west and the west, then in the south, though Stalin delayed
instructions to the south-western and south-eastern commands as long as possible.
By this time the final offensive operation of the winter campaign was launched
against the German Seventeenth Army in the Crimea, long shut off from the
main body of German troops. Reduction of the German redoubt in the Crimea
fell to Tolbukhin's 4th Ukrainian Front, entrenched in its bridgeheads on the
Sivash and at Perekop, while away to the eastern tip of the Crimea troops of
the Independent Coastal Army had landed on the Kerch peninsula.

Together with Marshal Vasilevskii, Tolbukhin and Biryuzov (commander and
chief of staff of 4th Ukrainian Army) had been summoned by Stalin in March

to attend a special briefing in Moscow on the proposed Crimean operations. Standing before a relief map of the Crimea which showed all known details of German deployment and defences, Stalin listened to an exposition of the attack plans involving the 4th Ukrainian Front, the Independent Coastal Army, the Azov Flotilla and the Black Sea Fleet. Tolbukhin proposed to attack across the Perekop isthmus and through the Sivash lagoons, using G. F. Zakharov's 2nd Guard and Kreizer's 51st Army; the main attack would come across the Sivash, bringing Soviet troops into the rear of the forces in the Perekop, followed by a drive on Simferopol and Sevastopol. At the other end of the Crimea, on the Kerch peninsula, men of the Coastal Army under General Yeremenko had established another bridgehead; Yeremenko now planned to drive into the interior, take Kerch, destroy the enemy garrisons, block the escape route through Ak-Monai and prevent any transfer of German troops north to counter Tolbukhin's push. For air support, Tolbukhin had Khryukin's 8th Air Army; Yeremenko, Vershinin's 4th. Marshal Vasilevskii remained *Stavka* 'representative' with 4th Ukrainian Front, and to supervize Yeremenko's operations Stalin sent Marshal Voroshilov, his post at the Central Partisan Staff now wound up. The old war-horse gradually came snorting back.

General Jänecke, commanding 150,000 mixed German–Rumanian forces (the bulk of the German Seventeenth Army brought off from Taman), rested considerable confidence in the fortifications behind which his eleven divisions manned the lines covering Perekop, the defences against Kerch, the Ak-Monai positions, and finally Sevastopol itself, where Soviet troops had held out against massive German attacks for almost a year. Mad and cruel though Hitler's decision was to immure his men in the Crimea, the winter waned and still no Russian attack materialized; the Sivash lagoons had not frozen and now they appeared to present a formidable barrier. The Perekop fortifications had a full complement of pill-boxes, anti-tank ditches and 'the Turkish Wall', itself a good defence line. In 1920 Red troops under Frunze had stormed Perekop and its fortifications held by the 'Black Baron', Wrangel, operations studied by the German command and utilized to base its present defences on the high ground not much beyond Ishun. German gunners with their batteries covered these 'impregnable' defences, though along the Sivash the Rumanian divisions took themselves off to the relative comfort of the hard, high ground, leaving only detachments to screen the salt-flats and the marshes. To stiffen a wilting morale, the German command paraded much of its strength, especially in artillery, and placarded its determination 'to bar the Crimea to the Bolsheviks'. But the stillness, rent only by occasional artillery exchanges (when Soviet reconnaissance planes carefully registered German gun positions), served merely to thicken the atmosphere of suspended doom.

On the morning of 8 April, beginning at 0800 hours, Soviet guns to the north along the Perekop isthmus opened fire in 2nd Guards area, where the infantry went into the attack under cover of smoke-screens. Soviet shells exploding in so constricted a space blew defensive positions to pieces, and two and a half hours later the guns in 51st Army opened fire, this time on the Sivash sector. Zakharov's Guardsmen pushed into Armyansk, while Kreizer's infantrymen and gunners manoeuvred their guns and light tanks on pontoons, the men working in biting salt water where no horse would go, through the small but treacherous Sivash 'sea'. On 9 April Yeremenko attacked from his bridgehead on the Kerch peninsula, fighting to capture Kerch itself, while Kreizer's men dragged their rafted guns and lorries to the southern end of the ruined Chongar bridge and went ashore in some strength, ready to strike out of the Sivash and into the rear of the Perekop defences. General Jänecke had already ordered his units out of Kerch and on to the Ak-Monai line: when Kreizer on 11-12 April burst out of the Sivash bog, Jänecke had no option but to pull his divisions out of Ishun. Two 'impregnable' lines were already breached or turned—Ishun and Ak-Monaiskii. When 4th Ukrainian crossed the Sivash and took Tomashevka, Biryuzov reported this to Vasilevskii and added to his signal: 'Permit me, in the name of the Front command, to present you, Alexander Mikhailovich [Vasilevskii] with the keys of the Crimea.'

Biryuzov did not exaggerate. Kreizer's 51st, with 19th Tank Corps in the lead, slashed through the Rumanians and on to Simferopol, from which Jänecke had hoped to launch a counter-blow. On his way Kreizer smashed up the three German divisions pulling back from Ishun. Yeremenko had meanwhile burst through the 'bottleneck' at Ak-Monai, cutting off two German divisions which now turned south along the coast road running from Sudak to Yalta. In less than a week, Soviet troops had rolled up the main defence lines, dispersed the Rumanians and hammered the German garrison; it remained now to subdue Sevastopol, to fight it out amidst the base's forts and trenches, for there was no chance of rushing the defences.

General Jänecke planned to hold the northern face of Sevastopol to keep Soviet guns out of range of the docks and wharfs, from which German ships were moving all spare equipment and even lifting off Rumanian troops. A smaller German force (two divisions) took up positions to the east and south-east, holding the formidable *Sapun-Gory* (Sapun Heights), a long exposed ridge dropping down into a valley, the same valley where the Light Brigade had charged the Russian guns ninety years before (the 'valley of death'). Here, along the south-eastern axis, Tolbukhin proposed to make his main thrust with 51st Army and units of the Coastal Army that passed under 4th Ukrainian Front command. Towards the end of April, more and more Russian artillery as well as air reinforcements moved up; Zakharov's 2nd Guards prepared to attack from the north across the Mackenzie Heights, but Tolbukhin shifted his main weight on to the left flank, against the Sapun Heights, and planned to use 19th Tank Corps in a sweep from the south into the German rear. Marshal Vasilevskii approved these plans and early in May preparations were almost complete. The *Stavka* demanded rapid action and immediate results; what had taken the Germans 250 days in 1941-42—the reduction of Sevastopol—must now be done in a few hours.

On the fair, fine morning of 5 May Zakharov's Guards, attacking in the north along the Mackenzie Heights, opened the Soviet assault on Sevastopol, where General Almedingen had taken Jänecke's place, though he left more or less undisturbed the earlier plans to fight to the north where most of the mobile artillery was deployed. In the face of heavy German fire, 2nd Guards fought its way up the Heights, extensive minefields slowing the advance. After two days of bloody combat, Tolbukhin unleashed his main attack from the east against Sapun Heights with 51st Army and the Coastal Army. Moving by night, Kreizer's 51st had crossed the Bakchisarai mountains and now lay in front of the northern slope of Sapun Heights; the Coastal Army to the south had taken Balaklava and waited to storm the southern end of Sapun. By dawn on 7 May Colonel Pavlov's 12th Assault Engineer Brigade had cleared a passage for Colonel Rodionov's 77th Rifle Division (51st Army); 11th Guards Rifle Corps (Coastal Army) was assigned to attack the southern sector. Tolbukhin and Vasilevskii installed themselves at forward HQ in Balaklava. Up with 51st Army, Biryuzov watched the opening barrage supported by dive-bombers cover the heights almost completely in smoke and dust. Kreizer's men were astride the ridge by mid-morning and a sapper from 12th Assault Brigade hoisted a Red banner. In the afternoon both Soviet armies, 51st and the Coastal, had fought up the western slopes and battled to break into the Inkerman valley. Once there, the route to Sevastopol lay open.

Within hours German troops had begun falling back in the northern sector, towards the ferries or the Inkerman bridge; 2nd Guards launched assault boats into the bay. From Sapun Heights Russian infantrymen pushed their way into the outskirts of Sevastopol and on to the main station, 10th Rifle Corps (51st Army) in the lead, and engaged in heavy street fighting. Tanks from 19th Corps swept along the coast from the south, on to the Kherson spit, to what Soviet intelligence identified as the German 'disaster line', the final point of German resistance. On the evening of 9 May Sevastopol had fallen entirely to Soviet troops; on 10 May Tolbukhin reported this to Stalin, who, even before Tolbukhin had finished speaking, demanded the complete clearance of the Crimea within the next twenty-four hours. Soviet dive-bombers, fighter-bombers and artillery relentlessly harried German troops fleeing by boat out of Sevastopol. Squadron after squadron bombed the last remaining airfield in German hands near Kherson. The remnants of the German Seventeenth Army withdrew into the Kherson spit, the long finger of land with the lighthouse at its point where in a last flicker of resistance German troops tried holding off the Coastal Army with AA guns depressed and firing over open sights. But the end had come. Soviet guns ranged freely over the trapped regiments, Soviet aircraft jumped boats and rafts making for the open sea, Soviet warships and motor-gunboats patrolled the coastline intercepting and sinking rescue ships. The long lines of dead bobbed in the water, inshore and out to sea, while the living shuddered under the final Russian bombardment. By noon on 12 May, 25,000 German troops surrendered at Kherson. Soviet estimates of total German losses—the virtual annihilation of

Seventeenth Army—reached 110,000 killed, wounded and captured. The revenge for 1942 had been both massive and swift.

While Tolbukhin's troops had been slicing through the Crimea, the Soviet high command had finally committed itself to a main strategic plan for operations in the summer. Previous offensive plans had fallen short in co-ordinating several fronts, in not providing proper aim and direction to Soviet operations. Since March the General Staff had been working on an exhaustive analysis of the Soviet–German front, inspecting each Soviet strategic unity in turn. Chief of Operations Shtemenko and Marshal Timoshenko, the latter acting for the *Stavka,* carried out a detailed inspection of the situation in the north-west, 1st and 2nd Baltic Fronts in particular; the 'main blow' could not be lauched here, nor further north, for though an offensive could lead to knocking Finland out of the war, this hardly meant mortal danger for Germany. On the 'western axis', the situation looked rather different. North of the Pripet marshes, in the Belorussian bulge, German forces covered the route to Warsaw and could mount a flank blow at Soviet armies aimed at East Prussia, as well as menacing the flank and rear of Soviet fronts on the 'south-west axis', seriously complicating a Soviet drive on Lvov and a thrust into Hungary. South of the Pripet marshes Soviet armies had struck deep along the 'Lublin axis', but their strength had suffered through unbroken commitment to offensive operations; to mount a 'main blow' here must involve extensive regrouping and reinforcement from interior reserves. North of the marshes lay Army. Group Centre, whose divisions tied down considerable Soviet strength; Moscow still lay within range of German bombers on their Belorussian airfields. The destruction of Army Group Centre seemed, therefore, both the logical and the desirable strategic objective to pursue. But was it feasible? Already Soviet armies on the 'western axis' had tried and failed too often, with grim losses, to pull down the Belorussian 'balcony' about Army Group Centre's head.

The General Staff thus arrived at two fundamental conclusions: that simultaneous offensive operations on all Soviet fronts were undesirable and impossible, and that the misfortunes of the Western Front could be attributed not merely to German strength but to 'organizational failures' on the Soviet side, the immediate corrective to which must be to split the Western Front into two entities. The Western Front disposed of five armies (thirty-three rifle divisions, three artillery, one AA and one mortar division), one air army, one tank corps and nine tank brigades; the front had previously attacked in the direction of Vitebsk, Orsha and Moghilev, thereby dissipating its striking power. The precise recommendation of the General Staff envisaged splitting the front, moving the headquarters further forward up to the fighting formations, and bringing in reinforcement. Front commanders had meanwhile completed the 'questionnaires' sent out to them on operational possibilities. Rokossovskii at the Belorussian Front had reported to Stalin (and also to the *Stavka* in writing) that his front should take in all formations operating in the Polesia sector and in the Kovel area, thus enabling him to deal with both the Bobruisk and the Lublin 'axes'. After a fierce argument, the *Stavka* approved this proposal and Rokossovskii received orders to plan operations on this basis. By 12 April, the investigation of the Western Front carried out by the *GKO* (the State Defence Committee) was complete, and the tally of 'subjective' and 'objective' shortcomings filled out.

Apparently at an early stage in its 'investigation' the *GKO* had itself plumped for splitting the Western Front into two new fronts, 2nd and 3rd Belorussian, since early in April Stalin was consulting Marshal Vasilevskii—then with 4th Ukrainian Front in the Crimea—about a possible commander for 3rd Belorussian. The new 2nd Belorussian Front (the command of the designation under Kurochkin had been wound up on 5 April) went to General I.E. Petrov, the able and energetic commander of the Independent Coastal Army, currently storming its way through the Crimea. But the 3rd Belorussian Front command was even more important. Vasilevskii nominated Chernyakhovskii, 60th Army commander on the 1st Ukrainian Front, whom Marshal Zhukov on 5 March in a special telegram to Stalin had recommended for immediate promotion to colonel-general. Ivan Danilovich Chernyakhovskii had already displayed exceptional ability; thirty-eight years old, a regular officer of Jewish origin, orphaned when typhus struck his family in the Civil War, he began his military career as a cadet at the Odessa Infantry School in 1924, serving with the tank forces in the 1930s. In 1941 he commanded the 28th Tank Division in the Baltic district, fought in the north-west until 1942, went to Voronezh to command 18th Tank Corps, and then to 60th Army, the army he commanded at Kursk and used like a rapier in 1st Ukrainian Front operations early in 1944. Stalin also consulted General Antonov, who confirmed Marshal Vasilevskii's choice. Chernyakhovskii became the youngest Front commander in the Red Army when his appointment was confirmed on 12 April. Two days later he took over the old Western Front administration at Krasnoe, while General Petrov set up his 2nd Belorussian HQ at Mstislavya. The old, battle-scarred Western Front, having survived for three years, died an official death on 24 April 1944.

By mid-April the General Staff had completed its outline plan for the 1944 summer offensive, involving 5-6 fronts extending from Idritsa in the north to Chernovitsy in the south, though operational planning considerably expanded this range. The General Staff plan envisaged the summer offensive being opened with the Leningrad Front attack, timed for the beginning of June and aimed at Vyborg, to be supplemented by the Karelian Front striking out for Svirsk–Petrozavodsk to knock Finland right out of the war. Once the Karelian attack began, the main operations of the summer campaign—the offensive in Belorussia—would open, with a fair prospect of attaining surprise and accomplishing the destruction of Army Group Centre. As this offensive unfolded, persuading the German command that this was the 'main blow' against which German reserves should be moved from the south, then the major offensive 'on the Lvov axis' mounted by the 1st Ukrainian Front would open. Meanwhile, 2nd Baltic Front would appear to be

on the point of launching its own operations, thus restraining Army Group North
from trying to help its neighbour on the right, Army Group Centre. With success
in these operations, it was reasonable to consider that the Soviet offensive could
be swung in new directions—to Rumania, Bulgaria and Yugoslavia, though not
excluding Hungary, Austria and Czechoslovakia.

In its final form the General Staff plan went to the *Stavka* for consideration
at the end of April. As such, it was used to define the main political objectives
of the summer campaign, which were spelt out in Stalin's May Day order. The
Soviet objective was to clear Soviet soil of remaining German troops, to strike
out in order to lift 'the Fascist yoke' from Poland, Czechoslovakia and the
'fraternal' Slav nations. These national and international flourishes had a place
all their own; now that the Allies were closing in on Germany they assumed
vast new importance, but the Soviet command worked feverishly to keep its
plans and planning absolutely secret, essential if the Belorussian attack was to
come as a stunning surprise to the German Army. The full outline of the summer
campaign was kept within the circle of five men only. All telephone and telegraph
traffic was rigorously controlled. At Front command the smallest possible number
of officers worked on operational plans and all draft orders were written out by
hand; the political administrations with fronts and armies received orders to lay
on 'defensive ideas' thick. Signal centres closed down their big transmitters, and
formations used only low-power sets, none of which must be located within 20–
30 miles of the front line.

The General Staff aimed to convince the German command that the Soviet
offensive would develop in the south and in the Baltic area. On 3 May the two
fronts selected to 'dis-inform' the German command, 3rd Ukrainian in the south
and 3rd Baltic in the north, received special orders on 'operational camouflage':
3rd Ukrainian was to 'concentrate' 8–9 rifle divisions, with supporting armour
and artillery, on its right flank (north of Kishinev), 3rd Baltic would 'concentrate'
east of the river Cherekh, all 'preparations' to be fully effective for the period
5–15 June. To lend greater credence to the idea of a southern attack the Soviet
tank armies remained in position in the south-west, but the bulk of the new
equipment and reinforcement went to armoured units about to regroup for the
Belorussian attack. None of the Belorussian fronts disposed of a tank army,
though a preliminary General Staff plan called for a powerful tank 'fist' to strike
towards Bobruisk–Minsk, principally to block the movement of German reserves.
Almost immediately Chernyakhovskii asked the *Stavka* for a tank army to be
assigned to his front, a request supported by the General Staff which resulted in
5th Guards Tank Army being moved up to 3rd Belorussian Front.

Between April and May the Soviet command drastically altered its distribution
of strategic unities north and south of the Pripet marshes. The splitting of the
Western Front now brought the total of major Front organizations north of Pripet
to eight (three Belorussian fronts, three Baltic fronts, two northern fronts), with
at first only three in the south—1st, 2nd and 3rd Ukrainian. Here the commanders

were rapidly changed round: Marshal Koniev took over 1st Ukrainian, Malinovskii 2nd Ukrainian, Tolbukhin 3rd Ukrainian (the armies of his old 4th Ukrainian Front were transferred from the Crimea to 2nd and 3rd Ukrainian). Somewhat later 4th Ukrainian Front reappeared, this time under General Petrov, whose fortunes suffered a blow almost as soon as he took over 2nd Belorussian: this new front was finally inserted on Koniev's left flank between 1st and 2nd Ukrainian, its purpose to operate with special mountain troops in the Carpathians.

Stavka 'co-ordination' of the four-front offensive (1st, 2nd, 3rd Belorussian, 1st Baltic) aimed at Army Group Centre presented difficulties and peculiarities. Neither Bagramyan (1st Baltic) nor Chernyakhovskii (3rd Belorussian) were experienced Front commanders; Marshal Vasilevskii took these two under his wing, while Marshal Zhukov assumed control of 1st and 2nd Belorussian. General Petrov's tenure at 2nd Belorussian was brief, thanks to Lev Mekhlis, the 'political member' of the Military Soviet. Mekhlis had denounced Petrov to Stalin as unfit for his present command, reporting that he was ill and always requiring medical attention, plus a pack of the usual Mekhlis lies. Mekhlis did not think Petrov— a commander at Odessa and Sevastopol, defender of the Terek, Coastal Army commander—'capable' of carrying out his present responsibilities. At Mekhlis's prompting Stalin therefore removed Petrov and appointed Col.-Gen. G.F. Zakharov (2nd Guards Army commander in the Crimea) as Front commander. Two months later Petrov, with his experience of mountain warfare, took over the new 4th Ukrainian Front. Also attached to 2nd Belorussian Front was a special 'General Staff group' under Shtemenko, Chief of Operations, subordinated in all operational questions to Marshal Zhukov but with special authority to contact the Chief of the General Staff directly in all questions of planning. By mid-May, however, the General Staff had finished its detailed planning for the Belorussian operation and on 20 May General Antonov signed the handwritten operational brief, a few sheets of paper with maps attached. On receiving the General Staff paper, Stalin asked what code-name the General Staff proposed for the operation. Hearing that none had been so far affixed, Stalin at once suggested *Bagration*, in honour of the Russian commander of 1812 mortally wounded at Borodino.

On 23 April General Antonov had written to Maj.-Gen. Deane that the Soviet General Staff was 'satisfied' with ' "R" date' (the timing of *Overlord*). Antonov then intimated with a brevity bordering on the enigmatic that the Red Army would attack simultaneously in the east, but he gave no hint of time or place. At this stage neither of these had, in fact, been decided. The General Staff plan submitted to the *Stavka* selected Belorussia as the best target for a Soviet attack but no specific date was mentioned. On the Soviet–German front the Soviet command took a whole series of measures to hide their intention of attacking in the centre and at the same time worked on an even larger deception scheme connected with the cross-Channel attack; the object was to persuade the Germans that an invasion would not come before July and that July was also the likeliest date for a Soviet attack. Under *Bodyguard* (the combined deception operation) the Russians worked to suggest a joint Allied attack on Norway, and went about concentrating ships and men to lend credence to the idea of an assault on Petsamo. Information was leaked about 'preparations' for a Russian concentration at the centre of the Soviet–German front, to be ready for action at the end of June and with reserves to be trained for July. Meanwhile the Soviet tank armies remained bunched up in the southern theatre, posing yet another apparent threat.

Gehlen at *Fremde Heere Ost* submitted a steady stream of reports and assessments of Soviet operational intentions and capabilities to the German high command. On the German side, an early Soviet thrust in the direction of Lvov—precisely the attack Marshal Zhukov had proposed in March—seemed as imminent as it was likely and, because 1st Ukrainian Front held an extended front from Kovel down to the Bukovina, late in April German–Hungarian troops launched their own attacks on the left flank of 1st Ukrainian to hinder Soviet concentrations for the presumed attack on Lvov. Hungarian troops went into action between the Carpathians and the upper Dniester. Soviet units pulled back a little but apart from these tactical adjustments held their positions intact.

In his major intelligence surveys, *Wichtige Abwehrmeldungen*, Gehlen drew on many sources of information to establish Soviet operational intentions—agents' reports, order-of-battle information, the neutral press, the Soviet press and Soviet broadcasts. Early in May Maj.-Gen. Gehlen presented an agent's report on a secret conference in the *Stavka* held under Stalin's presidency at the end of March where two offensive plans were discussed: either a major attack in the Kovel–Lvov area with a drive on Warsaw (and a Polish rising in the German rear), or an offensive in the Baltic with supporting attacks in the south. According to this agent, Stalin selected the second plan which also included a Polish rising. Tank strength was another indicator: on 3 May Gehlen reported 39 armoured corps (106 units) in the line, 1,200 Soviet tanks facing the German group *Süd-Ukraine*, 500 deployed against *Nord-Ukraine*, 423 against German Army Group North and a mere 41 at the centre—2,214 tanks, which could be reinforced to 2,437 in less than four weeks and more than 3,400 after one month, to give a grand Soviet tank strength (with reserves) of 8,117. The radio silence was duly noted, especially in the south, and the German command anticipated that it would be broken only when operations began. It looked on this evidence more and more like an attack in the Kovel–Lvov area, and possibly a major attack in the Baltic zone. Meanwhile German intelligence picked up *Bodyguard* rumours of 'Soviet–American naval planning' in Novorossiisk for a landing on the Rumanian coast.

By mid-May the first operational plan for Operation *Bagration*, the onslaught against Army Group Centre in Belorussia, had been completed: in this form it envisaged the elimination of the German salient in the Vitebsk–Bobruisk–Minsk area in order to reach a front running from Disna on to Molodechno, Strolbtsy and Starobin, thereby crushing the German flanks and breaking through the centre of the defensive front with concentric attacks aimed at Minsk. Current Soviet estimates of German strength reckoned on encountering 42 German divisions in the Belorussian salient, to be destroyed by 77 Soviet divisions, three tank corps, one mechanized corps, and one cavalry corps, six artillery divisions and three Guards *Katyusha* divisions. The General Staff proceeded to divide the four Soviet fronts involved in *Bagration* into two main components, Group A (1st Baltic and 3rd Belorussian Fronts) with 39 divisions and two tank corps, and Group B (2nd Belorussian and the right-flank armies of 1st Belorussian Fronts) with 38 divisions, one tank and one mechanized corps. For reserves the *Stavka* dipped at once into the Crimea, proposing to move out 51st Army to Gomel and 2nd Guards Army to Yartsevo; at the beginning of May a small General Staff group flew to the Crimea to arrange the movement of these armies and to hand over the defence of the Crimea to the remaining units of the Coastal Army.

Almost at once the General Staff discovered a flaw in its plan. German strength, fixed at forty-two divisions, was turning out in the light of fresh reports to be appreciably higher; though 2nd Baltic Front had the task of holding Army Group North, thereby eliminating the danger of a German attack in the Soviet flank, this Soviet Front appeared to be much too weak to restrain Army Group North, which might turn to help its neighbour on the right. But the attention of Marshals Zhukov and Vasilevskii was directed to ensuring one principal objective, the destruction of a 'significant' element of German fighting strength during the actual breakthrough operation in the German forward defences, which were heavily manned. Zhukov and Vasilevskii therefore proposed to concentrate a mass of artillery and aircraft with the Front commands, in particular 'artillery break-through divisions' with heavy-calibre guns. The need to pin down and to wipe out German troops in the tactical defensive zone, to wreak the greatest possible havoc here, arose from the supposed difficulties of 'encirclement' operations: only Vitebsk raised no problem, for there Soviet troops already held this German strong-point in a vice. Analysis of past Soviet experience, at Stalingrad and in other operations, confirmed that the actual encirclement and subsequent destruction of enemy troops on a major scale demanded no small amount of time; in Belorussia, the German command could use time to bring up reserves and could rely on the terrain, with its bogs and thick woods, to hinder any Soviet attempt to build a firm encirclement front. The problem for the Soviet command therefore involved not only smashing German divisions as they stood in their defensive positions but also preventing surviving units from fleeing to the abundant protection provided by the Belorussian swamp and forest.

Far away in the west 'D-Day' was fast approaching, though the Soviet high command had learned through the American and British Missions of several postponements in the date of the cross-Channel attack. To finalize Soviet preparations for Operation *Bagration,* Stalin summoned top Soviet commanders to a massive battle conference which lasted for two days, 22 and 23 May. General Antonov headed the General Staff party. Front commanders Rokossovskii and Bagramyan joined the two *Stavka* 'co-ordinators', Marshals Zhukov and Vasilevskii; Col.-Gen. Chernyakhovskii had also been summoned, but illness prevented his attending. The members of the Military Soviets of 1st Belorussian, 3rd Belorussian and 1st Baltic Fronts sat in with Novikov (air force commander), Voronov and Yakovlev (artillery), Khrulev (rear services), Peresypkin (signals) and Vorob'ev (engineers). Petrov had not as yet been relieved of his command, but he received no orders to attend the conference since his Front, 2nd Belorussian, had not been assigned a major attack role.

The conference opened with a presentation of the General Staff plan for *Bagration,* and in the subsequent discussion the main operational task was defined as the encirclement and destruction of the main force of Army Group Centre east of Minsk (although the General Staff disliked the term 'encirclement' for these operations). This raised at once the question of the rate of advance required both by infantry and mobile formations; here the General Staff formally supported Chernyakhovskii's 3rd Belorussian Front acquiring a tank army, and 5th Guards Tank Army was assigned to this Front command. The General Staff had also miscalculated over securing the right flank from possible attack by Army Group North. Here General Bagramyan, commander of 1st Baltic Front, proposed that, rather than commit all his Front armies to the main attack, he should operate to guarantee full security against interference by Army Group North. Bagramyan's suggestion was taken up and adopted, so that now 1st Baltic Front, instead of striking on to the east of Minsk after taking Vitebsk, would attack westwards to outflank Polotsk from the south and seal off Army Group North from German troops fighting at the centre. As additional security, 2nd Baltic Front would mount its own limited operations in the north. The southern flank presented no such comparable problem and did not require substantial forces to secure it.

The real row came over Rokossovskii's operational plan for 1st Belorussian Front. As far back as March, Rokossovskii, on learning from Stalin about possible offensive operations aimed at Bobruisk and Brest, asked that Soviet forces operating on 'the Kovel axis' (the old 2nd Belorussian Front) be brought under his own command, thereby extending his front by 300 miles with its flank armies scattered across the Polesian marshes. On 2 April the *Stavka* approved Rokossovskii's proposal: 1st Belorussian acquired 61st, 70th and 47th Armies from the defunct 2nd Belorussian Front and in turn handed over 10th and 50th Armies to the Western Front (itself soon to be wound up). At the same time Rokossovskii and his chief of staff General Malinin had worked out plans for the destruction of German forces in the Minsk–Baranovichi–Slonim–Brest–Kovel–Bobruisk area, to bring Soviet forces to the Minsk–Slonim–Brest line and thereby cut German road and rail links to a depth of 150 miles or more, thus paralysing the German defence on 'the western axis'. Rokossovskii envisaged a two-stage operation, the first lasting no more than twelve days, mounted by the four armies on the left flank and designed to destroy the German defences with a southerly attack. By seizing bridgeheads on the eastern bank of the western Bug from Brest to Vladimir–Volynsk, the way would be open to turn the whole right flank of Army Group Centre; the left-flank armies would move from Brest into the rear of the German armies, while the right flank simultaneously launched a second offensive, this time towards Bobruisk–Minsk, the whole operation taking thirty days and requiring a couple of tank armies to accomplish the full manoeuvre.

Rokossovskii's grand design fell through, because the *Stavka* ruled out any possibility of moving a tank army into the Kovel area, but the General Staff Operations Section took over the suggested lines of advance for its own *Bagration* plan. Five weeks later, on 11 May, Rokossovskii submitted a second plan for 1st Belorussian Front operations, proposing this time the elimination of German troops at Zhlobin, followed by an offensive in the direction of Bobruisk–Osipovichi–Minsk. The striking feature of this revised plan was the double attack on Bobruisk, one attack aimed along the northern bank of the Berezina, the second along the southern bank, with a supporting attack in the direction of Parichi–Slutsk–Baranovichi. This plan passed into the overall operational planning without any undue comment, but suddenly at Stalin's war council it became the centre of fierce argument. Stalin himself objected to the double attack on Bobruisk, seeking instead one single 'main blow'. Rokossovskii refused to consider only one attack. During the course of the argument, Stalin twice sent Rokossovskii into a neighbouring room 'to think it over', and on the second occasion Molotov and Malenkov followed Rokossovskii into his immediate exile. Both urged Rokossovskii to fall in with Stalin's suggestion—'Do you know who you are arguing with?', they asked. Rokossovskii stuck to his guns and intimated that, if the *Stavka* insisted on a single attack, he would ask to be relieved of his Front command. After the third presentation of his 'report', Rokossovskii convinced Stalin, who announced that he liked generals who knew their job and their own mind— there would be a double attack on Bobruisk.

Operation *Bagration* emerged in its final form from the *Stavka* conference: the destruction of Army Group Centre would open with simultaneous blows on the German flanks to flatten them in the areas of Vitebsk and Bobruisk, as well as wiping out German troops at Moghilev. The road to Minsk would then be open, and west of Minsk Soviet troops could sever the German escape route, entrap Army Group Centre and proceed to destroy it piecemeal by air attack, by ground attack launched from three fronts and by partisan operations. Though the 2nd Belorussian Front had not been assigned a primary attack role, it was to pin down as much German strength as possible to prevent its use against 1st and 3rd Belorussian Fronts. The one commander absent through illness, Chernyakhovskii of 3rd Belorussian, arrived in Moscow on 25 May and on being briefed by Zhukov and Vasilevskii on *Bagration* submitted his Front operational plans. Both marshals approved, but that same evening, during the *Stavka* examination, Chernyakhovskii received instructions to plan an additional attack, one directed along the Orsha–Minsk highway as well as the operation aimed at Bogushevsk; by way of compensation, Chernyakhovskii learned that 5th Guards Tank Army had been definitely assigned to his Front, plus one artillery breakthrough division. Throughout the night Chernyakhovskii, his chief of staff (V.E. Makarov) and Lt.-Gen. V.F. Mernov (General Staff officer responsible for this 'axis' and an old military schoolmate of Chernyakhovskii's from their days in the Kiev Artillery School) worked out a new Front plan. Early on 26 May Chernyakhovskii and Shtemenko (General Staff Operations) submitted the plans to the *Stavka* and that evening travelled out to Stalin's 'out-of-town' *dacha* on the Dmitrovsk highway. Here Stalin inspected the plan and approved it without further ado. But the last word on 5th Guards Tank Army had by no means been said, and Stalin played a very personal hand here.

The May conference set 15-20 June as the probable date for opening Operation *Bagration*. The General Staff on 21 May had set in train the first measures to regroup (that day Tolbukhin received a personal secret telegram prescribing the movement of the Crimean armies), but pulling armour and infantry from the interior districts and sliding out armies from the flanks was a gigantically complicated task. The railways worked furiously, overloaded and stretched to the limit. Front staffs received categorical instructions to maintain the strictest security of movement: all trains must be guarded, all de-training to be carefully controlled and done only under orders. Moving Rotmistrov's 5th Tank presented special difficulties. The Front command wanted to see it withdrawn in stages, but the General Staff considered this merely weakened the formation; 5th Tank's orders specified that two corps (Vovchenko's and Kirichenko's) must move out fully manned and with no less than 300 tanks. For some time reinforcements had been moving discreetly into the central area and the four fronts: 1st Tank Corps to 1st Baltic Front, 11th Guards Army and 2nd Guards Tank Corps to 3rd Belorussian, 81st Rifle Corps to 2nd Belorussian, 28th Army, 9th and 1st Guards Tank Corps, 1st Mechanized and 4th Guards Cavalry Corps to the right flank of 1st Belorussian Front, 8th Guards and 2nd Tank Army destined for the left flank, with 2nd Guards Cavalry Corps. Many of these formations were first pulled back into reserve, like Chuikov's 8th Guards Army withdrawn from the Dniester bridgehead of 3rd Ukrainian Front, then assigned to the central sector, though several weeks elapsed until they moved into position. For the moment, the *Stavka* assigned 51st Army and 2nd Guards (moving from the Crimea) to its special reserve. Marshal Novikov, air force commander-in-chief moved up dense masses of aircraft, no less than eleven aviation corps and five aviation divisions.

Although *Bagration* occupied pride of place as the hammer-blow aimed at Army Group Centre, the *Stavka* and the General Staff laboured simultaneously on the attack plans involving the outer flanks, with the offensive to knock Finland out of the war high on the list of operational priorities, involving the Leningrad and Karelian Fronts with a combined strength of forty-one rifle divisions, almost half a million men, 10,000 guns and over 800 tanks. During the month of

May Govorov on the Leningrad Front prepared an attack on Vyborg, to drive north of Leningrad across the Karelian isthmus; Meretskov on the Karelian Front planned an attack to seize Petrozavodsk. Govorov proposed to use Gusev's 21st Army for his main attack, a force of nine rifle divisons reinforced with tanks, to drive straight through the Finnish defences, along the Vyborg highway and the coastal railway all in a matter of ten days. To smash its way through, the Leningrad Front disposed of half the available artillery to fight across the old, bloody battlegrounds of the 1939-40 'Winter War'.

The decision for an all-out attack on Finland came speedily on the heels of the breakdown of the first sustained Soviet–Finnish peace probe. Towards the end of 1943 Mme Kollontai at the Soviet Embassy in Stockholm let the news seep out that the Russians would not be averse to talking to a Finnish delegation. This produced a cautious response from the Finns and a furious reaction from Germany now bent on a binding Finnish pledge not to sign a separate peace. Washington at the beginning of 1944 urged the Finns to talk terms, but when in February Paasikivi talked to Mme Kollontai he heard how chilling Russian 'terms' might be—the 1940 frontiers and the elimination of German troops in Finland. Late in March a two-man Finnish delegation, Paasikivi and Enckell, went to Moscow to test the truth of these terms, only to return on 1 April with the stunning news that they were, in fact, even harsher—the 1940 frontiers as a matter of principle, the internment or expulsion of German troops and the payment of a war indemnity of $600 million spread over five years. On 18 April the Finnish parliament rejected this 'peace offer'. In Germany General Heinrich, Chief of Staff, suffered some rough handling from Keitel and Jodl because the Finns had even dared to go to Moscow, but no German sound and fury could alter the basic Finnish conviction that catastrophe was looming in the east and Finland was on the edge of this terrible whirlpool.

The Russians now applied the lessons of 1940 with enormous energy and a menacing heartlessness. The war in the north had been savage and was to be brought to a savage end. To break through the Karelian isthmus and on to Vyborg, the Soviet command massed thousands upon thousands of guns and almost 1,000 *Katyusha* rocket-launchers, 536 bombers and ground-attack aircraft and almost 500 tanks; the Baltic Fleet added 175 guns (most of them 130mm and upwards) trained on the Finnish defences. The Baltic Fleet also lifted the main body of 21st Army from Oranienbaum across the gulf of Finland to the Karelian isthmus. The final operational plan committed two fronts (Leningrad and Karelian) to a double attack, the right wing of the Leningrad Front on the Karelian isthmus, and two armies of the left wing of the Karelian Front operating in southern Karelia, 7th Army fighting between lakes Onega and Ladoga and 32nd Army attacking north of lake Onega, supported by nineteen partisan detachments under orders to blow up enemy dumps and rail links. The *Stavka* set 10 June as the date for Govorov's attack with the Leningrad Front, with Meretskov's Karelian Front starting its own operations a few days later.

In the 'southern theatre' the command changes took effect in mid-May; Marshal Zhukov formally handed 1st Ukrainian Front to Marshal Koniev, who in turn relinquished 2nd Ukrainian Front to Malinovskii. The German command considered it almost axiomatic that the Russian summer offensive would be launched by 1st Ukrainian Front jutting out into the western Ukraine. For the defence of Lvov and its surrounding area—a valuable communications centre between German troops in Poland and Rumania, and the shortest route to the upper Vistula, thence into Silesia—fresh German divisions drew up in considerable strength throughout May and early June, until some thirty-eight divisions with a powerful tank force had been concentrated. The Lvov region also lent itself to defensive operations, covered as it was by the numerous tributary rivers of the Dniester, none formidable but a hindrance to an attacker. Here the Red Army would be fighting over one of the old battlefields of the Imperial Russian Army, which in August–September 1914 had launched the offensive in Galicia that smashed the Austro–Hungarian armies and opened the way for a drive into Silesia, though not before serious misjudgment on the part of the Russian command had allowed the Austrians to escape complete encirclement and thus to fight on west of Lvov. It was an instructive lesson, which Marshal Koniev evidently put to good use. After Stalin's April directive, 1st Ukrainian Front turned to the defensive along its 220-mile sector (running west of Lutsk, east of Brody, west of Kolomiya and Krasnoilsk) after fighting off German–Hungarian attacks which gradually petered out. German Army Group *Nord-Ukraine* meanwhile built up its strength in infantry and tank divisions.

On taking up his command Koniev went at once to 38th Army HQ at the centre of the front to examine plans for an offensive operation, whose form was dictated both by the terrain and by the location of German operational reserves. The northern sector was flat but marshy, the centre around Lvov hilly with numerous rivers and streams, the southern sector decidedly hilly; German reserves were grouped round Kovel, Lvov and Stanislav. At the very beginning of June Stalin telephoned Marshal Koniev and instructed him to present his plans to the *Stavka,* where he must report forthwith. Koniev's attack plan rested principally on the idea of a double blow, one launched from the Lutsk area and aimed at Lvov itself to destroy German forces in this area: at Lutsk, Koniev proposed to mass fourteen rifle divisions, two tank corps, a mechanized corps and a cavalry corps, all with concentrated artillery support, on a six-mile breakthrough sector; on the 'Lvov axis', fifteen rifle divisions, four tank corps, two mechanized corps and a cavalry corps on a seven-mile breakthrough front. The 'Lutsk assault group' would consist of 3rd Guards Army (Gordov), 13th Army (Pukhov), 1st Guards Tank Army (Katukov) and a 'cavalry-mechanized group' under Baranov; the 'Lvov group' comprised 60th Army (Kurochkin), 38th Army (Moskalenko), 3rd Guards Tank Army (Rybalko), 4th Tank Army (Lelyushenko) and another 'cavalry-mechanized group' under Lt.-Gen. Sokolov. Grechko's 1st Guards Army and Zhuravlev's 18th Army, supported by Poluboyarov's 4th Guards Tank Corps, would secure the left flank of 1st Ukrainian, with Zhadov's 5th Guards Army going into Front reserve. Koniev aimed to encircle German forces at Lvov, split Army Group *Nord-Ukraine* (hurling one part into Polesia, the other back to the Carpathians) and bring 1st Ukrainian Front to the Vistula.

The double thrust involved Koniev in both deception measures and regrouping: 1st Guards Tank Army had to be moved up against Lutsk, 4th Tank to Tarnopol, 38th Army and 18th Army were redeployed, with deception measures designed to give the impression that the tank armies were moving on to the left flank. Not that Koniev could do much to disguise either his forces or his intentions massed against Lvov, though an attack aimed towards Rava–Russkaya did stand some chance of being concealed. The double thrust had much to recommend it, and Koniev submitted his final operational plan to Stalin exactly on these lines. Stalin reacted to Koniev's double attack exactly as he had received Rokossovskii's proposals for Bobruisk—grave disapproval. Stalin argued that success before had been based on a single powerful thrust by fronts and now was no time to depart from this practice. Koniev, like Rokossovskii, argued back. Stalin insisted on one powerful attack in the direction of Lvov, and Koniev responded by emphasizing that a frontal attack on Lvov would merely give the German defence most of the advantages, the likeliest outcome of which must be that the Soviet offensive would fail. 'You are a very stubborn fellow. Very well, go ahead with your plan and put it into operation on your own responsibility.' With that, Stalin finally yielded and Marshal Koniev was free to fight as he saw fit, though he would personally suffer the consequences if the operation failed.

The day on which Stalin telephoned Marshal Koniev to prepare 1st Ukrainian Front plans, the Front commanders involved in Operation *Bagration* received the final *Stavka* directive (dated 31 May) specifying their lines of advance, objectives and the forces to be committed. The General Staff map had been finally marked up on 30 May with all the operations forming the full complex of the 1944 'summer offensive'. The tally of forces assigned to *Bagration* now comprised four Fronts, the Belorussian partisan formations, the Long-Range Air Force (*ADD*) and the Dnieper Flotilla (the old Volga Flotilla). Bagramyan's orders for 1st Baltic Front specified co-operation with Chernyakhovskii's 3rd Belorussian: after destroying forces at Vitebsk–Lepel, 1st Baltic would force the western Dvina and move into the Lepel–Chashniki area. Two armies must penetrate enemy defences south-west of Gorodka and invest the Beshenkovicha area, while other Front forces operating with right-flank armies of 3rd Belorussian Front seized Vitebsk and then moved to Lepel, covering themselves against possible German attack from Polotsk. Chernyakhovskii's 3rd Belorussian Front would conduct its operations linked with 1st Baltic to its right and 2nd Belorussian to its left. Joint Front operations must destroy German forces in the Vitebsk–Orsha area after which 3rd Belorussian forces would make for the Berezina. Chernyakhovskii already knew of the double thrust to which his front was committed, with one attack by two armies aimed at Senno (north-west of Vitebsk) and then moving north-west to trap the Vitebsk garrison, the second attack unrolling along the Minsk highway towards Borisov. Once Orsha and Senno fell, Chernyakhovskii was to get his armies on to the western bank of the Berezina. One reinforced army from 2nd Belorussian Front would take Moghilev, with Front forces pursuing the enemy along the Moghilev–Minsk highway as far as the Berezina. Rokossovskii's 1st Belorussian Front received formal orders to strike two blows with two armies committed to each attack, the first from Rogachev to Bobruisk and Osipovichi, the second from Ozaricha to Slutsk: the Front assignment included the encirclement and destruction of German forces at Bobruisk, the seizure of the Bobruisk–Glusha–Glussk area, and an advance on Osipovichi–Pukhovichi and Slutsk. Rokossovskii thus was committed to two main axes, Bobruisk–Minsk and Bobruisk–Baranovichi, but until his right flank armies reached a line running west of Slonim (north-east of Brest), his centre and left-flank armies would remain stationary.

At 1600 hours on 4 June Marshal Vasilevskii, Chief of the General Staff and *Stavka* 'co-ordinator' for 1st Baltic and 3rd Belorussian Fronts, arrived at Chernyakhovskii's HQ. During the small hours of 5 June Marshal Zhukov, Deputy to the Supreme Commander and 'co-ordinator' for 1st and 2nd Belorussian Fronts, flew out to Rokossovskii's HQ, arriving at 0500 hours and starting the operational planning three hours later. At the end of their first day's work, both Vasilevskii and Zhukov reported to Stalin in midnight calls. Vasilevskii intimated that the situation remained unchanged, but Zhukov complained in strong terms that rail movements were falling sharply behind schedule—would Stalin therefore urge Kaganovich (head of the railways) and Khrulev (head of rear services) to speed up the movements? For a week both marshals complained in increasingly exasperated terms to Stalin about delay with rail movements: tanks, artillery, ammunition and fuel all failed to arrive either on time or in the right quantities. Vasilevskii personally asked Kaganovich to get Rotmistrov's tank army into the area no later than 18 June. And now 2nd Belorussian Front was gasping for lorries and aircraft fuel.

During that first week in June when Zhukov and Vasilevskii worked to heave Soviet armies into the line for the enormous attack aimed at Army Group Centre, Govorov made final preparations for his attack on Vyborg (Viipuri) to wipe Finland out of the war. 'The vast naval and ground forces' committed to *Overlord* in the west had launched the cross-Channel invasion of 6 June. The night before the invasion the Prime Minister sent off a signal to Stalin (dated 5 June) explaining the reason for the last minute postponement, the weather conditions; now, finally, 'proper weather conditions' prevailed and 'tonight we go'—all 5,000 ships and 11,000 'fully mounted aircraft'. The Prime Minister's next signal followed on D-Day itself, 6 June: 'Everything has started well. The mines, obstacles and land batteries have been largely overcome. The air landings were very successful . . . Infantry landings are proceeding rapidly . . . The weather outlook is moderate to

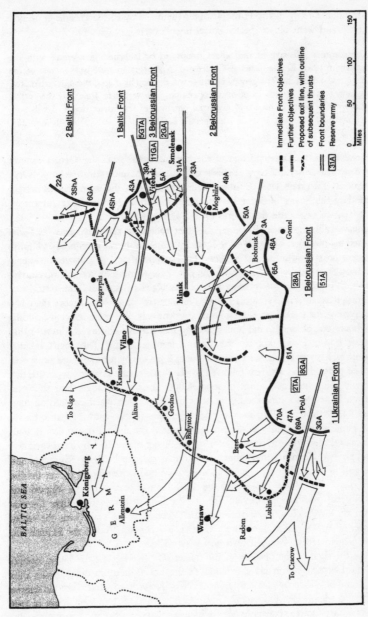

Map 7 The Belorussian offensive: 1944 General Staff planning map

good.' Stalin's reply to the Prime Minister (with a copy to the President) opened austerely and went on to specify Soviet intentions:

The summer offensive of the Soviet troops, to be launched in keeping with the agreement reached at the Teheran Conference, will begin in mid-June in one of the vital sectors of the front. The general offensive will develop by stages, through consecutive engagement of the armies in offensive operations. Between late June and the end of July the operations will turn into a general offensive of the Soviet troops. I will keep you posted about the course of the operations. [*Perepiska*. . . . , vol. 1, no. 274, p. 267.]

General Antonov, Deputy Chief of the General Staff, sent Maj.-Gen. Deane of the American Mission a copy of this text as a guide to and confirmation of Soviet intentions. Two days later (9 June) Stalin lifted one of the wrappings of secrecy shrouding the Soviet offensive by informing the Prime Minister that 'tomorrow, June 10, we begin the first round on the Leningrad Front'.

Heavy-calibre guns had opened the 'first round' in the north even as Stalin drafted his message. Throughout 9 June, 240 Russian heavy guns fired at Finnish defences on the isthmus, and at dawn on 10 June after 140 minutes of intense fire supplemented by ground-attack aircraft, 21st Army took the offensive across a nine-mile front on the western side of the Karelian isthmus. The thunder of the first Russian artillery barrage carried as far north as Helsinki, more than 150 miles away; the second pre-attack bombardment was even more ferocious, hurling pill-boxes out of the ground and smashing in defensive positions. Almost 1,000 aircraft bombed and shot up the Finnish front and rear. The Soviet infantry assault was massive and fierce: on 11 June, 23rd Army attacked and on special *Stavka* orders heavy artillery followed in the wake of the infantry, with 203mm mortars being fired at a range of some 1,000 yards at the larger Finnish block-houses. From 9–13 June the big guns of the Baltic Fleet warships fired off more than 11,000 rounds. Two reserve rifle corps were thrown into the battle for the first Finnish defence line, where Govorov pressed the fierce Russian attack along the coastal road. By the evening of 15 June Soviet troops had battered their way through two Finnish defence lines, torn out a passage between Kivenappi and the gulf of Finland and prepared to drive on Viipuri. Reinforced by yet another rifle corps, 21st Army broke into the third Finnish line, the main Viipuri line. As Russian columns approached Viipuri, the Finnish command sought German help. At 1900 hours on 20 June Viipuri (Vyborg) fell. On 21 June the second Soviet offensive opened in southern Karelia, but beyond Viipuri the Finnish line, stiffened now with German men and guns, held.

At the time of the opening of the Soviet offensive against the Finns, opinion in the German command still clung to the belief that the main Soviet blow must fall in Galicia against Army Group *Nord-Ukraine,* to which German reserves were accordingly directed. Army Group Centre, thought to be the object of mere diversionary attacks, had only one division in reserve with Fourth Army and one with Third *Panzer,* a dangerous state of affairs even for coping with a subsidiary Russian attack. At the end of May Hitler categorically forbade Army Group Centre to pull back to the Dnieper or Berezina lines. Worse was to come. Governed by the fixation about a Soviet offensive in Galicia, *OKH* withdrew LVI *Panzer* Corps in the Kovel sector from the control of Army Group Centre and subordinated in to Army Group *Nord-Ukraine,* thus gravely weakening the central sector. No longer could Army Group Centre hope to use its former tactics, so far successful, of moving up reinforcements to block or check Russian thrusts. Evidence was increasing of a massive Russian build-up against Army Group Centre, apparently deployed to smother Ninth Army at Bobruisk, concentrated against Fourth Army in the Moghilev and Orsha area, and again at Vitebsk to threaten Third *Panzer.* German intelligence was aware that divisions from the Crimea were moving up to the central sector and that 5th Guards Tank Army was also on the move to this front. There was a massive Soviet air presence. Third *Panzer* was identifying crack Soviet divisions closing on Vitebsk, a sure sign that something big was brewing. Yet even at the *OKH* conference on 14 June attended by all Army Group commanders, while Army Group Centre could point to enormous Soviet reinforcement against it, none of this evidence was taken as conclusive. *Feindbeurteilungen* and *Feindlage,* 'enemy intention' and 'enemy situation' assessments, conceded that a rapid build-up against Army Group Centre was feasible, but the idea of a Russian attack in Galicia still held sway. One intelligence report (*Agentmeldung*) dated 10 June mentioned 'a major attack in the next ten days' from Vitebsk and Orsha to Minsk, Baranovichi and even Vilno, but it also stated that an offensive would be directed from the Kishinev–Akermann area. As late as 20 June, *OKW* stuck to the declared view that the blow would come in the south and might be expected when the British and American armies had driven deeper from their coastal bridgeheads.

On the Soviet side of the front, Zhukov and Vasilevskii drove Front and army commanders relentlessly, hammering on the need to speed up the rail movements. On 13 June Vasilevskii countered Stalin's insistent queries about how the Front preparations were going and if his original timetable (15-20 June) would be kept, by stating categorically that 'once again I submit that the final date for beginning operations depends entirely on the work of the railway men: from our side we have done everything and we are continuing to do everything to keep to your timetable.' Roused at last, Stalin turned on Kaganovich and demanded an investigation of rail movement. Traffic did speed up as a result, but the original timetable for *Bagration* could no longer be maintained. Preparations were still not complete, and Stalin agreed to a four-day postponement. The opening of *Bagration* therefore coincided almost by chance with the third anniversary of the German attack on the Soviet Union. By mid-June, however, the ground-attack plans were almost complete. On 10 June Zhukov had asked Stalin to send out the Soviet Air Force commander, Marshal Novikov, to the operational area and on 19 June Zhukov, Novikov and yet another aviation marshal,

Golovanov (in command of Long-Range Aviation, the bomber force) worked on detailed plans for Soviet bomber and ground-attack squadrons.

The *Stavka* directive for *Bagration* (31 May), the basic directive, embodied a relatively new feature in Soviet strategic planning: for the Belorussian operation, immediate Front assignments were limited to a depth of 30–40 miles, and wider objectives were set at a range not exceeding 100 miles (in contrast to previous wildly ambitious, if unrealistic, *Stavka* operational directives). Working under the supervision of Zhukov and Vasilevskii, Front commanders completed their planning for 'immediate assignments' by mid-June: the diary of their respective *Stavka* activities with Front commands is a terse record of how these two marshals, each with his own distinctive style of command, bored into armies, corps, divisions on all four fronts (Shtemenko, *VIZ*, 1966 (2), pp. 72-7):

11 June   *Zhukov*

At 0548 hours reported to Stalin that movements of transport with ammunition for 1st Belorussian Front proceeding behind schedule. . . . At 0655 hours requested Stalin to authorize increased fuel for 16th Air Army which is receiving additional new units. During day proceeded with Rokossovskii to Luchinskii's formation. With him, as well as chief of staff of 28th Army Major-General Rogachevskii, artillery and engineer commanders also, examined operational plan in detail and issued orders on the spot . . .

Vasilevskii

Supervised preparations of 3rd Belorussian and 1st Baltic Fronts. Preparations work on these and other Fronts proceeding to plan. Dangers arise above all from railway movements. Today obliged to approach Kaganovich with request to chase up traffic, to get Rotmistrov in position not later than 18 June.

15 June   *Zhukov*

Present with commanders of corps, divisions, chiefs of arms of troops of 28th Army (Luchinskii) committed to attack.

Vasilevskii

Detailed inspection of combat preparation and supply services for presumed operations of 6th Guards and 43rd Army 1st Baltic Front. During inspection issued series of orders dealing mainly with employment of artillery, tanks, SP Gun regiments and aircraft.

16 June   *Zhukov*

With Rokossovskii and Yakovlev [head of Red Army Artillery Administration] up with corps, division and heads chiefs of arms of troops of 48th Army under Romanenko. Gave orders that by 17 and 18 June to eradicate shortcomings revealed during inspection concerning co-operation and organization of artillery offensive. At 0245 hours during night reported to Moscow on work undertaken during day.

Vasilevskii

Continued with work reported June 15. Ordered Rotmistrov as from 17

June with night marches to move combat ready units into area of Gusino into rear area of Galitskii's army, so as to have the army in this area in full state of readiness in the first days of the operation.

During night of 17.6 reported to Stalin: 'Good impression of new commander of 43rd Army Beloborodov. Corps commanders Vasilev and Ruchkin sent from south working excellently. Gave order allowing Vasilev, sent from Guards to non-Guards corps to retain Guards rate of pay. Request that you authorize my decision and give corresponding order to comrade Khrulev [Chief of Rear Services] . . .'

In its latter stages, much of this work involved the detailed 'Front co-ordination'.

The attack plans devised by the Front commands and supervised down to the last detail by the two marshals involved a considerable degree of 'inter-Front' co-operation in time and space. On 1st Baltic Front, Bagramyan decided to make his breakthrough on a twelve-mile sector south-west of Gorodka, with two mixed armies, Chistyakov's 6th Guards and Beloborodov's 43rd: after the breakthrough, the objective was Beshenkovichi and the forcing of the western Dvina. Elements of 43rd Army in co-operation with 39th Army (3rd Belorussian Front) would attack Vitebsk, while Front armies moved in the direction of Lepel covering the Front offensive operations against any incursion from Polotsk; 1st Tank Corps received orders to make for the western Dvina and Beshenkovichi, once the rifle armies had reached the Vitebsk–Polotsk railway line. Chernyakhovskii on 3rd Belorussian Front set up two 'assault groups' to carry out his immediate Front assignments: 'Northern Group' (39th, 5th Army and a 'cavalry-mechanized group' from 3rd Cavalry and 3rd Guards Mechanized Corps) to attack Bogushevsk, 'Southern Group' (11th Guards, 31st Army) to attack along the Orsha axis. 'Northern Group' received orders to attack on a nine-mile front south-east of Vitebsk, the right-flank divisions of Lyudnikov's 39th to operate with 43rd Army (1st Baltic) in the Vitebsk operation. Krylov's 5th Army would attack towards Bogushevsk–Senno, destroy enemy forces in the Bogushevsk–Orsha area in co-operation with 11th Guards and then move forward to the Berezina. The 'cavalry-mechanized group' had the task of seizing the Berezina crossings north-west of Borisov. 'Southern Group', Galitskii's 11th Guards and Glagolev's 31st Army, was aimed at Orsha and thence Borisov on the Minsk motorway; the 'mobile group' (Burdeinyi's 2nd Guards Tank Corps), having cut the communications of German troops at Orsha, would make for the Berezina at Chernyavki.

But when and where should Marshal Rotmistrov's 5th Guards Tank Army go into action? This crucial decision exercised the *Stavka*, the General Staff and the Front commands. On 17 June Vasilevskii presented the plans for 3rd Belorussian and 1st Baltic Fronts. For two days at *Stavka* meetings in Moscow 5th Guards Tank was tossed about on two possible axes, as a striking force in 11th Guards area aimed at Borisov, or in 5th Army area to attack towards Bogushevsk–Tolochin–Borisov. The *Stavka* proposed to give the *Stavka* co-ordinators, Zhukov and Vasilevskii, the right to decide on 5th Guards' line of advance, but the point at which it would pass under Front control must be subject to General Staff opinion and personally approved by Stalin himself.

South of Smolensk, Zakharov's 2nd Belorussian possessed no armoured force of any significance. On Stalin's orders, Zakharov displaced Petrov and caused consternation in the General Staff group attached to the Front when he disputed the line of advance prescribed in the *Stavka* directive. In the end, however, Zakharov came to accept both the *Stavka* requirement and Petrov's Front decisions. Grishin's 49th Army would strike for Moghilev and then on to the Berezina: Kryuchenkin's 33rd Army and Boldin's 50th Army received orders to hold their positions, though one corps from 50th Army must move into reserve to exploit 49th Army's success.

General Rokossovskii on 1st Belorussian Front, with full permission to mount his 'double attack' on Bobruisk, planned one breakthrough north of Rogachev and a second to the south of the village of Parichi with two 'assault groups' ('northern' and 'southern') mounting concentric attacks aimed at Bobruisk. The 'northern group' (or 'Rogachev group') included Gorbatov's 3rd Army, Romanenko's 48th Army and a 'mobile group' attached to 3rd Army (Maj.-Gen. Bakharov's 9th Tank Corps); 'southern group' also comprised two infantry armies, Batov's 65th and Luchinskii's 28th, with Maj.-Gen. Panov's 1st Guards Tank Corps supplying the 'mobile group' attached to 65th Army. The 'mobile group' would be introduced at the junction of 65th and 28th armies, with Slutsk, Osipovichi or Bobruisk as possible objectives. The five left-flank armies of 1st Belorussian Front (not counting the 1st Polish Army) were for the moment to remain in position, to inhibit any German movement on Minsk and to prepare a major attack in the direction of Kovel–Lublin. This plan Zhukov and Rokossovskii worked over on 20 June, giving orders for the final version to be prepared for submission to Stalin.

By 20 June the four Soviet Fronts assigned to *Bagration* mustered fourteen 'all-arms' armies, one tank army, four air armies, 118 rifle corps divisions, two cavalry corps and eight tank or mechanized corps—1,254,000 men (plus 416,000 of the left-flank armies of 1st Belorussian Front), a combined strength of 166 rifle divisions. Armoured and mechanized units disposed of 2,715 tanks, supported by 1,355 SP guns. Lined up practically hub to hub were 24,000 guns and mobile heavy mortars, supplemented by 2,306 *Katyusha* rocket-launchers. The four air armies deployed 5,327 aircraft (not including the 700 bombers of the Long-Range Bomber Force asigned to operate with 2nd and 3rd Belorussian Fronts). Between them, the four fronts had 70,000 lorries and 43,500 machine-guns. Each day 90-100 trains shifted fuel and ammunition up to the four fronts, while 12,000 lorries operating on Front supply duties hauled up to 25,000 tons in one run—one fifth of the ammunition, and one quarter of the fuel supply required for a 24-hour supply period under the 'norms' set for *Bagration*. The medical services, in addition to setting up their base hospitals, organized 294,000 forward aid stations. And atop this pyramid of men, tanks, guns and aircraft stood

Marshal Zhukov, waiting impatiently to lash Soviet armies forward in a savage attack on the one remaining bastion of German strength on the Eastern Front.

Three days before any Soviet unit crossed its start line, Soviet partisans opened the battle of Belorussia, laying and exploding their demolition charges in the *relsovaya voina*, 'the war of the railway tracks', which the Belorussian Communist Party ordered in the instruction radioed to all partisan units on the night of 8 June. Throughout the short summer night of 19 June more than 10,000 demolition charges ripped up German railway links west of Minsk. The next night, and for three successive nights, the partisans went back to the tracks, sidings and junctions, blasting away with 40,000 demolitions which spread the destruction as far as possible. The lines between Vitebsk and Orsha, Polotsk and Molodechno, suffered heavy damage; the partisans visited even greater destruction on the lines connecting Minsk with Brest and Pinsk, the routes German reinforcement might be expected to take.

The Soviet partisan brigades west of Vitebsk and south of Polotsk, 140,000 men lodged in the thick forest and screened by the swamp of the Ushachi, Lepel and Senno area, had long been the scourge of Third *Panzer* and Fourth Army. To be rid of this menace in the spring of 1944, SS anti-partisan units, assisted in the grim work of *Bandenkrieg* by the 'Kaminsky Brigade' (manned by Russian collaborators), launched two operations–*Frühlingsfest* and *Regenschauer* to wipe out the partisan strongholds in the Ushachi area: a third operation (*Komoran*) planned for June aimed to clear the area further south, to destroy partisan brigades between Lepel and Borisov. In mid-April the partisan hunt began, directed at flushing out and destroying the Ushachi units: the German estimate of Soviet losses reached 7,000 partisans killed. The SS men cut a swathe of blazing villages and massacre through the partisan 'blanket' laid over Third *Panzer*'s rear areas— and possible escape routes. The Soviet military command, by sending in Soviet planes to attack the partisan hunters and by mounting diversionary attacks at the front, did what it could to stave off destruction for the partisan brigades, but they were both mauled and scattered. Yet as thousands of demolitions in June disabled mile upon mile of railway track or knocked out precious rolling stock, it was plain that the German punitive actions had not eradicated the partisans as a force to reckon with.

The Red Army opened its offensive on 22 June 1944, three years to the day after the *Wehrmacht* had first loosed its stunning surprise attack on the Soviet Union. With the massive Soviet build-up now almost complete, all four Soviet Fronts rushed ahead with last-minute preparation. Delays in rail movement had already disrupted the initial Soviet timetable, and as late as 21 June Marshal Zhukov reported to Stalin that six trains were still due on Zakharov's 2nd Belorussian Front. The whole Soviet offensive was staggered, with 1st Baltic Front in the north leading off on 22-23 June, followed by 3rd Belorussian Front, then extending to 2nd and 1st Belorussian Fronts. The time differential was very small, a matter of forty-eight hours at the most from north to south (and to some degree owing to utilizing both tactical and long-range air forces), but its contribution to eventual Soviet success proved to be considerable, since the German command persisted in believing that Soviet troops were merely putting in 'holding attacks', an impression given greater substance since the first Soviet attacks involved only battalions, 'reconnaissance battalions' detached from first-echelon rifle divisions from each front.

At 0400 hours on 22 June Marshal Vasilevskii reported to Stalin that Bagramyan's 1st Baltic and Chernyakhovskii's 3rd Belorussian Fronts stood ready for action. Marshal Zhukov released the heavy bomber force for use by Vasilevskii against the German defences before the full attack of Vitebsk went in, mounted jointly by Bagramyan and Chernyakhovskii. North-west of Vitebsk—where the massive Soviet attack came as an overwhelming surprise to the German command— Bagramyan up at 1st Baltic Front forward command post watched the weather anxiously. Ahead lay the hummocks and the dark lines of forest, Belorussia's great expanse of trees, streams and hills. The recent heavy rain, if it continued, would ruin the going for both men and machines. At dawn, however, the sky cleared and at 0500 hours the morning mists began to disperse under the early sun. His fears set at rest on this score, Bagramyan on the stroke of the hour instructed the Front artillery commander, General Khlebnikov, to fire off the opening Soviet barrage, a sixteen-minute preparation. Now Bagramyan fretted over what forward units would find when they reached the German defences— possibly empty positions, the main force pulled back deep into the defensive zone, with only light forces to the front. The first battalions moved out. Committing battalions recommended itself strongly to Bagramyan as a means of saving artillery ammunition, which might only fall on empty trenches, and as a means of avoiding a possible trap; but his confidence was not shared by a number of officers who nursed private fears about this method of 'developing reconnaissance into battle'. The main attack by 1st Baltic was to be launched along a relatively broad front, a proposal that Marshal Vasilevskii at first rejected only to be won round subsequently by the arguments of the Front command.

Within three hours of the battalions going out, Bagramyan received the kind of battle reports he wanted: the 'reconnaissance battalions' of 6th Guards and 43rd Army signalled that they were involved in fierce hand-to-hand fighting as German troops counter-attacked to recover their forward positions. Maj.-Gen. Ruchkin, commander of 2nd Guards Rifle Corps (6th Guards Army), sent in more battalions and during the day pushed some three miles into the German defensive zone. With the coming of night Soviet formation commanders rushed special night-fighting squads into action to 'hold the Germans by the throat', though the Front command still suspected German disengagement and withdrawal deeper into the defensive system. Third *Panzer*, however, had expected 1st Baltic to drive almost due west on Polotsk, and the present Soviet attacks were falling on 9th Army Corps, holding an over-extended front with only minute reserves. From this small beginning grew the crisis that finally engulfed Col.-Gen. Reinhardt's Third *Panzer* Army.

During the night of 23 June Bagramyan had to decide whether or not to proceed with the full artillery barrage scheduled for the morning or simply to take advantage of the disruption in the German ranks and throw in the main infantry force, relying on ground-attack aircraft for support. At 0400 hours the Front commander issued orders to fire off the barrage against sectors where the German defences remained intact, but the infantry attack would go in mainly with air support. On 23 June German troops saw much evidence of new Soviet tactics. Soviet infantry assaulted the main defence line, opening breaches that they fought to extend in every direction: in the wake of the assault battalions came more infantry with artillery support to clear the area: once the infantry attack had broken through the defences, the big tank formations moved through the gaps, while ground-attack aircraft—in numbers never before seen—pounded German strong-points and gun positions. In this order Bagramyan rolled out his infantry, artillery, aircraft and armour. By mid-morning on 23 June, 23rd Guards Rifle Corps (6th Guards Army), supported by right-flank divisions of Beloborodov's 43rd Army, took Sirotino at the centre of the Soviet breakthrough sector. Bagramyan ordered up more air support, the Soviet infantry cleared the area about themselves while Butkov's 1st Tank Corps rolled towards the gap, though the tanks made slow progress along roads and tracks softened with rain. At Shumilino, where German troops put up stiff resistance, General Bazhanov brought up all available *Katyusha* rocket-launchers to smother the defenders with fire. Together 6th Guards and 43rd Army made up to ten miles into the positions held by IX Corps.

During the course of the day, Soviet air reconnaisance reported a large column of German vehicles moving from the south-west towards the western Dvina. Bagramyan's staff assumed that German troops meant to hold the Dvina line, and if they held it in strength 1st Baltic's offensive could come to a dangerous halt. The main mobile striking force, Butkov's tanks, were still struggling along the soaked roads and only late in the day closed on Shumilino. Bagramyan decided to make a dash for the Dvina with infantry—once the infantry armies got across the river, the tanks could follow. General Chistyakov (6th Guards) and General Beloborodov (43rd Army) received urgent orders to advance with all speed, to be astride the Dvina on the morning of 24 June and to take personal responsibility for moving up bridging equipment and boats as speedily as possible. Throughout the night Soviet engineers and infantrymen dragged pontoons back on to the wet roads from which they so frequently slipped, lorries took each other in tow and road movement officers (*dorozhno-komendantskie chasti*) sorted out the multiple traffic jams. At noon on 24 June General Chistyakov reported to Front HQ that the first Soviet units were over the western Dvina, making a hazardous crossing on improvized rafts, planks and any boat to hand; by the evening the pontoons finally arrived so that a start could be made ferrying over artillery and tanks. But without waiting for his heavy weapons General Beloborodov rushed two corps (1st and 60th) over the western Dvina, sending 60th Corps in the direction of Gnezdilovichi and straight into the rear of the German forces at Vitebsk.

There was need for a speedy crossing of the western Dvina. Marshal Vasilevskii, co-ordinating the operations of 1st Baltic and 3rd Belorussian Fronts, had telephoned to ask Bagramyan for a precise situation report, in particular the location of Beloborodov's corps. Bagramyan's last information was that two corps belonging to 43rd Army were on the western Dvina north-west of Beshenkovicha: General Beloborodov himself had gone up to 60th Corps to supervise the river crossing. Marshal Vasilevskii, rarely given to dramatization, stressed that it was vital to get Beloborodov's right-flank divisions over the river at top speed—'the whole course of the Vitebsk encirclement operation literally depends on this'. The reason for Marshal Vasilevskii's excitement was that the other arm of the pincer moving from the south-west, General Lyudnikov's 39th Army from Chernyakhovskii's 3rd Belorussian Front, had already closed in on Gnezdilovichi. Marshal Vasilevskii continued: 'We have information that the Fascist command has twice sought Hitler's permission to withdraw from the Vitebsk "bag" . . . but it is not Hitler, but us, who must decide the fate of this concentration of troops. In any case we mustn't let go of the Fascists. That depends on rapid operations on the part of comrade Beloborodov.'

Not long after this talk with Vasilevskii, Bagramyan made contact with Beloborodov himself. Revising his orders, the Front commander appointed noon on 25 June as the time limit for 43rd Army's link-up with 39th Army. Since Beloborodov could not now wait for all his artillery to be moved over the western Dvina, Bagramyan promised him full air support instead. Beloborodov was soon to need it. Striking on with 60th Corps, he was only about ten miles from units of 39th Army which were then to the south of Gnezdilovichi; on the evening of 24 June he promised Bagramyan that he would 'close the ring' at noon the following day. During the night of 24-25 June, as 60th Corps drove down from the north-west, German units tried hard to hold the Soviet advance; on the morning of 25 June the 246th German Infantry Division launched a full-scale attack to press 60th Corps right back, an enterprise smashed from the air when Bagramyan ordered 3rd Air Army commander to send in a complete division of *shturmovik* ground-attack planes to support Beleborodov.

On 24 June Third *Panzer* faced a highly critical situation. Bagramyan's assault armies closed on Vitebsk from the north-west, Beloborodov in the lead. The day before Chernyakhovskii had opened 3rd Belorussian Front offensive, attacking in force, and on the first day Lyudnikov's 39th Army, with Krylov's 5th, had broken into the German defences to a depth of some five miles across a 25-mile front. To the north-west of Vitebsk, Third *Panzer's* IX Corps had been badly hammered: to the south-west Lyudnikov was now pushing 6th Corps over the river Luchessa and striking on to the north-west. On 25 June Krylov's 5th took

Bogushevsk by storm, cutting the Vitebsk–Orsha railway line and biting deeper into 6th Corps on Third *Panzer's* right flank: the same day Chernyakhovskii ordered Lt.-Gen. Oslikovskii with his 'cavalry-mechanized group' to push as far and as fast as possible to the west of Bogushevsk.

The drive on Vitebsk was only one of Chernyakhovskii's Front assignments; the second involved a full-scale attack on Orsha itself. A huge battle had begun to unroll along the northern sector of Army Group Centre, but for the first twenty-four hours the drive towards Orsha was stalled: the attack mounted by 11th Guards Army and 31st Army failed to make much progress, largely because the preliminary bombardment fell on open ground, missing the German gun positions and leaving the German defences largely intact. The blame for this belonged to 5th Artillery Breakthrough Corps; their violation of camouflage discipline had long given the game away to the Germans, who methodically plotted the Soviet artillery deployment.

The delay with the second of Chernyakhovskii's attacks now opened a gap between the 'southern group', whose progress was rapid. To plug the breach, Marshal Vasilevskii proposed to use Marshal Rotmistrov's 5th Guards Tank Army, committing it along the 'Bogushevsk axis' with Krylov's 5th Army, a somewhat unwelcome surprise for the tank marshal, who had expected to operate with Lt.-Gen. Galitskii's 11th Guards: fortunately, in a quiet moment, Marshal Rotmistrov had gone over Krylov's plans and operational area, so that he was not wholly unfamiliar with 5th Army's commitments. Rotmistrov had already received orders from Chernyakhovskii to close on 11th Guards Army, but his latest instructions stipulated that the tank army must be ready for action with Krylov's 5th by noon on 25 June. On the morning of 25 June Rotmistrov's tanks were concentrating to the west of Liozno, with the bulk of 1st Air Army—four corps and two divisions under the command of Lt.-Gen. Ushakov—assigned to special support operations, a powerful armoured fist ready to drive deep into the German lines and with ground-attack aircraft available to blast a path for the tanks.

Crashing through woods or fighting over streams and rivulets, the Soviet 'pincers' closed on Vitebsk during the afternoon of 25 June, trapping four divisions of LIII Corps (Third *Panzer*): 5th Guards Rifle Corps from 39th Army—3rd Belorussian Front—linked up as planned with 60th Corps from Beloborodov's 43rd Army. Flank units of 39th Army began fighting their way into Vitebsk itself, Soviet machine-gunners worked their way into the rubble of the suburbs even as Hitler demanded that the town must be held 'at all costs'—a sentence of death passed on the 206th German Infantry Division. Reluctantly Hitler had given permission for LIII Corps to fight its way out to the south-west, but this decision came far too late, for 39th Army had already cut the main escape route for the corps at Ostrovno. In Vitebsk itself, where Soviet and German troops fought it out for possession of suburbs and squares, what the Soviet command wanted was possession of the main bridge over the western Dvina; as 43rd Army crashed into Vitebsk from the north, on the night of 25 June a squad of Soviet sappers under the command of Sergeant Blokhin worked their way to the bridge and killed the guard, whereupon the sergeant swung himself across to dismantle the demolition charges. The next morning Soviet armour and artillery rolled on to the west across the main bridge. Twenty-four hours later the German garrison surrendered to a Soviet ultimatum, leaving 20,000 dead in the shattered town: the commanding general and chief of staff of LIII Corps were taken prisoner. One force of 8,000 German troops did find a way out of Vitebsk, only to be surrounded once more and then wiped out almost to a man.

By the time the Soviet pincers had closed on Vitebsk—25 June—the whole massive Soviet offensive against Army Group Centre was fully and finally joined, a savage, relentless battle rolling across an enormous front. As Third *Panzer* was being dragged down in the north, Zakharov opened his attack on Fourth Army on 23 June and one day later, on the morning of 24 June, Rokossovskii launched a shattering attack against Ninth Army. If there was any moment of decision outweighing all others in the battle for Belorussia, it came on the morning of 24 June. Once Rokossovskii unleashed his armies against General Jordan's Ninth Army, there could be no further doubt that the whole of the German army group was under sustained and fierce attack. That morning, in the Minsk HQ of the army group, Field-Marshal von Busch (Army Group commander) and General Zeitzler (Chief of the General Staff) held a hurried and remarkably inconclusive conference, most of which turned on the subject of Vitebsk alone: Busch suggested pulling Third *Panzer* back to the Tiger Line and asked for reinforcements, but he drew back from discussing the whole situation building up round his army group. Zeitzler was presumably pleased not to have too drastic a list of proposals to present to the *Führer*, but on his return from the Minsk meeting, when he reported to Hitler, Zeitzler failed to get any agreement for a withdrawal by Third *Panzer*. All Hitler authorized was the movement of two *Panzer* divisions by way of reinforcement. From this point forward, Army Group Centre was caught in an impossible situation and progressively drenched with Russian fire, denied any degree of flexibility yet bereft of any effective reinforcement.

Zakharov's 2nd Belorussian Front, attacking with 49th Army east of Moghilev, was already grinding through Fourth Army's defences; the left flank of Fourth Army had to be pulled back to maintain contact with Third *Panzer*'s right, which was being pushed away from Bogushevsk. After three days of dragging battle, on 26 June, forward units of 49th Army crossed the Dnieper and established bridgeheads north of Moghilev; General von Tippelskirch, commander of Fourth Army, in a personal decision that flew in the face of all the 'stand fast' instructions emanating from Hitler, was already pulling his army away from the Dnieper. To rush heavy weapons over the broad Dnieper, the 92nd Soviet bridging battalion moved up its equipment quickly on lorries, laying down two bridges—30-ton and 16-ton—under heavy German fire. By noon on 27 June Soviet sappers had the bridges in position; tanks and artillery moved into the Soviet bridgehead which swelled to some fifteen miles in depth. In the wake of 49th Army came Boldin's 50th, and together on 28 June these two armies stormed Moghilev from the north and from the south-east, a bloody assault which left the Soviet armies reeling with their casualties.

Chernyakhovskii on 3rd Belorussian Front pushed Oslikovskii's mobile group on to Senno, moving as fast as possible towards the Berezina. Rotmistrov's tanks were now fighting their way along the Minsk motor-road and, supported by ground-attack aircraft, they blasted a passage to Tolochino by the evening of 26 June—thereby cutting the German escape route to the west of Orsha. Yet another of the strong-points that Hitler was determined to hold, Orsha, one of the anchors holding the German front in position, fell to 11th Guards and 31st Army on 27 June. Three days after Operation *Bagration* was fully engaged, with all four Soviet fronts in action, Russian armies had made deep penetrations along the entire length of Army Group Centre's front: three German armies, Third *Panzer*, Fourth Army and Ninth Army, were being sliced away from each other. Soviet operations so far followed the original plan: Bagramyan, having invested Vitebsk, was moving towards Lepel and also preparing to strike with his right-flank armies on Polotsk (thus isolating Army Group Centre from Army Group North, the operational variant Bagramyan had himself suggested to the General Staff): Chernyakhovskii's first thrust—the attack from the south-west on Vitebsk—had succeeded and now his second, aimed along the 'Borisov–Minsk axis', was pushing through the gap torn in the German line and reaching menacingly down Fourth Army's long' flank, all the way to the Berezina: Zakharov had closed in on Moghilev, thereby uprooting Fourth Army.

The situation of Third *Panzer* and Fourth Army was serious: for Ninth Army to the south, it rapidly became catastrophic. On the morning of 24 June Rokossovskii lashed out on his right with his 'double attack' on Bobruisk, the operation for which he had risked Stalin's wrath in arguments over operational planning. The basic aim of the Bobruisk operation was the encirclement of Ninth Army by moving along both banks of the Berezina and then destroying the trapped divisions in or near Bobruisk itself: four armies of 1st Belorussian Front, 3rd and 48th ('northern group') and 65th and 28th ('southern group') were committed to the attack. Rokossovskii planned the attack on Bobruisk with three powerful columns. Gorbatov's 3rd Army had orders to attack from the Dnieper bridgehead north of Rogachev in the direction of Bobruisk–Pukhovichi: 48th Army occupied the lower sector, but here marshes and dense woodland forced Rokossovskii to detach most of 48th's divisions to operate on Gorbatov's left flank. The two 'southern group' armies, Batov's 65th and Luchinskii's 28th, had orders to attack along the western bank of the Berezina; two mobile formations, Panov's 1st Guards Don Tank Corps and Pliev's 'cavalry-mechanized group', attached to 6th and 28th Army respectively, would be used to cut German communications west of Bobruisk.

Marsh, bog, woodland, innumerable small rivers and lakes—above all, the formidable river Drut—lay in profusion across Rokossovskii's proposed line of advance. The terrain made careful preparation indispensable, though Soviet commanders too often ignored details of this order. This time, however, they had an exacting task-master to supervise them—Marshal Zhukov, who inspected the terrain and the preparations with all commanders. Commanders who displeased him through carelessness or bad planning were ruthlessly sacked, and 'sacked' meant the threat of a penal battalion: 44th Guards Division commander was hauled unceremoniously out of his command post by Zhukov and virtually demoted on the spot. Marshal Zhukov bore down on General Batov in merciless fashion, interrogating him on every detail of planning and his proposed operations. In the armoured formations all tanks were equipped with brush and logs to carry them over the soft ground of this marshy region: all tank and self-propelled gun units had sappers attached to them as well as infantry. The tanks moved forward on roads of logs, the infantry carried brush 'mats' to ease them over the bogs.

At 0355 hours on the morning of 24 June the guns of 1st Belorussian Front began firing off a two-hour barrage. On the 'northern' sector, 3rd and 48th Armies attacked at 0600 hours, followed one hour later by the two on the 'southern' sector. During the night, bombers from Rudenko's 16th Air Army attacked targets in the German rear, but at dawn the weather worsened and closed down massed air operations. It was only later in the day that Rudenko could launch two big bombing raids, though all told 16th Air Army crews flew over 3,000 sorties on 24 June. During the first day the 'northern group', 3rd and 48th Armies, made little progress, fighting across swampy land on the Drut. But while it proved to be a dismal day for Gorbatov and Romanenko, Batov got off to a flying start: with 18th Rifle Corps in the lead, supported by ground-attack aircraft, 65th Army broke into the positions held by XLI *Panzer* Corps. At 1400 hours, 18th Corps was already on the line pre-selected to move in the armour. The lead battalions of 1st Guards Tank Corps were standing by to move off: Panov gave the order to advance—the code signal *reka techet* ('the river is flowing') transmitted three times—and the first tanks moved forward through the infantry, straightway fighting an action with Ferdinand self-propelled guns, and pushing on into the German lines. The Guards motorized troops, part of Panov's corps, fought alongside 65th Army infantrymen. And in Luchinskii's area, 28th Army, the time had come to move in Pliev's mobile units. By the end of the day both Batov and Luchinskii were five miles inside the positions of XLI *Panzer* Corps on a fifteen mile front, with Panov's tanks well ahead and closing on Knyshevicha. For a few hours the Soviet and German commands had an inverted image of the battle. Grievously dissatisfied with the 'northern' attack, Marshal Zhukov sent his own *Stavka* 'assistants' to take over the direction of Romanenko's 48th Army and Urbanovich's 41st Corps with 3rd Army— 'bad handling of troops' was what Zhukov reported to Stalin. General Jordan at Ninth Army, however, judged this northerly attack directed against 35th Corps on the Drut to be the most serious threat and decided to commit his reserve, 20th *Panzer* Division, to a counter-attack. Late in the day—too late as it proved— Ninth Army commander suddenly realized the proportion of Soviet success in the south against XLI *Panzer* Corps, south of the Berezina; 20th *Panzer* received orders to switch southward and counter-attack the Russian armour now piling in, but this diversion cost valuable time.

On the second day of the offensive the 'northern group' outflanked Zhlobin to the north, the 'southern group' took Parichi and pressed on to the river Ptich at Glutsk. South of the Berezina, Soviet columns cut the railway line leading from Bobruisk. The counter-attack finally launched by 20th *Panzer* into the Russian flank in the south brought no improvement whatsoever. Hauling their guns over the swamps, shoving lorries along clogged roads, building log roads to speed the tanks or picking their way through clumps of forests, Soviet units continued to push on west and north-west, slicing through the road links running out of Bobruisk to the west one by one. Late on 25 June the German command had no very firm picture of what was happening on the northern boundary between Fourth and Ninth Armies, but the growing pressure on Ninth Army placed Fourth Army in a dangerous position; Hitler finally permitted General von Tippelskirch to pull back to the Dnieper, the decision Tippelskirch had already taken for himself and his men, pulling the army out of the most imminent danger and starting a fighting retreat to the Berezina. To the north Third *Panzer* slowly collapsed and to the south Ninth Army had already begun to disintegrate; Fourth Army could be buried alive amidst this gathering landslide of battered corps and divisions.

Throughout the next twenty-four hours Pliev's mobile group and Panov's tanks struck on towards the north-west in the direction of Bobruisk, hacking at Ninth Army's rearward communications. On the evening of 26 June, though insisting that Moghilev must be held, Hitler was prepared to allow Fourth Army to fall back on the Berezina and Ninth Army to pull into the 'Bobruisk bridgehead': Bobruisk finally proved to be the grave of Ninth Army, though Hitler insisted that it must be held to anchor the Berezina line. Gorbatov's 3rd Army, backed by powerful artillery support and with a tank corps (the 9th) at its side, rammed its way to the Berezina and seized several bridgeheads on the western bank, to the north-east of Bobruisk: with the bridges over the river now captured or shelled by Russian guns, units of 35th Corps and XLI *Panzer* Corps trying to pull into Bobruisk were pinned on the eastern bank. Panov's tanks, with Batov's infantrymen in their wake, came striking up from the south-east. The trap closed on five German divisions in Bobruisk itself and to the south-east.

In an attempt to clear the bridges over the Berezina, 20th *Panzer* Division was smashed to pieces; 35th Corps struggled frantically to free itself by attempting to break out to the north where the Russian 'ring' was at its loosest, held mainly by 9th Tank Corps. Rokossovskii ordered three armies, 3rd, 48th and 65th, to hold the 40,000 Germans so far entrapped in the Bobruisk 'cauldron', while the fast units made for Slutsk to the west and for Osipovichi–Pukhovichi (on the road to Minsk). South-east of Bobruisk, between the main highway and Berezina, units of XLI *Panzer* and 35th Corps were stranded in the spreading woods, cut off from Bobruisk by Gorbatov, prodded from the south by Romanenko's 48th Army and now shelled from the western bank of the Berezina by Batov's guns. Inside Bobruisk the German garrison, swelled with troops who had managed to get back to the town, set up strong-points, laid barricades and positioned AA guns to fire at ground targets in readiness for the Russian assault. Towards evening on 27 June units of 35th Corps, with 150 tanks and self-propelled guns leading off, tried once again to blast their way through the Russian trap to the north, but Gorbatov's men turned the German column back. The troops still locked inside the ring set about destroying vehicles, equipment and stores, the smoke from the burning dumps billowing into the evening sky. Taking this as an indication that a major break-out was imminent, Rokossovskii ordered Rudenko to send in a mass of bombers from 16th Air Army: in just under an hour 526 planes—400 of them bombers—dropped 12,000 bombs across the few square miles in which the German corps were encased, a merciless aerial lashing which tore men and machines to pieces, ripping up the ground, smashing the remaining tanks and assault-guns with rocket attacks.

In the morning Romanenko's men moved into the forest to engage the survivors, who finally gave up the struggle by the evening: 6,000 men marched into captivity. The storming of Bobruisk began on the afternoon of 27 June with a Soviet tank attack which the defenders beat off. At dawn the next day, units of 48th Army crossed the Berezina and fought their way through the eastern outskirts of Bobruisk, while a German battle group 5,000 strong from XLI *Panzer* Corps, the commanding general at their head, battled to breakout on the northern edge of Bobruisk, only to be met by Gorbatov's troops. The final Soviet assault went in at 10 am on 29 June, Batov's men cooperating with Romanenko's units to clear the blazing town: further to the west Soviet mobile columns had already taken Osipovichi, the junction on the railway line to Minsk.

One week after the opening of the Soviet offensive, the first phase of the battle for Belorussia ended; with the fall of Vitebsk, Orsha, Moghilev and Bobruisk, the German defensive system of the central sector of the Soviet–German front had cracked wide open. The three German armies had lost over 130,000 men killed, 66,000 taken prisoner (almost half of them—32,000—falling to Rokossovskii), 900 tanks and thousands of motor vehicles. In the north, Third *Panzer* was left with only one badly weakened infantry corps, in the centre Fourth Army stood daily in greater danger of being cut off in its long retreat to Minsk and to the south Ninth Army could count only three or four dispersed and battered divisions from the wreckage of its corps. The whole Russian attack had been ruthlessly pressed home and on some sectors mounted with real fury; though

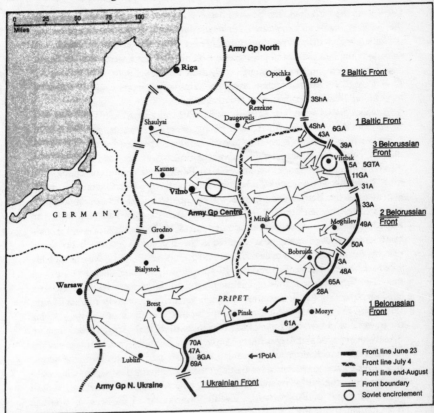

Map 8 Operation *Bagration*, June–August 1944

Soviet tactics had visibly improved, and co-ordination vastly bettered upon past performance, the cost in human life was appalling. General Bagramyan confessed himself shaken to the core by the losses incurred by his front: Zakharov's 2nd Belorussian Front, victor in the bloody immolation of Moghilev, was forced to refit and recoup.

At his headquarters in Obersalzberg, Hitler held high hopes of manning some rear defence line where the Soviet advance would be stemmed as it ran out of steam; on the evening of 28 June Field-Marshal Model assumed command of both Army Group Centre and Army Group North Ukraine, not least to facilitate the transfer of reserves from the concentrations of 'North Ukraine' to the centre.

Yet for all the casualties, the Soviet offensive showed no sign of slackening; on the contrary, as Model took over his new command, Soviet movement on the flanks suggested that something much greater than the capture of Minsk was afoot—to the south Rokossovskii pressed his mobile units westwards on Slutsk and in the north, moving through Lepel, more Soviet columns were making for Molodechno. As the outer claws swept on, the inner pincers could be expected to close on Minsk and thus trap Fourth Army.

Advance Soviet units were already within 50 miles of Minsk, north-east and south-east of the city; Fourth Army, fighting its way westwards, was still a good 75 miles from Minsk. With the 'Minsk meridian' specified by the operational plan of *Bagration* almost within reach, the *Stavka* on 28 June issued revised directives to all four Fronts: Bagramyan's 1st Baltic Front received orders to strike for Polotsk and westwards to Glubokoe; Chernyakhovskii's 3rd Belorussian Front was to force the Berezina, co-operate with Zakharov's 2nd Belorussian Front in taking Minsk no later than 7-8 July and advance its right-flank formations to Molodechno; Rokossovskii would also use part of his forces for a drive on Minsk, but his main strength must be committed in the direction of Slonim–Baranovichi, thereby cutting the German line of retreat to the south-west. Zakharov's orders specified his forcing the Berezina by 30 June/1 July, closing on Minsk no later than 7-8 July and then moving his main force to the western bank of the river Svisloch. The *Stavka* directives set the stage for a two-pronged drive on Minsk, from Borisov in the north-west and from Osipovichi in the south-west—keeping the Soviet line of advance more or less constant with Fourth Army's steady retreat; by advancing along the Moghilev–Minsk axis, Zakharov would maintain the frontal assault on Fourth Army, pushing it into the trap laid to north and south. Bagramyan's operations with 1st Baltic Front were intended to secure Chernyak-hovskii from the north; by swinging out Chernyakhovskii's right flank, as well as the left flank of Rokossovskii's assault force, as far to the west as possible, the German command could neither move up significant reserves nor stabilize the front as a whole.

Lt.-Gen. Oslikovskii's mobile group (made up of 3rd Cavalry Corps and 3rd Guards Mechanized Corps), following its original orders, pushed through Senno while the lead tanks of 3rd Guards Mechanized reached the Berezina north of lake Palik on 29 June, forced a crossing and pressed on to the west, cutting the Minsk–Vilno railway line. To the south of Oslikovskii, 11th Guards Army and the main force of Rotmistrov's 5th Guards Tank Army also bore down towards the Berezina—with Soviet formations and the retreating German Fourth Army all converging on Borisov. Holding off the Russians, a desperate German defence struggled to keep the Berezina bridges open for Fourth Army, the bulk of whose forces still threshed about on the eastern bank of the river in a desperate attempt to move back. Rescuing the Fourth Army meant keeping the Berezina crossing open for a further seventy-two hours, but on 1 July Russian units took Borisov in yet another storming action; two corps of Fourth Army—12th and 27th

Corps—were now wholly marooned to the east of the Berezina, though continuing to fight towards the west. South and south-west of Minsk, Pliev's mobile units took Slutsk on 30 June, then moved in the next two days to Stolbtsy and Gorodeyia, severing the Minsk–Baranovichi railway line and sealing off the escape route deep to the south-west.

On 2 July Model knew that there was now no hope of bringing surviving units of Fourth Army back in strength to Minsk. Minsk itself was directly threatened by Soviet columns to north and south, and the Berezina, against whose eastern bank Fourth Army was pinned, had been crossed in strength by Soviet forces to the west of Lepel. Virtually ignoring the situation at Minsk itself, Model threw his remaining strength into holding open escape routes to the north-west and south-west of the Belorussian capital. Chernyakhovskii—his eyes fixed on Vilno—swung his main force in the direction of Molodechno (north-west of Minsk), assigning the assault on Minsk itself to Glagolev's 31st Army and one corps of Rotmistrov's 5th Tank: Burdeinyi's 2nd Guards Tank Corps would also drive for Minsk and simultaneously cover the left flank. At dawn on 2 July Rotmistrov launched his tanks along the Minsk highway, making up to thirty miles and breaking into the north-eastern outskirts during the night: Burdeinyi's corps started the same day, guided over rough country by partisans and making good speed in the absence of enemy resistance. To the south-west Panov's 1st Guards tanks were within a dozen miles of Minsk on 2 July, having pushed through Pukhovichi; two tank brigades (15th and 16th) followed a battery of SP guns and a small infantry force, with 3rd Army and its supporting 9th Tank Corps also closing on Minsk. On 3 July, four hours after tanks from 3rd Belorussian Front rushed the city from the north, north-west and north-east, Panov's tanks and infantry were in the south-eastern suburbs. Minsk, its factories dynamited and its installations wrecked, stood mostly in ruins; throughout most of Belorussia Soviet troops advanced through burned villages and broken towns, the livestock gone and the population fearfully thinned. More than once Red Army units came upon trains loaded with children consigned to deportation to the *Reich*.

With the capture of Minsk, the Soviet encirclement locked round Fourth Army, trapping 105,000 men split into two bodies, one to the south-west and the other to the east of Volma. Almost on the site where in June 1941 the *Wehrmacht* had carried out a great encirclement of Soviet armies, a mass of German soldiers now awaited annihilation or capture in the great forests east of Minsk: more than 40,000 of them died either in attempting to break out of the ring or in fighting off the Russian reduction of the encirclement area. Save for air-dropping supplies—and the last attempt was made south of Minsk on 5 July—Army Group Centre could do nothing. Three days later the acting commander of 12th Corps ordered a general surrender, since lack of ammunition and fuel ruled out further organized resistance. The rounding up of the remnants of four German corps, a dwindling mass of hungry, hunted men with their wounded untended, lasted until 11 July: the mopping up fell to 49th Army of Zakharov's

2nd Belorussian Front, Rokossovskii's units having peeled off to drive on south-westwards.

On 4 July, when the battle for Belorussia was decided—the Red Army having torn a 250-mile gap in the German front and Army Group Centre left with eight scattered divisions—the *Stavka* set new target lines for the four fronts. The way ahead for the Red Army lay into Poland and Lithuania. Using two armies, 6th Guards and 4th Shock Army, Bagramyan had just taken Polotsk, another of Hitler's phantom fortresses from which he planned to lunge with Army Group North—a two-division attack to restore a situation which the power of more than a hundred Soviet divisons had produced: Model and Lindemann (Army Group North commander) managed to scotch this senseless plan. The *Stavka* meanwhile aimed Bagramyan's 1st Baltic Front at Kaunas; Chernyakhovskii's 3rd Belorussian at Vilno and Lida, thence the western bank of the Niemen; Zakharov's 2nd Belorussian at the Molchad and Niemen river lines and thence to Bialystok; and Rokossovskii's right-flank armies at Baranovichi–Brest, across the line running from Slonim to Pinsk and finally to the western Bug. The Soviet pursuit, as it unrolled along the axes specified by the *Stavka,* made an average speed of ten to fifteen miles per day. Baranovichi fell on 8 July, Vilno—already encircled—on 13 July, while Bagramyan with five armies advanced on a broad front towards Lithuania and eastern Latvia.

By mid-July Rokossovskii's right flank armies had passed the line running from Svisloch to Pruzany and west of Pinsk—a highly significant meridian, for now Rokossovskii could bring his powerful left-flank armies into action, 1st Belorussian Front being no longer cut into two widely separated entities by the vast Polesian swampland which lay well to the rear at this stage of the advance. The *Stavka* had already authorized the attack plan for the left-flank armies on 7 July; as the right-flank armies moved down on Brest from the north-east, the left prepared to attack towards Lublin in Poland and to sweep past Brest from the south. Rokossovskii's left hook disposed of great power—nine infantry armies (including 1st Polish Army), one tank army (the 2nd), two tank, one mechanized and one cavalry corps, two air armies: 70th, 47th, 8th Guards and 96th Armies formed the first echelon. Shortly after dawn on the morning of 17 July, preceded by a barrage of 170,000 shells fired off by Soviet guns, the lead armies of the left flank lashed out westwards from Kovel in a double drive on Siedlce and Lublin. Six days later Chuikov's 8th Guards Army, supported by 2nd Tank Army, broke into Lublin and then turned north-westwards towards Deblin on the Vistula—and Warsaw.

When Soviet armies shattered Army Group Centre, they achieved their greatest single military success on the Eastern Front. For the German army in the east it was a catastrophe of unbelievable proportions, greater than that of Stalingrad, obliterating between twenty-five and twenty-eight divisions, 350,000 men in all. On 17 July 57,000 German prisoners of war—with captured generals at their head—were marched in a great column through the streets of Moscow lined with Russian crowds: for the most part, the Russians masked their anger with silence, apart from jeering boys and saddened women. This chilling and unique display was prompted on the Russian side by the desire to ridicule German assertions that nothing 'unplanned' had happened in Belorussia and to underline to the Allies that the Belorussian victory had been hard-fought. Russians resented suggestions that German troops had been transferred from Belorussia westwards to fight off the invading Allied armies: the parade of prisoners was in part designed to stifle 'nonsensical talk' of this kind. The main battle-front, and here Soviet comentators quoted directly from German cries of anguish, lay in the east where battles of 'apocalyptic' dimensions raged.

After 9 July, in order to bring his 'personal touch' closer to the Eastern Front, Hitler moved his headquarters into East Prussia, and it was here on 20 July that the abortive attempt was made on his life. The 'bomb-plot' did much to confirm Russian feelings that the *Reich* was beginning to disintegrate, though too speedy a crack-up at this juncture—with the Red Army about to burst into Germany itself—might not have served Stalin's best interests, or even those of the Soviet Union. Yet the Soviet press did not scoff or minimize the importance of the 'bomb plot': *Freies Deutschland*, the *NKD* newspaper and mouthpiece of the 'Free German movement', took an equally positive line and called for 'common action' with the much unloved German generals to dispose of Hitler. The 'bomb plot', and the great German defeat in Belorussia, gave a fresh impetus to the activities of 'Free Germany', though it proved to be short-lived. Two days after the attempt on Hitler's life, sixteen of the generals recently captured issued an 'appeal'—authenticated by Lt.-Gen. Bambler, commanding officer of the 12th Infantry Divison—calling for a continuation of the struggle against Hitler, for Germans 'to use force against force, to resist Hitler, not to fulfil his orders, to finish Hitler's regime and the war with it . . . Do not wait until Hitler ruins you.' In the wake of the savagery inflicted on the German officer corps after 20 July on Hitler's orders, Field-Marshal Paulus, for long unwilling to form any association with the *Bund Deutscher Offiziere*, finally dropped his resistance and came out with his own personal summons to deal with Hitler and expressed his agreement with the programme advanced by the 'Free Germany' movement.

Before the Soviet offensive opened in Belorussia, and at a time when 'Free Germany' had accomplished very little to win over German troops in the field—at Korsun, Seydlitz and his companions, shunted down to the Soviet 'ring' to persuade the trapped divisions to surrender, failed dismally for all their loudspeaker broadcasts, leaflets and personal appeals—the NKD and the BDO were at each other's throats over their respective roles. Seydlitz objected to being merely a propaganda mouthpiece to subvert German soldiers: Lattmann, however, seized upon this, and Lattmann won. A few, a very few, German prisoners were trained to work behind the German lines, or else were hand-picked to form the nucleus of military units attached to the Red Army: small groups of ex-prisoners wearing Red Army uniforms made their appearance in the Ukraine that summer. Inside the German lines rumours flew fairly thick about the 'Seydlitz army' and there was talk of the 'German government' set up in Moscow, but the 'army' was virtually a phantom and the 'government' exercised no pull on German troops still fighting. Inevitably the role of the 'Free Germany' movement dwindled and its importance waned, though for the moment it flourished amidst the vast wreckage of the Belorussian defeat. How disastrous this defeat was, those who had just suffered it—sixteen of the chastened generals so recently captured—set out in their 'appeal':

. . . the destruction of 30 divisions, in other words almost the whole of the Army Group [Centre]: the whole of the Fourth Army, the bulk of Ninth Army and the Third Panzer Army. In these unequal battles 21 generals, including ourselves, were taken prisoner and more than 10 others killed. Reasons for this renewed defeat: a wrong interpretation of the enemy's strategic possibilities and intentions; our flank positions threatened ever since the winter; lack of reserves and Luftwaffe support. To put it briefly, Army Group Centre was sacrificed in a game of chance. [Lt.-Gen. Bambler, Cdr. 12th Infantry Div., pamphlet, 22 July 1944.]

As Army Group Centre crashed in ruins, spilling out its enormous debris of shattered units and broken divisions, the reverberations made themselves felt across the length of the Eastern Front, from the Baltic to the Balkans. The Red Army was now in a position to ram the German centre as far back as the Vistula and the East Prussian frontier; it could threaten German troops in the Baltic states with isolation from the main body and finally menace the German strongholds in the south-eastern theatre. This was more or less the order in which Soviet fronts and armies went about their strategic tasks in the summer of 1944. In mid-July, intent on denying the enemy either the time or the opportunity to build any kind of defensive front east of the Polish frontier, the Soviet command extended operations north and south of the Belorussian breakthrough area. With the capture of Vilno, Grodno, Baranovichi and Pinsk, together with the forcing of the Niemen and the seizure of bridgeheads on its western bank, the German 'strategic front' had been well and truly breached: the 'Niemen line' had gone and with Soviet troops once in Grodno, Olita and Kaunas the way would be open for an advance on a broad front towards the East Prussian border. In the 'gap' being ripped out between the Niemen and the Dvina, Chernyakhovskii's 3rd Belorussian Front raced on with a two-pronged thrust, from Minsk to the Niemen and through Vilna to Kaunas, in Lithuania; Bagramyan with 1st Baltic Front put five armies over the Dvina and advanced in his turn on Lithuania and Latvia. The main weight of Rokossovskii's attack was through Baranovichi and to the north of Brest-Litovsk, thence to the Bug which ran north-east of Warsaw, pressing into the Bialystok–Brest-Litovsk 'gap' and threatening to split the German defensive front down the middle.

At this stage the Soviet command jammed another great crowbar into the cracking German fronts. Marshal Koniev's 1st Ukrainian Front, the most powerful single Front entity in the Red Army, was now aimed at Lvov and at Army Group North Ukraine under Col.-Gen.Harpe, who was holding the front running from the Pripet marshes to the Carpathians. Though abutting on to Rokossovskii's left flank west of Kovel, the bulk of Army Group North Ukraine faced 1st Ukrainian Front and covered that area where the German command had originally anticipated that the main blow of the Soviet summer offensive would fall. Army Group North Ukraine held what was left to the Germans of the Ukraine; its function was to prevent a Soviet breakthrough to Lvov and into the valuable industrial region of Drohobych–Borislav, as well as to cover the approaches to southern Poland, Czechoslovakia and Silesia with their industrial resources.The disaster in Belorussia forced the transfer of six divisions (three of them armoured) to Army Group Centre, leaving North Ukraine with thirty-four infantry divisions, five *Panzer* divisions, one motorized division and two infantry brigades on the eve of Koniev's attack—900,000 men, 900 tanks and assault guns, over 6,000 guns and 700 aircraft. For all the collapse in the centre, Lvov retained great significance as a communications centre linking German forces to the north and those in Rumania; taking advantage of the favourable terrain (including natural defensive barriers formed by the several tributaries of the Dniester), the Germans established a powerful defence in depth, with three defensive belts reaching from twenty-five to thirty miles, fortifying the river lines of the Dniester, San and the Vistula and fitting out the towns of Vladimir—Volynsky, Brody, Zolochev, Rava Russkaya and Stanislav for protracted defence. The most powerful German force was deployed on the axis covering Lvov (from Brody to Zborov); the infantry was committed to holding the first two defensive lines, the armour held back some ten miles from the forward positions, a disposition forced on the German command by the lack of reserves.

Marshal Koniev had already battled with Stalin over his proposed plan which envisaged a double thrust, where Stalin insisted on only one main thrust in the direction of Lvov; Koniev proposed to strike along the Rava Russkaya axis and also from the centre of his front towards Lvov itself—proposals to which Stalin grudgingly agreed, though not without a warning to Koniev that if his 'stubborn attitude' failed to produce results then it would be 'on his own head'. The *Stavka* directive issued to the Front command on 24 June duly specified the two thrusts aimed at the destruction of enemy forces 'on the Lvov axis' and 'on the Rava Russkaya axis'; the first attack would be made from the area south-west of Lutsk in the direction of Sokal–Rava Russkaya, the second from the area of Tarnopol towards Lvov, the flank cover for this latter attack being provided by Front left-flank armies attacking towards Stanislav–Drohobych, all to bring Koniev's armies out onto a line running from Hrubieszow (south-east of Lublin)–Tomaszow–Yavorov–Galich. (The same directive also mentioned the possibility of the right-flank formations, operating between Hrubieszow and Zamosc, co-ordinating their operations with Rokossovskii's left-flank armies, which were due to launch their offensive on the heels of Koniev's attack.)

The *Stavka* did not stint Koniev over reinforcements. In addition to the nine rifle divisions and ten aviation divisions, Koniev received over 1,000 tanks and not far short of 3,000 guns and mortars. On the eve of the offensive 1st Ukrainian Front mustered seven infantry armies (3rd Guards, 13th, 60th, 38th Army, 1st Guards, 18th Guards and 5th Guards Army), three tank armies (1st and 3rd Guards, together with the 4th Tank Army), two air armies (2nd and 8th) plus two 'cavalry-mechanized groups'—Baranov's (1st Guards Cavalry Corps and 25th Tank Corps) and Sokolov's (6th Guards Cavalry Corps and 31st Tank Corps): this gave Koniev a grand combined strength of eighty divisions (six of them cavalry), ten tank and mechanized corps, four independent tank brigades, plus the 1st Czechoslovak Corps—843,000 men, 1,614 tanks and self-propelled guns, almost 14,000 guns and mortars, 2,806 aircraft. Koniev's own tally of his Front strength is, in fact, greater, setting his manpower at 1,200,000 and his strength in tanks and SP guns at 2,200. With this formidable force Marshal Koniev intended first to encircle and to destroy German forces in the Brody–Lvov area, then to split Army Group North Ukraine in two, driving one segment back into Polesia and the other into the Carpathians, and finally to bring the main forces of 1st Ukrainian Front on to the Vistula.

On his right flank, aimed along the 'Rava Russkaya axis', Koniev grouped 'the Lutsk assault group' consisting of Gordov's 3rd Guards Army, Pukhov's 13th Army, Katukov's 1st Guards Tank Army and Baranov's 'cavalry-mechanized group', supported by Lt.-Gen. (Aviation) Slyusarev's four corps from 2nd Air Army: fourteen rifle divisions, two tank corps and a mechanized corps, a cavalry corps and two artillery divisions were concentrated along this six-mile breakthrough sector. On the 'Lvov axis', with a seven-mile breakthrough sector, Koniev concentrated fifteen rifle divisions, four tank and two mechanized corps, a cavalry corps and two artillery divisions drawn from the 'Lvov assault group' with Kurochkin's 60th Army, Moskalenko's 38th Army, Rybalko's 3rd Guards Tank Army, Lelyushenko's 4th Tank Army and Sokolov's 'cavalry-mechanized group', supported by five corps of 2nd Air Army (commanded by the Air Army chief, Col.-Gen. Krasovskii).The two left-flank armies assigned to cover the flank of the Lvov 'assault group', Col.-Gen. Grechko's 1st Guards Army and Lt.-Gen. Zhuravlev's 18th Army, occupied a front of some one hundred miles; 1st Guards, exploiting the success of Moskalenko's 38th, was to set up its own assault group of five rifle divisions with Lt.-Gen. Poluboyarov's 4th Tank Corps to seize a bridgehead on the Dniester in the area of Galich, while Zhuravlev's 18th (with units of 1st Guards) was to be ready to attack in the direction of Stanislav. Zhadov's 5th Guards Army and 47th Corps remained as Front reserve.

Marshal Koniev and his chief of staff General V.D. Sokolovskii had good reason to plan the double thrust on Lvov: in August 1914 the Russian South-Western Front under General Ivanov had also fought for Lvov (Lemberg) with two armies, Brusilov's 8th and Ruzskii's 3rd; though the Austro-Hungarian forces were defeated east of Lvov, the failure to move the right-flank Russian armies in due time allowed Field-Marshal von Hötzendorf's battered troops to fall back on excellent positions to the west of Lvov and hold on at Rava Russkaya. Marshal Koniev intended no repetition of this mishap and pushed on with elaborate preparations for a double breach of the German defences, in particular to conceal the weight of the blow about to fall along the Rava Russkaya axis, where Koniev intended to mount a massive surprise attack. Front movements were planned to suggest to German observation that the weight was going to the left wing, where two tank armies and one tank corps would be 'located' amidst 1st Guards and 18th Army. Night movements hid the true concentration and the pattern of regrouping involving the three tank armies and Moskalenko's 38th Army: German intelligence was presumed to know about the attack building up in front of Lvov and against Stanislav, but the Soviet command worked to keep the other deployment secret. The Germans were not wholly deceived, though Koniev's command calculated that the movement of 1st Guards Tank Army to the south of Lutsk and 4th Tank Army into the Tarnopol area had gone largely unobserved.

The final attack plans went from 1st Ukrainian Front HQ on 7 July to the *Stavka* for inspection by the General Staff; after three days they were officially confirmed and approved, subject to the proviso that the tank armies and 'cavalry-mechanized groups' must not be used for the actual breakthrough but for exploiting success. Tank armies would be committed twenty-four hours after the beginning of the operation in the event of success, 'cavalry-mechanized groups' forty-eight hours later and in the wake of the tank armies. The scope of the infantry commitments for the first day of operations must also be increased. As a result Koniev altered the sequence in which he intended to commit his armoured armies and increased the depth to which infantry formations must operate, completing all Front preparations by 12 July. That evening the Front command considered the evidence of German awareness of impending Soviet attack; to preserve the defending German troops from destruction through artillery bombardment in the customary opening phase of a Soviet offensive, Army Group North Ukraine was pulling men out of the forward positions, away from the first defensive zone into the second, from which the defence would be maintained. Fourth *Panzer* and First *Panzer* Armies were no novices in Soviet attack methods; north of Brody and along the 'Rava Russkaya axis', Soviet reconnaissance detected signs of a planned German withdrawal to the second line, at which Marshal Koniev decided to dispense with artillery preparation and immediately to commit the forward battalions of 3rd Guards and 13th Army from the 'Lutsk assault group' on the right flank.

By the afternoon of 13 July Pukhov's riflemen from 13th Army were heavily engaged around Gorokhov; at the end of the day, the town fell to Soviet troops but it proved impossible to 'leapfrog' into the second German defence line, from which heavy German counter-attacks were being launched. On 14 July Marshal Koniev decided to commit the second-echelon formations of the rifle corps and to use his artillery, thereby bringing the main body of 3rd Guards and 13th

Armies into action at a time when 16th and 17th *Panzer* Divisions fought to hold off the Soviet advance and small groups of German bombers raided the Russian lines repeatedly. Having failed to rush the German defences, the right-flank offensive continued with air and artillery support on 15 July, with heavy fighting north-west of Brody. By the evening the assault armies had pierced the German lines to a depth of twelve miles, German reserves were exhausted and both *Panzer* divisons badly mauled. The same evening (15 July) and throughout the early hours of the following morning, the Front commander ordered Baranov's 'cavalry-mechanized group' into the battle in the Stoyanov breakthrough sector punched out by Pukhov's 13th Army. Baranov's orders specified that he must be fully committed by 16 July, capture Kamenka–Strumilevskaya by 17 July and cut off the escape route for German forces in the Brody area. Baranov and his staff, however, were not quick enough off the mark, and not until the evening of 16 July could the mobile group pass through the infantry units, coming out through 13th Army sector at Kholoyuv and then pressing on to the south-west, fighting off the German 20th Motorized Division. Between 17 and 18 July Baranov forced the western Bug off the march and the capture of Kamenka–Strumilevskaya and Derevlyany effectively cut the German escape route to the west for German troops fighting in the Brody area. While Baranov's tanks and cavalry moved to the western Bug, Col.-Gen. Katukov's 1st Guards Tank army—with orders to attack from Sokal in the direction of Rava Russkaya, force the western Bug and capture bridgeheads along the Sokal–Krystonopol sector—was committed on 17 July. That day 44th Guards Tank Brigade reached the western Bug, forced a crossing and established a bridgehead in the area of Dobrochin. The lead tanks of 1st Guards Tank Army had already crossed the Soviet frontier and were now on Polish soil; behind them came the main force of 1st Guards Tank Army, followed by 13th Army and 3rd Guards Army (whose right-flank units struck out for Vladimir–Volynsk, the left for the western Bug in the area of Sokal).

The attack along the 'Lvov axis' fared badly. Bad weather, combined with stiff German resistance, meant grinding through strong concentrations of infantry and armour. Reconnaissance and preliminary actions by forward battalions on 13 July showed that the Germans were occupying their positions in strength and intended to hold them; there was no alternative but to launch Kurochkin's 60th and Moskalenko's 38th Armies in a full-scale attack preceded by heavy artillery and air bombardment. But the morning of 14 July brought only thick mist and heavy rain. Not until the afternoon could the Soviet barrage open, and at 1600 hours the assault groups from both Soviet armies attacked. At the end of the day, across a ten-mile front, Soviet troops had made only a slight penetration, varying from one to five miles; the German command committed its tactical reserves at once, 1st and 8th *Panzer* Divisions with the SS Division *Galizien*. Moskalenko's 38th was particularly hard-pressed, being counter-attacked by assault groups from both *Panzer* divisions, and was actually being pushed back, with a strong force of German tanks battering the left flank of the Soviet assault armies committed east of Lvov. Krasovskii's ground-attack planes and bombers were called up, artillery mobilized and by the evening the German counter-attack was slowed down, but Marshal Koniev realized that 'it was time to bring up the tank armies'. Rybalko's 3rd Guards Tank Army moved up in strength on the morning of 16 July, although it had already begun to deploy the day before. At 0300 hours on the morning of 16 July Rybalko contacted the Front commander and asked for permission to push on with his main force, based on the success that his lead elements had enjoyed in the Zolochev area. Though Kurochkin's 60th Army still needed greater depth of penetration to justify this decision, Marshal Koniev decided to risk it and to authorize Rybalko to move forward, which meant passing the Soviet tank army through a narrow corridor (running between Koltuv and Trostyanets Maly)—the 'neck' of the present Soviet breakthrough—and driving north-west.

Rybalko's tanks drove through in a single unbroken column and by the evening of 16 July he reported to Koniev that one corps was to the north-west of Zolochev, with forward units racing for the river Peltev. South of the 'Koltuv corridor' a strong force of Geman armour and infantry tried to seal off the passage, isolate 3rd Guards Tank Army and thus eliminate the threat of encirclement building up in the Brody area. Koniev realized that at all costs the 'corridor' must be held and widened, and he decided to commit his second tank army (Lelyushenko's 4th Tank Army) once Kurochkin's infantry had taken Zolochev; Lelyushenko's armour would go in behind the left flank of 3rd Guards Tank Army and strike out for Gorodok, some fifteen miles west of Lvov. Lelyushenko received strict instructions not to commit his armour to a frontal attack on Lvov but to outflank it from the south and sever German escape routes to the west and south-west. The 4th Tank Army entered the battle on 17 July, but with heavy German pressure on the flanks of the Soviet breakthrough sector not all of 4th Tank could be detached to outflank Lvov; with tank formations still fighting the 60th Army south of Zolochev, only 10th Tank Corps moved towards Lvov. As the Germans fought desperately to seal off the 'Koltuv corridor' and entrap the Soviet tank armies, Rybalko's 3rd Guards had already crossed the Peltev and on 18 July reached the Busk–Derevlyany line, linking up with Baranov's mobile group and closing the ring round the German troops in the Brody area, eight divisions holding a sizeable area. That night 10th Tank Corps reached Olshanitsa (south-west of Lvov), deeply outflanking the German *Panzer* divisions from the west and the south.

It was on 18 July that Rokossovskii unleashed another powerful blow from 1st Belorussian Front when he set his left-flank armies in motion—70th, 47th Army, 8th Guards Army, 69th Army, 1st Polish Army in the second echelon, supported by 6th Air Army and with considerable armoured strength in 2nd Tank Army, as well as a 'mobile group' formed from 11th Tank Corps, 2nd and 7th Guards Cavalry Corps. The right-flank armies of 1st Belorussian Front were already on a line running from Sisloch in the north through Pruzhany and to the west of Pinsk, hanging menacingly over the north-east of Brest-Litovsk; the time had come to launch right and left flanks in an encirclement operation designed to close on German troops at Brest-Litovsk. Rokossovskii proposed to commit his left-flank armies in the direction of Kovel–Lublin. The operation as a whole envisaged the outflanking of Brest-Litovsk from the north and from the south, the destruction of German forces in the area of Brest-Litovsk and Lublin, after which the offensive would be developed along 'the Warsaw axis' to bring Soviet armies on a broad front to the Vistula, ready to strike into eastern Poland. The main blow was to come from the left flank, which three armies—Gusev's 47th, Chuikov's 8th Guards and Kilpachki's 69th—assigned to breaking the German defences east of Kovel and assuring the passage of the armoured formations, infantry and armour, then co-operating in an advance along two axes, in the direction of Siedlce and Lublin; elements of the left flank would also assist in outflanking Brest-Litovsk from the south-west. This attack was intended to slice into the left flank of Fourth *Panzer* from Army Group North Ukraine (which jutted north past Kovel) as well as achieving the destruction of the German Second Army in the area of Brest-Litovsk.

Chuikov's 8th Guards Army pulled out of the Dniester bridgehead of 3rd Ukrainian Front early in June 1944 and moved from the southern flank to the 1st Belorussian Front, starting out in trains on the morning of 12 July. In spite of all attempts to keep the army's destination secret, the 'buzz' was that 8th Guards was moving up to Rokossovskii's front, and it proved, like many military rumours, to be quite accurate. Three days later, after travelling by car, Chuikov and his military soviet reached Rokossovskii's Front HQ in the forest to the west of Korosten, were briefed by General Malinin (Rokossovskii's chief of staff) and then moved off to 8th Guards HQ, also sited in a wood just south of Rafaluvka station. Army units took up their positions only by night. Track and tyre marks left by tanks or vehicles on the move were carefully swept away; radio communication was forbidden and radio equipment sealed. The Guards regiments went through a rapid and intensive training course, learning how to fell trees, construct anti-tank defences and lay log-roads over the Belorussian marshes. Chuikov also had to devise a method of coping with the methods of 'elastic defence' adopted by the Germans, who fell back from their first line of defences to straighten their line and economize on forces, then dealt out a punishing counter-blow from secure, well-prepared positions further to the rear. Not much more than a week before, 47th Army, and more particularly 11th Tank Corps (then under Maj.-Gen. F.N. Rudkin), had raced into just such a trap; on 7 July, 47th Army attacked from the left flank in the Kovel area, with 11th Tank Corps under orders to pass through the breach and to make for Lyuboml–Opalin, and then for the western Bug, after which it was to press in the direction of Lublin. The infantry attacks on the morning of 8 July made little progress, and under the mistaken impression that German troops were pulling back to the western Bug

11th Tank Corps rushed in, only to take a savage beating from the well-timed German counter-blow. On Rokossovskii's orders the corps disengaged, pulled back to Kovel, came under the command of Maj.-Gen. Yushchuk and was subordinated to 8th Guards Army. Defective reconnaissance lead to this reverse and Chuikov took good note of it, determined not to expend 'trainloads of ammunition on empty space'.

Chuikov's 8th Guards duly undertook the main breakthrough operation on the left flank of 1st Belorussian Front: the Germans must receive no alert by extended Soviet reconnaissance; the blow must be 'decisive' and mounted without a protracted build-up in the rear. Rifle battalions would act as reconnaissance battalions, with infantry support and mine-clearing tanks; the preliminary bombardment was to be brief, a mere thirty minutes. Success by the reconnaissance battalions would bring on the main forces without further artillery preparation, but if the reconnaissance was halted the barrage would continue for an hour and forty minutes, followed by a main attack. Twenty-four hours before the attack opened Marshals Zhukov and Rokossovskii, Aviation Marshal Novikov and Peresypkin (signals) attended a full-scale rehearsal, an occasion for a clash between Zhukov and Chuikov, smoothed over by the tactful Rokossovskii. During the night of 17-18 July, when the staff of 1st Polish Army arrived at Chuikov's HQ (1st Polish being slated to follow 8th Guards), Guards divisions took over from 60th Rifle Division's units which held the forward positions until the last moment to deceive German intelligence. At 0530 hours on 18 July the guns duly fired off a thirty-minute barrage and the reconnaissance battalions moved out. Thirty minutes later Zhukov, Rokossovskii and Col.-Gen. V.I. Kazakov (Front artillery commmander) arrived at Chuikov's forward observation post and watched the 'reconnaissance in force' unroll under cover of the short but very heavy barrage using guns of up to 203mm calibre. The use of the heaviest guns in this kind of attack shook Kazakov, who remonstrated with Pozharski (8th Guards artillery commander), only to be told that Chuikov wanted it this way.

After two hours the infantry had broken into the first defences and taken the high ground: at 0730 hours Chuikov reported to Zhukov and Rokossovskii that he was committing his main forces. By the evening the first echelon of 8th Guards reached the eastern bank of the river Plysk. Yushchuk's tank corps received orders to move on the morning of the second day of operations through the infantry, outflank Lyuboml from the north and south, then advance with all speed to the western Bug to secure crossings in the Opalin–Gnishuv–Svezhe sector. Three lead brigades from 11th Corps (36th, 65th and 20th Tank Brigades) pushed on westwards, outflanking Lyubomyl, and at 1300 hours on 20 July 20th Tank Brigade reached the western Bug; towards evening the brigade had secured crossings, and by nightfall more units of 11th Tank Corps (with advanced elements of Glazunov's 4th Guards Cavalry Corps) were over, fighting to enlarge the Soviet bridgehead. Rokossovskii now issued orders to Chuikov to commit Bogdanov's 2nd Tank Army, which moved off for the western Bug at 1700 hours on 20 July, the tank columns driving ahead under fighter protection provided by 6th Air Army: at noon on 21 July, 2nd Tank was on the western Bug.

Marshal Rokossovskii and Lt.-Gen.Bulganin (the third member of the 1st Belorussian Front Military Soviet) arrived at Chuikov's forward HQ on 21 July. Bogdanov's tanks took ten hours to make their crossing of the Bug, 3rd Corps moving into the wooded area west of Stulno, 8th Guards Tank Corps to Bytyn while the second echelon (16th Corps) completed its crossing; Bogdanov received orders to cut loose from the infantry as from the morning of 22 July, attack in the direction of Savin–Pugachuv–Leczna, reach the line of the river Wieprz by the evening and capture Lublin the next day. Yushchuk's corps was meanwhile detached from 8th Guards Army and combined into a 'cavalry-mechanized group' with 2nd Guards Cavalry Corps, with orders to strike north-west along the line Parchev–Radzyn–Lukuv. At dawn on 22 July Bogdanov's tanks moved off for the attack on Lublin, where the wooded areas, swamps and numerous small rivers forced the tank columns to keep to the roads, themselves in none too good condition owing to the heavy rain. Lublin itself had also been fitted out for defence, with outlying defences made up of trenches, pill-boxes and firing-points and inner defences built round strong-points.

To clear the passage for his main body of armour along the approach to Lublin, Bogdanov pushed out strong 'forward detachments' consisting of a tank brigade, a section of self-propelled guns, two or three companies of infantry and a squad of sappers; 6th Air Army provided the air cover. As they fell back on Lublin, German troops set up tank ambushes in the woods bordering the roads, in the numerous villages and at the several bridges; while the 'forward detachments' dealt with these, 'pursuit detachments' (consisting of a tank section with tommy-gunners riding atop the machines) flushed out German units digging in along the line of the Soviet advance. On 22 July 107th Tank Brigade (16th Tank Corps), acting as 'forward detachment' with a motorcycle regiment, and units of 7th Guards Cavalry corps, cleared Chelm (forty miles south-east of Lublin). 3rd Tank Corps, disengaging from the infantry, moved on the right flank in two columns on Kiyany–Lublin, with 8th Guards Tank Corps on the left driving through Pugachuv, Leczna and on to the eastern outskirts of Lublin, where Bogdanov decided to attack from three sides. 'Forward detachments' received orders to bypass the outer defences of Lublin and make straight for the Vistula.

During the morning of 23 July Soviet tanks broke into the eastern suburb of Lublin, clearing it quickly but running into heavy resistance on the river Vyszczicsa which bisected the town. While Soviet tanks and SP guns fired over open sights across the river and into the stone houses held by German troops, 51st Tank Brigade crashed into Lublin from the west, where Soviet tanks and infantry fought fierce street battles. Here the German garrison attempted to break out to the west, using an armoured train and an infantry battalion to cover the break. Soviet tanks brought the armoured train under close and heavy fire, blowing it to pieces and killing many scores of German soldiers intent on escape; among the prisoners taken was the German commandant of Lublin. In the north-west, 3rd Tank Corps had taken the suburbs along with a stretch of the Lublin–Warsaw road, but in the south-eastern suburbs German resistance to 8th Tank Corps continued as fiercely as ever. Bogdanov decided to go to Maj.-Gen. Vedeneyev's HQ (3rd Corps) to see for himself, and he learned that only tanks were in action here; Vedeneyev intimated that until the infantry from 57th Brigade came in he could not get the German machine-gunners out of their lairs in the strongly built stone houses. Bogdanov thought that Vedeneyev was dragging his feet, that he overestimated German powers of resistance, and so he invited him to take a little tour of the town, with a single tank for escort leading the two jeeps holding Bogdanov, Vedeneyev, adjutants and intelligence officers. Nothing stirred as the tiny convoy moved down deserted streets past burning tanks and smashed German trucks: no shots, no sign of life in any house. A few yards further on, however, an anti-tank weapon opened fire and disabled the lead tank, killing the crew. Bogdanov gave orders to turn back, but when the jeeps swung round they at once came under more fire which brought Bogdanov's own jeep to a halt; the Army commander got out and then slumped to the pavement, his shoulder smashed by an explosive bullet. After they had walked more than a mile and a half, the remaining officers fighting off German attempts to trap the party, a Soviet truck picked up the general, whose command passed to Maj.-Gen. A.I. Radzievskii, chief of staff to 2nd Tank Army. At noon on 24 July the remnants of the German garrison in Lublin collected tanks and SP guns to support one last attempt to break out, an attempt that failed in a final spurt of heavy fighting. Lublin had been cleared; 2nd Tank Army now received orders to advance north-west on Pulawy and Deblin, taking bridgeheads on the Vistula to prepare for a further advance on Warsaw.

This north-westerly advance of 2nd Tank Army, through Pulawy and on to Praga, the part of Warsaw that lay on the eastern bank of the Vistula, promised to complete the encirclement of the German divisions that had been trapped in the region of Brest-Litovsk: this tank thrust would sever the German escape route in the direction of Warsaw. Chuikov's 8th Guards also received orders to move to the north-west, though Chuikov did not have instructions to force the Vistula (which one of his divisions reached on 26 July). While Rokossovskii's left flank thus curled round through Lublin and into the deep rear of German forces fighting eastwards at Brest-Litovsk, his right-wing armies—65th and 28th Armies—were closing on this vital junction and were established in some strength on the western Bug to the north of the town. General Pliev's 'cavalry-mechanized group', operating in the German rear, was already fighting close to Brest-Litovsk while 4th Guards Cavalry Corps from this group moved on to the western Bug in company with Batov's 65th Army. Soviet reconnaissance confirmed that, in addition to known German divisions in Brest-Litovsk, there were also the staffs of some fourteen formations that had been dispersed—a very favourable moment to strike and one that Batov hoped to exploit, but for which he needed reserves. Unfortunately Rokossovskii could supply none—'I have almost nothing left', he told Batov, who got orders to hang on to his bridgehead on the Bug. Nevertheless, Rokossovskii squeezed out 80th Corps, but on the understanding that this formation was moved up to Pliev who was 'having it hard on his own'. Batov sent his deputy commander Batinov to contact 80th Corps, but German bombers got there first, killing the corps commander and knocking out the headquarters. By 22 July Batov still had not made contact with Pliev's cavalry and that evening Marshal Zhukov came on the line to demand why; Batov explained that neither he nor Front staff had heard from Pliev, whereupon Zhukov cut him short, told him that the assignment was his, and not that of the Front staff, and then ordered reinforced attacks from Batov's southern flank. Preoccupied with the left-flank offensive on Lublin, Zhukov had no time to spare for operations near Brest-Litovsk and none for the predicament of Batov; all available reinforcement, especially armour, was going to the left flank.

On 23 July the Germans put in a heavy counter-attack against Batov's right flank, moving from north and south with strong tank support and crashing into the area of 65th Army forward HQ. Batov's signal to Rokossovskii was interrupted by the appearance of German tanks and left hanging in the air as shells burst on the badly camouflaged signals centre. From Front HQ Rokossovskii signalled: 'Where is Batov?' Receiving no reply, Rokossovskii sent fighter planes to scour the area between Kleshchela and Cheremkha; that evening Rokossovskii and Zhukov arrived at 65th Army HQ, where Zhukov showed himself less impatient and even offered reinforcement to eliminate the German breakthrough into Batov's corps. This German attack slowed the Soviet advance but could not prevent Brest-Litovsk from being closed off when, on 27 July, 28th Army and 70th Army (Lt.-Gen. V.S. Popov's formation from the left flank) lined up on the eastern bank of the western Bug north-west of Brest-Litovsk. Eight German divisions, the remnants of the German Second Army and Ninth Army, hung on to Brest-Litovsk for as long as possible, the garrison reinforced with tanks moved up from Warsaw. Rokossovskii had undertaken a giant encircling movement to cut all communications between Brest-Litovsk, Bialystok and Warsaw, using his right and left flanks, but in Brest-Litovsk itself Soviet units had to beat down strong German resistance before the town, with all its road and rail links, fell on 28 July. The gap between the left wing of 1st Belorussian Front, 2nd Tank Army and 8th Guards driving north-west to the Vistula and in the direction of Warsaw, and the forces clustered about Brest-Litovsk, was now considerable.

As Rokossovskii opened the battle for Lublin, Koniev ended the encirclement battle west of Brody: on the evening of 22 July more than 30,000 German troops had been killed and 17,000 made prisoner. Once the liquidation of the pocket was complete, Soviet divisions were free for operations directed against Lvov itself, where the Soviet assault force made only slow progress. Marshal Koniev hoped to seize Lvov off the march with his armoured units, before German

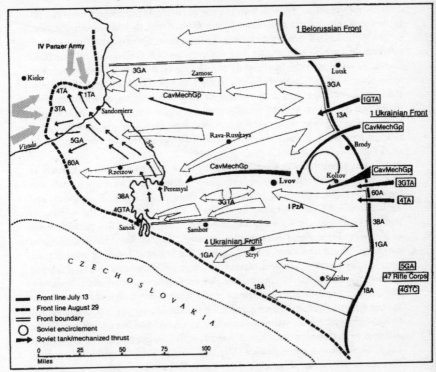

Map 9 Lvov–Sandomierz operations, July–August 1944

reinforcement could move up from Stanislav; on 18 July the situation seemed favourable for a *coup de main*, with 3rd Guards Tank Army and 13th Army not more than twenty miles from the city, and 10th Tank Corps (4th Tank Army) already at Olshanitsa to the south-east. Koniev therefore prepared to outflank the city from the north and south, then seize it by 20 July.

That this did not succeed Marshal Koniev attributed to the errors committed by Rybalko (though admitting the factor of the heavy rain, which slowed down 3rd Guards Tank Army's artillery and supplies). Rybalko took the shortest route, the Brasnoe–Lvov road, only to land his tanks in the peat bogs north-east of the city. All hope of manoeuvring the tank army due west of the city was lost, and 3rd Guards was tied up in heavy fighting close to Lvov. By 21 July three German divisions moved up from Stanislav and it needed more than a tank army to shift them. The Front command therefore decided to bring 3rd Guards

Tank Army round to the west and northwest, move Lelyushenko's 4th tank on from the south and advance Kurochkin's 60th Army to attack from the east, while Moskalenko's 38th Army would drive from Peremysl to the southern outskirts of Lvov. Radio contact had been lost with Rybalko, but his orders to disengage were dispatched by aircraft and carried by the chief of staff of the tank army, Maj.-Gen. D.D. Vakhmet'ev. The essence of the orders to Rybalko was that he should leave only a light force to cover Lvov, bringing his main body in an outflanking movement to the north-west and into the area of Yavorov, thus cutting the German escape route to the west and leaving a force from 3rd Guards free to co-operate with 60th and 38th Armies in the actual reduction of the city.

Marshal Koniev did not wish to see his most powerful forces tied down in front of Lvov while the Germans organized a defence line on the river San and the Vistula. The right-flank armies of the Front, 1st Guards Tank Army and 13th Army, were already racing for the San, coming down from the north-east, and on the evening of 23 July, Katukov's tanks reached the San near the town of Yaroslav. Twenty-four hours earlier Rybalko detached two tank brigades and two battalions of motorized infantry to hold the line near Lvov, setting his main body on the move to the area around Yavorov. By the evening of 24 July, 3rd Guards was deployed in the triangle Yavorov–Mostiska–Sudovaya Vyshnaya, from which it launched attacks from the east against Peremysl and from the west against Lvov. Lelyushenko's tank army, or at least one corps (10th), was already in Lvov; Lelyushenko's orders specified an attack on Sambor to the south-west of Lvov to cut another German escape route, but Lelyushenko decided to take Lvov 'on the way there'—*po puti*. The bulk of 4th Tank Army closed on Lvov by the evening of 22 July, while 10th Tank Corps was actually inside the city, though cut off from its fellows.

So the concentric attack on Lvov took shape and opened with all forces on 24 July: Kurochkin's 60th Army from the east and north-east, 10th Tank Corps in the southern suburbs, Rybalko's 6th Guards Tank Corps from the west, leaving only one escape route for the German troops, the south-westerly Lvov–Sambor road. It took three days and nights of heavy fighting to clear the ancient Ukrainian city. Kurochkin's riflemen fought their way in street by street, Poluboyarov's 4th Guards Tank Corps from the east linked up with 10th Tank Corps in the south, but to the west Rybalko's corps was held in check. On the evening of 26 July the Soviet commanders saw signs of a German withdrawal to the south-west and at dawn the next day Soviet armies attacked from all directions—from the west (3rd Guards Tank), from the north, east and south-east (60th Army) and from within the city itself (4th Guards Tank and 10th Tank Corps). Almost simultaneously 3rd Guards Tank Army, supported by units from 1st Guards Tank Army, stormed Peremysl during the night.

Smashing German resistance at Lvov, together with the capture of Rava Russkaya, Peremysl, and Vladimir–Volynskii, broke Army Group North Ukraine in two; Fourth *Panzer,* fighting off the Russians all the way, fell back on the Vistula, while First *Panzer* (with the 1st Hungarian Army) drew back to the south-west and down to the Carpathians. Rybalko's 3rd Guards Army now received orders to advance to the Vistula, to force a crossing on the night of 29 July, seize a bridgehead on the western bank and capture the town of Sandomierz. Katukov's tank army was directed to the Vistula just south of Sandomierz at Baranow, Sokolov's cavalry-mechanized group was to force the river to the north, at Annopol, and Pukhov's 13th Army was directed to the Vistula along 'the Sandomierz axis'. Zhadov's 5th Guards Army (Front reserve) was also moved to the Vistula, where Koniev's main strength was gathering—two infantry armies (5th Guards and 13th), two tank armies (1st Guards and 3rd Guards) and a 'cavalry-mechanized group'.

Koniev's armies took the Vistula at a rush. By the evening of 30 July Rybalko's tank crews, accompanied by Sokolov's cavalry, had crossed the river and taken three smallish bridgeheads north and south of Annopol, but these hastily improvised crossings failed to provide the requisite strength and impetus to enlarge the bridgeheads. Pukhov's 13th Army and the lead units of Katukov's 1st Guards Tank Army were more successful in the Baranow area; Pukhov got two divisions over, the boats and rafts carrying Soviet soldiers often racing side by side with the makeshift ferries laden with retreating German soldiers. By the evening, 305th Rifle Division (13th Army) had carved out a bridgehead five miles deep and with a frontage of some eight miles. Behind the infantry and the armour came the bridging units, the 20th Bridging Battalion and the 6th Bridging Brigade, which by 1 August put down, under persistent German air attack, heavy bridging equipment and pontoons capable of carrying loads up to fifty–sixty tons and sixteen tons respectively: these carried the men and equipment for two corps plus 182 tanks, 11 armoured carriers, 55 guns and 94 lorries across the Vistula into the 'Sandomierz' bridgehead.

On the left flank Koniev ordered Lelyushenko to swing 4th Tank Army to the south-west on to Sambor (where he should have been in the first place), to take Drohobych and Borislav off the march by the evening of 28 July, and in co-operation with the right-flank formations of Grechko's 1st Guards Army to seal off the German route to the San to the north-west. The German rearguards, fighting with great skill and very stubbornly, did not let Lelyushenko pass so easily and held 4th Tank Army at Drohobych. The infantry armies of the left flank, 1st Guards and 18th Army, did nevertheless enjoy some successes of their own; Grechko's 1st Guards took the regional centre of Stanislav on 26 July and by the end of the month 18th Army captured the rail junction of Dolina and cut the motor road leading through the Carpathians into the Hungarian plain. Though the main task of 1st Ukrainian Front lay now in a north-westerly direction towards the Vistula, Koniev ordered the two left-flank armies to seize the passes over the Carpathians leading to Hummene, Uzhorod and Mukachevo. If Army Group North Ukraine had been split down the middle, 1st Ukrainian Front was now operating on two diverging axes, the 'Sandomierz axis' and the 'Carpathian axis', thereby complicating the problem of controlling the separate armies; and with a massive battle building up for the Sandomierz bridgehead, Koniev at the end of July consulted the *Stavka*, suggesting that the armies on the Carpathian axis should come under independent command. He was informed that there was one unassigned Front administration, that of Col.-Gen. I.E. Petrov (lately in the Crimea), and within a few days Petrov's new command—4th Ukrainian Front—was officially activated to take control of operations in the foothills of the Carpathians.

Meanwhile Rokossovskii's left-flank armies—8th Guards, 69th Army, 1st Polish Army and 2nd Tank Army—raced on to the Vistula and up to Warsaw. Behind them lay the ghastly discovery of the 'death-factory' of Maidanek, lying just to the west of Lublin, where more than a million people died and many thousands more suffered the sub-human existence reserved for the inmates of the camps. Maidanek was only the first of such horrors upon which the advancing Red Army stumbled—Treblinka, Sobibor, Auschwitz–Birkenau, Belzec and Stutthof, all extermination camps with their mountains of dead. Maidanek was but a grisly foretaste. Chuikov's and Kolpakchi's mobile columns were advancing north-west but Chuikov was baffled by the apparently contradictory orders he received—'halt the advance', 'consolidate positions', 'resume the advance': the tempo of the Soviet advance as a whole was beginning to flag as the armies moved further and further from their bases, and now the confusion of instructions tended to slow 8th Guards and 2nd Tank Army in their sweep to the Vistula. Further to the east, on the outer edge of these left-flank armies, General Kryukov's 'cavalry-mechanized group' drove on towards Siedlce, which the Front command hoped to seize off the march towards the evening of 24 July. Siedlce, sixty miles west of Brest-Litovsk, was an important road and rail junction, one that played a significant part in supplying Brest-Litovsk itself—and, equally, could serve as an escape hatch for German units trapped at Brest; but before 11th Tank Corps could rush Siedlce, German armoured and infantry reinforcements moved in. With Soviet tanks in the suburbs at dawn on 25 July, German units swept in from the north and north-east, displaying every intention of holding the town. German bombers attacked the Soviet tank units and armoured counter-attacks forced 11th Corps to take up defensive positions; heavy fighting surged through the southern outskirts of Siedlce, while Kryukov detached 65th Tank Brigade to deal with a German armoured column moving down from the north-west. Though sections of the town were in Soviet hands by 26 July, the group commander decided to launch a concentric attack the next day, surround Siedlce completely and then storm it, a task assigned to 11th Corps and 2nd Guards Cavalry Corps. Though this cleared most of the town, it proved impossible to dislodge the SS troops and elements of three German infantry divisions holding the northern part of Siedlce. Only on 31 July, after a powerful barrage and the use of a regiment of bombers, could 11th Corps, cavalry units and riflemen from

47th Army clear the Siedlce area, giving Soviet troops undisputed possession of two major communication centres—Siedlce and Minsk–Masowiecki—on the approaches to Warsaw.

On the morning of 27 July the first echelon of 2nd Tank Army—3rd and 8th Guards Tank Corps—moved off in the general direction of Warsaw–Praga from the Deblin area. Chuikov's 8th Guards still received contradictory orders: on 26 July, Chuikov was ordered to reach the Vistula on the Garwolin–Deblin sector, keeping his army in 'compact order' and 'in full readiness for a major engagement', with forward detachments sent ahead to a considerable distance—only to be told a few hours later that '8th Guards Army will not become dispersed . . . the Army will have its main grouping on the right flank, bearing in mind that the activization of enemy operations is most likely in the direction of Siedlce–Lukow'. Col.-Gen. Chuikov nevertheless realized that sooner or later his formations must force the Vistula, even though they were coasting alongside it at the moment; Chuikov himself set out to choose a particular sector, and a little to the north-west of Magnuszew, in the village of Wilga, the Army commander conducted his own reconnaissance, driving into the middle of a Polish crowd in holiday mood, taking the air on the Vistula bank and enjoying the music of accordions. From observation of the western bank, it was clear that the Germans did not expect an attack here and Chuikov plumped for the Magnuszew sector to make his crossing of the Vistula. Returning to his own HQ, Chuikov reported to Rokossovskii about his decision, which the Front commander noted and promised to reply the next day. At noon on 30 July Rokossovskii came on the line and authorized Chuikov to prepare plans for forcing the Vistula on the Maciejowice–Stezyce sector (south of the sector Chuikov had himself chosen), giving him three days' notice; not unnaturally, Chuikov asked for 'the Wilga sector', the one he had already chosen, and pointed out that he could begin operations 'early tomorrow morning, not in three days' time, since all preparatory work has been done here'. He submitted at once plans specifying 1 August as the operational date, and this was approved. On the morning of 1 August Chuikov's men launched their boats into the darkness; the scouts reached the western bank and had cleared the first line of German trenches before the artillery opened fire, as the rifle battalions began their crossing.

On the first day of its renewed advance (27 July), 2nd Tank Army covered about thirty miles, driving between German units stretched from Garwolin to Stochek and pushing them back on Kolbel–Sennitsa–Kalyszyn, operations which 2nd Tank conducted under increasingly heavy air attack and with each corps running very low on fuel and ammunition. This compelled the army commander to slow his advance, move up the tankers and supply lorries, regroup and prepare to resume the attack on 29 July.

After a preliminary artillery bombardment and air attacks on the morning of 29 July, the tanks of 3rd Corps moved forward again, cutting clean through the German lines, capturing Stanislawow and drawing up to Radzymin. 8th

Corps outflanked Sennitsa from the east, took the town during the course of 29 July and by the evening was advancing on Okuniew. Dubovoi's 16th Corps, checked before Kolbel, set off on an outflanking move to the west of the Warsaw highway and broke into the rear of the 73rd German Infantry Division defending the Kolbel area, where a section of Soviet tanks captured the commanding general of the 73rd, General Franckel. As 2nd Tank Army raced up to Praga, with its right-flank columns (3rd Corps) cutting the road and rail links connecting Warsaw with Bialystok, 47th Army drew up to the Kalyszyn–Tsegluv line and 8th Guards Army to Tsegluv–Garwolin, the area into which German troops from Brest-Litovsk were retiring—only to find Soviet units at their back.

On 31 July the lead tanks of the Soviet armoured columns, together with some motorized infantry, suddenly burst into Otwock and Radzymin, not more than a dozen miles from Warsaw. This put Soviet tanks north-east and east of Praga, the Warsaw suburb on the eastern bank of the Vistula, which fairly bristled with defences—pill-boxes and fixed firing positions, field fortifications, numerous minefields, anti-tank and anti-infantry obstacles in profusion. By the evening, 2nd Tank Army command knew that the Soviet tank units had stumbled into a heavy and formidable concentration of German armour with at least five divisions, SS formations *Wiking, Herman Goering* and *Totenkopf* plus two *Panzer* divisions, the 19th and the 4th. To the east, in the area of Siedlce, Soviet mobile forces were still engaging strong concentrations of German armour (including SS units), with Yushchuk's 11th Tank Corps—also low on fuel and ammunition— along with cavalry units of the 'cavalry-mechanized group' trying to batter its way forward and clear the Germans out of Siedlce, all at a time when Rokossovskii's right flank was finally breaking down German resistance at Brest-Litovsk and the 2nd Belorussian Front—on Rokossovskii's right flank—fought for possession of Bialystok. One by one these German strong-points—Siedlce, Brest-Litovsk and Bialystok—fell to the advancing Soviet armies by the end of July, but the 1st Belorussian Front command showed a justifiable nervousness about the 'Praga concentration' of German forces. On 26 July Front HQ anticipated the weight of the German counter-attack falling in the Siedlce–Lukow area and urged Chuikov to hold his 'main grouping' on the right flank in order to counter the 'activization' of enemy operations. At that moment 2nd Tank army was advancing into the thick of a considerable concentration of German strength, into the midst of the SS divisions and the *Panzer* divisions deploying the latest heavy tanks, the 'Royal Tigers', when Soviet tank divisions were all feeling the hurt of their losses sustained in the drive from Lublin to the approaches to Warsaw—no less than 500 tanks and SP guns. During the night of 28 July the citizens of Warsaw could hear the sounds of the battle waged between German and Soviet tank forces at Wolomin, but once at Praga the commander of 2nd Tank issued orders that the suburb must not be assaulted by tank units; motorized infantry would first carry out a thorough reconnaissance and uncover the weak spots in the enemy defences, and only then could the armour be introduced.

Soviet tanks had definitely breached the southern perimeter of the German bridgehead on the eastern bank of the Vistula at the approaches to Warsaw, but—contrary to what the inhabitants of Warsaw imagined and the command of the 'Home Army *(Armija Krajowa, AK)* believed—the German defence was by no means disorganized. The precipitate withdrawal of German rear units, civilian bodies and military commands, begun on 21 July, had already been halted on 26 July when fresh German military forces began to move up to Warsaw and be deployed south of the city itself. *Luftwaffe* General Stahel took over military command of Warsaw on 27 July and the German authorities announced to the populace at large that the city would be defended, at the same time conscripting civilian labour to build fortifications. To the east, on the other side of the wide Vistula, Maj-Gen. Radzievskii, temporary commander of 2nd Tank Army, realized at the end of July that his formations were in contact with three, possibly four, *Panzer* divisions and with one infantry division; to meet the threat of a powerful counter-attack, 2nd Tank must concentrate and be gathered into a 'fist', with 3rd Tank Corps at Wolomin, 8th Guards Tank Corps at Okuniew, 16th Tank across a line running from Zbytki (near the Vistula) to Milosna Stara, some five miles north-west of Milosna Stara. All tank formations were to go over to the defensive as from midnight on 1 August.

Five hours after the Soviet tanks rolled into their defensive positions and Soviet infantry dug in, on that same day, 7 August, men of the *Armija Krajowa* launched their own offensive inside Warsaw, attacking German installations and strong points; the 'Warsaw rising' had begun, and the city was speedily plunged into a savage internal battle.

Throughout the late winter and early spring of 1944, as 'the tide of Teheran' fast spent itself, the Prime Minister and Marshal Stalin conducted their rasping correspondence over Poland. While the British government tried to steer the Polish government in London in the direction of a Russo-Polish 'settlement', Stalin took an unwavering stand on two issues—recognition of the Curzon line and the need to 'reorganize' the Polish government, 'the London clique' so bitterly assailed by Moscow. Towards the end of December 1943 members of the Polish government, while probing as deeply as they could into the nature of the Teheran 'agreement', pressed more evidence on the British government relating to 'the most energetic agitation' aimed at 'the Polish government and its organs in the home country' conducted by Communist agencies; the 'infiltration of Eastern and Central Poland' by Russian partisan detachments was proceeding apace, while 'communist bands at large' were provoking German reprisals against the civilian population and the same bands had even 'murdered a number of soldiers and members of the Polish Underground Movement'.

In a conversation on 20 December, Prime Minister Mikolajczyk and Mr Eden explored the implications of a Soviet advance into Poland. Mikolajczyk pointed

to what lay behind the Soviet accusations laid at the door of the Polish government—
'the threat of ruthless extermination of the leadership of our underground movement'
in the wake of the Soviet advance—while Eden, having read a note on Stalin's
declaration at Teheran regarding Poland, urged the Polish government to 'state
its position in order to show Stalin that he laboured under a mistake'. On the
question of frontiers, Eden told Mikolajczyk that his impression was 'that the
Soviets insist on the Curzon line, but I did not try to get to the core of the
matter'. Two days later, at dinner on 22 December, Eden took up all these
matters in greater detail with the Polish government. In an attempt to find a
way to resume Soviet–Polish diplomatic relations, he proposed that the Poles
should issue a statement 'denying all charges levelled against them' and proposing
'the co-ordination of military operations on Polish territory', whereupon Mikolajczyk
pointed to the fate of the previous agreement made in 1941 on 'co-ordination'
and demanded that British troops be sent to Poland once Red Army units crossed
into Polish territory. Eden did not find this a very useful suggestion, but Mikolajczyk
persisted with it; it was left to Sir Alexander Cadogan to propose separating
requests for resumption of diplomatic relations from proposals dealing with co-
operation. On the territorial settlement, the British members expounded the plan
for shifting the Polish frontiers from east to west, outlining the Soviet claims
which 'embraced all the territories up to the Curzon line and the "Botha Line"
in Galicia'.

At the end of December the Polish government issued its formal denial of
Soviet charges, referring to its 'instruction for the Home Country' issued on 27
October 1943 and rejecting charges that 'Communists in Poland were being
murdered' on the orders of the commander of the Secret Army; in spite of the
failure of previous attempts at 'co-ordination', the Polish government declared its
willingness for 'Polish armed action' to be included in 'the general strategic plan
of the Allies'. Within a week, the first Red Army units had crossed the former
Polish frontier and on 5 January 1944 the Polish government issued its own
statement, referring to itself as 'the only and legal steward and spokesman of
the Polish nation recognized by Poles at home and abroad' and asking for 'the
earliest re-establishment of sovereign Polish administration in the liberated territories
of the Republic of Poland' not 'in *all* the liberated territories', a formulation that
was deleted under pressure from the Foreign Office. This declaration, for all its
pruning, produced a sour reaction in some quarters of the British press and a
tart comment from Stalin in his letter of 7 January to the Prime Minister—'the
latest declaration of the Polish *émigré* government' did not encourage him to
think that 'these circles can be made to see reason . . . They are incorrigible.'

Three days later, on 10 January, Mikolajczyk learned at first hand from
President Benes (who had recently journeyed to Moscow) something of Stalin's
views. Stalin did not 'exclude Soviet–Polish agreement' if their present government
was changed (Stalin's ire being directed principally at Sosnkowski, the Polish
C-in-C); any agreement concerning eastern Poland was to be based on the Curzon

line; the western frontiers of Poland—which 'did not preclude the Oder line'—could involve a Russo–Polish–Czecho–Slovak–Anglo–American agreement; there would be no pressure and no 'proposal of adhesion' for Poland to join a Polish–Czech–Russian pact; Stalin's 'positive attitude' towards Poland resulted from his view that, though Germany was to be destroyed, there was no such thing as 'a communist Germany'; and finally, on fears about the 'Sovietization' of Poland and Europe, Stalin dismissed this by saying that 'we are not such fools as to undertake things we cannot achieve'. Peace would depend on co-operation with England and America; Germany 'must be disrupted'; Italy and France could be counted out, so that 'guarantees' for Poland must engage Poland itself, Czechoslovakia, England and America. None of this gave the Polish Prime Minister much comfort; in territorial terms Poland 'was to be deprived of half of her territory, including those two frontier-pillars, Lvov and Vilno'. President Benes seemed merely to be 'repeating Soviet arguments' and appeared 'mesmerized by Soviet strength'.

The very next day a *TASS* announcement, authorized by 'the Soviet government', threw up fresh alarms within the Polish government. It was a reply to the Polish statement of 5 January and aimed to counter 'a number of incorrect assertions . . . among them the incorrect assertion concerning the Soviet–Polish frontiers', all in a document which, while not totally hostile or wholly negative, introduced new and significant shifts in the Soviet position. The Soviet government no longer considered 'the frontiers of 1939 to be unchangeable', thus marking a change in the prevailing Soviet stance on the 'Ribbentrop–Molotov' line of 1939; the Soviet–Polish border could run approximately along the so-called 'Curzon line' with some corrections 'in favour of Poland', so that 'the eastern borders of Poland can be fixed by agreement with the Soviet Union'. The Soviet claim to the western Ukraine and western Belorussian districts was based on the plebiscite carried out 'according to broad democratic principles in 1941': if this was not enough, the Soviet statement referred to the 'injustice' worked by the treaty of Riga in 1921 which had been 'forced on the Soviet Union'—real revision of diplomatic history. The Polish government, which 'frequently plays into the hands of the German invaders' through 'its wrong policy', came in for abuse—'cut off from its people . . . incapable of establishing friendly relations with the Soviet Union . . . equally incapable of organizing an active struggle against the German invaders in Poland itself '—but the statement ended with a saving clause: '*at the same time,* the interests of Poland and the Soviet Union lie in the establishment of firm friendly relations between our two countries'.

The effect of this Soviet statement was to bring the British and Polish governments into immediate collision; the former found 'the Soviet proposals as a fair basis for negotiation', even 'a great step forward from the Teheran negotiations', while the latter insisted that there was 'no reason to believe in the sincerity of Soviet intentions'—indeed, 'all signs are to the contrary'. The exchanges between Eden and Mikolajczyk of 11 January were tense and not a little painful. At the close Mr Eden stipulated that the Polish reply to the Soviet statement must be agreed with him, and he painted a gloomy picture of the consequences of a Polish failure to respond to this Soviet initiative. Two days later Mikolajczyk read to Eden the draft of a reply to the Soviet statement of 11 January; the phrasing of the third point, protesting against 'unilateral decisions or *faits accomplis*' and arguments 'designed to justify the loss by Poland of about half of her territory', caused Eden to suggest a rephrasing, but this was not welcome to the Polish cabinet, which insisted on the retention of the original form of words. Only after lengthy discussion and Eden's assurance that the British press 'would be asked to produce as its own the arguments which have been removed from the Polish declaration', was the section amended and the text presented by Eden to the Soviet Ambassador on 14 January, with the injunction that the British government 'gave its support' to the document as a means to 'paving the way to an understanding'. That an 'understanding' was feasible at this juncture—a seeming break in the clouds of Soviet obduracy—appeared to be the overriding impression in London, nurtured by the reports from Moscow. Mr. Balfour (in charge of the British Embassy in Moscow in the absence of Sir Archibald Clark Kerr) reported that Molotov seemed to think the 11 January Soviet statement an 'initiative' likely to win British and American support, while Ambassador Harriman thought an agreement on the lines of the Soviet compact with President Benes was part of the Soviet plan, provided the Polish government was 'reorganized' and the Soviet position on boundaries given a form of recognition. Otherwise, in the opinion of Ambassador Averell Harriman, the deeper the Soviet advance into Poland, the less the likelihood of agreement acceptable to the Poles.

The Polish declaration of 14 January produced in turn the Soviet declaration of 17 January, a document that suggests that its predecessor of 11 January was more a manoeuvre than a real 'initiative': *TASS* on 17 January proclaimed that the Polish declaration of 14 January 'cannot be considered as other than the rejection of the Curzon Line', that the proposal to open 'official negotiations' between the Polish and Soviet governments is 'intended to mislead public opinion', and that 'in the opinion of Soviet circles' it was clear that 'the present Polish Government does not wish to establish good neighbourly relations with the Soviet Union'. This was a curious, alarmingly inflexible document, citing first 'the Soviet government' and then 'Soviet circles', and implying that if 'the *present* Polish government' did not want good relations then there could be a government (and one now existed in embryo—the *Krajowa Rada Narodowa*, recently founded under Communist sponsorship) that would. For good measure 'Soviet circles' threw in a reference to 'the active participation in the hostile anti-Soviet campaign of slander [connected with the] "Katyn murders" '. But whether it was 'the Soviet government' or 'Soviet circles', it was clearly Stalin's intention to have no truck with the Polish government as it stood. It had to be discredited, outflanked, isolated or forced to some final extravagant and ruinous act. Meanwhile the American government had instructed Ambassador Harriman to offer 'the good offices' of the United States in promoting a resumption of Soviet–Polish relations, an initiative firmly turned down by Molotov on 23 January. Though naturally given to wooden repetitiveness, Molotov twice insisted that 'conditions are not yet ripe' for mediation or for negotiation in any form, until there had been 'a radical improvement of the composition of the Polish government' involving the exclusion of 'the pro-fascist imperialist elements' and the inclusion of 'democratic elements'. Over Poland, Stalin appeared to believe with a sense of Shakespearian finality that ripeness is all.

On 20 January in London, the Prime Minister and Eden conferred with Mikolajczyk and Romer at this latest turn in the Soviet–Polish crisis. The Prime Minister chose not to mince his words on this occasion and began: 'I want the Polish government to accept the Curzon Line without Lvov as a basis for negotiations with the Russians. . . .', going on to ask for Polish acceptance not only in principle but 'with enthusiasm'. Poland would be cast for 'the responsibility of rendering great service to the future of Europe [as] the guardians of Europe against Germany on the east, and that would ensure a friendly Russia'. Poland would get compensation up to the Oder and East Prussia, but as for the eastern frontier it was unthinkable that Britain should go to war with the Soviet Union over such an issue and America 'would never do so'; Britain had not entered the war for 'the eastern frontiers of Poland' and it was groundless to think that 'we could embark on a conflict with Russia on that issue'. What the Prime Minister said now in private he was prepared to repeat in public. Mikolajczyk insisted that the Polish government was prepared to negotiate—the last Polish government declaration made this clear—a point the Prime Minister readily agreed, interrupting to say that the latest Soviet rejoinder (the text of 17 January) was 'brutal and not convincing'. Mikolajczyk tried to inject 'revision of the Riga treaty' (dating back to 1921, and the 'only valid instrument governing Polish frontiers') as the basis for negotiation and advocated that a solution be found in the exchange of populations rather than of territories (though keeping the population changes to a minimum). The Prime Minister reminded Mikolajczyk that in fact there was not much room for negotiation, that 'the starting point must be the Curzon line'—without any settlement, the Russian army would roll on, and the Pole in Lvov who might ultimately be transferred to Oppeln would merely suffer the automatic fate of having his future decided by the Soviet government. Without a settlement, Poland would be 'exposed to Russian wrath'; the war could not be won without Russia, Allied bombers alone could not do it and it was necessary to see the Russian point of view. The Prime Minister was ready to try to influence Stalin, to declare Polish readiness to talk on the basis of the Curzon line (subject to Polish compensation in the west) and to insist that it was 'inadmissible' to undermine the authority of the Polish government. On the question of Soviet co-operation with the Polish underground movement, Churchill saw the pressing need for an agreement but a prior Soviet–Polish settlement was necessary and 'the Curzon line leads to that'. In his message to Stalin the Prime Minister wished to explain the British point of view and to set out what the Polish government was prepared to accept, the principle of non-interference in the internal affairs of another government and 'a speedy understanding' concerning the Polish underground. The matter was urgent and the Prime Minister needed from the Poles 'as full a contribution as possible' to use in his telegram to Stalin: the moment for the Poles was 'tragic and decisive'. At Milolajczyk's question as to what Polish fighting men—many from the eastern territories, anticipating a return one day to their homes—would now think of 'Western pledges, slogans and declarations of principles', Churchill remained silent.

Before making its reply, the Polish government set out four questions on the British guarantee on Polish independence and territorial status (addressed by Count Raczynski to Eden on 23 January). Mikolajczyk put the position to the Delegate of the Polish Government in Poland in a signal dated 25–26 January and the process of sounding out the American government was put in train. On 25 January the War Cabinet had already decided to forward a message from Mr Churchill to Stalin, to be delivered by the British Ambassador on 1 February. That message informed Stalin of the Prime Minister's advice to the Polish government 'to accept the Curzon line as a basis for discussion. I spoke of the compensations which Poland would receive in the North and in the West. . . but I did not mention the point about Königsberg', and went on to point out that 'the Polish Ministers were very far from rejecting the prospects thus unfolded but asked for time to consider the matter. . . '.The message was 'a statement in broad outline of the position of His Majesty's Government in Great Britain' and sought from Stalin information on what steps he would be prepared to take to help 'resolve this serious problem'.

Stalin duly conveyed his impressions to the British Ambassador on 2 February, stating that he wanted a definite acceptance of the Curzon line from 'the Polish government in exile' and that there must be some 'reconstruction' of this government before relations with it could be resumed; he criticized the Polish government's methods of directing the underground movement, members of which would be attacked and disarmed if they obstructed the Russians—otherwise the Red Army would help. And with Soviet armies once west of the Curzon line, the Poles need not fear for their position, the Polish government could return and set up a broad-based government free of Russian interference. Stalin's letter of 4 February (received in London the next day) added little but emphasized that the 'Curzon line' was a Soviet concession to the Poles; what was now required involved a Polish declaration for a revision of the Riga treaty and the acceptance of the Curzon line as the new Soviet–Polish boundary; the 'northern' territorial concession to the Poles stood, save for the 'minimum claim' of the Soviet Union against German holdings, the ice-free port of Königsberg; and finally, 'I think you realize that we cannot re-establish relations with the present Polish government'—the composition of this government must be 'thoroughly improved', and without it 'no good can be expected'.

At the beginning of February the Polish government obtained some response to the questions it had put to the British and American governments about guarantees for the Polish frontiers: the British note could not specify 'any final answer' and the American memorandum offered support to 'Prime Minister Churchill's efforts to bring about the re-establishment of relations between the Polish and Soviet governments' but firmly eschewed guarantees. On 6 February the Polish ministers again met Churchill and Eden, who advised the Polish government to accept the Curzon line, together with the Soviet demands for Lvov and Königsberg. Eden read out the British Ambassador's telegrams of 3 February describing the course and content of his talk with Stalin and the replies Stalin had given to the Prime Minister's questions. Churchill also referred to Stalin's observation that the Polish underground was ordered not to co-operate with the Russians. This last point Mikolajczyk took up straight away and in his turn he referred to the orders given to the underground—in particular the instruction of 27 October 1943, which advised that if Polish–Soviet relations were re-established the underground was to come out with open support for Soviet troops, but that otherwise they should remain inactive though at no time had orders been given to oppose Soviet troops. Now, even though the re-establishment of relations looked unlikely, the underground commanders (who had been consulted) were quite prepared to come out 'and meet the requirements of the Soviet commanders'. The local Polish military commander, with the civilian underground authority, was to meet with and declare to the Soviet troops their willingness to 'co-ordinate their actions in the fight against the common foe'. This pleased the Prime Minister, but Mikolajczyk added that there was one reservation—the underground forces were not prepared to be press-ganged into the 'Polish formations created in Russia . . . under Berling's command'.

Thereafter the meeting drifted towards gloomier talk. Mikolajczyk disclosed the contents of messages from Warsaw, asserting Poland's territorial integrity and also confirming the establishment of a rival to the Polish underground by the Polish Workers Party (the *PPR*). The Soviet plan, Mikolajczyk continued, was to establish even before the Curzon line had been crossed a 'Committee of National Liberation' formed out of pro-Soviet elements in the Soviet Union, in the USA and if possible in Britain, followed by the creation, once over the Curzon line, of a 'Polish government' through the *Krajowa Rada Narodowa* already set up under Soviet auspices. This was taken by the Prime Minister to be merely the reinforcement of his own argument—if there were no agreement, then these things must inevitably and automatically come to pass. The Curzon line was 'the best that the Poles could expect and all that [the Prime Minister] would ask the British people to demand on their behalf'. Mikolajczyk, however, questioned Russian good faith—it seemed that they were trying to make the Polish government refuse their terms in advance, for it was a relatively simple matter 'to bring the Polish government into negotiations'. To this the Prime Minister could return only one answer: without the 'great victories' already won by the Russians, Poland would have had no future at all; he himself would do his 'utmost for Poland' but failing agreement with the Polish government he must then 'make [his] own position clear to the Russians and . . . come to an understanding with them'. There were only three choices: an agreement among all the parties, an Anglo–Russian agreement, or a decision 'to do nothing' and simply let the Russians roll over Poland, setting up their own government in Warsaw.

Against this background the Prime Minister drafted a message to Stalin dated 12 February, incorporating the instructions given to Polish underground commanders to disclose identities and 'meet the requirements' of Soviet commanders 'even in the absence of a resumption of Polish–Soviet relations', declaring the readiness of the Polish government to pronounce the treaty of Riga 'unalterable' and to negotiate a new frontier 'the basis of negotiations being the Curzon line as far as the old Austrian frontier and passing thence west of Lvov' (leaving Peremysl to Poland). In addition, the Polish government 'are ready to remove the commander-in-chief [Sosnkowski] from his post and to drop from the Cabinet the two members of it to whom you object, viz. General Kukiel and M. Kot'. Since the Polish government's abandonment of all territory to the east of the Curzon line 'is bound up with the transfer to Poland of what is now German territory', the Curzon line would be a 'temporary' demarcation, though until the time of 'final demarcation' the civil administration in liberated territory to the east of the Curzon line would be a Soviet responsibility and that to the west would fall to the Poles.

It was an ingenious scheme but one at once rendered unworkable by the refusal of the Polish government to 'go so far as this'. Just how far to go was debated in a tense meeting between the Prime Minister and the two Polish ministers on 16 February, when Mikolajczyk in place of the alternative draft message sought by the Prime Minister, produced a short paper and an explanation of the principles behind it. The Poles could not accept the Curzon line, nor could they take 'final decisions regarding future frontiers'; rather they suggested a demarcation line running east of Vilno and Lvov which should become effective immediately. The cession of Königsberg to the USSR would also mean an additional threat to Poland. Nor could the Polish government 'reconstitute' itself at the behest of a foreign power, however embittered the attacks. (*Pravda* on 12 February had just delivered another attack.) Little of this seemed to impress Churchill: did the Polish government now wish him to inform Stalin that 'no progress could be made'? For in that event nothing would be easier—the Russians were on the verge of a rapid advance; they could hold a plebiscite from which their opponents were excluded; 'Poland might be even affiliated to the Soviet Union'. There must be 'some *modus vivendi*'; this was, Churchill explained, 'a very powerful ally' to whom he was addressing himself on behalf of the Poles, an ally 'which had broken the German Army as no other nation would have done' and one with whom we must march through what must be 'a very bloody year'. He must reply to Stalin, and in the absence of Polish agreeement 'he would himself have to support the Soviet occupation and permanent annexation of all territory up to the Curzon line, including Lvov, on the understanding that the Poles received compensation in the north and south'. There must be 'an arrangement with Marshal Stalin' before the Russians occupied all Poland—'if the Polish government would not participate they would be the first to suffer'. What the Polish government presently offered would not satisfy Marshal Stalin: the 'brutal facts' could not be overlooked, the Prime Minister could 'no more stop the Russian advance than stop the tide coming in', it was 'no use saying something which would only make the Russians more angry and drive them to the solution of a puppet government in Warsaw'. The Polish government must make 'suggestions . . . on practical lines'—if the Russians rejected the settlement, the Poles lost nothing; if the Russians agreed, 'the Poles would gain a lot'. On 19 February (two days after Mikolajczyk and Romer told the Prime Minister that they favoured a message to Stalin on the lines discussed even though the Polish cabinet refused to agree, but Mikolajczyk sanctioned a message indicating his acquiescence now and his adherence in the future), Churchill told Stalin that he hoped soon—after 'wrestling continually with the Poles'—to send proposals for the Soviet leader's consideration. 'I must warn you that these proposals will very likely split the Polish government': in that phrase, meant as an earnest indication of the gravity of the situation, the Prime Minister signalled Stalin his victory and provided him with a cue for action. Conditions were 'ripening' apace.

The Prime Minister sent his message, with the amended draft, through the British Ambassador on 21 February: the Polish government were ready to discuss with the Soviet government 'a new frontier between Poland and the Soviet Union', together with future frontiers in the north and west; until the Polish government returned to Poland it could not 'formally abdicate its rights in any part of Poland as hitherto constituted', but the vigorous prosecution of the war in collaboration with Soviet armies would be greatly assisted by the Soviet government facilitating the speedy return of the Polish government to liberated territory 'at the earliest possible moment', there to take up the reins of civil administration in areas west of the Curzon line; the Polish government had ordered the full collaboration of the Polish underground with Soviet commanders, and the Polish government 'can . . . assure the Russian government that by the time they have entered into diplomatic relations with the Soviet Union' this government would include 'none but persons fully determined to co-operate with the Soviet Union'. The settlement the Prime Minister proposed would be supported 'at the Conférence after the defeat of Hitler' and would be guaranteed 'in after years to the best of our ability'. The day after this was sent, Churchill made his own statement in the House of Commons, supporting the Soviet stand on the Curzon line. To the growls of Poles and the anguished reception of this speech among the Polish underground, was added the blast of German propaganda aimed at Polish troops fighting in Italy and at the population in occupied Poland. Nor could the Polish government derive much comfort from information in the reports from its ambassador in the United States, to the effect that American passivity was due in no small degree to a deliberate policy of allowing the Prime Minister to handle the Soviet–Polish dispute. And if the British Prime Minister could not therefore be shifted by an appeal to the American President, there was less to be expected of Stalin who, according to the Soviet Ambassador to the Czech government in London, had laid down in 1941 (at the time of the first Polish–Soviet negotiations) 'directives' for dealing with the Polish question which were still operative: Stalin wanted an immovable grip on Belorussians and Ukrainians, the latter in particular, and aimed to cure their separatist tendencies by sealing them into the USSR.

At the end of February Stalin gave the British proposals for a settlement short shrift. During the night of 28–29 February, when he received the British Ambassador and discussed the Prime Minister's message of 20 February, all he could muster for the Polish government was 'a snigger' and a burst of sarcasm at being told that the Poles would not go back on the proposals presented by the British—'How handsome of them.' Stalin refused to admit that the Poles wanted a settlement, that the Polish government could not presently accept the Curzon line and that the 'reconstruction' of the government might best be done once it was back in Warsaw. For all practical purposes the British proposals were rejected, a point Stalin made unpleasantly plain in his reply of 3 March—'the time is not yet ripe for a solution of the problem of Soviet–Polish relations', a view he had also communicated to President Roosevelt, and 'the soundness' of which he was 'compelled to re-affirm'. The rejoinder from the Prime Minister on 7 March was almost as terse: the proposals gave the Russians *de facto* possession of the Curzon line 'as soon as you get there', with the promise of British support for it and most probably that of the Americans at the peace conference, while we should regret if 'nothing can be arranged' and the Soviet Union cannot enter into relations with the government we recognize. The British Ambassador in Moscow was carefully instructed to emphasize the danger of a divergence in policy between the Soviet and the Western powers, but to convey neither the hint of threats nor the suggestion of a change in policy towards the Soviet Union. The Ambassador's request for an interview with Stalin, however, went unanswered.

On 16 March Stalin acknowledged receipt of the Prime Minister's message of 7 March only to complain of leakages in the press of their 'secret and personal correspondence'. Five days later Churchill replied that the fault lay with the Soviet Ambassador, but that now he must announce to the Commons that negotiations for a Polish–Soviet settlement had broken down, that 'we will continue to recognize the Polish government' and that now all question of territorial change must 'await the armistice or peace conferences of the victorious powers'. The result of this, and of the British Ambassador's statement on 19 March to Molotov, was a furious retort from Stalin on 23 March: the statements from the British side 'bristle with threats against the Soviet Union', and threats 'may lead to opposite results'. Stalin was incensed that the Prime Minister should go back on his undertaking made at Teheran about the Curzon line, but 'as for me and the

Soviet government, we still adhere to the Teheran standpoint and we have no intention of going back on it': by his references to *'forcible* transferences of territory' the Prime Minister makes it appear that the Soviet Union is 'being hostile to Poland'.

To be sure, you are free to make any statement you like in the House of Commons— that is your business. But should you make a statement of this nature I shall consider that you have committed an unjust and unfriendly act in relation to the Soviet Union. [*Perepiska* . . . , vol. 1, no. 257, p. 255.]

A first reaction to this message was to consider the dispatch of a reply 'in the name of the British government' to the effect that the British position was not a rejection of the Teheran stipulations; that the Prime Minister had pressed the Poles to accept the Curzon line, while the British proposals embodied a working arrangement in the absence of a public declaration on the part of the Polish government, an arrangement made necessary to secure the co-operation of the Polish underground. Soviet rejection of the proposals meant a withdrawal of British mediation but no calumny of 'our Russian ally'.

That this mesage was never sent owed something to the situation in Poland itself, where Red Army units and Polish underground forces in Volhynia had each met in some strength. The *Armija Krajowa* and the Soviet command concluded an agreement towards the end of March, which—as Count Raczynski reported to Eden on 7 April—'did not bode so ill as had first been feared'. The Polish underground forces came under the local operational command of the Soviet military but were to be organized into the 27th Volhynian Infantry Division which would remain under the authority of the Polish underground commander (and thence to the Polish C-in-C in London): the new division, to be fitted out from Soviet stocks, would remain operationally subordinated to the Soviet command until such time as a 'mutual Polish–Soviet agreement' altered the arrangements. This came as more welcome news after earlier reports of men of the Polish underground being discovered, or revealing their identities, only to be shot out of hand, a state of affairs the Polish government hoped to circumvent by seeking the aid of British and American liaison officers who might be seconded to the Polish underground and also to 'the Polish Army within the Soviet lines'. And well ahead of regular Soviet military formations went Soviet partisan units, who were under instructions to push on regardless of frontiers; once on the frontier lines (according to partisan commanders operating from the Ukraine), the unit commander opened a sealed envelope given him by the Ukrainian Partisan Staff which advised him to 'act independently according to the existing conditions and the conscience of a Soviet citizen'. Soviet partisan units crashed into the underground forces of the London-led *Armija Krajowa,* and then the killing started: while the Soviet partisan groups flushed out the *Armija Krajowa* they also helped the small Communist-led *Gwardija Ludowa* to start to its feet. In the spring of 1944 Poles serving in three Soviet partisan brigades were moved out and sent to a special training camp run by Soviet officers, then assigned to a Polish partisan brigade, a programme much intensified in the summer and run under the auspices of the Ukrainian Staff of the Partisan Movement. In April 1944 the Polish Staff of the Partisan Movement was set up with control over all guerrilla units operating on Polish territory—three brigades and a detachment, with a total strength of 1,863 men. The training school attached to the Polish Partisan Staff went on to train over 1,500 men by July, while the Ukrainian Partisan Staff sent thirty experienced instructors to run courses in demolition and radio work; this school in Volhynia disposed of over fifty lorries, five aircraft and large quantities of weapons.

The establishment of communist-led Polish armed forces also included the raising of 1st Polish Corps to the status of 1st Polish Army, announced by the Soviet government on 18 March 1944. On the orders of the Soviet General Staff, 1st Corps was already on the move to the area of Berdichev and Zhitomir, where an army staff, staff services and arms commands, supply services and specialist units were built on to the burgeoning corps, now officially designated 1st Polish Army under the command of Brigadier-General Berling, with Brigadier-General Swierczewski as his deputy and Colonel Zawadzki the deputy commander for political affairs. On 29 April 1st Polish Army consisting of three infantry divisions was put under the operational command of Rokossovskii's 1st Belorussian Front, while at Suma—the base for recruiting and fitting out Polish divisions— the organization for setting up a 'Polish army' was rapidly expanded. In March the *Krajowa Rada Narodowa (KRN)* sent a delegation to Moscow from Poland— Osobka-Morawski, Spychalski, Sidor and Haneman—all of whom passed safely through the Front lines and arrived in Moscow on 16 March, not only to report on themselves but also to make requests for arms, ammunition and equipment— all of which they got, plus their own 'agreement' on the form of co-operation between the Red Army and the *Armija Ludowa*. This delegation also spent some time with the British Ambassador (and with Ambassador Harriman); Sir Archibald Clark Kerr questioned the members of the *KRN* about the general situation in Poland, on the relations between the *KRN* and the London government, on their attitude to the eastern frontier and on the position of the *Armija Krajowa* vis-à-vis the Red Army. Like the Polish army units, the guerrillas of the *Armija Ludowa* had to be rushed into existence and into action; the *Armija Ludowa* used the *Gwardija Ludowa* (the People's Guard) as the foundation on which to build and to expand, a process vastly speeded up by the establishment of the Polish Partisan Staff which worked from Rovno and which came under the control of Zawadzki, deputy commander of 1st Polish Army, a former officer of the *NKVD* and a party member reportedly sentenced after 1936 to ten years' imprisonment.

During the night of 9-10 February Maj.-Gen. Vershigora's 1st Ukrainian Partisan Brigade, a Soviet partisan force some 2,500 strong, crossed the Bug and pushed on to the west, penetrating as far as the river San. The presence of Soviet partisan units—not only Vershigora's, but those of Prokopyuk, Yakovlev, Nadelin, Sankov and many more—acted as a fillip for the *Armija Ludowa (AL)*, which issued its first main operational orders on 26 February. Soviet partisan units and men of the *Armija Ludowa* fought under 'joint command' (Soviet–Polish), a notable instance of which was Mieczyslaw Moczar's action with his *AL* detachment against *SS Wiking* in the Rembluv area in May. Soviet transport aircraft now began dropping arms, uniforms and equipment in systematic flights over eastern Poland, and the *Armija Ludowa* filled out from its first brigade in February to eleven within a few months (a dozen brigades having been initially planned). Soviet partisan commanders—who, even without specific orders, seemed to understand well enough what was required of them in the name of their 'liberation mission'—reported on the growing support for the guerrillas. In addition to its military significance, the Soviet command had never been blind to the role of the partisan movement as a means of winning political influence, not only for themselves but for their communist *protégés*, who were more immediately important. Partisan activity was a powerful means of 'radicalizing' the masses; it was also a means of uncovering the sources of anti-Soviet activity by forcing the hands of opponents.

The Polish underground led from London was the largest and the most powerful in Europe: the Polish national *Armija Krajowa (AK)* thus represented a special obstacle to Stalin, unlike anything he had so far encountered in the war. Though there were instances of 'agreements' between the *Armija Krajowa* and the *Armija Ludowa*, as well as between the *AK* and the Red Army, a savage fight was already on, with each side hunting down the other. The nature of the early agreements between the *AK* and the Red Army suggested that the Soviet military command found it useful to co-operate with Polish underground units in fighting German troops, not least because the *AK* could provide invaluable local support and local knowledge. But once the area was cleared of enemy troops, and the *AK* men were all revealed, they were wholly at the mercy of Soviet security forces. Sporadic, ragged fighting between Soviet or pro-Soviet groups and Polish guerrillas of extreme nationalist conviction—the *Narodowe sily zbrojne*, an ultra-rightist organization—had gone on for some time, as the Soviet command parachuted its own men behind the lines on sabotage assignments, quite separate from *AK* operations. The *Narodowe sily zbrojne*, itself unconnected with the *AK*, also took on organized Soviet partisan detachments and fought it out with them. Meanwhile Stalin rushed to get 'the true Polish resistance' led by the *KRN* installed and operational on Polish soil, while the *Armija Krajowa* pleaded for more air-lifts to drop arms (since only 28 flights had materialized out of a planned 301 in the period from October 1943 to March 1944).

In London Mikolajczyk and the Prime Minister studied the implications of the 'Volhynian agreement' enacted between the Red Army and the *AK*. The first stage had involved the Soviet military taking over and then lighting on more of the *Armija Krajowa*; with the establishment of the 1st Polish Army, an attempt was made to incorporate Polish units into the Soviet-sponsored army, an attempt that was resisted, leading to the shooting of the *AK* commander and the hanging of twenty men of the *AK*. Late in March the Soviet attitude changed, no doubt owing in part to the recognition of the military utility of the *AK,* and a more favourable 'agreement' was drawn up. Mikolajczyk suggested that now was the time to take 'a new initiative' and also to think about sending British and American military missions to Warsaw and the 'Volhynian division'. Churchill thought not: sending British officers would only enrage the Russians; it 'would not help but rather bring much harm'. As for 'activating' British policy, he had broken off his correspondence with Stalin—which also made the situation 'more acute'; at this juncture, while agreeing to an American proposal that there might be a joint Anglo-American 'plain-spoken approach' to Stalin, Churchill elected for 'a moody silence so far as Stalin is concerned'.

On the eve of Mikolajczyk's departure for the United States, a journey on which he embarked with high hopes of turning the tide of Allied policy in Poland's favour and with the Prime Minister's encouragement to seek out the President, Stalin made his own moves to blunt the impact of this development. With an election in the offing, President Roosevelt was not anxious to alienate 'the Polish vote', but (as Ambassador Ciechanowski subsequently pointed out to Mikolajczyk) there was 'no significance in the long run' now that the Polish problem had become part of American internal politics; it was a unique coincidence of events, unlikely to endure or to return. This had also not escaped Stalin's attention, and his reception in Moscow of Professor Oskar Lange, influential among left-wing Polish-Americans, and Father Orlemanski, a Catholic priest from Massachusetts who exercised similar influence, was calculated to have some effect on public opinion in the United States. It was thus a gesture in the direction of President Roosevelt, and a shaft aimed at Mikolajczyk.

Stalin talked at length to Professor Lange on 17 May, opening the discussion with an exchange about the Polish army and the political attitudes of the groups within the Polish 'patriotic' front. The Soviet leader listened to a deal of academic pomposity from Professor Lange, and on being told about 'the radicalism of the Polish people', which he underestimated, and the unrepresentative 'social composition of the Polish army' in the USSR, replied tongue in cheek, though he took note of Professor Lange's observations about the treatment of Poles in the USSR—when the refugees and deportees returned to Poland, tales of their harsh treatment would have an adverse effect on Polish public opinion. On 'the Polish problem', Stalin insisted that he wanted Poland as an ally, that he was ready to arm and equip a Polish army of a million men. He brushed aside arguments that Germany might be too deeply hurt by Polish territorial compensations and demands; he was indifferent to German feelings—the peace would either 'create no desire for German revenge, or it will be such as to make German revenge impossible'; in any event, 'Germany must be destroyed once and for all as a political power.' The co-operation between the Soviet Union, Britain and America, which he readily conceded to be the foundation of any lasting peace, was itself no mere 'temporary conjuncture' but rose from 'a fundamental community of historical interests'. And with the destruction of Germany—conceived at Teheran —'Poland will emerge as a major European power'.

In Poland itself 'the Poles must form their own administration': 'the Polish government must emerge out of Poland itself' and Stalin believed that 'such forces' existed within the Polish underground. While Soviet-sponsored bodies might play a part, an understanding with the London government could be desirable and the door to it 'is never closed'. Stalin was 'favourably disposed' towards Mikolajczyk and Romer, but as far as 'collaboration' between the Polish underground and the Red Army was concerned thought that Mikolajczyk should beware the 'fairy tales of his own intelligence service'. Over the Curzon line, Stalin conceded that there might be adjustments—'four kilometres to east or west'—but Professor Lange reminded him about Lvov and what this meant to 'Americans of Polish descent' and to those Polish refugees sympathetic to the Union of Polish Patriots, who had asked him specifically to raise the question. Any concession on Lvov, Stalin went on, meant he must 'make war on the Ukrainians and there are several millions of them in the Red Army': either the Poles or the Ukrainians 'must be hurt', therefore it must be that party that will mean the least hurt 'to the future of Polish–Soviet friendship'. Though reminded by Professor Lange that Lvov meant more to the Poles, and that surrendering it would be a 'constant source of anti-Soviet ill-feeling and agitation', Stalin would only commit himself to 'further study' of the question. On this occasion Stalin showed himself much more sympathetic to the London government; having told the Prime Minister that he saw no reason why the London government could not agree at once on a territorial settlement, in the presence of Professor Lange he mellowed and announced that 'to a certain degree' he understood their predicament—required as they were to cede territory in the east before the compensation in the west materialized. The western frontiers of Poland must therefore be settled first.

Finally Stalin urged Professor Lange to seek out Mikolajczyk and General Sosnkowski—'and find out what that man really wants'—but not to do this through official channels, not to arrange a trip to London through the British Ambassador, but to go to London from America. On being questioned by Stalin about the genuineness of Soviet assurances of not encroaching on Polish independence and sovereignty, Professor Lange replied that they could be 'political manoeuvres', but the fact that Stalin was arming a Polish force 'to win and protect Poland's independence' disposed of this argument, and was the basic 'proof' of Soviet intentions. From Stalin's point of view it had proved to be a very satisfactory exchange, underlining his reasonableness and the underlying honesty of his intentions. He did choke off a suggestion for direct talks between the Union of Polish Patriots with its seat in Moscow and the London government, with the excuse that this meant 'official negotiations' and thus required 'definite proposals', suggesting instead that Professor Lange as a 'private citizen' (and as an American) could do much on his own; within a very few days, however, Lebedev, the Soviet Ambassador to the Allied governments in London, made a confidential approach to Professor Grabski, president of the Polish National Council in London. This was followed a week later (on 31 May) by another meeting, all with Mikolajczyk's knowledge, to try to establish a new Soviet–Polish agreement designed also to secure military collaborations. To judge by his comments to the Prime Minister and Eden at the end of May, Mikolajczyk was not impressed, for he discerned in these moves the 'third phase' of Soviet policy designed to 'split the unity of Polish politicians, parties, soldiers and people'.

Once in Washington Mikolajczyk hoped to enlist the aid of the President to turn the tide of policy finally in Poland's favour. With the approach of the great fire-storm which the Soviet command planned to unleash on the Eastern Front, however, time was running short. From the outset the Polish Prime Minister found himself under pressure to accept the idea of a visit to Moscow, and though his first call upon the President went well, he was shaken to learn from President Roosevelt—in a talk laden with tales of Teheran—that it was Churchill who was the author of the Curzon line proposal. While advising Mikolajczyk to make some concessions to facilitate a Soviet–Polish agreement, the President intimated that it would be judicious to avoid 'final or definite' territorial settlements at this stage—and he so couched his opinion that Mikolajczyk quite justifiably drew the conclusion that the Curzon line was not to be the last territorial word. The changes in the government that President Roosevelt urged on the Polish Prime Minister were in reality a small concession—after all, only four people—but they might prove decisive. Over the possibility of Mikolajczyk visiting the Soviet Union (in which matter the Polish minister had already rejected the good offices of President Benes) and the question of American support, President Roosevelt indicated his willingness to act as 'moderator' in this matter, a good Presbyterian device which enabled him to forgo the role of prince or bishop in this election year and to confine himself to promoting the moral betterment of both parties, itself a form of support. Immediately after this talk, Mr Stettinius went so far as to offer Mikolajczyk some unofficial advice: with the war as it now ran, and in the midst of preparations for an election, the United States, like Great Britain, could not take a bolder line against the Soviet Union; but in palmier days—if the Poles could hold on and postpone a settlement—then 'the United States will come back to her fundamental moral principles' and support Poland 'strongly and successfully'.

With his hopes thus buoyed, Mikolajczyk launched on his encounter with Professor Lange, whose request to meet the Polish Prime Minister had been withheld by the Polish Embassy in Washington but reached him through a second channel, one furnished by Stettinius and Bohlen. Promptly at four in the afternoon of 13 June Professor Lange arrived at Blair House: in the course of the two-hour interview Mikolajczyk did not venture his own opinions nor did he 'disclose his own plans of action'. Professor Lange summed it up admirably himself: 'I was talking all the time and Mr Mikolajczyk was sitting with a poker face. . . .' Professor Lange produced an accurate summary of his talks with Stalin on the territorial settlement, on the nature of the Soviet military administration in Poland and on Stalin's wish for a 'Polish–Soviet understanding'. Professor Lange was at pains to express the conviction of the men within 'Berling's army' that they were fighting for Polish independence—'all of them were against Soviet interference in Polish internal affairs', and since the bulk of the Poles in the Soviet Union was made up of Poles from Galicia, then 'all the soldiers took the view that Lvov should remain with Poland'. Feelings ran so high that Berling was forced 'to intervene with Stalin on several occasions', though there was less passion spent over Vilno.

The next day Mikolajczyk paid his farewell call upon the President, the talk based on a memorandum drawn up on the evening of 13 June. President Roosevelt told his guest that 'he would approve the Polish Premier's journey to Moscow and his direct talks with Stalin': he adjured Mikolajczyk to come to terms with the Russians—'there are five or six times more Russians than Poles'—but pointed out that the concessions would involve 'prestige' rather than territory. In this 'political year' the President could not 'take an initiative and actively assist the Polish government', though he wished Mikolajczyk to leave America 'with a full conviction that he, Roosevelt, was willing to be helpful', indeed anxious 'to be a moderator', to which end he would prepare a telegram for Stalin. Whatever Mikolajczyk's feelings at this, a report from Ambassador Ciechanowski made sombre reading: President Roosevelt's 'pre-election promises' would never be put into effect; interest in 'the Polish case' would not last 'any longer than five or six weeks', by which time the Red Army would have struck deep into Poland. The next six weeks were crucial and were all that remained to Poland—without any settlement (either a Soviet–Polish agreement or some incorporation of Poland into a system of European security) then the Polish cause would suffer grave damage, even to the loss of independence: 'whatever we can secure in the next six weeks will be all that we should expect'.

While Mikolajczyk tried to work a miracle cure in Washington, General Tabor struggled to win more support for the *Armija Krajowa;* at a plenary meeting of the Combined Chiefs of Staff on 12 June the general presented a full report on the strength of the *AK*—approximately 250,000 men (6,500 platoons) of which only twelve per cent, or 32,000 men, were armed—and while putting the obvious arguments for greater arms deliveries, also stressed the advantages to be derived from synchronizing Polish underground operations with those of the 'general war effort of the Allies'. If the Allied air forces carried out 1,300 flights to Poland, delivering arms and equipment, then the requirements of the *Armija Krajowa* would be fully met and the Polish striking force made fully effective. On being asked by General Macready (head of the British Military Mission) whether a general rising in Poland would take place 'in co-operation with Russia', General

Tabor's reply caused a stir: 'It is our aim', he replied at once, 'to defeat the Germans in co-operation with the first Ally who comes near enough Polish territory'. How consonant this was with the Polish C-in-C's instructions issued in London did not seem clear. The next day (13 June) General Tabor went over some of the same ground at a meeting of the Planning Staff (Office of Strategic Services): for three years the equipping of the AK had lagged; at present plans were organized on a monthly basis but they could only be fulfilled if there was general co-ordination with Allied action and if the AK received a minimum quantity of arms and equipment. In April 1944 Operation JULA, a test of diversionist activity in southern Poland, had been successfully carried out at the British request. At the moment arms were flown in from the Italian bases, but General Tabor submitted that use of the 'northern bases'—British bases—was now imperative. Two days after the meeting with the Combined Chiefs of Staff (CCS) a Polish journalist (Mr Besterman) supplied the Polish Ambassador with information, apparently from a Pentagon source, that the CCS supported the proposal for more arms for the AK but that the reply received from the Soviet authorities—consulted in order to implement a common policy—was 'negative', to the effect that Poland was an 'operations area under Soviet responsibility': only the Soviet command could supply arms to the Polish underground. On 19 June Colonel Mitkiewicz and Brigadier Donovan (head of the American Office of Strategic Services–OSS) discussed arms deliveries, and Donovan suggested using American air bases, which would give the Poles a useful political lever, but Colonel Mitkiewicz returned to the point that the question was basically 'political' in view of that state of Soviet–Polish relations.

Polish representatives on the CCS had been struggling since July 1943 to win more supplies for the AK and a specific recognition of the need for operations 'co-ordinated with the military operations of the Allies'; British support had been contingent on the availability of suitable aircraft and on the start of operations on the Continent on a large scale. For its own planning purposes the Polish General Staff set the period during which the insurgent forces could hold on until the arrival of substantial outside assistance at twenty days, though Polish political leaders, weighing the consequences of the break in Soviet–Polish relations, thought Soviet assistance very problematical. The Joint Secretary of the CCS, Brigadier Redman, had talked in rather general terms to Colonel Mitkiewicz at the beginning of September 1943 about the Polish plans: in addition to the intrinsic military difficulties, the British Special Operations Executive (SOE) had reservations about the proposed Polish operations and the Soviet attitude, as well as doubts on the score of the Poles keeping to the 1939 frontier line. When the CCS convened on 19 September 1943 (with Colonel Mitkiewicz in attendance), to the consternation of the Polish representative, the Polish submissions about the AK were simply not discussed. All that Brigadier Redman could offer by way of explanation the next day to Colonel Mitkiewicz was the British opinion that 'the Russian snag' had obtruded itself. The official CCS reply of 23 September pleaded lack of aircraft and the absence of direct land or sea communications with the theatre, but no particular reason was given for cutting back the expansion of the *Armija Krajowa*. In mid-October the Poles tried again, only to receive a formal reply from the CCS on 20 January 1944 that the requisite equipment for the *AK* would not be forthcoming and that the CCS could only refer the Polish suggestion for joint American–British strategic responsibility over Polish territory to 'the Chiefs of State'.

The Polish submissions of June 1944 to the CCS again went unanswered (though the reception was sympathetic), and it was left to Colonel Mitkiewicz to dig out the subterranean details, part of which he managed to his own satisfaction in his talk with Brigadier Redman on 7 July. On the strength of this conversation, supported apparently by some documentary evidence produced by the Brigadier, Colonel Mitkiewicz concluded that no supply of arms by air sufficient for a general uprising could be expected, such a supply depending on land/sea links and integration within the context of Soviet operations. The timing of the rising was the responsibility of the Polish government, who in turn should co-ordinate with the Soviet Union as the ally directly interested; and the same requirement existed for operations aimed at the dislocation of German communications passing through Poland, for again this affected the Soviet forces most immediately. This was how Colonel Mitkiewicz construed the evidence that he encountered. Somewhat later in July General Kopanski, in a signal to the Polish C-in-C (then in Italy), intimated that as a result of a letter from the British CIGS there was no likelihood of any co-ordination of *Armija Krajowa* operations in Poland on an 'inter-Allied basis'. Whatever the basis of Colonel Mitkiewicz's conclusions, whether intuitive or rationally perceived, they proved correct; while Stalin expanded his *Armija Ludowa* (and Berling's regular formations) at top speed, the *AK* was left at an increasing disadvantge.

In mid-June Mikolajczyk returned to London, optimistic to a degree that the Foreign Office thought dangerously misplaced: the Polish Prime Minister referred to President Roosevelt's own conviction that the Soviet–Polish frontier should run east of Lvov and added that the President seemed to entertain hopes of retaining Vilno. In his account to the Delegate of the Government in Poland dated 21 June, Mikolajczyk underscored the President's opposition to the Curzon line but his approval for changes in government personnel which might facilitate a settlement: 'America would like the restoration of Polish–Soviet relations, the postponement of controversial matters and creation of a military and administrative *modus vivendi*. . . .' Though Mikolajczyk informed his colleagues in Poland that 'Roosevelt considers his own influence with Stalin . . . as greater than Churchill's,' this was scarcely apparent from Stalin's reply on 24 June to the President's message of 17 June, in which he played his role of 'moderator'. Stalin laid down massive conditions: one such 'vital condition' was the 'reconstruction' of the Polish government in London, plus recognition of the Curzon line—while at the present Stalin found it 'hard to express an opinion about a visit to Moscow by M.

Mikolajczyk'. The Soviet Ambassador Lebedev had already taken up where he left off on the eve of Mikolajczyk's journey to America. On 20 June both men met again to discuss 'principles of collaboration', defined by Mikolajczyk as a resumption of relations, co-ordination of the Soviet forces and the *AK*, joint Polish–Soviet administrative measures in liberated territory and territorial changes to be postponed until the end of war. Lebedev used a second meeting on 22 June to 'elucidate' the point about postponement of territorial settlements: Mikolajczyk explained that he was distinguishing between a demarcation line and a future frontier line. The next day Lebedev brought down the axe: he had 'no instructions' about a demarcation line, but he did have the Soviet terms—before any resumption of diplomatic relations, four men (President Raczkiewicz, General Sosnkowski, and the ministers Kot and Kukiel) were to be removed from 'posts enabling them to influence the policy of the Polish government'; the 'reconstructed' Cabinet was to include Poles from London, the USA, the USSR and the *Rada Narodowa* in Poland, whereupon this 'new' government would condemn its predecessor for its 'mistake in the Katyn affair'; and, finally, the Curzon line would mark the new Soviet–Polish frontier. It was to be all or nothing, at which Mikolajczyk terminated the talks.

As Operation *Bagration* ground Army Group Centre to pieces in early July, the likelihood of Poland becoming 'the theatre of fierce warfare' grew apace. With three Soviet fronts—1st, 2nd and 3rd Belorussian—on the move, General Sosnkowski on 7 July dispatched specific and revised instructions to General Bor-Komorowski on the proposed 'war preparations against the Germans' involving ' "intensified diversionist action" ' under the code-name *Tempest ('Burza')*. General Sosnkowski ruled out 'a general armed rising of the Nation' and 'resolutely opposed' any description of *Tempest* as an 'insurrectionist movement'; yet, if by 'happy conjunction of circumstances' as the Germans fell back, and before Soviet troops moved in, the *AK* could take even temporary possession of Vilno and Lvov, or any other important centre or 'small part of land', then this should be done so that the Poles appear as 'the rightful masters'. Before the dispatch of this instruction, Mikolajczyk, General Sosnkowski and General Kukiel tried to thrash out just what was involved. Mikolajczyk, in what looks like an excess of optimism, declared for intensifying *AK* activities, submitting proposals to Soviet commanders for co-operation in local administration and settling for this arrangement while postponing the main issues. General Sosnkowski wanted a direct assumption of administrative authority by *AK* representatives, intensification of 'diversionist action' but on no account an 'armed rising' without a previous understanding with the Soviet Union—any rising without 'the sincere and genuine co-operation of the Red Army' meant only an 'act of despair'. General Kukiel asked whether there was not a case for calling 'a rising', to which General Sosnkowski responded by admitting that *Tempest* could 'for political purposes' be defined as 'insurrectionist'.

The pressure from the British side upon the Polish government to make immediate and substantial concessions did not abate during these critical days:

a draft document covering the territorial issues, the composition of the government and the position of the Polish C-in-C was submitted by Ambassador O'Malley on 13 July, only to be rejected by Mikolajczyk. If these proposals were transmitted to Stalin by the Prime Minister (and it has been reported that they were), the fact of Mikolajczyk's dissent was evidently deleted from the message, since the only published signal dated 13 July deals with the Prime Minister's request to the Russians to seek out the German experimental base for flying-bombs in the area of Debica lying 'in the path of your victorious advancing armies'. Churchill's signal of 20 July did mention the possibility of Mikolajczyk asking 'to come to see you' and made a special point of emphasizing that nothing had been said previously 'because I [Churchill] trust in you [Stalin] to make comradeship with the underground if it really strikes hard and true against the Germans. . .'. The Foreign Office meanwhile nurtured growing fears that without some definite step by the Polish government the Russians would simply and inevitably take unilateral action, a view propounded within the State Department, where the Director of the Office of European Affairs (in a paper submitted on 20 July) predicted Soviet dealings with 'some rival Polish organization as the provisional representative of the Polish people', in all probability the 'National Council of Poland'. In such an eventuality the only possible American policy must be to avoid 'being stampeded by any propaganda campaign' into a hasty recognition of the 'new' government, but at the same time to avoid 'any positive statement' which bound the American government to irrevocable support of the 'Polish' government in exile *per se*'. This depressingly realistic paper wound on: the danger of civil war was obvious and real, with one side—'and probably the losing one'—fighting with the moral support (but little else) of the Western powers, and the other side receiving the active support of the Soviet Union.

That forecast was confirmed within forty-eight hours. Shortly after 8 am on the morning of 22 July Moscow Radio announced the establishment in Chelm, a small town in eastern Poland, of the 'Polish Committee for National Liberation' *(Polski Komitet Wyzwolenia Narodowego)*, which the *Krajowa Rada Narodowa* had actually brought into existence the day before. On 27 July this new Polish committee signed an agreement with the 'government of the Soviet Union' at a ceremony in which Stalin, Molotov and Zhukov participated, with Witos, the Polish vice-chairman, Morawski (in charge of the 'Foreign Affairs Department') and General Rola-Zymierski, the new C-in-C of the 'United Polish Armed Forces'. The *Rada Narodowa* had already made detailed provisions for the Polish armed forces: the *Armija Ludowa* was to be 'unified' with the Polish army formed in the Soviet Union. The unified armies would assume the designation 'the Polish Army' with its own supreme Command (a C-in-C, two deputies and two members of the Command); generals' ranks would be conferred by the presidium of the *Rada Narodowa*, but nothing enacted under these provisions would prejudice 'the operational subordination of the Polish army to the Supreme Command of the Red Army operating on the Soviet–German front'. In London the Polish government in its memorandum of 25 July to the Prime Minister demanded an immediate British disclaimer of this *fait accompli* and a restatement of the British declaration of 24 May. Events, however, were moving with even greater rapidity, and the agreement of 27 July concluded between the Russians and the Poles—members of the new committee, which came to be known as the 'Lublin Committee' and its adherents the 'Lublin Poles'—whittled away any chance of a diplomatic counter-stroke. General Bulganin, whose talent lay in discerning his master's real desires, was simultaneously appointed Soviet plenipotentiary to the new Polish committee. The stage was all but set.

On 23 July Stalin furnished the Prime Minister with a very plausible explanation of Soviet moves and motives in Poland; it was precisely because 'we do not want to, nor shall we, set up our own administration on Polish soil' that the Russians were in touch with the Polish Committee of National Liberation, which 'intends to set up an administration on Polish territory, and I [Stalin] hope this will be done'. The underground forces, 'so-called underground organizations led by the Polish government in London', have proved to be 'ephemeral and lacking influence'. At this moment Stalin was not prepared to consider the new Polish committee 'a Polish government', but in time it might form 'the core of a provisional Polish government made up of democratic forces'. 'As for Mikolajczyk,' it would be better if he approached the Polish national committee 'who are favourably disposed towards him', though Stalin would 'certainly not refuse to see him'—hardly an effusive welcome, a point Mikolajczyk made to Eden on 25 July in discussing Stalin's latest message. Indeed, it did not amount to 'a proper invitation' at all, though Eden urged the Polish Prime Minister to follow up this first sign of Stalin's readiness to meet him 'without asking him first to fulfil certain conditions'. In fact, by expressly excluding conditions, Stalin had imposed one major proviso, that the approach should be made through the Polish national committee. On the evening of 25 July Churchill saw Mikolajczyk for the second time that day and 'strongly insisted' on the Polish Prime Minister's 'speedy flight to Moscow' to discuss Soviet–Polish relations and to 'find a way out from the present blind alley'. Prime Minister Mikolajczyk, Minister Romer and Professor Grabski left the next night by air via Cairo for Moscow. Churchill sent Stalin a further message once the Polish party had departed, emphasizing that 'the Western democracies recognizing one body of Poles and you recognizing another' would be a disastrous turn of events.

While Mikolajczyk made his way to Moscow, and as Soviet armour began to fight its way to the approaches of Praga on the eastern bank of the Vistula, in London Count Raczynski sounded out Eden on the possibility of direct British aid 'with regard to the support of military operations in the Warsaw area by the Royal Air Force': though prepared to listen, Eden pointed out that Warsaw lay outside the range of British bombers while flights by Allied aircraft terminating on Soviet airfields were exclusively an American operation. The next day (28 July) a formal British reply absolutely precluded the type of assistance the Poles had requested 'to further a rising in Warsaw'; to fly the Polish Parachute Brigade across Germany might involve 'excessive losses'; dispatching RAF Mustangs and Spitfires to Polish airfields would need prior Soviet agreement, and since Warsaw lay beyond the normal operational range of RAF bombers 'bombarding Warsaw airfields' (which could be more efficiently executed from Soviet airfields) did not seem feasible.

Amidst all this diplomatic squirming, and with the leading personages of the Polish government in exile widely dispersed (the Prime Minister on his way to Moscow, C-in-C Sosnkowski absent on a singularly ill-timed inspection trip to Italy), the preparations for a rising in Warsaw were now moving into an advanced stage. A warning order to the 'Home Army' *(Armija Krajowa)* from the Home Commander, General Tadeusz Bor-Komorowski, went out on 19 July, alerting 'home units' to BBC transmissions bearing on the opening moves of a rising; a stand-by order, operative as from 25 July, went out on 21 July, accompanied by General Bor-Komorowski's own estimate of the situation—'the Soviet westward movement on this sector will be quick . . . [and will] continue in the westerly direction after crossing the Vistula', while the Germans will be unable to 'offer any effective resistance', having lost the initiative on the Eastern Front, thus demanding of the Poles that they be 'constantly and fully prepared for a rising'. Before leaving for Moscow, Mikolajczyk in consulation with his colleagues invested General Bor-Komorowski with full authority to decide in the light of local conditions on whether to order a rising and when to do so; the Home Commander had already submitted his 'operational and political conclusions' to the Delegate of the Government in Poland (and to the main commission of the Council of National Unity), obtaining in turn a decision that the moment for the rising would be fixed by mutual agreement.

'We are ready to fight for the liberation of Warsaw at any moment. . . . Be prepared to bomb the aerodromes round Warsaw at our request. I shall announce the moment of the beginning of the fight:' so ran General Bor-Komorowski's signal to the Polish C-in-C on 25 July, the signal which also intimated that the presence of the Polish Parachute Brigade promised to be of 'enormous political and tactical significance'. Signals now flew thick and fast (though some not fast enough, in particular C-in-C Sosnkowski's own dispatches, documents of no small importance). The Polish government in London decided on 25 July to empower its Delegate (Mr Jankowski) in Poland to take all decisions 'required by the progress of the Soviet offensive' without reference to London 'if the need arises'; Mikolajczyk's own specific delegation of authority, transmitted to the Delegate on 26 July, read quite simply: 'I authorize you [the Delegate] to proclaim the rising at the time chosen by you.' At once Count Raczynski plied Eden with requests for British assistance and the transfer of the parachute unit requested by the Home Army commander: on 29 July the Polish National Defence Ministry made a formal submission to General Sir Hastings Ismay for 'support'—the bombing of aerodromes, the dispatch of the Parachute Brigade and a Polish fighter wing: this *aide-mémoire* stressed that German armoured reinforcements were moving up to the city; the SS Division *Hermann Göring* had been identified and everything now pointed to a protracted struggle between the Germans and the Russians for possession of Warsaw.

A protracted fight: that was the course of events anticipated in the Polish paper of 29 July (to which the British returned a largely negative answer on 2 August, pleading that bombing operations were ruled out because they would come 'within the Russian tactical sphere' and rejecting any movement of paratroops or fighters since this presented 'an almost insuperable operational problem' as well as posing 'grave political implications'). C-in-C Sosnkowski expressed his implacable opposition to any 'general rising' and on 30 July—in a dispatch that took much too long to arrive in London—he stressed that the Parachute Brigade could scarcely be counted on since it was at the disposal of the British, the aircraft of the Polish Air Force could only serve limited purposes, and therefore that *'the support of the rising depended on British assistance'*. By the time these papers reached London the decision to attack the Germans in Warsaw had been taken and the rising was in full swing.

'For Warsaw, which never yielded and never gave up the struggle, the hour of action has now struck. . . : this unmistakable call to arms went out on the morning of 29 July to the people of Warsaw, who could at that moment *'hear the guns of the battle which is soon to bring liberation'*—transmitted not from the BBC in London and its Polish station *'Swit'*, but from Radio 'Kosciuszko' in the Soviet Union broadcasting to occupied Poland in the name of the Union of Polish Patriots. The sound of the guns thudded away to the east and north where Bogdanov's 2nd Tank Army crashed into the German XXXIX *Panzer* Corps. But amidst this distant rumble, the clatter of German armoured reinforcements and the roar of lorries moving into the city grew louder by the hour; inside Warsaw, where General Stahel had taken command, German tank patrols were much in evidence, assault guns stood at crossroads with crews at the ready and the loudspeakers in the streets summoned Poles to report for work on more defence positions. That appeal from Radio 'Kosciuszko', based as it seemed to be on enormous and ever rising optimism, coupled with what the German command was embarked upon inside Warsaw and the presence of Soviet armour not many miles from Warsaw, all combined to impel the Home Army command to take action. Not to act meant being stigmatized a virtual collaborator with the Nazis or else being written off as the nonentity which Stalin insisted the Polish underground was. But a general rising meant taking an enormous risk, the risk written into General Bor-Komorowski's decision to fight in any case, whether the Germans withdrew or elected to stand and fight. Polish resistance in any event would either help to shorten the struggle or it would install the Home Army as the men to come out and meet the advancing Red Army.

With Soviet tanks battling on the eastern edge of Warsaw on 31 July, two meetings held that day each in their own way vitally affected the fate of the city (and, with it, the fortunes of all Poland). Inside Warsaw, on an afternoon which seemed to hold so much promise when the Inner HQ of the Home Army assembled to consider the situation, Colonel Chrusciel (the Warsaw district commander known as Colonel 'Monter'), in the presence of the senior civilian and military command of the Polish underground, presented details of the Soviet breakthrough and submitted the latest reports on the Soviet capture of the outlying posts of Radosc, Milosna, Okuniew and Radzymin. General Bor-Komorowski then made his final decision committing the Poles to battle; with the Delegate to the Government, Deputy Prime Minister Jankowski, looking on, the Home Army commander instructed 'Monter' to go over to the attack at 5 pm on the afternoon of 1 August, whereupon 'Monter' set about transmitting orders to the AK men deployed throughout the city. General Bor-Komorowski did not err in thinking that the rapid capture of Warsaw was of immediate and important significance to the Soviet command. The capture of the Polish capital meant major political and operational gains. Soviet armour battering at the eastern walls of the city seemed to presage such a move and impelled the *Armija Krajowa* to urgent action, all on the basis that the morrow must be decisive.

But on and after 25 July, four days after General Bor-Komorowski submitted his optimistic assessment to London of an impending German rout, the situation had begun to change substantially, for all the disasters that befell three German armies. During their fighting retreat the remnants of these armies—more than a dozen divisions all told—were stiffened with German units brought up from Field-Marshal Model's area and from the Baltic command, with fresh formations at their back—armoured divisions moving in from western Europe and the Balkans, among them *Panzer* divisions in sufficient strength to give the German command no less than fifteen divisions to utilize along a much-shortened front. Model, who was no novice at dealing out punishing counter-blows, already planned to mount a skilful attack, using the three *Panzer* divisions available to him to slice into the Soviet columns forming Rokossovskii's flank and thus threaten Soviet communications running through Siedlce and Brest-Litovsk. Late in July part of that attack went in, but Model left it just too late to recapture Siedlce The pressure ultimately became so heavy, however, that Siedlce was quickly transformed by the Soviet command into the centre of its defensive front. It was presumably from such a general survey of the front that the Polish National Defence Ministry in London was talking just at this time (late July) of a protracted battle for Warsaw. In and around Warsaw the German command was not simply hanging on to a communications centre (for Model took the precaution of shifting his line of movement to the bridges at Modlin), but was safeguarding its entire right flank.

As 'Monter' sent out his orders to AK units on the evening of 31 July, Mikolajczyk finally met Molotov in Moscow for another talk which vitally affected the Poles. Molotov tried at once to steer Mikolajczyk into the arms of the Polish Committee for National Liberation, with whom Mikolajczyk should come 'to an agreement . . . in the first place'. The Polish Prime Minister did not 'discard' Molotov's suggestion, but thought he should have 'an exhaustive discussion with Marshal Stalin in the first place'. Molotov parried; 'of course', what Stalin said to Churchill about meeting Mikolajczyk was 'valid', but Stalin was preoccupied with 'military matters', so that a meeting must wait three or four days. Mikolajczyk then pointed out that he was in possession of 'direct, exact and up-to-date information from Poland', having met three delegates recently arrived from the country; to the mention of 'measures to be taken in connection with the outbreak of a general rising in the Warsaw area', Molotov returned a vague, almost noncommittal reply to the effect that Soviet troops were now ten kilometres from Warsaw. The conversation ended with Mikolajczyk pressing once more for an interview with Stalin and obtaining Molotov's undertaking to arrange one, but not before the lapse of three days. And so while Mikolajczyk kicked his heels in Moscow the Warsaw rising was passing through its first fiery stage.

At five o'clock on Tuesday, 1 August, Polish underground units poured down fire on German patrols and units inside Warsaw. From windows, doors and street corners small-arms fire caught the German troops in the open; Polish insurgents captured strong-points and installations that were thinly held or insufficiently guarded, with the fighting going on through the night to storm positions that did not fall in the first furious assault. For the next two days the *Armija Krajowa* threw itself into continuous attacks on the strong-points still held by the Germans, who had been split up into several groups fighting inside the city, cut off from each other. General Stahel, with a strong force of troops and SS men, held out in the Bruhl Palace in Plac Teatralny; in the suburb of Praga the Germans managed to contain the AK attacks and were holding on to the Citadel, the airfields at Okecie and Bielany, as well as the radio station at Bornerowo. The Poles—armed with sufficient light infantry weapons to equip only a quarter of the fighting men available—at once found themselves at a grave disadvantage in dealing with fixed defences without heavy weapons of any kind. With stocks of ammunition for seven days, they had planned to expand their supplies with captured German material, and they did during the first forty-eight hours seize quantities of arms and ammunition, only to expend more and more ammunition as the fighting grew very fierce and German resistance stiffened. Beyond the confines of Warsaw, German reinforcements speeded to the relief of the city under categorical orders from Himmler. Within twenty-four hours Hitler appointed a fearsome commander for the German units engaged in stamping out the rising, SS *Obergruppenführer* von dem Bach-Zelewski, a 'specialist' in partisan operations in the east, who was to have at his disposal not only regular army, police formations and the SS, but the brutish fellows of the '*Dirlewanger* brigade'—drawn from the prisons—and additional brigades of ex-Soviet soldiers who had defected to the Germans. Behind this human flail came a train of heavy guns, multiple mortars, flame-thrower units and finally deadly refinements such as the miniature cable-steered tanks packed with explosive, the 'Goliaths'. The German command fused ingenuity with bestiality to fight one of the ghastliest battles of the war.

As the first Polish onrush which cost many dead began to fall away, the rumble of the battle on the eastern bank of the Vistula grew all the while fainter. Marshal Rokossovskii reports that it was only on 2 August that Soviet intelligence received information about a proposed Polish attack on the German occupation forces in Warsaw—'this news put us in a great state of alarm'. The Belorussian Front staff at once set about trying to establish the scale and the nature of the rising, even working on the assumption that the Germans were the source of these rumours, which further set the Soviet command wondering. If it was a Polish decision, the Marshal was appalled at the timing. Two armies, 48th and 65th, were fighting about fifty miles east and north-east of Warsaw; the whole Soviet right flank, weakened by the *Stavka* pulling out two armies into reserve, was still under orders to go for the river Narew and seize a bridgehead on its western bank; 70th Army had just taken Brest-Litovsk and was clearing the area; 47th Army was fighting to the north of Siedlce; 2nd Tank Army—at the outskirts of Praga—was beating off fierce German armoured counter-attacks; while the left-wing armies (1st Polish, 8th Guards and 69th) set about forcing the Vistula at Magnuszew, their main operational task. The capture of Warsaw needed a full-scale offensive operation at a time when Rokossovskii's right-flank armies, almost at the end of their tether, were being pressed to carry out *Stavka* orders to cross the Narew and the left wing was seriously embattled—all at the end of a 300-mile supply line. With a group of officers Rokossovskii went up to a forward observation post with 2nd Tank Army. From this post, sited in a factory chimney, he looked out over a Warsaw covered with rolling clouds of smoke; the burning houses were clearly visible; the city was flecked with bomb bursts and evidently under shell-fire.

Model meanwhile was probing deeper into the weak spot in the Soviet line, the strip of land between Praga and Siedlce, an attack from which would hit the Soviet formations south of Warsaw in the flank and in the rear. The German *Panzer* divisions and one infantry division moved down from the north and north-west, only to crash into the 3rd Soviet Tank Corps (2nd Tank Army). Rokossovskii saw that one possible way to get the Red Army into Warsaw was to put the maximum insurgent effort into Praga, trying to take the bridges over the Vistula and hitting the German troops fighting off the Russians nearest to Warsaw in the rear. This, he felt, was the only way of helping Soviet troops to break into the city and to have any direct influence on events there. The Soviet command knew of no such plans, however, and under heavy German pressure they had already ordered 2nd Tank Army over to the defensive, with 47th Army following in its wake; Soviet tank units were taking up defensive positions along a line running from Kobylka through Ossuv, Milosna Stara and on to Zbytki (where 16th Tank Corps held flank positions close up to the Vistula). Both Soviet armoured and infantry units were committing their last reserves; 3rd Tank Corps had been pushed away from Wolomin and faced the danger of encirclement by elements of three *Panzer* divisions. Soviet armoured spearheads had been repulsed; the situation between Praga and Siedlce was deteriorating very rapidly, and Rokossovskii saw no way out but to speed up the advance of Batov's 65th and Romanenko's 70th Army through the Bielowieza forest and so to spear the Germans in their flank. But a move of this order demanded time, and Soviet units were now falling back. Rokossovskii's proposed counter-move demonstrated that it was not simply a matter of being checked before Praga, but of preparation for a bigger battle that barred the way to Warsaw. This confirmed the Polish estimate submitted to the British command in London, and it was the gloomy but all too real setting against which the Delegate's and the Home Army commander's signal of 1 August had to be read: 'As the battle for the capture of Warsaw has begun we ask you to ensure Soviet assistance for us *by means of an immediate attack from outside.*' With every hour, 'outside' became more distant from Warsaw.

After four days of fighting inside Warsaw between the Polish insurgents and the German forces, the areas controlled by both sides became more definitely demarcated. Poles and Germans set about building barricades round their respective perimeters, and out of the German sectors deep 'fingers' poked into the city, splitting up those parts of the city in Polish hands into three distinct sectors— Mokotow and Czerniakow in the south; the city centre and Powisle facing on the river bank, with the Old Town to the north; and finally Zoliborz—a situation that 'Monter' recognized for what it was by setting up three detached commands. Though hemmed in at various points, the German command concentrated on clearing the main routes leading from the west into Praga. This had been half accomplished already, after heavy air bombardment and tank attacks had opened the direct westerly road from Wola to the Kierbiedza bridge over the Vistula, but it remained a hazardous thoroughfare swept by Polish gunfire.

With Poles and Germans engaged in savage battles on every street and at every junction, the fighting degenerated into barbaric displays on the part of the Germans, aimed at ripping out Polish resistance wherever they came across it. Once an area was cleared, all Polish men were taken out and shot, civilians were pressed ahead of tanks to form living screens for German attacks, prisoners were shot out of hand, and the wounded lying in the hospitals, together with the doctors and nurses, were also summarily shot. Incendiary bombs, artillery fire, tank guns and flame-throwers, supported by heavier guns, moved into bombardment positions, turning streets, houses and buildings into a morass of fire or gaping ruins. After little more than a week German tanks, assault guns and infantrymen, assisted by the fearful fighting squads of Bach-Zelewski's licensed killers, smashed a great wedge through the Polish sectors and emerged on the Vistula, turning at once to capture and clear the Old Town by attacking it from three sides. *Reichsführer* Himmler, responsible for quelling the revolt in Warsaw, had assembled a miniature but monstrous army for this purpose. Dirlewanger's 4,000 convicts in his penal brigade were bad enough, but few could compare for ferocity with Kaminski's SS brigade, over 6,000 strong, formed from Russian prisoners of war, expert in every kind of atrocity and urged to live by fearful excesses by Kaminski himself, excited by his pathological hatred of the Poles. Faced with men such as these the Poles could expect no mercy, and they got none.

On the evening of 3 August, with the Warsaw rising in its first furious phase, Stalin and Mikolajczyk finally met in Moscow in an encounter that seemed far from unfriendly. Almost at once, in his exposition of his 'programme', Mikolajczyk asked Stalin 'to order help to be given to our units fighting in Warsaw', to which Stalin replied: 'I shall give the necessary orders.' Then Stalin pointed out Mikolajczyk's omission—'was this a deliberate omission?', he asked—of the Polish Committee for National Liberation, the body with which the Soviet government had already concluded an agreement 'on the provisional administration of the liberated Polish territories'. Stalin went on to explain his point of view; before any Soviet–Polish agreement, there must be an end to 'the present dualism of power, the Government in London on the one hand, and the Committee in Chelm on the other. I agree with Churchill that it would be proper to unite all the Poles in order to create a provisional government.' Nor could Stalin accept the argument that the men of the Polish Committee were nonentities, representing 'but a very small section of Polish public opinion,' as Mikolajczyk phrased it; there must be, Stalin continued 'very big and quite unforeseeable changes'. As for the *Armija Krajowa,* the Home Army, Stalin expressed the greatest scepticism of its fighting abilities: 'I was told that the Polish government has ordered these units to drive the Germans out of Warsaw. I wonder how they could possibly do this; their forces are not up to that task. As a matter of fact, these people do not fight against the Germans, but only hide in the woods, unable to do anything else.' Against Stalin's barrage of facts about the Home Army's incompetence and stupidity, Mikolajczyk put up a defence based on their record, though he admitted that he had not thought the subject would come up for discussion and had no specific reports to hand. But if the Home Army lacked arms, as Stalin insisted even as he admired it as human material, would not it be possible to contribute 'on your [Stalin's] part to the rearmament of the Home Army?' Stalin returned no direct answer but urged Mikolajczyk 'to take into consideration' that the Soviet Union did not want 'two authorities fighting each other' in Poland; that 'we shall never allow' the Poles to fight amongst themselves and that if the Polish government should 'prefer the existence in Poland of two different forces . . . in that event we shall be forced to continue to assist the Committee of National Liberation. Such is our position.'

With this exchange the conversation seemed to reach an impasse, broken by Mikolajczyk referring Stalin to the question of frontiers; this again triggered off differences over the Curzon line, with Mikolajczyk pleading for Lvov and Vilno but Stalin foreclosing arguments about the actual implications of the 'line' with the remark that 'it is a historical document, well known to everybody; there is no point in arguing about it; it was not we who invented it, at the time nobody asked us for our opinion.' Stalin refused to budge on either principle or on details; 'it is not a question of magnanimity or friendship and feeling. It is in the interest of the Russian state that Poland should be independent and strong.' It would be possible, Stalin intimated in his final statement, to come to a definitive agreement on frontiers 'with a new, united Polish government'. It was up to Mikolajczyk to bring about that unity and it was urgent that this be done. At the Polish Prime minister's prompting on how to proceed, Stalin suggested a meeting between 'both Polish groups', falling in with Mikolajczyk's suggestion that such a meeting be held in Moscow. On taking his leave Mikolajczyk asked Stalin 'privately to take a personal interest' in those men of the Home Army who revealed themselves to the Red Army and offered to co-operate in fighting the Germans, whereupon Stalin promised that they would not be harmed 'provided they did not play the fool'.

Not many hours later the British Prime Minister on 4 August sent Stalin his first signal dealing with the Warsaw rising: the British, in response to urgent Polish requests but subject to weather conditions, proposed to drop sixty tons of arms and ammunition over the south-western sector of the city 'where it is said that a Polish revolt against the Germans is in fierce struggle', and where 'they appeal for Russian aid which seems very near'. Stalin's reply made the next day was chilling and began ominously, after perfunctory thanks for the message about Warsaw: 'I think the information given to you by the Poles is greatly exaggerated and misleading,' at which he went on to chide the Poles for their claims in connection with the capture of Vilno and referred to 'the facts'—'the Home Army consists of a few detachments, misnamed divisions. . . . I cannot imagine detachments like these taking Warsaw, which the Germans are defending with four armoured divisions. . . .' As Stalin's reply went out to London, the Delegate of the Government in Warsaw sent his own signal to Mikolajczyk, stressing that 'a complete cessation [of Soviet operations] continues even now while for the second day the Germans heavily bombard the town from the air. . . . In other words there is no Soviet intervention.' The signal continued: the behaviour of the Soviet troops was 'incomprehensible, passive and ostentatious', all at 'a distance of a dozen kilometres from Warsaw', behaviour to which must attach a 'political significance' and as such be raised 'with the Allied quarters'.

On the following day, 6 August, another round was danced in this elaborate but grisly minuet: from London the Polish President Raczkiewicz instructed Ambassador Ciechanowski in the United States to press for 'authority for Eisenhower [to] render aid via air drop [of] ammunition [to] Warsaw combatants'—the British air drop had not yet gone in, 'due to so-called technical reasons', but 'everything is now a matter of hours'. Not a few of these valuable hours Mikolajczyk expended in Moscow, talking this time to the representatives of the

'Lublin Committee', the step Stalin had suggested on 3 August, a meeting that developed into a barely concealed political wrangle with Mikolajczyk intervening twice to ask for help in the Warsaw rising, only to be told—at his second attempt—that the Chairman of the National Committee arrived from Warsaw on 4 August. 'It was quite quiet there until the 4th of August. They mislead you in London . . . the Germans launched four armoured divisions against the Red Army in the Praga suburb,' and the attack on the Home Army was joined by General Rola-Zymierski, the new C-in-C of the Soviet-raised Polish armed forces, as well as Wanda Wassilewska, who insisted that 'the Home Army must be disbanded'. What the Committee was demanding amounted to the dissolution not only of the Home Army but also the London government. It was not, therefore, surprising that the meeting adjourned in the evening having reached no conclusion, only to reassemble the next day (7 August) at 11 o'clock in the morning.

This time Boleslaw Bierut, the chairman of the National Committee, the individual who had reportedly left Warsaw on 4 August and had seen no sign of a rising, attended the conference and called on General Zymierski to give 'some information about Warsaw'. The general began by denouncing how, 'lightheartedly, and without any understanding with the Red Army', the Home Army command had precipitated the rising: on 5 August General Zymierski approached Stalin, seeking arms supplies for the Polish insurgents and an assurance that the Red Army would treat Warsaw 'with consideration'. With General Zymierski standing by, Stalin issued orders to Marshal Rokossovskii to plan an outflanking attack from north and south, the position being presently that Rokossovskii had ten divisions between Deblin and Warsaw 'ready to turn the flanks of the Germans from the south and west'. Over supplies of arms, the general had 'intervened three days ago [4 August] at Soviet HQs', though he was bound to point out the difficulties of delivering arms 'to a city in the midst of battle'—dropping them by air could be done only in the neighbourhood of Warsaw (Skierniewice, Tomaszow and Lowicz) and in Praga, from where the arms must be transported into the city. 'Arms must be provided, but how?' Mikolajczyk pointed out that there had been 'several proposals relating to air-lifts', but Mr Bierut cut him short brutally: 'An agreement with the Western Allies does not suffice. It is an agreement with the Soviet Front Command that matters' and, 'as far as we know', there had been no attempt 'to come to an understanding with the Soviet commander in charge of the operations round Warsaw'. At this, the subject reverted to the possible composition of a 'government', so composed on the basis of present discussions that 'out of a total of eighteen posts you [the Committee] would assign only four to the representatives of the Government'. That was Mikolajczyk's quick calculation. 'Bierut nodded.' The plan, Mikolajczyk continued, meant having him represent the Polish Peasant Party, along with Professor Grabski as a member without specific political allegiance, and two more members to represent the Labour Party and the Polish Socialist Party. 'Bierut nodded.'

General Zymierski broke the silence by returning to the rising in Warsaw, saying that 'Stalin had issued orders to Rokossovskii that the Polish units should participate in the assault on Warsaw': General Berling's Polish Army was presently deployed between Deblin and Pulawy, but on the evening of 6 August General Zymierski had again called on Stalin, asking him to speed up operations against Warsaw. Stalin explained his own position in the light of what was happening not far from Warsaw itself: 'I shall do everything possible but this cannot be done within 2–3 days because the Germans have thrown into action four armoured SS divisions and because of this I shall have to make a deep outflanking manoeuvre.' At this disclosure, General Zymierski turned back to the question of 'the constitution of the government', one more inconclusive discussion which brought about an adjournment until the evening. Chairman Bierut was again brutally abrupt: 'A prompt decision is necessary. . . . If we do not come to an understanding, we shall form a government ourselves.'

More discussions and more entreaties followed on 8 August. In London, where 'the British authorities had little information about the position outside Warsaw' save for German claims about annihilating a Soviet armoured force, the Polish Deputy Prime Minister Mr Kwapinski sought out Eden and showed him messages from the insurgents that the Russians were doing nothing to help Warsaw, and elsewhere were disarming units of the Home Army as soon as fighting died down and arresting or even shooting Polish administrative officials. Kwapinski asked for a British declaration that Polish underground fighters possessed the rights of regular belligerents, to which Eden responded by saying that it was early days to assume a lack of Russian goodwill, that the Russians appeared to have suffered a military reverse near Warsaw, and that a unilateral British statement about belligerent status for the Home Army would be 'useless' and could even be misinterpreted by the Russians. From Warsaw itself General Chrusciel, commander of the Warsaw District of the Home Army, sent a signal to Marshal Rokossovskii urgently requesting supplies of ammunition—'speedy assistance by your forces, Marshal, is therefore an absolute necessity for us'. A Red Army officer, Captain Konstantin Kalugin, who had made contact with the Home Army staff and the underground HQ, sent out a signal through London incorporating Kalugin's own dispatch for his superiors and reporting his 'personal contact with the commander of the Warsaw garrison' who was conducting 'the heroic partisan fight by the nation against the Hitlerite bandits', and requesting small-arms ammunition, grenades and anti-tank weapons to be air-dropped on designated sectors of the city marked with white and red sheets for identification purposes. Captain Kalugin also requested artillery fire on 'Vistula bridges in the Warsaw area, on Saski Garden, Aleje Jerozolimski, as these are the main channels of movement for the German Army', and ended on an almost despairing note: 'Help me to get in touch with Marshal Rokossovskii.'

That evening (8 August) Mikolajczyk with his small party met Bierut and Osobka-Morawski in Molotov's room in the Kremlin for one more attempt to break the political deadlock. Both sides took up declaratory positions, Mikolajczyk standing on the 1935 constitution, the Polish Committee on the constitution of 1921, and both sides found wordy arguments to justify their respective stands. Towards the close of this session it was clear that no agreement on the post-war frontiers of Poland or on the setting up of a joint 'Polish government' was likely to emerge: Mikolajczyk conveyed his regrets to Molotov, adding that 'I myself and my colleagues have not lost hope that all will end well.' Stalin's message to the British Prime Minister of 8 August reflected this same feeling: 'I regret to say that the meetings have not yielded the desired results. . . . Still, [he continued] they were useful because they provided Mikolajczyk and Morawski, as well as Bierut who had just arrived from Warsaw, with the opportunity for an exchange of views and particularly for informing each other that both the Polish National Committee and Mikolajczyk are anxious to co-operate. . . . Let us hope that things will improve' (*Perepiska* . . . , vol. 1, p. 298).

On 9 August, the day on which the Germans smashed their way through the Polish barricades and broke out to the Vistula, Mikolajczyk and Stalin met in the evening for a final talk. After explaining the *impasse,* Mikolajczyk intimated that a solution might be found after his return to London, a sentiment that Stalin applauded. At this Mikolajczyk turned at once to the problem of rendering 'immediate assistance by the Soviet Union to Warsaw', whereupon Stalin asked, 'What kind of assistance is in question?' Arms, Mikolajczyk replied, for a city in which the Germans are trying at all costs to hold the main roads leading through the centre and to the Vistula bridges. On hearing this, Stalin gave Mikolajczyk a short, sharp lecture on the military aspects: for Stalin, the struggles in Warsaw seemed 'unreal', perhaps this might not be the case if the Soviet armies were approaching Warsaw, but 'unfortunately this is not the case. . . . I reckoned on our army occupying Warsaw on August 6th but we failed to do so'—and now several German armoured divisions were attacking the Red Army; the outflanking movement on Warsaw, begun by crossing the Vistula in the river Pilica area, had at first gone well, but on 8 August the Germans blocked this drive with more armour, thus barring the way to Warsaw with five armoured divisions, of which three 'are still posted round Praga'. 'What can an air-lift do?' Stalin asked, and proceeded to answer himself: it was possible to supply 'a certain quantity of rifles and machine-guns, but we cannot parachute cannon' and in any event, he asked Mikolajczyk, 'are you quite sure that arms parachuted from the air will reach the Poles? This might be easy in some outlying areas like Kielce or Radom, but in Warsaw, considering the big concentration of German forces, it would be an extremely difficult thing to do.' Nevertheless, Stalin continued, 'we must try', and he asked Mikolajczyk to be specific about quantities and dropping zones. Mikolajczyk mentioned Captain Kalugin and his pressing request to make contact directly with 'the Soviet Supreme Command'; in addition, those areas indicated for parachute drops were secured by barricades, so 'there is no danger that the arms could be intercepted by the enemy'.

After quizzing Mikolajczyk about the reliability of this information and on being told that Soviet aircraft could not land but that only air-drops were involved, Stalin then delved into the question of establishing contact with the Warsaw command and assured Mikolajczyk: '. . . in so far as we are concerned we shall try to do everything possible to help Warsaw'. At least Stalin knew more than mere generalities about the Warsaw situation; he was aware that Captain Kalugin lacked 'technical means' to set up contact (Stalin suggested parachuting a Soviet officer into Warsaw with a code and asked Mikolajczyk to make the necessary arrangements for his reception). His promise to the Polish premier semed quite unequivocal and was even repeated, sufficient to cause the inclusion of Churchill's thanks in his message of 10 August to Stalin, though these proved to be the last amiable words exchanged over the growing tragedy in Warsaw.

In Washington the Poles tried frantically to pull every lever that might set in motion a massive arms drop on Warsaw and facilitate the transportation of units of the Polish Parachute Brigade to the scene of the fighting. But the only response was a 'noncommittal promise' and a bluntly negative reply on 8 August from the Combined Chiefs of Staff. At General Sosnkowski's urging, Colonel Mitkiewicz again pressed the Combined Chiefs of Staff about using American aircraft flying from bases in Italy or England to drop arms, a submission made on 11 August and honoured with a formal reply only a week later (to the effect that London was handling the whole matter of support—more or less what was said on 9 August). On 12 August President Rackiewicz appealed directly to President Roosevelt to 'order the American Air Force in the European Theatre of War to give immediate support to the Garrison of Warsaw' by dropping arms, bombing airfields and 'transporting Polish airborne units'. More immediately ominous was the *TASS* communiqué of 12 August, relaying Moscow Radio's denials that 'they who rose up in Warsaw were allegedly in contact with the Soviet command, [and] that the latter did not render the necessary assistance'. *TASS* was 'authorized' to declare that such statements were either a 'misunderstanding' or else 'the manifestation of slander against the Soviet command'.

The secret tug-of-war had now become a public brawl, made the more ugly by the sickening background of destruction and killing in Warsaw itself. The Polish insurgents, surrounded now and bereft of all outside aid save for the arms dropped sporadically by RAF planes (manned by British, Dominion and Polish air crew) making the long and hazardous flight from Brindisi, maintained contact between their three 'sectors' by using the sewers as communication passages. Above ground, German assault squads and tanks fought to reduce the formidable Polish barricades one by one. German tank-gunners who could not subdue the living took their revenge on the dead by firing incendiary rounds into the corpses strewn about the steets or attempted to burn the populace alive by setting house after house alight.

During the first week in August, in his talks with Mikolajczyk and in his messages to the Prime Minister, Stalin did all he could to play down the scope and significance of the Warsaw rising. He impugned the sources of Mikolajczyk's information, stressed the unreality of the situation, pointed to the lack of co-ordination with the Red Army and even produced Mr Bierut out of Warsaw to attest to the 'quiet' reigning in the city early in August. But the Soviet leader did give a clue to what he had anticipated, that the Red Army would take possession of Warsaw by a *coup de main* and that Stalin 'reckoned on' the city falling by 6 August (which makes sense of a Soviet radio appeal to the Polish population on 29 July declaring that 'the hour for action' had arrived). *Stavka* orders issued to the Soviet Front commanders on 28 July tend to support this interpretation: Rokossovskii's orders specified that after the capture of Brest-Litovsk and Siedlce his right-flank armies were to push forward in the direction of Warsaw and 'not later than 5-8 August capture Praga [the Warsaw suburb]', then force the Narew and set up bridgeheads on its western bank in the area of Puluck–Seroc, with the left-flank armies forcing the Vistula in the area of Deblin–Zwolen–Solec. But while Rokossovskii's left flank pushed on, his right and centre had been held up, leaving a 120-mile salient jutting away to the right of those Soviet armoured units that had actually reached Praga. There was no possible solution, as Rokossovskii recognized, other than to move his right-flank armies up to the line running from the Narew, the mouths of the western Bug and on to Praga. Further south, on the Vistula, Chuikov had put his 8th Guards across, and set about expanding the Magnuszew bridgehead after 1 August, leaving three divisions on the eastern bank and committing six to the investment of the bridgehead. The first phase of this operation went on without sufficient air cover or even AA defence, since the bulk of the Soviet fighter aircraft were shifted further north and suffering at this time from a fuel shortage. To Chuikov's surprise and ill-concealed disappointment, just as the fighting began to intensify for the Magnuszew bridgehead, he received orders (on 3 August) from the Front command to detach three divisions, swing them north and deploy them defensively some twenty to twenty-five miles from the Vistula crossings, to help counter a German attack which was expected to roll southwards along the eastern bank of the Vistula. This seemed ludicrous to Chuikov, who scarcely saw any justification for supposing that the German command—having lost 'all Belorussia, half of Poland' in one operation—would try this southerly thrust when not only 1st Belorussian but also 1st Ukrainian Front were on the Vistula (at Sandomierz). The Vistula bridgeheads were vitally important, but now Chuikov lay straddled between the western and eastern banks, unable to operate really effectively on either; the mistake committed by Front HQ (and the Supreme Command, in Chuikov's view) was soon exposed, for two German divisions supposed to be south-east of Praga turned up on the western bank of the Vistula and forward of Chuikov's newly won bridgehead. Heavy attacks developed by 5 August and the next day the three regiments of 47th Guards Rifle Division lived through some critical hours: at noon a regiment of Stalin heavy tanks went over to the western bank, the Tiger tanks of the *Hermann Göring* Division were halted and the bridgehead held. But only by submitting detailed reports, air reconnaissance evidence and interrogation reports of tanks crews could Chuikov persuade Front command that two German *Panzer* formations (19th and 25th), with the *Hermann Göring* Division, were definitely in action on the west bank of the Vistula.

The Front command finally woke up over its Vistula bridgeheads, and Chuikov was gratified by the speed of the reaction. Kolpakchi's 69th Army received orders to leap the Vistula to the west of the Deblin–Pulawy sector, Chuikov acquired anti-aircraft divisions and artillery reinforcements to cover his own crossing area, and one corps from 2nd Tank Army was pulled over in to the Magnuszew bridgehead on the western bank, as well as the divisions that 8th Guards had been obliged to turn north. On the morning of 8 August Soviet engineers threw two more bridges over the Vistula for Chuikov's Guards units and 1st Polish Army units went over to hold the defensive perimeter at Studzianki, the northern bulge of the bridgehead which did not become 'stabilized' until mid-August. Though the Magnuszew bridgehead held, the chance to burst into Warsaw 'off the march' had long since vanished and Stalin was not exaggerating when he told Mikolajczyk that it would take some time to mount a new operation. It is possible that he thought the rising in Warsaw would be quickly liquidated or else would peter out when only rifles were available against tanks; his minimizing of the rising seems to suggest this. What is clear is that the very fact of a large-scale rising in Warsaw, a general rising, came as a surprise to the Soviet command, and this response to the 'London Poles' could only provide distinct embarrassments for Stalin who espoused the 'Lublin committee'. When the insurgents continued to fight against all odds, it became necessary to insulate Soviet policy and action, which explains the marked shift in attitude that took place after the first fortnight in August; already the *TASS* communiqué of 12 August was a straw in the wind, placing 'the responsibility for all that is taking place in Warsaw . . . *exclusively* on the Polish *émigré* circles in London'.

On 12-13 August both the Prime Minister and Mikolajczyk approached Stalin with requests for immediate Soviet help with arms-drops. Mikolajczyk reminded Stalin of his undertaking and specifically sought the bombing of airfields, daytime fighter patrols to check the *Luftwaffe* and arms-drops—'the most important areas for parachuting are: Krasinski Square and Napoleon Square'. The British reply of 14 August to the Polish request for a declaration of combatant rights for the Home Army and other assistance for Warsaw could scarcely cheer the Poles. The British letter pointed to the unfortunate consequences of 'the decision to start a general rising in Warsaw without any prior consultation with His Majesty's Government', dwelt on the major difficulties of organizing arms-drops from the Italian bases, ruled out the dispatch of parachute troops—scarcely 'militarily feasible since it would involve flying relatively defenceless troop carriers over great distances'—and finally urged the Poles 'to promote practical means of co-operation between the Polish and Soviet forces', though reminding them that 'Soviet operations in Poland are governed by their general strategy' which 'no doubt prevents the Soviet forces from improvizing immediate operations in the Warsaw neighbourhood' or co-ordinating with a rising 'of which neither they nor His Majesty's Government were informed in advance'. For all its cold comfort, the British suppositions about 'Soviet operations in Poland' were not mere idle speculation. Soviet plans, even allowing for that 'local' improvization of a dash into Warsaw, turned on possession of the line formed by the major rivers, the Vistula, the Narew and the Bobr, with the Bug–Narew theatre forming a vital objective of its own (which Soviet troops finally invested only in September). Having failed to implant themselves in this area by mid-August, the Soviet armies were hamstrung before Warsaw—a predicament to which Model's counter-thrusts substantially contributed—and Stalin simply recorded an unpalatable truth when on 22 August he stated somewhat raspingly that 'from the military point of view the situation which keeps German attention riveted to Warsaw is highly unfavourable both to the Red Army and to the Poles'. But by that time he had also formally and fiercely 'disassociated' himself and the Soviet command from 'the Warsaw adventure', thus consigning the Polish insurgents to inevitable death and inescapable destruction.

Throughout the first half of August the Soviet attitude seemed to waver. After the middle of the month it congealed into irreducible opposition and intractability. From Italy Churchill sent Eden a dispatch on 14 August, pointing out that it was 'very curious' for the Russian offensive to have halted and even drawn back 'at the moment when the Underground Army has revolted'. Russian aid to the insurgents would involve 'only a flight of 100 miles', whereas aircraft from the bases in Italy faced a flight of 700 miles and losses were mounting. Churchill therefore proposed bringing pressure to bear by 'referring to the implications that are afoot in many quarters' and requesting Russian help. Mikolajczyk had already sent his own message to Stalin on 13 August asking for Russian assistance, only to receive on that same day a chilling reply: orders to 'drop arms intensively in the Warsaw area' had gone out; a Soviet parachutist had been dropped (only to be killed by the Germans); but now, *'after a closer study of the problem'*, Stalin was convinced that the rising was 'a reckless adventure causing useless victims among the inhabitants. . . . In view of the foregoing the Soviet command decided openly to disclaim any responsibility for the Warsaw adventure.' The same charge of reckless adventurism came from Vyshinskii on 15 August in an official Soviet response to the American request made at President Roosevelt's prompting for landing facilities for American bombers flying from the west to Warsaw, there to drop supplies or bomb German airfields. Operating by day and at high altitude, with fighter escorts, the American aircraft would then overfly the Soviet battle-lines and land at the base already used for the return-trip 'shuttle bombing', Poltava (where on the night of 21-22 June German bombers, accompanied by planes of the Hungarian Air Force, carried out a devastating raid which burned out fifty Flying Fortresses on the ground, a disaster which, in the words of General Deane, 'sowed the seed of discontent', leaving the Russians 'smarting and sensitive' and the Americans 'forgiving but determined to send their own anti-aircraft defenses as protection for the future').

The brusque Soviet reply forwarded by Vyshinskii impelled both the British and American Ambassadors to seek an interview with Molotov. Not surprisingly, he proved to be unavailable, and it was Vyshinskii who again handled the western *démarche*. He restated the Soviet position as dourly as ever and simply refused to explain why Stalin had initially offered Mikolajczyk help for Warsaw, returning once more an obdurate refusal for facilities, which prompted Ambassador Harriman to report on 15 August that 'ruthless political considerations' alone must account for the Soviet attitude. The next day Vyshinskii gave both ambassadors a written explanation which blandly passed over the British and American dropping of arms over Warsaw as 'an American and British affair' to which the Soviet government could not object, but it could and would object to any landing on Soviet territory by these aircraft once they had finished their mission over the Polish capital. Eventually the ambassadors met up with the elusive Molotov and on the night of 17 August conducted another equally unrewarding exchange over Warsaw. While freely admitting a change in Soviet policy, and attributing it to the discovery on the part of the Soviet government of 'the real nature' of the rising, blaming the London government for the events in Warsaw and attacking them for slandering the Soviet government, Molotov held out no hope at all of intervention to save the insurgents even a part of their agonies. In his own dispatch of 18 August to Stalin, Mikolajczyk pleaded once more for Soviet help. He admitted that the rising, 'as it seems now, was premature' and uncoordinated with the Soviet command, but 'the timing could not have been agreed jointly', though the Polish commander did issue orders 'to start the fight in Warsaw when the Soviet armies were approaching the capital, and broadcast appeals from Moscow had expressly called the population to rise in arms'. Mikolajczyk was now 'warmly appealing for the resumption of technical contacts between the Red Army and the fighting in Warsaw', and again asking for help in 'arms-dropping, strafing of German centres and retaliating to the raids of the German Air Force'— and permission for American aircraft to use Russian bases.

From Italy Churchill sent the President a message proposing a joint message to Stalin, giving 'true counsels' even if Stalin resented it (though 'quite possibly he wouldn't'). In Moscow Ambassador Harriman received instructions to inform either Stalin or Molotov that American military forces would help the Polish insurgents as best they could. But the thrust for this type of intervention was appreciably diminished by State Department advice to the Ambassador (sent on 19 August) not to press the Russians too peremptorily over the use of Soviet bases for operations involving Warsaw, because this might prejudice the 'shuttle-bombing' arrangements which remained a prime consideration for the American military. Since this weighed less with the British, they would be inclined to push harder and certainly further than the President was prepared to go. Harriman nevertheless sent Molotov a letter setting out the American intention to help and this was followed within hours by the short but unequivocal appeal from Churchill and the President—'We hope that you will drop immediate supplies and ammunition to the patriot Poles of Warsaw, or will you agree to help our planes in doing it very quickly?' Eden discussed this 'second direct intervention' with the Polish ministers in London on 21 August, though the British minister took a pessimistic view of the possibilities of 'Marshal Stalin changing his mind'.

Such wisps of hope as did remain were blasted to nothing by Stalin's withering reply of 22 August, denouncing 'the handful of power-seeking criminals who launched the Warsaw adventure', throwing 'practically unarmed civilians' against German tanks and aircraft; since the military situation was bad for Poles and Russians alike, the only way to bring 'the best, really effective help to the anti-Nazi Poles' must be a new, large-scale Soviet offensive to crush the Germans and liberate the Poles. All reference to specific requests—Soviet air-drops or permission for Allied aircraft to land behind the Soviet lines—Stalin omitted from his curt, categorical message, a message suggesting either real conviction or a sense of immunity based possibly on knowledge that the Americans were not prepared to go to all lengths (demonstrated in the reluctance implicit in the signal of 19 August to Ambassador Harriman). Even if the latter was guesswork, Stalin's instinct did not fail him. The President on 24 August intimated that without the use of Soviet airfields nothing much could be done, and though importuned by the Prime Minister to send yet another joint message to Stalin, he replied on 26 August that such a move would not be 'advantageous to the long-range general war prospect'. If the Prime Minister wished to intervene, however, the President had no objections on that score.

In Warsaw itself the German ring round the Old Town tightened with each passing day, days filled with unending air and artillery bombardment. Polish attacks on 19 August, mounted from Zoliborz on Dworzec Gdanski and intended to pierce the German ring, brought little or no result, and more attacks from the direction of Zoliborz and the Old Town on the station at Dworzec Gdanski had no real effect. District by district the German troops set about clearing the insurgents, burning whole sections of the city to the ground and either killing or capturing the population. Reporting from the city late in August, General Bor-Komorowski admitted that the main German strongholds remained in German hands for all the Polish incursions, that Warsaw had become 'a city of ruins' where 'the dead are buried inside the ruins or alongside them', and where German aircraft rained down leaflets threatening the burning of the entire city—but that 'there are only ruins left to be burnt'. The Polish command was making preparations to conduct a fighting withdrawal from the Old Town and move into the city centre, using the sewers to withdraw into the centre and on Zoliborz. More than

2,500 combatants disengaged from the maelstrom of the Old Town, leaving only the wounded who could not be dragged through the sewers. All that the Germans found when they smashed their way in at the end of the month were these immovable wounded, who were promptly doused with petrol and burned alive where they lay. With German troops commanding a wide swathe of the city from the centre to Zoliborz, the third and final stage of the rising was about to begin, the obliteration of Polish resistance in the City Centre and the clearing of the river bank between the Poniatowski and the Kierbedzia bridges over the Vistula.

On 1 September Churchill met the Polish premier in London and discussed bringing aid to Warsaw. To Stalin's refusal of co-operation on 22 August Churchill confessed his own reaction—'I could not believe it'—and there was cause for regret when the American President had not associated himself more forcefully with the plan to launch a mass daylight raid over Warsaw and land the bombers on Soviet airfields, thus facing the Russians with a *fait accompli*. Now they should look into the possibilities of a mass flight organized by the Royal Air Force. On the night of 4 September the War Cabinet met to consider the situation produced by what Churchill called the 'extraordinary behaviour' on the part of the Russians, and decided upon another appeal to the Soviet leadership, with a copy forwarded to the President and begging the use of American aircraft to fly to Warsaw, 'landing, if necessary, on Russian airfields without their formal consent'. The note arrived amidst rumours that operations in Warsaw had actually ceased. President Roosevelt's reply (5 September) referred to information from American intelligence that 'the fighting Poles have departed from Warsaw', so that the problem 'has therefore been unfortunately solved by delay and by German action'. There was nothing more to be done. As for the Prime Minister's plan for a mass flight and a mass landing on Soviet airfields, Ambassador Harriman in Moscow had been brusquely informed that, not only was Soviet permission not forthcoming, but that 'even damaged aircraft' would be refused permission to land.

While the insurgents fought it out in Warsaw the Polish government in London slowly worked round to a compromise solution which would facilitate a political settlement with Moscow, offering the 'Lublin Committee' fourteen seats in a combined coalition government, proposals submitted to and debated by the Polish underground even in the vortex of the battle. But for many Poles the Warsaw rising lay blanketed in a conspiracy of silence. The Prime Minister late in August queried what looked like a 'stop in the publicity of the facts about the agony of Warsaw', and urged that, while there need be no mention of the 'strange and sinister behaviour' of the Russians, there was no case for being coy about the consequences. Anglo–Polish relations, already very tense, slumped sharply with General Sosnkowski's Order of the Day for 1 September, which castigated Great Britain for abandoning her Polish ally, thus prompting a British demand for his immediate resignation. Churchill advised Mikolajczyk not to submit his own resignation out of despair over Warsaw. Should this happen, the British 'will not support any other head of the Polish government', and in any event such a step would simply leave the field wide open for Moscow to work its will unopposed. Mikolajczyk seemed nevertheless bent on resignation and declared his inability to 'take appropriate measures with regard to General Sosnkowski' because he could not prove that 'the line of policy pursued by the Polish government was right and appropriate'.

The day after this conversation, on 6 September, the insurgent command in Warsaw telegraphed that 'Warsaw has lost all hope of help from Allied air deliveries or from a Soviet advance which would liberate the city'. The German troops in the city set about clearing the Vistula bank, pushing Polish fighting units back into the City Centre and severing any contact the Poles might have with Soviet troops fighting their way into the eastern-bank suburb of Praga, a precaution that speedily afforded the Germans several advantages. Already the glacial indifference and the unbending hostility of the Soviet leadership was melting. On 9 September the British Ambassador in Moscow received the Soviet reply to the War Cabinet's representations, a note that once more disassociated the Soviet government from any responsibility for what was happening in Warsaw and rounded on the British government for not warning the Soviet Union in advance about the rising (and referred to similarities with the 'Katyn massacre' denunciations of April 1943), but then went on to announce Soviet air-drops over Warsaw and Soviet agreement 'in principle' to the use of its airfields by Allied aircraft, provided the operational plans were agreed in advance by the Soviet authorities. This sign of co-operation prompted Mikolajczyk to send an immediate telegram to President Roosevelt asking him 'to give orders to General Eisenhower to carry out the operation of American air-squadrons in order to help Warsaw'.

Early in September Soviet troops, regrouped and reinforced, were on the move again. Rokossovskii ordered three Soviet armies, 48th, 65th and 70th, to make all possible speed towards the river Narew (Batov received 'categorical orders' from the *Stavka* to be on the Narew early in September). On 5 September Panov's Don Tank Corps' forced the Narew at Pulutsk and to the south of it, which eased the passage of 70th Army pushing on in the direction of Sokoluv, Radzymin and Modlin (north of Warsaw). To break into Praga Rokossovskii proposed to use divisions from both 70th and 47th Armies, with the latter attacking the south-eastern sector of the Praga perimeter; Gusev (commanding 47th Army) would acquire 8th Guards Tank Corps and Colonel Bewziuk 1st Polish Infantry Division as reinforcement. The aim of this Soviet operation was to clear German forces out of the reach of land stretching between the Vistula and the western Bug. If Soviet troops did take Praga, they would be fully drawn up on the Vistula facing Warsaw. Bewziuk's Polish riflemen changed positions with Soviet units at the beginning of September, coming under Gusev's operational command on the fifth; at this time the insurgents still held three main sectors, Zoliborz, the City Centre and Czerniakow (together with Mokotow), although only the battle groups in Czerniakow had direct access to the Vistula bank. During the night of 9 September units of 1st Polish Division concentrated in the Miedzylese area, the artillery already in position. The next night Soviet bombers, supported by Polish units of the *Krakow* squadron, bombed the German defences on the southern edge of Praga and at 0920 hours on the morning of 10 September Bewziuk sent in the assault battalion from 1st Regiment. After four days of heavy fighting Polish and Soviet troops cleared Praga, bringing them out on the Vistula bank opposite the Polish positions at Zoliborz, Solec and Czerniakow.

During the night of 13 September low-flying Soviet aircraft dropped arms, medicines and food supplies for the insurgents in Warsaw, but the weapons and food, dropped in canisters without parachutes, were either spilled or fell into German hands. Soviet AA guns moved up to the eastern bank and fighters covered the supply-dropping flights that went on for the next two weeks involving over 2,000 sorties delivering 505 anti-tank rifles, almost 1,500 machine-pistols and 130 tons of food, medicine and explosives. Meanwhile Malinin (chief of staff, 1st Belorussian Front) ordered Chuikov to hand over 1st Polish Army for deployment in the Garwolin area, effective as from dawn on 12 September. General Zymierski that same day instructed 4th Infantry Division to move with all speed from Lublin into the Garwolin area, the Polish reinforcement being intended for the Praga battle. Berling, 1st Polish Army commander, decided to make a forced crossing of the Vistula straight off the march to bring Polish units on to the western bank in the Czerniakow area, an operation that meant improvization all the way since equipment for the crossing and artillery ammunition was in short supply—but so was time, for a freshly arrived German *Panzer* division (25th) had already begun to attack the insurgents in Zoliborz and more German attacks directed against Czerniakow began to clear the Vistula bank of Polish fighting men, leaving only a narrow strip of land, cut off from the City Centre, defended by 400 insurgents.

Under cover of darkness on the nights of 16 and 17 September two battalions of the 9th (Polish) Infantry Regiment commanded by Major Mierzwinski crossed the Vistula to Czerniakow, only to be pinned down by heavy German fire in support of tank and infantry attacks. Colonel Goranin's 6th Infantry Regiment in an effort to reduce German pressure on Czerniakow sent over its 2nd Battalion in the direction of Zoliborz, where a small bridgehead was established on the western bank. Berling decided to try a third assault landing, this time just to the north of Czerniakow, putting down units of two regiments between the railway bridge and Poniatowski bridge with the object of bringing an attacking force into the rear of German troops assaulting Czerniakow. The first parties went over during the night of 19 September, covered by smoke-screens and artillery fire—two battalions (1st and 2nd from 8th Infantry Regiment) in all.

For all these fierce, fighting attempts to bring immediate aid to the insurgents, sorties which Berling launched on his own responsibility and for which he was subsequently punished, the situation of the insurgents deteriorated disastrously. On 22 September Rokossovskii, who earlier in the month had advised Stalin that his Front forces were in no condition to liberate Warsaw, ordered 1st Polish Army over to the defensive and the evacuation of Polish troops from the western bank, the last survivors of the bridgeheads moving over the Vistula during the night of 24 September. On 18 September American bombers, flying at high altitude, dropped supplies over the city and then proceeded to Soviet airfields, but again this isolated action could not affect the outcome; the altitude of the drop and the prevailing high wind robbed the insurgents of seventy per cent of the supplies dropped that day.

By mid-September, with Soviet policy visibly modified, Stalin could avoid both supporting a rising that meant underwriting a *fait accompli* devised by the 'London Poles' (thus discrediting his own policy based on the 'Lublin Poles') and also escape a growing breach with his allies and the odium implicit in total abandonment of the insurgents. The Warsaw rising was with each day nearer the point of being throttled, and the *Armija Krajowa*—the core of the Polish underground—lay decimated. Soviet troops were once more on the move immediately in front of the city but Stalin knew that they could not take it by frontal assault. On 23 September he passed on his gloomy views to Ambassador Harriman (who gave him news of the Anglo-American decisions taken at Quebec), referring to the weight of German fire that swept the Vistula crossings and thus held back the tanks—and without tanks, no frontal attack could clear the Germans from the high ground.

That same day, 23 September, German troops took up positions along the length of the Vistula bank, leaving the Polish commander north of Czerniakow (Colonel Radoslaw) no choice but to drag those men still able to fight back through the sewers to Mokotow and to put the wounded over the Vistula in boats. The next day, 24 September, German units reinforced from 19th *Panzer* began to fight their way from the south and west into Mokotow, forcing the Polish defence units into ever narrower lines until withdrawal through the sewers to the city centre became imperative. But this time the Germans were ready and waiting, blocking off the sewers and pitching gas grenades into those sections where the Poles tried to make good their escape, killing hundreds in these miasmic, slimy tunnels. After reducing Mokotow, it was the turn of Zoliborz in the north, and finally the forest of Kampinos. General Bor-Komorowski had failed to establish any operational link with the Red Army, hope of a Soviet assault on Warsaw had gone, and British and American aircraft had disappeared from the skies. After two months of merciless fighting, sixty-two days of unending horror and atrocity, with 15,000 men of the 30,000–40,000 of the *Armija Krajowa* dead, the population forcibly evacuated or murdered on the spot, 150,000–200,000 civilians immolated out of one million, the dead entombed in the ruins and the wounded lying untended on the roads or suffering their last agonies in cellars, surrender could no longer be delayed. On October 2 the fighting ceased: the

Poles were collected for deportation or extinction in the gas chambers, after which the Germans bent to the maniacal labour of levelling Warsaw to the ground. The German command reckoned its 10,000 dead, 7,000 missing and another 9,000 wounded.

During the last frenzied spurt of fighting, with Berling's men clinging to the embankment on the western edge of the Vistula inside Warsaw, Stalin sent Marshal Zhukov (latterly with the southern battle-fronts in Bulgaria) to investigate the situation of 1st and 2nd Belorussian Fronts. German pressure was forcing the Polish troops out of their precarious footholds: the two Soviet officers parachuted in to make contact with General Bor-Komorowski (who acknowledged their arrival in a signal to London on 21 September, announcing 'liaison' with the eastern bank) were, according to the Marshal, not received, 'nor did we ever hear from them after that'. With the Front command convinced of the impossibility of capturing Warsaw, the units on the western bank were pulled back to their original positions. Marshal Zhukov's impression of 47th Army, operating between Serock, Modlin and Praga, was not encouraging; advancing along flat terrain, the 47th was already worn down and suffering heavy casualties, and things looked no better with 70th Army at Pulutsk. For Zhukov, the 'operational aim' seemed far from clear, though Rokossovski referred to *Stavka* orders prescribing that 47th Army reach the Vistula between Modlin and Warsaw. Zhukov reported to Stalin and asked for permission to halt offensive operations in 1st Belorussian Front area 'because it led us nowhere', and for the right flank of 1st Belorussian and the left of 2nd Belorussian Front to go over to the defensive. Recalled to Moscow, both Zhukov and Rokossovskii faced a restless, discomfited Stalin, impatiently listening to an account of the German brake on Soviet movement which was presently incurring 'unjustifiably heavy losses'. Stalin proposed strengthening 47th Army to force a breakthrough between Modlin and Warsaw. Zhukov scotched this idea, suggesting instead a turning movement south-west of the city and a 'powerful splitting blow' in the direction of Lodz–Poznan, all demanding major reinforcement. Stalin took twenty minutes to think it over; he did not commit himself over the new attack but agreed to Soviet troops going over to the defensive. Warsaw, a gaunt, fire-blackened tomb for all its dead, still lay ahead of the Soviet troops.

Three hundred miles to the south, and not much more than three weeks after the start of the general insurrection in Warsaw, the small but strategically placed republic of Slovakia also took up arms against the Germans. Both risings, Polish and Slovak, finally came to the same bloody end. Both were hamstrung by the same fatal divisions in their ranks, the conflict between the 'bourgeois' military forces and those communist-led or communist-raised, the problem of the exile government's relations with Moscow and the crucial question of the Red Army's role in support of the rising.

Already on 8 April 1944 units of 1st Ukrainian Front had reached the eastern boundaries of Czechoslovakia. In his May Day broadcast Stalin promised the liberation of Czechs and Slovaks from the Germans, and from Moscow broadcasts in Czech urged the populace to form 'national committees' *(narodni vybory)*, a plan previously discussed in the talks between President Benes and the Czechoslovak Communists in December 1943, a measure designed to help in the fight against the Nazis and also to establish a means of participating in the administration of liberated territory. The planning of the Slovak rising also dated back to December 1943, when a secret meeting of all the Slovak underground organizations decided to form a 'Slovak National Council'. This body included representatives of all political groups engaged in the struggle against the Germans and incorporated a demand for the restoration of Czechoslovakia within its pre-Munich frontiers as a major part of the Council's political platform.

As the battlefronts drew closer to Slovakia itself, the National Council began shaping its own plans in the light of two obvious contingencies, that either the Red Army would come bursting through the Carpathian passes into Slovakia and the whole Danube basin, or the German Army would simply occupy this vital rear area and defend the Carpathian line. In either event the Slovak armed forces and the populace at large must take up arms and drive the Germans out of Slovakia, a struggle in which the Slovak field army (particularly the 22,000 men of the 'East Slovak Corps' with its two infantry divisions) would play a decisive part, aided by the 'Rear Army' with its garrison troops some 10,000 strong; the Rear Army must speed the full mobilization of the Slovaks and help set up partisan detachments. The 'independent state' of Slovakia was for the moment ruled by Mgr Tiso, a Nazi puppet manipulated as Hitler's whim and desire demanded, though latterly even the Slovak fascist leadership was growing discontented with the demands heaped upon them by the Germans. The activities of the underground Communists and pro-Czech middle-class politicians, if not entirely undetected, went increasingly undisturbed, leaving the army command to hatch its own schemes in the heart of the Slovak Ministry of National Defence. Preparations for revolt were both efficient and rapid. Officers known to be sympathetic to the Nazis were posted out of harm's way, stocks of fuel, weapons, ammunition and even aircraft were laid by. The command of the military *gendarmerie* was carefully posted to select strategic spots and the *gendarme* detachments given orders to join partisan units in the event of German occupation or else to assist Slovak army forces.

The motives behind the development of a Slovak resistance movement were mixed. The Czechoslovak government in London kept a close watch on the situation in Slovakia, hoping to add much-needed lustre to the Czechoslovak cause by an act of overt and successful rebellion. The plans of the London-based government hinged, therefore, on establishing a Czechoslovak fighting force, an insurgent army, within the confines of the country, to be supported if possible by military units raised abroad. In April 1944 talks began in London with the object of setting up Czechoslovak air transport squadrons which would give the government in exile means of direct communication with the 'liberated areas', including Slovakia. Early in May the London government also signed an agreement with the Soviet Union dealing with the problems of administrative authority in liberated Czechoslovak territory: in the area of military operations authority devolved directly upon the Soviet command, but the Czechoslovak government would then assume administrative responsibilities as rapidly as possible, affording the Soviet command all necessary assistance through its military and civil agencies.

Once Soviet troops appeared on the borders of Czechoslovakia, however, the Central Committee of the Czechoslovak Communist Party took a hand, 'appealing' to the Soviet Party for assistance in waging partisan warfare. The Soviet response was understandably rapid. In the middle of April 1944 the *Orgburo* of the Ukrainian Communist Party formally approved a decision to 'assist the Czechoslovak cause' by setting up special training courses for partisans and organizing partisan cadres for service in Slovakia. Operational responsibility was invested in the Ukrainian Partisan Staff, to which body Rudolf Slansky was seconded as a special plenipotentiary of the Czechoslovak Communist Party. About a hundred Czechs, most of them party members, joined the first partisan training course run by the Ukrainian Staff in a school also attended by Polish partisans under training; the initial plan called for the dispatch of some ten partisan groups (with fifteen to twenty men to a group) into eastern Slovakia. The Soviet command simultaneously hurried on with the organization of an expanded Czechoslovak regular military force raised and trained in the Soviet Union. Czechoslovak units had already played a distinguished part in the fighting for Kiev in 1943, and now the liberation of the western Ukraine placed many more potential recruits at the disposal of the Soviet authorities, who could also count on men who had deserted to the Red Army (including 4,000 Slovaks).

The 2nd Czechoslovak Parachute Brigade began to form up under Soviet supervision in January 1944; Slovaks made up the core of this formation. By mid-April the Czechoslovak paratroopers were sent off for special training. Under an agreement with the Soviet General Staff, the 1st Czechoslovak Army Corps was being raised at its depot in Yefremov (in the Tula *oblast*). This wholly new corps had an establishment of 16,000 men (plus 350 attached Soviet personnel and 800 women) organized as a motorized formation with four brigades and supporting arms, a regular force intended to serve as the basis of a 'new' Czechoslovak army.

Meanwhile the Soviet-trained partisans went into action. During the night of 26 July 1944 the first group of eleven men, equipped with weapons and two radio-transmitters, dropped by parachute into Slovakia in the Ruzomberok area. P.A. Velichko, a captain in the Red Army, commanded this detachment, which worked feverishly to set up base areas into which many more partisans were dropped during August, to be followed by partisan units coming over the land frontier. Soviet aircraft carried out supply-dropping flights, delivering arms, ammunition and additional equipment. These early flights used aircraft from the Ukrainian Partisan Staff, but regular supply-dropping missions required the services of a regular unit, an assignment handed to Colonel Yuzeyev's 208th Night Bomber Division attached to the 2nd Air Army (1st Ukrainian Front). The Soviet guerrillas speedily flung out a wide net of bases and inter-linked sub-units, making contact with communist and non-communist sympathizers, enlisting Czechs, Slovaks and foreigners (French prisoners-of-war finally formed a partisan detachment of their own), though the Soviet command built up its main base in the Kantorska valley near Sklabina and put it under a Soviet officer, Red Army lieutenant Vysotskii.

At the end of July the *Stavka* decided to create a new Front command. Following Marshal Koniev's recommendation, the 4th Ukrainian Front was formed from Koniev's left flank, out of which 1st Guards and 18th Army were withdrawn to form the first strength of the new front, the air support coming from 8th Air Army presently in *Stavka* reserve. The commander of 4th Ukrainian Front, Petrov, received a preliminary directive to prepare an offensive operation, designed to seize the eastern Carpathians and drive on in the direction of Uzhorod–Mukachevo in order to debouch on to the Hungarian plains. The Front command accordingly set about preparing its own plans, proposing to use 1st Guards and 38th Army to seize the Carpathian passes before attacking Uzhorod and Mukachevo, plans that received *Stavka* approval and full authorization to prepare an offensive operation for the period 25–30 August. The *Stavka* meanwhile moved up 3rd Corps (Mountain Troops), artillery and engineer units to reinforce 4th Ukrainian Front. Marshal Koniev's left-flank formations had also reached the foothills of the Carpathians, with Moskalenko's 38th Army fighting throughout August for possession of tactical footholds in the approaches to the Carpathians, each day bringing losses and the steady wearing down of the rifle divisions that were already badly in need of rest and reinforcement. Though the axis for 4th Ukrainian Front operations had been selected early in August and preparations went ahead to organize the Uzhorod–Mukachevo operations, designed principally to assist 2nd and 3rd Ukrainian Fronts operating in Rumania and Hungary, events late in August in Rumania suddenly facilitated Soviet movements, thus throwing the plans for 4th Ukrainian Front into the melting pot. Petrov at 4th Ukrainian Front HQ received orders from the *Stavka* to put his present plans aside and not to embark on any offensive operations without the express authorization of the *Stavka*.

Events in Slovakia were already impinging on Soviet plans shortly after the first week in August. Inside the Slovak Defence Ministry three colonels of the Slovak Army—Golian, Vesel and Ferencik—worked out detailed military plans for a rising, an operation that greatly interested the London-based Czechoslovak officers and politicians, already preoccupied with the question of how to raise an indigenous army and install a command inside liberated territory, particularly 'liberated Slovakia'. While the Czechoslovak government in London explored means of 'expanding' the Slovak Army into a force of four divisions and thus creating an indigenous Czechoslovak army (with units in Bohemia and Moravia to be armed if arms could be found), Lt.-Col. Golian as chief of staff of the Slovak Army attended his first meeting with the Slovak National Council in Bratislava on 27 April. Two months later, at the end of June, the Council set up its own 'Military Centre' with Golian as chief.

Golian quickly took up the question of the status of the Slovak Army. In mid-June, in his report to London, he stated categorically that 'we do not wish to go over to the Russians . . . above all we wish to take part in the liberation of the Czech lands'. This required that talks start at once with the Russians about the status of the Slovak Army as a possible 'co-belligerent' to prevent it being taken prisoner and disarmed. At the end of the month Golian submitted his operational plan (the second part of which arrived between 4 and 7 July); his plans envisaged the use of the field army (two divisions) in a joint operation with the Red Army to free the Carpathian passes, the Rear Army with its garrison troops being committed to holding central Slovakia, and the rising as a whole to be triggered off at a signal from the Russians. The Czechoslovak Defence Ministry in London at once asked Golian how he saw the Slovak Army's relations with the Red Army, to which Golian made a very specific reply on 4 August: on receipt of the pre-arranged signal, Soviet troops could pass through the Slovak lines and expect the co-operation of Slovak officers, for which reason it was vital that Soviet forces should come in strength, otherwise Slovakia would be occupied by the Hungarians. Equally, the Russians must know of the Slovak plans, they must be made aware of the need to cross the frontier in strength and the rendezvous for liaison officers must be fixed. Under these conditions Golian thought that the whole of Slovakia could be in Soviet hands practically overnight.

During the first week in August a considerable amount of information on Slovakia flowed into Moscow from a variety of sources, from Koniev's Front HQ, from the Ukrainian Partisan Staff, from the two representatives of the Slovak National Council (Karol Smidke and Colonel Ferencik, who were flown to the Soviet Union) and from General Heliodor Pika, the head of the Czechoslovak Military Mission in the Soviet Union. General Pika dealt with the details of possible co-operation between Slovak and Soviet troops. On 8 August he sent the Soviet high command a letter suggesting this co-ordinated role for Slovak troops and two days later followed it up with a memorandum entitled 'On the situation of the divisions in eastern Slovakia', the main point of which concerned Slovak–Soviet co-operation in the area of the Dukla pass, a key part of the terrain. What the secret minutes of the Czechoslovak Military Mission show then is a break in the contact between Pika and the Soviet command lasting for more than two weeks (from 10 to 28 August), but neither these minutes nor other available records explain why this connection with the Soviet command was not firmly and formally established. It is also far from clear just what was proposed in the way of 'co-operation' to the Soviet command. Colonel Golian was reportedly informed by the Czechoslovak Defence Ministry in London (responding to the Colonel's signal of 4 August) that his plan could not be submitted to the Russians as it stood, since it ruled out any significant operational role for Slovak troops. As for suggesting, as Golian had, 'a large Soviet force' for Slovakia, the London message rejected this idea completely on the grounds that the Soviet command needed all its men for 'more important strategic axes'.

Soviet–Czechoslovak arrangements at the governmental level seemed, therefore, to be conspicuously lacking in conciseness and commitment. But there were other channels. On 6 August Karol Smidke and Colonel Ferencik arrived in Moscow after being flown out of Slovakia as representatives of the Slovak National Council. Both men possessed detailed information about the proposed rising and reported presumably in the requisite detail both to the Czechoslovak Communist Party and to officers of the Soviet military command. For two days the Slovak delegates talked at length with Maj.-Gen. Slavin of the Soviet General Staff, who reported to General Antonov, who in turn submitted this material to Stalin on 10 August. Though a Communist, Smidke was also a Slovak nationalist, as were a number of his colleagues in the Party, including Dr G. Husak; such 'opportunism' and deviationist ways led to Slovak Communists embracing the so-called 'London concept' of the struggle for the liberation of Slovakia, a transgression that inevitably brought the wrath of Moscow upon their heads. Viewed from Moscow, Slovakia presented the spectacle of a strategic area presently devoid of German troops but ruled by a reactionary government, with a nationalistic population liberally sprinkled with 'opportunistic' non-Communist elements looking to the Benes government in London, and with even the communist leadership leaning in the direction of the 'London concept'—the label attached to the idea of delaying any rising until the Red Army was on Slovakia's doorstep, effecting a *coup* rather than pursuing a 'revolutionary struggle' and then consolidating a 'bourgeois' state system. To allow the proponents of the 'London concept' to triumph without any challenge would have been foolish and pointless political benevolence. Once a Soviet-controlled partisan movement was entrenched on Slovak territory there was an instrument in being to 'activate' the struggle, to place the leadership of this fight firmly in the hands of the 'progressives' and to pre-empt the bourgeois nationalists by precipitating revolt.

In the course of the talks with the Foreign Bureau of the Czechoslovak Communist Party (which avoided any direct contact with the Soviet government, a useful precaution aimed at warding off the protests of the Czechoslovak government in London who could be told that these were simply 'Party proceedings'), Smidke and his communist colleagues worked out the terms of a 'directive' covering the planned rebellion in Slovakia. In the event of a German occupation, the Slovak people along with the Slovak Army would fight the invaders, occupy or liberate as much territory as possible, set up a 'provisional national authority' and fight guerrilla actions until final liberation came with the entry of the Red Army. The second contingency envisaged by this document centred on Soviet troops entering the country first, in which event there would also be a national rising, the setting up of 'organs of revolutionary power' and a drive to expel the Germans and the Hungarians, to be followed by the participation of Slovak troops in the final liberation of all Czechoslovakia.

But while these various parties talked, Smidke and Ferencik in Moscow, Golian in his exchanges with London, Pika with the Soviet command, the situation in Slovakia blew up in their faces, precipitating an impromptu rising for which the Slovak Army was far from prepared. Acting under orders from the central Ukrainian Partisan Staff and ignoring the Slovak National Council, the Soviet-led guerrillas intensified their own operations early in August and tightened their grip on central Slovakia and the middle reaches of eastern Slovakia. The Slovak government took fright and appealed to Berlin for German help and German troops. On 12 August Golian informed London that a major anti-partisan operation was in the offing. He asked for the curtailing of these partisan activities, which could only bring German intervention and must mean the premature crushing of Slovak 'resistance'. The reply from London could scarcely have encouraged Colonel Golian. It was, the London signal affirmed, technically impossible to restrain the partisans since there was no direct communication with their command— but more important, it would be political madness for the Czechoslovak government in exile to call for a cessation of partisan operations on Czechoslovak soil when throughout all Europe calls were going out for nations to take up arms. The only solution London offered was that the Slovak military command should itself make contact with the partisans and should support partisan operations.

Twelve days later, on 24 August, Golian again reported that a German–Hungarian occupation of the country seemed to be imminent. This Axis military occupation had been fixed as the signal for the Slovaks to take up arms and fight. But the problem now looked much more complex. Should the Slovaks offer resistance on a purely local scale to the German–Hungarian troops, or would it be more effective for the Slovak Army to break through and go over to the Russians? In four days Golian received a reply to his questions: military resistance on any major scale was impossible, but London could not advise on the particular course to follow from the options presented by Golian. To break through to the Russians seemed on the face of it the best course; but if this promised no success, then there was nothing for it but to organize local resistance, to concentrate the bulk of the available forces in central Slovakia, to reinforce rear units and to fight alongside the partisans. The Czechoslovak Defence Minister in London promised nevertheless to inform the Soviet supreme command about the critical turn of events in Slovakia.

The partisans in Slovakia, however, moved first. After 25 August guerrilla actions intensified and the insurgents were already in control of one town, Turciansky Sv. Martin. During the next two days Slovak garrisons defected to the partisans in other towns, but it took the murder of the head of the German military mission in Rumania, passing through Slovakia on his way to Berlin, to trigger off the final explosion. Captain Velichko's partisans halted the German military train at Turciansky Sv. Martin, which lay no great distance from the main partisan base at Sklabina. The German general along with his staff was taken from the train; they were lodged in a local military barracks and then shot the following day, 27 August. Enraged at these killings and incensed with the Slovak government for its failure to maintain order, Hitler ordered the 357th German Infantry Division along with some supporting units—a force of some 20,000 men—to move immediately into Slovakia to put down the disorder. On 29 August German reinforcements entered Slovakia from Moravia and the first fighting with the Slovaks broke out at Zilina, Cadca, Povazska Bystrica and Trencin. The partisan units pressed on with their own attacks, closed in on Banska Bystrica and seized the radio station.

The 'military centre' run by Slovak officers sent out its own call sign for a military revolt—'Commence transfer'—to all army units earmarked for operations against the Germans. The 'Free Slovak Radio Station' broadcast an appeal to the nation at large, calling on the Slovaks to resist the German invasion. The Slovak National Council proceeded to proclaim a 'Czechoslovak Republic' and announced the establishment of six provisional ministries. For the defence of the new state the Council authorized the establishment of two 'defence areas', each with an independent headquarters, to operate under the general command of the '1st Czechoslovak Army': 'Defence Area 1' was centred on Banska Bystrica and disposed of three infantry regiments with artillery to defend the Zvolen–Banska Bystrica–Brezno area; 'Defence Area 2' had its own headquarters at Liptovy Sv. Mikulas and covered the area from Spiska Nova Ves-Kezmarok westwards to the Vah valley down to Dolny Kubin and Ruzomberok.

The Slovak rising, sudden as it was, flared up first in central Slovakia, but the main strength of the key force—the Slovak field army—lay in eastern Slovakia. To this geographical division was now added a much more gravely damaging factor, the confused and dangerous situation that built up as a result of the flight in the early hours of 31 August of the Slovak deputy corps commander, Colonel Talsky. Behind the Soviet lines information came in from partisan commanders about the capture of a number of large towns; V.I. Yagupov, a detachment commander, flew in to Koniev's HQ on 29 August to report on the situation in eastern Slovakia and to supply detailed information on the strength and disposition of the Eastern Slovak Corps. It was also on 29 August that Colonel Talsky summoned a council of war in Presov, at which he announced that steps must be taken to arrange contacts with the Soviet command. The colonel, without informing anyone else in the corps staff, arranged through A.A. Martynov's partisan detachment for flight paths and a landing site to be fixed by the Soviet command.

At 0530 hours on 31 August three Slovak aircraft with nineteen Slovak officers and soldiers landed at Kalinuv in 1st Ukrainian Front area. More Slovak aircraft began landing at Lvov an hour or so later, until twenty-two aircraft finally arrived on Soviet airfields and unloaded twelve officers with fifty-four soldiers. But while Talsky made his way to Marshal Koniev's headquarters, confusion began to pile up swiftly in eastern Slovakia. From Bratislava, the seat of the Tiso government, the East Slovak corps commander General Malar sent out radio messages to the corps announcing that German troops entering Slovakia intended to take no punitive action against Slovak army units. Without orders, bereft of its commander and deputy commander, badly deployed and hopelessly confused, the East Slovak Corps proved to be easy meat for the 108th *Panzer* Division which ripped into the Slovak units on 31 August. The bulk of the Slovak soldiers were simply disarmed on the spot; only a few small groups broke away to join up with the partisans. Within twenty-four hours the entire corps was completely disarmed, a number of Slovak officers went over to the Germans and not a few Slovak soldiers found themselves on the way to concentration camps.

This military collapse was by no means confined to eastern Slovakia. The garrison troops in the west, units in Bratislava, Nitra, Hlohovec, Trencin and Kezmatok, also failed to join the rising in any strength, with the result that almost from the outset the Slovak rising was more or less confined to central Slovakia, the region into which both soldiers and partisans began to withdraw, a variegated force of partisan units and some dozen battalions of the Slovak army, badly armed and with little or no artillery. From London the government in exile sent Golian an urgent signal on 30 August asking for information. Golian provided few hard facts, referring only to his 'solution' to the problem created by the entry of German troops. Talsky was about to make contact with the Russians, Golian himself was remaining behind to organize resistance with the Slovak army and the partisans, though Golian did include an urgent request for the dispatch of parachute troops who could be landed at *Tri Duba* ('Three Oaks') or Mokad aerodromes—'send help quickly, we need it badly, our situation is critical'. The Czechoslovak Defence Ministry in London, almost completely in the dark about Talsky's whereabouts and intentions, sent a message to General Pika in Moscow, asking him to contact the Soviet command and to seek the release of the Czechoslovak airborne brigade, or better still the Soviet parachute troops, for use in Slovakia.

The news on 1 September fluctuated wildly. First there was information that all was well with Talsky, that he was supporting Golian's men; this was followed by the disastrous revelation that Talsky had virtually abandoned the Slovak Corps to its fate. By this time the East Slovak Corps no longer existed. Talsky, however, was definitely at Marshal Koniev's headquarters, reporting on the German incursion, maintaining stoutly that if Soviet units began a south-westerly advance then two Slovak divisions would fight their way towards Krosno and link up with the Red Army. What Talsky did not know, or did not guess or did not reveal, is that those two divisions had already been obliterated. Marshal Koniev reported by telephone to Stalin on his talk with Colonel Talsky; at 0320 hours on 2 September he sent a written report to Stalin, outlining an operation with his own left flank and Petrov's right (4th Ukrainian Front) to break into Slovakia along the Krosno–Dukla–Tilyava axis:

In our conversation Colonel Talsky makes the point that in the event of an offensive operation by our troops in a westerly direction the Slovak 1st and 2nd Divisions which are deployed along the line of the frontier would be able to attack from the east and thus link up with the Red Army.

In the area of Krosno our front is about 30–40 kilometres from the Slovak frontier. To link up with Slovak army units and with the Slovak partisan movement, if you give your permission, it would be sensible to mount a simultaneous operation with the left flank of the 1st Ukrainian Front and the right flank of the 4th Ukrainian Front to come out on Slovak territory in the area of Stropkov–Medzilaborze.

For this operation 1st Ukrainian Front could commit four RDs [rifle divisions] 38th Army and 1 GDs. Cav. Corps [Guards cavalry corps]: attack along the axis Krosno–Dukla–Tilyava. On that axis also it would be desirable to use 1st Czechoslovak Corps. It would be possible to begin the operation in 7 days. I request your orders on this issue. [Koniev, *Zapiski komand. frontom*, p. 300.]

On the evening of 2 September the *Stavka* sent Koniev specific orders to commit Soviet troops for this operation, necessitated by a situation 'arising out of the activation of the partisan movement in Slovakia and the development of the armed struggle of independent regular units and formations of the Slovak Army against the German invaders'.

The *Stavka* directive instructed 1st Ukrainian Front to 'prepare and execute an operation at the junction of 1st and 4th Ukrainian Fronts striking from the Krosno–Sanok area and driving in the general direction of Presov to reach the Slovak frontier and to join up with the Slovak troops'. Koniev received permission to use 1st Czechoslovak Corps and was advised to exploit 'the presence of Slovak forces north-east of Presov, with whom consultations must take place'. To secure the operations of the left-flank armies of 1st Ukrainian Front, the *Stavka* sent Petrov at 4th Ukrainian Front orders to organize an attack on his right wing from the Sanok area towards Komanc, a supporting attack employing one rifle corps. The *Stavka* worked on the assumption that the Slovak Corps could still fight, and Marshal Koniev did the same in submitting his attack plans on 3 September. The main role fell to Moskalenko's 38th Army, with 1st Czechoslovak Corps attached: the Soviet plan envisaged the rapid destruction of enemy forces in the Carpathian foothills by Soviet rifle divisions, followed by a deeper penetration with 1st Guards Cavalry Corps, 25th Tank Corps and second-echelon units moving through the mountain range, to link up after three or four days with the Slovak partisans. The selection of the line of advance running along the road to Dukla and through the Dukla pass provided the shortest route into Slovakia and would enable Soviet troops, once they had broken through the German tactical defence zone, to use the motor-roads for rapid movement. Bringing out 38th Army on the southern slopes of the Carpathians in the direction of Dukla would also cut First *Panzer* Army's main lines of communication with the left flank of Army Group North Ukraine. Koniev's Front command, with Sokolovskii as chief of staff, worked on two assumptions in planning the Slovak operation: that on the third day after the opening of the Soviet offensive 1st and 2nd Slovak divisions would begin attacking to the north of Stropkov, thus fighting their way towards Moskalenko's 38th Army and forcing the main mountain passes, and that the whole Soviet operation would be concluded after five days, by which time 38th Army would have reached the line running from Stara Liubovna to Presov, some sixty miles deep inside Slovakia. Apparently still unaware that these Slovak divisions no longer existed, the *Stavka* approved Koniev's attack plans on 4 September and fixed 8 September as the last possible date for taking the offensive.

Under orders from the Czechoslovak government in London, General Pika submitted a formal request for Soviet military aid in the Slovak rising, a document that was in the hands of the Soviet military authorities by 2 September. The two representatives of the Slovak National Council in Moscow were meanwhile unable to discover anything definite about possible Soviet assistance and turned to the London government with an appeal of their own. The Czechoslovak government for its part instructed the Czechoslovak Ambassador, Zdenek Fierlinger, to seek some assurance of Soviet support, an application supplemented by Klement Gottwald's letter to Molotov stressing the significance of the Slovak rising for the whole communist cause. The Soviet government delivered an assurance of help without either delay or demur, and the first Soviet decisions seemed to promise speedy action: a *Stavka* directive went out to Koniev for military support for the rising and, in response to General Pika's request for arms (1,000 automatic weapons, 300 anti-tank rifles, 400 machine-guns, ammunition and a ton of explosives as a first consignment), the Soviet command detached two long-range bomber corps (4th and 5th) for air transport operations, a decision effective from 5 September. That same night nineteen Soviet planes from the thirty originally sent out landed at *Tri Duba* airfield near Banska Bystrica and unloaded their supplies, small arms plus 13,800 rounds of machine-pistol ammunition, 41,800 cartridges and 125,000 more for the automatic weapons. During the next two days more flights came in while the 'transplanting' of Soviet partisan units from their Ukrainian bases continued, bringing the total Soviet partisan strength in Slovakia up to some 3,000 men. On 5 September, Prokopyuk's partisan brigade, 600 men strong and the third large detachment sent into Slovakia, crossed the land frontier and began operating in the Medzilaborce area; two additional Soviet units, each of twenty men, later dropped into the base area set up by Prokopyuk.

'Free Slovakia' in these early September days attacked the invading German troops at a number of points and tried simultaneously to complete its emergency mobilization. Only 16,000 men of the 60,000-strong Slovak Army joined the insurgents during these first days of the rising, but the National Council decreed general mobilization and managed to add 25,000 more men, all organized into the '1st Czechoslovak Insurgent Army'. Other Slovaks joined the partisans. Soldiers and guerrillas alike put up stiff resistance, forcing General Berger and the German command to revise their calculations that the rising could be put down in a matter of days simply by rolling over the insurgents from the north-west (from Zilina to Turciansky Sv. Martin), from the north, the south-east and the south-west. *Reichsführer* Himmler, from whom Berger received his assignment in Slovakia (only to be unceremoniously ejected in less than a month and replaced by Höffle, a senior SS police commander), ordered nothing less than the total suppression of the rising and demanded the clearing of the rail links (the double-tracked Zilina–Bratislava line and the Zilina–Kostice line) that bisected the country. For this clearing operation the Tatra *Panzer* Division pushed through the Jablunkow pass making for the junction at Zilina and Cadca; units of 20th SS Security Division advanced on Trencin from Moravia; an improvised SS *Panzer* Regiment strung together from the training schools in Moravia struck into western Slovakia towards Nitra; units of 86th *Waffen SS* came in from the north; *Kampfgruppe Schäffer* advanced from the east along the line of the Vah with orders to close on Ruzomberok; and finally from the south-east came the tanks of the SS *Panzer* Division that had already disarmed the hapless East Slovak Corps.

At the end of the first week in September German troops took Liptovy Sv. Mikulas and Ruzomberok, trapping the Slovak insurgents north of the Vah. Less success attended the German drive towards the south-east which was held at Strecno; French prisoners of war fighting as partisans under Captain de Lanurienne, supported by Slovak troops and Soviet guerrillas, held off the German tanks and won time to reorganize the defences of the Turec valley. Checked in the north, the German command decided to penetrate from the south with an attack aimed through the Nitra valley at Prievidza and Handlova, while away to the south-east (on the eastern edge of Slovakia) German tanks reached Telgart on 4 September; Slovak troops under Captain Stanek and Soviet partisans commanded by Major Yegorov counter-attacked fiercely, pushing the Germans back and forcing a German withdrawal, *eastwards,* to Dobsina and Spisska Nova Ves. The subsequent withdrawal of German units from this sector to the Carpathian defence lines caused the fighting to die down here towards the middle of the month. The southern sector which adjoined Hungary remained quiet for the moment, because the Hungarians did not elect to intervene in Slovakia.

While the Slovaks fought erratically but not unsuccessfully against the first wave of German troops, Moskalenko's 38th Army with a 'mobile group' (1st Guards Cavalry and 25th Tank Corps, 1st Czechoslovak Corps) as reinforcement made final preparations for the attack into Slovakia, amassing three rifle corps (52nd, 101st and 67th) with a total of nine rifle divisions, though many of them were below strength and short of weapons. On this sector of the Carpathians only the Dukla and Lupkow passes afforded access through the heights up to 800 metres, with thickly wooded slopes and narrow valleys bisecting mountain valleys swept with small rivers and mountain torrents. The German defences on

which Slovak and Hungarian soldiers had toiled for many months stretched across
a 25-mile zone with the main positions sited in the foothills and the northerly
slopes fitted out to cover the main approaches and the few roads in particular.
Two German corps (11th from Seventeenth Army and XXIV *Panzer* from Fourth
Panzer Army) were presently holding the 'Krosno–Dukla axis': ahead of Moskalenko's 38th lay three German infantry divisions, an engineer training battalion,
police units and a regiment from 96th Division, in all 20,000 men with 200
guns using Krosno as their strong-point. Elsewhere all roads and the approaches
to the mountain passes were mined, tank-traps and obstacles laid with fire-points
and small positions strung out along the ridges and slopes.

At dawn on 8 September, as prescribed in the *Stavka* directive to Koniev,
Soviet guns cracked out over the Carpathians in a two-hour barrage, the prelude
to Moskalenko's attack with 38th Army. The first Soviet infantry attacks met
little or no resistance, and encouraged by the progress of the first few hours of
fighting Moskalenko decided at noon to commit units of the 1st Czechoslovak
Corps. For most of that day the Czechoslovak troops struggled along waterlogged
roads, a time-wasting march which kept them well away from the battle on 8
September. By the evening German resistance began to stiffen. Seventeenth Army
command pulled reinforcements into the Krosno area, an infantry division moved
on from Turka, armour rolled in from the Sandomierz bridgehead and other
units were brought up from the interior of Slovakia. Krosno held out stoutly
and the breach opened by Soviet troops was just as quickly closed on 9 September,
the day on which Grechko's 1st Guards Army began attacking on the right flank
of Petrov's 4th Ukrainian Front in an operation designed to break the German
defences at Sanok.

After two days of fighting at close quarters, Soviet riflemen managed to break
into Krosno after penetrating the second German defence zone. But the Soviet
advance snagged once again in the main defences covering Dukla, a delay exploited
by the German command to bring up more men and armour until their strength—
compared with 8 September—had almost doubled, amounting to six infantry
and two *Panzer* divisions. Marshal Koniev moved up to Moskalenko's HQ to
look into the situation at first hand. What he saw was far from encouraging:
the new German reinforcements could frustrate the entire Soviet operation, which
must now be conducted without any hope whatsoever of the Slovak troops striking
at the German rear and yet had to go ahead against a tight timetable. To provide
some reinforcement Koniev had earlier ordered 4th Tank Corps—low in strength,
with 59 T-34 tanks and nine SAU-85 SP guns—into action: some of this armour
put in a timely appearance in the storming of Krosno, but something more drastic
had to be done. Soviet troops were still a long way from the area held by the
Slovak insurgents, and Dukla remained to be cracked. Koniev decided to use a
small gap, 2,000 yards or less, opened in the German lines on Moskalenko's
left flank to the east of Dukla, a strip of land lying between the villages of Lysa
Gura and Gloitse covered by German machine-guns and mortars. 1st Guards

Cavalry received orders to push into the gap and move across the heights to drop down into the German rear, a risky undertaking which depended upon keeping the narrow 'corridor' open.

1st Guards moved off during the night of 12 September, picking its way across the slopes towards the heights. The corps left behind all its heavy equipment and carried only a minimum of ammunition, 300 rounds for the 76mm guns, 420 rounds for the 82mm mortars, 400 hand-grenades, sufficient for only a few hours of fighting. Behind the cavalry Moskalenko sent up the corps artillery as quickly as possible; the gunners manhandled their pieces over the slopes, fought off German machine-gunners covering the access to the roads while the 'cavalry caravans' fought their way forward with the limited supplies of ammunition. As the Soviet troops moved forward, the Germans closed in behind; during the night of 15 September the narrow 'corridor' was closed off behind 1st Guards Corps, which was now wholly isolated from the main body of 38th Army. From now on ammunition, food and medicines could only be dropped to the Soviet corps by transport aircraft.

Koniev's gamble had not come off and the Red Army did not break through to rebel-held territory in Slovakia, though the Soviet attacks in the Carpathians drew off German strength and eased some of the pressure on the insurgents in central Slovakia. Czechoslovak troops operating with 38th Army played a prominent part in these first Soviet relief attacks, and by mid-September Czechoslovak pilots and parachute troops joined the battle raging inside Slovakia. The appearance of Czechoslovak forces as such, the parachute troops in particular fighting as a single formation, may have been a comfort to the Slovaks but it precipitated a struggle for control over the entire 'Czechoslovak armed forces', including the guerrillas. The *Stavka* authorized the transfer on 13 September of the 1st Czechoslovak Fighter Regiment to Slovakia, a move General Pika had already requested. Marshal Koniev received information at his Front HQ that *Tri Duba* airfield could be used and therefore gave his own orders to 2nd Air Army to deploy the Czechoslovak fighter regiment directly to the Slovak front. The fighters arrived at *Tri Duba* on 17 September and during the night of the 18th, flying with a full complement of stores, ammunition, fuel and radio equipment. *Tri Duba* was also the scene of another infusion of Czechoslovak fighting men, 2nd Parachute Brigade (part of 1st Czechoslovak Corps) ordered into Slovakia by the *Stavka* in response to General Pika's request for these troops. On 13 September, along with the fighter regiment, the *Stavka* released the brigade and assigned the 5th Long-Range Air Transport Corps to lift the men and their equipment into Slovakia.

The first Soviet transport planes dropped twelve Czechoslovak paratroopers with two radio sets on 17 September, an advance party sent into *Tri Duba* to prepare the landings and unloadings at the airfield. Not for ten days did the first units land and then only companies showed up. The main body of the brigade—700 men and 104 tons of equipment—flew in during the first week in October, deploying at once to the west and south-west in the area of Banska

Stiavnica. For more than five weeks Soviet aircraft continued to fly in elements of the Czechoslovak brigade, landing 1,855 men, transporting 360 tons of supplies, and flying out 784 wounded partisans and soldiers. The Soviet air-lift ceased on 25 October, but well before that the flights had been at the mercy of unfavourable weather conditions with the autumn bringing mists and high, driving winds.

The mixture of partisans and regular troops, the entangling of lines running to London and to Moscow, and the military pressures of the revolt itself intensified the struggle for control of these miniature armies. As the first German rush into Slovakia was held, the rebel front contracted and the revolt was confined largely to central Slovakia, where the defence system was quickly reorganized; the two 'defence areas' were replaced by six 'tactical groups' affording greater flexibility and easier collaboration with the partisan units, but this still did not solve the problem of the regular military forces and the partisans fighting under what amounted to separate commands. In an effort to centralize partisan activities, the Slovak National Council on 16 September established its own 'Main Staff for Slovak Partisans', whereupon the leadership of the Czechoslovak Communist Party 'requested' the Ukrainian Staff of the Partisan Movement to fly in specialist Soviet officers. For quite some time Soviet transport planes continued to bring in Soviet partisan commanders and political officers, swelling an already considerable force, but the dispatch at the end of September of Colonel A.N. Asmolov from the Ukrainian Staff with Rudolf Slansky as his deputy (along with Jan Sverma, who was subsequently killed in Slovakia) marked a much more significant change, for it put the Slovak partisan movement under overt Soviet command. Towards the end of the month American and British liaison missions working through Marshal Koniev's Front command arrived at the headquarters of 1st Czechoslovak Army in Banska Bystrica; under the command of Major Sehmer and Lieutenant Green, the men of these two missions along with their two officers were shot out of hand by the Germans upon being captured, in spite of their being in regulation uniform.

Early in October the situation in Slovakia seemed to take a turn for the better in what proved to be a brief and heady interlude before the full storm broke over Slovakia. Moskalenko's 38th Army fought its way to the summit of the Carpathians late in September and was forcing the approaches to the Dukla pass. At the very end of the month, in the mists and heavy autumn rains, Soviet and Czechoslovak troops attacked and after five days of fierce fighting 1st Czechoslovak Corps took the pass in the celebrated action of 6 October. More units of the 2nd Parachute Brigade were coming into Slovakia from their Soviet bases, while from London General Viest came to take over the 1st Czechoslovak Army installing himself at his post in Banska Bystrica, the prelude to a determined attempt to bring all the Czechoslovak military units fighting in and for 'Free Slovakia' under a single command responsible to the London government. The Czechoslovak government had already instructed its ambassador in the Soviet Union to sound out the Soviet attitude over Czechoslovak discussions with the British and Americans about supplying arms to Slovakia, since the 'transportation of weapons from the Soviet Union is being delayed by bad weather conditions'. Ambassador Fierlinger replied that the Soviet attitude was wary in the extreme, but he supposed that 'if the British and Americans bring in only arms to Slovakia, then Moscow should not raise any objection . . .'. His own view, however, was that the Czechoslovak government should formally request the Soviet government to send 'an experienced Soviet general' to Slovakia, to act as 'Red Army supreme commander'; thus armed with the requisite authority, this commander could 'co-ordinate the operations of all forces . . . particularly those of the military units and the partisans'. Masaryk returned a plain negative to this proposal; the Soviet–Czechoslovak agreement stipulated that for those military units raised in the Soviet Union there should be a Czechoslovak commander, even if the units were operationally subordinated to the Russians; whereas the forces raised in Slovakia were not covered in any way by this agreement and there was consequently no need to seek the services of 'a Russian general'. Czechoslovak efforts to unify all their forces by seeking to bring 1st Czechoslovak Corps—which was now on Czechoslovak territory—into the framework of the 1st Czechoslovak Army under Viest and Golian led inevitably to strained relations, which became more embittered as the rebel state crashed in ruins once the Germans determined upon its complete destruction.

For all the momentary brightening of the scene early in October, with Czechoslovak troops at last fighting on their own soil, the portents were grim enough. Heinrich Himmler arrived in Bratislava at the end of September and took Höffle, the SS commander in Slovakia, to the special conference in Vienna that met during the first week in October, at which the German plans to crush Slovakia were laid. There were pressing reasons for this drastic action. The Soviet penetration of the Dukla pass gave the Russians access to Slovakia and the possibility of an eventual link-up with the rebel army, which, if suitably reinforced, could push on to the west, or even more likely could move north-westwards into Bohemia–Moravia or south-westwards into Hungary, the source of immediate German concern as the Hungarians set about negotiating their own surrender to the Allies. 'Free Slovakia' must be eliminated at top speed, and the task was assigned to a force of seven German divisions, 40,000–45,000 men with artillery, armour and aircraft at their disposal. The Szálasi *coup* in Hungary in mid-October greatly facilitated this operation, for German troops could attack from Hungarian territory and Slovakia lost the valuable asset of a quiet southern frontier. After 18 October German troops closed in on Slovakia from all sides, striking from eleven points on the perimeter. Among the new arrivals in Slovakia was the Dirlewanger Brigade, fresh from the butchery of Warsaw and eager for further 'anti-partisan' operations: the *Horst Wessel Panzer* Grenadier SS Division moved from reserve to the south for a strike towards Telgart, Banska Bystrica, Zvolenska Slatina and Zvolen, while to the north a *Waffen SS* division took over the *Kampfgruppe* Schäffer.

These fresh German troops struck into rebel territory between 18 and 20 October, leaving everywhere a trail of burning villages, mass graves or cowed civilians awaiting transportation to the concentration camps. Only on the northern slopes of the Low Tatras could the partisans and soldiers hold up German armour; elsewhere the SS slashed their way through the insurgent positions. From the north-west 14th *Waffen SS* cut its way to Brezno; *SS Horst Wessel* attacked from the south towards Tisovec; German tanks moved from Kremnica and Turciansky Sv. Martin towards Banska Bystrica, upon which other German units were converging. Brezno fell on 25 October, Zvolen two days later and Banska Bystrica, the governmental seat of 'Free Slovakia', on 27 October. Under this flail of converging attacks the Slovak National Council evacuated Banska Bystrica and fell back on Donovaly at the edge of the main range of the Low Tatras. Once German tanks appeared at *Tri Duba* airfield, the Czechoslovak Fighter Regiment lost its only base and was forced to fly back behind the Soviet lines. German aircraft then concentrated on the roads to the south of Banska Bystrica, finding a mass of targets in the jam of soldiers and civilians breaking out to the mountains.

In this final bloody round with its massacre and confusion, General Viest, mocked by the Communists as a 'drawing room general' (though he met his death in a concentration camp), made one last attempt to salvage the remnants of an army in what was left of 'Free Slovakia'. Viest issued his last order on 29 October; though anxious to preserve his army, Soviet officers insisted on breaking up the 1st Czechoslovak Army into guerrilla units in order to carry on the fight in the mountains. This issue of the control of the fighting forces in Slovakia both at this time and later provided each side, communist and anti-communist, with a great deal of ammunition to fire at one another. The Communists charged that 'bourgeois elements', including the 'deviationists' among the Slovak communists who were infected with nationalism, worked in the interests of the *émigré* Czechoslovak government to free Slovakia without Soviet help and were hoping to use the 1st Czechoslovak Army, plus the 1st Czechoslovak Corps raised in the Soviet Union, as the core of a new, bourgeois-type army. The counter-charges aimed at Soviet leadership and policies indicted the 'prohibition' on the supply of arms to the Slovak insurgents from the Western powers, the 'sabotage' of the transfer of the Czechoslovak Parachute Brigade to Slovakia, and the deliberate exploitation of the rift between the army and the partisans in Slovakia.

By the end of October 'Free Slovakia' was almost obliterated. Himmler quickened the pace of the sadistic 'pacification' he was visiting upon the Slovaks. General Viest and General Golian, who attempted to make their escape by plane, saw their machine burned before their eyes by embittered Slovak soldiers, and both officers fell into German hands. Partisans and the survivors of Colonel Prikryl's 2nd Czechoslovak Parachute Brigade trudged into the mountains and prepared to fight through all the fierce winter conditions.

The use of partisans in the Slovak rising provided the Soviet Union's most successful 'transplant' of the partisan movement across the Soviet frontiers, the only sustained example of Soviet-led partisans being used to precipitate a 'revolutionary struggle' on which even leading Slovak Communists turned their backs. In the field the Red Army did not succeed in breaking through to the rebel Slovak Army, but this force had been effectively eliminated by the Germans or disorganized by the antics of the Slovak officers long before the first Soviet soldier moved off for Slovakia. Soviet plans to break through to Presov proved to be unrealistic, though Soviet military pressure in the Carpathians did undoubtedly draw off over 12,000 German troops fighting the Slovak insurgents in the interior. The Soviet command, to the degree that it was actually culpable, made Slovakia the victim of its inflexibility; but equally the London-based government, even while trying to get control of all Czechoslovak fighting forces, failed to call out any more than a handful of its men from Bohemia and Moravia, from which only about a thousand appeared in Slovakia.

The Red Army continued its gruelling battle in the Carpathians until late November, though any hope of rescue for Slovakia had gone. Moskalenko's 38th Army set out its reasons for prolonging its operations in a staff submission at the end of October: to fight on could bring the encirclement of German units on the left flank, an eventual drive into eastern Slovakia to link up with forces on the 2nd Ukrainian Front striking north from the direction of Hungary, and also some relief for the Slovak guerrillas by drawing off German troops. Troops of the 38th continued to fight, therefore, through these dark days with winter already whipping in the wind until they reached the river Ondova. Whatever the deviousness of the politics of the Slovak rising, it had cost the Red Army dear. Behind Moskalenko's men presently on the Ondova lay the battles for the mountain passes and 80,000 casualties, with almost 20,000 men killed in action. General Ludwik Svoboda's 1st Czechoslovak Corps, fighting alongside the Soviet 38th Army, suffered even more fearfully in wresting a foothold on its native soil, of which many men of 1st Corps saw only a few metres. General Vedral, commander of 1st Czechoslovak Brigade, was only yards over the frontier line when he was blown to pieces by a German mine; he joined the lists of the Czechoslovak dead in this operation—6,500 men in all, almost half the original strength of the 1st Czechoslovak Corps.

Shortly before dawn on 17 August 1944 a section of Soviet riflemen led by Viktor Mikhailovich Zakabluk used the last of the morning dark to slip off the road into a clover field and crawl the final two hundred metres to the river Sheshupe, a line on which German and Soviet tanks had clashed in the past few days in small but fierce actions. To the left and right of Zakabluk's section, Captain Gubkin's 2nd Rifle Battalion from 184th Rifle Division (attached to 5th Army, operating with Chernyakhovskii's 3rd Belorussian Front) fought with tank and heavy mortar support to clear the German trenches running along the river bank. At five o'clock in the morning, with only a few metres more to go before reaching the frontier with East Prussia, Zakabluk gave the order to charge; his section scrambled to their feet and moved off at the double, raising as much of a cheer as they could. Half an hour later Alexander Afanasevich Tretyak—the first Soviet soldier to stand on the Soviet–German frontier—planted his red battle-flag on the site of Frontier Marker No. 56. Chernyakhovskii's Front armies had carried out *Stavka* orders to the letter.

With Vilno surrounded by Soviet armies as early as 9 July, Chernyakhovskii loosed his mobile columns in pursuit of the Germans and drove towards the river Niemen. Lt.-Gen. N.I. Krylov, 5th Army commander, demanded the surrender of the German garrison in Vilno now that 'you [the Germans] are trapped in our deep rear and it is useless to think of a break-out'. Chernyakhovskii's columns raced on to the Niemen, reaching the river on a broad front between the area west of Vilno and the approaches to Grodno. (Third *Panzer* held the Niemen sector from Kaunas to Alitus and Fourth Army was dug in along the southern reaches of the river as far as Grodno itself.)

While Krylov's riflemen assisted by units of the Polish underground finally cleared Vilno on 13 July after one last savage battle in the centre of the city, the *Stavka* set about regrouping to strengthen 3rd Belorussian Front for the coming assault on the Niemen line: 39th Army operating north of Vilno reverted to Chernyakhovskii's command, Bagramyan at 1st Baltic Front was relieved of the 'Kaunas axis', while 3rd Guards Mechanized Corps passed to Bagramyan from Chernyakhovskii and 3rd Guards Cavalry Corps, which was already engaged in fighting at Grodno came under Zakharov's direct command in 2nd Belorussian Front. Lyudnikov's 39th Army now extended Chernyakhovskii's right-flank operations up to Ukmerg; Krylov's 5th, after investing Vilno, was fighting off German units that had broken through north-west of the city, while 3rd Guards Tank Corps struck north-west, cutting the Vilno–Kaunas railway line and breaking into Kaisyadoris. Col.-Gen. Galitskii's 11th Guards Army pushed on for sixty miles between 9 and 13 July, his right-flank corps (Maj.-Gen. Gurev's 16th Guards) reaching the Niemen on 13 July and making immediate preparations to cross. First over in the Alitus area was Colonel Leshchenko's 95th Guards Regiment (31st Guards Division); by dawn on 14 July 11th Guards Army had two corps on the western bank north and south of Alitus. North of 11th Guards, 45th Corps of 5th Army also drew up to the Niemen within a few hours, followed by 31st Army whose forward elements forced the Niemen north of Grodno. The next day (15 July), under threat of encirclement, German troops pulled out of Alitus.

North-west of Vilno German armour and infantry attacked in an effort to hold the developing Soviet drive on Kaunas. On the western bank of the Niemen repeated attacks were launched on the Soviet bridgeheads. *Stavka* orders issued to Chernyakhovskii in the major directive of 28 July specified an attack from the north and south to take Kaunas not later than 1–2 August, to be followed by a drive towards the East Prussian frontier. Krylov's 5th Army accordingly received orders from Chernyakhovskii to outflank Kaunas from the north and south, destroy the German garrison and then drive on to the frontier. Within hours Krylov began his assault on Kaunas, using two assault formations, 72nd Guards Corps to break through to the north-west and 45th Corps fighting in the south-east. On 30 July, as Krylov's corps hacked their way into Kaunas German resistance along the whole Niemen line began to crumble. Chernyakhovskii's centre and left-wing armies moved forward in the direction of Vilkovyshki, with one tank corps—2nd Guards—racing for the railway station at Mariampol, thus threatening German communications leading out of Kaunas. During the night of 31 July two Soviet corps, 45th and 65th, put in a decisive attack against Kaunas from the south; one Soviet division, the 144th, fought its way through the old forts in the south into Kaunas itself. By the evening much of the city had been cleared, though the German command pulled 9th Army Corps out to the north-west, followed by the Soviet 72nd Corps in hot pursuit.

To cut off the German troops trying to withdraw along the railway line and motor-road from Kaunas to Mariampol, a fighting withdrawal covered by heavy tanks, assault guns and motorized infantry, the commander of 45th Rifle Corps Lt.-Gen. S.G. Poplawski—by birth a Pole, currently a career officer with the Red Army and subsequently transferred towards the end of 1944 to the command of 1st Polish Army—ordered a rifle regiment with tank support to move south-west and block both road and rail routes. Behind this blocking force came Burdeinyi's 2nd Guard Tank Corps operating with the infantry of 5th Army also south-west of Kaunas. With the tanks in the lead, the infantry of yet another army (the 33rd) moved in to occupy the railway station at Mariampol and then pushed on in the direction of Vilkovyshki.

For some time Chernyakhovskii maintained this momentum, some of his units crossing the Niemen bend (lying east of Kaunas), others striking out from the smaller bridgeheads at Druskeniki and Gozha (north of Grodno) into the great forest of Augustovo, the tanks racing along the main road to Suvalki and past Mariampol. Early in August units of 3rd Belorussian Front were over the Sheshupe, having captured Vilkovyshki and Kalvaria, with the fastest progress being made north-west of Mariampol. In the course of little more than three weeks, nine German divisions had been broken or flung aside, the 15,000-man garrison of Vilno wiped out or captured (Soviet troops counted 7,000 German dead), and almost 44,000 prisoners taken in the subsequent pursuit. Soviet armies, however, did not escape lightly. Rotmistrov's 5th Guards Tank Army could deploy only one brigade of twenty-eight tanks, all that was left of its tank force, with only the motorized infantry left to fight in the tank corps when the tank brigades were pulled back to Ionavi to refit. In 11th Guards Army the two-company battalions were reduced in many regiments to a single company per battalion. German troops still held considerable stretches of the region lying between the Niemen and the Sheshupe, German forces were gathering behind the Niemen north-west of Kaunas at Shaki, and at Vilkovyshki a German counter-attack at the end of the first week in August drove Soviet troops back. Though Chernyakhovskii was skirting the frontier with East Prussia—and formally implanted some units there on 17 August—behind the frontier line lay fixed German defences which could not be overcome with a rush. The *Stavka* directive of 28 July specified preparations for an attack in the direction of Gumbinnen–Insterburg–Preis–Eilau, a drive in the direction of the Kaunas–Eydtkuhnen railway line, but Chernyakhovskii had yet to clear the Niemen–Sheshupe area and then recoup sufficient strength to launch his front against the formidable defences of East Prussia. With Soviet troops on the frontier, just biting into East Prussia, the front settled into shape: German troops held Vladislavov (south-east of Schirwindt) on the Sheshupe, Soviet units Mariampol and thence southwards through Kalvaria and on to Seyny.

Chernyakhovskii's neighbour to the north, Bagramyan, in command of 1st Baltic Front, had orders to cut the communications between Army Group North and East Prussia, all part of a grand strategic design emanating from the *Stavka*. But the way in which the *Stavka* proposed to deal with Army Group North failed to impress Bagramyan, who on earlier occasions had voiced his scepticism over the high hopes so glibly entertained at the centre. This new offensive proved to be no exception. Bagramyan's own plans envisaged an attack in the direction of Riga with the main forces of his front, with a supporting attack on Shavli, a powerful offensive aimed at the entire southern flank of Army Group North with the object of rolling it up to the north-west and pushing the remaining German strength behind the western Dvina, where it would be pounded to pieces by 2nd and 3rd Baltic Fronts operating to the north of the river. In addition to endangering the German flank and rear, threatening land communications with East Prussia and thereby lowering the defensive capacity of the German divisions which would then be under attack by two other Soviet fronts (2nd and 3rd Baltic), Bagramyan reached for his greatest prize, finishing off Third *Panzer* Army once and for all in co-operation with the right-flank formations of 3rd Belorussian Front, leaving all Lithuania and Courland wide open to Soviet troops. The *Stavka* directive No. 220130 of 4 July, which prescribed Bagramyan's objectives, came as a rude shock to the Front commander, who was nurturing his own plans: the main line of the advance set by the *Stavka* ran along the Sventsyani–Kaunas axis, where five Soviet armies—6th Guards, 43rd, 39th, 2nd Guards and 51st— were to be committed, with part of the Front forces detached to attack in the direction of Panevezus–Shavli to secure the main offensive from the north. The 4th Shock Army, presently on Bagramyan's right flank, was transferred to Yeremenko's 2nd Baltic Front; in exchange Bagramyan acquired 39th Army which was almost free of the encirclement battle at Vitebsk.

The *Stavka* plans for eliminating Army Group North were based on a series of staggered blows involving the three Baltic fronts (1st, 2nd and 3rd), with Govorov's Leningrad Front driving into the Narva isthmus from the east. Bagramyan's 1st Baltic would move off first on 5 July in a westerly direction, attacking between the Niemen and the Dvina: next to go would be Yeremenko's 2nd Baltic Front, with orders to advance along the Polotsk–Dvina railway line and then develop a full-scale offensive to wipe out German units in the Idrits–Sebezh–Drissa area, with the Front forces advanced to the Rezenke line (north-east of Dvinsk) and ready to strike towards Riga. Col.-Gen. Maslennikov's 3rd Baltic Front would be the last of the Baltic fronts to attack, with its first objective the destruction of the German forces in the Pskov–Ostrov area, followed by an advance towards Tartu and Piarnu, thereby 'bottling up' German units defending the Narva area. Maslennikov and Govorov (Leningrad Front) would be jointly responsible for clearing Estonia of German troops.

The flaw in all this was plain enough to Bagramyan. Where German strength was greatest, on the northern wing, Soviet attacks would be 'relatively weaker' with fronts going over to the offensive 'considerably later'. Bagramyan evidently tried to persuade the *Stavka* to throw the main Soviet weight against the German southern wing, but all to no avail. The *Stavka* demanded an offensive in the direction of Kaunas as a means of 'isolating' Army Group North and as a protection for the Soviet offensive aimed at Warsaw, while the 2nd and 3rd Baltic Fronts would force a general withdrawal of Army Group North towards East Prussia. This was the grand design, but in Bagramyan's opinion the *Stavka* was deluding itself; how, he asked with characteristic bluntness, did the capture of Kaunas 'isolate' Army Group North? The whole 'Kaunas plan' posed a threat to the operations of 1st Baltic Front, whose flank and rear would be exposed to a danger 'hanging like the sword of Damocles' from Army Group North itself— the further west 1st Baltic advanced, the greater the danger of a German counter-blow. Worse still, Bagramyan had lost one army (4th Shock) without receiving a replacement, though 39th Army was promised him. The new army would not be in position, however, for at least another five days, and even with the exchange completed it scarcely favoured Bagramyan, who lost 4th Shock with ten divisions and got the 39th with only seven—and it would be mid-July before 2nd Guards and 51st Army arrived in full strength. His Front reserve consisted of a single tank corps (the 1st), equipped largely with battered tanks just out of the repair shops.

Unable to deflect or dissuade the *Stavka*, Bagramyan decided to attack without waiting for 39th Army to move up. The two armies available, 6th Guards (two corps) and 43rd (three corps) would be used in the first stage of the diverging attack aimed at Dvinsk and Kaunas. For the Dvinsk attack Chistyakov's 6th Guards was to co-operate with 4th Shock Army, now under Yeremenko's command on the 2nd Baltic Front.

Opening on the morning of 5 July, 1st Baltic Front offensive developed more or less as Bagramyan expected, with the heavier resistance developing on his right flank where 6th Guards fought its way towards Dvinsk; at the centre and on the left success came more easily, with Beloborodov's 43rd Army pushing ahead at some speed, cutting the Dvinsk–Vilno railway line along the entire length of its front on the morning of 9 July, severing the Dvinsk–Kaunas motorway in the area of Utena the following day and threatening the rail link running from Dvinsk to Shaulyai (Siauliai) and thence to Tilsit. By now Lyudnikov's 39th Army had moved up into 1st Baltic's left flank with orders to attack in the direction of Ukmerg, but Bagramyan seized the opportunity presented by Beloborodov's breakthrough to the Dvinsk–Kaunas road to order 43rd Army to move down this road from the west and south-west, into the rear of the German units holding up Chistyakov's advance on Dvinsk itself. Elements of 43rd Army would continue their north-westerly drive in the direction of Panevezius, with Butkov's 1st Tank Corps (attached to 43rd infantry for the attack) aimed at Dvinsk.

The tank-supported attack along the Dvinsk road failed, owing to defective reconnaissance, lack of artillery support and the use of frontal assaults. Through lack of fuel and too few forward airfields, 3rd Air Army could fly only a limited number of sorties in support of 43rd Army. On Chistyakov's 100-mile front his three rifle corps were splayed out, with German counter-thrusts poking between them and threatening even 6th Guards' rear; the losses sustained over the previous three weeks, diminished air support, shortage of lorries to move up supplies (only one 'motor transport brigade' operated over the bad roads) and the deficit in ammunition all contributed to slowing the advance of 6th Guards, facing fierce and well-organized German resistance. By the evening of 12 July, with three armies now in action across his whole front, Bagramyan had committed all his available forces, at the very moment when the *Stavka* signalled the Front command that the German armies of Army Group North were on the point of pulling out of the Baltic states—a mistaken view of German intentions, as it proved but reason enough for Marshal Vasilevskii, *Stavka* 'co-ordinator' with the Baltic fronts, to demand faster movement to the west with the main body of 1st Baltic Front.

Bagramyan realized that it would take the best part of a week for 51st and 2nd Guards Armies to move up to the front; what was to be done must be done with the armies presently engaged, without waiting. Chistyakov received orders to attack from the south and to work in with 4th Shock Army to capture Dvinsk, after which Chistyakov was to go for Rokiskis (thirty-five miles to the west of Dvinsk). Beloborodov's 43rd was aimed along the Utena–Panevezius axis, with 1st Tank Corps covering the attack from the north but needing Bagramyan's explicit permission to join an extended action. 39th Army would strike for Ukmerg, then attack with its main force towards Kedainia and also Kaunas with part of its strength.

Precisely at 1930 hours on 10 July scores of red signal rockets flared across fifty miles of front in General Yeremenko's 2nd Baltic command, bringing another four Soviet armies into action against Army Group North. Yeremenko's front faced the thirteen divisions of the German Sixteenth Army, and his line of advance reached into the southern extension of the 'Panther line', the fortifications south of Opochka built up by Field-Marshal Model at the close of the 1943–4 winter campaign. Behind these positions lay the 'Reiter line', with three further defensive lines—'Blue', 'Green' and 'Brown'—to the west; marshes, bog and wooded country added natural obstacles to those devised by men. Yeremenko proposed to develop a double attack, on his right (10th Guards and 3rd Shock Army) driving on Rezenka, and on his left 2nd and 4th Shock Armies striking along the eastern bank of the river Daugava in the direction of Dvinsk. The Front offensive would unroll in two stages, the first (10–17 July) involving a penetration of the German defensive system (with mobile units committed to the battle after penetration of 5,000 yards was achieved and with orders to reach the line Opochka–Sebezh–Osveya–Drissa) and the second (17–27 July) spoiling German attempts to establish a firm defence by pushing Soviet armies to a line running from Rezenke to Dvinsk. For a distance of over 150 miles German fortifications of one sort or another, fully fitted out or more hastily flung up, many skilfully adapted to the terrain, faced Yeremenko's 2nd Baltic Front. The rail junction of Idritsa and the town of Sebezh formed a powerful double bastion straight in the path of 3rd Shock Army, from whom, as from all other armies on this front, a major effort was required.

Within little more than forty-eight hours Yeremenko's assault armies ripped out a gap fifty miles wide and more than ten deep in the German defences. By 12 July Lt.-Gen. M.I. Kazakov's 10th Guards Army had cut the Pskov–Idritsa railway line and the Nevel–Opochka road, Lt.-Gen. A.V. Yushkevich's 3rd Shock Army had reached the eastern bank of the river Velikaya, captured the bridges with demolition charges already laid on them and pushed on to outflank Idritsa. Lt.-Gen. P.F. Malyshev's 4th Shock Army, after forcing the Drissa along a wide front, took the town of Drissa; and Lt.-Gen. G.P. Korotkov's 22nd Army was already more than ten miles into the German defences along a 100-mile front. With 2nd Baltic offensive developing northwards between Idritsa and the river Sorot and a mounting attack on the north side of the Dvina aimed at Dvinsk, Kazakov's 10th Guards Army registered a most significant gain on 15 July with the capture of Opochka. Two days later Yushkevich's 3rd Shock Army took Sebezh after a deep outflanking movement and that same day Korotkov's 22nd captured the strong-point of Osveya.

The fall of Opochka, a major strong-point in the Panther line, opened a gap in the whole German defensive system guarding the Latvian frontier—Kazakov was now fighting on the frontier itself and was engaged in the northern reaches of the Green line defence works, having broken through the Blue line in the rush to Ludza. To hold the Soviet penetration, the German command moved up the 126th Infantry Division from Pskov, units of the 58th Infantry Division from Narva and brought 87th Infantry Division from reserve. The German infantry in these northern armies were battle-hardened veterans, highly skilled in fighting rearguard and holding actions; with the terrain well suited to defensive operations, Soviet riflemen struggled through the bogs and marshes, fighting through the numerous defiles between the many lakes, crossing the multitude of small rivers and feeder streams, and at the larger river barriers racing for the bridges before German demolition crews blew them. The worst job remained for Soviet sappers in the forest paths and tracks, all of them liberally strewn with mines. On each road German rearguards planted four or five charges of high explosive every thousand yards.

Yeremenko's 2nd Baltic Front, fighting through the forests and swamps, had nevertheless staved in the Panther line with the capture of Idritsa, Sebezh and Opochka; 2nd Baltic armies were now penetrating Latvia, and on the left flank 4th Shock Army closed in on Dvinsk. Bagramyan at 1st Baltic Front, with two new armies and a mechanized corps under his command, now pleaded for permission to strike at Riga, but again the *Stavka* refused. Meanwhile Col.-Gen. Maslennikov in command of 3rd Baltic Front prepared to loose the third and final blow of the offensive against Army Group North, with an attack aimed at Pskov and Ostrov. Maslennikov's orders, laid down in the *Stavka* directive of 6 July, specified the destruction of the 'Pskov–Ostrov concentration of enemy forces'. The first stage of this offensive involved the capture of Ostrov, Liepna and Gulbene; the second an advance in the general direction of Verro (almost due west of Pskov), a penetration into the rear of the 'Pskov concentration' and the capture of both Pskov and Verro; followed by an attack on Parnu and Tartu, thus bringing Soviet troops into the rear of the 'Narva concentration of enemy troops'. The immediate task of Maslennikov's left-flank armies was to cut the Ostrov–Rezenke railway line, then to seize Liepna and Gulbene: not less than twelve or thirteen rifle divisions were to be employed on this line of advance running through Balvi and on to Gulbene. Maslennikov's own operational plans (built round the *Stavka*'s instructions) assigned the right-wing and centre armies (42nd and 67th, with seven divisions between them) a defensive role to pin down German forces, while the left flank—1st Shock Army and the 54th, with fifteen divisions—set about breaking into the German defences.

Not long after the *Stavka* directive was sent to Maslennikov, Stalin expressed much concern that 'no one had been even once up to Maslennikov'; here was 'a young commander, with a young staff and not enough experience', needing 'experienced gunners and airmen' but no tank officers, since Maslennikov had few tanks on his front. Shtemenko, Yakovlev and Vorozheikin—a high-powered team—flew out to Maslennikov's HQ the next day, working for much of the time on the small bridgehead on the western bank of the river Velikaya. The final operation plan, accepted by the *Stavka*, confirmed the use of 1st Shock Army and the 54th in an attack from the left wing in the direction of Ostrov–Liepna–Gulbene with the object of destroying German forces west and south-west of Ostrov and capturing Ostrov itself, a penetration of 100 miles in seven days; the second stage involved using two rifle corps of the same two armies to drive on Verro and, with three rifle corps, on Valga with the object of breaking into the rear of the German forces holding Pskov, an eight-day operation with a penetration of over sixty miles.

In the first half of July, 3rd Baltic regrouped its rifle formations and artillery units; the nine divisions 'deployed' on the 'Ostrov axis' exercised and trained with some deliberate show, while three dummy tank regiments and four radio transmitters 'worked' for 20th Army. One full decoy aerodrome operated fighter and training aircraft. By mid-July, of the twenty-five divisions available to 3rd Baltic, eighteen had been concentrated within the armies assigned to the main assault. After 11 July all armies north of Pushkinskie Gory carried out intensive battlefield reconnaissance, and on the late afternoon of 16 July left-flank units of 1st Shock Army were already on the attack. The next day both assault armies, 1st Shock and the 54th, were attacking and within two days they tore out a gap thirty-five miles wide and twenty-five deep in the German positions south of Ostrov. By 20 July two divisions of 1st Shock Army, 23rd Guards and 33rd Rifle Division, deeply outflanked the Ostrov positions in their drive to the west and south-west. As German units began to withdraw, on the morning of 21 July a Soviet rifle regiment with tank support broke into the north-eastern outskirts of Ostrov, another Soviet regiment was fighting on the southern outskirts, and shortly before noon elements of four Soviet divisions took Ostrov by storm. The same night, units of 42nd Army made ready to attack Pskov; by the evening of 22 July their forward units had reached the river Velikaya and with it the eastern and central areas of Pskov, which by 6 am on the morning of the twenty-third was cleared of German troops. The *Stavka* now intervened to redirect 3rd Baltic Front's assault formations towards Valga, a main junction of great importance, with the object of cutting the one link connecting all German forces in Estonia and northern Latvia with Riga—a 'variant' previously investigated by 3rd Baltic command but rejected for lack of sufficient troops.

Riga also drew Bagramyan like a magnet. By the middle of July, with his armies wholly bereft of reserves, with 2nd Guards and 51st Army still moving up (and not likely to be in position for at least another four days), two firm conclusions were forming in the Front commander's mind: that the German command showed not the slightest sign of ordering a pell-mell flight into East Prussia from the Baltic states, and that the continuation of 1st Baltic Front's offensive in the direction of Kaunas was not only pointless but downright dangerous. At least Bagramyan had some small consolation, since Marshal Vasilevskii undertook on his own responsibility to shift the axis of 1st Baltic's main attack towards Shaulyai once the two fresh armies arrived at the front. Bagramyan himself submitted proposals directly to the *Stavka* for a full-scale attack on Riga, using only a part of his Front forces against Shaulyai, but the *Stavka* refused to consider this. Behind the *Stavka's* resistance to Bagramyan's proposal lay its particular fear that by the time 1st Baltic actually reached the Shaulyai–Riga road, the offensives by 2nd and 3rd Baltic Fronts would have dislodged the main body of Army Group North from Estonia and eastern Latvia, German divisions would have pulled back into East Prussia and Bagramyan's great blow would simply meet 'empty space'.

Undeterred by this rebuff, Bagramyan set about dispelling the *Stavka* arguments: neither 2nd Baltic (seriously deficient in armour) nor 3rd Baltic, nor even the two fronts in combination, could 'eject' Army Group North, whose command showed every sign of hanging on grimly in the Baltic states where the terrain could tie up large Soviet forces. A 'voluntary withdrawal' on the part of the Germans was virtually unthinkable. In this case, Bagramyan would certainly not be thrusting into thin air, and what gave his plan added advantage was that he did not need to regroup in order to go for Riga—two of his three armies were already committed to the 'main axis', while the fresh formations (2nd Guards and 51st Armies plus 3rd Guards Mechanized Corps) could be deployed at will. The *Stavka*, however, remained wholly unconvinced, and Shaulyai remained as Bagramyan's immediate objective.

The drive for Shaulyai began on 20 July, preceded by a rapid regrouping as Kreizer's 51st Army and Lt.-Gen. P.G. Chanchibadze's 2nd Guards moved into the Front area. Kreizer's newly arrived divisions changed positions with 43rd Army, now under orders to cover the main drive on Shaulyai in a north-easterly direction by striking out for Birzha; 2nd Guards Army deployed on Kreizer's left with orders to move on Baisogala–Tituvenai, and further south 39th Army provided protection for the assault armies (though the 39th soon came under Chernyakhovskii's 3rd Belorussian Front command for the attack on Kaunas). The new armoured formation, Lt.-Gen. V.T. Obukhov's 3rd Guards Mechanized Corps, needed still more time to complete fitting out with men and tanks; Obukhov's orders specified that he would be held back until Panevezius fell and then be thrown straight into the attack on Shaulyai. On Bagramyan's right flank, however, the situation showed little sign of improvement as Chistyakov's 6th Guards slogged ahead in the attack aimed at Dvinsk, where fresh German reserves were already moving to block 6th Guards. The shortage of ammunition persisted and Soviet air support remained curtailed; for the moment Bagramyan committed Chistyakov's army on a line of advance to approach Dvinsk from the south, but the three corps of 6th Guards made only slight progress.

On Bagramyan's left flank, the advance by 51st and 2nd Guards Armies gathered speed, building up to a rapid drive on Shaulyai. On 22 July two rifle divisions from Kreizer's 51st (417th and 267th Divisions) burst into Panevezius and on the following day lead units on Kreizer's right flank took Bibalnikas and Pumpenai. Driving north-west, 43rd Army collided with units of the German 43rd Corps which slowed the Soviet advance in the direction of Birzha and thus opened a 'gap' between the faster-moving 51st Army and 43rd Army, a breach that Kreizer lost no time in covering with one of his rifle divisions. Bagramyan, who watched his Front deployments like a hawk, confirmed Kreizer's decision and moved a rifle division out of reserve up to 51st, with orders to use it in the event of real danger developing at the junction with 43rd Army. Apart from this potential danger, now headed off, events were moving favourably and at great speed; the Soviet command detected a perceptible German retirement in the general direction of Riga, slow at the moment, but attributable to the pressure built up by the attacks launched by 2nd and 3rd Baltic Fronts. The whole German front was beginning to sway and had cracked wide open further to the north once Yeremenko broke through the Panther line. Bagramyan reined in his forward armies for a few hours to adjust his line before loosing them, together with 3rd Guards Mechanized, on Shaulyai; the fruitless advance on Dvinsk to the south he called off, ordering Chistyakov to regroup as the 4th Shock Army fought its way to the western Dvina north of Dvinsk.

On the morning of 26 July Bagramyan's right flank opened its full drive for Shaulyai; 51st Army brought its second echelon (1st Guards Rifle Corps) into action and Obukhov's brigades swept west of Panevezius, covering over fifty miles that day. Soviet mechanized units had already raced to the south-east of Shaulyai, with armour and motorized infantry closing on the town from the north and the east. Major Sparykin's 44th Tank Regiment with a regiment of self-propelled guns in support was in contact with the main German garrison, but the first Soviet attempt to rush the town failed. As 35th Guards Tank Brigade worked its way to the south-west to cut the German escape route, General Obukhov decided to storm Shaulyai on the morning of 27 July with simultaneous attacks from the east and north-west. German counter-attacks rolled against the Soviet brigades, a situation that eased only when Soviet motorized infantry cleared Meskuachai to the north-east, the area from which the attacks were being launched in an effort to hold off 3rd Mechanized at any price. Joined now by rifle troops of 51st Army, the mechanized brigades fought throughout 27 July to clear Shaulyai and by evening the vital junction was in Soviet hands: 8th Guards Mechanized and 35th Guards Tank Brigade took Shaulyai as a battle-honour.

At the very end of July the whole German front in the north seemed in imminent danger of collapse as key positions tumbled one by one—Dvinsk (27 July), followed by Rezekne the same day and Shaulyai, then Narva (attacked by Govorov's Leningrad Front coming in from the east). The fate of the German armies east of the Dvina was hanging in the balance, now tipped in Soviet favour by the fast-moving invasion of Latvia and the successful elimination of the Dvinsk stronghold. The Soviet drive for Shaulyai came as a thoroughly unpleasant shock to the German command and a catastrophic situation seemed to be in the making. The Soviet seizure of Shaulyai pointed Soviet armies straight at the flank and rear of Army Group North, promising the eventual realization of Bagramyan's notion— to press the German divisions behind the Dvina where they could be pounded to pieces by the other two Baltic fronts, 2nd and 3rd. Bagramyan at once determined to strike among the 'Riga axis': 2nd Guards Army would push to the west of Shaulyai, but the main force of 1st Baltic would go for Riga, using 51st Army and 3rd Guards Mechanized Corps for a thrust to the gulf of Riga, while 6th Guards Army and the 43rd advanced to the western Dvina. Marshal

Vasilevskii approved these plans, at which 1st Baltic Front command flung their caps in the air. Bagramyan could issue orders for an advance on Riga with the overall situation vastly improved now that the destruction of the powerful German force at Dvinsk removed the threat of a thrust from the north into his flank; he was free to unleash 3rd Guards Mechanized Corps for a drive on Riga and at liberty to push in behind the tanks any rifle divisions he could lay his hands on. Kreizer therefore received orders to leave one rifle corps in the Shaulyai area and to push on for Jelgava (Mitau) with the remainder of his divisions: Obukhov's 3rd Mechanized Corps would take the lead.

Soviet armour moved off at high speed along the Shaulyai–Jelgava road. At 2 am on the morning of 28 July Captain Galuzo's armoured reconnaissance detachment from 9th Guards Mechanized Brigade roared into Ioniskis, scattering the few German guards posted beside vehicles and military dumps and waking German troops sleeping in the town square. Galuzo's tanks opened fire, cutting down infantrymen rushing out of the houses. Within minutes the fire-fight was over, the German garrison dispersed and Ioniskis in Soviet hands. Galuzo's column struck due north for Jelgava but this time the German garrison with its SS troops, supported by artillery on the bank of the river Lielupe, did not scatter so easily. The lead Soviet tanks could only wait for the main body of 3rd Mechanized Corps to close on Jelgava, where on the morning of 29 July the fighting began to intensify as more Soviet units arrived on the scene. Most of Obukhov's 3rd Mechanized was now tied down in front of Jelgava and Bagramyan's uneasiness was not diminished as heavier German reinforcement began converging on the town.

If the situation at Jelgava was confused, at least the morning of 29 July brought Bagramyan some relief in another direction when *Stavka* Directive No. 220159 arrived. This fresh set of orders authorized an attack with the main forces of 1st Baltic against Riga, supplemented by an assault of Memel—objectives that Bagramyan had already assigned to his assault armies forty-eight hours earlier, but with these new official orders it seemed at long last that 1st Baltic and the *Stavka* were fighting the same battle. Meanwhile in Jelgava Soviet riflemen with tank support were engaged in heavy street fighting in which 1st Guards Rifle Corps (51st Army) speedily joined, but lack of proper co-ordination with 3rd Mechanized hampered progress. Bagramyan therefore ordered Kreizer to take personal command of the battle, with 3rd Mechanized subordinated to him for the duration of the fight for Jelgava; to seal off the town, Bagramyan instructed Obukhov to advance an armoured force to the north-west as far as the gulf of Riga and to push another due west up to Dobele. The advance to the gulf of Riga was entrusted to Colonel S.D. Kremer's 8th Guards Mechanized Brigade whose tanks struck out along the road to Tukums. Tukums was captured on 30 July and forward units of the 8th rushed on to the gulf of Riga, coming out at Klapkalns. Colonel A.A. Aslanov's 35th Guards Tank Brigade simultaneously sent out armoured detachments in the direction of Dobele, thus isolating Jelgava from the west.

Army Group North was now completely cut off. The rapid Soviet tank thrust to the Gulf of Riga severed the last vital land communication link joining Army Group North with the main body of the German army on the Eastern Front and with its immediate rear, East Prussia. Colonel Kremer's tanks stationed on the shore of the gulf formed the point of an ever-thickening Soviet salient straddling the German overland route to the west from Estonia and Latvia, a salient with its eastern face running from Tukums to Jelgava, Bausk to Birzha, its western edge starting also at Tukums and running down to Aust (south-west of Jelgava) and as far as Shaulyai. Together with Marshal Vasilevskii and other *Stavka* officers with 1st Baltic—Aviation Marshal Falaleyev, Col.-Gen. of Artillery M.N. Chistyakov and Lt.-Gen. V.D. Ivanov—Bagramyan had cause to be not only pleased but downright relieved that the 'Riga thrust' undertaken without specific authorization from the *Stavka* was proving successful. There were, however, grounds for concern now that 1st Baltic extended itself day after day and moved further from its supply bases. Chanchibadze's 2nd Guards Army holding the extreme left flank was already fighting off German counter-attacks south of Shaulyai; mounted by 7th *Panzer* Division, these attacks were growing in strength and had pushed back at least one Soviet division, 32nd Guards, making for Rasieni. On the eastern face of the salient, 60th Rifle Corps (43rd Army) was holding Birzha but here too there were signs of an impending German attack. Early in August that attack materialized on some scale when elements of six German infantry divisions supported by over 100 tanks started a drive north-east of Birzha with the aim of breaking through to Panevezius.

This first assault on the eastern face of the Soviet salient was held by 43rd Army, assisted by 6th Guards Army and a tank corps (the 19th) moved from *Stavka* reserve. But fierce though these attacks were, they were only the prelude to very heavy fighting on the western face which developed in the middle of the month. The German command was now aiming for Shaulyai. Elsewhere, in the remainder of the Estonian–Latvian theatre—north of the Dvina—Yeremenko's and Maslennikov's armies battered away at the German defences but without winning success on any decisive scale. Towards the end of July Yeremenko's assault armies took Dvinsk and Rezekne, a feat for which Yeremenko himself received the decoration 'Hero of the Soviet Union' and a victory saluted in Moscow by twenty salvoes fired from 224 guns. By 25 July 2nd Baltic Front armies had broken through the last of the German defensive lines—the Brown line—covering Rezekne and Dvinsk from the east; on the right flank 10th Guards Army took Karsava and was advancing on Ludza from the east, bringing Soviet troops within easy striking distance of Rezekne. South of Rezekne 3rd Shock Army closed in on Kaunata, 22nd Army cut the Dvinsk–Rezekne railway line, while away on the left flank 4th Shock Army, supported by Maj.-Gen. M.G.

Sakhno's 5th Tank Corps, pushed along the river Dvina and was preparing to storm Dvinsk itself.

Malyshev, 4th Shock Army commander, took elaborate measures to cut off the German garrison in Dvinsk: 100th Rifle Corps and 5th Tank Corps were pushed to the north and west, two more corps (14th and 83rd) moved from the north-east along the Rezekne–Dvinsk railway line and also from the east. Preceded by a heavy artillery barrage and under cover of air attacks, Soviet infantry closed in hour by hour, cutting the Dvinsk–Riga road very quickly. Captain Moroz's 3rd Tank Battalion made the first interception of German columns pulling out to the west towards safety, the chance of which was much diminished on 26 July when 100th Corps captured the whole stretch of railway line north-west of Dvinsk and sealed off the motor-road. All the German escape routes to Riga were now cut.

Two Soviet armies, 4th Shock and 6th Guards, closed in to Dvinsk from the north and south, completely trapping the German garrison. To clear a route to the west, German units attacked the flank of 100th Corps, only to be beaten back and pinned against the Dvina. Malyshev's 4th Shock Army was now only a short distance from Dvinsk and in the early hours of 27 July two corps advanced under cover of artillery fire on the ancient town, breaking in from the east and west. At 8.30 am all German resistance ceased. Inside Dvinsk more than half the houses and factories lay in ruins, many more were swept by fire or destroyed by delayed-action bombs. The power station lay gutted, the water supply and sewers had been put out of action and every bridge over the Dvina blown up. The capture of Dvinsk was nevertheless a triumph much sought after and a victory that was compounded that same day when 10th Guards Army crossed the river Retupe north-west of lake Tsirma, pushed on for twenty miles and took Rezekne in one rush.

Central Latvia now lay ahead of Yeremenko's armies, great stretches of marsh in the area of lake Luban and the plain of Luban itself, a last natural barrier of bog and forest in front of Riga. With Dvinsk and Rezekne in Soviet hands, Yeremenko received orders to advance across the Luban plain, reach a line running west of Gulbene, through Madona and on to Plavinas, then to deploy for a 'decisive thrust' against Riga. To achieve these objectives Yeremenko's command decided to use 10th Guards to outflank lake Luban from the north and south, bringing this army up to the line formed by the river Aidikste (the Ewst) and to push it westwards to a line running from Madona itself on to the west of Gulbene: 3rd Shock Army would move south of lake Luban and to a line south of Madona, 22nd Army to an even more southerly sector (Martsiena–Yankalsnava) and 4th Shock—securing the left flank along the Dvina—to a line running from Yankalsnava to Plavinas. None of this terrain was easy, and the river Aidikste, 70 metres broad and over 2 metres deep in places, offered a natural defensive line; the Germans had blown every bridge and the lower reaches of the river formed one great expanse of swamp.

Having received their new orders, the armies of the 2nd Baltic Front moved off punctually at dawn on the morning of 1 August, preceded by heavy artillery barrages. Within three days all were engaged in sharp fighting in the central area of the Luban plain. After five days 10th Guards pushed the German rearguards back to the eastern bank of the Aidikste, and by the evening of 5 August established a small bridgehead on the western bank just below Lubana. Behind 10th Guards came 3rd Shock and 22nd Armies, moving up to their sectors on the river line and launching their infantry in assault crossings. With his left-flank and centre armies over the Aidikste, Yeremenko at once looked for some way of exploiting this success to the north and west. The situation with 4th Shock Army, however, was not so encouraging, since two corps bumped into strong German resistance in the reach of land between the Aidikste and the Dvina, where Krustpils and Plavinas had been turned into powerful fortified positions.

The task of reducing this bridgehead area fell to 22nd Army; two corps (100th and 44th) from 4th Shock Army were to join in this battle for the reduction of the German positions once the railway bridge over the Dvina just north-west of Krustpils was in Soviet hands. On the morning of 8 August infantry from 130th Latvian Rifle Corps with the tanks of 5th Tank Corps—supporting 22nd Army— cut the Krustpils–Plavinas road and the railway line, broke through to the railway bridge over the Dvina and fought their way into the railway station at Krustpils. The two rifle corps from 4th Shock Army were by this time coming in from the east and had penetrated the suburbs of the town. At noon the two bodies of Soviet troops linked up and Krustpils was cleared of Germans.

The capture of Krustpils, an important road and rail junction, was a very useful gain for Yeremenko, but his left-flank armies fought for the next ten days in the triangle formed by Gulbene–Madona–Luban without any real success. Soviet troops pushed across the Luban plain and finally forced the Aidikste along its whole length, capturing Tsetviane and Madona (west of the river) and Leigrade (on the Aidikste itself). Yet all attempts to break north and west achieved little or nothing; after Krustpils came Plavinas, and Plavinas proved to be a very tough nut to crack. The terrain almost everywhere lent itself very readily to effective defence; though Soviet troops were over the Aidikste, they then stumbled into a morass of swamp which gave way to the stretches of forest around Madona. To the north and west lay more uncongenial country with its hilly, broken ground.

Yeremenko was using the traditional route along the Dvina, exploited three hundred years earlier by the armies of Muscovy, but this passage became much less convenient the closer it came to Riga; the route contracted into a much narrower channel lying between the Dvina and its tributaries, the Oger and the Egel—a channel the Germans could certainly block. Moving into this funnel, Soviet armies were quickly stopped short: 3rd Shock Army forced the Oger on 19 August and then had to fight off three German divisions counter-attacking with heavy air support: at Ergli, north-west of Madona, Soviet divisions found their way effectively blocked and to the south, at Plavinas, Soviet attempts to reduce the German positions in the area lying between the Aidikste and the Dvina also proved to be fruitless. For the moment, Yeremenko found the way to Riga completely barred.

If Yeremenko was held before one bastion, Plavinas, so Maslennikov with 3rd Baltic Front was finally pinned down at another, Valk. At the end of July Maslennikov's armies, with Pskov and Ostrov in their hands, prepared to assault the 'Marienburg line' running from lake Pskov to Gulbene and then to break into Tartu and Valk. Izborsk had fallen on 30 July and for a few days in early August 3rd Baltic armies carried out a series of local operations to improve their positions; the capture of Laura on 6 August afforded another useful jumping-off position. Four days later the Front offensive began, mounted along a line running north-west of Izborsk–Laura at the junction of 67th and 1st Shock Army: the first objective was Verro. Pechory, north-west of Izborsk, fell on 11 August and Verro on 13 August, whereupon Maslennikov switched his attacks, committing 67th Army to an attack in the direction of Tartu and 1st Shock Army against Valk, a key position connecting both Estonia and Latvia. The right-flank attack on Tartu made slow but perceptible progress, boring its way along the Verro–Tartu road and also hugging the shore of lake Peipus, assisted in mid-August by an amphibious landing carried out by the small craft of the Baltic Fleet river flotilla. On 24 August Soviet troops were already in the south-western suburbs of Tartu, and the following day they cleared this ancient city and moved north, establishing a bridgehead on the northern bank of the river Emaiga. The formations on the centre and left flank meanwhile moved down the eastern shore of lake Virts Jarvi and to the east of Valk, all marshy ground well suited to defence and held by over four German divisions prepared to hold the 'Valk line'. As Yeremenko was halted before Plavinas, so was Maslennikov stalled before Valk, caught in the swamps and pinned by the Germans, unable to wrest this central bastion of the whole Estonian–Latvian theatre from its defenders.

The defence of the eastern regions of Latvia and Estonia, now entrusted along with the whole Army Group North to Col.-Gen. Schörner (the latest in the line of Hitler's special 'firemen' committed to averting further catastrophe), was greatly facilitated by the peculiar topography of the region stretching from the gulf of Finland to the river Dvina. Any east–west advance depended on forcing the few existing passes between the numerous obstacles—the spreading swamps, reaches of forest and the high ground running between the several rivers, each with oozing marshy valleys. Both Yeremenko and Maslennikov had run into difficulties in trying to force their way along their chosen routes. North and west of Madona, Yeremenko's armies bumped into heavy German resistance or were checked where the Aidikste joins the Dvina; Maslennikov's troops were caught in the marshy stretches south of lake Pskov whose tributary rivers meandered through swampy valleys, separated from each other by more high ground. One other east–west route remained to the Russians, the neck of land running between lake Peipus and the coast of the Gulf of Finland, a passage not more than thirty miles wide with its landward side largely screened by swamp; Narva covered the eastern approaches to this east–west 'bridge', the forcing of which was assigned to Marshal Govorov's Leningrad Front. Narva itself lay astride the river Narva, whose breadth varied all the way to the gulf of Finland from just under 200 yards to over 700, with a depth of ten feet and high, steep banks. Behind the Narva lay a marshy valley and, to the south of the Narva–Tallinn railway line, more impassable swampland. The only useful sector for Soviet operations was confined to the north of the railway line, but here the river Narva ran at its broadest.

Lt.-Gen. Fedyuninskii's 2nd Shock Army received orders to force the Narva passage. The German fortifications at Narva ruled out a frontal assault, but Fedyuninskii proposed to attack north of Narva and to strike from the south with 8th Army, breaking into the rear of German forces holding the town. *Armeeabteilung 'Narva'* consisted of some twelve German divisions at the end of May, strength that fell steadily as divisions moved to other sectors of the Soviet–German front until at the end of July in *Abteilung Narva* only five divisions and three brigades remained—the core of III *SS Panzer* Corps, three German infantry divisions, the *SS* Motorized Division *Nordland* and three *SS* motorized brigades (22,250 men). Leningrad Front HQ issued its operational directive in mid-July, laying down Kudrukiula–Vasa as the 'breakthrough sector' and specifying a southerly advance after the breakthrough to link up with units of the Soviet 8th Army; after the fall of Narva Soviet divisions would move westwards along the shore of the Gulf of Finland.

At 7 am on the morning of 25 July 1,000 guns and mortars in 2nd Shock Army area fired off an eighty-minute barrage as Lt.-Gen. Ivanov's 13th Air Army bombed forward German positions. Under cover of the artillery and air bombardment, two Soviet divisions, 191st and 131st, launched their makeshift rafts and boats on to the Narva, the steady roar of the barrage giving way to the strains of the Soviet national anthem and Aleksandrov's sombre battle hymn *Svyashchennaya voina* broadcast along the banks of the Narva by Soviet loudspeakers working at full blast. Hot and sweating under the July sun, with the Narva reflecting the light cloud skimming across the blue skies, Soviet riflemen, assault parties and assault engineers ploughed on through the shell-bursts to the western bank, unloaded artillery pieces set to fire over open sights and worked on constructing pontoon bridges. By eleven o'clock the sappers had the pontoon bridge laid; 76mm regimental artillery, anti-tank guns and finally tanks began to trundle across, followed by 109th Corps under the cover of darkness. Shortly after dawn on 26 July Soviet troops were fighting inside Narva itself, clearing both fortresses towards 8 am and linking up with the Soviet 8th Army moving up from the south-west. The 'gateway to Estonia', captured by Russian troops in 1558 during the Livonian wars and the scene under Peter the Great of a crushing Russian defeat, was again in Russian hands, though the town was in ruins, the streets strewn with German dead and littered with smashed vehicles, the ashes of burning papers blowing in the wind beside the gloomy building that housed the German headquarters. In the streets, girl traffic-controllers directed the swelling columns of Soviet artillery moving over the Narva, shunting them through the crossroads and on towards the 'Tannenberg line', where the Soviet offensive was momentarily halted by six German infantry divisions. Marshal Govorov finally decided to embark on an extensive outflanking movement through Tartu and into the rear of the 'Narva group', marching like the medieval Russian armies into the Livonian strongholds.

North of the river Dvina, entrenched in Balka, Plavinas and behind Narva, Schörner had won a temporary respite. To the south of the Dvina river line, the German commander now proposed to smash in Bagramyan's salient running up to the gulf of Riga by attacking Shaulyai from the west and the north-west, an ambitious plan which envisaged more than just slicing off the tip of the penetration at Tukums and Jelgava, and for which Schörner mustered the best part of ten divisions grouped under two corps administrations, XXXIX and XL *Panzer* Corps (operating with Third *Panzer* Army). The assault on the eastern face of the Soviet salient, directed against Birzha, was beaten off during the first week in August by 51st Army supported by aircraft, artillery and armour. Aware now that a German offensive against Shaulyai was in preparation, the *Stavka* put 4th Shock Army under Bagramyan's command, thus enabling him to solidify his right flank and to build up divisions on his left and centre. On the extreme left flank Chanchibadze's 2nd Guards Army forced the river Dubissa and pressed forward on the western bank, taking Rosieni on 10 August. But German resistance was stiffening with every hour, and German divisions were gathering for the blow aimed at Shaulyai: XL *Panzer* Corps (two *Panzer* divisions, *SS Gross Deutschland* and two infantry divisions) were to attack Shaulyai from the west and the south-west (from the area of Kelme), drive north-east and co-operate with 39th Corps in capturing Jelgava. East of Jelgava and Shlok (not far from the shore of the gulf of Riga) German units were to fight westwards to link up with the divisions cutting into the Soviet salient. For the moment the Soviet advance towards Riga from the central region of Latvia was brought to a complete halt.

Bagramyan's armies were sprawled across a huge area running from Rosieni in the south to Shaulyai in the centre, Tukums and Jelgava in the north and Birzha in the east. Where a month ago three armies on 1st Baltic Front attacked along a 100-mile front, now with only one additional army Bagramyan had to hold a 300-mile front. The imminence of a powerful German attack made concentration imperative. Already on the afternoon of 16 August a German infantry regiment with sixty tanks in support was driving from Kelme in the direction of Shaulyai, an operation designed to pin Soviet forces south-east of Shaulyai before the main attack came from the west. Rozhdestvenskii's 110th Guards Rifle Corps (2nd Guards Army) held the Kelme–Shaulyai road that first day, but during the night of 17 August 300 German tanks and assault guns rolled forward in the full attack on Jelgava and Shaulyai. West of Zhagar and south-west of Shaulyai, German units penetrated Soviet positions; 54th Rifle

Corps (2nd Guards Army) fought to hold the German advance west of Shaulyai, but the situation degenerated by the evening. German tank reinforcements crossed the river Venta and pressed on for another six miles to Smilgiai, not far from the western outskirts of Shaulyai. Bagramyan rushed artillery and armour into Shaulyai, sending up Volskii's 5th Guards Tank Army, units of 1st Tank Corps and heavy artillery, all with orders to stop the German advance.

In the attack aimed at Jelgava more than 180 German tanks from two German *Panzer* divisions (the 5th and 14th) advanced up to ten miles on 14 August, striking into the left flank of 51st Army holding the Soviet line at Zhagar. To hold off this German tank strength Bagramyan ordered 3rd Guards Mechanized Corps to close with 51st Army and sent up heavy artillery to beat back the German assault. After four days of heavy fighting, with the fate of Shaulyai hanging in the balance more than once, 51st and 2nd Guards Armies contained the attack on Jelgava–Shaulyai, but at the very tip of the Soviet salient General Missan's 1st Guards Rifle Corps (51st Army) could not deflect Battle Group *Strachwitz* from Tukums and on 21 August Soviet troops under orders from the Front command fell back to a line running from Jelgava to Dobele and Aust. German communications with Army Group North had been reopened, even if this remained a narrow and tenuous link.

Shaulyai, however, held out. By the morning of 18 August units of 5th Guards Tank Army were arriving in the town, accompanied by 16th (Latvian) Rifle Division under Maj.-Gen. Karvialis. As the day drew to a close, and after repeated German tank attacks, Shaulyai was still in Soviet hands. German tank losses and the lack of reserves brought the offensive to a halt. In a few days Bagramyan's divisions were reinforced and they launched their own counter-blow, which pushed German troops once more ten miles to the west of Shaulyai. One last attempt by German tanks to drive on Jelgava through Zhagar came to grief by 23 August, by which time Bagramyan had moved up two tank corps (1st and 19th), concentrated the bulk of 51st Army, redeployed the right flank of 2nd Guards Army and 3rd Guards Mechanized Corps, as well as emplacing 5th Guards Tank Army at Ioniskis.

Though Bagramyan held Shaulyai, Jelgava and the Jelgava–Birzha line (covered by the river Lielupe), the Soviet salient contracted to a narrow bulge. The spearhead that reached up to the Gulf of Riga was now blunted and the German attack on Tukums reopened a small corridor with Army Group North, a circuitous land route, but one that momentarily averted the total isolation of the German armies fighting in the Baltic states. The Soviet drive on Riga had been halted; in fifty days of fighting the three Soviet fronts, assisted by the left flank of the Leningrad Front, wrested only half of the Baltic territory from Army Group North but had prevented it going to the aid of Army Group Centre. Schörner broke open the 25-mile corridor through Tukums, but he had not dislodged Bagramyan or significantly affected the situation in Courland and northern Lithuania; nor had he averted the great and growing danger facing the Army Group which must with time be split within the Baltic states into one large body in the central theatre and another smaller grouping in the western extremities. Withdrawal from Estonia and Latvia, which must be a hazardous business now that only the 'Tukums gap' remained, could no longer be either avoided or delayed. Along a defensive line running from the gulf of Finland to the river Niemen—a line stretching for almost 600 miles—the German command deployed fifty-six divisions, among them five *Panzer* divisions and two motorized divisions, 700,000 men with over 1,000 tanks. A strong force of armour held the sector from Jelgava to Aust, with other powerful concentrations in the Narva isthmus, in the Valk 'bastion' south of lake Virts Jarvi and west of the Aidikste between Ergli and Plavinas. The Tannenberg line covered the approaches to Tallinn, but Riga became the focus of German attention.

Riga also preoccupied the Soviet command during the reappraisal of its plans for the 'second stage' of the Red Army offensive in the Baltic area: the *Stavka* ordered a careful regrouping of all Soviet armies on the four fronts involved, while after 26 August Front commands worked on plans and preparations for a massive concentric attack aimed at Riga, designed to isolate Army Group North once and for all.

The defeat of Army Group Centre, the seizure of vital bridgeheads on the western bank of the Vistula and the advance to the outskirts of Warsaw, the result of the giant offensive waged by five Soviet fronts, pushed Soviet armies as much as 350 miles along 'the road to Berlin'. On this, the shortest line of advance, Berlin was now less than 400 miles away. Two out of the four major German concentrations, Army Groups Centre and North Ukraine, were fiercely mauled in the battles which sucked in more than six million men on both sides and employed 85,000 guns (and heavy mortars) and over 11,000 tanks or assault guns supported by over 10,000 aircraft. Of the seventy German divisions facing 1st, 2nd, 3rd Belorussian and 1st Baltic Fronts, thirty were obliterated from the German order of battle and thirty more immolated in Koniev's drive with 1st Ukrainian Front to the Vistula. German formations were encircled five times, at Vitebsk, Bobruisk, Brody, Vilno and Brest–Litovsk; along the 'western strategic axis' the Soviet front advanced more than 300 miles to run from the west of Jelgava to Shaulyai, Suwalki, Ostrolenka, Pulutsk, on to the Warsaw suburb of Praga, to Magnuszew, Sandomierz, Drohobych and finally to the junction with 2nd Ukrainian Front at Chernovitsy, the line at which the offensive finally subsided in August. At the end of the month the *Stavka* ordered all five fronts on to the defensive.

After the German rout in Belorussia the Russian pursuit was relentless, ramming its way through towns and villages ripped to pieces by the deliberate devastation of the retreating German troops or all but demolished by the fierce fighting. One by one the last of the ancient cities of Russia, gutted as they were by fire or ruined by bombardment, returned to Soviet possession, but at fearful cost. Further west the dreadful enactment of the destruction of Warsaw took place before the eyes of Soviet troops who seemed on the point of bursting into the city at the end of July; then came the silence on the eastern bank of the Vistula and the inhuman fighting on the western side, the stillness to the east remaining unbroken through a fiery August followed by the furious spurt over the broad river and into the outposts of the underground army, much too late in September when the Warsaw rising was nearing its last horrifying gasp. Polish rashness and icy Soviet calculation combined in their own way to produce the monstrous wreckage of Warsaw, but this was not all Soviet deceit (or if it was, the reckoning is even grimmer); at the approaches to Warsaw, fending off German counter-attacks or trying finally to batter its way in, the 1st Belorussian Front also fighting on Polish soil lost almost 123,000 men in these same agonizing weeks. Further south in Slovakia yet another rising in the German rear ended before Soviet troops and rebel forces linked up, in an insurrection that Soviet-controlled partisans operating inside Slovakia and communist leaders outside the country did much to precipitate. The Soviet 38th Army lost 80,000 men in attempting to force the Carpathians, overall Soviet losses reached 90,000 and General Svoboda's 1st Czechoslovak Corps (raised in the Soviet Union) suffered very heavily in the fighting for the mountain passes. The Polish and Slovak insurgents, and the Red Army, incurred brutal losses as a result of the devious political manoeuvres, made worse by inflexibility and tardiness either in rendering aid or forcing access. Slovakia was the sole Soviet success in 'transplanting' its partisan movement across the frontiers, but as in Poland those patriots who enjoyed the political support if not large-scale material aid from the Western powers were viewed by Stalin as inherently and unalterably hostile to the Soviet Union. Those whom he could not discredit he set out to destroy, a policy that meant consigning many thousands of the brave political innocents of the anti-Nazi resistance movements to a grisly and untimely death. The Red Army however has angrily, even passionately, rebutted charges of any connivance in these massacres of the blameless, citing as proof of its own exertions the lengthening toll of the Soviet dead.

Though not decisive in its own right, the north-western flank occupied a significant place in Soviet strategic plans: the reduction of Army Group North's forty-seven divisions was a necessary preliminary to administering the *coup de grâce* to Army Group Centre. Army Group North, in addition to covering East Prussia from the north-east, hung over the flanks of any Soviet army driving into Poland and on to East Prussia. German occupation of Lithuania, Latvia and Estonia secured communications with Finland (and Sweden), thereby contributing to the supply of strategic war materials; German possession of the coastal states also imprisoned the Soviet Baltic Fleet in the eastern reaches of the gulf of Finland. Six weeks of offensive operations pushed German troops out of their defensive positions and back to the west, but the veterans of Army Group North, though thinned by casualties and transfers, did not give ground easily, fighting off Soviet troops with skilful counter-attacks over terrain that lent itself very readily to stubborn defence. Yeremenko's 2nd Baltic and Maslennikov's 3rd Baltic Fronts were slowed down and then held at Plavinas and Valk, while Bagramyan reached the sea to sever German communications only to be pressed back by Schörner, who managed to bring momentary relief to the situation in Courland and northern Lithuania. The left flank of Govorov's Leningrad Front stormed Narva and broke into north-east Estonia, only to be brought to a halt by more German resistance and impassable terrain. The Soviet invasion of Estonia nevertheless brought home to the Finns how perilous their plight had now become. The fall of Vyborg on 20 June produced a critical situation, but beyond the city the Finnish line held against heavy Russian attacks and the Germans, anxious to hold Finland within the German orbit, supplied men and equipment to assist the Finnish defence, provided it was maintained along the Vyborg–Vuoks line.

The blow unleashed by Govorov (appointed a Marshal of the Soviet Union within the month) against the Finns in the Karelian isthmus was both massive and fiercely sustained. One day after the fall of Viipuri yet another Soviet offensive opened, General Meretskov's Karelian Front attacking with 7th and 32nd Armies (twelve rifle divisions supported by three brigades of Naval Infantry and garrison troops) fighting in the passage of land between the lakes Ladoga and Onega and striking from the direction of Medvezhegorsk to cut off the Finnish 'Olonets Group'. Early in June Meretskov flew to Moscow for talks with the General Staff and for an interview with Stalin on what came to be known as the 'Svir–Petrozavodsk operation'. Intent on impressing on his listeners the strength of the enemy fortifications between the two lakes, Meretskov took with him an elaborate relief map which—against the advice of Shtemenko and Antonov at the General Staff—he insisted on producing in the talk with Stalin. The map only roused Stalin to anger, who asked Meretskov if 'the enemy has personally let him in on their plans' and whether he was trying to 'scare all of us' with this 'toy'. Meretskov had already been told that Stalin did not like detailed analyses of enemy plans and positions, nor would he countenance attempts to wheedle reinforcements out of him, which is precisely what Meretskov went on to do, asking for several regiments of heavy tanks and breakthrough artillery. At this Stalin broke off the interview and ordered the General Staff to draw up the necessary plans. The next day the review of these plans went by in the usual fashion; Stalin wished Meretskov success and dismissed him with an admonition about 'scaring the enemy yourselves'. For all his rough sarcasm at the outset, however, Stalin relented in the end. During the final investigation of the attack plans, Marshal Vasilevskii and Zhukov, supported by General Antonov, refused to make an additional rifle corps available to Meretskov, but Stalin invited Meretskov and his chief of staff to watch the artillery salutes fired off in honour of the Leningrad Front. When the Kremlin guns had ceased firing, Stalin spoke softly into Meretskov's ear: 'I will give you as additional strength that rifle corps you have been asking for.'

The destruction of enemy forces between lakes Ladoga and Onega fell to Lt.-Gen. A.N. Krutikov's 7th Army, which was to force the river Svir and attack in the direction of Olonets–Pitkiaranta–Sortavaala. One rifle corps with a tank brigade was detached to operate with 32nd Army in clearing the western shore of lake Onega and capturing Petrozavodsk. North of lake Onega Lt.-Gen. F.D. Gorolenko's 32nd Army received orders to destroy the 'Medvezhegorsk concentration' of enemy forces, to co-operate with 7th Army in taking Petrozavodsk and then advancing to the Soviet–Finnish frontier in the area of Kuolisma. Aware of an impending Soviet offensive, the Finns withdrew from their bridgehead on the Svir and from forward positions covering the 'Medvezhegorsk axis'; Meretskov ordered Soviet units from 7th Army to close on the southern bank of the Svir which they reached by the evening of 20 June, while further to the north 32nd Army made final preparations for its own attacks. On the morning of 21 June Meretskov watched the full offensive with Krutikov's 7th Army take shape, preceded by a massive artillery barrage fired off from over 1,500 guns and by heavy bombing of the northern bank of the Svir carried out by over 3,000 aircraft from 7th Air Army, three and a half hours of sustained shelling and bombing. The first assault troops then moved over the broad Svir. By the evening Soviet engineers had twenty pontoon bridges in position and within twenty-four hours 7th Army pushed across the river on a 35-mile front to a depth of some seven or eight miles; but failure to shift supplies and weapons over the Svir at the proper rate slowed the Soviet advance to such a degree as to bring *Stavka* intervention. *Stavka* orders demanded faster movement and required a rapid advance on Olonets using three corps (7th Army) with not less than one corps committed to the capture of Petrozavodsk in co-operation with 32nd Army.

Within a week 7th Army, assisted by marines of the Lake Ladoga Flotilla, landing on the eastern shore of the lake, took Olonets and were closing in on Pitkiaranta. Right-flank units of 7th Army and 32nd Army, assisted in turn by the Lake Onega Flotilla, struck out for Petrozavodsk, which fell on 29 June, a victory saluted like the crossing of the Svir by salvoes from the Kremlin guns. Within a month of the opening of the offensive in southern Karelia, units of 32nd Army reported early on the morning of 21 July that they had reached the Soviet–Finnish frontier, a signal relayed at once by Meretskov's command to Moscow.

The moment to tighten the screw on Finland had finally come; the first June attacks, though ultimately contained, virtually exhausted Finnish reserves (so Marshal Mannerheim reported to Hitler), and after another month of ceaseless hammering the situation had grown desperate. The Finns struggled furiously to seal up every path and passage from the defile between the two great lakes but it was, as Meretskov observed, a losing battle. Soviet troops bored on with Finnish resistance stiffening nearer to the frontier; roads were mined and barricaded, bridges blown, stretches of open country mined. The Red Army pounded the Finns into asking for an armistice and into repudiating the *Waffenbruderschaft* with Germany. Already on 28 July President Ryti appeared at Finnish Headquarters to inform Mannerheim of his decision to lay down his office and begged the Marshal to assume the presidency. President Ryti resigned on 1 August and Mannerheim took up his new post, intent on leading Finland out of the war. Though Keitel rushed to Finland on 17 August, showering decorations on Mannerheim and Heinrichs, desperate to keep Finland in the war, the German–Finnish compact was doomed and done. Mannerheim repudiated the agreement signed between President Ryti and Ribbentrop on 26 June as one not ratified by the *Eduskunta;* the Ryti–Ribbentrop agreement bound Finland not to conduct separate peace negotiations without the prior approval of Germany, but this was now a dead letter. On 25 August the Finnish Minister in Stockholm, through a note delivered to Mme Kollontai, formally asked the Soviet government for an armistice delegation to be received in Moscow. Moscow agreed and set out its terms: Finland must break absolutely with Germany and all German troops must be withdrawn from Finland by 15 September. If the Germans resisted the Finnish request, the Finns were to disarm the Germans and turn them over to the Allies as prisoners of war. These were the conditions agreed between the Soviet Union and Great Britain, together with the assent of the United States. The *Eduskunta* duly submitted and authorized the opening of talks on this basis.

The Finns, however were not the first to beat this hasty path to Moscow's door. Late in August, at the other end of the Soviet–German front, the Russians opened a massive attack on Rumania. Within hours the German–Rumanian positions crumbled and the Rumanians in the decisive *coup* of 23 August took themselves out of the war, abandoning their German allies and in the process tearing down the German defensive arch in south-east Europe. The armistice with Rumania was already signed when the Finnish delegation was finally received by the Russians.

6

Soviet Liberation, Soviet Conquest: August–December 1944

'Broadly speaking the issue is: are we going to acquiesce in the Communisation of the Balkans and perhaps of Italy?'

Preoccupied with this thought, the Prime Minister on 4 May demanded of Eden a short paper setting out 'the brute issues between us and the Soviet Government which are developing in Italy, in Roumania, in Bulgaria, in Yugoslavia and *above all* in Greece'. The turn of events in Greece, its resistance forces ripped apart by civil war, gave Churchill cause for acute concern. The communist-controlled *ELAS* ('National People's Liberation Army'), the fighting guerrilla arm of *EAM* (the 'National Liberation Front'), which served as a loose coalition of left-wing parties though it was essentially the executive of the Greek Communist Party, the *KKE*, turned its British-supplied weapons not only against the Germans but also on its political rivals, the few thousand anti-Communists of the *EDES* ('National Democratic People's Army') led by Colonel Zervas, an officer of pronounced republican conviction. Zervas operated in the western Pindus (his strength coming mainly from the Epirus); north of Athens there was also Colonel Psaros's resistance group, '5/42 Regiment' (also known as the *EKKA*, 'National and Social Liberation'), an organization finally wiped out by *ELAS* in the spring of 1944, leaving only Zervas in the field. By 1943 the sudden, savage raids launched by *ELAS* guerrillas on other independent resistance groups had drastically thinned the anti-communist ranks. The survivors of these murderous and stealthy assaults were usually pressed into the ranks of *ELAS* itself, while others took up arms against the Communists by enlisting in the security battalions raised by the collaborationist government. In March 1943 *ELAS* wiped out the *AAA*, a republican resistance organization led by General Saraphis; once captured, the general was duly accused of collaboration with the enemy and then at gun-point offered the post of military commander of *ELAS*. Throughout the summer of 1943 *EAM–ELAS* proffered a political olive branch, setting up a joint headquarters for all resistance groups, only to fall savagely on Zervas's *EDES* once the Italians had surrendered, a violent spasm of open civil war that ended with a rough-and-ready truce in March 1944.

The truce signalled a change in *EAM* tactics. In March 1944 *EAM* set up in the Greek mountains the 'Political Committee of National Liberation' *(PEEA)*, a provisional government in all but name and an acute embarrassment to the Greek government in exile, whose plight grew more serious with the mutiny of Greek troops serving under British command in the Middle East, a grave disturbance on the eve of the departure of the Greek brigade for Italy. British troops cordoned off the mutinous Greeks who finally surrendered at the end of April, but not before they had set up soldiers' committees, pressed their demands for a plebiscite before King George II of Greece might return to his country, and urged the recognition of the 'Political Committee of National Liberation' as the true provisional government. In Greece itself *EAM*, whose potent political influence had been so dramatically demonstrated among the soldiers, set about destroying the *EKKA* resistance organization in the belief that the end of the occupation was practically in sight, thus eliminating one more rival and clearing the ground for the seizure of power that had been planned as far back as 1943. Only *EDES* remained under Zervas, but by now *EAM–ELAS* knew full well that only small British forces would move into Greece once the Germans withdrew.

The installation of a communist government in Greece and the implanting of Russian influence in the eastern Mediterranean was anathema to the British government. Warned by the portents in Greece and prodded by the Prime Minister, Eden on 5 May put a specific suggestion to Mr Gusev, Soviet Ambassador in London: assuming that Rumanian affairs might be regarded as largely a Russian concern, the British could perhaps legitimately expect Soviet support for their policy in Greece. It took all of two weeks to elicit some response from the Soviet government, but on 18 May Gusev called on Eden to inform him that his government accepted the idea of a division of interests covering Greece and Rumania; but first Moscow must know whether or not the Americans had been consulted. The British Ambassador in Washington, Lord Halifax, was therefore instructed to sound State Department opinion on the advisability of making such an approach to the Russians, a proposal which basically rested on 'military realities'.

Though the British plan specifically disavowed any commitment to 'spheres of influence', Cordell Hull in his talk with Lord Halifax on 30 May showed some alarm at the implications of the proposals; the next day the Prime Minister sent his own message to the President, reaffirming that no return to or recognition of 'spheres of influence' was in any way involved, though the message did disclose that the British had made an approach to the Russians, a move dictated by 'the existing military situation since Rumania fell within the sphere of the Russian armies and Greece within the Allied command . . . in the Mediterranean'. In his first talk with Cordell Hull, Lord Halifax confined himself to Rumania and Greece. On 8 June the Prime Minister instructed the Ambassador to add Bulgaria and Yugoslavia to Rumania and Greece (making the apportionment Yugoslavia and Greece for the British, Rumania and Bulgaria for the Russians), an enlargement of the original scheme which served only to incense Secretary of State Hull still further.

In his first response (10 June) the President did not accept Churchill's main argument and suggested rather 'consultative machinery to dispel misunderstandings' and 'to restrain the tendency towards the development of exclusive spheres'. The Prime Minister returned to the attack at once, pressing upon the President his view that consultative machinery would end up as 'mere obstruction' and suggesting that the Anglo-Soviet arrangement be given a three-month trial run, to be followed by a 'Big Three' review. President Roosevelt agreed on 12 June to this proposal, adding that nevertheless this did not imply the establishment of 'post-war spheres of influence', cautious assent which was given without the knowledge of his Secretary of State who was taking a brief rest from his duties. Churchill thanked the President and on 19 June Eden gave Gusev the news of this presidential approbation, expressing the hope that Soviet agreement would duly follow.

At this point, however, Secretary of State Hull chose to insert himself rather forcefully into the train of events; though the President's agreement was given on 12 June, Hull on 17 June submitted a draft reply (to the British message of 8 June) which pointedly underscored the preliminary British approach to the Russians without first consulting the Americans. These strictures the President duly forwarded to Churchill on 22 June, only to have the Prime Minister rebut the charge of improper behaviour in first approaching the Russians, singling out the President's unilateral approach to Stalin over Mikolajczyk as a counter-argument.

In the midst of these strained messages the State Department learned from the American Ambassador to the exile Greek government that British sources in Cairo had informed him of prior American agreement to the proposed Anglo-Soviet plan for Greece and Rumania, a circuitous route indeed for the American Secretary of State to learn of a presidential decision. Hull very primly forwarded this ambassadorial disclosure to the President on 30 June, the day on which Gusev (answering Eden's communication of 19 June) brought up the uncertainty of the American position and announced an independent Soviet investigation of the American attitude. The very next day Gromyko in Washington presented Hull with a summary of the Eden–Gusev exchanges and then sat back to wait for results. Obstructed at this late stage in the negotiations, the Prime Minister spilled out an angry sentence about 'the pedantic interference of the United States'. In an attempt to win over Stalin without further ado, his message of 12 July referred to earlier conversations, emphasizing the need for a 'working arrangement to avoid . . . the awful business of triangular telegrams which paralyses action' and mentioning that 'the President agreed to a three-months trial'. Now it was Stalin's turn to find 'some difficulties'; his reply arrived on 5 July and was firm in its refusal to go any further until those 'certain doubts' entertained by the American government were finally clarified—'we shall do well to return to the matter when we get the US reply'.

That 'US reply' was already on its way, on 15 July as it proved, when Gromyko received a reply to his query of 1 July: this latest communication confirmed American agreement to the proposed Anglo-Soviet plan for Greece and Rumania but stipulated that it was no part of American policy to promote 'spheres of influence' in the Balkans and declined to admit any prejudice to American interests in a temporary division promoted by 'the present war strategy'. Though no actual agreement was as yet concluded between the Russians and the British, it was this all-important American assent that triggered off the first and far from insignificant diplomatic redeployment in eastern Europe. While the British struggled to keep the lid on the Greek situation, Soviet diplomacy explored the possibilities of contacts with Rumania. Already at the beginning of 1944 Rumanian Minister Nano and the Soviet *chargé* in Stockholm, Semeonov, had a series of meetings. In the spring another channel opened with the arrival in Cairo of Prince Barbu Stirbey (Cairo being chosen when a feeler put out in Ankara by the Rumanian minister for a meeting in London was rejected). Soviet, American and British diplomats engaged in the involved, dragging talks with Stirbey, while in Rumania the capitulationist plot thickened and drew King Michael more closely into it.

From the skilled and discreet men of the Rumanian Foreign Ministry, drawn mainly from the cipher department (and including Miculescu-Buzesti, son-in-law of Prince Stirbey), King Michael was kept informed of current negotiations with the Allies. From General Aldea he learned of the present temper of the army; from Iuliu Maniu he had news of the opposition, of their contacts with the Allies and with the Communist Party. Early in April Maniu discovered from Minister Cretzianu in Ankara that the Allied command in the Mediterranean promised negotiations from the Soviet side if Marshal Antonescu's government proved unwilling to break with the Germans and had to be forced out of power: where there were no Soviet troops to hand Rumanian forces must themselves engage the Germans, while Allied aircraft would mount air attacks as and when required.

On 2 April a Soviet note set out the Soviet position, reaffirming the claim to Bessarabia and the northern Bukovina, but ten days later the Soviet Ambassador in Cairo handed Prince Stirbey terms for an armistice which, though still insisting upon Soviet annexation of Bessarabia, promised the return of almost the whole of Transylvania to Rumania. Allied bombers were already raiding Rumania, putting in a massive attack on 5 May which knocked out half of the Rumanian oil production, but Maniu wanted Allied paratroops, not bombing raids which simply reduced Rumania's capacity to defend itself. He struggled to obtain a specific guarantee from the three Allied powers that none would interfere in Rumanian affairs once the country was freed, though the chances of striking a real bargain over Rumania's secession from the war were fast receding. Prince Stirbey advised speedy acceptance of the terms already offered, since they represented the best that could be obtained; Maniu, however, determined to try for more and sent out another emissary, Constantin Visoianu, towards the end of May.

The new negotiator brought with him plans for an Allied airborne operation in Rumania and tried to turn the terms of the armistice settlement even more generously in Rumania's favour, angling for an Allied presence by insisting that a successful break with the Axis required Allied (Anglo-American) help, with troops on the ground. Nothing came of this manoeuvre. Inside Rumania, Iuliu Maniu stepped up his contacts with the Communists, and in Moscow the exiled Communists pressed—equally unavailingly—for a speedy Soviet invasion followed by a straight communist 'takeover' involving the setting up of a communist government. This, however, did not conform to Stalin's style in 1944: there was no point in 'frightening' his allies for nothing, and what he wanted was control, not immediate and possibly troublesome 'communization'. To pull the Rumanian Communist Party together, Emil Bodnaras, a former lieutenant of the Rumanian Army who defected to the Soviet Union in 1937, was sent from Russia to Rumania with orders to put the Party on its feet, to forge links with the Rumanian military and to strengthen ties with the opposition. Early in April Bodnaras, Gheorghiu-Dej, Parvalescu and other communist leaders convened a meeting in a prison hospital, decided upon the dismissal of Foris as party leader and elected Gheorghiu-Dej in his place. Bodnaras, Parvalescu and Ranghet received 'authorization' to continue talks with the opposition groups committed to pulling Rumania out of the war—a sudden, unexpected resurgence of the Rumanian Communist Party which went ahead without any reference to the exile party group in Moscow and the party bureau headed by Ana Pauker and Vasile Luca.

In Cairo Visoianu met with no success in trying to pull the armistice negotiations his way, and time had practically run out. On 1 June the Soviet government demanded that Iuliu Maniu accept the terms as they stood before the talks went any further; Visoianu could only agree, but having agreed he then demanded that three Allied parachute divisions be dropped into Rumania. Coming at a time when there was heavy pressure for troops owing to landings in France and almost at the instant when Eden informed Gusev of American approval for the Anglo-Soviet plan for Greece and Rumania, the automatic rejection of the Visoianu plan was inevitable. For all practical purposes the Cairo talks closed down and the Soviet Union went about seeking an independent solution of the Rumanian question. The decline of Soviet interest in any further haggling with Iuliu Maniu was accompanied by fresh initiatives in Stockholm, where armistice talks had earlier slumped. Early in June Madame Kollontai presented favourable terms directed at the Antonescus themselves, though this fresh turn to events did nothing to stem Soviet suspicions even as Soviet diplomats worked to tug Rumania deftly out of the war on terms suggesting a direct act of capitulation to the USSR. An atmosphere becoming increasingly charged was not improved by the Soviet accusation aimed at the Prime Minister that a British mission had gone secretly to Rumania in pursuit of 'purposes unknown to the Soviet government'; the British Ambassador in Moscow presented an official denial to Molotov without visible effect or amelioration. And if the Russians suspected British double-dealing over Rumania, the British soon had cause to fear foul play over Soviet intervention in the Greek political situation.

The compulsion behind the Soviet attempt to seek its own 'separate' armistice agreement with Rumania lay in the overall weakness of Soviet political influence in the country, which in turn necessitated a disproportionate reliance on contacts cultivated through and by the British. Those contacts proved to be within a 'bourgeois' and pro-Western opposition, the very popularity of which obliged Antonescu to allow it to continue in existence. Of Rumanian anti-Russian feeling the Russians could be in no doubt; a persistent, historical anti-Russian sentiment within the Rumanian ruling group and the intelligentsia was intensified by the Soviet occupation of Bessarabia and the northern Bukovina in 1940. It was almost inevitable that the Soviet leadership should find in Maniu's procrastinations signs of a 'plot', complete with secret conspiracies and missions, to use Rumania as an instrument in an anti-Soviet power play, and the signal weakness of Soviet influence in the country (reflected in the depressed and divided condition of the Communist Party), increased these fears. The right move for Stalin was not to listen to the hysterical pleas for 'communization' advanced by the exiled Communists, but to get his own men into the country and on to the ground.

Soviet interest in achieving a separate diplomatic *coup* through negotiation with Antonescu, the irritation at their enforced dependence on British contacts and obvious scepticism over Iuliu Maniu's ability to deliver the goods he dangled so enticingly—all contributed to killing the Cairo talks as a means of drawing Rumania out of the war. Iuliu Maniu, the National Peasant Party leader imbued with pro-Western sentiments, placed little faith in underground activity and sabotage campaigns, thus giving slight assurance to those Communists who wished to 'activate' popular resistance to the government. The very foundation of his policy rested on one unwavering principle, that the clean sweep he planned and for which he tried to summon Allied—Western—help would not mean committing Rumania to an act of desperate resistance and revolt against Germany. He sought 'insurance' against Russian encroachment, the threat of which was real enough. The indecision which finally wrecked his policy fed on the illusion that he could actually talk terms with the Western Allies, a game that the Russians were not prepared to play; instead, they turned to hasty attempts to build up their own influence in the country as and when they could manage it, and tried negotiation not only with the opposition but with the Rumanian government itself.

Stalin's 'grand strategy' did not admit of much generosity towards his communist associates if they stood in the way of the 'accommodation' he sought temporarily with his major partners in the alliance. Over Poland he chose to use the Communists as wedges to force 'accommodation' on his terms; in Greece they became prime instruments in implementing the bargain with the British at the cost of all their hopes for a 'takeover'; and over Yugoslavia Stalin showed himself highly suspicious of the uncompromising attitude of the partisan leadership. Milovan Djilas, a member of the first Yugoslav communist mission to Moscow in the spring of

1944, found himself baffled by and deeply uneasy at Stalin's attitude, which showed all too brutally that 'he trusted nothing but what he held in his fist, and everyone beyond the control of his police was a potential enemy'. The total deviousness of these methods, compounded of unending suspicion of the British and complete contempt for the 'peasant' politicians of these small states, nevertheless worked to bring the whole Anglo-Soviet undertaking to the point of collapse. Late in July the Prime Minister, already smarting under 'American official reluctance' at the Anglo-Soviet deal, feared now that 'Russian bad faith' must be added to the catalogue of misfortune that had befallen it, an impression nourished by the 'subterfuge' so recently practised by the Russians in dispatching a military mission to *ELAS*.

On 25 July a Soviet aircraft cleared for a training flight from the base at Bari suddenly set course for Tito's headquarters in Yugoslavia; once at partisan headquarters, the aircraft picked up a number of officers from the Soviet mission working with the Yugoslav partisans and flew on to an airfield in Thessaly. The next day Colonel Popov and his colleagues arrived at *ELAS* headquarters, much to the anger and dismay of the British government, on whose behalf Eden delivered a sharp protest to Gusev. Molotov found the matter much too trifling to waste time on, an *hauteur* that hid the details of a complex Soviet operation, crammed with subterfuge and aimed not at the British interests but at the Greek militants themselves. The role of the Soviet mission to *ELAS* proved to be policing the unpalatable decision already made in Moscow, deferring all and any plans for a communist *coup* in Greece. Clearly the gears of Soviet policy began to grind more speedily after Stalin received news of official American acceptance of the Anglo-Soviet division of responsibility over Greece and Rumania. He was never inclined to look a gift horse in the mouth, and here was one with much to recommend it: in return for relinquishing 'responsibility' in the maelstrom of Greek politics, he could anticipate virtual freedom of action in Rumania, the same in Bulgaria and a powerful say in Yugoslav affairs, thus enclosing them 'in his fist' and being able at the same time to display his commitment to inter-Allied unity, no small consideration at a time when the Polish question was bringing dangerous discord in relations.

Soviet disengagement in Greece went forward brusquely and with blunt efficiency. Not long after the Soviet military mission received its orders to fly to *ELAS* and to cajole rather than incite (General Saraphis denied that the Soviet officers ever offered or supplied any effective assistance), Soviet diplomats in Cairo were reportedly advising members of *EAM* to show themselves more accommodating and to join the Papandhreou government. *EAM–ELAS* was being squeezed from both sides. The presence of the Soviet officers in Greece made itself felt (or so it was deduced by Colonel Woodhouse, commander of the British Military Mission) when the 'Committee of Liberation', the *PEEA*, dropped its demands for representation in any new government from seven to five possible members, though the Committee still insisted that Papandhreou was unacceptable as prime minister.

Within a few days the *PEEA* then turned a complete political somersault and agreed to enter the Papandhreou government, on those very terms it had so bitterly assailed and adamantly opposed. What Colonel Woodhouse described as 'the bellicose wing' of the Greek Communist Party (the *KKE*) was brought under a tight rein by Moscow: early in September six representatives of the *KKE*, heavily 'advised' by Soviet diplomats in Cairo, duly entered the Greek coalition government. The *PEEA* disappeared in a puff of smoke, and at the end of the month communist guerrilla forces (along with other guerrilla bands) placed themselves under formal government command (and thus effectively under British control). Soviet intervention in the affairs of *EAM–ELAS* contributed to postponing rather than provoking a head-on clash with the British, leaving the generals Saraphis and Zervas ironically and uneasily locked in a joint command.

Not long before this clamp was fastened on the *KKE*, the Yugoslav Communists were discovering the self-interested rigour that dominated Soviet policy and Stalin's outlook, much of it conveyed through Milovan Djilas's remarkable picture of the Soviet leader at war acquired at first hand during the visit of the Yugoslav mission to Moscow in the late spring of 1944. The British had already burned themselves badly in the fires of the Yugoslav domestic resistance movement, which at an early stage developed into a civil war between Mihailovic's anti-communist Cetniks and Tito's partisans with their pronounced communist leanings. Despairing of ever reconciling these two antagonistic groups, and aware that Tito's guerrillas were making a determined effort to fight the Germans, the Prime Minister in 1943 finally came round to the view that British support must be withdrawn from Draza Milhailovic and full backing given to Tito, even though this must in the long run bring complete communist control of Serbia. The Yugoslav government in exile (now lodged in Cairo to be nearer the fighting men) protested bitterly at the British decision, questioning the 'irrefutable' evidence of General Draza Mihailovic's collaboration with the Germans; the Yugoslav Prime Minister M. Puric insisted that the effect could only be to unleash communism in Yugoslavia and promote peasant resistance to it, at the same time putting the blame on British propaganda for the triumph of Tito's partisans.

This sombre situation, made more tragic by a terrifyingly brutal German war of extermination waged against the Yugoslav 'bandits' and by the atrocities perpetrated in a hideously unbridled civil war, produced political problems of great complexity. Already in October 1943, on hearing of the Foreign Ministers' meeting in Moscow, Tito nailed his colours to the mast, sending a signal to Moscow for the attention of 'the Soviet government' to the effect that 'the Anti-Fascist Council of Yugoslavia and Supreme Headquarters of the National Liberation Army have empowered me [Tito] to declare [that] we acknowledge neither the Yugoslav Government nor the King abroad . . .', followed by the categorical statement that 'we will not allow them to return to Yugoslavia because that would mean civil war', adding that 'the only legal government of the people at the present time is the National Liberation Committee led by the Anti-Fascist

Council'. The Moscow conference, however, scarcely had time to come to grips with the Yugoslav problem. Such talk of it as there was remained desultory, with Eden informing Molotov of the presence of a British mission to Tito's partisans and Molotov coming out with the intriguing news that the Soviet government might well send a mission to General Draza Mihailovic. Though the Russians passed over this first Yugoslav initiative in silence, ignoring the advertisement to 'the Soviet government', the subsequent step—the resolutions of the Anti-Fascist Council of Yugoslavia (AVNOJ) passed in the Bosnian town of Jajce in November 1943—did not escape the notice of Stalin who took it as almost a personal affront. On the eve of the Jajce conference Tito decided with his *Politburo* what it was politic to tell Moscow; the Yugoslavs mixed discretion with valour, disclosing that the Anti-Fascist Council proposed to form a national committee to act as a provisional executive but omitting any mention of the intention to declare the royalist government illegal and to ban the King from the country.

The Jajce conference duly set up a Supreme Legislative Council and an Executive Committee for the Liberation of Yugoslavia presided over by Tito himself upon whom the title 'Marshal of Yugoslavia' was bestowed; the National Council, which was for all practical purposes a provisional government, stipulated King Peter's exclusion from Yugoslavia until the Yugoslavs could themselves decide what form of government they wanted. The effect upon Stalin was to make him 'quite unusually angry', seeing in the Yugoslav initiative 'a stab in the back for the Soviet Union and for the Teheran decisions', in other words a threat to the arrangements he had so painstakingly concluded with the Western powers. But the latter did not take fright at the Jajce resolutions, and nothing ruffled that splendid, if momentary calm in the Big Power relations. The way was open for Stalin to make the necessary adjustment in his position. Late in December 'Free Yugoslavia' broadcasting from the Soviet Union demanded recognition for the National Committee and the winding up of the exile government. Early in 1944 a Soviet military mission headed by Lt.-Gen. Korneyev, with Maj.-Gen. Gorshkov second in command, finally appeared at Tito's headquarters, though the refusal of the Soviet officers to make use of the normal method of entry—a parachute drop—obliged the RAF to deliver the Soviet party in two Horsa gliders, the whole operation being covered by a fighter escort. General Korneyev and his colleagues arrived to a rapturous welcome, but all too soon it was apparent that they had brought nothing in the way of badly needed supplies. Since they could promise only the delivery of token loads, the enthusiasm cooled. The Russians for their part were chastened to find that they would not be taking command of the Yugoslav partisans (for all Gorshkov's disparagement of Tito's guerrillas compared with the Soviet brand), so that 'the disenchantment was mutual'.

The British government meanwhile tried to disengage itself from General Mihailovic and to use the break as a means of effecting a compromise between Tito and the King. Early in February 1944 the Prime Minister put a straight proposition to Tito: would the dismissal of Mihailovic facilitate 'friendly relations' between the King and the partisans, and might it permit the return of the King, though the fate of the monarchy itself must be decided after the complete liberation of Yugoslavia? Marshal Tito returned a resolute negative, insisting that the National Committee must be recognized as the sole government of the country, that the exile government in Cairo must be dissolved and Mihailovic dismissed for the traitor he was—then, perhaps, co-operation with the King might be considered, but not through any special arrangement, which would inevitably bring 'suspicion and anxiety'. At the end of March Tito repeated that the National Committee would not countenance the return of the King.

To provide greater security for the National Committee and Supreme Headquarters, Tito abandoned the little town of Jajce at the end of 1943 in favour of Drvar, further to the west. It was from this ruined Bosnian town that two Yugoslav military missions went out in the spring of 1944, one under Vladimir Velebit to London, the other headed by Milovan Djilas to Moscow. Of all the tasks assigned to the Djilas mission, which assumed both 'a military and party character', the most important was to discover whether the Soviet government was prepared to recognize the National Committee as 'the provisional legal government' of Yugoslavia and also to 'influence the Western allies to do so'. Passing through Bari and Cairo, ever on the alert for the fell hand of British intelligence (the Yugoslav mission was laden with the archives of the Supreme Command and the Central Committee, which included the exchanges between the Yugoslav Party and the Comintern), Djilas and his party flew on to Teheran, Baku and finally Moscow.

Djilas's first requests to be received by Molotov, possibly by Stalin, fell on deaf ears. All the talk was of Russia's great war against Hitler, the 'patriotic character' of the struggle and the decisive role of the Soviet Union. In the Pan-Slav Committee Djilas discovered an organization that was 'artificial' and 'quite hopeless', staffed with émigré Communists from other Slav nations who were basically unsympathetic to the idea of closer Pan-Slav ties. Neither this rather soggy group of tame ideologues nor the Yugoslav Party émigrés in Moscow, a group 'decimated by the purges' whose leading figure was Veljko Vlahovic, could help the impatient Djilas in his search for contact with the top Soviet leadership. In Manuilskii, former secretary of the Comintern, Milovan Djilas found only an apparatchik whose fortunes were fast fading, 'a lost, senile old man' sliding speedily into oblivion; Dimitrov, though a sick man and prematurely old in appearance, spoke out with greater vigour and frankness, but he too counselled caution in proclaiming 'the communist character' of the Yugoslav movement lest it damage relations between the Soviet Union and the Western allies. Djilas, burning with the reality of the Yugoslav revolution, thought it 'senseless' to insist upon a coalition of communist and bourgeois parties, for the resistance and the civil war in Yugoslavia had shown for all to see that 'the Communist Party was the only real political force'. Dimitrov was far from unsympathetic, and he understood the situation that prevailed in Yugoslavia: it was he who had personally interested Stalin in the question of helping the Yugoslav partisans back in 1941–2, though owing to the extreme range Soviet aircraft flew their hazardous missions in vain, failed to reach the partisan bases and returned carrying the frozen bodies of those Yugoslav Communists who set out on the flights in the hope of getting home. Dimitrov also enlarged on the circumstances surrounding the dissolution of the Comintern, first mooted in 1940 but abandoned lest it seem that the Soviet government was giving in to German pressure. Somewhat later Stalin gave Milovan Djilas his own version of how the Comintern met its end and was shovelled unceremoniously out of sight.

Their enforced wait upon the wishes, or the whims, of Stalin provided some opportunity for the Yugoslav mission to observe the Soviet Union at war and enabled them to clear up at least one mystery. What puzzled the Yugoslavs was where all the men had come from to form the 'Yugoslav Anti-Fascist Brigade', when so many of the Yugoslav communists resident in the Soviet Union had perished long before in the purges. Djilas discovered that the Brigade was manned largely by the collaborationist Croats from the ill-fated regiment sent by Ante Pavelic to serve on the Eastern Front. Like the Rumanians, Italians and Hungarians, the Croat soldiers along with their commander Mesic were sucked into the catastrophe of Stalingrad, taken prisoner and politically re-educated, to emerge as the 'Anti-Fascist Brigade', officered by Russians and with a few *émigré* Communists providing the political staff. It was even proposed that these mongrelly soldiers should wear the insignia of the Royal Yugoslav Army until Veljko Vlahovic protested and tried to devise a matching emblem with Tito's partisans, though he was hampered in never having seen the original. On finding the same commander still at the head of this regiment Djilas apparently could not restrain his criticism, a point the Russians blandly brushed aside by saying that Mesic had 'recanted'; there was nothing for the Yugoslav mission to do but leave 'everything as it was'.

Chastened as he was by this experience, by the sight of a 'Yugoslav Anti-Fascist Brigade' so strangely blended, Milovan Djilas was coming to understand that under the impact of war Soviet society was changing. Massive resistance had beaten off the German assault; Soviet citizens had shown their devotion to their country and to 'the basic achievements of the revolution' with every expectation of the slackening of 'political restrictions' and the dissolution of 'ideological monopolies held by little groups of leaders'. Deep down, however, the Soviet Communists felt that they were fighting alone. Their solicitude for the alliance with the Western powers was an act of self-interest, a manoeuvre, which scarcely dispelled the conviction that they were fighting 'for their own survival and for their way of life'. Until the opening of the Second Front, by which time the feeling was very deeply ingrained, the ordinary man and the fighting soldiers also shared this mood of embattled isolation.

At Marshal Koniev's headquarters the Yugoslav mission saw for itself the ravages of the fighting on the Eastern Front. Djilas and his colleagues inspected the destruction and carnage left in the wake of the Korsun–Shevchenkovskii operation with a horrified fascination while they listened to Marshal Koniev's account of how the Cossack troops cut the encircled Germans to pieces—legs, arms and even hands raised in surrender. From Koniev, Djilas learned something of the fate that befell the old heroes of the Red Army, Voroshilov and Budenny, in the first days of the war; though scathing in his comments about Budenny— he 'never knew much and he never studied anything'—Marshal Koniev preserved a very discreet silence on being asked about Stalin's role, confining himself to the innocuous but acceptable formula that Stalin was 'universally gifted . . . brilliantly able to see the war as a whole'.

The justification for such an encomium Djilas and his compatriot General Terzic were shortly able to test for themselves, when after all their waiting the summons came. The two Yugoslavs were whisked out of the premises of the Pan-Slav Committee, their lecture left unfinished, and driven in the company of an *NKVD* colonel to the Kremlin. For a Communist of Djilas's temper, devotion and commitment, the sense of occasion almost overpowered him—joy combined with agitation at the prospect of facing Stalin, the embodiment of 'the victorious battle today and the brotherhood of man tomorrow'. The implications of the meeting suddenly possessed Djilas—all that 'seemed unpleasant about the USSR' vanished and previous differences faded into nothing.

Nor did this first meeting, filled with comradely frankness and enlivened by Stalin's own incisiveness, disappoint Djilas. He was at the very fount of orthodoxy and the source of decisions—'I felt that I was in the right place . . .'—though he confessed himself surprised at the look of Stalin in the flesh, small in height, of 'ungainly build', with stiffened left arm and shoulder, paunchy, with thinning hair and yellow eyes, a restless, fidgety fellow who doodled and drew, 'not quiet for a moment', playing with his pipe, constantly moving his head. The talk, in which Molotov joined, lasted for about an hour. Almost at once Stalin broached the question of recognition for Tito's National Committee, asking Molotov by way of a joke if it might not be possible 'to trick the English into recognizing Tito'; with a self-satisfied smile Molotov replied that the English knew full well what was happening in Yugoslavia and could not be 'tricked'. Djilas obtained no undertaking from Stalin about recognition, only the impression that the Soviet government would take this step in due time, the moment 'it considered conditions ripe'. Stalin at the outset laid the blame on British obduracy and hinted that a 'temporary compromise' between the Soviet and British governments could well mean delay, requiring also a compromise between the Yugoslav Communists and the Royalists. What he did not tell Milovan Djilas was that such a 'temporary compromise' was already being fashioned, involving more than Yugoslavia. On the question of material aid Stalin spoke out much less ambiguously, offering an outright gift of the $200,000 that Tito had requested as a loan, promising to look into a Soviet air-lift for the partisans but insisting that an army—'and you are already an army'—needed supplies from the sea, an impossible undertaking for the Soviet Union with its Black Sea fleet destroyed.

Inconclusive though it was, this first meeting was a success, with Stalin all affability, understanding, shrewdness and decisiveness. At the second meeting, held on the eve of the landings in Normandy, much of the affability vanished to be replaced by rough impatience and spurts of unrestrained anger. The meeting to which Milovan Djilas was driven that June night was his real initiation into the world of the Soviet leaders, that nightly ritual of talk and supper but none the less a world of 'horrible unceasing struggle on all sides' which promised only 'victory or death', a world in which all policies must now bend to Stalin's own and all men must be bound to him. On the way to the *dacha*, Molotov quizzed Djilas on the situation brought about by the German surprise attack launched on 25 May against Tito's headquarters, an airborne assault preceded by a heavy bombing raid on Drvar. The cave in which Tito had taken shelter from the bombing was sealed off at the mouth, but the Marshal and Kardelj managed to make their escape from what seemed certain capture by using a deep inner passageway which led out to the plateau at the top of the cave. The Soviet Military Mission with the Yugoslav partisans gave Moscow news of the dangerous turn in the situation, and Soviet aircraft flew by night on supply-dropping missions to Tito's men, though the supplies dropped lay largely strewn about and uncollected in the woods that the partisans were forced to abandon under German pressure.

The danger to Tito and the predicament of the Yugoslav partisans formed Stalin's first questions to Milovan Djilas, once he had drawn him into a small, wholly unadorned room for a preliminary talk. 'They will starve to death': Djilas managed to assuage this particular fear of Stalin's, reminding him that the Yugoslav partisans had suffered and survived worse, but it was not easy to restrain Stalin on the subject of his own air crews—'cowards, by God, cowards', frightened to fly by day (a point Molotov rebutted by pointing to the great range, the lack of fighter cover and the small loads caused by the need to carry fuel). Djilas himself added that Soviet pilots had in fact volunteered to fly by day, without fighter escort. Only partly mollified, Stalin then argued that Tito must get himself to safety, an injunction that was not mere pious talk, for the Soviet Military Mission with the Yugoslav partisans speedily received instructions to expedite this move. General Korneyev personally urged Tito to leave Bosnia; he impressed on him that this was the wish of 'the Soviet government', and a Soviet Dakota, operating out of Bari, did finally fly Tito and his staff to the Italian mainland.

The main business, however, proved to be policy, in particular Tito's relations with the Western allies. The English must not be 'frightened', least of all by suggesting that Yugoslavia was in the grip of revolution. The 'form' did not matter: 'What do you want with red stars on your caps? . . . By God, there's no need for stars'—not a very vehement protest by Stalin, but he was serious in his warning to handle 'the English' carefully, reading Djilas a lecture on the quality of his allies, above all Churchill—'the kind of man who will pick your pocket for a kopeck if you don't watch him. . . . By God, pick your pocket for a kopeck'. Roosevelt was different, 'he dips his hand in only for bigger coins', but Churchill—he 'will do it for a kopeck'. Beware of British Intelligence, Stalin insisted, and take care for Tito's life: 'they [British Intelligence] were the ones who killed General Sikorski in a plane and then neatly shot down the plane— no proof, no witnesses.' On the question of recognition for the National Committee, Stalin also counselled caution and compromise: 'you cannot be recognized right away. You must take a halfway position.' King Peter of Yugoslavia had finally agreed under heavy British pressure to reorganize his government, with the Foreign Office recommending the appointment of Dr Ivan Subasic, a Croat politician and governor of Croatia until 1941, after which he lived in the United States. On 1 June the King appointed Dr Subasic prime minister and charged him with forming a small, non-political government. On his side Stalin pressed Djilas to advise Tito and the Yugoslav Central Committee to talk to Subasic, 'on no account' to refuse to talk to Subasic, and then to 'reach a compromise somehow'.

With the formal business concluded Stalin took Djilas to dinner, a meal that meandered well into the small hours of the morning. Amidst the eating, drinking and talking 'a significant part of Soviet policy was shaped', with the talk ranging over an enormous field. Stalin ate heavily but drank only moderately, mixing red wine and vodka, though the others indulged themselves with a will. Through all the anecdotes and cross-talk about the Slavs, the Turks and the Tsars, Stalin probed for information about the revolutionary movement in Yugoslavia, avoiding direct questions but building up his own picture of Yugoslav strength and political organization. Passing to the Comintern, Stalin made no reference to any plan to dissolve this body in 1940, stressing instead that the existence of 'a general Communist forum' created an 'abnormal' situation, generated friction and was wholly 'unnatural' at a time when all communist parties were better 'searching for a national language' and were more effective 'fighting under conditions prevailing in their own countries'. Stalin could work with Dimitrov, but 'with the others it was harder'. Nor could Stalin resist a dig at 'the Westerners', claiming that the dissolution of the Comintern was carried out in spite of them: '. . . had they mentioned it, we would not have dissolved at all!'

During the course of the evening two dispatches came to Stalin's hand, both of which he showed to Djilas. The first concerned Dr Subasic, who declared for the benefit of the State Department that 'pro-Russian traditions' counted for a great deal among the Yugoslavs, who would never be a party to an 'anti-Russian policy', sentiments that simply enraged Stalin, who demanded of his guests why Subasic was 'scaring the Americans. . . . Yes, scaring them. But why, why?' The second message from the Prime Minister announced the imminence of the landing in Normandy, which Stalin took as a cue to mock at the unfulfilled promises of the Allies: 'What if they meet with some Germans! Maybe there won't be a landing, but just promises as usual.' The sneering had a purpose—to play upon the 'anti-capitalist prejudices' of the Yugoslavs—and the hints of perfidy were designed to warn the Yugoslavs against the Western powers, even to frighten them. More Stalin could not do, for, as Milovan Djilas recognized, the Yugoslav revolution had already slipped out of Stalin's grasp.

Yet the talks with the Yugoslav mission in Moscow perfectly summed up Stalin's intentions and his frame of mind. He was, in short, prepared to bargain. What Churchill proposed in the summer of 1944 was a partition of Europe, or those parts of Europe upon which Anglo-American and Soviet armies were already encroaching. This Stalin was by all the signs ready to accept, and was determined to adhere to. He was fully deployed to negotiate, with the Rumanians, with the Finns, even with the Germans (his shadow political committee of captured generals gave him at least the outline of an option); in eastern Europe, over which the Red Army loomed large, he was prepared to encourage a nationalistic movement, but he insisted that it be deprived of its strong anti-Russian sentiment, its pre-war hallmark and distinguishing feature. It is probably true that Stalin was in earnest in declaring that the Soviet Union had no immediate interest in the kind of government the Poles or Rumanians intended to set up; the presence of the Red Army, with the *NKVD* in its wake, made this political largesse possible. Stalin gambled nothing and stood to gain a great deal. But he was not prepared to tolerate alarms and disturbances brought about by overt attempts at communist control, if only because he held the bunch of 'peasant politicians' with whom he was dealing in such low esteem. Building a formal 'communist bloc' in eastern Europe at this time does not seem to have figured in his plans: on the contrary, partition suited him down to the ground, promising as it did the prospect of the uninhibited exploitation of this relatively unscarred region in the interests of Soviet economic recovery, to be followed by a firm Soviet grip on Germany, whose resources would also be available to the Soviet Union. But to ease and speed the Red Army's advance to the west and south, Stalin was obviously prepared to strike almost any bargain—with the British, even though he mistrusted them deeply; with the petty dictators of south-eastern Europe; with the Germans, through his special 'Free Germany' committee (which could well have come in useful if the July plot against Hitler had enjoyed more success). Those who impeded this bargaining, either out of communist principles or national self-respect, inevitably incurred his wrath. Thus, in all these paradoxical policies whose import at first stunned men like Milovan Djilas (and many others), the Communists were urged to 'compromise' and the nationalists pressed to be realistic, which amounted to more or less the same thing. In Poland Stalin found a situation that taxed all the resources of this political Byzantinism. Yugoslavia puzzled him, and he may have half-suspected that real control was eluding him. Developments in Rumania, however, provided him with a signal and very serviceable triumph.

*   *   *

The formal order for the attack on Rumania went out from the *Stavka* on 2 August 1944. This terse directive, which came as no surprise to the commands of the two fronts involved—Malinovskii's 2nd Ukrainian and Tolbukhin's 3rd Ukrainian Front—alerted a further million Red Army troops for action in one more theatre where a huge cluster of men and machines waited to roll down on south-eastern Europe. The significance of the move however, lay as much with the timing as with the forces committed. This new Soviet offensive must be closely co-ordinated with the massive operations proceeding at the centre and in the northern theatre. Already the five fronts sent rolling forward in June and July in Belorussia and the western Ukraine were at the beginning of August on the Vistula and closing on the East Prussian frontier, having covered 300 miles or more in the previous two weeks. But now the *Stavka* realized that an operational 'pause' was inevitable in order to prepare for a massive push along the 'Warsaw–Berlin axis'. In the light of previous experience, and there was no reason to disregard it at this stage, such 'pauses' involving the movement of strategic reserves and the provisioning for a new offensive lasted not less than three months.

The offensive aimed through Warsaw on Berlin, the 'direct thrust', also remained dependent on destroying powerful German forces in the north-western and the south-western theatres, in the Baltic states and in south-eastern Europe. In committing all three Baltic fronts to action when the Belorussian fronts and Koniev's Ukrainian Front were deep in their own major offensive operations, the *Stavka* aimed successive blows at three of the four German army groups (North, Centre and North Ukraine). Now it was the turn of Army Group South Ukraine to come under the hammer. For the past three months the two fronts of the south-western theatre, 2nd and 3rd Ukrainian (presently threatening Moldavia and Rumania), had remained on the defensive after fighting off the joint German–Rumanian attacks mounted round Jassy in May, operations designed in part to reassure the Rumanians about German support in the field. The brunt of these attacks fell on the Soviet 52nd Army, but the *Stavka* permitted neither the army commander nor the Front commander (Malinovskii) to commit any reinforcement, hoping thereby to convince the German command that 2nd Ukrainian Front was already weakened by the transfer of troops to other Soviet fronts. After the opening of the Soviet offensive in Belorussia, the 'balance of forces' operated increasingly in the Red Army's favour. To bolster up Army Group Centre, Army Group South Ukraine was forced to hand over a dozen divisions (six of them armoured) and after Koniev's attack on Army Group North Ukraine there was little this force could do to help its southern neighbour, whose position was made much worse once Koniev's 1st Ukrainian Front fought its way to the foothills of the Carpathians and drove to the south-west of Lvov. Conversely, the creation of the new Soviet front (Petrov's 4th Ukrainian) could only benefit the two more southerly fronts (2nd and 3rd Ukrainian). No less than fifteen German divisions were tied up in the Carpathians facing Koniev's left flank and Petrov's 4th Ukrainian Front, and with a restless Slovakia in the rear of these

German troops, the country was stirred out of its acquiescence in fascist rule by plans for a national rising and by the growing presence of the Soviet-led partisans.

Without a shot being fired in any new Soviet offensive, the German armies in Rumania were facing catastrophe. The unfortunate formations of Col.-Gen. Friessner's Army Group South Ukraine were sandwiched between the Russians eager to attack them and the Rumanians no less eager to betray them, abandoning them to their enemies. Friessner's command comprised two main groups: 'Group Wöhler', with the German Eighth Army, the Rumanian 4th Army and the 17th German Corps, fourteen Rumanian divisions and seven German divisions, two-thirds of which were concentrated in the stretch of land between the Siret and the Prut; and 'Group Dumitrescu', including the German Sixth Army and the Rumanian 3rd Army, which held a line running from the Prut to the coast of the Black Sea with twenty-four divisions (seven of them Rumanian). Friessner's combined German–Rumanian strength amounted to something over 600,000 men with 400 tanks and 800 aircraft, a not unimpressive total after the battering these forces had taken in the winter and early spring. But the strength lay largely on paper. German divisions on a number of sectors were 'connected' by Rumanian units, a dangerous piece of 'corsetting', and now the position was made much worse by the withdrawal of the *Panzer* divisions which went north to help Model in his struggle with Koniev. Once the *Panzer* divisions and the motorized infantry moved north, the Eighth Army was left with only one armoured division (20th *Panzer*) and a couple of mobile formations to fight off massive Russian tank strength.

To his twenty-four regular German divisions, Friessner could add the police units, *SS* troops, air defence troops and a force of special naval infantry guarding Black Sea port installations, in all about 57,000 men. Two of the three Rumanian armies (3rd and 4th) formed part of the order of battle of Army Group South Ukraine, but an additional army—the 1st—with four infantry divisions remained at the disposal of the Rumanian command who put it to singular use, guarding the revised frontier line with Hungary set as a result of the Vienna Award of 1940 which ceded northern Transylvania to Hungary. Though the Hungarians held the Carpathian passes leading into Transylvania, the Rumanians guarded those providing access from southern Transylvania into Wallachia, an arrangement that seemed ideal to the Germans in 1940 when they acted as the diplomatic brokers of the Vienna Award but which in the late summer of 1944 finally produced quite disastrous consequences. Other Rumanian units were also scattered about the country, with a special force maintained in the capital (where all Rumanian troops came under the military commandant of Bucharest): on the lines facing the Russians, Rumanian units were interlaced with the German troops of the Eighth Army, as they were in Bessarabia where the Sixth Army held positions between the Prut and the Dniester.

The river Prut bisected the whole 350-mile front into two 'sectors', the northern one running from Cornesti to Husi held by the German Eighth Army and the

Rumanian 4th Army ('Group Wöhler', with General Wöhler in command of the Eighth Army). To cover the vital 'Focsani–Galatz gap' which led to Ploesti and Bucharest, Wöhler deployed the pick of Eighth Army in the valley of the river Siret and emplaced three Rumanian divisions between Targul Frumos and a German force just north of Jassy itself. On the southern sector, a 200-mile stretch running from Cornesti to the Black Sea, the German Sixth Army operated with the Rumanian 4th, 'Group Dumitrescu' (Dumitrescu commanding the Rumanian 4th Army): here German attention was concentrated on the 'Kishinev bastion', with German divisions holding sectors of some two miles, though the flanks were weak, especially the right flank and reserves marginal (two divisions at the disposal of the group commander). The Dniester, however, protected Kishinev—which screened the Focsani gap from the north-east—to the east, and in the area between Cornesti and the river Reut, German troops found excellent defensive positions in the hilly, wooded country west of Kishinev. Though Soviet troops had two small bridgeheads on the western bank of the Dniester, at Grigoriopol (east of Kishinev) and near Bendery (opposite the Russian town of Tiraspol), both seemed to be effectively compressed. The 'Tiraspol bridgehead' was established in swamp ground and overlooked by German-dominated high ground not far from Bendery itself. The defence of the Dniester line was entrusted to a Rumanian force under the general supervision of Sixth Army. With this deployment, the stage was set for a smaller but no less savage repetition of history: the Sixth Army had gone to its doom at Stalingrad similarly trussed with Rumanian divisions, except that now it was the Dniester rather than the Don.

Though both Soviet Front commanders were convinced of the feasibility of driving into the Kishinev salient, the *Stavka* could give absolutely no indication of when the offensive could take place, mentioning only that it would have to be the subject of special authorization. During the preparation of the great Belorussian attack, both fronts were ordered on to the defensive and instructed to assign a number of powerful formations—2nd and 5th Guards Tank Army, 5th Guards Army, artillery and aviation (2nd Ukrainian Front), plus 8th Guards Army (3rd Ukrainian Front)—to *Stavka* reserve. While the great battles roared across Belorussia and in the Baltic states, the South-Western Front remained absolutely quiet, with only diplomatic stirrings to ruffle the calm in Rumania, and even these seemed almost wholly inconclusive. Not until late on the evening of 15 July did General Antonov, deputy chief of the General Staff, telephone the two Front commands with instructions to start planning and preparing the 'Jassy–Kishinev operation' designed to accomplish the final destruction of Army Group South Ukraine.

For Malinovskii at 2nd Ukrainian Front, the choice of the direction of the 'main blow', though undoubtedly of critical importance, was less complex than with Tolbukhin to the south. Malinovskii and his chief of staff, Col.-Gen. M.V. Zakharov, planned the main attack in the direction of Vaslui–Focsàni, proposing to break through north-west of Jassy, then striking in the direction of Jassy–

Vaslui–Felciu. Although the valley of the Siret offered the most direct route to the Focsani gap, its lack of width would inevitably inhibit Soviet armoured movement and the terrain itself would enable German troops to carry out a fighting withdrawal: for this reason, Malinovskii's staff chose to attack north-west of Jassy, between the German troops and the Rumanian forces strung out to Targul Frumos, while a second thrust would move down the valley of the Prut, at the junction of a German–Rumanian force on the left flank of the Sixth Army. The first objective of 2nd Ukrainian Front was to gain the line Bacau–Vaslui–Felciu; a junction with the troops of 3rd Ukrainian Front would thus encircle the 'Jassy–Kishinev enemy concentration' and the encirclement line would prevent them making for Barlad–Focsani and freedom. The next objective was Focsani—the 'gap' leading to Ploesti and Bucharest—with the right flank of the 2nd Ukrainian Front secured by a force operating in the direction of the Carpathians.

General Tolbukhin's 3rd Ukrainian Front provided the other hook of the encirclement arm. In that first telephone talk on 15 July the *Stavka*, represented on this occasion by Antonov, evidently plumped for an all-out attack on Kishinev. As soon as the Front Military Soviet assembled on the morning of 16 July, Tolbukhin pointed out that this was not really feasible—it amounted to attacking once and then having to attack all over again. The Germans were expecting a Soviet attack from the Bendery bridgehead; with a pencil Tolbukhin traced the line of German fortifications on the map for the benefit of his staff gathered for the morning meeting in one of the peasant cottages that served as his headquarters. In the Tiraspol bridgehead area Tolbukhin suggested using Kitskan, where the Dniester bank was steep and the ground softened with swamp—a very unprepossessing site, but one that would guarantee surprise for the main attack. Though other axes were considered, the Military Soviet agreed to carry out a reconnaissance of the Kitskan bridgehead, an assignment given to Col.-Gen. Biryuzov (chief of staff), the Front artillery commander and the chief engineer. General Kotlyar, the Front engineer, was far from enthusiastic on surveying the swampland with its mass of rivulets: the problems would be formidable and he pointed out to Biryuzov that 'we are not so rich in engineering troops'. Col.-Gen. Nadelin, the artillery commander, was nevertheless impressed with the possibilities of mounting a surprise attack from Kitskan and supported Biryuzov: 'the enemy won't expect us from this direction and that's what matters'.

The selection of Kitskan signally affected the choice of the axis for the 'main blow': instead of making directly for Kishinev as the *Stavka* first insisted that Tolbukhin must, the Front command decided to slant the main attack towards Husi, lying on the western bank of the Prut. The bridgehead was undeniably small; movement would be difficult with the absence of good roads and the prevalence of swamps; the lack of high ground would inhibit observation and the engineers would have a massive job on their hands to position the tanks, artillery and troop carriers. But one advantage outweighed these drawbacks: an attack aimed from here could take the shortest route to link up with 2nd

Ukrainian Front in an encirclement operation. Such an attack could be launched without forcing the Dniester under heavy fire, and it would come as a complete surprise to the Germans. Having made his choice, Tolbukhin was not inclined to waver, and the use of the Kitskan bridgehead formed a major part of the provisional operational plan submitted to the *Stavka*, to which both Front commanders (Tolbukhin and Malinovskii) were summoned for a special conference on 31 July.

This conference confirmed the final form of the 'Jassy–Kishinev' operation; the results were then incorporated in the *Stavka* directive of 2 August. The two fronts were ordered to destroy German–Rumanian forces in the area of Jassy–Kishinev–Bendery, advance to a line running to Bacau–Leovo–Tarutino–Moldavka, with a view to striking on to Focsani, Galatz and Izmail. Malinovskii's orders specified that three infantry armies and one tank army—27th, 52nd and 53rd Armies, with 6th Tank Army—would breach the enemy defences and move towards Jassy–Vaslui–Felcui. In the first stage of the operation it was imperative to seize Bacau, Vaslui and Husi, capture the crossings over the Prut in the Husi–Felcui sector and co-operate with the 3rd Ukrainian Front in eliminating the 'Kishinev concentration' of enemy troops simultaneously cutting their escape route through Barlad and Focsani. With this encirclement complete, Malinovskii was to drive for Focsani, securing his right flank with 5th Guards Cavalry Corps (which was to force the river Siret and advance on Piatra). Malinovskii's main thrust was to go down the valley of the river Barlad, thus outflanking the German defences in the Siret: the capture of Jassy would open the road to Vaslui and the towns of Barlad and Tecuci, the latter little more than a dozen miles from Focsani. Once on the river Barlad, whose course began not far south of Jassy, Malinovskii's mobile troops were then within a score of miles of the lower Prut at which Tolbukhin was also aiming.

The *Stavka* accepted Tolbukhin's 'Kitskan plan' and abandoned the idea of a direct assault on Kishinev from the north; 3rd Ukrainian Front received orders to attack south of Bendery and, with three left-flank armies, to advance in the direction of Opach, Selemet and Husi (simultaneously protecting this assault force against attack from the south), to reach the Leovo–Tarutino–Moldavka line, and there to co-operate with 2nd Ukrainian Front in the encirclement. The second stage of the operation involved moving on Reni and Ismail to cut off the German line of retreat to the Prut and the Danube.

Within hours of the receipt of the *Stavka* directive the two Front commanders, together with their military soviets and army commanders, gathered at the junction of the two fronts for a conference devoted to detailed planning. Marshal Timoshenko, a figure from the seemingly far-off days of 1941–2 and one seen only infrequently on the battle-fronts, now re-emerged to act as *Stavka* 'co-ordinator' for the Jassy–Kishinev operation: in this capacity he attended the special conference. Of the two fronts, Malinovskii's was the stronger, with six infantry armies, one tank army, an air army in support and three independent corps; Tolbukhin disposed of four infantry armies but only one mechanized corps—the 7th—and even that he had had to plead for. Malinovskii proposed to use four armies (27th, 52nd and 53rd Armies, and 6th Tank Army) plus one tank corps (the 18th) for his main attack in the stretch of land between the rivers Siret and Prut: his breakthrough was planned across a ten-mile sector between Targul Frumos and Jassy, a sector with only field fortifications. A rapid breakthrough here would mean outflanking the stronger defences and would put him on the shortest route to the Prut crossings, deep in the rear of the main forces of Army Group South Ukraine: he was thus striking at the junction of the Eighth Army and 4th Rumanian Army and also isolating Sixth Army, deployed in the Kishinev salient. The main attack would be secured by a supporting operation mounted by 7th Guards Army, with 5th Guards Cavalry and 23rd Tank Corps operating as a 'cavalry-mechanized group', holding off any German attack from the Siret. The immediate Front task was to advance to the Bacau–Vaslui–Husi line, capture the Prut crossings in the Husi–Felcui sector and link up with the troops of the 3rd Ukrainian Front. The second assignment was to eliminate the encircled enemy forces and also to push on to Focsani; for the capture of the 'Focsani gate' would open the route to central Rumania and provide full freedom of manoeuvre to the west and south. To accomplish this Malinovskii disposed of eight armies, four independent corps, fifty-five rifle and cavalry divisions, eleven artillery and mortar divisions and eight aviation divisions—over 11,000 guns and mortars, 1,283 tanks and SP guns and almost 900 aircraft.

Tolbukhin's final operational plan was no less intricate. His main attack would come from south of Bendery, aimed at Husi to link up with Malinovskii; Lt.-Gen. M.N. Sharokhin's 37th Army, supported by Gagen's 57th and Shlemin's 46th, was to make the main thrust, with two mechanized corps also committed to the drive on Husi, thus outflanking the main German force from the south. The destruction of the 3rd Rumanian Army holding the lower reaches of the Dniester was entrusted to a force from 46th Army operating with units of the Soviet Black Sea Fleet and the Danube Flotilla: the left-flank divisions of Shlemin's 46th Army were to force the Dniester estuary at Akkerman, complete the encirclement of the Rumanians and seize the mouth of the Danube. Tolbukhin's strength for these operations amounted to five armies (including an air army), two mechanized corps and a mechanized brigade, thirty-seven rifle divisions, two brigades of naval infantry, six artillery and seven aviation divisions, 8,000 guns, about 600 tanks and 1,000 aircraft.

Operations in the Dnieper estuary called for special planning and the co-operation of the naval command. At the beginning of August the Black Sea Fleet command began gathering light craft and aircraft in bases on the north-west coast of the Black Sea. The command itself moved to Odessa and set up a 'co-ordinating staff' to work with 3rd Ukrainian Front on the joint operations and to supervise naval actions against enemy naval forces. For the Dniester estuary assault, Rear-Admiral Gorshkov's Danube Flotilla would operate with the left-flank units of 46th Army, which were organized into a separate force under the command of Lt.-Gen. A.N. Bakhtin (deputy commander, 46th Army). General Shlemin, the army commander, planned to use three infantry corps and a mechanized corps in a right-flank attack designed to out-flank the Rumanian 3rd Army from the north-west: on the second day of these operations Bakhtin's special left-flank units and Gorshkov's Danube Flotilla were to attack the Dniester estuary and capture Akkerman, after which 46th Army would complete the encirclement of the Rumanians between the river Kogilnik and the Dniester estuary before advancing towards the Danube delta and the river Prut.

The final planning of the amphibious assault began on 11–12 August at a special conference held at Tolbukhin's headquarters. General Bakhtin opened with a review of the strength and role of the troops involved: the assault on the Dniester estuary was to begin on the second day after 46th Army's main attack and would be made under cover of darkness, with two groups landed south-east and north-west of Akkerman. After pushing on to Moldavka to surround the Rumanians north-west of the estuary, the assault group would drive south-westwards to the river Kogilnik to complete the main encirclement in co-operation with the rest of 46th Army. The army men of the Front command then listened to Gorshkov, who arrived with his full military soviet, Captain Matushkin and Captain Sverdlov (chief of staff) as well as General Ermachenkov, air force commander for the Black Sea Fleet. Gorshkov did not waste words, and his terseness impressed the soldiers. The general naval plan called for the suppression of all enemy interference from the sea by using submarines, torpedo boats and naval aircraft to attack the bases of Constanza and Sulina, plus all surface targets. For the assault on the estuary Gorshkov was assembling a force of twenty-eight amphibious vehicles, thirty-five cutters and 450 boats for landing troops: the support consisted of six motor gunboats, two small craft equipped with mortars and three small minesweepers, together with sixteen guns from coastal artillery.

Both Front commands held operational reviews at which all army commanders, heads of arms and services (plus the naval personnel in Tolbukhin's case) reported on their plans and received specific directions from the Front commander or the chief of staff, the armoured and artillery preparations coming in for special notice. The political administration of both fronts also found itself faced with a considerable task in dealing with the mass of raw recruits brought in by the mobilizations carried out in the recently liberated areas of the western Ukraine. The General Staff record shows that only 8,224 men reached 2nd and 3rd Ukrainian Fronts between April and August 1944, but in the same period the 2nd Ukrainian Front acquired no less than 265,000 recruits from the conscriptions in the liberated areas, all of them needing basic military training and political re-education after their years under German rule. Tolbukhin's front received 80,000 conscripts. And for veterans and recruits alike the political administration prepared special political lectures to impress upon them that they were now abroad, on 'foreign soil', and must exercise the requisite 'vigilance'; towards the Rumanian population they must act in accordance with 'Soviet dignity', respecting the land and explaining to farmers that 'when abroad the soldier must live only out of his own pack'.

Though Malinovskii's men had been 'abroad' for some months after crossing the frontier, substantial forces of the Red Army were about to cross that great divide, the line between the communist and the capitalist world. The troops listened to hundreds of lectures on the aim of the Soviet invasion, the 'criminal activities of the Antonescu clique', the squalor in which the Rumanian peasants lived and the unjust oppression of the Rumanian working class, exploited by their German occupiers and native capitalists alike. Nor did the enemy escape the attentions of the political administration; the Rumanian lines were blasted with loudspeaker broadcasts urging the Rumanian soldiers to abandon their German allies and were showered with leaflets encouraging them to leave the front for their own homes.

The Soviet troops also trained. After the first phase of the Belorussian operations the *Stavka* issued on 6 July a special directive devoted to the shortcomings in Soviet organization—violation of the procedures for setting up staff headquarters and command posts (which were not to change positions until signal links with lower and higher echelons had been set up in the new site), the failure to exploit radio communication and the use of first-echelon troops for secondary tasks, thus slowing up the whole pace of the attack. On 9 July Malinovskii ordered staff training in all armies and independent corps until 25 July; at the end of the month a Front order prescribed training for infantry, artillery and tank crews, a 50-hour programme for the first echelon troops, 100 hours for second echelon units and 300 hours for armoured troops, with forty per cent of the training time taken up with night exercises. Tolbukhin's command ordered a similar programme: Tolbukhin himself, with other army and corps commanders, took part in the exercises with 37th Army. Malinovskii supervised the two-day exercise with 2nd Ukrainian Front staffs devoted to the control of formations during the 'manoeuvre stage' of operations. Reconnaissance aircraft brought back air photos of the terrain along the line, of advance marked out for the armoured forces, material indispensable for Kravchenko with 6th Tank Army and for 18th Corps commander in planning their movement down the river valleys. In the estuaries near Odessa, where conditions resembled the Dniester estuary, the naval infantry also rehearsed their assault.

The most gruelling labour, however, lay with the material preparations for the Soviet attack, and none was more taxing than Tolbukhin's commitment on the Kitskan bridgehead, into which 37th Army, artillery and armour was being steadily crammed—three rifle corps, a mechanized corps, fifty-one artillery regiments and thirty specialist units. The bridgehead lacked any good road, save for a single track running along the eastern bank of the Dniester; the earth roads could be used by transport only when the weather was fine. Elsewhere in the bridgehead the various units settled down amidst the small lakes and swamps, one company at a time taking up their positions; most of the trenches required embankments and the armour had to be moved by means of logs lashed to make a kind of planking. The service units installed themselves in the three small villages of Merineshti, Kitskan and Kopanka. The sweat of moving in the machines and the acute discomforts of the bridgehead were real enough when one company would have to skirt a five-mile swamp to keep in touch with the other, but all this was offset by the knowledge that none of the formations need force the Dniester under fire.

Waiting for the inevitable—the Russian military landslide which must fall sooner or later upon all Rumania—the government and the people in Bucharest were feeling the strain by early August. The Communist Party showed signs of stirring, even embarking on plans for a national rising: on 13–14 July a meeting between Communists and army officers resulted in the formation of a Military Revolutionary Committee which discussed plans for a rising in Bucharest, even a turn-about at the front, with the Rumanian troops linking up with the Russians and turning on the German troops. Any rising in Bucharest would mean finding arms for some 2,000 insurgents, the arrest of the German authorities and the existing Rumanian government, and the freeing of all imprisoned 'anti-Fascists'. The Committee all too soon discovered, however, that the Germans enjoyed great numerical superiority, not least in Bucharest itself, and they therefore set afoot various conspiratorial schemes to increase Rumanian troop strength in the capital and to maintain Rumanian forces in the interior of the country. While this plan grew, Iuliu Maniu showed himself less enthusiastic for the kind of action the Communists presently proposed, street demonstrations and strikes designed to undermine the government. And what the Communists really wanted of Maniu, an undertaking that the army would not shoot in these circumstances, he was unable to provide. Much stranger, however, was the fact that the Soviet command was not informed of plans for an armed rising in Bucharest.

While these contacts between Iuliu Maniu and the Communists flickered on and off, Marshal Antonescu paid what proved to be his last visit to Hitler at Rastenberg where the *Führer's* train was standing. Antonescu took with him his brother Mihai and General Steflea, the Rumanian chief of staff. In an atmosphere heavy with Hitler's suspiciousness, expressing itself in his barbed questions about Rumania's role, Marshal Antonescu faced the *Führer* in a four-hour interview on 5 August. The military talks lasted longer and were conducted by Steflea, but to Hitler's savage probing Antonescu returned with questions of his own about the German response in the event of the Moldavian Front caving in, about what the *Luftwaffe* might do to hold off the increasingly heavy Allied air attacks, and about how Germany proposed to protect the Black Sea coast, a new preoccupation prompted by the all too recent Turkish rupture of diplomatic relations with Germany. Whatever the satisfactions he sought—and Steflea spelt these out in military terms to the German command—Antonescu did not get them from Hitler. What comfort he drew from all the talk about secret weapons and changing the course of the war was probably minimal, though for the moment Rumania stayed in the war at Germany's side. There still remained that other option, one that Marshal Antonescu chose to exercise a little later—the armistice terms already suggested to him from the Soviet side through Mme Kollontai. The Marshal may have reckoned that all was not lost.

Towards the middle of August the German command in Rumania began to take a much more serious view of the whole situation; Col.-Gen. Friessner sent out orders to put all three *Wehrmachtteile* in a greater state of readiness and under full command. Marshal Antonescu may have promised to fight on, but this scarcely settled anything. During the first week in August the Germans detected signs of considerable Soviet reinforcement along the Prut to the north of Jassy, but the General Staff was not inclined to change its view that a major Russian effort in Rumania was unlikely, if only because in July several armies had been withdrawn from the Soviet fronts facing Army Group South Ukraine to fight on the central sector of the front. The general summary of possible developments on 15 August repeated the view that an offensive on a major scale was unlikely in this theatre; any Soviet operation in the Balkans would have a purely limited objective—to prevent the transfer of fresh German forces to the battle-fronts at the centre. But by 18 August the signs of much increased Soviet activity were as unmistakable as they were disturbing. Col.-Gen. Friessner reported to *OKH* that now was the time to order German forces back to the line of the Carpathians, for a major attack against Group Wöhler north-west of Jassy was pending and a supporting attack against Group Dumitrescu must also be expected. It was also at this time that the army group command realized that those mobile formations that Antonescu demanded and Friessner hoped for were never going to materialize. All that Friessner could do was to issue a call to his mixed bag of troops, urging a fight to the finish in which German troops would stand 'shoulder to shoulder with our tested Rumanian comrades'.

On the evening of 19 August Marshal Timoshenko, Marshal of Aviation Khudaykov, General Malinovskii and the 'operations staff' of 2nd Ukrainian Front moved to the forward command post situated on Height 195: at first the evening was still but later the quiet was broken by a German bombing attack on the heights. On the 3rd Ukrainian Front Tolbukhin called together all arms commanders and supply officers, questioning them once again on their state of readiness and ordering them to get some rest, after seeing that their men were resting properly. Once darkness came, the Front 'operational group' set off for the forward command post, located in the Kitskan bridgehead. Biryuzov checked the command posts and looked up General Tolstikov, the aviation corps commander, who reported that his 'rippers'—special aircraft used to cut telephone lines— were already flying out over the German lines. The late evening was full of the usual noises, machine-gun bursts and isolated shots, and was lit by the flares over the enemy lines. In the Front command post General Tolbukhin was asleep, 'snoring in heroic style'. The guns of 3rd Ukrainian Front were set to fire at

0800 hours, those on Malinovskii's at 0600 hours on the morning of 20 August, the day of the great offensive.

On the first day of the offensive Malinovskii's assault armies fought their way to some depth into the German defences north-west of Jassy: Trofimenko's 27th Army and Koroteyev's 52nd, supported by Soviet ground-attack planes, drove ten miles into the enemy positions along a fifteen-mile front. Here, as on Tolbukhin's front, the initial artillery barrage wreaked great havoc, smashing in the defensive system and inflicting heavy casualties on the defenders. At noon Malinovskii loosed Kravchenko's tanks into the breach and the armour pushed on to the third line of defences. The German command, at first unaware of the weight of the Russian attack, tried to localize the penetration, but the mass of Russian infantry and armour proved too much. At the end of the first day the Soviet command was reckoning on the destruction of five enemy divisions and 3,000 prisoners. The Rumanian divisions stationed along Eighth Army's front began to crumble almost at once and nothing the German officers might do could raise their fighting spirit. The Rumanian army commander, General Abramescu, had pleaded with Antonescu to pull the 4th Army back to enable it to make some defence of Moldavia and to defend the line of the Prut: this would also secure passage for the Rumanian divisions in Bessarabia. Abramescu pleaded on 20 August to be allowed to retire to the 'Trajan line', but this was summarily rejected and the Rumanian troops finally perished singly or in groups amidst the fury of Malinovskii's first attack.

The next day, 21 August, Trofimenko's 27th Army pushed on deeper into Eighth Army's positions, with orders to clear the Mara heights and open up a path for 6th Tank Army: Koroteyev's 52nd Army received orders to go for Jassy itself and then to advance in the direction of Husi. To the right of his front, Malinovskii broadened his offensive by committing Shumilov's 7th Guards Army and the 'cavalry-mechanized group' in a supporting attack to clear the flank. By this time Group Wöhler was in a precarious position: the Rumanian positions between Jassy and Targul Frumos had been completely smashed in, and Soviet troops were thrusting down the valley of the Prut preceded by the remnants of the Rumanian divisions in full retreat. Kravchenko's tanks were now more than fifty miles to the south, German positions at Jassy had been outflanked from the west and east, while Koroteyev's troops had already turned east and were making for the town of Husi on the way to the link-up with 3rd Ukrainian Front.

Tolbukhin's success during these first hours of the offensive was equally striking. Sharokhin's 37th Army, supported by heavy artillery and air strikes, along with Shlemin's 46th, broke through the defences along a front of twenty-five miles by the evening of 20 August. Though German resistance on the heights south of Bendery scarcely slackened, the Rumanians covering Causani collapsed completely and by the evening this road junction was in Russian hands enabling the mobile forces to strike in several directions. The German command still thought this a 'supporting attack', deceived as it was by Tolbukhin's demonstrative concentration north of Kishinev and further confused by Berzarin's 5th Shock Army preparations for an attack from this area. Within twenty-four hours Rumanian resistance was almost at end, the reserves of Group Dumitrescu wholly expended. With Sharokhin and Shlemin's divisions already more than twenty miles deep into the enemy defensive zone, the Front command ordered 4th Guards Mechanized Corps to move up into Sharokhin's zone and 7th Mechanized into Shlemin's. Tolbukhin's three armies—37th, 46th and 57th—had broken right across the Dniester in a number of places, though Gagen's 57th Army faced continuing German resistance, prompted by fear for the flank and rear of the Sixth Army.

While Tolbukhin began pushing in his mobile formations, Malinovskii feared that Kravchenko's tanks might remain tangled up with Koroteyev's infantrymen fighting in the hilly area around the Mara height. At noon on 21 August the Front commander categorically ordered Kravchenko to break off all action with the infantry and to speed up his drive to the south. Kravchenko took the hint and turned all his forces south; Koroteyev continued to fight his way eastwards. On the evening of 21 August the *Stavka* sent out a revised directive to both Front commands, emphasizing that their task remained the rapid conclusion of the encirclement of the 'Kishinev group', to which end the main forces must be committed and should not be dispersed on 'other tasks'—'you have all the means for the successful accomplishment of your orders and you must carry out this assignment.' General Antonov telephoned Biryuzov at Tolbukhin's headquarters to give him verbally the substance of the new directive and also the latest news of Malinovskii's movements.

In the region of Jassy, German and Rumanian forces faced a hopeless situation: though the German positions in the valley of the Siret still held, Soviet columns were pushing past the troops holding Jassy on two sides. On 22 August Kravchenko's tanks were closing in on Vaslui and making for Husi after striking down the road in the valley of the Barlad. The only way of escape for the Germans was to make for the Siret and somehow to link up with what was left of the Eighth Army, but many men were trapped by Russian units as they tried to break away or else were put to even faster flight. The mobile forces from 2nd and 3rd Ukrainian Fronts were now closing on the Prut: Jassy was abandoned and the Sixth Army given orders to fall back, but it would only find the Russians already south of the line upon which the Germans proposed to retire. From east and west Soviet pincers fastened on the river Prut: while Malinovskii's armour sliced into Group Wöhler, Tolbukhin's two mechanized corps burst into the rear of three corps of the Sixth Army causing so much disruption that the commander of Group Dumitrescu lost contact with them. Withdrawal would not save the Germans now, since they had to cover fifty miles at least to the Prut and Soviet armour was only twenty miles away from the river.

Bakhtin's special group meanwhile set out to seize the estuary. Once the naval infantry captured bridgeheads for the Red Army riflemen, the troops were ferried ashore or towed to their positions in small boats; the Danube Flotilla put more than 8,000 men ashore together with heavy equipment including tanks and artillery. At Akkerman the Rumanians showed no fight and only one of the two German divisions stayed to resist with any force. Once the town was taken, Bakhtin's columns struck out south-west, while the left-flank and centre divisions of 46th Army began to sweep round the Rumanians to the north and north-west, breaking through to the river Kogilnik and into the rear of the main body of the 3rd Rumanian Army. While the encirclement of this Rumanian Army to the south-west was almost complete, the German Sixth Army began to disintegrate at alarming speed and the German command tried desperate measures to save what it could of the army. Hastily assembled units set up defences at Leuseni, Leovo and Felcui on the Prut, in order to secure the crossings. But already the two encirclement arms of the 2nd and 3rd Ukrainian Fronts—the inner encirclement—were not far from closing; on the western bank of the Prut the Germans tried to hold off 52nd Army and the 18th Tank Corps, both under orders from Malinovskii to take Husi with all speed and at any cost. Tolbukhin had broken right across Sixth Army area from Bendery, on the Dniester, to Leovo, on the Prut, and was now starting an attack on Kishinev itself from the north. The tanks from 6th Tank Army also continued to drive south, on to Tecuci and eventually to the 'Focsani gap', thus sealing off the entire German escape route.

The little Rumanian country town of Husi became for a few hours the focus of the massive battle waged across Moldavia and Bessarabia. The command of Army Group South Ukraine tried to pull its troops from the south-west of Kishinev towards the river Prut, struggling at the same time to hold a few crossings over the river, a task assigned to a force passed from Eighth to Sixth Army command. Husi, a road junction and the area of the most convenient crossing points over the Prut, occupied all the attention of both the Soviet and the German command. Meanwhile on the 2nd Ukrainian Front the rapid sequence of events at the centre forced the Germans to retire from their well-prepared positions in the valley of the Siret: the fortified position of Tirgu Frumos had been in Shumilov's hands for several hours and the town of Roman was already threatened. Units of the left flank of Eighth Army in the valley of the Siret were left with only one way out, along the road leading to Focsani, but this too was to be cut by more Russian columns. From left, right and centre, Army Group South Ukraine shuddered under these multiple blows. By the evening of the twenty-fourth the situation was entirely and uncontrollably catastrophic.

From dawn onwards on 23 August, 18th Tank Corps (2nd Ukrainian Front) was engaged in heavy fighting with elements of Sixth Army falling back on Husi and units of 52nd Army followed in the wake of 18th Corps tanks. German troops from Jassy and Kishinev were also converging on Husi and the wooded country to the south-west, the remnants of three German and four Rumanian

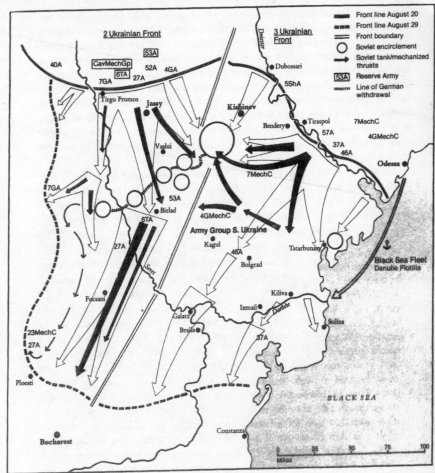

Map 10 Jassy–Kishinev operations, July–August 1944

divisions, whose fighting troops tried to organize some kind of defence on the eastern bank of the Prut. As Soviet tank units began to fight their way into Husi well ahead of the infantry, on the eastern bank of the Prut the forward armoured units of 3rd Ukrainian Front on August 23 were also closing on the river line at Leusini and a little to the south of it—Colonel Marshev's 16th Mechanized Brigade and Colonel Shutov's 64th Brigade, both belonging to 7th

Mechanized Corps; Colonel Zhukov's 36th Guards Tank Brigade from 4th Mechanized Corps captured the Prut crossing north of Leovo at about the same time. Once on the river the tank crews, baked in their hot machines, stopped long enough to strip off their overalls and bathe, looking like a group of village lads as they splashed about. The brief rest was well earned: the Soviet pincers forming the inner encirclement had all but met, trapping five German corps, the bulk of them pinned on the eastern bank of the Prut. In the woods south of Kishinev the remnants of ten German divisions sought what cover and protection they could find; on Tolbukhin's left flank the Rumanian 3rd Army was by now completely encircled. Soviet troops finally cleared Bendery on 23 August and hoisted the red flag of victory.

23 August 1944 proved to be one of the decisive days of the entire war. With Russian tanks on the Prut and more racing south for the 'Focsani gap', the fate of an entire German Army Group hung in the balance, proof of the massive and effective Russian battlefield performance in Moldavia and Bessarabia. That alone, however, could not make one single day so momentous. What changed the fortune of Germany's entire south-eastern theatre was the *coup* carried out that day in Bucharest, when King Michael had the Antonescu brothers arrested and Rumania ceased to fight alongside Germany. Rumanian troops were instructed to cease firing on the Red Army and King Michael surrendered unconditionally to the Allies. Hitler had already confessed at the end of July that 'the Balkans are my major worry', yet on 22 August General Warlimont could scarcely believe his ears when the Balkan crisis was discussed without any reference to the dangerous situation in Rumania. Hitler treated the German commander-in-chief in the south-eastern theatre to a ranting attack on 'the danger of a greater Serbia', concentrating on Tito at a time when the Russians were over the Dniester and the Prut and about to drive through 'the coastal front' in the south-east. German opinion about Rumania persisted in the belief that the Soviet invasion would force the Rumanians to fight on to the end. Nor was anything said of Bulgaria, Germany's other ailing ally, save for an almost inconsequential remark that the Bulgarians might pull their troops out of Serbia and must be replaced by German troops.

The Rumanian defection of 23 August turned Germany's military defeat into a welling catastrophe which made itself felt far beyond the bounds of a single Army Group. What was left of the two Rumanian armies fighting with Army Group South Ukraine laid down their arms: one German army, the Sixth, was being slowly throttled at Kishinev and was inside the encirclement ring: the whole of southern Bessarabia, the Danube delta and the passes through the Carpathians lay wide open to the Red Army. Neither the Danube nor the Carpathians could bar the Russian advance. Ahead of the Soviet armies lay the route to the Hungarian plains, the gateway to Czechoslovakia and Austria, as well as the road to Bulgaria and Yugoslavia, the collapse of the entire German defensive system in the south-eastern theatre. All this was precipitated by the Bucharest *coup*.

The date originally fixed by the Rumanian conspirators for their *coup* was 26 August, but the rapid deterioration of the situation in view of the disasters at the front made keeping to a 'timetable' pointless. Iuliu Maniu nevertheless seemed inclined to wait still longer but the senior officers associated with the opposition pressed for action even without informing the Rumanian representatives in Cairo. The Communists and their Military–Revolutionary Committee were also sounding out the possibility of immediate action. At one of the last sessions of the Council of Ministers Marshal Antonescu found himself finally forced to confess that the army was slipping out of his control and the troops could scarcely be blamed for not fighting as energetically as they might against the Russians; threats of dire punishment no longer produced any effect upon the Rumanian soldiers who were facing far greater terrors at the front. Shortly after 9 o'clock on the morning of 23 August Colonel Dragomir, chief of staff to 4th Army, telephoned General Sanatescu at the palace with the news that the front was wholly shattered: Russian tanks were pouring through a sixty-mile gap, and the hope of any effective resistance was utterly gone. The German command forbade Rumanian officers to give orders but nothing was being done to save the army. Dragomir appealed for help and for 'influence' to be brought upon the Germans.

General Sanatescu expressed great astonishment at this news, which acted as one more stimulus to change Rumania's course. A communist emissary to Iuliu Maniu was evidently brushed off somewhat abruptly with the observation that armistice talks should be initiated by the Antonescus: Constantin Bratianu of the National Liberals did not even attend this hasty council of war. But on the morning of 23 August Maniu, Petrescu and Bratianu did meet to plan their approach to Marshal Antonescu; Bratianu was selected as the spokesman for the 'historical' parties, who now pressed the Marshal to seek an armistice or else retire from the political scene. The position of the king now assumed extraordinary importance. He had already advised Cairo through his private channels of the intention to act in a few days' time, but the arrival at the palace of the Antonescu brothers on the afternoon of the 23rd produced an unforeseen climax: Ion Antonescu informed the king that he intended to seek an armistice though he would tell the Germans of his plans to do so. Aware that this could only prolong the agony and must inevitably bring down the wrath of both Russians and Germans upon Rumania, the king made his own decision on the spot. Going into an adjoining room he instructed his friends to arrest the Antonescu brothers.

In place of the Antonescus, King Michael established his own government with General Sanatescu at its head, a non-political figure who represented the armed forces: Niculescu-Buzesti took over foreign affairs, General Aldea internal affairs, and four representatives of the main parties joined the government—Maniu, Bratianu, Petrescu and Patrascanu (the latter for the Communists and, as a lawyer, installed as minister of justice). In the evening the king spoke to the nation and to the outside world over the radio, announcing an end to all fighting and hostile acts. Through a British officer in Bucharest he addressed an urgent appeal for three parachute brigades to be dropped near the Rumanian capital. On behalf of the new government, Niculescu-Buzesti sent a signal to the Rumanian representatives in Cairo authorizing them to sign an armistice on the terms originally proposed by the Allies on 12 April, though the new foreign minister drew attention to the concessions mentioned by Mme Kollontai—the Rumanian economy could not bear excessive reparations and the Rumanian government must be left an integral piece of Rumanian territory from which Soviet troops would be barred.

The day's developments in Bucharest took the Germans completely unawares. Hitler that evening ordered all military units, SS units and German citizens to work for the re-establishment of order and to throw back the Russian offensive. The military command still hoped to pull the German armies back to a defensive line which might also cover the oil-producing regions and to 'clean out' the 'putschists' in Bucharest, thus restoring the political conditions that would keep German troops in Rumania. The German commander in Bucharest reported that the coup, which had come out of the blue, was only the work of a 'palace clique'; with 5th Flak Division about to take over the city he reported at 0415 hours on 24 August that all the immediate steps to carry out Hitler's orders had been taken. But the news in mid-morning was undoubtedly bad. Bucharest was in the grip of 'heavy fighting'—schwere Kämpfe—in which a strong force supporting the 'palace clique' was besieging several German installations; the German Embassy was threatened by mobs and the German Ambassador had committed suicide. German reinforcements from Ploesti were moving on the capital and at 11 am a force of 150 German aircraft mounted an immediate bombing attack, singling out the palace as one of their prime targets. Hitler was bent on taking full and furious revenge.

While the Stukas were attacking Bucharest, the two Soviet fronts driving through Moldavia and Bessarabia completed the first stage of their offensive: in the area of Leovo the armoured units of 2nd and 3rd Ukrainian Fronts finally linked up, sealing the inner encirclement line. Berzarin's 5th Shock Army was already in possession of Kishinev on the morning of 24 August. Malinovskii's mobile columns pushed on to Bacau, Barlad and Tecuci—less than forty miles to the 'Focsani gap', while German troops had still twice this distance to cover in order to escape. Almost fifty miles separated the inner from the outer Soviet encirclement lines, and eighteen German divisions were trapped inside the inner ring.

In the course of 24 August the Stavka issued revised orders through Marshal Timoshenko to Malinovskii and Tolbukhin: the offensive was to continue on the outer encirclement line, with 'explanations' to the Rumanian troops—now abiding by the cease-fire order—that 'the Red Army cannot cease military operations until such time as those German forces which continue to remain in Rumania have been eliminated'. The Stavka also intimated that Rumanian units which surrendered voluntarily and came over to the Soviet lines in a body should not be disarmed, provided they agreed to wage 'a common struggle' against the Germans and the Hungarians. The unfortunate Rumanians were now caught between the Russians and the Germans, who also forced them to choose, though none could be found to turn traitor to the king and support the Germans: the OKW War Diary recorded that all the Rumanian generals remained *'königstreu'*. The hasty attempt to bring back Horia Sima and install an 'Iron Guard' regime flopped almost at once. The bombing of Bucharest failed to produce the panic and subservience the Germans hoped for and even anticipated; rather, the German attack on the capital (and the fighting at Ploesti) brought Rumanian soldiers into action against the *Wehrmacht,* whose attempts to 'restore order' failed and simply helped to precipitate Rumania's formal declaration of war on Germany on 26 August.

On the day that Rumania officially entered the war, Tolbukhin's columns were completing the conquest of all southern Bessarabia, where Bolgrad, Kilia and Remi fell to Shlemin's tanks, while Malinovskii's armoured forces raced for the 'Focsani gap'. Of the four German divisions concentrated to hold this escape route open, two were speedily withdrawn to protect German interests deeper inside Rumania, leaving only two infantry divisions to hold off Malinovskii's rush, a hopeless task in the face of Soviet tank strength sweeping on to the 'gap'. Inside the Soviet ring German troops, formed into three columns and covered by powerful rearguards to the north, east and south, prepared to break out, aiming to punch their way through to Husi. Malinovskii's orders, in addition to prescribing co-operation with Tolbukhin in dealing with this sizeable German force in his rear, specified further movement to the west and south-west towards the eatern Carpathians, together with a high-speed drive through the 'Focsani gap' and into the central regions of Rumania.

The last chance of escape for the German divisions trapped by Malinovskii and Tolbukhin lay in holding a crossing over the Prut, a desperate enterprise which was inadvertently aided by a costly Soviet mistake: 4th Guards Army from Malinovskii's front, driving down the Prut, became tangled with Berzarin's 5th Army under Tolbukhin, a mix-up over army boundaries which led to 4th Guards being too quickly disengaged. The *Stavka* and the Deputy Chief of the General Staff, General Antonov, 'categorically ordered' Malinovskii to pull back 4th Guards, away from the eastern bank of the Prut—out of contact with the bulk of the trapped enemy formations. Dispersed and weak as it was, Berzarin's 5th even after two days of heavy fighting could not beat down the fierce German resistance at the northerly crossings of the Prut. Desperate to escape the Soviet trap, German troops managed to prise open a small gap in the 'pincers' formed by 5th and 37th Armies, slipping the elements of two corps through this passage, over the Prut and into the woods round Husi. Here this large body of Germans fought it out with the rear units of 52nd Army, causing a considerable crisis to flare in Malinovskii's rear. Bakers, drivers and mechanics rushed to man what suddenly became front-line positions as the Germans, supported by the tanks and heavy weapons brought over the Prut, burst into their midst. Among the Soviet casualties was Maj.-Gen. V.I. Polozkov, 18th Tank Corps commander, killed in action on 28 August.

Altogether 70,000 German soldiers had broken across the Prut, determined to force their way to the Carpathians and into Hungary. Those divisions on the eastern bank of the Prut were, however, wholly marooned and doomed either to destruction or captivity. In Malinovskii's rear the situation nevertheless assumed alarming proportions as the elements of five German divisions roamed through 52nd Army's positions, aiming to break out to the south-west. There was nothing for it but to move up Front reserves and part of the second echelon, with 25th Guards Rifle Division rushed in to block the German drive that was to lead them to safety. On the night of 28 August the German command issued final orders for one last break-out attack, the dash for the Carpathian passes. At dawn German guns opened fire and the infantry launched themselves on Krivolapov's 25th Guards Division. On 29 August the main body of 52nd Army began to close in on the Germans concentrated in the area of Husi: 25th Guards fought to hold off the break-out attack, and gradually whittled down the attacking Germans. No more than 25,000 German troops managed to break out of the 'tactical' encirclement but they were still deep within the strategic encirclement, bumping into the rear positions of 27th Army; deep in Malinovskii's rear 38,000 Germans were made prisoner and their equipment captured. Slowly, but not without a whole series of fierce engagements with smaller parties of Germans, the Husi cauldron began to cool. Early in September the German command gave Sixth Army up for lost: five corps and eighteen divisions had been swallowed up in the Soviet encirclement, with four more divisions battered in the battles to cut their way free. The Soviet command claimed 98,000 prisoners and 100,000 German dead for the period 20–31 August; by Soviet reckoning, about 25,000 men made their way out of the trap. At the beginning of September the *Wehrmacht* no longer disposed of any substantial and organized body of troops on Rumanian territory.

Late in August Soviet columns fanned out and sped into the central districts of Rumania. Malinovskii strengthened his right-flank drive in the direction of the Carpathian passes, though the main body of the Front rushed the 'Focsani gap' and made for Ploesti and Bucharest; Tolbukhin's Front cleared the remainder of south-eastern Moldavia, the line of the Danube from Izmail down to the Black Sea, and occupied Constanza on 29 August. Within a very short time Tolbukhin's troops were on the frontier of the Bulgarian Dobrudja. In a sweep on his right flank, Malinovskii swung 40th and 7th Guards Armies, supported by a 'cavalry-mechanized group', towards Brasov (Kronstadt) in southern Transylvania, where Rumanian troops were mounting guard to prevent any Hungarian invasion; 6th Tank Army received orders to go for the oilfield area at Buzeu, after which it was to strike for Ploesti and Bucharest, with 27th Army moving its infantry in the wake of the Soviet tanks. At the end of August Malinovskii captured Ploesti itself and the surrounding oilfields, trapping three or four German divisions in the process. Kravchenko (6th Tank Army commander) received special orders from Malinovskii specifying the use of one corps for the Ploesti operation and two for the capture of Bucharest, though on receiving a copy of this order the *Stavka* decided for the moment to hold back Soviet troops from an all-out thrust against the Rumanian capital.

One Soviet mechanized corps (the 5th), two rifle divisions from 53rd Army together with the 1st Rumanian Tudor Vladimirescu Infantry Division (raised in the Soviet Union and recruited from men taken prisoner in southern Russia) already lay in a semi-circle not more than ten miles to the east and north-east of Bucharest. To ensure that the Soviet entry into the Rumanian capital would be made in proper style—'organized and disciplined . . . the infantry with bands playing . . . divisional and regimental commanders on horseback, at the head of their columns'—Malinovskii flew on 28 August to Managarov's HQ (53rd Army). On the return flight the small machine passed over Husi, where the encircled German troops were still fighting; heavy anti-aircraft fire wounded Malinovskii and only the skill of the pilot prevented a disaster. Back at Front HQ Malinovskii found several disquieting reports awaiting him from Soviet army commanders. At Ploesti General Sanatescu had approached the commander of 6th Tank Army with a formula designed to contain the Soviet advance (the same approach was made to the commander of 46th Army), suggesting that the Rumanian government should deal with German forces left on territory 'not yet occupied by the Red Army' and that in effect the Red Army should halt along a line running from the Carpathians to the Danube, making no further southerly movement. The *Stavka* naturally refused this and ordered Malinovskii to move into Bucharest as from 10 am on the morning of 31 August, a move designed to stifle the 'intrigues' of the 'internal and external reactionaries', which meant bringing the nationalist politicians to heel and forestalling any Anglo-American 'intervention'.

The Red Army's entry into Bucharest provided the briefest carnival, with the Soviet press recording Rumanian 'wonder and surprise' at the sight of Soviet soldiers, at their youth and at the quality of their guns and tanks. With the German Sixth Army all but smashed to pieces, there was now nothing to hold the Russians from flooding into the whole of Rumania. On 29 August the Military Soviet of the 2nd Ukrainian Front met for an extended discussion of future operations. The head of Front intelligence, Maj.-Gen. F.F. Povetkin, reported that only the remnants of seven divisions now faced Soviet forces along the right flank and centre of the 2nd Ukrainian Front; to the left and at the junction with 3rd Ukrainian Front no organized German force existed at all. The German southern flank, which had hitherto rested on the Black Sea, had now disintegrated; the German command could in no sense rely on Bulgarian forces— if they had not used Bulgarian troops before on the Soviet-German front, they would hardly use them now. On Malinovskii's left and at the centre, however, there was some enemy force—elements of those seven German divisions and Hungarian units—in Bystritsa and Cluj, plus eight Hungarian divisions (shortly to be formed into the 2nd Hungarian Army), and in Transylvania up to 30 battalions of frontier guards on the present Rumanian–Hungarian border. In Hungary itself up to nine divisions were presently identified.

From forward Front HQ in the small village of Ipatele, Malinovskii's command reported to the *Stavka* that the enemy in Rumania was completely 'demoralized', a verdict with which the *Stavka* agreed wholeheartedly and promptly issued a fresh set of directives to Malinovskii and Tolbukhin that same day (29 August). There were more than reasonable grounds for optimism, with the Slovak rising just beginning deep in the German rear, with Hungary showing signs of wavering and Bulgaria on the point of wobbling out of the war. The new *Stavka* orders set Malinovskii and Tolbukhin moving in disparate directions, with 2nd Ukrainian Front advancing through the central and western areas of Rumania towards the frontiers with Hungary, Yugoslavia and Bulgaria, all west of Giurgiu; and 3rd Ukrainian Front moving down the coast towards the Rumanian-Bulgarian frontier east of Giurgiu. Malinovskii's front was also 'split', into left-flank operations (27th, 53rd and 6th Tank Armies) driving into the southern Carpathians (from Turnu-Severin to Giurgiu) and the right flank (40th, 7th Guards Army and a 'cavalry-mechanized group') making for the eastern Carpathians, to reach the line Bystritsa–Cluj–Aoud–Sibiu by mid-September. The ultimate objective of Malinovskii's right-flank drive was Satu-Mare, with the idea of 'co-operating with the forces of 4th Ukrainian Front forcing the Carpathians and driving for the Uzhorod-Mukachevo area'. That latter refinement was amplified in a revised directive sent out by the *Stavka* early in September.

For Malinovskii the invasion and investment of Transylvania presented some difficulties, not least the need to split his forces into several columns and the distance involved in keeping them supplied; at the same time the presence of substantial Rumanian forces and the absence of any appreciable German strength clearly favoured rapid Russian exploitation of the situation. For the moment the remnants of Eighth Army—three or four battered divisions—could scarcely fill out the 'front' running along the line of the Transylvanian Alps (southern Carpathians) from Brailov westwards on to the Danube, which the German command hoped to hold. In southern Transylvania, in the towns of Brasov, Sibiu, Arad and Timosoara, the Rumanian army was in control, and it kept more of its forces along the Rumanian–Hungarian frontier: two full Rumanian armies (4th and 1st) with two additional corps came under Soviet operational command when the Rumanian government agreed (as indeed it had no choice but to agree) that Rumanian forces should come under Soviet control, thus giving Malinovskii some twenty Rumanian divisions, indifferently equipped but infantrymen at least who knew the ground on which they were to fight.

Stunned by events in Rumania, the Hungarians now faced an obvious and immediate threat to northern Transylvania, though their reaction was surprisingly sluggish. At this point Hungarian forces were scattered from Galicia to the Carpathians, with the 1st Hungarian Army holding the Carpathian passes from Dukla to Yablonitsa. The 2nd Hungarian Army was still forming up and was about to be rushed to the scene of the gravest crisis, the Rumanian–Hungarian border, to which divisions of the 1st Hungarian Army were also being directed, thus producing a combined German–Hungarian force (some five German divisions and about eight Hungarian). Malinovskii was already moving with some speed into western Rumania and turning north-west, reaching Pitesti and Craiova by 5 September and taking Turnu-Severin and Giurgiu on the Danube the following day. By this time strong forces were through the passes in the Transylvanian Alps and already Brasov and Sibiu were in Russian hands, thereby giving the Red Army a firm grip on southern Transylvania. The lead units of 6th Tank Army were on the Danube at Turnu-Severin, the junction with Yugoslavia and not more than 100 miles east of Belgrade.

At dawn on the morning of 5 September a mixed German-Hungarian force five divisions strong suddenly struck back, launching an attack from the Cluj–Turda area against the 4th Rumanian Army, which had just begun to deploy in the area to the north of the southern Carpathians to cover this south-eastern approach and to block just such an attack as was now developing. Ill-prepared as they were, the Rumanians fell back to the line of the river Muresul, while Kravchenko's 6th Tank Army moved into the Sibiu area, having swung north on Malinovskii's orders. Kravchenko's tank army was showing all the signs of its recent travels and battles: tank strength was down to 130 tanks and 56 self-propelled guns, with the majority of the machines in need of substantial maintenance, the tanks having covered almost 600 miles and the engines run well over the 200-hour mark. By the evening of 11 September Kravchenko had moved his tank army into positions to mount a counter-attack and started to push the German-Hungarian troops away from the Maros; on 12 September the tank troops celebrated not only their successful counter-thrust but also their elevation to 'Guards' status.

Towards the middle of September Malinovskii's front had almost cleared southern Transylvania, an operation conducted amidst one of the most formidable mountainous regions of Europe. On the extreme right flank of 2nd Ukrainian Front, 40th, 7th Guards Army and a 'mobile group' pushed through the eastern Carpathians, occupying the upper valley of the Moldava and reaching a line running from Dorna–Vatra to Targul–Mores, capturing Toplita at the eastern end of the upper Maros gorge on 15 September. At the centre Malinovskii's forces made the fastest progress, with 6th Tank Army moving across the southern Carpathians and driving north to support the Rumanian troops pressed by the German-Hungarian attacks from the Cluj-Turda area: the Soviet 27th Army finally closed with the Rumanian 4th Army and by 15 September moved up to the line running from Turda to Targul–Mores. On the left flank, 18th Tank Corps striking from Slatina made for Deva in the valley of the Maros, from

which point Malinovskii switched the tanks north-west in the direction of Arad.
Managarov's 53rd Army was moving at 'a record pace' in a north-westerly
direction towards Arad and Timosoara, two important towns from which the
Rumanian garrisons were on the point of being ejected by another German–
Hungarian force. Left-flank Soviet units joined by the Rumanians retreating from
Arad and Timosoara prepared to fight it out for the possession of these two key
towns, which must serve as bases for any advance into the middle reaches of the
Danubian plain. Meanwhile at the centre, in the area of Cluj, a bout of heavy
fighting set in as the Germans moved up *Panzer* reinforcements, bringing these
divisions from Moravia through the chaos and collisions in Slovakia where the
insurgents slowed down the passage of the German armour but did not manage
to halt it completely.

At this point the *Stavka* intervened to modify Malinovskii's previous orders
outlined in the directive of 29 August. Although 2nd Ukrainian Front had
advanced more than 150 miles at the centre and on the left flank in those nine
days between 6 and 15 September, German resistance on the Targul Mures–Turda
sector prevented Malinovskii's troops reaching all their objectives: Cluj was still
in German–Hungarian hands, while at Arad and Timosoara German–Hungarian
troops also managed to build something like a firm front. So far these forces
effectively blocked the passages leading from the southern Carpathians into Cluj
and thence to the Hungarian plains. The *Stavka* had also to reckon with
developments to the north and south of Malinovskii; Petrov's 4th Ukrainian
Front launched its attack towards Mukachevo and Uzhorod on 9 September—
though progress was slow on this front—while Tolbukhin on 8 September
proceeded with the occupation of Bulgaria, which abandoned its allegiance to
Germany. The situation seemed ripe for a co-ordinated operation involving the
final sweep in Rumania, the invasion of Hungary and a thrust into Yugoslavia.

Ahead of Malinovskii lay the plains of Hungary. His latest orders from the
Stavka, embodied in the directive of 15 September, instructed him to move up
to the Bystritsa–Cluj–Lugo line by 19 September, continue his advance in the
direction of Cluj–Debrecen–Miskolcz and by 7–10 October to bring his main
force to the line of the river Tisza in the area of Chop–Szolnok, thus advancing
himself to assist Petrov's 4th Ukrainian Front in its struggle for the Carpathian
passes and for possession of the Uzhorod area. The essence of the *Stavka* plan
lay in maintaining the momentum on all of Malinovskii's sectors but to mount
the main attack along the Cluj–Debrecen–Miskolcz axis in order to bring Soviet
forces into Hungary along the line of the river Tisza, an advance of some 300
kilometres. The new line of advance was also dictated by the fact that Malinovskii's
central forces had not managed to reach Satu-Mare, the original objective set on
29 August: now the attack was shifted further to the south. But the most
important implication of the *Stavka* plan lay in connecting Malinovskii's and
Petrov's operations—and all without due regard for the difficulties facing Malinovskii, whose offensive had now run for twenty-seven days and covered distances

ranging from 250 to 400 miles, doubling his frontage and drawing him ever further from the supply bases. Malinovskii, however, could scarcely disregard these orders even though they did not allow him time even to regroup. Once again the *Stavka* underestimated the difficulties on the ground.

To bring his armies into the rear of those German forces fighting off Petrov's 4th Ukrainian Front, Malinovskii planned to use three infantry armies on his right and centre, plus Gorshkov's 'cavalry-mechanized group' and Kravchenko's tank army in an attack aimed to the north-west in the direction of Bystritsa–Cluj–Targul Muros. Denied any chance to regroup, Malinovskii's right-flank and centre armies moved off on 16 September in their attempt to break right through northern Transylvania. For the next seven days, armour and infantry tried to smash down heavy German resistance, stiffened with *Panzer* reinforcements moved into the area of Cluj and along the Targul Muros–Turda sector. By 24 September it was plain that the Soviet attack could not manage a breakthrough. Gloom on this score, however, was relieved by the rapid advance on the left flank, where 53rd Army, 18th Tank Corps and the Rumanian 1st Army took Arad, only ten miles from the Hungarian frontier, and pushed along the Orad–Timosoara road in the direction of the frontier. On 24 September Soviet–Rumanian forces were on the Hungarian frontier at Mako and had pushed a few miles to the north-east of the town.

Further to the north the Slovak rising was already entering its final crisis, while Soviet and Czechoslovak troops tried to force their way through the Carpathian passes to link up with the Slovak insurgents: it still remained to force the Dukla pass. To the south Malinovskii could only conclude that it was no longer feasible to think of fighting forward to Miszkolc; on 24 September he reported his conclusions to the *Stavka*, emphasizing the resistance encountered by 40th, 7th Guards and 27th Armies but also stressing that the successes of 53rd Army on his left flank now made it possible to turn the whole attack along the 'Oradea–Mare, Debrecen axis'. Malinovskii asked for permission to swing 6th Guards Tank Army on to this axis, to halt his offensive at the centre until the divisions there could be supplied and better reconnaissance of enemy positions undertaken, and finally to complete the concentration of reinforcements for his left flank (46th Army and Pliev's 'cavalry-mechanized group'). The *Stavka* agreed but insisted that the offensive involving the three armies of the right and centre be kept up, otherwise the Germans would simply transfer their forces to check Malinovskii's left: the new 'Debrecen operation' was to begin on 6 October. For the moment, save for the holding attacks on his right, Malinovskii's operations came to a brief halt, the last respite for both sides before the storm broke over all of eastern Hungary.

Early in September, as Malinovskii's columns began cutting their way deeper into Transylvania, the Rumanian armistice delegation arrived in Moscow. Headed by Prince Stirbey, the Rumanian delegation was received with deliberate and obvious pomp, but all too soon the Rumanians discovered that they were in Moscow simply to sign what the Soviet government set before them, not to talk terms. Though present at the 'negotiations', the American and British Ambassadors played no active part and took great care to avoid personal contacts with the Rumanians, a precaution designed to prevent these hapless visitors being compromised in Soviet eyes. Minister Patrascanu, the communist representative and the mouthpiece of the delegation, did much of the talking, betraying nevertheless considerable nervousness and confiding to at least one member of his own delegation his fears for the future of a 'collaboration' which already seemed so ominously one-sided.

On 12 September 1944 the Armistice convention was signed, hammered home with all of Molotov's obduracy. The document was important not only for Rumania but, as subsequent events showed, for Hungary and Bulgaria, Germany's other Axis allies in Europe: the Soviet–Rumanian armistice served as a model upon which to base future transactions and stipulations. With its three signatures the convention bore some inter-Allied impress, but in practical terms Rumania was handed to the Soviet Union, lock, stock and barrel, in a very literal sense. Rumanian troops were placed at the service of the Soviet Union, Rumania formally ceded Bessarabia and the northern Bukovina (in return for northern Transylvania under the Soviet cancellation of the Vienna Award), and Rumanian indemnities— payable to the Soviet Union—were fixed at \$300 million spread over six years (to be delivered in goods and raw materials), in addition to occupation costs imposed on Rumania. It was an armistice that stung the Rumanians with its injustice and left them with a rankling sense of grievance against Western powers who remained completely inert in the face of Soviet demands on Rumania, applying no pressure of any kind to sustain the Rumanian case for concessions.

For the nationalists among the political leaders, perhaps for the Rumanians at large, regaining northern Transylvania could conceivably offset the loss of Bessarabia, but this faint sentimental glow was extinguished by the realities of Article 11 of the Armistice Convention dealing with indemnities, for all this meant heavier economic burdens. The fiercest sting, however, lay in Articles 10 and 12, covering Soviet requisitioning and Rumanian restitution of 'goods taken from Soviet territory during the war'. Red Army requisition quickly proved to be a costly affair for Rumania, involving the whole of the navy and a large part of the merchant fleet, equipment from the oil fields and the petroleum industry, railway rolling stock and every motorcar to hand, all commandeered and taken into Soviet 'service'. With fresh Soviet troops moving into the country and without any effective arrangement for contact between the Soviet command and the Rumanian authorities, Sanatescu's government found itself faced from the outset with a situation bordering on the chaotic. Once the first friction was engendered over implementing the 'economic' aspects of the Armistice Convention, the Russians quickly demonstrated their suspicions of the 'historic parties' and the nationalist leaders, while the

Communist Party—its ranks swelled with a horde of place-seekers, collaborationists and men on the run from their Iron Guard past—began to flex its muscles. Ana Pauker's achievement was the creation of a vastly expanded party, though it was one bloated with elements which only weeks earlier had manned or supported the Antonescu dictatorship—the same thugs, secret policemen and soldiers, swelled with the riff-raff signed up by the new communist leadership. Sizeable contingents of these recruits were quickly used to fill out the membership of the political groups affiliated to the National Democratic Front consisting of the Communists and the Social Democrats; there were also men to spare for the special task of penetrating the Social Democrats.

Reports reaching Moscow (if that submitted by the political member of the Military Soviet of the 2nd Ukrainian Front at the end of September is a fair example) could only exacerbate the situation and stiffen the Soviet attitude. Malinovskii's headquarters, reporting to the Central Committee and the Political Administration, emphasized the continuing presence of 'reactionary elements' in the state machine, stressing the activity of 'several ministers, especially Maniu, who surround themselves with similar elements'; the 'Green Guards' were mustering in civil and military administrations; officials inclined to co-operate with the Red Army were persecuted. In Bucharest the press came under only partial control; and in the schools the teachers still filled the pupils with 'Hitlerite propaganda and slander against the Soviet Union'. That this was not an isolated complaint is shown by Soviet reports on the Rumanian army, whose senior officers came in for a blasting from the Soviet command: General Mikhail, chief of the General Staff and a 'thorough-going reactionary', closely connected with Maniu, was the chief target of Soviet criticisms and his vacillations were trenchantly denounced. Even worse, though there were 'progressive elements' in the Rumanian officer corps, 'German agents' held important posts in several divisions sent to fight the Germans. None of this augured well for the future and the prospect grew bleaker with each passing week. As for Rumania's one positive gain, northern Transylvania, that territory still remained to be cleared; and even when finally cleared, the problems of Transylvania were added to a fast degenerating situation.

Clearing Rumania cost the Red Army 46,783 dead, 171,426 wounded, 2,000 guns and mortars, over 2,200 tanks and 528 aircraft (casualties and losses recorded during the weeks from April to October 1944). Meanwhile Bulgaria fell without a shot being fired or a man being lost. On the morning of 8 September, three days after the Soviet declaration of war on Bulgaria, Soviet gunners with the 3rd Ukrainian Front stood ready to open fire, but 'from our observation posts we did not see any target we could shell'. Georgi Dimitrov, the exiled Bulgarian communist leader in Moscow and hero of the *Reichstag* fire trial of 1933, had assured Marshal Zhukov late in August that there would be no war with Bulgaria: 'You will not be met with artillery and machine-gun fire but with bread and salt—according to our old Slav custom. I don't think the Bulgarian troops will risk engaging the Red Army.' Georgi Dimitrov proved to be right. When elements of 57th Army crossed the Bulgarian frontier in force, they were met by a Bulgarian infantry division lined up on both sides of the road, 'welcoming our [Soviet] troops with unfurled red banners and music'.

Late in August, after Rumania's defection from the Axis, Bulgaria succumbed to panic. Though an ally of Germany and a formal enemy of Britain and the United States, Bulgaria had never declared war on the Soviet Union; all attempts to send a volunteer force to the Eastern Front had failed and even war against the Anglo-Americans was both remote and virtually a token act, at least in Bulgarian eyes. The real Bulgarian effort lay in sending occupation troops into Yugoslav territory (Yugoslav Macedonia, which the Bulgarians regarded as theirs by right) as well as Greek Thrace and Macedonia, which was also considered rightfully to belong to Bulgaria. Though German pressure for naval and military facilities increased after 1942, German troops did not occupy the country and the Bulgarian government remained master in its own house, the king—Boris, who died in August 1943—resisting all and any German pressure to involve Bulgaria in the war against the Soviet Union. Of the right-wing extremists who were not so averse to an anti-Bolshevik crusade, General Lukov was the most important in the General Staff, but he was assassinated in February 1942. Pro-German policies persisted within the government; Bulgaria supplied Germany with raw materials and foodstuffs and Bulgarian troops did indirectly aid the German effort by supplying occupation troops, yet none would go to war against the Soviet Union, whose diplomats remained on the spot in Sofia.

The underground political opposition, a coalition that was reputed to have its origins in talks in 1941 between the Communists and the Agrarians, finally assumed the name of the 'Fatherland Front'. As early as 1942 in his broadcasts from the Soviet Union Dimitrov found much to praise in the idea of this political association, which would be at once an inter-party group and the force behind the Bulgarian resistance movement. Four parties—Communists, Left-Wing Agrarians, the 'Zveno Party' (republicans and socialists) and the Social Democrats—finally forged this loose political alliance, which came to enjoy both the support of the Soviet Union and the approval of the Western powers, at least in broadcasts beamed to Bulgaria. The Front also overlapped with other political organizations, the Democratic Party and the Right-Wing Agrarians, who shared a common anti-German viewpoint but were not members of the 'Fatherland Front' coalition. It was the Front, however, that exercised the main control over the Bulgarian partisans, and it was the Communists who provided the underground organization necessary to start up and to pursue effective resistance. Yet neither the Front's political leaders nor the partisan units themselves could organize a national liberation movement on a large scale, if only because there was no overwhelming German presence to galvanize the country to fervent resistance. The partisan bands turned instead against their own countrymen, the police and in a few cases the army itself. Operating in small groups, they raided villages, killed officials and harangued the villagers, frequently destroying official records; trains carrying supplies to Germany were prime targets, but the very paucity of factories made industrial sabotage an isolated business.

The partisans' forces in Bulgaria remained small, never rising above 15–18,000 men (organized finally into eleven brigades and thirty-eight detachments)—though by adducing the strength of their 'helpers', this figure is boosted to over 200,000; that army, however, was a wraith and a propaganda fiction. Nevertheless, the raids and incursions of the partisans stung the government to mounting frenzy. In the autumn of 1943, after the death of the king and by authority of the new Regency Council, fresh and powerful forces were thrown against the partisans in campaigns conducted with ferocity and efficiency and involving the Bulgarian army. Fifteen thousand men of the *gendarmerie* equipped with heavy weapons, 30,000 men of the police, 8,000 forest wardens and four army divisions hunted the partisans down, a measure which only served to increase the unpopularity of the pro-German government. The growing turbulence also attracted outside aid, from the British and the Yugoslav partisans, who helped the Bulgarians operating in the frontier area, and at a very late stage from the Russians, who dropped arms and ammunition at the request of the 'Main Staff of the National Liberation Army'.

Late in the spring of 1944 the Bulgarians started out of their political dream-world: the Russians were closing in. A new government under Bagrianov, one much less professedly pro-German, took over from the Bozhilov cabinet and adopted a more lenient policy towards the partisans (or at least the hostages taken for them), as well as modifying the prevailing anti-Jewish measures. This occurred just as a Soviet diplomatic offensive aimed at Bulgaria began to take effect, and it remained for Bagrianov to solve this acutely difficult problem. On 17 April a Soviet official note to the Bulgarians had drawn 'attention' to Bulgaria's aid to Germany and to the German use of the ports of Varna, Burgas and Ruschuk. This had been followed by another note on 26 April demanding the opening of Soviet consulates in these towns, and by yet a third note—peremptory in tone—delivered on 18 May, pointing out that without satisfaction of the Soviet demands 'it will be impossible to maintain relations with Bulgaria, since this is a state which helps and deliberately helps Hitlerite Germany in the war against the Soviet Union'. The next day Bozhilov's government retired from the scene and Bagrianov took office, a shuffle which the Russians seem to have considered nothing more than a manoeuvre. It took Bagrianov more than two months to frame a reply to the Soviet demands and then the outcome, presented to the Russians on 29 July, promised merely a 'considered' approach to the Soviet request. In turn, the Soviet reply of 12 August brushed aside the question of consulates and counselled the Bulgarians to think of their position—the only way out of 'the blind alley' was to break with Germany: 'the Soviet Government is asking the Bulgarian government whether it is ready to make the break with Germany.'

If Bagrianov thought that a soft answer might turn away Russian wrath, he was mistaken. His speech of 17 August, promising a programme of reform and stressing the Bulgarian desire for peace, struck the Russians as sheer demagoguery. Nor did his assurance to the Soviet plenipotentiary in Sofia that Bulgaria would break with Germany at the first favourable opportunity—though not at the price of precipitating an armed clash—cut much ice with the Russians. The Red Army stood poised for the Jassy–Kishinev operation and, given any success, Soviet troops should soon be on the Danube. What then followed in Bulgaria was of necessity overshadowed by the course of military operations in Rumania, with the Bulgarians forced to do something to head off what looked like impending disaster. Whatever complacency existed about Russian indulgence born of long historical association or Slav kinship was shattered, not least on the day when King Michael took Rumania out of the war.

It was the turn of the Fatherland Front to act. On 24 August the Front demanded that the government hand over power, a demand that Bagrianov's government refused outright, though it promised the Front a few seats in the cabinet, an offer that was duly spurned. The pro-Western and the pro-Soviet politicians now tried each in their own way to advance their separate causes. Bagrianov decided to send emissaries to Cairo to sue for peace with the Western powers (with whom Bulgaria was officially at war); Stoicho Moshanov and Colonel Zhelezkov were dispatched on this mission, though they did not reach Cairo until the end of the month (30 August). It was necessary to hold off both the Russians and the Fatherland Front, though the Bulgarian government had left everything much too late. On 26 August the Bulgarian government officially informed the Soviet plenipotentiary in Sofia that Bulgaria would now conform to 'full neutrality', that German troops crossing from Rumania would be disarmed according to the Hague Convention and that the German government had been asked to remove its troops, failing which they would be disarmed. That same evening Sofia radio informed the populace that Bulgaria had entered into contact with those states with whom Bulgaria was presently at war (Britain and the United States), while maintaining 'a state of neutrality' towards the Soviet–German conflict.

The Regency Council, desperately anxious to light upon some formula that would maximize Bulgaria's supposed advantages, proposed joint consultations with all the opposition parties, pro-Western (such as Gichev and Muraviev of the Right Agrarians) or pro-Soviet from the ranks of the Fatherland Front. Whatever the seriousness of the intention to form a joint government, however, it all came to nothing, precisely because the Fatherland Front refused to participate, an outcome that gravely disturbed the pro-Western moderates who would have felt safer with some communist representation, the better perhaps to fend off the Russians. The Front, however, had already decided on insurrection, the Central Committee circular No. 4 of the Bulgarian Party announcing on 26 August that 'for Bulgaria the twelfth hour has come!' In his letter of 27 August to the Bulgarian Central Committee, the Fatherland Front and the Staff of the National

Liberation Army—a text transmitted by radio—Dimitrov urged concentration of all 'democratic and progressive forces' around the Fatherland Front, the disarming of German units, the summoning of the people to the struggle against 'the Hitlerites and their agents', the establishment of the greatest freedom of action for the 'National Committees' of the Fatherland Front, and finally the creation of a state of readiness to pass over to the side of the Red Army, the army of liberation from 'the German yoke'. While Moshanov argued in Cairo, the Fatherland Front issued its own sixteen-point manifesto, demanding a break with Germany and friendship with the Soviet Union, the cessation of all military operations and the withdrawal of Bulgarian troops from Greece and Yugoslavia, and the restoration of all civil rights within the country.

On 30 August a *TASS* announcement vigorously denied 'rumours' that the Soviet Union recognized Bulgarian 'neutrality' in the form or on the terms stipulated by the Bulgarian government. Side by side with this semi-official and somewhat ominous announcement, a Soviet note delivered the same day to the Bulgarian government referred to 'confirmed reports' of German troops using Bulgaria as a means of access to Rumania where 'Soviet troops are located', an attitude on the part of the Bulgarians that could only be regarded as 'direct aid to the Germans in their war against the Soviet Union'. In the most peremptory terms the Soviet government demanded termination of this transit. Within twenty-four hours the Bagrianov government toppled, to be replaced by one formed by Muraviev representing the 'democratic opposition'—parties (like the Right-Wing Agrarians) that were by no means enamoured of Bulgaria's pro-German course but which also out of persistent mistrust refused to join the Fatherland Front. The advent of the Muraviev government thus brought 'pro-Western' and 'pro-Soviet' elements face to face. For both, time was running out, but the advantage turned increasingly in favour of the latter, for the Red Army was now almost concentrated on the Bulgarian border.

Muraviev's last attempt on 4 September to manage the kind of extrication he favoured failed within hours; the government statement made that day included a denunciation of the Tripartite Pact and the Anti-Comintern Pact, a declaration that Bulgarian troops would be pulled out of Axis-occupied territories and a commitment to speed up talks with the British and Americans in order to bring about an armistice. Bulgarian policy was one of firm and unconditional neutrality in the Soviet–German war. As for a final rupture with Germany, this would undoubtedly come if German troops on Bulgarian territory refused to be disarmed. Muraviev thus withdrew Bulgaria from the war against the Anglo-Americans and promised neutrality to the Soviet Union. But this did not suffice—indeed, it was the reverse of Moscow's preference, since it excluded the Soviet Union from a direct act of peace-making. The next day, without consulting its allies, the Soviet Union promptly declared war on Bulgaria, citing as justification Muraviev's declaration of neutrality which was nothing less than '*de facto* waging of war in the camp of Germany against the Soviet Union'. With frantic speed

Muraviev informed the Soviet Legation in Sofia during the night of 6 September that the Bulgarian government had severed relations with Germany—for that seemed the nub of the matter—and promptly asked Moscow for an armistice. But again Muraviev was baulked: Moscow pointed to the Bulgarian public statement about seeking an armistice of the Russians, yet 'nothing was said about a break with Germany'. Convinced of Bulgarian 'perfidy', Moscow stood by its declaration of war. The Fatherland Front meanwhile prepared its final plans for a *coup d'état*.

During the first few days of September Tolbukhin's armies closed on the Rumanian–Bulgarian frontier: 46th Army moved along the Giurgiu–Silistra sector, 57th and 37th Armies with two mechanized corps (4th Guards and 7th) occupied the sector between the Danube and the Black Sea. Tolbukhin, now a Marshal of the Soviet Union (like Malinovskii, who was also promoted for his part in the Jassy–Kishinev operation), disposed of twenty-eight divisions with 169,000 infantrymen. The Bulgarian army, deploying five armies and two corps of 'occupation forces', could field 450,000 men; eleven divisions were on 'occupation duties' in Yugoslavia and Greece, with one corps administration in Yugoslavia (together with the headquarters of 5th Army) and the other in Greece. Late in August Stalin sent Marshal Zhukov down to 3rd Ukrainian Front to supervise the operations aimed against Bulgaria. Zhukov's first stop was at Fetesti to discuss general Front co-ordination with Marshal Timoshenko. Zhukov had already talked with Dimitrov about developments in the Bulgarian situation and at the end of July, when the Jassy–Kishinev operation was undergoing its final scrutiny, Tolbukhin and Zheltov—on Stalin's recommendation—also talked with Dimitrov about the problem of Bulgaria. The plan worked out by Tolbukhin's command for the invasion of Bulgaria called for 46th Army to advance in the direction of Esechoi–Kubrat, 57th Army towards Kocmar–Shumen and 37th towards Dobrich–Provadiya, while the mechanized corps struck towards Karnobat–Burgas.

While Tolbukhin's front made its last preparations, the partisans inside Bulgaria were rushing to form the 1st Division of the 'National Liberation Army', a task made almost impossible by the shortage of weapons. Early in September the Bulgarian Party Central Committee and the 'Main Staff' of the Revolutionary Army sought the help of 3rd Ukrainian Front: on 4 September seventy-five Soviet transport planes dropped rifles, machine-guns and ammunition to the Bulgarian partisans in the area of Kalna, thereby providing the 1st Division with weapons. Three days later this division began its march on Sofia. During the morning of 8 September Tolbukhin's armies began their operations against Bulgaria and the first Soviet units crossed the frontier. It was as Dimitrov had forecast—no fighting and no war. Though perhaps the 'bread and salt' was a romantic exaggeration, Bulgarian soldiers and civilians turned out to greet the Red Army with banners and placards—in Silistra the townspeople came on to the streets in their best clothes and the fire-brigade hosed the streets clean for the Red Army's procession. Not a shot was exchanged between Soviet and

Bulgarian units, whereupon Zhukov telephoned Stalin, who advised against disarming the Bulgarian troops—'let them be while they are waiting for orders from their government'.

The first Soviet units crossed the Bulgarian frontier at 11 am on the morning of 8 September; twelve hours later, after driving through unusual heat for the time of the year, advance detachments were well south of the Tutrakan–Sakalli–Emirkei line, over forty miles into Bulgaria and still driving south-west. In the absence of any resistance, Tolbukhin ordered 4th Guards Mechanized Corps and a motorized rifle brigade to move off at once, though their orders called for them to advance as from 9 September; at 3 pm the motorized infantry reached the port of Varna, followed by Soviet marines brought in first by aircraft and then landed from three motor-torpedo boats. At dawn the next day (9 September) a thousand men from 83rd Marine Brigade descended on Varna, where Bulgarian warships offered no resistance and German naval units in the port scuttled themselves on the orders of the German commander. Further south Soviet marines landed at Burgas, with more men brought in by aircraft. By the evening Tolbukhin's right and centre were already astride the line—running from Rushcuk on the Danube to Palatitsa, Karnobat and Burgas—specified as the first objective in the Front plan (which laid down 12 September as the deadline for the advance, after which Soviet movement would halt until a decision had been made about further operations, depending on the course of the insurrection planned inside Bulgaria). The orders about not crossing this line without 'special authorization' nevertheless still held; when a mobile unit of 31st Rifle Corps (46th Army) did push on, the army commander received an immediate reprimand from Front HQ and a categorical order to bring the unit back 'to the line specified'.

At 2100 hours on 9 September Soviet troops in Bulgaria received orders to suspend all military operations: the Fatherland Front had seized power inside Bulgaria and the war was at an end. During the early hours of 9 September the Front carried out a smooth and silent *coup* in Sofia; partisan units together with 'patriotic' elements of the Bulgarian army seized post offices, the radio station and government buildings, including the War Ministry. The police, who did not venture out of their barracks, were disarmed. Further afield in the country almost 700 'National Committees' of the Fatherland Front began to take power into their own hands; the partisans moved down from the mountains, were handed arms and formed in many places a 'people's militia'. In the larger towns and cities strikes had already begun some time before the *coup* and by 8 September the Fatherland Front had set up its own administration in a few towns. The Muraviev government fell and was replaced by one headed by Colonel Kimon Georgiev (former premier of the Military League government set up in 1934), with two Communists (Tarpeshev and Yugov), Petkov (Agrarian), two Social Democrats and two 'independents' in the new government. Already at 6.25 am on 9 September the government announced its programme, one based largely on that of the Fatherland Front—a break with Germany, friendship for the Soviet

Union, the restoration of civil liberties. Later in the day Georgiev's government decreed the arrest of the Regency Council and all 'pro-German members' of the previous government. That evening Dimitrov, still in Moscow, asked Tolbukhin's HQ to receive a 'plenipotentiary delegate' of the Fatherland Front government, Ganev of the Bulgarian Communist Party. Ganev duly arrived and 'reported' to the Soviet command on the course of the insurrection, at the same time voicing his fears about German Army Group F attacking Sofia, pointing to the German concentration at Vidin north-west of Sofia and also in Yugoslavia at Nis and Bela-Palanka. For Tolbukhin, who was about to lose 46th Army and 7th Mechanized Corps to Malinovskii fighting in Transylvania, this was not perhaps the best of news, though it provided a ready justification for moving on Sofia. Bulgarian partisans were sent to cover the western frontier, and the new government 'requested' the Soviet government to authorize 3rd Ukrainian Front to organize Red Army and Bulgarian Army 'co-operation'. On 13 September the *Stavka* issued a formal directive to this effect, assigning Col.-Gen. Biryuzov (Front chief of staff) directly to Sofia to handle this Soviet–Bulgarian military effort.

In the countryside at large, within hundreds of small towns and villages, the partisans and local Communists now set up 'national committees', establishing a rough administration and meting out rough-and-ready justice, revenging themselves on the officials and policemen who had harried them in the past years. Though each committee was supposed to include representatives of all the Fatherland Front parties, only the Communists had maintained an effective provincial organization, with the result that Communists inevitably dominated the local committees, the Agrarians and Social Democrats falling a long way behind. In Sofia the partisans who moved into the capital and the 'People's Militia' hastily flung together after the *coup* enjoyed their new authority to the full, taking over private property and commandeering cars, but there was little of the vengeance visited upon the countryside. Only at the beginning of 1945, with the opening of the trial of war criminals and the arraignment of the Regents, members of all governments since 1941 (including the Muraviev government, for all its attempt to bring Bulgaria out of the war) and assorted political lackeys, did the People's Court mete out its own retribution. By that time the Fatherland Front had cracked wide open, setting in motion a running battle between the Communists and the Agrarians, but in September the profusion of partisans and committees served to spread the power and influence of the Front right across the country, even into the most isolated areas.

To secure Sofia against all surprises, Tolbukhin proposed to advance one corps (the 34th from 57th Army) with all speed; Soviet troops closed in on the Bulgarian capital from the north-west and the south-west, blocking the main roads. On 17 September the Bulgarian army came under formal Soviet command, duly arranged with the Bulgarian General Staff by Biryuzov. Meanwhile the planning of the Trans-Danubian campaign had just begun, the sense of urgency dictated by German troop movements through Yugoslav territory so recently occupied by Bulgarian troops (who received orders to go over to the Yugoslav partisans) and by German troops who had pulled out of Greece concentrating in the area of Nis and Belgrade. On 20 September Tolbukhin received a fresh *Stavka* directive setting out the lines on which 3rd Ukrainian Front was to regroup: Soviet troops in the area of the Bulgarian capital were designated 'the independent Sofia operational group'; 57th Army (with two corps) was to move up to the Bulgarian–Yugoslav frontier towards the Negotin–Belogradchik sector; 37th Army would make for the Sliven–Yambol area and south of Burgas, with 4th Guards Mechanized Corps concentrating at Yambol.

With this deployment the *Stavka* intended to move one Soviet army into north-western Bulgaria and to mount an operation aimed at Belgrade in co-operation with Bulgarian and Yugoslav forces: the southerly concentration was intended to cover the Soviet southern flank and to guard against 'any unexpected moves from the direction of Turkey'. In view of the distances and difficulties involved—Tolbukhin's forces were spread all the way back into Rumania—this redeployment would require some time; much of 3rd Ukrainian Front was either on the roads or shifting men and equipment down the Danube, with almost 600 kilometres to cover before the deployment on the Yugoslav frontier could be complete. An 'operational group' of 17th Air Army arrived at Sofia aerodrome on 14 September and in the next week two aviation divisions installed themselves at airfields in the area of Lom, Sofia and Plovdiv. For the forthcoming Belgrade operation, the *Stavka* proposed to commit almost the entire strength of 3rd Ukrainian Front, left-flank units of Malinovskii's 2nd Ukrainian Front, 17th Air Army and elements of 5th Air Army (a total of thirteen air divisions) and the Danube Flotilla, altogether nineteen rifle divisions from 46th and 57th Armies, over 500 tanks and SP guns supported by 2,000 aircraft. For operations aimed at Nis, Leskovac, Kocana and Velec, the Soviet command intended to use three Bulgarian armies (1st, 2nd and 4th, with a strength of nine divisions); the Yugoslav National Liberation Army would employ two 'army groups'—four corps—with Peko Dapcevic's 1st Proletarian and 12th Corps fighting their way into Belgrade and Koca Popovic's 13th and 14th Corps linked up with Soviet troops coming in from Rumania and Bulgaria.

The overall Soviet plan committed Tolbukhin's 3rd Ukrainian Front to an attack aimed at Belgrade and to the clearing of the eastern regions of Yugoslavia, with the main thrust coming from the region of Vidin and directed towards Palanka–Belgrade: Malinovskii received instructions to use his left-flank units in an attack aligned from Vrsac to Pancevo and Belgrade. The *Stavka* proposed to start the Red Army's attack at the end of September, with Yugoslav operations aimed at Belgrade timed for 9–10 October, the Bulgarian attack on Nis timed for 8 October and the additional Yugoslav operations in this southerly area set for 10–11 October. Meanwhile the German divisions from Army Groups F (Yugoslavia) and E (Greece and Albania) remained in positions that became steadily more dangerously exposed, their lines of communication threatened most immediately by the defection of Bulgaria and the deterioration of the situation in Yugoslavia. As a precaution against Bulgaria abandoning Germany, Hitler had ordered the manning of a new 'front' running along the Yugoslav–Bulgarian border, and proposed to fight off invasion with the troops of Group 'Serbia', but his elaborate plans to reverse the Bulgarian *coup* proved to be nothing but military fantasies. Rumania and Bulgaria were irretrievably lost, though this did not prevent the *Führer* from clinging to the Balkans, or pieces of it, such as the chrome-ore mines of northern Greece to which he detached a strong force of *Luftwaffe* personnel; orders for the final evacuation of Greece, southern Albania and southern Macedonia he delayed until the beginning of October.

During the first half of September Hitler persuaded himself that all was not lost in the Balkans. The entry of Soviet troops into Bulgaria could only speed the prospect of an Anglo-Soviet collision, for it was not inconceivable that the Red Army would itself strike down to the Aegean and make for the Dardanelles, in which event the British would advance to bar the way to the Russians—and in such a situation Army Group E might act as a buffer or screen, all with British approval. German troops would constitute 'a kind of police force'—*eine Art Polizeitruppe*—and would hold the line against Bolshevism both within and beyond Greece. But the devastating air attack by British and American aircraft on German airfields and the transports earmarked to lift German troops from the Aegean islands put paid on 15 September to any hopes of British 'disinterest' in German dispositions; it could only be assumed within the *Führer's* staff that the British made their attack on the retreating German army 'conditional' on the Russians denying themselves the Aegean and Dardanelles. By this time also it was plain that 'Possibility No. 2'—a Soviet thrust to Nis, coupled with an attack aimed at Belgrade and into Croatia, or north-westwards to Budapest and the Vienna basin—represented real Soviet intentions.

For all the eager German scrutiny, no sign of Soviet 'military interest' in the Aegean could be discerned. On the contrary, everything now pointed to the dangerous situation building up in southern Serbia and Macedonia, presenting a 'mortal threat' to Army Group E lines of communication; instead of striking on to the south, as Hitler had first anticipated, Soviet troops in Bulgaria were now swinging north-west towards the Yugoslav frontier, while the Soviet command in Sofia piled on the pressure to put the Bulgarian army in the field, stiffening Bulgarian divisions with 'highly experienced' Soviet officers, remedying the shortages of equipment and clamping on commissar control, all with a speed that plainly disconcerted the Germans.

During the first week in September—on the sixth, at 1700 hours, according to Soviet battle reports—Red Army troops liberated the first few yards of Yugoslav territory. The 4th Independent Motorcycle Regiment (6th Tank Army) had reached Turnu–Severin on 4 September, forced the Danube in the ensuing twenty-four hours and cleared enemy troops out of the area of Kladovo, after which a section of Soviet riflemen entered a Yugoslav village. With the prospect of the Red Army rolling forward into Yugoslavia, the time had come for Tito to act, for Soviet troops would be entering the territory of an ally, not some craven and cringing ex-German satellite. The master now of a formidable partisan army which had already liberated sizeable areas of Yugoslavia from German occupation and torn great gaps in the German divisions holding down the country—the Yugoslav estimate of German losses in the latest offensive to wipe out the partisans amounted to 43,000 officers and men killed, wounded, or taken prisoner—Tito prudently resolved to discuss the terms of the Red Army's entry into Yugoslavia with the Soviet command, even with Stalin himself. It was a proposal submitted in good time and well in advance of the inevitable Soviet entry into Yugoslavia, for at Tito's prompting General Korneyev flew to Moscow at the beginning of July to sound 'the Soviet government' about a possible visit. Early in September Stalin presumably agreed; on hearing of this confirmation, General Korneyev expressed his satisfaction to Tito, but advised him to keep the time of departure 'strictly secret', one result of which was to enrage the British when Tito's 'disappearing act' was discovered. Few Yugoslavs and none of the Soviet military mission learned of the impending visit; the Soviet pilot Mikhailov, flying the Dakota from Bari to the airfield on the island of Vis, then under British control, knew nothing about the passengers he was to take aboard. Shortly before midnight on 21 September, having evaded the RAF security guards, the Soviet Dakota carrying Tito, Korneyev, Ivan Milutinovic (from Yugoslav Supreme Headquarters), Mitar Bakic and Tito's dog Tigar suitably muffled in a sack, left Vis for the Soviet lines in Rumania.

This 'spiriting away' of Tito—*ischesnovenie,* as General Korneyev called it subsequently—went without a hitch (though Molotov later attributed all the fuss about secrecy to Tito himself and dismissed the furore as something to be expected in any dealings with a 'Balkan peasant'). From Tolbukhin's Front HQ Marshal Tito, now wearing a high Soviet decoration—the Order of Suvorov, First Class— flew on to Moscow accompanied by an escort of Soviet fighters. The style (and the uniform) were a signal contrast to his last visit to the Soviet Union in 1940, when he used a forged passport and an assumed name, his business that of a Comintern agent representing a far from successful illegal communist party which was held to be of little account.

The first meeting between Tito and Stalin proved to be something of an encounter. Tito himself described it as being 'very cool'. Though the details of joint Soviet–Yugoslav operations, plus the form of Soviet aid to the partisans, were worked out in some depth, if Stalin assumed that the Red Army would simply crash into Yugoslavia and bring all the 'anti-fascist' forces under immediate and unquestionable Soviet command, then he was speedily disabused by Tito, who spoke not merely for himself but also for the National Committee of Liberation—about which Stalin and Djilas had wrangled a few weeks earlier—

and for Supreme Headquarters. The public statement issued in Moscow on 28 September referred to the Soviet 'request' to the Yugoslav National Liberation Committee, which in turn consented to the 'temporary entry of Soviet troops into Yugoslav territory', with the proviso that the Red Army would leave Yugoslav soil once the 'operational task' was completed. The Soviet command also 'accepted the condition advanced by the Yugoslav side' that the civil administration in areas containing Soviet troops would remain in Yugoslav hands. For the forthcoming Belgrade operation Stalin promised Tito a tank corps and evidently agreed to the withdrawal of Soviet troops once the Yugoslav capital had been liberated. The Yugoslav partisans were to remain under Marshal Tito's direct command, and the Russians were specifically denied the exercise of any power once they crossed into Yugoslavia.

The temperature rose uncomfortably and the tension increased visibly when Stalin insisted on advising Tito (whom he addressed as 'Walter', using Tito's pre-war Comintern pseudonym) about what course he should adopt in Yugoslavia's internal political affairs. Tito's wartime telegrams to Moscow had already angered Stalin, not least the signal reading 'If you cannot send us assistance, then at least do not hamper us . . .', which put Stalin into a terrible rage. Now Tito talked back to Stalin in his own office, astonishing Molotov, Malenkov and Beria with his defiance of 'the boss'. With the atmosphere already strained to the point of becoming 'painful', Stalin suffered another rebuff when he tried to urge Tito to take King Peter back. After listening to Tito's passionately indignant outburst denouncing the 'corruption and terror' practised by the Karageorgevic dynasty, for which the people hated them, Stalin fell silent and then spoke quite tersely— 'take him back temporarily, and then you can slip a knife in his back at a suitable moment'. Whatever the eventual outcome of this line of conversation, it was interrupted by Molotov bringing news of a British landing in Yugoslavia, an item that brought Tito to his feet with a cry that this was impossible, whereupon Stalin rounded on him and proclaimed it 'a fact'. A moment later Tito explained that the 'British invasion' was evidently the arrival of the artillery he had requested from General Alexander, but Stalin pressed him for an answer about his attitude 'if the British really forced a landing': the Yugoslavs would fight, Tito announced quite unequivocally.

By now in a thoroughly unpleasant mood, Stalin telephoned Malinovskii, who was trying to smash his way into northern Transylvania, berating the newly promoted Marshal for his slow progress and scoffing at his request for more armour—'my grandma would know how to fight with tanks. It's time you moved.' Having worked off a little of his spleen, Stalin then invited Tito to his *dacha* for a supper that turned into a drinking bout, much to Tito's discomfort and self-disgust when, at one stage, he made for the fresh air in a surge of sickness. It was no consolation that Beria, who followed him through the door, dismissed it all as of no consequence and as just one of the facts of life. When the alcoholic mists lifted and cold day came once again, neither Stalin nor Tito could claim that their meeting had been either mutually congenial or wholly successful; the overbearing Stalin and the impenitently insubordinate Tito came into direct collision, though from his sessions with Milovan Djilas Stalin must have gathered that he was dealing with 'Balkan peasants' of more distinctive breed. But for the moment, both men chose to nurse their grudges in silence and in secret.

On his way back to Yugoslavia from the Soviet Union Marshal Tito stopped at Craiova, which became a temporary command post for the Yugoslav National Liberation Army and also the site of joint Soviet–Yugoslav–Bulgarian talks during the first week in October. The preliminary phase of the Soviet offensive into Yugoslavia had already begun late in September, with Akimenko's 75th Corps (on Tolbukhin's left flank) fighting its way towards the Yugoslav frontier from the Danube bend, a series of actions that cost the corps 340 dead and 900 wounded for nine days of operations; on 28 September 75th Corps reached the frontier and Gorshkov's gunboats from the Danube Flotilla moved up into the area of Negotin, the first Soviet objective, which finally fell on the afternoon of 30 September. The road into Yugoslavia was now open and the chances of a Soviet–Yugoslav link-up much increased, though on that same day Tito sent a special signal to his 1st Army Group with instructions not to start out on the proposed 'Belgrade operation' without his express authorization.

Though Soviet troops were now on the move in the opening phase of the Belgrade attack, much still remained to be done to co-ordinate the actions of the Russian, Yugoslav and Bulgarian forces involved in the whole offensive. Under orders from the *Stavka*, Biryuzov flew into Craiova on the morning of 5 October, where, in addition to Marshal Tito, a Bulgarian delegation headed by Dobri Terpeshev of the Fatherland Front waited to complete the political formalities for the tripartite operation. High on the agenda was the conclusion of a Yugoslav–Bulgarian armistice. Though broached earlier and pressed by the Russians, the Yugoslav command insisted that they needed more time in which to persuade their own people, who had suffered drastically at the hands of the Bulgarian occupation troops, that this was a 'new' Bulgaria and its army an ally rather than a cruel enemy. The Craiova meeting also provided the occasion for a review of the final attack plans involving the troops of all three nations; none, according to Biryuzov, disputed that Bulgarian troops were needed, and no one wished to brand the Bulgarian people with 'the mark of Cain', holding them responsible for 'the criminal acts of the former royalist government'. The talks lasted the whole day. Biryuzov gave details of the Soviet strength to be committed, Terpeshev the Bulgarian and Tito the Yugoslav strength. For operations in the area of Nis, Leskovac and Belets the Bulgarians proposed to use three armies—1st, 2nd and 4th, nine divisions in all, plus three brigades (one of them armoured)—on Yugoslav territory; Tito in turn supplied the latest information on the strength and deployment of his two 'army groups' committed to the offensive.

It was plain from the outset that the Yugoslavs were woefully short of weapons and in desperate need of heavy weapons. The political sections of 3rd Ukrainian Front submitted reports earlier in September about the need to arm the Yugoslav units and stressed partisan expectations of receiving Soviet arms. On 7 September the State Defence Committee (*GKO*) in Moscow granted formal permission for 500 men of the Yugoslav National Liberation Army to be trained as tank-crews in the Soviet Union, but this did not solve the immediate question of the Yugoslav divisions thrown in against well-equipped German troops. Nearer the front the Soviet command agreed to stockpile equipment and ammunition for twelve Yugoslav divisions in the region of Craiova and Sofia; this prompted a Yugoslav request for Soviet instructors to be sent to Yugoslav units, while with the approval of 'the Soviet government' two Soviet air divisions (with an 'air-base' contingent) were earmarked for service in Yugoslavia. Slowly at first, but speeding up in the ensuing weeks, Soviet weapons found their way to the troops under Tito's command—100,000 rifles, 68,000 machine-guns, over 800 anti-tank and field guns of various calibres, 491 aircraft, 65 tanks and equipment for seven field hospitals and four surgical units.

By the evening of 5 October, when the conversation came down to reminiscences and the mood turned to mutual back-slapping, the prime business of the Craiova meeting was concluded; Terpeshev got his armistice and thus refurbished the honour of Bulgaria, Biryuzov pocketed the tripartite military agreement now signed and sealed, while Tito could be well satisfied that this self-same document safeguarded the independent status of each national army and in no way infringed national sovereignty. Meanwhile General Korneyev, that obedient if somewhat bibulous officer, received instructions from the *Stavka* to pass on details about the Belgrade operation to the Yugoslav command, though at this stage—before the joint plan was mutually agreed—Tito also sent an order to his 1st Army Group not to move any units towards Belgrade without express authorization. But the day after the signing of the agreements, 6 October, Tito sent another signal from Craiova instructing Peko Dapcevic of 1st Army Group that his units should now move on Obrenovac (south-west of Belgrade)—the Belgrade offensive was now fully agreed with the Red Army and the Yugoslav command must wait for Tito's final directive: '. . . the whole of your [1st] group with a strength of nine divisions will take part in the Belgrade offensive. It is desirable that our troops enter Belgrade first, and the Russians are of the same opinion.' Dapcevic attacked at once that same day, but the Yugoslav troops were immediately pushed back, after which they waited another four days before renewing their push.

After the capture of Negotin, Gagen's 57th Army (with 75th Corps attached) fought its way for a week through the eastern Serbian uplands and towards the river Morava; on 4 October 75th Corps finally made contact with a Yugoslav brigade from the 25th Division and Gagen received orders to co-ordinate the operations of two Soviet rifle corps (75th and 68th) with the two Yugoslav divisions in immediate contact with the Red Army, with the aim of cutting off the German escape route. At the centre of his front Gagen made good progress, but on the flanks German resistance proved to be stiff and effective; along the mountain roads German troops from Group Müller held on to slow the Soviet advance, but again at the centre 68th Corps ground its way to the river Morava by 8 October and seized a bridgehead in the area of Velika Plana. General Shkodunovich's success with 68th Corps in reaching the Morava galvanized Tolbukhin's command into action; Tolbukhin himself doubted if tanks and artillery could negotiate the gorges and ravines in due time, but his staff assured him that they would make it and on the morning of 9 October 4th Guards Mechanized Corps received its orders to pass through the gap punched by 68th Corps. These orders to 4th Guards specified that 'not later than noon on 14.10' Belgrade must be taken and held until the arrival of 57th Infantry Army: the tanks were to move off for Belgrade itself on 11 October, which meant first heaving them over 120 miles of rugged country up to the start line for the attack.

General V.I. Zhdanov's 4th Guards Mechanized, with 17,000 men and 180 tanks, was presently deployed in the area of Archar, a small Bulgarian village south of Vidin, having crossed almost the whole of Bulgaria from east to west after receiving orders on 30 September to move up to the Yugoslav frontier. Zhdanov decided to advance his corps towards the Morava in a single column through the heights, with 'powerful combat echelons' along the whole length of the column; 36th Guards Tank Brigade took the lead, supported by special groups of tommy-gunners mounted on tanks to take on any opposition encountered *en route*. Once committed to the main action, the corps would split into two echelons, a main attack force and the 'artillery anti-tank reserve': three brigades operating on the left flank were to be put in the main attack. The bulk of the fuel and supplies needed would be carried by the forward units, loaded on to the tanks and self-propelled guns, hampering their manoeuvrability but ensuring at least that they did not run short of fuel and ammunition; the tank-crews and riflemen were issued with two days' rations. The only other way to shift 2,000 tons of fuel, 800 tons of ammunition and 400 tons of supplies was to use 1,600 two-ton lorries, but since 4th Mechanized did not possess transport on anything like this scale, it had to be loaded on the tanks. By the evening of 10 October 4th Mechanized had completed much of its mountain march and was concentrating in the area of Petrovac, preparing to attack on the following day in the direction of Palanka–Belgrade.

Once at Velika Plana, Tolbukhin's columns cut the Nis–Belgrade railway line and the motor-road: on 8 October Marshal Tolbukhin ordered General Stanchev's 2nd Bulgarian Army to start its attack aimed at Nis itself, an action co-ordinated with the 13th Corps of the Yugoslav National Liberation Army. While Tolbukhin smashed his way forward at the centre, splitting the German forces in two once Soviet troops reached the Morava, and as the Bulgarians started their attacks on the left, Malinovskii's 2nd Ukrainian Front on the right flank launched a fast-moving attack with Shlemin's 46th Army using three mobile columns operating north of Belgrade. Striking through Vrsac, 10th Rifle Corps brushed past weak German opposition and made for Pancevo, clearing it on 5 October.

Soviet troops were now only a few miles to the east of Belgrade, though the formidable stretch of the Danube still lay between them and the Yugoslav capital. During the next three days more units from 10th Corps closed in on Belgrade from the north and the north-east, establishing themselves along a broad sector of the Danube bank; further north, a column from 31st Rifle Corps struck into the great rolling plain of the Voivodina, making for Petrovgrad and the lower Tisza, while a third column—from 37th Rifle Corps—drove from the area of Timosoara towards Velika Kikinda, rolling up the units of 4th SS Division and a force of Hungarians in three days of continuous fighting. By the evening of 8 October Red Army troops, assisted in many places by the 'main Voivodina staff' of the Yugoslav army, had cleared all Yugoslav territory east of the Tisza from Kanjiza in the north to the source of the river Tisza, not many miles from Belgrade.

Malinovskii's armies were now in action along the entire length of the Tisza, from the area where this river runs into the Danube in the north to its source in the south; having cleared the valley of the Maros, Malinovskii turned at once for the Tisza, whose course lay right across the approaches to Budapest. The 'Debrecen operation', the revised line of advance decided upon when German troops blocked 2nd Ukrainian Front at Cluj, brought Soviet troops across the Hungarian frontier west and north of Arad on 5 October; Mako, directly ahead of Szeged, was captured within twenty-four hours and with every hour stronger Soviet forces were piling over the middle and lower reaches of the Tisza. Szeged was captured on 11 October, giving Malinovskii control of a major rail and road junction and one more crossing over the Tisza. Meanwhile 37th Corps, which had moved straight over the Yugoslav frontier and taken Velika Kikinda, also crossed the Tisza lower down at Senta and Stari Becej, swinging then a little to the north and liberating Subotica—the chief town of the Banat—in co-operation with those units that had taken Szeged not many hours before.

As Malinovskii swept across the plain to the north, Tolbukhin's columns were on the point of opening the battle for Belgrade from the south. Covered by elements of 68th Corps and 5th Independent Motorized Brigade, Zhdanov's tanks crossed the Morava by the morning of 12 October and started their advance in the direction of Topola and Mladenovac, to the south of Belgrade. The German command, desperate to hold its lines of communication with the south until its divisions pulled right out of Serbia and Macedonia, was determined to hold Belgrade against all comers, reinforcing the defence with every available man. No longer were the German troops fighting only partisans, staunch fighters but so often short of weapons and supplies; a Soviet Guards mechanized corps was closing on Belgrade, several Soviet rifle corps disposed of their own complement of heavy weapons, and to the north of Belgrade more Soviet tanks and artillery rolled in day after day. With Bulgarian and Yugoslav units advancing on Nis, and with the lines connecting Nis with Belgrade cut, the divisions of Army Group E could only swing away in their withdrawal through the valley of the Ibar; but at Kraljevo—a vital point of access for both the Ibar and Morava valleys—heavy fighting was already in progress. Everywhere German units fought with the greatest tenacity. They were fighting to stave off annihilation, and they knew it: along each road German commanders formed mobile and powerful 'screening forces' equipped with infantry, tanks and assault guns, allowing Soviet tanks to move up to point-blank range and then blasting them to pieces. Fighting off 4th Mechanized on the road leading through Markovac and Topola to Belgrade, German anti-tank gunners, supported by a few Tiger tanks or by groups of tommy-gunners in half-tracks, savaged the Soviet columns until they were themselves completely destroyed.

To spare the inhabitants of Belgrade the terrors of a major battle in the city, and to save the city itself as far as possible (though British and American bombers pounded it heavily in the raids of mid-April and May), Tolbukhin planned to head off the Germans falling back on Belgrade and to finish them off to the south. While Soviet aircraft harried the retreating German units, 4th Mechanized Corps, which had already linked up with the Yugoslav 1st Proletarian Corps at Velika Plana, swept on to the heights of Avala, ten miles south of the city; here Soviet tanks made contact with Peko Dapcevic's 1st Army Group. With Soviet tanks in the southern outskirts, the German front was split down the middle; units of Gagen's 57th Army surrounded a strong force of Army Group F south-east of Belgrade, and those German troops retreating towards the city now faced a full circle of Soviet divisions in position, with Malinovskii's 2nd Ukrainian Front to the north and east and Tolbukhin to the south and south-east. In Belgrade itself the German command put the city in a state of siege and mustered 22,000 men with a few dozen tanks in order to fight off attacks to the bitter end. To the south-east another force of 20,000 men was trying to smash its way into the city and to safety, struggling to escape Soviet encirclement at Pozarevac and further south at Kucevo. Still another force, 15,000 men in all, managed to break through the right flank of 57th Army, crossed the Morava and began moving along the southern bank of the Danube towards Belgrade, aiming for the bridge over the river Sava and thence to freedom towards the north-west.

The storming of Belgrade and the destruction of the German units trapped to the south-east occupied the week of 14–20 October. On the eve of the attack on the city Marshal Tito again reminded the Soviet command of his request to 'make it possible for troops of the Yugoslav National Liberation Army, supported by tanks and artillery, to be the first to enter Belgrade'. The Soviet plan for the assault involved a frontal attack on a narrow sector to break through the German defences and into the rear of the defenders, followed by a rush for the bridge over the river Sava, thus depriving the Germans of any chance to move up reinforcements or to escape to the north-west; 4th Guards Mechanized Corps supported by two rifle divisions would carry out the assault, with Gorshkov's gunboats fighting on the Danube. To get the Yugoslav troops into the city, Zhdanov instructed the commanders of 4th Mechanized to lift the men of 1st Proletarian Corps on to the Soviet tanks moving into and through the German defences.

In the small hours of 14 October Soviet guns fired off a short but intensive artillery barrage against the German positions, after which the assault on the Avala heights began, still under cover of darkness. During the course of the day Soviet and Yugoslav troops broke through this first line of defences. Once inside the city itself, Tolbukhin ordered Soviet units to avoid using their heavy weapons to blast their way through from building to building or from street to street, many of which had to be wrested from the Germans in hand-to-hand and close-quarter fighting. Behind the assault troops came the sappers—seven battalions—under orders to clear buildings of the thousands of mines or booby-traps, literally to clear the path for the Yugoslav authorities and military staffs to move in. As the street fighting intensified, by 16 October the Soviet–Yugoslav troops pressing towards the centre of the city were suddenly threatened to the rear by a strong force of Germans bearing down from the direction of Smederovo; if they gained the city limits they would provide substantial reinforcement for the defence. With Soviet troops turned to face south-east, this force of Germans was kept within encirclement and was finally wiped out on 19 October after rejecting a Soviet ultimatum to surrender. At Kragujevac another fierce battle raged to keep the Germans hemmed in.

Inside Belgrade with the Germans fighting desperately to hold each house, street and square, Soviet tanks, artillery and aircraft were continuously in action to flatten the defence. Gunboats of the Danube Flotilla also poured their fire into German strong-points and on 19 October seized the island of Ratno, severing the German escape route over the Sava and the Danube. On the evening of 20 October the Yugoslav 1st Proletarian Division fought its way along one of the main boulevards leading to the old Turkish fortress, the Kalemegdan; Yugoslav troops cleared it of Germans, and Soviet sappers cleared the mines, at which Peko Dapcevic and General Zhdanov of 4th Mechanized met and embraced to signal joint victory over Army Group F. Throughout Belgrade, Soviet and Yugoslav soldiers fired off their own victory salute, loosing off signal rockets to proclaim the end of the assault. German units were already falling back across the river Sava and making for Zemun, trying to break westwards; for the past two days Soviet aircraft had been attacking both Zemun and the concentrations of lorries spotted in the area. Hot on the heels of the retreating Germans came more Yugoslavs and Russians, who cleared Zemun on 22 October and then moved on north-westwards.

Further south at Kragujevac, German resistance also collapsed by the afternoon of 21 October, though here too German troops held on until the last possible moment, fighting to keep Soviet units away from the Kraljevo–Cacak–Sarajevo road, the last remaining trunk route for the German divisions on their way from

Greece, deprived by now of the Athens–Belgrade railway line. But at Kraljevo the 117th German Infantry Division was still fighting, a fiercely dogged action to win a few more hours though Soviet troops had already cut the Krusevac–Kraljevo railway line. The Morava valleys were now virtually closed to the retreating Germans: the *OKW* recognized that, with the Bulgarians in Nis and the Soviet–Yugoslav breakthrough to Belgrade, Army Group E was 'in fact cut off', with only the road running from Skopje through Mitrovica and Kraljevo on to Sarajevo still in use. Col.-Gen. Löhr 'never for a moment doubted' that the loss of this road and 'its key point of Kraljevo' meant catastrophe for the men under his command: to shunt them into the mountains of Albania and Montenegro meant almost certain death with winter fast coming on. Kraljevo had to be defended to the limit of German exertions. Immediate orders went out to fly one battalion of 22nd Infantry Division from Salonika (and a battalion from Rhodes) into Kraljevo, where *General der Infanterie* Müller took command of a motley group of German regiments unable to make their way out of the Soviet trap. Kraljevo had become the German *Schwerpunkt,* and Müller 'the very man' to fight a defensive battle with his highly variegated forces. Kraljevo continued to hold out for many more days and nights, while an additional screen for the Ibar valley was provided by the German command mobilizing Albanian units, stiffened where necessary with German troops.

Elsewhere, in groups large and small, the units of Army Group F were ground to pieces or taken prisoner: the battles in and around Belgrade cost the German army 15,000 dead and 9,000 prisoners. South and south-east of the city the last of the German anti-tank gunners and the infantrymen fought their last-ditch actions, waiting with no hope of escape to be blown apart by massed Russian guns. Inside Belgrade the Yugoslav partisans and the Red Army counted their dead; though justly proud of their part in liberating Belgrade, the partisans had suffered heavy casualties. On 22 October the bodies of Yugoslav and Soviet soldiers killed in the city were drawn in a massed procession through the gashed and scarred streets, a final journey to the communal graves. Somewhat later, in a Belgrade suburb not far from the site of the German concentration camp of Banjica, Marshal Tito held his victory parade for Yugoslav units; among the ragged soldiers but veteran units was the 'Belgrade battalion', which three years earlier had begun fighting in Serbia, had criss-crossed the whole of Yugoslavia in the many partisan campaigns and was now returning home, though with only two men of its original complement left in its ranks.

In the celebration parade held to salute the liberation of the city the Soviet 36th Guards Tank Brigade led off, the T-34 tanks rolling past the saluting base and then making straight for the temporary bridges over the Danube to drive northwards to Hungary, where 4th Mechanized was to join the coming battle for Budapest. More armour followed this first brigade, the drab-green T-34s spurting along the flat if bumpy roads of the Voivodina to the frontier in the north, followed by lorried infantry and the *Katyusha* rocket-launchers shrouded in canvas wraps. At a slower pace other Soviet infantry formations began to pull northwards from the more southerly reaches of Yugoslavia, though one Soviet rifle corps on the move—Lt.-Gen. G.P. Kotov's 13th—came in for some rough handling from American aircraft as it crossed the mountain road out of Nis; the American planes shot up Soviet aircraft on the local airfield while another group strafed the Soviet infantry columns, killing Kotov and a number of his men. Displaying recognition signs did nothing to diminish the American attacks, but— in the words of a Soviet commander who watched this melancholy incident— 'decisive measures' by the Russians finally did.

The 'Belgrade operation' was conducted and concluded more or less simultaneously with Soviet offensives aimed at Debrecen and Uzhorod, thus bringing all four Ukrainian fronts into action—the left flank of 1st Ukrainian and 4th Ukrainian Front (Uzhorod), 2nd Ukrainian Front (Debrecen), the left flank of 2nd Ukrainian and the 3rd Ukrainian Front (Belgrade). Malinovskii's immediate objective was to clear northern Transylvania and eastern Hungary; Petrov with 4th Ukrainian Front battled his way into Slovakia and sub-Carpathian Rus, taking Mukachevo on 26 October and Uzhorod one day later, a tough campaign over rugged country—the main Carpathian range, through which Petrov passed 1st Guards, 18th and 38th Armies. To the rigour of the terrain was added the tension within the command generated by the mutual hostility between Moskalenko and Grechko who were commanding adjacent armies, the 38th and the 1st Guards.

During the first half of October Petrov's armies made agonizingly slow progress, fighting the terrain, the elements and a stubborn enemy: Grechko's 1st Guards Army came grinding to a halt by 18 October; at the centre 18th Army registered local successes but on a limited scale, while on the left the 17th Guards Rifle Corps found itself facing determined resistance in the area of Yasina. The unrelieved gloom of the situation, however, was about to be lifted, endowing Petrov's efforts with ultimate success. Though Grechko with 1st Guards and Moskalenko with 38th Army made little progress in terms of ground gained, they did nevertheless draw off a great deal of German–Hungarian strength to hold them; as a result the force facing Petrov's left flank was weakened and Petrov was quick to take advantage of this development, setting up a 'mobile group' to strike towards Mukachevo and Uzhorod.

Meanwhile the threat of Soviet invasion was enough to throw the Hungarian political and military leadership into a turmoil, though the Germans had learned enough from Rumania's defection and the Bulgarian *débâcle* to act more speedily in Hungary, instigating their own *coup* this time and making use of a much stronger local pro-Nazi element. German troops had already installed themselves in Hungary as an occupation force since March when the Kallay government was replaced by one under Szotaj, a most pliable puppet amenable to every German pressure, intent on demonstrating fidelity to the German cause by introducing among other repressions a virulent and murderous anti-Jewish programme.

Regent Miklos Horthy and his political circle showed little liking for the Szotaj government. Emboldened by Anglo-American successes after the cross-Channel landing in Europe, Horthy removed the extreme pro-German representatives on 7 August and on 29 August, in the wake of Rumania's defection from Germany, dismissed Szotaj in favour of General Lakatos. Horthy was now aware that, in abandoning Germany, he must come to terms with the Soviet Union; throughout August contacts with the Western powers were resumed through Gyorgy Bakach-Bessenyei (formerly Hungarian minister in Bern) but the Hungarians were given to understand on 29 August that a request for an armistice must be directed towards the Soviet Union. It was a full month before Horthy exercised this option, while exploring other possibilities, not least negotiations with the Hungarian underground to arm the workers against German reprisals when Hungary left the war and also an application to the Germans for increased military assistance to hold off the Russians. As late as August the Hungarian Cabinet Council buoyed up its hopes with the expectations of a landing by the 'Anglo-Saxons' on the Adriatic coast, at which the Hungarians would fight to hold up the Russians 'until the Anglo-Saxons would occupy Hungary'. There was no landing in Dalmatia, however; there would be no 'Anglo-Saxon' protectorate in Hungary, nor could the German forces presently deployed in Hungary prevent the Soviet advance beyond the Carpathians or turn back the threat to Budapest. A break with Germany and submission for an armistice in Moscow could no longer be postponed.

The Hungarian armistice delegation arrived in Moscow on 1 October, at a time when the Soviet breakthrough to the line of the river Tisza brought home the reality of destruction at Soviet hands. Eleven days later, and on the sixth day of Malinovskii's Debrecen operation, the Hungarian delegation signed the armistice terms, which General Antonov of the Soviet General Staff communicated to Malinovskii on 12 October—Hungarian troops would evacuate the territory of neighbouring states; the three Allied powers would send their military representatives to Hungary to supervise these arrangements, but this 'military mission' would operate under the chairmanship of the Soviet representative; Hungary would at once break with Germany and declare war on Germany, in which event the Soviet Union would lend all aid. Though committed to surrender, Horthy still waited out the days and failed to make adequate preparations to cover Hungarian withdrawal from the war. Dislike of the Russians and bitter memories of 1918—revolution and the short-lived communist republic—reinforced by real fears for the stability of an outmoded social system all contributed to this procrastination.

By the end of the first week in October Malinovskii's tanks had broken into Mezö Tür, Szentes and Hödmezo Vasarhely, bringing his Front forces to within a few miles of the Tisza. His mobile units then pressed on in the direction of Debrecen, with Szeged falling to the Russians on 11 October. Further to the south, on Malinovskii's left, Soviet units operating beyond the Yugoslav frontier crossed the lower Tisza at Zenta and Stari Becej and, linking up with the forces which had already taken Szeged, captured Subotica on 12 October. Meanwhile the Soviet attack in northern Transylvania was making greater progress and was rolling towards Cluj (Koloszvar), the important traffic centre which had so far eluded them; a complicated outflanking manoeuvre in difficult terrain finally succeeded and Cluj fell on 11 October after a burst of fierce fighting. German and Hungarian troops began pulling back to the north, since the road to the west was already cut in two places. From the north, Petrov's 4th Ukrainian Front was pressing down steadily through the Carpathian front (in Galicia), along a sector running from Sanok to the Yablonitsa pass. With the first phase of his 'Debrecen operation' working so far successfully, Malinovskii on 13 October submitted plans for the next stage to the *Stavka*: with 53rd and 46th Armies on the Tisza, he proposed to use a 'cavalry-mechanized group' under Pliev to attack towards Nyiregyhaza–Cop (Csop) with the object of speeding the movement of his forces into the Hungarian plain north of the Tisza, at the same time pushing another 'cavalry' mechanized group' under Gorshkov from Orad towards Karoly and Satu Mare, a sweep designed to trap the German-Hungarian forces withdrawing through northern Transylvania.

General Farago, the Hungarian negotiator in Moscow, signed the text of an armistice, which Molotov abruptly put in front of him, on 11 October; Admiral Horthy agreed to accept the terms, though he asked the Soviet government to halt their military operations on 'the Budapest axis' in order to give the Hungarians time to carry out the terms. Antonov at the Soviet General Staff sent Malinovskii a signal on these lines on 12 October, but this time the Germans acted first, their plans having been laid well in advance. The creation of the Lakatos government at the end of August showed the Germans which way the wind was blowing, clearly indicating Hungarian withdrawal from the war. Almost simultaneously Ferenc Szalasi, the fanatically pro-Nazi Hungarian, stood by to seize power, supported by the men and the machinery of the SS. In Budapest *SS-Obergruppenführer* Winkelmann, chief of the SS in Hungary and head of the special police squads, resolved to 'clarify the situation' which had built up since the Lakatos government came to power. That 'clarification' was simplicity itself—to arrest the Horthy group with all possible speed and to nip further 'treachery' in the bud. Winkelmann, Geschke (*Sicherheitspolizei* commander in Hungary) and Skorzeny, the man who had rescued one dictator, Mussolini, on the Führer's orders and was now assigned to eliminate another, drew up a joint plan to deal with Horthy and his supporters. 'Action Horthy', or 'Operation *Panzerfaust*' as Skorzeny christened it (as a joking reminder that he had failed to tell his para-commandos to bring their bazookas), sprang to life on 10 October, when first Field-Marshal Bakay was kidnapped; Aggteleki, Bakay's replacement, was then speedily removed.

The *Sicherheitsdienst* (SD) now proceeded with an elaborate decoy operation to trap Horthy's son, suspected of dealings with Tito in an attempt to arrange an armistice; the SD proposed to impersonate two officers of Tito's entourage and catch the young Horthy 'red-handed', kidnap him and use the hostage to exert pressure on the elder Horthy to remain on Germany's side. The first attempt to carry through this cloak-and-dagger job fizzled out when the young Horthy became suspicious; on 15 October he agreed to a meeting but took a company of Hungarian troops and a group of Hungarian officers with him. In what suddenly developed into a running gun-fight between the SD men and the Hungarians, Skorzeny's body-snatchers managed to seize Horthy and rush him into a car and off to a waiting aircraft, which transported him to the concentration camp that was his destination.

The *coup*, for all its complicated details carried out with a dash becoming its Al Capone style, proved to be something of a damp squib. The German Minister in Hungary, Dr Veesenmayer, also an officer of the SS, suddenly quailed at the prospect of bargaining with Admiral Horthy for the life of his son; that interview took place at noon when young Horthy had been in German hands for two hours, but Veesenmayer did not 'fire the biggest gun' at the Admiral—the news of the successful kidnapping—and early in the afternoon Radio Budapest broadcast its own news about the conclusion of an armistice with the Soviet Union. News of his son's disappearance did not unnerve Admiral Horthy in the fashion that Hitler and Ribbentrop expected. With more than forty Tiger tanks making a menacing show in the city, Winkelmann and Skorzeny set about taking over Budapest completely, and in another feat of derring-do Skorzeny's commandos assaulted the Burgberg, Horthy's redoubt, an action completed by 6.30 am on 16 October. Yet half an hour before Skorzeny's men went into action, Horthy had indicated his willingness to abdicate and to hand over power to Szalasi. This brought a hoodlum government to rule over Hungary, stiffened with German troops and given over to a final rampage against the Jews when the Eichmann commando won a free hand to conduct its mass round-ups and exterminations.

The road to Budapest was now barred to the Russians, as the Germans intended that it should be. On 7 September Veesenmayer and the German military attaché von Greiffenberg had informed the Hungarian Prime Minister quite bluntly that 'the Germans are intent on holding the Eastern Front will all their forces, and if they lost the war, they would not let the collapse take place on the Eastern Front' but would rather surrender the Western Front. Budapest was becoming the key point of a ferocious defence of southern Europe, and the Hungarians were dragged by the heels into the holocaust of one of the most savage battles of the war, a siege operation of great cruelty and raging ferocity on both sides. The Political Administration of the 2nd Ukrainian Front reported after the *coup* that some Hungarian officers and a large part of the rank and file of the Hungarian Army took the view that further resistance was really futile. Within three days of the Germans taking over, two Hungarian generals, Varos Dalnoki and Miklos Bela, went over to the Russians—Miklos, commander of the 1st Hungarian Army, offered to bring his army over to the Russians but the Germans quickly stepped in to stop the rot. On 24 October the *Stavka* issued a formal order to the commanders of the 2nd and 4th Ukrainian Fronts instructing them to treat German and Hungarian troops alike, since Hungarian troops were continuing to fight.

In the latter half of October, with Hungary dragged back into the German camp, fierce straggling engagements took place on the plain to the north of Debrecen. The German command struggled to secure the safe withdrawal of their own Eighth Army and the two Hungarian armies (the 1st and 2nd), jabbing the Russians in the Orad and Debrecen areas with repeated attacks mounted in battalion or regimental strength supported by anything from 10 to 50 tanks and SP guns; in the area of Szolnok, two German divisions (24th *Panzer* and an *SS* division), with a battalion of heavy tanks rushed in from the interior, attacked on 19 October to free the German lines of communication and managed to push the Soviet troops back a distance of some twenty miles, retaking Mezö Tür and Turkev in the process. Meanwhile Pliev's mobile group was outflanking Debreczen, held by a force of three divisions made up of Hungarian and German troops; Soviet pressure drove the defenders westwards to the Tisza and northwards to Nyiregyhaza, only to be pursued by Pliev whose units took Nyiregyhaza on 22 October and pushed on for another fifteen miles, reaching the Tisza at Dombrad and Rakamaz in the northerly bend of the river. The enemy escape route was now well and truly cut, sealing off divisions to the east of Debrecen and on the southern bank of the Tisza. To support what was left of the Debrecen garrison, now rammed back to the Tisza, German tank units crossed the Tisza at Tokaj and struck out for Nyiregyhaza, striking the Soviet troops in the flank, recapturing the town on 25 October and reopening the westerly escape route. In this see-saw struggle, Pliev's men recaptured Nyiregyhaza five days later, but by this time a far larger battle had opened as Malinovskii launched his armour in a fast-moving drive between the Tisza and the Danube, fighting the battle of the Great Alföld and striking in the direction of Budapest.

The conclusion of the Debrecen operation brought Soviet forces into eastern Hungary (almost one-third of the country) and marked the clearing of northern Transylvania, once Satu Mare and Carei Mare had been taken on 25 October. With the capture of Mukachevo on 27 October and Uzhorod the following day, Petrov's 4th Ukrainian Front brought its 'Carpathian-Uzhorod' operations to a close, moving up to a line running through Starina to Sobrante and Cop, and 'sharing' a boundary line with Malinovskii's 2nd Ukrainian Front on the river Tisza. On Malinovskii's left, Tolbukhin's 3rd Ukrainian Front fought its way into Belgrade alongside Tito's troops, but instead of striking westwards and helping to free considerable areas of Croatia and Bosnia in Axis hands, these Soviet units moved only a little to west of Belgrade and halted on *Stavka* orders: after three days (on 18 October) the *Stavka* instructed Tolbukhin to move one rifle corps to the northern bank of the Danube and into the Sambor–Novi Sad sector, in order to cover Malinovskii's flank (where Tolbukhin's 75th Corps finally locked flanks with the 46th Army of Malinovskii's 2nd Ukrainian Front). There was never any intention of swinging Tolbukhin's Front forces to the west; at the beginning of November Tolbukhin began to regroup along the middle reaches of the Danube in order to strike into Hungary from the south-east, operating with Malinovskii's 2nd Ukrainian Front along the 'Budapest–Vienna axis'— keeping Soviet troops well clear of the 'demarcation line' marked out between Churchill and Stalin at their Moscow conference in mid-October.

Malinovskii found himself well placed at the conclusion of the Debrecen operation to jump rapidly into the second phase, the attack between the Tisza and the Danube. The bulk of his forces were already concentrated on his right flank and on the centre, facing Army Group South with its thirty-five divisions (nine motorized or armoured), the bulk of them deployed along the Nyiregy-haza–Miskolcz axis where Malinovskii had already concentrated his main strength: the bulk of the remaining enemy forces were largely Hungarian and facing Malinovskii's left. As yet no great concentration of German force had appeared to defend Budapest, though this was quickly remedied when the German command began pulling units back from the northern sector on the western bank of the Tisza towards the Hungarian capital, improvising a hasty defence between Budapest and Jaszbereny. The *Stavka* orders transmitted to Malinovskii on 28 October envisaged a frontal attack towards Budapest and its capture 'with relatively small forces': on 29 October 46th Army and 2nd Guards Mechanized Corps would start their attack into the Great Alföld with the object of turning the German defences on the Tisza line and bringing 7th Guards Army up to the river, with 46th Army reinforced by two mechanized corps (2nd and 4th Guards) assaulting enemy forces defending Budapest itself. Petrov's 4th Ukrainian Front received orders to prepare a drive deep into Czechoslovakia to tie down First *Panzer*, which must not be permitted to divert forces to Budapest. Tolbukhin would simultaneously proceed to regroup, concentrating the bulk of his forces in the Banat and consolidating the bridgehead on the Danube, and then drive into Hungarian territory. Malinovskii proposed, therefore, to use Shlemin's 46th Army and Sviridov's 2nd Mechanized Corps in an attack aimed first at Kecskemet, followed by Shumilov's 7th Guards Army attacking south-east of Szolnok, forcing the Tisza and making way for 6th Guards Tank Army—the Front reserve—aimed directly at Budapest; the right-flank formations (40th, 27th and 53rd Armies) with Rumanian divisions and Pliev's mobile group would continue to drive along the 'Nyiregyhaza–Miskolcz axis'.

Up at Shlemin's HQ, Malinovskii received a rude jolting from Stalin in the wake of the *Stavka* directive. Stalin wanted Budapest and he wanted it within hours, not least to make sense of his moves to bring a 'democratic government' to life: a triumphant sweep into Budapest would be a *coup de main* which would silence the 'bourgeois' waverers. This he now proceeded to impress upon Malinovskii in no uncertain terms, opening his telephone conversation with a question which was more a categorical statement:

It is absolutely essential that in the shortest possible time, in days even, you capture the capital of Hungary—Budapest. This has to be done no matter what it costs you. Can you do this?

MALINOVSKII: This assignment could be carried out within five days, once 4th Guards Mechanized Corps moves up to 46th Army. This movement is expected to be complete by November 1. Then 46th Army, reinforced by two Guards mechanized corps—2nd and 4th—would be able to mount a powerful attack, which would come as a complete surprise to the enemy and in two to three days take Budapest.

STALIN: The *Stavka* cannot give you five days. You understand that it is because of political considerations that we have got to take Budapest as quickly as possible.

MALINOVSKII: I very definitely understand that we have to take Budapest in view of these political considerations. However we should wait for the arrival of 4th Guards Mechanized Corps. Only under these considerations will it be possible to count on success.

STALIN: We cannot consider postponing the offensive for five days. It is necessary to go over to the offensive for Budapest at once.

MALINOVSKII: If you give me, as of now, five days, five days as an absolute maximum, Budapest will be taken. If we go over to the offensive without delay, then 46th Army, for sheer lack of forces, will not be able to develop its blow quickly, it will inevitably get bogged down in heavy fighting at the very approaches to the Hungarian capital. Putting it briefly, it cannot seize Budapest off the march.

STALIN: You are arguing all to no purpose. You do not understand the political necessity of mounting an immediate attack on Budapest.

MALINOVSKII: I understand all the political importance of taking Budapest and for that very reason I am asking five days. . . .

STALIN: I categorically order you to go over to the offensive for Budapest tomorrow. [Malinovskii, *Budapesht Vena Praga*, pp. 81–2.]

The conversation ended abruptly. A few minutes later the telephone rang once more, and this time it was General Antonov of the General Staff on the line, seeking from Malinovskii confirmation of 46th Army's attack timetable. There on the spot, in 46th Army HQ, Malinovskii issued orders for an immediate attack on the morning of 29 October.

Shlemin with 46th Army opened his attack on time and within twenty-four hours had driven up to twenty miles into the German positions: 7th Guards attacked and seized a substantial bridgehead on the western bank of the Tisza. German attempts to hold Kecskemet with elements of XXIV *Panzer* were crushed and on 1 November the town was in Soviet hands. The Budapest attack, mounted with two mechanized and four rifle corps, seemed to bring rapid success within the first hours, but it also brought immediate complications connected with Malinovskii's sudden offensive lunge which left the regrouping incomplete. More than a dozen formations, including four German *Panzer* divisions and a motorized division, were moving to positions lying across 46th Army's line of advance, though 4th Mechanized Corps had finally joined Shlemin's rifle army and, with the two mechanized corps in the lead—2nd and 4th—and the infantrymen of 23rd Independent Guards Rifle Corps moving forward in lorries, the Soviet command was pressing its advance units on to the south-easterly approaches of Budapest.

On 4 November lead tanks of 4th Guards Mechanized Corps reached the southern and eastern suburbs of Budapest, but as the tank units waited for the Soviet infantry to catch up with them the chance to break into the Hungarian capital slipped away. Worse still, their right flank now lay open to German attack and the Soviet command had to add this danger to the risks of assaulting Budapest on an extremely narrow front. Though Shumilov's 7th Guards Army took Szolnok and Czegled, the area to the north was still in German hands and here a powerful armoured force was assembling, threatening the Soviet flank. Repeated tank engagements were being fought in the heavy rain and amidst the flooded fields north of the Szolnok–Czegled–Budapest highway, but the German armour was not beaten back. On 4 November the *Stavka* signalled to Malinovskii that 'an attack on Budapest along a narrow front with only two mechanized corps together with an insignificant body of infantry can lead to unjustified losses and expose the troops operating along this axis to the danger of an enemy blow against their flanks from the north-east'. The *Stavka* signal suggested expanding the Soviet attack by pushing forward the right-flank armies—7th Guards, 53rd, 27th and 40th Armies—and mounting an attack from the north and north-east in conjunction with one launched from 46th Army on the left. Pliev was therefore ordered 'not later than 7.11.44' to force the Tisza and slice the German units away from the river. The new Soviet plan involved one more frontal attack with the object of cutting up the German formations to the east of Budapest, outflanking the city from the north and then assaulting it from three directions, the north, the north-east and the south.

The second Soviet bid for Budapest began on 11 November and lasted for sixteen days. It brought the capture by Pliev's columns of Miskolcz, thus snapping the link between Hungary and Slovakia, but it failed to bring the fall of Budapest. Malinovskii's prediction proved to be accurate. Stalin had won his race for five days, but in so doing he lost five months. Hungary was fearfully ravaged and the twin cities of Buda and Pest subjected to a horrible fate, seared by fire and bombardment, turned into a nightmarish scene of killing, looting, murder and rape. For Stalin, Budapest became so sensitive a topic that he shunned any further mention of it in his telephonic visitations upon his commanders.

In the autumn of 1944 the thoughts of most men within the Allied and the Axis camps alike turned increasingly to the prospect of the war coming to an end. This was reflected in the Soviet Union by small but significant hints of better things to come and a general expectation of kindlier policies once the present rigours were done; while the Nazi leadership, thrown deeper into its own chaos, threw up Himmler as its latest warlord and stepped up draconian measures of mobilization which brought 'the new slave warfare' to the Eastern Front, already surfeited with horrors.

The frenzied application of Hitler's maniac dictum of 'the last man and the last round' gave it one final, fearful dimension and provided the human grist for Himmler's military mill. Himmler's power seemed to mushroom almost endlessly in the wake of the 20 July bomb plot; in addition to being head of the SS, the Secret Police and the state police, supervisor of the Nazi racial policy as 'Reichskommissar for the Strengthening of Germanism', overlord of important sections of the armaments industry (including the 'revenge weapons') and commander of thirty-eight *Waffen SS* divisions, he was now commander-in-chief of the 'Replacement Army'. Under orders from Hitler to form fifteen new divisions, Himmler seized the chance to assemble a new army in the image of a 'people's army', officered by Nazis and stiffened with the Nazi version of the Soviet commissar, the National–Socialist '*Führungs-Offizier*', in fresh formations boasting their origin in 'the people', *Volksgrenadiere* in the van, to wage what Himmler himself called 'the sacred war of the people'. But to be forced into waging it, 'the people' were put in front of summary court-martial. The *Wehrmacht* watched for any sign of wavering; to encourage that last-ditch resistance, trees and bridges were turned into wayside gallows with their complement of corpses hung with warning signs that as deserters they had suffered Himmler's justice. The 'real swine', however, and the true object of Himmler's hatred, were 'the people who belong to the officers' clique' and these men Himmler was determined to break.

For this last-ditch defence Himmler drew upon Soviet experience, extolling Soviet methods and singling out the defence of Leningrad as a model that his officers should study and emulate. The search for more men also brought about a spectacular volte-face on Himmler's part—a 'reconciliation' with Vlasov, whom he had hitherto damned as a 'hired Bolshevik butcher', refusing to recognize the 'Russian liberation movement' that sprouted under the patronage of the *Wehrmacht*. All this changed on 16 September 1944, when Vlasov and Himmler met: the date (and the significant mix-up over press releases) suggest that Himmler had finally despaired of the outcome of the secret negotiations he had set afoot with the Russians in Stockholm, tenuous contacts which had been maintained since the middle of 1943 but which towards the end of September 1944 came to a dead end. Dr Peter Kleist's return to Berlin from Stockholm on 21 September signalled the final collapse of this precarious and preposterous venture. Himmler and Vlasov met at Rastenburg, Himmler's HQ. The *Wehrmacht* officers who supported Vlasov and his cause thought the decisive hour had struck, for with Himmler in command of the 'Replacement Army' there seemed a greater chance of forming and fielding large-size units composed of the Soviet PWs in German hands. Much depended, therefore, on Vlasov making his case to Himmler. On the surface, the meeting was a success, with Himmler weeping into his beer about his unfortunate errors in believing in '*Untermensch* theories': the *Ostpolitik* must go into reverse and provide the basis for a political and psychological onslaught against Stalin and his system. Vlasov was to get ten divisions and enjoy 'the rights of an ally'; Himmler even proposed the rank of 'Head of Government' for Vlasov, though the latter tactfully declined. For a brief moment Vlasov enjoyed the status of a 'wonder weapon' in his own right, but the glitter was soon gone. Himmler suddenly revised his figure of 'ten divisions' to three; Keitel and Jodl at the *OKW* firmly squashed talk of 'building up Vlasov', Rosenberg was furious at the Himmler-Vlasov compact and his *Ostministerium* vigorously pressed the claims of other national minorities to block Vlasov's 'Great Russian chauvinism'. The new 'wonder weapon' flopped almost from the start.

Between them, Himmler and Goebbels (recently nominated the 'Reich Plenipotentiary for Total War') raised half a million men and dispatched them, half-trained and ill-equipped, to the front; in the rear Goebbels filled up the barracks, and just as fast Himmler emptied them. At first Goebbels thought in terms of a grand alliance between Himmler and himself—the army for Himmler, the civilian direction of the whole war effort for Goebbels—but Martin Bormann was not prepared to stand idly by while Himmler took over the *Reich*. Over the creation of the *Volkssturm*, the local defence force or 'home guard' formally established on 18 October, Bormann ensured that the party organization retained a tight grip, thus diminishing Himmler's prerogatives as head of the Replacement Army; the *Volkssturm* emerged as a *levée en masse* conducted under the aegis of the *Gauleiters*—and Bormann controlled the *Gauleiters*. To bypass this barrier to his authority, Himmler inevitably channelled as many men as possible into the *Waffen SS*, the military empire which was closed to the intrusions of Bormann and his satraps; of the fourteen new *SS* divisions being formed, only two—*SS Götz von Berlichingen* and *SS Horst Wessel*—were truly German and therefore even faintly Nordic, while seven drew their recruits from south-eastern Europe. Vlasov's prisoner-legions never materialized. Himmler coveted the mass of deserters for himself and drew Latvian, Estonian, Ukrainian and White Russian units into the *Waffen SS*, which already enclosed special brigades of Turkomen and Caucasian prisoners or deserters. The *Wehrmacht* refused to hand over its own special Cossack divisions to this phantom army for 'Russian liberation'; General Köstring, commander of the *Wehrmacht*'s own 'Volunteer Formations'—the *Osttruppen*—drawn from Russian prisoners and deserters, refused to have anything to do with Vlasov and a contrived meeting in Prague in November 1944 proved to be extremely 'uncordial', barely preserving basic civilities. The occasion of this fleeting Köstring–Vlasov meeting was provided by the Prague congress, the scene of some elaborate ceremonial and junketing, but Vlasov was unable to offer much more than a congratulatory telegram from Himmler. The Russian civilian labourers, the *Ostarbeiter*, for whom Vlasov had pleaded, were not represented nor were their slave-labour conditions improving in any way, though Himmler promised not only this but their eventual freedom, while on the German side there were some studied absences.

The manifesto of the 'Committee for the Liberation of the Peoples of Russia', read amidst an elaborate ceremony on the afternoon of 14 November in the Spanish Hall of the Hradcin in Prague, at long last legitimized the 'liberation movement' and made it clear that this was no mere collection of Quislings. The document made no mention of national socialism and implicitly rejected the Nazi system. But equally, without the bayonets to back it up and relying as it did on the power of a regime dedicated to a stupefyingly inhuman *Ostpolitik,* the manifesto remained a collection of phrases and finally transformed political farce into personal tragedy. Himmler's opportunist support for Vlasov, weak though it was, proved to be the kiss of death. Rosenberg counter-attacked fiercely, denouncing Vlasov's plan as 'a Great Russian dictatorship' full of 'subversive intentions'. In agreeing with Vlasov on one cardinal point, that the 'liberation movement' needed a 'unified command', Rosenberg also uncovered the fatal weakness in Vlasov's whole position: 'such unity could be secured only through the German High Command'. It was also only through the co-operation of the high command that Vlasov could organize any Russian fighting units, and this proved to be difficult.

The first two divisions, the 600th and the 650th, were to be raised at Münsingen and Heuberg, but the *Wehrmacht* command refused to part with its best surviving Russian troops, preferring to transfer only the remnants of mangled units—*SS Sigling* with its Russian troops battered in France, and the men of the 'Kaminsky Brigade' presently under Belai, a former Red Army lieutenant (Kaminsky himself having been shot for his ferocity and insubordination in the Warsaw rising, justice and discretion delivered by the *SS* itself in one blow suitably faked as a Polish ambush—a bullet-ridden car and a liberal application of animal blood—to conceal the truth from Kaminsky's officers). Vlasov finally appointed the former Soviet colonel Bunyachenko, a divisional commander in the Far East in 1939 and subsequently a staff officer with Timoshenko, as the new commander of 600th Division with the rank of major-general. Under Bunyachenko, who fought for every man and scrap of equipment, the division began to take shape. But the case for the Vlasov 'wonder weapon' rested not on one or even two divisions, but on the massive psychological impact that a large Russian-manned army led by Vlasov might have (indeed, in the opinion of Vlasov's German protagonists, must have) on the Soviet armed forces and their will to fight. Questionable though that assumption was, with the Red Army scenting victory Vlasov's droplets meant nothing in the whole tide flooding up to Germany's eastern frontiers.

Whatever the German fantasies about the state of Soviet morale, the Soviet leadership responded to the prevailing mood in the Soviet Union by adopting a 'carrot-and-stick' policy: a certain buoyancy was maintained by encouraging the belief in far-reaching post-war changes, but already certain steps were being taken to produce an ideological tightening-up. The huge bout of officially encouraged patriotism had gone far enough and now the Party embodying the Party 'line' was about to make its presence felt once again. Amidst the escapism of popular songs and sentimental plays, or the sensational success of a Deanna Durbin film shown along with other American films, the Party journal *Bol'shevik* in October sounded a warning against these 'bourgeois' tendencies: 'light comedies and other forms of thoughtless entertainment' would not be allowed to predominate at the expense of 'big and serious subjects' in literature and the arts. The Communist Party, however, had first to attend to the strains which three years of war imposed upon it. The demands of the front and the impact of the German occupation wrought havoc with the civilian party organizations, the strength of which fell from some three and a half million to just under two million during the first six months of the war, a declining curve which did not show signs of recovery until 1943. At the same time the armed forces, the Red Army above all, drew in a mass of Communist Party members and candidate members. Slightly more than half—56 per cent—of the entire strength of the Communist Party was in uniform by the end of 1943. In 1944 the pace of this expansion had begun to slacken, but between January and August 1944 party organizations in the Red Army admitted 460,780 full members and accepted 557,590 candidate members. The pace of this admission was accelerated by the 1941 decrees admitting Soviet servicemen who had distinguished themselves in action to full membership after only three months as candidate members, but there was also the heavy casualty rate among party members to offset this. On 14 October 1944 the Central Commission turned its attention to party admission for 'the best Soviet servicemen', at a time when the Red Army mustered 1,810,000 full members and 965,930 candidate members: two thirds of the party members (and an even greater proportion of candidate members) were on active service with fronts and armies. In sum, for three years and two months of war the grand total of admissions to the party organizations in the Red Army amounted to 1,802,410 full members and 3,196,580 candidate members (four-fifths with fighting formations).

The danger now loomed that there might be not too few party members in the armed services but rather too many. The Central Committee tried to apply the brakes, yet the total party membership in the armed forces reached its highest wartime peak as 1944 drew to a close—3,030,775 members and candidate members. Almost 23 per cent of the Red Army were party members, and it was even higher in the Navy (31 per cent), with the fastest rate of growth in the specialist arms and services, though even in the infantry units (with their heavy rate of casualties) 10 per cent of all riflemen were party members. In particular formations, however, the percentage of party members among infantrymen was falling due to battle casualties, and new recruits to the Party were not restoring the figures. The flood of new party members inevitably meant an expansion of the organization to handle them, in particular the divisional party commission, comprising some nine to eleven senior and long-service party members; the basic unit of the party-political apparatus also came to rest in the battalion party organization.

With the Red Army now fighting well beyond the Soviet borders and open to the contagion of 'bourgeois' contacts, the work of ideological preparation and surveillance took on a new dimension. In addition, as the Red Army liberated Belorussia and the Ukraine, the male population of military age was conscripted into the field armies as they passed through the towns and countryside, a motley collection of former soldiers, ex-prisoners and semi-literate country boys, all of whom required both political and ordinary education. Baffled as much as ignorant, these new recruits asked political officers such questions as 'Who are our allies?' and 'Who can become an officer in the Red Army?' The Main Political Administration directive of 22 March 1944 stressed that the youth under German occupation had been exposed to 'bourgeois-nationalist' propaganda and other influences, demanding an intensive effort at re-education which must take 'the highest priority'. At a meeting of the Military Propaganda Soviet in July, Shcherbakov (head of the Main Political Administration) emphasized that 'other methods' would have to be used in work dealing with conscripts unfamiliar with what 'every Soviet man' knows. The conscript from the newly-liberated western areas of the Soviet Union was to be taken in hand by the field commanders, political officers and propaganda staff well before he was sent to an operational unit; in the reserve regiments the new recruit relearned the business of being a Soviet citizen, and veteran soldiers did their best to impart some military skills to those without any previous military training. At the other end of this vast manpower spectrum, the political administration was facing the problems of increasing war-weariness and combat fatigue among front-line troops, the veterans in particular. Armies and divisions set up 'leave houses' for officers, sergeants and rank-and-file soldiers, trying at the same time to counter this lassitude by treating men with unbroken front-line service in a special manner.

The 'tendency of the Party to get lost in the crowd', as Alexander Werth put it, underwent a sharp and visible change. In the armed forces the *Orgburo* on 14 October put its weight behind the Political Administration directive on tightening up the 'ideological–political education' of prospective party members and their effective absorption into party work, while the democratization in recruitment for civilian party organizations was similarly slowed. Though still weakened and with a preponderance of young, wartime recruits (two-thirds of the total strength in 1944), the Party speedily showed its teeth. A stream of Central Committee decrees hammered in the need to improve 'mass political and ideological work' in many areas; the party *aktivy* received categorical instructions to take 'concrete measures' to improve instruction and indoctrination. To correct the drift from Marxism–Leninism, the party organs set about organizing a mass lecture programme; but the newly liberated areas presented special difficulties for not only were there 'material' deficiencies—the devastation left in the wake of the Germans—but also 'moral–political consequences' of occupation, a euphemism for the property owning instinct which flourished among the peasants who had seen the collective-farm system broken up. Soviet propagandists now took up the fight against 'individualism' and the consequences of the 'capitalist order' introduced by the Germans.

The popular expectation that the whole *kolkhoz* (collective farm) system would somehow 'emerge' in a different form, a belief widely spread in the liberated areas and shared by the peasants now entering the army as conscripts, obviously gave the Party cause for great concern. During the 'anti-Vlasov campaign' in 1943 the rumours and whispers deliberately fed into the rural population spoke of the eventual abolition of the collectives; part of the general anticipation of post-war changes, the 'relaxation', included this crucial question of the transformation in the countryside. In Belorussia and the western Ukraine the party massed its propagandists and educators to persuade the peasants to return to the 'sole correct road—to break with privately owned, small-scale farming'. A special effort was directed towards peasant women, whose heads had been filled with 'lies' about the *kolkhozy;* thousands of peasants were lectured about the evils of private property and the virtues of the collectives. At the same time the Party and the administration grappled with yet another infusion of problems, the forced labour and prisoners of war freed by the Soviet advance. Colonel-General F.I. Golikov assumed control of a special organization, established under the authority of *Sovnarkom,* to deal with repatriated Soviet civilians and soldiers. But Beria struck first. His *NKVD* troops and agents rounded up the repatriates for screening and interrogation, the preliminary in many thousands of cases to deportation to a Soviet forced labour camp, there to purge the monstrous crime of simply having fallen into German hands.

Free of any military threat, Stalin could now turn his morbid attention to settling the scores for all the rankling insubordination and indiscipline he had detected during the months of greatest danger. The non-Russian nationalities had already paid in horrible fashion for their own derelictions. The Chechens of the Chechen–Ingush Autonomous Republic in the North Caucasus had been brutally rounded up by the *NKVD* and the survivors transported from their homes; in 1944 Stalin completed this obliteration by abolishing the Republic and establishing the Groznyi *oblast* in the place of the burnt and blasted Chechen settlements. The same fate lay in store for the Crimean Tartars—deportation, punishment and finally obliteration. While they had never stopped, the wheels of the devious and cruel Stalinist system were already speeding up: the concentration of immense power in the hands of a relatively small group within the State Defence Committee, though essential for survival, scarcely conformed to Stalin's liking, and he proceeded to break it up. The clash between Stalin, Beria and Malenkov was possibly (and reportedly) triggered off by the reaction of the latter to Stalin's illness in the spring of 1944, when he was found unconscious at his desk. Old feuds flared anew when Zhdanov was recalled from Leningrad to resume his duties in Moscow; Leningrad's ambitious plans to rebuild were abruptly shoved aside in favour of concentrating on restitution of its military–industrial capacities. This proved to be the lightest of the punishments subsequently inflicted on insubordinate Leningrad.

The Party had already begun to tighten up in the armed forces, reasserting its somewhat tarnished authority. Bravery no longer sufficed. The Communist in the forces needed more than his proficiency in combat (and there were complaints that soldiers were admitted to the Party who had never seen any action); the emphasis was passing to ideological fitness and political maturity, which meant both knowing and toeing the Party line. Stalin acquiesced readily enough in the diminution of the Party's role in the army in order to promote military efficiency, but he was not prepared to countenance any erosion of his own authority. The cult of Stalin as an outstanding military leader was by now well under way, and the troops were fed a diet of Stalin's 'Orders of the Day'. The re-imposition of his absolute authority, however, required still more drastic measures, and this task fell to Bulganin, promoted in November 1944 to Stalin's deputy for defence at the cost of displacing Voroshilov. It was Bulganin's assignment to prepare for the 'purge of the heroes' designed to cut down to size the generals and other personalities connected with defence matters who trod too heavily on the Party's prerogatives or on Stalin's susceptibilities.

Yet throughout 1944 the country continued to mobilize. The labour force grew from 19,400,000 in 1943 to over 23,000,000 in 1944, of which almost ten million were employed in industry and on building work or construction. Women, girls and youths figured largely among these contingents set to work for the first time—women in 1944 formed over 50 per cent of the labour force in industry and 36 per cent of the labour in building and construction work. Not many months before, in 1941–2, the trains had sped east carrying factories out of the range of the German armies, a massive industrial migration that had torn whole regions out by the roots. Now in 1944 the 're-evacuation' was in full swing, bringing machines back to the western industrial regions where brigades of young people were already working to rebuild the shattered factories and plants. 'Re-evacuation', reconstruction in the liberated areas and the need to maintain production in the eastern hinterland meant careful deployment of skilled labour, above all keeping a balance between the western and eastern regions, though high priority went to putting the Donbas and the metallurgical industries of the south into full production.

Coal, petroleum, ferrous metals, machine tools and cement were among the more critical shortages in a country stretched to the limit, with its underfed and drastically overworked population. Prices of foodstuffs continued to rise. Tens of thousands of villages, thousands of worker settlements and towns, several large cities and the railway system were for the most part hideously ruined. Factories, plants and urban installations had been blown up or destroyed in the fighting, mines flooded and railways wrecked. In April 1944 the State Defence Committee concentrated on key improvements to raise output in the rear areas and the newly liberated regions, giving priority to the supply of electric power and the mining of coal. New electric power stations were planned for the Kuzbas and the northern Urals, as well as for the central industrial region and the Ukraine. The mines of the Donbas were already contributing coal to the Soviet war effort, where the production of weapons continued to climb—29,000 tanks and self-propelled guns (24,000 in 1943); 40,300 aircraft (34,900 in 1943); 122,500 guns of all types and calibres (a drop when compared with 130,300 in 1943, but the smaller output was due to the withdrawal of older models); 184,000,000 shells, mines and aerial bombs (compared with 175,000,000 in 1943); almost 7.5 milliard rounds of small-arms ammunition. The IS-2 heavy tank (the 'Joseph Stalin') with its 122mm gun was now in serial production and over two thousand were built in 1944 (only 102 in 1943); over 11,000 of the new modernized T-34s (the T-34/85 with an 85mm gun) were produced, together with the first 500 SU-100 self-propelled guns built on a T-34 tank chassis; and 2,510 of the new ISU-122 and ISU-152 (using the IS-2 tank chassis) compared with only 35 in 1943. Lend-lease delivery of weapons fell in comparison with 1943 (2,613 tanks in 1944 compared with 3,123 in 1943; 5,749 aircraft in place of 6,371 in 1943), though the shipment of raw materials played an important part in building up Soviet reserves: of the half million tons of steel, more than half consisted of rails, which, together with 129,000 lorries and over 1,000 locomotives, served to alleviate difficulties in restoring the transport system.

In October the Russians received another substantial bonus, less tangible than tanks or aircraft but no less significant as a psychological boost to their feelings of the surety of the 'grand alliance', which was yet one more harbinger of better post-war days to come based on 'Big Three' co-operation. Between 9 and 18 October the Prime Minister held a series of talks in Moscow with Stalin, conversations that surpassed any other in affability and mutual esteem—or so it appeared on the surface and to the world at large. Churchill, though worried about the prospect of Soviet control being fastened over the whole of south-eastern Europe, did not come to Moscow this time entirely devoid of bargaining power; the Allied armies in the west, for all the earlier Soviet mocking, pushed on with gathering speed and already on 11 September had crossed into German territory, giving them a head start in the race for Berlin. The suggestion for a meeting came from the Prime Minister on 27 September and for once Stalin made neither objection nor demur. As soon as Stalin indicated his willingness to meet, the Prime Minister was in Moscow within a week.

In Moscow Churchill found 'an extraordinary atmosphere of goodwill . . .' (such was his description of his reception to President Roosevelt) and at his first meeting with Stalin on 9 October he seized the opportunity to 'settle our affairs in the Balkans', outlining on a piece of paper a scheme of sharing out south-eastern Europe between the Soviet Union and Great Britain, or 'the others'. In Rumania the Russians were to have ninety per cent of the predominance (ten per cent for 'the others'); in Greece 'Great Britain in accord with USA' would in turn take ninety per cent predominance with Russia taking ten per cent; in Yugoslavia and Hungary honours were even at fifty per cent each; while in Bulgaria the Soviet Union would acquire seventy-five per cent. It was perhaps something of an improvement upon the matchsticks of Teheran. Stalin returned the paper to Churchill with a large blue tick inscribed upon it. 'It was all settled', Churchill remarked, 'in no more time than it takes to set down.'

It was not, however, 'all settled'. Molotov and Eden haggled throughout 10 October over the precise meaning of these percentages, curious exchanges with these two pertinacious foreign ministers bargaining for what amounted to a ten per cent increase in Russian influence in Yugoslavia as against a larger British share in Bulgaria. This quasi-mathematical disputation was resumed in the afternoon, when Molotov suggested a figure of eighty per cent for Hungary and Bulgaria, fifty per cent for Yugoslavia, by which he meant that until the German surrender Bulgaria would come under Soviet control, but after the German surrender British and American participation would be allowed. This led, in turn, to a settlement over the terms of the Bulgarian armistice and to a balance sheet 'flogged out', in Churchill's phrase, between the two foreign ministers. The Russians pressed for predominance in Bulgaria, took 'great interest in Hungary', claimed the 'fullest responsibility' in Rumania but were prepared 'largely to disinterest themselves in Greece'. The explanatory letter the Prime Minister drafted for Stalin on British policy and the significance of the percentage sliding-scale was not sent, since Churchill thought it 'wiser to let well alone'; to the War Cabinet he sent a message stressing that 'the system of percentage' did not mean specific numbers on particular commissions in the various Balkan countries but rather it expressed 'the interest and sentiment with which the British and Soviet Governments approach the problems of these countries. . . .' Nor did this agreement in principle commit the United States or represent in any way 'a rigid system of spheres of influence'.

The problem of Poland, however, could not be settled with slips of paper. At his first meeting with Stalin, Churchill proposed that Mikolajczyk, Grabski and Romer be invited to take part in the present talks; after some considerable pressure from the British, the London Poles agreed to travel to Moscow and left on 10 October. Though Mikolajczyk's memorandum of 7 October stipulated that the Polish delegation should know in advance 'what terms for a settlement will be put forward by the Soviet Government', Eden (according to the Polish record) insisted that 'this is the last chance for the Polish Government to come to an agreement with the Soviets at an auspicious moment . . .' while 'both Churchill and Eden see no possibility of setting any preliminary conditions for entering into negotiations' but insist that to miss this opportunity would be 'unforgivable'. When the Polish delegation arrived in Moscow, Ambassador Harriman also emphasized that in his view this was 'the last and sole chance to reach an agreement on the Polish question'.

Late in the afternoon on 13 October the first talks on the Polish question began in the Spiridonovka Palace. On entering, Stalin informed the Prime Minister that Soviet troops had taken Riga and several German divisions had been cut off in Hungary and he was in turn offered the Prime Minister's congratulations.

Ten minutes later Molotov officially opened the proceedings and invited Mikolajczyk to open his case. In essence, Mikolajczyk argued that the nature of the Polish political system precluded any forced fusion of the London government and the Committee for National Liberation (the 'Lublin Committee'): the Memorandum of 29 August ruled out participation by Fascist and 'non-democratic groups'. Mikolajczyk proposed a Polish government based on the five political parties, 'each of which would receive a fifth of the ministries'. The Polish memorandum must be the basis for further discussion.

Stalin proceeded to kick this aside. The memorandum had two important defects: first that it ignored the Lublin Committee—'a government must be formed on the basis of a compromise between the two authorities which claim to be the government'—and, second, it failed to settle the problem of the eastern frontiers of Poland on the basis of the 'Curzon line'. It had to be the Curzon line or nothing. Mikolajczyk refused to agree to 'ceding 40 per cent of the territory of Poland and 5 million Poles'. Stalin intervened to point out that it was 'Ukrainian territory and a non-Polish population' which was in dispute. The Prime Minister cooled this wrangle for the moment, but Mikolajczyk refused to accept his proposal that 'the frontier solution' should be adopted at once, with the right of appeal at a subsequent peace conference; the Polish Prime Minister would not countenance 'a new partition of Poland' while Stalin rejected a 'partition of the Ukraine and White Ruthenia'. This time Churchill appealed 'for a great gesture in the interests of European peace' from the Poles, intimating that for the Polish government 'to estrange' themselves from the British at this juncture would be unwise: specifically he proposed that the Curzon line be accepted as the *de facto* frontier with the right of 'final discussion' at the Peace Conference, and also that 'a friendly agreement with the Committee of National Liberation . . .' be concluded.

Stalin, who had been on his feet for some time, spoke with great deliberation in what was effectively the final statement: 'I want to state categorically that the Soviet Government cannot accept Premier Churchill's formula concerning the Curzon line.' At this the Prime Minister threw up his hands in despair. Furthermore, Stalin continued, the Curzon line must be accepted as the future eastern frontier: as in the case of Rumania and Finland, so in the case of Poland, the Soviet Union aimed at 'determining a definite frontier'. 'I repeat once more: the Curzon line as the basis of the frontier.' Faced with such intractability, Mikolajczyk could only note in his personal observations on the meeting that 'the Polish government is expected to commit suicide of its own volition', a role he was not persuaded to adopt and for which he and his government would be 'inept'. Later in the evening the British ministers together with Stalin met the leaders of the 'Lublin Committee', who at once agreed to the Curzon line, whereupon Stalin's interest rapidly faded and could not be aroused by Osobka-Morawski's disquisition on the internal policies of the Committee. All Stalin wanted was a 'definite frontier' of his own determining.

Towards noon on the morning of 14 October the Prime Minister met Mikolajczyk in order to clear up 'the Polish position' before talking to Stalin that same afternoon. Churchill opened a furious attack—'It is the crisis of the fortunes of Poland'; the damage would be 'irreparable' if agreement could not be reached; the Russians would back the rival government; there was 'unlimited means' at the disposal of the Russians to liquidate opposition; Mikolajczyk would have to go to Poland and form a united government; ideas such as those of General Anders, who hoped that after Germany was defeated 'the Russians will be beaten', were 'crazy—you cannot defeat the Russians'. But Mikolajczyk was not to be moved, and in a burst of anger the Prime Minister rounded on him: 'I wash my hands of it . . . because of quarrels between Poles we are going to wreck the peace of Europe. . . . You will start another war in which 25 million lives will be lost. But you don't care.' Mikolajczyk countered this outburst by retorting that the fate of Poland was sealed at Teheran, to which Churchill retorted that, on the contrary, Poland was saved. As this storm subsided a draft paper on the territorial question was prepared, recommending the Curzon line in the east and Poland's compensation from lands 'to the east of the line of the Oder', their possession by Poland to be guaranteed by Great Britain and the Soviet Union.

At 2.30 pm the Polish delegation called on the Prime Minister, who was waiting to fix an appointment with Stalin, who, he was told, was 'away from town' (which simply meant he was having a nap, or so the Prime Minister divined from his own habits). This Anglo-Polish encounter was 'very violent'. Churchill lashed out at the delegation: 'you have no sense of responsibility . . . you do not care about the future of Europe . . . . it is cowardice on your part.' It was impossible for Churchill to present this draft text as his own proposal, from which the Poles would formally dissent: 'I am not going to worry Stalin . . . I feel as if I were in a lunatic asylum. I don't know whether the British government will continue to recognize you.' Great Britain stood powerless in the face of Russia, but the Poles talked of beating the Russians. The Poles, Churchill continued, 'hate the Russians—I know you hate them.' At this the meeting ended in some confusion as the Prime Minister hurried off to meet Stalin, bearing a draft British proposal which dealt with the western and eastern frontiers of Poland. Stalin did accept the proposed draft, but on 15 October the Polish delegation returned to their previous insistence on 'Line B' for eastern Galicia, which meant Polish retention of Lvov; inevitably this was rejected by Stalin, and Mikolajczyk refused to countenance public confirmation of the Curzon line. The British draft proposal of 16 October adopted the old formula of a 'line of demarcation' and applied it to the Curzon line, specifying also the formation of a 'Polish Government of National Unity under Prime Minister Mikolajczyk': Stalin simply scored out the term 'line of demarcation' and substituted 'basis for the frontier' and slid in an amendment making the new Polish government the product of an 'agreement' between the London Poles and the Lublin Committee. Everything came back to square one.

Since the Teheran conference the Americans had tried to push the idea of preliminary studies and even preliminary moves for Soviet–American collaboration against the time when the Soviet Union entered the war against Japan. While Stalin held out tantalizing hints about talks with Soviet air and ground forces commanders in the Soviet Far East, nothing of any consequence had transpired. The American attempt to trade four-engined bombers (which Stalin requested in large numbers to give the Soviet air force a strategic arm) for air bases in Siberia also had come to nothing, all on the eve of the British ministers' visit to Moscow. On being given an account of the proceedings of the Quebec conference late in September, Stalin had at once pointed out that projected operations in the Pacific made no mention of eventual Soviet participation and asked whether the President still thought it essential that the Soviet Union should enter the war against Japan—if not, then he was prepared to abide by that decision. Both the British and American ambassadors had assured him that Soviet help was important, whereupon Stalin had intimated that he would arrange for General Deane to meet Soviet commanders to discuss problems relating to Far Eastern operations. Further American prodding had still not produced any tangible result when the Prime Minister and his party appeared in Moscow.

On the evening of 14 October, 'All Poles day' as Churchill described it, the two leaders and their staffs sat down to a review of the military situation, with Field-Marshal Alanbrooke presenting the Allied operations in Europe and General Deane covering the Japanese situation, outlining the American view of the Soviet role—their principal task being the defeat of the Japanese army in Manchuria. For planning purposes the American chiefs of staff needed information on the timing of Soviet-Japanese hostilities once Germany was defeated, the length of time needed for the offensive build-up of Soviet forces in the Far East and the capacity available on the Trans-Siberian railway to organize and support an American strategic air force. All Stalin wanted to know in response to this was how many divisions the Japanese possessed. The meeting then broke up, on the assumption that Red Army operations would be reviewed the following evening. The Prime Minister, however, was somewhat sceptical. At the end of September Stalin had evidently called for a full analysis of the requirements for concentrating and supporting Soviet troops in the Far East: since 1942 the post of deputy chief of the General Staff (Far East) had been in existence and in the Operations Administration Maj.-Gen. Shevchenko ran the 'Far Eastern section' until June 1943 when he changed places with the chief of staff of the Far Eastern Front, Maj.-Gen. P.A. Lomov, who moved back to the General Staff while Shevchenko went out to the Far Eastern command. The requisite data on Far Eastern operations had been assembled at the beginning of October and used by Stalin on the evening of 15 October, when General Antonov and Lt.-Gen. Shevchenko attended him. In a detailed reply to the American questions posed the night before, Stalin submitted that the Red Army would need sixty divisions in the Far East (thus doubling present strength), requiring three months to concentrate all the Soviet forces once the war in the west was over: in view of the limitations on the capacity of the Trans-Siberian, even running it at full stretch (thirty-six trains a day) would not supply sixty divisions, for which reason two or three months' stocks must be built up in advance. Though vague about the date, Stalin repeated to Harriman that once Germany was defeated Russia would take the offensive against Japan, subject to the Americans helping to stock reserve supplies and to 'the clarification' of certain political aspects of Soviet participation, a reference to Soviet claims. The Americans could also have air bases in the Soviet Maritime Provinces and the use of Petropavlovsk as a naval base. Field-Marshal Alanbrooke put Antonov through his paces during the briefing, and more than once Stalin fished his deputy Chief of the General Staff out of the difficulties posed by Alanbrooke's leading questions. Stalin argued the supply problem rigorously, he 'displayed an astounding knowledge of technical railway details', he showed detailed knowledge of past campaigns in the theatre from which he drew 'very sound deductions'. The Field-Marshal came away 'more than ever impressed by his military ability'.

When a brief position paper, compiled at the prompting of Eden with the reluctant agreement of Harriman, reached Stalin, his indignation at this 'disregard of secrecy' boiled over; committing the discussions to paper could mean a leakage and that might in turn trigger off a Japanese attack resulting in the loss of Vladivostok: secretaries might well talk, whereas Stalin preferred his own style— 'I am a cautious old man.' Yet the Prime Minister discerned that Stalin was not unduly anxious about the effect of his preparations on the Japanese; on the contrary, he seemed to relish the prospect of a 'premature attack' by the Japanese, if only to make the Russians fight the harder. A Japanese pre-emptive attack could have spelt disaster for the Soviet plans, but, for all his fury about the 'breach of secrecy', on 17 October at a third and final meeting Stalin enlarged in detail on Soviet strategic plans for the Far Eastern attack: Soviet forces would pin the Kwantung Army from the north and the east in Manchuria, while powerful mobile forces struck down from the area of lake Baikal through Mongolia in the direction of Kalgan and northern China, thus isolating the Kwantung Army from Japanese troops in China. Air bases in the Maritime provinces would be available to the Americans, who could start secret surveys in the area and at Petropavlovsk, the naval base also available to them; joint planning could begin at once. In return, the United States would supply the Soviet Union with the supplies necessary to sustain a two-month reserve for a million and a half men with 3,000 tanks and 5,000 aircraft—the equivalent of 860,410 tons of dry cargo and over 200,000 tons of liquid cargo, to be delivered by 30 June 1945. The bargain was astutely driven home.

The Moscow conference ended in a gush of good feeling. Even the talk between Stalin and Mikolajczyk engineered by the Prime Minister passed off smoothly on 18 October, though Stalin made it unpalatably plain that the Curzon line—'this line, by the way, was not invented by us but by the then Allied powers . . . by the Americans, French, English, that is to say, by our enemies at that time'—

must stand as the frontier: there could be no quibble about 'a line of demarcation'. The composition of the new government provided further cause for misgiving and dissension when the chairman of the Lublin committee, Bierut, demanded seventy-five per cent of the Cabinet posts in return for Mikolajczyk becoming premier. On this point Stalin remained studiously vague, but he made a point of reminding the British Prime Minister that only he and Molotov could be counted on to resist applying the big stick to Mikolajczyk. Even that did not damp Churchill's optimism that a settlement might be promoted within the coming two weeks. Such was his report to the President on 22 October, though the euphoria quickly evaporated. For all practical purposes the British and the London Poles returned from Moscow empty-handed: the tactic of winning Stalin's friendship to save the Poles had not worked. The signs of friendship were assiduously and ostentatiously cultivated, even on the part of Stalin, who made the almost unprecedented gesture of seeing the Prime Minister off at the airport, a rare compliment once bestowed on Matsuoka in April 1941. Stalin was also open-handed with his gifts of caviar, but no other concession was to be prized out of him.

Towards the end of August the Soviet fronts in the north—1st, 2nd and 3rd Baltic, together with Govorov's Leningrad Front—ground their way slowly through Estonia and Latvia, fighting off heavy German counter-attacks mounted with great skill amidst the rivers, marshes and thick forests of this northern theatre. The veterans of Army Group North provided some of the toughest and most experienced German battle groups on the Eastern Front. With Finland out of the war, both the Germans and Russians could devote their full attention and greater resources to this southerly basin of the northern theatre, a change that affected Estonia almost at once, for more men were available to Govorov on the Leningrad Front (thus diminishing his dependence on Maslennikov's 3rd Baltic Front) and Schörner could contemplate evacuating Estonia now that the need to prop up Finland had gone: additional troops were freed to fight off the main Russian threat to the Baltic bastions the German command intended to hold. The *Stavka* meanwhile concluded that the time had come to deliver the *coup de grâce* to Army Group North: between 26 August and 2 September fresh directives descended on the Soviet Front commanders, instructing them to prepare a major offensive designed to clear the Baltic states and, above all, to take Riga.

Under these revised schedules and assignments, Govorov took over the Tartu sector from 3rd Baltic Front, the prelude to an attack aimed in the direction of Rakevere–Taps, breaking into the German rear and driving on Tallinn. The three remaining Baltic fronts were committed to a series of concentric attacks aimed at Riga: Maslennikov's 3rd Baltic would attack on both flanks, co-operating with the 10th Guards Army of 2nd Baltic Front to destroy German forces east of Smiltene (with the *Stavka* supplying an additional army, the 61st, plus one rifle corps from Govorov's front); Yeremenko's 2nd Baltic Front was aimed at Riga itself, an offensive to be carried through in co-operation with Maslennikov and Bagramyan whose task it was with 1st Baltic Front to wear down German forces east of Dobele, to block any breakthrough in the direction of Jelgava and Shaulyai—the axis of the fierce fighting in the past month—while attacking on the left flank with the object of reaching Vetsmuzhei and the mouth of the western Dvina. This would push Soviet armies on to the shore of the gulf of Riga in the general area of Riga itself and thus isolate Army Group North from East Prussia. The *Stavka* orders prescribed that the three Baltic Fronts were to go over to the offensive on 14 September, followed three days later by the Leningrad Front, where regrouping needed more time.

The size of this offensive indicated that the *Stavka* intended to go for the kill. The concentric attacks were designed to encircle the bulk of the German divisions in the Baltic states, with Bagramyan's thrust severing Army Group North from the rest of the German forces and driving the Germans to the sea, where a sea-borne blockade would keep them sealed off while deep frontal attacks destroyed the entire Army Group. Along the 500-kilometre front, the *Stavka* proposed to deploy 125 rifle divisions and seven tank corps—900,000 men, 17,483 guns and mortars, 3,081 tanks and 2,643 aircraft (supplemented by the naval aircraft of the Baltic Fleet). On the first days of the Soviet offensive the *Stavka* plan called for the commitment of ten 'all-arms' armies and three armoured corps, the equivalent of 95 rifle divisions of which 74 were to be employed on the 'breakthrough sectors' (with a total frontage of 76 kilometres), which meant committing more than three-quarters of the available Soviet strength to the breakthrough, leaving the secondary sectors under relatively light attack—a blunder which cost the Soviet command dear almost from the outset, since it left the Germans free to transfer units in strength to threatened lines and positions.

For the forthcoming offensive, Soviet armoured strength almost doubled, with Bagramyan disposing of 1,328 tanks and SP guns. Ths *Stavka* directive stipulated that Bagramyan's armour must be used to 'develop gains along the Riga axis', to which Bagramyan responded by deploying 5th Guards Tank Army and two tank corps (1st and 19th) on his left and at the centre. Yeremenko disposed of 287 tanks, more than half of which were assembled into 'mobile groups', 133 being assigned to the infantry-support role: Maslennikov used most of his 290 tanks and SP guns in an infantry-support role, leaving only 53 in reserve or for use with 'mobile groups'. Splitting up the armour in this fashion proved to be a very unsatisfactory solution, largely because it left insufficient tanks for use in infantry-support roles. This weakened the infantry, many of whose units and formations consisted of newly conscripted men taken into the army on the line of march through Belorussia and the Baltic states, raw recruits without any previous military training who were about to be committed to the most searing and intensive infantry fighting in any theatre. Many of the German defensive positions were protected by rivers, which meant assault crossings. Across the length of the front the terrain also assisted the tenacious German defence, which relied on preserving men and equipment by 'emptying' the forward positions during the preliminary Soviet bombardment, and holding units in reserve to put in counter-attacks which blunted or deflected the Soviet infantry attacks in the wake of the barrage. Bagramyan's unit and formation commanders seemed to have a good idea of what faced them on the German side, but Maslennikov and Yeremenko failed to register the German defences properly: reconnaissance on the 2nd Baltic Front began only a few hours before the main attack was due, and on the 3rd Baltic Front (in the area of 67th Army) it was thought that the German defences consisted of only a couple of lines of trenches, ignoring completely the defensive positions on the heights and the heavily fortified villages.

Preceded by an hour's artillery bombardment (extended to two on some sectors), the three Baltic fronts renewed the Soviet offensive on 14 September. Bagramyan's attack, preparations for which had been carefully camouflaged, came as an unpleasant surprise for units of the German Sixteenth Army transferred to the southern side of the Dvina. Striking out along a seven-mile sector, the assault groups penetrated several miles on the first day, with Beloborodov's 43rd Army fighting north of Bausk making the greatest progress and breaking into the second zone of the German defences, bringing 3rd Guards Mechanized Corps into the action. Fighting off a score of German counter-attacks, the Soviet assault divisions pushed forward to the 'eastern Jelgava defence line', capturing Bausk, Jelgava on the Dvina and Eckau; by the evening of 16 September advanced units of the mobile formations were drawing up to Baldon and reaching for the western Dvina, bringing Soviet units closer to the southern suburbs of Riga.

Attacking on the northern bank of the Dvina, Maslennikov and Yeremenko ran into stiff German opposition which slowed the Soviet advance very considerably. On 15 September Maslennikov's Front, aimed from the north-east in the general direction of Riga, began a converging attack on Valk, the fortified communications centre given additional protection by the marshes and thick forest surrounding it. Possession of Valk and the 'Valk line' secured the communications of the German force in Estonia (Operational Group 'Narva'), which meant that the German defenders would not lightly give it up. After four days of bitter fighting between units of the German Eighteenth Army and Maslennikov's units, Valk fell to the Russians. Yeremenko's 2nd Baltic Front armies were meanwhile attacking to the north-west of Madona and in the area of Plavinas on the Dvina, another German bastion which had to be toppled. The new offensive got off to a bad start, much as Yeremenko feared; the initial artillery bombardment was mounted in insufficient depth, the German positions were not destroyed in any depth and the Soviet attack came as no surprise to the German command. German units retired methodically from one system of defences to another, forcing Soviet troops to reorganize for each new step in this 'offensive' when as little as 2–3 miles separated the defensive lines. Three times Yeremenko introduced 5th Tank Corps to finish off the 'breakthrough', only to have it effectively beaten back. The broken terrain, small rivers, innumerable lakes and dense clumps of forest all gave the German commanders ample cover for ambushes and for camouflaging their defences. Col.-Gen. Sandalov, Yeremenko's chief of staff, also deplored the tactics of making single attacks where the Germans were ready and waiting, but such was the nature of *Stavka* directives (and Stalin's own refusal to countenance even tactical modifications) that outflanking could not be practised on any scale. Soviet units could only try to batter their way through the deeply echeloned German defences, admirably fitted out with weapon-pits, machine-gun positions, artillery and mortar firing points; command and observation posts, many of them substantial stone structures, were liberally distributed throughout the whole area and served as additional fortification when necessary. Minefields created an extra hazard, laid not in large fields but in clumps both at the forward edge of the German defences and throughout the depth of the positions.

With only forty miles separating Yeremenko from Riga, the German command lost no time in organizing a series of powerful counter-attacks to block the Soviet thrusts. With progress measured only in a few thousand yards, Soviet infantrymen faced the attacks of five German divisions supported by well over a hundred tanks, stabbing at every Soviet move. During 15–16 September the 3rd Shock Army and 22nd Army beat off one attack after another finally pushing the Germans back to the western bank of the Oger but making only a few thousand yards of ground. In the area of Ergli a powerful German armoured force drawn from 14th *Panzer* Division launched a series of attacks on 15 September, committing up to 200 tanks. But as Schörner fought off Yeremenko and threw in more armour against Bagramyan to the west of Jelgava and in the area of Baldon, Govorov's delayed offensive with the Leningrad Front finally opened on 17 September and resulted in very rapid gains, putting Group 'Narva' at risk and speeding up the decision to pull back the whole Army Group along a line running from the gulf of Finland to the western Dvina.

Govorov's front attacked from the Tartu sector, aiming to break through the German defences by means of concentric attacks: Fedyuninskii's 2nd Shock Army was already in its new position by 12 September, having moved southwards through Gdov and across the neck of land between the Peipus and Pskov lakes to take the place of 8th Army south of Tartu, deploying five rifle corps (including the 8th Estonian Corps) and one 'fortified district' unit, the 14th, a new unit for 2nd Shock and one whose commander scarcely impressed Fedyuninskii. The Front plan called for Fedyuninskii to strike north and north-west, destroying German units in the Tartu area, followed by the destruction of the whole 'Narva' Group as the 8th Army struck from the line of the Narva and advanced on Rakevere. Ahead of Fedyuninskii lay some five German divisions, their fortified lines by no means complete but the defence again facilitated by marsh and forest. On 17 September Fedyuninskii attacked with two corps in the lead—Simonyak's 30th Guards and Pern's 8th Estonian: by the end of the day, Soviet troops were ten miles deep into the German defences along a fifteen-mile front. To exploit

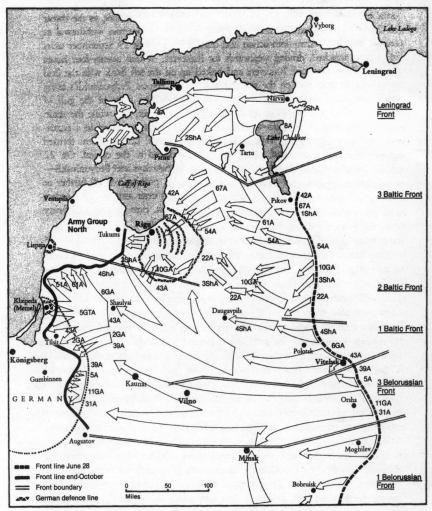

Leningrad Front

3 Baltic Front

2 Baltic Front

1 Baltic Front

3 Belorussian Front

1 Belorussian Front

Vyborg
Lake Ladoga
Leningrad
Tallinn
Narva
8A 2ShA
8A
2ShA
Lake Chudskoe
Parnu
Tartu
Gulf of Riga
Ventspils
42A
67A
Pskov
42A
67A
1ShA
Army Group North
Tukums
67A
61A
Riga
54A
54A
Liepaja
1ShA
10GA
22A
54A
4ShA
43A
3ShA
10GA
3ShA
51A 6TA
6GA
Shaulyai
43A
3ShA
22A
22A
Daugavpils
10GA
22A
Klaipeda (Memel)
5GTA
43A
4ShA
4ShA
6GA
Tilsit
2GA
Polotsk
43A
Königsberg
39A
Vitebsk
39A
Gumbinnen
5A
Kaunas
5A
3 Belorussian Front
GERMANY
11GA
Vilno
Orsha
11GA
31A
31A
Augustov
Moghilev
Minsk
Bobruisk

	Front line June 28
	Front line end-October
	Front boundary
	German defence line

0   50   100
Miles

Map 11 The Soviet drive into the Baltic states, July–November 1944

this success Fedyuninskii committed Colonel Kovalevskii's 'mobile group' made up of tank brigades and tank regiments, followed by another group under Colonel Protsenko on 19 September. The German command was already pulling its SS units back from the Narva sector on the evening of 18 September, as the threat to their rear from Fedyuninskii grew by the hour. The German withdrawal at once brought 8th Army into action and during the night of 19 September units of the 8th attacked, driving westwards for Rakevere. Within twenty-four hours Soviet mobile units took Rakevere and linked up on the left flank with the 2nd Shock Army at Lokusu on the western side of lake Peipus. Fedyuninskii's army now received orders to swing south in order to clear the shore of the gulf of Riga and to capture Parnue not later than 25 September, but while the main body swung south and south-west Pern's Estonian corps continued in a north-westerly direction, towards Tallinn, the Estonian capital. Lt.-Gen. Pern formed his own 'mobile group' and pushed on with all speed to the capital. On 22 September the city was cleared of German troops and two days later Fedyuninskii—forty-eight hours ahead of schedule—reached Parnu, pushing on still further to cross the frontier into Latvia. Then, to Fedyuninskii's utter astonishment, orders from the Front command brought his pursuit to a halt, even as his lead infantry formations seemed to be within striking distance of Riga.

Even before Fedyuninskii was halted in his tracks, it was plain that the attempt to take Riga by direct assault could not succeed. Maslennikov and Yeremenko were pinned down by heavy German attacks, their progress drastically reduced. Though Bagramyan had fought his way to the southern outskirts of Riga (Soviet units were only about fifteen miles from the city), to assault the city while the Germans held the right bank of the Dvina and the coast covered from the east by the lower reaches of the river Aa presented formidable problems. Schörner, while pulling his Army Group back to the final defence lines, smashed into the Soviet positions with two major counter-blows from the region of Baldon itself and once again in the area to the south-west of Dobele. On Bagramyan's left flank, in the Dobele area, the newly constituted Third *Panzer* Army (moved from Army Group Centre) hurled a dozen motorized battalions and almost 400 tanks into fierce attacks which lasted for a full five days, hammering at Bagramyan's flank armies (51st Guards and 5th Tank Army). From 16–22 September German tank units fought furiously to stave in the Soviet defences but only managed to dent the lines held by 6th Guards Army south of Dobele, all at the cost of 131 tanks and 14 assault guns. The German attacks did nevertheless prevent Bagramyan loosing his second assault group in a northerly attack from Jelgava towards Kemeri (to the west of Riga) and the Gulf of Riga.

The main assault group from 1st Baltic Front (43rd Army and 4th Shock Army) had already run into more German attacks in an effort to close the gap opening up on the southerly approaches to Riga. In the area of Baldon 14th *Panzer* Division put in yet another appearance, supported by two divisions pulled out of Group 'Narva'. Beloborodov's 43rd Army on the left flank took the brunt of these attacks mounted by at least six German divisions, but by the evening of 22 September Soviet divisions were still pushing on to a point not much more than ten miles from Riga. Bagramyan's progress with the 1st Baltic Front could not, however, hide the obvious fact that German forces still held substantial areas of the Baltic states. Destroying the enemy north of the Dvina was evidently beyond the capacity of the 2nd and 3rd Baltic Fronts until they were reinforced and regrouped. The slow rate of advance allowed the German command to make systematic and orderly withdrawals, falling back on Riga to turn it into a key fortified area; possession of Riga and the Moon islands also gave German warships freedom of the gulf of Riga and the middle reaches of the Baltic. Schörner still disposed of a formidable force on the northern bank of the Dvina—up to seventeen divisions—and drawing them into a much shorter line on this northern arc enabled him to start moving larger contingents into Courland and western Lithuania, anchoring himself against East Prussia without depending on the narrow 'gap' between Jelgava and the sea where only one road could be used.

The race to form a new front was on. If Schörner won it, he could count on building up a stable front line between Jelgava and Tilsit, firmly secured to East Prussia and anchored from Tukum in the north to Kelmy south-west of Shaulyai. In the event of a Soviet attack across the East Prussian border, the German command could riposte by attacking in the direction of Kaunas and striking the Russians deep in the flank. Neither side had a moment to lose. The *Stavka* ordered an immediate halt to all operations aimed at Riga and on 24 September issued a radically revised offensive plan, one which finally recognized the merits of Bagramyan's earlier pleading to put his weight on the left flank in order to strike the decisive blow. The concentration of German forces at Riga and in the 'Riga corridor', from which they could be syphoned westwards, demanded that the main Soviet attack be shifted from 'the Riga axis' to the 'Memel axis'. Bagramyan's 1st Baltic Front would transfer its right-flank armies presently engaged south of Riga to the region of Shaulyai, in order to strike in the direction of the coast and towards Memel, aiming for the mouth of the Niemen and thereby severing once and for all Army Group North's land connections with East Prussia. Riga itself was to be left to Maslennikov and Yeremenko, whose progress was slow but sure. In order to achieve maximum surprise Bagramyan's new offensive was timed for the very beginning of October.

The projected attack along the 'Memel axis' presented the rare spectacle of an entire Front being swung on to a completely new alignment. It was also an enterprise that commanded Stalin's closest personal attention: he alone conducted the discussions with Marshal Vasilevskii, *Stavka* representative with the Baltic Fronts, checking on the forces required, the problems of the massive regrouping, and the difficulties of concealing a manoeuvre on this scale. Attaining surprise— the indispensable condition of success—caused Stalin much misgiving, but the information available to the Soviet General Staff suggested that the *Stavka* had chosen a good moment in which to launch this enterprise: the maximum distance over which formations must be moved did not exceed 120 miles and the Soviet command disposed of more than twenty-five separate routes along which they could be shifted. Soviet command of the air also guaranteed a minimum, if not the total absence, of German observation. In six days Bagramyan's right-flank and centre army formations—three infantry armies, a tank army and three armoured corps, together with equipment and supplies—moved into the new deployment area to the north of Shaulyai; south of the Dvina Yeremenko's 3rd Shock Army took over what had been 1st Baltic sector. Late in September more than half a million men, 10,000 guns and mortars, and well over a thousand tanks criss-crossed Front, army and divisional boundaries. From Dobele, Bagramyan transferred 5th Guards Tank Army, three armoured corps (1st and 19th Tank, 3rd Mechanized) and two rifle crops detached from 2nd Baltic Front: the new concentration area lay to the north of Shaulyai, making use of the woods and thick forest for concealment. Further south Chernyakhovskii with the 3rd Belorussian Front received orders to use his right-flank 39th Army in an attack from the Rasieni area towards Tauroggen, with an additional thrust south of the Niemen aimed at Gumbinnen, designed to block German attempts to move reinforcements up to Memel.

Bagramyan planned to break into the German defences on his left along two sectors, with a distance of some twenty miles separating the two attacks: 6th Guards, 43rd, 51st and 5th Guards Tank Armies would launch the main blow. Where the flanks of 6th Guards and 43rd Armies locked, along a ten-mile breakthrough sector, Bagramyan concentrated twenty-nine rifle divisions (half the force available to the Front); 6th Guards was to strike north-westwards, 43rd Army west and south-west, with Volskii's tank army moving into the junction of the two infantry armies with orders to clear a path to the west by the end of the first day of offensive operations. Since 6th Guards and 43rd would be moving on divergent axes, Bagramyan planned to bring his second-echelon army— the 51st—up to the junction as additional stiffening and protection. The second thrust was aimed at Kelme–Tilsit and assigned to 2nd Guards Army, whose breakthrough sector ran for five miles: the objective was the river Niemen and the aim to cover the main Soviet striking force from any attack coming from the south. General Chernyakhovskii would meanwhile employ 39th Army with six divisions to break out on a two-mile sector south of Rasieni with the object of capturing Tauroggen and linking up with 2nd Guards Army in the drive for the Niemen, thereby encircling German forces to the east of Tauroggen itself.

To screen this massive deployment on his left flank, Bagramyan moved infantry and tank formations only by night. Infantry units travelled usually about twenty miles, towed artillery and armour almost twice that distance, with the infantry moving out first, followed by armour taking separate roads and then concealed or camouflaged in the Shaulyai woods. Only on 2 October did the German command discern what was happening on Bagramyan's left. By that time it was too late. From Aut to the Niemen there were about eight German divisions, five of them facing Bagramyan's assault armies. Schörner's divisions, also on the move, lay straddled between the gulf of Riga and the railway line running from Shaulyai to Libau, falling back into Courland. Further east the two Baltic Fronts, 2nd and 3rd, continued to batter at the last German defence line, 'Sigulda', blind and almost purposeless attacks save for the fact that they prevented Schörner pulling more troops out. Marshal Govorov was assigned by the *Stavka* to act as 'co-ordinator' for this two-front operation and planned a massive break-in for 7 October, but a rapid change in the situation further west brought another abrupt change in plans.

For the first few days in October thick fog had hung over Bagramyan's left flank, hampering his reconnaissance battalions. On 5 October the fog still lingered and only at 11 o'clock could reconnaissance parties move forward. Ten minutes later the guns opened fire and the forward parties rushed for the first line of German trenches. In 6th Guards and 43rd Army area, the forward units made for crossings over the river Venta; on 2nd Guards front for the river Dubissa. After ninety minutes the attack roared into high gear. Chistyakov's 6th Guards and Beloborodov's 43rd drove on for about five miles, but the fog tied Soviet aircraft to their airfields and blinded the artillery. The short October day ended before the tank formations could be brought into the action. On 6 October Volskii's tanks drove through rain and slush to join the battle which was unrolling across a 120-mile front: Chanchibadze's 2nd Guards Army had already driven several thousand yards into the German lines and now 39th Army, supported by the 1st Air Army, extended the Soviet offensive across the length of the front.

With all of Bagramyan's armies engaged and Chernyakhovskii's right-flank army committed, the German command—well aware of the danger of encirclement—began withdrawing divisions from the north-west of Riga during the night of 6 October. On the morning of 7 October 2nd and 3rd Baltic Fronts pushed forward in the wake of the retreating German troops and advanced up to seven miles during that same day. In this effort to compress Army Group North still further, units of the Leningrad Front landed on the islands of Dago and Osel. To hold off the Soviet pressure Schörner needed more men, but with East Prussia now visibly threatened by 3rd Belorussian Front the German command could not release a single division. With the Soviet offensive developing along multiple axes—towards Memel, Riga and the Moon islands—the available German forces were pinned down across a huge arc, facing an additional threat developing in the direction of Gumbinnen. No longer could reserves be switched almost at will. By the evening of 8 October, 43rd Army was closing on the first defensive positions covering Memel, an indication that Bagramyan was on the verge of decisive success. Advancing at high speed, Volskii's 5th Guards Tank Army also drew up to the defences at the approach to Memel, the assault formations of 1st Baltic Front having torn a gap forty-five miles deep across a front of over 120 miles and rolling up the few German divisions in their path.

With his left-flank armies Bagramyan pressed on towards the lower reaches of the Niemen, at the centre towards the sea and on the right in a north-westerly direction, though on this axis the Soviet advance slowed down in the face of growing German resistance. Kreizer's 51st Army made the fastest progress and on 10 October captured the small Lithuanian port of Palanga, twenty miles to the north of Memel itself; Volskii's tanks forced the river Minija and also reached the sea in the area of Palanga. Beloborodov's 43rd, with the Minija already behind it, pressed even closer to Memel. On the left flank 2nd Guards Army, moving to the south-west in the direction of Tilsit, reached Tauroggen, taking over a sector from 39th Army which was to strike on to the south of the Niemen. With this mass of Soviet divisions implanted on the coast and north of Memel, the trap finally swung shut and cut Army Group North off from any land link with East Prussia.

Meanwhile, in the direction of Riga, Maslennikov's units fought the German rearguards on the 'Sigulda line', while Yeremenko's 2nd Baltic Front took Oger (where the river Oger joins the Dvina) on 8 October. Schörner's plea to retire to the Tukums line west of Riga fell on deaf ears at Hitler's headquarters; German divisions north and south of the Dvina fought on. The first Soviet attempt on 10 October to storm the outer defences of Riga failed, but the morning attacks were renewed in the afternoon, piercing the German lines in a number of places. Fierce German counter-attacks then restored the position within a few hours. The next day the pattern repeated itself, full of bloody actions amidst the marshes and lesser lakes, but Soviet infantrymen pushed as far as the perimeter defences covering the city itself. Schörner again appealed for permission to withdraw from what was rapidly becoming a hopeless situation, and this time was authorized to retire to the 'Tukums line'—but not before the evening of 12 October. On the morning of 12 October, however, Soviet units finally battered their way through the first line of defence inside Riga, and by the afternoon were fighting within the second line. The end was a matter of hours. Piece by piece the German defences disintegrated and the garrison sought what safety it could in flight. Riga fell to Soviet troops on 13 October. The campaign to liberate the Baltic states was over, and in Moscow Stalin announced the fall of Riga to the accompaniment of the Prime Minister's plaudits.

After ten weeks the Soviet armies finally succeeded in isolating Army Group North holding the Baltic states from East Prussia. With the fall of Riga the *Stavka* disbanded Maslennikov's 3rd Baltic Front: 1st Shock Army and the 14th Air Army went to Yeremenko's command, 61st Army to Bagramyan's 1st Baltic Front. The German forces were now grouped into two 'bridgeheads', a smaller one at Memel and a much larger force blockaded within Courland, remnants of the German Sixteenth and Eighteenth Armies amounting to some thirty divisions which dwindled through evacuation by sea: a few divisions escaped to East Prussia, using Tilsit itself or the ferries on the Niemen. The *Stavka* nevertheless decided upon the destruction of these trapped divisions, a task which fell to 2nd Baltic

and 1st Baltic Fronts. Yeremenko's 2nd Baltic would attack wc
Dobele, and Bagramyan would strike to the north-west, using the re
his Front forces to clear Memel and to occupy the northern bank of the
in the area of Tilsit. Chernyakhovskii would attack simultaneously in the dir
of Gumbinnen to prevent any transfer of troops to Courland. The main Sov
objective was the isolation of Schörner's Courland group and the investment o
the northern bank of the Niemen, a prerequisite for any offensive across the East
Prussian border.

Thirty or so German divisions were jammed into Courland between Tukums
and Libau (Liepaja): four German divisions were holding Memel and several
more—two *Panzer* divisions, four infantry divisions and a motorized brigade
(assigned to Third *Panzer* Army)—faced Bagramyan's left-flank units converging
on Tilsit. Chernyakhovskii had to reckon with some ten German divisions from
Fourth Army (Army Group Centre). To eliminate these forces the *Stavka* approved
plans which called for 2nd Baltic Front to attack from Dobele with three armies
(3rd Shock, 42nd and 22nd Armies) in a westerly direction, assisted by a secondary
attack rolling along the coastline to Tukums and bringing Soviet units to a line
running from Tukums to Aut; Bagramyan would make his main effort to the
north, with the object of destroying the trapped divisions in Courland, striking
to Skrunda with 6th Guards Army and towards Liepaja with 51st Army. Two
armies, 61st and 5th Tank Armies, moved up to support this attack, while the
flank armies moving to the Niemen and presently investing Memel would prevent
any German attempt to link up with the Courland garrisons. To tie down German
units in East Prussia, Chernyakhovskii's 3rd Belorussian Front prepared an attack
from the area of Volkovishki aimed at Insterburg with the object of bringing
Soviet troops to the Gumbinnen–Goldap line.

On the morning of 16 October the two Baltic fronts and the 3rd Belorussian
Front launched their several attacks. Lt.-Gen. Zakhvatayev's 1st Shock Army on
the right flank of Yeremenko's 2nd Baltic Front made the best progress during
the next few days, forcing the Lielupe and taking Kemery on 18 October, but
on reaching the defensive positions covering Tukums 1st Shock Army was halted
in its tracks. The offensive finally stalled in the face of heavy German resistance
making great use of the marshes and bogs which abounded. Bagramyan's attack
along the 'Liepaja axis' also ran into sustained German resistance, where counter-
attacks at full divisional strength supported by substantial numbers of tanks held
off the Soviet armies. In spite of a further attempt late in October to burst
through the German defences and deal the final blow to the trapped divisions,
Bagramyan's men could not manage it and this offensive inevitably came to a
halt. Nor did Soviet troops succeed in rushing the defences at Memel. On the
East Prussian frontier, Chernyakhovskii pressed home a powerful attack, penetrating
two German defensive lines and capturing Goldap, only to bump into a third
line running from Angerapp to Gumbinnen and on to Pilkallen. The way to the
'Insterburg gap' was barred except for a frontal assault on Gumbinnen or a

allen. Both, for the moment, were impossible, and
o was called off at the end of October.
iuary 1945: the Courland divisions remained locked
ng but a wasting asset. Their war came to an end
rrendered to the Red Army.

...ng already surveyed the outcome of the gigantic
offensive operations conducted by the Red Army during the summer and early
autumn, senior officers of the Soviet General Staff in Moscow bent over their
maps and pored over their calculations to complete the operational plan for the
final campaign of the war, the Soviet invasion of Hitler's *Reich*. This was the
preparation of nothing less than the greatest campaign in military history, a
campaign that was to unleash men in their millions and machines in their
thousands, fusing massed battlefield efficiency with an elemental appetite for
revenge, combining at the end cruel, unrelenting fighting with a rampage of
almost animalistic fury. Behind the Soviet armies lay mile upon mile of stupefying
ruination and the terrible, staggering weight of their own dead; ahead, at long
last, 'the lair of the Fascist beast', the approaches to which were emblazoned
with savage propaganda signs and slogans, designed to ravage the soldier's memory
with the evocation of past crimes committed by a now shuddering enemy on
him and his own. From the top to the bottom, from the *Stavka* and the General
Staff to the platoons and sections, the scent of the great kill sharpened with each
day. 'As before', wrote a Soviet soldier towards the end of 1944, 'I am on my
way to Berlin . . . Berlin is precisely the place we *must* reach . . . we deserve
the right to enter Berlin'. Stalin's mind apparently ran on exactly the same lines.
Within days, therefore, he nominated the Soviet field commander and selected
the Front forces for the capture of Berlin. The task of 'co-ordination' (normally
assigned to *Stavka* 'representatives') he reserved exclusively for himself.

The balance sheet for the year's operations proved to be more rewarding than
the Soviet command's own expectations. All the German army groups—North,
Centre, North Ukraine (A) and South Ukraine (Group South)—had suffered
drastic losses. The Red Army destroyed on Soviet calculations 96 divisions and
24 brigades (killed or captured), battering another 219 divisions and 22 brigades,
of which 33 divisions and 17 brigades were so severely mauled that they were
disbanded. On this reckoning the German armies in the east lost more than a
million and a half men, 6,700 tanks, 28,000 guns and mortars, and over 12,000
aircraft; during the months of August, September and October the *Ostheer* suffered
672,000 casualties, receiving 201,000 men as replacements—cutting German
strength in the east during this single three-month period by almost half a million
men.

With the offensive unrolling across the entire arc from the Barents to the Black
Sea, Soviet armies fought on not only their own territory but also on that of

eight foreign countries. The greatest depth of operations was re
western theatre' (south-eastern Europe), which stretched for 750 miles
of double envelopments increased—Vitebsk, Bobruisk, Minsk, Brody and K
with a marked reduction in the time taken for the elimination of the encirc
divisions (which at Stalingrad lasted two months but at Kishinev not much more
than five days and east of Minsk a week). Of all the German units knocked
out during the years 1941–4, more than half (sixty-five per cent) were eliminated
in the course of 1944. The scale of these operations also showed in the effort to
maintain supplies to the fronts: in 1943 the central supply system delivered the
equivalent of 1,164,000 million railway wagon loads, in 1944 the figure rose
to 1,465,000 (of which 118,000 consisted of ammunition loads alone). The
three services consumed almost 4 million tons of fuel (almost one-third of the
entire wartime consumption) compared with 3.2 million tons in 1943. Production
of weapons continued to climb towards the end of 1944, rising to the peak of
almost 30,000 tanks and SP guns, together with 40,000 aircraft.

Save for Courland, the Soviet frontier was now everywhere restored. At the
end of October, Soviet troops reached the northern frontier of Finland, with
whom the Soviet Union formally signed an armistice on 19 September, and were
pushing into northern Norway. With the Baltic states now virtually cleared, the
Soviet advance reached into East Prussia itself as far as a line running from
Goldap to Augusto, on the eastern and south-eastern borders. Somewhat to the
south, Soviet armies established a number of bridgeheads on the Narew and the
Vistula, the most important being Serock (2nd Belorussian) and three at Magnuszew, Pulawy and Sandomierz, held by the 1st Belorussian and 1st Ukrainian
Fronts emplaced along the line of Praga (Warsaw)—the Vistula–Jaslo; in Hungary
the 3rd Ukrainian Front was fighting on the outskirts of Budapest. The decisive
zone of operations—that which contained the shortest direct route to Germany—
lay between the Niemen and the Carpathians, but the whole slanting of the
Soviet fronts at the end of October placed considerable strength to the north,
with many armies deployed between the Niemen and the Gulf of Finland, and
Meretskov's army group committed between the Gulf of Finland and the Arctic
Ocean. Of those Soviet army groups deployed along this shortest route (Chernyakhovskii's 3rd Belorussian, Zakharov's 2nd Belorussian, Rokossovskii's 1st
Belorussian and Koniev's 1st Ukrainian Front), two—3rd and 2nd Belorussian—
faced the formidable obstacle of East Prussia. They required reinforcement, but
time was needed to redeploy them in the 'northern zone' even though the surrender
of Finland and the reduction of the Baltic states released several armies to join
the Niemen–Carpathians concentration. It was not simply a question of storming
on into the *Reich,* or even of redeploying: the whole balance of the eastern front
had to be taken into consideration.

At first sight, a thrust straight through East Prussia seemed to offer the most
favourable opportunity, not least because the 3rd Belorussian Front outnumbered
the enemy, with 40 Soviet infantry divisions to the German army's 11, 2 Soviet

...ns, in all 17 German formations against 47 ...aff submitted, therefore, that with reinforcement ... possible to drive in strength through East Prussia ...n to the mouth of the Vistula. On closer inspection, ... optimistic, since in the first instance Soviet superiority ... divisional strengths (a German infantry division disposed ... its Soviet counterpart and a Soviet armoured corps was ...t of a *Panzer* division). As for the 'Warsaw–Poznan axis' ano ... ', where the 'battle for Berlin' was to be decided, the Soviet General ... ...cipated very heavy resistance. They calculated that even with maximum en... , the 1st Belorussian and 1st Ukrainian Fronts could drive only as deep as 90–100 miles.

There remained yet another radical alternative—to use the 'southern' fronts, 4th, 3rd and 2nd Ukrainian Fronts, in a deep penetration aimed at the *Reich*, passing through Budapest, Bratislava and Vienna. In Rumania enemy armies had been dispersed and destroyed, while war-weary Hungarian divisions (as they were depicted by Soviet intelligence) formed a large part of the defending force in Hungary, the 'breakwater' of the *Reich*. The events of mid-October in Hungary dispelled that illusion: Hungary was held tight within the German grip, the fighting for Budapest took a desperate turn, and by the end of October the Soviet command reckoned with the presence of thirty-nine enemy formations in action against Malinovskii's 2nd Ukrainian Front battling at the approaches to Budapest, and on a 350-mile front running from Miskolcz in the north to Subotica in the south.

The Soviet General Staff could not ignore the fact that the Soviet offensive was slowly running down. It was time to give the divisions some respite, to regroup, to reorganize the supply and rear services, and to build up reserves of men and weapons to ensure that the coming breakthrough operations could be successfully carried through. Marshal Zhukov and Marshal Rokossovskii on the 1st Belorussian Front put these points plainly to Stalin towards the end of October: the offensive operations between Seroch, Modlin and Praga entrusted to the 47th and 70th Armies were producing no results at all, except for inflicting heavy casualties on the tired and depleted Soviet armies. Perkhorovich's 47th was fighting under orders from the *Stavka* to reach the Vistula between Warsaw and Modlin, with instructions to expand the bridgeheads on the river Narew. Zhukov could see no point whatsoever in these fruitless and exhausting operations. Stalin, however, was not so persuaded, and when the two Soviet commanders reported to him personally in Moscow he suggested armoured and aviation reinforcement for 47th Army to ram it on to the Vistula. Though Molotov bleated about stopping a successful offensive, Zhukov pointed out that the Germans were clearly holding up the Soviet advance and insisted to Stalin that 'our offensive will yield us nothing but casualties'. Zhukov then continued with a typical strategic résumé that went to the heart of the matter—the Soviet armies did not need the area

Map 12 Overall Soviet offensive operations in eastern Europe, 1944

north-west of Warsaw; the city must be turned from the south-west, and at the same time 'a powerful splitting blow' must be delivered in the direction of Lodz-Poznan. This would inevitably smash in the German Vistula Front and open the way for deep penetrations by Soviet mobile columns. After ushering out Zhukov and Rokossovski, urging them 'to think some more', Stalin recalled them after twenty minutes and informed them that Soviet forces would go over to the defensive: as for future plans, these would be discussed later. The next day Stalin consulted Zhukov on another matter, asking whether the fronts could be controlled directly from the *Stavka* (without the use of 'co-ordinators' such as Zhukov himself or Marshal Vasilevskii). Zhukov agreed that the smaller number of operational fronts and the shortening of the front as a whole made this quite feasible. That evening Stalin telephoned Zhukov to inform him that the 1st Belorussian Front would be operating in what he called 'the Berlin strategic zone' and that he, Zhukov, would assume command of the front. Zhukov agreed.

At the beginning of November the three Belorussian fronts (1st, 2nd and 3rd) were obliged to turn to the defensive in 'the entire western zone of operations'. General Antonov of the General Staff and Shtemenko at the head of Operations along with A.A. Gryzlov and N.A. Lomov (the officers responsible for planning particular strategic axes) now elaborated the draft plan for submission to Stalin and the *Stavka*. In line with what had now become standard procedure, this draft plan concentrated on the initial phases of the offensive and simply sketched in subsequent Front assignments. The broad outlines derived from an 'all-round assessment of the situation and capabilities of all the combatants', Allied and Axis: at this point the Red Army in the east and the Allied armies in the west stood roughly the same distance from Berlin, with 74 German divisions in the west, supported by 1,600 tanks, facing 87 Allied divisions and over 6,000 tanks, while in the east the German command retained over 3 million men, about 4,000 tanks and 2,000 aircraft. With such a balance sheet before them, the Soviet planners drew some obvious conclusions about the 'race for Berlin'. Clearly, for the Red Army the 'central sector' (or the 'western zone') was of decisive importance, providing the most direct route into Germany. But here the German armies must offer the stiffest resistance. To weaken this German concentration at the centre, the Red Army would have to operate with maximum effectiveness on the flanks, involving not only Hungary and Austria but also East Prussia. In brief, a powerful thrust into Budapest and against Vienna meant a simultaneous attack on Königsberg, thus draining German strength away from the 'western axis'.

Prescribing the particular assignments of the fronts proved to be both complicated and taxing, since the offensive along the western axis brought the General Staff face to face with the problem of East Prussia with its well-organized defence system. The threat of a German thrust from East Prussia against the right flank of Marshal Zhukov's armies striking along the Berlin axis could only be neutralized by the Red Army itself driving into East Prussia and sealing it off from contact with the remainder of the front. To accomplish this, two Soviet fronts would be needed, one for an attack on Königsberg from the east and a second for isolating German forces in East Prussia from Army Group A defending the Berlin axis. The deep outflanking of East Prussia from the south and south-west would at the same time secure the flank of the Soviet armies deployed along the Warsaw–Poznan–Berlin approach. The 2nd and 3rd Belorussian Fronts were promptly assigned to the East Prussian operation. For the 'main task', the offensive designed to breach the German strategic front followed by a rapid drive to the west, the two fronts on the Vistula—1st Belorussian and 1st Ukrainian—were selected, subject to massive armoured reinforcement, especially tank armies and independent tank corps.

At the beginning of November 1944 the General Staff plan was ready, the Front assignments delineated, the direction of their thrusts fixed, together with Front boundaries and the depth of their immediate objectives set, followed by their subsequent assignments. The General Staff plan submitted that within forty-five days the German war machine could be smashed by offensive operations reaching a depth of 375–440 miles, a two-stage operation but with no 'operational pause' between phases. The first stage would occupy fifteen days, the second thirty. The rate of advance was deliberately not fixed too high, for heavy German resistance was expected, particularly in these 'closing battles'. The prospect of such resistance stamped itself on the particular Front assignments: Chernyakhovskii's 3rd Belorussian, facing the defences of East Prussia, was assigned immediate objectives to a depth of 100–120 miles. The 1st Belorussian Front was to attack in the general direction of Poznan, the 1st Ukrainian Front to reach the Oder north-west of Glogau, Breslau and Ratibor; the immediate objective for 1st Belorussian Front became the breaking of enemy defences in two separate areas in a simultaneous attack, moving to the Lodz line once the German forces in the Warsaw–Radom area were eliminated, advancing after this stage in the direction of Poznan to a line running through Bromberg–Poznan and enlarging the attack to the south until 1st Belorussian linked up with 1st Ukrainian Front. With 1st Ukrainian Front disposing of massive strength, any southerly 'extension' of 1st Belorussian Front commitments seemed on the face of it unlikely; the greater probability was that 2nd Belorussian Front battering its way into East Prussia might need help and in this event Zhukov would have to move part of his forces to the north.

From the outset the final campaign directed against the *Reich* was conceived as a two-stage operation, with the 'old' axis—the southern-flank offensive aimed at Budapest—taking the brunt in the very first instance: the General Staff planners counted on using the brief breathing space to move up Tolbukhin's 3rd Ukrainian Front (that entity which seemed for so long to have disappeared from the Soviet order of battle) into the region between the Tisza and the Danube, bringing the bulk of its forces to the south of Kecskemet. With 2nd and 3rd Ukrainian Fronts so closed up, it should be possible so to increase the rate of advance that within twenty or twenty-five days Soviet armies would reach a line running from Banska Bystrica through Komarno and on to Nagykanizsa (west of Budapest), and within one month after that push on to the outskirts of Vienna. The General Staff calculated that the threat of the destruction of the vital southern flank must impel the German command to move troops from the central sector to defend it, thereby easing the task of the fronts attacking to the north of the Carpathians.

Nor did the General Staff planners entertain any doubts about the possibility of Soviet armies on the lower reaches of the Vistula being able to reach Bromberg and capture Poznan, thus bringing them out on a line running from Breslau to Pardbitse on the Elbe and further south closing on Vienna, advancing the Soviet front from its October disposition anything from 75 to 220 miles. Once on this line, the second stage would open and lead to the final capitulation of the *Reich*.

At the beginning of November Stalin summoned Marshal Zhukov and General Antonov for a discussion of the proposed operational plans. Already Stalin had to be persuaded of the futility of prolonging further offensive operations, agreeing with obvious reluctance to countermand the existing directives. Zhukov came out unequivocally against a frontal attack across the Vistula and again, with the same reluctance, Stalin finally agreed. Yet on the question of reinforcing the assault on East Prussia—where, in Zhukov's opinion, the *Stavka* had blundered not so many weeks earlier—Stalin seemed unwilling to face facts by strengthening the 2nd Belorussian Front with an additional army to undertake this offensive, though the obvious solution was to take that reinforcement from the Baltic fronts due to go over to the defensive.

A few days later, on 7 November and during the October Revolution holiday, Marshals Tolbukhin, Rokossovskii and Koniev together with General Chernyak-hovskii worked over the plans in the General Staff, a secret and select assembly since the *Stavka* did not propose this time to hold a general conference of commanders such as was convened on the eve of the Belorussian offensive, Operation *Bagration*. Each front worked out its own requirements and then submitted requests for reinforcements and supplies to the General Staff. Though no major modification to the main operational plan emerged in these preliminary discussions, the *Stavka* did not give it formal approval until late in November. Stalin let it be known that 'D-day' would be somewhere between 15 and 20 January 1945, but for the moment Front planning went ahead without the *Stavka* issuing formal directives or even without the main plan being authorized in the usual fashion. The crucial decision, however, emerged with some rapidity—the nomination of the commander of the troops assigned to capture Berlin. The man nominated was Zhukov, Stalin's deputy, an appointment made official on 16 November when Zhukov took command of the 1st Belorussian Front and Rokossovskii assumed command of the 2nd Belorussian Front from G.F. Zakharov: both Zhukov and Rokossovskii received the news personally from Stalin, who passed it to them by telephone.

The singular innovation of the Berlin operation lay not in the reshuffle of the commanders but in Stalin assuming the role of 'co-ordinator' for all four fronts involved. With Zhukov emplaced as the senior field commander in charge of the operations, and with Stalin acting as his own *Stavka* 'co-ordinator', it was Marshal Vasilevskii who was rudely displaced, leaving him only 1st and 2nd Baltic Fronts to occupy his considerable talents: in effect, the chief of the General Staff (a position Vasilevskii still held) was marooned in a military backwater. (That he was rescued from it owed nothing to Stalin but was due to a twist of fate which killed General Chernyakhovskii, 3rd Belorussian Front commander.)

Even with the general acceptance of the operational plan, much remained to be done in the way of specifying Front assignments, above all the operations of 1st Belorussian Front. The original General Staff plan envisaged 1st Belorussian Front attacking from the Magnuszew and Pulawy bridgeheads, breaking through the German defences at great speed, a concept that required adjustments to the attack assignments for Zhukov's left-hand neighbour, Koniev's 1st Ukrainian Front. Here the General Staff proposed that Koniev's Front should not take 'the shortest route into Germany' but should rather shift its attack a little to the north, in the direction of Kalisz, since taking the shortest route meant crashing into the Upper Silesian industrial region—ideally fitted for defence with its massive structures and installations. Further ahead lay German Silesia, also a formidable defensive obstacle. After discussing the problem with Marshal Koniev himself and submitting it to the *Stavka*, the General Staff substituted a plan to outflank Silesia from the north and north-east. This variant brought the double advantage of preserving Silesian industry from destruction and introducing Koniev's troops into the rear of German forces covering Poznan. Stalin himself impressed on Koniev the need to spare the factories of Silesia.

Zhukov arrived at *Stavka* on 27 November to discuss his own operations. The latest intelligence assessments confirmed that any Soviet thrust due west would be met by heavy German resistance on well-defended lines. To guarantee speedy success with the breakthrough operation and the subsequent westerly drive, Zhukov proposed that his armies strike first for Lodz and then shift their attack towards Poznan. Stalin agreed, this time without demur, and the revised attack assignments for 1st Belorussian Front were duly affixed to the master plan. Once this decision was accepted, the need to adjust Koniev's attack to the north disappeared and Breslau rather than Kalisz became the prime target for the 1st Ukrainian Front. At the end of November the General Staff had completed the full plot of the forthcoming offensive. Apart from some minor changes, the plan remained unaltered. Though formal *Stavka* directives had not yet been issued, the normal pre-offensive preparations went ahead, with a significant build-up in reserves and the stockpiling of supplies, especially ammunition. Even the simplest military tally suggested the scale of the storm about to break over the eastern front: Soviet strength in the field climbed to over six and a half million men, supported by more than 100,000 guns and mortars, 13,000 tanks and SP guns, over 15,000 aircraft—fifty-five 'all-arms' armies, six tank armies and thirteen air armies, no less than 500 rifle divisions being prepared for the final apocalyptic battle.

On 20 November, when the Soviet attack plan for a massive eruption into Germany was largely complete, Hitler left the barely finished towers of the *Wolfsschanze* for his 'western' headquarters at Ziegenberg. The move from East Prussia was dictated by the imminence of the German attack in the west, the

'Ardennes offensive' designed to 'eliminate the danger in the West'. With that accomplished, there was 'every possibility of holding out and sticking it through'— so Hitler informed his officers when explaining his decision to go over to the offensive in the west. To win time and to frustrate the hope among his enemies of winning total victory, Hitler intended first to strike in the west and still to have time to move armies to the east to beat back the Soviet offensive directed at 'Fortress Germany'. Devastating though the military impact of the Ardennes offensive proved to be in the beginning, it worked the one effect that Hitler refused to countenance as reality, triggering the very Soviet offensive which at the end of 1944 he dismissed angrily as a mere figment of the imagination of the officers in *Fremde Heere Ost*. Nor was the *Reich*'s new martinet Himmler any more persuaded by the facts and the figures, scoffing at the whole idea of a Soviet attack to Guderian's face in a rush of condescension and conceit—'. . . I don't really believe that the Russians will attack at all. It's all an enormous bluff. . . .'

7

The Assault on the *Reich*: January–March 1945

Shortly before dawn on the morning of 16 December 1944, with their final deployment concealed by the prevailing fog and snow showers, twenty-five divisions from three German armies swept into the attack along a seventy-mile front in the Ardennes held only by a handful of American divisions. The 'Battle of the Bulge', which lasted well into January 1945, opened with this thunderbolt blow and enjoyed considerable success in the beginning. Aimed at Antwerp, with the object of splitting the Allied armies and destroying four of them in the northern sector, the *Panzer* divisions struck out for the river Meuse. In the north Sepp Dietrich's Sixth *Panzer* Army struggled to reach the roads it so desperately needed, though *Kampfgruppe Peiper* managed to break out, butchering soldiers, prisoners and civilians in its path. At the centre, south of Saint-Vith, two corps of Manteuffel's Fifth *Panzer* Army burst through the thin screen of Americans, crashed into Luxemburg and raced for the Meuse using the route running through the Belgian town of Bastogne. Having surrounded Bastogne the German tanks continued their drive for the Meuse, only to be caught on 23 December by the Allied air forces when the skies suddenly cleared.

On Christmas Day, when lead German armour was only three miles from the Meuse at Celle but already bumping into the American 2nd Armoured Division, a despondent Col.-Gen. Guderian drove from his headquarters in Zossen to the 'Adlerhorst' redoubt near Giessen for a conference with Hitler and his other military advisers. Convinced by now of the futility of pressing the attack in the west which could not lead to a decisive German success, Guderian intended to ask the *Führer* to break off the Ardennes offensive and move all available forces to the eastern front, where the warning lights were already flashing. Though Chernyakhovskii's hammering at the doors of East Prussia had ceased for the moment and a relative calm had settled on the Narew and Vistula lines, the battle in Hungary had intensified when Tolbukhin's 3rd Ukrainian Front joined Malinovskii's 2nd, and fierce fighting was now raging for Budapest, as the two Soviet fronts battled under hard winter conditions to close the ring on the German defenders. The trap was all but closed.

Guderian went well armed for this confrontation with the *Führer*. Gehlen, head of *Fremde Heere Ost,* prepared a formidable brief indicating that a huge wave of Soviet armies must shortly break over the *Reich* from the east. The Soviet and German armies presently faced each other across a drastically shortened front, cut from 4,400 kilometres to little more than 2,000; the line ran from Memel on the Baltic, along the border of East Prussia to the line of the Vistula east of Warsaw, thence across Poland and eastern Czechoslovakia to the river Danube north of Budapest, lake Balaton and the river Drava, at which junction the Red Army gave way to Marshal Tito's Yugoslav 'National-Liberation Army' holding its own line running east of Sarajevo and on to the shore of the Adriatic at Zadar. Only the German divisions bottled up in Courland remained on Soviet territory, a useful reserve but one imprisoned by Soviet troops. Massed along the eastern borders of Germany was a gigantic Soviet force made up of almost six million men, deployed on nine fronts each of which was preparing its own operations for the final campaign. Gehlen's report, based on interrogation of prisoners and an assessment of Soviet operational intentions (dated 5 and 22 December respectively), made grim reading. It announced a major Soviet attack 'towards the middle of January' at the latest; and the tabulation of Soviet Front strength left no doubt what was in store for the *Ostheer,* destined for destruction by the Red Army. The essence of the Soviet plan consisted of drawing German reserves away from Army Group A and from the centre by heavy attacks in Hungary, after which the Soviet command would be free to develop its main assault on Germany's vitals.

Though the front had shortened, it was still too long for Guderian's peace of mind. The divisions in Courland had remained on Hitler's express insistence; he ruled out 'timely evacuation' of the Balkans and of Norway, and he overruled the proposal that the *Hauptkampflinie (HKL)* should be separated by several miles from the *Grosskampflinie* (the 'main battle line'), thus forcing the Russians to waste men and munitions on assaulting the first line—the *HKL*—only to crash into the real German strength at the second. The result of ignoring this advice was simply an invitation to disaster: major defensive positions and the few available reserves were bunched up to present one prime target, all under the barrels of the Russian guns. Not content with throwing out Guderian's arguments on tactical methods, Hitler also debunked the talk of a forthcoming Soviet attack as so much rubbish, dismissing Gehlen's reports out of hand and ridiculing the idea of a mass of Soviet armies about to fall on the *Reich*. In the *Führer's* opinion, a Soviet rifle division fielded no more than 7,000 men—an estimate not far off the mark, as it proved; but to assert that Soviet tank armies lacked tanks was nothing but insane self-delusion. Yet this stubborn refusal to face even a modicum of facts enabled Hitler to discount any Soviet attack in the east for the immediate future, whatever Gehlen might indicate to the contrary. Predictably, Himmler held to the same view out of the conviction that the *Führer* could do no wrong nor even think it; a line of thought which scarcely applied to Jodl, who was no military ignoramus, though he too clung to the idea of persisting with the German attack in the west, whatever the consequences for Germany's eastern frontier and the vulnerable eastern provinces. None of Guderian's pleading could deflect Hitler, who was already contemplating yet another blow at the Anglo-American armies—Operation *Nordwind,* designed to recover Alsace.

Yet for all this obsession with the offensive in the west and the quest for 'the decision', Hitler perforce threw more than a backward glance at the eastern front, forced to do so by the Soviet pressure in Hungary. Throughout November Malinovskii's 2nd Ukrainian Front kept up its slogging attacks, fighting its way to the north of Budapest by the end of the month only to become snagged in the Matra hills to the north-east of the Hungarian capital. Once again Malinovskii broke off his offensive. Meanwhile Tolbukhin's 3rd Ukrainian Front, which had begun its crossing to the western bank of the Danube in the Mohacs–Batina–Apatin area during the first week in November, was slowly fighting its way out of its hard-won bridgeheads, though the sodden ground badly hampered the Russians and their attacks were not helped by the piecemeal manner in which Tolbukhin deployed his forces. Only towards the end of November did Tolbukhin commit substantial forces to the Batina and Apatin Bridgeheads, reinforcement which finally altered the situation and enabled Soviet units to break out in a drive towards lake Balaton and lake Velencze (situated roughly halfway between the northern tip of lake Balaton and the Danube).

While Tolbukhin moved up from the south-west, Malinovskii on 5 December launched his armies in a brief but powerful thrust designed to cut a path into Budapest from the north-west: Shumilov's 7th Guards Army was to attack from north-west of Hatvan, with Kravchenko's 6th Guards Tank Army and Pliev's 'mobile group' following through to the north-east of Budapest; while 53rd Army advanced on Sezcen and 46th Army made for Csepel island, thus outflanking Budapest from the south-west. Tolbukhin's part in this preliminary manoeuvre consisted of pushing on from his own Danube bridgehead in two directions— towards Szkesfehervar with 4th Guards Army, 18th Tank Corps and Gorshkov's cavalry corps, and towards Nagykanizsa with 57th Army. This double thrust to the west and the north by Tolbukhin was designed to confuse the German command, who might well assume that the main Soviet objective on the left was to drive on to Austria in the 'gap' between the Drava and lake Balaton; the northerly drive into the area of lake Velencze would nevertheless bring 3rd Ukrainian Front to within some thirty miles of Budapest.

On the morning of 5 December, under cover of a 45-minute artillery barrage, Malinovskii's 2nd Ukrainian Front renewed its attack on Budapest, with Shumilov's 7th Guards in the lead, striking at the junction between the Sixth and Eighth German Armies. For a week Shumilov's infantrymen and Kravchenko's tanks fought their way across the ditches and canals, steadily outflanking Budapest to the north and severing every road linking the Hungarian capital with the northern industrial region. Advancing along the boundary line between the two German

armies Soviet armour made for Vac, a strongly fortified point of great importance
in the bend of the Danube which ran to the north of Budapest. The drive on
Vac, secured by the capture of Nagyszal and the Tepekh hills (separating the
valley of the Danube from that of the rivel Ipel), was the first stage of the
operation aimed at the complete encirclement of Budapest, for to the south-east
troops of the 46th Army began forcing the Danube just before midnight on 4
December. By morning eleven Soviet rifle battalions were across and rapidly
expanding the bridgehead, though frequent German counter-attacks tried to hold
this Soviet passage of the Danube in the Ercsi region. On 9 December rifle units
of the 46th Army cleared Ercsi, and in the area of lake Velencze linked up with
the lead elements of 3rd Ukrainian Front. On the previous day Tolbukhin's
divisions had cleared German troops from the southern edge of lake Balaton and
driven to the outskirts of Szekesfehervar and Nagykanizsa; by the evening, 4th
Guards Army was approaching the German defence line between lakes Balaton
and Velencze, with the left-flank units closing on the south-eastern shore of lake
Velencze to link up with Malinovskii's 46th Army from 2nd Ukrainian Front.
On Tolbukhin's extreme left flank, 57th Army pushed on to the southern shore
of lake Balaton and also swept south-westwards to the Drava, seizing a bridgehead
on the western bank at Barcs.

Shlemin's 46th Army, fighting its way south of Budapest, inevitably suffered
heavy losses. To complete the 'western encirclement' with only one weakened
army was obviously impossible, and on 12 December the *Stavka* intervened with
a revised directive assigning this task to the right flank of Tolbukhin's 3rd
Ukrainian Front, to which 46th Army was transferred (its sector being taken
over by the 18th Independent Guards Rifle Corps from Malinovskii's reserve.)
The same *Stavka* directive also prescribed the form that the Soviet encirclement
operation must now take: Malinovskii's 2nd Ukrainian Front (with twenty-eight
rifle divisions, six mobile cavalry, armoured and mechanized corps plus some
fifteen Rumanian divisions) received formal orders to hold the enemy garrison in
Pest on the eastern bank of the Danube as the northerly encirclement drive
continued, cutting off the German escape route to the north-west; while Tolbukhin's
3rd Ukrainian Front with some thirty rifle divisions and four mobile corps was
to strike northwards from lake Velencze in the direction of Bicske, to reach the
southern bank of the Danube in the area of Esztergom, thereby severing the
German escape route to the west. Part of Tolbukhin's Front was also to attack
directly from Bicske towards Budapest, co-operating with Malinovskii's 2nd
Ukrainian Front in seizing the Hungarian capital. The two armies on Malinovskii's
right flank (40th and 27th, together with one Rumanian army) were detached
from the battle for Budapest, receiving orders to make a wide outflanking
movement to the north in order to cross the old Hungarian–Czechoslovak frontier,
advancing to the slopes of the Lower Tatra mountains and further to the south-
west, as far as the river Nitra.

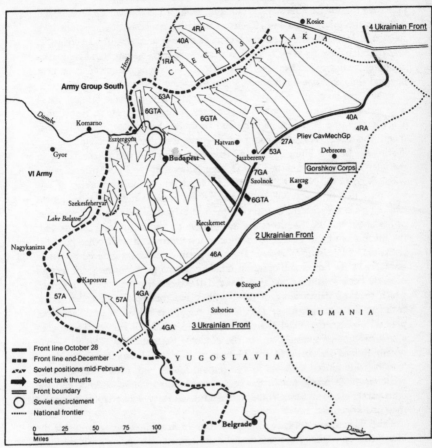

Map 13 The Budapest operation, October 1944–February 1945

Malinovskii planned to use 53rd, 7th Guards and 6th Tank Armies in the attack directed against Vac and the northerly bend of the Danube, concentric attacks aimed to the north-west, west and south-west and designed to encircle Budapest completely in co-operation with Tolbukhin's 3rd Ukrainian. By the evening of 23 December 1944 three corps must be in possession of Pest itself. The right-flank armies, driving into Slovakia and on to the river Nitra, were to make for the route leading from the Moravian Gap to Budapest; in co-operation with Pliev's 'mobile group' advancing from the area of Komarno, this Soviet force was to aim for Bratislava. Tolbukhin with 3rd Ukrainian Front intended to pierce the 'Margareten line' (German defensive positions running from lake Balaton to Hatvan) on two narrow sectors to the east and west of lake Velencze. Once through these defences, Tolbukhin's armies would co-operate with Malinovskii in closing the ring round Budapest, with 46th Army forming the inner encirclement line and the outer line established by thrusts to the west and north-west.

Behind the lines, in Soviet-occupied Hungarian territory, Stalin hurried ahead with setting up a new Hungarian government, although his plan to rush it into a newly captured Budapest had misfired badly in October. At the end of that month the exiled Hungarian communists—several of them survivors of the first 'Soviet republic' in Hungary, many others men who had fled to the USSR in the inter-war period—returned in the baggage train of the Red Army, together with officers of the NKVD and the usual complement of former prisoners of war now converted to a new political creed. For the moment this proto-government had to be content with the cramped quarters of Szeged rather than the splendours of Budapest, but the 'Szeged centre' soon began to operate, making contact with the organizers of the Hungarian resistance movement and with other potential sympathizers in eastern Hungary. The Hungarian communists received the ready assistance of the Soviet authorities in building up the party organization, though precisely because current policy demanded the creation of the 'Popular Front', which required the presence of other parties and the creation of a democratic coalition, the same groups of agitators and organizers helped to stimulate other political bodies—the Social Democrat Party and the Small Farmers Party, with a smaller agrarian ginger-group in the National Peasant Party. This four-party system formed the basis of the Hungarian National Liberation Front. Local 'national committees' sprouted in villages and towns, with communist influence predominant in many, but in the beginning the Communists did not find the other parties—and in particular the National Peasant Party—the pliable instruments they had hoped for.

On 3 December 1944, at a mass meeting in Szeged, the programme of the Hungarian Liberation Front was formally proclaimed, demanding the elimination of all fascist and 'anti-national' organizations, the purging from the state apparatus of such elements, the institution of political rights and freedom, a comprehensive programme of land reform, state control of the banks, the nationalization of the petroleum industry, coal and bauxite mines, and the guarantee of an eight-hour working day. The 'Szeged programme' also called for the establishment in every town and village of a 'national committee' acting as an organ of the Liberation Front, as well as the summoning of a 'national assembly' to draft a constitution and to set up a provisional government. Two days later, another mass meeting in Debrecen adopted this programme. A 'national committee' was set up in Debrecen, which became the seat of the provisional government later in the month, though the Szeged centre continued to exercise considerable influence. Within a week elections were afoot for the 'provisional national assembly', which convened on 21 December in Debrecen with its 237 delegates (71 of them Communists). On 22 December this assembly voted a 'political council' into power, which in turn selected Col.-Gen. Miklos (former commander of the 1st Hungarian Army) as prime minister and head of a provisional government with its coalition component (three Communists, three representatives of the Small Farmers, one National Peasant Party man and four 'Horthy-ists', including General Miklos himself). Amidst the ruin brought about by military operations and the havoc wrought within the administration, a new socialist order began to emerge and beside it a form of government, a 'provisional government', with which Stalin could talk armistice terms. The Hungarian delegation duly arrived in Moscow at the beginning of January 1945.

But even as the national committees in 'liberated' Hungary set about organizing elections for the National Assembly, Hitler determined to fight on and fight back in Hungary, issuing orders in mid-December that Budapest was to be turned into a fortress and defended building by building. In addition to this defensive investment, he proposed to launch an armoured counter-stroke between lake Balaton and lake Velencze, with the object of driving south-eastwards to the Danube. Three *Panzer* divisions and two infantry divisions from East Prussia were to be transferred to Friessner in Hungary in order to carry out these missions. Both of these tasks brought fresh problems for Friessner: the armoured attack with the three *Panzer* divisions (attached to Sixth Army) was to be launched across ground already soggy or crisscrossed with ditches, while the defence of Budapest as envisaged by Hitler meant tying down a large force in the eastern side of the city (Pest) and making much more effective provision for a defensive battle, few signs of which showed in Budapest even at this late hour. Buda on the western bank of the Danube formed a natural fortress, dominated by the Gelerthegy heights dropping precipitously into the Danube itself and honeycombed with underground caverns, passages and casements hewn into the rock. Further to the north lay another height, the Palace Hill, similarly mined and tunnelled; these twin heights of Buda were protected in turn by the Buda Hills proper. To the east, on the other side of the Danube and on the low-lying land dominated by the heights of Buda, lay Pest with its several industrial suburbs—Ujpest, Pestujhel, Kobanya, Kispest and Erzsebetfalva, each with solid, massive structures and a variety of public buildings which lent themselves readily to conversion into formidable urban fortresses.

While the inhabitants of Budapest prepared for Christmas in a city which was not yet fitted out for war, with everyday life not so far removed from the usual, the two Soviet fronts closed in on the Hungarian capital. A German tank attack with 8th *Panzer* Division to the north of Budapest failed to deflect Kravchenko's 6th Guards Tank Army; the *Dirlewanger* Brigade, which had the barbarous suppression of the Warsaw rising to its dubious credit, broke up almost to a man and fled. To plug the gap the German command, no less than Guderian and Hitler in person, ordered the two *Panzer* divisions to the south of Budapest to shift their infantry northwards, leaving the armour in the Balaton area on the Margareten line—a decision which left III *Panzer* Corps in this southern region without infantry and thus at the mercy of the Soviet divisions facing it. Guderian had not long to wait for the inevitable reckoning. On the morning of 20 December Malinovskii and Tolbukhin renewed their offensive in line with the *Stavka* directive of 12 December. Kravchenko's tanks from 6th Guards Army pushed on to the north-west, covering up to twenty miles and reaching the river Hron on the first day of the attack. Shumilov's infantry from 7th Guards gained up to ten miles and approached the valley of the river Ipel, the signal for heavy German counter-attacks with strong tank forces—the armour brought up from Balaton, launching repeated attacks which lasted for more than a week in the strip of land between the rivers Ipel and Hron. On the evening of 24 December Malinovskii instructed Kravchenko to attack towards Esztergom (involving a turn to the south) and Shumilov was ordered to break through to the river Hron with his left-flank divisions. Covered from the north by a corps from Pliev's 'mobile group', Kravchenko duly swung south, only to meet stiff German opposition; fighting now almost side by side, the tanks of 6th Guards and the infantry of 7th Guards pressed southwards and reached the Danube to the north of Esztergom on 26 December. Tolbukhin had also started his main offensive effort on 20 December, driving from south-west of Budapest to link up with Malinovskii coming from the north and north-west. German resistance was also heavy in this southern sector, with fierce fighting in the area of Szekesfehervar; Tolbukhin committed two armoured formations (2nd Guards Mechanized and 7th Mechanized) on this first day, followed by a second (18th Tank Corps) on 21 December. Soviet rifle formations made slow progress at first, since their infantry-support tanks had been taken away to fight the considerable numbers of German tanks; the mechanized formations also became snagged in the infantry fighting for many hours.

After three days, Tolbukhin's front had broken through the German positions along a sixty-mile front, with only Szekesfehervar holding out (though the Soviet advance made further resistance pointless and German troops pulled out). Once through the German defences Tolbukhin now unleashed 18th Tank Corps on his right flank and sent it northwards towards Esztergom. Govorunenko, 18th Corps commander, decided to outflank Bicske from the three sides and then rush the town with a motorized infantry brigade. On the afternoon of 24 December Bicske was cleared, and two brigades, with a third guarding the left flank, struck out for Esztergom, also cleared after some five hours of fighting. Tolbukhin and Malinovskii linked up on 26 December when 2nd and 3rd Ukrainian Fronts joined hands. Budapest was now completely sealed off.

The line of the river Hron had caved in. In the bend of the Danube north of Budapest Tolbukhin had also trapped a sizeable force of German troops and his lead elements were pushing on to a point less than twenty miles from Komarno, the main German base. As rapidly as possible the Soviet command thickened the 'ring', with Malinovskii clamping his divisions round Budapest and Tolbukhin strengthening his own line from the Danube to the east of Komarno on to lake Balaton. But once again Malinovskii's 'Budapest group' (a rifle corps from 7th Guards Army, 7th Rumanian Corps and 18th Independent Guards Rifle Corps) found the task of breaking right into the city completely beyond their resources, and four days of heavy fighting from 26–31 December brought only heavy casualties and little progress in the suburbs. Soviet troops stood between seven and ten miles from the city centre, with the greater distance on the Pest side, though Pest with its level ground and good road system offered better facilities for organizing an assault. Inside the 'ring' the Soviet command reckoned that as many as twelve German divisions had been trapped, in all 188,000 men; within the city itself four German divisions (13th *Panzer*, *SS Feldherrnhalle* and two *SS* cavalry divisions) together with Hungarian units were locked in and became perforce the defending garrison. Throughout the night and on the morning of 29 December loudspeakers in Soviet front-line positions relayed in German and Hungarian the Soviet terms for the capitulation of Budapest. Soviet guns ceased firing and emissaries from both Fronts, 2nd and 3rd Ukrainian, went forward to parley with the German command about surrender, Captain Miklos Shteinmetz (a Hungarian by birth) from Malinovskii's command and Captain Ostapenko from Tolbukhin's front. Shteinmetz's truck, carrying a large white flag, came under heavy fire from the German positions and was blown up by mines, killing Shteinmetz and a sergeant. Ostapenko passed through the German lines and was taken blindfolded to a headquarters, where the senior German officer refused to accept the text of the Soviet terms and declined to enter into any talks. Blindfolded once more, Ostapenko and his two companions were taken back, but the moment he passed the German forward positions a burst of fire struck him in the back; his companions Orlov and Gorbatyuk, however, escaped with their lives.

Hitler had no intention of giving up Budapest and was now planning to wrest it from the Russians. Having summarily dismissed Friessner and Fretter-Pico (GOC Sixth Army) and replaced them with Wöhler and Balck, he ordered Guderian to shift IV *SS Panzer* Corps from Army Group Centre to Hungary (a deployment which was discovered by the Soviet command, though they could not discover on what sector this tank formation would be committed). Gille's *Panzer* corps de-trained at Komarno, going straight into an attack aimed at Bicske–Budapest, a south-easterly thrust which hit Zakharov's 4th Guards Army full in the flank; Bobruk's 31st Guards Rifle Corps took the full weight of the German attack, which burst on the Soviet troops at 2230 hours on 1 January 1945. German aircraft appeared in some strength to support the counter-attack, which gathered momentum in the next few days, causing Tolbukhin considerable anxiety. The *Panzer* divisions, attacking along narrow sectors with up to a hundred tanks, drove on to Bicske junction—a mere fifteen miles from Soviet troops who were fending off German attacks mounted from Buda itself. To relieve the pressure on Tolbukhin, the *Stavka* on 4 January issued orders to Malinovskii to launch an attack on Komarno with 6th Guards Tank Army and 7th Guards, a Soviet thrust aimed at the rear of IV *Panzer*. Tolbukhin also received orders to attack towards Komarno, a joint operation with Malinovskii designed to encircle the German *Panzer* corps.

Early on the morning of 6 January Malinovskii's left-flank armies (6th and 7th Guards) attacked from the line of the river Hron, carving out a large bridgehead on the western bank by midday. In the evening, however, German units blocked the Soviet advance and pushed along the southern bank of the Danube, taking Esztergom and threatening the rear of Kravchenko's Guards tank army. Heavy fighting went on in the area between the rivers Hron and Nitra, where German reserves managed to stem any further Soviet advance for the moment. While Soviet troops struggled to roll back this first German attempt to break through to the garrisons in Budapest, a second attack unrolled from the salient south of Mor, mounted in this area by III *Panzer* Corps and aimed at Zamoja; this second force with three *Panzer* divisions was to link up with German troops fighting north of Bicske. For five days, from 7–11 January, Biryukov's 20th Guards Corps supported by 7th Mechanized Corps fought off Breith's III *Panzer* Corps, which made only a few miles and then fell back on the defensive after suffering heavy losses in tanks. The German attempt to smash a way in through Bicske had failed, but a third attack—designed to slice Tolbukhin's 3rd Ukrainian Front in two—produced a much more dangerous situation. Gille's IV *Panzer* quickly disengaged from the battle and fell back on Komarno, where it was loaded on to trains and appeared to withdraw further west. The command of 4th Guards Army, wholly deceived by the move, were anxious to organize the pursuit of the 'beaten' enemy, who nevertheless did not disappear to the west but suddenly appeared further to the south in the area of lake Balaton, south-west of Szekesfehervar.

Out of the winter gloom on the morning of 18 January, IV *Panzer's* tanks crashed into Gnedin's 135th Rifle Corps, which was itself bereft of either tanks or SP guns. Moving off at 0830 hours, German armour made rapid progress during the course of the day, leaving the wreckage of 135th Corps behind it. Driving to the east, IV *Panzer* made for Dunapentele and covered up to twenty miles on the first day, brushing aside 7th Mechanized Corps hastily moved up to block the German advance. Two more Soviet corps, 18th Tank and 133rd Rifle Corps, also failed to hold off the German tanks, which by the evening of 19 January had reached the Szarviz canal, making a successful assault crossing at first light and reaching Dunapentele by the afternoon. On the morning of 20 January German units were on the Danube. Tolbukhin's Front on the western bank of the Danube had been split in two, a situation which caused the Soviet command some very anxious moments. At Szekesfehervar Soviet troops were also battling to hang on to this vital road and rail junction; the Soviet defence was holding for the moment, supported by 18th and 133rd Corps even though they were fighting whilst encircled. On the evening of 20 January, with his southern flank ripped wide open and the threat of encirclement facing 57th Army (together with the 1st Bulgarian Army and 12th Yugoslav Corps), Tolbukhin spoke to Sharokhin, commander of the 57th, by radio, asking for his opinion about pulling all Soviet units back to the eastern bank of the Danube. Somewhat laconically Sharokhin pointed out that, since the Germans could now get to the Danube crossings first, 57th Army would be in a worse plight if it tried to pull back— the only course was to stay put, and fight in encirclement if necessary. Tolbukhin agreed and presumably reported this opinion to Stalin, who had ordered him to look into the question of a Soviet withdrawal behind the Danube.

Gille's IV *Panzer* was, however, only starting on its rampage amidst the Soviet positions. While Tolbukhin tried feverishly to shore up the southern face of his front, German armour turned north and north-west towards Soviet units located between lake Velencze and the Danube—the shortest route to Budapest. Starting on the morning of 22 January German tanks again battered 4th Guards Army, the main German force moving into the Velencze–Danube area with a second attack developing against Szekesfehervar, which Soviet troops abandoned that same evening after holding on for four days. It was now plain that Tolbukhin's 3rd Ukrainian Front could not hold the German drive towards Budapest. During the night of 24 January a strong force of German tanks broke through the defensive positions held by 5th Guards Cavalry and 1st Guards Mechanized Corps, striking on to the north-west and approaching a point only twenty-five kilometres from the southern suburbs of Budapest, from which at least one German corps could have fought its way out to meet the relieving tank force. That moment was never realized, simply because Hitler did not want it so—he wanted Budapest recaptured rather than the defenders rescued. Malinovskii also stepped in with a remarkable show of initiative, transferring 23rd Tank Corps to the western bank of the Danube and putting it in a blocking position across the southerly route to the city, a decision and a redeployment made without the authorization of the Soviet General Staff. Unauthorized or not (though *Stavka* instructions of 22 January proposed the movement of this tank corps), this deployment shored up the Soviet defences south-west of Budapest and saved 4th Guards Army from further punishment. Slowly but surely IV *Panzer* Corps was running out of steam.

While German tanks flailed away west and south of Budapest, Malinovskii's assault units were fighting their savage battles inside the city, already under heavy Russian shellfire and now bombed by Russian aircraft seeking to destroy strong-points across the length of Budapest. On the western bank of the Danube Soviet guns closed in on Buda, hammering defensive positions in the hills—Gelerthey in particular—while to the north Matyas Hill fell to the Russians and from this vantage-point fire could be directed not only against Buda but also against Pest. By the beginning of the New Year Malinovskii's forward detachments were already in the outer suburbs—Ujpest, Rakospalota, Pestujhel and Kobanya— and it was on this easterly bank of the Danube that Malinovskii proposed to open his assault on the city with his Budapest group (30th Rifle, 18th Guards and 7th Rumanian Corps); the western sector of the city, Buda, was assigned by the preliminary plan to 46th Army of 3rd Ukrainian Front, but the heavy fighting on the approaches to the city virtually eliminated this formation from taking any part in the protracted and bitter operations to clear the city street by street.

After being encircled, the German garrison had worked frenziedly to fit out the city for a siege: buildings were fortified and the massive multi-storey dwelling houses, railway stations, industrial installations, together with the pompous but solidly built public buildings, each received its complement of defenders and weapons. The underground passages and caverns promised special advantages to the defenders, who could use this extensive underground system to link one miniature fortress with another; up above, at street level, German tanks, SP guns and armoured troop-carriers could tackle Soviet assault squads, but only for so long as the fuel lasted.

At the end of the first week in January, with the necessary artillery concentrated and the special *shturmovye gruppy* formed up, Malinovskii opened the first purposeful and preplanned attack on the eastern suburbs. On the outer edge of the city the German command was not prepared to fight last-ditch actions—*Kampf Haus um Haus*—which must lead almost inevitably to German combat groups being encircled by swift Soviet tank raids and thrusts. These first few days of fighting brought Soviet troops deeper into the eastern sector of the city—the suburbs of Ujpest, Rakospalota, Palotaujfalu, Pestujhel, Kobanya and Kispest—but already the Soviet General Staff was concerned at the straggling nature of the operation. On 10 January a General Staff signal to Malinovskii pointed to the absence of 'unified direction' for the Soviet units committed (the two rifle corps operated under the command of the 7th Guards Army commander, 18th Rifle Corps under direct Front command), and proposed the establishment of a special combat group under Front control. The next day the *Budapeshtskaya gruppa voisk* formally came into being and was put under the command of Maj.-Gen. I.M. Afonin, 18th Independent Guards Corps commander.

Afonin's special operational group received orders to begin a double attack from the morning of 12 January with the object of splitting the defences in Pest in two: by the evening of 14 January Soviet units were to break right through to the Danube. The Soviet command was well aware that the real struggle for Budapest was about to open, now that the ring had tightened in the eastern and northern suburbs—in Pest—and Soviet troops had also taken O-Buda (to the north of Buda), as well as occupying the industrial installations on Csepel Island. From this point forward the ring would have to be tightened by brute force. Rifle divisions were assigned attack sectors of some 400–800 metres, with regiments fighting across 150–300 metres; the flanks were especially vulnerable and the special reserves played a vital part in the clearing operations, with the regimental commander usually keeping a company of tommy-gunners, an engineer and a reconnaissance squad to hand in order to secure cellars (or roofs) and to cover the immediate rear of the lead detachments. Corps and divisional artillery engaged long-range targets, but the rest of the guns were kept ready for instant firing over open sights, often hidden in lower floors of buildings (though some were positioned on the roofs). Heavy guns—132mm, 152mm and 203mm—also fired over open sights when barricades or strong-points had to be blasted away by shellfire. But in Buda, with its narrow, winding streets and the solid stone structures of imposing houses or villas, Soviet troops found the greatest difficulty in deploying their guns, which had to be grouped to give covering and supporting fire.

After 11 January 1945 the fighting for Pest intensified. The wintry days brought mists thickened with snow, shrouding streets and buildings. Soviet assault squads could not advance along the streets swept by German guns, but instead closed on their objectives by passing through holes blown in walls or by using less exposed spaces. If holes did not exist, heavy guns blasted passages for the infantry or sappers moved up and deployed their own 'sapper artillery' (simple launchers for captured German shells) to reduce enemy positions and firing-points. The debris of these fierce exchanges littered the approaches to the central section of Pest. In the ceramics factory German troops took up a circular defence, using the windows as firing-points for machine-guns, forcing Soviet infantry to take the buildings by storm, fighting their way first into the shattered interior and from the outside shooting down the Germans who tried to leap to safety through the windows. In the neighbouring textile factory most of the German garrison was wiped out.

German tanks tried fighting off Soviet assault units on the patches of open ground, in the parks and gardens, but with the loss of the factories, already heavily bombarded from the air, supplies fell off drastically and artillery ammunition was running short. Fuel ran out all too quickly, leaving German tanks immobilized and marooned, firing off the last of their ammunition as fixed-gun positions. The German command organized a last desperate defence to hold the racecourse, where Ju-52s used the grass track as an emergency landing strip to bring in ammunition, the same planes then flying out the wounded. A full German artillery brigade deployed to cover the landing strip, but the growing shortage of ammunition and casualties among the gun crews made the situation more critical with each hour. On 12 January Soviet infantry finally burst through the ring of burning tanks, assault guns and assorted vehicles to capture the racecourse, thus cutting the tenuous supply line for the German garrison. With Varosliget Park in their hands on 13 January, Soviet units then cleared Negpliget Park and pressed on towards the hospitals. At the Ferencz Station, the Germans held on desperately, fighting off a Soviet attack which came at them from two sides, from the park and from the engineering works which had just been captured. Railway wagons in the sidings served as machine-gun positions, assault guns and tanks fired across the railway lines to hold off the Russians moving in from the park, but the East Station and the Ferencz Station finally fell. By now the Russians were near the railway bridge over the Danube, though the heaviest fighting still raged in the centre of Pest, round the parliament building, the Opera House and the University.

After five days of uninterrupted street fighting, on 17 January, almost all of Pest was in Soviet hands and the German defence was split into three parts. Hungarian soldiers surrendered more readily, but German units hung on in ferocious style, only to be pressed back to the Danube, where the bridges, which might have led to safety, had already been blown up. The remnants of the Pest garrison fell back to within a thousand yards of the river bank, only to find the Russians already ahead of them, with more men using the sewers and the underground passages to break out to the bank, from which they covered the few available crossings with machine-guns. After 18 January, trapped in a hopeless position with their backs to the Danube, German troops could do nothing but surrender. Malinovskii's command put German losses at 35,840 killed, 62,000 taken prisoner and large quantities of equipment destroyed or captured—almost 300 tanks, over 200 light armoured vehicles and 20,000 rifles. The 'Budapest operational group' reported that the whole of Pest (with the exception of Margit Island) was now cleared of the enemy. Pest itself had almost ceased to exist: the close-packed urban and industrial suburbs were a mass of flaming wreckage, with streets reduced to total ruin and fires roaring through innumerable buildings, leaving only burnt-out shells. The rationing system for the civilian population broke down completely on 16 January, the supply system was smashed to pieces, and even the defending Germans were getting only seventy-five grammes of bread per day (just short of three ounces.)

The *Stavka* now issued orders for the reduction of Buda, the other half of the twin city. With this order went a show of generosity in assigning to the Budapest group two rifle corps as reinforcement (75th and 37th, taken from 3rd Ukrainian Front). This magnanimity proved to be short-lived, for no sooner had the German garrison surrendered in Pest on 18 January than that same night German armour fell on Tolbukhin's southern flank, cutting deep into 3rd Ukrainian Front defences before turning north-west to drive on Buda itself. The reinforcement for Malinovskii was hurriedly cancelled. The *Stavka* made 2nd Ukrainian Front solely responsible for the capture of Buda in its order of 20 January and left Tolbukhin's 3rd Ukrainian Front to fight defensively along the outer encirclement line. Malinovskii's troops therefore set about clearing Margit Island, lying in mid-Danube to the north-west of Buda, a preliminary operation which was an essential to the asault on Buda itself. Ahead of these Soviet troops lay the winding streets and catacombs of Buda, an uninviting prospect of natural deathtraps for the assault formations upon whom this task was laid. At the same time Malinovskii's right-flank armies—40th, 20th, 53rd and 7th Guards, together with Pliev's 1st Cavalry Mechanized Group—were trying to push into eastern Slovakia, where

Petrov's operations with his 4th Ukrainian Front had made only slow progress. Having fought his way to the Topola–Ondava line, Petrov faced some formidable obstacles on his way to Kosice.

Malinovskii's right-flank armies were aimed at Komarno, but in the process of striking towards it they took a heavy battering, though they did finally break through to the river Nitra. Losses told heavily in all armies. By 11 January all three corps of 6th Guards Tank Army mustered only seventy-two tanks between them, the strength of the rifle division of 7th Guards dropped to under 4,000 men and in some divisions only a thousand men were left alive and whole. The swollen waters of the river Hron and heavy snowfalls stopped all movement of supplies. Soviet engineers could not repair key bridges until 14 January, working amidst these icy conditions to join shattered supply lines. In spite of these shortcomings Soviet units managed to capture Lucenec on 14 January and continued to advance on Zvolen from two directions, but having to fight amidst the heights of the Slovenska Krusnohori without either air or artillery support inflicted a painfully slow rate of progress and brought heavy casualties. Malinovskii found himself in a difficult position indeed: his Front was committed to a full-scale assault on Buda and obliged to parry the third relieving attack mounted by the Germans, while at the same time he needed to reinforce his right flank. But the right flank fighting in the Slovak uplands was not reinforced; on the contrary it was drawn back to refit, 6th Guards Tank with less than forty tanks to its name and Pliev's mobile group being pulled back into the interior of the Front, leaving three Soviet armies (40th, 53rd and 7th Guards) and two Rumanian armies (1st and 4th) to the north of the Danube.

Unable to attack along a broad front, Soviet infantry armies launched a series of separate attacks which cut German escape roads, except for the perilous mountainous routes of the Slovenska Krusnohori. Meanwhile Petrov's armies occupied Kosice and Presov between 18 and 20 January and though German units were able to make their escape down the valley of the river Vah, by the end of January the greater part of the German force operating between the rivers Hernad and Ipel had been wiped out. At about the same time, towards the end of the third week in January, it was also plain that the German defenders of Buda would not be relieved by their fellows fighting towards them from the south. The Soviet Budapest operational group nevertheless faced ferocious German resistance in the western sector of the city, and decided on one last, all-out effort to crush it. During the fighting on 22 January the Soviet group commander, Afonin, was severely wounded and Col.-Gen. Managarov (53rd Army commander) took his place, though the change in commanders did not bring about any radically improved conduct in the assault. Reporting to the General Staff, a specialist Soviet officer complained of the 'unsatisfactory' organization of operations, the dispersal of men and equipment, the lack of co-ordination between assault groups, the separation of the supporting artillery from the infantry and the emplacement of command posts in houses still occupied by civilians.

This type of criticism had some effect. Early in February, at Malinovskii's express orders, the Soviet formations fighting in and for Buda regrouped. On 3 February 1945 Malinovskii issued a Front directive stipulating that a fresh, decisive effort must be made to reduce the encircled German garrison no later than the evening of 7 February. On the morning of 5 February Managarov's assault formations duly opened their attack on the remaining German strongholds in Buda, with heavy Russian fire marking the points from which the ring was steadily narrowed. For four days heavy fighting went on in Buda for the possession of Sashegy Hill, the cemetery at Nemetvölgy and the area of the south station. Once Soviet units took Sashegy Hill, the next embattled step took them to the Gelerthey Heights and thence to Palace Hill. In this area the narrow twisting streets made the use of heavy artillery impossible, but elsewhere heavy guns fired at little more than ranges of 150 metres to blast away the concrete and iron barricades holding up the Russian advance.

By 11 February more than a hundred buildings had fallen to the Soviet troops, together with 25,000 prisoners. The Hungarians now fell away from the side of the Germans as the Russians literally hacked their way on to and into the heights which also comprised a whole network of caverns. The remnants of the German garrison fought one last desperate action to break out of Buda as the ring closed on them, with the German commander Pfeffer-Wildenbruch taking to the sewers only to emerge in the midst of a Soviet unit. During the night of 16 February some 16,000 German troops tried to fight their way out to the north-west; they cut a corridor through the Soviet 180th Rifle Division and made their escape— or so it seemed—along the Lipotmező valley. Within forty-eight hours, however, this force was encircled in the area of Ferbal and wiped out almost to a man. Inside Buda itself, organized resistance ceased at 10am on the morning of 13 February, with the Red Army claiming over 30,000 prisoners. The entire Soviet tally for the period 27 October–14 February amounted to 50,000 'enemy troops' (German and Hungarian) killed and 138,000 made prisoner.

The battle for Budapest had ended, though the fight for Hungary had yet to run its full course. Hitler not only intended that this should be so, but virtually conspired to produce such an outcome. After mid-January the German army in the west went over to the defensive, but the troops available for transfer to the east—in particular Sixth *Panzer* Army— were destined for Hungary, which for all the ferocity of the fighting had become a relatively unimportant theatre. The fate of the *Reich* hung on the Rhine and on the Oder rather than on the defence of the Danube. Clinging to the few oil-fields in Hungary could in no way compensate for the catastrophic weakness in German armoured forces to the north of the Carpathians. Out of a total of eighteen *Panzer* divisions operating with the *Ostheer,* no less than seven were committed in Hungary, four were located in East Prussia, two in Courland and only five on the all-important central sector covering Brandenburg. Along the line of the major Soviet thrust—the Warsaw–Berlin axis—German armoured forces were demonstrably at their very weakest, despite

Guderian's pleading and cajoling. Armed with more of Gehlen's chillingly precise reports, Guderian tried once more on 9 January to persuade Hitler of the enormous danger in the east. General Gehlen pinpointed the timing and probable objectives of the coming Soviet offensive (accurately, as it transpired) and announced its overall aim as the complete destruction of the German will and capacity to carry on the war—'*Das Ziel . . . ist in der völligen Zerschlagung der deutschen Widerstandskraft*', nothing less than the destruction of the *Ostheer* and the obliteration of the central industrial regions of Germany.

The *Führer* rounded on Guderian in a fury and described Gehlen's reports as 'completely idiotic'; the place for the man who compiled such drivel was a lunatic asylum. In a matching rage Guderian refused Hitler's demand that Gehlen be relieved of his duties, at which the storm passed, but nothing further could be done to bolster the German armies in the east. Guderian lamented that 'ostrich politics' went hand in hand with 'ostrich strategy' and to Hitler's soothing assurance that the reserves in the east had never been so powerful, Guderian could only reply that twelve and a half divisions in reserve simply invited disaster; in truth, the eastern front was nothing but a 'house of cards'—one breakthrough and it must collapse.

Three days later, on 12 January 1945, the attack which Hitler and his circle had dismissed as Soviet 'bluff', or the lunatic ravings of an unhinged intelligence staff, materialized on a scale which grew more massive with each hour—after a mere seven days the Red Army was fighting inside the boundaries of the *Reich*, signalling what Guderian called 'the beginning of the last act'.

For what was demonstrably one of the mightiest strategic operations of the whole war—the massive thrust into the *Reich* along the Warsaw–Berlin axis—the Soviet command assembled a force of infantry, armour, artillery and aircraft on an appropriate scale. Marshal Zhukov's 1st Belorussian and Marshal Koniev's 1st Ukrainian Front disposed of no less than 163 rifle divisions, 32,143 guns and heavy mortars, almost 6,500 tanks, and 4,772 aircraft, involving in all just under two and a quarter million men. These two fronts alone disposed between them of almost one-third of all Soviet infantry formations and almost a half (43 per cent) of all Soviet armour committed at that time on the Soviet–German front. Both fronts deployed ten armies (eight infantry, two tank), a full air army and 4–5 mobile formations (tank, mechanized and cavalry corps). Soviet superiority was both absolute and awesome, fivefold in manpower, fivefold in armour, over sevenfold in artillery and seventeen times the German strength in the air. The average density in infantry formations was one rifle division per 3.7 kilometres, with 64 guns and 12 tanks to a kilometre, all along an offensive front which stretched for some 300 miles. The Soviet objective, an advance to the river Oder, lay more or less the same distance—300 miles—from the start line on the middle reaches of the Vistula.

In addition to the 1st Belorussian and 1st Ukrainian Fronts committed to the two massive and parallel armoured offensives aimed at the Oder, the full picture of this strategic assault on Germany also involved Col.-Gen. Chernyakhovskii's 3rd Belorussian Front in an operation to destroy the 'Tilsit–Insterburg group' of German forces (with 1st Baltic Front co-operating in the reduction of the Tilsit group) and an advance along the river Pregel in the direction of Königsberg; while Marshal Rokossovskii's 2nd Belorussian Front—heavily reinforced for the purpose—was to attack from the north-east of Warsaw in a north-westerly direction and drive to the Baltic in the area of Danzig. Rokossovskii's operations would thus seal off East Prussia from the remainder of Germany and also furnish some protection for Zhukov's right flank. Such a design set almost every Soviet army on the move from the Carpathians to the Baltic, and in the Baltic Soviet naval forces were ordered to intensify submarine and naval air activity against German lines of communication. The very accumulation of fronts, however, demanded careful planning and effective execution of inter-front operations. No one was more conscious of this than Zhukov himself, who ever since the inception of the main operational plan in November had kept the possible threat to his right flank from East Prussia under careful and constant review. Events quickly proved him correct and justified all his misgivings over the defective co-ordination of operations on his right.

The regrouping of 3rd and 2nd Belorussian Fronts, together with transfers from 1st Baltic Front, went on throughout December 1944 and into early January 1945. Rokossovskii, who took over 2nd Belorussian Front command from General G.F. Zakharov, (who was effectively demoted and dispatched as a mere army commander to another front), was left in no doubt by Stalin as to the importance of his new command: 1st Belorussian, 1st Ukrainian and 2nd Belorussian Fronts were 'probably the ones destined to end the war in the West'. In his briefing, Stalin concentrated exclusively on Rokossovskii's co-operation with Zhukov's 1st Belorussian Front; as yet nothing was said about co-ordination with Rokossovskii's neighbour to the north, Chernyakovskii's 3rd Belorussian, which would 'deal' with German forces in East Prussia. In Rokossovskii's own words, 'no complications' were expected on his northern flank, an assumption which turned out to be wishful thinking. Rokossovskii's Front command comprised three field armies— 3rd, 48th and 50th Armies—as its basic strength, to which were added the 2nd Shock Army transferred from the 3rd Baltic Front and Volskii's 5th Guards Tank Army which had previously been attached to the 1st Baltic Front. Grishin's 49th Army was also transferred to Rokossovskii, while he received the 65th and 70th Armies when his Front boundary was shifted southwards to take in the confluence of the rivers Narew and Vistula. This gave him seven field armies, one tank army and 4th Air Army under Vershinin. Meanwhile on the 3rd Belorussian Front Chernyakhovskii deployed five armies—the 5th, 11th Guards, 28th, 31st and 39th—as the main attacking force, supported by 1st Air Army. The total strength of these two Fronts—2nd and 3rd Belorussian—finally amounted to fourteen field armies, one tank army, two air armies and six mobile corps (tank, mechanized and cavalry), with a combined strength of 1,670,000 men, 28,360 guns and heavy mortars (including more than 1,000 *Katyusha* rocket-launchers), 3,300 tanks and SP guns, and some 3,000 aircraft.

In sum, for the four major breakthrough operations—in the direction of Königsberg (Chernyakhovskii), in the direction of Danzig (Rokossovskii), across the Vistula south of Warsaw (Zhukov) and from the Sandomierz bridgehead (Koniev)—the Soviet command concentrated thirty field armies, five tank armies and four air armies, as well as independent mobile formations and special artillery 'breakthrough divisions' equipped with heavy guns.

Of the five German army groups holding the Eastern Front in January 1945, two—Reinhardt's Army Group Centre and Harpe's Army Group A—lay directly in the path of this mass of men and machines. Army Group North with its Sixteenth and Eighteenth Armies lay locked in Soviet encirclement in Courland and thus could do nothing to influence the defensive battle. Reinhardt's Group (with Third *Panzer*, Fourth and Second Armies) held East Prussia and an area of northern Poland along the river Narew to its junction with the Vistula. Harpe's Group A with Fourth *Panzer*, Ninth and Seventeenth Army was deployed along the middle reaches of the Vistula from the north of Warsaw down to the Carpathians, German strength consisting of thirty divisions (four of them *Panzer* divisions plus two motorized divisions), two brigades and numerous independent battalions—400,000 men, 1,136 tanks and SP guns, and 270 aircraft. Reinhardt's Centre Group holding East Prussia had forty-one divisions (thirty-four infantry, three *Panzer* and four motorized) at its disposal, with 580,000 men, 700 tanks and SP guns, and 515 aircraft.

The principal features and main objectives of the coming Soviet offensive had already been established during the first half of November 1944. The 'main effort' was to be made along the Warsaw–Berlin axis, thus assigning the major task to Zhukov's 1st Belorussian Front. At the end of November, Stalin accepted not only the basic strategic plan but also the related Front plans and proposals submitted to him, though apparently not without several individual briefings and consultations with Front commanders. No opening date for the offensive had been fixed, but Stalin let it be known that it should be within the period 15–20 January 1945. (Some small mystery attends this question of the timing, for particular operational records and testimony by individual commanders—Marshal Koniev among them—cite 20 January 1945 as the specific date set for launching the offensive.) It is also apparent that a final review and the ultimate approval of the general plan was conducted by Stalin at the end of December 1944, with Marshal Zhukov in attendance at this crucial meeting. Unlike previous offensive planning, however, Front commanders were not on this occasion summoned to a single conference but rather reported individually to the General Staff—and to Stalin—on their own Front assignments.

The formal *Stavka* directives to the Front commanders took full account of these many consultations and the singular role of Stalin as '*Stavka* co-ordinator' for all four fronts concerned with the offensive along the 'Berlin axis'. At the end of November Marshal Zhukov reported to Stalin that an advance by 1st Belorussian Front due west would be well-nigh impossible owing to the existence of what appeared to reconnaissance to be well-manned defensive positions. Zhukov, therefore, recommended swinging the main attack in the direction of Lodz with the subsequent blow aimed at Poznan. (Zhukov's offensive operations were initially designated the 'Warsaw–Poznan Operation'.) Stalin did not disagree: the axis of Zhukov's advance was aligned to Poznan, and in the light of this decision Marshal Koniev's 1st Ukrainian Front was given Breslau rather than Kalisz as its main objective. A special feature of Koniev's operations was the need to preserve the Silesian industrial area intact. When Koniev presented his operational proposals to Stalin at the end of November, Stalin's finger carefully traced the outline of the massive Silesian industrial basin, at which he uttered only a single word: 'Gold'. Koniev needed no further explanation; liberating this region must at all costs preclude destroying it.

Marshal Zhukov's formal instructions from the *Stavka* prescribed the launching of the main attack from the Magnuszew bridgehead with a force of no less than four field armies, two tank armies and one cavalry corps striking westwards in the direction of Kutno–Lodz, moving thereafter on Bydgoszcz–Poznan. A secondary attack launched from the Pulawy bridgehead by two field armies, two tank corps and one cavalry corps was to be aimed along the Radom–Lodz axis, with units of 1st Belorussian Front co-operating with the right-flank units of 1st Ukrainian Front to destroy the 'Kielce–Radom grouping' of enemy forces. A supporting attack was also to be carried out from the region north of Warsaw by the Soviet 47th Army co-operating with the left-flank units of 2nd Belorussian Front designed to clear German troops from the area between the Vistula and the western Bug, thereby outflanking Warsaw from the north-west. Troops of the 1st Polish Army, which came under Zhukov's Front command, would be used for the liberation of Warsaw itself. The direction of Rokossovskii's main attack with 2nd Belorussian Front was fixed in a north-westerly direction and aimed at Marienburg, on the Baltic and within reach of Danzig. This great sweeping movement was designed to isolate East Prussia from Germany proper, while left-flank units of Rokossovskii's outflanked Modlin from the west, took positions to cross the Vistula and thus cut the escape route for German troops holding Warsaw.

Marshal Koniev's 1st Ukrainian Front was assigned Breslau as its primary objective. The main attack would be launched from the Sandomierz bridgehead with five field armies, two tank armies and four independent tank and mechanized corps in the direction of Radomsko; in ten to eleven days Koniev's forces were to reach a line running from Radom–Czestochowa–Miechow, after which the offensive would be developed in the direction of Breslau. The break-out from the bridgehead would be made on a narrow twenty-mile front by three armies, supported by six artillery divisions; two field armies would be held in the second echelon, one of them supported by a tank corps to be used for an attack on Szydlowiec, outflanking German units in Ostrowiec from the west and co-operating with troops of the 1st Belorussian Front in the capture of Radom, the second army to be employed along the axis of the main attack. The tank armies would be committed once the enemy defences had been shattered along the line of the main thrust. To the south Petrov's 4th Ukrainian Front was ordered to prepare Moskalenko's 38th Army for joint operations with the 60th Army of Koniev's 1st Ukrainian Front in order to capture Cracow.

With Poznan and Breslau pinpointed as their major objectives, Zhukov and Koniev set about preparing their own operational–tactical variants. Marshal Zhukov decided on three breakthrough sectors—from the Magnuszew and Pulawy bridgeheads, and from Jablonna to the north of Warsaw. In conformity with the *Stavka* directive, Zhukov planned his main attack from Magnuszew bridgehead with three field armies (5th Shock, 8th Guards and 61st Armies) committed to breaking through the German defences on a narrow ten-mile sector and driving in the direction of Kutno–Poznan; right-flank units of 61st Army would outflank Warsaw from the west and south, while the 3rd Shock Army—a second-echelon formation—would also attack in the direction of Poznan. The two tank armies— Katukov's 1st Guards and Bogdanov's 2nd Guards—plus 2nd Guards Cavalry Corps were to be introduced into the gaps torn in the German defences; 2nd Guards Tank Army and 2nd Cavalry Corps would move into the gap on the third day in 5th Shock Army's zone and drive on Sochaczew with the aim of cutting escape routes from Warsaw. Katukov's 1st Guards Tank Army would be committed in Chuikov's 8th Guards Army zone of operations, to push on in the direction first of Lodz and then Poznan. The secondary attack from the Pulawy bridgehead would be launched by 69th and 33rd Armies supported by two tank corps, and aimed first in the general direction of Radom and then on Lodz; left-flank units of 33rd Army would co-operate with 1st Ukrainian Front forces in reducing the Kielce–Radom group of German forces. The attack on Warsaw would be mounted by Perkhorovich's 47th Army operating to the north of the Polish capital, while the 1st Polish Army would be introduced on the fourth day of the operation and co-operate with 47th, 61st and 2nd Guards Tank Armies in clearing the city.

Marshal Koniev decided on one massive blow from the Sandomierz bridgehead aimed along the Radom–Breslau axis. The breakthrough sector was some twenty miles wide and here Koniev intended to use 13th, 52nd and 5th Guards Armies, together with elements of 3rd Guards and 60th Armies, all reinforced with three tank corps (25th, 31st and 4th Guards). The second echelon consisted of two field armies, the 21st and 59th, the first destined to be used for an attack on Radom, the second for operations in the direction of Cracow. With over 3,000 tanks at his disposal, Koniev planned to commit Lelyushenko's 4th Tank Army on 13th Army's sector to drive in a north-westerly direction, cut the escape route of the enemy's Kielce–Radom group and then link up with 1st Belorussian Front in the area of Lodz; Rybalko's 3rd Guards Tank Army would attack in 52nd Army's sector, strike on to Radom and frustrate any attempts by enemy forces to take up defensive positions on the rivers Nida and Pilica. Right-flank formations (6th and 3rd Guards Armies) would attack in the direction of Szydlowiec, while the left-flank armies (60th and 59th) were to advance along the Vistula and co-operate with the 38th Army of 4th Ukrainian Front in an attack on Cracow.

The offensive operations to which Rokossovskii and Chernyakhovskii were committed—the conquest of East Prussia and the elimination of German forces in that region—involved a co-ordinated attack from the east and the south on the defensive bastion formed by the Masurian lakes. This offensive intention inevitably recalled the days of August 1914 and the Imperial Russian Army, when Rennenkampf and Samsonov attempted the invasion and conquest of East Prussia in a simultaneous drive from the east and the south; Hindenburg and Ludendorff had rallied a shaken German defence, turned on Samsonov moving from the south and defeated him, while Rennenkampf stood by inexplicably inactive, though he had already approached the outer defences of Königsberg. Rennenkampf had marched through Insterburg, Samsonov through Allenstein; though the Russian threat was finally deflected, here was a lesson the German military did not easily forget. In addition to securing the 'Insterburg gap' and the 'Allenstein gap', the German army made provision for a defensive system deeper within East Prussia. In 1945 Rokossovskii took up the role of Samsonov and once again much depended on the speed of his advance; Chernyakhovskii for his part was faced with smashing his way through the fortifications of the 'Insterburg gap'.

The *Stavka* directive to Rokossovskii stipulated an initial offensive operation designed to destroy enemy forces in the Przasnysz–Mlawa area and, after ten to eleven days of operations, a drive in a north-westerly direction to the Neidenburg–Myszynec line and thence to Marienburg and the Baltic. The main attack would be launched from the Rozan bridgehead on the Narew with four field armies, one tank army and one tank corps, with the breakthrough sector fixed at some twelve to fourteen miles where three armies and three artillery breakthrough divisions would be committed, giving a density of some 220 guns and heavy mortars to each kilometre of front. A second attack with two field armies and one tank corps would be launched from the Serotsk bridgehead in the direction of Belsk, while one army and one tank or mechanized corps was to be used for joint operations with the 1st Belorussian Front in eliminating German forces in Warsaw. Rokossovskii's formations would outflank Modlin from the west and prevent the Germans falling back on the Vistula.

Rokossovski accordingly planned to use three armies—3rd, 48th and 2nd Shock Armies—striking from the Rozan bridgehead along the Mlawa–Marienburg axis. To widen the breach 3rd Army would make its main attack in the direction of Allenstein, with a secondary thrust in a northerly direction. 2nd Shock Army would use part of its forces to outflank Pulutsk from the west and co-operate with 65th Army (attacking from the Serotsk bridgehead) in eliminating the 'Pulutsk group'. Volskii's 5th Guards Tank Army would be introduced in the gap made by 48th Army and drive through Mlawa in a north-westerly direction. The main attack would thus be launched from the left wing of 2nd Belorussian Front, with four field armies and one tank army assigned to this primary assault, advancing in two echelons. Two field armies—the 50th on a broad front from along the Augustov canal from Augustov to Lomza, and the 3rd in closer formation north of Rozan—were deployed to provide protection against possible German counter-attacks from the north, 49th Army being assigned to the second echelon of this force.

Chernyakhovskii's 3rd Belorussian Front received *Stavka* instructions which specified the destruction of the 'Tilsit–Insterburg group' of German forces as its initial objective and, after ten to eleven days of operation, the seizure of the Nemonien–Darkehmen–Goldap line. Thereafter 3rd Belorussian would develop its attack along the river Pregel in the direction of Königsberg, with the main attack force operating on the southern bank of the river. The main assault would be launched with four field armies and two tank corps from the area to the north of Gumbinnen in the direction of Wehlau. Faced by extensive German defences, manned and ready and waiting, Chernyakhovskii had no choice but to grind his way forward step by step. He proposed to destroy the Tilsit forces at the outset and reach the Tilsit–Insterburg line; then the Insterburg group would have to be reduced and eliminated, followed by an advance in the direction of Wehlau–Königsberg. Three field armies—39th, 5th and 28th—would make the initial breakthrough north of Gumbinnen; Galitskii's 11th Guards Army would operate in the second echelon, following 5th and 28th Armies, and on the fifth day of the offensive 11th Guards would join action with 1st Tank Corps on the line of the river Inster, make a sudden thrust on Wehlau and use part of its force to co-operate with 28th Army in the capture of Insterburg. Chernyakhovskii envisaged one deep and massive thrust in the direction of Königsberg, reducing the Ilmenhorst and Heilsberg fortified regions and finally storming the fortress city of Königsberg. In the process German forces at Tilsit and Insterburg would be encircled and destroyed. The task was formidable indeed, taxing all the skill and tenacity of the brilliant Chernyakhovskii: the accomplishment of it was all too soon to cost him his life.

The Soviet build-up for the offensive on all four fronts proceeded apace during the late autumn and early winter. An enormous effort went into repairing the shattered railway networks running eastwards from the Vistula; the rail bridge over the Vistula at Sandomierz, destroyed by German shellfire, was also fully repaired and thus facilitated a more rapid movement of supplies to the western bank. More than 1,200 train loads served to fill out the supply dumps on the 1st Belorussian Front and virtually the same number served Koniev. Red Army lorries shifted more than 920,000 tons of supplies to Zhukov's Front command

and over 100,000 reinforcements. In order to keep this stream of transport flowing, 22,000 trucks were overhauled and put into service with 1st Belorussian Front. The attack from the Vistula bridgeheads inevitably presented difficult problems. Zhukov's Magnuszew bridgehead was relatively constricted, being no more than fifteen miles long and seven deep, served by inadequate dirt roads: here Zhukov concentrated 400,000 men and 1,700 tanks and SP guns. Over the question of the supply of ammunition and fuel, nerves frayed and tempers snapped. Commanders, such as General Chuikov of 8th Guards Army, were incensed at the notion of Front 'rear services' (logistics) under Antipenko dumping their supplies with the forward assault formations and then leaving them to it, putting an immense strain on individual army rear services to maintain the flow of supplies. Fuel for 2,500 aircraft, 4,000 tanks and SP guns, 7,000 lorries and 3,000 heavy tractors proved to be a vastly difficult problem, and even food supplies—never the highest priority—could not be entirely ignored; the Front required a daily supply of 25,000 tons, including 1,150 tons of bread and 220 tons of meat, 1,500 tons of vegetables and 44 tons of sugar. Difficulties with meat supply already demanded a second meatless day for the Front armies.

Marshal Koniev was a little more fortunate with his bridgehead dispositions. The Sandomierz bridgehead on the western bank of the Vistula stretched for some forty-five miles and was almost forty miles deep, which facilitated the concentration of large forces. To persuade the German command that his front would mount a major offensive from the left flank, Koniev made no secret of the preparations going forward on the eastern bank of the Vistula or of massing near Sandomierz, largely concentrated amidst Kurochkin's 60th Army and designed to suggest that the main Soviet thrust would be in the direction of Cracow. An impressive force of 400 wooden tanks and dummy SP guns, plus 1,000 dummy guns—all served by a network of newly built roads for this 'important' sector—served some notice that a major attack could be expected on the left flank of Koniev's front. On the bridgehead itself more than 1,160 command posts were set up, 11,000 gun and mortar emplacements made ready, and more than 2,000 kilometres of motorroad repaired or built from scratch to give each division and tank brigade two roads in order to avoid traffic jams. Red Army engineers laid no less than thirty bridges over the Vistula and put three heavy-duty ferries into service. Half the ammunition available to the front was concentrated in forward dumps in the Sandomierz bridgehead on the eve of the offensive in order to cope uninterruptedly with the heavy demand the initial barrage would make.

The preliminary German dispositions caused Marshal Koniev unconcealed satisfaction. The German command, not unnaturally, concentrated substantial reserves facing the Sandomierz bridgehead—two *Panzer* and two motorized divisions, drawn closely into the tactical defensive zone. Koniev's Front artillery plan was designed to neutralize the whole of the enemy's tactical defensive zone and his operational reserves all to a depth of some ten miles. In addition, it seemed that Army Group A had taken the bait about an attack to be developed from the left flank of his front, to the east of the Wisloka and on the south side of the Vistula. On Zhukov's front, German infantry divisions held fortified positions in front of the Magnuszew and Pulawy bridgeheads, with other units garrisoning Ostrowiec. Col.-Gen. Harpe was also holding a mobile reserve of two German divisions at the Skarzisko road junction, a 'fire-brigade' force able to move on any threatened sector, be it Radom, Kielce or up against the Sandomierz bridgehead. The key to the battle for Malopolska eventually proved to be Kielce, but the German command discovered that far too late in the day.

During the first week of January 1945 events in the western European theatre impinged directly on the Soviet preparations to attack in the east. Amidst a tense and sordid wrangle over the Polish question, with Stalin wringing his hands that he had not succeeded in persuading Churchill of the 'correctness of the Soviet Government's stand', the British Prime Minister on 6 January 1945 sounded out the Soviet leader on the prospects of a Soviet attack in the east to ease the burden in the west, where Allied armies were being beaten bloody by the German offensive launched from the Ardennes. 'I shall be grateful if you can tell me whether we can count on a major Russian offensive on the Vistula front, or elsewhere . . .'; Stalin was only too pleased to reply on 7 January that preparations would go ahead 'at a rapid rate' and *'regardless of weather'* for launching the Soviet offensive not later than the second half of January. Twenty-four hours later Marshal Koniev received a radio-telephone call from General Antonov, Chief of the Soviet General Staff, who informed him that in view of the 'difficult position' of the Allies due to the Ardennes offensive the Soviet attack would now begin as soon as possible: 1st Ukrainian Front would accordingly attack on 12 January, not the 20th as previously understood. This order emanated from Stalin himself. Koniev agreed at once, though he realized almost immediately that due to the prevailing as well as anticipated weather conditions his offensive would have to rely on artillery alone, with Soviet aircraft grounded. Somewhat inexplicable (and still unexplained) is the instruction to Zhukov to open his attack on 14 January, but judging from the adjustments in the timing of other offensive operations it would appear that some kind of synchronization was being attempted. Koniev would attack first with 1st Ukrainian, Chernyakhovskii on the following day, 13 January, with 3rd Belorussian, followed in turn by Zhukov with 1st Belorussian and Rokossovskii with 2nd Belorussian on 14 January. And while Stalin could make the grand gesture to his Allies by advancing the date of the Soviet offensive, this accelerated pace also had the advantage of setting Soviet armies on the move before the German command could bring substantial reserves to bear in the east. The prevailing weather promised poor flying conditions, but at least the cold would facilitate the ground movement and offer firm going for some days.

Contemplating the high ground enclosing the areas of Kielce and Cracow, with the multiple intersections of river valleys and the dense screen of ancient forest to the north along the line of the river Pilica, the German command concluded with some confidence that Malopolska was no place for a high-speed offensive with mobile forces. Once before, in November 1914, this natural redoubt had halted two Russian armies in their tracks as they attempted to march on the Silesian border. Following this reasoning, General Harpe duly focused his attention on defences to the south of the upper Vistula, which suited Marshal Koniev perfectly. To encourage this, Koniev assiduously and obviously 'massed' his forces to the south of the Vistula, all the while slipping armour, infantry and artillery across the Vistula by night into his old bridgehead to the east of Czarna, aiming to strike directly at Kielce with his right-flank forces and to cross the river Nida with divisions on his centre and left.

At 5 o'clock on the morning of Friday 12 January 1945, deploying as many as 300 heavy- and medium-calibre guns for each kilometre of front, Koniev opened his 'artillery attack', simultaneously pushing reconnaissance battalions forward amidst this fierce rolling fire. Driven on by the desperation of the penal units—the *strafbats*—in their midst, these forward battalions took the first line of German trenches and went to ground ahead of the second, whereupon the Soviet guns opened fire once again, an hour and forty-seven minutes of sustained bombardment which blasted away everything in its path, with fearful physical and psychological consequences. The gunfire battered in Fourth *Panzer* Army's command post and broke up the German mobile reserves that were deployed in the immediate vicinity of the main battle line, the *Hauptkampflinie*, on Hitler's express instruction—whatever tactical ingenuity or flexibility the German command might have shown had been brutally extinguished by the *Führer's* own meddling in front-line dispositions. This chaos was also compounded by the damage done by Koniev's guns which reached into the German rear and also ripped away huge gaps in the first line of German defences: pounded now by Soviet long-range guns, dazed and bludgeoned by the incessant bombardment, the defenders fell back on their second line in order to meet the impending Russian attack just as Koniev loosed his armour into the breaches torn in their lines. Shortly after noon Lelyushenko stood ready with his 4th Tank Army and learned that Pukhov's 13th Army was already through the first line of German defences. The first German prisoners, ashen and trembling, babbled out the details of what horror the Russian bombardment had brought to the German trenches, with the dead flung over the screaming wounded. At 1350 hours Lelyushenko asked Koniev for permission to launch his tank formations; Koniev replied in seven minutes, authorizing the armoured advance, and at 1400 hours 10th Tank and 6th Guards Mechanized Corps (4th Tank Army) moved off, each with a regiment reinforced with the newer heavy IS 'Stalin' tanks mounting 122mm guns. Shortly before three o'clock in the afternoon Soviet tank units were in action against the 168th Infantry Division and 51st *Panzer* Battalion with its own heavy tanks, all elements of the German tactical reserve.

By the evening of 12 January Koniev's tank and infantry formations had broken through Fourth *Panzer* Army's defences to a depth of over twelve miles along a 25-mile front, with Lelyushenko's tanks at least twenty miles into the German positions though now about to collide with Nehring's XXIV *Panzer* Corps aimed at the Soviet northern flank. In 36 hours of heavy fighting, which brought over two hundred German tanks and assault guns into action, Lelyushenko and Pukhov drove to the river Nida on a broad front, while Rybalko's 3rd Guards Tank Army with two infantry armies—Koroteyev's 52nd and Zhadov's 5th Guards—held off more German counter-attacks in the area of Chmielnik. With three Soviet armies closing on Kielce—4th and 3rd Guards Tank Armies, with the sturdy 13th under the imperturbable Pukhov—the fate of XXIV *Panzer* Corps was sealed, trapped as it was to the south of Czarna Nida. Pinczow, an important junction, had already fallen to Soviet troops, despite desperate German attempts to hold it. Koniev had meanwhile launched his left-flank army, Kurochin's 60th, on a drive for Cracow and, to keep up the momentum of his main attack as the front broadened, he slid Korovnikov's 59th Army and Poluboyarov's 4th Guards Tank Corps into the gap between 60th and 5th Guards Army; both of these formations were also speedily aimed at Cracow.

As Lelyushenko outflanked Kielce from the west in a drive across the Nida, Soviet infantry fought a final fierce battle for the town, losing it briefly to *Panzer* troops who were eventually destroyed, together with remnants of XXIV *Panzer* Corps. The capture of Kielce secured the whole of Koniev's right flank and brought his armies into open country; Zhadov and Rybalko struck out in pursuit, taking their infantry well beyond the Nida and towards the foothills of Cracow, while to the north Soviet tanks reached the Pilica. This deep penetration brought imminent danger to the German XLII Corps, already half encircled, but the attempt at withdrawal degenerated into hopeless chaos as Soviet tank units broke into Corps HQ, killing or capturing the German staff; the Corps commander, General Recknagel, fell into the hands of Polish partisans. In a wild and ill-considered move, which ran counter to Guderian's urgent advice, Hitler ordered the *Gross Deutschland Panzer* Corps from East Prussia to Lodz in order to stiffen the defence of Kielce—but Kielce had already fallen to the Russians. The *Panzer* corps found itself fighting not for Kielce but in Lodz itself, which all too soon came under attack.

The fall of Kielce and the growing threat to Cracow finally brought signs of movement to that strangely inert German force deployed in the Wisloka area on the southern side of the Vistula—all in expectation of that Soviet attack which never materialized. On 16 January the withdrawal began, prompted by the beginning of an attack aimed at Jaslo (mounted by Moskalenko's 38th Army on the extreme right flank of Petrov's 4th Ukrainian Front) and nudged on its way by Gusev's 21st Army (Koniev's Front); with luck these German divisions would be eventually outflanked from north and south, but next day the German command suddenly speeded the withdrawal, pulling units towards the south of Cracow and into the Myslenice area.

As the evening of 17 January drew on, Koniev's left-flank armies were drawing up on Cracow; Zhadov's 5th Guards and Rybalko's tanks, operating along the 'Czestochowa axis', had already outflanked the city far to the north, while 59th and 60th Army closed on the city. Koniev determined on a rapid operation to seize this ancient Polish city. Up with 59th Army on the morning of 19 January, he ordered Poluboyarov's tank corps to envelop the city from the west and thus threaten encirclement in company with Kurochkin's 60th Army operating to the south and south-east. Korovnikov's 59th would attack from the north and north-west in a special bid to take the bridges over the Vistula. But that same evening the city was cleared and spared all-out bombardment, the threat of encirclement precipitating a German retreat; for once, the usually merciless Koniev let them go on their way. The fall of Cracow completed the battle for Malopolska. The way to the Oder was open, for which Koniev intended to use Rybalko's tanks, while the infantry armies would envelop the Silesian industrial area from the north, north-west and south. In the course of a week Koniev's Front had achieved major successes and a victory of strategic proportions, comparable to earlier resounding Soviet triumphs.

If Koniev toppled the pillars of the German defensive system, Zhukov pulled down the entire roof. On 17 January, the sixth day of Koniev's offensive and the fourth of Zhukov's, the situation had become plainly catastrophic; every vestige of a front line running from the Pilica in the north to the Nida in the south had been totally obliterated. Marshal Zhukov proposed to attack out of his two bridgeheads at Magnuszew and Pulawy, north-east and east of Radom— an unlikely axis of advance at first sight due to the heavy forestation between the Pilica and the Radomka rivers. Zhukov carefully fostered this impression by appearing to aim directly at Warsaw, but steadily cramming the Magnuszew bridgehead—a mere seven miles deep with a frontage of fifteen miles—with almost half a million men and well over a thousand tanks.

On the morning of 14 January Zhukov unleashed his Front forces in what proved to be a savage and relentless offensive, achieving stunning tactical surprise from the outset. Under cover of a pulverizing artillery barrage lasting twenty-five minutes, forward assault battalions moved out of the Magnuszew bridgehead and along the 'fire lanes' in what Zhukov called 'the reconnaissance action'— but one conducted with such punch and power that German units fell back from their first line in confusion. To exploit this momentum Zhukov sent in his main assault forces virtually on the heels of the assault battalions, their passage secured by double 'fire lanes' reaching up to three kilometres into the German positions. The leading tank corps were committed shortly after noon, deepening the penetration along the southern bank of the Pilica and the northern bank of the Radomka; 26th Rifle Corps took the Pilica in its stride, established a small bridgehead near Warka—whose garrison fled in the direction of Warsaw—and secured a bridge capable of taking sixty tons, mined but not blown. Bogdanov's 2nd Guards Tank Army speedily made full use of this godsend from the infantry: by the evening of 14 January Russian tanks were driving at will as much as twenty miles beyond the breakthrough line. Even greater success attended the attack from the Pulawy bridgehead, which brought a Soviet tank corps (the 11th) into striking distance of Radom.

Having punched this double hole in the German positions, Zhukov pressed his advance by night and day. Heavy barrages fired off for up to forty minutes on 15 January preceded Berzarin's 5th Shock Army's attack across the Pilica. Chuikov's 8th Guards Army struck out for the Warka–Radom railway line and final German defensive positions, with Katukov's 1st Guards Tank Army sent in to pursue retreating German units. The right flank of Zhukov's Front now went into action, when on the morning of 15 January under cover of a 55-minute bombardment Perkhorovich's 47th Army north of Warsaw began clearing the reach between the Vistula and western Bug. To this envelopment from the north was added another building up from the south, where Belov's 61st Army was approaching Warsaw from the south-west—while Bogdanov's tanks were sweeping in a north-westerly direction on Sochaczow to cut the main German escape route. Faced with the imminence of encirclement, the German command decided on the hasty evacuation of the Polish capital; if the city could not be held as one of the 'fortresses' specifically designated by Hitler, it could at least be burned, blown up, mined and even looted in a revolting spasm of vengeful destruction. The German withdrawal began during the night of 17 January whereupon the task of breaking into the city was assigned to the 1st Polish Army operating with 1st Belorussian Front; the 6th Polish Division crossed the Vistula near Praga (supported by the gunfire of the Soviet 31st Special Armoured Train Artillery Battalion), as the 2nd Polish Division fought its way into the city from the north, eliminating the German rearguards amidst these fearful and tragic ruins. By noon on 17 January 1945 Warsaw was cleared of German troops.

The fall of Warsaw triggered off reaction in both Berlin and Moscow. Maddened by the abandonment of the city in spite of categorical orders to hold, Hitler lashed out at his military commanders, removing Harpe from Army Group A and replacing him with a man supposedly after his own heart, Schörner, at the same time dismissing von Lüttwitz as GOC Ninth Army and putting Busse in command. Vindictive though this fiat directed against the General Staff was, its irrationality paled into insignificance compared with Hitler's other decision—to transfer the powerful Sixth SS *Panzer* Army from the Ardennes to Hungary, of all places. For the sake of the paltry Hungarian oilfields, the *Führer* dismissed the actual and impending loss of two army groups (A and, latterly, Centre), ignored the massive threat building up in the direction of the Oder and derided the imminent peril to the German population. Guderian could make no impression with his pleading to bring Sixth *Panzer* to bear in the battle for the Oder— shunting an entire *Panzer* army half way across Europe must in any event keep it out of action for many weeks—nor was he able to persuade Hitler to bring Army Group North back into the battle for the *Reich* by evacuating it from Courland. If Hitler's decisions were extravagant and even unreal, Stalin at the *Stavka* showed a marked disposition to caution. The *Stavka* directive of 17 January issued to 1st Ukrainian and 1st Belorussian Fronts redefined their respective objectives: Koniev would make his main effort in the direction of Breslau in order to reach the Oder not later than 30 January, with the left-flank armies taking Cracow by 20–22 January and thereafter outflanking the Dabrowa coalmining area from the north and south, using second-echelon armies for that latter move; Zhukov's primary target was fixed at Poznan and his final objective to secure the Poznan–Bydgoszcz line 'not later than 2–4 February'.

Events soon outpaced both Hitler and Stalin. In not much more than a hundred hours after these various decisions, by 20 January at the latest, the gigantic Soviet breakthrough reaching from East Prussia to the foothills of the Carpathians—a huge rent almost 350 miles across—was an accomplished fact. After one week's fighting, the German defensive system had been staved in, overrun or bypassed, Fourth *Panzer* and Ninth Armies reduced to a drifting mass of men and mangled machines, left far to the rear and oozing in a glutinous military mass in the direction of the Oder and hopefully home. On the day that Koniev took Cracow, 19 January, the large industrial city of Lodz fell to Chuikov's 8th Guards Army on Zhukov's Front. Without any specific orders from Front HQ, Chuikov had decided to take Lodz, which lay spread out before him in the winter sunshine on the morning of the 19th, smoke coming from the factory chimneys and without visible signs of preparation for a determined defence. The first hazard came from the Soviet air force, bent on a bombing and strafing mission and completely unaware that the Soviet 8th Guards Army lay beneath its bomb-line; only frantic ground signals and the desperate firing of green rockets caused the aircraft to sheer off. The city remained wholly intact. Soviet tanks broke into the western suburbs and forward units reached the road along which German units were pulling out to the south-west. Further to the north Zhukov's tank columns were fanning out across Mazovia, racing along the good road network in western Poland. Meanwhile, the locking of Zhukov's left flank (33rd Army and a tank corps) with Koniev's right in the region of Ilza (south-west of the Pulawy bridgehead) finally eliminated the Opatow–Ostrowiec salient and scooped up further remnants of Fourth *Panzer* Army near Skarzisko and Konsk.

German attempts to hold the Soviet advance on the river lines of the Bzura and Rawka came to nothing as Bogdanov's tank army—now bearing the battle honour 'Warsaw'—crashed ahead along a north-westerly axis, though stiffer resistance meant moving up Krivoshein's 1st Mechanized Corps as reinforcement. Taking Kutno and Gostynin, Bogdanov's tanks drove ahead west and north-west, bumping into 'the Netze line' where the Germans hoped to make something of a stand. 34th Guards Rifle Brigade operating with the lead units of 12th Guards Tank Corps took Inowroclaw on 21 January, and the frozen Netze with

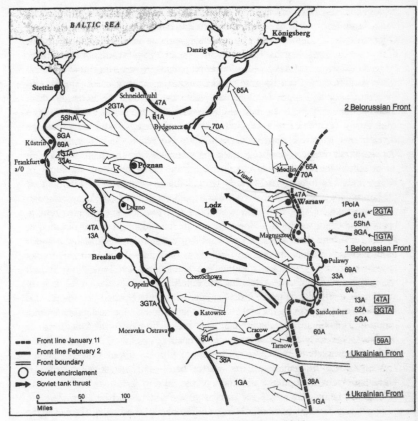

Map 14 From the Vistula to the Oder, January–February 1945

its lakes similarly turned into ice passages was crossed the next day by 9th Guards Tank Corps. While the main body of the tank army pressed on towards Samochin and Schneidemühl, 9th Tank Corps launched a sudden attack on Bydgoszcz (Bromberg) and had cleared it by the evening of 23 January, opening the road to the *Reich* frontier, now just over forty miles away.

The honour of being the first to cross that frontier, however, fell to Marshal Koniev and the formations of the 1st Ukrainian Front. After 17 January, in response to the *Stavka's* instructions, Koniev turned his main armoured attack north-westwards in the direction of Breslau, but the looming battle for the major industrial region of Silesia caused the Front command to make some radical re-dispositions, the most dramatic of which was to swing Rybalko's 3rd Guards Tank Army from north to south, thus taking it finally along the line of the river Oder. In order to dislodge the German forces without literally blasting them out of the factory towns, Marshal Koniev decided on a very skilful series of manoeuvres designed to move his armies round—rather than through—this industrial complex: while armour carried out its wide envelopment, the infantry would attack from the north, east and south in order to squeeze the German garrisons into open country where they might be more easily destroyed. North of the Vistula, Gusev's 21st Army (reinforced with a tank and cavalry corps) would carry out the envelopment from the north and north-west, Korovnikov's 59th Army (with Poluboyarov's tank corps) would attack towards Katowice, and Kurochkin's 60th Army effect the southern envelopment. In the north the lead battalions of Koroteyev's 52nd Army had already crossed the *Reich* frontier at Namslau on 20 January together with Rybalko's tanks from 3rd Guards Tank Army, although the main body of that formation was about to make its ninety-degree turn to bring it sweeping southwards along the line of the Oder and in the direction of Katowice. Behind them was Pukhov's 13th Army making up the distance between Piotrkow and Wielun, driving on until they, too, crossed the German frontier near Militsch on 23 January. Meanwhile Lelyushenko's 4th Tank Army moved westwards ahead of Pukhov, entering the Polish town of Rawicz on 22 January and pushing brigades on to the Oder—17th Guards Mechanized Brigade reached Göben on the Oder during the night of 22–23 January and a forward reconnaissance group of 16th Guards Mechanized Brigade broke through to the Oder north of Steinau (some forty miles north-west of Breslau). Zhadov's 5th Guards Army had also advanced to the Oder north-west of Oppeln (Opole) on 22 January and captured a bridgehead on the western bank—the first seized by the 1st Ukrainian Front, though the reduction of the Silesian industrial region had to be resolved before any large-scale crossing of the Oder could be attempted.

By 25–26 January, as both Zhukov and Koniev pushed on to the Oder, the problem of co-ordinating this advance—within each separate front and between the fronts themselves—assumed new urgency. Stalin on 25 January telephoned Zhukov to interrogate him on his immediate plans: Zhukov intimated that he proposed to advance with all speed towards Küstrin on the Oder, while his right-flank forces would swing north and north-west to fend off any possible threat from East Pomerania, though as yet no immediate danger presented itself. Stalin seemed to be far from convinced, pointing out that Zhukov's 1st Belorussian Front would be separated by 'more than 150 kilometres' from Rokossovskii's 2nd Belorussian Front: Zhukov must wait until Rokossovskii completed the 'East Prussia operation' and had his forces 'out beyond the Vistula', a task requiring all of ten days—nor could Koniev cover Zhukov's left flank since his main forces were still engaged in reducing the Silesian industrial region. Zhukov pleaded at once with Stalin to be allowed to continue his offensive without any break or pause, if only to penetrate the 'Miedzyrzecz fortified line' at speed; an additional army as reinforcement would secure the right flank. To this Stalin made no specific reply, save for an undertaking to 'think it over'. Zhukov heard no more.

Undeterred for the moment, Zhukov pressed his attack, pushing Katukov's 1st Guards Tank Army into the Miedzyrzecz fortified line, which proved to be disorganized and still largely unmanned. To protect these forces now advancing on the Oder from any assault from the direction of East Pomerania and to cover his right flank, Zhukov redeployed 3rd Shock Army, 47th and 61st Armies, 2nd Cavalry Corps and the Polish 1st Army to face northwards. Chuikov's 8th Guards Army, 69th Army and part of 1st Guards Tank Army were assigned to the 'reduction' of Poznan, which, as Chuikov sardonically noted, was not a lightly defended city to be seized off the march, but a formidable fortress.

At this point in time all those imperfections and imprecisions of the *Stavka* directives issued at the end of November 1944 now came home to roost. On the day that Stalin telephoned Zhukov about his next moves, Marshal Rokossovskii had all but won the battle for East Prussia. Yet a gnawing crisis was building up on Rokossovskii's left flank as he tried desperately to keep pace with Zhukov's advance to the Oder. Zhukov's forces remained 'poorly protected on the north, from the direction of East Pomerania' (which is how Rokossovskii himself described the situation) while he, in turn, was thoroughly bemused by the situation on his northern flank where Chernyakhovskii was operating. Stalin was right in pinpointing possible danger for Zhukov, but he remained ominously silent on the possible remedy and, naturally enough, did not refer to the root cause of the impending crisis.

On 14 January, as Zhukov's 1st Belorussian Front went into action, Rokossovskii's 2nd Belorussian Front opened its own offensive along the line of the river Narew, mounting the main attack northwestwards from the left flank with four infantry armies (70th, 65th, 2nd Shock and 48th Armies) and one tank army (Volskii's 5th Guards Tank), plus one army (Gorbatov's 3rd) in immediate reserve; on the right flank Rokossovskii deployed two armies, Grishin's 49th and Boldin's 50th, for an attack on Lomza and an advance through the Masurian lakes to link with Chernyakhovskii's 3rd Belorussian Front. Rokossovskii needed speedy success above all else, yet the river Narew itself—at least 300 yards across and four yards deep—posed a formidable barrier; the late-winter frosts had laid only the thinnest screen of ice, passable for small groups rather than large bodies of men, but at least the marshes on the Russian side were frozen hard and could support a goodly force. North and south of Pulutsk Soviet troops had earlier captured two small bridgeheads, holding them for several weeks though under constant German artillery fire; from the Soviet side of the river heavy guns had duelled daily with German batteries, steadily building up their firepower. On the morning of 14 January, when mist and swirling snow storms cut visibility to a hundred yards, Rokossovskii's Front fired off an artillery barrage at 10 o'clock, heavy gunfire which lasted for most of the day and was concentrated for the most part against Pulutsk. But the same foul weather kept Soviet aircraft grounded. Deprived of air support and with tank operations limited by dense mist, the brunt of the fighting fell on the infantry. Rokossovskii disposed of much armour and many guns but was seriously short of infantry, in spite of his divisions having been filled out on the eve of the attack with 120,000 men— 10,000 were liberated POWs, 39,000 returned from field hospitals and 20,000 flushed out of rear services and supply units, with many more local conscripts pressed into the Red Army.

Progress was disappointingly slow on this first day and, on the next day, Gorbatov's 3rd Army had to hold off powerful attacks launched by *Grossdeutschland Panzer* units (shortly to be transferred south to Kielce, to fight against Koniev) with all the danger that German troops might break into the flank and rear of the main Soviet assault force. Gorbatov held on, the attacks slackened and Rokossovskii, for all his reluctance, decided to commit two tank corps alongside 48th, 2nd Shock and 65th Armies to smash in the German defences.

With the Pulutsk fortified area outflanked, the defenders fell back, though the German command rushed up reinforcements to cover the approaches to Mlawa. The weather improved on 16 January, Soviet ground-attack aircraft joined the battle and N.I. Gusev's 48th Army, supported by 8th Mechanized Corps, battered its way forward. Ciechanow, more than thirty miles to the west of the Narew, fell to Soviet troops, and the capture of this important road junction began to signal a major breakthrough. The next day, 17 January, Volskii's 5th Guards Tank Army was committed into the breach effected by 48th Army; Soviet columns were now advancing on Mlawa and had crossed the river Wkra on a wide front. Prasznysz at the centre of the front was captured on 18 January, Popov's 70th Army took the old fortress town of Modlin, and German attempts to escape along the motor-road to Plonsk were dashed as Batov's 65th Army took Naselsk and Plonsk. Within twenty-four hours the 2nd Belorussian Front had broken through the German defences along a sixty-mile front running from Modlin to Ostrolenka, to a depth of some 35–40 miles. Mlawa itself fell on 19 January and the way was cleared for Rokossovskii to lunge far beyond the Vistula.

The next day, 20 January, produced a major shock for Rokossovskii. The *Stavka* ordered him to turn three infantry armies—3rd, 48th and 2nd Shock— plus 5th Guards Tank Army to the north and north-east against German forces in East Prussia, aiming at the Frisches Haff. These revised operational orders clearly cut across the formal provisions (and informal understandings) of the main *Stavka* directive of 28 November 1944, which had envisaged close and effective co-ordination between the 1st and 2nd Belorussian Fronts in the entire 'Vistula–Oder operation'. Rokossovskii was left with his initial assignment—co-operation with 1st Belorussian Front—but now burdened with the task of surrounding German forces in East Prussia. In view of the *Stavka's* latest orders, Rokossovskii could commit only two armies on his left flank in support of Zhukov's drive on the Oder, a state of affairs which brought a burst of fierce anger from Zhukov himself.

Chernyakhovskii's offensive with 3rd Belorussian Front had already begun on 13 January, when assault battalions moved forward on the eastern frontier of East Prussia at 6 o'clock in the morning, screened by dense mist—though the same mist drastically reduced the effectiveness of the massive artillery barrage, involving an expenditure of almost 120,000 shells, fired off against the fortified lines between Pilkallen and the river Goldap. The Front attack plan called for an assault from the centre of the Front and a westerly drive to destroy the 'Tilsit–Insterburg' group of German forces; Königsberg, capital and 'citadel of East Prussia', was the final objective. The assault armies were drawn from Lyudnikov's 39th, Krylov's 5th and Luchinskii's 28th, with Galitskii's 11th Guards Army as a second-echelon formation assigned to eliminate German defences north of the Masurian lakes. P.G. Chanchibadze's 2nd Guards Army was allotted the task of securing the left flank of this assault force, which might be attacked from the direction of the Masurian lakes; Shafranov's 31st Army was deployed on the extreme left flank to hold German units in a covering action. The Front command determined that it was opposed by thirteen German infantry divisions and one motorized division, part of Third *Panzer* and Fourth Armies.

Chernyakhovskii's formations had literally to batter in German defences, slogging bloody battles in the midst of prepared German defences, from which Soviet assault troops were met by fierce counter-attacks. Both sides suffered heavy losses. The main Soviet thrust was concentrated north of Pilkallen, though the German command waited for an attack to develop south of Gumbinnen. On 16 January Chernyakhovskii loosed his main attack in full force, when Soviet tanks crossed the frozen marsh between Schillehnen and the river Sheshupe. Schillehnen was outflanked and Lasdehnen taken. A sudden improvement in the weather brought the Soviet air force on to the battlefield and in support of Burdeinyi's 2nd Guards Tank Corps. Kyudinikov's 39th Army, with close air support provided by Khryukin's 1st Air Army, took Schillehnen and pressed on over the Sheshupe; Lt.-Gen. V.V. Butkov's 1st Tank Corps was committed alongside 39th Army and moved to outflank Tilsit from the south. On 19 January the *Stavka* handed over Lt.-Gen. A.P. Beloborodov's 43rd Army (1st Baltic Front) to Chernyakhovskii, for use in operations against Tilsit and the subsequent drive on Königsberg. Pilkallen, attacked now from three sides, fell on 18 January, having resisted so many Soviet frontal attacks, and the next day Tilsit was in Soviet hands, after which Soviet tank columns struck along the Königsberg road and were well on their way to Insterburg.

Taking account of this situation Chernyakhovskii decided to shift the axis of 11th Guards operations from the area of 5th Army to the junction between 39th and 5th Armies. Together with 1st and 2nd Guards Tank Corps, 11th Guards Army went into action on the line of the river Inster and was committed to advancing to the south-west. In this fashion the famous 'Insterburg gap' was turned from the west as 11th Guards advanced on Wehlau, outflanking these long-established fortifications; 5th Army bypassed Insterburg to the east, and 28th Army using its artillery and air support took Gumbinnen.

Now Chernyakhovskii could only slog his way forward to Königsberg, battering down one line of defences after another. At this stage the *Stavka* stepped in and ordered Rokossovskii to complete the job of isolating East Prussia from the *Reich* at large—to the near fury of Rokossovskii, who evidently considered the whole East Prussian campaign ill-planned from the outset, in that it had meant throwing armies against the well-defended eastern and south-eastern areas when the assault should have come from south to north, starting from the Lomza line and aiming directly at Frisches Haff. An operation on these lines would have combined almost automatically with 2nd Belorussian Front plans and would have meant a more rapid penetration of German defences, particularly if 50th and 3rd Armies had been handed over to Chernyakhovskii.

Disgruntled or not, Rokossovskii flung himself with a will into his new assignment, launching tank columns and lorried infantry in a swift and savage attack which brought the modern mechanized equivalent of 'fire and sword' to East Prussia, though the pillage and rape was as old as warfare itself. The operation, however, began badly and involved serious loss of time since the commander of 50th Army, holding the line of the Augustov canal, failed to detect that the Germans had pulled back to the north. Two days were lost, and 50th Army—whose commander, Boldin, was summarily replaced by his chief of staff, F.P. Ozerov—had to struggle hard to catch up with the enemy, while 49th Army's efforts were frittered away in premature attacks. Meanwhile Rokossovskii's armies were swinging north and north-west in response to *Stavka* orders of 21 January, driving along the Deutsch-Eylau/Marienburg axis and aiming for a line running from Elbing to Marienburg and the lower reaches of the Vistula down to Torun (Thorn). Gorbatov's 3rd and Gusev's 48th Armies turned north-west and crashed through the barrier of the old frontier defences, bypassing isolated strong-points; N.S. Oslikovskii's 3rd Guards Cavalry Corps drove deeper into the German positions, bursting into Allenstein amidst all the bustle of German trains unloading tank and artillery reinforcements. In the bout of furious fighting only the timely arrival of the 48th Army in strength saved Oslikovskii. But the second-defence line had now been staved in, and the central region of East Prussia, hitherto covered from the south, now lay open to the Red Army.

Speed, frenzy and savagery characterized this advance. Villages and small towns burned, while Soviet soldiers raped at will and wreaked an atavistic vengeance in those houses and homes decked out with any of the insignia or symbols of Nazism. German officials lay strewn in the street with a bullet in the head, small-town functionaries and local burgomasters flung about by bursts of automatic fire; some fussily bedecked Nazi Party portrait photograph, seen as a sign of obeisance to the *Führer* himself, would be the signal to mow down the entire family amidst their table, chairs and kitchenware. Columns of refugees, combined with groups of Allied prisoners uprooted from their camps, and slave labour no longer enslaved in farm or factory, trudged on foot or rode in farm carts, some to be charged down or crushed into a bloody smear of humans and horses by the juggernaut Soviet tank columns racing ahead with assault infantry astride the T-34s. Raped women were nailed by their hands to the farmcarts carrying their families. Under these lowering January skies and the gloom of late winter, families huddled in ditches or by the roadside, fathers intent on shooting their own children or waiting whimpering for what seemed like the wrath of God to pass. The Soviet Front command finally intervened, with an order insisting on the restoration of military discipline and the implementation of the 'norms of conduct' towards the enemy population. But this elemental tide surged on, impelled by the searing language of roadside posters and crudely daubed slogans proclaiming this and the land ahead 'the lair of the Fascist beast', a continuous incitement to brutalized ex-prisoners of war now in the Soviet ranks or to the reluctant peasant conscripts dragged into the Red Army in its march through the Baltic states, men with pity for no one.

On 21 January one memory of German militarism had been erased when Tannenberg fell. The scene of Hindenburg's crucial battle in August 1914 and the symbol of earlier Russian disgrace and defeat, the town was evacuated by German units who also carried away with them the remains of Hindenburg and his wife, blowing up the huge memorial behind them. The Soviet units involved in a battle that was less ferocious than symbolic and psychological, took 'Tannenberg' as a battle honour. The fall of the Allenstein fortified zone, however, on 23 January opened up greater vistas for Rokossovskii; he ordered Volskii's 5th Guards Tank Army into the gap and instructed this formation to strike for the sea. Gusev's 48th and Fedyuninskii's 2nd Shock Army meanwhile won the race to occupy the Deutsch-Eylau/Osterode line, heading off the vanguard of Third *Panzer* which might have checked the Soviet advance in the direction of Marienburg–Elbing. Volskii unleashed his armoured columns: 10th Tank Corps took Mohrungen on 23 January and Mülhausen the next day, trapping German reserves moving along the Königsberg–Elbing autobahn. The 29th Tank Corps swept even further ahead with 31st Tank Brigade in the lead. The forward battalion, Captain Dyachenko's 3rd with seven tanks and a group of tommy-gunners, received orders to push on to outflank Elbing from the east, cutting road and rail links east of Elbing at Gross-Robern.

Driving on Elbing from the east, Dyachenko found it easier to race straight through the city, headlamps full on in the gathering gloom, lighting up trams lumbering about and shoppers going about the streets; taken at first for a German tank training unit, panic-stricken realization that these were Soviet tanks gave way to bursts of gunfire but Dyachenko pressed on and towards midnight reached the Frisches Haff. Colonel Pokolov's 31st Brigade was following behind Dyachenko, but finding the defences fully alerted he too swung to the east and linked up with his 3rd Tank Battalion on the morning of 24 January. The main body of the tank army now drew up on Tolkemit east of Elbing, broke through to the sea and trapped German forces who might try to make their way to the Vistula. Meanwhile Fedyuninskii's 2nd Shock Army was closing on Marienburg, that time-honoured fortress of the Teutonic Knights; 8th Mechanized Corps forced the river Nogat off the march, while Fedyuninskii's troops attacked to the north and set about storming the city, which fell on 26 January. At the same time Batov's 65th and Popov's 70th Armies made for Grudziadz (Graudenz) and Torun, the 70th fighting in the 'Kulmland', that reach of land between Grudziadz and Torun.

With his armies at the sea and on the lower Vistula, Rokossovskii had severed the land communications of German forces in East Prussia: Third *Panzer* Army, Fourth Army and six infantry divisions plus two motorized divisions of Second Army were trapped. In a desperate attempt to re-establish the land link in the direction of Marienburg, the command of Fourth Army decided on a powerful break-out attempt from the west of Heilsberg, assembling seven infantry divisions and a *Panzer* division to fight this deblockading action. The idea was originally Reinhardt's, commander of Army Group Centre in East Prussia; while Hitler raged that the line in the Masurian lakes must be held at all costs, Reinhardt saw the only hope of salvation in withdrawal and in an attempt to smash through to the Nogat and the Vistula, taking as many civilians with the German troops as could be managed. Hossbach, commander of Fourth Army, agreed and had fallen back behind the Heilsberg line to launch the attack. Two infantry divisions, a motorized and a *Panzer* division would attack from Wormditt, two infantry divisions from Mehlsack and two from Braunsberg towards the south-west.

On 27 January a short but powerful artillery barrage preceded the German attack, which unrolled against Soviet units at the height of a fierce blizzard and tearing winter winds. Rokossovskii's armies were stretched thin, all the way from Tolkemit to Allenstein, supplies were low and reserves at some distance from the front-line units; Gusev's 48th Army was particularly exposed and not a little complacent, thinking the enemy beaten into the ground. On that blizzard-swept night German infantry, driven by desperation, fell on the 96th Rifle Division of 48th Army; heavily damaged and short of ammunition, the division fell back to the south-west. The alarm bells rang in every sense at Rokossovskii's HQ, where he was holding a supper for his generals: Volskii's 5th Guards' tanks, 8th Tank Corps and Oslikovskii's 3rd Guards Cavalry Corps were alerted at once, with instructions to Fedyuninskii to redeploy 2nd Shock Army in a blocking position to the east, from its present location south of Elbing.

The German attack pushed ten miles into the Soviet positions, recapturing Liebstadt and encircling the 17th Rifle Division of 48th Army, though Colonel Grebnev hung on grimly with his 17th. During the next forty-eight hours Fourth Army fought furiously to break through to Marienburg, driving more than fifteen miles into 48th Army positions and recapturing Mühlhausen and Pr.-Holland. With lead German units only about six miles from Elbing the threat of a German breakthrough to the Vistula had suddenly become very real, forcing Rokossovskii to mass four corps (one rifle, one mechanized and two tank), the elements of a cavalry corps, a mechanised brigade, five anti-tank artillery brigades and a rifle division (3rd Guards Tank Corps, assigned as the Front reserve, was too short of equipment to be committed). These formations rushed to build up a firm battle-line between Allenstein and Frisches Haff.

On 30 January Fourth Army made its last attempt east of Elbing to break out to the Vistula, only to be met by Volskii's tanks: Grebnev's 17th Division was freed from its encirclement, while Gorbatov's 3rd Army and the unfortunate 50th attacked the fortifications of Heilsberg, threatening the left flank of the German force. One by one, German units were smashed to pieces, grimy Soviet soldiers and battle-worn divisions grappling with desperate German soldiers whose salvation lay so near and yet so far. Stirred by suspicions that here was yet more treason in unauthorized withdrawal, Hitler had removed Reinhardt and Hossbach (Fourth Army commander) on 26 January; Rendulic, successor to Reinhardt, received the strictest injunction from Hitler to hold the East Prussian capital Königsberg at all costs. Having switched commanders, Hitler also juggled with their commands, turning Army Group North into Army Group *Kurland*, Centre into a new Army Group North, and Army Group A into Army Group Centre. Two of these groups, North and *Kurland*, were now completely isolated and marooned with their backs to the Baltic, unable to take any part in the battle for the *Reich*. For the defence of north Germany Hitler now raised a new army group—Vistula—made up of Second Army and Ninth Army, or what remained of them. Command of this key force went to none other than Heinrich Himmler, *Reichsführer SS* and Chief of Police. The chief hangman had finally arrived among his minions at the front.

The encirclement of East Prussia was complete, though the reduction of the string of *Festungen*, 'Führer fortresses'—meant to hold out to the bitter end however improvised or impoverished the defences and whatever the hazard to the civilian population—took many weeks of ferocious fighting and a horrendous toll in lives. The greatest and grimmest of these *Festungen* was Königsberg, which by the end of January 1945 was encircled by Soviet armies and seemed likely at one moment to fall speedily to Soviet troops. On 27 January Bagramyan's 1st Baltic Front took Memel, from which the German garrison fell back on the Kurische Nehrung and took up positions to the north of Königsberg. Chernyakhovskii's 3rd Belorussian Front was striking due west, hammering its way through the fortifications of Heilsberg and closing on the eastern edge of Königsberg, while the left flank steered its way through the Masurian lakes (capturing in its passage Hitler's old headquarters at Rastenburg). Once Beloborodov's 43rd Army encircled the city from the north, capturing Cranz at the exit to the Kurische Nehrung and advancing to the Frisches Haff (thus isolating the city from Samland

and Pillau), it seemed that the end could not be long delayed, since Galitskii's 11th Guards Army advancing along the Pregel had by now cut the road link between the city and those German troops still fighting south of the Frisches Haff. German forces still fighting in East Prussia were now splintered into three isolated groups.

But Königsberg did not fall with a rush. Attacking from Brandenburg, south of the city, panzer grenadiers of the *Grossdeutschland* Division, the *Hermann Göring* Division motorized infantry and other units beat back 11th Guards' left flank, making contact with the city from this southerly point. What then remained to the German army consisted of a long, narrow, formidable pocket, packed with the elements of twenty-three divisions, extending for some forty miles from the southern shore of the Frisches Haff to include Königsberg itself and varying in depth, though nowhere greater than twelve miles; west of Königsberg, but separated from the city by a narrow strip of land held by Soviet divisions, were the nine divisions of 'Group Samland', the erstwhile defenders of Memel now holding the port of Pillau at the tip of the peninsula. (In mid-February a sudden and highly successful blow linked Samland with Königsberg, furnished a narrow land corridor and kept the city out of Soviet hands for a further two months.) Rokossovskii's right flank, fighting to hold off the attempted breakout to the Nogat and Vistula, had suffered badly: Elbing had yet to be subjugated and Grudziadz (Graudenz) was transformed into yet another *Festung,* while on the left at Torun—famed in its own right as a 'Vistula fortress'—V.S. Popov with 70th Army made the foolish blunder of thinking that he could rush a supposedly small garrison with one under-strength rifle division and a single rifle regiment woefully short of artillery. Nine days of fighting (1–9 February) were needed to smoke out this 'hornets' nest', from which only 3,000 men escaped from a garrison of 30,000.

As the pounding of East Prussia proceeded, Marshal Zhukov was pushing his right flank at top speed towards the middle Oder with the cognizance of Stalin, who nonetheless warned him to keep a wary eye open to the north. Bogdanov's tanks were already over the Netze, crossing the German frontier at noon on 26 January and under orders to reach the Oder by 30 January; Katukov's 1st Guards Tank Army forced both the 'Netze line' and the 'Obra line' at speed and also received orders to make for the Oder in the region of Frankfurt. Zhukov pressed at the same time to bring Chuikov's 8th Guards in strength across to the northern side of the Netze and the Warte, leaving a blockading force at Poznan—yet another *Festung,* one held by over 60,000 men manning the well-prepared and well-stocked armoured forts. The main body of the forces of 1st Belorussian Front passed the frontier of the *Reich* on 29 January. While right-flank armies stabbed into western Pomerania and advanced against dwindling resistance as far as Arnswalde and Deutsch-Krone, at the centre Berzarin's 5th Shock Army and Bogdanov's tanks forced their way to the Oder. Colonel Yesipenko's battle group from the 89th Rifle Division (5th Shock)—a forward unit made up of rifle troops, heavy tanks, an anti-tank regiment and a mortar regiment—made the first assault crossing of the Oder on the morning of 31 January, capturing a bridgehead in the area of Kienitz, Neuendorf and Refeld; the surprise assault on Kienitz caught German soldiers walking the streets as if nothing had happened, and trains were running on the Kienitz–Berlin line.

Bogdanov's tank army, with Colonel Vainrub's 219th Tank Brigade from 1st Mechanized Corps in the lead, reached the Oder at 10 am on the morning of 31 January. The next day 1st Mechanized drew up in strength and fighting went on in the eastern approaches to Küstrin. At three o'clock in the afternoon of 1 February, 20th Guards Mechanized Brigade from 8th Guards Mechanized Corps (1st Guards Tank Army) also reached the Oder; 40th Guards Tank Brigade spurted along for the last fifteen miles, drawing up to the Oder late in the evening. 1st Guards Tank Brigade had meanwhile crossed the Kunnersdorf battlefield, where Russian troops long years before had defeated Frederick II of Prussia, and closed on the Oder. Frankfurt seemed only 'a hop, skip and a jump' away, but 1st Brigade had run out of fuel and was almost without ammunition, so in Kunnersdorf it stayed. Meanwhile Colonel A.Kh. Babadzhanyan with 11th Guards Tank Corps (1st Guards Tank Army) made its initial crossing of the Oder on 2 February, the same day as Chuikov's 4th Guards Corps started its own assault, crossing to seize a bridgehead on the western bank and gain control of Kietz in the southern suburbs of Küstrin. Treacherously thin ice, the lack of any proper bridging equipment and the sudden arrival of the *Luftwaffe* all severely inhibited this first ambitious attempt to cross. The arrival of AA guns on 3 February kept the German fighter-bombers at bay, but the lack of heavy bridging meant that neither guns nor tanks could be ferried across the Oder.

During this last week in January five of Marshal Koniev's armies were either astride or across the Oder, though the lack of firm ice caused by the swift-flowing current made it difficult to transfer large bodies of men and equipment. Lelyushenko's 4th Tank Army had reached Göben north of Steinau on 22 January; improvised and hazardous crossings brought men and tanks to the western bank, with Göben being cleared completely on 25 January and Steinau captured on 30 January, the day that V.N. Gordov's 3rd Guards Army took up its own positions on the Oder and thus secured Lelyushenko's right flank. D.N. Gusev's 21st Army had reached Oppeln and the Oder on 23 January, followed in short order by the 13th, 52nd and 5th Guards Armies. A week of furious labour and strenuous fighting brought Koniev's armies two large bridgeheads, the first to the north in the region of Steinau, between Breslau and Glogau, the second further to the south at Brieg, between Breslau and Oppeln.

On Koniev's left flank, which was committed to the capture of the Silesian industrial region, 'everything turned out exactly as planned'. Gusev's 21st Army, rather than persisting with its outflanking movement to the north-west, received orders to launch a frontal attack on the German garrisons, while one corps of Rybalko's tank army was to make for Ratibor. Wryly accepting the need for yet another turn, Rybalko re-routed his armour and watched his tanks move off, many festooned with silk netting captured in some textile mill as camouflage against the snowy ground. Gusev took Gleiwitz first and then advanced along a west-to-east axis, closing on Hindenburg before taking Beuten and Katowice. On their southerly encircling drive, 59th and 60th Armies, accompanied on their extreme left by 38th Army from 4th Ukrainian Front covering difficult terrain in the direction of the river Skawa, moved towards Rybnik, which they reached on 27 January. In this drive Kurochkin's riflemen stumbled on the gigantic death camp at Auschwitz (Oswiecim) with all its hideously perverted industrial processes of mass extermination—the rail unloading ramps and assembly points, the gas-chambers and crematoria, the giant's staircase of piled suitcases and the ghastly mountain of a full seven tons of women's hair, bulging bales of suits and dresses, plus the grotesque pyramids of dentures and spectacles removed from those consigned to the death-chambers.

By 29 January the Silesian industrial region was cleared. German units falling back to the south-west towards the Oder were caught—as Koniev planned they should be— by Rybalko's tanks and Kurochkin's riflemen. Only one-third, 30,000 out of 100,000 men, escaped the Silesian trap. Now Marshal Koniev began shifting the main weight of his assault to the right flank in order to invest the Oder line; the area north of Breslau offered a much more favourable deployment area and was in any event much nearer to Zhukov's 1st Belorussian Front, as well as being closer to Berlin itself. Both Pukhov's 13th Army and Gordov's 3rd Guards Army had to battle their way to the Oder against stiff opposition from XXIV *Panzer* Corps and XLII Corps, battered though these formations were. German troops failed to eliminate the Soviet bridgehead at Steinau, but Koniev for his part failed to encircle enemy units squeezed southwards by 1st Belorussian Front and intent on escaping across the Oder. The German bridgehead at Glogau on the eastern bank survived yet awhile, though Gordov and Lelyushenko managed a limited encirclement at Leszno, eliminating about 15,000 German troops. Tattered though the German divisions had become, Koniev's assault armies were also severely worn down; Lelyushenko had outpaced his supply and was running short of fuel and ammunition, with air-drops scarcely making up for the shortfall. But the bridgehead at Steinau held and, in spite of furious German resistance at Brieg, a large consolidated bridgehead fifty miles long and fifteen deep was built up south of Breslau. Breslau itself, however, set about manning its elderly forts and improvised anti-tank defences, transforming itself into a fortress of astonishing resilience and extraordinary tenacity.

As their armies drew up to and massed along the river Oder, both Marshal Zhukov and Marshal Koniev fixed their gaze on one compelling and commanding target—Berlin. Only forty-eight miles separated the capital of the *Reich* from the Küstrin Bridgehead at the tip of Zhukov's massive salient driven into the eastern reaches of Germany. The capture of Berlin now loomed increasingly large in the minds of the Soviet military commanders, persuaded that one final all-out, high-speed attack was feasible in view of the present pace and scope of the Soviet offensive. That view was also shared at the centre: as Soviet armies drew up to the Mlawa–Lodz–Czestochowa–Cracow line, the Soviet General Staff on 19 January formally plotted the capture of Berlin on its working operations map as Zhukov's next assignment with 1st Belorussian Front. The final decision to go for Berlin would not be taken, however, without consulting the two Front commanders themselves.

Marshal Zhukov evidently decided on 26 January to go flat out for Berlin; that same day he submitted his plans for a non-stop offensive aiming at the capture of Berlin. Zhukov's plan involved reaching the Berlinchen (Barlinek) –Landsberg–Grätz line, concentrating his Front forces, replenishing ammunition stocks and bringing his armour into a full state of readiness, moving 3rd Shock Army and 1st Polish Army into the first echelon of the Front and, on the morning of 1 or 2 February, opening a non-stop offensive to force the Oder off the march and then strike along 'the Berlin axis'; 2nd Guards and 1st Guards Tank Army would converge on Berlin from the north-west and north-east respectively. Hot on the heels of Marshal Zhukov's plan came that of Marshal Koniev: the first phase of his operations, timed for 5 or 6 February, envisaged eliminating German forces at Breslau by an attack launched from the two large bridgeheads north and south of the city, followed by an advance to the river Elbe which was to be reached by 25–26 February. Koniev's right-flank armies would then co-operate with Zhukov's 1st Belorussian Front in the capture of Berlin, while left-flank armies advanced in the direction of Dresden, relying for support in this operation on 4th Ukrainian Front. At this juncture these plans clearly coincided with Stalin's own view of the situation, for they were approved without demur and without delay, Zhukov's on 27 January, Koniev's on 29 January. Both Fronts, 1st Belorussian and 1st Ukrainian, were apparently free to strike out for Berlin.

For all the forthrightness of these decisions, a certain confusion began to prevail both within the Front commands and at the centre. There were unmistakable signs that the *Stavka* was no longer entirely abreast of the pace and extent of the Soviet advance: Koniev's 1st Ukrainian Front had speedily outstripped its *Stavka* directives, while Zhukov's Front was almost five days ahead of schedule when it reached the Kutno–Lodz line, yet no great thought seems to have been given to re-examining rates of advance and possible objectives. As they outran *Stavka* directives, so also were Soviet armies overreaching themselves in terms of supplies of fuel and ammunition; in the onward armoured rush, Soviet tank crews would fill up from one or two vehicles, leave them stranded and press on with the remainder of the battalion or company, but this could not solve the problem of ammunition. At the same time Marshal Zhukov was looking with growing anxiety at his northern flank—and yet again at his southern flank, where he depended on Marshal Koniev. On 31 January he sent an urgent signal to Stalin stressing that the frontage of 1st Belorussian Front had now reached 500 kilometres, that Rokossovskii's left flank was lagging appreciably behind the right flank of 1st Belorussian Front—Rokossovskii *must* push his 70th Army forward—and Marshal Koniev should gain the Oder line as speedily as possible. Marshal Zhukov received no reply to this urgent signal, and thus was faced with the dilemma of buttressing his outstretched right flank and at the same time concentrating all his armies for the advance on Berlin. Meanwhile the General Staff was trying to resolve an impossible military conundrum, in which Stalin had designated Marshal Zhukov alone as 'the victor of Berlin', yet Marshal Koniev was to participate in the operation. The General Staff simply closed its eyes to this problem for the moment and took solace in the fact that Berlin was still some way off.

Confusion and contradiction now began to creep into Soviet orders at all levels. Zhukov had already pointed out the danger on his right flank but received no hint of any response from the *Stavka* and, more important, no indication that reinforcement would be forthcoming. He was trying to pull all his armies into one main striking force directed against Berlin, yet he had to make provision to defend his right flank, 'a huge and almost unprotected gap' opening wider with each day between 1st Belorussian and 2nd Belorussian Front; it proved impossible, for example, to regroup 47th Army with the main striking force. On 1 February, 8th Guards and 5th Shock Armies had reached and crossed the Oder, taking small bridgeheads near the fortress of Küstrin; 69th Army had also reached the Oder, but German troops still held a bridgehead of their own near Frankfurt. For his immediate purposes Zhukov could count on four rifle armies and two tank armies drawn up along 'the Berlin axis', but two of the rifle armies—8th Guards and 69th—had detached part of their forces to deal with the fortress of Poznan, while Berzarin's 5th Shock was besieging Küstrin with elements of that army. On the embattled right flank the 1st Polish, 3rd Shock and 61st Armies were forced to leave more divisions to reduce the 'fortress' of Schneidermühl and other strong-points.

Losses and shortages further denuded Zhukov's assault forces. Chuikov could only commit fifty per cent of 8th Guards for the proposed attack on Berlin (the other half of his army was presently held back at Poznan); battle losses had made heavy inroads into Chuikov's strength, with regiments down to two battalions and the companies reduced to an average strength of 22–45 men. Ammunition was becoming alarmingly scarce and Chuikov had fallen back on using captured German guns with captured ammunition. Berzarin's 5th Shock Army and the 33rd and 69th Armies also reported growing shortages of ammunition and depleted ranks. Katukov's 1st Guards Tank Army mustered 737 tanks and SP guns at the time of breaking through to the Oder, of which 567 were in working order with 750–1,000 miles on the clock and 180–200 engine-hours piled up. All Soviet formations were calling for increased air support, but poor weather and the difficulties in moving up Soviet squadrons kept the Soviet air force out of the battle; heavy snow and rain turned grass airfields into quagmires, making take-off and landing impossible. A great clamour went up from all sides for AA guns in order to provide some kind of air defence.

Faced with growing German resistance on the Oder, with the appearance of German reinforcements along 'the Berlin axis' and with growing German strength in East Pomerania—directed against the right flank of 1st Belorussian Front and the left of 2nd Belorussian—Marshal Zhukov, caught up in the ambiguity and imprecision of the *Stavka's* stance, followed one set of orders by instructing his armies to dig in and honoured the other by issuing a provisional attack order for the Berlin operation. Zhukov specifically ordered 5th Shock Army to hold on, at the same time issuing a general brief—*orientirovka*—covering the proposed attack on Berlin to the military soviets of all armies, to all arms commanders and to the chief of Front logistics. Divided into two main sections, this operational document described German dispositions and detailed Soviet tasks:

1. Enemy forces facing 1st Belorussian Front do not dispose of sufficient forces for a counter-attack and cannot maintain a continuous defence line.

   The enemy has moved four Panzer divisions and five-six infantry divisions from the Western Theatre to the east, continuing at the same time to transfer troops from the Baltic and East Prussia.

   During the next six-seven days enemy forces on the move will be deployed along the Schwedt–Stargard–Neustettin line in order to cover Pomerania and to deny Soviet forces Stettin and access to the Bay of Pomerania.

   Enemy troops transferred from the west will be deployed in the Berlin area to cover the approaches to the city.

2. The Front assignment for the *next six days* is to consolidate gains, move supplies from the rear, concentrate two 'fills' of fuel and two of ammunition and in a high-speed assault—*stremitel'nym broskom*—*capture Berlin by February 15–16.*

   The consolidation of gains between February 4–8 will require

   (a) 5th, 8th, 69th and 33rd Army to sieze the bridgeheads on the western bank of the Oder, with 8th Guards and 69th having a common bridgehead between Küstrin and Frankfurt and also, if possible, combining the bridgeheads of the 5th and 8th Army;

   (b) Polish 1st Army, 47th and 61st Army, 2nd Tank Army and 2nd Cavalry Corps to push the enemy back beyond the Ratzeburg–Falkenburg–Stargard–Altdamm–river Oder line, leaving a covering force in position until 2nd Belorussian Front troops move up and regroup along the Oder line for a breakthrough;

   (c) the complete elimination of the enemy forces at Poznan–Schneidemühl by February 7–8;

   (d) recognition of the fact that breakthrough reinforcement will be precisely what the armies possess as of now;

   (e) return to service of tanks and SP guns presently undergoing running repairs or medium refit by February 10;

   (f) the completion of air force re-deployment, with at least six 'fills' of aviation fuel at forward airfields;

(g) a state of full readiness for Front, army and unit rear services [logistics] by February 9–10, for the decisive stage of the operation.
[Zhukov, *Vosp* . . . (2), 304–5.]

As both Marshals Zhukov and Koniev struggled to build up their main striking forces (with divisional strengths dwindling now to an average of 4,000 men), even as their armies grappled on the Oder, the *Stavka* mulled over the implications of German reinforcement, order of battle and the problem of the two flanks— Zhukov's right and Koniev's right, though the latter stirred less apprehension. Was that gap in the north between Zhukov and Rokossovskii really 'huge', or was it simply 'a visual impression' induced by poring over maps in the distant calm of Moscow? Was the right flank of 1st Belorussian Front so desperately and dangerously open? Soviet intelligence had estimated at the outset that only eleven German divisions 'and a few detachments' opposed the Red Army along 'the Berlin axis', but growing German resistance fostered serious doubt and air reconnaissance was now reporting a German build-up in East Pomerania. The *Luftwaffe's* local air superiority also impinged quite dramatically upon General Staff calculations. In essence, their appreciation pointed to the growing Soviet disadvantage in the 'balance of forces', the lack of adequate air support, the growing shortage of artillery munitions and the danger to the flanks emanating from East Pomerania and Silesia. The first priority was to fend off the threat of 'converging attacks' from East Pomerania and Silesia; removing the threat from the flanks was manifestly beyond the resources of 1st Belorussian Front alone and necessitated a new design involving three fronts—1st Belorussian, 2nd Belorussian and 1st Ukrainian. Whatever the inclination of Front and army commanders, the centre—which, in the person of Stalin, was all-powerful—took a simple but forthright motto for itself: no risks.

Marshal Zhukov had yet to learn officially that he was not to drive immediately and directly for Berlin, but Stalin knew this even as he joked over a wager with President Roosevelt at the Yalta conference that an immediate attack on Berlin was off, for the moment. In the absence of disclaimers or formal orders of any kind, however, Stalin could still hedge his bets.

Shortly before midnight on Friday, 2 February 1945, the first of twenty Skymaster and five York transport planes lifted off from Luqa in Malta and headed away on the 1,400-mile flight to Saki airfield on the Crimea, there to disgorge some 700 assorted officers and officials of the party destined for the 'Crimea Conference' and its actual venue at Yalta. In the deeper, darker hours after midnight the two planes carrying President Roosevelt and the Prime Minister duly took off, retracing the route earlier reconnoitred by Lt.-Col. Myers whose aircraft on this test run had come under fire of a sort from anti-aircraft guns, either German or Turkish. Blacked out and observing strict radio silence, the President's transport bored its way towards Soviet territory, icing up steadily and dragging this same dangerous load as the six P-38 fighters flying escort over Greece. The Prime Minister slept on in his own C-54, flying a little behind the President's aircraft.

Behind both men lay the previous day spent in talk of the forthcoming conference, though the brevity of these exchanges troubled Churchill, whose constant plea had been for more extensive preparation and consultation. The Prime Minister confided his misgivings in a signal to the President on 5 January, filled with the foreboding that 'this may well be a fateful Conference, coming at a time when the Great Allies are so divided and the shadow of the war lengthens out before us'. Nor were the combined chiefs of staff presently assembled in Malta and engaged in a review of Anglo-American strategy in any more optimistic or amiable mood. The discussions over General Eisenhower's 'Appreciation' brought on a blustery session, with a deal of British huffing and puffing over the ambiguity of the Supreme Commander's operational outline, which promised a main thrust in the north across the Rhine yet seemed to support substantial offensive action to the south; the 'Appreciation,' in a dismissive British judgement, 'points to no decisive action'. The ensuing debate, pursued in closed session, brought General Marshall out fighting, insisting on the validity of Eisenhower's plan and simultaneously denouncing Montgomery in no uncertain terms.

The arrival of the President in Malta aboard the US cruiser *Quincy* brought an affectionate reunion on 2 February with the Prime Minister. The President perforce listened to General Marshall and Fleet Admiral King recount their collisions with the British and British opposition to a Rhine crossing by General Bradley, but both senior officers cut their tale short at the sight of a much tired and worn President. At an evening meeting with the combined chiefs and in the presence of the Prime Minister, the wrangle over Anglo-American strategy was swiftly resolved. In the event the Americans understood the need for concentration in the north, even if this did not mean denying General Bradley his supporting attack in the south, while once again the Americans approved the transfer of British and Canadian divisions from Italy to swell Montgomery's forces, with US troops remaining in place. On one question, however, General Marshall remained unyielding: he refused to countenance either giving Eisenhower a British 'deputy' for ground operations or handing over greater powers of command to Montgomery once the Rhine had been crossed.

Still on the *Quincy,* the President and the Prime Minister sat down to dinner and to a review of yet another series of talks, those conducted between Edward Stettinius Jr, replacement as Secretary of State for Cordell Hull, and Anthony Eden. This working dinner left Eden in a despondent frame of mind, fearing that too little had been done to prepare negotiation with 'a Bear who would certainly know his own mind'. In their earlier talks, this time on the British cruiser *Sirius,* Eden came to understand the depth of American resistance to recognizing the 'Lublin government' in Poland and promptly urged his American counterpart to take up this particular cause, since 'a change of bowling' might work the desired effect on Stalin. Eden worried that the Americans were too eagerly bent on bringing about a world security organization, the United Nations, possibly at the expense of attending to the Polish question—and it could not be gainsaid that if the Russians would not treat Poland with 'some decency', then little value could attach to any 'United Nations' organization. Perturbed and bemused, gloomily disposed, Eden turned to Harry Hopkins, the real power behind the Presidential seat, with a plea to inject some sense of urgency and cogency of business into these last-minute discussions—but to little or no avail.

The swirl of transports and escorting fighters, after making a right-angle turn for identification, touched down at Saki a little after midday on 3 February. With the immediate reception ceremonies over, the President and the Prime Minister went their separate ways in motor cavalcades along the seventy-mile route to Yalta, passing through the battle damage strewn about in the wake of the German retreat from the Crimea only a short ten months ago. Stalin, who had stipulated from the outset his total aversion to air travel to any destination, trundled down by train and arrived on Sunday, 4 February. At 4 pm he called on the Prime Minister, starting up an 'agreeable discussion' about the progress of the war. The talk was agreeable because it was largely desultory. Stalin exuded optimism, stressing the damage inflicted on Germany—blood drawn by the Red Army as a consequence of total Soviet commitment of its manpower and the will to win. Interested, Churchill asked Stalin what might happen if Hitler moved south, to entrench himself there in some last-ditch redoubt: 'We shall follow him!' Stalin answered without hesitation. The Oder no longer posed any barrier for the Red Army: Soviet troops had swept past German units pulled back from the Vistula to hold this river line and were now astride the Oder at several points. The German Army disposed now of a strategic reserve reduced to a mere twenty or thirty divisions, the bulk ill prepared, though some good divisions were still available in Scandinavia, Italy and the west. Stalin ridiculed the Rundstedt offensive, a vain venture mounted only for prestige: the German Army had harmed itself irrevocably, the most able commanders had been swept away leaving only Guderian, who was at best 'an adventurer'. The divisions isolated in East Prussia could have been used to defend Berlin but these, too, had been squandered; eleven *Panzer* divisions still clung to Budapest but were simply hostages to fortune; Germany's role as a world power was done. While looking at the Prime Minister's map room Stalin suddenly brought to life a suggestion made by Churchill himself at an earlier stage in the war, that British divisions should be transferred from Italy to Yugoslavia and Hungary and then aimed at Vienna, thus linking up with the Red Army and outflanking the Germans south of the Alps. At some cost Churchill bit back his words, contenting himself with observing that 'the Red Army may not give us time to complete this operation'. It must have tasted bitter to Churchill that the Red Army was indeed on the verge of consummating his own cherished strategic design; all that was left to him was what he had emphasized in the flurry of the Malta talks with the President, that as much of

Austria as possible should be occupied and no more than was strictly necessary of western Europe should be invested by Soviet troops. If Stalin's comment was mere gratuitous insult, the Prime Minister let it pass.

Calling next on the President at the Livadia Palace (the location of the full plenary sessions of the conference), Stalin assumed quite a different pose and came not so much as a self-confident conqueror but almost as a hard-pressed supplicant. The Red Army was certainly on the Oder, but meeting with stiff German resistance; the Americans must surely be in Manila before the Russians were in Berlin and Stalin dismissed any bets on the outcome with a laugh. At the President's expressions of shock and dismay at the destruction he had just seen in the Crimea, Stalin remarked that this was nothing compared to the planned ruination worked in the Ukraine. Turning to the western front Stalin learned with obvious pleasure that a limited offensive would begin on 8 February, followed by a second on the 12th and a full-scale attack in approximately one month, even if the President hedged all this about with talk of ice on the Rhine and hinted at Anglo-American divergence over the location of the major assault crossing. The advance of the Allies into Germany nevertheless gave the President the opportunity to propose to Stalin direct communication between General Eisenhower and the Soviet military command, a proposal cordially received by Stalin. In a free and easy exchange over matters more specifically political, the President gave Stalin to understand that the British and American positions were by no means one in relation to France and the question of the treatment of Germany. Stalin at once joined the President in mocking the pretensions of the French and in emphasizing French weakness—but the British were intent on recreating French power. Once more the British were proving troublesome over the question of a possible occupation zone in Germany prescribed for France; to Stalin's direct question about the President's own attitude to this, Roosevelt returned an evasive answer, intimating that any gesture in this direction would merely be one of charity. Stalin and Molotov for their part signalled the same identity of feeling.

At this juncture, shortly before 5 pm, the 'Crimea Conference' was about to assemble for its first plenary session, devoted to a review of the military situation, following the agenda tabled on Stalin's behalf the day before. At the outset Marshal Stalin proposed that President Roosevelt should once more preside over the proceedings, to which request Roosevelt gracefully acceded. Conforming to an agreed order of business, the President called at once on General Antonov to make his report on the military situation and to present the Soviet assessment. Antonov carefully recounted the course of Soviet operations since 12 January, when—under favourable weather conditions—the Red Army had gone over to the offensive across a mighty battle front ranging from the Niemen in the north to the Carpathians in the south, all in response to the plea of the Western allies for aid in a difficult situation. The Soviet operational plan, based on a recognition of German strength on the central sector, called for the diversion of these forces to the flanks, hence Soviet offensive operations in East Prussia and Hungary, both of which had had the desired effect in drawing off German armour—with as many as twenty out of twenty-four *Panzer* divisions being so diverted; even now eleven *Panzer* divisions were marooned in the area of Budapest. On the vital central sector the Red Army had established superiority in infantry and crushing strength in armour, artillery and aircraft. In a matter of eighteen days the Red Army had advanced some 500 kilometres, averaging thirty kilometres per day, investing the Silesian industrial region, reaching the eastern bank of the Oder and slicing East Prussia off from the *Reich,* and inflicting drastic losses upon the German Army, to the tune of 400,000 men and the destruction of no less than forty-five divisions.

General Antonov asserted with some vigour that the Germans would stiffen and strengthen the defences of Berlin with all the resources at their command, drawing on the strength of other fronts to accomplish this objective and transferring divisions from western Europe and Italy. Vienna also would be heavily defended, with possible reinforcement from Italy. The Red Army had already identified sixteen divisions (nine from Germany, six from western Europe and one from Italy) on the Eastern Front; a further five (four *Panzer* and one motorized) were already being transferred and no less than 30–35 divisions were available from the Western Front, Norway, Italy and the interior of Germany—making an impressive total of 35–40 divisions upon which the Soviet command must reckon as German reinforcement in the east. In view of these figures General Antonov urged action to inhibit the movement of German divisions, especially from Italy; in addition, Allied co-operation could take the form of mounting air attacks against both Berlin and Leipzig in order to stifle this military traffic. At the conclusion of Antonov's report Stalin sought the reaction of the President and the Prime Minister: brushing aside some remark by the President about changing the gauge of German railways—a total irrelevance, in Stalin's view—the talk turned on how to prevent the movement of up to eight German divisions from Italy, with the Prime Minister also bringing up the question of British forces attacking through the 'Ljubljana gap' and thus linking up with the Red Army's left flank. Though he himself had mentioned it earlier in private, this time Stalin did not deign to comment. The Prime Minister and the President had to be satisfied with Stalin's assertion that he was in favour of military co-ordination and closer liaison, and would support such moves.

General Marshall then reported on the Western front, pointing to the defeat of the German offensive in the Ardennes and emphasizing present preparations for an Allied attack in the north with a second envisaged for the southern reaches, scheduled for 8 February. The crossing of the Rhine would take place in March, an operational pace which was admittedly slow but one governed by the flow of supplies—and here German V-2 weapons posed a threat, not least to the port facilities at Antwerp. Stalin brushed all this aside with a remark about the notorious inaccuracy of bombs and rockets alike. General Marshall would not allow this to pass without commenting on the destruction wrought by the Allied air forces, whether in hammering German rail communications or by reducing German oil production by as much as eighty per cent. Air superiority was also a major factor in Italy, where Allied and German ground forces were more or less equal (thirty-two divisions each). Nor could the submarine threat be discounted now that the German navy was bringing improved U-boats into service and the Allied navies must cope with the difficulties of detection in shallow waters swept by varying tides.

In the ensuing debate, sharp questions and tart comments steadily dissipated the prevailing cordiality. The Prime Minister obtained a promise of help from Stalin in dealing with Danzig—lying in the path of the Soviet advance—and other centres of submarine production, but a request for details of Soviet river-crossing assault operations elicited no immediate response. Stalin took up the cudgels on his own behalf, probing deeply into Western plans and performance. The burden of this exchange was to stress the Red Army's contribution and Stalin's own military foresight. Pressed by Stalin, General Marshall set the length of the Allied breakthrough front at some 50–60 miles—the Red Army front had stretched more than ten times this distance—and though the Allies expected to breach prepared fortifications, they possessed the necessary reserves to carry through the operation. Stalin was gratified to hear that, for one of his own cardinal principles was the importance of reserves. And what about tank strength? The Red Army had employed as many as 9,000 tanks on the main breakthrough operation in the centre. General Marshall could only estimate that about 10–12 armoured divisions would be committed for every thirty-five divisions, a figure which Stalin found wanting in detail and accurate measure. The Prime Minister intervened in the tussle about tank figures to assert that in western Europe the Allies disposed of 10,000 tanks. A large number, Stalin observed.

Continuing his steady probing of the Allied position, Stalin turned to air strength and was given these figures as a comparison with 8,000–9,000 deployed with the Soviet air force. The wrangle over superiority in manpower grew out of misunderstanding and mistranslation, with the Prime Minister denying any Anglo-American superiority save that in the air, while General Marshall pointed out the balance of seventy-nine German divisions facing seventy-eight from among the Allies. At this point, conscious of rising tension, Stalin contented himself with remarking on Soviet artillery superiority and by way of mollification treated his listeners to a short discourse on the Soviet artillery offensive and the use of 'artillery breakthrough divisions' with their very large density of guns per kilometre. This overture to exchanging operational experience led Stalin to stress the manner in which the Soviet Union had fulfilled its obligations to its allies and now stood ready to discharge yet more—let the Allies but indicate their requirements. The Prime Minister at once proffered thanks for Soviet aid and congratulation on Soviet achievement, only to have Stalin turn on him in a spasm of annoyance at this obtuseness—the Red Army did not take the field either to earn mere thanks or to carry out a formal commitment underwritten at Teheran but to discharge its *moral* duty as from one ally to others.

President Roosevelt took the sting out of this exchange by expressing his agreement with Stalin that Teheran had not meant formal commitment, embodying rather common agreement to strike at the common enemy. Quickly turning the point, the President went on to raise the question of co-operation and co-ordination among the Allies, receiving support at this juncture from Churchill, who speedily repaired the breach with Stalin by repudiating any notion of a bargain with the Soviet Union. With the three staffs presently in attendance, the Prime Minister thought it timely to embark on a review of 'the whole question of military co-ordination between the Allies'. Such collaboration, already underlined by the President, could mean the pursuit of operations on one front even if the other were hindered or halted. Stalin protested: this was neither collaboration nor co-ordination; it was in fact the opposite, with no better illustration than the Soviet offensive in the autumn of 1944 coming to a close just at a time when the Allies unleashed their own in the west.

Towards the close of this meeting, with harmony and good humour restored, Stalin took note of some specific requests made by his allies, particularly the capture of Danzig and the reduction of the U-boat threat. President Roosevelt enquired of Stalin whether Danzig could be within Soviet reach, to which Stalin replied that 'hopefully' it might well be. The company found that remark a huge and enjoyable joke. Stalin could congratulate himself on that deft touch, as he could derive considerable satisfaction from what he had learned of Anglo-American plans and their possible implementation, particularly in terms of 'co-ordination' which would synchronize Anglo-American operations in the west with Soviet operations directed at Berlin in the east. Co-ordination was to be taken up in greater detail at the meeting of the chiefs of staff scheduled for the morning of the 5th; for the moment, however, Stalin had learned sufficient for his immediate purposes.

The dinner which followed at the Livadia palace, with the President as host, carried this bonhomie through into the evening, though the proceedings were not without their awkward moments. One such was the exchange between Bohlen and Vyshinskii, who refused to countenance any argument which would accord to small nations the right to judge the actions of the great powers, a point of view not unnaturally contested by Bohlen who stressed the American popular support for the rights of small nations. Vyshinskii replied that the American people should 'learn to obey their leaders', a remark as acidulous as it was inept. Otherwise, the humour was heavy indeed, and at one juncture even unfortunate: encouraged by the apparently relaxed atmosphere, the President told Stalin to his face that he was commonly known as 'Uncle Joe', at which Stalin, stung by the very commonness of the sobriquet, at once made to leave the dinner. The Prime Minister drew Stalin back to the circle of the dinner with a toast which emphasized the importance of the present conference and the commanding role of the three major allies in waging the war and sustaining the peace to come. Stalin responded in prim but powerful style, making absolute assertion of the rights of the 'Big Three' against all the bleating of the small powers that their rights were at risk; he, Stalin, served the interests of the Soviet Union and its people, this he could neither disguise nor conceal, though this did not preclude participation in a concert of the 'Big Three' to protect the rights of the smaller— but without that right to sit in judgement on the great.

Having slithered to the point of acute embarrassment, if not actual disaster, the dinner party steered its way through a series of stern and unambiguous statements by Stalin: the small must be ruled by the great, the delinquents brought to book—one such delinquent being Argentina, but since this miscreant was within the American orbit, Stalin would forbear. The President reminded Stalin that Poland was just such a small power in the Soviet area yet he was a President who had to take account of the opinion of Poles living in the United States; Stalin dismissed this argument with a quick statistical flick, pointing out that of seven million American Poles only 7,000 actually voted. The President could demonstrably rest easy.

None could complain that Stalin had not made himself plain, even brutally plain. His was no mere table talk, but intended for real effect. He was clearly not inclined to compromise on Poland and had presented a clear picture of the role of the great powers in any future world security organization; the prestige, power and authority of the Soviet Union were at stake and Stalin forcefully impressed upon his listeners his iron determination to sustain and nurture these above all else. The company dispersed in a mood of general well-being bordering almost on euphoria, with Stalin himself making a late departure in spite of his earlier fit of huffiness. Eden, however, did not share the prevailing mood; for him the dinner party had been little short of a disaster—'a terrible party, I thought'—marred by the President's vagueness and the Prime Minister's long-windedness, though neither was as devastating as the brutally stark opinions expressed by Stalin who did not mince words about the subordination of the small nations to the will and the requirements of the great.

On the morning of 5 February the Anglo-American Combined Chiefs of Staff met with the Soviet General Staff to discuss military planning and military co-ordination, a session held at General Antonov's HQ on the road to Yalta. Field-Marshal Sir Alan Brooke in the chair opened the discussions by raising the issue of co-ordination and made a general appeal for Soviet help while Anglo-American forces forced the Rhine, operations which would continue throughout March and April—would the Russians be able to maintain their own operations in spite of the thaw and their extended lines of communication? General Marshall took up this theme, stressing the peculiar conditions under which the Allied armies operated, in particular their lack of overall superiority and the problems presented by their lines of communications; air power was the winning Allied card, but Soviet help was critical in keeping the Germans off balance at those times when poor weather grounded Allied planes, thus nullifying the sole Allied superiority.

General Antonov made a reasoned response. Obviously the Soviet command wished to know how the Germans would be prevented from transferring divisions from the west to the eastern front: German divisions had moved westwards at the time of the Allied landings in 1944 and the Soviet command wanted them held there. For its part the Red Army would continue its own operations in the east as long as 'circumstances permitted', operational pauses would be kept to a minimum and the Soviet advance would continue to the very limit of Soviet resources. The immediate Soviet concern centred on the Italian front and Antonov again put the case for Allied forces operating through the 'Ljubljana gap' in the direction of Vienna: Brooke had already tagged this subject 'a bore' and referred General Antonov to the difficulties—brought on by the weather—of Allied operations in Italy and the present plan to withdraw divisions from Italy to reinforce the Anglo-American offensive on the Western Front. Inevitably, what the Allies could do in the way of moving troops was also open to the German command under Kesselring and there was nothing anyone could do about that.

Probing deeper, Antonov enquired just what all this would mean in actual numbers of divisions; he received the rather disconcerting answer that up to ten German divisions could be involved in such transfers. The senior British and American officers joined a chorus of praise to Allied air power, pointing to the havoc it had wreaked on German oil supply and the possibilities it presented for hampering German troop transfers, from Italy in particular. Aviation Marshal Khudyakov, not to be outdone, heaped fulsome praise on the Soviet air force for its role in Soviet operations, but pressed Field-Marshal Alexander for an assurance that this much-vaunted Allied air superiority would be directed against German troop movement. Alexander duly gave this undertaking, evoking a certain satisfaction on the Soviet side though not enough to offset Antonov's obvious despondency over the futility of trying to interest the Anglo-American command in a drive through the 'Ljubljana gap' and thus supporting the Soviet offensive aimed at Vienna. Brooke hammered the final nail into that military coffin: in view of the absence of Allied superiority in ground troops, every effort must be made to concentrate maximum forces on the Western Front to deliver the *coup de grâce* against Germany, and such was the paucity of Allied strength that it would not even be possible to exploit any German withdrawal from Italy, assuming that this took place. Headed off in this fashion, Antonov turned to the possibility of Allied action to prevent German troop movements from Norway, only to be told once again that lack of force precluded any Allied action on the ground, in Norway itself, while Allied operations against German movement by sea would at once encounter those difficulties presented by extensive mining. Inevitably, Antonov let the whole matter drop.

The issue of co-ordination and co-operation brought a sudden intervention from Admiral Leahy, to the effect that General Eisenhower should have his own mission in Moscow, this being his own 'very frank' opinion—which came as quite a surprise to the British. Brooke intervened deftly, insisting that the British and Americans shared the same view about the need for effective liaison, but the whole thing must be soundly based in a proper commission whose function would be to settle all questions of 'higher strategy' with the British and American Chiefs of Staff. At a lower level there should be liaison between theatre and army group commanders. Antonov made no objection to the principle of closer liaison but insisted that it would have to be handled through the several military missions in Moscow and with the Soviet General Staff; General Marshall protested vigorously at such an amputation of liaison, insisting on the need for tactical as well as strategic co-ordination. Antonov dismissed this out of hand, arguing in turn that confusion and collision in air operations had been brought on by blunders in navigation rather than deficiencies in co-ordination. In any event, since Soviet air force operations were directed centrally from Moscow, that was where co-ordination should be effected. The Chief of the Air Staff (Royal Air Force) Sir Charles Portal agreed that strategic air missions could be handled at the highest level, but this did not dispose of tactical co-ordination for air operations in Italy and the Balkans. Khudyakov came straight to the point and told the Allied officers that any question of immediate tactical liaison would have to be approved by Stalin himself.

In an attempt to repair the situation, Antonov proposed an 'arbitrary line' running through Berlin, Leipzig, Vienna and Zagreb as an operational limit for Allied strategic bombing operations. This, Brooke observed, 'did not suit us' and the fixing of a bombing line was held over to the next meeting. At this juncture and towards the close of the conference Admiral Leahy abruptly demanded a planning date for the end of the war from Antonov. Nonplussed, Antonov scouted any idea of firm predictions and would not commit himself to mere supposition, in spite of pressure from Admiral Leahy and General Marshall, who stressed that planning for shipping must be set afoot. Allied assumptions reckoned on the beginning of July or the end of December as likely terminal dates. Antonov did not disagree, mentioning in turn summer as the likeliest early date and winter as the latest. (Stalin himself had earlier mentioned that the war 'might well go on till the summer' and Antonov was in no position to contradict or to amplify.)

Whatever his private thoughts about the duration of these final operations and the ending of the war, Antonov could scarcely draw much encouragement from this meeting. The Allies could give no firm assurance that German troop movement would be effectively hampered, much less inhibited. The Soviet General Staff must now calculate that appreciable German reinforcement could and would reach the Eastern Front—a preliminary impression which received doleful and definite confirmation the next day, 6 February, at a subsequent meeting of the Chiefs of Staff, when Antonov patiently winkled out the unpalatable truth that much of the German armour used in the abortive Ardennes offensive was presently speeding eastwards to meet the Red Army. Nor would help be forthcoming for the Soviet drive on the southern flank, presently locked in fierce fighting in

Hungary but aimed eventually at Vienna. German troops held in Norway would also inevitably join the main battle for the *Reich*. Any idea of a 'non-stop' offensive on Berlin, if not actually dead, was dying on its feet. The Soviet General Staff was reckoning on full-strength German divisions, while Soviet divisions had fallen as low as 4,000 men, a weakness compounded by the shortage of fuel and ammunition; local air superiority enjoyed by the *Luftwaffe* also made life hard for the Red Army. The conclusion to which the Soviet General Staff was increasingly drawn envisaged large enemy forces available for the defence of Berlin, with the prospect of these forces being appreciably reinforced. In this context Antonov could have little by way of encouragement to report to Stalin.

If the immediate military future seemed murky, this did not deter the three Allied leaders from embarking in the late afternoon of 5 February on a discussion of 'the German question' and the fate of a defeated Germany; rather, they were impelled in this direction, by Molotov insisting to Eden that the division of Germany must be discussed, and by Stalin, who steered the meeting unerringly towards the issue of dismemberment. President Roosevelt opened the plenary session by suggesting a discussion of the occupation zones delineated by the European Advisory Commission (EAC), the proposal from the British side to allocate France its own zone and the question of French participation in the Allied control machinery. Stalin overrode this at once, virtually recasting the agenda. He wanted dismemberment discussed in full, both as a matter of principle and what it would mean in practice, the form of government—or administration—to be fastened upon Germany and what the actual terms of surrender would involve, bearing in mind that 'unconditional surrender' had not meant the absence of special conditions, at least in the case of Italy. What would happen in the case of Germany? Would unconditional surrender go hand in hand with the continued existence of 'the Hitler government'? There was no option but to prescribe the terms of surrender in wholly unequivocal fashion. Finally, the issue of reparations must be decided.

Stalin argued relentlessly and in brilliant command of his facts. The President's device of substituting talk of occupation zones was abruptly swept aside: dismemberment could not be called by any other name save that of dismemberment. At the Teheran Conference dismemberment had been agreed in principle, albeit not put to any strict legal tests and binding agreements; in Moscow in October 1944 the British Prime Minister had proposed the division of Germany into two states (Prussia and Bavaria), with the Ruhr and Westphalia internationalized. Stalin now required decisions. Here the Prime Minister swung into the attack: dismemberment was commonly agreed in principle, but so complex a matter could not be decided in days. Much remained to be considered in detail by some 'special committee', whose report would be needed before any decision could be reached. There would be no negotiation with the war criminals; in the most likely event of the death or disappearance of Hitler and Himmler, then others would treat for unconditional surrender and in this instance the Allies must consult on whether to treat with them or not. The terms of surrender would be laid before them.

Stalin seized on that latter point, the surrender terms. They were far too vague. He proceeded to argue that the surrender terms automatically subsumed dismemberment and suggested simply adding a specific clause to that effect, though without spelling out the geographical details. Stalin and Churchill fell into a kind of truce in agreeing that the right to impose dismemberment, rather than the actual details of the political severance, was the paramount issue. While the Prime Minister fell back on suggesting that the problem be left to a future peace conference, the President intervened to reinforce his view that dismemberment was, in fact, fundamental to the act and instrument of surrender; he also accepted the idea that a study of the problem must be undertaken. He referred to Stalin's own point about informing the Germans of their future at the hands of the Allies and then, at the prompting of Harry Hopkins, charged the Foreign Ministers with preparing a plan for dismemberment. Stalin stuck grimly to the fact of dismemberment and to its mandatory inclusion in the surrender terms with forthright visceral import and, with Roosevelt's help, won his point. Reluctantly, the Prime Minister signified his assent to adding 'dismemberment' all unvarnished into Article 12 of the surrender instrument.

The President then swung the meeting towards a consideration of a place in the sun for France by allocating her a zone of occupation in Germany. This time Churchill pressed the attack and Stalin fought a stubborn delaying action. The Prime Minister went straight for the main question—the allocation to France of a specific zone of occupation and a prescribed place within the Allied control machinery for occupied Germany. The British government held this dear; a French zone could be formed out of the apportionment to the United Kingdom and the United States, leaving the Soviet share unaffected. The Prime Minister refuted Stalin's objections that the introduction of France to 'Big Three' arrangements would open the door to other states: France and France alone was to be admitted. Moreover, Great Britain looked for a France restored to its traditional place as a counterweight to Germany, conceivably a resurgent Germany; an American military presence in Europe might not be a permanent feature of the post-war scene. President Roosevelt came speedily to the Prime Minister's aid but in so doing loosed off a thunderbolt all his own. American troops, as he foresaw the situation, would remain in Europe for little more than two years after the war. The Prime Minister started, and Stalin listened the more intently. Now Churchill urged his case afresh, reminding Stalin that France was to Great Britain what Poland and its role *vis-à-vis* Germany represented for the Soviet Union. Giving way on this point, Stalin nevertheless fought against any idea of giving France access to the inter-Allied control commission, which must be confined to those powers which had stood firm against Germany from the very beginning: 'so far' France did not belong by right to this group. That was a strange mixture of tactical dexterity and self-delusion about past events. Suddenly recalling and reviving the Franco-Soviet agreement, concluded only a matter of weeks ago, Stalin was content to call France ally and he found rather bizarre support for his opposition to French participation in the control commission from President Roosevelt. The President had to be reminded in another of Harry Hopkins' sage and pithy notes that France was presently a full member of the European Advisory Commission—'that is only body [sic] considering German affairs now'—and a decision about the control commission would be better postponed.

To end this plenary session Stalin called on Maiskii to present the Soviet position on reparations, a plan envisaging both the removal of industrial plant and equipment from Germany as well as ten annual payments, also to be made in kind. German heavy industry would be reduced to one-fifth of its present size, with all arms factories and synthetic oil plants to be dismantled within two years and a tripartite international control commission taking command of the entire German economy after ten years of such payments. Since payments would not of themselves cover wartime losses, the Soviet plan also called for monetary compensation to separate claimants based on their respective contributions to winning the war and on the losses incurred in war; the Soviet Union duly laid claim to 10,000 million dollars. The Prime Minister, while agreeing to the Soviet suggestion of a Reparations Commission, pointed to the fiasco of reparations after the First World War and voiced immediate doubt that Germany could furnish even the sum of money the Soviet Union demanded for itself. Great Britain faced a debt of £3,000 million for its wartime exertions, yet present and future British burdens would scarcely be relieved by German reparations. Other countries had suffered and their accounts must be rendered, but who would profit from a Germany reduced to starvation? Should the Germans be left to starve?

Stalin interposed calmly enough that there would indeed be food for Germans; as for British problems, they would follow their course wholly unaffected by any Soviet plan for reparations. Finally the Prime Minister came round to the idea of a Reparations Committee whose work would be secret, and he supported President Roosevelt when he in turn accepted the proposal for a Reparations Commission located in Moscow and charged with looking at the claims of a number of countries. Maiskii returned to his charge once more, pointing out that the Soviet reparations plan had nothing in common with the post-1918 schemes—reparations *in kind* ruled out the financial jiggery-pokery which had ruined that earlier design. Germany could assuredly pay the indemnity demanded by the Soviet Union and would not starve into the bargain. If the Germans ceased their colossal expenditure on weapons, the money would be to hand: *quod erat demonstrandum*. For the moment, however, Maiskii was content to leave matters in the hands of the proposed Commission.

Stalin seized on the points developed by Maiskii. All parties seemed to be agreed upon the establishment of a Commission, but it must have specific instructions: a principle which recommended itself to him was that those nations who had borne the greatest heat and heaviest burden of the battle should be the prime claimants to compensation, signifying the Soviet Union, the United States and Great Britain. The Soviet Union should not be the sole recipient of reparations—let each nation decide upon the particular form of exaction they wished to implement. France again loomed disproportionately large in Stalin's mind: the French contributed a mere eight divisions to the common war effort while the Yugoslavs fielded twelve but Stalin sought nothing in the name of the Yugoslavs. The conference must agree, and to this end the matter should be handed over to the foreign ministers rather than to some Reparations Commission. Churchill waved this away as a mere gesture and indicated that his own hold on elective office was questionable, only to be told peremptorily that victors would not be so easily vanquished. In a final rally the Prime Minister both referred to and deferred to a Soviet prescription, arguing that exertion in war should mean less than 'from each according to his abilities and to each according to his needs'. Stalin revised Marxist–Leninist principles on the spot and refurbished this to read 'to each according to his deserts'. The reparations question was, therefore, assigned to the Foreign Ministers for their deliberations.

From the outset a strange but intrusive dialectic involving the President's commitment to a World Organization and Stalin's preoccupation with Poland flickered like St Elmo's fire over the proceedings at Yalta.

The conference at Dumbarton Oaks, convened on 21 August 1944, had settled the main outlines of what was to become the United Nations Organization, but two substantial issues remained to be solved—the voting formula to be adopted in the Security Council and the actual membership of the General Assembly. The principle of the right of veto ascribed to each Permanent Member of the Security Council, for all the complex and involved arguments which proliferated about it, had attained general acceptance: in fact, the Russians through Gromyko insisted on 13 September on nothing less than unanimity among the great powers—a 'final and unalterable' decision, one which was not appreciably altered by President Roosevelt's request to Stalin for some qualification. Stalin for his part insisted on the principle of unanimity based on his understanding of what had passed at Teheran. Moreover, American military opinion seemed to be swinging behind the Soviet stance and none other than Field-Marshal Smuts in his message of 20 September to the Prime Minister stressed that the chance should not be missed of treating the Russians as equals and worthy of trust: the principle of unanimity among the great powers could even act as a brake upon 'people drunk with new-won power'.

Gromyko was blunt enough. When advised that Soviet obduracy might seal the fate of the World Organization before it saw the light of day, he replied that such an organization could in no wise exist if a great power were to be denied the right to vote in any dispute, irrespective of its role in that dispute. The voting formula for the Security Council clearly involved major issues and major decisions for the Soviet Union: behind the legalism and the obduracy lay current preoccupations with new-found status and past memories of isolation and even expulsion from the world community, combined with fears of some repetition in the future.

In addition to being isolated in the Council it also appeared that the Soviet Union might be outnumbered in the General Assembly, with the Soviet Union assuming that only twenty-six signatories of the United Nations Declaration would be members, while the United States proposed the addition of six Latin American republics together with Iceland and Egypt; behind Great Britain were ranged six additional votes derived from the Dominions. The abrupt Soviet counter was to suggest all sixteen constituent republics of the USSR as members; though abruptly presented on 19 August and brusquely rejected by the President and Cordell Hull, the question lingered on and formed the basis of the President's observation in January 1945 that he hoped to 'trade' the problem of voting against this Soviet claim for separate representation for the several Soviet republics.

On 6 February at Yalta President Roosevelt turned to the matter closest to his heart and nearest to his aspirations for the post-war world, the World Organization, transmuted now into the United Nations. His warning over the problem of the voting formula for the Security Council was nonetheless plain: failure to agree upon the American plan could prejudice American assistance in holding down a beaten Germany. However, the President had not come unprepared and unarmed. Stettinius proceeded to unfold a revised American plan, referring to a 'minor clarification' of Chapter VIII, Section C of the proposed United Nations Charter. Instantly alert, Stalin queried this 'minor clarification'; amidst a considerable flurry, Gromyko managed to convince both Stalin and Molotov that nothing of substance was as yet involved, whereupon Stettinius proceeded with his elaboration of the voting formula, stressing now that nations other than the great powers might present their views to the Security Council, all as protection for the smaller countries. For a settlement by peaceful methods, seven votes would be needed plus the unanimous 'agreement of the permanent members of the Security Council; in the event of a dispute involving any member of the Security Council (including any permanent member), that same member might discuss the problem but not vote upon it.

Stalin declared himself puzzled by this new proposal. He defended the principle of absolute unanimity doggedly and with flashes of passion, pointing to the danger of a situation ten years hence when a new generation, unmindful of what war meant, might fall to blows and precipitate 'conflict among ourselves'; with unanimity prevailing among the great powers, the German menace could be discounted. The Prime Minister's intervention served to support the President's plan and, as if to counter Stalin's obvious reservations, he emphasized that the rights of the three great powers remained intact—as indeed the guarantee afforded to the Dominions secured British rights at large. No one would wish to appear to be bent on ruling the world, yet to deny the smaller nations the elementary right of expression of their opinion might raise precisely those suspicions.

Wrapped up in his own suspicions, Stalin began to unwind these arguments for his own purposes. The new proposals would require study, though he asked for a copy of Stettinius' paper at once. Clearly, the argument was not about any right to express an opinion—rather the real issue lay with making and taking decisions; as for countries so far brought up in the discussion, with China and Egypt having been cited, neither of these would simply rest content with expressing an opinion. Wherefore this argument about dominating the world and which power specifically was aiming at this? Great Britain had in an impromptu gesture sided with the United States over the voting formula: this could only leave the Soviet Union as the candidate for seeker after dominance. The Prime Minister intervened to deny this outright and repeated that it was simply a matter of avoiding giving such an impression on the part of the great powers. Stalin returned at once to what he found to be the true substance, the crucial implication, of this rather spurious argument about some phantom world domination: the great powers had to keep the peace at large by keeping the peace between themselves. Though pressure of work had prevented him from being fully acquainted with the Dumbarton Oaks proposals, he understood all too well what was involved in the United Nations Charter and the need to solve problems in such a way as to preserve the unity of the Big Three.

With his points thus hammered home, Stalin became rather more expansive. Having begun to align himself with the President, he suggested quite suddenly that out of recognition of America's interests China should indeed be accorded some distinctive position of its own, a move which prompted the Prime Minister to add France to this list of favoured and favourite nations.

All this was but a prelude to further probing, however. Reverting to the revised formula, Stalin asked if he was right in assuming that there would be two categories of disputes, the first entailing sanctions (economic, political or military) and the second involving peaceful solutions. Thus far Stalin had understood everything correctly. That being the case, he went on to ask about procedures: in the event of sanctions being involved, all permanent members could vote even if one were a party to the actual dispute, whereas in the case of a peaceful settlement no party to the dispute—even if a permanent member—could vote? Once again, his view was confirmed. Assured now of his position, Stalin pointed out that if it appeared that the Russians seemed to talk too much about voting, this was because of overriding Soviet interest in voting which would decide everything. Suppose that China demanded the return of Hong Kong or Egypt claimed the Suez Canal? Neither country would be alone and would have 'friends and protectors' in the Council and Assembly. The Prime Minister countered this by insisting that the powers of the World Organization could not be used against Great Britain, which held the power of the veto. Eden reinforced the point by repeating that member nations might talk but could not decide of themselves; China and Egypt might complain, but the use of force must have the approval of the British government. Stettinius weighed in, to assert that even economic sanctions would require the unanimous support of the permanent members of the Security Council.

Both Molotov and Maiskii tried to clarify this strange boundary between types of decisions and the operation of unanimity. The technical gyrations failed to persuade Stalin. The prospects for great-power unity could be endangered and even isolation visited upon particular nations through the manipulation of world opinion. Seizing once again on Hong Kong, Stalin pointed out that any discussion of that question could in effect damage great-power unity. Churchill hastily added that in this event normal diplomacy was still available for use by all states, great or small, with the Big Three having a special responsibility to discuss among themselves issues which might otherwise fracture their unity. Stalin returned a blunt reply: he pointed to what had happened in the Russo–Finnish war of 1939, when the British and French mobilized the League of Nations against Soviet Russia, first isolating and then actually expelling the Russians. What guarantee was there that 'this kind of thing' will not happen again? Both the Prime Minister and Eden assured Stalin that the American proposal made such an eventuality wholly impossible. But why not even more barriers, Stalin asked? The Prime Minister explained patiently that the expulsion of the Soviet Union from the United Nations Organization—unlike the League—could not be managed under any circumstance, since expulsion would mean a unanimous vote and any great power could simply veto it. It was, Stalin grumbled, the first time he had heard of that. The President confirmed the accuracy of what the Prime Minister had just said: here was the heart of the veto. Churchill admitted the risk of 'agitation' being worked up against any one great power—the British, for example— but here orthodox diplomacy would come into play; the President would scarcely open or support an attack on Great Britain, while Marshal Stalin would not launch some verbal assault on us without some preliminary consultation and without recourse to a friendly solution. Stalin tersely signified his agreement and signalled his alignment with the President's sentiments about 'Big Three' unanimity combined with freedom of discussion, but he suggested that the discussion be carried over to the following day.

The business of the day, however, was far from done. Though there had just been a spate of talk about great-power unanimity, the next item on the agenda— Poland—embodied the most immediate threat to Allied unity. The fate of Poland, rather than Hong Kong or the Canal, rawed the nerves and jarred the amity of the three Allied leaders. Stalin needed to do nothing, save to sit, wait and watch while both the President and the Prime Minister impaled themselves on the spikes of their own discomfiture and impotence. President Roosevelt as chairman opened the discussion with a statement about his own objectivity, taking 'a more distant view of the problem', though identifying himself with the several million Poles in the United States who 'like the Chinese, want to save face'. He reiterated the position he had adopted in Teheran: 'In general, I am in favour of the Curzon

Line'. However, here was a place for a 'gesture' from Stalin, one which would leave Lvov and the eastern oilfields to the Poles, all to balance the loss of Königsberg. To settle the frontier issue on Soviet terms must mean that the Poles, the government in exile, must lose face. Stalin could only snort: true Poles for him were the Lublin Poles, who had already expressed themselves in favour of the Curzon Line. Shifting his ground, the President asked for the concession for his own electoral purposes, to give the Poles, all Poles, something with which to save face. Even so, he would not insist.

The question of the frontier line, however, did not compare in importance with the future government of Poland. The President recognized that any Polish government must be one 'thoroughly friendly to the Soviet Union' for the foreseeable future, but he stated quite bluntly that American public opinion would not countenance the recognition of the present Lublin government, rooted as it was in a small unrepresentative minority. He would suggest, in response to general demand, a 'government of national unity', which could well include representatives of the five main Polish parties; a small presidential council would appear to be a desirable innovation at this stage (a reflection of the proposal made by Stettinius to Eden at the Malta meeting on 1 February). As for Mikolajczyk, the President had met him during his visit to Washington and had found him an honest man. This was the limit of his acquaintance with either the London or Lublin governments.

At this the President opened the general discussion. The Prime Minister took up the cudgels at once, affirming his support for the Curzon line ('that is to say, leaving Lvov with Russia') and justifying the Soviet Union's claim as one of right rather than might. For this he had been criticized not merely in Parliament but by the Conservative Party itself, yet even now a gesture on the part of the Soviet Union, some magnanimity, would not come amiss; such a move would bring both admiration and acclaim. However, the main issue lay not with some frontier line but with a Poland which would be free, strong and independent: 'that is an objective which I have always heard Marshal Stalin proclaim with the utmost firmness'. Great Britain harboured no special designs: it was for a free and independent Poland that we had gone to war in 1939, ill-armed as we were, and risked everything not only as an empire but also as a nation. Honour had dictated that we draw the sword against Hitler and honour dictated a settlement for Poland bringing freedom and independence.

In the matter of the disputed governments, his own hands were as free as they were untainted. For some time he had not seen the present London government—'we recognize them but have not sought their company'. Nevertheless, Mikolajczyk, Romer and Grabski were men of good sense and the British had confidence in them. The Polish question should not be the cause of a rift between the Big Three; the obvious move was to create some interim government or governmental instrument—'pending full and free elections'—which recognized that Stalin must ensure the Red Army's lines of communications in their advance into Germany and any 'temporary government' would have to be acceptable to him under these special conditions.

During the short recess white-coated waiters, headed by the President's butler, brought on the trays of sandwiches, cake and hot Russian tea in glasses, too hot to hold and hence the object of inexpert and indecorous juggling. When the session resumed, Stalin set out his position in a speech as impassioned as it was implacable. Both the United States and Great Britain had insisted that Poland represented no material interest for them, but for the Soviet Union vital security was at stake—honour was only one element, though for the Soviet Union honour too was involved. Security and honour demanded a free and independent Poland, closing the traditional invasion route from the west and also reversing the 'Tsarist policy of the abolition of Poland'. Twice in thirty years the Germans had passed through Poland to invade Russia; this was because Poland was weak; Russia wanted in turn a powerful Poland so that this invasion route could be secured since Russia itself could not close it from the outside. Polish independence and Soviet security were inextricably bonded: honour certainly, but it must be security above all else, and here was a life-and-death matter for the Soviet state.

Relentlessly pressing his case—much of it related to the intrinsic weakness of the Anglo-American position—Stalin turned to the Curzon line, protesting that this demarcation was 'invented not by Russians but by foreigners . . . Russia was not invited and did not participate . . . Lenin opposed it'. This was a *minimum* Soviet demand and configured to some foreign formula, for that matter. Honour, that quality much paraded by his Anglo-American allies, was clearly at stake here: must he settle for less than what Curzon and Clemenceau had conceded? Rising most astonishingly to his feet, Stalin warned that in this event he must face the wrath of the Ukrainians and return together with Molotov to Moscow branded as a 'less trustworthy defender' of Russia than Curzon and Clemenceau. Better that the war should continue even longer, that Russia should pay with yet more blood and Poland find compensation in the west at the expense of Germany.

Having adroitly managed this tactical shift of emphasis (and location), he presented the Soviet view that it was the western Neisse and the Oder which should form Poland's western frontier. In this he called upon the Prime Minister and the President to support him—incidentally, had not Mikolajczyk himself during his visit to Moscow in October declared himself delighted with a frontier pushed to the Oder–Neisse line? Switching his theme once again, Stalin turned to the problem of the government of Poland and, without committing himself to a reply about a 'Presidential Council', concentrated his attack on the Prime Minister. 'The Prime Minister has said that he wants to create a Polish government here [in Yalta]'. Stalin could only hold that this was 'a slip of the tongue', for without the participation of the Poles themselves there could be no 'Polish government'. Men called him dictator, yet he retained enough 'democratic feeling' not to thrust some government on the Poles without their participation. If the

Prime Minister could adopt a high moral tone, then so could Stalin.

Coming directly to the issue of the two governments, Stalin ruled out any idea of a coalition, with the London government calling the Lublin government bandits and criminals, with a consequent exchange of vituperation, thus ruling out any kind of agreement. The Lublin government—which should now be called the Warsaw government, for that was where it was to be found—would not traffic with the London government: they would, according to Stalin, accept General Zeligowski and Grabski as a concession but in no wise make any place for Mikolajczyk. Why not, Stalin interjected suddenly, invite the 'Warsaw Poles' to Yalta, even better to Moscow, to a conference? If this was meant to soothe, he quickly sharpened the edge of his remarks by saying that 'frankly, the Warsaw government has as great a democratic basis in Poland as De Gaulle has in France'. Moreover, and this harked back to one of the Prime Minister's own arguments, the Warsaw government alone could help to secure the Red Army's lines of communications: agents of the London government had killed more than two hundred Soviet soldiers, raided dumps and broken Soviet regulations on radio traffic. Speaking as a military man, Stalin must perforce support that government which afforded the Red Army secure rear areas; his allies should surely support him in this.

It had been a masterly performance, leaving no loophole and no hope of genuine negotiation. He disclaimed any Soviet responsibility for the stalemate, appealed to 'democratic' processes and, in the final resort, pleaded operational requirements for Allied acceptance of a Soviet solution. The President had taken no direct part in these discussions and, looking grey and drawn, suggested an adjournment. The Prime Minister, however, insisted on placing before the meeting the difference in information about the situation in Poland received by the British and Soviet governments: only one-third of the Poles supported the Lublin government, but the British government—even if mistaken in some particulars— could only fear for the outcome of any clash between the Polish Underground Army and the Lublin government, bringing 'bitterness, bloodshed, arrests and deportations'. It was this which prompted the British desire for a joint arrangement, though attacks on the Red Army could not be tolerated. Yet on the facts presently available the Lublin government could not pretend to represent the Polish nation. Obviously wearied, the President referred to Poland as a cause of trouble for more than five hundred years, at which the Prime Minister answered pertly that there was more need than ever to end such a state of affairs.

That same evening President Roosevelt, with the help of Harry Hopkins and State Department officials, drafted a letter to Stalin, showing it first to the Prime Minister and Eden. The presidential letter set out three main points: the unity and unanimity of the Big Three must be maintained, hence the lament for the lack among the three Allied powers of 'a meeting of minds about the political set-up in Poland'; the United States could not recognize the Lublin government in its present form (a formulation inserted at Eden's prompting); lastly, the desirability, following Stalin's own suggestion, of bringing Bierut and Osobka-Morawski from the Lublin government to Yalta, plus two or three representatives of other elements from the Polish people, names drawn from a list including Archbishop Sapieha, Wincenty Witos, Z. Zulawski, Professor Buyak and Professor Kutrzeba. Joint agreement might result in a provisional government, one including—again at Eden's suggestion—Mikolajczyk, Romer and Grabski. Given such an eventuality, the United States and Great Britain would be prepared to examine with Stalin an act of disassociation from the London government and hence recognition of the provisional government. Finally, the United States would in no way lend support to a provisional government in Poland which 'would be inimical to your interests'; an interim government would be pledged to hold free elections, but that also conformed with Stalin's expressed preference for a free and democratic Poland.

On the following afternoon, 7 February, the talk turned once again to Poland, though not before the Prime Minister had managed to whisper somewhat conspiratorially to the President that 'Uncle Joe will take Dumbarton Oaks'. The import of that remark was soon to become plain. The President turned at once to the Polish question, repeating his concern and the overriding importance of finding a solution—'I am not so concerned with frontiers. I am likewise not so concerned with the question of the continuity of the Government. . . . I discard the ideal of continuity. I think we want something new and drastic—like a breath of fresh air.' For a moment it looked as if Stalin had been hoisted by his own petard: it was he who had pleaded Allied unanimity throughout and was now being asked to concede in the interests of that self-same unity, not to mention the democratic principle which he also professed to address. Wholly in command of the situation, Stalin played the scene with consummate skill and admirable timing. He pleaded at once that he had received the President's letter only an hour and a half before the meeting began; he had at once given instructions for Bierut and Osobka-Morawski to be traced and put on the telephone to him. Unfortunately, the two men were presently in Cracow and Lodz and not to be reached; as for the opposition, Witos and Sapieha, he simply did not know their addresses. Time could well run out before they could be found and brought to Yalta. However, without yielding his obliging tone, Stalin suggested that Molotov should now present a draft document which might well meet the President's own proposals—though this meant waiting for the translation to be finished, time which could be usefully occupied with more talk of Dumbarton Oaks. The Soviet delegation then announced in a trice that the Soviet Union would accept the American voting formula and would relinquish its earlier insistence on representation for the sixteen Soviet constituent republics, seeking now for the admission of only two or three. Delighted at the initial announcement of acceptance, the President winced at the mention of even two Soviet republics—'This is not so good', he scribbled hurriedly in a note to Stettinius. He mixed congratulation with a certain reproof to Molotov, only to be held in check by Harry Hopkins who urged him to refer the matter at once to the Foreign Ministers. The President, anxious to speed the business of the United Nations, proposed March as a possible date for its first meeting, only to be interrupted this time by the Prime Minister who thought March too early.

Stalin had managed his *coup de théâtre* to perfection. The British already knew of the Soviet intention to accept the American voting formula. Molotov had deftly sidestepped a suggestion from Stettinius that they discuss this very question, with Molotov making vague reference to some projected observations he would make soon. This Soviet concession, designed to preserve hallowed unanimity, immediately preceded Molotov's draft statement on the Polish question. The Soviet Union had tried for 'maximum unity' in accepting the American voting proposal (ostensibly guided in this decision by Stettinius's explanation and British clarification), but by the same token 'maximum unity' could be preserved by an Anglo-American acceptance of the Soviet draft on Poland, configured as it was to accommodate the President's proposals. Molotov's draft simply codified Stalin's propositions of the previous day, incorporating only some minor concessions—a 5–8km shift of the Curzon line in favour of Poland, the addition of 'some democratic leaders from Polish *émigré* circles' to the provisional government, and a call to the polls 'as soon as possible' for the establishment of permanent organs of government. For all practical purposes, the Lublin government (or the Warsaw government) remained intact: 'technical difficulties' precluded bringing Polish leaders to Yalta and such 'difficulties' virtually ruled out any implementation of the President's plan. For practically nothing, Stalin had acquired the Curzon line, a definition of Poland's western frontier and an indeterminate commitment to an enlarged government, even if a sting lay in the use of that term *émigré*. In spite of the President's talk of the Poles 'saving face', it was essentially Stalin who seemed bent on saving face for the western Allies.

Both the Prime Minister and the President objected to the use of '*émigré*'; obligingly, Stalin removed it, and also added a reference to Polish democratic leaders inside as well as outside Poland. When Churchill launched into a discussion of the frontier question the President braced himself for another Churchillian discourse—'Now we are in for half an hour of it'—but the Prime Minister was anxious that Poland should not be awarded so much territory in the west that 'the Polish goose dies of German indigestion' or that millions of Germans be displaced in a forced population transfer. Stalin took little time to dispose of the latter objections: the lands under discussion were already emptying of Germans as the Red Army advanced, driving gigantic refugee columns before it. Amidst some brutal badinage about how many Germans remained to be killed, the Prime Minister slid in his reference to democratic Poles 'from inside Poland' and Stalin quickly agreed, having disposed of the question of population transfer. At this juncture all agreed to adjourn, each satisfied in his own way and ready to renew the discussion on the following day.

On 8 February the Allied leaders met for their fourth plenary session and again took up the Polish question, with the President advancing a revised draft of Molotov's proposals. The American draft approved extension of the Polish western frontier to the Oder but not as far as the *western* Neisse, and proposed a 'Polish Government of National Unity', with a Presidential Committee of three ('possibly M. Bierut, M. Grabski and Archbishop Sapieha') committed to forming a government of 'representative leaders from the present Provisional Government in Warsaw, from other democratic leaders inside Poland, and from Polish democratic leaders abroad'. This provisional government would hold elections to a Constituent Assembly to enact a new Polish constitution under which a permanent government would be elected. After a preliminary probe about the eventual American and British attitude to the London government of the Poles, Stalin let Molotov launch the first phase of the Soviet counter-attack, which was facilitated by that tactical clumsiness which placed both American and British counter-proposals on the table. Molotov pursued one aim and one alone: to prove that a 'Polish government'—the Lublin (or Warsaw) government—existed here and now, a government which enjoyed prestige and popularity and was presently emplaced in Warsaw itself. If a start were made on enlarging *this* provisional government, then the chances of success were good; the resulting government might well prove to be only a temporary institution, but there could be a start at organizing free elections in Poland. As for the President's proposal for a presidential committee, this collided with the existence of a National Council in Poland, which could also simply be enlarged.

Molotov's admission of the incongruity of two bodies—the Lublin government and the presidential committee—gave the Prime Minister his cue and he lunged directly at Molotov and Soviet obfuscation: 'This is the crucial point of the Conference. The whole world is waiting for a settlement and if we separate still recognizing different Polish governments, the whole world will see that fundamental differences between us still exist. The consequences will be most lamentable. . . .' British information on Poland differed from Soviet information. The Lublin government did not represent the Polish people; a world outcry would result from setting aside the London government in favour of the men of Lublin. Nor could the British government countenance an act of betrayal in the transfer of British recognition from the London government. Certainly, the London government had acted foolishly at times, but to abandon it would signify to Parliament that Britain had altogether forsaken the cause of Poland. Great Britain had already yielded on the question of the frontiers; she could not surrender completely by transferring recognition until there was surety that the new government represented the Polish nation. 'Our doubts would be removed by elections with full secret ballot and free candidacies to be held in Poland. But it is the transfer before then which is causing so much anxiety to us. That is all I have to say.' Unabashed, Molotov pointed to the possible outcome of the discussions in Moscow and pleaded in pursuit of democratic principles that to 'consider the Polish question without the presence of Poles' was difficult.

The President spoke up to support the Prime Minister in his plea for early free elections in Poland, adding his own hope that there might be elections before the end of the year. Now came Stalin's turn, an intervention which he exploited neatly by reversing Molotov's arguments in an even more powerful negativistic sense—if Molotov had argued that any settlement must be on Soviet terms, Stalin threatened that there might be no agreement at all. But first he challenged the Prime Minister on his information about the state of affairs in Poland: British and American information clearly differed from that available to the Soviet government, whereupon he launched into a lengthy speech. The men of the Lublin government were indubitably popular, with a special place for Bierut, Osobka-Morawski and Rola-Zymierski who had not left the country during its occupation, who had lived in Warsaw and worked through the underground movement. There might be clever men in the London government, but they had not lived under the German occupation and were not liked—a peculiar and even primitive view, but occupation nurtured such feelings.

The liberation of Poland by the Red Army had almost certainly revolutionized the old antagonistic Russo–Polish relations, where Russia had formerly taken part in three partitions of the country. 'Now there is goodwill towards Russia. . . .' The Poles had seen members of the provisional government, but where, they asked, were the London Poles? The Lublin government was not composed of great men, but they did enjoy great popularity. Certainly, the Lublin government had not been elected—but then De Gaulle's government had not been elected; it was unreasonable to demand more of Poland than was asked of France, and it should be noted that while the French government had done nothing to generate enthusiasm in France, the provisional government in Poland had embarked on land reforms which had evoked a popular response. In Stalin's view, the situation was not so tragic—the Prime Minister pressed for a settlement, so let there be concentration on essentials rather than on secondary matters: take up Molotov's suggestion, reconstruct the present provisional government rather than create a wholly new government. As for the presidential committee, the Poles might or might not agree with it.

The dissension died away and the discussions flickered out. Seemingly much wearied, the President asked how long it might be before elections took place in Poland: barring some military catastrophe, Stalin submitted that they might be only a month away, a statement which capped all the discussion about interim arrangements, for the elections were intended to decide Poland's future government. The Prime Minister found this more reassuring and in placatory mood assured Stalin that Great Britain would not seek steps which might interfere with Soviet military operations. On the President's suggestion, the Polish problem was turned over to the foreign ministers, who should consult Sir Archibald Clark Kerr and Mr Harriman.

However, Stalin was not quite done. In informal fashion, he raised two issues, Yugoslavia and Greece. On Yugoslavia he was anxious to know why the United Government (already agreed by the British) had not yet materialized, and on Greece he was simply asking for information. He had no criticism of British policy in Greece, he simply wanted news of the situation. After the wrangle over information about conditions in Poland, the hint was broad and crude: if the British did not break the rules, the situation in Greece would continue, and likewise there would be no accusation of British bad faith over Yugoslavia if there was no such charge levelled against the Soviet Union *vis-à-vis* Poland.

Thus far the President and his delegation could feel a certain satisfaction with the course of the conference. For all the friction over Poland there had been no actual breach with the Soviet Union, the President and Stalin seemed to see eye to eye over Germany, and no doubt the same reasonableness would prevail over the issue of the United Nations. The United Nations embodied one of the President's major objectives, totally overshadowing parochial and pettifogging European politics. Now a second major objective—Soviet commitment to the war against Japan—came close to realization. At Teheran in 1943 Stalin had skirted the question warily, but in December 1944 he had already begun to deploy his arguments about Soviet claims by outlining them to Harriman. Eden remained sceptical, and in suggesting before the Yalta conference that Britain and the United States pursue a joint negotiating strategy he emphasized that the Soviet Union would scarcely wish to stand by idly while Japan was vanquished, so that there was no need to meet every stiff concession demanded by Stalin as the price for his own self-interested entry into the Pacific war; concessions to Stalin over the Far East must be balanced by Soviet moderation in other areas.

This counsel went unheeded. On the afternoon of 8 February the President and Stalin met privately to discuss Soviet entry into the war against Japan; here was collaboration at its closest, so close as to assume well-nigh conspiratorial form. Already prodded by the American chiefs of staff, the President at once broached the question of military co-operation, agreed in principle but dragging woefully in practice. The Kamchatka survey, approved in December 1944, stood stalled. Although the Americans had assembled their men and measured them for the Russian uniforms the Soviet government insisted they must wear, the whole project was now subject to indefinite delay. General Antonov, Chief of the Soviet General Staff, had agreed in December to nominate four Soviet officers to work with the American planning group. Six weeks passed without any development, only to have the first meeting virtually collide with the Yalta conference. General Slavin from the General Staff, Marshal of Aviation Khudyakov (Chief of Staff to Novikov, Air Force C-in-C), Rear-Admiral Kucherov and General Semichastnov made up this Soviet military delegation, who busied themselves with procedure rather than planning in any real sense.

The President came armed with a list of questions, seven specific points upon which the American Chiefs of Staff required answe.s to facilitate their own planning. While the substance of this list took up a .ur:her day of discussion, Stalin in a show of immediate amiability and pron.pt willingness agreed to the establishment of American air bases in the Nikolay⌣vsk–Komsomolsk area and the Pacific supply line running into Siberia; by way of emphasis, Stalin stressed the importance of the first, the forward bases, which General Antonov had been unable to authorize on his own, though he had from the first shown keen interest in the supply question. In the same spirit Stalin agreed to the establishment of bases for US bombers in the Budapest area, thus eliminating the dangerous run from Italy to Germany, and he readily acceded to the request for American experts to investigate bomb damage in those areas of south-eastern Europe now in the hands of the Red Army.

To start the trading, Stalin asked about the possibility of buying shipping after the war. The President, anxious to encourage any Soviet initiative which would bring them out into the wide world—in this case, international trade—responded by saying that he hoped to transfer shipping on interest-free credit terms, whereas the British, imbued with crude commercialism, would simply sell. All this pleased Stalin enormously, who lavished praise on the President's handling of economic problems of this kind: Lend-Lease itself had been a spectacular contribution to the common cause. There was nothing, however, interest-free in Stalin's terms for Soviet entry into the war against Japan. Fully cognizant of these claims, the President made no demur over the Soviet acquisition of the Kuriles and the southern reaches of Sakhalin, but on the two ports (Port Arthur and Darien) and the two railways, the Chinese–Eastern and the South Manchurian, he was reluctant to commit himself without some reference to the Chinese. Several possibilities suggested themselves: for example, the Soviet Union could lease Port Arthur, as it could also lease the railways or even operate a joint Sino–Soviet commission; as for Darien, the President made it plain that he preferred an internationalized status for the port, more or less on the lines of his proposals for Hong Kong. At this Stalin made his first, faint but firm protest: summoning up Soviet 'public opinion' as sudden and subtle reinforcement, he pointed out that he could scarcely call for war against Japan without holding out the promise of Port Arthur and Darien. Given these political pre-conditions, there should be no difficulties. The President countered by referring to the need to consult Chiang Kai-shek, but this step might mean compromising vital secrecy; Stalin agreed with this point, but insisted that the Soviet Union must have its claims formally set down in writing before the end of the conference. To this the President made no objection.

On the question of China, Stalin went out of his way to assure the President that the Soviet Union would in no way overturn the prevailing situation; after all, had not he, Stalin, always supported a united front between the *Kuomintang* and the Communists? The only pity was that the *Kuomintang* seemed to ignore the best men in its ranks. President Roosevelt paid little heed to this or to any praise of Chiang Kai-shek, implying that it was Chiang Kai-shek who was impeding his own efforts to build up this united front. Stalin murmured that this, a united front, echoed his own sentiments exactly. Scanning the future face of Asia, the President let Stalin deeper into his thoughts. Over Korea he proposed, not the quadripartite body (Russian, American, Chinese and British) recommended by his own State Department, but an American–Soviet–Chinese trusteeship; in mock tragic tones Stalin pleaded for the British, but he was more concerned to discover whether there would be foreign troops in Korea, to which the President returned a resolute no. The President also proposed extending the idea of trusteeship into Indochina, thus prising France out of Asia and displacing the colonial presence even further; Soviet–American co-operation in the Far East would fill the vacuum brought on by the defeat of Japan and the eradication of the colonial powers.

The question of military co-operation took up much of the talk on 8–9 February. General Antonov found his position easier now that Stalin had spoken, agreeing to the establishment of American bomber bases and to the establishment of the Pacific supply line, keeping it open even after Soviet–Japanese hostilities had begun, largely for petrol. To the seven leading questions presented by the Americans, Antonov—prompted by Stalin—returned his best answers. The Chief of the Soviet General Staff made it clear that there had been no change in Soviet operational plans since October 1944: the Soviet command expected heavy resistance to the Red Army by the Japanese and a sea-air route would be necessary to secure supplies in view of the vulnerability of the Trans-Siberian Railway to attack. As yet no redeployment of Soviet troops to the Far Eastern theatre had been set in motion, owing to the weight of the fighting on the Soviet–German front.

General Antonov confirmed Stalin's ruling on bomber bases: the Soviet Union would, therefore, handle the initial construction work necessary to prepare bases in the Nikolayevsk–Komsomolsk area. On 8 February he affirmed that American help in the defence of Kamchatka 'would be useful' and he repeated this the following day, adding an authorization for American survey parties to proceed to the Amur area but excluding them—for reasons of secrecy—from Kamchatka. General Marshall learned on 8 February that the capture of southern Sakhalin came high on the list of Soviet operational priorities, a point confirmed on the 9th, though General Antonov added that while La Perouse Strait was denied to Japanese ships Allied vessels would have to wait upon the construction of a suitable base. On the question of additional weather stations, General Antonov could satisfy the Americans that these would be available, a decision endorsed by Stalin. But one American question, more by way of a pointed rejoinder and reminder, stung General Antonov to the quick: how effective and 'vigorous' would be this joint planning? With Soviet troops not as yet on the move to or deployed in the Far East, General Antonov asserted with some heat, joint planning must be necessarily limited. The Red Army needed to establish its own bases.

General Marshall failed to find satisfaction in this argument and stressed the needs of American planners. A ruffled Antonov calmed himself on being told that none of this impugned either Soviet competence or good faith, and he undertook to ensure nothing less than 'vigorous' combined planning in Moscow.

On 10 February, after some final adjustments, the Soviet–American compact was formally sealed. Over the signatures of President Roosevelt, Marshal Stalin and the Prime Minister (who signed against the advice of Eden), the Soviet Union agreed to enter the war against Japan two or three months after the defeat of Germany, subject to the following conditions: the preservation of the *status quo* in Outer Mongolia, the restoration to Russia of 'former rights violated by the treacherous attack of Japan in 1904' (the recovery of southern Sakhalin, the internationalization of Darien and the restoration of the lease of Port Arthur as a Soviet naval base, joint Sino-Soviet operation of the two railways subject to recognition of the pre-eminence of Soviet interests and Chinese sovereignty over Manchuria), and Soviet acquisition of the Kuriles. Ambassador Harriman had been obliged to clarify certain points with Molotov before the draft agreement could be accepted: the Soviet draft mentioned leases on the two ports and the two railways, which the Ambassador modified to confirm the status of Port Arthur and Darien as free ports, simultaneously bringing the railways under the joint commission and stipulating prior Chinese agreement. Stalin objected over Port Arthur, which he bluntly demanded as a naval base, after which he fell in with the plan for joint control of the railways and even suggested obtaining the Chinese view on the status of Outer Mongolia. Whatever Eden's protestations, supported by Sir Alexander Cadogan, the Prime Minister could only put the best face on the compact, disclaiming it as a necessary American initiative; to Stalin he affirmed the justice of making good Russia's historical losses and extended a welcome to Russian ships in the Pacific.

Meanwhile the remaining business of the conference flowed on amidst these secret conclaves. On 8 February, after a tense and complicated meeting of the foreign ministers, the plenary session attended to the question of membership of the United Nations, with the President facing solid Anglo–Soviet opposition to the manifest ambiguity of his ideas. Having reduced the Soviet request to two republics (Lithuania had been quietly dropped) as signatories of the United Nations Declaration, Stalin faced further prevarication from the President and finally asked him that if he (the President) would just explain his difficulties, then something might be done about them. On the President's earnest pleading, Stalin withdrew his formal proposition that the two Soviet republics (the Ukraine and Belorussia) sign the United Nations Declaration, in return for American and British support for them at the actual UN Conference and specific reference to them in the text of the foreign ministers' decisions.

Over the question of trusteeships, Stalin could watch with undisguised delight as the Prime Minister, refusing to be restrained by the President, lashed out in defence of the British empire: he agreed to the practice of trusteeship being applied to former enemy territories, but the British empire should remain inviolate, a point on which Stettinius hastened to reassure him. Since he was in the process of recovering Imperial Russia's 'rights' lost to Japan in 1904–5, Stalin must have relished this fierce defence of the imperial principle and could store it away for future use, combining this with an assertion of 'democratic principles' to legitimize his hold on newly won gains in eastern Europe. But the talk over Yugoslavia took on a grimmer note, with the Prime Minister and Stalin on opposing sides: the Soviet side suspected British duplicity in undermining the Tito–Subasic agreement by detaining Subasic in London, and Stalin charged the Prime Minister with delaying the formation of a Yugoslav government. Though Stalin actually supported the British amendments to the original agreement, he demanded unequivocal three-power support—in the form of a telegram to the Yugoslav leaders—for the compact. Once the government was formed, the Russians would underwrite two of the British stipulations, a National Council enlarged to include former members of the last Yugoslav parliament who had not been compromised by collaboration, and ratification of legislative acts by the Constituent Assembly. Molotov rejected as a 'humiliation' to the Yugoslavs the proposal that the government formed out of the Tito–Subasic agreement should continue only until the free will of the people was declared.

Iran also proved to be another stumbling block and came up for discussion at the foreign ministers' meeting on 8 February. Backed by Stettinius, Eden submitted that no pressure be put upon Iran to grant oil concessions and the withdrawal of Allied troops should be set in train once the truck route to Russia was closed down. Molotov at his most intractable responded by arguing that the withdrawal of troops was quite a new issue and that, although the Soviet Union had not been well treated, oil concessions scarcely warranted all this attention; matters could wait. In the face of the Prime Minister's reluctance to raise this question in plenary session, and equal American indifference, Eden went directly to Stalin on 10 February, to be met with every show of accommodation to 'think about' eventual withdrawal of Allied troops and a waving away of Molotov's dour resistance with a heavy-handed jibe about the latter's hurt feelings in the negotiations over oil concessions. Iran got but passing mention in the proceedings of the conference. The same deliberate indecisiveness attended Soviet attempts to revise the Montreux Convention and the status of the Dardanelles, for all Stalin's protestations about the outmoded nature of existing arrangements.

Compared to Poland, however, these were both literally and figuratively peripheral matters. The struggle over verbal formulae and political commitment reached its climax in the closing phase of the conference, centred on guarantees for free elections in Poland—which must be, as the President observed, as free of suspicion as was Caesar's wife (though Stalin interjected that she was not above suspicion)—and a specific Anglo–American commitment to the western frontier. On the evening of 9 February at the meeting of foreign ministers, Eden dropped his own bombshell: the British War Cabinet referred to growing public criticism of the territorial demands of the Lublin government and therefore suggested couching the terms of Poland's western frontier to read 'and such other lands to the east of the Oder as at the Peace Conference it shall be considered desirable to transfer to Poland'. Moreover, in the period between the formation of a new provisional government and the proposed elections, the non-Communists would simply be eliminated—hence the political balance of the government should be maintained beyond the period of elections. It had to be a draft on these lines, Eden insisted, or nothing. Molotov proceeded to juggle with words, referring again to the 'reorganization' of the government 'now acting in Poland' and this whole body to be recognized by the three great powers. Eden did not want a 'reorganization', he demanded something wholly new; equally, he rejected Molotov's objections to the three ambassadors reporting on the elections—and, in any event, they would do this whatever the present conference decided.

This British draft overrode the previous American formulation, but it was treated in the sense of an 'amendment' to the American text. Molotov worked mightily to align these two versions yet to retain the cogency and purpose of the Soviet arguments. For all practical purposes he succeeded. He expunged reference to a 'fully representative' government from the final text, reinstated the 'Polish Provisional Government' (a synonym for the Lublin government) and hung on grimly to the 'reorganization' of the existing government; and, like Stalin, he skilfully used the proposed 'Declaration on Liberated Europe' to insert a caveat about 'anti-Nazi' as well as democratic parties, thus driving a coach and horses through any specific interpretation of party political affiliations.

The result, in essence, was a conundrum: when is a new government not a new government? Everything hung on the significance of 'reorganization'. The British and Americans might expect a new government to emerge from 'reorganization', while the Soviet Union could take it to mean that 'reorganization' meant recognition of a government in being—the Lublin government. The British and Americans, however, refused to take the step of affording that specific recognition, in spite of Molotov's pressure to this end. There remained the question of the guarantee over elections. Wearied by Molotov's total obduracy, the American delegation gave up its demand for ambassadorial reporting on the elections and settled for an inconclusive formula on the role of ambassadors—more presumptive than real. However, the Prime Minister and Eden resolved not to surrender so easily and met with Stalin privately to discuss the elections, all on the eve of the plenary session of 10 February. The Prime Minister asserted that he must give Parliament a guarantee of fair elections in Poland, to which end there must be British representatives at hand. Stalin proffered an immediate solution: recognize the Polish government and an ambassador would have no difficulty whatsoever. The Red Army would not interfere but it depended on what arrangements the British made with the Polish government; after all, General de Gaulle had his representative in Poland. The Prime Minister was nudged to the edge of recognition.

Hurrying into the final plenary session after this consultation with Stalin, Eden laid the final document before the conference. It bore all the signs of having been cobbled together by many hands, as indeed it had been: it embodied the original American proposal (buttressed by the Soviet submission), subject to Soviet revision, drastically revised by the British and revised in turn by Molotov. The Prime Minister's latest exchange with Stalin had also to be slid into the document. The President gave his agreement at once. However, the Prime Minister brought up the subject of the western frontiers, referring to his telegram from the War Cabinet which opposed the extension of the frontier to the western Neisse, the same telegram proposing that no mention be made of the Poles going beyond the Oder. President Roosevelt for his part wanted no mention whatsoever of frontiers and suggested consulting the Poles; nor could he by American constitutional practice commit his government without the ratification of the Senate. Stalin objected. The eastern frontier must be mentioned. The Prime Minister now held fast to his refusal to commit his government. Nevertheless, Stalin squeezed out a reference to the Curzon line—'the eastern frontier of Poland should follow the Curzon line with digressions from it in some regions of 5 to 8 km in favour of Poland', and Poland should receive 'substantial accessions of territory' in the north and west. The new Polish government would be duly consulted and a final decision delayed until 'the Peace Conference'.

The Declaration on Liberated Europe, presented in its final form to the plenary session on 10 February, occupied less of the attention of the conference. Designed to bind the wartime allies to commitments of common policy, the original document urged the three governments to assist the liberated nations of Europe to 'solve by democratic means their pressing political and economic problems'. Stettinius, who introduced this document, did not proceed with the proposal to set up an Emergency High Commission for Liberated Europe, which would hold sway until the World Organization came into being. Discussions over the document became a stalking horse for other issues—the President's faith in democratic guarantees, the Prime Minister's suspicion of any move directed against the British empire, Stalin manipulating the terms 'fascist' and 'non-fascist' in the context of Poland. Soviet attempts at amendment, meant to broaden Allied support for those active in the struggle against German occupation, were rejected: 'mutual consultation' was transmuted into the more stilted and stiffer 'joint machinery' for the received text, and after some resistance the Russians agreed to Eden's proposal to invite the French government to associate themselves with the Declaration. Stalin was not averse to supporting this document, and its 'anti-fascist' theme seemed to strike a responsive chord in him: sound sentiments and good words, drawing the line between fascist and non-fascist.

Behind the 'spirit of Yalta', which had undoubtedly triumphed and justified much of the euphoria, lay the reality of Soviet military victories, the epitome of which was represented by Poland; the United States and Great Britain could seek but they could not demand. Yalta tested the alliance to its limits. The underlying issue was the degree to which the Soviet Union under Stalin would or would not pursue a path of co-operation. Within very strict and formally prescribed conditions Stalin indicated that he had chosen the path of collaboration, subject to a proper (and at times seemingly exaggerated) recognition of Russia's rights; to this end he engineered compromises and offered concessions of a minimum order, but concessions nevertheless. He had gained his prime objective, the establishment of a pro-Soviet Polish government, the Lublin government, and then warded off all efforts to encumber it with 'democratic' appurtenances, though the issue of Poland's western frontier still remained to be solved. He was also denied immediate satisfaction over reparations from a defeated Germany: the sum of 20.000 million US dollars set for full reparation from Germany was split down the middle in favour of the Soviet Union, but the final protocol of the Yalta conference mentioned this only as a *basis for discussion*. In a burst of genuine anger at the plenary session of 10 February, Stalin demanded to know of the Prime Minister whether the British wanted the Soviet Union to get reparations or not. A secret protocol permitted the Soviet Union to put its own figures before the Moscow Reparations Commission; other nations might do the same. Otherwise Stalin seems to have been well satisfied with the de-militarization and de-Nazification proposals for Germany.

Although sceptical in the beginning, Stalin also came to view the proposed World Security Organization as a serious venture and went markedly out of his way to help the President out of the manifest muddle over membership and voting. The vista of this kind of co-operation may have stretched even further, to thoughts of an American loan to aid Russian reconstruction—certainly Stalin pointedly referred to the outstanding contribution made, at the President's instance, through Lend-Lease. In the Far East he obtained handsome restitution of Russia's historical losses and a grip on Manchuria which was generosity, at China's expense, taken to extremes—it was a strange turn of events which persuaded the President to enter into a binding commitment in Asia while so skilfully avoiding any such constraint in Europe. The President's bald announcement that the United States was unlikely to keep its troops in Europe for more than two years after the defeat of Germany must have worked the same deep impression on Stalin as it did on the Prime Minister. Stalin could also express his unbounded enthusiasm for the Declaration on Liberated Europe, which, contrary to the President's expectations, could in no wise alter or interfere with the Soviet hold on eastern Europe.

In terms of big three unity, Stalin had held out the prospect of collaboration. Since the alternative was too gloomy to contemplate, his partners seized avidly upon this sense of compatibility, forgetful that the terms were strict and prescribed. There were no outright 'surrenders' enacted at Yalta, for nothing slipped out of Stalin's iron fist; nor could it be prised open. However, ambiguity was piled on ambiguity, most of which went unchecked at the time. And Stalin was a past-master at exploiting ambiguities.

Two days after the close of the Yalta conference, as the grandees went their separate ways in their cruisers and aircraft, the battle for Budapest ended in a welter of butchery, looting and rape. Battle-weary but triumphant Soviet soldiers machine-gunned the limping, broken German survivors and their Hungarian helpmates, or went about rounding up stunned civilians to swell the total of 'prisoners' taken in this ferocious fighting which spilled over the Danube and spewed into the tunnels and the cellars of Buda's rock. Pest burned fiercely, slabs of buildings crashing into ruins and spreading a fiery rain in the city. Successive Soviet combat echelons moved through these twin hazards, killing and looting at will as ferocity alternated with childishness—taking women or seizing toys to hoard as presents for children. To give pleasure and yet inflict excruciating pain, to remember home but ravage foreign families, was all part of the mood of the Soviet soldier. It took a little time for sheer criminality to gain the upper hand, stimulated by the deliberate, bloodthirsty and horrifyingly vengeful language of the propagandist Ilya Ehrenburg, a slur and stain on Slav honour but a reflection of the degradation which all Slavs had suffered—not an eye for an eye, but two eyes for one eye, all rising to a hysterical frenzied crescendo which the Party felt impelled to check. Words, however, meant little, and while Red Army troops might mouth the slogans of death and vengeance, their conduct was governed by their immediate memories. The first-line fighting troops might pass without molesting anyone, but the second echelons—recruited *en route*, pulled out of prison camps or freed from forced labour, given a machine-pistol and a uniform— were brutalized from the outset. Even then there was a bewildering admixture of the maudlin with the bestial—the collective, guttural croak of *'Frau komm'* with sweets and dollies for the children.

Though Budapest had fallen, the battle for western Hungary was far from over. Undismayed by Soviet armies massing on the Oder and piling up their reserves in Poland,.Hitler determined late in January to switch Sepp Dietrich's Sixth *SS Panzer* Army, recently withdrawn from the Ardennes and refitting in southern Germany, to Hungary; during the second half of February Sixth *Panzer* began to appear in the area of Vienna and further east, at Györ in Hungary. Impervious to Guderian's arguments that the armour was desperately needed on the Oder, the *Führer* contemplated an offensive designed to drive a deep wedge between Malinovskii and Tolbukhin, having reached the Danube south of Budapest; the envelopment of part of Tolbukhin's 3rd Ukrainian Front between the Danube and the Drava would lead to the establishment of fresh German bridgeheads over the Danube, the recapture of Budapest and the recovery of eastern Hungary. Economic considerations also dictated this counter-offensive, for the Hungarian and Austrian oilfields were now producing four-fifths of Germany's needs; even if the counter-blow failed, it might still delay a Soviet offensive directed against Vienna. And, finally, what Sixth *SS Panzer* had failed to achieve in the Ardennes it might accomplish in Hungary, thus raising the spirits of defending armies in the east and on the Rhine alike.

Hitler may also have drawn some encouragement, even if misplaced, from the limited success of Hungarian divisions attacking in the direction of Szekesfehervar: possibly, the Soviet forces were not as strong as might appear, with Tolbukhin's troops under heavy pressure and Malinovskii's command weakened by the heavy, brutal fighting for Pest, with Buda still to be reduced. Smashing into 3rd Ukrainian Front might work, splitting it and driving to the Danube. The German plan called for an offensive by Wöhler's Army Group South assisted by a supplementary attack from General Löhr's Army Group E in Yugoslavia; the German Sixth Army under Balck, with 8th Hungarian Corps and Sepp Dietrich's 6th *SS Panzer* (amounting in all to ten *Panzer* and five infantry divisions), would attack between lake Balaton and lake Velencze, splitting Tolbukhin's 3rd Ukrainian Front in two. Meanwhile Second *Panzer* Army—a *Panzer* army in name only, equipped with assault guns—would use its four infantry divisions to strike in an easterly direction from the south of lake Balaton, an operation generally co-ordinated with Army Group E attacking with three divisions from the direction of the Drava. Admirable in conception, this plan took little account of the terrain, for here the Hungarian plain between the northern extremity of lake Balaton and the Danube was intersected by canals and ditches—soft, squashy and watery ground which caused German tank commanders to yell into their telephones that they were equipped with tanks, not U-boats. But by way of compensation Sixth *SS Panzer* mustered the newer 'King Tigers', underpowered and mechanically unreliable, but massively armoured and mounting an 88mm gun. Sixth *SS Panzer* Army was a formidable foe by any reckoning.

Tolbukhin's 3rd Ukrainian Front consisted at this time of five field armies—4th Guards, 26th, 27th and 57th, plus the 1st Bulgarian Army—supported by 17th Air Army; south-east of Budapest 9th Guards Army formed the Supreme Commander's Reserve. Lt.-Gen. Kosta Nadj with the 3rd Yugoslav Army (formed from 12th Corps in the Vojvodina) held the lower reaches of the Drava on Tolbukhin's left; the Danube Flotilla with its gunboats and naval infantry also came under Tolbukhin's operational control. Further north Malinovskii's 2nd Ukrainian Front disposed of five armies (40th, 53rd, 7th Guards and 46th Armies, plus 6th Guards Tank Army) and 5th Air Army, reinforced with 1st and 4th Rumanian Armies; Malinovskii's armies were holding a front which reached down from Zvolen to the river Hron in Hungary. Shumilov's 7th Guards Army occupied the important bridgehead east of Komarno on the western bank of the Hron, preparing all the while to take the offensive. German–Hungarian forces pounded away at this bridgehead in an effort to eliminate it, while away at the southern end of the Danube front German troops crossed the Drava at the junction with the Danube and cut their way to the Mohacs–Pecs road. Something was brewing, but the Soviet command could not quite determine what. Fresh German armour was on the move, but moving so obviously—with tanks laden on railway flat-cars and taken westwards while the air filled with rumours about them going north—that Soviet intelligence became ever more suspicious.

On 17 February the *Stavka* issued an operational directive to Malinovskii and Tolbukhin instructing them to prepare and execute an offensive designed to destroy the German Army Group South and occupy the area running from Bratislava to Brno, Vienna and Nagykanizsa. Striking from the Hron bridgehead and from the western bank of the Danube, Soviet forces would move on Brno, Vienna and Graz, complete the liberation of Hungary, deprive the Germans of the use of the Nagykanizsa oilfields, occupy Vienna and threaten the approaches to southern Germany. This sweep towards southern Germany would cut the escape route for German forces operating in Yugoslavia and simultaneously force the speedier capitulation of German troops in northern Italy. 9th Guards Army was specifically earmarked for the Vienna operation; the formation was drawn from reserve and assigned at once to the 2nd Ukrainian Front. Malinovskii's 2nd Ukrainian Front also acquired operational control of the Danube Flotilla and the 83rd Independent Naval Infantry Brigade. The Soviet offensive would open on 15 March.

Tolbukhin and Malinovskii regrouped and reinforced, but the SS struck first, Tiger, King Tiger and Panther tanks to the fore. The German plan called for maximum effort between lakes Balaton and Velencze, using the German Sixth Army and Sixth SS *Panzer* to break through to the Danube in the Dunapentele–Szegzard sector, splitting Tolbukhin's Front in two and then striking north and south along the banks of the Danube; Second *Panzer* Army would attack from Nagykanizsa in the direction of Kaposvar, while Army Group E attacked from the Drava in the area of Donji–Miholjac to link up with Sixth SS *Panzer*. Sepp Dietrich's SS tank army fielded five *Panzer* divisions, two infantry and two cavalry divisions, two heavy battalions and SS units; Sixth Army mustered three infantry and five *Panzer* divisions; and 3rd Hungarian Army one tank division, two infantry divisions and a cavalry division. Second *Panzer* Army could count on four divisions, a motorized brigade and three 'combat groups', swelled with a motorized division which arrived on the eve of the counter-offensive; Army Group E deployed eight divisions and two brigades. The full German–Hungarian force committed against Tolbukhin amounted to thirty-one divisions (eleven of them tank divisions), five 'combat groups' and motorized brigades and four assault-gun brigades—431,000 officers and men, 5,630 guns and mortars, 877 tanks and assault guns, supported by 850 aircraft. The main assault force accounted for almost 150,000 men, 807 tanks and assault guns, and more than 3,000 guns and mortars. Malinovskii faced Eighth German Army on his left flank, a force of some nine infantry and two tank divisions.

On 17 February, as the *Stavka* advised Front commanders to prepare offensive operations, I *Panzer* Corps of Sixth *Panzer* fell on Shumilov's 7th Guards holding the Hron bridgehead, striking at Kruze's 24th Guards Rifle Corps with three infantry divisions and SS *'Adolf Hitler'* and *'Hitlerjugend' Panzer* divisions. As many as 150 German tanks and assault guns rolled over the Soviet positions, driving up to five miles into the Soviet defences. Taken completely by surprise, Shumilov rammed 93rd Guards Rifle Division into a counter-attack, but this only weakened his defensive force. During the night of 18 February German armour forced the Danube from the south and threatened the rear of Safiulin's 25th Guards Rifle Corps, ploughing on for another five miles. Too late the Front command began to react, moving up reserve formations—18th Guards Rifle Corps, 4th Guards Cavalry Corps and units of 6th Guards Tank Army—but all in vain. With left-flank formations threatened with encirclement, Shumilov could only withdraw. During the next four days, from 19–23 February, I *Panzer* Corps flayed Shumilov's rifle army and succeeded by the morning of 24 February in clearing the bridgehead of Soviet troops; during this period Shumilov lost about 8,800 men and much equipment, leaving him no option but to abandon the bridgehead and pull over to the eastern bank. The German offensive also came to a sudden halt.

Shumilov had only himself to blame, having organized his defence badly, neglected any proper reconnaissance and ignored the proper deployment of reserves, as well as failing to maintain effective vigilance. Nor did the Front command escape censure: with their attention fixed on the fighting in Budapest, they had failed to notice the operational importance of the Hron bridgehead, were tardy in reinforcing the forces holding the bridgehead, and had completely misunderstood the scope and scale of German activity on 'the Komarno axis'. It began to dawn on the Soviet high command that something drastic was afoot. On 20 February General Antonov received a signal from General Marshall that the German command proposed to launch two major attacks on the Eastern Front—the first from Pomerania in the direction of Torun, the second from Vienna and Moravska–Ostrava towards Lodz. For this southerly blow Sixth *SS Panzer* Army had been redeployed from the western theatre. (Colonel Brinkman of the army section of the British Military Mission had already passed information on Sixth *Panzer's* transfer to the Soviet command on 12 February.) Clearly the situation of Soviet troops along the northern reaches of the Danube had worsened, and this required immediate changes in Soviet operational planning, but not until the end of February—certainly after the loss of the Hron bridgehead—did the Soviet high command decide that Sixth *Panzer* would launch its attack in the area of lake Balaton and strike at 3rd Ukrainian Front.

Little time remained to Tolbukhin, whose orders from the *Stavka* prescribed fighting a defensive action against a German thrust between lakes Balaton and Velencze while continuing to prepare a major Soviet offensive. Marshal Tolbukhin, a calm and skilful commander well versed in the arts of war, went about his job in measured fashion; it was not the first time the Red Army had had to hold off a massed tank assault and grapple with the *SS*, hard-driving and daring tank men. He deployed his Front in two echelons, 4th Guards, 57th and 1st Bulgarian army in the first army, 27th Army in the second, supported by all available tank and mechanized formations deployed on the right flank. On the left, where a German supporting unit could be expected, Tolbukhin put in 133rd Rifle Corps from his main reserve. The terrain itself·presented problems, the ground low and water-logged, dissected with canals and rivers to the front and rear of Tolbukhin's formations. The Danube itself stood astride Soviet communications, causing Tolbukhin to take special measures to maintain contact with Malinovskii.

Soviet soldiers dug in, now under increasing German artillery fire and air attack. Tolbukhin's men set up three main defence lines, two Front defensive lines and interconnecting defence lines: on the bridgehead west of the Danube these lines were set close together due to lack of space, but the main defence belt was 3–4 miles thick, the second line five miles from the forward edge of the main defence line, and the third as much as fifteen miles. Heavy-calibre guns would tackle the King Tigers, while each army, corps and division set up its 'anti-tank reserve', which could be switched to threatened sectors. Mines went down by the thousand, both anti-personnel and anti-tank. Col.-Gen. Nadelin co-ordinated Front artillery resources, while separate formations deployed their available guns—57th Army adopted a centralized fire-control plan codenamed *Shtorm,* which allowed the infantry commander to bring down fire as the situation required, subject to the authorization of his immediate superior.

The weather played havoc with Tolbukhin's supply services. Ice-floes on the Danube threatened the pontoon bridges and ferry points. An overhead cable railway went into service to supply forward units with essentials—principally ammunition—able to deliver 1,200 tons per day across the river on to the western bank of the Danube; for the first time in the war, the Red Army delivered fuel via a pipeline to forward units. The 1st Bulgarian Army stood in urgent need of supplies, since it was now operating at some distance from its bases; Soviet instructors also went to the Bulgarian units to teach officers and men how to handle Soviet weapons and follow Soviet tactical practice. Soviet officers spoke Russian but were well enough understood by the Bulgarians. Tolbukhin himself went to the Bulgarian HQ at Szigetvar on 5 March to look over the final details of the defensive battle to which 1st Bulgarian Army was committed.

Tolbukhin's Front, with its five armies (thirty-seven Soviet rifle divisions, plus six Bulgarian infantry divisions), numbered 407,000 officers and men, almost 7,000 guns and mortars, and 407 tanks and SP guns; 3rd Ukrainian Front also included two tank corps, one mechanized and one cavalry corps. The 17th Air Army comprised 965 aircraft, though some frenzied work had to be put in hand to improve the network of forward airfields available to Soviet squadrons. The wear and tear of the earlier fighting in February, however, still showed in the Front command. In 14th Guards Army, average divisional strength had fallen to 5,100 men, in 26th Army to 4,250, in 57th Army to 5,300, and to 4,100 men in 27th Army; tank and mechanized formations had suffered correspondingly, leaving 18th and 23rd Tank Corps plus 1st Guards Mechanized Corps only 166 tanks and SP guns between them. Some tank regiments could only field 2–8 tanks.

Neither the time nor the place of the German counter-offensive came as a surprise to Marshal Tolbukhin. During the night of 2 March three Hungarian soldiers deserted to the Russians and talked about a German attack due to be launched in three days' time in the Balaton–Velencze sector; a Hungarian deserter to 57th Army also spoke about a forthcoming German attack on 5–6 March, an offensive which would also develop to the south of lake Balaton. (Further interrogation and additional reconnaissance in 57th Army established that this attack would materialize in the sector between Nagy Bajom and Kaposvar.) Tolbukhin meanwhile received additional intelligence from the Yugoslavs, indicating that the German offensive would unroll along three axes—from Szekesfehervar in an easterly direction, from Nagykanizsa towards Pecs, and from Osijek and Donji-Miholjac towards the north.

Strictly according to plan, entirely in line with the information given to Tolbukhin's command, the German attack began on the night of 5–6 March, jabbing into the Soviet 57th Army and the 1st Bulgarian and 3rd Yugoslav Armies. But this was a mere prelude south of lake Balaton. On the morning of 6 March, preceded by a thirty-minute artillery barrage supported by air attacks, Sixth *SS Panzer* and Sixth Armies smashed into Tolbukhin's main force: III *Panzer* Corps moved against the junction between Zakhvateyev's 4th Guards Army and Gagen's 26th, while I *SS Panzer* Corps and 1st Cavalry Corps went for the centre and right flank of Gagen's army. Soviet riflemen and gunners fought off the *SS*, who were supported by formidable waves of tanks. The *SS* troops ground forward slowly but steadily, cutting into Gagen's 26th. Soviet artillery fired over open sights at the mighty German tanks, using the most modern equipment and manned by superb crews inured to any hardship of the battlefield. Gagen's men faced a fresh assault on 7 March when two infantry divisions and 170 tanks and SP guns moved up in attack; Tolbukhin responded by moving 5th Guards Cavalry Corps and a brigade of SP guns from his reserve to stiffen the 26th. Nadelin also massed his guns, bringing 160 guns and mortars to bear across a 3,000-metre field of fire. To step up the air support the *Stavka* authorized the transfer of aircraft from 2nd Ukrainian Front to operate with Sudet's 17th Air Army.

After two days the *SS* had cut its way some four miles into the Soviet defences, south of lake Velencze; on 8 March the German command committed 2nd *SS Panzer* division, bringing more than 250 tanks into action in the reach between Balaton and Velencze. Both sides suffered heavily and at this stage Soviet AA guns joined the battle, fighting off German tanks which threatened to break into the depth of the Soviet positions. The next day 9th *SS Panzer* Division joined the battle, bringing more than 600 German tanks and SP guns into action south of lake Velencze and steadily widening the breach in the Soviet defences, pierced now to a depth of some fifteen miles.

Tolbukhin, faced with a situation growing more serious as his reserves began to dwindle, moved Trofimenko's 27th Army—reinforced with the three armoured formations (23rd Tank Corps, 18th Tank Corps and 1st Guards Mechanized Corps)—into the first echelon to close the gap in the Soviet defences. Meanwhile the *Stavka* ordered 9th Guards Army to deploy south-west of Budapest, bringing it under Tolbukhin's command. Tolbukhin at once asked permission of the *Stavka* to bring 9th Guards into the defensive battle but this was peremptorily refused— 9th Guards was not to be drawn into the defensive fighting and would be held back for the offensive operations. That signal went out on 9 March and four days of heavy fighting still faced Tolbukhin. The *Stavka* took the view that the German counter-offensive was beginning to lose its impetus and Tolbukhin could hold with his existing forces, leaving 9th Guards intact, fresh and fully reinforced.

German armour battered away at Trofimenko's right flank, where on 14 March Wöhler threw in his last reserve formation, built out of 6th *SS Panzer* Division and fielding 200 tanks and SP guns, in one final desperate push to the Danube. General Goryachev's 35th Guards Rifle Corps on Trofimenko's right flank, supported by 23rd Tank Corps and two SP-gun brigades from *Stavka* reserve, fought fiercely to hold the German tanks from the rear defence line, halting them just short of it; on the left flank 30th Rifle Corps and 18th Tank Corps kept the SS back even though outflanked to the east. Gagen's 26th Army and 5th Cavalry Corps were also fighting to keep the rear defence line intact.

No great success attended the other supporting German attacks. Sharokin's 57th Army, using its guns to great effect, smashed up Second *Panzer* Army attacking from east of Nagykanizsa in an effort to draw Soviet forces from the main axis of the German assault. Army Group E struck out at the 1st Bulgarian Army and 3rd Yugoslav Army on the night of 6 March, using three divisions in the region of Donji–Miholjac and driving to the north. Once across the Drava, German divisions moved on to break into the rear of the Soviet 47th Army and 1st Bulgarian Army. Sharokin decided to use General Artyushenko's 133rd Rifle Corps to eliminate the German threat to the junction between the Bulgarians and Yugoslavs. Maj.-Gen. A.E. Breido, artillery commander of 57th Army, worked the *Shtorm* artillery plan to manoeuvre his sixteen artillery units—with 150 guns and mortars—to break up German attacks. Worn down after days of fighting, the German divisions fell back to the southern bank of the Drava.

The main German assault lumbered to a final halt on 15 March, the tanks badly shot up or marooned in the muddy wash of the low-lying ground of central Hungary. Starved of fuel, the heaviest battle tanks lay immobile and presented easy targets to Soviet ground-attack planes. Over 500 tanks and assault guns, 300 guns and 40,000 men had been pounded to pieces in this last abortive offensive, all to no avail. Sepp Dietrich pulled his surviving tanks away from the Danube as fast as possible, using the pretext of protecting Vienna. Now the Russians were on the move with a thundering charge of tanks, unleashed in the wake of the defeat of the German attack and overwhelming the remnants of

Sixth *Panzer* Army in a pell-mell engagement where the few German Panthers fired into the massed ranks of Soviet heavy tanks in a fruitless attempt to hold this armoured rush.

The loss of the Hron bridgehead and the German offensive in the Balaton area caused the *Stavka* to reconsider its original plan for offensive operations designed to capture Vienna. The main axis of the forthcoming Soviet offensive was now shifted from north of the Danube to the south, into Tolbukhin's command: 3rd Ukrainian Front would now mount the main attack. In holding back 9th Guards from the defensive battle, the *Stavka* also issued attack orders to Tolbukhin: once the German assault force had been worn down, 3rd Ukrainian Front would take the offensive not later than 15–16 March, using right-flank armies to destroy the enemy north of lake Balaton and then to drive on in the direction of Papa and Sopron. This shifted the main axis of advance to the north-west rather than the westerly advance prescribed in the directive of 17 February. Malinovskii's 2nd Ukrainian Front would move its right flank on to the Hron and use left-flank armies south of the Danube to attack no later than 17–18 March in the direction of Györ.

While Tolbukhin held off the German counter-offensive, Malinovskii fought his way to the river Hron using 53rd and 40th Armies and his two Rumanian armies, the 1st and 4th. Zvolen in Slovakia also fell to Soviet troops, operating in the difficult mountainous country. Malinovskii's front was spreadeagled between Czechoslovakia and Hungary; south of the Danube Malinovskii planned to use Kravchenko's 6th Guards Tank Army, Petrushevskii's 46th Army and 2nd Guards Mechanized Corps in a drive on Györ, but on 16 March 6th Guards Tank Army with 406 tanks and SP guns was handed over to Tolbukhin. The reasons for this transfer were compelling: though 4th and 9th Guards Armies were to carry the main attack on 3rd Ukrainian Front, they could only muster some 200 tanks between them and they would inevitably run into German *Panzer* units equipped with 270 tanks and SP guns. Kravchenko received orders to concentrate his tanks in the area of 9th Guards Army, to the west of Budapest. The Soviet 6th Guards Tank Army would thus grapple with Sixth *SS Panzer*, smashing the German tank force once and for all.

Malinovskii's Front committed only one reinforced army to operations on Hungarian soil: out of thirty-six divisions (Soviet and Rumanian alike), he deployed only twelve for offensive operations connected with the drive on Vienna. Tolbukhin decided to use two infantry armies on his right flank (9th and 4th Guards), drive into the flank and rear of the German armour, cut its escape route to the west and destroy these remnants with 27th and 26th Armies, thereby opening up a route for a speedy advance to the frontiers of Hungary. Glagolev's 9th Guards Army was to isolate and destroy the enemy north of lake Balaton, assigned to cover twenty-five miles in five days; although fully manned (with divisions swelled to 11,000 men and more, plus a heavier complement of guns), 9th Guards had not been blooded, lacked infantry support tanks and possessed only small-calibre SP guns, in spite of having to tackle German armoured units. Zakhvateyev's 4th Guards received orders to break the German lines north of lake Velencze, outflanking Szekesfehervar to the north and south, and drive to the south-west. The two remaining Soviet armies, 27th and 57th (with 1st Bulgarian Army), would wait on the success of 9th and 4th Guards before moving off themselves.

On 16 March Tolbukhin's troops began that gigantic heave which quickly toppled the entire German southern flank. Two armies, 9th and 4th Guards, jumped off in the attack and steadily widened a gap for Soviet armour, while Malinovskii launched 46th Army on the following day in his own Front offensive. Heavy fighting centred on Szekesfehervar, which the German command determined to hold at all costs. On the morning of 19 March, Kravchenko's tank army went into action, and both Malinovskii and Tolbukhin raced to encircle the German *Panzer* army, Malinovskii attacking from the north and Tolbukhin bringing three armies to bear against Szekesfehervar. By the evening of 22 March the bulk of Sixth *Panzer* faced the threat of complete encirclement south of Szekesfehervar, with only a narrow corridor less than a mile wide and already swept by guns and machine-gun fire providing a hazardous route to safety. Four *Panzer* divisions and a German infantry division fought fiercely to keep this lifeline open, throwing in tanks to keep the Soviet 'pincers' apart, straining, sweating, infantry fighting agonized actions to keep contact with islands of German soldiers sinking beneath this sea of Soviet attacks. Home was not so far away, but thousands of German soldiers died in this Hungarian *débâcle* as Tolbukhin rolled on relentlessly. Szekesfehervar fell on 23 March, the Bakony Hills came under Soviet attack and the flimsy defence lines at Vesprzem collapsed under increasing Soviet pressure. But Sixth *Panzer* had escaped encirclement. Shortage of ammunition to pound the German defenders into dazed insensibility, lack of infantry support tanks, the slow progress of the main assault group and the absence of overwhelming superiority in armour all contributed to the failure; Kravchenko's 6th Guards Tank Army should also have been brought to battle much more rapidly.

The pursuit, however, quickly became a rout. The much-vaunted SS took to their heels and now the Soviet tanks ground on, smashing down the German defences and turning to the road junction at Papa. German forces west of lake Balaton milled about in total confusion. Malinovskii battered the German positions north of the Danube, taking Komarno, so that by 23 March the German defences were on the point of collapse; Esztergom was surrounded and stormed, the Vertesz Hills pierced and Totis captured. By 25 March Malinovskii's troops had pushed more than twenty miles into the German positions and ripped a sixty-mile gap in the defences. Having cleared the valley of the Hron, Malinovskii prepared to strike in the direction of Bratislava, following fleeing German troops.

Tolbukhin's successes north of lake Balaton also gave 57th Army its chance, operating on the left flank of the 3rd Ukrainian Front. Pitted against Second *Panzer* Army, a staunch enemy which gave ground only slowly, Sharokhin closed on the oilfields at Nagykanizsa and encircled them completely towards the end of March. To the west, the main body of 3rd Ukrainian Front swept on, taking Papa and then driving to the north-west towards the river Raab and the Austrian frontier: on 28 March Soviet troops forced the Raab on a broad front, brushing aside the attempts of Sixth *Panzer* and Sixth Army to hold the river line. The last town of importance in Hungary—Sopron—fell on 1 April, Soviet lead units were already across the Austrian frontier near Keszeg and the Red Army was poised to strike on Vienna from two directions. German resistance in Hungary was at an end, leaving in its wake a great litter of shattered tanks and doomed men. Faced with a hopeless situation, Hungarian troops and even some German units abandoned a wholly unequal struggle and began to surrender in large numbers, with 40–45,000 men giving themselves up to Tolbukhin's units towards the end of the month.

On 1 April the *Stavka* issued revised battle orders for the speedy capture of Vienna. The city was to be encircled from the east and attacked from the west and south-west in a joint operation mounted by 2nd and 3rd Ukrainian Fronts.

Though a mere thirty-five miles from Berlin early in February, Zhukov's armies closing on the Oder learned quickly enough that they were not about to launch a high-speed attack on the German capital, taking the city off the march with a couple of rifle armies and two tank armies. German resistance stiffened everywhere, even if the days of fielding mighty armies had passed. Scratch units, stragglers, impressed deserters, the ageing and enfeebled *Volkssturm* enrolled as an embattled Home Guard, merciless *SS* holding detachments, regular *Wehrmacht* formations and the remnants of the *Luftwaffe*—all fought bitter battles in desperate attempts to hold off the Bolshevik hordes whose fearsome reputation went before them. The ferocity of the fighting took inevitable toll of the Red Army, which now all too frequently hurled men with fatalistic recklessness and in a veritable passion of destructiveness against German redoubts. German defenders hung on grimly to their Oder fortresses of Küstrin, Glogau, Breslau and Ratibor; in the rear of the advancing Soviet armies, garrisons at Elbing, Poznan, Deutsche-Krone and Schneidemühl continued their resistance, tying down much artillery and many Soviet battalions. Losses bit deep on both sides. Rokossovskii's 2nd Belorussian Front, which had carved its way through East Prussia, fielded scarecrow divisions ground down to 3–4,000 men supported by 297 patched-up tanks. Mud, rain, sleet and snow slowed the movement of Soviet supplies and reinforcement, with traffic further hampered by the need to shift from the broad Russian railway gauge to narrower European tracks.

The *Stavka* meanwhile stared long and hard at the hundred-mile gap opening up between Zhukov's right flank and Rokossovskii's 2nd Belorussian Front, concentrating its gaze on East Pomerania which hung menacingly over 1st Belorussian Front. To the rear lay two considerable bodies of German troops surrounded in East Prussia and Courland, their land links with the *Reich* cut. Seen from Moscow, Zhukov's open flank was no simple 'visual' phenomenon derived from General Staff maps but a dangerous gap filling at an alarming rate with German divisions, thirty-three of which were piling up in Pomerania and only thirteen diverted to the 'Berlin axis' itself. The buffeting which Soviet divisions suffered early in February was real enough—the air attacks came from the fighters Hitler ordered eastwards (and at Hitler's insistence German fighters had in most cases been designed to carry a bombload). AA guns were rushed to the Oder to provide some anti-tank defence, though this meant stripping German cities of protection as Anglo–American bombing raids increased in intensity, striking harder at Germany's rail communications. Fierce though that onslaught was, Hitler derived some phantasmagorial comfort from such a shift in targets when *Luftwaffe* intelligence presented him with the intercept of an American directive issued late in January, prescribing these air attacks apparently to assist the Soviet advance but in reality aimed at slowing it down. Himmler, whose jellied military nerve gave way so often, also began to speak of a miracle, as the impetus of the Soviet attack on the Oder began to die away. The highway of ice, too, would soon be gone.

Guderian pressed repeatedly for a major and timely German counter-stroke from the Glogau–Kottbus area and from Pomerania across the Oder to strike at the weakened Soviet lead armies. Hitler showed himself remarkably reluctant to consider this plan and persisted with the transfer of Sixth *SS Panzer* Army to Hungary, thus not only removing it from a decisive axis but also rendering it useless until its extensive movement was done. Guderian pleaded for the evacuation of German troops from Courland, locked up to no purpose, together with the transfer of German forces from Italy, Norway and the Balkans, all to build up effective counter-attack forces. Hitler rejected these proposals out of hand and in a wild meeting full of tempestuous tantrum—with Himmler's dismal military competence dredged up in front of him—the *Führer* clung to his refusal to move one man or a single gun from Courland and reduced Guderian's plans to a limited attack from the Stargard area to strike at the Soviet forces north of the Warthe and thus hold Pomerania in German hands. To the accompaniment of more frantic screaming Hitler gave his permission for this counter-stroke to be launched in a few days and for General Wenck, Guderian's own deputy, to be attached to Himmler's HQ as a guarantee of sensible military leadership.

Guderian was right to press for an immediate German counter-attack. Time had almost run out. On 10 February, the day on which Hitler held his hysterical meeting with Guderian and Himmler, two Soviet fronts—2nd and 3rd Belorussian—launched fresh attacks conforming to the revised operational orders issued by the *Stavka* on 8 February. Rokossovskii's 2nd Belorussian Front received orders to destroy German forces in East Pomerania, launching an offensive with left-flank and centre formations to reach a line running from the mouth of the Vistula to Dirchau–Rummelsburg–Neustettin by 20 February, thereafter using 19th Army to drive straight on Stettin, and with right-flank formations to capture Danzig and Gdynia, as well as clearing the Baltic coast from Frisches Haff in the east to the Pomeranian bight in the west. On 9 February the *Stavka* instructed 3rd Belorussian Front to speed up and accomplish the destruction of the Fourth German Army in East Prussia not later than 20–25 February, thus eliminating the 'Heilsberg group' south of Königsberg.

The very heavy fighting in East Prussia and the battles to reduce German strongholds wrought a certain havoc with Soviet timetables. At the beginning of February the *Stavka* decided to turn the Soviet Baltic Fronts to the defensive; with Stalin and Antonov on their way to the Yalta conference, Marshal Vasilevskii resumed his duties as Chief of the General Staff and Deputy Defence Commissar, handing over the co-ordination of the Baltic Front operations to L.A. Govorov, commander of the Leningrad Front. The *Stavka* also set in motion an intensive military shunting operation, regrouping 2nd and 3rd Belorussian Fronts together with the Baltic Fronts. On 6 February on *Stavka* instructions, 2nd Baltic Front took over the forces operating with 1st Baltic, whose command received three armies (43rd, 39th and 11th Guards) from 3rd Belorussian Front. To compensate, Chernyakhovskii at 3rd Belorussian Front acquired three armies (including 5th Guards Tank Army) and one tank corps (the 8th) from Rokossovskii. The intention behind this extensive reshuffle of armies and commands was to free Rokossovskii entirely for operations in East Pomerania, while Chernyakhovskii's 3rd Belorussian Front and Bagramyan's 1st Baltic Front went about clearing East Prussia, Chernyakhovskii destroying the German Fourth Army south of Frisches Haff and Bagramyan reducing Königsberg itself and German troops in Samland. Simultaneously, 3rd Air Army received orders to move up to Insterburg. Marshal Vasilevskii himself, having received Stalin's authorization by telephone from Yalta, informed Rokossovskii on 8 February about his new operational assignment. In this complicated fashion the *Stavka* set about wrenching these several Soviet fronts back to their main axes of advance and thus eliminating growing deviations from the original master plan.

Vasilevskii's instructions placed Rokossovskii in an unenviable position: his operational responsibilities were reduced, with Chernyakhovskii taking over operations in East Prussia, but half of his fighting strength went to Chernyakhovskii. Now, without halt or pause, he faced a new offensive operation, with forty-five rifle divisions of 2nd Belorussian Front facing thirteen German infantry divisions, two *Panzer* divisions and the several battle groups of the German Second Army. Rokossovskii at once requested reinforcement, receiving the promise of 19th Army (presently deployed near Torun) and one tank corps. Meanwhile Zhukov at 1st Belorussian Front proposed to continue with his preparations for the main attack on Berlin, leaving only light forces facing East Pomerania; by 12–13 February the beleaguered German garrisons at Schneidemühl, Deutsche Krone and Arnswalde should have been eliminated, right-flank formations on 1st Belorussian Front would move to the Stargard–Falkenburg line and then leave defensive forces in position while Front regrouping continued.

Attacking simultaneously on 10 February, neither Rokossovskii nor Chernyakhovskii achieved any substantial result. Rokossovskii's left-flank 70th Army made some progress, but on his right encircled German garrisons still snagged Soviet armies, or else, like 2nd Shock Army, they were on the move to new positions, struggling at the same time with the ice-laden Vistula. In five days Batov's 65th Army and the 49th Army covered only ten miles at the centre of 2nd Belorussian Front, grappling with fierce German resistance and struggling with the mud and flooded ground. Further to the east Chernyakhovskii with sixty-three divisions (four rifle armies reinforced by three transferred from Rokossovskii and one tank army, 5th Guards) planned concentric attacks to reduce the 'Heilsberg group', ordering Volskii's tank army to isolate German forces from Frisches Haff and prevent any attempted evacuation in the direction of Frische-Nehring. Two air armies—1st and 3rd—supported by naval aircraft from the Baltic Fleet pounded away at the German defences, but stubborn resistance from well-prepared defences slowed the Soviet advance to a painful and bloody crawl covering less than a mile a day. Bagramyan also hammered in vain and at much cost at the approaches to Königsberg.

The situation was beginning to deteriorate sharply. On his right flank Zhukov now faced stronger German attacks merging into a powerful counterstroke launched by Third *Panzer* Army on 15 February, an attack supervised by Guderian's own man, Wenck. German troops succeeded in piercing the Soviet blockade of Arnswalde, releasing the German garrison and then slicing into Bogdanov's 2nd Tank Army to the south, recapturing Pyritz. However, Zhukov considered that his right-flank armies were strong enough to hold off this German thrust and also to help Rokossovskii's attack. Fate came unexpectedly to Zhukov's aid when Wenck, driving back from the *Führer's* evening briefing on 17 February took the wheel of his staff car from a tired driver and then crashed into a bridge parapet; with Wenck incapacitated, the German attack sputtered out. Rokossovskii, for his part, had already talked to Vasilevskii on 15 February about modifying his attack plans, proposing that the scale of the offensive be reduced and replacing frontal attack with a manoeuvre to squeeze the German Second Army to the sea. Two days later Zhukov added his own views, suggesting that his right-flank armies mount their own attack on 19 February in the direction of Stettin, with 2nd Guards Tank Army, 61st Army and 7th Guards Cavalry Corps carrying through this stroke, supported by 3rd Shock Army and the 1st Polish Army.

The following day, 18 February, Stalin consulted Vasilevskii about the situation in East Prussia, suggesting that Vasilevskii proceed to the front to lend his assistance to 1st Belorussian and 1st Baltic Front commanders. Stalin explained that these forces would be needed to reinforce the main strike force for the attack on Berlin, but, equally important, he wanted to know what forces could be released for transfer to the Far East. Vasilevskii learned that Stalin wanted two or three of the best armies pinpointed for the move to the Far East—where, Stalin continued, Vasilevskii himself would most likely be going to direct operations, roughly two or three months after the German surrender. Vasilevskii then asked to be relieved of his post as Chief of the General Staff, which Antonov presently discharged in all but formal rank. Stalin approved, leaving Vasilevskii his official post as Deputy Defence Commissar and signed the *Stavka* directive covering the 'co-ordination' of 1st Belorussian and 1st Baltic Fronts. Within hours Vasilevskii received an urgent summons to report to Stalin once again. The youngest Front commander in the Red Army, General Chernyakhovskii, had just died of wounds at Mehlsack in East Prussia. Stalin signed the *Stavka* order appointing Vasilevskii Front commander to replace this brilliant young general; on the evening of 19 February Stalin gave Vasilevskii his orders, some advice and his best wishes. Poskrebyshev gave Vasilevskii another document, containing a revised version of the GKO decree of 10 July 1941 appointing members of the *Stavka*. Vasilevskii had never been an official member of the *Stavka* but this revision of the decree duly nominated him; Zhukov alone of Front commanders served on the *Stavka* and Vasilevskii asked Poskrebyshev just what this new move meant. All he got by way of reply was a smile and the remark that Vasilevskii knew as much as anyone else.

As Vasilevskii took over his operational command, Zhukov tried to launch his right-flank attack. Two Soviet corps began to encircle Arnswalde once again and the 311th Rifle Division fought hand-to-hand actions in the town itself, but if German troops here were falling back to the north-east and the north-west, Bogdanov's 2nd Guards Tank Army could not turn to the attack since this formation was still fighting off German assaults. Zhukov pulled all these units over to the defensive. The *Stavka*, however, had other ideas. Between 17 and 22 February fresh orders went out to both Rokossovskii and Zhukov, prescribing a joint attack on East Pomerania with the flanks of 1st and 2nd Belorussian Front locked. The new offensive was aimed in the general direction of Kolberg, striking from the south towards the north and bringing both fronts to the Baltic coast, first slicing the German forces in two and isolating them from the main body of German troops. Once on the Baltic, Rokossovskii would turn east and seize both Danzig and Gdynia; Zhukov's right-flank armies were charged with developing a high-speed offensive in the direction of Kolberg, breaking out to the Baltic and clearing the western region of Pomerania, as well as investing the western bank of the Oder. *Stavka* orders fixed 24 February as the date for Rokossovskii's offensive and 1 March as the latest date for Zhukov to open his attack, though he should move off when 19th Army on 2nd Belorussian Front reached the Baldenburg–Neustettin line. Vasilevskii with 3rd Belorussian Front was instructed to move his left flank towards the gulf of Danzig to the east of the Vistula and block an enemy escape from Frische Nehring; this gave Rokossovskii the chance to use Fedyuninskii's 2nd Shock Army in his main assault force, rather than holding it back.

On the morning of 24 February, after a thirty-minute artillery barrage, Rokossovskii launched his new offensive, designed to exploit manoeuvre—his true *métier*. In two days 2nd Belorussian Front ripped a 35-mile gap in the German defences and penetrated to a depth of thirty miles. The infantry needed tank support and Rokossovskii decided to commit 3rd Tank Corps ahead of schedule. Unfortunately 19th Army lagged behind, failing to take advantage of the situation created by the advancing armour. With Stalin's permission, Rokossovskii removed the commander, G.A. Kozlov, and replaced him with V.Z. Romanovskii. This, however, was the least of Rokossovskii's worries: his left-flank formations were advancing slowly, moving across marshy ground towards the coast, but the Front lacked any reserves to supplement this thrust. This nervousness at the lack of any Front reserve increased as Rokossovskii watched his left flank being uncovered since Zhukov had not budged. On being told of this situation Stalin asked Rokossovskii if Zhukov was 'up to something'? Rokossovskii denied this but stressed the danger to his left flank, whereupon Stalin promised to jog Zhukov's elbow. Meanwhile Rokossovskii would have to take Neustettin on his own.

Zhukov attacked on the morning of 1 March, launching 3rd Shock Army and 1st Polish Army under cover of a fifty-minute artillery barrage supported by ground-attack aircraft. To the complete astonishment of the German General Staff, Zhukov's tanks swung northwards instead of streaking towards Berlin as they had expected. Katukhov's 1st Guards Tank Army smashed into the German defences, forcing troops and refugees to flee northwards in helpless, vulnerable columns. 2nd Guards Tank Army with 61st Army had meanwhile to fight its way through Stargard, but Katukhov pressed on to the north, reaching Kolberg on 4–5 March accompanied by units of 3rd Shock Army and 1st Polish Army. On 5 March, 61st Army finally broke into Stargard and uncovered German defences screening Stettin, but 47th Army was fighting hard to cover the ground towards Altdamm.

Zhukov and Rokossovskii swept on to the Baltic coast, closing on Danzig and Gdynia. Refugees crowded on to the roads, trying to escape to the west and east, facing the trials of the spring flooding and the terror of Soviet tank columns on the move. German ships moved party officials and some wounded from Danzig; to cope with the German warships lying off the gulf of Danzig, the Soviet command rushed up heavy guns to counter this sea-borne fire support for the German defences, while Soviet aircraft attacked both the ground troops and the German navy.

On 8 March the *Stavka* assigned Katukhov's 1st Guards Tank Army to Rokossovskii's Front command, a move which prompted Zhukov to telephone Rokossovskii and inform him that he wanted the tank army 'returned in the same state as you received it'. Rokossovskii duly promised, tongue in cheek. The Soviet plan now envisaged splitting the Danzig–Gdynia fortified area in two, separating Danzig from Gdynia. Rokossovskii was also encouraged by the fact that the frontage of his divisions shrank considerably, adding power to their attack as losses made themselves felt. The first attack was aimed at Sopot, a seaside resort. Soviet troops broke into the suburb of Oliwa late in March. On 25 March, having reached the Gulf of Danzig, Rokossovskii reported that the German defenders had been split into three pockets, one at Danzig, another at Gdynia and a third at the Putziger–Nehring spit.

Katukhov's tanks, with 19th Army, struck along the coast towards Gdynia. Fedyuninskii's 2nd Shock Army moved towards the southern suburb of Danzig. The attack on Danzig was easier from the north, but Gdynia fell first, stormed on 26 March. Some days were needed to clear the port of remnants, by which time the assault on Danzig began, preceded by a rejection of the Soviet offer of surrender. Attacked from three sides on 26 March, the garrison fought from building to building, calling once more on German warships for fire support. After a few days it was all over; the survivors fled to the mouth of the Vistula and on 30 March Danzig was cleared of German troops. True to his promise, Rokossovskii had already handed back 1st Guards Tank Army, not much the worse for wear.

Far to the rear on Zhukov's 1st Belorussian Front, German fortresses and strong-points fell one by one. Chuikov with 8th Guards Army fixed 20 February as the final date for the storming of the citadel in Poznan. That morning, at 9 o'clock, the Soviet assault began, followed by two days of hand-to-hand fighting. The storm operation recalled the breaking of a medieval siege, filling the moat with fascines and mining the outer wall, though a modern touch was supplied by tanks and SP guns making their way through the breach in the walls. The German command rejected Chuikov's radio appeal to surrender, but late at night on 22 February General Bakanov with 74th Rifle Division reported that German emissaries were moving out to parley. Thirty minutes later the German garrison surrendered, their commander having committed suicide; the defeated troops marched out in good order, a marked contrast to what Chuikov had seen at Stalingrad when pathetic crippled columns of starving men dragged themselves away to captivity. The fall of Poznan unlocked the floodgates of Soviet supplies, sending men and ammunition racing to the Oder bridgeheads.

Chuikov's 8th Guards now closed on the Oder, all formations—nine divisions, with combat support—up to strength, deployed between Frankfurt and Küstrin. The preliminary operations closed the gap between 8th Guards and 5th Shock Armies, isolating the German garrison in Küstrin. Berzarin with 5th Shock and Chuikov with 8th Guards planned to close on this famous fortress town from the south and north. Already the old forts covered by streams and marshes had fallen, but a hand-picked German garrison still held the town. Berzarin and Chuikov duly linked up, and the assault on the town began on 22 March. The irony was that Küstrin had already 'fallen', at least in Front reports, early in February; Chuikov sarcastically told the Front chief of staff that since 5th Shock had already captured Küstrin, a feat proclaimed by an artillery salute in Moscow, why bother to do the job again? Marshal Zhukov interrupted the conversation to say that things go wrong in war and they must be put right.

Chuikov's men fought their way along narrow roads and the tops of dykes to crack German resistance. Soviet guns pounded the fortifications, aiming to drive the defenders out of the fixed defences and into the earthworks where Soviet aircraft waited to attack them. On the morning of 29 March the final assault began, as the guns now shifted to the field works and assault troops landed on the island formed by the Oder and the Warta. Soviet infantrymen stormed the fortress itself, racing to the fortress wall and breaking into the fortress yard. By noon the fiercest of the fighting was over and resistance ended, the dead lying strewn throughout the fortress and prisoners being collected. Chuikov reported the news to Marshal Zhukov in Moscow. This was Zhukov's second visit to Moscow during the month of March; during the first week in March Stalin summoned him for a meeting during the course of the East Pomeranian operation. Stalin was tired, dispirited and far from well. During the course of a long talk Zhukov finally asked him about the fate of his son, Yakob, who had been captured in 1941; Stalin remained silent for a long while and then remarked that the Germans were bound to shoot him, for he would never betray his country. Zhukov also learned some details of the Yalta conference, laying much stress on the importance of having a Poland friendly to the Soviet Union. After giving Zhukov some information about the administration of Germany after the capitulation, Stalin instructed him to discuss the attack on Berlin with Antonov.

Further south Zhukov's arch-rival Marshal Koniev, also poised along the 'Berlin axis', renewed his offensive in order to occupy western Silesia and to close on the Neisse in Brandenburg, thus bringing him fully abreast of the 1st Belorussian Front. On his two bridgeheads north and south of Breslau, Koniev concentrated three rifle armies and two tank armies (to the north) and two rifle armies supported by two tank corps to the south; a third assault group with two rifle armies and a cavalry corps deployed along the left flank, south-west of Oppeln. Like other Soviet fronts, Koniev faced serious supply problems, lack of reinforcements and battle-weary troops; shortage of ammunition and bad weather added to the Front commander's difficulties. To maintain as much 'shock power' as possible, Koniev ordered his two tank armies to concentrate closely behind the rifle armies and break through enemy defences in a single echelon.

At 6 am on 8 February Koniev's guns opened fire, laying down a fifty-minute barrage and signalling the attack from the Steinau bridgehead north of Breslau. After three days the Soviet breakthrough reached a depth of forty miles across a front of more than ninety, encircling the German garrison at Glogau and, after forcing the Bobr, approached the river Neisse. Though Gordov's 3rd Army had trapped the German garrison in Glogau, Koniev became increasingly concerned about German resistance at the centre, at Breslau, which blocked the advance of Zhadov's 5th Guards and 21st Armies. Gluzdovskii's 6th Army was also stuck and the left-flank armies of the Front had failed to manage a breakthrough. German counter-attacks flailed away at 6th Army in an attempt to fend off the danger to Breslau, but on 15 February Zhadov's 5th Guards linked up with 6th Army to the west of Breslau, sealing the encirclement and shutting up 40,000 German troops. To make assurance doubly sure Koniev routed Rybalko's 3rd Guards Tank Army towards Breslau, putting in armour to secure the infantry encirclement.

Facing the formidable Soviet ring of steel to the west, the refugees piling out of Breslau hastily turned back and sought safety in the city. Two German infantry divisions received orders to break out, leaving only one—the 609th—to hold the fortress, a puny garrison supplemented by an assortment of SS units, *Luftwaffe* personnel and *Volkssturm* battalions. Elsewhere the population fled headlong before the Soviet advance, denuding Silesia of its population. (Somewhat later the Soviet *kommandatura* registered only 620,000 Germans remaining out of what had been almost five million a year before.) Koniev's immediate gains, however, consisted of the advance to the Neisse and the encirclement of both Glogau and Breslau, all by 15 February. More he could not do, as he pointedly emphasized in his Front report of 16 February. The *Stavka* approved his plan to drive for the Neisse but Stalin throughout the Yalta conference prodded him about his southern flank—the German command had every intention of retaking the Silesian industrial basin and would strike in the direction of Ratibor. 'You had better look out', Stalin advised Koniev, and asked for details of his operational plan to cope with the situation.

On 15 March Koniev struck again, this time with his left-flank armies in an operation designed to seize Upper Silesia as far as the Czechoslovak frontier. Koniev planned to use two assault forces to encircle German forces in the Oppeln bulge and in Oppeln itself: one force (with 21st Army and 4th Tank Army, plus two corps) would attack from the area of Grottkau in a south-westerly direction, while the other with two armies (59th and 60th) supported by one tank and one mechanized corps received orders to attack from the north of Ratibor in a westerly direction. At least Koniev did not have to face Sixth SS *Panzer* Army—expected hourly, only to materialize in Hungary.

Aiming concentric blows at Neustadt, Koniev first encircled the Oppeln group, with two armies linking up in the Neustadt area. The *Hermann Göring Panzer* Division tried to break into the encirclement but was beaten off by Belov's 10th Guards Tank Corps. The following day, 20 March, a German army corps, two *Panzer* and one infantry division tried again to break the Soviet ring, only to be engaged by three Soviet corps. Inside the ring 30,000 German officers and men fell to the Soviet onslaught, with 15,000 finally taken prisoner. Kurochkin with 60th Army now received orders to take Ratibor, for which task he was given four tank and mechanized corps together with two artillery 'breakthrough divisions'. To speed the blow Koniev sent two more tank corps from 4th Guards Tank

Army in the wake of 60th Army with orders to attack from the north; but speed itself failed to materialize as Soviet troops battered their way through villages, across road junctions and over hill after hill. Suddenly, away to Koniev's left on the 4th Ukrainian Front, Moskalenko's 38th Army resumed its own offensive and faced the German forces with the spectre of yet another encirclement in the area of Rybnik and Ratibor. Kurochkin seized the chance to storm both cities, taking Rybnik off the march and putting one corps across the Oder to the south of Ratibor. For an hour heavy guns bombarded Ratibor, after which two rifle corps of 60th Army and 4th Guards Tank Army launched their assault on 30 March, clearing the Germans from the city. Upper Silesia had fallen to the Red Army, there could be no German recovery and Breslau was completely sealed off.

In less than a month the euphoria generated by the Yalta conference had all but vanished. The Moscow Commission, set up to implement the conference decisions on Poland, met for the first time on 23 February and immediately set off a fresh and bitter wrangle with the Russians. In spite of the representations of Ambassadors Harriman and Sir Archibald Clark Kerr, urging that three Poles should be invited from outside Poland, Molotov in a stinging rebuff charged that the Yalta agreement stipulated consultation only with the 'Warsaw Poles' in the first place, without intruders. On the vexed question of British and American observers in Poland, Molotov agreed four days later to such a move, a step welcomed by the British government provided that it did not imply recognition of the 'Warsaw Poles'. At this Molotov suggested a postponement of discussions but was visibly taken aback when the two ambassadors agreed with the dispatch of observers—whereupon the Soviet government abruptly withdrew this facility on 1 March. As the impasse deepened the Prime Minister prepared a special message for Stalin but was persuaded to wait on the results of one more attempt to cajole Molotov into accepting the Anglo–American interpretation of the Yalta agreement. On 19 March the British and American ambassadors presented separate but identical notes setting out the Anglo–American position, but Molotov on 23 March rejected them outright, with a show of high dudgeon at the 'insult' to the Poles if outsiders were brought in, and repeated with iron insistence that the 'Warsaw Poles' had a right to prior consultation.

This embitterment on both sides lurched suddenly to the edge of estrangement over the Soviet attitude to Anglo–American contacts with the German command, a highly secret undertaking engineered by Allen Dulles in Berne and involving the possible surrender of German forces in Italy. The hidden German hand behind this belonged to none other than Himmler himself, who used Karl Wolff (head of the SS in Italy) to pursue these probes. Field-Marshal Alexander warily obtained the authorization of the Joint Chiefs of Staff in Washington to send two senior officers to Switzerland to hear Wolff out, but they advised the Field-Marshal that the Russians must be informed. The British Chiefs of Staff urged not only notification to the Soviet government but also an invitation for Soviet officers to participate in the talks. By way of compromise the British and American ambassadors broke the news of the proposed talks to Molotov on 12 March; Molotov raised no objection but proposed the attendance of three Soviet senior officers. General Deane, the head of the American Military Mission in Moscow, strenuously opposed the idea of Soviet officers joining this enterprise, whereupon Molotov was told that the object of the talks was to facilitate the passage of a German plenipotentiary to Caserta, Field-Marshal Alexander's HQ—and here Soviet officers would be most welcome.

Molotov lashed out at once. In demanding that the talks in Switzerland be broken off at once, he went on to state brusquely that the Soviet government found it 'inexplicable and incomprehensible' that no place had been found for a Soviet military representative in these first exchanges, a view also pressed on the American ambassador. On 21 March Sir Archibald Clark Kerr informed the Soviet government that no negotiations as such had taken place, only to trigger off a furious Soviet reaction in a written note of 22 March which charged that negotiations had certainly taken place 'behind the back of the Soviet Union', the nation bearing the whole brunt of the war: here was no mere 'misunderstanding' and must be construed as 'something worse', an insinuation that this was nothing short of an attempt to conclude a separate peace with Nazi Germany, excluding the Soviet Union. The Prime Minister advised Eden that no reply need be forthcoming to this brutally insulting note, though a copy should go to the State Department in view of American insistence that no Soviet officers attend the first talks; meanwhile 'let Molotov and his master wait'.

Molotov's master, however, was not prepared to wait and his displeasure involved Molotov at once. In an abrupt withdrawal of co-operation Stalin removed Molotov from the Soviet delegation due to attend the San Francisco conference and substituted Gromyko, a decision which prompted the President in his message of 25 March to ask that Molotov be allowed to attend at least 'for the vital opening sessions'. On the same day the President tried to stifle a growing storm with Stalin, but intimated that he could not call off the contacts designed to seek a German surrender in Italy on the grounds of Molotov's objections, which were 'for some reason completely beyond my comprehension'. This tone was reasonable and the reproof mild enough, but Stalin refused to give ground. He reported on 27 March that due to vital duties and the 'imperative' need for his services at the coming session of the Supreme Soviet, Molotov would not attend the San Francisco conference. Let the world think what it might.

The turbulence of these tripartite relations became even more agitated with the onset of a major Anglo–American argument, brought to sudden life when General Eisenhower addressed a telegram directly to Stalin on 28 March, a signal which ruled out any direct Anglo–American advance on Berlin. The Supreme Commander intimated that after the destruction of German forces in the Ruhr encirclement, the main Allied thrust would be in the direction of Erfurt–Leipzig–Dresden, thus splitting the German defence in two once a junction with the Red Army had been effected; a supporting attack aimed at the Regensburg–Linz area would deal with the suspected 'National Redoubt' envisaged by Hitler as a final centre of resistance. General Eisenhower now waited on information about Soviet plans so that the operations of the armies advancing from west and east could be co-ordinated.

If this signal caused consternation in London, it brought Stalin substantial satisfaction. After pondering the telegram and its contents, he told General Deane that it met with his approval. Stalin asked about the starting point of the supporting attack and was told that it would also come from the Western Front rather than from Italy. To Ambassador Harriman's query about the delay imposed on Soviet offensive operations until the end of March, Stalin responded by saying that things had improved remarkably, with early spring flooding and the roads already drying out. Though he must perforce consult with his staff, Stalin promised an early reply to General Eisenhower. That reply, duly sent on 1 April, lauded the Eisenhower plan as one entirely in conformity with the perceptions of the Soviet Command. Stalin agreed with the proposal to effect a junction in the Erfurt–Leipzig–Dresden area—Soviet forces would, therefore, launch their main attack in that direction. 'Berlin has lost its former strategic importance', for which reason the Soviet command would commit only secondary forces towards that objective. Subject to the dictates of changing circumstances, the Soviet command planned to launch its offensive in the second half of May.

Conceivably General Eisenhower intended through this confirmation of his plans to allay or smother Stalin's suspicions aroused by the Anglo–American contacts with the German command, but the move misfired and may indeed have had the opposite effect. Even before replying to General Eisenhower, Stalin advised General Marshall in a message dated 30 March that the information passed to the Soviet command on 20 February concerning the movement of Sixth *Panzer* Army proved to be 'at variance with the actual course of events on the Eastern Front in March'. Bluff of a deliberate and damaging kind from 'certain sources of information' could not be discounted. This time it was Stalin's turn to bluff on his terms.

On the day Stalin received General Eisenhower's communication about the line of the Allied advance Marshal Zhukov was in the process of presenting to the Soviet General Staff detailed plans—Plan A and Plan B—for an offensive operation aimed at Berlin. The following day, 29 March, Zhukov flew into Moscow at the urgent bidding of Stalin and joined him late that night in a preliminary discussion of the Berlin operation. On 31 March Marshal Koniev duly arrived in Moscow bearing his own Front plans for the Berlin operation and went at once to a General Staff conference for a review of the overall attack plan. On the very day, 1 April, he sent his reply to General Eisenhower, a document dismissing Berlin as a major objective and fixing the Soviet offensive for later in May, Stalin convened a major command conference in order to finalize all plans and preparations for a gigantic Soviet offensive aimed directly at the very heart of the German capital—a mighty offensive to be launched *no later* than 16 April and to be carried through in the span of 12–15 days.

8

No Time to Die:
April–May 1945

'Tak kto zhe budet brat Berlin, my ili soyuzniki?' ('Well, now, who is going to take Berlin, will we or the Allies?') Stalin exploded this question in his office on 1 April 1945 against the intense quiet of the main planning conference, which was made up of the seven members of the State Defence Committee (the *GKO*), Marshal Zhukov and Marshal Koniev, together with General Antonov from the General Staff and Col.-Gen. Shtemenko, Chief of the Main Operations Directorate. As usual, Stalin set the scene carefully. The conference opened with a survey of the situation on the Soviet–German front and an appreciation of both Allied operations and their intentions. Summarizing the position, Stalin then called on Shtemenko to read aloud a telegram to the meeting: Anglo–American forces, Shtemenko intoned, were about to mount an operation designed to capture Berlin before the Red Army, Field-Marshal Montgomery was even now assuming command of these forces, which would attack to the north of the Ruhr and thus take the shortest route to Berlin, with assault forces presently being readied since the Allied command believed the operation to be eminently feasible. At that Stalin fired his question, aimed directly at the two Marshals. Koniev recovered first and assured Stalin that the Red Army would be the first to take Berlin. Koniev had risen too readily to the bait and Stalin swung on him, asking him how he could regroup his forces in time when the bulk of his striking power was dispersed to the southern, left flank. Koniev promised timely reorganization, while Zhukov tersely reported that his Front was ready to take Berlin and pointed straight at the city.

General Antonov then presented the main operational plan to the conference. From Stettin to just north of Görlitz three Soviet fronts, supported by Long-Range Aviation bombers, would pierce the German defences by striking along several axes, cut the enemy 'Berlin grouping' into a few isolated elements, destroy them and then seize Berlin: between the twelfth and fifteenth day of operations Soviet assault forces should reach the Elbe on a broad front and link up with Anglo–American troops. In view of the urgency of the situation, all fronts would have only 12–14 days in which to prepare. Seen in greater detail, this General Staff plan called for Zhukov's 1st Belorussian Front to mount three simultaneous attacks to destroy German opposition on a 55-mile sector between the Hohenzollern canal and the Oder–Spree rivers, eliminating the bulk of the German Ninth Army at the approaches to Berlin, storming the German capital and then developing this offensive westwards to reach the Elbe not later than twelve or fifteen days after the beginning of the offensive. Zhukov's main attack would be carried by four rifle armies and two tank armies, launched from the bridgehead on the western bank of the Oder west of Küstrin. (This corresponded to Zhukov's own Plan A, while Plan B envisaged improving the general operational position of 1st Belorussian Front, followed by the capture of a fresh bridgehead south of Schwedt from which three rifle armies would be launched, while the Frankfurt bridgehead was expanded in order to accommodate the Front's main striking force made up of three rifle and two tank armies.)

Two supporting attacks were designed to cover Zhukov's main assault force from the north and south, each attack utilizing two armies: the first would strike along a northerly route in the direction of Eberswalde–Fehrbellin, the second would come from the Oder north and south of Frankfurt and aim in the general direction of Fürstenwalde, Potsdam and Brandenburg, thus outflanking Berlin from the south and isolating the German 'Frankfurt–Guben grouping' from the main body of German defenders. Artillery densities were fixed at not less than 250 guns per kilometre of attack frontage, a stupefying concentration designed to put one gun in position every thirteen feet across this front. By way of reinforcement Zhukov was to receive an additional rifle army (the 3rd), eight artillery 'breakthrough divisions' and more combat support.

Koniev's 1st Ukrainian Front received formal orders to carry out the speedy destruction of Fourth *Panzer* Army in the areas of Cottbus and to the south of Berlin; this accomplished, Koniev would drive west and north-west to reach the Belzig–Wittenberg line and the river Elbe up to Dresden no later than the 10th–12th day of operations. The main attack would be mounted with five rifle and two tank armies from the area of Triebel in the general direction of Spremberg–Belzig, with elements of right-flank forces co-operating with 1st Belorussian Front in the capture of Berlin. The same artillery densities—250 guns per kilometre—would prevail as on 1st Belorussian Front, for which the *Stavka* would provide an additional seven artillery divisions. Meanwhile forces on the left flank would cover Breslau; cover for the main striking force would be provided by a supporting attack with two rifle armies in the direction of Dresden.

Now Antonov broached a very delicate subject, virtually a taboo. In November 1944 Stalin had dictated that Zhukov with 1st Belorussian Front should undertake the conquest of Berlin. The present attack plans certainly accorded this role to Zhukov's Front, but for weeks—even months—the General Staff had wrestled with the problem of co-ordinating the operations of 1st Belorussian with 1st Ukrainian Front. How should the demarcation line between these fronts be fixed? The line which the General Staff had tentatively delineated on its own operational map shut Koniev out of the Berlin operation for all practical purposes, but this could mean major difficulties in carrying through the attack as planned. Koniev himself not unnaturally argued fiercely against this exclusion, suggesting that he aim his tank armies specifically in the direction of Berlin's south-western suburbs. Only Stalin could decide a matter of this magnitude. The result was a cunning compromise. He deleted the boundary line between 1st Belorussian and 1st Ukrainian Fronts running from the Neisse to Potsdam, the line pencilled in on the General Staff operations map and which effectively barred Koniev from Berlin. Stalin now let it run only as far as Lübben, just short of forty miles from the German capital and then announced: 'Kto pervyi vorvetsya, tot pust i beret Berlin'— 'Whoever breaks in first, let him take Berlin.' He also officially advised Koniev to work out an 'operational variant' which would utilize 3rd and 4th Guards Tank Armies in an attack on Berlin from the south, once they had broken through the German lines on the Neisse. In effect, Stalin left Zhukov and Koniev to race each other, all without nullifying his November edict. The odds were on Zhukov, but Koniev had—literally—a fighting chance.

Although the General Staff specified an offensive involving three fronts, the commander of the third front—2nd Belorussian—did not take part in this conference. The Stavka merely sent Rokossovskii at 2nd Belorussian Front a warning order to begin an urgent regrouping of his forces, the four rifle armies, three tank and one mechanized corps as well as the reinforcements deployed in the Stettin area, in order to facilitate a change of sectors with Zhukov's right flank; this would have to be carried through no later than 15–18 April. Following Stalin's original directive that the 1st Belorussian Front should play a decisive part in the capture of Berlin, the Stavka intended to reduce Zhukov's frontage by at least 100 miles. This would enable him to concentrate his main assault force as Rokossovskii took over the sector running from Kolberg to Schwedt; the boundary line between the fronts (1st and 2nd Belorussian) now ran through Schneidemühl–Arnswalde–Pyritz–Schwedt–Angermunde–Wittenberg.

This relatively brief instruction from the Stavka, when translated into action, thrust Rokossovskii into intense and complicated activity. His Front, so recently advancing to the east, now had to swing westwards and traverse almost 200 miles of devastated countryside, villages still aflame, towns blocked and river crossings impassable. Trains could only proceed at a snail's pace, even if the rolling stock could be assembled. The tanks would have to go by rail, but other formations took to the roads using lorries and horses; 49th and 70th Armies received the first orders to redeploy, followed by Batov's 65th and Fedyuninskii's 2nd Shock Armies, with 5th Tank Army taking up Fedyuninskii's positions. Lorries carrying troops, ammunition and food, and towing regimental artillery, moved by day and night; rifle units also followed on foot, walking arsenals with riflemen festooned with machine-pistols, ammunition, grenades, fighting knives, a pouch with dry rations—all at a pace of twenty or so miles a day. The loot also went on the lorries.

Stalin signed Zhukov's operational directive on 1 April. Koniev received his signed orders the next day, stipulating that the main task of 1st Ukrainian Front was to destroy enemy forces in the Cottbus area and to the south of Berlin, with the principal assault aimed along the Spremberg–Belzig axis; Koniev's two tank armies might be swung on Berlin, but only after they had passed Lübben. Though drafted, the directive to Rokossovskii was not issued until 6 April; Rokossovskii would not participate directly in the capture of Berlin, but 2nd Belorussian Front would attack in a westerly direction towards Berlin, destroying German forces at Stettin and securing the whole Berlin operation on this northerly sector. The attack plan specified that 2nd Belorussian—once regrouped—would force the Oder north of Schwedt, destroy the Third *Panzer* Army and seal its escape route in the direction of Berlin. Having thus secured Zhukov's assault from the north, Rokossovskii would drive west and north-west to reach the Anklam–Pritzwalk–Wittenberg line not later than the 12th–15th day of operations. The main attack would be mounted with three rifle armies, three tank corps and a mechanized corps from the area north of Schwedt, aimed at Neustrelitz.

Complete now in every detail, including regrouping and reinforcement, the main Soviet plan committed three Fronts to action on 'the Berlin axis', mounting six powerful attacks designed to break through the German defences on a wide front in order to split the defending forces and destroy them piecemeal. The encirclement of the German forces committed directly to the defence of Berlin—Ninth Army and Fourth *Panzer*—would be accomplished by the right-flank operations of 1st Belorussian Front, outflanking Berlin from the north and north-west, while right-flank formations of 1st Ukrainian Front outflanked the city from the south and south-west. The splitting of the encircled defenders into two isolated groups would be carried out by Zhukov's left-flank armies attacking towards the southern suburbs of Berlin and Brandenburg; if successful, this manoeuvre would greatly facilitate the task of capturing Berlin itself, for the bulk of the defending force—Ninth Army—would be isolated from the fighting for the city. The 2nd Belorussian Front, operating to the north of Berlin and advancing on western and north-western axes with its left-flank formations, would engage Third *Panzer* Army and push the German defence north of the city back to the sea. Third *Panzer* would be cut off from Berlin and its escape route to the Elbe would also be severed.

In spite of their brave bold words to Stalin and the *Stavka*, both Zhukov and Koniev could only reel privately at the enormity of their tasks—not the actual operations but the logistical effort. Stalin had already prodded Koniev about his present deployment: two armies—the 28th and 31st from 3rd Belorussian Front—were earmarked as reinforcement for Koniev, but they had a long way to travel and could not possibly arrive in time for the opening of the attack. Koniev could only propose that he would launch his offensive without this reinforcement, a suggestion which Stalin approved, assigning 16 April as 'D-Day, H-hour' for Koniev. Zhukov received Gorbatov's 3rd Army as immediate reinforcement, assigned to the 1st Belorussian Front's second echelon with the forces operating along the main line of attack. A few days later Rokossovskii flew into Moscow to receive his briefing and his operational orders. Only after protracted argument did he succeed in having the date of his offensive operations fixed at 20 April, a plea supported by data showing that 2nd Belorussian Front had not yet completed the East Pomeranian operation, that it must now swing from east to west, redeploy across a couple of hundred miles and then prepare to force the lower reaches of the Oder. Four days at the very most was all that Rokossovskii could win by way of time; his urgent request for more lorries to speed his movement simply went unanswered.

Zhukov and Koniev left Moscow in aircraft which left within minutes of each other, both marshals bent on exploiting the limited time available to them. To save precious time Marshal Zhukov had already telephoned his Chief of Staff, Col.-Gen. M.S. Malinin, on the evening of 1 April, telling him that the main operational plan had been accepted more or less without change but 'we haven't much time', hence Malinin must start things moving at once. Laid out on maps and seen from the air—Soviet aircraft flew six special reconnaissance missions to photograph the city and its defences—Berlin presented a formidable obstacle, 320 square miles of urban sprawl, a giant 'hedgehog' with a huge number of strong points provided by the substantial buildings as well as the underground facilities and installations which could be put to good use by the defenders. Improvised anti-tank barriers sprouted from the jumble of bomb-blasted concrete, rubble and abandoned vehicles, linking up the lakes and rivers which formed natural tank traps. Immediately ahead of Zhukov lay the Seelow Heights, two hundred feet high in places, with carefully prepared fortifications and German guns sited atop the plateau to cover all approaches, particularly the valley intersected with numerous streams and filled with soft ground.

Developing his original plan, Plan A, Zhukov worked on the details of the assault to be launched from the Küstrin bridgehead with six armies (four rifle armies and two tank armies), all with the aim of smashing in the German defence to the east of the capital and then embarking on the storming of the city itself. The three armies at the centre of the front in the Küstrin bridgehead—3rd and 5th Shock Army, with 8th Guards Army—received orders to break the German defences, open up a passage for the armour and by the sixth day of operations reach the eastern edge of the Havel lake in the Henningsdorf–Gatow sector; 47th Army was to outflank the city from the north-west, attacking towards Nauen–Rathenow and on the eleventh day of operations reach the area of Schönhausen on the river Elbe. The two tank armies were deployed with the main strike force, but Zhukov now planned to use them to outflank Berlin from the north and from the south—a change in the role of 1st Guards Tank Army which Stalin personally sanctioned; Katukov's 1st Guards would now make a southerly swing rather than operating to the north with 2nd Guards Tank Army. Katukov's tank army, together with Yushchuk's 11th Tank Corps, received orders to move into the breach opened by Chuikov's 8th Guards Army, advance in the direction of Seelow–Karlshorst and on the second day after moving off seize the Köpenick–Friedrichshafen–Neuenhagen area; having outflanked the city from the south, 1st Guards Tank Army would then co-operate with 2nd Guards Tank Army in seizing the Charlottenburg area (in western Berlin) and Zehlendorf. Bogdanov with 2nd Guards Tank Army would exploit 5th Shock Army's breakthrough, driving finally to the river Havel in the Oranienburg–Henningsdorf sector and then turning to the south to operate with 1st Guards Tank Army in reducing the north-western suburbs of the city.

Zhukov also planned two supporting attacks designed to cover his main striking force from the north and the south. Two armies, 61st and 1st Polish Army, would mount the northerly attack to sweep to the north-west across Liebenwalde and thence to the Elbe on the eleventh day of operations. The second attack, launched by 69th and 33rd Armies, would sweep in from the south driving in the general direction of Fürstenwalde–Potsdam–Brandenburg; these two armies received orders to break the German defence in the Frankfurt area and drive to the southern and south-western suburbs of Berlin, thus completely isolating the German Ninth Army. Gorbatov's 3rd Army, furnished as reinforcement, would be committed along the line of the main attack, operating as the Front second echelon.

With his Front not as favourably inclined to the 'Berlin axis', Marshal Koniev faced some complex planning problems, to which was added the complication of incorporating Stalin's suggested 'variant'—moving the tank armies into the battle for Berlin. On closer inspection of the situation, Koniev began to realize that his position was far from unpromising: if he planned *from the outset* to include the 'manoeuvre' which would bring him to Berlin into his operational plan and aimed for a rapid breakthrough, his right-flank forces could be committed to the Berlin operation. After all, this was in full conformity with the *Stavka*'s own appreciation of the possible turn of events. Accordingly, Koniev pinpointed the force to accomplish this—a reinforced tank corps from 3rd Guards Tank Army and a rifle division from 3rd Guards Army. With that fixed in his mind's eye, Koniev could proceed to plan the whole operation. He intended to launch his main attack with five armies (three rifle, two tank: 3rd Guards, 13th and 5th Guards Army, 3rd and 4th Tank Army) from Triebel in the direction of Spremberg–Belzig in order to destroy German forces in the Cottbus area and to the south of Berlin; Koniev planned to break through to the Beelitz–Wittenberg line by the 10th–12th day of operations and then push on to the river Elbe as far as Dresden. The main striking force received specific orders to break through the entire German tactical defence in the Forst–Muskau sector by the second day and drive for the river Spree.

Once on the Spree, both tank armies would go into action, Rybalko's 3rd Guards Tank Army under orders to move through the breach opened by 3rd Guards Army, south of Cottbus, and drive on Luckenwalde, seizing the Trebbin–Treuenbritzen–Luckenwalde area by the fifth day and using reinforced lead elements to take Brandenburg on the sixth day. Rybalko should also 'bear in mind' the possibility of attacking Berlin itself with a tank corps and a rifle corps. Also jumping off from the Spree, Lelyushenko's 4th Guards Tank Army would drive with all speed towards Schlieben, invest the whole Finsterwalde area by the third day, seize the Niemegk–Wittenberg–Arsndorf line by the fifth day, and on the sixth day capture Rathenow and Dessau with reinforced lead elements. Operating at the centre of the Front, it seemed that Lelyushenko must cover a lot of ground, but having passed through 5th Guards Army he would then be swinging north-west, as indeed would the entire Front once the breakthrough was accomplished. Finally, to screen his main assault force, Koniev planned a supporting attack with 2nd Polish Army and right-flank divisions of 52nd Army, an attack aimed in the general direction of Dresden.

Losing no time, Zhukov set about preparing his army commanders for the attack. The Front command held two days of special briefings and exercises between 5–7 April, using for this purpose a huge scale model of Berlin and its suburbs. According to Soviet intelligence, straddling the route from Küstrin to Berlin the German command had constructed five defence lines, which beyond Müncheberg linked up with the three defence belts covering Berlin; German reserves were on the move, concentrating principally against 1st Belorussian Front and its Oder bridgeheads. Zhukov also knew that he would have to launch his attack without Rokossovskii providing cover from the north in the opening stages of the offensive—but no one could wait. He was also still in the process of recovering his two tank armies from East Pomerania, adding to the supply and movement difficulties which beset his Front.

The main problem, however, centred on the organization of the attack. To attain maximum shock power, Zhukov decided this time on a night attack, to jump off two hours before dawn and to light the German positions with no less than 143 searchlights providing artificial moonlight to illuminate the battlefield and confuse the defenders. (To test this idea, searchlights were used against Soviet troops and seemed to blind or daze them effectively.) But ahead of Zhukov, rising out of the sandy ground some five miles or so behind the forward German positions, lay the Seelow Heights, heavily invested by the German defenders. How should the two tank armies be best employed in view of this barrier? Tactical exercises showed clearly that the tanks should go in only when the heights had been captured—but in the event that the initial attack did not pierce the enemy positions quickly enough, the tanks must move at once and 'rip the defences wide open'. Zhukov accordingly decided upon an adjustment to the *Stavka* plan, which specified using both tank armies in a northerly outflanking drive: he now planned to deploy Katukov's 1st Guards Tank Army directly behind Chuikov's 8th Guards riflemen, so that both armies could go into action together should the need arise. Stalin agreed upon this change without argument, though it proved to be not the happiest of solutions.

If Zhukov demanded masses of blinding searing lights on the battlefield, Koniev chose the dark and the concealment of dense smokescreens to cloak his assault crossing of the Neisse: all formation commanders (and 2nd Air Army commander) received this instruction in Koniev's operational directive No. 00211, issued on 8 April. Zhukov opted for only thirty minutes of artillery preparation; Koniev planned a lengthy barrage lasting 145 minutes. At least Zhukov was across the Oder at Küstrin—though the bridges and crossings suffered continuous shelling and bombing, even the hazard of floating mines—while Koniev had to force the Neisse from its eastern bank, flat and sloping as opposed to the steep western side. The Neisse was fast and formidable, forcing on Koniev an assault crossing on an enormous scale all under the German guns located in concrete forts and strong-points.

Across an arc of 235 miles the three Soviet fronts committed to the Berlin attack piled up massive stocks of ammunition, deployed hundreds of units and sited thousands of guns. Zhukov's divisions fought a losing battle against the weather and the terrain when it came to concealment: the sodden ground, oozing water from the spring floods and local springs, made it impossible to dig in properly and effective camouflage was ruined by the bare trees as yet without leaf. Ammunition by the thousands of tons—seven million shells finally—came up by rail, with the tracks now replaced by broad Russian gauge and the wagons bypassing intermediate dumps to unload near the front-line positions. Tanks and SP guns were shifted by rail on flat-cars, covered by great bundles of hay and bulging sacks, while units moved by night as a rule, halting by day and moving at once under what camouflage they could devise; the guns moved into the spiky forests, a giant array growing day by day and stepped in ranks by calibre, an artificial forest in its own right dominated by the massive 203mm guns draped in their camouflage nets. The searchlights came in from the Front Searchlight Company and from 5th Air Defence (*PVO*) Corps, the lights sited in intervals of 200 yards from each other and at varying distances from the front line, anything from four hundred to almost a thousand yards: the girl crews did not arrive in the forward positions until 15 April, cheered on their way by a deal of front-line humour. The Germans also used searchlights, which poked and prodded from the Seelow Heights into the valley where Soviet assault units steadily piled up; when the lights went out, German aircraft dropped flares to continue the illumination. Under strict orders Soviet guns did not fire and the units in the bridgehead froze or squirmed flat as the lights swept over them.

As the guns massed in incredible numbers—8,983 on Zhukov's main attack axis, 7,733 mustered by Koniev on his attack line—the engineer troops also crowded the bridgeheads and assault positions. Rokossovskii and Koniev faced assault crossings of the Oder and the Neisse, while Zhukov's men in the Küstrin bridgehead would have to deal with strong German fortifications and fixed defences. The *Stavka* rushed up all the reinforcement it could muster, in all 485 battalions of combat engineers and bridge-building (pontoon) troops, of which

360 battalions were to be used directly in the breakthrough operations. On Zhukov's Front, bridge-building over the Oder went on ceaselessly and under heavy fire, with thirteen pontoon bridge and twenty-seven engineer battalions working like demons to keep the damaged bridges and crossings open; twenty-five bridges went into position, linking the Küstrin bridgehead to the eastern bank of the Oder, thus emplacing two bridges for each mile and a half of front in the actual assault area, plus three ferries. Then, on 10 April, the Dnieper River Flotilla sailed into this flurry of river activity, the gunboats of the 1st and 2nd Brigade taking up positions on the Oder near Küstrin; the 3rd Brigade received orders to prevent the destruction of the power installations at Fürstenberg.

Koniev planned to bring his infantry and light guns over the Neisse in the first assault, followed by tanks and SP guns, but both tank army commanders were warned not to use their river-crossing equipment on the Neisse and to hold it back for the Spree. Each rifle regiment took delivery of a couple of light assault bridges, divisions had two three-ton bridges and corps a sixteen-ton pontoon bridge: armies would deploy their own thirty-ton and sixty-ton bridges. Elsewhere Koniev's engineers laboured on, preparing 136 bridges, digging out 14,700 bunkers and armoured command posts, and setting up 11,780 gun-pits. Five Motor-Transport Regiments put 3,000 lorries to work shifting fuel and ammunition, as well as redeploying troops; 15,000 Lend-Lease lorries crisscrossed the Front area delivering more food and above all, ammunition.

While his front-line troops struggled manfully to complete the preparations for the mammoth attack on Berlin involving over 190 Soviet divisions, Stalin battled in dour style with his two partners within the Big Three to secure all his political gains: wariness was necessary, for as he told Zhukov at the end of March, President Roosevelt would not violate the Yalta agreement, 'but as for that Churchill—*vot Cherchill*—he can get up to anything'. Over Poland truculence turned to trickery. At the end of March, under cover of a specific safe-conduct, fifteen leading Polish political and military figures travelled to Pruszkow near Warsaw for consultations with Marshal Zhukov. Two groups made this journey, the first on 27 March and the second following a day later. None ever returned. In any event it would have been difficult to talk with Marshal Zhukov, who was already on his way to Moscow to confer with Stalin on the Berlin offensive. The Poles, it is true, did follow him but under *NKVD* guard. This spoliation of the opposition in Poland was also accompanied by yet another manoeuvre, an attempt on the part of one Jagodzinski as an 'unofficial' representative of the Lublin Committee to negotiate a direct settlement with Professor Grabski, the former Speaker of the Polish Parliament in London. Jagodzinski dismissed the 'Moscow Commission' as unimportant, he scorned all the business of 'intermediaries' and proposed that Professor Grabski, Mikolajczyk and three others join 'his' government. Forget the Moscow Commission, Jagodzinski counselled; it was 'only window dressing. Stalin will decide all.' Mikolajczyk was also subject to these same blandishments by yet another 'Lublin Pole'.

Such news dismayed the Prime Minister, who was not inclined to accept a Foreign Office appreciation that Stalin's aims were limited. Nor was he inclined to acquiesce in Soviet control of eastern Europe. His letter of 27 March to President Roosevelt spelled out this growing anxiety, with a plea for 'the strongest appeal to Stalin about Poland'. But Stalin was also nursing his own grievances and responded to the President's message of 25 March about the 'Berne negotiations' with a growling signal on 29 March, complaining about the movement of German divisions to the Soviet–German front from Italy and hinting that 'some other, more far-reaching aims affecting the destiny of Germany' must have been involved in a German move to 'open the front' to Allied armies in Italy. On 1 April, the day on which Stalin was finalizing the military arrangements to guarantee his portion of Germany and Berlin to boot, the President and the Prime Minister launched two lengthy messages to Moscow, both letters conveying obvious misgivings particularly over Poland. A further message from the President also responded to Stalin's views, expressed on 29 March, about the 'Berne negotiations': no negotiation had taken place, the President repeated, and German troop movements from Italy—with two divisions sent to the Eastern Front—took place well before this contact was made.

Stalin had already fired his shot about the erroneous intelligence supplied about Sixth *Panzer*. Now he sent direct contradiction to the President in a letter on 3 April: there were indeed negotiations at Berne—'Apparently you are not fully informed'—all ending in an agreement to open the front to Anglo–American troops and allow German forces to move east. In return, the British and Americans will ease the armistice terms for Germany. Such was the information from Stalin's 'military colleagues' and, he added, 'I think that my colleagues are not very far from the truth.' The Germans on the Western front have practically ceased the war against Britain and America; they fight on only against Russia. Stung and angered, a physically weakened President left it to General Marshall to send a reply on 5 April: rebutting the charges, the message ended with undisguised bitterness, castigating Stalin's informers 'whoever they are' for 'vile misrepresentations' of the President himself and his subordinates—his trusted subordinates. The Prime Minister also sent a message in similar vein.

Unabashed, Stalin would have none of this. 'The Russian point of view'— that other allies should be invited to surrender talks—is 'the only correct one'; the Germans could easily withdraw 15–20 divisions from the east to aid their western front, but this does not happen. They fight furiously in the east for 'an obscure station', about as much use to them as a poultice to a dead man, but they surrender Mannheim and Kassel without a shot . . . 'strange and unaccountable behaviour'. As for Stalin's informers he pointed again to the information on Sixth *Panzer*: they may have been late with the news, but they were right. To the Prime Minister he was offhandedly brusque: no one was trying to 'blacken' (*'chernit'*) anyone, certainly neither he (Stalin) nor Molotov was casting slurs, for the matter boiled down to 'the duties and rights of an ally'. As for those rights

Stalin referred to them in his communication of 7 April to the President and the Prime Minister, answering their complaints about the handling of the Polish question. Certainly, 'the Polish question has indeed reached an impasse', Stalin agreed somewhat grimly, but only because the Western ambassadors were departing 'from the instructions of the Crimea conference' and introducing 'new elements': they have ignored the Provisional Government, they demand that an 'unlimited number' of persons from Poland and London be invited by each member of the Moscow Commission for consultations rather than the five from Poland and three from London, and they ignore the 'Crimea decision' that only those Poles willing to accept the Yalta agreement (in particular, the Curzon line demarcation) and anxious to implement 'friendly relations' with the Soviet Union should be invited for consultation. Given the presence of Poles committed to 'friendly relations' with the Soviet Union, the provisional government could be enlarged with the understanding that it formed the 'core of the future Polish Government of National Unity', with a restriction on the numbers invited for consultation and a ratio of old to new ministers in this future government based on the Yugoslav model.

At the beginning of April, in one momentous week, Stalin sieved the whole of his strategy through his fingers. Showing the strain of war, Stalin seemed a prey to conflicting pressures and contradictory emotions—the vengeful mood which filled the Russian mind at large; the rights of Russia and the honour due to her, the freedom to secure Russia's security interests in eastern Europe born of massive military presence and power, a gnawing suspiciousness that the British would clamp a *cordon sanitaire* once again round the Soviet Union, and paranoia about secret deals which would deprive Russia of the spoils of Germany and sabotage Russia's claim to power and prestige in a morass of intrigue and dingy dealing. Stalin was right about Yalta and the Polish question: the British and Americans were now pinned on the ambiguities they had encouraged, but Yalta could not be renegotiated, certainly not when Stalin insisted on a legalistic and strict interpretation of what had been agreed. In view of the grip fastened by the Red Army and the *NKVD* on Poland, Stalin could even afford a certain insouciance in disputing the Prime Minister's charge about too much secrecy in Poland—'Actually there is no secrecy at all', he wrote on 7 April.

Having drawn up his armies for a mighty assault on Berlin, sucking in at least two and a half million Soviet fighting men for a grand if gruesome finale by way of chastisement to the strutting *Herrenvolk*—the butchers of the common folk of Russia when they were not acting out the part of supercilious slavers—Stalin set about discharging his remaining obligations under the Yalta agreement. He sent orders to begin strengthening the command staffs in the Trans-Baikal and Far Eastern military districts, as well as the Far Eastern Coastal group; Soviet armies in the European theatre should shortly begin their move to the Far East. The former Karelian Front had already been disbanded, and at the end of March Meretskov found himself on the way to Yaroslavl where his staff was assembled ready for fresh orders. Ahead of Meretskov, the 'wily man' in whom Stalin reposed an unwavering confidence, went 670 T-34 tanks and some of the latest equipment to stiffen the Far Eastern armies.

On 5 April, implementing Paragraph 3, the Soviet government served notice of its denunciation of the Non-Aggression Pact with Japan, signed in April 1941. It had run for four years, short of eight days.

In the middle of March Marshal Vasilevskii, in immediate command of the 3rd Belorussian Front and with Bagramyan's 'Samland Group' (formerly 1st Baltic Front) directly subordinated to him, gathered his battered forces for the final attack on Königsberg, though a necessary and costly prelude proved to be the reduction of the German bridgehead to the south and south-west, a defensive system with Heiligenbeil at its centre and manned resolutely by the German Fourth Army. By Soviet reckoning nineteen German divisions were deployed in this bridgehead, with only eleven in Samland and Königsberg itself, but Vasilevskii envisaged three stages to the Königsberg operation—the destruction of the Heiligenbeil defensive force, a powerful attack on Königsberg itself and finally the elimination of German forces in Samland. To split the Heiligenbeil defence Vasilevskii proposed to mount two attacks from the east and the south-east, realizing full well that this would inevitably delay the final assault but unable to see any other way to solve what had become a formidable problem.

The *Stavka* confirmed Vasilevskii's operational plan but resolutely refused to supply him with additional reinforcement in spite of the heavy losses suffered by 3rd Belorussian Front. Fuel and ammunition were in short supply, delay piled on delay with roads clogged increasingly with mud, holding up armour, artillery and lorries moving from the more distant dumps. Meanwhile Bagramyan was preparing Operation *Samland,* the codename for the storming of Königsberg itself, for which Vasilevskii promised nothing less than *all* Soviet aircraft operating in East Prussia (two tactical air armies, 1st and 3rd, reinforced with divisions from 18th Air Army, a heavy bomber formation), together with the very heaviest artillery from the High Command reserve, including 305mm-calibre siege guns. Bagramyan was under no illusions about the enormity of the task facing him, nothing less than the largest and most complex urban assault operation undertaken by the Red Army, facing powerful forts, innumerable pillboxes, well-constructed fortified buildings and obstacles at every turn. To assist the planning a model of the city in 1:3000 scale was built, detailing the external and internal fortifications, particularly the forts. Three lines of defences ringed Königsberg, with fifteen forts presenting a major threat to the Soviet assault; the second line of defences followed the outline of the suburbs and the third covered the centre, also fitted out with its own forts. Having studied the defensive system on the model, Bagramyan marked out the attack sectors for 43rd, 50th and 11th Guards Armies, with 39th Army also committed, a 'psychological stroke' suggested by Vasilevskii, for its was Lyudnikov's 39th which had failed to hold the German attack from the city and also from Samland on 18 February, thus establishing a land link which breathed fresh life into German resistance. Lyudnikov might now get his revenge.

On 13 March Vasilevskii told Bagramyan that in spite of the rain, sleet and poor visibility the assault on the Heiligenbeil defences must open on time; it was also time for Bagramyan to move. Bagramyan could at least report that 16th Guards Rifle Division was in action and had cut the road linking Brandenburg with Königsberg. Three days later, on 16 March, Vasilevskii submitted a lengthy report to Stalin on the situation in East Prussia, specifying the details of the planning for the assault on Königsberg; but the official *Stavka* reply stipulated that the Heiligenbeil operation must be concluded by 22 March and the assault on Königsberg begun no later than 28 March. Vasilevskii turned at once to Stalin and pointed out that this timetable simply could not be carried out, since the Heiligenbeil operation could not be concluded before the 25–28 March and it would take three or four days to regroup, thus delaying the artillery and air bombardment of Königsberg until early in April. Stalin not only agreed but promised major reinforcements and the dispatch of two senior air officers, Air Chief Marshal A.A. Novikov and A.E. Golovanov, to assist Vasilevskii.

Fighting for every foot of its bridgehead, the German Fourth Army was pushed steadily back to the sea, jammed into the cramped Balga peninsula which poked out into the Frisches Haff in the direction of Pillau. Heiligenbeil itself fell on 25 March in a welter of hand-to-hand fighting, while on the beaches at Balga the remnants of German divisions came under sustained Soviet air attack. Hitler at first refused to permit any evacuation and only agreed on 26 March, provided the heavy equipment had been rescued, a decision which came too late to save either the equipment or the men. Only small groups made their escape to Frische Nehrung and Pillau; on 29 March the German bridgehead to the south had been completely eliminated, leaving Vasilevskii free to unleash all his forces on Königsberg, which the Soviet command intended to smother in a giant wave of fire. Meanwhile, the *Stavka* ordered the disbanding of Bagramyan's Samland Group, the divisions being assigned to reserve at Insterburg, though Bagramyan himself remained as deputy commander of the 3rd Belorussian Front.

The preliminary bombardment of Königsberg began early in April but low cloud and driving rain impeded Soviet pilots and gunners. Vasilevskii telephoned Stalin and found him fretting over any possible delay to the Berlin operation; a glance out of the window revealed only more fog and rain, but Vasilevskii knew he could delay no longer. The guns would have to take the main weight at the moment, though Novikov promised an all-out air effort even with a marginal improvement in the weather. All Soviet armies were on their start lines, prepared if necessary to rely on artillery alone. Marshal Novikov could give no firm indication when his air armies would be committed and pointed out drily that he did not command the weather, only the planes and pilots. The Soviet assault force with its four armies numbered 137,250 men (more or less equal to the German garrison) but massively reinforced with fire-power—5,000 guns and heavy mortars, 538 tanks and SP guns, and 2,444 aircraft. The *Stavka* directed guns and aircraft from a variety of sources. The Baltic Fleet contributed its naval aircraft, river gunboats brought from the gulf of Finland, the 404th Railway Artillery Division, naval infantry to strike at Samland, a naval component organized into the 'South-Western Naval Defence Zone' under the command of Rear-Admiral N.I. Vinogradov. Almost half the artillery strength consisted of large-calibre guns, including the heaviest pieces (203mm to 305mm) and the naval railway artillery with 130mm and 180mm guns; rifle-division commanders could call on 152mm and 203mm guns, as well as 160mm mortars supplemented by 300 multiple rocket launchers.

The weather cleared appreciably on 6 April, whereupon Vasilevskii launched infantry and armour on the storming operation, driving into the German perimeter at eight separate points on the north-western and south-western sectors of Königsberg. The Soviet regiments had earlier set up their 'assault squads', made up of a rifle battalion, a company of engineers, a section of 76mm guns, one flamethrower section, a battery of 120mm mortars, a tank company and SP guns; battalions and companies formed similar assault groups supported by two anti-tank guns, two guns and two or three tanks. Every rifleman in the assault groups was equipped with six grenades and rigged out with all the kit that arduous experience of street fighting dictated. The Soviet artillery fire never slackened, and in the afternoon Soviet aircraft joined the assault as the weather improved, 1st Air Army attacking from the east, 15th Air from the north, Baltic Fleet naval aircraft coming from the west and bombers of Long-Range Aviation striking from every direction. Against these swarms of aircraft the *Luftwaffe* could do little or nothing with a hundred or so fighters desperately trying to fly off from airfields under heavy bombing or even using the main streets in Königsberg.

As the evening arrived, Soviet assault units had already pushed their way into the city, blockading or blowing up several forts, cutting the Königsberg–Pillau railway line and piercing the entire defensive system. Night brought no respite. Vasilevskii ordered all army commanders to fight on without pause, a fiery prelude to the storm of fire poured over the city the following day. Königsberg was doomed and the mass of civilians, mixed with the fighting troops, could not fail to be seized with terror amidst this military cremation stoked quite mercilessly by the Red Army. 7 April dawned with clearer skies, the morning mists dispersing quickly, but dense smoke piled over Königsberg. The Soviet guns fired off their covering barrages and the aircraft of 11th Guards Fighter Corps swept in to attack what remained of aerodromes and AA positions. At ground level, forts, fortifications and buildings fell to Soviet fighting squads leaping, running, squirming, climbing, firing, dynamiting and burning out German garrisons in the fearful drills of street fighting. The heavy guns continued to batter down the defences, some of which proved to be astonishingly durable—Fort Nos. 5 and 5a survived a rain of 500–600 shells from heavy-calibre guns (203mm and 280mm) and even then crippled the German gun-crews fought Soviet riflemen from the covered passageways crisscrossing the ditches and moats ringing the forts.

That massed formation of Soviet fighter-bombers, however, signalled fresh frenzy about to be injected into the battle. Bad weather had kept Novikov's air armies grounded on 6 April, with the bombers managing only 85 sorties of a planned 1,218; out of the grand total of 4,000 planned sorties, only 1,000 were flown. But at 10 am on 7 April Novikov launched 246 bombers to carry out three waves of attacks and decided to use the heavy bombers of Long-Range Aviation in daylight attacks, much to Golovanov's consternation. Golovanov argued that Soviet bomber crews, used to operating only at night, were not trained for daylight formation flying and would be easy meat for German fighters. Novikov dismissed that last point with derision: 'Don't fret yourself on that score. I will give your bombers an escort of 125 fighters, so not a single "Messer" will touch you. In addition, 200–300 *shturmoviki* with heavy fighter escort will cover the city constantly and in co-operation with our artillery will make sure that German AA guns won't utter a peep. . . .' Golovanov tried to argue back but Novikov, Soviet Air Force C-in-C, told him to get on with it. More than 500 bombers duly dropped 550 tons of bombs on the defences, knocking down whole buildings and blocking street after street, piling a huge shroud of dust over the defenders.

This devastating attack spread the ruin but it did not crack German resistance, which continued from underground shelters and heavily reinforced strong-points. Through the passages blasted by Soviet dive-bombers and cleared by sappers, Soviet armies cut their way street by street into the city: Beloborodov's 43rd Army ground its way from the north-west, Galitskii's 11th Guards from the south, crossing the river Pregel in its path. On 8 April, as Beloborodov and Galitskii fought to link up, Novikov put in a maximum air effort with Soviet aircraft flying 6,000 sorties, but as Soviet troops closed on each other from the north-west and from the south there was growing danger of Soviet air attacks and artillery fire engulfing Soviet units. General Lasch, the German commander of *Festung Königsberg,* could see no point in this continued carnage. He had already asked General Müller, Fourth Army commander, for permission to withdraw into Samland but this was refused. Now Königsberg was cut off from Samland, making a mockery of Müller's belated permission for a withdrawal.

Engulfed in horrible destruction and trapped in a morass of flame under continuous bombardment inflicted on soldiers and civilians alike, Lasch reluctantly signed an act of capitulation with the Soviet command at 2130 hours on 9 April. At dawn on the following day columns of Geman prisoners assembled in the ruined city centre, senior German officers much in evidence and Lasch himself in the van. Lasch, interviewed by Marshal Vasilevskii, complimented the Soviet command on the speed with which the final storming of the fortress had been carried through. His own defensive operations, largely improvised as they were, also commanded respect, though all he received from Hitler was an accusation of a 'premature' surrender, the death sentence and the arrest of his family. The

Red Army claimed 42,000 German officers and men killed, 92,000 prisoners (including 1,800 officers and generals) and a lengthy tally of weapons and equipment. The civilians suffered cruelly and one quarter—25,000 people—perished, trapped as they were without any means of escape, a situation deliberately planned by East Prussia's *Gauleiter*.

It remained now to deal with the German Group Samland, which Vasilevskii's chief of intelligence reported to consist of eight infantry divisions and one *Panzer* division. He also reported that Müller had been dismissed as commander of Fourth Army, being replaced by von Saucken. The whole German force amounted to about 65,000 men, with 1,200 guns and 166 patched-up tanks. To eliminate this group and to reduce Pillau, the Soviet command proposed to use five armies, with the main attack directed on Fischausen. The Soviet attack opened on 13 April and ushered in a final bout of savage fighting as German rearguards fought regardless of cost to themselves to hold off the Russian attacks and to cover the withdrawal on Pillau. Group Samland, battered out of all recognition, ceased to exist formally in the German order of battle after 15 April, but orders went out to hold Pillau at all costs in order to permit every available German ship to take off refugees and soldiers. A fighting force of 20,000 German troops manned an improvised but fanatically fought defence at Pillau, grappling with Soviet assault units and grinding them to pieces, piling loss on loss until Vasilevskii was forced to commit his second echelon—11th Guards Army—in a last furious effort to overwhelm the German defences. Six long, drawn-out bloody days ensued, costing both sides dear before the fighting died away amidst the mounds of shattered equipment and the litter of corpses strewn across the sands and heaped in the pine forests, the last spasm in 105 days of butchery, ferocity and almost ceaseless bombardment which had stamped the East Prussian campaign, culminating in the fiery reduction of Königsberg.

Nor did events to the west and the south fail to have an impact on the mood of the defenders and the eventual fate of the defence of Königsberg: the fall of Danzig, followed by the capture of Vienna by the Red Army, brought great gloom to the civilians and soldiers trapped in the mighty circle of Russian guns clamped round Königsberg. Surveying this scene, becoming increasingly nightmarish with each day, Hitler divined at the end of March that the massive Soviet build-up at the approaches to Berlin was nothing but a feint and that, when it came, the main Russian attack would fall in the south with a drive into Czechoslovakia in order to lay hands on vital and extensive industrial resources. The *Führer* accordingly ordered the transfer of SS *Panzer* divisions from Army Group Vistula to the south, all to stiffen Schörner's forces defending Czechoslovakia. Soviet plans did indeed call for a major offensive directed against Czechoslovakia, though the execution in March proved to be a costly and disappointing affair. The operational plan submitted by 4th Ukrainian Front in mid-February envisaged an initial stage designed to improve the Front's general position, followed by a thrust to a depth of 250 miles and reaching as far as the line of the river Vltava—and

Prague itself; the first stage of the operations would involve the capture of the Moravska-Ostrava industrial region, a mission assigned to 38th Army. Malinovskii's 2nd Ukrainian Front received orders to use its main force to capture Bratislava and Brno, diverting elements of the Front at the same time to co-operate with 3rd Ukrainian Front in the seizure of Vienna.

This grand design all too speedily came to grief. General Petrov's 4th Ukrainian Front ran into difficulties at once, attacking on 10 March and colliding straightway with a well-organized German defence; poor weather conditions deprived Petrov of air support and the artillery failed to dent the German defensive positions. On the eighth day, 17 March, Petrov called a halt; his troops had advanced only a mile or so each day, were only about 6–7 miles into the German positions and no breach had been opened to introduce 5th Guards Mechanized Corps as a 'mobile group'. The *Stavka* proceeded at once to vent its fury on Petrov and his command: Petrov himself and his Chief of Staff, Lt.-Gen. F.K. Korzhenevich, were relieved of their commands and replaced with Army General A.I. Yeremenko and Col.-Gen. L.M. Sandalov (as Chief of Staff). The *Stavka* accused Petrov of failing to make proper preparation for the offensive, of failing to inform GHQ of the inadequate planning, of ignoring measures to conceal his offensive and of failing to request further time to prepare.

Within a week, on 24 March, the 4th Ukrainian Front resumed its offensive after a 45-minute artillery barrage. 38th Army again launched the main attack, reinforced with 127th Mountain Troops and 101st Rifle Corps (bringing the total strength of the army to five corps, plus four independent tank brigades); 5th Mechanized Corps went on the *Stavka*'s orders to the 1st Ukrainian Front in order to stiffen 60th Army. Yeremenko took command and under his direction 38th Army battered its way forward, pushing German troops back to the Oder north-east of Moravska-Ostrava, fighting hundreds of actions amidst the stout and sturdy buildings which abounded; 1st Guards Army pushed on towards Friestadt but 18th Army failed to fight its way through the German defences in the Carpathians. In all the twelve days of the rejuvenated offensive, 4th Ukrainian Front had advanced a mere twenty miles in the direction of Moravska-Ostrava

At least the *Stavka* could calculate that the 4th Ukrainian Front operations, even if they had failed to achieve any substantial success, contributed to drawing off German strength from other sectors. At the same time Malinovskii's 2nd Ukrainian Front produced some promising results: on the night of 25 March a dozen assault battalions from 53rd and 7th Guards Armies forced the river Hron across a ten-mile front and fell upon an unsuspecting enemy. Alert to this growing threat the German command threw in two divisions of the *Feldherrnhalle Panzer* corps, to which Malinovskii responded by committing Pliev's 1st Guards Cavalry Mechanized Group (with its two cavalry divisions, six tank and two SP-gun regiments, all amounting to 83 tanks and 63 SP guns). Driving fast and deep, with air support provided by Goryunov's 5th Air Army, Pliev's 1st Guards and

7th Guards Armies forced the Nitra and the Vah in turn, driving on Banska Bystrica and Trencin. By the evening of 1 April 25th Rifle Corps (7th Guards Army) was closing on Bratislava, though on receipt of partisan intelligence that the town was well fitted out for defence, Shumilov with 7th Guards decided on outflanking moves to south-east and north-east, assigning the final assault to 23rd Guards Rifle Corps (seconded from 46th Army). Faced with a rapidly changing situation, the *Stavka* on 1 April issued fresh orders to Malinovskii and 2nd Ukrainian Front, instructing him to continue operations north of the Danube with the object of striking in the direction of Malacky-Iiglava, capturing Bratislava no later than 5–6 April and moving on to the Nove Mesto–Malack–river Morava line; Malinovskii's next objective would be Brno (together with Znojmo and Stokkerau), for which he was to use 1st Guards Cavalry Mechanized Group while he earmarked 46th Army (reinforced with 2nd Guards Mechanized Corps and 23rd Tank Corps transferred from 3rd Ukrainian Front) for the attack aimed at Bruck and Vienna—the latter to be carried out in co-operation with the right flank of 3rd Ukrainian Front. The final stage of Malinovskii's Front operation involved driving north after the capture of Brno and linking up with 4th Ukrainian Front in the area of Olomouc, thereby isolating those German forces to the south-east and south of Moravska-Ostrava.

Tolbukhin in command of 3rd Ukrainian Front also received special *Stavka* orders on 1 April, specifying that 4th and 9th Guards Armies (with 6th Guards Tank Army) should reach the Tuln/Sankt-Polten/Lillienfeld line no later than 12–15 April, while 26th, 27th, 57th and 1st Bulgarian Armies in advance of these dates would capture Glognitz, Bruck, Graz, Maribor and then dig in along the Mürz, Mur and Drava river lines. While the main body of 2nd Ukrainian Front would attack in the direction of Brno and Bratislava, Petrushevskii's 46th Army received orders to encircle Vienna from the east, while 4th and 9th Guards Armies swept in from the south and west. These same *Stavka* orders also extended Tolbukhin's frontage on his right, which from 2400 hours on 1 April ran along a line which brought the southern reaches of Vienna into the operational zone of 3rd Ukrainian Front, an adjustment which obliged Tolbukhin to redeploy 4th Guards and align it with 46th Army.

While adding the final touches to the plan for the Soviet drive on Vienna, the *Stavka* also made some last-minute adjustments to the plan for the destruction of German forces in eastern Czechoslovakia, thereby synchronizing the operations of all four Ukrainian Fronts (1st, 2nd, 3rd and 4th). It was the lack of progress with 4th Ukrainian Front which produced the problem, for while 1st Ukrainian and 2nd Ukrainian had struck to some depth to the west, 4th Ukrainian had yet to crack the Moravska-Ostrava redoubt. On 3 April the *Stavka* issued its formal directive to Yeremenko at 4th Ukrainian Front, specifying the capture of Opava and Moravska-Ostrava as immediate objectives, followed by an attack in the direction of Olomouc to link up with 2nd Ukrainian Front; Malinovskii had already received corresponding orders (Directive No. 11051) to drive on Olomouc.

Taking no chances this time, the *Stavka* proceeded to reinforce 4th Ukrainian and handed over Kurochkin's 60th Army from 1st Ukrainian Front to Yeremenko, bringing his total strength to 265,000 men, 6,000 guns and mortars, more than 300 tanks and SP guns, supported by 435 aircraft. Both of the assault armies, 60th and 38th, were reinforced with two artillery breakthrough divisions and a tank corps, a total of forty Soviet rifle divisions (and six aviation divisions) facing twenty German divisions with 300 tanks and 280 aircraft.

While Yeremenko made preparations for his offensive, Malinovskii and Tolbukhin struck out for Bratislava and Vienna. On Malinovskii's Front, Soviet troops were astride the river Vah in a single day (1 April) and Pliev's mobile group pressed on to Trnava and the 'Little Carpathians'. While Pliev moved on Malacky and the Morava, swinging an encircling arm round Bratislava from the west, two Soviet divisions (409th Rifle and 4th Guards Parachute/25th Guards Rifle Corps) closed in on Bratislava from the north-east, followed on 3 April by 23rd Rifle Corps attacking from the east. During the night of 4 April Soviet riflemen and paratroopers began their final assault, joined in the morning by 23rd Corps and 19th Rifle Division moving along the bank of the Danube supported by the gunboats of the Danube Flotilla. At 1800 hours on 4 April what remained of the German garrison abandoned Bratislava and fell back behind the river Morava.

While Malinovskii's men cleared Bratislava, Tolbukhin's armies raced for Vienna, attacking along several axes: 4th Guards Army received orders to strike for the centre of the city and then advance towards Florisdorf, Kravchenko's 6th Guards Tank Army (reinforced with 18th Tank Corps and 12th Engineer Brigade) was instructed to use 5th Guards Tank Corps to strike into the south-western sector of Vienna, while 9th Guards Mechanized Corps outflanked the city from the west in order to seal off the western and north-western escape routes. One corps (39th Guards) of 9th Guards Army would follow in the wake of Kravchenko's tanks and join the assault on the south-western sector, while yet another corps (38th Guards) must sever the Vienna–Linz motor road and employ two divisions to secure the Soviet assault from the west; 37th Guards Corps (also from 9th Guards Army) was allocated to protect the open left flank of the main assault force.

Nothing like the formidable defensive systems of Buda and Pest existed in Vienna, but rearguard detachments of Sixth *SS Panzer,* with elements of *SS Wiking, Adolf Hitler* and 17th Infantry Division, set up frequent ambushes, mined roads and blew bridges in order to hold off Kravchenko's armour. A stand of sorts was made on the river Leithe line, inflicting more losses on Soviet 6th Guards Tank Army and reducing some tank brigades to a mere 7–10 tanks, but Kravchenko pushed on towards Wiener Neustadt. Soviet infantry pushed in to the east and south of Vienna, while the armour tried to sweep round to the west only to find German resistance stiffening and the whole Soviet advance appreciably slowed. Inside the city, over Easter, fires spread in profusion and streets became impassable with rubble after American bombing attacks. Baldur von Schirach, *Gauleiter* and newly appointed Defence Commissioner, duly declared Vienna a *Festung* even as party officials and Nazi sympathizers struggled to get clear of the city before the Russians broke in. Von Schirach called out the population to work on defences in the suburbs, digging trenches, barricading streets and setting up anti-tank barriers, though the Viennese at large showed less than enthusiasm for a bitter fight to the death involving the ruination of their city. An Austrian resistance movement—hidden under the code '0-5'—devised a plan to circumvent a desperate German defence of the city and managed to make contact with the Soviet command, which received the Austrians with obvious and unallayed suspicion, fearing a devious trap. On 5 April, for those privy to this desperate and complicated manoeuvre on the part of '0-5', it seemed that the mission might well have succeeded, for the sky cleared of aircraft and the Soviet advance appeared to have halted abruptly, two conditions suggested by the Austrian emissaries to Tolbukhin.

It was not, however, Austrian persuasiveness but stiffening German resistance which slowed the Soviet columns. On the evening of 5 April Tolbukhin reviewed operations on his right flank, assigning 4th Guards Army to the eastern and south-eastern sectors of the city, and 9th Guards to an assault from the south as well as an outflanking movement to the west. Kravchenko's tank army received orders to regroup, then to strike northwards in order to cut escape routes leading from the city in a north-westerly direction, and finally to assault the city from the west in conjunction with 9th Guards Army. The *Stavka* also took a hand, instructing Malinovskii to transfer 46th Army to the eastern bank of the Danube in order to outflank Vienna from the north, while Tolbukhin's right-flank armies operated to the south of the Danube and completed their outflanking movements from the south-west. The Danube Flotilla promptly set about the task of ferrying some 72,000 men and more than 500 guns to this new deployment.

The Soviet assault on the city opened on the morning of 6 April. Reinforced with 1st Guards Mechanized Corps and operating with 39th Guards Rifle Corps (9th Guards Army), 4th Guards fought its way towards and into the western and southern outskirts of Vienna, starting the first of many street battles fought in winding streets, across small canals and ditches or through factory buildings. Kravchenko's tanks ground on, with 9th Guards Mechanized Corps sweeping round the city to the west and south-west, after which the corps swung round and launched its own attack from a westerly direction. But losses were biting deep: 46th Guards Tank Brigade making now for the western suburbs mustered a mere thirteen tanks and the heavy SP-gun regiment (the 364th) sent as reinforcement could only provide 4–5 ISU-152s. With a reconnaissance detachment in the lead, 46th Brigade, consisting of thirteen tanks, four SP guns and twenty-six riflemen mounted on the tanks, crossed the Wiener Wald and entered the western suburbs of the Austrian capital, advancing towards the West Station.

For the moment, however, the Soviet tank troops found their way to the centre barred.

By 8 April the fighting moved closer to the centre. Together with the Arsenal, the South and East Stations were in Russian hands; 5th Guards Tank Corps regrouped in the northern suburbs and attacked to the south-east in order to link up with 1st Guards Mechanized and 4th Guards Army, fighting their way in from the south and south-west. Attempts to set up a hasty defence to the west of Vienna—whence the Russians had appeared as if by magic—failed hopelessly. Members of the Austrian resistance tried to guide Soviet tanks into the centre of the city, others took up rifles to fire at German troops and beleaguered civilians angrily fended off troops trying to set up strong-points in houses and basements. In an attempt to smother this mutiny, Gestapo officers and SS troops activated their grim procedures of public hangings, but nothing could now stem the panic, disorder and milling flight.

In an attempt to cover the withdrawal of their tanks across the Danube and the Danube canal, German squads fought fierce street battles with Soviet infantry in the area of the Ringstrasse, with Soviet gunners dragging their guns into the second storeys of buildings in order to fire through windows or gaps in the walls. Artillery and mortar bombardment set scores of buildings ablaze, inflicting heavy damage on the Ring itself, Kärntnerstrasse, the Graben and gutting the Burgtheater and the Opera House. In the centre 20th Guards Rifle Corps (4th Guards Army) fought its way along the Danube through the Prater, meeting heavy resistance as German units tried to block any Soviet advance to the Danube bridges and the sole escape route. The Soviet 46th Army was also pressing down from the north, adding a fresh menace and giving frenzied urgency to this last German defensive effort. During the night of 11 April 4th Guards Army forced the Danube canal and fought a final savage battle on the island created by the Danube and the Danube canal. Only the massive structure of the *Reichsbrücke* remained intact, held until the bitter end to bring the German survivors to the northern bank of the Danube. Behind them Vienna burned, the dead lying out in streets choked with charred and crippled tanks or smashed equipment. At 1400 hours on 13 April the Soviet command declared Vienna cleared of enemy troops and the *Stavka* simultaneously issued fresh operational directives to Tolbukhin's 3rd Ukrainian Front: the centre and left flank were to move in the direction of Graz, while the right flank invested Sankt-Pölten, whereupon 9th Guards Army was brought into reserve and deployed in the wooded area to the west and south-west of Vienna. Kravchenko's 6th Guards Tank Army reverted to Malinovskii's 2nd Ukrainian Front, while Tolbukhin acquired operational control of the Danube Flotilla.

Within forty-eight hours Soviet troops moved forward and occupied a line running from the river Morava, through Stockerau and Sankt-Pölten, on to the west of Glognitz and the east of Maribor. This breakthrough to the junction of the frontiers of Hungary, Austria and Yugoslavia, coupled with the capture of

Vienna itself, effectively trapped German armies in Yugoslavia and northern Italy. The immediate Soviet advance to the west of Vienna also contributed to a deep outflanking of the German army group defending Czechoslovakia and thus prepared the way for the Soviet drive on Prague. Hitler correctly divined Prague as a Soviet objective but he was disastrously deceived by his 'intuition' in not identifying Berlin as *the* Soviet target, a prize which outshone all others and one for which Stalin had amassed mighty numbers of men and a stupefying quantity of war material. Prague could wait.

'We're not going to Berlin, Sid. This is the end of the war for us.' Completely stunned, Brigadier-General Sidney R. Hinds commanding the US 2nd Armoured Division—with his men already on the eastern bank of the Elbe—learned this directly from General Simpson, US Ninth Army commander. The instruction came through General Omar Bradley at Twelfth Army Group and emanated from the very highest level of the Allied command, none other than General Eisenhower himself. There could be no contravention or slightest insubordination. During the night of 14 April the Supreme Commander went on to transmit his operational plans to Washington, delineating his intentions now that the thrust into the centre of Germany had been successfully concluded: pursuing the aim of destroying the remaining German forces and capturing those areas where the enemy might mount a 'last stand', he proposed to hold a firm front on the Elbe, strike towards Denmark and Lübeck, and also drive into the Danube valley to link up with Soviet troops as well as overwhelming the 'National Redoubt'. The capture of Berlin simply did not figure in these operational assignments.

On the evening of 11 April American tanks had reached the Elbe, the columns of the US 2nd Armoured Division slicing through German positions and startled defenders with immense speed. In the van of the tanks hurtling forward like cavalry, an American reconnaissance group driving at an astonishing pace swept into the suburbs of Magdeburg on the western bank of the Elbe, careering into terrified shopping crowds and jammed traffic. With the city defences now alerted, it was no longer possible to seize the *autobahn* bridge to the north of the city off the march. Meanwhile further south Major Hollingsworth raced for the bridge at Schönebeck, only to see it disintegrate at dawn on 12 April when German engineers blew it up, but General Hinds with Combat Command D (2nd Armoured Division) forced a crossing of the Elbe at Westerhüsen, south of Magdeburg. By the evening of 12 April three battalions were across the Elbe and digging in. To the north of Magdeburg the US 5th Armoured Division closed on Tangermünde shortly after noon on 12 April, but even more dramatically at Barby, about fifteen miles south-east of Magdeburg, the men of the US 83rd Infantry Division launched an immediate assault crossing of the Elbe, put one battalion across the river and set about building their pontoon bridge to serve in place of the local bridge demolished by the Germans. Upstream at Westerhüsen

General Hinds with 2nd Armoured laboured prodigiously to improvise crossing equipment, using a cable ferry in a furious attempt to stiffen his eastern bridgehead with armour and artillery, only to be swept off the eastern bank by a sudden, slashing attack by General Wenck's ardent young men, striplings from cadet battalions thirsting for action and undaunted by any odds in men or equipment. The shock blow proved to be decisive; 2nd Armoured rolled back and turned towards 38th Division's crossing points at Barby, where a second bridge now supplemented the first. Armour and infantry piled over the Elbe during the night of 14 April and the omens appeared to be good: the commanders assumed that the momentum of the American drive could be speedily resumed and already patrols from the 83rd had pushed as far as Zerbst, less than fifty miles from Berlin. Yet within hours the order to hold fast on the eastern bank of the Elbe was clamped on the US Ninth Army and any idea of a drive on Berlin abandoned.

Proud of its achievement, 83rd Infantry Division ostentatiously signposted 'their' bridge at Barby the 'Truman Bridge', doing a little highway decorating in their flamboyant style and also saluting the new President of the United States, Harry S. Truman. On 12 April President Roosevelt had died suddenly, a signal for unrestrained grief among friends and wild exultation within the *Führer's* circle (where Goebbels sent up the manic cry, 'this *is* the turning point!'). News of Wenck's sudden success on the Elbe served only to add substance to these weird and fevered fancies, nurtured already on the expectation of a military clash between Anglo–American forces and the Red Army, or if not that, then anticipation of victory on both the Oder and the Elbe, or yet again triumph secured by new and terrible secret 'revenge weapons'.

Unable or unwilling at one moment to entertain the very idea of a battle for Berlin, Hitler nevertheless sat down on the morning of 13 April to pen his proclamation to the troops of the *Ostfront,* an envenomed document breathing hatred of the 'Jewish Bolsheviks', predicting the martyrdom of Germany at their hands but promising deliverance with the defeat of the enemy at the very gates of the capital of the German *Reich.* Berlin would remain German and Vienna— which had only that day fallen to the Red Army—would once more be German. This order of the day, intended to be released the moment the Soviet offensive broke, was committed to paper at a time when reports of the imminence of the Red Army attack on Berlin grew apace, information culled from field reconnaissance, agents and interrogation of prisoners or deserters, all artfully compiled by Colonel Wessel (successor to Gehlen as head of *Fremde Heere Ost*) and laced with enticing hints of Soviet–American discord, anti-Soviet British military moves and common talk in Soviet ranks of drenching American units with shellfire just 'by mistake' to teach them their place. General Heinrici, commanding Army Group Vistula, was neither impressed by this devious piffle nor deceived when on 14 April Soviet guns opened fire on General Busse's Ninth Army, shelling accompanied by attacks with reinforced rifle battalions. The artillery fire and battalion attacks signalled standard Soviet reconnaissance missions, but Heinrici waited to divine the true timing of the main assault, a critically important factor which would enable him to pull back Ninth Army into a second, secret defence line and leave Soviet guns to pulverize the vacant ground to the front.

News of President Roosevelt's death produced its own effect in the Soviet Union and upon Stalin. Black-bordered newspapers carrying this sombre announcement were no mere formality, for the sorrow and dismay proved to be both genuine and widespread. To the astonishment of Ambassador Harriman it was an emotional Molotov who intruded on a dinner party to deliver news of the death of the President and the same Molotov who expressed great sympathy and a deep sense of loss at the passing of a true friend of Russia. In the company of Stalin, at a meeting attended by General Patrick Hurley and Molotov, Ambassador Harriman roundly countered charges about a 'conspiracy' on the part of Americans with the Polish underground against the Red Army—the details involved the indiscretions of some American airmen—but with admirable self-control and promptitude he responded to Stalin's show of 'immediate assurance' of Soviet willingness to continue a 'co-operative policy' with the United States by suggesting the attendance of Molotov at the San Francisco Conference. Molotov squirmed visibly, but Stalin agreed to the proposal and peremptorily ordered the discomfited Molotov to San Francisco.

With this new man in the White House and with the Polish question at such a critical impasse Stalin no doubt felt that he must tread softly, if not warily. The reassurance he received from Ambassador Harriman must needs be put to some practical test: President Truman proposed to continue those policies clearly ordained and delineated by President Roosevelt, he learned, but what precisely did that mean, in view of the late President's political vagaries? In addition, Stalin was bemused (according to General Shtemenko) by the flood of reports on German shuttling to the 'National Redoubt' in the south, and immersed in reports from Soviet intelligence agents about the transfer of German troops to the Eastern Front, a process speeded by the suspiciously high incidence of 'surrenders by telephone' enacted by German units in contact with the American army. What larger design lay behind these all too casual surrenders? Was there indeed a secret Anglo–American plan to seize Berlin by *coup de main* using those two airborne divisions, or yet again might the Germans contrive to surrender the capital to Anglo–American troops and thus head off the Red Army? Another 'surrender by telephone'. . . . Might the Fascist leaders make a final dash for, and a last stand in, the Alpine redoubt? What did these trains loaded with cement and heavy construction equipment signify as they thundered daily through Czechoslovakia, making for mountainous country? (Stalin was well served with intelligence from the heart of Czechoslovakia.) There was also the matter of Winston Churchill's letter to General Eisenhower written at the end of March, urging a rapid advance to the Elbe and a thrust on Berlin. What exactly was happening in Italy with the devious armistice talks and what significance attached to all the muffled rumours of wider peace negotiations and surrender parleys?

It was, therefore, with the utmost wariness that Stalin parried Harriman's carefully modulated query about the imminence of a Red Army attack directed against Berlin. His response was studiously offhand, even dismissive: a Soviet offensive was indeed in the offing, it might or might not be successful, but the main axis was directed towards Dresden rather than Berlin, a fact already well known to General Eisenhower. Yet almost at that same hour the thousands of Soviet guns massed along the Oder–Neisse front were being readied and loaded, all positioned to fire off a stupendous opening barrage heralding the Red Army's assault on Berlin. What Stalin himself would not tell the Ambassador of the United States of America was confided at once by a lowly Red Army soldier, captured south of Küstrin, to his German captors—that a gigantic attack on Berlin was timed to open early the next day, 16 April. Hitler found this credible, Heinrici was convinced and so during what was left of the night of 15–16 April Busse's Ninth Army pulled back to its second defensive line, the fortifications sited and fitted out in accordance with Hitler's previous instructions.

While Soviet armies were gouging their way into Königsberg and hammering a path into Vienna, the final operational planning and preparation for the attack on Berlin went ahead at a feverish pace. The tension mounted, with the masses of men on both main fronts—1st Belorussian and 1st Ukrainian—sensing and seeing that a gigantic operation was in the offing. Crack armies jammed ever more tightly into bridgeheads or assault positions, armadas of tanks crammed the Front areas and on Zhukov's Front in particular the miles of guns snugged under camouflage or screened in woods and forest lengthened day by day. Both fronts set about extensive reconnaissance, using ground observation posts and aerial photographs; Soviet aircraft photographed German defences to a depth of 50–60 miles, covering certain sectors eight times over and flying more than 2,500 sorties for the 1st Belorussian Front alone. Marshal Koniev used not only two photo-reconnaissance regiments but also the 10th Artillery Observation Balloon Squadron to build up a complete aerial survey of the first line of German defences. Nor did the *Luftwaffe* escape the attention of Soviet aerial reconnaissance, which aimed to locate enemy air bases and establish the German air order of battle.

The immensity of the artillery resources available, as well as the complexity of the operational tasks, demanded major consideration. The density of guns and mortars (all over 76mm calibre) per kilometre of frontage varied between 233 and 295. Zhukov determined upon a density of 189 guns for each kilometre of front, increasing this to 295 on the frontages of the assault armies; during the breakthrough operation each first-echelon rifle regiment would have 4–5 artillery regiments in support with the regimental artillery group supplying about seventy guns. While army commanders controlled regimental, divisional and corps artillery groups, army artillery groups—243 guns and mortars, including 152mm howitzers, 203mm howitzers, 160mm mortars, M-13 and M-12-31 multiple-rocket launchers—could be called on for further support. Each army also included mobile anti-tank reserves formed from two 'tank-killer' brigades with 136 guns.

In order to achieve maximum surprise, Zhukov planned a very powerful but relatively short opening barrage. The Front fire plan, confirmed on 8 April, stipulated a ten-minute artillery strike, followed by ten minutes of battery fire followed in turn by a second ten-minute artillery strike. The infantry and tank attacks would be supported to a depth of 2,000 yards by a double rolling barrage and up to 4,000 yards with a single barrage. To support 8th Guards Army in storming the Seelow Heights, the double rolling barrage would be followed by massed fire as the assault opened. The night attack, however, posed a number of problems for Soviet gunners. On some sectors Soviet infantry would be within 100–150 yards of the enemy's forward positions, requiring very careful artillery registration. To improve their techniques Soviet gunners retired to training areas in the rear and worked on practising night-firing procedures.

Not all would be total darkness, in spite of the hour of the attack. Marshal Zhukov planned to illuminate the battlefield with 143 searchlights, sited some 150–200 yards from each other along the length of the front and about 400–500 yards from the forward edge of the German positions, the beams shining out for a distance of three miles and more. The sight of all these searchlights caused tongues to wag and heads to shake in disbelief or sheer bemusement, and few divined the purpose behind this extraordinary array. Even senior commanders found themselves at something of a loss to understand what was intended, simply siting the lights and their crews according to instructions.

Facing the river Neisse and the Spree further ahead of him, Marshal Koniev adopted a very different solution for his artillery. He planned an artillery preparation lasting 145 minutes, divided into three phases, the first a forty-minute artillery strike before the launching of the assault crossing of the Neisse, the second following the laying down of the smokescreens (in which the artillery would also fire smoke) and lasting an hour, and a final 45-minute barrage beyond the Neisse river line. No artillery preparation would precede committing the tank armies for Koniev argued that most of the enemy opposition would have been suppressed; artillery would support the tank armies to a depth of ten miles, using converging fire along nine lines and assigning artillery officers to the tank armies to spot for the guns. To provide artillery support for mobile formations and units, Koniev organized powerful regimental and divisional artillery groups (including 203mm howitzers) in all armies, with divisional artillery groups also operating special counter-mortar sections. To facilitate the army commander's direct control of his artillery resources no corps artillery groups were formed, and army artillery groups varied quite widely in strength and composition depending on the operational tasks to be carried out, but it was assumed that for most of the time artillery would be firing over open sights.

Four Soviet air armies—4th, 16th and 2nd, with the 13th (Long-Range Aviation)—and elements of the Polish air force were already deployed for the Berlin operation, a huge array of 7,500 combat aircraft. One air army operated with each front (4th with 2nd Belorussian, 16th with 1st Belorussian—plus the

18th—and 2nd with 1st Ukrainian Front), committed to attaining air superiority, covering the movement to assault positions, co-operating with the ground troops in breaking through the Oder–Neisse defensive positions and securing the commitment of the mobile formations once the German defensive lines had been broken.

In Rokossovskii's planning on 2nd Belorussian Front Vershinin's 4th Army with 1,360 aircraft occupied a vitally important place in supporting the assault crossing of the Oder, for it would be impossible to transfer any quantity of artillery with any speed; Vershinin's aircraft must supply the necessary fire support and cover. During the night preceding the actual assault, air attacks would be aimed at destroying defensive positions and disrupting the work of German staffs, all with five ground-attack air divisions flying 272 sorties. The effective co-operation of air units and ground troops was of singular importance, so that each assault army—65th, 70th and 49th—acquired one ground-attack aviation division, though ultimate control of the use of air resources was left to the discretion of 4th Air Army commander himself. Vershinin planned a total of 4,079 sorties on the first day of the offensive, 1,408 fighter sorties, 1,305 ground-attack and 1,366 bomber sorties.

On the 1st Belorussian Front S.I. Rudenko in command of 16th Air Army calculated that he faced 1,700 German aircraft: his own air army consisted of 3,188 combat aircraft deployed on 165 airfields, a force supplemented with the 800 bombers from Golovanov's 18th Air Army (Long-Range Aviation). To facilitate ground–air co-operation, air divisional and corps commanders received orders to join the staffs of infantry and tank armies, with forward air controllers attached to the mobile units. Zhukov demanded three ground-attack aviation corps and one ground-attack air division to support the main blow, with operational control assigned to the infantry commanders during the breakthrough and to the armoured forces once the breakthrough was achieved. Once the opening artillery barrage lifted, night bombers (Po-2s from 16th Air Army and Il-4s from 18th Air) would continue the bombardment until dawn, taking the attack to the second line of the German defences. From dawn on 16 April until 1950 hours, bombers and ground-attack aircraft would maintain their assault on German troops and positions. To facilitate tight control of air operations 1st Belorussian Front established an 'army radar net', enabling the Front command to monitor Soviet flights, German incursions and Anglo–American air operations.

Further south S.A. Krasovskii's 2nd Air Army with 2,150 aircraft operating from eighty-two airfields deployed to support Koniev's 1st Ukrainian Front. Koniev planned to use six aviation corps and one night-bomber air division to support his main attack, leaving two aviation corps for other sectors. During the first day of operations four massed air strikes would be directed against the German defences, using 800 aircraft in the first wave, 570 in the second, 420 in the third, and 370 in the fourth and final attack, with strong forces committed to further attacks in the intervals between the massed strikes—in all, a planned total of 3,400 sorties on the first day. Soviet aircraft also received assignments to help laying those smokescreens which figured so prominently in Koniev's plans to force the Neisse.

The final stockpiling of the vast quantities of ammunition, fuel and that all-important bridging equipment went forward with a rush. To carry out his plan to 'stun and shake' the German defenders from the very beginning of the operation and to carry through the full assault, Zhukov needed 7,147,000 artillery rounds. Ammunition poured in from Front depots to the gun positions themselves, bypassing both army and division dumps, using almost 4,000 lorries from army motor-transport units and falling back where necessary on the five motor-transport regiments and two battalions—a further 3,772 lorries—with the Front reserve. Zhukov proceeded to organize his engineer support into four echelons, sappers up with the assault infantry in the first echelon, Front and army engineer units as a second echelon operating with the first-echelon divisions, a third echelon of combat engineers and construction troops and a fourth for specialist tasks such as setting up Front and Army command posts. The engineer troops also built their own model of Berlin to study the street-fighting problems.

Unlike Zhukov with his bridgehead on the western bank of the Oder, Koniev lacked any foothold on the western bank on the Neisse and everything depended on a successful assault crossing. From the 120 engineer battalions and thirteen bridging battalions assigned to his Front, Koniev detached twenty-five engineer battalions to support his left-flank armies committed to defensive operations and proceeded to plan a two-stage assault crossing of the Neisse. The first stage involved the capture of a bridgehead on the western bank and the transfer of first-echelon infantry with supporting artillery; the second involved bringing over infantry-support tanks, the bulk of the artillery and second-echelon rifle divisions. But this was only one half of the problem. Koniev's armour must get over the Neisse in strength and with all speed in order to foil any German attempt to fall back on the line of the river Spree (20–25 miles to the west) and block the Soviet advance. The first draft of the Front operational plan called for Lelyushenko's 4th Guards Tank Army to move only when Zhadov's 5th Guards riflemen had taken a bridgehead on the western bank of the Neisse, but Zhadov's army possessed only a limited number of infantry-support tanks and could not develop a high-speed attack. This became a subject for much heated debate.

On the 2nd Belorussian Front—scheduled to join the attack on Berlin on 20 April, four days after the opening of the general offensive—Rokossovskii faced not only the complicated labour of redeploying his entire Front but also the daunting task of forcing the lower reaches of the Oder, where the river forked into two channels, the East and West Oder. Two armies, 49th and 70th, moved off on 4–5 April to cover the 170–215 miles to the area of Altdamm–Schwedt, followed by Batov's 65th Army, tanks and heavy artillery trundling by rail along damaged and dangerous track, the infantry moving in columns of lorries. But before this redeployment was complete Rokossovskii together with the three army commanders and their chiefs of staff on 10 April looked over the ground earmarked for their operations. To their dismay it was largely water and marsh rather than solid ground which met their eyes, for where the Oder split into the West and East Oder, the land between them was heavily flooded and presented an expanse of water at least 3,000 yards wide. Nor could the Soviet officers make out much of the detail of the steep western bank. A single assault crossing would not work here, because ferries and pontoons would ground in the shallow water of the flooded interval between the two rivers.

Rokossovskii decided to attack on a wide front using all three armies; in the event of success on any one sector, all available resources would be flung in there. The main attack would be mounted across a thirty-mile front with 65th, 70th and 49th Armies supported by three tank corps, one mechanized and one cavalry corps. Once through the German defences on the West Oder, the offensive would develop in the direction of Neustrelitz and reach the Elbe between the twelfth and fifteenth day of the offensive; in this phase of the offensive each rifle army would be reinforced with a tank corps, while 3rd Guards Cavalry Corps acted as Front reserve, taking station on the left flank of 49th Army. In view of the terrain the provision of artillery support presented special problems. During the assault crossing of the Oder, the guns would be firing at long range and would be forced to wait for crossings to be opened before getting to the west bank, hence the need for Vershinin's 4th Air Army to fill this fire gap.

Front intelligence also supplied the disconcerting news that the German defences were strongest in those very sectors where Rokossovskii planned to launch his attack. Col.-Gen. Manteuffel's Third *Panzer* Army was holding a sector running up to the western bank of the West Oder, with three infantry divisions deployed forward, reinforced with two fortress regiments, two independent infantry regiments, one battalion and one combat group, supported by a second echelon consisting of three infantry and two motorized divisions, four brigades, independent regiments, battle groups and an officers' school. Vershinin's aerial reconnaissance disclosed that the German defences on the west bank of the West Oder stretched to a depth of 6–7 miles and consisted of strong-points surrounded by continuous lines of trenches, while on the riverbank itself slit trenches and machine-gun pits had their own communication trenches linking them with the main trench system. A second German defence line had been established on the Randow, about twelve miles from the Oder, and further aerial reconnaissance uncovered a third defence line.

As the first of Rokossovskii's assault armies drew up to its new positions— Batov's 65th Army began deploying along the Altdamm–Ferdinandstein line on 13 April—the operational planning on 1st Belorussian and 1st Ukrainian Front had entered its final stage, giving way to the distribution of attack orders. None of the Army commanders who attended Marshal Zhukov's first briefing on 5 April could forget the scene when the Front commander unveiled the huge model of Berlin and pointed out the several objectives, each carefully flagged—'I ask you to turn your attention to Objective 105. That is the *Reichstag*. Who is going to get there first? Katukov? Chuikov? Maybe Bogdanov or Berzarin?' No one replied, and Marshal Zhukov passed to Objective 106. The Marshal stifled any doubts or misgivings on the spot—when General Bogdanov, commanding 2nd Guards Tank Army, pointed to the need for more room for manoeuvre to complete the outflanking move to the north, Zhukov asked sarcastically whether he intended to take part in the assault on Berlin or go off on his own northwards for most of the time. Nor would he entertain the idea, advanced by several senior commanders, that the main German defences lay on the second line and that the Soviet artillery strike should be directed against this rather than the immediate front-line positions.

Staff studies and war-games conducted in the wake of this initial briefing evidently gave Zhukov much food for thought, particularly the question of using his two tank armies. The original *Stavka* directive stipulated that both tank armies—1st and 2nd Guards—should be used in an outflanking drive to the north of Berlin as well as striking into the city itself from the north-east, but Zhukov now decided to alter the operational assignment of Katukov's 1st Guards Tank Army, deploying it directly behind Chuikov's 8th Guards and directing that on the *second* day of the offensive the tank army should seize the eastern suburbs of Berlin, then outflank the city from the south and also capture the southern and south-western suburbs. On being informed by Zhukov of this major revision, Stalin merely told him to do what he thought best, since he was on the spot. Katukov received his final operational directive on 12 April, committing 1st Guards to this easterly thrust on Berlin followed by a move south-westwards; these orders prescribed a thirty-mile advance on the first day of operations, up to eighteen miles on the second—an assumption based on encountering fierce resistance at the approaches to the city. On 14 April Katukov issued his own orders to his corps commanders, 11th Guards and 11th Tank Corps with 8th Guards Mechanized Corps. Topped up with its reinforcement of 290 tanks and SP guns, all with crews, by the evening of 15 April 1st Guards Tank Army had swelled to 45,000 officers and men, 709 tanks and SP guns, 700 guns and 44 multiple-rocket launchers. Bogdanov's 2nd Guards Tank Army with three corps (9th and 12th Guards Tank Corps, 1st Mechanized Corps) remained committed to its original task, exploiting the breach opened by 5th Shock Army, driving to the north-west and seizing the north-western suburbs of Berlin.

Few doubts lingered in the mind of Marshal Koniev about where and how he wanted his two tank armies to operate. Rybalko with 3rd Guards and Lelyushenko with 4th Guards Army from the outset received the firmest instructions to cut loose from the infantry with all speed, to move by day and by night and to bypass German strong-points. It was a 'large-scale manoeuvre' Koniev sought and he was confident that they could manage this, given a successful and speedy breakthrough. Koniev had his gaze fixed on Lübben, fifty miles south-east of Berlin, for here the formal demarcation between 1st Belorussian and 1st Ukrainian

Front ended; after that, it would be 'initiative' all the way. Already in his Front directive of 8 April Koniev had mentioned 'the possibility' of using 'some forces' from the right flank to assist in the capture of Berlin: Rybalko received a specific instruction to 'bear in mind' a strongly recommended 'possibility' of attacking Berlin with a reinforced tank corps and a rifle division from Gordov's 3rd Guards Army. Moscow made no demur.

Three rifle armies, Gordov's 3rd Guards, Pukhov's 13th and Zhadov's 5th Guards made up Koniev's main infantry assault force. Gordov was assigned 25th Tank Corps and Zhdanov 4th Guards Tank Corps, the armoured formations coming under their immediate command during the breakthrough, after which they would operate as 'mobile groups'. The first operational plan called for the main assault force to break through the depth of the enemy's tactical defence along the Forst–Muskau sector and by the second day of operations reach the river Spree. The two tank armies would be introduced once the line of the Spree had been gained, with Rybalko's 3rd Guards attacking from south of Cottbus and Lelyushenko's 4th Guards from north of Spremberg, after which both would drive north-westwards in the general direction of Treuenbrietzen. The implications of this plan were plain—two days could be lost before the armour really moved off.

Zhdanov, Lelyushenko and Rybalko put their heads together, coming up with a plan to commit lead elements of the armoured armies the moment one sixty-ton bridge was open, though two such bridges would help. Forward elements from the two tank armies could then race across the 20–25 miles of ground stretching between the Neisse and the Spree, thus disrupting any German attempt to meet the Soviet thrust with a prepared defence stiffened with reserves. If all went well with the bridging operation on the Neisse, Lelyushenko was even prepared to throw in his entire first echelon. However, the new chief of staff of 1st Ukrainian Front, General I.E. Petrov (the recently disgraced commander of the 4th Ukrainian Front, sent to Koniev as a replacement for Sokolovskii, whom Zhukov had commandeered to be his own deputy with 1st Belorussian) was aghast at this suggestion. According to his book, tank armies simply did not waste themselves on trifling with the enemy's tactical defence and should be held back for deep operational penetration, which meant waiting for the infantry to force both the Neisse and the Spree.

Marshal Koniev, seeing all the possibilities, took a very different view. On 14 April Lelyushenko received orders to the effect that the moment Zhadov had two bridges open, two forward detachments of 4th Guards Tank Army would cross the Neisse and break into the enemy's tactical defences. Lelyushenko got it both ways: using the instruction about forward detachments to ram much of his first echelon forward, he selected two brigades from 10th Guards Tank Corps and one reinforced brigade from 6th Guards Mechanized Corps to operate with 95th Guards Rifle Division and with 13th and 58th Guards Rifle Divisions, respectively. Both armoured corps would make an assault crossing on the Spree, with 10th Corps driving on Sonnenwalde and the 6th on Finsterwalde; 5th Guards Mechanized Corps, which formed the second echelon, would follow in the wake of 6th Mechanized towards Finsterwalde and screen the left flank of 4th Guards Tank Army from possible counter-attacks. Koniev, however, stipulated that the tank armies must not use any of their river-crossing equipment on the Neisse, all bridging and ferries to be saved for the Spree.

In the space of the forty-eight hours between 12 and 14 April both Front commanders, Zhukov and Koniev, had drastically revised the original operational plan for the attack on Berlin. Katukov, commanding 1st Guards Tank Army, received his final orders from 1st Belorussian Front command on 12 April, which stipulated that the tank army would operate from the Küstrin bridgehead in the wake of Chuikov's 8th Guards Army, with Bogdanov's 2nd Guards Tank Army to the north and fighting with Berzarin's 5th Shock Army. Katukov's orders prescribed in detail that his tanks should go into action only when Chuikov's infantry reached the Seelow–Dolgelin–Alt Malisch line, whereupon 1st Guards would drive westwards and on the second day of operations reach the eastern outskirts of Berlin, switching then to a south-westerly axis in order to outflank the city from the south as well as seizing those southerly suburbs. The prospect of committing his tanks to heavy street fighting scarcely filled Katukov with elation and there was the uncomfortable thought of throwing in two tank armies before the defences of the Seelow Heights had been thoroughly neutralized. Meanwhile he prepared to move his tank divisions from the cover of the woods on the eastern bank of the Oder and into the Küstrin bridgehead.

On 14 April, as Marshal Koniev gave his personal approval to the plans for speedy movement of armour across the Neisse, Zhukov launched his reconnaissance in force in the areas of 47th, 3rd Shock, 5th Shock and 8th Guards Armies— the frontage of his main attack. First-echelon divisions received orders to use reinforced rifle battalions for this purpose, all covered by heavy artillery fire. Supported by tanks, Soviet units pushed into the forward German positions covering the Seelow Heights, driving in places as far as three miles and apparently disorganizing the German fire system, as well as plotting the location of large minefields. Appearances, however, were deceptive, almost fatally so as events were to prove. The German command was not fooled, and one Soviet prisoner blithely told German officers that the present attacks were only for reconnaissance. What this prisoner did not know was that the reconnaissance, put forth with such vigour, had for all practical purposes failed, since neither Front nor army staffs drew the 'correct conclusions' about the existence of the second line of German defences—the main defensive positions to which Soviet officers had drawn Zhukov's attention as early as 5 April, suggesting that the main artillery and air strikes should be directed here.

As Sunday, 15 April, drew to a close the Soviet attacks slackened and died away. The dark came, screening frantic activity on both sides of the line as German troops started on their night movement to man the second, main defensive line on the Seelow Heights while Soviet soldiers gathered round to hear last-minute, fiery exhortations from political officers, clustered at pre-attack Party meetings, trundled weapons forward, topped up tanks, filled magazines, adjusted the hundreds of guns and mortars, and lugged great quantities of bridging equipment up to the Oder bank. For all the bustle and sweaty work, there was little noise; the entire Front seemed to be creeping forward, rustling, creaking, stepping out of natural cover and from under camouflage netting, a military monster in the making and coming more alive with each minute. Closer now to zero hour and in the deep night the Guards battle-standards were taken up to front-line positions and Guards units repeated their oath to fight with honour. Two hours before the opening of the artillery barrage—timed for 5 am (Moscow time)—Marshal Zhukov appeared at Chuikov's command post, having carried out last-minute checks with several army commanders while en route to 8th Guards. Chuikov, with Marshal Zhukov uncomfortably close at his elbow, waited out the final minutes drinking tea, while across the entire Front masses of Soviet soldiers tensed up.

On the stroke of five, with the dawn not yet come, three red flares shot up and at that moment thousands of Soviet guns, *Katyusha* rocket-launchers and mortars tore the darkness apart in great gouts of muzzle flashes followed by a rolling thunder throbbing more intensely with the engine noise of the Soviet bombers and *shturmoviki* making for their targets. Not only the ground itself heaved and whirled in repeated spouts, but the very air set up its own screeching and whirring, sending its own storm of blast-whipped wind in a fresh vortex of destruction. As the guns fired on for twenty minutes, earth and what passed for sky slowly merged, a vast curtain raised by half a million shells, rockets and mortar bombs falling to a depth of five miles on the forward German positions. Three minutes before the end of this opening bombardent one searchlight shone its beam vertically into the sky, at which 143 searchlights in the sectors of the assault armies switched on, to light up the ground in front of the advancing infantry, while the artillery moved its main fire deeper into the German positions.

The searchlight beams lit up an eerie, pulsating world hung with a great pall of smoke, dust and spewing earth. Under cover of a double moving barrage the assault troops moved out of the Küstrin bridgehead, while to the north and south Soviet troops literally flung themselves at the Oder, sometimes swimming where there were as yet no bridges or paddling their way across on improvised rafts or even clinging to tree trunks amidst the great litter of guns and supplies being floated over. Ahead, the assault infantry and tanks moved forward for more than a thousand yards only to find themselves unnerved by their own lights throwing up strange reliefs or simply failing to pierce the gloom thickened with dust. Frantic orders to switch off the lights were as quickly countermanded, bringing fresh confusion as light gave way to sudden total darkness, only to be lit again with fresh beams. Chuikov's riflemen supported by forward detachments of Katukov's tank army, lurched forward searching out the terrain and, where the lights failed, simply waiting for daylight to tackle the numerous streams and canals intersecting the Oder valley. But now the tanks and SP guns began to flounder, falling further behind the infantry and steadily unwinding the co-ordination of the attack. Closing on the flooded Haupt canal at the foot of the Seelow Heights, with the only bridges under German fire, Chuikov's attack came to a complete stop until Soviet engineers could set up their own bridges. Behind, the roads began to clog with more and more traffic, piling up remorselessly and unable to move elsewhere owing to the marshy ground—and the minefields.

To the south Koniev's guns opened fire at 0615 hours on the morning of 16 April, the artillery bombardment combined with laying down smoke across 250 miles of front. From his observation post with Pukhov's 13th Army, Koniev noted with great satisfaction that the smoke laid by the guns and by aircraft—at least in this sector—was both dense and at just the right height, following the line of the Neisse exactly. With the good weather and a light but adequate wind, the smoke was beginning to fill the entire valley of the Neisse and to drift into the depth of the German defences, this artificial screen thickened now by smoke from burning forests. After forty minutes of artillery bombardment, supplemented by air strikes, Koniev set in motion the second crucial stage of his plan, launching the first-echelon assault battalions over the Neisse across a relatively narrow frontage between Forst and Muskau, and with three armies in the lead—13th, 3rd and 5th Guards.

Brought to the eastern bank of the Neisse in broad daylight, the assault troops plunged across under cover of artillery fire and the drifting smokescreens. Neither could last very long and speed was vital. Planned on a massive scale, the main assault on the Neisse involved no less than 150 different sites where engineers held bridges and ferries in readiness. The lead battalions made their crossing in boats, towing small assault bridges behind them; with a bridge laid down, infantry raced over while the engineers plunged shoulder-deep into the ice-cold water to put prefabricated wooden bridge sections in position, bolt them together and speed more infantry on its way. Within fifteen minutes of the infantry reaching the western bank, the water crossing whipped by machine-gun fire and the air slashed by Soviet weapons firing towards the German positions to make the defenders 'keep their heads down', 85mm anti-tank guns were brought over pell-mell to stiffen the tiny bridgeheads, followed by tanks and SP guns lashed to ferries. It took just under an hour to launch the light pontoon bridges, but with the tanks presently on their way to the western bank Koniev knew towards eight o'clock in the morning that his first echelon was well astride the Neisse and had secured numerous crossings. With the smoke slowly dissipating but still under the cover of the bombardment, which roared away into indeterminate distances, Soviet tanks squatted in the bridgeheads and field guns went into action. At nine o'clock the first of the heavier bridges carrying thirty-ton loads opened, but furious work went on to lay down the sixty-ton bridges capable of passing armour and heavy artillery to the western bank.

At the stroke of noon the first sixty-ton bridge in Zhdanov's 5th Guards sector opened, and in high good humour Lelyushenko prepared his two 'forward detachments' for action on the western bank, the lead tanks moving off at exactly 1300 hours—the first 'detachment' made up from 62nd Guards Tank Brigade (10th Mechanized Corps) reinforced with heavy tanks, anti-tank guns and the lorried infantry from 29th Guards Motor-Rifle Brigade, followed by a second 'detachment' comprising 16th Guards Mechanized Brigade (16th Mechanized Corps) with substantial reinforcement. Both brigade commanders received orders to cut loose from the infantry with all speed and to move ahead at a cracking pace, orders enthusiastically noted as hatches slammed, engines roared and gears crashed in, with the riflemen mounting up to follow the tank columns.

Lelyushenko and Rybalko might well rub their hands in glee as they unleashed what amounted to their first armoured echelon. But to the north, on Zhukov's front, a mighty traffic jam was building up, much to the Marshal's consternation and mounting rage. Brought to a halt on the Haupt canal, Chuikov's 8th Guards clawed its way forward, using air support to silence some of the German guns sited to the rear of the forward defence lines. Soviet infantry cleared two lines but a third, reaching to the steep slope of the Seelow Heights where the going was impossible for tanks and SP guns, remained intact. Battalion after battalion piled into this soggy, swampy, churned-up morass, with 47th Army pushing ahead for a few thousand yards, 5th Shock trying to batter its way ahead while fighting off small but ferocious counter-attacks, and 3rd Shock throwing in Kirichenko's 9th Tank Corps in an attempt to speed the breakthrough. The tanks and SP guns were forced to fan out, seeking easier ways up the Seelow escarpment but in the process slamming into German strong-points along the roads leading to Seelow itself, Friedersdorf and Dolgelin—the shout went up for artillery support and the guns were forced to redeploy to support this movement.

Fretting and fuming, Zhukov decided at noon that he could wait no longer and against the protests of the infantry commanders decided to call on both of his tank armies. Chuikov had already issued fresh orders for a renewed infantry assault, timed to go in at 1400 hours after a twenty-minute artillery bombardment and aimed at the capture of Seelow, Friedersdorf and Dolgelin, thus securing the heights. Brooking no opposition Zhukov brushed this aside and peremptorily demanded that the tanks take the field, disregarding the battle plan which expressly stipulated that the armour would go in only when the heights had been taken and the breakthrough accomplished. In a transport of rage, with little to show for nine hours of infantry actions, Zhukov now intended to loose 1,377 tanks and SP guns—six armoured corps—in order to smash his way to the heights.

Looking ahead of him, Katukov, 1st Guards Tank commander, felt his spirits droop at the prospect of committing his armour amidst the countless ditches and widespread minefields, all combining to limit his movement and deny him any manoeuvre. He at once issued orders to three corps—Yushchuk's 11th, Babad-

zhanyan's 11th Guards and Dremov's 8th Guards Mechanized—to deploy into
the Küstrin bridgehead. Zhukov issued formal attack orders to 1st and 2nd
Guards Tank Army at 1630 hours, with 1st Guards Tank committed now to
fighting with 8th Guards in order to overwhelm the German defences on the
heights, while 2nd Guards Tank would operate with 5th Shock Army and attack
towards Neu-Hardenberg-Bernau. In the late afternoon, both tank armies moved
off, with Colonel I.I. Gusakovskii's 44th Guards Tank Brigade leading for 1st
Guards Tank Army (followed by the 40th and 45th Guards Brigades), crashing
into the infantry units of 8th Guards and jamming the few roads open for
movement. The tank columns pushed their way forward, only to hamper the
transit of the artillery which Chuikov badly needed for his infantry assault on
the heights. Shouting, sweating and cursing, the tanks edged forward but the
supporting elements for rifle corps and division were hopelessly bogged down,
forced off the roads and sent sprawling into the soft, sticky ground of the valley.

Chuikov could make progress only on his right flank, where the armour did
not entirely monopolize the roads: 4th Guards Corps drew up to the town of
Seelow itself and cut the railway line together with two motor-roads. Soviet tanks
poked cautiously round bends and from corners, only to be reduced to burning
wrecks by German 88s or *Panzerfausts*, while the infantry loping beside them
were cut down by small-arms fire. Bogdanov's two tank corps, 9th and 12th
Guards, moved off to support both 3rd and 5th Shock Army, but in a very
short time—7 o'clock in the evening—they could make no further progress,
meeting heavy fire from 88s and the even heavier 155mm guns firing over open
sights. Shortly before midnight on 16 April three houses in the northern part of
Seelow had been captured by Chuikov's infantry, and Katukov's tanks continued
their fight for the heights. On Zhukov's express orders the attack continued by
night, with more tanks crowding in, roaring and grinding towards German
positions, only to be met by point-blank fire which sent them reeling and blazing
out of control. The Soviet advance had reached a distance varying between two
and five miles, but no breakthrough was as yet in sight. Zhukov, therefore,
issued fresh attack orders for 17 April, when the assault on the second line of
German defences would open with a 30–40 minute artillery bombardment and
the tank armies would continue to fight with the infantry.

This disastrous day closed on yet another unnerving note for Zhukov when
he encountered Stalin's obvious displeasure in the course of a late-night conversation
by radio telephone. Earlier in the day, at three o'clock in the afternoon, Zhukov
duly called the *Stavka* and reported that enemy defences had been breached by
Soviet troops but that they were encountering stiff resistance on the Seelow
Heights, hence the decision to send in both tank armies. Apparently unmoved,
Stalin told Zhukov that Koniev had managed to force the Neisse 'without
difficulty' and was already pressing ahead, whereas Zhukov should support his
tank armies with bombers and then report later at night to describe the outcome.
When Zhukov duly called in, late in the evening, his reception was less than

cordial and Stalin became increasingly roused at his tale of failure. Stalin rounded on Zhukov for having committed 1st Guards Tank Army on 8th Guards Army sector, all against the *Stavka's* original instructions, and demanded of the Front commander with what certainty he could state that the Seelow Heights would be captured on 17 April. Taking a firm grip on himself, Zhukov spoke as calmly as he could, promising Stalin that the heights would indeed be taken the next day and there was at least the advantage that the more troops the Germans threw in now, the quicker Berlin would fall, for it would be easier to destroy the enemy in the open rather than in protracted street fighting. Obviously unconvinced, Stalin proceeded to tell Zhukov that 'we'—the *Stavka* and himself—were toying with the idea of ordering Koniev to swing both his tank armies on to Berlin from the south, at the same time instructing Rokossovskii to speed up his attack on the Oder and then outflank Berlin from the north. The point was not lost on Zhukov. He agreed perforce that Koniev's tank armies might be moved towards Berlin, but Rokossovskii could not attack before 23 April because he would be held up forcing the Oder. *Do svidaniya*—'goodbye'—said Stalin tersely, and abruptly ended the conversation. At least Zhukov knew what he was up against.

On the 1st Ukrainian Front, Koniev could not fail to feel extraordinarily pleased at the day's outcome. Though his first-echelon troops had not quite reached the target line running through Drewitz–Komptendorf–Weisswasser, the main breakthrough on the Forst—Muskau sector—preceded by the forcing of the Neisse—brought three armies (3rd Guards, 5th Guards and 13th Army) into the German defences to a depth of almost nine miles across a seventeen-mile front. During the evening the main body of the two tank armies proceeded to cross the Neisse and moved steadily towards the breach torn in the German defences, a breach which Koniev laboured to widen with every hour. German reserves moved up to check the Soviet advance and one operational order, which fell into Soviet hands, mentioned a stand on the 'Matilda' line—something of a surprise for the Soviet command, but Koniev was far from displeased that the Germans were now committing not only their tactical but also their operational reserves. For all the resistance put up by 21st *Panzer* Division, by the evening first-echelon divisions were fighting in the second line of enemy defences, roughly halfway between the Neisse and the Spree. A further cause for satisfaction lay with the progress made by the supporting attack mounted by the Polish 2nd Army and the Soviet 52nd Army driving in the direction of Dresden, all masking the direction of the main blow; after forcing the Neisse, both armies were now between three to six miles inside the German defences on the western bank of the river.

News of the 'Matilda' line, with two German tank divisions piling up against it, as well as the need to attain those first operational objectives, caused Koniev to issue immediate orders for night attacks, both to pile on the pressure and to increase the pace of his offensive. His orders for operations on 17 April prescribed the penetration of the second line of enemy defences, the forcing of the Spree and an advance by the evening to a line running from Heide (north-west of Cottbus) to Rensdorf, Burghammer and Scheln. In addition, Koniev now alerted General Luchinskii with 28th Army to move forward in the wake of 3rd Guards Tank Army and advance along 'the Berlin axis', without waiting for the full concentration of the army. The two armies striking towards Dresden would also break through the second line of German defences and by the evening of 17 April reach a line some twelve miles east of Görlitz; 1st Guards Cavalry Corps was instructed to operate in the rear of the German forces, strike on through Kamenz and to the north-west of Bautzen, after which 1st Corps would make for the Elbe and thus secure the main assault armies from any German attack launched from the south-west.

Now unabashedly racing each other towards Berlin, Zhukov and Koniev renewed full-scale offensive operations on the morning of 17 April. During the night, in preparation for the breakthrough operation aimed at the second main line of German defences on the Seelow Heights, Zhukov regrouped artillery and armour, much of it scattered and disorganized as a result of the previous day's frenzied but abortive fighting. To prepare the fresh offensive Zhukov launched 800 bombers from Long-Range Aviation in heavy night attacks on the German positions, while the artillery redeployed to support the infantry and tank assaults. At 10 o'clock on the morning of 17 April massed Soviet artillery again rained down shells on the German defences on the heights, thirty minutes of heavy bombardment supplemented by bombing attacks with wave after wave of Soviet aircraft. Once again huge columns of smoke and dust climbed over the Seelow Heights, with the first tanks and sections of assault infantry moving up before the barrage ceased; the main body of 8th Guards and 1st Guards Tank Army jumped off at exactly 1015 hours. In the broad morning light, hundreds of Soviet tanks were on the move with Soviet riflemen clinging to the T-34s lumbering along the roads to the heights. Some tanks burst into flames, slewed sideways or stopped, but more came on, and crunched over the trenches and gun-pits, facing dwindling fire from the 88s and *Panzerfausts* while heavy machine-guns cut into the Soviet infantry. Towards noon 11th Guards Tank Corps and 8th Guards Mechanized Corps straddled the railway line and captured both Friedersdorf and Dolgelin, only to be heavily attacked by units of the *Kurmark* division.

Operating with the 35th Guards Rifle Division from 4th Guards Corps (8th Guards Army), Yushchuk's 11th Tank Corps enjoyed some substantial success on the morning of 17 April: jumping off at 1030 hours, the tanks and infantry fought their way to the north of Seelow, smashing down German resistance by noon, with tank brigades assaulting Seelow from the north and the south. The village of Seelow was a vital point in the German defences, since it was located close to the southern extremity of the defensive system near the western bank of the Oder. The Küstrin-Berlin motorway ran along the crest of the heights and through Seelow itself, so that once Soviet troops occupied the crest of the ridge an open highway stretched away into Berlin itself. Yushchuk, a bluff and genial veteran, pushed his tanks forward as best he could, hamstrung as he was by all the clutter of infantry and menaced by the over-enthusiasm of Soviet gunners— already one of his brigade commanders had remonstrated in very earthy Russian with 5th Shock Army about just where they were putting down their shells, much to the fury of General Sokolovskii, a real stickler for discipline, who witnessed this distinctly uncultured scene. The *Panzerfausts* presented continuous dangers, but Yushchuk was intrigued to see Soviet tank crews grabbing wire mattresses from German houses and wrapping them round the front of the tanks to deflect the bazooka rounds.

Seizing on this chance, Katukov directed Babadzhanyan's 11th Guards Tank Corps into the gap ripped open by Yushchuk's two brigades, the 20th and 65th. But still the armour could not break out and cut loose from the infantry, since heavy German opposition from numerous strong-points and terrain chopped up with small lakes, little rivers and canals constantly slowed movement. Elsewhere Zhukov's assault armies edged their way into the main German defences, with the 3rd Shock Army supported by 9th Guards Tank Corps driving on Kunersdorf and 5th Shock Army supported by two armoured corps (12th Guards Tank and 1st Mechanized Corps) also biting into this defensive line, having forced the Alt-Oder. Towards the end of the day Chuikov's 8th Guards with Babadzhanyan's tanks managed to take the village of Seelow, and the German lines, hammered mercilessly by ground fire and air bombardment, began to crack—though the flanks still held against the assaults of 3rd Shock and 47th Army.

Koniev's main assault force went into the attack promptly at 0900 hours on the morning of 17 April, preceded by a short but powerful artillery bombardment. With the woods burning about them, Soviet tank columns raced for the river Spree, fighting off German counter-attacks and leaving scores of small but ferocious battles in their wake as German tanks and infantry tried to stem the Soviet advance. As he hurried on to the Spree in order to watch 3rd Guards Tank Army take this obstacle in its stride, Koniev passed a great litter of gutted and burning machines, the forests hiding most of the dead jammed into the small streams and strewn haphazardly across the line of advance. The gaunt frames of tanks and the spiky remnants of guns presented a whole panoply of battle, but the fight was over here. Only the thunder of artillery ahead and the continuous roar of Soviet aircraft reminded Koniev of the unfinished battle as he pushed along the corridor carved out by Soviet troops, the sappers having cleared paths through the spreading minefields.

To his disappointment Koniev discovered that his lead elements had not been able to beat the Germans to the Spree, though sporadic preliminary fire indicated a defence as yet uncoordinated. There was no time wasted in forcing the Spree, an expanse of water 50–60 yards wide in places. Without waiting for bridging equipment and after talking with Rybalko, 3rd Guards Tank commander, Koniev proposed that a single tank, with a handpicked crew, try a rush-crossing in view of rumours about a ford. The lead tank hit the water and ploughed ahead in water only about three feet deep, the water washing merely up to its tracks; the light German weapons simply pinged against and bounced off the T-34. Tank after tank followed, until the lead brigades were over the Spree and the German line broken with exemplary speed. Koniev knew at last that the crunch had come and lost no time in reporting his striking gains to Stalin.

Quartered for the moment in a castle near Cottbus, fitted out with all the baronial accoutrements, Koniev pondered his final talk with Lelyushenko and Rybalko—both of whom knew that the Front commander was talking about Berlin, for all the general injunctions about pressing ahead, outflanking, manoeuvring, conserving equipment. The offensive was rolling forward at speed, but Koniev was obliged to think about the fact that the tank formations were about to enter a deep gap ahead of 13th Army, while Gordov's 3rd Guards to the right and Zhadov's 5th Guards to the left held off furious German counter-attacks. The corridor was narrow, the flanks were under heavy pressure but the tanks must press on. At least, however, Koniev had planted himself in the centre of the breakthrough zone and here was token enough that he would see his tank commanders through, come what may. All this went unspoken but it sufficed. Koniev was now in a position to consult with Stalin.

Assured finally that his tank units were advancing west of the Spree, Koniev contacted the *Stavka*. The Front commander reported his progress to Stalin, who listened for a moment and then suddenly broke in with a statement about Zhukov's relatively slow progress, only to fall into an abrupt silence. Koniev also held his tongue, wisely as it proved. After a moment or so Stalin returned with a proposal to redeploy Zhukov's mobile forces and send them through the gap opened by Koniev. Punctilious as ever, Marshal Koniev rendered a considered reply: 'Comrade Stalin, this will take too much time and will add considerable confusion . . . the situation on our Front is developing favourably, we have adequate forces and we can turn both tank armies towards Berlin.' Koniev went on to describe the axis on which the tank armies would operate and cited Zossen as a reference point. Silent for a moment, Stalin asked Koniev whether he knew that Zossen was the headquarters of the German General Staff and what scale of map he was using. Koniev replied that he was using a 1:200 map and that he was perfectly well aware that Zossen housed the German General Staff. Stalin spoke quite decisively: '*Ochen khorosho. Ya soglasen. Povernite tankovye armii na Berlin*'—'Good. I agree. Turn your tank armies on Berlin.' At that the line went dead.

Koniev lost no time at all in making radio contact with his tank army commanders—what had earlier gone unsaid could now be spelled out in detailed operational orders specifying Berlin as the objective. Rybalko at 3rd Guards received orders to force the Spree in strength on the night of 17 April, drive towards Fetschau–Golsen–Barut–Teltow and break into the southern outskirts of Berlin on the night of 20 April; Lelyushenko at 4th Guards was instructed to force the Spree north of Spremberg during the night of 17 April, strike towards Drebkau–Calau–Danne–Luckenwalde, capture the Beelitz–Treuenbrietzen–Luckenwalde area, and invest Potsdam and the south-western suburbs of Berlin, also securing the Treuenbrietzen area with 5th Mechanized Corps. The tank armies must bypass towns and avoid frontal attacks, for Koniev demanded speed above all—'I demand a firm understanding that the success of the tank armies depends on boldness of manoeuvre and swiftness of operations.' This Front directive, numbered 00215 and dated 17 April, was issued at 0247 hours on 18 April, by which time both Lelyushenko and Rybalko were already turning their tank columns to the north-west with all possible speed, confident that the flanks would hold.

Suffused with anger Zhukov heard from Stalin of the new demarcation line between 1st Belorussian and 1st Ukrainian Fronts, all a reflection of Koniev's rapid progress. More than ever he was intent on ramming his armies on to Berlin, but Stalin demanded of him those 'requisite measures' for speeding up his attack and in galling fashion offered help from the *Stavka*. In fact there was some cause for concern that Zhukov's forces would expend themselves before they embarked on the actual storming of Berlin. Stalin now envisaged two outflanking movements against the Germans, from the south and south-west with Koniev's front and from the north when Rokossovskii took the offensive on 20 April. The reproof to Zhukov was very plain and the Marshal had no intention of taking it lying down. Warning signals went out from the Front staff to army commanders, demanding an acceleration in the pace of the offensive—otherwise the main strength and reserves of the armies would be consumed in this battle—and requiring that all army commanders proceed forthwith to those corps mounting the main attacks, an order accompanied by Zhukov's own categorical refusal to allow any to the rear. All artillery would be moved up to the first echelon, even the heaviest siege guns, and under no circumstances should it be held back more than a few thousand yards from the echelon engaged in the assault; artillery fire must be concentrated on the decisive breakthrough sectors. The attack must be relentless, the Front must fight by day and by night—then the sooner would Berlin be theirs.

Zhukov proceeded to lay the lash across the backs of his commanders. Nor was he a novice in this practice. Inadequate knowledge of the German defensive system and inefficient use of artillery and air resources contributed substantially to Zhukov's failure—a costly one in terms of men, machines and time—but he now thrust the responsibility on to subordinate commanders. In a stern and menacing order issued on 18 April Zhukov demanded that all commanders from army down to brigade personally inspect forward units and investigate the situation, to establish exactly where the Germans were and in what strength, where Soviet forces were and just what they with their supporting arms were doing and how much ammunition supporting units had at their disposal. Further, how was the control of supporting units organized? The Front formations were given until 1200 hours on 19 April to put their units in order, to issue precise operational orders and replenish ammunition; at 1200 hours on that day the offensive would be renewed and the advance 'developed *according to plan*'. The commanders of 8th Guards and 5th Shock Armies would be responsible for co-ordinating infantry and armour; strict traffic control would be enforced, transport vehicles would be taken off the roads and mechanized infantry must move on foot. To implement co-ordination between rifle divisions and tank brigades, 5th Shock and 8th Guards must send their own officers to the tank brigades of 1st and 2nd Guards Tank Army, while the tank armies would send officers to the rifle divisions. Officers who showed themselves 'incapable of carrying out assignments' or displayed 'lack of resolution' faced immediate dismissal. Advance or face dire consequences: such was Zhukov's dictum.

This order had yet to filter throughout the assault armies, but whatever 'lack of resolution' and crass inability had been so far displayed, the sheer weight of metal and gross numbers now began to tell on the German defenders. Ominous cracks started to appear in the German lines as units were simply obliterated in storms of fire or were slaughtered to a man, as troops on the move found themselves boxed in by refugee columns and as contact between units was slowly lost. On the morning of 18 April, after yet another heavy barrage, Zhukov renewed the assault on the Seelow defences, more than ever determined to break through, though the infantry was red-eyed and like Soviet tank units drastically thinned—the price of frontal assault on the 500 feet of the Seelow Heights. Busse's Ninth Army still held its positions but his left flank was beginning to buckle and the right was now seriously menaced by Koniev's sweeping drive from the south. To the north, von Manteuffel in command of the Third *Panzer* Army cruised in his reconnaissance plane over Rokossovskii's front, noting all the preparations for an attack and the obvious unconcern at the appearance of a German aircraft: this additional blow must fall soon. On the Seelow Heights Weidling's LVI *Panzer* Corps—now a shadow of that famous formation—desperately needed reinforcement and waited expectantly on *SS Nordland* and 18th *Panzer* Division. Neither arrived; the *SS* troops milled about trying to obtain fuel and the heavily armed 18th Division arrived just in time to join an enforced retreat. By this time also the 9th Parachute Division, which had already taken the brunt of that first furious Soviet assault, could no longer hold and was breaking into pieces. Much to Weidling's disgust and anger, the unctuous leader of the *Hitler Jugend,* Axmann, promised him schoolboys to hold the rear of LVI Corps, an order the corps commander rescinded at once: if the *SS* frittered away vital time and the *Wehrmacht* fumbled, then mere boys should not die in their place.

Pouring on the fire, Zhukov's assault armies waged a furious battle on 18 April across the Seelow positions, rutted and gashed by constant bombardment.

At 1000 hours 47th Army, after a forty-minute artillery barrage, jumped off with three corps in the first echelon in an attack aimed at Wriezen. An hour earlier 3rd Shock with 9th Guards Tank Corps in support launched another attack in the direction of Kunersdorf, probing towards open country; fighting near Batzlow Soviet tanks bumped into the third line of German defences and found their operations once again cramped by lack of space. Striking early in the morning, at 7 am, 5th Shock attacked under cover of a short artillery bombardment—ten minutes—and cut its way through wooded ridges towards Reichenberg and Münchehof, only to be brought to a halt by infantry counter-attacks and *Panzerfaust* fire.

Chuikov's 8th Guards also struck at 7 am after a short artillery barrage. Yushchuk's 11th Tank Corps supporting 4th Guards Rifle Corps ground its way forward, beating off repeated German counter-attacks and driving inexorably towards Müncheberg, though slowly. Chuikov was becoming increasingly concerned about his left flank where 69th Army seemed scarcely to have moved for the past seventy-two hours. Clearly the German plan was to deflect 8th Guards southwards—away from Berlin—and any complaint on Chuikov's part about the inertia of 69th Army would have meant diverting his own troops in that very direction southwards. Chuikov decided to press on without pointing up the dangers on his left flank, and rammed his divisions on to Müncheberg, covering the eastern approaches to Berlin itself. By the evening of 18 April 8th Guards were on the Treibutz–Jahnsfelde line and fighting for Marxdorf and Lietzen, while to his right Soviet troops had reached the Marxwalde–Wulkov line; the left flank remained a problem, with 69th Army stalled, so that Chuikov sent in two divisions from his own 28th Corps to stiffen the flank. North-west of Seelow, 3rd Shock Army found itself engaged in very heavy fighting for Batzlow, with every approach road covered by artillery and mortar fire, literally rained down on the Soviet troops from the surrounding high ground; Lt.-Gen. A.F. Kazankin commanding 12th Guards Rifle Corps decided to mount a night attack after a thirty-minute artillery bombardment, with two divisions fighting their way through gaps in the German defences to the north of Batzlow itself. Under cover of the guns, the infantry, with tanks and SP guns in support, started the attack at 11 o'clock at night, but it was almost dawn before the village was cleared of German troops. Berzarin's 5th Shock Army took over the business of ripping open this breach in the defences where they stretched into 5th Shock's operational area.

Now fully two days late, Zhukov could only hope that on this fourth day of offensive operations he would attain the objectives prescribed for the second. The Soviet offensive was cutting deeply into the third line of German defences, with fierce fighting taking place at Müncheberg, a key position: two corps (4th and 29th Guards) from 8th Guards Army used a reinforced battalion from each division to crack this strong-point, with the attack going in shortly after noon on 19 April and preceded by a thirty-minute barrage. Outflanked by 11th Guards Tank Corps to the south and 11th Tank Corps to the north-west, Müncheberg

finally fell towards 9 o'clock on the evening of 19 April, when 82nd Guards
Rifle Division burst into the town from the east and cleared it of Germans. The
fall of Müncheberg, east of Berlin, and the capture of Wriezen to the north
clearly marked the beginning of the end. By the evening of 19 April Zhukov's
forces had cracked all three German defence lines across a 45-mile front running
from the Alt-Oder to Kunersdorf, and were eighteen miles further on their way
to the west and to Berlin.

That same night, 19 April, Marshal Rokossovskii reported to Stalin that 2nd
Belorussian Front stood ready to take the offensive. Von Manteuffel's misgivings
were fully justified. During the night of 19–20 April Soviet bombers with the
Women's Night Bomber Regiment in the van, attacked the German defences,
while the three assault armies—65th, 70th and 49th—made their last-minute
preparations, sending out hand-picked fighting squads and patrols to stiffen the
positions already won on the western bank of the West Oder, as well as investing
those all-important dykes which crisscrossed the floodland. Rokossovskii intended
to launch his attack across a thirty-mile front from Altdamm to Schwedt, with
each army allocated a relatively narrow breakthrough sector (little more than
2–2½ miles); the artillery barrage would be fired off at 0700 hours on 20 April
and last one hour exactly. Like Koniev, Rokossovskii intended to make considerable
use of smokescreens and included a large-scale diversionary attack by 19th and
2nd Shock Armies to the north of Stettin, an assault crossing of the river in this
area which was designed to mislead the German command about the main axis
of the offensive.

The actual timing of the offensive had been the cause of considerable debate
at 2nd Belorussian Front. Batov commanding 65th Army did not care for the
original plan, which called for an opening barrage at 9 o'clock, preferring a dawn
attack which could take advantage of the morning mists; the duration of the
barrage should also be reduced from 90 minutes to 45, since staff calculations
at 65th Army showed that the assault troops should be astride the West Oder
in 45 minutes. Rokossovskii took his time to ponder this problem, which involved
timing the attacks of 49th and 70th Armies and only at the last minute decided
in favour of Batov's suggestions. Meanwhile Batov became much concerned with
the level of the water in the flood valley, a level which had been rising during
the past few days when reconnaissance activity was being intensified, but now an
added hazard came from strong winds forcing more water into Batov's path; to
allay Batov's growing anxiety and to allow him to provide the speediest possible
support to his detachments already on the western bank, Rokossovskii authorized
him to attack even earlier. At 0630 hours Batov's guns opened fire and laid
smoke in the sector of the 37th Guards Rifle Division. Grishin and Popov with
49th and 70th Armies elected to stick to the original plan and waited—a less
than happy decision, as events all too soon showed.

Batov's 65th Army opened the assault crossing and under cover of smoke the
109th Guards Rifle Regiment (37th Guards Rifle Division) made for the western

bank of the West Oder in a motley fleet of small boats and rafts. Fierce struggles broke out for the dykes on the western bank as Soviet troops tried to invest them in order to land the tanks and guns being ferried over by pontoon, but by 8 o'clock units already on the western bank began to strike out at the German defences. The thick morning mist, made the more dense by smoke, dispersed only slowly and the air support which was promised failed to materialize until after 9 o'clock, but Batov's first bridgehead expanded yard by yard, the main divisional force making ready to follow the lead battalions. Though a few 45mm guns were ferried over to the bridgehead the great need was for tanks and artillery in some quantity; finally, at 1300 hours, two sixteen-ton ferry crossings were in operation and delivering artillery and SP guns to the western bank. By the evening Batov had 31 battalions across the river, together with 50 artillery pieces, 70 mortars and 15 SU-76 SP guns, all in a bridgehead now holding four divisions and extending for more than three miles and a mile or so deep.

Concerned at the progress of the attack, Rokossovskii asked Batov for a report and decided to come to 65th Army to see for himself, accompanied by the air force commander, K.A. Vershinin, the Front engineer B.V. Blagoslavov and the Front artillery commander A.K. Sokolskii. The scene which greeted him laid most of his fears to rest and he was able to watch by telescope Soviet units on the western bank beating off a German counter-attack mounted with about one battalion. Confident that Batov's divisions were well established, Rokossovskii proposed to exploit this bridgehead in the interests of the entire Front assault. Popov's 70th Army had begun its attack at 0700 hours, covered by an hour-long artillery bombardment; using two ferry crossings and 150 small boats, lead battalions from 47th Rifle Corps managed to gain a foothold on the opposite bank of the West Oder but the crossing was covered by German guns at Greifenhagen and the dykes—vital for the movement of artillery and heavy equipment—were covered by German machine-guns and anti-tank weapons. Popov's guns had failed to knock out these defences, and the infantry suffered. Only the intervention of Soviet aircraft saved the situation, enabling the engineers to move pontoons up to the dykes and start the movement of artillery.

Small though his bridgeheads were and as yet bereft of artillery, at least Popov was across the West Oder. The same could not be said for Grishin's 49th Army, a formation specially reinforced to launch an attack designed to push Third *Panzer* back to the north and the north-west where 70th Army would finish the German divisions off—an operation closely linked with the right flank of Zhukov's 1st Belorussian Front. To Rokossovskii's consternation Grishin had not moved an inch: attacking at the same hour as 70th Army, 49th Army's assault crossing had been beaten back decisively. Thanks to poor reconnaissance before the attack, a secondary canal had been mistaken for the main stream of the West Oder, so that the opening artillery barrage fell on a few insignificant German positions, leaving the main defences untouched. Once the rifle units launched their crossing, they were met by devastating machine-gun fire. Only handfuls of men managed to get ashore on the West Oder, hanging on to the minute bridgeheads by their fingertips and suffering heavy casualties in their attempt to remain on the opposite bank.

Rokossovskii ordered Grishin to renew his attack in the morning, since he feared that further delay might allow the German command to transfer troops from this sector to block the 65th and 70th Armies, but this did not appreciably alter a serious situation. Ironically, the formation in the least favourable position— Batov's 65th, whose flank was exposed to long-range German guns in Stettin— had scored the greatest success, a situation Rokossovskii now intended to exploit to the full. There was nothing for it but to shift the main effort of 2nd Belorussian Front to the right flank, using Batov's substantial bridgehead; 70th Army could be directed to these crossings, though by the evening of 20 April Popov had twelve battalions across on his own sector, while the reinforcement supplied to Grishin's 49th could also be rerouted into this area. Should Grishin fail again, Rokossovskii intended to redeploy these resources. Meanwhile he had offered Batov Panov's 1st Guards Don Tank Corps—Panov was an old comrade of Batov's—and possibly 3rd Guards Tank Corps, as well as reinforcements in bridging equipment to take the increased traffic. Already reconnaissance units from 136th Rifle Division (70th Army) were drawing up in Batov's area, and Grishin sent along two pontoon bridges and two regiments of SP guns. Batov certainly stood in need of some reinforcement, for the slow progress of 70th Army and the unsuccessful 'demonstration' by 2nd Shock Army north of Stettin enabled the German command to bring more forces to bear against the 65th Army. During the night of 20–21 April the units in Batov's bridgehead fought off more than thirty German counter-attacks and two German divisions (27th *Langemark* and the 281st Infantry Division) were on their way to swell the attacks, which grew steadily to fifty and more, sometimes in regimental strength with tank support.

For the moment Soviet units on the western bank of the West Oder could only 'nibble' at the German defences, since they lacked sufficient strength to launch a break-out; furious work went on to build up the crossings in Batov's zone, with thirty-ton and fifty-ton bridges going down and large sixteen-ton ferries in operation, much of this equipment coming from 49th Army. In the course of operations on 21 April Batov continued to reinforce his bridgehead, with 105th Rifle Corps extending the front to the right, but 70th Army made little or no progress, the sum total of its gains amounting to the capture of a clump of woods north of Pargov; however, units of 70th Army did manage to clear some of the dykes in the flooded stretch between the two Oders and began at last to move heavy equipment. Grishin's 49th continued to fare dismally, managing only small footholds on the western bank of the West Oder, which had to be maintained against heavy Germany pressure. Rokossovskii's offensive must now proceed almost wholly along the right flank, using Batov's enlarged bridgehead now five miles across and over two miles deep.

On 20 April, the *Führer's* fifty-sixth birthday, the reality of the threat to Berlin hit the city like a shock wave. By way of vengeful and sardonic salutation, Allied bombers mounted their last massive raid on the German capital, setting off a huge round of fires. Rumours began to spread, affirming that Soviet troops were now at Müncheberg and Strausberg—a mere fifteen miles to the east of Berlin—and another major Soviet thrust was developing with great rapidity from the south; encirclement could not be far away. The ruination brought about by repeated heavy bomber raids abounded in the city. Now, familiar daily routines terminated abruptly: the trams stopped, the underground closed, refuse lay uncollected, mail undelivered, and electric power died. Nazi potentates made ready to pack and depart without further ceremony, though not without their large and impressive official cars; senior officers were not slow to follow this example, adding to the convoys of cars now speeding to the north and to the south. The Commandant's office in Berlin freely handed out passes to those officials who wished to leave, deliberately fuelling the stampede. But there was to be no escape for the mass of the citizenry denied transport or for those already hanging limp from lamp-posts, hanged for supposed desertion when their masters practised it in reality.

At 11 o'clock on the morning of 20 April Zhukov's guns opened fire directly on Berlin: Guards Major A.I. Zyukin commanding a battery of the 30th Guards Artillery Brigade attached to General Perkhorovich's 47th Army fired off a salvo in salute to the capture of Bernau. In the course of the morning's fighting 125th Rifle Corps (47th Army) had stormed and captured Bernau; Kuznetsov's 3rd Shock was through the third belt of German defences, and Bogdanov's 2nd Guards Tank Army after its agonizing entanglement among the German position had now reached open country and raced ahead of the infantry to the outskirts of Berlin at Ladenburg and Zepernick, the latter in the north-eastern suburbs of the city. Two of Bogdanov's corps—9th Guards Tank and 1st Mechanized—continued their drive to outflank the German capital from the north. Berzarin's 5th Shock Army with 12th Guards Tank Corps and elements of 11th Tank Corps in support fought its way through the remnants of the third defence line and aimed to wipe out the defenders of Strausberg.

Koniev's tanks continued to race upon Berlin from the south, a fact much to the fore of Zhukov's mind. Cutting right away from the infantry, Lelyushenko and Rybalko had sliced their way north-westwards for about thirty-eight miles isolating Gräser's Fourth *Panzer* Army and cutting right across Busse's lines of communication in the drive for Zossen and Potsdam. Towards midday on 20 April the 6th Tank Corps (3rd Guards Tank Army) raced towards Barut in an attempt to rush this small town. The attempt failed, whereupon the Corps commander selected two brigades—the 53rd and 52nd—to attack Barut from the south-east and west; at 1300 hours Barut fell to Soviet troops and the road to Zossen was open. Lelyushenko operating a little to the south meanwhile pressed on towards Luckenwalde and Jüterborg, swinging the left flank of the tank army to the west. Further to the rear Gordov's 3rd Guards Army was trying desperately to eliminate the German 'Cottbus group', having already broken into the eastern suburbs and outflanked the town to the south-west. Koniev, however, could scarcely ignore the fact that from Cottbus to Zossen his right flank was open and vulnerable—it was necessary to have a little 'educational talk' with Gordov in order to impress on him the urgency of eliminating the Cottbus group, while at the same time pushing Luchinskii's 28th Army forward to close this gap and to complete the encirclement of German forces south-east of Berlin. Part of Luchinskii's army also moved forward to support Rybalko's tank divisions.

However, Marshal Koniev was far from satisfied. In the morning a heavy artillery barrage, preceded by bombing attacks, opened against Spremberg—a threat to his left flank, as Cottbus was to his right—and Zhadov's infantry attacked at 11 o'clock; Lebedenko's 33rd Guards Rifle Corps managed to clear the town and even advanced about four miles to the west. Two corps from Pukhov's 13th Army continued to advance westwards in the wake of the tank armies and covered about twenty miles on 20 April, drawing up to Finsterwalde. In effect, Koniev had cut the entire German front in two. But this achievement was not enough. A Front order instructed army commanders that henceforth only fuel and ammunition would be shipped west of the Spree. Koniev, voicing his dissatisfaction, ordered Bogdanov to speed up his investment of the Barut–Luckenwalde line, the quicker to strike on Berlin. On 20 April both tank army commanders received a blunt radiogram from Koniev: 'Personal to Comrades Rybalko and Lelyushenko. Order you categorically to break into Berlin tonight. Report execution. 1940 hours 20.4.45, Koniev.' The import was plain.

The moment for urgent, demanding signals had clearly come. Within an hour of Koniev's radiogram to his tank armies Marshal Zhukov radioed the commander and staff of 1st Guards Tank Army with special instructions of his own:

Katukov, Popiel. 1st Guards Tank has been assigned a historic mission: to be the first to break into Berlin and hoist the Victory Banner. Personally charge you with organizing and execution. From each corps send up to one of the best brigades into Berlin and issue following orders: no later than 0400 hours morning 21 April at any cost to break into the outskirts of Berlin and report at once for transmission to Comrade Stalin and press announcement. Zhukov. Telegin. [A. Babadzhanyan, *Dorogi pobedy*, p. 271.}

This order left nothing to the imagination. Zhukov intended to be the first into Berlin and not only Stalin but the world press would know it. Since 1430 hours on 20 April the 207th Field Artillery Regiment of the 10th Artillery Brigade (6th Breakthrough Artillery Division) had been systematically shelling Berlin, but Zhukov wanted his men on the ground in undisputed first possession. Katukov knew what was required of him, though time was short to prepare. Choosing the best brigades presented no problem—1st and 44th, obviously, the latter commanded by Colonel Gusakovskii—but very little time remained in which to plan the operation in detail. The woods were burning, sending out thick smoke and cutting down visibility; the tanks could use one road, but boys with *Panzerfausts* waited at almost every turn.

With Soviet shells falling directly and uninterruptedly on Berlin, Hitler emerged from the bunker in the afternoon of 20 April to dust-laden air and the virtual rubbish dump of the *Reichskanzlei* garden, littered with old cans and torn branches. It was a bent, trembling *Führer* who inspected soldiers of the *SS Frundsberg* Division and the boys of the *Hitler Jugend*, teenagers who might sob with fright but still fired their *Panzerfausts* with determination. Wishing the men and the boys well, Hitler turned his back on the daylight and went underground, there to greet well-wishers gathered for his birthday and then to debate the fate of Berlin in a weird, writhing, hopeless war conference. The situation bore every sign of impending catastrophe: Busse's Ninth Army, particularly his right flank, faced encirclement and speedy destruction, a great and growing gap had opened between Ninth Army and Fourth *Panzer*, Koniev's tanks were at the approaches to Zossen, von Manteuffel's Third *Panzer* was isolated from the main body of the defence and Ninth Army, and Berlin itself was under threat of immediate attack. Of his own plans Hitler confided privately that he intended to stay in Berlin. Discussing a reorganization of the Nazi command, he authorized Dönitz and part of the OKW staff to leave for the north and others to depart to the south—even hinting that he might follow—though his own decision was well nigh made. Heinrici had battled all day to save Busse's Ninth Army; shortly after midnight, on 21 April, he argued again for permission to pull the Ninth back, conscious that a 'front line' scarcely existed, only to encounter an unyielding refusal on the part of the *Führer*. Indeed, Hitler for his part now demanded that Ninth Army hold its positions and Heinrici bend all his efforts to plugging the gaps to the east of Berlin in order to re-establish a continuous front. Ninth Army was clearly doomed, but the grandiose war game with arrows stabbing the maps and lines coiling round supposed positions, where none but the dead now lay, must be played out to the end.

On Saturday morning, 21 April, the scream of shells and the dull veinous red of shell bursts, scattering shoppers, blowing passers-by to pieces or ripping them horribly with shrapnel on the open streets, were the first intimations that Berlin was under close and sustained attack. 'Mother cannon' announced it in traditional Russian style, forcing Berliners into the grim, crowded bunkers which all too soon stank of overloaded humanity. Berlin scrambled underground to fight this pitiful, sordid, dirty, filth-laden battle, shunning the light of day like the *Führer* who had already abandoned the open skies. During the night, as Hiler dementedly condemned Ninth Army to death, Zhukov's tanks and infantry closed on the northern and north-eastern suburbs of the city, driving past the remnants of SS units and skirting the *Panzerfaust* ambushes laid by old men and schoolboys. The tanks steered gingerly through wooded areas and passed warily through hamlets and small villages, alert for that sudden burst of fire which signalled a German rearguard. Towards 6 o'clock in the morning of 21

April Kuznetsov's 3rd Shock Army with 1st Mechanized Corps closed on the north-eastern suburbs of Berlin, with Colonel A.I. Negoda's 171st Rifle Division in the lead. Driving down the Lindenberg–Malchow road, units of Krivoshein's 1st Mechanized Corps tried during the morning to take Malchow off the march, but two brigades—19th and 35th—ran into heavy opposition and stopped short. Krivoshein decided to sidestep to the east and drive on Weissensee. One regiment (9th Tank) fought its way into Weissensee and opened up a route for the whole corps to push deeper into Berlin as well as investing this outer suburb. Karow had already fallen to 79th Corps during the afternoon.

Zhukov intended to strike as speedily as possible into the very centre of Berlin. Kuznetsov's 3rd Shock Army was already following its changed orders, which directed it into the heart of the city rather than merely outflanking it from the north. All armies, in addition to adjusting their line of advance, were also reorganizing into battle groups and assault detachments ready for the street fighting which now faced them; assault groups formed up with their complement of riflemen, tanks, artillery and the ubiquitous combat engineers—such groups usually about company strength with two or three 76mm guns, a couple of 45mm guns, a handful of tanks or SP guns, two or three platoons of sappers, and a flame-thrower platoon. Those flame-throwers came in for extensive use when spraying bunkers and strong-points—turning men, women and children into blazing, writhing torches screaming their way to death. Everywhere Soviet gunners laid down their barrages or else fired off the *Katyusha* multiple rocket launchers; with undisguised glee, army and divisional artillery commanders fired salvo after salvo into Berlin, a sustained bombardment augmented by the short-range fire of tank guns blasting away at houses and prominent buildings. To support 3rd Shock's assault General Ignatov commanding 4th Artillery Break-through Corps let loose with the heaviest-calibre guns, opening fire at 10 o'clock in the morning.

During the course of 21 April Berzarin's 5th Shock Army, with 12th Guards Tank Corps in support, also broke into Berlin from the north, smashing its way towards Hohenschönhausen by the evening, with one corps—32nd Rifle—fighting in Mahrzahn; 9th Rifle Corps held the left flank and was engaged south of Altlandsberg. Though Zhukov's right-flank armies—3rd Shock, 47th Army and 2nd Guards Army—made considerable progress, Chuikov's 8th Guards and Katukov's 1st Tank Army found their way barred in the area of Fürstenwalde, Erkner and Petershagen to the east of Berlin, fighting off infantry counter-attacks and steering carefully through minefields.

Zhukov's plan using three armies (47th, 3rd Shock and 2nd Guards Tank Army) to attack from the north-east and three armies (5th Shock, 8th Guards and 1st Guards Tank Army) to strike from the east and south-east aimed to split the defence into two parts, with Chuikov aiming at Bohnsdorf. The dire threat, however, seemed to come from the direction of Koniev's front, sweeping from the south towards Berlin with two tank armies, slashing its way through

Gräser's Fourth *Panzer* Army—Hitler moaned desperately about 'treachery' here—
and amputating Ninth Army's right flank. Finally Zhadov's 5th Guards eliminated
the Spremberg threat, while the imperturbable Pukhov with 13th Army followed
in the wake of the tank armies, slicing away the German Army Group 'Vistula'
from Army Group Centre. Koniev pushed Luchinskii's 28th Army forward as
fast as possible, but the lead formation of 28th Army—128th Rifle Corps—
still lagged a good sixty miles behind the fast-moving tanks of Rybalko's 3rd
Guards Tank Army. To the astonishment of the Germans, Soviet tanks halted
inexplicably at Barut, giving them time to organize the evacuation of the massive
headquarters at Zossen, though the column of *Wehrmacht* vehicles transporting
files and staff to Berlin found itself under violent attack from Soviet fighter-
bombers. Rybalko's 6th Tank Corps did press the attack on Zossen, using three
tank brigades—51st, 52nd and 53rd. Soviet tank troops had captured the German
High Command headquarters on 21 April, stumbling into an underground world
of bewildering complexity, the floors, offices and galleries strewn with papers,
maps and discarded uniforms.

Here was a genuine lair of the Fascist beast, with teleprinters still clacking
and telephones ringing. The consoles carried large printed notices in elementary
Russian, reading 'not to damage the installations'. A telephone rang, a voice
peremptorily demanded some general or other and with huge delight a Russian
reply was returned—'Ivan is here, you can - - - -'. Four fat and drunken German
soldiers watched this scene with astonishment, taking care to raise their hands
high in the air. The engineer in charge, Hans Beltow, obliged his captors with
a short tour of the communications set-up, where phones continued to ring and
teleprinters spewed tape: 'What would be your attitude to our attempts to get
in touch with the Allies' (message from the north), with the reply, 'Fools, don't
you know the real state of affairs? The Ivans are on top of us . . .' The Soviet
girl interpreters picked up more tapes, began to translate and left off, blushing.
The capture of Zossen, the very brain of the fearsome and dreaded *Wehrmacht*,
was finally consummated with one extremely intoxicated German soldier being
carried off on a stretcher.

While the tanks raced on north-westwards to Berlin, Koniev once more urged
the speediest possible reduction of the entire German 'Cottbus group'. Gordov
at 3rd Guards Army had used his available tanks too slowly and had not
manoeuvred with sufficient dexterity, but Zhadov's operation at Spremberg was
proceeding more or less according to plan and in co-operation with 13th Army;
the main body of 5th Guards now deployed for the drive towards the Elbe.
While Koniev continued to reinforce 3rd Guards in order to complete the
envelopment of Ninth Army's right flank—the 'Frankfurt-Guben group'—he
also became increasingly concerned about the gap opening between 3rd and 4th
Guards tank armies, a gap which now reached for almost twenty miles and was
growing with each hour. The only solution was to rush part of Luchinskii's 28th
Army into the Barut area and seal the breach. Given every available lorry, on

21 April Luchinskii rushed Colonel Shatskov's 61st Rifle Division ahead with all possible speed and by late evening the division had closed up with Rybalko's tank army. Lelyushenko continued his own drive, taking Calau, Luckau and Babelsberg and sweeping up to the south-western suburbs of Berlin. At Babelsberg 63rd Guards Tank Brigade, acting as forward detachment for the entire tank army, stumbled on a concentration camp with its many nationalities and managed to free Monsieur Herriot, former French Prime Minister, and his wife. By the evening of 21 April both Lelyushenko and Rybalko were within striking distance of the outer defences of Berlin and had already cut the ring-road. Koniev now decided to reinforce Rybalko with one artillery breakthrough corps (the 10th), an artillery breakthrough division and an AA artillery division, plus the 2nd Fighter Corps which came under Rybalko's own operational control. The scene was thus set for Koniev's own assault on the capital; within a matter of hours the whole of Rybalko's 3rd Guards Tank Army was drawn up before Berlin, about to break into the city.

During the course of 22 April, with five rifle and four tank armies now engaged, the Soviet noose tightened perceptibly round the city. Kuznetsov's 3rd Shock and Bogdanov's 2nd Guards Tank Army (minus 9th Guards Tank Corps) attacked from the north, Chuikov's 8th Guards and Katukov's 1st Guards Tank Army (minus 11th Tank Corps) struck from the east, together with Berzarin's 5th Shock Army; Perkhorovich's 47th Army swept northwards and then struck back into Berlin from the west, using 9th Guards Tank Corps. From the south came Koniev's tanks and infantry: Rybalko's 3rd Guards Tank Army with three rifle divisions from Luchinskii's 28th striking straight from the south, and Lelyushenko's 4th Guards Tank Army (minus 5th Guards Mechanized Corps) also sweeping round to the south-west. Any idea on the part of Kuznetsov and Bogdanov that they might take the city in a rush—straight off the march— vanished for the pipe-dream it was when both rifle and tank formations became involved with the complicated business of street fighting. Marshal Zhukov at once marked out an offensive zone for 2nd Guards, assigning 1st Mechanized Corps to an assault on Rosenthal–Wittenau and thence into the western part of Siemensstadt, while 12th Guards Tank Corps would attack towards Pankow–Reinickendorf, cut into the eastern sector of Siemensstadt and make for Charlottenburg; 9th Guards Tank Corps would drive north-westwards and cut the German escape route to the west.

The northerly sweep succeeded admirably. Towards 7 o'clock on the evening of 22 April, 9th Guards Tank Corps, after a day's fighting, crossed the Havel and established a useful bridgehead to the east of Hennigsdorf. 125th Rifle Corps with the tanks of 9th Guards were now in a position to attack southwards on Potsdam in order to link up with Koniev's units—thus providing a northerly encircling arm—while 129th Rifle Corps continued to fight for the Tegel area. Kuznetsov, commanding 3rd Shock, decided to regroup during the night of 21–22 April, having received orders to direct the axis of his attack from the north towards the centre of Berlin; he proposed to advance towards a line running from Rosenthal, through Wilhelmsruh, Schönholz and into the southern sector of Weissensee, using three rifle corps to chop through the defences of northern Berlin and wipe out the remnants of the 11th *SS* Motorized Division, police units drafted to fight in the front line and some *Volkssturm* battalions, those elderly Home Guards facing battle-tested Soviet divisions with only an armband, a rifle or a *Panzerfaust*.

Deploying into assault squads and assault groups—with each corps holding at least one division in reserve—3rd Shock units proceeded to lay down massive artillery fire, blasting away yard by yard, siting guns in any open space and lining up the *Katyusha* rocket-launchers to fire phosphorus into strong-points and buildings, setting off chains of fires. Rather than fight for separate buildings the tanks would go forward and blow them to pieces section by section, eliminating snipers; the improvised barricades crumpled and splintered as more tanks heaved them aside, while anything more substantial was blasted away by guns firing over open sights and at close range. As buildings collapsed in a fiery rain of burning timber and blazing frontages, piling mounds of rubble in the streets, Soviet infantry took to tunnelling their way from cellar to cellar, blowing aside walls and doors with anti-tank rifles; the sappers laid the heavier charges to clear more passages. Sheltering civilians, huddled in basements and underground shelters, found themselves in the thick of this ferocious fighting, choked, blinded and maimed amidst the thunder of explosive charges or swept by the terrifying spurts of flame-throwers. Dragging the dead and dying out of the rubble at street level exposed the inhabitants to the sportive habits of Soviet airmen, diving down to rake streets, soldiers, fire-fighters and anything that moved. Soviet planes also cruised higher, spotting for the guns.

Striking towards Weissensee at 10 o'clock on the morning of 22 April, after a short and murderous artillery bombardment, 3rd Shock Army renewed its attack, skirmishing with small groups of *Volkssturm,* some *SS* squads and battling with the anti-aircraft guns firing with depressed barrels at Soviet tanks. Weissensee— once noted for its Communist loyalty—threw out surrender flags quickly enough, strips of red torn from Nazi banners. The officers and men of the forward fighting units, dressed for combat in several varieties of uniform but laden with automatic weapons and ammunition, seemed to have nothing on their minds but clearing the area under attack, bursting into cellars and buildings, searching for German soldiers and weapons, pocketing the odd watch but leaving the women alone. The majority of these first-echelon units were well turned out and even properly shaved, clearly under the control of their officers, some speaking excellent German or otherwise relying on their girl interpreters. Some rapid screening took place, men were rounded up—or released on a show of genuine anti-Nazi credentials— and the women set to cleaning up the shattered buildings. But the loutish, drunken, indisciplined murderous second echelon—much of it manned with brutalized men taken from German slave camps liberated on the Red Army's line of march, erstwhile captives given a machine-pistol and pressed immediately into the Soviet ranks—had yet to hit Berlin, an uncontrollable mob intent on pillage and rape, though not without those same contradictions of the maudlin and the bestial consuming them.

Berzarin's 5th Shock, supported by 12th Guards and 11th Tank Corps, drove on into Kaulsdorf, Biesdorf and towards Karlshorst, cutting into the eastern defences. Chuikov's 8th Guards, with Katukov's tank army, ran into heavy opposition at Erkner and Petershagen, but in the afternoon of 22 April the infantry and tanks had reached the river Dahme, with the right flank fighting in the woods east of Mahlsdorf and Uhlenhorst. Ahead lay the Spree, with an assault crossing planned for 23 April under cover of a thirty-minute artillery barrage. Tank army commander Katukov during the course of the day received a bizarre and disconcerting call from one of his corps commanders, Babadzhanyan, who reported that he had some Japanese on his hands. An incredulous Katukov repeated 'Japanese' in dazed tones, only to be told that Soviet tank troops had run into a Japanese mission near Erkner; Katukov, who found himself burdened with a number of diplomatic incidents that day, instructed Babadzhanyan to bring the Japanese to his HQ at once. Then there was the affair of the mineral water: scorched and thirsty Soviet troops had 'liberated' several cases of mineral water from a neutral embassy, gulping it all down, only to have protests rain down on the head of the army commander. Katukov could only wonder what mean attitude prompted protests like this.

Meanwhile Berlin burned, raked by Soviet guns and torn into sprawling ruins by Soviet assault squads, blasting their own passage. Lelyushenko's 4th Guards tanks, driving on relentlessly, swept along on their south-westerly path and on 22 April were only twenty miles from Perkhorovich's 47th Army hammering down from the north, closing a giant outer encirclement round the city to the west. Crashing on its way to the west, 5th Guards Mechanized Corps suddenly came upon another German concentration camp at Treuenbrietzen holding large numbers of Allied prisoners of war; Red Army Lieutenant Zharchinskii leading a reconnaissance group opened fire on the SS guards and was himself mortally wounded in the exchange of fire, but in a final gallant last stand he cut down the camp commandant and could see German resistance collapsing. Among the liberated prisoners was Maj.-Gen. Otto Ruge, commander of the Norwegian Army. Picking up speed, 5th Mechanized raced on to Jüterborg and drove on to an aerodrome packed with aircraft (144 damaged machines, 362 aircraft engines and 3,000 bombs, all duly handed over to the 9th Guards Fighter Division), colliding with a German division in the process of forming up on the Jüterborg Parade Ground. The sudden appearance of Soviet tanks sent men and machines scattering in all directions, though the guns fell at once into the hands of the Russians. With the Beelitz–Treuenbrietzen line in their hands, Soviet tanks continued to drive forward and once in the area of Saarmund there was every prospect of closing on Potsdam and Brandenburg—and completing the encirclement of the city, as well as sealing it off from any attempt to mount a relief attack from the west.

Rybalko's tanks, reinforced by heavy artillery rushed up from the Spremberg area, crossed the Nuthe canal and continued their advance from the Mitten-walde–Zossen sector, with 9th Mechanized Corps in the lead and closing on the Berlin ring-road. Towards the evening of 22 April 9th Mechanized, accompanied by the 61st Rifle Division (28th Army), broke into the southern suburbs of Marienfelde and Lankwitz; elements of the corps also drew up to the Teltow canal, only to be met by heavy fire from the northern bank. By the evening of 22 April the tanks of 3rd Guards were only about seven miles from Chuikov's 8th Guards, fighting in the south-eastern suburbs. Meanwhile Marshal Koniev ordered Rybalko to prepare the assault of the Teltow canal, a water barrier lined with factories whose reinforced concrete walls formed an unbroken rampart well suited to defence. The Germans had already blown the bridges, leaving the Soviet commanders no option but to force a crossing and to mass artillery—3,000 guns, SP guns and mortars—on a narrow sector, in addition to all the direct-fire guns that formation commanders could lay their hands on. In this fashion Koniev intended to smash his way straight into the heart of Berlin.

The whole gigantic trap was almost sprung. Lelyushenko was a mere twenty miles from Perkhorovich driving down from the north; Rybalko would shortly make contact with Chuikov and Katukov, only a few miles separating the two fronts in the southern suburbs of Berlin. During the course of 22 April Gordov's 3rd Guards Army finally took Cottbus and completely bottled up the German 'Frankfurt-Guben group' from the south, while Pukhov's 13th and Zhadov's 5th Guards Army cut the German escape route to the Elbe, the junction between the two armies being sealed by 4th Guards Tank Corps. Luchinskii continued his advance towards Berlin, pushing 128th Corps towards the Teltow canal and Rybalko's 3rd Guards Tank Army, while the 152nd Rifle Division moving towards Mittenwalde held off a small group of German troops from the Frankfurt-Guben group as they tried to break towards Berlin; Luchinskii also deployed one corps in the Barut area as added insurance against any breakout by the Frankfurt-Guben group. Chuikov's advance into the south-eastern suburbs and Rybalko's thrust with 28th Army into the southern suburbs presented the possibility of splitting the Berlin garrison into two separate entities, while the main body of Ninth Army had also been encircled and might be kept isolated in the woods to the south-east of Berlin. The distance between the outer and inner lines of encirclement was some fifty miles to the west and a little more than thirty miles in the south.

Both Hitler and Stalin bent over their maps at this critical juncture in the battle for Berlin, though the contrast in their approach to reality was its own cruel commentary—Hitler manipulating phantom forces and decimated divisions, Stalin and the *Stavka* calmly supervising the movement of score upon score of divisions, massed batteries of artillery and huge columns of tanks. On 22 April

Hitler suffered a total nervous collapse, raving at what he conceived to be more treachery. His best hope had centred on *SS* General Steiner, whose 'Army Group' would attack from its positions near Eberswalde in a southerly direction, cutting off Zhukov's offensive on Berlin and slicing right into his northern flank. To swell this force Hitler ordered Göring's private army to be placed under Steiner's command and the bulk of the *Luftwaffe*'s ground staff. But Steiner could neither command the means nor summon the will to attack. The explosion came not on the battle lines but in the *Führerbunker* on the afternoon of 22 April, when a deranged and hysterical Hitler learned that Steiner had not attacked, in spite of the soothing reassurance of the *SS*. To the amazement of his entourage Hitler declared the war lost and his own life forfeit, his fate being to remain in Berlin and if needs be end his life with a pistol shot. He refused adamantly to alter his decision to remain in Berlin and announced his intention to broadcast the fact; the entreaties of his intimates made no impression. It was left to Jodl to point out that a dead *Führer* would leave the German army leaderless and even as the thudding of Soviet shells reverberated through the bunker Jodl pointed to some remaining reserves—Schörner's army group and especially Wenck's Twelfth Army, which could be turned about from the Elbe and directed eastwards towards Potsdam, there to link up with Busse's Ninth Army. In addition, Steiner and von Manteuffel could strike towards Berlin from the north. In the early hours of 23 April Field-Marshal Keitel reached Wenck's HQ and ordered him, amidst much brandishing of a field-marshal's baton, to abandon his positions on the Elbe and drive towards Jüterborg and Potsdam.

Shortly before 1 am on 23 April—a mere fifteen minutes or so before Keitel reached Wenck's HQ in the Weisenburg forest south-west of Berlin—Stalin issued a definitive order setting the boundary line between 1st Belorussian and 1st Ukrainian Fronts, Stavka Directive No. 11074, classified secret and timed for 0045 hours 23 April. Stalin's cut was deep and decisive. The revised frontal boundary line ran from Lübben, on to Teupitz, Mittenwalde, Mariendorf and thence to the Anhalter Station in Berlin—a line which sliced right through Berlin and placed Marshal Koniev's 1st Ukrainian Front just 150 yards to the west of the *Reichstag,* thus disbarring him from any attempt to seize the outstanding prize which would signify the capture of Berlin and the defeat of the *Reich*. The palm was to go to Zhukov, who might wear the title of 'conqueror of Berlin', exactly as Stalin had insisted he should as long ago as November 1944. The new boundary line was to come into effect from 0600 hours on 23 April.

Koniev had already flung almost the full weight of his right flank into the battle for the south-western and southern suburbs of Berlin, while his centre and left-flank armies pushed on westwards and to the Elbe. Rybalko's 3rd Guards Tank Army was drawn up on the banks of the Teltow canal, waiting for the arrival of the heavy guns and carrying out a thorough reconnaissance. Soviet officers could see lines of trenches, pill-boxes and tanks buried in the ground, bridges clearly mined or already blown; but since there was little attempt to

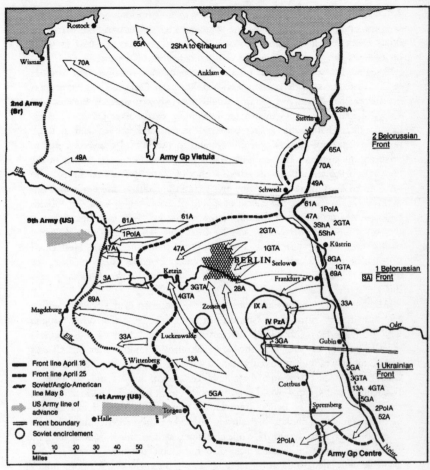

Map 15 The Berlin operation, 16 April–8 May 1945

camouflage or conceal these defences, guns could be brought right up to the forward positions and simply blast away, with aimed fire reserved for certain street crossings, gardens and specific buildings. This concentration of Soviet fire-power beggared even the imagination of Koniev—650 guns per kilometre of front for the assault, 55 minutes of massed fire timed for 0620 hours on 24 April and supporting the three corps committed to the attack. No less than

1,420 guns were brought up to this sector with 400 (including 122mm pieces) sited for firing over open sights. The staggered hour for opening the barrage— 0620 hours, rather than the orthodox clockwork precision of 0600 or 0700 hours—was designed to throw the German defenders off balance.

Rybalko also received orders to take the greatest care with his right flank, in order to effect a smooth junction with Katukov's 1st Guards Tank Army from 1st Belorussian Front; 3rd Guards would now advance towards Buckow and render assistance as 1st Guards made its crossing of the river Dahme. Already liaison officers had made contact between the two tank armies, and at 0125 hours on 23 April Koniev ordered Rybalko to use 9th Mechanized Corps to drive on Buckow and link up with Katukov's tanks, facing the barrier of the Spree. Rybalko accordingly detached 70th and 71st Mechanized Brigades to drive up to 1st Guards Tank Army and secure the requisite street crossings east of Marienfelde. During the course of 23 April Lelyushenko with 4th Guards tanks pressed on towards Potsdam, narrowing the gap with each hour between the two fronts—1st Belorussian and 1st Ukrainian—in order to close the outer encirclement, the gap now being only about fifteen miles; 6th Guards Mechanized Corps continued its push towards Brandenburg, covering fifteen miles in the course of 23 April and completely smashing up the *Friederich Ludwig Jahn* division in the process.

Marshal Zhukov meanwhile attended to the execution of the *Stavka*'s orders. He pushed 47th Army on to Spandau, ordering one division to break through with a brigade from 9th Guards Mechanized Corps and drive towards Potsdam in order to link up with Lelyushenko's tank army. Chuikov with 8th Guards and Katukov's tank army received categorical orders to force the Spree and not later than 24 April drive into the area of Tempelhof, Steglitz and Marienfelde; Bogdanov's 2nd Guards would simultaneously attack towards Charlottenburg in the western districts of Berlin. Impatient as ever and determined to crack the German resistance, Zhukov had already ordered his formation commanders on 22 April to organize round-the-clock operations with assault squads fighting by day and by night and with tanks included in the assault companies. To supplement available tank strength for street fighting, during the night of 23 April Zhukov regrouped some of the armoured formations, subordinating 9th Tank Corps to 3rd Shock Army, 11th Tank Corps to 5th Shock Army, and a tank brigade to Chuikov's 8th Guards. Perkhorovich's 47th Army with 9th Guards Tank Corps continued its northerly sweep, with two corps—125th and 129th—across the Havel and investing Tegel. Kuznetsov's 3rd Shock with two armoured corps (1st Mechanized and 12th Guards Tank Corps) cut its way into the northern and north-eastern suburbs, clearing several apartment blocks and reaching the Wittenau–Lichtenberg railway line. Berzarin's 5th Shock drew up to the Spree and managed to win some footholds on the western bank, ready to make a full assault crossing west of Karlshorst.

At long last Chuikov's 8th Guards enjoyed a stroke of luck. Moving up to the Spree and the Dahme, units of two corps (28th and 29th Guards Corps) found a variety of boats and barges, even motorboats, on the eastern bank and promptly pressed them into Red Army service. The sailors of the Dnieper Flotilla were also much to the fore, managing to ferry forward elements of 9th Guards Rifle Corps (5th Shock Army) across the Spree. Chuikov smashed down the resistance in his area and taking the Wuhlheide moved his corps across the Spree, pushing on to Adlershof in the afternoon. By the evening of 23 April one corps (28th Rifle Corps) was fighting in Alt-Glieicke and Bohnsdorf. Chuikov was now in a good position to link up with Rybalko's tanks also drawing up to this south-eastern sector.

There was every reason for the salutes of gunfire in Moscow on the evening of 23 April, salvoes celebrating the successes of both the 1st Belorussian and the 1st Ukrainian Fronts. The great link-up was about to take place, with 8th Guards and 1st Guards Tank Army making contact with Rybalko's 3rd Guards Tank Army and Luchinskii's 28th Army in the south-eastern sector of Berlin. Soviet armies had closed on Berlin from three sides, leaving only three roads open to the west and these were being harried constantly by Soviet aircraft. The net had almost closed on the 'Frankfurt-Guben group', with the *Stavka* ordering its rapid liquidation. A gap wavered to the west of Berlin but a rifle division from 47th Army and a tank brigade from 2nd Guards Tank Army were racing to link up with 6th Guards Mechanized Corps from Lelyushenko's tank army. After days and hours of agonized, bitter fighting the grand plan was about to be consummated. However, the wounds inflicted on the Red Army were deep and they hurt: companies were down to 20–30 men, regiments were fielding only two battalions rather than three, the battalions pressing men into companies consisting of a mere fifty men. The Russians could only bury their dead in gardens and sundry open spaces, all the while counting the cost of this massive assault.

Much to his dismay Col.-Gen. Chuikov received a telephone call on the evening of 24 April from Marshal Zhukov, who peremptorily demanded to know the source of the news of Koniev's advance into Berlin—who had reported this? Taken aback, Chuikov replied that units on the left flank of 28th Rifle Corps had made contact at 0600 hours in the area of the Schonefeld aerodrome with Rybalko's tanks from 3rd Guards, contact duly confirmed by the corps commander himself, General Ryzhov. A querulous and sceptical Zhukov ordered Chuikov to send out 'reliable staff officers' and find out which units from 1st Ukrainian were in Berlin and what their orders were. Chuikov dispatched three officers, but in a matter of hours Rybalko himself turned up at Chuikov's command post and telephoned Zhukov—proof positive of the presence of 1st Ukrainian Front, if Zhukov wanted proof. Not only had the link-up taken place between the two fronts inside Berlin but close operational liaison brought left-flank units of 28th

Rifle Corps (8th Guards Army) to the Teltow canal and into the districts of
Britz, Buckow and Rudow. Units of 29th Rifle Corps meanwhile invested
Johannisthal and the aerodrome at Adlershof.

While this encircling knot was drawn tighter and tighter, pulling on the inner
noose draped round Ninth Army, the outer ring was closing fast: Colonel Turkin's
35th Guards Mechanized Brigade, the lead element in 8th Mechanized Corps
from Lelyushenko's 4th Guards Tank Army, raced towards the north-west from
Potsdam in the direction of Ketzin. At noon on 25 April, here at Ketzin, the
two outer encircling wings from 1st Ukrainian and 1st Belorussian Fronts finally
linked up. This junction was effected by 6th Guards Mechanized Corps, from
1st Ukrainian Front, and the 328th Rifle Division from General Poznyak's 77th
Rifle Corps (47th Army) and 65th Guards Tank Brigade (2nd Guards Tank
Army) from 1st Belorussian Front. Intent on isolating and then chopping up the
Berlin defences, the Soviet command could now count on an encirclement line
manned by at least nine armies—47th, 3rd and 5th Shock, 8th Guards, elements
of 28th Army and four tank armies (1st, 2nd, 3rd and 4th Guards); in the
wooded country to the south-east of Berlin, the 'Frankfurt-Guben group' was
hemmed in by another five armies—3rd, 69th, 33rd, 3rd Guards and more
units from 28th Army.

The encirclement of Berlin was complete by 25 April. On the same day, some
time during the afternoon, Soviet and United States troops linked up on the
river Elbe, the final consummation of a cleaving blow which shattered the German
front in its entirety and tore Hitler's *Reich* apart, slicing it into two isolated
segments to north and south. Marshal Koniev's report to Stalin and the *Stavka*
was very explicit with respect to time and place: at 1330 hours on 25 April in
the area of Strela, units of 58th Guards Rifle Division from Zhadov's 5th Guards
Army made contact with a reconnaissance group from the United States 69th
Infantry Division, attached to the 5th Army Corps of the US First Army, while
on the same day the lead 2nd Battalion—commanded by Captain V.P. Neda—
from the 173rd Guards Rifle Regiment (also with 58th Division) linked up with
another United States Army patrol in the area of Torgau. Shortly after one o'clock
that afternoon Lieutenant Albert Kotzebue of the US Army's 69th Infantry
Division had met a solitary Soviet soldier near the village of Leckwitz and crossing
the river—the riverbank strewn with dead civilians, cut down in some unexplained
butchery—had met more Red Army soldiers near Strehla. Both parties exchanged
formal salutes, both groups of soldiers finding themselves thousands of miles
from home, separated by steppe and ocean. Later in the afternoon another US
patrol led by Lieutenant William D. Robinson from 69th Division came upon
more Red Army soldiers at Torgau, some twenty miles north of Strehla, and
thus an 'official' US-Soviet link-up was celebrated at 4.40 pm on 25 April 1945.

Whatever the euphoria about the US–Soviet junction, it was relatively short-
lived since Marshal Koniev discovered that he had a major battle on his hands,
a crisis developing along the 'Dresden axis' and which first burst upon him during

the night of 22 April. A German taskforce consisting of two divisions and supported by 100 tanks from Gräser's Fourth *Panzer*, attacking from the area south-east of Bautzen, drove cleanly into the junction between Korotoyev's 52nd Army and Swierczewski's 2nd Polish Army; driving towards Spremberg, the German divisions broke through 48th Rifle Corps (52nd Army) and crashed on into the rear of the Polish army. Those Polish divisions advancing westwards with their right flank resting on Zhadov's 5th Guards Army found themselves in serious trouble as the *Panzers* ripped into the supply columns and destroyed divisional communications.

Faced with a chaotic situation, Koniev sent his chief of staff, Petrov, to sort out the mess. The first task was to re-establish contact with General Swierczewski at 2nd Polish Army, a mission assigned to General Kostylëv, Chief of the Operations Administration, and one executed admirably under the circumstances. Petrov was charged with supervising the whole situation, checking the German breakthrough and then mounting a counter-attack. Genuinely weighed down with staff work at Front HQ Petrov could do little but drive out, survey the scene and then race back to HQ for his evening labour of co-ordinating all the reports on 1st Ukrainian Front operations for that day. It fell to Kostylëv to do all the spadework, co-ordinating the defensive operations of 52nd, 5th Guards and 2nd Polish Army, as well as bringing in the 2nd Air Army to beat back the German columns. The German breakthrough, skillfully timed and aimed with admirable precision at a weak Soviet junction, made some progress in the direction of Spremberg but, inevitably, the thrust was checked and by the evening of 24 April the German 'Görlitz group' had been brought to a complete halt.

The German armies thrashed about inside the Soviet encirclement ring and struggled to break the Soviet line from the outside. Recovered from his deranged spasms of 22 April, Hitler now pinned his faith on relief attacks aimed at Berlin from north-west, west and south, with Wenck and Twelfth Army driving from the south-west to link up with Busse's Ninth Army surrounded in the Spree forests to the south-east of Berlin; to the north there was the ghost of SS General Steiner and what passed for his army, already ordered to attack towards Spandau. In the boiling battles around Berlin whole formations disappeared from sight, only to re-emerge battered and dreadfully thinned but still extant—as was the case with Weidling's LVI *Panzer* Corps, nominally obliterated but actually on the outskirts of Berlin. Hitler had already ordered Weidling's arrest for desertion, but the enraged corps commander reported his position by public telephone, rushed to the *Führer*'s headquarters and vehemently protested his innocence of this base charge. In a whirl of fortune typical of these frantic days—either promotion or the firing squad—Weidling found himself appointed the Battle Commandant of Berlin itself.

Koniev kept a very wary eye on Wenck's Twelfth Army and the growing pressure along the Beelitz–Treuenbrietzen sector: intelligence reported that Twelfth Army was somewhat battered but could still muster a substantial force, made up of 41st and 48th *Panzer* Corps plus 39th and 20th Army Corps. Working at this moment on the final orders to be issued to Zhadov's 5th Guards Army as it approached the Elbe and preoccupied with eliminating the disorder created by the 'Görlitz group's' thrust—a German blow which certainly delayed the advance on Dresden—Koniev was also obliged to ponder the implications of the German pressure on his left between Wittenberg and Jüterborg. Wenck was stirring, much as Koniev expected that he might; in the course of 24 April the first *Panzer* attacks fell on the Beelitz–Treuenbrietzen sector, striking into Yermakov's 5th Guards Mechanized Corps and units from Pukhov's 13th Army—the long left flank of Lelyushenko's 4th Guards Tank Army.

Yermakov's corps rushed to strengthen its defensive positions, setting up a mobile anti-tank reserve with a tank company from 51st Guards Tank Regiment, siting anti-tank positions and tank or artillery ambush positions: to fill out these defences the corps command mobilized those prisoners just released from German concentration camps, issued them with captured *Panzerfausts* and gave them some rudimentary training in how to use them. Some 20–25 men usually manned an anti-tank strong-point, making plentiful use of *Panzerfausts*. Elements of three divisions from the German 20th Army Corps attacked under cover of an artillery barrage on 24 April, aiming the thrust at Treuenbrietzen and trying to break through to Lückenwalde. Beaten back by day, German troops then put in a night attack in an attempt to take Treuenbrietzen, only to meet fierce Soviet resistance: the Soviet units allowed German units to come within close range, then cut loose with heavy machine-guns and speeded the tanks out of the ambushes to grind the infantry to pieces under their tracks, with 10th Guards Mechanized Brigade holding Treuenbrietzen fast.

On the morning of 25 April elements of two German divisions supported by the 243rd Assault Gun Regiment again fell on 10th Mechanized Brigade, with another attack developing on the Beelitz–Buchholz sector defended by two mechanized brigades. This time the mechanized troops called in Lt.-Gen. V.G. Ryazanov's 1st Guards Ground-Attack Air Corps, attacking at low altitude and unloading their anti-tank bombs on the German tanks. At the same time the 147th Rifle Division from 102nd Rifle Corps (13th Army) was drawing up to Treuenbrietzen; though 10th Mechanized had been fighting in semi-encirclement, during the afternoon of 25 April the Soviet 15th Rifle Regiment moved into the southern part of Treuenbrietzen and linked up with 10th Mechanized, breaking the encirclement. The advance of the main body of 147th Rifle Division then secured the main defence line and stiffened the entire left flank of 5th Guards Mechanized Corps. Holding off Wenck, however, was only part of Koniev's problem: together with Marshal Zhukov he had yet to deal with the 'Frankfurt-Guben group', the remnants of Ninth and Fourth *Panzer* Army, trapped in the woods to the south-east of Berlin and presently preparing to break out in order to fight towards Wenck. The German force amounted to at least 200,000 men with 300 tanks and 2,000 guns—not to be either despised or ignored, as Koniev himself recognized, 'especially when they fight purposefully and desperately'. The Soviet armies hemming in Ninth and Fourth *Panzer* included three armies from Zhukov's front (3rd, 69th and 33rd) and two armies (3rd Guards and 28th Army) from Koniev's front, amounting in all to 277,000 men with over 7,000 guns, and 280 tanks and SP guns.

With so much at stake, both sides prepared for hard and desperate fighting. Ninth Army command planned to use 5th *Jäger* and XI *SS Panzer* Corps to cover the movement of the encircled units from the north and south-east, while 5th Army Corps attacked in the direction of Halbe and Baruth. As much as possible of the available ammunition would be used in the opening artillery barrage, with guns being jettisoned once no ammunition was to hand for them; fuel for the tanks was syphoned from wrecked lorries and every man carrying a weapon was assigned to a battle group. Some supply drops had been made by the *Luftwaffe*, but there were too few planes and the drops simply failed to reach the Ninth, certainly never enough to remedy the critical supply position. The night of 26 April passed in making final preparations for the break-out attempt in which a battle group formed from 21st *Panzer*, the *Kurmark* motorized and 712th Infantry Division would take the lead.

Zhukov had already made his own plans to deal with the Frankfurt-Guben group: at 1600 hours on 25 April he ordered 3rd Army, 2nd Guards Cavalry Corps, 69th and 33rd Armies to start their own attack from the north and north-west to split the German divisions, with 3rd Army driving towards Mittenwalde in order to link up with Koniev's formations, 69th Army aiming to the south and south-east, and 33rd Army advancing from Beeskow in a westerly direction. Koniev also issued a flurry of orders and redeployed as fast as possible to build up a barrier against the German thrust which would no doubt be directed towards Baruth; he moved Aleksandrov's 3rd Rifle Corps from 28th Army into the Baruth area, at the same time organizing a second defensive line behind 3rd Guards Army, while one corps (24th Rifle) with three divisions from 13th Army took up defensive and reserve positions. Koniev's orders to Gordov's 3rd Guards Army emphasized the danger of a German breakthrough on the Schönewalde–Teupitz–Mittenwalde sector and instructed the Army commander to hold one division in reserve at Teupitz, block roads through the woods leading to the west and organize strong-points supported by artillery along the Berlin–Cottbus road. By way of further insurance Koniev also called in most of the available bomber, ground-attack and fighter strength of 2nd Air Army, reinforced with one corps and one division from the 16th Air Army.

Flanked by tanks and SP guns, the first German columns moved off at 0800 hours on 26 April and struck at the junction between 3rd Guards and 28th Army in the area of Halbe. Within a matter of two hours German battle groups pounded on towards Baruth and had cut the main Baruth–Zossen road—the main supply line for 3rd Guards Tank and 28th Army. Hand-to-hand fighting and strenuous defensive actions failed to hold the German thrust, which was slowed but not halted by bombing attacks launched by 4th Bomber Corps; 395th Rifle Division managed to hold on in Baruth, while two more rifle divisions—50th and 96th—attacked from the south and slowly pushed the German units into the woods north-east of Baruth, where they were again encircled. The breach in 3rd Guards Army's front near Halbe was momentarily sealed and the German troops involved in this attack once again cut off from the main body.

To the west and south-west Wenck's attacks with Twelfth Army slackened appreciably on 26 April. Koniev felt that Wenck was fighting 'by the book', virtually going through the motions, while Ninth Army was fighting with all the fury and tenacity of doomed but determined men. Beleaguered in his bunker, Hitler fed on fragments of fact and the concoctions of his military command: he placed an undimmed hope in Wenck and was momentarily elated by the success of Busse's Ninth Army to the south-east of Berlin, but towards the close of 26 April a gnawing doubt entered his mind—Ninth Army was assuredly moving westwards but its track could well take it past Berlin and thence into some void away from the decisive battle. Inflamed with suspicion Hitler instructed Jodl to insist that Ninth Army swing to the north and close on Berlin. There was a hint of disobedience here, but north of the city, where Steiner dallied and temporised insubordination was blatant. The threat from Rokossovskii's 2nd Belorussian Front had finally materialized, placing von Manteuffel's Third *Panzer* in mortal danger; after a slow start and a struggle against soggy terrain, Rokossovskii's assault armies managed finally to build a front out of Batov's bridgehead—three corps from 65th Army, two corps from Popov's army and two tank corps (3rd Guards and 1st Don Guards) well over to the western bank of the West Oder.

On 23 April the *Stavka* cancelled its instruction of 18 April to Rokossovskii to outflank Berlin from the north—already accomplished by Zhukov's right-flank armies—and re-instated the original operational objectives set out in the *Stavka* directive of 6 April, a drive to the west and the destruction of German forces at Stettin. Assigning the reduction of Stettin to Fedyuninskii's 2nd Shock Army, Rokossovskii pushed Batov and Popov to the west, breaking von Manteuffel's front and reaching the river Randow. On the morning of 25 April both Rokossovskii and von Manteuffel had reached an identical conclusion: with the front-line units battered to pieces and reserves all but expended, Third *Panzer* could not hold for more than a day at the most. Rokossovskii now intended to envelop Third *Panzer* from the south and south-west, to cut it off from Berlin and also to cut its escape route to the west. He accordingly instructed Batov with 1st Don Guards tanks to advance to the north-west and isolate German troops located north-east of the Stettin–Neubrandenburg–Rostock line. All that now remained of Heinrici's shattered Army Group Vistula was Third *Panzer*, and this army Heinrici determined to save by hook or by crook. Against every express order of the *Führer*, Heinrici authorized von Manteuffel to withdraw—on a sudden visit to the front, Field-Marshal Keitel to his stupefaction stumbled upon a steady, systematic, premeditated retreat instead of discovering well-manned and orderly defences supposedly running along the Angermünde–Ückerheim sector.

While the carnage in the south raged on and the chaos in the north multiplied, on 26 April 464,000 Soviet troops—supported by 12,700 guns and mortars, 21,000 *Katyusha* multiple rocket launchers, and 1,500 tanks and SP guns—swarmed forward for the final assault on the centre of the blazing, shell-torn city. Two Soviet air armies, the 16th and the 18th, launched hundreds of aircraft in repeated bombing raids and added to the holocaust already created by the guns and rocket launchers. The guns continued relentlessly, ploughing up the streets, carving up squares and gardens, and piling up masses of rubble as buildings crashed down in great slabs; with windows and doors barred or walled up, the Soviet gunners simply blasted away to destroy any firing ports and send German snipers or machine-gunners toppling into the crazed ruins. The bunkers, some multi-storeyed with thick walls and equally thick roofs, presented difficult targets and added dangers to Soviet assault groups since they mounted AA guns on the concrete platforms—a menace to Soviet tanks and SP guns. The streets, strewn with dead, were also littered with burning tanks and shattered vehicles; the wounded who could not crawl away died in their bloodied tracks. The women scuttled from their shelters and cellars to collect what water they could from the standpipes in the streets, but the shells ripped into them and flung more bodies against walls and into doorways; when none would venture out of doors, the dead were packed into cupboards or shunted into passage ways.

Casualties multiplied at a horrendous rate, the hospitals were crammed and still refugees closed on the centre or clawed their way to the western districts. In 'G Tower', one of the two massive 130-foot-high Flak towers in the central district, troops and civilians by the thousand jammed its floors and stairways, the resolute and the sane trapped with the dead, the dying and demented. Soviet shells thudded into the massive concrete walls of this modern ziggurat and shrapnel rattled piercingly on the steel-shuttered windows. Outside on the streets the dust raised by the bombardment hung in a persistent fog and beneath the Flak towers the open space of the *Tiergarten,* Berlin's famous zoo, was a nightmare of flapping, screeching birds and broken, battered animals. The 'cellar tribes' who dominated the life of the city crept and crawled about, but adding to the horror of these tribalized communities clinging to life, sharing a little warmth and desperately improvised feeding, when the shelling stopped and the assault troops rolled through the houses and across the squares there followed a brute, drunken, capricious mob of rapists and ignorant plunderers. Doors crashed open: a flashlight illuminated some cellar or shelter, the beam passing across the faces of assorted women, the rough search for and seizure of women inmates, held fast and then pinioned by groups of soldiers or trapped singly at the point of a gun. Where the Russians did not as yet rampage, the SS hunted down deserters and lynching commandos hanged simple soldiers on the orders of young, hawk-faced officers who brooked no resistance or excuse.

The jagged yellow bomb-bursts pointed the way forward for the Red Army covered by yet more guns and the roaring ripple of the *Katyushas*. The newest and heaviest tanks, the 'Joseph Stalins', were in action, mighty and virtually invulnerable to German gunfire. Massed batteries—including the heaviest-calibre pieces sent up at Koniev's special and urgent request—blasted a path across the Teltow canal for Rybalko's tanks and Luchinskii's riflemen; raising great palls of smoke, the guns steadily shattered the houses on the northern bank, throwing huge lumps of concrete, stone and timber high in the air, a cascade of broken masonry and tumbling structures pounded into smaller dust by the bombing attack supplementing the artillery. In the Lankwitz area 9th Mechanized Corps took a bloody knock from the defenders, with tanks and infantry retiring to the southern bank to recoup, but 6th Guards Tank Corps made the northern bank and the 22nd Guards Motorized Rifle Brigade used a demolished bridge to gain a foothold on the opposite bank; within a matter of hours assault engineers had one pontoon bridge in position, followed by a second and the tanks were over the Teltow canal. Rybalko sensibly decided to use these crossings to transfer 7th and 9th Corps across the Teltow; Koniev for his part ordered Lelyushenko— trying to force the Teltow canal to the west of Rybalko—to shunt his divisions sideways and use Rybalko's crossings. Lelyushenko then swung west and turned towards the Havel.

During the course of 25 April Rybalko's tanks with infantry support cleared Zehlendorf and Lichterfelde, with Lelyushenko's 4th Guards fighting for the crossings over the Havel. Koniev's troops were driving through the southern suburbs and on to the central districts when the *Stavka* guillotine fell with a sudden but irresistible rush, chopping away Rybalko's corps from the centre of Berlin with the new demarcation line set between 1st Belorussian and 1st Ukrainian Front. Towards the close of 25 April—on the eve of the storming of the central districts—eight Soviet armies were throttling Berlin, crushing the resistance and much of the life out of one sector after another: Perkhorovich's 47th Army with 9th Guards Tank Corps was now well to the west and south, fighting in the north-west approaches to Potsdam; Bogdanov's 2nd Guards Tank Army (operating with two corps, 1st Mechanized and 12th Guards Tank), finding an open zone between 47th and 3rd Shock Army, fought its way south-westwards through Siemensstadt and on to the Spree; while Kuznetsov's 3rd Shock Army cut through the northern suburbs with a front running from the eastern edge of Siemens- stadt–Weissensee–Friedrichshain and was about to assault the centre of the city. Berzarin's 5th Shock Army with Yushchuk's 11th Tank Corps pushed along both banks of the Spree in a westerly direction to the Silesian Station, while Chuikov's riflemen from 8th Guards with Katukov's tanks had already sliced into the south-eastern edge of the central district—closing on the *Tiergarten*— as left-flank divisions invested Mariendorf and linked up with Rybalko's tank troops. Meanwhile Rybalko with his tank army supported by three divisions of Luchinskii's 28th Army was well astride the Teltow canal and making for

Schmargendorf to link up with the Soviet tanks carving their way from the north-west.

On 26 April all the honours went to Rybalko, who scored considerable success on his left flank. His 7th Tank Corps pushed through the woods bordering the Havel and were within a couple of thousand yards of Bogdanov's tanks to the north-west. The tanks cleared Steglitz, Schmargendorf and the southern reaches of Grunewald, and swept round to Pichelsdorf, cutting the lines of communication between the Berlin defence and those German troops holding Potsdam and the island of Wannsee, plunging a Soviet dagger in the back of the whole Berlin garrison. Chuikov's Guardsmen also forced the Teltow canal on their drive to the Tempelhof airfield, from which the Soviet command suspected that the Nazi leadership might make a bolt for freedom and fly out of the Soviet ring. Masked by the smoke from blazing buildings, units of the 39th Guards Rifle Division drove on the Spree; using the remnants of a shattered bridge Soviet rifle units got a foothold on the western bank and broke into a large building, clearing some rooms in hand-to-hand fighting and bursting into a neighbouring house.

Unaware of the immediate whereabouts and possible escape plans of Hitler and his entourage, the Soviet command determined to deny him Tempelhof. The airfield was defended by AA guns, SS troops and dug-in tanks—prisoners reported that all available fuel was assigned to the *Luftwaffe* for the aircraft in the underground hangars. Chuikov ordered units of the 39th and 79th Guards Rifle Divisions to outflank the aerodrome from the east and west before opening the main attack from the southern perimeter, when tanks and infantry raced across runways to block any access to them from the underground hangars, at the same time sweeping the area with machine-gun fire and bombardment with tank guns. By noon on 26 April the runways and the airport buildings were firmly in Soviet hands. Chuikov's assault groups pressed on, blasting their way forward by dynamiting gaps in walls to pass from street to street, a tunnelling operation obstructed by the massive ruins and also by the demolition set in train by the defenders, bent on destroying everything in the path of the Soviet armies—though the Berlin garrison soon ran short of explosives and had to use improvised aerial bombs as charges; demolition plans were further frustrated by Speer's failure to hand over the bridge plans. Weidling pleaded for air drops, and a few Me 109s appeared and parachuted medical supplies into the city, but desperately needed ammunition was not forthcoming. Some Ju-52s managed to use the 'East–West axis' as a runway much to Speer's apoplectic displeasure since the ornamental bronze lamp-standards had to be removed to clear a flight path—but only a small quantity of anti-tank ammunition was brought in.

Fewer Soviet aircraft flew over Berlin on 26 April—while a few German planes tried to fly in, making a last desperate use of Gatow and the hair-raising route to the 'East–West axis'. Soviet activity was dictated by the diminished visibility, with columns of smoke rising more than a thousand feet and visibility on the ground reduced, by more smoke, to a few hundred yards in most places;

only hand-picked crews were selected for ground-support operations instead of the massed air onslaughts of previous days. As the fighting swept up to the heart of the city with its tall imposing buildings, every available gun was brought to bear, with assault squads supported by at least 3–4 guns; the Soviet gunners also went for targets on the flanks and to the rear, aiming to cut off any outside support for the garrisons holding strong-points and buildings—and then switching to knocking out fire-points. Flame-throwers burned out desperadoes who refused to surrender or who holed up in basements, cellars and even sewers. As the attack sectors narrowed, both Zhukov and Koniev urged their commanders to speed up the elimination of trapped garrisons. Koniev vented his anger on Lelyushenko at 4th Guards for taking too much time to reduce the German forces on Wannsee island. While grudgingly recognizing that Lelyushenko could scarcely ignore 20,000 German troops on Wannsee, Koniev categorically insisted that 4th Guards use 10th Mechanized Corps to take the island by 28 April and push 6th Mechanized Corps on to Brandenburg to the west. Within his own boundary Zhukov ordered Kuznetsov's 3rd Shock to drive towards the *Tiergarten,* attacking south-eastwards in order to link up with Chuikov whose units had closed on the *Landwehr* canal. Meanwhile Berzarin's 5th Shock Army also advanced on the *Tiergarten* from the east, hacking its way along a very narrow sector—with two corps operating along a front not much more than a quarter of a mile wide.

At the end of 27 April only a drastically reduced strip of Berlin—running for some ten miles from east to west and a mere three and a half miles across at its widest—remained to the defenders, though General Krebs assured the *Führer* that all defence lines were holding and that south of the Picheldorf bridge (to the west, on the Havel) preparations were in hand to cover Wenck's arrival, the long-awaited relief. The *Luftwaffe* was standing by to fly in more troops, though Soviet fighters and AA guns were covering the approaches along the 'East–West axis' which, in any event, was temporarily blocked since a Ju-52 had careered into a house. There were plans to air-drop ammunition, but this could scarcely match the near-catastrophic supply situation, which not only starved the guns but also deprived the populace of food—and water—and the wounded of medicines. Fires raged on all sides and thick smoke rolled along the streets, shells exploded on and around the *Reichskanzlei,* the reverberations reaching into Hitler's bunker where the ventilators drew in air reeking with fumes from shell bursts. In addition to this hot sulphurous blast, the wraith of Wenck—'*Wo ist Wenck?*'— hung in the air, fed with wisps of news about Wenck's approach towards the Potsdam garrison, even as Hitler began to realize that time was running out.

To the north it had run out completely. Rokossovskii's 2nd Belorussian Front was fully free of its bridgeheads, making for Prenzlau and slicing through von Manteuffel's Third *Panzer,* which was withdrawing in the best possible order to the west—away from the Russians, towards the Americans. A relief attack on Berlin from the north was no longer feasible in any form and Steiner's two armoured divisions, long a bone of contention, were not even attempting to close the gap at Prenzlau but had joined in the defiance of the *Führer's* orders.

The retreat on the ground had its counterpart in the retreat from reality in the *Führerbunker,* though the former aimed to save lives while the latter drove yet more men, women and children to their deaths. Hitler's world, ringed now with Russian tanks and pounded by Russian guns, shrank malignantly on 28 April when he learned the news of Himmler's treachery in contacting Britain and the United States to offer Germany's unconditional surrender. Aghast at this report, the *Führer* then roused himself to a fury of revenge made more intense by the fact that the SS was the source of this betrayal, not the ever-suspect officer corps: within hours SS General Fegelein, liaison officer to Himmler and husband of Eva Braun's sister, was summarily shot. At 2200 hours at the evening conference on 28 April General Karl Weidling, Battle Commandant of Berlin, reported to the *Führer* on the rapidly deteriorating situation throughout the city, with ammunition left for only two days' fighting, supply dumps now largely in Russian hands, masses of wounded lying untended and food virtually unavailable. Weidling proposed a final break-out to the west, using three echelons: the first, stiffened with those tanks and guns still left, would consist of 9th Parachute and 18th Motorized Division, the second—including Hitler's own headquarters staff—would be formed from 'Group Mohnke' and a Marine battalion, and the third, from the remnants of the Müncheberg *Panzer* Division, the Bährenfänger battle group, 11th SS Nordland Division and a rearguard of 9th Parachute. Adamantly Hitler refused to entertain any idea of escape.

Soviet tanks now closed in for the kill. Chuikov's divisions hammered their way across the *Landwehr* canal, attacking in countless small assault groups, swimming, rafting or storming those bridges still accessible; the guns blazed away at the *Tiergarten,* raising columns of smoke and clouds of brick dust as buildings came under sustained fire, with mortars bombarding German machine-gun positions which the guns could not reach. Scouts reported that it would be possible to penetrate the *Tiergarten* by using the underground railway tunnels but only with small groups. Chuikov urgently needed to get possession of the bridge on the Potsdamerstrasse in order to get at least a few tanks through to the *Tiergarten,* an operation he was supervising personally. Beaten back several times, Soviet infantry rigged up one tank with sandbags soaked in diesel fuel; the tank moved forward to the bridge, spectacularly caught fire but continued to move and fire. Taking advantage of the confusion among the SS gunners, other tanks at once rushed the bridge and broke through to the courtyard of the corner building, from which the entire block was cleared. The storming of the *Tiergarten* then started from the southern edge; at the western tip of the zoo the two giant Flak towers reared up high in the air.

On the northern edge of the *Tiergarten* Old Moabit fell to General S.N. Perevertkin's 79th Rifle Corps from 3rd Shock Army—the formation leading the attack on that prime Soviet objective, the *Reichstag.* Breaking down German resistance in the narrow reach of land between the Spree and the *Verbindungs-*

kanal, Shatilov's 150th Rifle Division (79th Corps) struck from the east and on the morning of 28 April had taken the factory district to the south of the *Kleiner Tiergarten.* Ahead lay the Moabit Prison, a grim building with a grim reputation, forbidding in appearance with high brick walls and massive iron gates. Colonel Zinchenko, commander of the 756th Rifle Regiment (150th Division), carried through the assault on the prison, though his men needed little urging for rumour had it that Goebbels himself was in command here and could well be among the prisoners. Soviet troops frantically scanned the German prisoners but Goebbels failed to materialize—the popular assumption being that he had escaped. Jailer and captive now exchanged places as 7,000 prisoners, including Allied prisoners of war, were freed by Zinchenko's men, from whom many begged just for a rifle and the chance of revenge.

Zeroing in on the *Reichstag,* Chuikov's 8th Guards advanced on the *Tiergarten* from the south, Berzarin's 5th Shock Army with 11th Tank Corps pressed on from the east, and Kuznetsov's 3rd Shock Army bore down from the north-west, narrowing the range to this supreme target to not much more than a thousand yards or so. The *Reichstag* building had a lure all its own, for it would be not only a symbol of Soviet victory but also a signal to end the war, to finish the fighting. Not to be outdone in this contest for the real prize, Koniev ordered Rybalko with 3rd Guards Army to advance towards the *Landwehr* canal and in co-operation with General Shvarev's 20th Rifle Corps (from 28th Army) to clear the whole of the south-eastern districts of Berlin. By the evening of 28 April Koniev wanted Rybalko on the western edge of the *Tiergarten* with the main body of 7th Guards Tank Corps and 20th Rifle Division. But as the day progressed new danger loomed when it became apparent that with Chuikov driving on the *Landwehr* canal there was every possibility of Rybalko's tanks colliding with Chuikov's riflemen as the attack sectors continued to narrow. Koniev ordered Rybalko—much to the latter's fury and disgust—to turn back westwards once he had reached the line of the *Landwehr* canal, a deployment which meant pulling 3rd Guards tanks well away from the coveted prizes in the central district of Berlin. The front boundary between 1st Ukrainian and 1st Belorussian continued to run as before through Mariendorf, but it was now adjusted to slant north-westwards from the Tempelhof station, Viktoria-Luise-Platz, on to the Savigny station and thence along the railway line to the Charlottenburg, Westkrauz and Ruhleben stations. In spite of his passionate and insubordinate protests, Rybalko received categorical orders to shift the axis of his attack from the Schöneberg district in the direction of the Savigny station, that is, to the north-west and well away from the *Tiergarten.* Koniev's 1st Ukrainian Front, whose tank armies had done so much to rip the German defences apart, was now shut out from the centre of Berlin, a bitter pill which Koniev and Rybalko had to swallow.

On the south-western limits of the city 10th Guards Tank Corps from Lelyushenko's tank army and the 350th Rifle Division (from 13th Army) continued to fight for Wannsee island, forcing their way into the southern reaches of the island which housed a considerable German force. Potsdam had fallen on 27 April and Lelyushenko then directed 6th Mechanized Corps towards Brandenburg further to the west, but 6th Mechanized suddenly crashed into the forward elements of Wenck's Twelfth Army trying to break through to Berlin. Wenck pressed more attacks on the Beelitz–Treuenbrietzen line and here Yermakov's 5th Mechanized Corps found itself in an increasingly difficult position. Lelyushenko's orders were quite specific: 4th Guards Tank Army must close the German escape route to the south-west of Berlin, block any attempt by Wenck to break into Berlin with Twelfth Army and also eliminate the remnants of Busse's Ninth Army in the Luckenwalde area. But it was Yermakov's corps which was taking a hammering and forced at this stage to fight on a reversed front, with the main body deployed to the west in order to hold off Wenck but part of the corps facing east to counter Ninth Army. By way of reinforcement Lelyushenko rushed 63rd Guards Tank Brigade to Luckenwalde, followed by the 72nd Guards Heavy Tank Regiment, an independent SP-gun regiment and, finally, 68th Guards Tank Brigade.

This bitter and bloody fighting, with German battle groups trying to break the Soviet ring, inflicted heavy losses on both sides. Inside Berlin on 28 April Rybalko's 3rd Guards pushed its attack into Charlottenburg, leaving only one tank brigade—the 57th—on its left flank and holding the centre. Three German battle groups, with tanks and SP guns, seized this chance to fight their way to the Havel—only to encounter units of Perkhorovich's 47th Army and find themselves enmeshed in another fire trap. As Lelyushenko launched his assault attack on Wannsee island late on the evening of 28 April—a plan Koniev did not much care for, since the tanks could be at a severe disadvantage—in the heart of Berlin General Perevertkin with 79th Rifle Corps prepared its attack on the *Reichstag*. Perevertkin's battle orders specified that the commander of that unit or section which first raised the 'Victory Banner' over the *Reichstag* would be made a Hero of the Soviet Union. With his corps reinforced with artillery, tanks and SP guns, Perevertkin ordered the 171st Rifle Division to seize the Moltke bridge over the Spree and on the morning of 29 April clear the Germans from the corner building on the Kronprinzenufer, then to co-operate with 150th Division in taking the Ministry of Internal Affairs—'Himmler's house'—and take up positions for the storming of the *Reichstag* itself. Each battalion would organize two assault groups supported by SP guns; heavy-calibre artillery received orders to fire over open sights and the *Katyusha* crews to bombard the whole area of the *Reichstag*.

A thunderous explosion signalled a German attempt to blow the Moltke bridge, but the bridge remained hanging by the centre section. A Soviet attempt to rush the bridge failed, first foiled by the barricades and finally beaten back by fire from German pill-boxes on the southern bank. Shortly after midnight on 29 April Captain Neustroyev's 1st Battalion (756th Rifle Regiment) and the 1st Battalion from 380th Rifle Regiment smashed through the barricades and across the bridge, but a crossing in force had to wait until the buildings on the corner were cleared. General Shatilov commanding 150th Rifle Division assaulting the Spree encountered two German generals taken prisoner in the recent burst of fighting: with 'detestable civility' both senior officers dropped to their knees with the remark, 'The German generals bow their knee before the Soviet general . . .' —and then asked if they might smoke. The Soviet divisional commander showed them from his observation post the panorama of flaming ruins, with the dark outlines of large buildings showing up through the columns of smoke—and there it was, the *Reichstag* with its battered outer shell and the cupola atop, well suited as a tactical strong-point. But before tackling the *Reichstag* the Spree had to be forced in strength.

A mere quarter of a mile away in the *Führerbunker* the first of several eerie scenes was enacted. Not much after Neustroyev's battalion had clawed its way across the Spree, in the early hours of 29 April Hitler turned to dictating his 'political testament', with the heavy thud of Soviet shells as background: casting out Göring and Himmler from the Party, the *Führer* went on to dismiss Speer and appoint Dönitz his successor, entrusting command of the German Army to Field-Marshal Schörner. Having acquitted himself before history, the Nazi Party and the German people, Hitler then arranged to be married, now that his 'mortal span' had all but ended and his public duties were about to be laid down. The ceremony with Eva Braun as bride was a model of middle-class decorum. Ensconced in the bunker along with Hitler was Goebbels (together with his wife and children) and it was to Goebbels that Hitler turned frequently during the wedding breakfast in order to fill out the details of the cabinet he would bequeath to Dönitz; Bormann enjoyed more of Hitler's confidences and proceeded to transmit stern messages to Dönitz in Flensburg. Orders to those still faithful or professing faith, threats against those engaged in treason or on the verge of it, and ever more frantic requests for information from mangled armies went out over the wavering wireless network (silenced suddenly when a barrage balloon carrying the antenna was shot down), while enemy broadcasts brought news of fresh calamities. Outside the fighting raged for 'Himmler's house'.

At 7 am on the morning of 29 April Soviet guns fired off a ten-minute barrage at 'Himmler's house': infantrymen dragged mortars to the second floor of the building cornering Alt-Moabit Strasse and Kronprinzenufer and fired point-blank at their targets. Towards noon two Soviet regiments—the 756th and the 380th—broke into the courtyard of the Ministry and even took a few rooms on the first floor. This was mad, protracted fighting at very close range, enveloped in its own murk, dust and smoke, lit with gun flashes and filled with a steady roaring noise. Elsewhere throughout the city Soviet assault squads cleared their allotted sectors or made steady advances, breaking into the Zoo and firing up at the Flak towers from the Hippopotamus House. To the east, Berzarin's 5th Shock Army was operating with its right flank in the southern sector of Prenzlauerberg and fighting a fierce battle for the Anhalt station with left-flank units, while over to the west Rybalko's reconnaissance troops reported preparations by a German battle group to break out from the Ruhleben area in an attempt to push south, whereupon the main body of 7th Guards Tank Corps moved into a blocking position. On Wannsee island Lelyushenko's 10th Guards Tank Corps fought all day for control of the south-western reaches but failed to bottle up a sizeable German force. As these short stabbing battles continued, more Soviet troops and support units moved into the blocks of the burned and blackened city, settling into cellars, camping in gardens, rummaging through rooms, pillaging in bizarre style, hunting down women, mixing acts of ferocity with sudden generosity and compassion—or wild revels—in bewildering, brutal, fearsome, unexpected behaviour. To the women they raped Soviet soldiers would bring presents of bread, fish, alcohol. Drunken squad rapes might end in murder and Soviet officers with a tighter grip on their soldiers sometimes exacted rough justice with their side-arms—shooting the culprit—while in places affronted, agonized victims pleaded for the lives of soldiers standing at the point of a gun. In the horrible crawl out of and through the ruins in search of the bare necessities of life, Red Army soldiers lent their own aid by distributing what food they themselves had or by 'requisitioning' boarded-up shops.

The Red Army soldier straddling Berlin, gun in hand and flanked by massive, mighty battle tanks as well as the nimble T-34s, with Soviet fighters flicking and rolling over the city in the company of the black scarecrow squadrons of ground-attack planes, felt himself to be not only a victor but also a victim— victim of a series of horrible, bestial outrages inflicted on himself, his family and his country. Soviet front-line propaganda certainly stirred the blood and rammed home in short, thudding phrases what the enemy was—a beast: the average Soviet soldier, however, needed no great instruction on this theme. Riflemen in Captain Neustroyev's battalion attacking the *Reichstag*, crouching in corners to storm 'Himmler's house' and stalking *SS* machine-gunners, knew that here in front of their eyes was 'the lair of the Fascist beast'. Though conscious of the historical mission of the Red Army to root out Fascism, confident that they alone had broken the back of the *Wehrmacht*, many commanders were revolted at having to shoot down ranks of schoolboys in *Hitlerjugend* garb carrying *Panzerfausts*, the *faustniki;* many of the same commanders, when it came to marshalling and corralling prisoners, let the red-eyed youths go from the columns with little more than a cuff round the ear, if that. Sentimentality and simple-mindedness there was, often turned to murderous anger and irrational rage by alcohol, stores of which were locked up by German military order and thus discovered intact in magical largesse by oncoming Russian troops. The fighting drained both sides, though Russian lustiness won through.

On the evening of 29 April, at the final battle conference in the *Führerbunker,* General Weidling painted a stark picture: no *Panzerfausts,* no means to repair tanks, no ammunition, no air-drops and no hope. The fighting in Berlin must inevitably come to an end within the next twenty-four hours, by 30 April at the latest. No one appeared keen to break the silence which followed Weidling's report, but at last Hitler asked 'in a tired voice' what SS Colonel Mohnke (the commandant of the 'Citadel') thought: Mohnke replied that he could only agree with Weidling's assessment. General Weidling then returned to the theme of a breakout, at which Hitler 'looking like a man completely resigned to his fate', pointed to a map, a map marked up only through reports from enemy radio stations since German staffs no longer replied and which showed formations which no longer obeyed Hitler's orders. Completely nonplussed, Weidling went on to ask what was to happen when his troops ran out of ammunition. Hitler turned to consult General Krebs and after a few moments told Weidling that his troops might break out 'in small groups' but he, Hitler, categorically forbade the surrender of Berlin. (Later in the day Weidling received from an *SS Sturmführer* a letter written by Hitler in the early hours repeating that there was to be no surrender: if ammunition ran out, then 'small groups' might make their escape.) Not long after the conference with Weidling whatever hopes Hitler entertained of relief from outside vanished when Keitel reported the answers to urgent queries made during the evening. Hitler had demanded to know the location of Wenck's spearheads, the time of their attack, the location of Ninth Army and the direction of its breakthrough and, finally, the location of 'Corps Holste' spearheads. Keitel at 1 am on 30 April at length returned answers which signalled the crack of doom: Wenck's spearhead was stalled south of the Schwielow lake, Twelfth Army could no longer continue its attack towards Berlin, Ninth Army was completely encircled and 'Corps Holste' had been forced on to the defensive. This was the end. Hitler prepared to kill himself within a matter of hours.

Towards midday on 30 April, as the regiments of the 150th and 171st Rifle Divisions took up their positions for the final assault on the *Reichstag,* a hush settled over the squares in front of this gaunt and battered building. 'Himmler's house' had been finally captured at 0430 hours in the morning, and Soviet units proceeded to entrench themselves in the lower parts of the structure to prepare for the next assault. Soviet military maps showed green belts ahead of the infantry but all the squads could see was pock-marked earth and stumps of trees wrenched out of the ground; by way of unpleasant surprise there was also a large trench, part of the city's expanding underground railway, with bridges of steel beams overlaid with planks, most of which had been destroyed. The assault sections from 150th Division began to deploy round the trench and settled into their start positions for the attack. Though the day was generally sunny, the assault battalions could see little or nothing of the sun or the sky through the smoke blowing down on them. But first came the battle ceremonial. At the beginning of the offensive against Berlin the military soviet of the 3rd Shock Army had distributed nine Red Victory Banners to divisions for hoisting over the *Reichstag:* now the 150th Division stood on the very threshold of the *Reichstag* and up in the forward positions Maj.-Gen. Shatilov as divisional commander assigned Banner No. 5 to Colonel Zinchenko's 756th Rifle Regiment and this it passed to the best battalion, Captain Neustroyev's 1st. More banners went to units deployed for the assault—to Captain Davydov's 1st Battalion from the 674th Regiment, to Senior Lieutenant Samsonov's 1st Battalion from the 380th Regiment, and to the two special assault squads formed by 79th Rifle Corps command, one commanded by Major Bondar and the other by Captain Makov, both squads manned predominantly by volunteer Party and *Komsomol* members.

At 1300 hours eighty-nine Soviet guns opened fire on the *Reichstag,* heavy-calibre 152mm and 203mm howitzers joined by tank guns, SP guns, *Katyusha* rocket launchers and even Soviet soldiers firing captured *Panzerfausts* at point-blank range. The *Reichstag* vanished under rolling clouds of smoke as the three Soviet battalions received orders to attack. In his best military style Sergeant Ishchanov crouched next to Captain Neustroyev and asked: 'Permission to be the first to break into the *Reichstag* with my section?' Permission granted, Ishchanov's section slipped from a window on the first floor of 'Himmler's house' and crawled across the open ground: Neustroyev took the reconnaissance troop—with the precious Red Banner—with him and the forward company literally bounded to the *Reichstag,* broke through doors and breaches in the wall and rushed the central staircase. The assault party cleared the first storey, only to discover that the substantial German garrison held both the extensive underground chambers and the upper storeys. Almost at once the Germans counter-attacked, fighting off a battalion from the Soviet 380th Regiment deploying amidst the half-smashed concrete installation to the north-west corner of the building; the 380th was forced to call urgently for help from an anti-tank battalion to beat off the German tanks.

Meanwhile Neustroyev's battalion was fighting for possession of the second storey. Sergeants Yegorov and Kantariya from the reconnaissance troop blasted their way forward with hand-grenades and raised the Red banner on the half-ruined staircase only to be brought to a halt at the third storey by extensive damage and German machine-gun fire. The Red banner waved from the second floor of the *Reichstag* at 1425 hours but the Soviet attempt to rush the whole building had not succeeded. Neustroyev called up a combat group to support the standard bearers, put Lieutenant Berest in command and ordered him to clear the German tommy-gunners from the whole second storey. '*Gde Znamiya?*'— 'Where is the Banner?': Colonel Zinchenko's repeated question was answered with the report that it was in good hands, everyone in the battalion knew Yegorov and Kantariya and that the Banner was well on the way to being raised over the *Reichstag.* In the thick and murky atmosphere of the entrance hall to the *Reichstag* Zinchenko summoned Yegorov and Kantariya, talked briefly with them and then addressed them in very homely terms: 'Well then, off you go, lads and stick the Banner up there.' At 1800 hours on the evening of 30 April a second assault went in, bursting through the machine-gunners in the upper levels and succeeding at 2250 hours in planting the Victory Banner high over the *Reichstag*, though it was many hours before the entire building was cleared. The garrison entrenched in the basement was powerful and well armed, as Soviet scouts soon discovered, bringing about a weird and tense situation as 300 Soviet riflemen literally sat on a much larger enemy force clustered round their machine-guns.

Not much more than an hour after Sergeant Kantariya managed to brandish the Victory Banner from the second floor of the *Reichstag*, Hitler accompanied by Eva Braun retired to his study in the *Führerbunker* and, seated side by side, both committed suicide by biting on their cyanide ampoules. Soviet tanks continued to crunch through the city, blasting their way forward against a wearied, decimated, disorganized and dispirited defence, running low on ammunition and bereft of information. To the west Perkhorovich's 47th Army was holding a line running from Potsdam to Spandau, including the western bank of the Havel; the 125th Rifle Division was now engaged on reducing German resistance at Kladow and clearing Pichelsdorf. Bogdanov's 2nd Guards Tank Army continued to fight in the south-eastern sector of Charlottenburg and the western edge of the *Tiergarten*, while Chuikov's 8th Guards Army also cut its way into the *Tiergarten*, though the main progress was on the flanks—with 4th Guards Rifle Corps on the right breaking into the Potsdam station and closing on the *Reichskanzlei*, while on the left 28th Guards Rifle Corps reached the southern edge of the Zoological Gardens and was within striking distance of 2nd Guards Tank. Although the Zoological Gardens were held by at least 5,000 German troops with substantial artillery and the approaches covered by bunkers and barricades, Kuznetsov's 3rd Shock Army had already reached the *Reichstag* and in a matter of hours must link up with Chuikov's 8th Guards, leaving the German troops in the *Tiergarten* with only a strip extending for a thousand yards or so—and entirely covered by Soviet guns. Rybalko's 3rd Guards Tank Army worked its way north-west, attacking the Wilmersdorf district with tank and infantry units; on Koniev's orders 7th Guards Tank Corps—reinforced with the 55th Rifle Division (28th Army) speeded all the way from Zossen—attacked German units holding Westend but failed for the moment to close the 500-yard gap separating Rybalko's tanks from 2nd Guards Tank Army.

The fighting intensified in the *Tiergarten* and throughout the Zoo; Soviet heavy tanks began their approach to the Unter den Linden and Soviet guns were deploying along the 'East–West axis'. In the shell of the *Reichstag* Soviet and German assault parties still stalked each other in the gloom, while the Soviet companies hurriedly set about organizing a defence. Berlin was set in a red, purplish glow of seething fires and the flash of guns, hammering at a garrison which had now been cut into four isolated groups. General Weidling found himself facing an almost hopeless situation and an anguishing dilemma about the nature of his orders: it could only be a matter of hours before the Soviet formations striking from the north and the south linked up at the Zoo station, Soviet divisions had crashed into the Potsdamerplatz and the Anhalt station, and had ripped a great hole in the German line running from the Alexanderplatz to the Spittalmarkt—yet was he to order a breakout or carry on fighting? The *Führer*'s letter seemed to countenance a breakout in small groups but this instruction or authorization was countermanded later in the evening. His plight was momentarily resolved by a summons to the *Führerbunker*, a 1,500-yard journey from the Bendlerstrasse which took him almost an hour. In the *Führer*'s room in the bunker Goebbels, Bormann and Krebs met Weidling, who learned almost at once that Hitler was dead and his body burned. Sworn to secrecy, Weidling was told that only Marshal Stalin would be informed of Hitler's death and meanwhile Colonel Seifert, commander of Sector Z, had been empowered to negotiate a time and place with the Soviet command for General Krebs to cross the lines and explain the new developments. General Krebs intended to inform the Soviet command about the death of Hitler and the contents of his testament appointing a new government, while seeking a cease-fire which would enable the new government to assemble in Berlin and negotiate terms of capitulation with the Russians.

At 2330 hours on the evening of 30 April Lt.-Col. Seifert appeared as a German emissary at the junction of 5th Shock and 8th Guards. Conducted to the staff of the 102nd Guards Rifle Regiment, Seifert informed the Soviet officers that he was bearing important papers for the attention of the Soviet command, information passed up the Soviet chain of command from 35th Guards Rifle Division to 4th Guards Rifle Corps. Conditions were arranged for General Krebs and Weidling's chief of staff, the newly promoted Colonel von Dufving, accompanied by an interpreter (*Sonderführer* Neilandis) and a single soldier to cross the Russian lines; one by one they left the bunker, rushed across the road and made for the subway, making their way to Sector Z command post by way of an underground tunnel. General Chuikov had already been informed of the train of events involving Seifert and the arrangements to allow General Krebs through the Soviet positions. He instructed General Glazunov (commanding 4th Corps) to cease fire on the allotted sector and to pass the German emissaries to his forward command post. Chuikov, enjoying some of the immediate fruits of victory, had sat down to supper with his political staff and some prominent Soviet war correspondents—Vishnevskii, the poet Dolmatovskii and Blanter, the composer sent to Berlin to pen the victory hymn. At 0350 hours on 1 May the German plenipotentiaries finally appeared, at which Blanter was at once bundled into a cupboard since he was the only one not wearing military uniform; the others Chuikov passed off as part of his staff. General Krebs entered, wearing the Iron Cross round his neck and with a swastika on his sleeve. He made a form of salute with his right hand and proffered his service book. Colonel von Dufving and the interpreter accompanied him. Soviet soldiers attempted to strip Krebs of his side-arms but stiffly Krebs refused, demanding that an honourable opponent under the rules of war be allowed to keep his personal weapons. This the Russians somewhat shamefacedly allowed. The talk began at once, without any preliminaries:

Krebs: I am going to tell you something top secret: you are the first foreigner to whom I am giving the news that on 30 April Hitler committed suicide.

Chuikov: We know that.

Krebs: According to the *Führer's* testament . . . [at this point Krebs read out Hitler's testament and Goebbels' declaration]. The aim of this declaration—to find the most favourable way out for those peoples who have borne the greatest losses in the war. The document may be passed to your command.

Chuikov: Is this document concerned with Berlin or with the whole of Germany?

Krebs: I am empowered to speak on behalf of the entire German Army. I am Goebbels' plenipotentiary.

Chuikov: I shall report to Marshal Zhukov.

Krebs: My first question: there will be no firing during the talks?

Chuikov (picking up the telephone): Connect me with Marshal Zhukov. Chuikov reporting. General of Infantry Krebs is here. He has been authorized by the German authorities to hold talks with us. He states that Hitler ended his life by suicide. I ask you to inform Comrade Stalin that power is now in the hands of Goebbels, Bormann and Admiral Dönitz (under the terms of Hitler's testament). Krebs is empowered to hold talks with us on a cease-fire. Krebs suggests a cessation of military operations during these talks. I will ask at once.

Chuikov to Krebs: When did Hitler kill himself?

Krebs: Today at 1550 hours. I beg your pardon, that was yesterday. . . .

Chuikov (repeating the statement): Yesterday at 1550 hours. About peace? No, he has said nothing about that. I will ask him straight away. Yes, of course, understood.

Chuikov to Krebs: Marshal Zhukov is asking if you wish to discuss capitulation?

Krebs: No. There are other possibilities.

Chuikov to Zhukov: No, he says that there are other ways of making peace. No. This other government is approaching the allies and exploring other possibilities. Does Krebs know about this? He hasn't mentioned it so far. They have no communications with the allies.

Chuikov, listening to Zhukov's instructions: . . . Yes . . . Yes. He is Goebbels' plenipotentiary—the *Reichskanzler,* but Bormann remains secretary of the Party. He says that we are the first to be told about the death of Hitler and his testament. You, Comrade Marshal and I. . . .

. . . You will consult Moscow? I will wait by the telephone. Understood. Krebs is not a plenipotentiary, but we can talk this matter over.

Understood, Comrade Marshal! And what about the rest? Clear, I understand.
[Text and translations from author's 'Moscow Notebooks', 1963–65.]

Marshal Zhukov lost no time in telephoning Stalin, only to be told by the duty general in Moscow that Stalin had just gone to bed. Then wake him, ordered Zhukov, for here was news that could not wait. Once on the telephone Stalin listened to Zhukov's report on the arrival of Krebs, notification of Hitler's suicide, Goebbels' letter and the proposal for a cease-fire. Stalin replied in his own fashion:

'*Doigralsya, podlets!*' ('So—that's the end of the bastard'). 'Too bad that we did not manage to take him alive. Where is Hitler's body?' Zhukov informed him that Krebs had said that the body was burned. As to the talks, Stalin required that General Sokolovskii should rule out any kind of negotiation and stick only to unconditional surrender—'no negotiation with Krebs or any other Hitlerites'. Should nothing out of the ordinary happen, Zhukov could report in the morning; Stalin was going back to bed, to rest for the May Day parade.

Zhukov made sure that Chuikov was left in no doubt about the Soviet requirement. Chuikov put the point bluntly to Krebs:

Chuikov: We can hold talks with you only in the event of complete capitulation to the USSR, the USA and England.

Krebs: In order to satisfy your demands, I request a temporary cease-fire.

Chuikov, into the telephone to Zhukov: He cannot discuss complete capitulation until he has become acquainted with the general situation of the new German government. When he has found out, then he will report. He is empowered only for talks. Yes, I will ask.

Chuikov to Krebs: Will you surrender right away?

Krebs: I must have the agreement of my government. Perhaps a new government will be established in the south. So far there is only a government in Berlin. We are asking for a cease-fire.

Chuikov, into the telephone: They are asking for a truce—for talks. Possibly, there may be a general German government. . . . Yes, understood, good. . . . I can hear you [Zhukov], I understand. .. . . What? Good, I will.

Chuikov to Krebs: The question of a truce can only be decided on the basis of a general capitulation.

Krebs: Then you will overrun the area where the German government is and you will wipe out all Germans.

Chuikov: We did not set out to destroy the German people.

Krebs: The Germans will not be able to work. . . .

Chuikov: Germans are already working with us.

Krebs: We are asking you to recognize the German government till [*do*] full capitulation, get in touch with it and give us the possibility of contacting your government. . . .

Chuikov: We have only one condition—*general surrender.*

Krebs: But we were thinking that the USSR would consider the new legal German government. That would be favourable and acceptable to both sides.

At this point, shortly after 4.30 am, Krebs broke into Russian and again asked for a temporary cease-fire. He explained that he could not conduct any other kind of negotiation. 'Sir', he said, 'I am only a plenipotentiary. I cannot answer for my government.' Chuikov returned an abrupt answer: 'My suggestion is plain enough.' Krebs took the point and even admitted that the German government was *passé*—'You, you are powerful, we know this and you also think the same thing.' Chuikov rounded on Krebs at this juncture and challenged him directly: 'Of course we know this and you *must* get it clear. You will go on fighting in this futile fashion and squander people. Now let me ask you a question: what is the point of this struggle?' General Krebs wasted no words with his reply: 'We will fight to the very end (*do poslednevo*).' Chuikov repeated once more: 'I am waiting for a general surrender.' General Krebs replied tersely, 'No'. Softening this blow, Krebs went on to explain that in the event of complete and total capitulation, 'we would not legally exist as a government'.

Aching for sleep, Chuikov kept the talks going. After a desultory exchange Chuikov told Krebs that resistance was ending of its own accord, with the Berlin garrison downing arms, at which Krebs denied that this was mass surrender—only isolated incidents. Turning to the situation at large Chuikov showed Krebs the latest editions of the Soviet newspapers which carried reports of Himmler's negotiations with the United States and Great Britain. Krebs responded by saying that Himmler was not authorized to do this, that all feared him and that, in any event, he knows nothing of Hitler's suicide. But surely, Chuikov interposed, German radio transmitters are working and Himmler actually offered unilateral negotiations by radio. Krebs could only shrug and say that this was a 'partial measure, based on other considerations', but he reacted angrily to a report brought to Chuikov that Hitler was at this moment in the *Tiergarten: 'Eto lozh'* ('That's a lie'). Increasingly irritated, Chuikov pointed out that spilling more blood was pointless, and Krebs again asked for a truce and communications with the Allies. Chuikov could not enact this on his own authority, while Krebs continued to insist that in the event of general capitulation it would be impossible to form the new government. *Sonderführer* Neilandis took it on himself not only to translate this statement but added—much to Krebs' fury—the phrase 'Berlin decides for the whole of Germany'. Dispensing summarily with his services Krebs continued himself in Russian: 'I will speak Russian myself. I fear that another government will be formed, which will be contrary to Hitler's decision. I have only heard Stockholm radio, but it seems to me that Himmler's talks with the Allies have gone quite some way.' Chuikov refuted that categorically: the Allies worked by mutual consultation and this was only a case of unsuccessful diplomatic blackmail. But were not the Russians interested in forming a new government, Krebs asked? Chuikov asked in turn just what was Krebs counting on—the most popular government now would be one which concluded peace—only to have Krebs counter with his insistent plea that the present task was to form a government and conclude peace with the 'victor-power'—the USSR. Patiently Chuikov explained once again: the Russians and the Allies demanded unconditional surrender.

Maj.-Gen. Semenov, the political member of 8th Guards Army Military Soviet, arrived at this point. Chuikov and Krebs talked about their military careers and Krebs for the first time learned that he was facing the renowned 'Tschuikov', the commander of the 62nd Army at Stalingrad. A little later Chuikov turned

to Krebs and suggested that perhaps they might lay on a telephone link to
Goebbels. Krebs accepted with alacrity—possibly Chuikov could talk directly
with Goebbels. With a large map of Berlin spread before him Chuikov took
telephone reports on the battle situation and then telephoned Marshal Zhukov:
he informed him that Guderian had been ill since 15 March, that Krebs was
now Chief of the General Staff and in turn listened to some instructions from
Zhukov. Krebs now learned that Zhukov wished to have more details of the
German proposals and spoke at once in Russian: 'My document is signed by
Goebbels.' Chuikov proceeded to relay this to Zhukov by telephone:

We empower General Hans Krebs as follows: We inform the leader of the Soviet
people that today at 15 hours 50 minutes the *Führer* voluntarily quitted this life. On
the basis of his legal right the *Führer* conferred all power through the testament he
left to Dönitz, myself and Bormann. I am empowered by Bormann to establish contact
with the leader of the Soviet people. This contact is essential for peace talks between
the two powers who suffered the heaviest losses.

                                                                        Goebbels

Outside a *Katyusha* rocket-launcher fired off a salvo.

Krebs then launched into a general denunciation of Himmler, who had worked
against the *Führer* and now plotted to conclude a separate peace with the western
allies and bring disunity. The *Führer* had felt this treason keenly, indeed this had
been one of the reasons for his suicide. The *Führer*'s way had been to search out
a path to peace, above all with Russia. Chuikov probed as best he might into
these intrigues and divisions within the Nazi leadership, hazarding a few guesses
of his own and learning in the process that all German units would be transferred
'from there'—just where Krebs did not specify—to fight in Berlin and in the
east. Krebs supplied more details on the composition of the new government
and the location of its several members, whereupon Chuikov asked who would
be empowered to conduct final talks with the Soviet Union and the western
allies. Krebs replied that, it would be Goebbels and Bormann, presently in Berlin—
and what would the other members of the government do in this case, Chuikov
asked? 'They would fulfil the *Führer*'s order', Krebs replied equitably. Would
the troops recognize the new government? Given the broadcasting of the *Führer*'s
testament, Krebs thought this acceptance most likely—but this step should be
taken without delay before the appearance of 'another government'. 'You are
really afraid of this other government?', Chuikov asked Krebs, who repeated
again the talk of Himmler's treason and the possibility of his organizing a new
government.

This bizarre dialogue now came full circle. Chuikov asked Krebs how he
proposed to get in touch with the other areas of Germany, since they were
presently isolated. Krebs responded at once: through a temporary cease-fire,
whereupon everything would be announced. Chuikov confessed himself baffled
at this. Krebs went on to elaborate, stressing that with Soviet co-operation they
could get in touch with other areas by 'air and other means'. The implications

struck Chuikov forcefully: a German government was to be brought into existence in order to collect all its forces and then continue the war. Krebs denied this vehemently, since the object would be to start talks and end the war. Why not the opposite, Chuikov suggested, first end the war and then start talks? Krebs was quite unable to respond: 'My government can answer that, but not me.'

The pointless wrangle continued, interrupted as Chuikov reported more details to Marshal Zhukov. Krebs clung frantically to the argument that this new government—sanctioned by Hitler's testament and then recognized by the Russians—would stop the war, but only after recognition. Chuikov protested: this was neither war nor peace. Krebs retorted that he would stop the firing on that sector where it occurred, but above all he was concerned to prevent the emergence in Germany of 'a new illegal government'. A truce, Krebs suggested; capitulate, Chuikov repeated once more. There was little else Chuikov could say or do until instruction arrived from Moscow and at this juncture requests for additional information rained down from Marshal Zuhkov, who had already dispatched his deputy commander, General Sokolovskii, to attend the talks. The mire, however, only seemed to deepen. Krebs produced an appendix of names included in the government nominated in Hitler's testament, a paper Chuikov ordered to be dispatched at once to Zhukov, after which he turned to Krebs yet again with a question—'The object of your trip here—to have talks only with the USSR?' Krebs agreed that this was so, talks only with the USSR. 'But through us and with our other allies?', Chuikov prompted. Given an extension of his authority—then with the other allies, was all the reply Krebs would make; in an effort to be helpful, he went on to explain his own 'firm conviction' that in the event of capitulation in Berlin, the new government would never meet, and this would be in breach of the *Führer's* testament. General surrender cannot be enacted until the new government has been recognized.

The arrival of General Sokolovskii helped to relieve the monotony but it did not break the deadlock, which, Chuikov thought, was assuming a farcical aspect. Sokolovskii failed to persuade Krebs that surrender and only surrender would meet the situation. Chuikov reported Krebs's refusal to modify his position to Zhukov, retailing details of the argument that surrender would be impossible without Dönitz and at present Dönitz knew nothing of the turn of events. After a brief talk with von Dufving, Krebs returned to his theme, pointing to Germany's present plight but stressing that Hitler's authority—even if diminished—still held and the new government would be based on that authority; the new government might conceivably be more broadly based, though all must now fear Britain and France fastening a 'capitalist order'—*kapitalisticheskii stroi*—on the country and then woe betide Germany. Stalin by himself did not desire the destruction of Germany, but Anglo-American plans to dismember Germany promised only a terrible prospect. This display of fantastic, fanatical argumentation was cut short at 10.15 am when Moscow finally signalled its decision: general capitulation or the capitulation of Berlin, or else the renewal of the full artillery bombardment.

Lt.-Gen. Dukhanov announced that he was issuing the requisite orders. Krebs could only sit wringing his hands, deploring the bloody dénouement, repeating that surrender was ruled out and insisting that Goebbels could not authorize it without Dönitz.

General Sokolovskii determined to put an end to this pointless equivocation. He proposed to Krebs an act of surrender and the announcement of the formation of a new government; the Soviet command would provide a radio transmitter in Berlin and the new government could also contact the western allies. Krebs thought that this proposal might conceivably recommend itself to Goebbels and asked to be allowed to make his way back to the *Führerbunker*. Sokolovskii pointed out that this was hardly necessary, since on Zhukov's instructions von Dufving and the interpreter had already returned to the German lines in order to confirm Krebs' own safety; when they returned 'everything will be cleared up', so there was no need for Krebs to brave the artillery fire. Von Dufving's journey had been both hazardous and fruitless: the lack of cable—just fifty yards short—prevented the establishment of a direct link between Chuikov's headquarters and the *Führerbunker*, while von Dufving found himself held by the SS the moment he reached the German lines. It took Bormann's own order to have him released and brought to the bunker where he faced Goebbels.

What von Dufving reported came as no great surprise to Goebbels, who remained cool, calm and collected. Krebs's mission stood little chance of success and the Russians continued to insist unwaveringly on immediate unconditional surrender. With his calm evaporated, Goebbels heatedly refused to entertain this in any form, sending von Dufving back to bring Krebs once more into the German lines. While von Dufving repeated his dangerous journey, reported to Krebs by telephone from a Soviet post—and tried once more to lay a telephone cable, only to have it severed by a shell—the talks at Chuikov's headquarters were taking their final turn, with Sokolovskii 'speaking plainly': the German position was hopeless, Goebbels and Dönitz were not in contact but, after surrender, the Soviet command would make aircraft, trucks and radio transmitters available. With more details spelled out, Krebs proposed that he consult Goebbels and inform him of the 'variant' in the terms of capitulation. By telephone he made contact with his own command and set about reporting the capitulation terms— in particular, a radio announcement about Hitler's death.

Goebbels now requested that Krebs return at once to report in person, as Krebs noted the Soviet terms and read them aloud for confirmation: (1) the surrender of Berlin; (2) all those surrendering to give up their arms; (3) officers and men alike to be spared their lives; (4) the wounded to receive medical care; and (5) the possibility of talks with the Allies to be secured by radio. Chuikov then rammed the point home with a final injunction.

Your government will be given the possibility of announcing that Hitler is dead, that Himmler is a traitor and to treat with the three governments—USSR, USA and England

[Angliya]—on *complete capitulation*. Thus we are acceding partly to your request. Will we help you establish a government? Absolutely not! *[Nyet!]* But we will give you the right to furnish a list of those persons whom you do not wish to see regarded as prisoners of war. We give you the right after capitulation to present a statement to the United Nations. The ultimate fate of your government will depend on them.

General Sokolovskii made his own report by telephone:

Greetings on the First of May. General Krebs has been here. I have been dealing with this business. Krebs asked that we help him to establish a government. The list of members is with the Marshal [Zhukov]. We could not go along with that. We demand the capitulation of Berlin—after which we will give them means of communication for an announcement to the United Nations about *complete* capitulation and a radio transmitter—to announce Himmler's treason and that power is being taken by a provisional government. Goebbels will not agree—he wants *first of all* to establish a new government, he squirmed around. . . . But it didn't come off! Goebbels has asked to talk with Krebs. General Krebs is now on his way back to Goebbels. Krebs, I will spell it—K-R-E-B-S, General of Infantry. Report this at once to the Marshal. Any reply from Moscow yet?

Taking up another telephone, Chuikov pronounced the epitaph on these futile talks: 'Pour on the *"fausts"*, and the shells. And no more talks. Storm the place!'

Soviet guns and *Katyushas* fired massive salvoes into the frames of the solidly built government offices, into the *Reichskanzlei* and at the *Reichstag;* Chuikov's 8th Guards were fighting for possession of the centre of the *Tiergarten,* while Bogdanov's 2nd Guards Tank Army—supported by a Polish infantry division—pushed on towards the eastern edge of Charlottenburg in order to link up with 8th Guards in the Zoological Gardens. In the midst of this fiery conflagration an *SS* colonel appeared at 1600 hours at the crossing point in the front line used by Krebs, announced himself as an emissary of Goebbels and presented a package for Col.-Gen. Chuikov; the papers contained the German reply, signed by Krebs and Bormann, rejecting the Soviet demands for unconditional surrender and announcing the resumption of operations. Since the early afternoon the telephone link with the German lines had been kept open and operations suspended on that sector. The *SS* officer was hurriedly returned to his own side, the telephone cable cut and the sector made operational once more.

At 1830 hours on 1 May the Soviet command returned its reply. Every Soviet gun and *Katyusha* in Berlin reopened fire in a stunning, smothering barrage. Under orders to carry through a final storming attack, Soviet formations pushed forward and closed the trap tight. 3rd Shock Army coming in from the north linked up just south of the *Reichstag* with units of 8th Guards; Bogdanov's 2nd Guards Tank Army also effected a junction with 8th Guards and 1st Tank Army in the *Tiergarten.* Rybalko's 3rd Guards Tank Army had cleared the area of Wilmersdorf and Halensee, while Lelyushenko's tanks with infantry from the 350th Rifle Division broke the German resistance on Wannsee island. Inside the

Reichstag itself Neustroyev's assault units had opened tentative negotiations for the surrender of the German garrison blockaded in the cellars and lower chambers: the Germans demanded to speak to a Soviet colonel, and Lieutenant Berest—wearing a captured sheepskin cape to hide his lieutenant's shoulder-boards—found himself suddenly 'promoted' to fill the role of this indispensable colonel.

At Chuikov's command post General Sokolovskii complained about the slow progress—'a hop, skip and a jump and we would do it, only about 300–400 metres remain but we seem to be crawling along'. Chuikov pointed out that with the war as good as won his troops were not taking any chances and had no desire to die in Berlin at this point. Snatching what rest he could in a series of cat-naps, Chuikov was roused at 0125 hours on the morning of 2 May with a relay from 79th Guards Rifle Division recording a transmission from LVI *Panzer* Corps timed at 0040 hours: 'Hello, hello. LVI *Panzer* Corps speaking. We request a cease-fire. At 1250 hours Berlin time will send emissaries to the Potsdam Bridge. Recognition sign—white flag. We await reply.' The signal was sent five times in Russian. The Russians signalled in turn: 'Understand you. Understand you. Am forwarding your request to higher authority', and was answered, 'Russian radio station, hear you. You are reporting to higher authority.' These signals were also picked up by 39th Guards Rifle Division and 4th Guards Rifle Corps. Intensely irritated at the thought of yet another round of talks with Krebs, Chuikov settled down to sleep a little more but it was soon apparent that something quite different was afoot. Once alert to this, Chuikov sent two staff officers to meet the German emissaries, though with strict instructions to discuss nothing but unconditional surrender and an immediate laying down of arms. The German officers would be allowed through the lines of 47th Rifle Division.

At the Potsdamer Brücke Colonel von Dufving, accompanied by two majors, informed Colonel Semchenko commanding 47th Division of General Weidling's decision to capitulate with LVI *Panzer* Corps. Von Dufving handed over a document to this effect signed by Weidling himself. Semchenko asked von Dufving how long it would take to enact this surrender: a minimum of 3–4 hours, replied von Dufving, though speed was absolutely essential to take full advantage of the darkness and circumvent Goebbels's order that anyone going over to the Russians would be shot in the back. On hearing this, Colonel Semchenko, with Chuikov's permission, decided to send von Dufving back to his own lines at once with notification of the acceptance of the surrender of LVI *Panzer*, instructions to organize the surrender of men and laying down of weapons at 0700 hours, while the commander of LVI *Panzer* with his staff would cross the lines at 0600 hours to be taken prisoner first. The two majors with von Dufving would remain behind as hostages.

Precisely at 0600 hours General Weidling with his senior staff officers surrendered to the Russians and within an hour Weidling was brought before Chuikov. However, even before Weidling had crossed the lines Chuikov received a report of yet another delegation bent on talking with him, a delegation 'from Goebbels'. This deluge of delegations swept the sleep from him, and he ordered that they should be brought to his command post. Hans Fritzsche, Goebbels's deputy, had decided to intervene himself, sending a three-man delegation accompanied by a single soldier to the Soviet command. There was the inevitable letter and explanation, addressed this time to 'Gospodin Marshal Zhukov':

As you have already been told by General Krebs, the former *Reichskanzler* Göring—not to be found. Dr Goebbels is no longer among the living. I, as one of those remaining alive, beg you to take Berlin under your protection. My name is well known. [Signed:] Director of the Propaganda Ministry, Dr Fritzsche.

Chuikov eyed his visitors—one formally attired in morning dress—with some astonishment. *'Was wollen Sie?'*, was all he could manage; *'Berlin retten'*, replied his visitors. The letter read, Chuikov then asked when Goebbels committed suicide and was told that same evening (1 May), his body also being burned. Where is Krebs? No one knew, except that there seemed to be a new Chief of the General Staff. Chuikov then reminded the delegation of the Soviet terms—unconditional surrender. The Germans did not demur. Did this Fritzsche know that the Berlin garrison was on the point of surrendering? No, neither he nor the present delegation were aware of this. Would the German troops accept Fritzsche's order? Indubitably, came the reply, for Fritzsche's name was a byword in Germany and in Berlin. Marshal Zhukov had Fritzsche's letter relayed to him by telephone, while Chuikov tried to find out about the fate of Krebs and Bormann; it was rumoured that Krebs had committed suicide and Bormann had been killed in a gas explosion in the *Führerbunker*.

At 0645 hours, 2 May, after his talk with Zhukov, Chuikov confronted the German delegation:

Marshal Zhukov accepts the surrender of Berlin and is issuing orders for the cessation of military operations—that is the first thing. Second: inform all soldiers, officers and civilians that all military property, buildings and communal valuables must be intact. And no demolitions! Especially of military installations! Third: you will proceed with one of our officers to Herr Fritzsche, he can then make his broadcast and then be brought back here. Fourth: I affirm—we guarantee the lives of soldiers, officers and generals, medical aid to the wounded. Fifth: see that there is no provocative shooting and other sabotage.

Chuikov then ordered Colonel Vaigachev to escort the delegation back to Fritzsche, arrange the broadcast and then have Fritzsche and his staff back at Chuikov's HQ.

On the way out Fritzsche's delegation came face to face with General Weidling—an icy encounter. Chuikov opened the interrogation at once:

Chuikov: You are the commander of the Berlin garrison?

Weidling: Yes, I am the commander of the LVI *Panzer* Corps.

Chuikov: Where is Krebs? What did he say?

Weidling: I saw him yesterday in the *Reichskanzlei*. I assumed that he was going to commit suicide. At first he upbraided me for the fact that unofficially surrender had started yesterday. Today the order to surrender was issued to all troops. Krebs, Goebbels and Bormann rejected capitulation, but quite soon Krebs himself was convinced of the tightness of the encirclement and decided—in spite of Goebbels—to put an end to senseless bloodshed. Let me repeat: I have issued orders for surrender to my corps.

General Sokolovskii then took a hand in the proceedings, asking Weidling about the whereabouts of Hitler and Goebbels. Weidling replied that both had committed suicide, Goebbels with his family, Hitler with his wife. So this, remarked Chuikov, is really the end. Weidling agreed; to waste more life would be sheer madness, criminality. On being asked about his military service, Weidling pointed out that he had been in the army since 1911, starting in the ranks, at which point Weidling was wholly overcome by his feelings. Chuikov busied himself with a telephone call to Zhukov, followed by Sokolovskii who pointed out that Weidling's authority was 'relative', that the German surrender was proceeding in the sector of 3rd Shock Army and 8th Guards but not elsewhere. Sokolovskii turned at once to Weidling and suggested that he write out an order for a general surrender.

Weidling explained that he could not issue an order for general surrender since he lacked communications: isolated groups might continue to fight, many had no knowledge of Hitler's death since Goebbels forbade any announcement of it. SS troops did not come under his authority and they had plans to break out to the north. Sokolovskii persisted, urging Weidling to sign a surrender order—'better late than never'. Weidling finally sat down and wrote:

On 30 April 1945 the *Führer* took his own life and thus it is that we who remain—having sworn him an oath of loyalty—are left alone. According to the *Führer's* order, you, German soldiers, were to fight on for Berlin, in spite of the fact that ammunition has run out and in spite of the general situation, which makes further resistance on our part senseless.

My orders are: to cease resistance forthwith. [Signed:] Weidling, General of Artillery, former Commandant of the Berlin defence zone.

Save for removing the word 'former' from Weidling's designation of himself, Sokolovskii and Chuikov were content to let the order stand in its entirety.

The morning of 2 May brought with it a low fog and light, chilling rain. Columns of German prisoners formed up in the shattered streets and ruined squares. At about 5 am, after one more Soviet attack, the German garrison in the basement of the *Reichstag* began its surrender: a whole column of men moved out in the morning. To the west of the city a vast traffic of military vehicles, civilian trucks, horse-drawn carriages and pedestrians made its way to the bridges leading to Spandau, a huge throng which pushed and struggled forward amidst sporadic firing and random shelling. The buildings burned on in the city, the glare lighting up the jagged edges of ruined facades and shattered walls. The

Unter den Linden presented an unrelieved panoply of ruins, patrolled by Soviet tanks; the *Tiergarten*, wreathed in more smoke, presented a spectacle of shattered and uprooted trees, muddied and bloodied slit-trenches and pulverised masonry. The *Reichskanzlei* had been pounded into rubble, though here as elsewhere scores of red Soviet flags dotted the wreckage. Lt.-Col. Gumerov's 150th Rifle Regiment from the 301st Rifle Division (5th Shock Army) reported the capture of the *Reichskanzlei*, stumbling upon a great array of Nazi symbols—the massive bronze eagle, the *Adolf Hitler* standard, Field-Marshal Rommel's baton and more heraldic trophies. In the garden the Soviet officers finally came upon the *Führerbunker* itself, giving off an overpowering stench which discouraged a thorough inspection, but in the courtyard at the western entry Colonel Shevtsov showed Maj.-Gen. Antonov, 301st commander, the burned bodies of Goebbels and his wife. Antonov meanwhile placed the whole area under special guard, appointing Shevtsov commandant of the *Reichskanzlei*.

At 3 pm on the afternoon of 2 May Soviet guns ceased fire in Berlin. A great enveloping silence fell. Soviet troops cheered and shouted, breaking out the food and drink. Along what had once been Hitler's own parade route, columns of Soviet tanks were drawn up as if for inspection, the crews jumping from their machines to embrace all and sundry at this new-found cease-fire. Something like the great clean-up had already begun in several sectors with the establishment of a *komendatura*, a town-major's office under a Soviet officer, and the installation where possible of local German administrators and officials. Every item of value was to be catalogued, every file faithfully scrutinized and hoarded—except, ironically, a giant card-index compilation of the Nazi government's suspects, flung about in gay abandon by gleeful Soviet soldiers. *SMERSH*, Soviet counter-intelligence, did not neglect its duties and its passion for uncovering sabotage and subversion. Lt.-Gen. Krivoshein, commanding 1st Mechanized Corps (2nd Guards Tank Army), experienced an uncomfortable moment: in a box of photographs *SMERSH* came across a picture of General Guderian, a *Panzer* commander much feared by the Red Army, in the company of a Soviet tank officer, none other than Krivoshein, seen smiling broadly. Called on to explain this highly suspicious photograph, Krivoshein swore that he had had no secret contacts with Guderian though he had promised him to come as a guest to Berlin—and he was doing exactly that, right now. The photograph dated back to 1939, to the Nazi-Soviet pact, when in the partition of Poland his own 29th Independent Tank Brigade made for Brest-Litovsk and linked up with German motorized troops under Guderian's command. After a formal parade, both officers mounted a small reviewing stand and were duly photographed. Nothing serious came of Krivoshein's encounter with *SMERSH*; others were not so lucky.

SMERSH had other pressing duties, the most urgent being the search for Hitler and other Nazi leaders. The Red Army not only brought its tanks and guns to Berlin but also a great train of experts, all uniformed but all specialists, whether doctors, scientists, diplomats or historians: a political entourage moved in complete as the 'Ulbricht group', while the 'Mikoyan group' attended immediately to the dismantling and transfer of German factories and industrial plant to the Soviet Union. Stalin had been informed at once about the Goebbels–Bormann letter announcing Hitler's suicide—indeed, the express intention was to inform Stalin first as part of the strategy to gain Soviet acceptance of the 'new' German government. Lt.-Gen. Telegin, the political member of the military soviet of 1st Belorussian Front, had already asked Moscow for an expert in forensic medicine to be dispatched to the front to deal with 'a highly important matter'. Medical Colonel Dr Faust Shkaravskii was immediately ordered to Berlin, towards Buch and 3rd Shock Army area. Lt.-Col. Ivan Klimenko, commander of the *SMERSH* unit with Perevertkin's 79th Rifle Corps (3rd Shock Army), was much nearer—he was presently in the courtyard of the *Reichskanzlei* on the afternoon of 2 May. Klimenko had only travelled from his temporary headquarters in the Plötzensee Prison, where he had been interrogating German prisoners taken in the area of the *Reichskanzlei*, probing for information on the fate of Hitler and Goebbels—some mentioned the suicides and four prisoners were taken along with Klimenko to the actual site.

How Klimenko—an officer from 3rd Shock Army—managed to invade 5th Shock's bailiwick, bring his party into the garden of the *Reichskanzlei*, have one of his German prisoners excitedly identify the corpses of Goebbels and his wife and then transport the remains to Plötzensee Prison, has never been explained. During the night Klimenko continued his several interrogations in an effort to locate Hitler's body, a process interrupted by news that Hitler's body had now been found. Vice-Admiral Voss, Dönitz's representative on Hitler's staff, had helped to identify the Goebbels family (the bodies of the children having been found in the bunker) and he, too, was questioned closely about Hitler: all the Admiral could say was that the corpse had been burned in the garden, but that was enough to send Klimenko racing back to the *Reichskanzlei* and resume the search. A body taken from an emergency watertank bore an astonishing resemblance to Hitler, an appearance so plausible that Admiral Voss readily took it for the *Führer*. Closer inspection revealed that the body—Hitler's double, whether officially or unofficially so—was wearing darned socks and thus disqualified himself as the real *Führer*. Admiral Voss now voiced his own doubts.

Klimenko renewed his questioning, roping in any prisoner who could help. Ironically, one of Klimenko's own men had already discovered the two corpses, that of Hitler and Eva Braun. Private Churakov tugged Hitler's corpse partly out of a crater and also spotted Eva Braun's legs, but in the excitement over the 'double' and in view of Klimenko's conviction that the bodies must be in the *Reichskanzlei* these corpses were simply reburied. Belatedly (and after a senior Soviet diplomat brought to Berlin rejected the 'double' on the basis of his personal recollection of the *Führer*) Klimenko ruminated on Churakov's discovery of those two bodies in the bomb crater—his concern increased by the fact that his original 'Hitler corpse', the discarded double as it now proved to be, had mysteriously vanished. On the morning of 5 May, Klimenko returned with two soldiers from his detachment to the *Reichskanzlei* garden, located the crater and dug up the two bodies, at the same time coming upon the corpses of two dogs buried a little deeper. The four bodies, human and animal, were wrapped in blankets, placed in wooden boxes and lodged—under guard—in a room in the *Reichskanzlei* until nightfall, when a lorry transferred everything to 3rd Shock Army HQ at Buch on the north-eastern outskirts of Berlin. Meanwhile Klimenko enjoyed a little luck: he stumbled across *SS* soldier Mengershausen, who had watched the cremation and could specify the site of the crater where the bodies had been buried. Churakov's find and Mengershausen's testimony matched in every respect.

The autopsies began on 8 May in the mortuary of the military hospital at Berlin-Buch. Meanwhile the search for witnesses intensified, the first task being to confirm that the two corpses found in the crater were indeed those of Adolf Hitler and Eva Braun. Colonel Mirozhnichenko, head of *SMERSH* (3rd Shock Army), and his deputy Vasili Gorbushin were charged with this mission and set to work checking on the medical evidence which the Soviet military doctors provided through their grisly labours. The result was interminable interrogation and an endless search for confirmation, in some ways a strangely contradictory process since it involved establishing that here indeed was the corpse of Hitler and yet at the same time exploring the possibility that Hitler might have escaped. Soviet interrogators hammered away relentlessly at two questions: could Hitler have escaped from Berlin and what truth was there in the stories of Hitler's suicide—how was this actually carried out?

While *SMERSH* officers raked over this macabre rubbish of the *Reich* and in spite of the cease-fire enacted in Berlin itself, German units continued to fight desperately to escape the Soviet trap closing on them from many directions. In the early hours of 2 May 3rd Shock Army in Berlin held off an attempt by some 300 troops to break through to Pankow; Bogdanov's 2nd Guards Tank Army fought off a similar attempt by a battle group of roughly the same size. But in the area of 125th Rifle Corps—holding the western bank of the river Havel—a powerful German column some 17,000 strong with armoured vehicles made a bid for freedom, striking from the Ruhleben area and aiming for the bridges over the Havel, a running battle which lasted until 5 May as Soviet troops pursued retreating Germans through Staaken and on to Ketzin. A column almost twice as strong also struck out from Spandau on the morning of 2 May, making its way to the west and causing a hurried evacuation of its airfield by the Soviet 265th Fighter Division.

The fury of these attacks launched by men often on the verge of total exhaustion took more than one Soviet unit by surprise. To the south-west of Berlin, Lelyushenko experienced one such encounter: taking a nap towards midnight on 30 April at his tank army HQ near Schankensdorf, he was awakened abruptly by shouts from his staff—'Enemy! Look, hordes of them . . . bring the guns to bear.' Those German troops who had managed to escape from Wannsee island to the mainland had now broken through the Soviet lines and were bearing down in columns on Lelyushenko's vulnerable HQ. Soviet staff officers scrambled for their weapons as an urgent call for help went out to the nearest unit, 7th Guards Motorcycle Regiment equipped with ten tanks, a battery of guns and 200 men with machine-pistols. Fierce though this attack was, it did not compare in savagery with the fighting to hold off Wenck and hold back Busse, the one pressing on Yermakov's 5th Mechanized Corps from the west and the other from the east.

Wenck's left flank could not hold much longer but he was determined to stay as long as possible to effect a junction with Busse's Ninth, or the remnants of it. By 10 am on the morning of 1 May only a little more than 2,000 yards separated the two German armies, with 12th Guards Mechanized Brigade struggling to hold them off from each other. With only two Tiger tanks left and those fuelled for the last time from abandoned vehicles, as men literally crawled from overwhelming fatigue and women took up the load of the remaining weapons, Busse urged one last superhuman effort to make contact with Wenck. On the morning of that same 1 May Busse's lead troops heard firing from behind the Russians facing them and suddenly, incredibly, found themselves within arm's reach of Wenck's Twelfth. Behind them lay the ghastliest route strewn with dead, dying and wounded men, men who had been savagely mutilated and men no longer able to march, plus the trudging columns of civilians—the wreckage of an army once 200,000 strong.

While Lelyushenko struggled furiously to spring the trap shut on Busse, further to the north Rokossovskii with 2nd Belorussian Front raced to trap von Manteuffel's Third *Panzer*—and also raced the British Army into Lübeck. Fedyuninskii's 2nd Shock Army and Batov's 65th drove north-westwards towards the Baltic coast, taking Anklam, Greifswald and making for Stralsund; 70th and 49th Army pushed on to the west, rolling over a bout of German resistance in the Waren–Neustrelitz–Fürstenberg area. On 3 May forward elements of 70th Army made contact with the British 2nd Army south-west of Wismar, after which the main body closed up to the Baltic coast along a sector running from Wismar to Warnemunde and taking in the eastern edge of the Schweriner-See. In the ensuing twenty-four hours both 70th and 49th Army, with 8th Mechanized Corps and 3rd Guards Cavalry Corps, had reached the demarcation line with the British, and Soviet cavalry were already on the Elbe. Romanovskii's 19th Army and Fedyuninskii's 2nd Shock launched their several expeditions to clear German forces from the islands of Wollin, Usedom and Rügen—two divisions from 19th Army were also dispatched to the Danish island of Bornholm—but by 4–5 May Rokossovskii's main offensive operations had begun to die away.

At the close of this gigantic effort put forth by the Red Army—the capture of Berlin, the drive to the Elbe and to the Baltic—the Soviet command reckoned that it had destroyed no less than seventy German infantry divisions, twelve *Panzer* divisions and eleven motorized divisions: 480,000 German officers and men were tallied as prisoners of war, 1,500 tanks and SP guns captured, plus

10,000 guns and mortars and a massive array of aircraft. In Berlin itself on 2 May Zhukov's armies made 100,000 men prisoner, and Koniev's troops took 34,000. The cost to Berlin: probably 100,000 civilian and an undetermined number of German military casualties; to the three Soviet Fronts—1st and 2nd Belorussian, 1st Ukrainian—for the three weeks from 16 April to 8 May: 304,887 men killed, wounded and missing, 2,156 tanks and SP guns (with Koniev losing over 800), 1,220 guns and mortars, and 527 combat aircraft lost. By the most conservative calculation, the battle for Berlin thus cost half a million human beings their lives, their well-being or their sanity.

'Who do you think is going to take Prague?' There was an all too familiar ring about the question Stalin put to Koniev on 28 April even as 1st Ukrainian Front was deeply involved in gnawing its way through the Berlin defences. Stalin did not need to elaborate; in the briefest space of time Koniev reported that 1st Ukrainian Front could execute this operation, switching its offensive effort from north to south and mounting an attack on Prague from the west of Dresden. Earlier in the year, before the storm broke over Berlin itself, Hitler had assumed that Prague must be a prime Soviet objective, an accurate assessment though the *Führer*'s calculations of the Soviet timetable were somewhat mistaken—first Berlin and then Prague proved to be Stalin's order of priorities, not the reverse. Since the beginning of 1945 the Red Army had been pushing its attack into Czecho-slovakia from the east, utilizing two fronts (4th Ukrainian Front with three rifle armies and 2nd Ukrainian Front with four rifle armies and one tank army)—a grand total of almost three-quarters of a million men (751,000), with 8,300 guns and mortars, 580 patched-up tanks and SP guns, and about 1,400 aircraft similarly repaired for first-line duty. In addition, the 1st Czechoslovak Corps mustered 21,000 men, 168 guns and mortars and 10 tanks, supplemented in turn by two Rumanian armies—1st and 4th—adding 81,500 men to the strength of the 2nd Ukrainian Front.

The poor performance of the 4th Ukrainian Front had brought about Petrov's dismissal as Front commander towards the end of March. The new Front commander, A.I. Yeremenko, pleaded with Stalin for some postponement in the renewal of the offensive aimed at the Moravska-Ostrava industrial region, but Stalin angrily insisted that the operation must go forward with all speed, whatever the shortages of ammunition; Moravska-Ostrava must be taken without delay. The *Stavka* also brooked no delay, issuing its attack orders on 3 April in a joint directive to Yeremenko and to Malinovskii, commanding 2nd Ukrainian Front:

With the aim of destroying enemy formations defending the high ground south-east and south of Moravska–Ostrava, the *Stavka* of the Supreme Commander orders:
1. the commander of 4th Ukrainian Front to mount his main attack with 60th and 38th Army plus two artillery breakthrough divisions and 31st Tank Corps towards the

western bank of the Oder with the immediate objective of occupying—not later than 12-15.4.45—Opava, Moravska–Ostrava and then striking in the general direction of Olomouc, thus linking up with the southerly attack launched by 2nd Ukrainian Front.

2. after the capture of Brno as specified by *Stavka* directive dated 1.4.1945 No. 11051 the commander of 2nd Ukrainian Front will develop his offensive operations in a northerly direction in order to link up with 4th Ukrainian Front with the aim of closing on the Olomouc region. [Koniev, *Za osvobozh. Chekoslovakii,* pp. 194–5.]

The *Stavka* intended to encircle the main forces of the German Army Group Centre in the area of the Carpathians in order to prevent prolonged resistance in the interior of Czechoslovakia—a sound plan, though one which proved difficult in the execution, for all the reinforcement poured into the two Ukrainian fronts, with Kurochkin's 60th Army now detached from Koniev's 1st Ukrainian Front and assigned to Yeremenko's 4th Ukrainian.

Timed to coincide more or less with the main Soviet offensive directed against Berlin, Yeremenko's attack duly opened on 15 April with the launching of forty rifle divisions, six air divisions, 6,000 guns and mortars with more than 300 tanks and SP guns, all supported by 435 aircraft across a 125-mile front; the Soviet command estimated enemy forces at twenty divisions with 300 tanks and 280 aircraft. Two armies—60th and 38th—led the attack, striking across a seven-mile front north-east of Opava with the aim of outflanking Moravska–Ostrava from the north-west; 1st Guards Army also attacked along the eastern bank of the Oder and was under orders to co-operate with 38th Army in taking Moravska–Ostrava no later than three days after the beginning of the offensive. Stiff German resistance, however, sent Yeremenko's timetables spinning into disarray. By 18 April the two lead armies had expanded their bridgehead on the southern bank of the river Opava and pushed an edge between the German forces holding Opava itself and Moravska–Ostrava, but Soviet troops had to batter their way through the old Czech fortifications—modernized by the Germans—and the heaviest guns were needed to reduce the concrete forts and pillboxes, stout installations which even resisted twenty shells fired at close range by 122mm howitzers. Four days later, on 22 April, two rifle divisions from 60th Army with one brigade from 31st Tank Corps finally broke into Opava and cleared the town after a day of heavy street fighting, while left-flank divisions of 38th Army and Grechko's 1st Guards Army closed on Moravska-Ostrava.

To speed up the capture of this substantial industrial centre Yeremenko decided on 24 April to mount a series of concentric attacks on narrow sectors to the north-west, using three armies—60th, 38th and 1st Guards—and then strike at the town from the west. After two days of preparation these three armies launched their attacks, though Kurochkin's 60th Army had already struck out on 25 April with a drive aimed to the south-west of Moravska-Ostrava. Slowly but surely the Soviet ring tightened, and by the evening of 29 April Moskalenko's 38th Army had closed on the western suburbs, while Grechko's 1st Guards was approaching the northern outskirts. The assault on the town began at 10 o'clock on the morning of 30 April with only a minimum of artillery fire in order to preserve as many as possible of the mines, factories and industrial installations. Towards 1 o'clock both Moskalenko and Grechko reported good progress; Soviet air reconnaissance spotted precipitate German withdrawals and after a final burst of fighting both Soviet army commanders could signal on the evening of 30 April that the entire town had been taken.

While Yeremenko battered his way towards Moravska-Ostrava, Malinovskii with 2nd Ukrainian Front pressed forward to Brno, having forded the river Morava in mid-April. To capture Brno, Malinovskii proposed a double outflanking movement with his mobile forces combined with a frontal attack launched by rifle units: 53rd Army received orders to launch an attack on the morning of 23 April with the object of securing a passage for 6th Guards Tank Army— now back with 2nd Ukrainian Front—and then to drive on Brno from the east while the tank army outflanked the town from the north-east. The badly battered 6th Guards Tank Army could only muster 164 hastily repaired tanks and SP guns, but Malinovskii stiffened the striking force with Pliev's 1st Guards Cavalry-Mechanized Group—with 132 tanks and SP guns—and then added one rifle corps from 53rd Army to this group, which was ordered to outflank Brno from the south-west. Supported by Goryunov's 5th Air Army, Lt.-Gen. I.M. Managarov with 53rd Army and Pliev's cavalry-mechanized group opened the attack at 10.30 am on the morning of 23 April, under the watchful eye of Malinovskii himself. At noon the German tactical defence had been overwhelmed and Malinovskii at once ordered Kravchenko's 6th Guards Tank Army to move out with the 120 tanks of the first echelon (2nd and 9th Guards Mechanized Corps).

Kravchenko's tanks and Pliev's mobile group moved north and south respectively, with the infantry making straight for Brno—and crossing the famous battleground of Austerlitz in the process. Already on 24 April Kravchenko committed his second echelon (5th Guards Tank Corps), which pushed into the eastern and the south-eastern suburbs only to lose more than thirty tanks to German counter-attacks; this armoured fist now needed reinforcement from 9th Mechanized Corps. Colonel Boldynov's 109th Rifle Division from 18th Guards Rifle Corps also succeeded in breaking through to the suburbs and reached the river Svitava, improvising a crossing since the bridges had been blown; three Soviet rifle divisions followed the 109th in rapid succession. Pliev's mobile group cut the German escape to the west, while Kravchenko's tanks took up a blocking position to the north-east. During the night of 26 April Soviet units set about clearing the town, with Kamkov's 4th Guards Cavalry Corps operating with Katkov's 7th Guards Mechanized Corps fighting in the south-western part, Afonin's 18th Guards Rifle Corps coming in from the east and two armoured corps (5th Tank and 9th Mechanized) fighting in the north-east.

The capture of Brno was saluted by the Soviet command with a shower of battle honours and high decorations. The German defences in eastern Czechoslovakia had been finally cracked and both Soviet fronts now swung on Olomouc, forcing a hasty withdrawal by First *Panzer* Army to escape encirclement. Yeremenko employed three of his four armies to press forward to Olomouc, while Malinovskii used his right-flank armies to strike towards Olomouc and link up with 4th Ukrainian Front. Soviet success at long last was undisputed, but the price was high—38,400 killed in action, 140,000 wounded; while the 1st Czechoslovak Corps fighting under Soviet command lost 774 killed and 3,730 wounded. Nor was Stalin satisfied, for all the thunder of the salutes in Moscow and the lavish distribution of medals. Beyond the battle lines a struggle of larger proportions was being waged for Czechoslovakia, involving not only Schörner's German Army Group Centre but also American divisions racing now to the Czechoslovak border from the west and promising to be the first to reach Prague. Stalin had not the least intention of allowing this to happen.

Prague also loomed no less large in Churchill's mind at this juncture, though the sombre drift of his thought encompassed the entire face of Europe. German armies in the west crumbled one by one, speeding the advance of Allied divisions to the north—and on to the Elbe—and into Austria in the south, but wherever the Red Army trod one steely portcullis after another dropped upon the liberated and the conquered alike with chilling abruptness. Writing on 30 April to President Truman, Churchill insisted that 'the liberation of Prague and as much as possible of the territory of western Czechoslovakia' by US forces could make an appreciable difference not only to Czechoslovakia itself but to 'near-by countries', which might otherwise 'go the way of Yugoslavia'. Mention of Yugoslavia simply turned the knife in a deeper hurt, the suppurating sore of Poland. On 18 April both the Prime Minister and President Truman pressed on Stalin the urgency of a fair settlement to the question of forming a Government of National Unity consonant with consultations with Polish leaders and excluding an automatic application of 'the Yugoslav precedent', only to receive a hard rebuff from Stalin, who argued that the present Polish Provisional Government should be 'the core, that is, the main part' of a new, reconstructed Polish Government of National Unity. By rejecting 'the Yugoslav example', the British and Americans were saying in effect that the Polish Provisional Government could not be regarded as 'the basis for, and the core of, a future Government of National Unity'. Marshal Stalin in his signal of 24 April made his point bluntly plain: accept the Yugoslav precedent as a model for Poland and, as soon as this is done, we shall be able to make progress on the Polish question.

It was not, however, the London and Lublin governments which were swept away but the Prime Minister's hopes for an amicable and democratic settlement. Stalin wanted no new government brought into being beyond his own creation, scheming to trap Polish representatives with General Okulicki at their head and pinion them with the *NKVD*. In an extraordinary, passionate, importuning but despairing message on 29 April the Prime Minister played his final card, opening with a categorical statement that none would ever favour 'a Polish Government hostile to the Soviet Union'. 'The Yugoslav precedent' was in no way applicable to Poland: the process of consultation had been cut short even though it was agreed upon at Yalta, with the Soviet government signing its own treaty with the Bierut government and producing a feeling on the Western side that 'it is we who have been dictated to and brought up against a stone wall. . . .' In any event, Marshal Tito in Yugoslavia broke the 'fifty-fifty rule', proclaiming at once that his prime loyalties lay with the Soviet Union and rigging the business of consultation, so that only six members of the Royal Yugoslav government entered the government as opposed to twenty-five of his own nominees. What was now proposed for Poland meant that for every four representatives of the present 'Warsaw Provisional Government' there would be only one from 'the other democratic elements'—a position wholly unacceptable to the British government:

there is not much comfort in looking into a future where you and the countries you dominate plus the Communist parties in many other states are all drawn up on one side, and those who rally to the English-speaking nations and their Associates or Dominions are on the other. It is quite obvious that their quarrel would tear the world to pieces and that all of us leading men on either side who had anything to do with that would be shamed before history. [*Perepiska*, vol. 1, p. 407.]

There may be cause for offence here—'but . . . , I beg you, my friend Stalin (*moi drug Stalin*), do not underrate those matters which you may think small to us but which remain symbolic of the way the English-speaking democracies look at life'.

The reply, when it came on 4 May, was crude, rude and curt: 'I must say frankly', wrote Stalin, 'that this attitude [the refusal to consider the Provisional Government as a basis for a future Government of National Unity] precludes the possibility of an agreed decision on the Polish question.' Even as Stalin's message fell upon his desk the Prime Minister outlined a nightmarish prospect to Eden in a message sent the same day: 'terrible things' had undoubtedly happened in the course of the Soviet advance through Germany to the Elbe, an American withdrawal to the demarcation lines sketched in at Quebec could only mean a mighty Russian advance for 120 miles across a massive 300/400-mile front, fastening upon Europe a frontier running from the North Cape in Norway to the Baltic east of Lübeck along the agreed line of occupation and thence in Austria as far as the Isonzo river—to the east of which 'Tito and Russia will claim everything'. Russia would inherit the Baltic provinces, Germany as far as the demarcation line, Czechoslovakia, much of Austria, all of Yugoslavia, Hungary, Rumania and Bulgaria. The great capitals of central Europe—Berlin, Vienna, Budapest, Belgrade, Bucharest and Sofia—would have come under complete Soviet sway, 'an event in the history of Europe to which there has been no parallel. . . .' Vienna, occupied by the Red Army, was already closed to the visitations of Allied missions, in spite of vigorous protest to the Russians and energetic reminders about the stipulations of the European Advisory Commission.

Lübeck might yet be saved and the British Army 'head off our Soviet friends', thus barring the road to Scandinavia. Prague alone, it seemed, was still within the reach of the Western allies.

Stalin wasted neither time nor words. At 0130 hours on 1 May he issued operational orders to Marshal Zhukov with 1st Belorussian Front to take up Koniev's 1st Ukrainian Front positions in Berlin and south of the city to the Lubben–Wittenberg line no later than 4 May, while Koniev received categorical orders to finish off the German forces encircled east of Luckenwalde no later than 3 May, complete the exchange of positions with Zhukov and then swing his right-flank forces on to the river Mulde. Within a matter of hours (at 1940 hours, 2 May) Malinovskii received a separate but complementary set of orders for 2nd Ukrainian Front: he was to deploy his Front to the west in the direction of Prague in order to bring his formations on to the line of the river Vltava and capture Prague, all no later than 12–14 May, with his right flank continuing the attack towards Olomouc. The German Army Group Centre and remnants of Group 'Austria'—estimated by the Soviet command at sixty-two divisions— lay athwart the Soviet route to Prague, but between Potsdam and the Danube three Soviet fronts (1st, 2nd and 4th Ukrainian) mustered eighteen rifle armies, three tank and three air armies, five independent tank and two independent mechanized corps with three cavalry corps, a grand total of 153 divisions and seven rifle brigades, with 24,500 guns and mortars, and more than 2,100 tanks and SP guns, plus 4,000 combat aircraft—as well as the 1st Czechoslovak Corps, the 1st Independent Czechoslovak Tank Brigade, the 2nd Polish Army and two Rumanian armies (the 1st and 4th). The *Stavka* plan envisaged two powerful attacks aimed at both flanks of Army Group Centre, fusing into a general attack in the direction of Prague designed to complete the encirclement of German forces to the east of the Czech capital, thus cutting off the enemy escape route to the west and south-west. The main attacks would be developed from the area north-west of Dresden by 1st Ukrainian Front and from south of Brno by 2nd Ukrainian Front, while the main body of 4th Ukrainian Front and the right-flank armies of 2nd Ukrainian Front squeezed First *Panzer* Army tighter and tighter in the Olomouc encirclement operation. *Stavka* orders transmitted on 1–2 May laid down the essentials of the Prague operation—timed to begin on 7 May—leaving the three Front commanders to issue their own detailed instructions.

The Prime Minister's message of 30 April to President Truman had urged that General Eisenhower be made aware of 'the highly important political considerations' involved in the liberation of Prague, though nothing should impede the success of the primary operations against the German Army. While Stalin raced to issue the first major operational orders for the drive on Prague, the President consulted his own military commanders about the feasibility of a drive on Prague: General Patton with the US Third Army had already crossed the Czechoslovak frontier and pushed south-eastwards, with another column advancing eastwards towards the Karlsbad–Pilsen–Budejovice line. Cleaving to the side of the Prime Minister, the British Chiefs of Staff at the end of April naturally urged the combined Chiefs to press the wisdom of a continued advance in Czechoslovakia on General Eisenhower, provided that he could also maintain his pressure on the Germans in Denmark and Austria. General Marshall was less than enthusiastic about driving deep into Czechoslovakia merely for 'highly important political considerations' and was inclined to advise that General Eisenhower's resources would be fully committed throughout the theatre, though the final defeat of the German Army might mean some move into Czechoslovakia. This left the final operational decision to General Eisenhower himself and it was in this vein that President Truman replied to Churchill on 1 May: since the Soviet command envisaged operations into the Vltava valley, General Eisenhower proposed first to move on Pilsen and Karlsbad but not to proceed to further action which might be 'militarily unwise' all for the sake of some political prize.

Stalin showed no comparable disdain for or delicacy about political prizes: here was the very essence of his war-making and his fervour in ramming the Red Army forward. One such prize, the province of Sub-Carpathian Ruthenia, had already fallen into his lap—or rather, had been forced into the lap of the Soviet Ukraine at Red Army gun-point. Although the Czechoslovak–Soviet agreement of 8 May 1944 stipulated that Czechoslovak territory would be treated as that of a liberated ally, reports reaching Dr Benes in London towards the end of 1944 added up to an alarming picture of Soviet coercion in Ruthenia, in spite of formal permission for a Czechoslovak government mission to establish itself in Užhorod. Though the darkest suspicions roused by Soviet deviousness over the Slovak rising in the early autumn of 1944 seemed to have been allayed, they were now given fresh life and uncomfortable vigour by more reports that Soviet 'non-interference' in Czechoslovak affairs was a blatant fiction.

Stalin took the deliberate step in January 1945 of trying to calm the fears of Benes. In a personal letter dated 23 January Stalin explained to Benes that the Soviet Union had no intention whatsoever of solving the question of Sub-Carpathian Ukraine 'unilaterally': of course, the Soviet Union could not prevent Sub-Carpathians 'expressing their will' but this did not signify any Soviet intention to break the Soviet–Czechoslovak agreeent. Dr Benes replied to this profuse expression of goodwill in the same kind, asserting that none could suspect the Soviet government of unilateral action in the matter of the Sub-Carpathian Ukraine and that the matter would be settled 'in complete friendship with you' long before any peace conference convened. Nevertheless, the signs of degeneration in Soviet–Czechoslovak relations were plain: the Red Army was already deeply implanted in eastern Czechoslovakia, the forcible suppression of opposition in Slovakia could not be denied, and Czech and Slovak communist leaders were standing by to execute orders emanating from Moscow—though those Slovak Communists inadvertently pressing for a 'Slovak Soviet Republic' had to be reined in since this was no part of the Soviet design.

On 11 March 1945 Benes left London for Moscow, with the desperate hope—as he confided to Churchill—that he could 'keep matters under control'. As if by way of gloomy portent Benes was suddenly stricken in health just before his departure recovering sufficiently to travel but with his energies much impaired. Though received by Stalin on 19 March, when both men reviewed the military situation and discussed the build-up of the Czechoslovak Army, it was left to Molotov to handle much of the subsequent business. The main item concerned Ruthenia, which Benes could only cede in principle but try to postpone the actual act of cession until he could return to Prague, while Klement Gottwald and his communist associates urged him to yield immediately. Equally anguishing was the question of the Red Army's attitude to industrial plant and raw materials in Czechoslovakia, equipment seized at once on the pretext that it was held by Germans although it was essentially Czechoslovak property in the beginning. Grudgingly Molotov agreed to a review of this situation.

Yet flashes of encouragement lit this gathering gloom. As if to revive some of the euphoria of 1943 and genuine warmth in Soviet–Czechoslovak relations, Stalin spoke out at a farewell banquet in blunt but far from menacing terms. He reminded Benes that the Red Army—guilty of 'acts of wantonness'—clearly was not composed of angels, the soldiers having been fed on a diet of a heroic image and, being heroes, expecting to be excused as heroes, the uneducated especially abusing this honour. 'Grasp this and forgive them.' In a second and significant speech Stalin outlined his view of 'neo-Slavism', not Tsarist Slavism which had meant brute subordination to the Tsarist regime. 'I hate Germans', Stalin continued, Germans who made the Slavs pay both for the First World War and for the present war, Germans put back on their feet to form 'the so-called European balance of power'—'but this time we will break the Germans so that never again will attacks against Slavs be repeated'. The Germans would be neutered. As for the Soviet Union, there were people—some actually present on this occasion—who had their doubts about Soviet promises and undertakings, but the Soviet Union had no intention whatsoever of interfering in the internal affairs of its allies and there could be no question of 'the hegemony of the Soviet Union'.

It remained to work out the details of a new Czechoslovakia, one which would soon return to a liberated country. The communist leaders in exile—Gottwald, Slansky, Sverma and Kopecky—had earlier refused the offer by Benes of places in his London government, arguing instead for a wholly new cabinet with a pronounced leftist complexion: now, two years later, a new government began to take shape in Moscow, comprising representatives of the four parties in exile plus representatives for the two Slovak parties, superficially democratic but quickly overwhelmed by Gottwald's 'programme' for a National Front of Czechs and Slovaks. Gottwald's list of cabinet posts reserved the key ministries—all save the Ministry of Justice—for Czech and Slovak communist nominees, though with much-publicized generosity they ceded the premiership to 'social democrat'

Fierlinger: Jan Masaryk remained Foreign Minister but with a communist watchdog in the person of his deputy minister, Clementis. On 4 April 1945 the new government was installed and unveiled in Košice in eastern Slovakia, proceeding at once to unfurl its programme under the banner of the 'National Front of Czechs and Slovaks'. Benes could only acquiesce or face the possibility of fierce civil war.

While this avowedly pro-Soviet group sought to entrench itself in Czechoslovakia, an anti-Soviet movement—the 'Vlasov movement'—set out on a feverish search for salvation also in Czechoslovakia, living out a grim cycle of hope and despair in a matter of months and all within the compass of that ancient Slav city, Prague. Six months earlier, on 14 November 1944, Lt.-Gen. Andrei Vlasov in the company of five hundred delegates assembled in the Spanish Hall of the Hradcany palace to inaugurate the 'Committee for the Liberation of the Peoples of Russia' *(KONR);* a German guard of honour was drawn up in front of the Alcron Hotel for Vlasov and *Reichsminister* Frank entertained the Russian general and selected guests to lunch. The 'Prague Manifesto' was adopted as the *KONR*'s political creed of struggle against the Bolshevik dictatorship and the promise of a future 'free, democratic order'. But the odds were already hopelessly stacked against Vlasov; the *KONR* could neither engage the effective support of Hitler's Germany—least of all, of Hitler himself—or imprint any trace of political legitimacy on the mind of the western allies.

After the Prague meeting, the *KONR* 'government' repaired to its old haunts in Berlin, only to be bombed out and transferred to Karlsbad in February 1945. This was a 'government' in title only and even that was suspect, a dispiriting prospect made deeply disagreeable by the growing dependence of the movement on Himmler, though General Vlasov used this sinister patronage to raise and arm the first of three divisions—a far cry from the fully-fledged army Vlasov envisaged, but this was all Himmler would countenance. Maj.-Gen. Bunyachenko, an erstwhile officer on Timoshenko's staff in 1942, took command of the 1st Division but refused to allow it to be committed against the Red Army until it had been trained and equipped; instead, in order to show the paces and the possibilities of these Russian soldiers, a volunteer unit fought an action in February on the Oder and performed most creditably, enough to convince Himmler. At the beginning of March General Bunyachenko received orders to proceed forthwith to the *Ostfront* and deploy along a sector between Stettin and Berlin, a move at once protested by Bunyachenko who insisted that he obeyed only Vlasov, not the *Wehrmacht*. Vlasov raced up from Karlsbad and duly authorized the move, whereupon the 1st Division set off on a 120-mile march, footslogging it towards Nuremberg. As the Division, now swelled with several thousand volunteers from the *Ostarbeiter* picked up along the line of march, loaded itself on to troop trains, Vlasov paid the troops a visit—only to stumble upon a very drunk Bunyachenko and his equally drunk chief of staff. Understandably Vlasov feared for the impression this must have made on the Germans.

Finally deployed north of Cottbus at the end of March, Bunyachenko's 1st Division was assigned to a hazardous attack on Soviet positions near Frankfurt-on-Oder, an assault necessitating substantial artillery and air support. Neither was forthcoming. The 1st Division was cut to ribbons on the morning of 14 April and Bunyachenko broke off the murderous action, withdrawing to stem his losses and brood on a bleak future. The 1st Division never returned to the German front line, since to remain there only invited certain death. If not actually instructed by Vlasov, Bunyachenko read the former's mind aright, arguing with General Busse of Ninth Army for permission to turn 1st Division south, away from the front but down a perilous corridor with the Red Army to its left and ahead Schörner's Army Group Centre ready to pounce in its search for fighting men.

General Vlasov himself arrived in Prague on 16 April and tried at once to breathe some life into the idea of a 'third force', including non-communist Czechs who might help to hold Bohemia against the Red Army until the arrival of American troops. The *KONR* movement had so far managed to draw in von Pannwitz's Cossack troops and those of Domanov, as well as Rogozhin's 'Serbian Defence Corps', though the Ukrainians remained aloof. Through contacts arranged with the Czech underground by Russian *émigrés,* one of Vlasov's emissaries discussed the future with General Klecanda, an officer who had fought under Kolchak in the Russian Civil War and who now worked with the resistance forces. Klecanda saw no hope either for Vlasov's cause or for his person: the western allies would do nothing for Vlasov and much as they had dismissed any idea of war with Hitler, so they could see no possibility of a collision with the Soviet Union. The Czechs would welcome the Red Army with open arms because Benes would be borne home along with the Soviet troops; only later would they learn what fate really awaited them.

Meanwhile Bunyachenko in a remarkable exercise of generalship, determination and low cunning marched southwards, standing his ground against Schörner who threatened to have him shot; skirting German units, or slipping through them—at one point striding right across them—Bunyachenko eluded Schörner, kept the 1st Division out of the battle line and, towards the end of April, by dint of some ferocious forced marching crossed the Czechoslovak frontier. Suddenly Field-Marshal Schörner in person descended on the 1st Division, enquired about its battle readiness and abruptly left Bunyachenko and his 25,000 men to their own devices. While the 1st Division encamped north of Prague, another *KONR* force—2nd Division—pulled out of southern Germany, passed through Austria and also made for Prague, taking up positions to the south of the city. Here they might perhaps await the arrival of American troops.

Almost as soon as he arrived near Prague, Czech partisans sought out Bunyachenko and made him privy to their plans for an armed uprising in Prague: could they count on the 1st Division in this eventuality? While Bunyachenko saw some honour—and some hope—in this venture, other *KONR* units tried to rescue themselves as best they might from a nightmarish situation; the KONR 'Air Corps' managed to make contact with the Americans and received honourable treatment at the hands of General Kennedy. Others, their numbers running into many thousands, found no such response and were abandoned—or worse, forcibly handed over—to horrible Soviet retribution. Vlasov sent out his own emissaries in an attempt to make contact with the American authorities, waiting out the hours for a reply in his temporary headquarters at Kosojedi near Prague and witnessing the baleful erosion of relations between the Vlasovite Russians and the Germans. He had been instrumental in staying Schörner's hand levelled yet again at Bunyachenko, whose 1st Division had now moved to Beroun south-west of Prague. Schörner gave up his nominal hold on the 1st Division, the German military hoping at least for the neutrality of the KONR troops, but to Vlasov's shock his Russian troops were taking matters into their own hands and cutting down German soldiers, a base betrayal of honourable allies in Vlasov's view. Back in his own headquarters Vlasov confronted Bunyachenko over the issue of supporting the Czech insurgents and breaking openly with the Germans. Bunyachenko advocated supporting the Czechs and turning on the Germans, an act which the Czechs would repay within their new-found state by affording shelter to the KONR men. Vlasov disputed this violently, arguing that breaking with the Germans would be odious treachery aimed at German soldiers who had at least kept their word, while assisting the Czechs could avail little or nothing since the Red Army would soon be in Prague. Bunyachenko waved this aside, asserting that the Germans deserved their fate and KONR commanders must now act to save their men, a view supported vehemently by other officers of the 1st Division. Vlasov could do no more.

On 4 May, at about the time of this confrontation between Vlasov and Bunyachenko, Marshal Koniev summoned his army commanders to a conference. His attack orders had already been issued at 0110 hours that morning and now he added a personal briefing on the forthcoming Prague operation. He planned to launch three attacks: on the right flank north-west of Dresden, three rifle armies (3rd and 5th Guards, 13th Army) with the two tank armies (3rd and 4th Guards), reinforced with two tank corps and five artillery divisions, would strike along the western bank of the Elbe and the Vltava, developing the attack in the direction of Teplice–Sanow–Prague, thus partly enveloping the Czech capital from the west and south-west; a second attack would unroll from the area north-west of Görlitz with two rifle armies (28th and 52nd) advancing towards Zittau–Mlada Boleslava–Prague. A third attack was assigned to the 2nd Polish Army in order to outflank Dresden from the south-east, though Zhadov's 5th Guards Army was entrusted with the actual reduction of Dresden. Koniev gave explicit orders that the tank armies were not to become bogged down in the fighting for Dresden, impressing on Rybalko and Lelyushenko the need for the utmost speed during the first two days of the offensive—after the punishing battles of the Dukla pass Koniev had little taste for fighting in mountains and

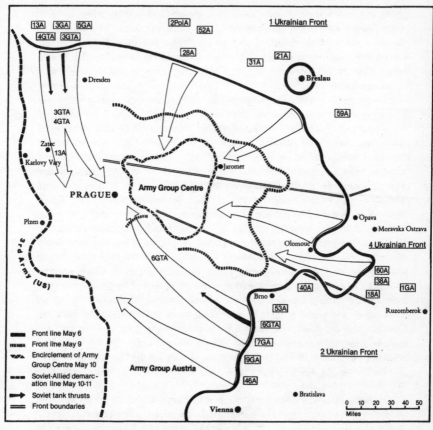

Map 16 The Soviet drive on Prague, May 1945

therefore he wanted the Krusnehory mountains 'vaulted' with all possible speed. All armies, save for 28th and 52nd, must be ready to jump off by the evening of 6 May.

General Eisenhower also reviewed his plans at this time, deciding finally that once the Karlsbad–Pilsen area had been secured an advance to the Vltava—and thus to Prague—was now both feasible and desirable. The Supreme Commander duly notified General Antonov, Chief of the Soviet General Staff, of this decision, only to receive a sharp reaction from the Soviet side, 'requesting' that Allied forces should not move east of the designated line—after all, had not the Red Army earlier halted its own advance on the lower Elbe at General Eisenhower's specific request? Marshal Koniev underlined the point on 5 May when General Omar Bradley visited the headquarters of 1st Ukrainian Front. In answer to a question about possible American help for the Prague operation, Koniev insisted that no help was necessary and that to avoid 'muddling things up' US troops should keep to the demarcation line. The road to Prague was definitely and deliberately barred.

Unaware of this profound change in the situation but excited by news of the American advance into Bohemia, the citizens of Prague took to the streets in sponaneous fashion on the afternoon of 4 May, tearing down German street signs or daubing them with patriotic slogans. Radio Prague under German control thundered out threats of reprisals combined with orders to desist, but the street demonstrations continued. Such was the speed, spontaneity and extent of this mass demonstration that the insurgent planners were taken by surprise and their carefully nurtured schemes for an organized rising thrown into disarray. The Czech resistance movement counted both Communists and nationalists within its ranks, with the former compensating for their lack of numbers by superior organization; for all practical purposes the rising had already begun, though it had been timed originally for 7 May. On the morning of 5 May (at 11.38 am local time) Prague Radio broadcast a dramatic appeal, urging all Czech police, all Czech soldiers, all Czechs to report to the radio station—'We need help!' The population, once more on the streets, set to work with a will building barricades, tearing up cobblestones and pushing trams over to block roads and avenues. The National Council (Narodny Rada) met in hurried session, voting to a man to lead the rising in spite of the absence of the air-drop of arms which the British had earlier promised—the rumours that the aircraft had already left Bari proved to be false, as were the reports that General Patton's tanks were only mere miles away from Prague.

This beautiful unscarred city, so far unhurt by bombing and not yet pockmarked by artillery fire, prepared to make war. The radio continued to direct the insurrection, announcing the proclamation of the National Council at 6.15 pm on the evening of 5 May that Greater Prague had been taken; ten minutes later, Station 'Prague, Czechoslovakia' instructed the population to set up barricades along the road from Benesov to Prague because German tanks were starting to move towards the city. In English and Russian, Station 'Prague, Czechoslovakia' also broadcast an appeal for air support in order to hold off the German armour.

Listeners to 'Station Prague, Czechoslovak Radio' had already learned that the National Council had assumed the direction of the rising. Hurriedly convened and struggling to control a confused situation, the Council selected Professor Albert Prazak as its president, with Josef Smirkovsky as his deputy and representative of the communist minority. Titular military command went to General Kutlwasr, though the Czechoslovak government in London at once dispatched Captain Nechansky as its own military nominee and delivered him to the scene in a parachute drop. The initial German reaction was slow and almost half-hearted, with troops and police trying to chase off the demonstrators, but the *Waffen SS* gathered its strength to strike back with customary ferocity. Towards ten o'clock on the evening of 5 May 'Station Prague' announced that the *Protektorat* and the German administration no longer existed and that the National Council held many of these men prisoner. But at 0053 hours on 6 May the assuredness of this tone was shattered by a frantic call to the US Army—'Send your tanks, send tanks and aircraft. Help us save Prague', repeated in a broadcast transmitted in Russian and English an hour or so later announcing the German encirclement of Prague—'Prague needs help. For God's sake help!' At 0210 hours 'Station Prague' sent out one particular signal to Lt.-Col. Sidorov of the 4th Department, Commissariat for State Security in Kiev: this plea in Russian urged both the dispatch of air cover and parachutists who could be dropped on the Olsany cemetery in Prague. Throughout the night more appeals went out by radio, begging for help and asking for confirmation of receipt. The BBC replied, Soviet transmitters remained silent.

Another broadcast in Russian went out at 0328 hours but addressed this time to 'Vlasov's Army' rather than the Red Army. The Czechs appealed to the Vlasov troops 'as Russian and Soviet citizens' to support the rising in Prague. Bunyachenko with his 1st Division kept close contact with the staff officers of the Czech insurrection and knew now that the National Council had assumed political responsibility for the operation in Prague. The issue of Bunyachenko's active participation—since 1st Division was the crucial military counterweight in this situation—brought dismay to the Germans and confusion within the Czech ranks. A Czech broadcast on the evening of 6 May stated exuberantly that not only were Allied divisions on the way to Prague but that 'General Vlasov's units arrived here today', countered in turn by an appeal from the German command broadcast in Russian shortly after midnight on 7 May to the Vlasov troops, 'first allies of the German people in its heroic struggle against Bolshevism', not to desert the German cause. Further discouragement for the 'Vlasov army' came from a somewhat unexpected quarter, from the Czechoslovak government in London, one of whose ministers—Dr Ripka—advised his compatriots in a broadcast that they should shun 'help from traitors' and refrain from staining the escutcheon of anti-German resistance by association with 'Vlasov traitors'.

Bunyachenko's troops had already lent considerable aid to the insurgents, ignoring German pleas and responding to the appeal of the National Council. Taking on the *Waffen SS,* the 1st Division hammered its way into the city and occupied the aerodrome, the radio station and other key positions; in the early hours of 7 May (at 0507 hours) Vlasov made the break complete and called on German troops in Greater Prague to surrender unconditionally or else face annihilation. Brave words these and substantially justified, but a shock awaited Bunyachenko that morning: having assumed he was operating with the cognizance of the National Council, Josef Smirkovsky informed him that the political authority of the Council did not extend to the *KONR,* the Council would have nothing to do with traitors and mercenaries—moreover, many men of the Council were Communists, the Vlasov men were declared enemies of Communism and thus became enemies themselves.

As if by magic, however, three US Army vehicles had reached the suburbs of Prague, a harbinger which Prague Radio announced as the prelude to a full-scale advance by American and British troops. But the trickle never became a flood, since observance of Soviet stipulations brought all troops back behind the Pilsen line, a shattering revelation which caused Bunyachenko to think at once of a speedy withdrawal and possible salvation at the hands of the Americans. The German command was equally confused and as intent on flight as the Vlasov men. The fighting in the city had all but died away by the night of 7 May, leaving German units—and the *KONR*—ensnared by Czech barricades and harried by partisan groups. In a bitter renewed brotherhood of arms Bunyachenko's men and the *SS* again closed ranks to punch their way through Czech cordons and fight their way free of a fate both dreaded above all else, capture by the Red Army.

During the night of 7–8 May the National Council and the German command talked their way towards a form of agreement, announced at 0504 hours on the morning of 8 May as the unconditional surrender of German forces in Prague. Bunyachenko was pulling back on Beroun and making ready to march south with all haste. Lacking real information about Bunyachenko's plans to aid the Czechs, the command of the *KONR* 2nd Division and General Vlasov's Chief of Staff, Fedor Trukhin, had already opened negotiations with the Americans and were ordered to pass over to the American lines, lay down their arms and surrender within thirty-six hours. News of this was sent to Bunyachenko but no reply came: first Boyarskii and then Trukhin set out in search of Bunyachenko, only to encounter a Czech partisan unit in Pribram—with a Red Army captain in command. Boyarskii was hanged on the spot, Trukhin consigned to the Red Army. Blagoveshchenskii, sent out to search for Trukhin, also fell headlong into this Red Army death-pit. These were among the first of many thousands to be bludgeoned, hanged, shot, bestially tortured, transported to slave camps or forced to suicide, all in the name of the fair principle of 'repatriation'.

Mightier events, however, were already shaping each battlefront and settling the fate of every army group, army division and unit, naval and air fleet. On taking up his heritage handed on from Hitler, *Gross-Admiral* Karl Dönitz had pledged himself to continue the fight against Bolshevism, whatever the odds and even if this meant further fighting with the British and Americans should they stand in his way of rescuing German troops and civilians from 'slavery or destruction' in the east. To this end he manoeuvred with increasing desperation to avoid a general capitulation on all battle fronts, seeking to delay any surrender in the east for as long a period as possible, his tactics centring on offering surrender on behalf of individual German armies to Western commanders. Elaborating carefully on this plan German plenipotentiaries sent to Field-Marshal Montgomery's

HQ on 3 May offered surrender on behalf of the three German armies in contact with the Red Army between Rostock and Berlin, a proposal which the Field-Marshal properly deflected and directed towards the Soviet command. A purely tactical surrender could be enacted but General Eisenhower advised that anything further would require the presence of German emissaries at his own headquarters.

On 6 May General Jodl joined Admiral Friedeburg at Rheims. In the presence of the Soviet liaison officer, General Susloparov, the German Admiral had already been shown a copy of an Act of Military Surrender: Jodl, empowered to offer simultaneous surrender on all fronts, hoped at least to gain acceptance of a surrender in two phases, capitulating only in full on the western fronts. General Eisenhower insisted on full and instantaneous capitulation, a position re-affirmed by General Walter Bedell Smith who pointed out that in the absence of agreement the talks must end and the Western Front would be fully sealed to all comers. Jodl reported this adamantine insistence and was authorized to sign, with the proviso that fighting would cease forty-eight hours later. The Act of Military Surrender was signed at 0241 hours on 7 May, General Susloparov adding his signature for the Soviet command.

Within hours irate Soviet reaction drilled upon General Eisenhower. General Antonov at the Soviet General Staff complained that though the surrender talks were designed to effect simultaneous capitulation, Admiral Dönitz was ordering further fighting in the east—the impression remained that here, in effect, was a separate truce with the West rather than general capitulation. Moreover, the Act of Military Surrender should have been concluded in Berlin and should bear the signature of Marshal Zhukov: General Susloparov had no authority to sign any act of surrender. Stalin made himself brusquely plain in a telephone call to Zhukov in Berlin. It was the Soviet people rather than the Allies who had borne the main brunt of the war and, therefore, the Germans should sign their surrender before the Supreme Command of the entire anti-Hitler coalition and not merely in the presence of the western Supreme Commander: nor had he agreed to the signing of surrender in some tuppeny-ha'penny town, only in Berlin itself—the Rheims document could be only a 'preliminary protocol of surrender', while the formal signing would take place in Berlin on 8 May, with the German High Command in attendance and in the presence of the Supreme Command of the Allies. Vyshinskii would fly to Berlin at once and act as Zhukov's 'assistant for political affairs'.

On the night of 7 May 'Station Prague' broadcast to the German military commander, disclosing the contents of the German surrender document signed at Rheims earlier in the day, a document reportedly delivered to the Czechs by an American officer from the US 1st Division. The document finally made it clear that the act of surrender applied to the Western and Eastern fronts alike. German unconditional surrender in Prague was enacted with some speed and accompanied by a protocol which promised Czech assistance in speeding the German withdrawal. Meanwhile Koniev's tanks were closing on Prague, following

through the offensive which had been launched a day earlier than planned, the
Stavka having decided that both Fronts—1st and 2nd Ukrainian—would move
off before they had completed their regrouping. In this quest for as much speed
as possible the *Stavka* on 5 May ordered Glagolev's 9th Guards Army from
3rd Ukrainian Front to join Malinovskii, who received specific *Stavka* orders to
use this additional army between 7th Guards and 46th Army in the attack aimed
at Pilsen; the main attack would be executed by four rifle armies, one tank army
(6th Guards) and a cavalry-mechanized group, leaving only 40th Army and 4th
Rumanian Army to continue operations along the 'Olomouc axis'. Yeremenko's
4th Ukrainian Front would also concentrate against Olomouc, but in the event
of a speedy collapse of German resistance Yeremenko had prepared several 'mobile
groups' including one rifle battalion earmarked for an air-lift to Prague in transport
planes. North of Opava 60th Army organized its own 'mobile group' to carry
out a deep raid, an operation deemed of such significance that the Deputy Front
commander, General G.F. Zakharov, took personal control of the planning and
preparations.

Wasting no time Koniev decided at 10 o'clock on the morning of 6 May to
launch his main assault force once lead battalions had discovered that there was
no continuous line of German defences ahead and that west of Meissen German
units were already retiring to the south. Attacking off the march, Koniev committed
his two tank armies that same afternoon after a brief but powerful 32-minute
artillery barrage, holding the tanks as yet within the infantry formations; to
Koniev's relief the German command had not detected the massive force on the
extreme right flank of 1st Ukrainian Front—two tank armies (3rd and 4th
Guards) and two rifle armies (13th and 3rd Guards)—and aligned to the west
and north-west of Dresden. Zhadov's 5th Guards Army, assigned to reduce
Dresden, required more time to deploy and Koniev was forced to postpone that
attack until the evening and leave Zhadov to a night assault. Pukhov with 13th
Army provided some compensation, having pushed on for about fifteen miles;
at this news Koniev ordered Pukhov to cut loose and make all speed for Prague,
at the same time informing all commanders that he demanded an advance rate
of at least twenty miles per day from the infantry and 30–35 miles from the
tank formations.

One undisputed success on 6 May was the surrender of Breslau, the *Festung*
which had held out for almost three months and suffered grievous casualties
among soldiers and civilians alike. In the evening at 1800 hours General Nickhoff
finally accepted terms of surrender presented by General Gluzdovskii, the commander of the Soviet 6th Army who had more than once badgered Koniev to
be allowed to carry out a storming attack on the city. The Soviet surrender terms
were generous on paper but malignant in practice. Koniev refused to see Nickhoff
and ordered that he be given the same treatment as other German prisoners.
During the night Koniev kept his mobile columns on the move along the western

bank of the Elbe, though heavy rain made the going difficult. During the course of the day Meissen fell to 3rd Guards Army, while Lelyushenko and Pukhov each raced for the German–Czech frontier and the routes through the Krusnehory mountains. As Zhadov continued to batter his way into Dresden supported by Rybalko's tanks, to the south-east of Prague Malinovskii launched his own attack with Shumilov's 7th Guards Army in the lead and assigned to open a path for 6th Guards Tank Army which still showed all the signs and retained the scars of the heavy fighting in Hungary—9th Guards Mechanized Corps could now only field twenty-one tanks.

As an abject and defeated German High Command proceeded under guard on 8 May to Berlin, there to re-enact their full capitulation in the presence of the Russians and on a site of Russian choosing, Lelyushenko's tanks and Pukhov's lorried infantry were already over the Czechoslovak frontier as Zhadov closed tightly on Dresden. Marshal Koniev found the situation somewhat bemusing, for while Field-Marshal Keitel signed away Germany's surrender in Berlin 1st Ukrainian Front was still fighting Field-Marshal Schörner. The *Stavka* had already informed Front commanders of the act of military surrender signed in Rheims in the early hours of 7 May and instructed Soviet commanders to use radio and leaflets in order to inform German troops of the act of capitulation and the need to lay down their arms; failure to comply would be met by a 'decisive response'. Stalin was not over-eager to meet British and American wishes for a speedy announcement of the German surrender. On 7 May he intimated, to the Prime Minister that there was no certainty as yet that the German armies on the Eastern Front would obey their own High Command and capitulate—on the contrary, there were signs that a 'considerable grouping of German troops' to the east had openly declared their intention of ignoring the capitulation call. Accordingly Stalin suggested that all wait 'until the German surrender takes effect' and announce the surrender on 9 May at 7 pm Moscow time. The Allies, however, could not wait: none could hide a surrender transmitted *en clair* to German troops in so many locations. Western capitals erupted in immediate jubilation but in Moscow the guns fired off just one more salute—greeting the capture of Dresden.

Marshal Koniev duly transmitted details of the capitulation order at 2000 hours on 8 May to all German units in western Czechoslovakia, allowing the German command three hours in which to submit. When no reply came, at 2300 hours Koniev fired off a massive barrage from his guns and ordered every army under his Front command—twelve armies in all—to resume military operations. Travelling at breakneck speed Lelyushenko's tanks reached Prague in the early hours of the morning of 9 May. At 0300 hours Belov's 10th Guards Tank Corps was in the north-western suburbs, followed by the 70th Guards Self-Propelled Gun Brigade and Rybalko's 3rd Guards Tank Army drawing into the northern suburbs at about six o'clock that morning. The rifle armies also drew up to the city somewhat later when the lead elements of two corps from

3rd Guards and 13th Army took their place alongside the tank columns. Shortly after noon the 22nd Guards Tank Brigade (6th Guards Tank Army) leading Malinovskii's attack from 2nd Ukrainian Front linked up in Prague with Koniev's units.

The very last Soviet trap had snapped shut.

References and Sources

This compilation needs some little explanation. As I explained in my Preface, here is virtually a second book, presenting a profile of the materials and literature relevant to the operational narrative, with each set of references related to the sub-sections of the chapters. The main division is between non-Soviet and Soviet materials (with an additional classification for East European items, where this is relevant). Equally, I have made separate provision for identifying diplomatic documents and materials, where necessary. Finally the Bibliography, which follows, can be used either independently or as a supplement to these notes and references.

While it is my earnest hope that the classification and presentation is self-explanatory, perhaps it is not out of place to specify the treatment of the German materials, particularly the documentary assemblies. In general, I have divided these into two sections: first, the printed volumes of the War Diary of the *Wehrmacht* High Command (*Kriegstagebuch des Oberkommandos der Wehrmacht*, vols. I–IV, abbreviated to *KTB/ OKW*, with volume/page number); and second, the microfilmed records, filmed at Alexandria, Virginia, USA, and held in the National Archives (USA)—duly administered by the National Archives and Records Service (General Services Administration). The microfilmed records present some complexities of their own. The reader will notice that I have first identified the source of the document under the general description of *German Military Documents (GMD)*, followed by a note of the title of the document or a brief description and, in turn, by its provenance—the microcopy number (for example, T-78), the roll number (R488 and the like) plus the frame numbers from that same roll: T-78/R499, 6487746-788 is an illustration.

This, however, does not end the need for further explanation. Inevitably there is the problem of abbreviation and identification. While it is impossible to provide an exhaustive list of German military abbreviations, I have selected those which occur most frequently and where amplification will assist the reader in evaluating the significance of the document, particularly the level of command at which it originated. I have already referred to the *OKW—Oberkommando der Wehrmacht* (the *Wehrmacht* High Command)—to which must be added *OKH, Oberkommando des Heeres* (Army High Command). Next comes Hgr. *(Heeresgruppe)*, with a specific designation (*Süd*—South, *Mitte*—Centre, etc.) identifying Army Group(s); the army/army commands (*AOK: Armee Oberkommando*, with the requisite number, *AOK 9* thus identifying the German Ninth Army); *Pz. A. (Panzer Army*, with its appropriate number); and *AK (Army Corps*, with its number).

For further convenience I have listed below all the 'Record Groups' which I consulted:

Records of Headquarters, German Armed Forces High Command

Records of Headquarters, German Armed Forces
Records of Headquarters, German Army High Command
Records of Headquarters, German Navy High Command (OKM)
Records of German Field Commands—Army Groups, Army, Division
Records of the Reich Leader of the SS and Chief of the German Police
Records of the Reich Ministry for the Occupied Eastern Territories 1941–1945
Records of Former German and Japanese Embassies and Consulates, 1890–1945
Records of Nazi Cultural and Research Institutes

Last, but very far from least, comes *FHO, Fremde Heere Ost* (Foreign Armies East), with its counterpart, *Fremde Heere West* (Foreign Armies West). The correct designation of this major intelligence organization is *OKH/GenStdH/Abt. FHO:* Army High Command/Army General Staff/Section-Foreign Armies East, which I have duly foreshortened to *FHO* to avoid cumbersome repetition. Nevertheless, I have in many instances added what I might best call the 'branch identification' after the notation *FHO*, as in *FHO*(Ia). This is not mere pedantry but indicates the type of material, as in:

FHO(Ia) Führungsabteilung/taktischer Führungsstab *(Operations)*
FHO(Ia/Mess)/Karten/Vermessungswesen *(Maps/Surveys)*
FHO(Ic) Feindnachrichten *(Intelligence* (Ic/A.O. denotes *Abwehroffizier))*
FHO(Id) Ausbildungsoffizier *(Training)*

Following standard German staff organization, other numbers (Roman numerals) and designations proliferated, though here I have confined myself to the most prominent and usual; for those interested in looking more closely into *Fremde Heere Ost*, procedures and internal administration are detailed in one folder covering the period 8 February 1941 to 4 December 1944 (see T-78/R480, 6463933–4331). I have also made substantial reference to the collection *Lageberichte Ost* (compiled under the auspices of *FHO*), the daily Situation Reports for the Eastern Front, not to be confused with the *Lageberichte OKH* printed in the volumes of the *OKW* War Diary, situation reports which cover every war front as well as the east *(Osten)*.

Soviet materials do not present the same problem and I trust that simply giving the full title or description, followed by an abbreviated form (as with the military newspaper *Krasnaya Zvezda*, hence *KZ*) will suffice. Such titles and descriptions are also expanded in the Bibliography.

1 'SURRENDER IS RULED OUT': THE END AT STALINGRAD

Introduction: Encirclement pp. 1–22

Adam, Colonel Wilhelm, *Der schwere Entschluss* (E. Berlin: Verlag der Nation 1965). See 'Finale des Schreckens', pp. 277–344.

Doerr, Hans, *Der Feldzug nach Stalingrad, Versuch eines operativen Überblickes* (Darmstadt: E.S. Mittler 1955; Russian translation, *Pokhod na Stalingrad*, Moscow, 1957).

Guillaume, General A., *La guerre germano-soviétique (1941–1945)* (Paris: Payot 1949), pt 1, pp. 33–57, on Stalingard.

Irving, David, *Hitler's War* (London: Hodder & Stoughton 1977), pt 4, 'Total War', pp. 453–70 (on Stalingrad). This work is invaluable for the precision of its treatment of contemporary German documentation.

Jacobsen, H.A. and Rohrwer, J. (eds), *Decisive Battles of World War II: The German View* (London: Deutsch 1965; orig., *Entscheidungsschlachten des Zweiten Weltkrieges*, Frankfurt, 1960). See W. Görlitz, 'The Battle for Stalingrad 1942–3', pp. 219–51.

Kehrig, M., *Stalingrad. Analyse und Dokumentation einer Schlacht* (Stuttgart: DVA 1974). Virtually unrivalled sources/documentation plus eye-witness evidence, establishing this volume as the most authoritative and comprehensive account of German operations in the offensive and defensive phase.

Manstein, F.M. Erich von, *Lost Victories* (Chicago: Regnery 1958; orig., *Verlorene Siege*, Bonn: Athenäum-Verlag), ch. 12, 'The Tragedy at Stalingrad', pp. 289–366.

Philippi, Alfred and Heim, Ferdinand, *Der Feldzug gegen Sowjetrussland 1941 bis 1945* (Stuttgart: Kohlhammer 1962). See pt 2 (F. Heim), Stalingrad und der Verlauf des Feldzuges der Jahre 1943–1945, pp. 179–200.

Schröter, Heinz, *Stalingrad* (trans. C. Fitzgibbon) (London: Michael Joseph 1958; orig., *Stalingrad . . . bis zur letzten Patrone*, Lengerich, 1953).

Seaton, Albert, *The Russo–German War 1941–45* (London: Arthur Barker 1971), ch. 20, 'Defeat at Stalingrad', pp. 306–40.

Warlimont, Walter, *Inside Hitler's Headquarters* (London: Weidenfeld and Nicolson; New York: Praeger, 1964; orig., *Im Hauptquartier der deutschen Wehrmacht 1939–45*, Frankfurt, 1962), pt V, ch. 2, 'Stalingrad to Tunis', pp. 282–96.

Werth, Alexander, *The Year of Stalingrad* (London: Hamish Hamilton 1946), bk IV, 'The German Rout', pp. 342ff. Much important contemporary Soviet material.

German materials

Kriegstagebuch des Oberkommandos der Wehrmacht (Wehrmachtführungsstab) 1940–1945, ed. Greiner, H. and Schramm, P.E. In 4 vols (also part volumes). Cited henceforth as *KTB*, with volume identification and publication date. See *KTB, II/2.1942*, ed. A. Hillgruber (Frankfurt: Bernard & Graefe 1963), pp. 1018–1212, for 25 Nov.–31 Dec. 1942.

German Military Documents (GMD)

FHO (I) *Kurze Beurteilung der Feindlage vom 26.8.43–31.12.42*. Microcopy T-78/Roll 467, frame nos. 6447108–7653. Esp.: Feindlage vor Gruppe Hollidt, 5.12.42 (6447115); Feindlage vor 3 rum. Armee, 22.11.42 (6447117); Feindlage vom 29.12.42 (6447129–31); Interrogation: Maj.-Gen. Krupennikov, Deputy Cdr, 3rd Guards Army. Rostov as main Soviet objective, 22.12.42 (6447163).

FHO Nr 1000/45 Beilage 1, *Teil A. Zusammenstellung (1942–1944). Beurteilung der Feindlage . . .* , T-78/R466, 6445899–5939 (for period Nov. 1942–Feb. 1943).

FHO (I) *Gesamtbeurteilungen bis 3.6.43*. T-78/R466, 6446293–6320. Esp. Soviet reserves Feb. 1943 (6446293); diagrams, maps (Soviet intentions) (6446316–6320).

FHO Nr 5845/42 (Ic-Dienstes/Ost), *Erfahrungen bei dem russischen Angriff im Donbogen u. südlich Stalingrad*, 26.12.1942, 8 pp.

FHO Nr 5734/42 (Ic-Dienstes/Ost), *Entwicklung der neuen sowjetischen Angriffsgrund-saetze* . . . , 24.11.1942, 15 pp. (Infantry attack method prescribed by Stalin Order No. 306.)

FHO (II) *Sonderakte Verhalten der Rumänen*. T-78/R459, 6437425–7470. Esp.: Haltung der Rumänen bei der russischen Angriffsoperation beiderseits Stalingrad, 26.12.42 (6437465–70); über den Zusammenbruch der 3. rumänischen Armee, 13.1.43 (6437428–34).

Reichsführer SS/Records

Interrogation reports: Maj.-Gen. P. Privalov (Cdr, 15th Rifle Corps). Fegelein to Hitler: also Generalkommando XXIV *Panzer* Corps, Ic 1230/42, 23.12.42. T-175/R66, 2582895–948.

Soviet sources and materials

Official histories

Istoriya Velikoi Otechestvennoi voiny Sovetskovo Soyuza 1941–1945 (Pospelov, P.N., Chairman Editorial Commission), 6 vols. Cited henceforth as *IVOVSS*, with volume number and publication date. See vol. 3 (Moscow: Voenizdat 1961), Soviet encirclement operation, pp. 32–42.

Istoriya Vtoroi Mirovoi voiny 1939–1945 (Grechko, Marshal SU A.A., Chairman Main Editorial Commission), 12 vols. Cited henceforth as *IVMV*, with volume number and publication date. See vol. 6 (Moscow: Voenizdat 1976), on Soviet strategic planning, pp. 26–31; build-up of Soviet reserves, pp. 31–4; relative Soviet–German strength, pp. 34–8; Soviet encirclement operation, pp. 43–61.

Wartime press

Soobshcheniya Sovetskovo Informbyuro, vols 1–8 (Moscow, 1944–5). Here vol. 3, entries 19 Nov.–31 Dec. 1942, pp. 316–427. (Cited henceforth as *Sovinformburo*.)

'Itogi 6-nedel'novo nastupleniya nashikh voisk na podstupakh Stalingrada', *Krasnaya Zvezda*, 1 Jan. 1943. (Also map.) (Cited henceforth as *KZ*.)

Soviet War News, published by press dept, Soviet Embassy, London. 'Stalingrad over Hitler', see nos. 420–50 (24 Nov.–31 Dec. 1942). (Cited henceforth as *SWN*.)

Histories, monographs, memoirs

For Soviet publications on Stalingrad, see *Istoriya SSSR. Ukazatel Sovetskoi literatury za 1917–1967 gg.*, vol. III: 'SSSR v gody Velikoi Otechestvennoi voiny' (Moscow: Nauka 1977), pp. 228–39 (bibliographical entries nos. 2405–2600). (Cited henceforth as *Istoriya SSSR*, 'SSSR v gody VOV' 1977.)

For wartime literature, see Lt.-Gen. V.F. Vorob'ev (ed.), *Sbornik materialov po istorii Sovetskovo voennovo iskusstva v Velikoi Otechestvennoi voine* (Frunze Academy) (Moscow: Voenizdat 1956), pp. 137–55. See also: Talenskii, Col. N.A., *Velikoe srazhenie pod Stalingradom* (Moscow: Gospolitizdat 1943), 32 pp.; Zamyatin, Col. N.M., *Srazhenie pod Stalingradom* (Moscow: Voenizdat 1943), 44 pp.

Pushkash, A.I., *Vengriya v gody vtoroi mirovoi voiny* (Moscow: Nauka 1966), ch. 7, 'Razgrom Vengerskoi armii na Donu', pp. 299–337. (Hungary in WWII, extensive use of archives, ample bibliography; Soviet and Hungarian archives.)

Rokossovskii, Marshal SU K.K. (ed.), *Velikaya pobeda na Volge* (Moscow: Voenizdat 1965), pt 2, pp. 261–310, Soviet offensive/encirclement. An authoritative operational narrative/analysis.

Samsonov, A.M., *Stalingradskaya bitva* (Moscow: Nauka, 2nd edn 1968), pp. 339–415, offensive and encirclement. This is the most authoritative Soviet historical work; see also appendix on Soviet Front/Army commands, pp. 525–66.

Two Hundred Days of Fire (Moscow: Progress Pub. 1970). Participants' accounts, Stalingrad; this is a Soviet translation of *Dvesti ognennykh dnei* (Moscow: Voenizdat 1968). See under Marshals Vasilevskii, Voronov, Yeremenko, Air Marshal Rudenko, General Batov.

Gurkin, Col. V., 'Kontrnastuplenie pod Stalingradom v tsifrakh (operatsiya "Uran")', *Voenno-istoricheskii Zhurnal*, 1968 (3), pp. 64–76. Soviet strengths, deployments, Front compositions, armour/artillery densities. (Cited henceforth as *VIZ*.)

'Artilleriiskoe nastuplenie (Tsifry i fakty)', *VIZ*, 1972 (11), pp. 37–9. (Data on Soviet artillery, Nov. 42–Feb. 43.)

East European publications and materials

Horvath, Miklos (ed.), *A 2. magyar hadsereg megsemmisülése a Donnál* (Budapest, 1959). Documents, operations and destruction, Hungarian 2nd Army: April 1942–March 1943.

Kljakić, Dragan, *Ustaško–Domobranska Legija pod Stalingradom* (Zagreb: August Cesarec 1979). Croat Legion at Stalingrad.

Ránki, György, *A második világháború története* (Budapest: Gondolat 1976), 'Sztalingrad', pp. 208–24. Hungary, Hungarian troops and Stalingrad. See also under A.I. Pushkash, above.

'Iskra' (planning), 'Saturn', 'Small Saturn', 'Koltso' (first phase) pp. 22–27

IVOVSS, 3 (Voenizdat 1961), pp. 42–54. *Saturn* planning, defensive operations 2nd Guards and 51st Army Kotelnikovo axis, destruction Italian 8th Army, 2nd Guards Army counter-blow end December 1942, transition to general Soviet offensive. Note also pp. 124–33, planning for *Iskra* (Leningrad), does not mention Zhukov's role.

IVMV, 6 (Voenizdat 1976), pp. 61–73. Operations on Kotelnikovo axis, *Saturn* planning, objective Rostov and SW Front offensive, 2nd Guards Army operations, opening SW Front offensive, Soviet Kotelnikovo counter-blow, destruction Italian 8th Army, also Group Hollidt, remnants Rumanian 3rd Army, achievements of Stalingrad Front. Note also planning for *Iskra* (Leningrad), request for postponement to 10–12 January 1943, Zhukov's role, pp. 117–22.

Operatsiya 'Malyi Saturn' (Rostov-on-Don: Rostizdat 1973). Collected memoirs up to liberation of Rostov.

Rokossovski, K.K. (ed.), *Velikaya pobeda na Volge*, pp. 368–423. Destruction of 'Group Hoth', Kotelnikovo operations, 2nd Guards, 51st Army (12–23 December), commitment main force 2nd Guards Kotelnikovo axis, operations (24–31 December).

Samsonov, A.M. (ed.), *Stalingradskaya epopeya* (Moscow: Nauka 1968). Major collection of material by senior commanders; see separate citations below.

Samsonov, A.M., *Stalingradskaya bitva*, pp. 435–85. Planning for *Saturn*, repulse of German deblocking attempts, evolution of *Small Saturn*.

Documentary-memoir materials

Badanov, Lt.-Gen. V.M., 'Glubokii tankovyi reid' in Samsonov (ed.), *Stalingradskaya epopeya*, pp. 625–40; see also Vasilev, Col. N., 'Glubokii reid tankistov', *VIZ*, 1972 (11), pp. 40–46.

Biryuzov, Marshal SU S.S., *Surovye gody* (Moscow: Nauka 1966), pp. 96–132. Chief of Staff 2nd Guards Army, Kotelnikovo operations. (Earlier version, *Kogda gremeli pushki*, Moskow: Voenizdat (VM) 1962.)

Domnikov, Lt.-Gen. V.M. (ed.), *V nastuplenii Gvardiya* (Moscow: Voenizdat 1971). History of 2nd Guards Army: see pp. 29–46, first operational commitment; pp. 47–60, Kotelnikovo operations.

Filatov, G., 'Razgrom ital'yanskoi ekspeditsionnoi armii na sovetskogo-germanskom fronte', *VIZ*, 1968 (4), pp. 44–54. Destruction of Italian 8th Army.

Gurkin, V., 'Razgrom nemetsko-fashistskikh voisk na srednem Donu (Operatsiya "Malyi Saturn")', *VIZ*, 1972 (5), pp. 21–7. Statistical data, comparative strengths, *Small Saturn*.

Golikov, Marshal SU F., 'Ostrogozhsko-Rossoshanskaya operatsiya', *VIZ*, 1973 (1), pp. 62–7.

Kazakov, General M.I., 'Operatsiya "Saturn" ', in Samsonov (ed.) *Stalingradskaya epopeya*, pp. 501–16.

Kazakov, M.I., *Nad kartoi bylykh srazhenii* (Moscow: Voenizdat (VM) 1965), pp. 148–58, from *Large Saturn* to *Small Saturn*.

Lelyushenko, General D.D., *Moskva–Stalingrad–Berlin–Praga. Zapiski komandarma* (Moscow: Nauka 1970), ch. 3, 'Operation "Small Saturn" ', pp. 134–48.

Popov, General M.M., 'Yuzhnee Stalingrada' in Samsonov (ed.), *Stalingradskaya epopeya*, pp. 659–68; see also his article (same title) *VIZ*, 1961 (2), pp. 67–98 (operations, 5th Shock Army).

Samsonov, A.M., *Ot Volgi do Baltiki* (Moscow: Akad. Nauk, 1st edn 1963—here 2nd edn, Nauka 1973), history of 4th/3rd Guards Mechanized Corps. Kotelnikovo operations, pp. 64–93 (text, Zakharov signal to Volskii, p. 92).

Vasilevskii, Marshal SU A.M. For narrative/memoirs on *Saturn* and Kotelnikovo, see *Delo vsei zhizni* (Moscow: Politizdat, 1st edn 1974—here 2nd edn 1975), pp. 249–87. Contains some documentation, also refutation of Yeremenko's version of Kotelnikovo operations and (p. 269) openly rejects Khrushchev's criticism of Stalin as a military leader.

For *operational reports, Stavka directives*, Stalin-Vasilevskii conversations/signals, see Vasilevskii, 'Nezabyvaemye dni', *VIZ*, 1966 (1), pp. 14–25 and *VIZ*, 1966 (3), pp. 24–44. Indispensable primary materials.

Voronov, Chief Artillery Marshal N.N., *Na sluzhbe voennoi* (Moscow: Voenizdat (VM) 1963), on *Koltso*, pp. 308–38. For further detail and documentation (directives, signals, orders, Stalin's instructions), see Voronov, 'Operatsiya "Koltso" ', *VIZ*, 1962 (5), pp. 71–84 (continued in (6), pp. 67–76). See also 'Koltso in figures', V. Gurkin in *VIZ*,, 1973 (2), pp. 34–42; and Vorob'ev, Col. F., 'Ob operatsii

"Koltso" ', *VIZ*, 1962 (11), pp. 52–8 (important critique of Voronov's own memoir on *Koltso*, with further documents from military archives).

Yeremenko, Marshal SU A.I., *Stalingrad. Zapiski komanduyushchevo frontom* (Moscow: Voenizdat 1961), pt 2, pp. 387–426, destruction of the 'Hoth-Manstein grouping'. Heavily slanted to inflate role of Yeremenko and Khrushchev, criticized by Vasilevskii.

Zheltov, Col.-Gen. A., 'Yugo–Zapadnyi front v kontrnastuplenii pod Stalingradom', *VIZ*, 1967 (11), pp. 57–69. Vatutin's SW Front operations.

Zhukov, Marshal SU G.K., *Vospominaniya i razmyshleniya* (Moscow: Novosti 1969, 1970 and 1971); also *The Memoirs of Marshal Zhukov* (Novosti translation) (London: Jonathan Cape; New York: Delacorte Press 1971). See here 2nd Soviet edition, *Vospominaniya i razmyshleniya* (Novosti 1975), in two volumes: see vol. 2, pp. 116–29, for documents, directives, signals on *Saturn/Small Saturn*. (See *Memoirs*, pp. 410–22 for translations.) Note: Zhukov's involvement with *Iskra* (Leningrad) is detailed in a further memoir contribution in *Operatsiya 'Iskra'* (Leningrad: Lenizdat 1973), pp. 28–36.

Air operations

Collective authorship, *17-ya Vozdushnaya armiya v boyakh ot Stalingrad do Veny* (Moscow: Voenizdat 1977), pp. 5–31, 17th Air Army operations, Stalingrad.

Collective authorship, *16-ya vozdushnaya* (Moscow: Voenizdat 1973), pp. 42–57, 16th Air Army operations, Stalingrad, 'aerial blockade'.

Caucasus, South and South-West Fronts, Upper Don, 'Koltso' (final phase) pp. 27–38

IVOVSS, 3 (Voenizdat 1961). N. Caucasus operations, pp. 81–91; Soviet offensive, Upper Don, pp. 99–106.

IVMV, 6 (Voenizdat 1976). Final stage *Koltso*, pp. 73–80; Southern and Trans-Caucasus Front operations, pp. 95–101; Ostrogozhsk-Rossosh operations, pp. 110–17.

Morozov, Col. V.P., *Zapadnee Voronezha* (Moscow: Voenizdat 1956), pp. 23–89, Ostrogozh-Rosossh operations; pp. 93–111, Voronezh-Kastornoe operations. (A highly detailed and important military monograph; see also appendices.)

Documentary-memoir materials

Bitva za Kavkaz (Moscow: Voenizdat, 1st edn 1967—here 2nd edn 1971), pt 2, pp. 253–302, operations *Gory* and *More*. See Soviet translation and publication (Moscow: Progress 1971), *Battle for the Caucasus*, ch. 4, 'Turning Point', pp. 199–238, offensive aimed at Krasnodar-Tikhoretsk, Black Sea and Northern Group assignments, Stalin rebuke to Maslennikov (p. 208), Krasnodar axis, Tyulenev–Petrov (p. 219); *Gory* and Grechko's 56th Army, *Stavka* directive to Black Sea Group, 23 January 1943 (pp. 234–5), 46th Army operations.

Gody voiny 1941–1943 (Moscow: Voenizdat 1976), pt 2, pp. 404–19, Operations *Gory* and *More*, *Stavka* plans, Black Sea/Northern Group operations, difficulties with 56th Army offensive, German plans to fall back on Taman peninsula.

Kazakov, M.I., *Nad kartoi bylykh srazhenii*, pp. 159–70, Ostrogozhsk–Rossosh operation, planning Voronezh–Kastornoe operation.

Kirin, I.D., *Chernomorskii flot v bitve za Kavkaz* (Moscow: Voenizdat 1958), pp. 151–65, naval support for Black Sea Group, January–February 1943.

Moskalenko, Marshal SU K.S., *Na Yugo–zapadnom napravlenii*. Vospominaniya komandarm (Moscow: Nauka 1969). See here the fully revised and expanded edition, *Na Yugo–zapadnom napravlenii 1941–43*, Book 1 (Nauka 1973), pp. 372–95, 40th Army and Ostrogozhsk–Rossosh operation. This edition contains much important documentary/archival material. Also useful summary in Moskalenko, 'Ot Voronezha do Khar'kova', *VIZ*, 1963 (4), pp. 25–9 (and to p. 32).

Shtemenko, General S.M., *Generalnyi shtab v gody voiny* (Moscow: Voenizdat (VM) 1968). See Soviet translation and publication, *The Soviet General Staff at War 1941–1945* (Moscow: Progress 1970), pp. 70–80, Stalin instructions to General Staff (4 January 1943, pp. 72–3), General Staff planning, Stalin rebuke to Maslennikov (p. 76), Stalin to General Staff (8 January, p. 78), approval of *Gory* plan, *Stavka* instructions to Southern Front (23 January, p. 80), co-ordination of Southern Front and Black Sea Group.

Shtemenko, S.M. 'Vtoraya voennaya zima na Yuge', *VIZ*, 1967 (12), pp. 63–70: on plans to cut off First *Panzer* Army, Southern Front objectives, planned isolation of N Caucasus, Stalin's orders to General Staff (4 January, p. 65), Stalin rebuke to Maslennikov (p. 66), *Gory/More* operations and Stalin's directions (pp. 66–8).

Tyulenev, General I.V., *Cherez tri voiny* (Moscow: Voenizdat (VM) 1960), pp. 246–52, Operations *Gory/More*, Stalin's personal instructions about Petrov (p. 250), Northern Group reorganized into N Caucasus Front (24 January).

Vasilevskii, A.M., *Delo vsei zhizni* (2nd edn), pp. 294–308, 'Na Verkhnem Donu', Ostrogozhsk–Rossosh operation, report to Stalin (6 January, p. 301), submission of Voronezh–Kastornoe plan to Stalin (18 January, p. 307).

Zavyalov, A.S. and Kalyadin, T.E., *Bitva za Kavkaz 1942–1943 gg. Voen. ist. ocherk.* (Moscow: Voenizdat 1957), also *Die Schlacht um den Kaukasus* (E. Berlin: Verlag d. Min. Nat. Verteidigung 1959).

'Koltso': final phase

Laskin, Lt.-Gen. I.A., *Na puti k perelomu* (Moscow: Voenizdat (VM) 1977), pt 2, Laskin receives surrender of von Paulus, pp. 324–41.

Rokossovskii, K.K., *Velikaya pobeda na Volge*, pp. 429–67, preparations for final assault, Don Front decisions/planning operations, 10–12 January, 13–17 January and to German capitulation.

Rokossovskii, K.K., *Soldatskii dolg*. (Moscow: Voenizdat (VM), 1st edn 1968, 2nd edn 1972). Soviet translation and publication (Moscow: Progress 1970), *A Soldier's Duty*, see 'Finale at Stalingrad', pp. 157–74.

Voronov, N., 'Operatsiya "Koltso" ', *VIZ*, 1962 (6), pp. 67–76 (final phase).

Stavka, General Staff, Stalin's promotions   pp. 38–44

IVOVSS, 3 (Voenizdat, 1961), pp. 210–27, on strengthening Soviet forces, orders and decorations, Party-political work.

KZ, 19 January 1943. Appointment of Zhukov as Marshal SU.

KZ, 16 February 1943. Details of *pogon* (illustrations).

Evseyev, Maj.-Gen. A., 'Organizatsiya informatsionnoi raboty v General'nom shtabe, shtabakh frontov i armii', *VIZ*, 1981 (3), pp. 10–18.

Gaglov, I.I., *General Antonov* (Moscow: Voenizdat 1973). See 'V General'nom shtabe', pp. 64–75.

Khrulev, General A., 'K istorii vvedeniya pogon', *VIZ*, 1963 (1), pp. 109–16: introduction of shoulder-boards (*pogon*), NKO Order No. 25, 15 January 1943.

Lomov, Col.-Gen. N., 'Ob organizatsii i metodakh raboty General'novo shtaba', *VIZ*, 1981 (2), pp. 12–19 (working methods of General Staff).

Saltykov, Maj.-Gen. N., 'Predstaviteli General'novo shtaba . . .', *VIZ*, 1971 (9), pp. 54–9 (on General Staff 'representatives').

Vasilevskii, A.M., *Delo vsei zhizni* (2nd edn), see 'V General'nom shtabe', pp. 515–51 (on the General Staff, Stalin and command procedures).

2 THE DUEL IN THE SOUTH: FEBRUARY–MARCH 1943

Soviet offensive, Operations 'Zvezda' and 'Skachok', Kharkov battle pp. 45–55

Carell, Paul, *Scorched Earth* ('Hitler's War on Russia', vol. 2) (London: Harrap 1970), pt 2: Manstein, 'Third Battle of Kharkov', pp. 173–204.

Jukes, Geoffrey, *Kursk. The Clash of Armour* (London, 1968—Purnell History of World War II, bk no. 7), see 'The Salient is formed', pp. 8–24 (on Soviet winter offensive).

Manstein, Erich von, *Lost Victories*, pt III: battles second half January 1943, pp. 393–401; plan to hold Donets basin, pp. 401–4; Hitler–Manstein conference 6 February, pp. 414–20; planning 'German counter-stroke', pp. 420–28; Donets–Dnieper success 19 February–2 March, pp. 428–33; battle of Kharkov, pp. 433–42.

Philippi, A. and Heim, F., *Der Feldzug gegen Sowjetrussland*, pp. 201–8 (Soviet offensive, German counter-blow).

Read, Anthony and Fisher, David, *Operation Lucy* (London: Hodder & Stoughton 1980). See ch. 10, 'Success and Failure', on reduced flow of material from *ULTRA*, Stalin's conviction of German retreat, supposed success of encirclement plan, pp. 147–50.

Seaton, Albert, *The Russo–German War*, pp. 341–50, German withdrawal into the Ukraine.

German materials

KTB, III/1: entries/Ostfront/1 February–9 March 1943, pp. 90–197.

KTB, III/2: see App. c/VIII: *Führung der Operationen*, 'Stalingrad und die Abstützung der Ostfront von Januar bis März 1943', pp. 1598–1602 (also bibliographical footnote, p. 1602).

GMD

FHO Intelligence assessments/agents' reports:

Feindlage: 28.1.43. T-78/R466, 6445929.

    Kräftebild/weitere russ. Operationsmöglichkeiten/Südbereich/Ostfront: 19.1.43. R466, 6446303–6.

    Vermütete Feindabsichten: 3.3.43. R466, 6446284–6.

Feindlage: Mitte, Nord, Süd, Mitte 7-12.3.43. R466, 6445942-6 (5947–8 to 15.3).

'Gesamtbild der Feindlage' (Hgr. Süd, signed Manstein), 26.3.43 (note on movement of Soviet 64th Army). R466, 6446277–8.

Feindlagebeurteilung vor deutscher Ostfront (tabulation of Soviet reserves): 19.2.43. R466, 6446293–6.

Beurteilung der Feindabsichten vor der deutschen Ostfront im Grossen: 22.2.43. R466, 6445936–39 (also Zusammenfassung: agent reports, Stalin's military conference . . .). R466, 6445951–6.

Soviet materials

IVOVSS, 3 (1961), ch. 2, 'Borba za osvobozhdenie Ukrainy'. Front organization and forces, German strength, offensive aimed at Kharkov, SW Front operations, German counter-offensive planning, mistaken Soviet estimates of German moves (p. 118), depleted Soviet tank strength (p. 118), breach between 69th Army and 3rd Tank Army, development of German attack, pp. 111–23.

IVMV, 6 (1976), ch. 5, 'The SW axis', offensive into Donbas codenamed *Skachok* ('Leap'), plan to seize Dnieper crossings, Voronezh Front operations, German withdrawal, fall of Kharkov, SW Front operations (no second echelon, weak reserves), pp. 127–34; German counter-blow, Popov refused permission by Vatutin to break off offensive (p. 136), Popov left with only 25 tanks, *Stavka* fails to perceive German threat (p. 137), Vassilevskii assigned to Voronezh Front (where only 70 tanks left), no operational reserves, tardy movement of 64th Army from Stalingrad, mid-March *Stavka* moves strategic reserves to Voronezh Front, Soviet reverses due to weakness, lack of air cover and mistaken assessment by Front command of German intentions and Soviet capabilities, pp. 134–41. (*IVMV* is more cautious than *IVOVSS* in apportioning blame for Soviet reverses; adds some detail on Soviet strength, involves Stalin less directly.)

Wartime press

Sovinformbyuro. Reports/communiqués for period 1.2.43–9.3.43, vol. 4, pp. 87–170.

SWN. No. 473: Stalin's Order of the Day, 25.1.43.

No. 497: Stalin's Order of the Day, 23.2.43.

No. 500: G. Alexandrov's 'Decisive stage of the War', 1.3.43.

No. 507: Stalin's appointment as Marshal SU, 9.3.43.

No. 509: German counter-offensive held, 11.3.43.

Documentary-memoir materials

Collective authorship, *Zarozhdenie narodnykh armii stran-uchastnits Varshavskovo dogovora 1941–1949 gg.* (Moskow: Nauka 1975), pp. 33–50, Czechoslovak People's Army.

Grachev, S.I. (ed.), *Rozhdenie Chekhoslovatskoi narodnoi armii* (translated from Czechoslovak) (Moscow: Voenizdat 1959), pp. 82–133 (origins/raising of Czech units in USSR).

Kazakov, M.I., *Nad kartoi bylykh srazhenii*, see 'Operatsiya "Zvezda" . . .', pp. 172–88 (Golikov's signal on distance to Dnieper and spring mud, p. 187).

Kazakov, M.I., 'Ot verkhnevo Dona k Dnepru', *VIZ*, 1965 (11), pp. 62–70: Voronezh Front and *Zvezda*.

Lelyushenko, D.D., *Moskva–Stalingrad . . .* , pp. 157–68, on Donbas operations.

Morozov, V.P., *Zapadnee Voronezha*, chs 3–5 *passim*. (Very detailed, indispensable operational study of Soviet offensive, Voronezh/Bryansk Fronts, Kharkov offensive.)

Morozov, V.P., 'Pochemu ne zavershilos nastuplenie v Donbasse vesnoi 1943 goda', *VIZ*, 1963 (3), pp. 14–43: article of singular importance analysing failure of Soviet Donbas operations, with intelligence assessments (e.g. Bogolyubov, 21 February, p. 17, Golikov's September report, *ibid*.), Popov–Vatutin (pp. 26–7), Vatutin to *Stavka* February (p. 31), Stalin's decisions, summary (pp. 33–4).

Moskalenko, K.S., *Na Yugo-zapadnom napravlenii*, vol. 1 (2nd edn), ch. 14, 'forming south face of the Kursk salient', pp. 431–49. (Important for operational directives, also Front report to Stalin 16 February, pp. 432–3.)

Moskalenko, K.S., 'Ot Voronezha do Khar'kova', *VIZ*, 1963 (4), pp. 30–33, directives for Kharkov offensive, Donbas, N Caucasus, Kharkov operation, lack of Soviet reserves.

Svoboda, General Lyudvik, *Ot Buzuluka do Pragi* (Moscow: Voenizdat, 1st edn 1963; here 2nd edn 1969) (translated from Czech), pp. 110–47.

East European materials (Czechoslovak military units in USSR)

Svoboda, General Ludvik, *Z Buzuluku do Prahy* (Prague: Naše Vojsko 1967).

Za armádu lidu, Sborník dokumentů k bojovým tradicim našeho lidu a vojenske politice KSČ, 1918–1945 (Prague, 1960).

Soviet offensive operations centre, 'Iskra' (Leningrad), north-west pp. 55–63

Carell, Paul, *Scorched Earth*, pt 3, 'Battles on the Northern Wing': Leningrad siege, pp. 205–14; south of Ladoga, pp. 214–19; Demyansk, pp. 248–66; Rzhev and Operation 'Buffalo' *(Büffel)*, pp. 266–75.

Goure, Leon, *The Siege of Leningrad* (Oxford UP/Stanford UP, 1962), pt II, ch. 9, 'The Fortress City, March 1942–January 1943', pp. 254–99. Detailed and definitive account.

Salisbury, Harrison E., *The Siege of Leningrad* (US title: *The 900 Days*) (London: Secker & Warburg 1969), pt III, 'Leningrad in Blockade', pp. 273–393; pt V, 'Operation *Iskra*', pp. 535–50. Authoritative and vivid account, bitterly assailed by Soviet critics.

KTB/GMD

KTB, III/1, Lageberichte/Ostfront entries 15 February–23 March 1943, pp. 127–236.

FHO (IIa), Beurteilung der Feindabsichten vor der deutschen Ostfront im grossen: 22.2.43. T-78/R466, 6445936–39.

FHO (IIa) Nr 574/43. Beurteilung der Feindabsichten vor der deutschen Ostfront im Grossen (auf Grund der neuesten Abwehrmeldungen): 23.3.43. T-78/R466, 6445951–56.

OKH/General der Eisenbahntruppen. Soviet railway construction: copious material on Soviet efforts to supply Leningrad (reports, air photos, maps). T-78/R119, 6044128ff.

Hgr. Nord. Feldzug gegen die Sowjetunion der Heeresgruppe Nord. Kriegsjahr 1943: Entwicklung der Lage 1.1 bis 31.1.43 (Bound volume). T-311/R136, 7181737–60.

AOK 9 (9th Army). Orders/appreciations relating to Operation *Büffel* (Buffalo): Army Group/Corps orders *'Büffel* Bewegung': January–March 1943, T-312/R320, 7888896–993.

Soviet materials

IVOVSS, 3 (1961), (i) pp. 142–9, Soviet offensive operations, central and north-west sectors: *Stavka* plans for NW, Kalinin, W, Bryansk and Central Fronts, aim to destroy Second Panzer Army and drive from Bryansk to Smolensk, encirclement of AGp Centre, NW Front to destroy enemy forces at Demyansk and introduce mobile group into rear of German forces operating against Leningrad/Volkhov Fronts, Bryansk Front operations, German countermoves, Central Front operations 15 February, inability to concentrate full Front forces, operations 65A and 2nd Tank Army, 21 March Central and Bryansk Fronts form northern face of Kursk salient, Kalinin and West Front operations liberate Rzhev and Vyazma (3–12 March), NW Front offensive delayed, poor command and control, Germans withdraw from Demyansk, Kalinin Front offensive (3rd Shock Army) north of Velikie Luki, summary of Red Army winter offensive, German losses (October 1942–March 1943) 1,324,000 officers and men.

(ii) pp. 124–39, *Iskra* (Leningrad): *Stavka* directive 8 December 1942, Soviet deployments, organization of two assault groups, Voroshilov as *Stavka* representative, artillery reinforcement for 67A and 2nd Shock Army, operations 12–18 January, junction of Leningrad and Volkhov Fronts (0930 hours, 18 January 1943), impossible to push offensive south of Mga.

IVMV, 6 (1976), (i) pp. 141–6. Western, NW offensive operations February–March 1943, *Stavka* plans to destroy Army Group North (Operation *Polyarnaya Zvezda,* pp. 141–2) using Leningrad, Volkhov and NW Fronts, Germans anticipate Soviet offensive, Central Front operations at least force Germans to commit reserves, Western Front offensive makes only slow progress, NW Front offensive begins without full concentration of forces, Germans evacuate Demyansk, Stalin orders Zhukov to speed up operations of 27th Army and 1st Shock Army (signal, p. 145), limited results of NW offensive. (This version supplies more detail on *Polyarnaya Zvezda* ('Pole Star'), Zhukov's role as *Stavka* co-ordinator in NW theatre.)

(ii) pp. 117–24, *'Iskra'* (Leningrad): operational planning, Leningrad Front plan 22 November 1942 (p. 119), *Stavka* confirmation 2 December, directive 8 December, Stalin sanctions delay due to ice conditions (p. 120), Voroshilov supervises co-ordination, Zhukov takes over on eve of offensive, role of Ladoga flotilla, Leningrad/Volkhov Front operations 12–18 January, decision to build rail link Leningrad–Volkhov. (Slightly more detail on operational planning.)

Diplomatic collections/wartime correspondence

Perepiska Predsedatelya Soveta Ministrov SSSR s Prezidentam SShA i Prem'er–Ministrami Velikobritanii . . . 1941–1945 gg. (Moscow: Politizdat, 2nd edn 1976), vols 1 and 2. Cited henceforth as *Perepiska* . . . ; see here vol. 1, no. 114, pp. 114–15, Stalin to Churchill, 16 February 1943.

Documentary-memoir materials

Bagramyan, Marshal SU I.Kh., *Tak shli my k pobede* (Moscow: Voenizdat (VM) 1977), pp. 163–73, 16th Army operations/W Front February–March 1943. (See also Bagramyan, *KZ*, 21 February 1965, on Sokolovskii as Front commander and failure of Orel–Bryansk operation due to insufficient allocation of forces.)

Batov, General P.I., *V pokhodakh i boyakh* (Moscow: Voenizdat (VM), 3rd edn 1974), pp. 276–92, 65A operations Central Front February–March 1943, Kryukov–Sankovskii enquiry Rokossovskii rejects field court-martial (pp. 289–90), Malenkov inspects army for GKO, Central Front forms north face of Kursk salient. (Note: In the 2nd edn (Voenizdat 1966) of Batov's memoirs, Malenkov is not mentioned, merely a 'GKO representative'.)

Burov, A.V., *Blokada den za dnem* (Leningrad: Leninzdat 1979). Daily record: see January 1943, pp. 291–308. (Note: Zhukov appointed Marshal SU 18 January 1943, the day blockade was breached.)

Fedyuninskii, General I.I., *Podnyatye po trevoge* (Moscow: Voenizdat (VM), 2nd edn 1964), pp. 128–41, Fedyuninskii appointed deputy commander Volkhov Front, made personally responsible for success of right-flank operations/Volkhov Front, operations of 2nd Shock Army, casualties among Soviet senior officers.

Frolov, M.I., *Artilleristy v boyakh za gorod Lenina* (Leningrad: Lenizdat 1978), pp. 149–84, artillery planning, operations in *Iskra*.

Inozemtsev, Lt.-Col. I., 'Deistviya aviatsii Leningradskovo i Volkhovskovo frontov v yanvare 1943 goda', *VIZ*, 1973 (1), pp. 26–31 (air operations, 13th Air Army, 14th Air Army/Leningrad).

Karaseyev, A.V., *Leningradtsy v gody blokady* (Moscow: Akad. Nauk 1959), pp. 271–85, breaching blockade. (Remains an invaluable work.)

Katukov, Marshal Tank Troops M.E., *Na ostrie glavnovo udara* (Moscow: Voenizdat (VM), 1st edn 1974, here 2nd edn 1976), pp. 191–7, raising of 1st Tank Army/ NW Front (February 1943), Khozin's 'special group' (1st Tank and 68th Army), tank army disengaged and ordered to Moscow, thence Kursk.

Kovalchuk, V.M., *Leningrad i Bol'shaya Zemlya* (Leningrad: Nauka 1975), pp. 290–321, Ladoga road/rail systems, winter 1942–3. (Detailed research monograph.)

Mikoyan, A., 'V dni blokady', *VIZ*, 1977 (2), pp. 45–54 (supplying besieged Leningrad).

Platonov, Lt.-Gen. S.P. (ed.), *Bitva za Leningrad 1941–1944* (Moscow: Voenizdat 1964), pp. 230–70, situation December 1942, operational planning, *Stavka* directive 8 December, deployment/strength 67A and 2nd Shock Army, operations 12–18 January 1943. (Detailed operational narrative, though omits any mention of Zhukov's role.)

Rokossovskii, K.K., *Soldatskii dolg*: see *A Soldier's Duty*, pp. 175–81, assumes command Central Front, logistics difficulties, 65A and 2nd Tank Army operations, *Stavka* miscalculation over planned deep envelopment of German 'Orel group', 'grave blunder' in not studying terrain, mid-March offensive halted.

Romanovskii, Col.-Gen. V.Z., 'Deistvuyet 2-ya udarnaya . . .' in *Operatsiya 'Iskra'*, pp. 233–48. (Lt.-Gen. Romanovskii, cdr. 2nd Shock Army, on breaching blockade, January 1943.)

Shumilov, N.D., *V dni blokady* (Moscow: Mysl 1977), pp. 250–59, on breaching blockade. (Author—Party propagandist, later editor *Leningradskaya Pravda*.)

Tkachev, Maj.-Gen. F. and Komarov, Col. N., 'Proryv blokady Leningrada', *VIZ*, 1973 (1), pp. 18–25 (Soviet planning, strength/deployment, operations 67th Army, 2nd Shock Army).

Vasilevskii, A.M., *Delo vsei zhizni* (2nd edn), pp. 308–17, reports to Stalin (16 February), Stalin retails contents of letter to Churchill, surprise at appointment to Marshal SU, recalled by Stalin to co-ordinate offensive against AGp Centre, *Stavka* directive for Central Front (p. 315), recalled to Moscow.

Vysotskii, F.I. *et al.*, *Gvardeiskaya tankovaya* (Moscow: Voenizdat 1963), pp. 10–23, raising of 2nd Tank Army, assigned to Central Front, Sevsk operations, turns to defensive 19 March 1943.

Yarkhunov, Colonel V.M., *Cherez Nevu* (Moscow: Voenizdat 1960). 67th Army operations and *Iskra*: operational narrative, chs 1–3.

Zhukov, G.K., 'V bor'be za gorod Lenina' in *Operatsiya 'Iskra'*, pp. 27–37, Zhukov assigned to *Iskra* operation (5 January), special report to Stalin (document 11 January 1943, printed pp. 32–3), capture and testing of Tiger tank, Leningrad/Volkhov Front link-up.

The build-up in the Kursk salient   pp. 63–76

Boelcke, Willi A. (ed.), *Deutschlands Rüstung im Zweiten Weltkrieg. Hitlers Konferenzen mit Albert Speer 1942–1945.* (Frankfurt: Athenaion 1969), pt IV, 'Das Kriegsjahr 1943', entries January–May 1943, pp. 209–65.

Jukes, Geoffrey, *Kursk. Clash of Armour*, 'The Germans prepare', 'The Red Army prepares', pp. 32–61. (Detailed account, excellent sketches of personalities/commanders.)

Klink, E., *Das Gesetz des Handelns 'Zitadelle' 1943* (Stuttgart: DVA 1966). Basic authoritative work on *Citadel* documentation/decision-making, *passim*.

Read, Anthony and Fisher, David, *Operation Lucy*, ch. 11, ULTRA, benefits from 'long preparation periods', also disagreements in commands, larger number of signals, Rado to Moscow 8 April (postponement of German attack), Moscow informed of new German tanks, 29 April Rado informed Moscow of attack date as 12 June, 9 May 'Director' in Moscow received 120 cypher groups on German plans: see pp. 151–3. (Note: Soviet sources have made no reference to *ULTRA*. The 'Ziebert' episode is described in a dramatized version in *Front bez linii fronta*, Moscow, Novosti 1965, pp. 134–9.)

Seaton, Albert, *The Russo–German War*, pp. 353–61, on Kursk, German and Soviet planning/preparations.

Bibliographical note

Parrish, Michael, *The U.S.S.R. in World War II. An Annotated Bibliography of Books Published in the Soviet Union 1945–1975* (Addenda 1975–1980) (New York and London: Garland Publishing 1981), pt 1 (10), 'The Battle of Kursk', pp. 97–102.

Istoriya SSSR, III, pp. 247–54, Bibliography (publications 1941–67) on Kursk (entries nos. 2695–2795).

KTB/GMD

KTB, III/2, Operationsbefehl Nr 5: 13.3.43, pp. 1420–22; Operationsbefehl Nr 6 (Zitadelle): 15.4.54, pp. 1425–7.

FHO, Beurteilungen/Feindlage: 7.4.43–27.5.43 (Intelligence reports and appreciations, Soviet expectations of Anglo-American operations, growing Soviet military-industrial capability.) T-78/R466, 6445957–978.

FHO (I), Übersicht uber die Verwendung der sowt.-russ. Panzer-u. mech. Korps seit März 1943. (Table of Soviet deployment, tank/mechanised formations.) T-78/R462, 6441617–21.

FHO (IIc), Kriegsgliederungen der Roten Armee (Organization/establishments Soviet formations and units: winter 1942–3, 1943–4.) T-78/R462, 6440637–1465.

Hgr. Mitte (AGp Centre), Neugliederung der russ. Mot.-Truppen (June/July 1943); also detail on rifle and artillery units; Stalin Order 038 15.1.43 on setting up Motor Transport Administration. T-78/R486, 6470777–803.

AOK 9 (9th Army). Anlage zu KTB Nr 8: orders, preparations for *Citadel* (Operationsbefehl Nr 6); see also, as example, 'Gliederung der feindl. Pz–Abwehr und ihre Bekämpfung', 18.4.43 (Soviet anti-tank defence). T-312/R320, 7888473–682 (also 7888747–51).

(Origin ?), Entwicklung der russ. Wehrmacht . . . (A manpower study, covering period pre-1941 to August 1943.) T-78/R486, 6470898–906.

Soviet sources

IVOVSS, 3, pt 2, pp. 245–53, Soviet planning for Kursk battle, Front command appreciations, planning for summer/autumn operations, planning of attack on German Orel group, Soviet reinforcements and reserves, defensive lines and systems, Party-political work. (A certain prominence is allotted to the Voronezh Front, where Khrushchev was a member of the Front military soviet.) Role of the civilian population, pp. 254–8.

IVMV, 7 (1976), pt 1, pp. 114–21, Soviet planning spring 1943, Stalin's meeting 12 April, decision for defensive operation/Kursk, Steppe MD as strategic reserve, Soviet strengths on N, NW, W, SW and Caucasus sectors (table, p. 120); pp. 128–33, Soviet air operations (six air armies); pp. 390–99, Kuban air operations, Soviet air attack on German communications, German air attack on Soviet airfields.

Koltunov, Col. G.A. and Solov'ev, Col. B.G., *Kurskaya bitva* (Moscow: Voenizdat 1970). This remains the standard Soviet work on Kursk. See Soviet military literature and Kursk, pp. 5–12; Soviet planning for summer–autumn campaign 1943, pp. 27–40; Central Front planning/command decisions, pp. 48–51; Voronezh Front planning/command decisions, pp. 51–5; Steppe Front planning/command decisions, pp. 55–6; strength and deployment of artillery, armour, aviation, pp. 64–79; utilization of local population in defensive works/measures, pp. 95–100.

Documentary-memoir materials

Bagramyan, I. Kh., *Tak shli my k pobede*, pp. 183–91, on meeting with Stalin, alteration of assignment of 11th Guards Army.

Bagramyan, I.Kh., 'Flangovy udar 11-i gvardeiskoi armii', *VIZ*, 1963 (7), pp. 81–90 (changes in operational plan).

Collective authorship, *Sovetskie voenno-vozdushnye sily v VOV 1941–1945 gg.* (Moscow: Voenizdat 1968), pp. 155–78, Soviet air operations Kuban, air attacks on German communications/Kursk.

Collective authorship, *16-ya vozdushnaya,* pp. 71–90, 16th Air Army operations, April–May 1943.

Getman, General A.L., *Tanki idut na Berlin (1941–1945)* (Moscow: Nauka 1973), pp. 78–83, Getman's 6th Tank Corps assigned to 1st Tank Army, transferred to Voronezh Front, defensive positions on river Psël.

Golushko, Lt.-Gen. I., 'Rabota tyla v vazhneishikh operatsiyakh vtorovo perioda voiny', *VIZ,* 1974 (11), pp. 35–42 ('Rear Services'/logistics, defensive preparations at Kursk).

Golushko I., 'Instruktsiya po rekognosstirovke i stroitel'stvu polevykh oboronitelnykh rubezhei' (GS instruction 27 April 1943: construction of fortifications, Kursk), *VIZ,* 1976 (6), pp. 66–70.

Katukov, M.E., *Na ostrie glavnovo udara,* pp. 198–207, 1st Tank Army (631 tanks) to Kursk salient, in *Stavka* reserve, Stalin–Katukov (p. 204) on raising additional corps, co-operation with Chistyakov's 6th Guards Army.

Koltunov, G., 'Kurskaya bitva v tsifrakh', *VIZ,* 1968 (6), pp. 58–68. (Defensive preparations, defensive phase, strengths, deployments, extent of defensive systems.)

Koniev, Marshal SU I.S., *Zapiski komanduyushchevo frontom 1943–1944* (Moscow: Nauka 1972). See pp. 8–11, *Stavka* decision to establish strategic reserve, Reserve Front formed into Steppe Military District (15 April), Steppe Front (as from July), Mekhlis member of Military Soviet, conversation with Stalin and Zhukov (p. 9), *Stavka* directive (23 April, p. 10), appointment of experienced commanders to formations.

Kozhevnikov, M.N., *Komandovanie i shtab VVS Sovetskoi Armii v VOV 1941–1945 gg.* (Moscow: Nauka 1977), pp. 119–39, battle for air superiority, Kuban attack on German air strength, *Stavka* directive 4 May for air attack on German communications, target assignments (table, p. 138). (Important, detailed and documented study.)

Kumanev, G.A., *Na sluzhbe fronta i tyla. Zheleznodorozhnyi transport SSSR . . . 1938–1945* (Moscow: Nauka 1976), pp. 230–38, Soviet railways and Soviet defensive preparations, Kursk. (Very detailed monograph.)

Markin, Col. I.I., *Kurskaya bitva* (Moscow: Voenizdat 1958). See 'Dva plana, dve strategii', pp. 13–31. (Earlier account, now superseded.)

Parotkin, Maj.-Gen. I.V. (ed.), *Kurskaya bitva* (Moscow: Nauka 1970). Memoirs, documents, tables of strengths/ deployments. Soviet translation, *The Battle of Kursk* (Moscow: Progress Pub. 1974). (*Note:* Soviet translation omits some memoir material, German military documents, detailed tables on Soviet deployments/ tactical densities, appendices 5–31. See supplements 2–4, pp. 341–3, for translations of Zhukov's appreciation to Stalin (0530 hours 8 April 1942); pp. 344–5, Central Front appreciation 10 April to General Antonov; pp. 346–7, Voronezh Front to General Staff 12 April. (Translations in the text are my own.)

Plotnikov, V.M., *Rol tyla v pobede na Kurskoi duge* (Kharkov: Kharkov Univ. 1969). Detailed study of the rear, 'rear services', construction of massive defensive system.

Plotnikov, V.M., 'Pomoshch naseleniya prifrontovykh raionov sovetskim voiskam nak-anune i v period bitvy pod Kurskom', *VIZ*, 1968 (8), pp. 20–28. (Civilian population: assistance to Red Army.)

Popel, Lt.-Gen. N.K., *Tanki povernuli na zapad* (Moscow: Voenizdat (VM) 1960), pp. 75–103, on 1st Guards Tank Army deploying at Kursk. (Highly personalized memoir, criticized for 'subjectivism'.)

Rokossovskii, K.K., *A Soldier's Duty (Soldatskii dolg.)* pp. 184–93, defensive preparations/ Central Front.

Rokossovskii, K.K., 'Bitva, ne imeyushchaya sebe ravnykh' in *Na ognennoi duge*, ed. Col. V.S. Lokshin (Moscow: Voenizdat 1963), pp. 8–27, on German and Soviet strengths, Soviet divisional strengths (p. 26).

Rokossovskii, K.K., 'On the Central Front . . .', in *The Battle of Kursk*, pp. 77–86 (Soviet plans, strength, deployment).

Rudenko, Air Marshal S. and Braiko, Col.-Gen. (Air) P., '16-ya vozdushnaya armiya v bitve pod Kurskom', *VIZ*, 1963 (7), pp. 21–6 (planning air operations, strengths/ deployments: 16th Air Army).

Ryazanskii, Maj.-Gen. A.P., *V ogne tankovykh srazhenii* (Moscow: Nauka 1975), pp. 52–64, 5th Guards Mech. Corps assigned 5th Guards Tank Army, deployed with Steppe MD (Steppe Front). (Detailed formation history.)

Shtemenko, S.M., *Generalnyi shtab v gody voiny*, see Soviet translation, *The Soviet General Staff at War*, ch. 7, 'Before the battle of Kursk', pp. 148–67, problem of offensive/ defensive, Zhukov's appreciation (8 April), Central Front decisions, air operations, intelligence reports on German attack plans and timing, Vatutin proposes pre-emptive blow, instructions to Steppe Front, uncertainty about deployment of German armour.

Solov'ev, Col. B.G., *Vermakht na puti k gibeli* (Moscow: Nauka 1973), ch. 3, 'Dva plana, dve strategii', pp. 63–93, German planning for *Citadel*; pp. 93–101, Soviet planning. (Extensive bibliographical references.)

Vasilevskii, A.M., *Delo vsei zhizni* (2nd edn), pp. 321–37. See 'Na Kurskoi duge', strengthening of reserve armies, 9 armies in reserve by 1 April, creation of Reserve Front under Lt.-Gen. M.M. Popov, offensive or defensive decision, General Staff supports Zhukov's appreciation (p. 332), Stalin's conference 12 April, Soviet deployments and order of battle (pp. 335–6), Stalin's instructions for Operation *Kutuzov* (attack on German Orel group), Vasilevskii sent by Stalin to Bryansk Front and left-flank W Front, mid-May.

Vershinin, Air Chief Marshal K.A., *Chetvertaya vozdushnaya* (Moscow: Voenizdat (VM) 1975), pp. 208–33, 4th Air Army operations, Kuban April–May 1943, *Stavka* plans for massive air strikes, battle for air superiority. (Detail on command and control of Soviet air operations.)

Yakubovskii, Marshal SU I.I., *Zemlya v ogne* (Moscow: Voenizdat (VM) 1975), pp. 114–25, formation of 3rd Guards Tank Army.

Zakharov, Marshal SU M., 'O sovetskom voennom iskusstve r bitve pod Kurskom', *VIZ*, 1963 (6), pp. 15–25 (planning, defensive preparations).

Zhukov, G.K., *Vospominaniya i razmyshleniya*, vol. 2, pp. 138–63. 8 April appreciation (pp. 139–41), Central Front appreciation, Voronezh Front appreciation, decision to assume *defensive*, sent by Stalin to Grechko's 56th Army, planning of attack on Crimea, increase in Soviet armour, artillery, air strength, Front response to Stalin's demand for reconnaissance/readiness (Central Front report 8 May, No. 00219, p. 155), refutation of Vatutin's proposal for pre-emptive blow, Zhukov's report to Stalin on state of Central Front 22 May (pp. 158–60), Soviet deployments including Steppe Front. (See *Memoirs of Marshal Zhukov*, pp. 427–51, for translation of above text, translation of orders and directives.)

Zhukov, G.K., 'Na Kurskoi duge', *VIZ*, 1967 (8), pp. 69–83.

Organization, production, armament   pp. 76–86

Alexander, Jean, *Russian Aircraft since 1940* (London: Putnam 1975).

Green, William and Swanborough, Gordon, *Soviet Air Force Fighters*, pts 1 and 2 (London: Macdonald and Jane's 1977–8).

Milsom, John, *Russian Tanks 1900–1970* (London: Arms and Armour Press 1970). (Not always entirely accurate: see wartime *FHO* files.)

Norman, Major Michael, *AFV*, No. 17, Russian KV and IS (Windsor: Profile Publns nd.). Also No. 47, Russian T-34/76B.

GMD materials on Soviet war economy, production, weapons (select items)

FHO to *OKW/Feldwirtschaftsamt*. File: on Soviet war economy, war industry, for 1943, also to 1944. T-78/R478, 6461656–816.

FHO (IId). Folder: tables, charts, maps showing location/volume of Soviet production of tanks and assault guns, also losses 1941/42/43. Total losses for this period 56,780 tanks/assault guns. T-78/R479, 6462293–300/on to 335.

FHO (IId). Folder: Soviet aircraft production, losses, Lend-Lease deliveries, monthly output aircraft factories. T-78/R479, 6462305–311. Gun production: tables for 1941/42/43, *ibid.*, 6462447–450.

FHO (IId). Composite folder: on Soviet logistics, food supply, clothing, tank maintenance, captured equipment, PW reports on supply/rations, 1941/2, 1943/4. T-78/R481, 6465470–6023.

FHO (IId). File: on Soviet tanks, photographs, engineering drawings, evaluations. A very important collection, materials running through 1942–3 and to 1944. T-78/R478, 6461818–2116.

Also File (*FHO*/IId) copied to Chef der Heeresrüstung on Soviet armour, assault guns, weapons. T-78/R478, 6461092–1518.

OKW/Feldwirtschaftsamt: Heeresgruppe Süd (Army Group South), Folder: data on Soviet tanks, assault guns, artillery (152mm), production rates, photographs, evaluations. T -78/R477, 6460740–1092 (compilations for 1943/4).

Obkdo. der Heeresgruppe Mitte (Army Group Centre), Mech. Verbände der Roten Armee (29.1.43), also *Pz AOK3: Entwicklung und Gliederung der russischen Panzerwaffe*. (On development of Soviet armoured/mechanized forces.) T-78/R486, 6470843–47/804–808.

Paper. 'Wehrkraft, Rüstungsumfang und Wehrmacht der Sowjetunion im Frühjahr 1943.' (Text of lecture by General Gehlen 16 April 1943 on Soviet war economy, potential and performance.) T-78/R478, 6462126–164.

Soviet materials, war economy, 'Rear Services',
organization/structure field forces

Ananev, Col. I., 'Sozdanie tankovykh armii i sovershenstvovanie ikh organizatsionnoi struktury', *VIZ*, 1972 (10), pp. 38–47. (Important article on tank armies: GKO Order No. 2791 28.1.43 on 'homogeneous' tank armies.)

Bakhirev, V.V. and Kirillov, I.I., *Konstruktor V.A. Degtyarev, Za strokami biografii* (Moscow: Voenizdat 1979). See 'Dyla fronta, dlya pobedy', AT weapons and weapon development, pp. 149–71.

Bokov, Lt.-Gen. F., 'Soveshchanie v Stavke or reorganizatsii tankovykh armii', *VIZ*, 1979 (3), pp. 38–41. (Stalin's conference January 1943 on reorganizing tank armies.)

Komkov, G.D. *et al.*, *Akademiya Nauk SSSR, Kratkii istoricheskii ocherk.* (Moscow: Nauka 1974), pp. 341–88, Soviet scientists and the war effort.

Kurkotkin, General S.K., *Tyl Sovetskikh vooruzhennykh sil v VOV 1941–1945 gg.* (Moscow: Voenizdat 1977), pp. 105–28, 'Rear Services'/logistics 1942–3.

Latukhin, Col. A.N. (ed.), *Bog voiny* (Moscow: Mol. Gvard. 1979), pp. 71–158. Popular but illuminating account of Soviet artillery developments.

Levshin, B.V., *Akademiya Nauk SSSR v gody VOV* (Moscow: Nauka 1966). Soviet scientists and the Soviet war effort.

Losik, Marshal Tank Troops O.A. (ed.), *Stroitel'stvo i boevoe primenenie sovetskikh tankovykh voisk v VOV* (Moscow: Voenizdat 1979). See pp. 59–78 on structure/organization tank forces 1943–5. (Essential, detailed study.)

Malinin, Col. K., 'Razvitie organizatsionnykh form Sukhoputnykh voisk v VOV', *VIZ*, 1967 (8), pp. 28–39 (wartime changes in organization of Red Army).

Obraztsov, I.F. (Editor-in-Chief), *Razvitie aviatsionnoi nauki i tekhniki v SSSR* (Moscow: Nauka 1980). Wartime aircraft production, pp. 52–60; aero-engines, pp. 180–84; aircraft armament, pp. 437–49. (Authoritative technical study.)

Petrov, Yu. P., *Partiinoe stroitel'stvo v Sovetskoi Armii i Flote (1918–1961 gg.)* (Moscow: Voenizdat 1964), pt III, note to p. 377, V.N. Gordov's letter to Stalin and Zhukov on military soviets, also proposing political sections be converted into sections within the staff. (On military soviets, functions and organization, some detail supplied in interrogation report on Lt.-Gen. Mazanov, captured July 1943.)

Pospelov, N.P. (ed.), *Sovetskii tyl v VOV* (Moscow: Mysl 1974), vols 1–2. Collected studies on industrial war effort, also 'rear services'/logistics; on tank/weapons production, see for example vol. 2, pp. 107–27.

Smirnov, E.I., *Voina i voennaya meditsina 1939–1945 gody* (Moscow: Meditsina, 2nd edn 1979), pt III, pp. 267ff, on Red Army medical services.

Sukhomlin, Col. I.M. On Soviet tank armies, 'mixed' and 'homogeneous' establishments, also table of tank army operations, *VIZ*, 1973 (9), pp. 121–7. (Indispensable information.)

Soviet wartime nuclear research programme

On Kurchatov (and Flërov), see P.T. Astashenkov, *Akademik I.V. Kurchatov* (Moscow: Voenizdat 1971) and I.N. Golovin, *I.V. Kurchatov* (Moscow: 3rd edn 1978). Also *International Herald Tribune* report, 27 July 1980, on David Holloway's study of the Soviet decision to build an atomic bomb.

3 BREAKING THE EQUILIBRIUM: KURSK AND ITS AFTERMATH

Kursk: the prelude   **pp. 87–97**

Ainsztein, Reuben, *Jewish Resistance in Nazi-Occupied Eastern Europe* (London: Elek Books 1974). See pt 5, 'Jewish Partisans', pp. 279–388. (Very important study on Jewish role in partisan movement/operations.)

Armstrong, John A. (ed.), *Soviet Partisans in World War II* (Madison: Univ. Wisconsin Press 1964). See pt I/III on organization (pp. 89–139), also IV on psychological warfare and popular attitudes, pp. 197–337. (A massively documented and indispensable work; see also pt II, 'Case Studies', and Appendix on Soviet sources.)

Churchill, Winston S., *The Second World War,* Vol. IV, 'The Hinge of Fate', bk II, ch. XVIII, 'Russia and the Western Allies' (including the Soviet–Polish rupture).

Dallin, Alexander, *German Rule in Russia 1941–1945* (London: Macmillan 1957, revised reprint, London: Macmillan, Boulder: Westview, 1981), *passim*. (A brilliant pioneer research study which retains its fundamental importance and from which I have derived countless insights.)

Fischer, Alexander, *Sowjetische Deutschlandpolitik im Zweiten Weltkrieg 1941–45* (Stuttgart: DVA 1975). See under II, 'Alternativen zur Anti-Hitler Koalition 42/43,' —peace feelers, Soviet–German 'separate peace' explorations, pp. 39–45; also 'Die Bewegung "Freies Deutschland" ', pp. 53–9. (Detailed scholarly investigation of Soviet–German wartime contacts, evolution of Soviet 'German policy'.)

Fischer George, *Soviet Opposition to Stalin. A case study in World War II* (Cambridge: Harvard UP 1952), pp. 58–63 on the 'Smolensk Proclamation'.

Hesse, Erich, *Der sowjetrussische Partisanenkrieg 1941 bis 1944* (Göttingen: Musterschmidt–Verlag 1969), *passim*.

Howard, Michael, *Grand Strategy* (vol. IV, History of the Second World War) (London: HMSO 1972). See bk IV, ch. XVII, 'The Russian Ally January–April 1943', pp. 325–34.

Howell, Edgar, M., *The Soviet Partisan Movement 1941–1944* (US Department Army, Pamphlet No. 20-244, 1956), 'Partisans and Zitadelle', p. 157.

Kleist, Peter, *Zwischen Hitler und Stalin* (Bonn: Athenäum-Verlag 1950). Documentary appendices (IV), Wlassow-Bewegung: offener Brief Lt.-Gen. Vlasov, 3 March 1943 (pp. 318–23), 'erste antibolschewistische Tagung . . . Smolensk', 12 April 1943, pp. 323–6.

Lochner, L.P. (ed.), *The Goebbels Diaries* (London: Hamish Hamilton 1948). See p. 276, entry for 8 May 1943.

Schofield, Admiral B.B., *The Russian Convoys* (London: Batsford 1964).

Sherwood, Robert E., *Roosevelt and Hopkins. An Intimate History* (New York: Grosset & Dunlop 1950), pt IV, '1943—the Second Front', ch. XXVIII, 'The Political Sector', Davies mission to Moscow, pp. 733–4.

Steenberg, Sven, *Vlasov* (New York: Knopf 1970) (German original, *Wlassow, Verräter oder Patriot?* 1968), pp. 68–91, Smolensk visit (also Pskov 1943).

Strik-Strikfeldt, W., *Against Stalin and Hitler* (London: Macmillan 1970). See ch. 7, 'The Smolensk Proclamation', pp. 103–11.

Werth, Alexander, *Russia at War 1941–1945* (London: Barrie & Rockliff 1964). See pt 6, ch. VI, 'Building a New Poland' and ch. VII, 'Dissolution of the Comintern and Other Curious Events . . . ', pp. 635–78.

Wartime press: SWN

No. 544, 21 April 1943, 'Saga of Northern Convoys' (Maiskii awards Soviet decorations to Royal Navy/Merchant Navy officers).

No. 547, 28 April 1943, 'The USSR's reply to Hitler's Polish Accomplices' (on Katyn).

No. 548, 29 April 1943, 'Treachery of Polish Imperialists' (diplomatic break with London Polish Government).

Diplomatic exchanges, documents, studies

Perepiska . . . (2nd edn), vol. 1, No. 163 (Churchill–Stalin 19 June), pp. 160–63; No. 165 (Stalin–Churchill 24 June), pp. 164–7; No. 166 (Stalin–Churchill 26 June), pp. 167–8; No. 167 (Churchill–Stalin 27 June), pp. 168–9; No. 174 (Stalin–Churchill 22 August), pp. 178–9 (on Italian surrender). Vol. 2, No. 83 (Roosevelt–Stalin 5 May), pp. 62–3; No. 88 (Stalin–Roosevelt 26 May), pp. 65–6.

Documents on Soviet-Polish Relations 1939–1945, ed. General Sikorski, Historical Institute vol. II (London: Heinemann 1967). See No. 1, Eden on 'unfortunate difficulties (re Katyn) in Soviet–Polish relations, p. 1; No. 2, Stalin–Churchill exchange, May 4, pp. 2–3; No. 7, Vyshinskii on Soviet–Polish relations, May 6, pp. 7–10; No. 12, Polish Government on Union of Polish Patriots, May 12, pp. 14–17; No. 20, Ciechanowski on dissolution of Comintern, May 27, pp. 23–4.

Sovetsko-frantsuzskie otnosheniya v vremya VOV 1941–1945 gg. (Moscow: Politizdat 1959). Documents/materials, Soviet-French wartime relations.

Israelyan, V.L., *Antigitlerovskaya koalitsiya* (Moscow: Mezh. Otnosh. 1964), pt 2, ch. XI, 'Vtorovo fronta ne budet i v 1943 godu' (Second Front controversy), pp. 222–51.

Kundyuba, I.D., *Sovetsko-polskie otnosheniya (1939–1945 gg.)* (Kiev: Kiev Univ. 1963), pp. 35–80, Soviet–Polish partisan operations.

Rozek, Edward J., *Allied Wartime Diplomacy. A Pattern in Poland* (New York: John Wiley 1958), pp. 115–31, under 'Increased Pressure and Katyn . . . ', General Kukiel's statement on Katyn, Soviet severance of relations with Polish Government in London.

Woodward, Sir Llewellyn, *British Foreign Policy in the Second World War* (vol. 2, History of the Second World War) (London: HMSO 1971). See ch. XXXIV, Anglo-Russian relations in 1943 (Russian demands for second front in France, north Russian convoys . . .), pp. 546–64, also pp. 564–70.

GMD, German documentary materials

Reichsministerium für die besetzten Ostgebiete. Reports on population, 'Agrarordnung . . . ', partisans 1942–3. T-454/R98, 48–380.

OKH/Gen. Stab (Fremde Heere West). *Chefsache:* reports on Pacific war, German pressure on Japan for 'second front' against USSR, estimates of Japanese forces available (7.43). T-82/R93, 0250062–90. (For Hitler's own *démarche* 1943, see also T-82/R90, 246898–7214.)

OKH/Gen Std H. Bandenlage im Osten. Anlagen. (Reports, maps, tables, statistics: partisan movement, May–June 1943.) T-78/R489, 6475171–229.

OKH/General der Osttruppen. *Anti-Wlassow Propaganda No. 8*. (Collection of Soviet anti-Vlasov leaflets/materials, originals and translations; also interrogation of Kapustin, *Soviet plans to liquidate Vlasov*.) T-78/R491, 6477761–889.

AOK 9 (9th Army). Anlage zu KTB Nr 8: von Kluge letter to Army Chief of Staff, collaboration with Vlasov and 'Plan für die Einsetzung eines National-Komitees im Bereich der Heeresgruppe Mitte'. T-312/R320, 7888682–710.

FHO Nachrichten über Bandenkrieg Nr 7. Geschichte des Polk "Grischin" (1941–3). T-78/R491, 6478224–235.

FHO (IIa): Nr 668/43. Subject: *Fernost* (transfer of Soviet forces in Far East to European theatre, Soviet order of battle/Far East): 1.4.43. T-78/R486, 6470809–842. (Note: for Soviet data on transfer from FE to Soviet-German Front, see *VIZ*, 1979 (8), pp. 73–7, tabulation p. 74.)

Die Behandlung des russischen Problems während der Zeit des ns. Regimes in Deutschland. See Teil B. 'Die Aktion des Generals Wlassow'. (Manuscript/report on Vlasov: personal holding.)

Soviet materials (partisan movement)

Beluga, Z.I. *et al.*, *Prestupleniya nemetsko-fashistskikh okkupantov v Belorussii 1941–1944* (Minsk: Belarus 1965). German atrocities, Belorussia.

Bychkov, L.N., *Partizanskoe dvizhenie v gody VOV* (Moscow: Mysl 1965). See ch. 3, partisan movement 1943.

Kalinin, Col. P., 'Uchastie sovetskikh voinov v partizanskom dvizhenii Belorussii', *VIZ*, 1962 (10), pp. 34–7, on Gil-Radionov.

Kasatkin, M.A., *V tyly nemetsko-fashistskikh armii 'Tsentr'* (Moscow: Mysl 1980). Partisan movement in AGp Centre area.

Katskevich, A.F. and Kryuchok, R.R., *Stanovlenie partizanskovo dvizheniya v Belorussii i druzhba narodov SSSR* (Minsk: Nauka i Tekhnika 1980). Belorussian partisans, co-operation with other movements.

Rudenko, N.N., *Slovo pravdy v bor'be s fashizmom* (Kiev: Naukova Dumka 1980). Detailed monograph/dissertation on Soviet propaganda aimed at German troops (offset print, 800 copies only).

Smirnova, V.A. (ed.), *Partizany Bryanshchiny* (Tula: Priok. Kn. Izd., 2nd edn. 1970), Bryansk partisans, reports (docs. nos. 147–74, January–March 1943), pp. 270–324.

Wolff, Willy, *Na storone Krasnoi Armii* (Moscow: Voenizdat 1976). Soviet translation of *An der Seite der Roten Armee* (Berlin: Militärverlag) "Freies Deutschland".

Zalesski, A.I., *V partizanskikh krayakh i zonakh* (Moscow: Sotsekgiz 1962). Partisan movement, considerable use of Party archives.

East European materials on Polish military/USSR

Bibliografia wojny wyzwolenczej narodu polskiego 1939–1945, (Warsaw: MON 1973). On Polish military units in USSR, entries nos 4854–958 (pp. 429–37).

Poplawski, General Stanislaw, *Towarzysze frontowych dróg*, (Warsaw: MON 1965). Ch. 4, 'Kosciuszkowcy', Polish units in USSR, pp. 59–68. (See also *Tovarishchi v bor'be*, Moscow: Voenizdat (VM) 1963).

Przygonski, A., *Z zagadnien strategii frontu narodowego PPR 1942–1945* (Warsaw: Książka i Wiedza 1976), pp. 116–28, Polish political organization, Polish military units in USSR.

Rawski, T., Stapor, Z., Zamojski, J., *Wojna wyzwoleńcza narodu polskiego w latach 1939–1945* (Warsaw: MON 1966), pt 4, pp. 403–16, organization of Polish forces in USSR.

Z zagadnień rozwoju Ludowego Wojska Polskiego (Warsaw: MON 1964). On formation of Polish Kosciuszko Division (1943), details of organization and equipment, pp. 160–222.

Kursk: the first phase 5–11/12 July pp. 97–105

Jukes, Geoffrey, *Kursk: the Clash of Armour*, 'The German offensive', pp. 80–103.

Klink, E., *Das Gesetz des Handelns 'Zitadelle'*, pp. 339–47, German intelligence appreciations of Soviet order of battle.

Manstein, Erich von, *Lost Victories*, ch. 14, 'Citadel', pp. 443–8.

Read, Anthony and Fisher, David, *Operation Lucy*, pp. 162–4, for Lucy's signals to Moscow on *Citadel*, Soviet queries to Lucy and Werther on German operational intentions, forces, direction of main thrust.

Seaton, Albert, *The Russo–German War*, pp. 354–65, on German preparations, Soviet strength, opening phase.

German documentation

KTB/OKW 1940–1945, III/2, Lagebericht WFSt . . . 5 July 1943, 'Am 5.7 früh hat bei der Armeeabt. Kempf, der 4 Pz—und der 9 Armee das Unternehmen "Zitadelle" planmässig begonnen'—to entry 12 July, pp. 748–72.

FHO (I): Tabulation of Soviet strength, 11.7.1943 (3 pp.).

Soviet materials

Wartime press

Sovinformbyuro. See vol. 5 (Moscow, 1944), July–December 1943: under *Operativnaya svodka*, 7–10 July, pp. 1–24.

SWN. Nos. 600–609, 1–12 July 1943: Kursk. 8 July, 'The truth about the German offensive'; 10 July, 'Men against "Tigers" '.

Official histories

IVOVSS, 3, pp. 258–72, Kursk, 'Oboronitel'noe srazhenie', defensive phase, Soviet artillery *kontrpodgotovka*, Central Front engaged 0530 hrs 5 July, assault on Ponyr, destruction of Rukosuev's 3rd Anti-tank Brigade (p. 263), heavy losses to German Ninth Army, German offensive halted; on southern face Vatutin covering Oboyan axis, 6th Guards Army heavily engaged, *1st Guards Tank dug in (p. 269) as fixed defensive barrier*, German advance on Prokhorovka.

IVMV, 7, pp. 144–54, defensive phase of Kursk operations, confirmation of timing of German offensive (0300 hours, 5 July) from prisoners, organization of *kontrpodgotovka*, attacks on 13th Army and flanks 48th and 70th Army, general offensive against Voronezh Front developed 5 July, pressure on Chistyakov's 6th Guards

Army, Vatutin redeploys 1st Guards Tank Army, *Stavka* moves up 5th Guards Tank Army, German pressure on Prokhorovka.

Military-operational analysis/personal accounts

Antipenko, Lt.-Gen. N.A., *Na glavnom napravlenii* (Moscow: Nauka, 2nd edn 1971), pp. 91–108. See 'Na Kurskoi duge', logistics in Kursk battle, operation and security of rail supply, little-known role of air transport/supply (flew out 21,000 wounded), ammunition expenditure/resupply.

Babadzhanyan, Marshal (Tank Troops) A.Kh., Popel, Lt.-Gen. N.K. *et al.*, *Lyuki otkryli v Berline. Boevoi put 1-i gvardeiskoi tankovoi armii* (Moscow: Voenizdat 1973), pp. 7–54, organization, strength, deployment 1st Guards Tank Army, Kursk, defensive operations. Detailed narrative.

Babadzhanyan, A.Kh., '1-ya tankovaya armiya v oboronitel'nom srazhenii', *VIZ*, 1973 (7), pp. 41–50. Compact but detailed account/analysis of 1st Tank Army, Voronezh Front, defensive operations.

Biryukov, Maj.-Gen. (Artillery) G., 'Artilleriya v oborone 13-i armii', *VIZ*, 1973 (8), pp. 41–8. Detailed study of artillery in 13th Army (Central Front) defensive operations.

Collective authorship, *16-ya vozdushnaya*, pp. 90–106, air support for Red Army operations, defensive phase, Kursk.

Danishevskii, I.M. (ed.), *Proval operatsii 'Tsitadel'* (Moscow: Politizdat, 2nd edn 1967). See, in this collection, M. Enshin (commander of 307th RD), 'Trista sed'maya-v boyakh za Ponyri', pp. 50–70; S. Rudenko and P. Braiko (commander and chief of staff 16th Air Army respectively), 'Tak zavoevyvalos gospodstvo v vozdukhe', pp. 85–95 (air operations); G. Rodin (commander Urals Volunteer Tank Corps), 'Ural'skii dobrovol'cheskii . . . ', pp. 120–33.

Getman, A.L., *Tanki idut na Berlin*, ch. 3, 'Na Oboyan'skom napravlenii', pp. 84–108, operations 6th Tank Corps (with 1st Guards Tank Army and 69th Army) as Voronezh Front second echelon, moved from Oboyan, heavy losses after five days, only 50 tanks left 10 July and three batteries of anti-tank guns, reinforcements equally weakened.

Ivanov, Army General S., 'Oboronitel'naya operatsiya Voronezhskovo fronta', *VIZ*, 1973 (8), pp. 11–22. Important, highly detailed, archivally based study by General Ivanov on Voronezh Front defensive operations; also excellent portrayal of General Vatutin, Front commander.

Katukov, M.E., *Na ostrie glavnovo udara* (2nd edn), pp. 202–36, Katukov in command 1st Guards Tank Army, deployment at Kursk, intensity of defensive fighting, losses to tank army.

Kazakov, Artillery Marshal K.P., *Vsegda s pekhotoi, vsegda s tankami* (Moscow: Voenizdat 1969) (Soviet artillery in the GPW), pp. 129–62, Soviet artillery at Kursk, strength, deployment, densities, Central and Voronezh Fronts: in defensive phase 2,424,600 artillery rounds and mines expended, 1,132,800 anti-tank rifle rounds, 1,861 German tanks and SP guns destroyed or disabled (800 on Central front, 1,049 Voronezh Front) (see also diagram Central Front anti-tank deployment, pp. 136–7).

Koltunov, G.A., and Solov'ev, B.G., *Kurskaya bitva* (Moscow, 1970). In this highly detailed, standard work see pp. 101–34, defensive operations, northern face of salient (artillery *kontrpodgotovka*, fighting in main defensive system, Central Front counter-blow, fighting at Ponyr and Olkhovatka, summary of results, defensive phase); pp. 135–66, defensive operations, southern face (artillery *kontrpodgotovka*, fighting in main defensive zone, operations 6 July, fighting in second defensive zone 7–9 July, operations on Prokhorovka axis).

Koltunov, G.A., *Ognennaya duga* (Moscow: Voenizdat 1973), pp. 48–102, narrative of Soviet defensive operations, Central and Voronezh Fronts 5–11/12 July. Useful diagrams of Soviet deployment patterns, types of defensive systems.

Koniev, I.S., *Zapiski komanduyushchevo frontom* pp. 9–17. Steppe MD (Steppe Front) in *Stavka* reserve, Zhukov, Stalin instructions to Koniev, *Stavka* directions (p. 10), *Stavka* directive to Steppe Front 10 July (p. 11), Soviet artillery *kontrpodgotovka*, German penetration Soviet defences Voronezh Front, advance on Prokhorovka, *Stavka* transfers 5th Guards Tank Army and 5th Guards Army to Voronezh Front, 27th Army deploys on Belgorod-Kursk axis.

Markin, Colonel I.I., *Kurskaya bitva* (Moscow: Voenizdat 1958). Useful general account: defensive operations Belgorod-Kursk axis, pp. 50–102; also Orel-Kursk axis, pp. 103–29.

Moskalenko, K.S., *Na Yugo-zapadnom napravlenii*, vol. 2, pp. 47–59. *Stavka* warning order 2 July (German offensive 3–6 July), Vatutin's command conference 4 July, preparation for artillery *kontrpodgotovka*, 40th Army intelligence summary 3 July (pp. 49–50), German offensive against Soviet 6th Guards Army, Vasilevskii-Vatutin decision to block German advance on Prokhorovka and Oboyan, deployment of strategic reserves.

Moskalenko, K.S. (ed.), *Bitva na Kurskoi duge* (Moscow: Nauka 1975). This is an extremely detailed and informative compendium, though little remarked as yet. See General E.E. Mal'tsev on the work of military soviets/Front, pp. 37–47; General S.P. Ivanov on the work of the Voronezh Front staff, pp. 58–64; Lt.-Gen. (Artillery) M.D. Sidorov on the massing of artillery and the manoeuvres of artillery anti-tank reserves in the defensive phase, pp. 96–104; and Colonel G.A. Koltunov on special features of the Soviet defensive at Kursk, pp. 112–21.

Parotkin, Maj.-Gen. I.V., *Kurskaya bitva* (Moscow: Nauka 1970). See translation, *The Battle of Kursk* (Moscow: Progress Pub. 1974), for memoir accounts: Zhukov, pp. 33–47 (defensive operations); Vasilevskii on strategic planning, pp. 59–74; Rokossovskii (Central Front), pp. 77–90; Col.-Gen. Fomin on artillery, pp. 196–205; Lt.-Gen. Antipenko on logistics, pp. 236–48 (ammunition expenditure, defensive battle, p. 245).

Peresypkin, Marshal (Signal Troops) I., 'Organizatsiya svyazi', *VIZ*, 1973 (7), pp. 51–61. Signals/communications systems, General Staff and Front staffs, army staffs and independent tank/mechanized formations, Kursk battle.

Rotmistrov, P., 'Bronetankovye i mekhanizirovannye voiska v bitve pod Kurskom', *VIZ*, 1970 (1), pp. 12–22. Critique of employment of Soviet armoured/mobile formations in defensive and offensive phases, Kursk.

Rudenko, Air Marshal S.I., *Krylya pobedy* (Moscow: Voenizdat (VM) 1976) pp. 156–80. Operations 16th Air Army in support of Central Front, struggle for air superiority, Zhukov proposes fighter reinforcement for 16th Air 7 July, planning for Soviet counter-blow.

Ryazanskii, Maj.-Gen. A.P., *V ogne tankovykh srazhenii* (Moscow: Nauka 1975) pp. 60–84, 5th Guards Mechanized Corps operations with 5th Guards Tank Army, Kursk, defensive operations. Highly detailed account of 5th Corps training, deployment, operations.

Solov'ev, B.G., *Vermakht na puti k gibeli,* pp. 103–25, Soviet defensive operations, Kursk, 5–12 July, narrative and analysis closely linked with footnoted commentary on German (and other) versions.

Tsukanov, Colonel F., 'Manevr silami i sredstvami Voronezhskovo fronta v oboronitel'noi operatsii pod Kurskom', *VIZ,* 1963 (6), pp. 35–42. Informative study of redeployment and manoeuvre, Voronezh Front (tables and diagrams).

Vasilevskii, A.M., *Delo vsei zhizni* (2nd edn), pp. 340–44. On Stalin's uneasiness, expectation of German offensive 26 May, Vatutin continues to urge Soviet offensive action, Stalin advises Vatutin to prepare offensive not later than first week in July, night of 2 July General Staff receives intelligence information that German attack timed for *not later than 6 July,* draft *Stavka* instruction to Front commands, Vasilevskii to Voronezh Front, German reconnaissance, offensive opens, first defensive phase.

Vysotskii, F.I. *et al., Gvardeiskaya tankovaya,* pp. 25–40, 2nd Guards Tank Army, in reserve Central Front, reinforced with 3rd Tank Corps, planning for tank army counter-blow, operations 6 July, Rokossovskii orders 2nd Tank Army on to defensive.

Zhukov, G.K., *Vospominaniya i razmyshleniya,* vol. 2, pp. 163–78, on defensive operations. (See translation, *The Battle of Kursk.*)

Kursk/Prokhorovka and Soviet riposte   pp. 105–113

German documentation

KTB/OKW, III/2, Lagebericht WFSt, entries 11–19 July (1943): 19 July 'Offensive erscheint die weitere Durchführung von "Zitadelle" *nicht mehr möglich . . .*', pp. 769–804.

Soviet materials

IVOVSS, 3, (i) pp. 272–5, German failure to break through to Oboyan, thrust against Prokhorovka on narrow front, Voronezh Front plan—approved by *Stavka*—to mount powerful counterblow with 1st Tank, 6th and 7th Guards Army, 5th Guards Tank and 5th Guards Army 12 July, plan frustrated by German forces cutting links between Soviet armies, German bombing attack on II *SS Panzer* Corps, Prokhorovka tank battle, T-34s fight at close range, German losses 350 tanks and 10,000 men, heavy fighting south of Prokhorovka against *Abteilung Kempf,* Soviet 69th Army goes over to defensive, 6th Guards Army and 1st Tank develop offensive along Oboyan-Belgorod motor-road southwards, *Stavka* 18 July orders 53rd, 47th, 4th Guards Army (Steppe Front) into action, German miscalculation that Soviet armies would need more time to recover.

(ii) pp. 276–81, *Orel offensive:* 11th Guards Army, *Stavka* plan to attack against Orel and Belgorod-Kharkov, Bryansk and left-flank Western Front to attack 12 July, four attacks aimed at Orel, assault groups formed in 11th Guards Army, 250 tanks attached, 7 engineer battalions to clear minefields (lifted 42,000 mines),

11th Guards Army penetrated up to 70 km by July 19, 4th Tank Army, 11th Army (Fedyuninskii) and 2nd Guards Cavalry Corps committed, 11th Army only committed piecemeal due to logistics problems, 4th Tank Army offensive on Bolkhov halted.

IVMV, 17, (i) pp. 152–6. Midnight 9 July Steppe MD activated as Steppe Front, Koniev to assign 4th Guards, 27th and 53rd Army to Belgorod-Kharkov axis with 5th Guards and 5th Guards Tank Army to Voronezh Front, Prokhorovka tank battle, German withdrawal begun, summary of results of Kursk defensive battle—heaviest attacks against Central Front but this already reinforced with an artillery corps, Voronezh Front by comparison had 2,740 *less* guns and mortars, use of strategic reserve (at Prokhorovka) halted German attack but weakened subsequent Soviet pursuit.

(ii) pp. 159–62. Soviet offensive aimed at Orel opened July 12 with 11th Guards and 61st Army (Belov) with 1st Air Army (M.M. Gromov) in support, Soviet concentration for Orel attack with left-flank Western Front, Bryansk and Central Fronts amounted to 1,286,000 men, 2,400 tanks, 21,000 guns and mortars, 3,000 aircraft, Bryansk Front operations slowed by German resistance, 15 July right-flank armies Central Front opened their offensive, though these armies (48th, 13th, 70th and 2nd Tank) much weakened in defensive fighting on northern face Kursk salient, 18 July *Stavka* committed Badanov's 4th Tank Army and 2nd Guards Cavalry Corps, though much delay and difficulty in committing strategic reserve.

Bagramyan, I.Kh., *Tak my shli k pobede*, pp. 196–237, reinforced reconnaissance (9–10 July), ADD bombing raids night July 11, Soviet surprise offensive 11 July, assault on Second *Panzer* Army, 50th Army offensive held up (July 13), conversation with Stalin (evening 14 July) reserves promised, threat to flank and rear of Second *Panzer* and Ninth Army, argument with Front commander Sokolovskii over commitment of 4th Tank Army, transfer of 11th Guards Army to Bryansk Front (29 July).

Bagramyan, I.Kh., 'Flangovyi udar 11-i gvardeiskoi armii', *VIZ*, 1963 (7), pp. 83–95.

Collective authorship, *Sovetskie tankovye voiska 1941–1945* (Moscow: Voenizdat 1973), pp. 131–43, role of Soviet *tank armies* in Soviet counter-offensive, beginning with Orel operation (12 July–18 August). (*Note:* the most comprehensive and indispensable work on Soviet tank operations is Army General A.I. Radzievskii, *Tankovyi udar*, Moscow: Voenizdat 1977, 271 pp. with maps, tables, diagrams.)

'*Commanders recall . . .* '/Kursk, I.M. Chistyakov (6th Guards Army), M.S. Shumilov (7th Guards Army), N.P. Pukhov (13th Army), K.S. Moskalenko (40th Army), P.A. Rotmistrov (5th Guards Tank Army), A.S. Zhadov (5th Guards Army), *VIZ*, 1963 (7), pp. 62–82.

Koltunov, G.A. and Solov'ev, B.G., *Kurskaya bitva*, ch. 4, 'Boevye deistviya na prokhorovskom napravlenii', German attack on Prokhorovka, unable to make complete breakthrough (pp. 162–6): tank battle at Prokhorovka, counter-blow assigned to 5th Guards Tank and 5th Guards Army, Rotmistrov deploys west and south-west Prokhorovka on a 15-km front, 18th, 29th, 2nd Guards Tank Corps in first echelon, 1,500 armoured vehicles (German and Soviet) in action (see note p. 174), 13–14 July final German attempt at breakthrough, Vasilevskii's personal report to Stalin (p. 176), 16 July Vatutin orders Front forces on to the defensive, need to build up ammunition stocks, German withdrawal begun under cover of powerful rearguards, pp. 166–77.

Koniev, I.S. *Zapiski komanduyushchevo frontom,* pp. 16–20, transfer of 5th Guards Tank Army and 5th Guards Army, Prokhorovka battle, Koniev fails to persuade *Stavka* to commit Steppe Front as *one strategic entity,* 30 July report to Zhukov on weakening of front due to transferring armies to Voronezh Front (pp. 19–20), Koniev's observation that it would have been better to commit the Steppe Front *en masse* and 'leap on the back' of the retreating Germans.

Rotmistrov, P.A., *Tankovoe srazhenie pod Prokhorovkoi* (Moscow: Voenizdat 1960) 107 pp. The gigantic tank battle 11–12 July, Rotmistrov commanding 5th Guards Tank Army.

Rotmistrov, P.A. 'Tankovoe srazhenie 12 iyulya' in V.S. Lokshin (ed.), *Na ognennoi duge* (Moscow: Voenizdat 1963), pp. 40–59 (tank battle at Prokhorovka).

Sandalov, Col.-Gen. L., 'Bryanskii front v Orlovskoi operatsii', *VIZ,* 1963 (8), pp. 62–72. Bryansk Front and the *Orel operation,* Stalin's instructions for use of 3rd Guards Tank Army 18 July (p. 70), Stalin's displeasure at lack of success with tank army operations (p. 71).

Vasilevskii, A., *Delo vsei zhizni,* pp. 344–5. Personal report to Stalin (document dated 14 July) on Prokhorovka tank battle: in Rotmistrov's 5th Guards Tank Army 29th Tank Corps lost 60 per cent of its tanks, 18th Tank Corps 30 per cent losses, 5th Mechanized Corps insignificant loss.

Vorozheikin, Maj.-Gen. (Air) A.V., *Nad Kurskoi dugoi* (Moscow: Voenizdat (VM) 1962). Fighter-pilot memoir, Kursk air combat (squadron commander, 728th Fighter Regiment).

The Soviet autumn offensive drive to the Dnieper   pp. 113–129

Armstrong, John A., *Ukrainian Nationalism* (Columbia Univ. Press, 2nd edn 1963), pp. 130–65. Ukrainian resistance/partisan movement.

Philippi, A. and Heim, F., *Der Feldzug gegen Sowjetrussland . . . ,* pt 2 (F. Heim), 'Der Feldzug des Jahres 1943', /III, 'Die sowjetische Sommeroffensive im südlichen und mittleren Abschnitt . . . ', pp. 212–23.

Seaton, Albert, *The Russo-German War,* ch. 23, 'The Soviet 1943 Autumn Offensives', pp. 369–91. (This is an excellent and truly comprehensive narrative and analysis, covering the full range of the Soviet offensive design and German reactions.)

German documentation

Gen. St. d. H.: Kräftegegenüberstellung 20.7.43
German strength: Ostfront

> 151 infantry divisions
> 22 Panzer divisions
> 3,064,000 men
> 2,088 tanks
> 8,063 guns

Soviet strength:

Field	Reserves	Total
365 Rifle Divisions	107 Rifle Divisions	506 Rifle Divisions
150 Tank/mech. divs.	92 Tank/mech. divs.	275 Tank/mech. divs.
4,067,000 men	1,275,000 men	5,755,000 men
4,348 tanks	2,951 tanks	7,855 tanks
15,310 guns	4,380 guns	21,050 guns

FHO Intelligence Appreciations:

Teil A., *Beurteilungen der Feindlage vor deutscher Ostfront im Grossen*. Reports for July (11, 12, 27, 28th), August (2, 18, 28th), September (8, 19, 21, 25, 27, 30th), also 11 October: report 19 September on Soviet field strength/deployment, 25 September on Soviet planning for winter offensive. T-78/R466, 6445988–6025.

FHO (I): also (Wirtschaftsstab Ost.). Bandenlage im Osten (1943), including 'Banden-Statistik', maps, tables: Soviet partisan movement. T-78/R489, 6475168–213.

Reichsführer-SS

Interrogation of Captain Boris Russanow (sic), 'General Staff officer'/Soviet partisans; Ukrainian partisan movement, under Col.-Gen. Strokatsch (Chief of Staff of Ukrainian partisan movement). T-175/R38, 1548473–487.

Soviet materials

IVOVSS, 3, pt 2, ch. 5 (5), Soviet counter-offensive, attack on Orel, pp. 276–85; ch. 5 (6), offensive on Belgorod/Kharkov, pp. 286–93; ch. 6, the Soviet drive to the Dnieper, pp. 305–13; ch. 6 (2), liberation of the Donbas, pp. 314–22.

IVMV, 7, (i) pp. 157–78, Soviet counter-offensive/Kursk, attack on Orel (1,286,000 men, 21,000 guns, 2,400 tanks, 3,000 aircraft), Belgorod-Kharkov operation, Voronezh Front outflanking of Kharkov, Steppe Front closes on Kharkov 17 August, liberation of Kharkov 23 August; pp. 193–210, Donbas operation (1,053,000 men, 21,000 guns, 1,257 tanks, 1,400 aircraft), Vasilevskii co-ordinating S and SW Front operations, defeat of German forces on Mius Line, Central Front offensive sweep into northern Ukraine (60th Army), opening of battle for Dnieper river line, 6 September *Stavka* assigns Voronezh Front to attack on Kiev (with reinforcement of 3rd Guards Tank Army), Steppe Front to Poltava and Kremenchug (reinforced with 5th Guards Army and 46th Army from SW Front), planning for Kiev attack (p. 200), German withdrawal to 'Eastern Wall', Soviet pursuit under Stalin's order to break through to Dnieper on a broad front, Pukhov's 13th Army first to cross Dnieper 22 September.

(ii) pp. 238–48, *Smolensk/Bryansk-Gomel operation* (codename *Suvorov I*), W and Kalinin Fronts, offensive designed to penetrate deeper into Belorussia (note: *Stalin's visit to 'Smolensk axis' beginning August (p. 241)*, lack of camouflage and deception discloses Soviet intentions to German defenders, slow progress, 17 September Bryansk liberated, German withdrawal from river Desna.

Biryuzov, Marshal SU S.S., *Surovye gody 1941–1945*, pp. 175–204, liberation of the Donbas, Biryuzov chief of staff to Tolbukhin, Southern Front operations.

Bychkov, L.N., *Partizanskoe dvizhenie v gody VOV*, pp. 303–26, partisan operations during Kursk battle, Smolensk region and Ukraine.

Chuikov, Marshal SU V.I., *Ot Stalingrada do Berlina* (Moscow: Voenizdat (VM) 1980), pt 2 (1), 'Zaporozhe . . .', pp. 360–83, 8th Guards Army (62nd Army from Stalingrad) in SW Front operations (Zhukov's request for 8th Guards to be transferred to Steppe Front under Koniev resisted by Malinovskii), fall of Zaporozhe, advance on Nikopol. (This edition—the latest—is a compound of the innumerable versions and editions of Chuikov's 'memoirs': e. g., *Gvardeitsy Stalingrada idut na zapad*, 1972, and *V boyakh za Ukrainu*, Kiev, 1972.)

Domnikov, Lt.-Gen. V.M. (ed.), *V nastuplenii Gvardiya* (Moscow: Voenizdat 1971), pp. 105–43, 'Krushenie "Mius-Fronta" ', 2nd Guards Army/Southern Front operations, liberation of the Donbas.

Fedyuninskii, I.I., *Podnyatve po trevoge* (2nd edn), pp. 148–52, Fedyuninskii assumes command 11th Army (14 July), explanations to Front commander (and *Stavka*) for slow rate of advance.

Istomin, Colonel V.P., *Smolenskaya nastupel'naya operatsiya (1943 g.)* (Moscow: Voenizdat 1975), *passim*. This highly detailed monograph on the 'Smolensk operation' (7 August–2 October) is an indispensable source, based largely on Soviet military archives and objectively critical of Soviet performance.

Istomin V.P., 'Smolenskaya nastupel'naya operatsiya 1943 goda', *VIZ*, 1973 (10), pp. 11–23. (Summary version.)

Kolos, Ivan, *Rel'sovaya voina v Poles'e* (Moscow: Voenizdat 1962). Popular account of partisan railway sabotage.

Koniev, I.S., *Zapiski komanduyushchevo frontom*, pp. 22–46, Belgorod-Kharkov offensive, operational plan submitted to Stalin (pp. 23–5), deployment of 53rd Army and 1st Mech. Corps, directive for capture of Kharkov, 53rd and 57th Army close on Kharkov from west and south-west, 22 August Koniev orders for night attack on Kharkov, insists on wakening Stalin with news of fall of Kharkov; pp. 51–80, drive to the Dnieper.

Koniev I.S., 'Na Kharkovskom napravlenii', *VIZ*, 1963 (8), pp. 49–61. Koniev's account of the assault on Kharkov (with fulsome tribute to N. Khrushchev, judiciously removed from the volume of memoirs published in 1972).

Koltunov, G.A. and Solov'ev, B.G., *Kurskaya bitva*, pt. Two, pp. 185–272, the Orel operation (12 July–18 August 1943), operations of 11th Guards and 50th Army, Central Front offensive operations, Soviet operations NW Orel, capture of Bolkhov, liberation of Orel, advance on Bryansk; pp. 275–352, Belgorod-Kharkov operation (3–23 August), liberation of Belgorod, Steppe Front advance on Kharkov axis, Voronezh Front operations, fighting at approaches to Kharkov, right-flank operations/Voronezh Front, repulse of German counter-attacks Akhtyrka (17–23 August), fall of Kharkov. (Immensely detailed day-by-day (also hour-by-hour) operational narrative, with extensive use of Soviet military archives.)

Krylov, Marshal SU N.I. *et al., Navstrechu pobede. Boevoi put 5-i armii*, (Moscow: Nauka 1970), pp. 146–71, 5th Army (commander Lt.-Gen. V.S. Polenov) in Smolensk operations. (See also V.P. Istomin, *op. cit.*).

Kuzmin, A.T. (ed.), *Vsenarodnoe partizanskoe dvizhenie v Belorussi*, (Minsk: Belarus 1978), vol. 2/2. Important documentary material on Belorussian partisans, July–December 1943.

Kuznetsov, Lt.-Gen. P.G., *Marshal Tolbukhin* (Moscow: Voenizdat 1966), pp. 79–97, 'Na Yuzhnom Fronte', Tolbukhin promoted colonel-general April 1943, given Front command (with Biryuzov as chief of staff), Tolbukhin's disappointment with July offensive but Stalin satisfied, 11 August Tolbukhin and Biryuzov in Moscow, planning for Donbas operation, capture of Taganrog, September offensive with SW Front, Tolbukhin promoted full general.

Managarov, Col.-Gen. I.M., *V srazhenii za Khar'kov* (Kharkov: Prapor, 2nd edn 1978), pp. 54–90, 53rd Army (Steppe Front) alerted 0400 hours 9 July, deployed defensively, preparation for Soviet counter-offensive on Belgorod-Kharkov axis (codenamed Operation *Commander Rumyantsev*), Zhukov's inspection 27 July, Zhukov's instructions for proposed attack and further visit, failure to meet Marshal Zhukov (who was *not* pleased), advance on Kharkov, 23 August broke into Kharkov from the west, liberation of Kharkov. (Illuminating comments on the style of Zhukov and Koniev.)

Moiseyev, O.V., *Velikaya bitva za Dnepre* (Kiev: Akad. Nauk, 1963), pp. 44–132, 'Forsirovanie Dnepra', establishment of Bukrin bridgehead, Kremenchug and Zaporozhe bridgeheads, contribution of partisans.

Popel, Lt.-Gen. (Tank Troops) N.K., *Tanki povernuli na zapad* (Moscow: Voenizdat (VM) 1960), pp. 184–6, 1st Guards Tank Army in Soviet counter-offensive, co-operation with Kulik's 4th Guards Army; Kulik, erstwhile Marshal SU, was demoted in 1941 for losing an army, re-instated as a lieutenant-general in 1943 but abruptly dismissed by Marshal Zhukov after a ferocious denunciation.

Sandalov, Col.-Gen. L.M., *Na moskovskom napravlenii* (Moscow: Nauka 1970), ch. 5, offensive on Orel, Bryansk Front operations ,(Sandalov as chief of staff).

Solomatin, Col.-Gen. (Tank Troops) M.D., *Krasnogradtsy* (Moscow: Voenizdat 1963), pp. 51–69, *1st Mechanized Corps*/Steppe Front operations, assigned as 'mobile group' to 53rd Army, preparations for offensive 23 July–2 August, 3 August on Koniev's own orders 1st Mech. committed to assist in breaching German defences (thus weakening 'shock power' of the corps), slow progress through defences, capture of Belgorod, operations with first echelon of 53rd Army, liberation of Kharkov.

Vasilevskii, A.M., *Delo vsei zhizni*, pp. 347–74, 'Osvobozhdenie Donbassa', Zhukov and Vasilevskii co-ordinate offensive on Kharkov, discussions with Malinovskii and role of SW Front for liberation of Donbas, report to *Stavka* on planning talks with Tolbukhin/Southern Front, 10 August *Stavka* confirms plans for SW and S Fronts, S Front offensive on the Mius timed for 18 August, 12 August Zhukov and Vasilevskii received *Stavka* directive for Voronezh, Steppe and SW Front operations, Kulik's 4th Guards Army to reinforce Voronezh Front (Vasilevskii's extreme dislike of ex-Marshal Kulik), heavy resistance to SW Front offensive across N Donets, 17 August Stalin threatens to dismiss Vasilevskii for failing to report in due time to *Stavka* (signal, p. 356), *Stavka* signal to Zhukov (evening 22 August) on Kharkov operation, Vasilevskii report to Stalin 26 August, 2 September Stalin reinforces S Front to exploit success, German withdrawal to the Dnieper, operations to isolate German forces in the Crimea, 28 September conversation with Stalin to review further offensives of Voronezh, Steppe, SW Fronts, fresh *Stavka* orders for Malinovskii (SW Front), redesignation of Fronts.

Vasilevskii, A.M., 'Osvobozhdenie Donbassa i levoberezhnoi Ukrainy. Bor'ba za Dnepr', *Istoriya SSSR*, 1970, No. 3, pp. 3–45. An extremely important collection of operational orders, reports to Stalin, operational directives to SW and S Fronts: this article is an indispensable adjunct to Marshal Vasilevskii's memoir account *(Delo vsei zhizni)* which supplies much personal detail.

Voronov, N.N., *Na sluzhbe voennoi*, pp. 381–99, Voronev, *Stavka* representative with Western Front, Smolensk offensive.

Yakubovskii, Marshal SU I.I., *Zemlya v ogne* (Moscow: Voenizdat (VM) 1975), ch. 2, 'Ot Kursha k Dnepru', pp. 124–51, operations of 3rd Guards Tank Army assigned to Bryansk front, deployed 17 July (with 40,000 men, 731 tanks and SP guns, 700 guns and mortars), Front commander M.M. Popov assigns mission but this altered by *Stavka* 18 July, end July 3rd Guards Tank transferred to Central Front to co-operate with Romanenko's 48th Army, capture of Orel, Yakubovskii's commentary on tank operations. (Though a memoir, Yakubovskii's work is a substantial contribution to the history of 3rd Guards Tank—he commanded 91st Independent Tank Brigade—also excellent pen portraits of Soviet commanders, as well as reviewing the organization and battlefield employment of Soviet tank armies.)

Yeremenko, Marshal SU A.I., *Gody vozmezdiya 1943–1945* (Moscow: Nauka 1969), Yeremenko's Kalinin Front co-operation with W Front, Smolensk operation, Kalinin Front strength, deployment, pp. 37–44; August operations, Lt.-Gen. A.I. Zygin (39th Army) relieved of command, lack of results, pp. 45–61.

Zhukov, G.K., *Vospominaniya i razmyshleniya*, vol. 2, pp. 195–201, the battle for the Ukraine, General Staff appreciation that Germany incapable of further *offensive* action, Stalin in agreement but demanded immediate *frontal blows* against German forces, Zhukov disagreed with this method, Stalin (August 25) demanded rapid seizure of Dnieper and river Molochnaya, Zhukov's request for reinforcements cut substantially by Stalin—'The rest we will give you when the Fronts reach the Dnieper'—reinforcement of Voronezh Front with 3rd Guards Tank Army, end September Soviet troops across Dnieper on 750-km front.

Soviet drive to the Dnieper
(Central, Voronezh, Steppe, SW and S Fronts)

See composite study G. Utkin, *Shturm 'Vostochnovo vala'*. Osvobozhdenie levoberezhnoi Ukrainy i forsirovanie Dnepra (Moscow: Voenizdat 1967). Central Front operations, assault crossing of Dnieper, completion of Chernigovsk-Pripyat operation, pp. 27–76; Voronezh Front offensive, forcing of Dnieper south of Kiev, crossing north of Kiev, pp. 84–175; Steppe Front operations, establishment of bridgehead SW Kremenchug, 37th Army operations SE Kremenchug, offensive on Kirovograd and Krivoi Rog, pp. 197–233, operations SW and S Fronts, liberation of Donbas, pp. 242–70; SW Front operations/Zaporozhe, fighting for Dnepropetrovsk, pp. 278–310; S Front operations, fall of Melitopol, destruction of German forces, pp. 320–48. (This is a highly detailed, day-by-day operational narrative based largely on Soviet military archives.)

Airborne operations: Kanev, September–October 1943

Lisov, Lt.-Gen. I.I., *Desantniki* (Vozdushnye desanty) (Moscow: Voenizdat 1968), ch. 6, 'Na pravom beregu Dnepra', pp. 153–78, planning, organization of airborne assault, airborne drop, ground action.

Sofronov, G.P., *Vozdushnye desanty vo vtoroi mirovoi voine* (Moscow: Voenizdat 1962), pp. 27–36.

Sukhorukhov, D.S. (C-in-C/Soviet Airborne Troops) *et al., Sovetskie vozdushno-desantnye* (Moscow: Voenizdat 1980). pp. 194–209, airborne forces and Dnieper battle.

Diplomatic complexities and complications   pp. 129–135

Fischer, Alexander, *Sowjetische Deutschlandpolitik im Zweiten Weltkrieg* . . . , ch. 2 (c), 'Die Bewegung "Freies Deutschland" ', pp. 53–9 (with extensive notes and references, pp. 186–90). See also:

Zur Geschichte der deutschen antifaschistischen Widerstandsbewegung 1933 bis 1945. Materialien: Berichte und Dokumente (E. Berlin Min. Nat. Verteidigung 1957). See under 'Nationalkomitee "Freies Deutschland" ', pp. 213–76; also facsimiles, 'Das Freie Wort (10.7.43)', p. 257; also 'Freies Deutschland', 24 November, 27 December 1943, p. 273– '1944. Beginn einer neuen Epoche' (editorial); also 'Manifest des Nationalkomitees "Freies Deutschland" an die Wehrmacht und an das deutsche Volk', pp. 233–6; Gründung des 'Bundes deutscher Offiziere' (September 1943), p. 245. (For a *Soviet* appraisal of the German anti-Fascist movement, including BDO, see Maj.-Gen. M. Burtsev, *VIZ,* 1969 (10), pp. 41–9.)

Irving, David, *Hitler's War,* pp. 565–77, Hitler's strategic thinking, 'feelers to Stalin', Hitler's confidence in the future, recognized difficulties in Allied coalition, 'internal collapse among our enemies', also Stalin's commanding position (and Hitler's preference for possible dealing with him). (There may be some point in recording a contemporary rumour that Berlin in 1943 contemplated the possible exchange of Stalin's son (a Red Army major, captured in 1941) for Field-Marshal von Paulus.)

Werth, Alexander, *Russia at War,* ch. 12, 'The "Free German Committee" ', pp. 732–7, which proved to be of 'small practical importance' (along with BDO) but which Alexander Werth saw as a form of Soviet 'insurance'.

German materials

OKW/WFSt: VO Ag. Ausland

German–Japanese exchanges: Geheime Reichssache, Hitler's démarché and that of Ribbentrop, October 1943, German criticism of Soviet troop transfers from Far East to European theatre, German pressure on Japan to maintain 'military threat' against USSR; also 2.11.43 WFSt/Ic report on transfer of Soviet Far East forces, Japanese report (30.10.43) pointing out—correctly—that fewer troops moved westwards in 1943. T-82/R90, 246961–966, 970, 971–973.

FHO: Intelligence appreciations

Teil A: Zusammenstellung . . . (FHO, Nr 1000/45g Kdos). Rpt No. 80/43, 17.10.43, major study comparing German and Soviet strength; Rpt No. 87/43, 9.11.43, appreciation of Soviet order of battle and intentions (360 RDs, 83 tank formations at brigade strength deployed, 159 RDs and 192 brigade-strength tank formations in reserve); Rpt No. 3102/43 on 'Feindliche Kräftelage' (order of battle) dated 4.12.43. T-78/R466, 6446031–045, 6052–58 and 6060–65, respectively.

FHO (IIa): Fernost 1.4.43. Report on Soviet Far Eastern forces, troop transfers to the European war theatre, Soviet commands/order of battle, Far East. T-78/R486, 6470809–842. Cf. for *complete Soviet data* on wartime troop transfer from the Far East, S. Isayev, 'Vklad voisk Dalnevo Vostoka v razgrom nemetsko-fashistskikh zakhvatchikov', *VIZ,* 1979 (8), pp. 73–7: a total of *39 divisions* were moved to the European theatre 1941–5 (the highest number, 30, in the period 21.6.41–18.11.42), with *21 brigades* (with *14 artillery brigades,* the highest single number, moved westwards in the period 19.11.42–31.12.43).

Diplomatic documents/diplomatic memoirs/materials

Gromyko, A.A. (Editorial chief), *Moskovskaya konferentsiya ministrov inostrannykh del SSSR, SShA i Velikobritanii (19–30 obtyabrya 1943 g.).* Sbornik dokumentov (Moscow: Politizdat 1978). Soviet protocols and stenographic record of the Moscow conference, pts II and III; for agenda, pt III, doc. no. 57, pp. 273–4 (also note 35, pp. 386–7, for projected Soviet agenda).

Wartime press

SWN. No. 691, 18 October 1943, 'The Moscow Conference' (from *Izvestiya*)—'the problem of the resolute shortening of the war . . . is inseparably bound up with the problem of opening the Second Front in Western Europe'. No. 709, 8 November 1943, Report by J.V. Stalin. Also, award of Order of Suvorov to Marshal Stalin (6 November).

Avon (Anthony Eden, Earl of), *The Eden Memoirs,* vol. 2: *The Reckoning* (London: Cassell 1965), bk 3, 'A Russian fortnight' (the Moscow conference), pp. 407–21.

Woodward, Sir Llewellyn, *British Foreign Policy in the Second World War,* pp. 581–93, Foreign Ministers' Conference in Moscow (19–30 October 1943), Foreign Office proposals for agenda and Soviet proposals (September 29), Soviet concern for 'war-shortening measures', 'urgent measures taken in 1943' by British and Americans to secure invasion of Europe plus Red Army operations would lead to German collapse, War Cabinet discussion of agenda, Moscow Conference to prepare way for Teheran conference, Soviet military questions answered (October 20), exposition of difficulties in organizing cross-Channel attack (shipping, US reinforcement), General Ismay on German air fighter force, Eden unable to answer about possible postponement of invasion, possible entry of Turkey into war, Russian claims to Italian fleet, proposal for European Advisory Commission by Eden generally accepted, Soviet reservations about handling of Italian armistice, question of treatment of Germany.

Israelyan, V.L. and Kutakov, L.N., *Diplomatiya agressorov* (Moscow: Nauka 1967), ch. 8, 'the crisis in the Fascist bloc', pp. 262–91, military-diplomatic repercussions of German defeats in the east, the Italian surrender.

Israelyan, V.L., *Antigitlerovskaya koalitsiya 1941–1945* (Moscow: Mezh. Otnosheniya 1964), ch. 14, pp. 301–21, problems of postwar reconstruction and the Moscow Conference. (See also, *Diplomaticheskaya istoriya VoV 1941–1945 gg.* (Moscow: Institut. Mezh. Otnoshenii 1959), ch. III (11), Moscow Conference, pp. 176–84.)

Kulish, V.M., *Raskrytaya taina*. Predystoriya vtorovo fronta v Evrope (Moscow: Nauka 1965), pp. 379–89, the Moscow Conference and the issue of the Second Front.

Strel'nikov, V.S. and Cherepanov, N.M., *Voina bez riska* (Moscow: Voenizdat 1965), pp. 57–76, Allied landings in Sicily; pp. 89–96, the Italian capitulation. (Soviet view of Mediterranean operations.)

The North Russian convoys/Soviet naval operations

Meister, J., *Soviet Warships of the Second World War* (London: Macdonald and Jane's, 1977). (Invaluable reference work on ship types and operational roles.)

Meister, J., *Der Seekriege in osteuropäischen Gewässern* (Munich, 1958), *passim*.

Mitchell, Donald W., *A History of Russian and Soviet Sea Power* (London: Deutsch 1974), pp. 422–34, WWII, Arctic and Pacific waters, Northern Fleet (and White Sea Flotilla) operations.

Ruge, Vice-Admiral Friederich, *The Soviets as Naval Opponents 1941–1945* (Naval Institute Press, Annapolis, 1979). See 'The Northern Theater', pp. 135–72 (Soviet surface unit, submarine, naval air and MTB operations). The Soviet Russians as opponents at Sea: Analysis of German and Russian Naval operations in the Second World War (4 vols, Tambach Collection). Vice-Admiral Ruge headed German specialists compiling this study.

Schofield, Vice-Admiral B.B., *The Russian Convoys*. Appendix I identifies 40 convoys to north Russia (1941–5), involving 811 ships (with 98 sunk).

Woodward, Sir Llewellyn, *British Foreign Policy . . .*, vol. II, pp. 564–74, 'The question of the North Russian convoys'.

Achkasov, V.I. and Pavlovich, N.B., *Sovetskoe voenno-morskoe iskusstvo v VOV*, Moscow, Voenizdat, 1973. On Soviet 'naval art': see ch. 8 for naval operations and maritime communications, pp. 216–324.

Basov, A.V., *Flot v Velikoi Otechestvennoi voine 1941–1945*. Opyt operativno-strate-gicheskovo primeneniya (Moscow, Nauka, 1980). (Part of present special pleading for the vital role of Soviet sea power, this monograph examines Soviet wartime naval operations in an 'operational-strategic' context: on sea lines of communications and the northern convoys, pp. 193–200.)

Golovko, Admiral A.G., *Vmeste s flotom* (Moscow: Voenizdat (VM) 1979), (2nd edn with foreword by Admiral Grishanov), pp. 174–6, Golovko's exchanges with Stalin over convoys, Northern Fleet operations in the Kara Sea. See also, *With the Red Fleet. The War Memoirs of Admiral Arseni Golovko* (London: Putnam 1965), pp. 159–64 (translated from 1st edn).

Kolyshkin, Rear-Admiral I., *Submarines in Arctic Waters* (Moscow: Progress Pub. 1966) (Soviet translation).

Kozlov, I.A. and Shlomin, V.S., *Severnyi flot* (Moscow: Voenizdat 1966). 2nd edn, Krasnoznamennyi Severnyi flot (1977). Somewhat flimsy history of Northern Fleet.

Vainer, B.A., *Severnyi flot v VOV* (Moscow: Voenizdat 1964), pp. 307–19, securing the northern convoys.

Additional note on British intelligence, the Eastern Front and prelude to 'Zitadelle', 1943
See F.H. Hinsley *et al.*, *British Intelligence in the Second World War* (London: HMSO 1981), vol. 2, pp. 623–7: first intelligence of German preparations discovered by Whitehall in third week in March (from *Luftwaffe* ENIGMA), 16 April report to Churchill about possible attack on north face of Kursk salient (but doubt as to ground or air operation), end April decrypt of von Weichs's appreciation of Soviet capabilities passed to Moscow, plus warning of German attack in near future, 3 May SIGINT note on 2 Pz. A in Orel area and 4 Pz. A at Kharkov, in June *Luftwaffe* ENIGMA disclosed movement of aircraft *from* Russia, propaganda 'line' that Hitler would postpone decisive offensive until 1944, Air Intelligence (AI) noted cessation of German preparatory bombing in Kursk sector, otherwise 'intelligence gave no advance notice of the opening of the much-delayed German offensive': Whitehall's intelligence confined to *Luftwaffe* ENIGMA and reports of British Military Mission, only on 10 July clear from *Luftwaffe* ENIGMA that *Zitadelle* being carried through.

4 THE DRIVE TO THE WESTERN FRONTIERS: OCTOBER 1943–MARCH 1944

In the 1960s a growing number of substantial and authoritative *Soviet military monographs* (dealing mainly with the period 1944–5) appeared. The material for this chapter, particularly Soviet operations in the western Ukraine, has been drawn largely from such studies, perhaps best exemplified by the work of Colonel (now Major-General) A.N. Grylev, whose first study of the Ukrainian offensive appeared in 1953 but which was superseded by his *Za Dneprom* (Voenizdat 1963, 228 pp.) and latterly *Dnepr Karpaty Krim. Osvobozhdenie Pravoberezhnoi Ukrainy i Kryma v 1944 goda* (Nauka 1970, 352 pp.). Both are immensely detailed operational narratives based largely on Soviet military records (as befits General Grylev's position as a chief General Staff historical analyst); they may not be very readable but they are invaluable, as is a work such as G.M. Utkin's *Shturm 'Vostochnovo vala'*. Nor am I alone in acknowledging the high standard of such work. (Equally, I should point to the comprehensiveness of the *Fremde Heere Ost (FHO)* material, which seems in 1944 to have exhibited increasing acuity.)

Allen, W.E.D. and Muratoff, Paul, *The Russian Campaigns of 1944–45* (Harmondsworth: Penguin Books 1946), pp. 22–69, the third Russian winter campaign. (Though sometimes disparaged and more often simply ignored, this is good exploitation of Soviet war communiqué material.)
Heidkämper, Otto, *Witebsk. Kampf und Untergang der 3. Panzerarmee* (Heidelberg: K. Vowinckel 1954), ch. XI, 'Vermutete Feindabsichten . . .', pp. 62–4; ch. XII, 'Die erste Winterabwehrschlacht um Witebsk', pp. 65–94, also pp. 94–101,

'Abwehrkämpfe nordwestlich Witebsk', pp. 117–20; ch. XVI, 'Auflockerung der 3. Panzerarmee', pp. 124–7.

Ionescu, Ghita, *Communism in Rumania 1944–1962* (London: OUP 1964). See ch. 2, from Teheran to the 1944 *coup*, here pp. 71–81 on Rumanian attempts to disengage from the war, an excellently informed and referenced account.

Manstein, Erich von, *Lost Victories*. See ch. 15 on the defensive battles 1943–4, beginning (p. 486) with the battle for Kiev, moving to the second battle of the Dnieper bend (Hitler's refusal to countenance withdrawal of German southern wing, German plan to concentrate at Rovno), pp. 490–508; German counter-stroke against Soviet breakthrough in direction of Uman, pp. 508–9; Hitler's agreement to abandonment positions east of Dnieper bend and Nikopol, pp. 512–17; the Cherkassy pocket, position of Fourth *Panzer* Army and loss of Rovno, pp. 518–19; comparison of Soviet and German strength, spring 1944, pp. 520–22. (This is an indispensable analysis and operational narrative, upon which I have drawn heavily to depict the German side.)

Philippi, Alfred and Heim, Ferdinand, *Der Feldzug gegen Sowjetrussland*, pt 2, 'Der Feldzug des Jahres', I, 'Fortgang der sowjetischen Winteroffensive . . .', loss of the Dnieper line, Soviet offensive (Leningrad), AGp Centre defensive battles, 'die höchst kritische Lage der Ostfront Ende Februar 1944', collapse of German front south of the Pripet, formation of new German front on the borders of Galicia and Rumania, pp. 230–45.

Seaton, Albert, *The Russo–German War*, ch. 25, German defeat at Leningrad and in the Ukraine: Soviet offensive/Leningrad, pp. 408–12; offensive into western Ukraine, pp. 412–31 (including Soviet attack on the Crimea). This is a very comprehensive treatment, leading up to April 1944.

Werth, Alexander, *Russia at War*, pt 7, ch. II, Ukrainian microcosm, Werth's eyewitness account of the Korsum battlefield, very vivid in its own right, pp. 771–812; also ch. III, Odessa and the effects of Rumanian occupation, pp. 813–26. (While assisting in the editing of Alexander Werth's manuscript for *Russia at War*, I was able to delve much more deeply into this remarkable collection of contemporary reporting and contemporary records.)

South and South-West Fronts, Kiev, Belorussia, Soviet strength and Soviet plans pp. 137–149

IVMV, 7, pp. 229–38, reduction of German forces Taman peninsula, clearing of the North Caucasus, preparations to attack the Crimea, planning of Kerch assault landing, Marshal Timoshenko *Stavka* co-ordinator (p. 234), 20.11.43 North Caucasus front redesignated Independent Coastal Army (note to p. 237), investment of bridgehead north-east of Kerch a move to recover the Crimea, but front stabilized here until April 1944.

IVMV, 7, pp. 257–71, liberation of Kiev, forcing the Dnieper and the Sivash.

Alferov, Colonel S., 'Peregruppirovka 3-i gvardeiskoi tankovoi armii v bitve za Dnepr (oktyabr 1943), *VIZ*, 1980 (3), pp. 16–24. (Redeployment of 3rd Guards Tank Army.)

Bagramyan, I.Kh., *Tak shli my k pobede*, pp. 261–85, Stalin promotes Bagramyan to full general and appointment Front commander (1st Baltic) 18 November 1943,

Front offensive aimed at Gorodok and Vitebsk, Gorodok taken 24 December, only partial fulfilment of *Stavka* plan.

Collective authorship, *Na vechnye vremena. Na věčne časy* (Moscow: Voenzidat 1975), pp. 96–104, Czech Brigade (1-ya OChBr), Kiev operations. (Also *SWN*, No. 717, 18.11.43, Major-General Jan Kratochvil, 'Czechs at Kiev'.)

Grylev, A.N.,. *Za Dneprom*, pp. 44–53, Kirovograd operation (2nd Ukrainian Front). Also *Dnepr. Karpaty . . .* , *op. cit.*, pp. 47–55.

Gorbatov, General A., 'Nastuplenie 3-i armii severnee Gomelya', *VIZ*, 1962 (8), pp. 30–43. (3rd Army, Gomel operations, with a disclaimer about the role of 3rd Army by Marshal Rokossovskii.)

Grechko, A.A., *Gody voiny 1941–1943*, pt 2, 'Taman svobodna' (Taman operation), pp. 540–58.

Grechko, A.A., 'V boyakh za stolitsu Ukrainy', *VIZ*, 1963 (11), pp. 3–17: liberation of Kiev (November 1943).

Koniev, I.S., *Zapiski komanduyushchevo frontom*, pp. 82–93, the Kirovograd operation.

Koniev, I.S., 'Kirovogradskaya operatsiya', *VIZ*, 1969 (5), pp. 66–74: 2nd Ukrainian Front operations (Koniev, Front commander), Kirovograd, January 1944.

Krainyukov, Lt.-Gen. K., 'Osvobozhdenie Kieva', *VIZ*, 1963 (10), pp. 67–79. (Liberation of Kiev, version advertising Khrushchev.)

Kreizer, General Ya., 'Sivash–Sevastopol', *VIZ*, 1969 (5), pp. 75–7, opening stages of developing Sivash bridgehead (10th Rifle Corps/51st Army), Tolbukhin's operational plan for further offensive, Voroshilov as *Stavka* 'representative'. (See also *Shtemenko*.)

Malinovskii, Marshal SU R.Ya., 'V boyakh za osvobozhdenie Sovetskoi Ukrainy' in *V bol'shom nastuplenii* (Moscow: Voenizdat 1964), pp. 22–38. Cf. G.M. Utkin, *Shturm 'Vostochnovo vala'*, ch. 5, Zaporozhe operation (pp. 288–300), also Dnepropetrovsk (pp. 300–10).

Monin, Colonel M., 'Iz istorii boevovo sodrushestva sovetskikh i chekhoslovatskikh voisk, *VIZ*, 1969 (2), pp. 31–41 (Czechoslovak units in Red Army operations).

Moskalenko, K., 'Kievskaya operatsiya', *VIZ*, 1973 (12), pp. 51–8 (Kiev operation).

Utkin, G.M., *Shturm 'Vostochnovo vala'*, pp. 365–402, liberation of Kiev.

Vaneyev, G.I., *Chernomortsy v Velikoi Otechestvennoi voine* (Moscow: Voenizdat 1978), pp. 270–95, Kerch amphibious landing operation, planning, landing of assault elements 18th and 56th Army, bridgehead operations.

Partisan movement/re-organization

IVMV, 8, pp. 156–63, *GKO* (State Defence committee) decree 13 January 1944 (p. 160), abolishing *Partisan Central Staff (TsShPD)*, intensifying partisan operations and 'political work' among population.

Note on Soviet strength January 1944

IVOVSS, 4, table p. 20: total Soviet manpower 6,736,000 (including 331,000 navy, 266,000 air force and 571,000 reserves; note also, in the figure for reserves, 75,000 airborne troops/*Stavka* reserve).

Soviet Plan operatsii/directives for winter offensive, 1944
IVOVSS, 4, pp. 18–26; also S.M. Shtemenko, *General'ny shtab* . . . , pp. 199–202
(translation, *The Soviet General Staff*, pp. 198–201).

Teheran Conference (1943)   pp. 149–162

Diplomatic history/diplomatic documents. The indispensable material is supplied in
The Conferences of Cairo and Teheran (US Department of State, Washington, 1961)
and most expressly Winston S. Churchill, *Closing the Ring*, vol. V of *The Second World
War*. These have been extensively utilized and analysed elsewhere, my purpose here
being to highlight Soviet materials and interpretation.

Wheeler-Bennett, Sir John W. and Nicholls, Antony, *The Semblance of Peace* (London:
Macmillan 1972 and 1974). See pp. 143–67, Teheran and Second Cairo. (This
is perhaps the most astringent view of Teheran, based on a very wide range of
sources.)

Woodward, Sir Llewellyn, *British Foreign Policy*, vol. II, ch. XXXIV (VI), the Teheran
Conference, pp. 599–603; see also ch. XXXV, Great Britain and Soviet–Polish
relations to end 1943, here pp. 635–50, and the Polish question at Teheran, pp.
650–51.

Soviet documentation/analysis

Gromyko, A.A. (Chief Editor), *Tegeranskaya konferentsiya rukovoditelei trekh soyuznikh
derzhav—SSSR, SShA i Velikobritanii*, Sbornik dokumentov. (Moscow: Politizdat
1978.) This collection is intended to be definitive, being correlated with US
publication and UK PRO holdings: as such, it supersedes the version published
in the journal *Mezh. Zhizn* (1961) and amends the composite volume *Tegeran–
Yalta–Potsdam* (1967, 1970 and 1971 edns). After an introduction (pp. 6–40),
pt 1 consists of correspondence exchanges between the 'Big Three' (pp. 43–86),
minutes of conversations in pt 2 (pp. 89–170, note publication from Soviet archives
of Stalin–Roosevelt talk, 1.12 at 1520 hrs, pp. 168–70), pt 3 covering the
communiqué and declarations.

IVMV, 8, *Teheran conference*, pp. 30–39; Second Cairo Conference, pp. 39–42.
(*Note:* I do not know of any substantive Soviet *documentation* relating to German
plans to assassinate the 'Big Three' at Teheran—reportedly Operation *Long Jump*.
There are two examples of 'documentary fiction': Viktor Egorov, *Zagovor protiv
Evriki* (Moscow: Sov. Rossiya 1968) and A. Lukin, 'Zagovor ne sostoyalsya' in
Front bez linii fronta (Moscow: Mosk. Rabochii 1970), pp. 328–49.)

Berezhkov, V.M., 'Tegeran, 1943 god', *Novaya i noveishaya istoriya*, 1967, no. 6, pp.
87–99.

Israelyan, V.L., *Antigitlerovskaya koalitsiya*, ch. XV, on the Teheran conference, emergence
of a genuine 'coalition strategy' based on Soviet–American agreement on the course
of military operations in 1944 (priority for *Overlord*), pp. 322–49.

Polish Government (London): documents

Documents on Polish–Soviet Relations 1939–1945, vol. 2 (1943–5) (General Sikorski
Historical Institute). See doc. no. 55, Mikolajczyk (22.11) on impending Teheran

conference and Polish question (pp. 90–93); Teheran conversations and Poland, docs. no. 58–60 (pp. 96–100); see also doc. no. 65, London Polish government memorandum on situation in Poland and early entry of Soviet troops, 16.12.43 (pp. 106–12).

Polish materials

Kowalski, W.T., *Wielka koalicja 1941–1945*, vol. 1: 1941–1943 (Warsaw: MON 1973), ch. VIII, 'Kair–Teheran–Kair', on the Teheran conference, pp. 639–715. (A very comprehensive analysis, as lively as it is sardonic in many places.)

On the Polish *Krajowa Rada Narodowa (KRN)*, see A. Przygoński, *Z zagadnień strategii frontu narodowego PPR*, ch. 5, on the creation of the *KRN*, arguing that the *KRN* 'Manifesto' was drafted before Teheran, even before the Moscow conference, pp. 195–212 (especially note to pp. 209–10).

The 'Zhitomir attack', Nikopol and Krivoi Rog (January 1944)   pp. 163–167

GMDs

FHO Beurteilung der Feindlage . . . Anlagenband zur Zusammenstellung (4.42–12.44), intelligence reports, information from Soviet PWs: see Nr 3102/43 (4.12.43) on location of reported *eight* Soviet tank armies (7th Tank Army in Far East, 6th and 8th Tank Armies forming up), also reports to 30.3.44. T-78/R498, 6485801–828. See also the diagrammatic maps on projected Soviet offensive operations (all Fronts, up to 29.3.44), plus statistical presentation of comparative Soviet–German strength (12.43–2.44): R497, 6485587–602, with duplicates.

FHO Feindkräfteberechnung. Daily statistical presentation of location of Soviet forces (German front, Caucasus, Iran, Far East) for period January–March 1944. T-78/R483, 6468469–8587.

Soviet materials

Babadzhanyan, A. and Kravchenko, I., '1-ya tankovaya armiya v Zhitomirsko–Berdichevskoi operatsii', *VIZ*, 1972 (9), pp. 21–31, 1st Guards Tank Army operations, December 1943–January 1944.

Belkin, Colonel I.M., *13-ya Armiya v Lutsko–Rovenskoi operatsii 1944 g.* (Moscow: Voenizdat 1960). (Detailed monograph 13th Army operations, Lutsk/Rovno, January/February 1944.) (See also Grylev, *Za Dneprom*, pp. 79–89.) Pukhov commanded 13th Army.

Biryuzov, S.S., *Surovye gody*, pp. 236–40, fate of generals Khomenko and Bobkov (artillery commander, 44th Army). General Bobkov was killed outright by German shellfire, Khomenko died without regaining consciousness (both officers having lost their way). German troops confined the corpses in a weapons packing case, from which they were recovered finally by the Red Army and returned to Melitopol for a military funeral.

Grylev, A.N., *Za Dneprom*, pp. 34–44, Zhitomir–Berdichev operation (1st Ukrainian Front). Also *Dnepr. Karpaty* . . . , pp. 36–47.

Grylev, A.N., *Za Dneprom*, pp. 89–102, Nikopol–Krivoi Rog operation (3rd and 4th Ukrainian Fronts). Also *Dnepr. Karpaty* . . . , pp. 102–22.

Koltunov, Colonel G., 'Udar voisk 1-vo Ukrainskovo fronta na zhitomirskom napravlenii zimoi 1943/44 goda', *VIZ*, 1967 (2), pp. 12–23.

Vasilevskii, A.M., 'Osvobozhdenie Pravoberezhnoi Ukrainy', *VIZ*, 1971 (1), pp. 59–73: acting as *Stavka* representative with 3rd and 4th Ukrainian Fronts for the drive into the western Ukraine, Vasilevskii here supplies a terse operational narrative, replete with *Stavka* directives, personal reports to Stalin, Front directives—Vasilevskii report to Stalin (29.12.43), pp. 61–3; Stalin to Vasilevskii (30.12.43), p. 63; (operational orders for 3rd and 4th Ukrainian Fronts), operational plans submitted by Zhukov and Vatutin, pp. 63–4; *Stavka* directive to Zhukov (12.1.44), pp. 64–5; the Korsun encirclement, *Stavka* directive 12.2.44 to Zhukov, p. 66; the drive on Nikopol, Vasilevskii's report to Stalin 6.2.44, p. 68; Stalin's directive to Vasilevskii, Malinovskii (3rd Ukrainian Front) No. 220019 7.2.44, p. 69; Vasilevskii's operational order to 4th Ukrainian Front 8.2.44, p. 70 (also to 3rd Ukrainian Front), p. 71. Results of the successful Nikopol–Krivoi Rog operation. (*Delo vsei zhizni, op. cit.,* pp. 380–96 is essentially a narrative but the detailed operational-documentary material presented here in *VIZ* has been removed.)

Zhukov, G.K., *Vospominaniya* . . . , vol. 2, pp. 202–35. Fighting for the Ukraine, liberation of Kiev, GHQ conference (December 1943), Stalin's comment on Teheran (p. 211), Stalin's work pattern and lifestyle, agreement to execute encirclement operations (p. 213), preparation of Zhitomir–Berdichev operation (1st Ukrainian Front) and advance to southern Bug, Koniev and Kirovograd operation, trapping of German Korsun–Shevchenkovskii forces, Zhukov report to Stalin 9 February (pp. 224–5), Stalin's directive on command of encirclement operation 12 February (p. 229), 1st Ukrainian Front ignored in saluting Korsun success, *Stavka* planning for operations 1st, 2nd, 3rd Ukrainian Fronts, death of Vatutin and Zhukov assumes command 1st Ukrainian Front (p. 233), attempted encirclement of First *Panzer* Army but Soviet forces short of men, guns and ammunition. (See here translation, *Memoirs,* ch. XVI.)

Soviet offensive operations, Leningrad, NW theatre   pp. 167–176

German materials

OKH/Gen. Std. H.: Op. Abt./IN., Army Group North: Hitler's signal (6.2.44), 'Ich sehe bei der H.Gr. Nord im Augenblick die grösste Gefahr bei Narwa', Army Group North 'Beurteilung der Lage' (Rpt Ia, Nr 38/44, 1.3.44), Dönitz on naval tasks/Baltic. T-78/R337, 6292849–947 (Hitler's signal, 6292905–910).

FHO (I/N) Beurteilung der Feindlage vor den finnischen Fronten . . . 15.12.1943 bis 20.3.1944 (Nr 935/44 g. Kdos): 22.3.1944 (Finnish fronts). T-78/R466, 6446414–423.

FHO. Anlagen to Rpt No. 500/44. Organization, strength Finnish army, air force, navy, also war economy: 12.43–2.44. T-78/R483, 6468104–214.

OKH/Allgemeines Heeresamt: Abwicklungsstab. Report on destruction of 9 *Luftwaffe-Felddivision,* eliminated January–February 1944 in Soviet operations from Oranienburg pocket. T-78/R139, 6068273–282.

Soviet materials

IVOVSS, 4, pt 1, pp. 29–53, Soviet offensive operations, Leningrad/Novgorod (January–February 1944).

IVMV, 8, pp. 112–20, Soviet offensive operations in North-West and West theatres, weakened position of Army Group North but powerful defensive positions, Soviet Leningrad and Volkhov Fronts to attack from north and north-east towards Luga to encircle German 18th Army, Soviet strength 716,000 men, 12,165 guns/mortars, 1,132 tanks and SP guns; pp. 121–7, Soviet offensive, 14–15 January 1945, 2nd Shock Army attacking 14 January, 42nd Army (Maslennikov) 15 January, capture of Novgorod 20 January, Leningrad and Volkhov Fronts 30 January closing on German defence line on Luga, 18th Army pulled back west and south-west to avoid encirclement.

Fedyuninskii, I.I., *Podnyatye po trevoge* (2nd edn), ch. VIII, 'Snova pod Leningradom', 2nd Shock Army operations, Leningrad, January 1944, advance to river Luga end January, ordered to close on Narva, pp. 166–184.

Inozemtsev, Lt.-Col. I., 'Deistviya aviatsii po razgromu gruppy armii "Sever" ', *VIZ,* 1974 (1), pp. 37–43. (Soviet air operations against Army Group North, January–February 1944.)

Kazakov, General M., 'Velikaya pobeda pod Leningradom', *VIZ,* 1964 (1), pp. 3–15.

Korovnikov, Col.-Gen. I.T., *Novgorodsko–Luzhskaya operatsiya. Nastuplenie voisk 59-i armii . . .* (Moscow: Voenizdat 1960). Detailed monograph, operations 59th Army, January–February 1944.

Petrov, Yu.P., *Partizanskoe dvizhenie Leningradskoi oblasti 1941–1944,* pp. 338–432, the partisan offensive in the Leningrad region. (A detailed analysis, utilizing both Soviet and non-Soviet sources.)

Platonov, S.P. (ed.), *Bitva za Leningrad,* pp. 331–80, ending of the blockade, clearing Leningrad *oblast* (January–February 1944): opening of Soviet offensive (14 January), 2nd Shock Army operations, Volkhov Front operations on Novgorod–Luga axis (14–20 January), 8th and 54th Army operations, developments of Soviet offensive end January 1944. (An operational narrative making extensive use of Soviet military records.)

Rakitskii, Colonel A., 'Udar pod Leningradom', *VIZ,* 1974 (1), pp. 26–36 (2nd Shock Army operations, January 1944, with critical comments on 2nd Shock performance due to prolonged period in defence).

'42-ya Armiya v boyakh za Leningrad', *Istoricheskii Arkiv,* 1959, no. 2, pp. 68–88. (War Diary, 42nd Army: see under offensive operations, January 1944, Maslennikov's analysis of reasons for heavy losses, lack of success, 109th and 86th RDs.)

The Korsun–Shevchenkovskii salient   pp. 176–179

IVOVSS, 4, pt 1, pp. 58–69, Soviet encirclement operation, Korsun–Shevchenkovskii.

Grylev, A.N., *Za Dneprom,* pp. 53–79, Korsun–Shevchenkovskii encirclement. Also *Dnepr. Karpaty . . . ,* pp. 55–91, Korsun operation (see table of Soviet–German strength, p. 61, also explanatory footnote p. 67, on external encirclement line 1st Ukrainian Front).

Koniev, I.S., 'Korsun–Shevchenkovskaya operatsiya', *VIZ,* 1969 (2), pp. 49–65. (The Korsun encirclement, promotion of Koniev and Rotmistrov.)

Koniev, I.S., *Zapiski Komanduyushchevo frontom,* pp. 94–143, Korsun encirclement: essentially as in the *VIZ* article, but much more detail, Stalin's disquiet at German breakthrough (12 February) and call to Koniev (p. 120), Koniev reassures Stalin that encirclement will hold, rejects idea of taking command of all Soviet forces (including 27th Army) on encirclement fronts, Stalin's rebuke to Zhukov 12 February that orders disregarded (pp. 121–2), Stalin's directive (12 February) that Koniev assume overall command (p. 122), repulse of German break-out, discovery of General Stemmerman's body, Stalin's order of the day to Koniev (p. 136), Koniev and Rotmistrov appointed Marshals.

Krainyukov, Col.-Gen. K.V., *Oruzhie osobovo roda* (Moscow: Voenizdat (VM) 1977), pt 2, operations in the western Ukraine, see Krainyukov's account of Vatutin's death, pp. 156–60. (An earlier version appeared in the magazine *Ogonëk.*)

Sukhovershko, G.V. (ed director), *Geroi-osvoboditeli Cherkasshchiny* (Dnepropetrovsk: Promin, 2nd edn 1980). See 'Podvigi Korsun–Shevchenkovskoi bitvy', pp. 232–78.

Zavizion, Maj.-Gen. (Tank Troops) G.T. and Kornyushin, Colonel P.A., *I na Tikhom Okeane . . .* (Moscow: Voenizdat 1967), pp. 13–29, 6th Tank Army committed/ Korsun–Shevchenkovskii encirclement.

From the Dnieper to the Dniester   pp. 176–182

German materials

KTB/OKW, IV/1: 3. Abschnitt. 'Der Fall "Margarethe" ' (Besetzung Ungarns): I. Teil, A, B, pp. 180–210, also II, implementation of "Margarethe", pp. 210–37 (and '. . . weitere Behandlung der ungar. Wehrmacht, pp. 240–43). 6 Abschnitt, 'Der südöstliche Kriegsschauplatz' II Teil, Anhänge (3) Rumänian, pp. 758–75 ''Margarethe—II'', operational plan/occupation of Rumania (also Briefwechsel Hitler–Antonescu, pp. 769–74). Also *KTB/OKW,* IV/2: 9. Abschnitt, 'Der Finnische Kriegsschauplatz' (1) and (2) 'Finnlands Verhandlungen mit der Sowjet-Union . . .', pp. 1917–21.

OKH/GenStdH. 'Chefs. Ungarn 21.3–6.4.44'; also 'Ungarn-Chefs. v. 29.3–2.4.44'. Defense of Hungary east of river Tisa,'mobilization of Hungarian troops for defence. (Operations-Abteilung materials.) T-78/R333, 6290844–1120.

OKH/GenStdH: Op. Abt. II, Chefsache: policies, operation in Bulgaria, Soviet–Bulgarian relations 2.43–5.44. T-78/R333, 6290413–480.

FHO. Teil A. *Zusammenstellung . . . Beurteilungen der Feindlage (1942–44):* important, detailed reports on Soviet strength/deployment (as Anlage Nr 1 to report 19.12.43), graphs and statistics, Soviet rifle and armoured strength (15.1.44), Report No. 103/44 on Soviet operational intentions dated 10.2.44 (10 pp.), intelligence data on Soviet intentions dated 4.3.44, Gehlen appreciation of overall operational and strategic situation 30.3.44. T-78/R466, 6446070–6135.

Soviet materials

IVMV, 8, pp. 133–7, Soviet operations, Western theatre, Soviet plan to drive on to Vitebsk, 13 January 1st Baltic Front offensive, failure to outflank Vitebsk from south-east, combined operation of 1st Baltic and Western Fronts, deep outflanking of Vitebsk and threat to Third *Panzer* Army: operations of 1st Baltic, Western and 1st Belorussian Fronts not wholly successful (these Fronts received only 19 per cent of field reinforcements, 4.2 per cent of tanks and SP guns), State Defence Committee (GKO) commission of enquiry into failure, blamed poor command and co-ordination.

Grylev, A.N., *Za Dneprom*, pp. 110–17, situation in western Ukraine, beginning March 1944. Also *Dnepr. Karpaty . . .* , pp. 123–30.

Grylev, A.N., *Za Dneprom*, pp. 117–51, Proskurov–Chernovtsy operation (4.3–17.4.44). Also *Dnepr. Karpaty . . .* , pp. 130–60.

Grylev, A.N., *Za Dneprom*, pp. 151–66, Uman operation (2nd Ukrainian Front).

Grylev, A.N., *Za Dneprom*, pp. 166–75, Bereznegotavo–Snigerevka operation (3rd Ukrainian Front: 6–18.3.44). Also *Dnepr. Karpaty . . .* , pp. 178–87.

Grylev, A.N., *Za Dneprom*, pp. 175–82, Odessa operation (28.3–14.4.44). Also *Dnepr. Karpaty . . .* , pp. 187–200.

Grylev, A.N., *Dnepr. Karpaty Krym*, pp. 219–42, planning of assault on *Crimea* (4th Ukrainian Front), breakthrough to Sevastopol.

Israelyan, V.L., *Diplomaticheskaya istoriya VOV*, ch. IV(2), ' "Mirnyi" zondazh satellitov gitlerovskoi Germanii vesnoi 1944 goda', pp. 198–205, satellite peace-feelers, spring 1944.

Svetlishin, Colonel N., 'O nekotorykh osobennostyakh zimnei kampanii 1944 goda', *VIZ*, 1969 (2), pp. 15–30, operational characteristics of Soviet winter offensive 1944 (see table, p. 29).

Yakubovskii, I., 'Na proskurovsko-chernovitskom naprevlenii', *VIZ*, 1969 (4), pp. 18–29, 1st Ukrainian Front operations, Proskurov offensive, March 1944.

Zakharov, Marshal SU M.V., 'Umanskaya nastupatel'naya operatsiya 2-vo ukrainskovo fronta', *VIZ*, 1962 (4), pp. 12–32, Uman offensive operations, March 1944, 2nd Ukrainian Front.

Strategic appreciations, Soviet and German   pp. 182–190

GMDs

FHO. Beurteilung im Grossen . . . , General Gehlen's appreciation *Nr 112/44 30.3.1944* (12 pp.), also letter of transmittal to Generalquartiermeister Wagner adjuring great secrecy, restricted circulation. T-78/R497, 6485544–556.

Note: *FHO report 1428/44* (dated 3.5.44), version of *conference held by Stalin* between 24.3 and 30.3 (44) to review operational plans, two variants with Stalin adopting Plan No. 2—to open access to the Balkans, also to push German forces back to the line of the San–Vistula; German reserves would be heavily strained due to the Anglo–American threat in the west and the dangers posed by a Polish rising (hence the Soviet command discounted the threat of a German counterblow from Galicia to the Dnieper and into the Soviet flank). T-78/R498, 6485829–832.

FHO (IIc), *Führerstellenbesetzung der Roten Armee* (1943–1944): alphabetic listing of senior Soviet commanders (down to lieutenant-colonel), positions held, identification of Soviet formations with commanders, commanders' fronts, armies, corps, divisions, brigades (also chiefs of staff). T-78/R463, 6442178–3155.

FHO (IIc), *Unterlagen für grosse Kräftegegenüberstellung*. Compilations of comparative Soviet–German strength, autumn 43 to summer 44. T-78/R463, 6441975–2002.

Soviet materials

IVOVSS, 4, pt 2, pp. 123–8, Soviet strategic planning, 12 April GKO investigation of W Front, 17–19 April Stalin orders turn to defensive all fronts (except 2nd and 3rd Ukrainian Fronts), outline of main operational plan.

Zhukov, G.K., *Vospominaniya . . . ,* vol. 2, pp. 237–42, summons to Moscow, April 22, discussion with Stalin on summer/autumn campaign plans, correctness of decision to give priority to attack Army Group Centre (Belorussia), Stalin announces that 'Second Front' will come in June, Zhukov emphasizes importance of 'enemy group in Belorussia', Stalin suggests opening with 1st Ukrainian Front offensive to achieve deeper envelopment of Army Group Centre (and draw off German reserves), Antonov argues better to begin in the north and then attack in Belorussia, some two to three days later Stalin agrees to this (also *Memoirs,* pp. 515–20).

5 BREAKING THE BACK OF THE *WEHRMACHT:* APRIL–AUGUST 1944

For Operation *Bagration,* the Red Army offensive directed against Army Group Centre, I have relied on much Soviet memoir material, hence the repeated reference to *Voenno-istoricheskii Zhurnal (VIZ)* and also the collection edited by Professor A.M. Samsonov, *Osvobozhdenie Belorussii* (Moscow: Nauka, 2nd edn 1974, 799 pp.), supplemented by my own notes taken in exchanges with Soviet commanders. Note also two collections from *GMD* which span several operations: (i) marked maps, updated daily, *OKH* 'Kriegsgeschichtliche Abteilung', T-78/R136; (ii) *OKH* 'Allgemeines Heeresamt. Ab-wicklungsstab', after-action reports from survivors of destroyed German divisions, T-78/R139, *passim.*

The recovery of the Crimea, Stavka planning   pp. 191–199

Allen, W.E.D. and Muratoff, Paul, *The Russian Campaigns of 1944–45,* ch. III, 'Reconquest of the Crimea', pp. 69–86, particularly the storming of the Sapun Heights with its descent into the valley where the Light Brigade charged in 1854 (pp. 84–5).

Deane, John R., *The Strange Alliance* (London: John Murray 1947), ch. IX, 'Co-ordinating the European Land Battle', 'Bodyguard' deception plan, visit of Colonel J.H. Beran and Lt.-Col. W.H. Baumer to Moscow, January 1944, meetings with Col.-Gen. F.F. Kuznetsov (Soviet General Staff).

Hillgruber, A., *Die Räumung der Krim 1944* (Berlin and Frankfurt: E.S. Mittler 1959).

Philippi, Alfred and Heim, Ferdinand, *Der Feldzug gegen Sowjetrussland,* pt 2, 'Die Katastrophe auf der Krim', pp. 242–5.

Seaton, Albert, *The Russo–German War,* ch. 25, Soviet recovery of the Crimea, 'the final in the succession of German defeats in the Ukraine . . . probably the greatest', pp. 427–31; ch. 26, planning and preparation for *Bagration,* pp. 432–7.

Werth, Alexander, *Russia at War,* pt 7, ch. IV, 'Hitler's Crimean Catastrophe', pp. 827–40.

Soviet materials

Badanin, Colonel B., 'Na perepravakh cherez Sivash', *VIZ*, 1964 (4), pp. 32–8 (engineer support, Sivash crossings).

Biryuzov, S.S., *Surovye gody,* pt 1, pp. 254–82, planning and execution of Crimea attack, fall of Sevastopol. (As well as being very informative, this is an extremely well-written account.)

Domnikov, V.M., *V nastuplenii Gvardiya,* 2nd Guards Army operations, Perekop and storming of Sevastopol—'Daesh Krym!', pp. 186–214.

Grylev, A.N., *Dnepr Karpaty Krym,* ch. 4, recovery of the Crimea, operational planning and preparation, pp. 219–27; breaching German defences and advance on Sevastopol, pp. 227–42; storming of Sevastopol, pp. 242–53. (Extremely detailed operational narrative.)

Koltunov, G. and Isaev, S., 'Krymskaya operatsiya v tsifrakh', *VIZ*, 1974 (5), pp. 35–41. (Tabulations of Soviet strength/Crimea operations; includes air strength, also partisan formations.)

Korotkov, I.S. and Koltunov, G.A., *Osvobozhdenie Kryma* (Moscow: Voenizdat 1959). See Soviet offensive, 51st Army (Sivash), 2nd Guards Army (Perekop), pursuit in northern Crimea, pp. 29–64; storming of Sevastopol, pp. 65–82.

Koshevoi, Marshal SU P., 'Na Sivashe', *VIZ*, 1976 (3), pp. 57–65. (P. Koshevoi commanded 63rd Rifle Corps assigned to Kreizer's 51st Army; here, on planning Sivash crossings, also Tolbukhin's planning for Sivash. Perekop attack on broad front.)

Kreizer, General Ya., 'Sivash–Sevastopol', *VIZ*, 1969 (5), pp. 75–92. (General Kreizer's 51st Army operations.)

Kuznetsov, P.G., *Marshal Tolbukhin.* See 'V Krymu', on Tolbukhin's planning/Crimean operation, 51st Army and 2nd Guards Army attack plans, summary of operations, pp. 117–34.

Luchinskii, General A., 'V boyakh pod Sevastopolem', *VIZ*, 1964 (5), pp. 17–30. (Independent Coastal Army operations, Crimea.)

Shavrov, General I., '19-a tankovyi korpus v boyakh za Krym', *VIZ*, 1974 (4), pp. 62–72. (Operations 19th Tank Corps, Crimea.)

Shtemenko, S.M., 'Pered udarom v Belorussi', *VIZ*, 1965 (9), pp. 44–59. (Unlike his 'memoirs', this account by Shtemenko supplies a close narrative with documentary support on the first phase of planning for *Bagration*.) Hitherto, operations in Belorussia had not attained the desired results, resulting in extensive analysis of previous failures by the Soviet command; Marshal S.K. Timoshenko confirmed that 1st and 2nd Baltic Fronts could not themselves mount the main blow, General Staff analysis of total situation on the Soviet–German front, recommendation for a provisional turn to the defensive (*Stavka* directive No. 202947, 7 May), submission of plans by Front commanders, *GKO* decision to split the Western Front, importance of operational deception (*operativnaya maskirovka*), GS operations completed draft planning by 14 May, aim to destroy bulk of Army Group Centre (importance of blows at the flanks), 22–23 May review of General Staff operational plans, offensive fixed for 15–20 June (provisional), 3rd Belorussian plans submitted, planning also for Leningrad and 1st Ukrainian Front offensive operations.

Vaneyev, G., 'Deistviya Chernomorskovo flota na kommunikatsiyakh protivnika v Krymskoi operatsii', *VIZ,* 1974 (5), pp. 28–34. (Black Sea Fleet operations, Crimea.)

Vasilevskii, A.M., 'Osvobozhdenie Kryma ot nemetsko-fashistskikh zakhvatchikov v 1944 godu', *VIZ,* 1971 (5), pp. 71–85 and (6), pp. 57–73. In contrast to Vasilevskii's memoirs proper *(Delo vsei zhizni),* these two accounts of the Crimean operation are filled out with a great deal of operational documentation and details of reporting to Stalin and the *Stavka;* in particular, *VIZ,* 1971 (6), p. 57, *Stavka* directive to Black Sea Fleet (11 April), Vasilevskii to Stalin 12 April (pp. 58–9), *Stavka* orders for Independent Coastal Army 16 April, re-assignment of Yeremenko (p. 61), Vasilevskii to Stalin 18 April (p. 64), Vasilevskii to Stalin 23 April (p. 65) Stalin's insistence on *rapid operations,* Tolbukhin's operational directives 29 April (pp. 66–7), Vasilevskii's written report to Stalin 5 May (p. 68), and report on storming of Sevastopol (pp. 69–70).

Vasilevskii, A.M., 'Belorusskaya strategicheskaya operatsiya', *VIZ,* 1969 (9), pp. 47–58. First stage of planning/co-ordination Belorussian offensive, 4-Front operation including Dnieper flotilla, partisan operations, decision *(GKO)* on splitting Western front, 20 May Antonov presents General Staff plan to Stalin for Belorussian offensive, confirmed by Stalin 30 May, decision on reinforcements, reports to Stalin 14 June (p. 55), final reports to Stalin on attack preparations.

Yeremenko, A.I., *Gody vozmezdiya,* pp. 180–205, Independent Coastal Army operations, Kerch peninsula, 16 April Independent Coastal Army assigned to 4th Ukrainian Front as Germans fell back on Sevastopol, Yeremenko recalled to Moscow, succeeded by Lt.-Gen. K.S. Melnik; pp. 145–50, transmission of information to Soviet command on revised timings for *Overlord,* Soviet suspicion that May (1944) date agreed in Teheran part of deception plan by Western powers directed against USSR.

The Second Front, Karelian offensive, planning/preparation *'Bagration'* pp. 199–215

Diplomatic correspondence

Perepiska . . . vol. 1, Churchill to Stalin, 5 June (1944), no. 271, pp. 265–66; Churchill to Stalin, 6 June, no. 273, p. 268; Stalin to Churchill, 6 June, no. 274, p. 267; Stalin to Churchill, 9 June, no. 276, p. 269.

GMD

FHO (I) *Feindliches Kräftebild vor der Finnland–Front* (24.4.44). T-78/R466, 6446408.

FHO (I) *Beurteilung im Grossen,* 30.3.1944. See maps, projected Soviet operations against Finnish Front, also detailed map 'Wichtige Abwehrmeldungen über sow.-russ. Operationsabsichten'. T-78/R497, 6485597–98 (for maps; otherwise 6485573–602).

Hgr. Nord (Army Group North). Tätigkeitsbericht. Ic/AO Teil 1. Feindlage. 1 Ausfertigung vom 16.5–20.6.44. (Intelligence, Army Group North, daily reports 16th, 18th Army, Army Group Narwa.) T-311/R90, 7117702–8070.

FHO (I) *Anlagenband zur Zusammenstellung* . . . abgefassten Beurteilungen (4.42–12.44). 'Wichtige Abwehrmeldungen . . .', Stalin's command conference (with attendance of head of Polish resistance), discussion of two offensive designs (dated 3.5.44). T-78/R498, 6485829–35.

FHO (I) *Notiz* (Soviet battalions deployed against Army Group Centre and N Ukraine, 28.4.44). Against N Ukraine: frontage 500 km, 420 Soviet battalions deployed; against Army Group Centre: frontage 1,200 km, 448 Soviet battalions deployed. T-78/T466, 6446403.

FHO (IIc) *Panzerlage vor deutscher Ostfront* (for 1 June 1944). Total, *deployed* Soviet tank/mechanized forces: 38 corps, plus 106 independent brigades, 8,073 tanks. T-78/R493, 6480814.

FHO (IIc) Booklet: *Truppen-Übersicht und Kriegsgliederungen der Roten Armee* Stand August 1944. Soviet divisions/regiments, place of origin, appearance on Soviet–German Front, current deployments. T-78/R459, 6437543–38066.

Planning/preparation, Soviet offensive, Karelia

IVOVSS, 4, pt 2, pp. 133–45, planning, execution of Soviet offensive Karelian isthmus.

IVMV, 9, pt 1, pp. 26–32, Soviet offensive Karelian isthmus, capture of Vyborg, preparations to drive on Petrozavodsk.

Inozemtsev, I.G., *Pod krylom–Leningrad*, pp. 208–26, 13th Air Army operations, Soviet offensive Karelian isthmus, to capture of Vyborg.

Mironov, Lt.-Gen. N., 'Proryv ukreplennovo raiona na Karel'skom peresheike', *VIZ*, 1974 (6), pp. 10–17. 21st Army operations, Karelia. Total Soviet strength committed to Vyborg operation—260,000 men, 7,500 guns/mortars (including naval guns), 628 tanks and SP guns, 1,000 aircraft (220 from Baltic Fleet naval air force).

Platonov, S.P., *Bitva za Leningrad 1941–1944*, pt 2, ch. 7, 'Razgrom vraga na Karel'skom peresheike', 1944, pp. 418–74. Govorov's operational directive (Leningrad Front) 3 May 1944, offensive against Karelian isthmus with 21st, 23rd Army and 13th Air Army, Baltic Fleet operational planning, fire support directive 23 May, organization artillery/engineer/air support, opening of Soviet offensive 10–12 June, operations D.N. Gusev's 21st Army, breaching main Finnish defences 14–17 June, operations 21st and 23rd Army, advance on Vyborg, capture of Vyborg 18–20 June, *Stavka* orders to continue Soviet advance 21 June, Govorov's plan for two-stage operation. (Extensive use of Soviet military archival material.)

Shtemenko, S.M., 'Na severnom flange sovetsko-germanskovo fronta letom i osenyu 1944 goda', *VIZ*, 1972 (6), pp. 59–66. Planning for offensive on northern flank, Stalin's concern over which force to hit first (German or Finnish), detailed planning for Karelian offensive, Stalin's instruction not to waste Soviet resources in order to preserve enough force to encounter German troops in the north.

Terekhov, P.V., *Boevye deistviya tankov na severo-zapade v 1944 g.*, (Moscow: Voenizdat 1965), pp. 10–74, planning of Karelian attack, use of armour in offensive on Vyborg, use of tanks and SP guns with 21st Army, 379 tanks and 164 SP guns used in first stage of offensive, increased to 464 tanks and 182 SP guns in second stage, armoured support for 23rd Army operations, approach to third line of defences 17 June, rifle corps commanders employing tank-mounted infantry and SP guns as 'forward detachments'. (Extremely detailed monograph.)

Tributs, Admiral V.F., *Baltiitsy nastupayut* (Kalingrad, Kalinin: Knizh. Izd. 1968), pp. 77–99. Tributs summoned to *Stavka*, naval support (Baltic Fleet, Ladoga Flotilla) planning, Baltic Fleet to support seaward flank 21st Army, problem posed by extensive mining in Gulf of Finland, Ladoga Flotilla to cover flank of 23rd Army, coordination of naval/ground forces command (co-location of artillery/fleet gunnery commanders), sinking of U-250, extracts from Tributs's diary (12–19 June, pp. 99–102).

Zubakov, Colonel V., '21-ya armiya v Vyborgskoi nastupatel'noi operatsii (10–20 iyunya 1944 g.)', *VIZ*, 1971 (6), pp. 23–33. 21st Army offensive, capture of Vyborg.

Planning/preparation 'Bagration'

Gaskenholz, Hermann, 'The Collapse of Army Group Centre in 1944' in *Decisive Battles of World War II: the German View* (eds H-A. Jacobsen and J. Rohwer) (London: Deutsch 1965), here p. 361, OKH conference, 14 June, warnings from Army Group Centre, but conviction of Soviet offensive in Galicia, operations against Army Group Centre would be of secondary nature.

Soviet materials

IVMV, 9, pt 1, pp. 40–47, planning, preparation for Soviet offensive, Belorussia.

IVOVSS, 4, pt 2, pp. 152–68, planning, preparation of *Bagration*.

Bagramyan, I.Kh., *Kak shli my k pobede*, pp. 287–306, planning for *Bagration* (note his comment that Stalin had special feeling for Rokossovskii, whom he compared to Dzerzhinskii—*osobaya simpatiya*, pp. 300–1), acceptance of Bagramyan's modification to initial attack plan, operational assignments to Front armies.

Chernyaev, Maj.-Gen. V., 'Operativnaya maskirovka voisk v Belorusskoi operatsii', *VIZ*, 1974 (8), pp. 11–21. Soviet camouflage/deception measures, Operation *Bagration*; extract from instructions for camouflage.

Patyka, Colonel F., 'Tylovoe obespechenie frontov v operatsii 'Bagration' ', *VIZ*, 1974 (8), pp. 22–9. Logistics/supply problems, rail movements, tonnages, fuel/ammunition *boekomplekty* (fills), medical services, Rear Services organization.

Rokossovskii, K.K., 'Dva glavnykh udara', *VIZ*, 1964 (6), pp. 13–18. Rokossovskii's own account of his insistence on a 'double blow' from his right flank (a version much disputed by Zhukov), attempts by Malenkov and Molotov to dissuade him from pressing the point with Stalin, plan finally accepted on its third submission.

Shtemenko, S., 'Pered udarom v Belorussi', *VIZ*, 1965 (9), pp. 43–59. *Stavka* and General Staff planning, logistical problems, Stalin's refusal to contemplate total if temporary shift to defensive operations—*podumaem eshchë*—17–19 April NW and W axes allowed to take up defensive, submissions 11 May, Stalin himself proposes codename *Bagration*, full *Stavka* session with Front and arms commanders (except Chernyakhovskii, absent through illness, and Petrov) 22–23 May, Bagramyan's proposal for modification of 1st Baltic Front plan accepted, agreement to time other fronts to transition gradually to defensive, *Stavka* directive issued only 1–7 May, first drafts of General Staff plan submitted to *Stavka* end April, importance of disinformation/camouflage (*maskirovka*), Plan *Bagration* and operational assignments, 1st Belorussian Front offensive for 15–20 June, Chernyakhovskii finally arrives in Moscow, assigned 5th Guards Tank Army and heavy artillery, further planning for Leningrad and 1st Ukrainian Front operations.

Shtemenko, S. 'Pered udarom v Belorussii', *VIZ*, 1966 (2), pp. 58–71. Mekhlis denounces Petrov as unsuitable to command 2nd Belorussian Front, Stalin replaces Petrov by G.F. Zakharov, Shtemenko sent to support Zakharov who then tried to effect alterations in *Stavka* plan, work of *Stavka* representatives with Front commands, Vasilevskii report to *Stavka* on operational plans 1st Baltic and 3rd Belorussian Fronts, 5th Guards Tank Army now subordinated directly to *Stavka*, 10 June Zhukov asks for air force commanders to define air tasks in person, reconnaissance of German positions begins, organization of command/control systems and procedures, great delays with rail movements, Stalin's categorical instructions to Kaganovich.

  Note: Tabulation of work schedules/assignments of *Stavka* representatives Zhukov and Vasilevskii (for period 4.6–24.6.44) *VIZ*, 1966 (2), pp. 72–82 (follows Shtemenko article).

Vasilevskii, A.M., 'Belorusskaya strategicheskaya operatsiya', *VIZ*, 1969 (9), pp. 47–58. Planning of *Bagration*, *Stavka* assignments to Fronts (1st Baltic, 1st, 2nd, 3rd Belorussian Fronts), relations with Antonov (Chief of General Staff), visits to Front/army commands early June as *Stavka* representative, 9 June report to Stalin on planning work, serious delays with rail movements, 14 June Stalin postpones offensive to 23 June, 17 June Antonov discusses Leningrad Front operations with Stalin, 21 June Vasilevskii report to Stalin (quoted p. 57), report on final readiness.

Vasilevskii, A.M., *Delo vsei zhizni*, pp. 432–55, under 'Pered Belorusskoi operatsii', *Stavka* planning for *Bagration*, operational concepts, Zhukov-Vasilevskii consultations with Stalin, 20 May General Staff plan presented to Stalin, 30 May *Stavka* approves final version of offensive plan, Stalin assigns Zhukov and Vasilevskii to Front commands as *Stavka* representatives (30 May), Front decisions, 9 June Vasilevskii to Stalin on completion of 1st Baltic Front preparations, Stalin signal on enforced postponement of offensive, report to Stalin 16 June, return to Moscow and review of Leningrad Front operations, deployment of Long-Range Aviation (ADD), summary of Stalin's role in preparation of *Bagration*.

Vasilevskii, A.M., 'Vospominaniya o Belorusskoi operatsii', in Samsonov, *Osvobozhdenie Belorussii*, pp. 40–65. Genesis of *Bagration* plan and entire summer offensive, consultations with Antonov, detailed planning with 3rd Belorussian Front, planning with 1st Baltic Front (Bagramyan), meeting with Stalin and Antonov 17 June, Zhukov's request for postponement of offensive.

Zhukov, G.K., *Vospominaniya . . .*, vol. 2, pp. 238–52. Hands over command of 1st Ukrainian Front to Koniev, Stalin instructs Antonov to prepare plan for summer offensive (end April), mid-May in Moscow with Vasilevskii, 20 May review of offensive plans with Stalin, Vasilevskii and Antonov assigned co-ordinating mission with 1st and 2nd Belorussian Fronts, dismisses Rokossovskii's version of 'two main blows' from 1st Belorussian Front as unfounded (p. 246), Front assignments, logistical/supply problems, key role of 1st Belorussian Front, Zhukov's supervision of 1st Belorussian planning/preparations, planning of air operations. (See also *Memoirs*, translation, pp. 517–29.)

Operation 'Bagration'/Belorussia   pp. 215–231

Allen, W.E.D., and Muratoff, Paul, *The Russian Campaigns of 1944–1945*, Ch. V, 'The Russian Summer Offensive', 23 June–end of August, pp. 104–63. (Derived largely from Soviet wartime communiqués—operational narrative, with special reference to terrain features.)

Armstrong, John A. (ed.), *Soviet Partisans in World War II*, ch. IX, the Polotsk lowland, pp. 544–6: operations of the Kaminsky Brigade, Soviet orders to partisan brigades in Ushachi area, German operations *Frühlingsfest* and *Regenschauer*, partisan losses estimated at 7,000 dead, mass demolitions by partisans, paralysis of German rail system.

Carell, Paul, *Scorched Earth* (Hitler's War on Russia, vol. 2), pt 8, 'The Cannae of Army Group Centre',—deployment (German expectation of an attack in Galicia), attack (Bobruisk, Vitebsk), breakthrough (the gigantic pocket), pp. 479–510.

Gackenholz, Hermann, *The Collapse of Army Group Centre in 1944, loc. cit.* See section 'Battle of White Russia', opened by extensive partisan actions, Soviet deployment opposite Fourth Army, Ninth Army, Third *Panzer* Army, new Soviet tactics surprise German command, also brigading of Soviet armour; 'Destruction of the German Front', penetration at Vitebsk, Busch refuses to allow withdrawal to Dnieper, conference June 24 at Army Group Centre HQ in Minsk, Zeitzlev (CGS) present, discussion of danger to Third *Panzer* Army, 24 June 'last chance of saving Army Group Centre by "changing its battle instructions"' (p. 368), Zeitzler fails to persuade Hitler for withdrawal, 'Fortress Vitebsk' a trap for Third *Panzer*, Hitler refuses permission for Fourth Army to withdraw to Dnieper line, 1st Belorussian Front assault on Ninth Army June 24, Army Group Centre HQ June 25 report to OKH request to abandon Vitebsk and withdrawal to Dnieper, Hitler again refused, Hitler insists on holding Vitebsk, June 26 danger of double envelopment of Army Group, Busch's personal visit to Hitler, Army Group still bound by restrictive orders, desperate situation of Ninth Army by June 27, Hitler's operational order No. 8 did nothing to change orders or properly estimate situation; 'The Russian Drive in Depth', Soviet plans to exploit success at Minsk, mass of Ninth Army encircled at Bobruisk, communications with Army Group North cut, Model assumes command of Army Group Centre, Hitler agrees to all measures proposed by Model (June 28–29), pp. 364–76.

Heidkämper, Otto, *Witebsk. Kampf und Untergang der 3 Panzerarmee*, ch. XXI, Soviet summer offensive 1944, Soviet assault on Third *Panzer* Army, first battles NW Vitebsk, breakout, withdrawal actions, pp. 144–62.

Hesse, Erich, *Der sowjetrussische Partisanenkrieg 1941–1944*, ch. 13, under 'Säuberungsunternehmen der Heeresgruppe Mitte im Jahre 1944', anti-partisan operations 'Regenschauer', 'Komoran', pp. 242–4.

Seaton, Albert, *The Russo-German War*, ch. 26, Belorussia and East Poland, pp. 432–42: Soviet strength/deployment, preparations for *Bagration*, opening of Soviet offensive, encirclement at Vitebsk, attempted German breakout, disappearance of German 53rd Corps, encirclement of Bobruisk, reshuffling of German command, Model replaces Busch (but Model retains command of Army Group North Ukraine), desperate commitment of small German reserves, 5th Guards Tank Army crosses Berezina, drive on Minsk.

GMD

RSHA (Reichssicherheitsamt): Amt IV. *Funkspiele:* German intelligence deception, exchanges of German agents with 'Centre' (Moscow), queries from 'Centre' on German order of battle/troop movements: signals for May–June/44 (21 pp.). T-78/R488, 6473443–66.

FHO (IIc), Feindkräfteberechnung: tables, daily estimates Soviet forces on European (Soviet–German) front, Soviet reserves, Caucasus, Finland, Far East: 2 January–23 August 1944. T-78/R483, 6468345–580.

FHO (I). Teil A. *Zusammenstellung der in der zeit von April 1942–Dezember 1944 ... abgefassten Beurteilungen ...* No. 1794/44: Kurze Beurteilung der Feindlage der Heeresgruppe, Mitte vom 2.6.44 (T-78/R466, 6446155); No. 1931/44: Feindlage vor deutscher Ostfront und vermutete Feindabsichten im grossen. (See final note on Finland/Finnish front) T-78/R466, 6446158–167. See also Kurze Beurteilung 14.6.44 (No. 1951/44), 6446168–69.

FHO (I). Teil A. *Zusammenstellung ... abgefassten Beurteilung der Feindlage.* Rpt No. 2096/44 27.6: early success in Soviet breakthrough as much as a surprise for the Soviet as for the German command; Nr 2163/44 2.7: transfer of Rotmistrov's 5th Guards Tank Army to Belorussian Front most likely, but this still leaves adequate Soviet armoured strength against Army Group South Ukraine for offensive into Rumania. T-78/R466, 6446170–174.

OKH/Allgemeines Heeresamt: Abwicklungsstab. Reports on German units destroyed in Soviet summer offensive, 1944: units of Heeresgruppe Mitte, 4th Army and 9th Army. T-78/R139, from 6068417 to 6068999.

OKH/Kriegsgeschichtliche Abteilung. Map collection: Der grosse Durchbruch bei Hgr. Mitte (21.6–10.8.44). Soviet breakthrough, Army Group Centre. T-78/R136, 6065394–5436.

Soviet materials

Wartime press

Sovinformbyuro. See Vol. 7 (June–Dec. 44): Moscow, 1945. Communiqués (*operativnaya svodka*), from 23.6 to 30.6, pp. 1–21; the same, 1.7 to 15.7, pp. 22–47.

SWN (date/number of issue)

Stalin: Order(s) of the Day.

To Bagramyan, Chernyakhovskii, 28 June, No. 895.

To Rokossovskii, 28 June, No. 905.

To Zakharov (2 BF), Rokossovskii, 30 June, No. 897.

To Meretskov and Rokossovskii (Karelian Front), 1 July, No. 898.

To Chernyakhovskii, 3 July, No. 899.

To Chernyakhovskii and Rokossovskii (cutting German links from Minsk to Vilno and Lida): 4 July, No. 900.

To the same, 5 July, No. 901.

To Bagramyan, 6 July, No. 902.

To Chernyakhovskii, 7 July, No. 903.

To Rokossovskii (capture of Kovel), 8 July, No. 904.

(Cf. *SWN*, 21 July 1944, No. 915. Account by Lt.-Gen. E. Hofmeister, captured commander of XLI *Panzer* Corps.)

Soviet official histories/statistics
IVOVSS, 4, pt 2, pp. 168–86, encirclement of German forces at Vitebsk/Bobruisk, threat to and encirclement of Fourth Army.
IVMV, 9, pt 1, pp. 48–55, destruction of Army Group Centre. Brief operational narrative based on Soviet military archives.
'Belorusskaya operatsiya v tsifrakh', *VIZ*, 1964 (6), pp. 74–86. *Bagration*, tabulation of strength, listing of Front/army commanders.

Collected memoir accounts, Belorussian operations
(1) *Osvobozhdenie Belorussii* (ed. A.M. Samsanov).
    See under:
    Bagramyan, I.Kh., 'Voiny-pribaltiitsy v srazheniyakh za Belorussiyu', pp. 109–37.
    Pokrovskii, A.P., '3-i Belorusskii Front v operatsii "Bagration" ', pp. 184–218
        (Pokrovskii was Chief of Staff, 3 BF).
    Krylov, N.I., 'Na glavnom napravlenii', pp. 276–310 (Krylov commanded 5th
        Army).
    Beloborodov, A.P., 'Vitebskii "Kotel" ', pp. 311–40.
    Rotmistrov, P.A., 'Udar nebyvaloi sily', pp. 404–27 (commander 5th Guards
        Tank Army, assigned 3 BF area, committed on direct *Stavka* orders).
    Pliev, I.A. 'Na ostrie udara', pp. 425–45 (commander, Cavalry-Mechanized Group,
        KMG).
    Galitskii, K.N., 'Gvardeitsy 11-i v boyakh za Belorussiyu', pp. 446–93.
    Note also: Appendix 1, complete Soviet order of battle, 23 June, pp. 741–7.
(2) Malanin, Colonel K.A. (ed.), *Polki idut na zapad*. (Moscow: Voenizdat 1964)
    (memoir material, Soviet Belorussian offensive).
    See esp.: Rokossovskii, K.K., 'Ot Gomelya do Bresta', pp. 21–47.
    Bagramyan, I.Kh., 'Skvoz v'yugu ognevu', pp. 48–71.
    Beloborodov, A.P., 'V raione Vitebska', pp. 99–116.
    Panov, M.F., 'Tanki vkhodyat v proryv', pp. 117–28 (commander 1st Independent
        Guards Don Tank Corps).
(3) 'Velikaya pobeda v Belorussii', *VIZ*, 1964 (6), pp. 3–35. Collection of personal
    accounts, Bagramyan, Rokossovskii, Pokrovskii, Rotmistrov, Vershinin (on 4th
    Air Army), Antipenko (logistics).

Antipenko, Lt.-Gen. N.A., *Na glavnom napravlenii* (Moscow: Nauka, 2nd edn 1971),
    foreword by Marshal Zhukov. See 'Osvobozhdenie Belorussii', assignments as Chief
    Rear Services/1st Belorussian Front, organization and operation supply services,
    transport, medical units, repair services, pp. 127–59.
Batov, P.A., '65-ya armiya v boyakh za Belorussiyu', *VIZ*, 1970 (9), pp. 65–72.
    Account by commander, 65th Army, first stages Soviet offensive.
Bychkov, L.N., *Partizanskoe dvizhenie . . . 1941–1945*, pp. 349–61, Belorussian
    partisan operations, co-ordination with Red Army summer offensive, effect of
    German anti-partisan operations, growth in partisan strength.

Eliseyev, E.P., *Na Belostokskom napravlenii* (Moskow: Nauka 1971), 229 pp., *passim*. An immensely detailed monograph dealing with 2nd Belorussian Front operations, Zakharov's command which carried through the Bialystok operation but suffered such heavy casualties that it could not conduct further operations; Zakharov was subsequently *demoted* to army commander. Tabulation of command appointments for 2 BF, also a comprehensive index.

  (Further to *G.F. Zakharov* as a Front commander, see S.M. Shtemenko, *The Soviet General Staff at War*, pp. 244–6, with Shtemenko present at Zakharov's first inspection and early command conference. Without having inspected the terrain, Zakharov queried the *Stavka* directive and at his command conference stated without ceremony that 'I'm the one who does the talking here . . .', finally trying to force the tactics he used in the Crimea on commanders facing the complex terrain of Belorussia—no one could just 'dash into the enemy trenches'.)

Kiryukhin, S.P., *43-ya Armiya v Vitebskoi operatsii* (Moscow: Voenizdat 1961), 143 pp., *passim*. Detailed monograph on 43rd Army operations (1st Baltic Front), Vitebsk operations.

Krylov, N.I., Alekseyev, N.I., Dragan, I.G., *Navstrechu pobede. Boevoi put 5-i armii* (Moscow: Nauka 1970), ch. 8, 'Za svobodnuyu Belorussiyu', pp. 205–35, 5th Army operations (3rd Belorussian Front).

Kuznetsov, Lt.-Gen. P.G., *General Chernyakhovskii* (Moscow: Voenizdat 1969). Biography: see under 'Komanduyushchii frontom', pp. 143–86, Chernyakhovskii's operations as commander, 3rd Belorussian Front, June 1944.

Lyudnikov, Col.-Gen. I.I., *Pod Vitebskom* (Moscow: Voenizdat 1962), 112 pp., *passim*. General Lyudnikov's own analysis of 39th Army operations (3rd Belorussian Front), Vitebsk operations.

Malinin, General M., 'O deistriyakh voisk 1-go Belorusskovo fronta v Belorusskoi nastupatel'noi operatsii', *VIZ*, 1959 (7), pp. 18–32.

Panov, Maj.-Gen. B., 'Okruzhenie i unichtozhenie krupnykh gruppirovok protivnika v Belorusskoi operatsii', *VIZ*, 1974 (6), pp. 18–26. Analysis of Soviet encirclement operations, Belorussia.

Rudenko, Air Marshal S., 'Osobennosti boevykh deistvii aviatsii v Belorusskoi operatsii', *VIZ*, 1971 (2), pp. 22–31. Air operations, Belorussian offensive; tabulation of sorties flown by air armies, p. 30.

Shimanskii, Colonel A., 'Organizatsiya operativno-strategicheskovo vzaimodeistviya v Belorusskoi operatsii 1944 goda', *VIZ*, 1973 (6), pp. 13–22. An important detailed analysis of planning for and implementation of 'co-ordination/inter-action' of four Fronts, plus aviation, air defence (PVO), partisans, Dnieper Flotilla in Operation *Bagration*, June–July.

Vasilevskii, A.M., 'Belorusskaya strategicheskaya operatsiya', *VIZ*, 1969 (10), pp. 63–71. With 3 BF 24 June, text of report to Stalin 24 June (pp. 63–4) with proposal over timing of committing 5th Guards Tank Army, report to Stalin 26 June on 1st Baltic Front operations (pp. 65–6), composite report on 3rd Belorussian and 1st Baltic Front operations 1300 hours 27 June (pp. 67–8), liquidation of enemy forces encircled at Vitebsk, Chernyakhovskii outflanks Orsha during night 26–27 June, interrogation of captured German generals.

Vasilevskii, A.M., *Delo vsei zhizni* (2nd edn). See 'Za zemlyu Belorusskuyu', pp. 456–64: further account of *Bagration*, operational reports to Stalin not included, problem of committing 5th Guards Tank Army and Rotmistrov's lack of enthusiasm at assignment to 3rd Belorussian Front, 5th Guards Tank performed 'worse than hitherto', Stalin's disquiet and dissatisfaction, demanded 28 June decisiveness in 5th Guards Tank operations, Chernyakhovskii promoted full general on Vasilevskii's recommendation, problems of rail movement and supply, signal to Stalin 27 June on requirements for effective rail traffic, continued concern over *low tempo* of 5th Guards Tank Army advance, orders to Rotmistrov to close on Minsk, considerations relating to further development of Soviet offensive.

Vasilevskii, A.M. For further version, see also 'Vospominaniya o Belorusskoi operatsii' in *Osvobozhdenie Belorussii* (ed. A.M. Samsonov), pp. 69–83. This account includes Vasilevskii's daily reports to Stalin on 3rd Belorussian Front operations dated 24 June (pp. 69–70), report 25 June (pp. 73–5), report 26 June (pp. 75–6), report for 27 June (pp. 78–9), signal on rail traffic 27 June (pp. 80–1), disquiet on slow progress of 5th Guards Tank Army, Stalin's directive (No. 220124) 28 June further orders for 3rd Belorussian Front, also insistence on decisiveness from 5th Guards Tank.

Zagorul'ko, M.M. and Yudenkov, A.F., *Krakh plana 'Ol'denburg'* (Moscow: Ekonomika 1980), ch. 6, under 'Rel'sovaya voina', pp. 252–65, Soviet partisan operations against German rail communications, detailed tabulations by type of operation (mining) and geographical area, extensive use of archival records. (A detailed monograph on the disruption of German plans for economic exploitation, also some military aspects.)

'Freies Deutschland': 20 July bomb plot

Irving, David, *Hitler's War*, pp. 657–77. See ' "Do you recognize my voice?" ', on the bomb plot and attempted assassination of Hitler, with its consequences.

Soviet War News, TASS report: 'Rebellion against Hitler', 24 July 1944, No. 917 (on the bomb plot).

On *Freies Deutschland*, see documents/facsimiles, *Zur Gesch. der deutschen Antifas-chistischen Widerstandsbewegung,* and on Paulus in summer 1944, see Willy Wolff in Soviet translation, *Na storone Krasnoi Armii,* pp. 128–38 (orig. German, *An der Seite der Roten Armee*).

For Soviet evaluation of German resistance to Hitler, see V.I. Israelyan, *Diplomaticheskaya istoriya VOV,* ch. IV(5), 'Razlozhenie germanskovo tyla', pp. 215–19; see also *Sovinformbyuro,* VII, p. 151, for 9 September 1944, secret German document captured from 28th Corps (doc. no. 40/44 for 4 August) explaining events of 20 July and great distrust now of German officer corps, also new role for Nazi Party—with instruction 'Burn after reading'.

Lvov–Sandomierz operation:
Rokossovskii's left-flank drive pp. 231–247

Seaton, Albert, *The Russo–German War,* pp. 444–54, Koniev's 1st Ukrainian Front offensive, Soviet drive to the Vistula and approaches to Warsaw.

GMD

FHO (I), Stellungnahme zur Beurteilung der Lage der Hgr. Nordukraine v. 17.6.44. T-78/R466, 6446349.

Obkdo. Heeresgr. Nordukraine, Ia, Nr 0823/44 g. Kdos. chefs. 8.6.44 *Feindbeurteilung.* Estimate of Soviet intentions: see also map, Kräftebild/German and Soviet forces, deployment, strength. T-78/R466, 6446386–89.

Obkdo. Heeresgr. Nordukraine Abt. Ic/AO, Garde-Panzer-Korps. Rpt Nr 21282/44 geh. Dated 30.6.44, Soviet order of battle—Guards tank/mech. corps, cavalry, artillery, anti-tank brigades, AA divisions: composition, deployment as of 20.6.44. T-78/ R486, 6470724–766.

Soviet materials

IVMV, 9, pt 1, pp. 81–92, encirclement of German forces at Brody, Soviet advance into SE Poland. (*Note:* figures for 1st Guards Tank Army strength 14 August (p. 92): 184 tanks/SP guns; strength on 12 July, beginning of operation, 416 tanks/ SP guns.)

IVOVSS, 4, pt 2, pp. 210–23, Brody encirclement, fall of Lvov, drive to Vistula, Sandomierz bridgehead, push to Drohobych. (Also p. 224: armed suppression of 'bourgeois nationalist bands', NKVD units—one cavalry, two motorcycle regiments—brought in for rear security duties, 'accounting for' 36 bands, 4,315 individuals.)

Babadzhanyan, A.Kh., *et al., Lyuki otkryli v Berline, op. cit.,* (Combat history of 1st Guards Tank Army). 1st Guards Tank operations 'from the Bug to the San', 13 July–28 July, 1st Ukrainian Front, pp. 185–97.

Batov, General P.I., *V pokhodakh i boyakh.* (Moscow: Voenizdat (VM), 3rd edn 1974). See 'K granitsam Pol'shi', 65th Army drive to W Bug, stormy relations with Zhukov (p. 420), pp. 416–32.

Collective authorship, *V srazheniyakh za pobedu.* Boevoi put 38-i armii . . . (Moscow: Nauka 1974), pp. 368–99, 38th Army operations, Lvov offensive, operational narrative.

Chuikov, Marshal SU V.I., *Ot Stalingrada do Berlina* (Moscow: Voenizdat (VM) 1980). (A composite version of previous memoir compilations, all heavily ghosted.) Pt 3, pp. 455–77, 8th Guards Army assigned to 1st Belorussian Front, drive to the Berezina, offensive on Lublin, liberation of Maidanek concentration camp.

Galitskii, General K.N., *Gody surovykh ispytanii 1941–1944.* Zapiski komandarma (Moskow: Nauka 1973). Ch. 16, 'Razgrom gruppy armii "Tsentr" ', 11th Guards Army operations, Belorussian offensive, drive on Orsha, advance to the Berezina, Borisov–Minsk, advance on Molodechno, movement to line west of Minsk–Molodechno, pp. 512–45. Ch. 17, drive to the Niemen, 3 BF directive 3 July to advance to Vilno/Lida, 11th Guards to operate at centre reaching Neimen at Alitus, 16th Guards Rifle Corps closes on river line dawn 13 July, pp. 546–53.

Getman, A.L., *Tanki idut na Berlin,* pp. 202–27, operations 11th Guards Tank Corps (1st Guards Tank Army), Corps not fully manned in July (1944)—only 38 per cent T-34s, 60–70 per cent SP guns—17 July moved up to new start line, attacked in two-echelon formation, forcing of W Bug, fighting for bridgehead 17–19 July, 1st Guards Tank Army now ordered to move westwards and on to river San, 24

July 11th Guards Tank Corps deepened San bridgehead, entire force across river by July 25, drive on Przemysl, captured July 27.

Katukov, M.E., *Na ostrie glavnovo udara*, pp. 314–22, operations with 1st Ukrainian Front (843,000 men, 19,300 guns and mortars, 2,200 tanks/SP guns, 3,000 aircraft): orders for 1st Guards Tank Army—on 2nd day of operations to enter breakthrough at junction of 3rd Guards and 13th Army, then drive for W Bug, on 4th day to capture Rava–Russkaya; July 19 Germans encircled at Brody, eliminated July 22, 1st Guards Tank driving for river San, crossing into Polish territory, threat to German rear, July 24 Koniev orders 1st Guards to assist 3rd Guards Tank Army assaulting Przemysl, Katukov duly detached Gusakovskii's 11th Guards Tank Corps.

Kazakov, Artillery Marshal K.P., *Vsegda s pekhotoi, vsegda s tankami* (Moscow: Voenizdat 1969), ch. 5, Soviet artillery operations, Lublin–Brest offensive, left-flank formations 1st Belorussian Front.

Koniev, I.S., 'Zavershenie osvobozhdeniya sovetskoi Ukrainy i vykhod na Vislu', *VIZ*, 1964 (7), pp. 3–21 (Koniev's earlier personal account). Discussions with army/divisional commanders, summons to *Stavka* early June, Koniev's decision to mount two main blows (Rava–Russkaya/Lvov), Koniev and Krainyukov in Moscow with Stalin, Stalin's objections to Koniev's plan, Koniev in this version pays fulsome tribute to Khrushchev and his assistance, Koniev presents his own view of the battle for Lvov, impossibility of taking Lvov off the march, urgency of having Rybalko (3rd Guards Tank Army) break off fruitless action for Lvov, Koniev's request to the *Stavka* end July to set up independent field administration for forces driving on Carpathians, this assigned to I.E. Petrov with command of 1st Guards and 18th Army (forming 4th Ukrainian Front on 5 August 1944).

Koniev, I.S., *Zapiski komanduyushchevo frontom 1943–1944*, ch. 6, 'Lvovsko–Sandomirskaya operatsiya', pp. 223–64: *Stavka* fixed mid-July as date for 1st Ukrainian Front offensive, preparatory work Front/army commands, assessment of previous Front operations, Koniev's discussions with commanders (down to division), Moskalenko kept record of these discussions (see pp. 227–9), conversation with Stalin early June, operational aim to eliminate Army Group North Ukraine, initial plan for two blows on two axes, composition of assault forces (shock groups), mid-June conference with Stalin, Stalin's objections to two blows, cited experience of other fronts, Stalin finally yielded but told Koniev that he must assume responsibility; Front operational plan developed 7 July, submitted to *Stavka*, confirmed almost intact, two-echelon deployment for armies, Front deployed 7 tank and 3 mechanized corps, 4 independent tank brigades, 18 tank regiments, 24 SP-gun regiments, 90 per cent tank/SP gun strength committed on main attacks (to Lvov and Rava–Russkaya), air support from 2nd Air Army, German intelligence knew of direction of Soviet attacks also Soviet deployments, Koniev personally supervised preparations of Rybalko's *3 Guards Tank Army*, all forces ready by July 12; 1st Ukrainian Front operations—begun 12–13 July, 3rd Guards and 13th Army on Rava–Russkaya axis, forces W Bug and enters Polish territory 17 July, Lvov attack more difficult, 3rd Guards Tank Army committed 16 July, encirclement of 8 German divisions at Brody, advance continued on Koniev's right flank, Katukov's 1st Guards Tank Army ordered to swing SW, force river San and cut

German escape route to west, evening July 18 Koniev's special orders to 3rd Guards Tank and 4th Tank Army to outflank and capture Lvov (p. 255), Rybalko drives into peat-bogs, impossible to seize Lvov off the march with only one tank army, heavy fighting for Lvov 24–26 July, finally cleared 27 July. Army Group North Ukraine now split in two, *Stavka* orders to seize bridgehead south of Warsaw, operations to be co-ordinated with 1st Belorussian Front.

Krainyukov, Col.-Gen. K.V., *Oruzhie osobovo roda* (Moscow: Voenizdat (VM) 1977). See pt 3 under 'V Stavke', pp. 214–23: *Stavka* instructions for 1st Ukrainian Front offensive early June, Front operational plan prepared in draft, submitted to Front military soviet before transmission to *Stavka*, summoned by Stalin 23 July, questions double blow, asserts that Koniev stubborn in clinging to this plan but thinks it 'not a bad idea', Krainyukov asserts that Stalin would and did listen 'attentively and patiently' to the opinions of front-line commanders, General Staff alters 'unreal' rate of advance for infantry units, Stalin shows both a 'victory salute' fired off in Moscow—'not just fireworks' but a salute to heroism—Krainyukov visits Shcherbakov, Chief of Main Political Administration.

Krasovskii, Air Marshal S., '2-ya vozdushnaya armiya v Lvovsko–Sandomirskoi operatsii', *VIZ*, 1964 (7), pp. 31–41. 2nd Air Army operations, 1st Ukrainian Front.

Kurochkin, General P., 'Proryv oborony protivnika na L'vovskom napravlenii', *VIZ*, 1964 (7), pp. 22–30. Composition 60th Army (four corps), co-operation with 3rd Guards Tank Army, characteristics of breakthrough operations, danger presented by difficult situation of neighbour to the left (38th Army), morning 17 July 3rd Guards Tank committed followed by 4th Tank Army, operations in the 'Koltuv corridor', tank formations make for Lvov after deep penetration, conclusion of Brody encirclement.

Moskalenko, K.S., *Na yugo-zapradnom napravlenii*, 2, ch. 12, Lvov-Sandomierz operation, pp. 392–414: three corps operating with 38th Army (10 divisions), assignment to co-operate with 4th Tank and 60th Army in destroying enemy forces at Lvov, offensive timed for 2100 hours 13 July, shortcomings of artillery/ air opening bombardments, co-operation with armour (4th Tank Army), Maj.-Gen. A.A. Yepishev (member military soviet, 38th Army) wounded 22 July, operations to capture Lvov, concentric attacks by 4th Tank, 3rd Guards Tank, 38th and 60th Army.

Panov, Colonel B. and Anov, Lt.-Col. S., 'K voprosu o proryve na rava-russkom napravlenii', *VIZ*, 1970 (2), pp. 94–9. Detailed analysis of breakthrough operation, Rava–Russkaya (1st Ukrainian Front), making particular use of captured German documents (especially *Fourth Panzer Army* records) *held in the Soviet General Staff*.

Polushkin, Colonel M., 'Lvovsko–Sandomirskaya nastupatel'naya operatsiya 1-vo Ukrain-skovo fronta v tseifrakh (13.7–29.8.1944 g.)', *VIZ*, 1969 (8), pp. 54–67. Lvov–Sandomierz operation, statistics, list of commanders (to corps).

Polushkin, M. *Na sandomirskom napravlenii Lvovsko–Sandomirskaya operatsiya (iyul–avgust 1944 g.)* (Moscow: Voenizdat 1969). Detailed monograph, 1st Ukrainian Front operations: ch. 2, Front planning/operational decisions, Koniev's double attack plan (pp. 17–22), assignments to rifle armies (pp. 22–5), role of armoured/ mechanized forces (pp. 25–31), air support (pp. 35–9); ch. 3, operational narrative, first stage of operations (13–27 July), breakthrough operations (pp. 55–66), commitment of Front mobile forces (3rd Guards Tank and 4th Tank Army , Guards Tank committed with 2nd Air Army in support (pp. 66–72), Brody encirclement, advance on Lvov (pp. 72–80), right-flank offensive operations, advance to W Bug, bridgeheads secure by 24 July (pp. 80–87), assault on Lvov (pp. 87–104).

Rakitskii, Colonel A., 'Nastupatel'naya operatsiya 3-i gvardeiskoi armii (iyul 1944 g.)', *VIZ*, 1978 (9), pp. 70–78. Detailed operational narrative 3rd Guards Army, 1st Ukrainian Front (article in series 'little known operations'—*maloizvestnye operatsii*).

Vysotskii, F.I. *et al.*, *Gvardeiskaya tankovaya* (2nd Guards Tank Army), pp. 113–28, 2nd Guards Tank in Lublin–Brest operation, assigned Lublin-Warsaw axis operating as mobile group for left flank 1st Belorussian Front, forcing of W Bug (21 July), capture of Lublin 24 July, drive towards the Vistula; pp. 128–34, 2nd Guards, 27 July, first-echelon units pushing to Warsaw suburbs (Praga), 31 July approach to Praga but contact with elements of five German divisions, 2nd Guards Tank had already lost 500 tanks and SP guns, decision not to attack Praga.

Yushchuk, Maj.-Gen. I.I., *Odinnadtsatyi tankovyi korpus v boyakh za Rodinu* (Moscow: Voenizdat 1962), pt IV, pp. 64–92, from Kovel to the Vistula, 11th Tank Corps operations 1st Belorussian Front, operating with 8th Guards Army as 'mobile group' (corps strength 233 tanks and SP guns), to advance to W Bug, corps committed 19 July, force crossing of W Bug 20 July, tanks refuelled and re-armed, advance on Siedlce, counter-attacks by *SS Panzer*, 31 July final attack for Siedlce, 11th Tank Corps had covered average of 57 km per day after crossing W Bug.

Zukov, G.K., *Vospominaniya . . .*, 2, pp. 259–71, summoned by Stalin July 7, Stalin in very good humour, Molotov joins conversation, discussion of Hitler's prospects and his possible attempts to secure separate peace with Great Britain and USA, Stalin insists Churchill and Roosevelt will not do separate deal with Hitler, Stalin also argues that Germans will fight to the end in E Prussia, hence need to take Lvov and E Poland first, Zhukov to meet Bierut, Bulganin to be representative with the Poles, Zhukov to 1st Ukrainian Front July 11, Zhukov meanwhile argued that success in the Belorussian operation and along the 'Berlin axis' meant that the Red Army should strike without delay at E Prussia—'off the march'—with three Belorussian fronts, aim for E Prussia and the Vistula in the Gulf of Danzig (or at least cut off E Prussia from central Germany), Zhukov's draft 'E Prussia attack plan'—see pp. 264–6 for full text—submitted July 19, rejected by Stalin even though reserves were available, this 'a serious blunder by the Supreme Commander' in Zhukov's view, necessitating a complex costly operation later (see p. 266), discussion of 1st Ukrainian Front operation, Zhukov's criticism of poor planning, poor reconnaissance, ineffective artillery/air support, Zhukov cannot understand why these mistakes 'never mentioned' by historians, talk with Koniev July 22, Stalin insists on taking Lvov first followed by drive to Vistula—'it won't run away from you'—Khrushchev agreed with Stalin, capture of Lvov, drive to Sandomierz. (*Note*: Zhukov's 'E. Prussia attack plan', no. 316, 19 July, is not cited in the single-volume edition of his memoirs and is perforce missing from *The Memoirs of Marshal Zhukov*.)

P-τ
669

zwolenie Polski 1944–1945 (Warsaw: MON 1971), ch. 2—
⟨ 1 frontu Bialoruskiego i oddzialów ludowego Wojska Polskiego
⟨ding 1st Polish Army operations), pp. 32–53. On *1st Polish Army*
⟨s, July 1944, see also *Boevye deistviya narodnovo voiska pol'skovo 1943–1945*
⟨ns. from Polish, *Wybrane operacje i walki Ludowego Wojska Polskiego*), pp.
⟨-103.

'The Polish question':
diplomacy, politics and insurrection   pp. 247–274

It is an all too obvious point that there is a mass of material relevant to 'the Polish question' at large and the anguished circumstances of the Warsaw rising in particular. However, here I have confined myself largely to documentary collections/diplomatic records and to the limited range of Soviet expositions of policy towards Poland and the Warsaw rising. I did broach the latter aspect with Marshal Rokossovskii and received from him (as from other Soviet commanders) vehement denials that the Red Army deliberately and as part of a specific plan abandoned the Poles in Warsaw—not mere apologias but much detailed explanation with operational maps, tables, logistics records and signals traffic. In addition, emphasis was laid on Soviet battle casualties (1st Belorussian and 1st Ukrainian Fronts) for August–September—*166,808 and 122,578 killed and wounded respectively, a total of 289,386 men*. I was told that whatever interpretation I might place on the evidence, the figures were absolutely correct and in no way manipulated.

Alan Clark in *Barbarossa: The Russian–German Conflict 1941–1945* (London: Hutchinson 1965) tended also to the view that to speak of a deliberate decision is to attribute such a move (or the lack of it) to circumstances 'largely accidental'.

I must also record my deep appreciation for the opportunity to discuss select Polish records and materials with Professor Rozek, who could illuminate this documentation from his personal interviews.

Diplomatic correspondence, diplomatic documents
Correspondence: Stalin–Churchill–Roosevelt

Perepiska . . . , vol. 1, *Stalin–Churchill:* see No. 235, 1 Feb., Churchill–Stalin, British urging settlement on Poles, pp. 230–34; No. 236, 4 Feb., Stalin–Churchill, emphasizes frontier question, pp. 234–6; No. 243, 27 Feb., Churchill–Stalin, Polish government abandons Riga line, composition of Polish government, pp. 240–4; No. 249, March 3, Stalin–Churchill denounces London Polish government, p. 247; No. 250, March 7, Churchill–Stalin, dangers of rift over Polish question, pp. 247–8; No. 257, March 23, Stalin–Churchill, claim to Curzon line in accordance with Teheran meeting, pp. 253–5; No. 299, July 20, Churchill–Stalin, suggest Mikolajczyk visit, p. 286; No. 301, July 23, Stalin–Churchill, on Poland, setting up of National Council of Poland, plans for administration, pp. 287–8; Nos 305–6, July 27–28, Mikolajczyk visit to Moscow, pp. 292–3.

Perepiska . . . , vol. 2, *Stalin–Roosevelt:* No. 159, February 11, Roosevelt–Stalin, on Polish question, pp. 124–5; No. 171, Feb. 28, Roosevelt–Stalin, outline of tentative settlement, p. 133; No. 172; March 3, Stalin–Roosevelt, Polish government rejects

Curzon line, p. 133; No. 203, June 19, Roosevelt–Stalin, impressions of Mikolajczyk visit, pp. 153–5; No. 206, June 24, Stalin–Roosevelt, need for 'reconstruction' of London Polish government, pp. 155–6.

Documents on Polish–Soviet Relations 1939–1945. General Sikorski Historical Institute, vol. II: *1943–1945* (London: Heinemann 1967). Doc. No. 68, Polish *aide-mémoire*, 30 Dec. 1943, on conditions for Soviet–Polish collaboration, pp. 121–2; No. 69, Sir Owen O'Malley to Mikolajczyk, 3 Jan. 1944, pp. 122–3; No. 71, Romer–Eden talk on co-operation of Polish Underground with Soviet troops, Jan. 6, pp. 125–7; No. 72, Mikolajczyk broadcast to Poland, Jan. 6, pp. 127–8; No. 73, Mikolajczyk–Beneš talk, Jan. 10, pp. 129–32; No. 74, Soviet statement on Soviet–Polish frontier, Jan. 11, pp. 132–4 (proposed Polish reply, pp. 134–6, Eden–Mikolajczyk), Polish reply, Jan. 14, pp. 138–9; No. 79, Raczynski to FO on situation in Poland/ entry of Soviet troops, Jan. 16, pp. 140–42; No. 83, Churchill–Mikolajczk–Eden, possible revision of Treaty of Riga, Jan. 20, pp. 144–9; No. 85, Raczynski to Eden four questions about British guarantee of Polish independence, Jan. 23, pp. 150–51; No. 87, Mikolajczyk on British proposal for new Polish frontier/Curzon line, Jan. 25–26, pp. 153–5; No. 93, Churchill to Stalin, frontier problem, Feb. 1, pp. 160–62, and Stalin to Churchill, Feb. 4, pp. 163–4; No. 96, Churchill–Mikolajczyk talk, eventuality of Polish rejection of Soviet terms, Feb. 6, pp. 166–71; No. 97, Roosevelt to Stalin, Feb. 7, pp. 171–2; No. 99, draft message, Churchill to Stalin changes in Polish government, Feb. 12, pp. 173–6; No. 103, Churchill–Mikolajczyk on reply to Soviet demands, Feb. 16, pp. 180–7; No. 107, Churchill to Stalin on frontiers, Feb. 20, pp. 191–3; No. 113, Churchill to Stalin, March 7, pp. 199–200; No. 117, Mikolajczyk to Roosevelt, March 18, pp. 207–11; Nos 118–19, Churchill to Stalin, March 21, Stalin to Churchill, March 23, pp. 212–14; No. 123, Raczynski–Eden, 'Volhynia division' agreement, April 7, pp. 218–20; No. 124, Mikolajczyk–Churchill and Stettinius–Winant: behaviour of Soviet troops, April 9, pp.220–24; No. 130, Romer–Stettinius, need for US co-operation, April 30, pp. 229–33; No. 132, Stalin–Professor Lange–Molotov, territory/future of Poland, May 17, pp. 235–40; No. 136, Churchill–Mikolajczyk–Eden–Romer, Polish governmental changes, May 31, pp. 243–6; No. 143, Ciechanowski note on Mikolajczyk–Lange talks, June 13, pp. 258–63; No. 144, conversation, Planning Group (OSS) supplies for AK, June 13, pp. 263–6; No. 145, Mikolajczyk farewell visit to Roosevelt, June 14, pp. 266–8; No. 152, Mikolajczyk–Raczkiewicz–Sosnkowski conference, instructions to AK during 'Tempest', July 6, pp. 274–6; No. 155, Romer–Eden on Mikolajczyk's visit to Moscow, July 11, pp. 279–80; No. 161, Mikolajczyk–Churchill, request for British Liaison Mission to Poland, July 18, pp. 288–90; No. 171,Churchill–Stalin, proposing Mikolajczyk visit to Moscow, July 27, pp. 301–2.

Diplomatic histories

Israelyan, V.L., *Diplomaticheskaya istoriya VOV*, ch. IV (6), 'Polski vopros v 1944 godu . . .', a general review reiterating the Soviet position, also emphasizing the reactionary attitudes and policies of the London Polish government, pp. 215–24.

Rozek, Edward J., *Allied Wartime Diplomacy. A Pattern in Poland*, ch. 6, 'The Soviets transform the Lublin Committee into the Provisional Government of Poland

. . .', detailed discussion with extensive documentation (plus personal interview material) on Polish problem, January–21 July 1944, pp. 183–235.

Woodward, Sir Llewellyn, *British Foreign Policy in the Second World War* (London: HMSO 1962, single volume), ch. XII, question of Soviet–Polish frontier, Soviet attitude to London Polish government and Polish Underground, British attempts to persuade Polish government to accept Soviet demands (to December 1943) (pp. 249–55); ch. XIV, Anglo–Russian relations to September 1944, further British attempts to secure settlement of Soviet–Polish frontier dispute, Churchill to Stalin January 28 and February 21, Soviet allegations against Polish underground (pp. 278–85); Stalin's refusal to accept settlement, Mikolajczyk to United States, secret Soviet–Polish talks in London, Soviet demands increase (to June 1944) (pp. 285–90).

Woodward, Sir L., *British Foreign Policy in the Second World War* (London: HMSO 1971, multi-volume series). See vol. II (1971), Ch. XXXV (vi), on British attempts to secure Soviet–Polish understanding, Polish *aide-mémoire* 30 Dec. 1943, pp. 652–7. See also additional note 'The Curzon Line', pp. 657–62. See vol. III (1971), ch. XXXIV (1) Polish and Soviet statements, January 1944 (pp. 154–60); (11) British attempts to secure settlement, Churchill to Stalin 28 January 1944, Stalin's reply Feb. 2, discussions with Polish ministers 6–20 February 1944 (pp. 161–74); (111) Churchill to Stalin Feb. 21, Stalin's rejection of proposals, Stalin's letter March 23 (pp. 174–83); (IV) draft reply to Stalin, War Cabinet decision to delay reply, discussions over replacement of General Sosnkowski, Soviet progress in building up Polish Army in USSR, Grabski–Lebedev meetings in London, Mikolajczyk to Washington (pp. 174–91); (V) Polish–Soviet talks in London collapse, proposal for Mikolajczyk to visit Moscow, Foreign Office view that Roosevelt dangerously vague and optimistic, Churchill emphasizes that Poles must give up Vilna and Lvov, further exchanges with Stalin, Polish ministers to Moscow (June–August 1944) (pp. 191–202).

Select Polish materials

Jurgeliewicz, W., *Organizacja Ludowego Wojska Polskiego* (22.7. 1944–9.5.1945) (Warsaw: MON 1968), pt 1, ch. 2: 'political circumstances' and creation of the Polish Army (in USSR: AP w ZSRR), merger with *Armia Ludowa (AL)*, pp. 41–61.

Margules, J. (ed.), *Z. zagadnień rozwoju Ludowego Wojska Polskiego* (Warsaw: MON 1964). See F. Zbiniewicz, 'Z zagadnień politycznych Armii Polskiej w ZSRR', *KRN* delegation to Polish Army in USSR, proposals for merger with *AL*, material from archives and contemporary press (e.g. *Wolna Polska*), pp. 7–32.

Przygoński, A., *Z zagadnień strategii frontu narodowego PRR*, pp. 278–96, delegation of *KRN* to Moscow 16 May, visit to Polish military units in Ukraine, creation of Provisional Government, exchanges with Stalin, acceptance of Curzon line for frontier, establishment of *Polski Komitet Wyzwolenia Narodowego (PKWN)*. (Przygonski draws extensively on Polish Party archives, much unpublished material.)

Rawski, T., *et al.*, *Wojna wyzwoleńcza narodu polskiego w latach 1939–1945* (Warsaw: MON 1966), section IV, pp. 555–65, position of Polish Army in USSR, proposals of KRN to fuse AL with Polish Army; organization, command appointments.

Wojewódzki, M., *Akcja V-1, V-2* (Warsaw: PAX, 2nd edn 1972). Polish underground/ intelligence and detection of V-1/V-2 weapons, German 'flying-bomb'/ballistic missile: *(Vergeltungswaffen)*.

The Warsaw Rising and the Red Army

Churchill, Winston S., *The Second World War*, Vol. 6: *Triumph and Tragedy*. See ch. IX, 'The Martyrdom of Warsaw', heavily documented, indispensable, pp. 116–29.

Lukas, Richard C., *Eagles East. The Army Air Forces and the Soviet Union, 1941–1945* (Florida State UP, Tallahassee, 1970), ch. XIII, (B), 'The AAF and the Warsaw Uprising', on attempts to fly in supplies to Warsaw, American and British diplomatic pressures, Soviet obstruction, pp. 201–7.

Reitlinger, Gerald, *The SS. Alibi of a Nation 1922–1945*, London, Heinemann, 1956. Ch. 13(3), on Erich von dem Bach-Zelewski, Dirlewanger penal brigade, SS Kaminski Brigade, Himmler's Posen speech (Aug. 3) praising Kaminski and Dirlewanger, Fegelein reports Kaminski atrocities, death of Kaminski, pp. 372–7.

Diplomatic histories/diplomatic documents

Woodward, Sir Llewellyn, *British Foreign Policy in the Second World War* (1962, single volume), pp. 301–6. Soviet refusal to assist Poles, Mikolajczyk request to Stalin, Churchill–Stalin (Aug. 4), Stalin on Polish 'exaggeration', Mikolajczyk plea to Stalin (Aug. 9), Stalin's promise but no aid forthcoming, Anglo-American pressure, problems of air-lift, final Soviet 'climb-down' but also denunciation of 'Warsaw adventure'.

Woodward, Sir L., *British Foreign Policy in the Second World War*, vol. III, ch. XXXIX(VI), the Polish rising in Warsaw, rising *not* an unplanned outbreak, British Chiefs of Staff emphasized need for agreement and co-operation with Russians, Moscow broadcast *July 29* calling for 'direct, active struggle' in Warsaw, Stalin's view that rising premature (pp. 202–4); Stalin–Churchill Aug. 5, lack of armament in *AK*, German check to Soviet advance on Warsaw (German claim Aug. 6), Eden on lack of information about rising, Stalin promises Mikolajczyk help (Aug. 9), Kalugin's message passed to Stalin (Aug. 5), Polish appeal to Churchill and Roosevelt, little chance of favourable Soviet response, Clark Kerr and Harriman see Vyshinskii who denounced rising, Clark Kerr and Harriman see Molotov (Aug. 17), Stalin–Churchill (Aug. 17) dissociating Soviet command from 'Warsaw adventure', Eden–Gusev talk with Gusev also disclaiming responsibility (Aug. 18), joint Churchill–Roosevelt message to Stalin (Aug. 20), Stalin reply (Aug. 22) again denouncing Warsaw rising, problem of air lift to Poland and Soviet bases (pp. 204–12); difficulties of air lift, impossibility of sending expedition, Mikolajczyk amends programme for reconstituted Polish Government, problem of the frontiers (pp. 212–15); possibility of 'gate-crashing' on Soviet airfields, Mikolajczyk threatens resignation, Sosnkowki's assertions that no help from Russia and only inadequate help from the West (pp. 215–17). Chapter XL: Soviet 'climb-down' (Sept. 9), agreement to drop supplies on Warsaw, discussions about 'shuttle service' of aircraft, Polish Army under Berling forces Vistula but obliged to withdraw, Eden intimates that Sosnkowski must be dismissed, Bor-Komorowski to replace him, situation in Warsaw desperate, Soviet refusal for further US air operation, Polish surrender in Warsaw (5 am, Oct. 4), Mikolajczyk once again invited to Moscow (pp. 218–23).

Documents on Polish–Soviet Relations 1939–1945, vol. 2, on the Warsaw rising: No. 173, Sir Orme Sargent-Raczynski, impossible to send Parachute Brigade or fighter squadrons to Poland, July 28, pp. 303–4; No. 175, Stalin–Churchill, émigré government alienated from democratic trends, July 28, p. 305; No. 177, Mikolajczyk–Molotov, demand for agreement between London government and Polish Committee of National Liberation, July 31, pp. 306–8; No. 180, Mikolajczyk–Stalin, on Polish frontiers and future, Aug. 3, pp. 309–22; No. 182, Churchill–Stalin, appeal for aid to Warsaw, Aug. 4, p. 323; No. 183, Stalin–Churchill, disparaging Polish rising, Aug. 5, p. 324; No. 186, Mikolajczyk–Bierut–Molotov on working to agreement with Committee of National Liberation, Aug. 8, pp. 325–33; No. 187, Stalin–Churchill, report on Mikolajczyk, Aug. 8, p. 333; No. 188, General Chruściel to Rokossovskii, requesting aid, Capt. Kalugin, in Warsaw, Aug. 8, p. 334; No. 189, Stalin–Mikolajczyk, further attempts at Polish understanding, Aug. 9, pp. 334–9; No. 192, TASS on responsibility of 'London Poles' for rising, pp. 340–41; No. 193, Churchill–Stalin, urgent plea for Soviet help, Aug. 12, p. 341; No. 194, Mikolajczyk–Stalin, pleading for air support, parachuted supplies, Aug. 13, p. 342; No. 198, Stalin–Mikolajczyk, rising 'a reckless adventure', cannot assume responsibility for 'Warsaw affair', Aug. 16, pp. 346–7; No. 201, Mikolajczyk–Stalin, request for US aircraft to use Soviet bases, Aug. 18, pp. 351–2; No. 203, Churchill and Roosevelt to Stalin, plea for aid to Warsaw, Aug. 20, p. 353; No. 204, Mikolajczyk–Eden *et al.*, ineffectiveness of Anglo–American intervention, Aug. 21, pp. 354–6; No. 205, Stalin message, mentions new large Soviet offensive, Aug. 22, p. 356; No. 232, Churchill–Mikolajczyk *et al.*, developments in Warsaw, dismissal of Sosnkowski as C-in-C, Sept. 29, pp. 395–8; No. 234, Churchill–Mikolajczyk, air-lift to be discontinued unless Soviet bases arranged, Oct. 7, p. 399.

Select Soviet materials

IVOVSS, 4, ch. 8(1), on the politics of the *Krajowa Rada Narodowa (KRN)*, planning for *Burza* ('Tempest'), quotations from Bor-Komorowski, *The Secret Army*, supplementary secret plan for struggle by *AK* against Red Army forces on Polish soil (pp. 228–37); (2) decision for rising by *AK* taken 24 July, aim to establish Polish 'political and administrative authority' before arrival of Soviet troops, Mikolajczyk in Moscow demands 80 per cent of seats for the *émigré* government in any future government and also affirmation of the 'Fascist constitution' of 1935, the rising badly planned and prepared—only 16 heavy mortars, 47 machineguns, 2,629 rifles, 44,000 grenades, ammunition for only two/three days—only 40 per cent of *AK* committed at beginning of rising, heavy losses due to lack of experience and supporting weapons, Soviet denunciation of this 'adventure', Soviet troops checked before Warsaw, urgent need to redeploy Soviet aircraft to forward bases, heavy losses (500 tanks) in 2nd Tank Army, Soviet offensive operation (47th Army, 1st Belorussian Front) captures Praga, 3rd Polish Infantry Division assault crossing of Vistula, 16–19 Sept. six battalions of 3rd and 2nd Polish Infantry

Divisions in action, pulled back 23 Sept. to easte
drops (p. 246), *Monter* (General Chruściel, comman
refuses to discuss the co-ordination of *AK* operations w
command finally suggests *AK* breaking out to the Vistu.
air and artillery support, this refused, final Polish capitulati

IVMV, 9, pp. 70–2, Warsaw rising, plans not disclosed to Sov.
command, Bor-Komorowski counted on panic in German forc   .ich
of Red Army, inferior armament of insurgents, Stalin's instructions   .tov for
forcing Vistula with Berling's Polish troops, repulse of Polish troops, Soviet air-
drops over Warsaw.

Collective authorship, *16-ya vozdushnaya* (16th Air Army). See pp. 204–37, aid to
Warsaw, air cover for Soviet bridgeheads, air combat over Warsaw, co-operation
with 1st Aviation Division (Polish armed forces), logistics problems, 2 *AK* emissaries
to Soviet command (Sept. 17), Soviet air-drops (figures of supplies, p. 223), 16th
Air total of 13,034 sorties in September, air support for Soviet ground operations.

Radzievskii, General A., 'Na puti k Varshave', *VIZ*, 1971 (10), pp. 68–77. Operations
of 2nd Tank Army, Brest–Lublin, July 1944: Radzievskii, Chief of Staff 2nd
Tank Army, assumed command from Bogdanov wounded.

Rokossovskii, K.K., *A Soldier's Duty*, pp. 254–63. Under 'Warsaw', no information
about rising, 48th and 65th Armies still 100km E and NE Warsaw, 2nd Tank
Army bogged down, no contact with *AK* insurgents, internal disputes among
insurgents followed by appeal to Soviet command, Flying Fortress supply-drop
largely useless, no *AK* attempt to capture bridges over Vistula, further Soviet attack
towards Narew, German attempts to destroy Soviet bridgeheads on Vistula and
Narew, Soviet troops take Praga (this the point at which rising should have begun),
in report to Stalin Rokossovskii emphasizes that offensive impossible, Soviet air
drops (4,821 sorties, 2,535 to drop supplies), 1st Polish Army's assault crossing
of Vistula (Sept. 16), withdrawn (Sept. 23).

Shtemenko, General S.M., *General'nyi shtab v gody voiny* (Bk 2) (Moscow: Voenizdat
(VM) 1973), pp. 78–104, on the Warsaw axis, initial Soviet optimism about
success near Warsaw, Rokossovskii and Zhukov fear powerful German blow at
left flank 1 BF, no information on rising available to Soviet command or Soviet
government, Rokossovskii received no reply to telegram to Bor-Komorowski,
Churchill to Stalin, Stalin orders Zhukov, Rokossovskii and General Staff to report
(Aug. 6: partial text, impossible to attack off the march, p. 87), draft operational
plan (pp. 88–9)—impossible to launch full offensive before Aug. 25—Stalin–
Mikolajczyk exchange, Stalin's disclaimers to Churchill, 47th Army offensive Sept.
10 followed by 1st Polish Army, assault on Praga, Polish Army assault crossing
of Vistula, General Staff sets up signals link with Bor-Komorowski, arrangements
to drop supplies, 20 Sept. 7 *AK* officers contact Red Army, one officer reports
that Bor-Komorowski issued secret orders to 'forcefully restrain' those insurgents
associated with the Lublin government, Polish Army bridgehead in serious state,
Stalin's agreement to put Polish army on defensive on Vistula *eastern* bank. (Highly
personalized account, stressing Soviet plans to relieve Warsaw, some material from
Rokossovskii memoirs.)

References and Sources

Select Polish materials

…omorowski, T., *The Secret Army* (London: Gollancz 1950), 407 pp., *passim*. On the Polish 'Home Army' *(AK)*, the Underground and the Warsaw rising.

Garlinski, J., *Poland, SOE and the Allies* (London: Allen & Unwin, 1969), pt IV, 'Into the Abyss', pp. 167–206, decision to launch rising, Polish efforts to secure Western aid, Soviet attitude, airlift problems, belated Soviet agreement. (Very critical of Polish planning in general and of Sosnkowski in particular; nor did the political situation justify improvisation.)

Bibliography

See *Polski czyn zbrojny w II wojnie światowej. Bibliografia wojny wyzwoleńczej narodu polskiego 1939–1945* (Warsaw: MON 1973), vol. VI, pt V, 'Ruch oporu', section 8, 'Powstanie warszawskie', with seven sub-sections dealing with general aspects, the insurrection itself, Allied aid/air drops, insurgent armament, conditions, German atrocities (pp. 646–79). (See also pt V, section 2, 'Armia Krajowa', including *Burza* ('Tempest'), pp. 509–51.)

Bartelski, L.M., *Mokotów 1944* (Warsaw: MON 1972) (English summary, pp. 701–2).

Karpinski, A., *Pod Dęblinem, Pulawy i Warka* (Warsaw: MON 1967) (1st Polish Army operations, Dęblin, Pulawy and Magnuszew area, 18.7–12.9.44). See ch. II, situation on the 'Warsaw axis', 18.7–15.9 (pp. 18–56); also ch. III, 1st Army (Polish) operations, Dęblin, Pulawy, 28.7–4.8 (pp. 60–80), assault crossing of the Vistula (pp. 80–121), operations in Magnuszew area (1st Tank Brigade), assault crossing of Vistula (pp. 199–232).

Kowalski, W.T., *Wielka Koalicja 1941–1945*. Vol. 2: *Rok 1944*. See ch. IV, ' "Bagration" and the Polish question', course of the Soviet offensive, Red Army–*AK* relations, draft Operation *Burza* and the hallucinations of a general-philosopher—*'Plan "Burza" i majaczenia general-filozofa'* (pp. 252–4)—SOE and Poland, Mikolajczyk in Moscow, struggle to help Warsaw rising, Praga operation, Stalin's assessments, Churchill's manoeuvres, pp. 219–324.

Margules, J., *Boje 1 Armii WP w obszarze Warszawy (sierpień-wrzesień 1944)* (Warsaw: MON 1967), *passim*. A massive monograph devoted to 1st Polish Army operations in context of Warsaw rising, with five appendices on military operations (pp. 315–27) and three documentary appendices (Polish—1st Polish Army documents, *AK* documents—Soviet documents and German documents, pp. 331–522): on the mystery surrounding Captain Kalugin, see pp. 238–9, with Przyoński's assertion that *Kalugin* was not a 'representative of the Soviet 1st Belorussian Front' but a PW who had joined the Vlasov forces; Soviet sources remain silent on Kalugin. Also 'Monter's' attempts to send emissaries to the Soviet command, pp. 239–41.

Rawski, T. *et al.*, *Wojna wyzwoleńcza . . . 1939–1945*, pt V, Ch. XXX, 'Powstanie warszawskie', decision for rising, Polish plans, German plans, opposing strengths, first phase, defensive fighting in western sectors, German counter-blows, attacks along Vistula bank, capitulation, pp. 566–92. (Narrative and analysis based on memoirs, WIH—Wojskowy Instytut Historyczny—archives also citing H.v.Krannhals, *Der Warschauer Aufstand 1944*, Frankfurt, 1962.)

Sęk-Malecki, J., *Armia Ludowa w powstaniu warszawskim. Wspomnienia* (Warsaw: Iskry 1962). Under 'Powstanie', pp. 61ff., see footnote to p. 100 on *Captain Kalugin*, with reference (pp. 102–3) on article by Captain Ryszard Nazarewics (printed in *Rzeczpospolita,* Nr 217, 1946) to the effect that Kalugin had been in Poland since Dec. 1943 and was, in fact, an officer of the Vlasov army (ROA).

The Dukla–Carpathians operation and the Slovak rising pp. 290–307

Táborsky, E., 'Beneš and Stalin—Moscow, 1943 and 1945', *Journal Central European Affairs,* XIII, July 1953, No. 2, pp. 169–70, on Red Army entry on to Czechoslovak territory. C-in-C of puppet Slovak Army, General Catloš proposed secret deal with Stalin for 'Slovak political matters' to be 'solved in accordance with the interests of the USSR', Colonel Pika informed secretly, protest by Beneš.

Soviet materials

IVOVSS, 4, pt 2, pp. 313–32, beginning of Slovak rising, Soviet push into eastern Carpathians, course of Slovak rising and partisan operations (October–November 1944).

IVMV, 9, pt 1, pp. 154–70, Slovak rising, Soviet operations in eastern Carpathians.

Collective authorship (joint Soviet–Czechoslovak work), *Na vechnye vremena. Na věčné časy* (Moscow: Voenizdat 1975), pp. 135–56, on the Slovak rising (utilizing largely Husak's account, documentary collections and some archival material—*Vojenský historický archiv*/VNA).

Grachev, Colonel S.I. (ed.), *Rozhdenie chekhoslovatskoi narodnoi armii.* See O. Janaček, 'Sozdanie naterritorii SSSR 1-vo chekhoslovatskovo armeiskovo korpusa' (also 'reactionary plans' of 'Czechkslovak émigré government' to form 'bourgeois army' in Slovakia), pp. 198–241. Also 'frustration of plans of Czechoslovak émigré government to wind up 1st Czechoslovak Army Corps', pp. 242–73. (Cf. Shtemenko's account of the Slovak rising.)

Grechko, Marshal SU A.A., *Cherez Karpaty* (Moscow: Voenizdat 1970), pp. 78–239. Combined memoir-monograph (Grechko commanded 1st Guards Army), Soviet operations in Carpathians: operations 1st Guards Army, 18th Army, 4th Ukrainian Front; 38th Army, 1st Ukrainian Front, Sept.–Oct. 1944. Extensive use of Soviet military archives.

Grylev, Maj.-Gen. A. and Vyrodov, Colonel I., 'Vernost internatsional' nomu dolgu', *VIZ,* 1968 (10), pp. 44–57. Soviet assistance to Slovak partisans, Soviet aid for Slovak rising (account based largely on Soviet archival materials).

Koniev, I.S. (ed.), *Za osvobozhdenie Chekhoslovakii* (Moscow: Voenizdat 1965) (a collective work, with contributions/advice from senior Soviet commanders—M.V. Zakharov, Moskalenko, Lelyushenko, Sandalov, A.N. Asmolov and others). See pp. 104–9, aid to Slovak rising, advance into eastern Slovakia: beginning of Slovak rising, Golian's agreement with London, partisan organization, threat of German occupation, Colonel A.N. Asmolov sent into Slovakia by Ukrainian partisans, German attacks on Slovak insurgents, capture of Banska Bystrica, Viest abandons further resistance, Golian and Viest made prisoner ultimately shot, results of Soviet campaign.

Note: A singular feature of this study is the regular record of *Soviet casualties.* For 1st and 4th Ukrainian Fronts: 21,000 killed, 89,000 wounded (losses for 1st Ukrainian Front being 11,550 killed, 47,200 wounded); 1st Czechoslovak Corps: 844 killed, 4,068 wounded. (See p. 108.) *IVOVSS,* 4, p. 324, gives the figure of

6,500 for total casualties in 1st Czechoslovak Corps, while the detailed article in *VIZ*, 1968 (10), p. 52 (note 42) repeats the figures in *Za osvobozhdenie Chekhoslovakii*.

Moskalenko, K., 'O Karpatsko–Duklinskoi operatsii', *VIZ*, 1965 (7), pp. 16–23. To demonstrate that this was a Front operation, not merely an army operation involving only 38th Army.

Moskalenko, K., *Na yugo-zapadnom napravlenii*, vol. 2, ch. 13, 'V glub Karpat', Sept. 2 Koniev orders 38th Army for Carpathian operation to assist Slovak insurgents, establishment of 4th Ukrainian Front (1st Guards Army, 18th Army, 8th Air Army), Koniev's report to Stalin who demanded speedy breakthrough to insurgents (pp. 432–3), preparations/deployment 38th Army, German movement into Slovakia and attempt to build new front in S Carpathians, tragedy of East Slovak Corps, promotion of Svoboda, difficulties in 38th Army operations, pp. 428–62. Ch. 14, advance through Dukla pass, 38th Army operations in detail, pp. 463–90.

Nedorov, A.I., *Natsional'no-osvoboditel'noe dvizhenie v Chekhoslovakii 1938–1945* (Moscow: Sots–Ekon. Lit. 1961). See pp. 254–92, on Slovak rising 1944, on partisan organization and Soviet assistance, German military moves, Soviet advance into Carpathians, political aspects of the rising. (Based on memoirs/accounts by Communist leadership, extensive use of Czechoslovak military archives.)

Proektor, Colonel A.M., *Cherez duklinskii pereval* (Moscow: Voenizdat 1960). (Monograph on Carpathian–Dukla operations Sept.–Nov. 1944.) See ch. 2, on planning of Soviet offensive, 38th Army preparations, pp. 39–78; ch. 3, operations 8–14 Sept., pp. 80–115; ch. 4, second stage 15–25 Sept., pp. 116–51.

Shtemenko, S.M., *General'nyi shtab* . . . , bk 2, pp. 318–46, Shtemenko and General A.A. Gryzlov ordered by Stalin to work on plan to assist Slovak rising, difficulties in idea of dropping two Soviet divisions (only 170 transports available, would mean five/six trips), Antonov accepts idea of Slovakia becoming major *partisan* operational area, 53 Soviet 'organizational groups' for partisan warfare infiltrated into Slovakia, on Čatloš and Golian (pp. 327–9), unreal planning for rising, Stalin–Koniev (Sept. 1–2) on rising and Red Army operations, draft directive to Koniev (1st Ukrainian Front), Slovak Army divisions disarmed by Germans, heavier resistance to 38th Army, Baranov's 1st Guards Cavalry Corps cut off (Sept. 14), Czechoslovak units in storming of Dukla pass Oct. 6, Czech government in London proposes dissolution of 1st Czechoslovak Corps, Stalin–Koniev on reinforcement for 1st Corps, Svoboda's quest for volunteers to replenish Corps. (Some interesting material on Soviet planning but no documentation.)

Kožnar, Lt.-Col. V. (ed.), *Dukla v dokumentech* (Prague: Naše vojsko 1970). Collection of photostats of operational orders/materials/awards Dukla operation, 246 pp.

Svoboda, General Ludvik, *Z Buzuluku do Prahy* (Prague, 1967). Soviet translation (2nd edn), Moscow: Voenizdat 1969. See under 'Korpus', (3), Slovak rising, pp. 267–75, (4) briefing from Marshal Koniev, co-operation between 38th Army and Czechoslovak Corps, pp. 275–8, (6) launching of Dukla–Carpathian Sept. 8, pp. 281–95.

Soviet operations in the Baltic states pp. 307–326

OKH Kriegsgesch. Abt. (Maps): Die Einkesselung der Hgr. Nord (10.7–14.8.44); Schlacht um Tuckum (15.8–27.8); Schlacht um Estland u. Absetzen Hgr. Nord

(14.8–28.9.44). T-78/R136, 6065135–73, 6065175–86 and 6065187–206.

IVOVSS, 4, pt 2, pp. 348–53, Soviet advance towards Riga, final stage of operations beg. Sept. 14, success of right-flank 'shock group' of 1st Baltic Front, threat to Army Group North, German counter-blows (Sept. 16–22), 3rd Baltic Front operations, 2nd Baltic Front thrust towards Riga, Leningrad Front drive into Estonia, operations of 8th Estonian Rifle Corps (see L.A. Pern), failure to isolate Army Group North completely, due to lack of power in initial attacks of 2nd and 3rd Baltic Fronts, German concentration in Riga area, revised Soviet planning for fresh attack.

IVMV, 9, pt 1, pp. 139–48, Soviet operations, Baltic states, breakthrough on Tallin and Riga axes, severing of communications between Army Group North and East Prussia.

Altukhov, P.K. *et al., Nezabyvaemye dorogi. Boevoi put 10-i gvardeiskoi armii* (Moscow: Voenizdat 1974). See pp. 156–96, 10th Guards Army and drive on Riga.

Bagramyan, Marshal SU I.Kh., 'Shaulyaisko–Mitavskaya operatsiya voisk 1-vo Pribaltiiskovo fronta', *VIZ*, 1962 (10), pp. 3–23. Bagramyan's highly personalized account, Shauliya operation.

Bagramyan, I.Kh., *Kak shli my k pobede*, pp. 339–418, early July consideration of further operations (drive on Riga–Shaulyai), liberation of Polotsk (July 4), Vasilevskii proposes drive on Kaunas and Shaulyai to cut Army Group North escape route to NE frontier of E Prussia, Kaunas fixed as prime objective, July 11 orders to Front armies, problems of co-ordination with Yeremenko/2nd Baltic Front, fall of Shaulyai and Daugavpils—'our road to the sea open!'—Vasilevskii assumes operational direction, German concentration in the Riga area, *Stavka* plans for 4-front offensive (1st, 2nd, 3rd Baltic and Leningrad Fronts) to destroy Army Group North.

Collective authorship, *Bor'ba za Sovetskuyu Pribaltiku v Velikoi Otechest. voine 1941–1945* (Riga: Liesma 1967), vol. 2 (this is a 3-vol. series), ch. 2, operational narrative, 3rd Belorussian Front offensive, Vilna–Kaunas, 5–31 July, pp. 39–60 (note on heavy Soviet losses, p. 60—11 Guards Army battalions reduced to two-company strength, in some regiments battalions with only one company); 1st Baltic Front offensive, operational narrative, 5–31 July, breakthrough to Gulf of Riga, cut communications of German Army Group North with East Prussia, pp. 60–73.

Collective authorship, *Rizhskie Gvardeiskie*. Sbornik voenno-istoricheskikh ocherkov (Riga: Liesma 1972). Detailed memoir-monograph studies, 52nd Guards, 30th Guards, 85th Guards, 43rd Guards, 22nd Guards, 65th Guards Rifle Divisions ('Riga' divisions), 315th 'Riga' Fighter Aviation Div.

Kazakov, General M., 'V boyakh za sovetskuyu Pribaltiku', *VIZ*, 1967 (2), pp. 62–75: Soviet attack towards Riga, *Stavka* planning, operations of 2nd Baltic Front, Govorov's co-ordinating role.

Krasnov, V.I. *et al., Gimn ratnym podvigam* (Moscow: Mosk. Rabochii 1966), under 'Vyshli na granitsu', pp. 128–34, Zakabluk's unit on the frontier line with E Prussia, Frontier Marker No. 56; Zakabluk himself was to receive Hero of the Soviet Union decoration but was killed in action three days later.

Pern, Lt.-Gen. L.A., *V vikhre voennykh let* (Tallin: Eesti Raamat 1976), pp. 172–210. Operations of Estonian Rifle Corps (operating with 2nd Shock Army), Sept. 1944. (Previous edition: Tallin, 1969.)

Portnov, Maj.-Gen. S.I. (ed.), *V srazheniyakh za Sovetskuyu Latviyu* (Riga: Liesma 1975), pp. 29–120, operations in Soviet Latvia, July–Aug. 1944. Extremely detailed operational narrative based almost exclusively on Soviet military archives. Note also one of contributing authors, Admiral of the Fleet S.G. Gorshkov.

Sandalov, Col.-Gen. L., 'Osvobozhdenie Sovetskoi Pribaltiki', *VIZ*, 1969 (10), pp. 14–26. Sandalov Chief of Staff, 2nd Baltic Front, detailed operational narrative, drive on Riga, Tallin.

Vasilevskii, A.M., *Delo vsei zhizni* (2nd edn), pp. 471–84. See 'Bor'ba za Pribaltiku', *Stavka* directive (July 29) to co-ordinate and direct operations of 1st, 2nd Baltic and 3rd Belorussian Fronts (p. 475), *Stavka* order to eliminate shortcomings in command/control—breakdown in communications, poor movement control—*Stavka*'s direct criticism of 2nd Baltic Front operational order of July 6 (p. 479), *Stavka* criticism of other Front commands (excerpts—1st Ukrainian Front, Leningrad Front, 4th Ukrainian Front, further signals to Belorussian and 1st Ukrainian Front, end Dec. 1944 to 2nd Ukrainian Front—Vasilevskii admits 'running ahead of myself'—pp. 480–83), Baltic offensive involved *four* Front operations, Vasilevskii's main attention fixed on 1st Baltic Front, fresh Soviet general offensive timed for Sept. 14, each army 1st Baltic given specific operational axis and 'tank-mechanized fist' built up—'the Riga express'.

Yeremenko, Marshal SU A.I., *Gody vozmezdiya 1943–1945* (Moscow: Nauka 1969), ch. 9, Yeremenko's 2nd Baltic Front operations opening 21 July, Rezekne–Daugavpils, pp. 341–90; ch. 10, Front directive July 29 (pp. 394–6), heavy fighting Luban–Madona–Gulbene triangle, capture of Krustpils (Aug. 8), investment of Luban plain and crossing of river Aidikste placed Front in position to close on Riga, pp. 393–436.

Finland leaves the war   pp. 327–330

Seaton, Albert, *The Russo–German War*, pp. 460–66, on Finland leaving the war, military and diplomatic analysis—an excellent, incisive and comprehensive account, utilizing: Marshal Mannerheim's *Memoirs*; W. Erfurth, *Der finnische Krieg 1941–1944* (Wiesbaden, 1950); L. Rendulic, *Gekämpft, Gesiegt, Geschlagen* (Munich, 1957); and Soviet materials.

Warner, Oliver, *Marshal Mannerheim and the Finns* (London: Weidenfeld, 1967), pp. 195–204, the continuation war, Jodl–Mannerheim Oct. 1943, Kollontai messages, German riposte, Finnish representatives to Moscow March 1944, Soviet terms, Keitel–Heinrichs, Soviet offensive June 10—'the black day in our war history' (Mannerheim)—Keitel visit to Mannerheim (Aug. 17), *Eduskunta* approves negotiation for ceasefire.

GMD/KTB
OKH/GenStdH/Op. Abt. I/N, Band II, Finnland. See signals, items 440 092/44, 117/44, 133/44, 211/44, 213/44: Finnish moves for peace, Soviet–Finnish relations/Soviet conditions. T-78/R337, 6293167–177.

KTB/OKW, IV/1, *KTB* 1944, 9 Abschnitt. Der nördliche Kriegsschauplatz . . . II Teil. A. Finnland (12), 'Der Abfall Finnlands' (31 Aug.–15 Sept.), pp. 893–900.

IVOVSS, 4, pt 2, pp. 143–51, Soviet offensive in S Karelia, advance to frontiers, Finland leaves the war.

IVMV, 9, pt 1, pp. 34–8, Finnish moves to leave the war, Soviet–Finnish armistice, setting up of Soviet Control Commission under Zhdanov.

Meretskov, Marshal SU K.A., *Na sluzbe narodu* (Moscow: Politizdat 1969), pp. 376–91. See 'Karel'skii front', 30 May summoned to Moscow, Stalin's sarcasm about Meretskov's relief model (p. 377), to 7th Army for attack across Svir, 9 June to Kremlin, planning to destroy enemy force Svir–Petrozavodsk area, discussion with Stalin, Vasilevskii, Antonov, Zhukov, request for additional corps, Zhukov–Vasilevskii objections, Stalin's whispered promise of the extra corps (p. 379), frontier line reached, Soviet–Finnish armistice talks.

Noskov, A.M. *Skandinavskii platsdarm vo vtoroi mirovoi voine* (Moscow: Nauka 1977), pp. 202–15, German–Finnish tensions, Finnish moves to leave the war. (A specialist monograph, using Soviet and non-Soviet archives, also extensive bibliography again citing non-Soviet publications.)

6 SOVIET LIBERATION, SOVIET CONQUEST: AUGUST–DECEMBER 1944

Wartime events in east-central and south-east Europe present immense complexity, being compounded of heavy German military and political investment, multiple civil wars, irredentism and ethnic warfare, competition between 'the Big Three' and the further upheavals brought on by the massive Soviet military irruption into the region in 1944.

One of the few composite Soviet views of military-political developments is presented in M.M. Minasyan, *Osvobozhdenie narodov Yugo–vostochnoi Evropy* (Moscow, 1967); Maj.-Gen. Minasyan evidently first embarked on this work not long after the war during his assignment to the Department of the History of Soviet Military Art in the Frunze Academy. I have perforce relied heavily on this work, supplemented by the insights gained by discussing these Soviet operations with Soviet military historians. As for the diplomatic intricacies, here I could find no substitute for Sir Llewellyn Woodward's history of British wartime foreign policy with its superb clarity and cool elucidation. Much remains to be explained amidst this wider murkiness, but an indispensable guide is part II of Professor Hugh Seton-Watson's *The East European Revolution* (London: Methuen, New York: Praeger 1950) dealing with the wartime history of Axis satellites, the Resistance movements and 'Great and small allies' (pp. 83–166). My own purpose here has been to review *Soviet* policies and *Soviet* actions, the course of military operations being a significant component.

Balkan upheavals   pp. 331–356

Barker, Elisabeth, *Truce in the Balkans* (London: Percival Marshall 1948), ch. 8 on the Rumanian political scene, pp. 129–40, and ch. 10, on Greek resistance/political movements, pp. 171–80. (Excellently vivid pen-portraits of political personalities.)

Campbell, John and Sherrard, Philip, *Modern Greece* (London: Benn 1969), pt 2(VI), pp. 173–80, on the Greek guerrilla/resistance movements, *EAM–ELAS* aim for political control over mountain Greece, on Saraphis (p. 176), 'National Bands Agreement', Lebanon conference, Soviet military mission/Colonel Popov in Greece, July 44—instructions to *KKE* to avoid open opposition.

Churchill, Winston S., *The Second World War*, vol. 6: *Triumph and Tragedy*. See ch. V, 'Balkan convulsions', pp. 72–9, Churchill to Eden May 4—'. . . are we going to acquiesce in the Communisation of the Balkans . . .' (p. 72)—Soviet discussion of 'sharing' over Greece vs. Rumania, Church to Roosevelt (p. 73), American response (June 11–13), Churchill to Stalin July 11, Stalin to Churchill July 15 insisting on American approval, Soviet mission to *ELAS* and British suspicious; ch. VII, pp. 101–5, on the Greek problem: *EAM* repudiation of Lebanon agreement, Churchill consultation with Colonel Woodhouse, Churchill to Eden Aug. 6, British force for Greece planned, Churchill to Roosevelt Aug. 17, meeting with Papandreou, position of Greek king.

Deakin, F.W.D., *The Embattled Mountain* (London: OUP 1971). See pt 2, pp. 123–227, on British policy, role of SOE, the contacts with Tito and the British mission, supporting Tito, view of Middle East Command on importance of the partisan movement.

Ionescu, Ghita, *Communism in Rumania 1944–1962*. See pt 1, pp. 73–80, Soviet plans for conquest of Rumania, opening of diplomatic contacts (Nano in Stockholm), contacts in Cairo (Stirbey mission), Hitler–Antonescu, Soviet assertion of rights over Bessarabia and B. Bukovina, Maniu sends Visoianu to Cairo (May 27), divisions within Rumanian CP, 'Tudor Vladimirescu Division' in USSR, Bodnaras sent to Rumania by *NKVD;* pp. 81–3, breakdown of negotiations between Allies and Rumanian opposition, Roosevelt's opposition to any creation of 'spheres of influence', Soviet attempts to bring about direct capitulation of Rumania, Kollontai's offer of an armistice (June 2), Rumanian decision to overthrow Antonescu.

MacLean, Fitzroy, *Disputed Barricade. The Life and Times of Josip Broz-Tito* (London: Cape 1957). See pt 2, 'In the woods', pp. 131–289, on the Serbian rising, the partisan movement, relations with the British and the Russians (esp. ch. X, 'How many miles to Babylon?').

Kiszling, Rudolf, *Die Kroaten* (Graz/Cologne: Böhlau 1956). See 'Das unabhängige Kroatien 1941–1945', esp. pp. 179–94 on partisan warfare. (Cf. *KTB/OKW*, IV/1, 6 Abschnitt (d) 'Aufbau der kroatischen Wehrmacht—1944', *SS* divisions (14th Mussulman *SS* Div. . . .), *Ustaša* and *Domobran*, police/security/gendarmerie units, pp. 742–7).

Diplomatic correspondence/diplomatic history

Diplomatic correspondence

Perepiska . . . , vol. 1, No. 294, Churchill to Stalin, on 'working arrangement' for Russians to 'take the lead' in Rumania, the British to do the same in Greece, Roosevelt's agreement to a three-months trial, July 12, pp. 280–81; No. 297, Stalin to Churchill, requires US reply and resolution of 'certain doubts' by US government, July 15, p. 283.

Woodward, Sir Llewellyn, *British Foreign Policy* (single-volume), see ch. XVII, British policy towards Yugoslavia, pp. 332–48; also ch. XVIII, on Greece, to the Caserta agreement and the ELAS rebellion, pp. 350–58.

Woodward, Sir L., *British Foreign Policy in the Second World War*, vol. III, (1) British policy towards Yugoslavia: see ch. XLI (iii–vi), pp. 296–335, Brigadier MacLean's report on the partisans, issue of withdrawing British support for Mihailovic: Churchill–Tito correspondence (Dec. 43–March 44), Tito's refusal to co-operate with King Peter, dismissal of Puric government, appointment of Subasic, Tito–Subasic, Tito's attitude to King Peter. See also ch. XLII (i–ii), pp. 336–50, Brig. MacLean's suggestion to Tito that his movement be extended into Serbia, Churchill opposes 'grovelling to Tito', Churchill meeting with Tito (Aug. 12), British memorandum on British views (pp. 340–41), Tito–Subasic meeting, Churchill meeting with Tito and Subasic together (Aug. 13), British concern for *Serb* interests to prevent civil war, Tito 'disappears' (Sept. 18–19) *en route* for USSR, Molotov on Soviet views of Yugoslav question (pp. 348–9), imminence of entry of Red Army into Yugoslav territory, Moscow conference and the Balkans.

(2) British policy and *Greece*. See ch. XLIII (i–ii), pp. 383–402, *EAM* and *ELAS*, Greek guerrilla groups, role of Greek Communist Party *(KKE)*, the anti-Communist *EDES, EKKA* and Col. Psarros, problems for British policy, role and importance of SOE operations, reports of Major Wallace emphasizing unpopularity of the King, renewal of civil war in Greece, British force designated for liberated Greece, *EAM–ELAS* plans to seize control after German withdrawal, Roosevelt fails to support British proposals to put to King, King finally agrees to compromise on his possible return. Also (iii–iv), pp. 410–11, Merekovo conference to reunite guerrilla groups (Feb. 44), Col. Woodhouse in attendance with US Major Win, plans to broaden Greek government but the King rejects idea of a regency, meeting of Greek units at Alexandria (April 3), *EAM* and the Lebanon conference, Churchill–Papandreou meeting in Italy, Caserta agreement, *EAM–ELAS* rebellion in Athens, *ELAS* rejection of Caserta agreement designed to prevent civil war, British troops enter 14 Oct. 1944.

KTB/GMD

KTB/OKW, IV (1): 6. Abschnitt, 'Der südöstliche Kriegsschauplatz'/II Teil. On Yugoslav and Greek partisan/resistance movements, pp. 632–712. See also *Anhänge*, 'Kroatien', pp. 732–57; 'Rumänien' (Jan.–Aug. 44), Antonescu–Hitler, Allied air attacks on Rumanian oilfields, negotiations May 44, pp. 757–97.

OKH/GenStdH/Op. Abt. II, Tagesmeldungen Ob. Südost. (For 1 Jan.–24 July 1944.) T-78/R330, 6288099–6289114. Also 'Balkan–Blb–Allgemein' (Balkans, Greece, Crete: Yugoslav situation, Mihailovic and Četniks, Pavelič and Croats/1943) T-78/R332, 6289729–845. Also Balkan I (c) politisch, Band I, Lagebeurteilungen/ Ob. Südost, partisan operations, Tito, Mihailović, Greek guerrillas (1943), 6289845–6290105.

Bulletins

Forschungsdienst Ost. Politische Informationen. (Printed bulletins—1944/Jan. 1945—on a wide variety of subjects: personalities, politics, organizations in the east.) See

'Allslavismus in Rahmen der bolschew. Aussenpolitik' (pp. 145–62) and 'Die Tito–Bewegung und ihr Ziel' (pp. 277–90), T-78/R493, 6480045.

Soviet materials

Biryuzov, Marshal SU S.S. (ed.), *Sovetskie vooruzhennye sily v bor'be za osvobozhdenie narodov Yugoslavii* (Moscow: Voenizdat 1960). See pt 1, pp. 47–53, Soviet aid to the Yugoslav partisan movement (table of deliveries for 1944, p. 52); also pt 2, pp. 201–5, Lt.-Gen. N.V. Korneyev, 'Voennaya missiya SSSR v Yugoslavii', Soviet military mission sent 17 Jan. 1944, 'spiriting Tito away'—*ischeznovenie*—to Moscow (p. 205). (A remarkably terse and primly discreet account of the Soviet mission.)

Kir'yakidis, G.K., *Gretsiya no vtoroi mirovoi voine* (Moscow: Nauka 1967). Detailed monograph on *EAM–ELAS*, the 'reactionary offensive' against *EAM* (extensive use of 'documents and materials' of the Greek Communist Party, *EAM–ELAS, EPON* and *PEEA*).

Kir'yakidis, G.K., 'Dvizhenie soprotivleniya v Gretsii (1940–1944). See *Sovetskii Soyuz i bor'ba narodov Tsentral'noi i Yugo–Vostochnoi Evropy za svobodu i nezavisimost' 1941–1945 gg.* (Moscow: Nauka 1978), pp. 384–439. (A detailed account of *EAM/ELAS,* extensive use of Greek sources, Soviet accounts, also some Western memoir literature.)

Yugoslav materials

Documents: Mihailović trial

Dokumenti o izdajstvu Draže Mihajlovića, Vol. 1 (in Serb), (Belgrade, Sept. 1945). 'Državna komisija . . .' 735 pp. (Text of documents, also facsimiles.)

Bibliography

Dedijer, Vladimir, *Tito Speaks. His Self-Portrait and Struggle with Stalin* (London: Weidenfeld 1955). Pt III, 'War of Liberation', see ch. 11, pp. 169–80, partisan resentment of publicity for Mihailović, Stalin's displeasure, lack of Soviet aid, Stalin and King Peter's government; ch. 13, pp. 201–14, Stalin's displeasure over Jajce decisions, cessation of British aid to Mihailović, Djilas mission to Moscow, Soviet supplies to partisans; ch. 14, pp. 215–30, Tito–Šubašić meeting, two meetings between Tito and Churchill.

Djilas, Milovan, *Conversations with Stalin* (New York: Harcourt, Brace 1952; London: Rupert Hart-Davis 1962 and Penguin Books 1963). On Djilas's first mission to Moscow, see under 'Raptures': this section and the book as a whole is generally and justifiably regarded as one of the most remarkable political portraits of Stalin ever penned. (On Mesić, see note below under Klajkić.)

Djonlagić, Ahmet et al., *Yugoslavia in the Second World War* (English text) (Belgrade, 1967). See First and Second AVNOJ sessions, pp. 101–41; on the Teheran Conference, pp. 145–50: Tito–Šubašic agreement, pp. 162–7; agreement between the National Commmittee of AVNOJ and the Soviet government, pp. 173–7.

Kijakić, Dragan, *Ustaško Domobranska Legija. . . .* See note, pp. 193–4, on Artillery Colonel Marko Mesić and the formation in the USSR of the 'Odred jugoslavenske vojske u SSSR', with Mesić as commander and Prišlin as chief of staff: in 1943 the force was redesignated 'Odred NOVJ, formiran u SSSR'.

Pajović, B. and Radević, M., *Bibliografija o ratu i revoluciji u Jugoslaviji*, Posebna izdanja 1945–1965 (Belgrade, 1969). See pt 1, 'Dokumenti, Nauka Publicistika', pp. 25–303.

Terzić, Col.-Gen. V. (ed.), *Oslobodilački rat naroda Jugoslavije 1941–1945*, vol. 2 (Belgrade, 1958). See pt 1, chs I–VIII, 'Od drugog zasedanja AVNOJ-a do oslobodjenja Beograda', pp. 7–344 (operational narrative, also ch. VIII on 'Sporazum Tito–Šubašić . . .').

Planning the Jassy–Kishinev operation
(2nd and 3rd Ukrainian Fronts) pp. 356–369

IVOVSS, 4, pt 2, pp. 254–67, planning/preparation of Jassy–Kishinev operation: role of the Rumanian Communist Party in organizing anti-Fascist front, reactionary, bourgeois support for Antonescu, in Soviet military planning need to complete destruction of German forces on the flanks before striking along the 'Warsaw–Berlin axis', German defences/strength in Rumania, additional German units (security, SS units), strength of Soviet 2nd and 3rd Ukrainian Fronts, total of 90 divisions, *Stavka* conference July, decisions of the Front commanders, 6th Tank Army assignment, assignments to 18th Tank, 4th Guards and 7th Mech. Corps, air support 5th and 17th Air Armies, logistics problems and solutions (p. 263), success of Soviet deception measures and German conviction that little likelihood of major Soviet attack, even at late date mistakenly assessed role of 3rd Ukrainian Front.

IVMV, 9, pt 1, pp. 97–104, operational planning for Jassy–Kishinev operation: *Stavka* directive, Front planning, table of comparative strength (p. 104).

Antosyak, Colonel A.V., *V boyakh za svobodu Rumynii* (Moscow: Voenizdat 1974). Ch. 2, Soviet victories, influence on the Rumanian anti-fascist movement (pp. 32–49), formation in USSR of '1st Rumanian Volunteer Division' (Oct. 43)—'Tudor Vladimirescu Division'—(pp. 49–56), Soviet entry on to Rumanian territory, repulse of German counter-attacks, Soviet losses May 30–June 5 (52nd, 27th Army, 2nd and 6th Tank Army) 14,871 men (2,800 killed), 96 tanks and SP guns, 132 aircraft (p. 60).

Biryuzov, Marshal SU S.S., *Surovye gody* (Moscow: Nauka 1966), pt 2 (published earlier in VM series as *Sovetskii soldat na Balkanakh*), pp. 313–52, Antonov issues warning order July 15 for offensive, Tolbukhin assembles military soviet July 16, discussion of 'Kitskan bridgehead', *Stavka* directive Aug. 2 (text, pp. 344–6), Malinovskii–Tolbukhin conference, Gorshkov and planning of amphibious operation. (Many pen-portraits of commanders involved.)

Biryuzov, S.S., 'Poiski pravil'novo resheniya', *VIZ*, 1963 (5), pp. 59–77. Detailed, at times racy, account of operational planning 2nd and 3rd Ukrainian Fronts, special reference to Tolbukhin's decision on the 'Kitskan Bridgehead'.

Cupsa, Colonel I. *et al.*, *Vklad Rumynii v razgrom fashistskoi Germanii* (Moscow: Voenizdat 1959). (Soviet translation of *Contributia Romîniei la războiul antihitlerist*, Bucharest, 1958). Pt 1, pp. 42–7, planning for a national rising, Communist Party planning, note to p. 45 on two possible courses of action (to attack the Germans, or to link up with the Red Army and then initiate actions against the Germans).

Kuznetsov, P.G., *Marshal Tolbukhin*, pp. 137–59. See 'Udar s Dnestra', planning for Jassy–Kishinev operation, decision for 'Kitskan bridgehead', *Stavka* order/directive, assignments to Front armies.

Malinovskii, Marshal SU R.Ya., *Yassko–Kishinevskie Kanny* (Moscow: Nauka 1964) (a collective work, bearing Malinovskii's name), pp. 45–82, planning the operation, German command deliberately misled over 'weakness' of 2nd Ukrainian Front (*Stavka* forbade heavy counter-blows in May–June to confirm this impression), German strength and defences, *Stavka* instruction to prepare offensive July 44, Tolbukhin and the 'Kitskan bridgehead', *Stavka* meeting, Tolbukhin gets more tanks (elements of 7th Mech. Corps), delineation of Front assignments Aug. 2, offensive provisionally timed for Aug. 20, Front planning/command appointments, Tolbukhin's liaison with Black Sea Fleet commander F.S. Oktyabrskii, role of Danube Flotilla. (I have made extensive use of this work, largely because of its detail; I had occasion to discuss this book at length with one of the authors.)

Matsulenko, Colonel V.A., *Udar s dnestrovskovo platsdarma* (Moscow: Voenizdat 1961). (Operations of 37th Army, 3rd Ukrainian Front). Ch. 2, pp. 23–86, command decisions, operational planning 37th Army. (Immensely detailed monograph, utilizing largely Soviet military archives.)

Minasyan, M.M., *Osvobozhdenie narodov Yugo–vostochnoi Evropy*, pp. 108–28, planning/ preparation Jassy–Kishinev operation, German strength and deployment, Soviet strength (87 rifle divs., 1 tank army, 2 air armies), *Stavka* meeting July 31, political aim to take Rumania out of the war, Stalin's insistence on a rapid breakthrough, Front planning/military measures, Front planning/political to use recruits from freshly liberated areas (400,000 men brought into the two Fronts).

Shtemenko, S.M., *General'nyi shtab v gody voiny*, vol. 2, pp. 118–28, initial instruction to 2nd and 3rd Ukrainian Fronts to plan attack May 44, command changes (Malinovskii to 2nd Ukrainian Front), aim to destroy German Army Group South Ukraine, regrouping complete early July, Tolbukhin argues for 'Kitskan' bridgehead, *Stavka* meeting July 3 Timoshenko present, Stalin's emphasis on both military and political aspects, final *Stavka* directive signed at 2300 hours Aug. 2.

Zakharov, Marshal SU M.V. (ed.), *Osvozhdenie Yugo–vostochnoi i Tsentral'noi Evropy voiskami 2-vo i 3-vo Ukrainskikh frontov* (Moscow: Nauka 1970). See ch. 2, 'Zamysli i plany', pp. 47–97, on German plans and intentions, Soviet planning for Jassy–Kishinev operation: ,very detailed study of planning/preparation, emphasizing Soviet deception measures and the risk in the Soviet plan—if the Germans discerned the Soviet plan, the flanks of the assault armies would be exposed and particularly the assault force of 3rd Ukrainian Front in the 'Kitskan bridgehead' (see p. 93), German assessment Aug. 15 that only a *limited* Soviet operation likely and feasible. (Compiled by 'collective authorship'. This is an important study drawing both on Soviet military records and the recollections of commanders, as well as utilizing some captured German documentation.)

Zavizion, G.T. and Kornyushin, P.A., *I na Tikhom Okeane . . .* (16th Guards Tank Army), pp. 60–66, intensive training for 6th Tank, army commander Kravchenko and A.V. Kurkin (chief of armoured forces, 2nd Ukrainian Front) supervise exercises, training concluded end July, 6th Tank Army equipped with 398 medium tanks and 153 SP guns, movement to concentration area Aug. 16, army assignment for rapid exploitation of breakthrough.

Jassy–Kishinev operation, drive into Rumania   pp. 369–380

Allen, W.E.D. and Muratoff, Paul, *The Russian Campaigns of 1944–1945*, ch. VI, 'Catastrophe in Rumania', pp. 163–76. (Emphasizing the importance of Tolbukhin's attack from the 'Kitskan bridgehead', even though it involved crossing a wide river and deploying first in apparently unfavourable ground.)

Ionescu, Ghita, *Communism in Rumania*, pt 1, pp. 83–93, on the coup Aug. 23, armistice, first Sanatescu government, collaboration and resistance.

Philippi, Alfred and Heim, Ferdinand, *Der Feldzug gegen Sowjetrussland*, pt 2, pp. 257–60, Soviet offensive operations, Rumania/Hungary: position of H.Gr. Südukraine, the Army Group in the wake of the Rumanian defection.

Seaton, Albert, *The Russo–German War*, ch. 28, Rumania: emphasizes elements of Soviet–Rumanian conspiracy before the attack (deliberate transfer of Rumanian commanders who 'might put old loyalties before new ones'—p. 474—Alea, confidant of the King, in touch with Malinovskii after Aug. 21: see also Hillgruber, *Hitler, König Carol und Marschall Antonescu*), also Soviet accounts over-emphasize success of *maskirovka* (deception); yet Friessner did consider Tolbukhin's attack merely to 'pin Axis forces on the lower Dniester', pp. 467–8. (See also Friessner, H., *Verratene Schlachten*, Hamburg, 1956, translated into Russian as *Proigrannye srazheniya*, Voenizdat, 1966; Kissel, H., *Die Katastrophe in Rumänien 1944*, Darmstadt, Wehr u. Wiss. Verlag, 1964; A. Rehm, *Jassy*, Neckargemünd, Vowinckel, 1959.)

GMD

OKH/Kriegsgesch. Abt. Maps, Hgr. Südukraine: 'Schlacht um Rumänien u. den Beskiden v. 20.8–29.9.44'. T-78/R136, 6065352–392.

FHO (I), Teil A: Zusammenstellung . . . , Assessment Nr 2494/44: 30.7.44 Kurze Beurteilung . . . Hgr. Südukraine, Soviet build-up 2nd and 3rd Ukrainian Fronts. Nr 2683/44 15.8.44 Gesamtfeindlage under para. 5, air recon. shows enemy build-up south of Tiraspol and north of Jassy. Nr 2713/44/17.8.44 Beurteilung: Hgr. Südukraine, anticipation of Soviet attack in *sector Jassy. Targul Frumos*. Nr 2896/44 31.8.44. Beurteilung/Hgr. Südukraine, possible Soviet moves hard to predict—could either aim for Bulgaria, or to drive west, to the 'Iron gates', on to Transylvania. T-78/R466, 6446183–191.

Soviet materials

Sovinformbyuro. 'Itogi Yassko–Kishinevskoi operatsii', vol. 3, 1945, pp. 157–8: list of German losses (106,600 German prisoners, including 2 corps commanders, 11 divisional commanders).

Eronin, Colonel N. and Shinkarev, Colonel I., 'Razgrom nemetsko-fashistskikh voisk v Rumynii (mart-oktyabr. 1944 goda)', *VIZ*, 1967 (9), pp. 51–63. (Review of Soviet operations against Rumania; considerable assembly of figures and statistics.)

Loktionov, I.I., *Dunaiskaya flotiliya v Velik. Otech. Voine (1941–1945 gg.)* (Moscow: Voenizdat 1962), pp. 63–114, Danube Flotilla operations (Aug.–Sept.), planning of Jassy–Kishinev operation, assignments to Black Sea Fleet and Danube Flotilla, Flotilla co-operation/co-ordination with 46th Army Aug. 21–23, also on the Lower Danube. (Note: Rear-Admiral Gorshkov—presently C-in-C, Soviet Navy—commanded the Danube Flotilla.)

Malinovskii, R.Ya., *Yassko–Kishinevskie Kanny*, ch. 3, pp. 106–67, Soviet offensive, 27th Army/52nd Army operations, 37th Army (3rd Ukrainian Front) operations, *Stavka* instruction Aug. 21 (p. 134), first stage completed Aug. 22, encirclement of 3rd Rumanian Army, 6th Guards Tank Army and 18th Tank Corps at Vaslui and Husi, Dragomir-Sanatescu (p. 148), 18 enemy divs. encircled Aug. 24; ch. 4, pp. 168–206, second stage of offensive, battle in rear of 52nd Army, commander of 18th Tank Corps killed, heavy fighting in rear of 2nd Ukrainian Front, necessary reserves badly deployed, General Staff largely responsible (p. 172), German attempt to break through to Prut, elimination of encircled German divisions, Sanatescu plea to commander 6th Tank Army (also to 46th Army) but rejected by 2nd Ukrainian Front command (p. 195), plans to enter Bucharest, Malinovskii wounded in flight over Husi (p. 201).

Matsulenko, V.A., *Udar s dnestrovskovo platsdarma*, ch. 3, pp. 87–159, 37th Army operations, breakthrough and pursuit; also ch. 4, on 'operational-tactical' lessons.

Matsulenko, Colonel V.A. and Pchelkin, Colonel V.D., 'Proryv oborony protivnika voiskami 35-vo Gvardeiskovo strelkovo korpusa 27-i Armii 2-vo Ukrainskovo fronta v Yassko–Kishinevskoi operatsii'. See *Proryv podgotovlennoi oborony strelkovymi soedineniyami*, Sbornik statei (Voenizdat 1957) (Frunze Academy), pp. 165–93 (text), pp. 350–58 (operational documents, 35th Corps). An important, highly technical study of 35th Corps, Trofimenko's 27th Army, 2nd Ukrainian Front.

Matsulenko, V.A., 'Nekotorye osobennosti voennovo iskusstva v Yassko–Kishinevskoi operatsii', *VIZ*, 1969 (8), pp. 12–30. (Analysis of operational features.)

Minasyan, M.M., *Osvobozhdenie . . .* , pp. 128–63, Jassy–Kishinev operation, Rumanian coup: operational narrative 2nd and 3rd Ukrainian Fronts (also material from *KTB/ OKW* H.Gr. Südukraine, Soviet captured German documents—Mil.-Hist. Section/ General Staff): German losses (from captured documents) recorded as 5 Corps HQs, 18 divisions (note to p. 161).

Sharokhin, Col.-Gen. M., '37-ya armiya v Yassko–Kishinevskoi operatsii', *VIZ*, 1969 (8), pp. 100–8. (Commander, 37th Army, on operations.)

Tolubko, General V.F. and Baryshev, N.I., *Na yuzhnom flange* (Moscow: Nauka 1973). (Combat history of 4th Guards Mech. Corps 1942–45.) See ch. 5, pp. 186–210, extremely detailed record of 4th Corps operations (3rd Ukrainian Front), Jassy–Kishinev operation, much emphasis on performance of sub-units.

Tolubko, V.F., 'Artilleriya 3-vo Ukrainskovo Fronta v Yassko–Kishinevskoi operatsii', *VIZ*, 1979 (8), pp. 37–42. (Artillery in Jassy–Kishinev operation.)

Zakharov, M.V. (ed.), *Osvobozhdenie. . . .* See ch. 3, Jassy–Kishinev encirclement, pp. 98–147; ch. 4, from Kishinev to Bucharest, pp. 148–94. (Detailed operational narrative, less breezy than the study bearing Malinovskii's name: much cross-referencing with Minasyan, though here I have relied on the Zakharov chapters for precise dating/timing of *Stavka* instructions and revised directives.)

Zavizion, G.T. and Kornyushin, P.A., *I na Tikhom Okeane . . .* , pp. 64–87, 6th Tank Army operations, committed into breakthrough zone of 27th Army—sole instance in entire war when a complete tank army passed through in the middle of the first day of the attack—Aug. 21 5th Mech. Corps in open country, capture of Vaslui, army moving 40–50 km per day, commander of 5th Tank Corps killed, Kravchenko orders drive for Focsani, 5th Mech. Corps turned south-west to drive on Bucharest Aug. 26, one corps to take Ploesti by Aug. 29, third corps to position north of Bucharest, at 0530 hrs Aug. 31 5th Mech Corps driving into Bucharest, 18th Tank Corps coming in from the east, 5th Tank Corps cleared Ploesti Aug. 29.

IVMV, 9, pt 1, pp. 104–19, Jassy–Kishinev operations, liberation of Soviet Moldavia, eastern Rumania, Rumanian national armed rising, further Soviet operations.

IVOVSS, 4, pt 2, pp. 267–82, Soviet offensive, *Stavka* directive Aug. 21 (p. 269), encirclement of Axis forces, *Stavka* to Timoshenko Aug. 24 to continue operations along external front (p. 271), resistance ceases east of Pruti, 'August anti-Fascist rising of the Rumanian people' (pp. 275–80), *Stavka* directive Aug. 29 to 2nd and 3rd Ukrainian Fronts (p. 281), Rumanian forces moving over to Soviet side.

Rumanian materials

Ilie, Lt.-Col. P. and Stoean, Lt.-Col. Gh., *România in războiul antihitlerist*. Contribuţii bibliografice (Bucharest: Editura Militara 1971). See index under IV, Rumanian army operations (also III, index to material on the Aug. 23 *coup*).

Romanescu, Colonel G. and Loghin, Colonel L., *Cronica participării Armatei Române la războiul antihitlerist* (Bucharest: Editura Militara 1971). Documented chronology of Rumanian Army operations, transition under Soviet command, with details (appendices) Rumanian armament, operational diary, command/field organization.

Rumanian armistice, Bulgarian defection pp. 369–380

Ionescu, Ghita, *Communism in Rumania*, pt I, pp. 87–99, armistice terms, 'Rumania: 90 per cent', first Sanatescu government.

Irving, David, *Hitler's War*, pt 5, pp. 731–2, Hitler's expectation of collision between Russia and Allies, British permitting withdrawal of *Wehrmacht* to S Hungary, Soviet troop movements presage thrust on Dardanelles (Eastern Thrace), British 'standing by' to protect vital interests.

MacLean, Fitzroy, *Disputed Barricade*, pp. 279–89. On Tito's visit to Moscow, preparation for liberation of Belgrade.

Oren, Nissan, *Revolution Administered: Agrarianism and Communism in Bulgaria* (Baltimore/London: Johns Hopkins Press 1973). See esp. ch. 3 on the war years, pp. 62–78, and ch. 4 on the Soviet entry/Bulgarian Communists, pp. 79–86. (Extensive use of a wide range of Bulgarian sources: see also Nissan Oren, *Bulgarian Communism: The Road to Power, 1934–1944*, New York, 1971.)

Sweet-Escott, Bickham, *Baker Street Irregular* (London: Methuen 1965), ch. VII, 'Mediterranean Maelstrom', pp. 214–20, details of Rumanian and Bulgarian armistice negotiations, SOE interests.

Warlimont, Walter, *Inside Hitler's Headquarters*, pt VI, pp. 470–71, collapse of fronts and alliances, Bulgarian defection, Hitler's reaction, delay in orders for general withdrawal.

KTB/GMD

KTB/OKW, IV/1, 6 Abschnitt, on Bulgaria, pp. 809–10; also 'Die grosse Absetzbewegung im Südosten . . .', see pp. 816ff. (Cf. Warlimont, above.)

OKH/GenStdH/Op. Abt., File: 'Bulgaria' (43–44), German policies, question of Turkish entry into war, Soviet–Bulgarian relations T-78/R333, 6290413–480.

FHO, Anlagenband: Beurteilung d. Feindlage. Feindlage. Report No. 2937/44, 2.9.44: 'Wichtige Meldungen über Bulgarien'. (Expectation of declaration of war on Germany.) Report No. 3508/44, 7.10.44, 'Wichtige Frontaufklärungsmeldungen'. (Anticipated Soviet thrust, Serbia/Belgrade.) T-78/R498, 6485847–48 and 6485849–53.

Soviet materials

IVOVSS, 4, pt 2, pp. 302–11, Soviet entry into Bulgaria, success of the 'September insurrection', Bulgarian participation in the 'anti-Fascist struggle'.

IVMV, 9, pt 1, pp. 119–32, Soviet entry into Bulgaria, success of the Bulgarian 'popular insurrection'.

Kuznetsov, P.G., *Marshal Tolbukhin*. See 'Na Balkanakh', 3rd Ukrainian Front investment of Bulgaria, Tolbukhin's decisions, pp. 172–83; preparation for Belgrade operation, pp. 183–96.

Zhukov, G.K., *Vospominaniya . . .* , vol. 2, pp. 275–7, Zhukov to 3rd Ukrainian Front, conversation with Dimitrov, planning of Soviet operations, peaceful entry, Stalin's ruling not to disarm Bulgarians.

Biryuzov, S.S., *Surovye gody*, ch. 13, pp. 424–54, Soviet operations in Bulgaria, preparation of Soviet–Yugoslav–Bulgarian co-operation.

Minasyan, M.M., *Osvobozhdenie. . . .* See ch. 2(7), implementing the Rumanian armistice (report of military soviet, 2nd Ukrainian Front, p. 191), pp. 187–207; also ch. 3 (1–3), 3rd Ukrainian Front operations in Bulgaria, the 'September rising' and its aftermath, pp. 208–43.

Zheltov, Col.-Gen. A., 'Osvobozhdenie Bolgarii', *VIZ*, 1969 (9), pp. 59–69. Soviet operations in Bulgaria; listing of forces (to division) involved (pp. 66–9).

Shtemenko, S.M., *General'nyi shtab v gody voiny*, vol. 2, ch. 5, pp. 157–94, Soviet operations in Bulgaria, instructions to Zhukov, role of Biryuzov, Anglo-American 'meddling', diplomatic manoeuvre; ch. 6, pp. 195–220, Tito's visit to Moscow, military agreements and military co-ordination, planning/preparation of Belgrade operations.

Tolubko, V.F. and Baryshev, N.I., *Na yuzhnom flange*, pp. 211–31, 4th Guards Mech. Corps drive into Bulgaria.

Note on Soviet casualties, operations in Rumania

The figure for Soviet losses April–Oct. 1944 (46,783 killed in action) is taken from Colonel Eronin, *VIZ*, 1967 (9), p. 63. Other sources such as Minasyan, *op. cit.*, p. 204 or *IVOVSS*, 4, p. 291 give a *composite* figure of 76,000 for Soviet operations in the period Aug. 20–Sept. 20 including both Fronts, 2nd and 3rd Ukrainian. However, *Yassko–Kishinevskie Kanny* refers to 'relatively small losses' on the Soviet side for the Jassy–Kishinev operation, citing (p. 251) the figure of *12,500 for both Fronts* (presumably the total for killed in action). In sum, for the period April–Oct. 1944 Soviet operations in Rumania cost almost 220,000 men (killed and wounded). (*IVOVSS*, 4, p. 284 also provides the figure of 'more than 75,000' for Rumanian losses between Aug. 23–Oct. 30.)

Zakharov, M.V. (ed.), *Osvobozhdenie . . .* , Ch. 6, 'Na zemle Bolgarii', Soviet entry into Bulgaria, pp. 215–39.

Bulgarian materials

Spasitelniyam za B'lgariya Otechestven Front. Stati i rechi, spomeni (Sofia: Izd. Otechest. Front 1975). Speeches, articles, memoir material—Dimitrov, Zhivkov, Traikov *et al.*—military/political activities, Fatherland Front.

Gornenskii, Nikiforov, *V'or'zhenata borba 1941–1944* (Sofia: Izd. na B'lgar. kom. partiya, 2nd edn 1971). See chs 5 and 6 on partisan movement, on Jassy–Kishinev operation and Bulgarian political scene.

Trunski, General Slavcho, *From the Tactics of Partisan Warfare in Bulgaria* (Sofia Press 1970) (in English). See ch. III, partisan warfare in Bulgaria, pp. 36–191 (also on the Fatherland Front, pp. 75–81).

Yugoslav materials

Dedijer, Vladimir, *Tito Speaks,* pp. 231–7, Tito's visit to Moscow, Craiova meeting with Bulgarians, exchanges with Stalin (Tito's own account), Stalin's rebuke to Malinovskii (p. 235), liberation of Belgrade.

Belgrade-Budapest ${}$ pp. 380–397

Allen, W.E.D. and Muratoff, Paul, *The Russian Campaigns,* ch. VII, the Danubian–Carpathian campaign (Sept.–Nov. 44), pp. 176–206.

Reitlinger, Gerald, *The SS. Alibi of a Nation.* See ch. 13, 'Rebellion in Eastern Europe', pp. 358–65, on Hungary, Lakatos replaces Szotaj, Farago mission to Moscow, plot to arrest Horthy's son, abdication of Admiral Horthy, Szalasi government, role of Skorzeny and 'operation *Panzerfaust*', Jewish deportations renewed.

Seaton, Albert, *The Russo–German War,* pp. 487–98, German–Hungarian relations, German grip on Hungary, Soviet advance to outskirts of Budapest, 3rd Ukrainian Front operations, Hitler's determination to defend Budapest.

Woodward, Sir Llewellyn, *British Foreign Policy,* vol. III, ch. XXXVIII(v), pp. 141–6, Hungarian peace-feelers, Foreign Office view of possible developments in Hungary, Veres contacts in Istanbul (Aug. 43), Soviet reaction, General Naday's visit to Italy 1944, Molotov proposes talks in Moscow, Hungarian acceptance of Soviet terms but second German coup, denunciation of armistice negotiations.

KTB/GMD

KTB/OKW, IV/1, 7 Abschnitt, 'Die Ereignisse in Ungarn von Anfang April bis zum Ende der Schlacht um Budapest . . .', (events March–Sept. 44, also Oct. 44), pp. 828–51.

OKH/GenStdH/Op. Abt., File: *Ungarn,* III (43–44), operations in Hungary, Hungarian forces, German–Hungarian relations; contd., III, also IV, military-political developments, also *Ungarn/Chefsache,* defence of Hungary, additional mobilization Hungarian forces (4/44). T-78/R333, 6290687–6291120.

Soviet materials

IVOVSS, 4, pt 2, pp. 379–93, Soviet operations in E Hungary, *Stavka* planning (pp. 381–2), Soviet success Debreczen and Szeged, Hungarian peace overtures; 2nd Ukrainian Front operations and attempt to capture Budapest, 3rd Ukrainian Front operations (largely operational narrative). Also pp. 424–30, liberation of Belgrade.

IVMV, 9, pt 1, pp. 163–202, East Carpathian operations, liberation of Belgrade, Debreczen operation, advance on Budapest. (One 'compound chapter'—as opposed to *IVOVSS* treatment—mainly operational narrative using Soviet military archives.)

Biryuzov, S.S., *Surovye gody*, ch. 13, Soviet operations in Bulgaria, pp. 424–54; ch. 14, Soviet–Yugoslav (also Bulgaria) operations, liberation of Belgrade, pp. 455–80.

Biryuzov, S.S. (ed.), *Sov. Voor. Sily v bor'be za osvobozhdenie narodov Yugoslavii*, pt 1, ch. 3, Belgrade operation pp. 54–63. Also pt 2, Nedelin (artillery), pp. 115–21; Gorshkov (Danube Flotilla), pp. 131–5; Sharokhin (57th Army), pp. 153–7; Zhdanov (4th Guards Mech. Corps), pp. 177–82; Korneyev (head of Soviet Military Mission), pp. 201–5; 'spiriting Tito away' (p. 205).

Chizh, Col.-Gen. V.F., *Ot Vidina do Belgrada* (Moscow: Nauka 1968) (4th Guards Mech. Corps operations). Detailed 'memoir-monograph', using in many instances primary military records (e.g. operational directives, 3rd Ukrainian Front); listing of Soviet and Yugoslav formations, with command staffs (also index of names).

Koniev, I.S. (ed.), *Za osvobozhdenie Chekhoslovakii*. See ch. 2(2), pp. 89–110, Eastern Carpathian operations, 1st and 4th Ukrainian Fronts (38th Army, 1st Guards and 18th Army, 17th Guards Rifle Corps operations), fall of Mukachevo, German counter-blows in Slovakia, results of Soviet operations.

Kupsha (Cupşa), I., *Vklad Rumynii v razgrom fash. Germanii*, pt 3, Rumanian troops in N Transylvania operations, pp. 162–89; pt 4, Rumanian troops in Debreczen operation, pp. 195–218; first stage of Budapest operations, pp. 219–33. (See also *Cronica participarii . . .*).

Loktionov, I.I., *Dunaiskaya flotiliya v VOV*, pp. 126–58, Danube flotilla (Gorshkov commanding) in Belgrade operation.

Malakhov, Colonel M.M., *Osvobozhdenie Vengrii i vostochnoi Avstrii* (Moscow: Voenizdat 1965), pp. 19–90, Debreczen operation, launching of Budapest operation, encirclement. (Terse, extremely compact operational chronology/narrative.)

Malinovskii, Marshal SU R.Ya. (ed.), *Budapest Vena Praga* (Moscow: Nauka 1965), ch. 2, 2nd Ukrainian Front, Transylvanian operations, pp. 37–76; ch. 3, drive for Budapest (see pp. 81–2, Stalin's *demand* for capture of Budapest); *Shtemenko*, on influence of over-optimistic reports by *Mekhlis*, pp. 77–97. (A fast-moving but informative narrative.)

Minasyan, M.M., *Osvodozhdenie . . .*, ch. 5(1–2), Soviet–Yugoslav operations, Bulgarian role, liberation of Belgrade, pp. 414–38; also ch. 4 (1–3), Soviet operations in eastern Hungary, pp. 255–97; Soviet policy towards Hungary, military regime in occupied territory, pp. 297–308.

Pushkas, A.I., *Vengriya v gody VMV*, pp. 421–73, Soviet military operations in Hungary, fall of Horthy, Soviet movement into E Hungary, Hungarian Communist Party, formation of National Independence Front.

Shtemenko, S.M., *General'nyi shtab v gody voiny*, vol. 2, pp. 227–58, *Stavka* instructions to Petrov (4th Ukrainian), critical nature of events in Hungary, planning of

Debreczen operation, negotiations (public and secret) with Hungarians, negotiations with 1st Hungarian Army, 24 Oct. directive to treat Hungarians as the enemy (p. 248), launching of Debreczen operation, *Mekhlis* submits wildly optimistic reports to Stalin about Hungarian demoralization (p. 253) thus encouraging Stalin to demand early seizure of Budapest, *Timoshenko*'s personal report to the *Stavka* Nov. 24 (pp. 256–7), revised *Stavka* directive for Budapest operations Nov. 26 (p. 258).

Tolubko, V.F. and Baryshev, N.I., *Na yuzhnom flange*, pp. 241–331, 4th Guards Mech. Corps operations, Belgrade. (Detailed operational narrative, continued emphasis on unit/sub-unit performance.)

Zavizion, G.T. and Kornyushin, P.A. *I na Tikhom Okeane* . . . (6th Guards Tank Army), pp. 94–125, from Bucharest to Budapest, liberation of first Yugoslav territory, operations on right flanks 2nd Ukrainian Front, N Transylvania, heavy wear and tear on Soviet tanks, drive from Bucharest to Oradea–Mare, planning for Budapest operation, 6th Tank Army fielding 325 tanks and SP guns (p. 116), operations against German IV *Panzer* Corps.

Zubakov, Colonel V. and Malakhov, Colonel M., 'Belgradskaya operatsiya', *VIZ*, 1964 (10), pp. 52–61 (operational narrative).

Yugoslav materials

Oslobodilački rat . . . 1941–1945, vol. 2. See ch. VII, 'Beogradska operacija' (1 NOVJ Army Group and Soviet 4th Guards Mech. Corps), Belgrade, liberation of Voivodina, pp. 314–30.

Djonlagic, Ahmet *et al.*, *Yugoslavia in the Second World War*, pp. 177–82, liberation of Belgrade.

Soviet–Jugoslav collective work, *Beogradska operacija* (Belgrade: Vojnoist. Institut 1964), pp. 83–266, preparation and execution of Belgrade operation.

Hungarian materials

The Confidential Papers of Admiral Horthy (Budapest: Corvina Press 1965). See Documents Nos. 62–5 (June–July 1944), Horthy to Hitler, proposed dismissal of Szótaj administration, pp. 300–19. (See also 'Concluding Remarks', bitterly anti-Horthy, pp. 320–22.)

Vengriya i vtoraya mirovaya voina. (Soviet translation of Hungarian secret diplomatic papers: *Magyarország és a második világyháború*, Budapest, 1959; Moscow, 1962). Pt IX, German occupation of Hungary, pp. 312–42.

The Soviet war effort (1944)   pp. 397–411

Soviet war effort/Soviet society at war

Soviet material on the Soviet war effort in its widest framework is massive and still growing. At the moment I know of no comprehensive non-Soviet study of Soviet society at war embracing these materials, which are at once highly variegated and highly informative. My purpose here is simply to furnish a rudimentary profile of subjects and sources, though in the Bibliography I have attempted to widen the compilation.

Dunnigan, James F. (ed.), *The Russian Front. Germany's War in the East 1941–45* (London/Melbourne: AAP 1978). Ch. IV on Soviet army organization (J. Dunnigan), pp. 87–106. (Text and organization charts.)

Fischer, George, *Soviet Opposition to Stalin.* See pt II, ch. VI, the 'Himmler stage' in the Vlasov movement, Himmler–Vlasov 1944, pp. 72–83; ch. VII, *KONR,* Prague assembly, *KONR* apparatus, pp. 84–93.

Millar, James R., 'Financing the Soviet Effort in World War II', *Soviet Studies* (Univ. Glasgow), vol. XXXII(1), Jan. 1980, pp. 106–23. (An exceptionally important study.)

Nicolaevsky, Boris I. (ed. Janet D. Zagoria), *Power and the Soviet Elite* (London: Pall Mall, New York: Praeger, 1965). See ch. 5, biographical essay on N.A. Bulganin, Stalin's illness (1944), p. 238.

Reitlinger, Gerald, *The SS. Alibi of a Nation,* ch. 14, 'Himmler the War Lord', in command of the Replacement Army, Himmler and Vlasov, pp. 381–91.

Rigby, T.E., *Communist Party Membership in the USSR 1917–1967* (Princeton UP 1968). See ch. 7, the army and the Party in wartime (numbers, composition Party membership), esp. pp. 250–72.

Steenberg, Sven., *Vlasov,* pp. 143–64, Himmler–Vlasov meeting, *KONR* manifesto (pp. 158–60), Prague conference, Vlasov and the Ukrainian movement.

Strik–Strikfeldt, W., *Against Stalin and Hitler, op. cit.* See pp. 206–21, Himmler–Vlasov meeting 1944 (author's eyewitness account), *KONR,* Prague manifesto, Prague conference.

Tolstoy, Nikolai, *Victims of Yalta* (London: Hodder & Stoughton 1977). Ch. 3 'Tolstoy' conference, Eden in Moscow (1944), on repatriation of Russian prisoners, pp. 62–76. See also *Stalin's Secret War* (London: Cape 1981), *passim.* (Also on repressions and deportations, the GULAG system, deportation of nationalities.)

Werth, A., *Russia at War,* ch. XIII, on 'alternative policies and ideologies . . .', pp. 932–48. (This is an excellent, first-hand analysis of changing Soviet moods and policies, including ideological/Party tightening up; there is also much contemporary material in *Soviet War News.*)

On *Vlasov,* see also: 'Die Behandlungen des russischen Problems während der Zeit des ns. Regimes in Deutschland (unpublished MS), Teil B, 'Die Aktion des Generals Wlassow', ch. VIII, 'Die Lage 1944 . . . eine neue Wlassow–Aktion', Himmler–Vlasov meeting; ch. IX, 'Weiterentwicklung der Aktion', *KONR* founded, manifesto, problem of the non-Russian nationalities, the Ukrainian problem, pp. 171–245.

Bibliography

Parrish, M., *The USSR in World War II* (New York/London: Gartland Pub. 1981), vol. II. See pt V, economic aspects—agriculture, economy, energy, labour, transport, pp. 685–785. (Books published in the USSR.)

GMD

Captured German military materials contain a mass of information on Red Army organization, weapons, the war economy and social conditions; here I have attempted to outline and identify some of these 'main collections' emanating largely from *Fremde Heere Ost (FHO)*.

OKW/Feldwirtschaftsamt. Feldpostbriefe . . . Extracts from many regions in USSR (captured mail), dealing with *rationing and food supplies*, Feb.–Dec. 1944. T-78/ R477, 6460649–740.

FHO (II). File: *Kriegsgliederungen der Roten Armee* . . . (Tables of organization, equipment of Red Army divisions and units—armour, rifle, naval infantry, air assault—PW interrogations, captured documents, 1943–4.) T-78/R460, 6438639–39110.

FHO. Reports to OKW/Feldwirtschaftsamt (Ausl. ost), material on *Soviet war industry*, war economy (1943–4). T-78/R478, 6461656–1816.

FHO (IId). Reports to Chef der Heeresrüstung, on Soviet tanks, SP guns, small arms (with photographs, technical drawings, 1942 onwards). T-78/R478, 64641092–1522.

FHO (IId). File: studies of *Soviet armour*, excellent photographs, technical drawings, intelligence assessments and reports. T-78/R478, 6461818–2119.

FHO (I). File: *Beute und Verluste* . . . Statistical presentations, Soviet losses men/ equipment, daily reports 1942 onwards to July 1944. T-78/R489, 6474667–7580.

FHO (IId). File: *Gefangene erbeutete u. vernichtete Panzer* . . . Statistical material, charts on Soviet losses, manpower, weapons, beg. Jan. 1942. T-78/R481, 6464699–950.

File: *(FHO)* on Soviet tank maintenance, Soviet logistics, rations, Red Army supply in non-Soviet countries . . . (variegated material, 1941 onwards). Captured Soviet orders also. T-78/R481, 6465470–6023.

OKW/Feldwirtschaftsamt (Hgr. Süd). File: on Soviet tank development, SP guns, tables of production, maps of production centres, photographs. Nov. 1943 onwards. T-78/R477, 6460740–1092.

Bibliography

Narodnoe khozyaistvo SSSR v gody VOV (Moscow: Nauka 1971). (Soviet publications on wartime economy, works 1941–68).

SSSR v gody VOV, Ukazatel' sov. literatury 1941–67 (Moscow: Nauka 1977). See ch. V, support for the front (pp. 463–521); ch. VI, trade/labour unions, the *Komsomol*, voluntary organizations (pp. 523–52); ch. VII, the war economy (pp. 553–86; see pp. 585–6 on finances); ch. VIII, the state structure/state apparatus (pp. 588–92).

Soviet materials

IVOVSS, 4 (on 1944), pt 4, chs 19–20: industrial production, Soviet economy 1944, agriculture, transport, food and welfare, recovery and reconstruction, pp. 580–627; Party organization, ideological work, literature and art in 'educational work', pp. 628–55.

IVMV, 9 (on 1944). See pt 3, ch. 14, on Party-political work, pp. 359–83; ch. 15, industrial production, recovery/reconstruction, pp. 384–406; ch. 19, Soviet military forces and Soviet 'military art', pp. 499–516.

General

Kim, M.P. (ed.), *Sovetskaya kultura v gody VOV* (Moscow: Nauka 1976). (24 essays on Soviet wartime science, education, propaganda, the cinema, front-line filming, the Hermitage and the blockade, cultural life in Siberia, the Ukraine, Belorussia. . . .)

Danishevskii, I.M. (ed.), *Voina Narod Pobeda 1941–1945* (Moscow: Politizdat 1976), vols 1–3. (Miscellany of reports, articles, short memoir pieces.)

Gladkov, I.A., *Sovetskaya ekonomika v period VOV 1941–1945 gg* (Moscow: Nauka 1970), 503 pp. (A comprehensive monograph, including a section on finances, pp. 415–43.)

Party organization/Party-political work

Krainyukov, K.V. (ed.), *Partiino-politicheskaya rabota v Sovetskikh voor. silakh v gody VOV 1941–1945* (Moscow: Voenizdat 1968), 583 pp.

Kommunisticheskaya partiya v VOV 1941–1945. Dokumenty i materialy (Moscow: Voenizdat 1970), 494 pp.

Petrov, Yu.P., *Partiinoe stroitelstvo . . . (1918–1961).* See pt III (6), on Party membership/composition in the armed forces in wartime, pp. 387–97; also on the *Komsomol*, pp. 420ff; on intensification of 'political work' among Party members 1944, pp. 431–6. (Petrov puts casualties among Party members at more than 1,500,000 killed at the front.)

Kirsanov, N.A., *Partiinye mobilizatsii na front v gody VOV* (Moscow: Moscow Univ. 1972). (General and local Party/*Komsomol* wartime mobilizations; detailed studies, much tabulation.)

Zhukov, S.I., *Frontovaya pechat' v gody VOV* (Moscow: Moscow Univ. 1968). (Useful, broadly based study of front-line newspapers—see listing for 1944, pp. 7–11.)

'Rear Services' (logistics), the Soviet rear

Kurkotkin, General S.K. (ed.), *Tyl Sovetskikh vooruzhennyk sil v VOV 1941–1945 gg.* (Moscow: Voenizdat 1977), 559 pp. (Immensely detailed and comprehensive work on Soviet wartime logistics.)

Pospelov, P.N. (ed.), *Sovetskii tyl v VOV*, vol. 1: 'Obsche problemy'; vol. 2: 'Trudovoi podvig naroda' (Moscow: Mysl 1974). (Collected essays and studies, with valuable reference and source material on the war effort.)

Transport/railways

Kovalev, I.V., *Transport v VOV (1941–1945 gg.)* (Moscow: Nauka 1981), 480 pp. (Detailed narrative and analysis Soviet wartime transportation—chiefly railways—by Lt.-Gen. Kovalev, wartime chief of the Main Admin./Military Communications, VOSO, member of the Transportation Committee/GKO.)

Kumanev, G.A., *Na sluzhbe fronta i tyla* (Moscow: Nauka 1976), 456 pp. (Detailed study of Soviet railway organization and operations, on the eve of the war and in wartime, for whole period 1938–45; detailed bibliography, tables, index.)

Industrial labour force/trade unions' role

Belonosov, I. (ed.), *Sovetskie profsoyuzy v VOV 1941–1945* (Moscow: Profizdat 1975). (14 memoir-essays on Soviet trade unions in wartime.)

Kotlyar, E.S., *Gosudarstvennye trudovye rezervy SSSR v gody VOV* (Moscow: Vysh. shkola 1975), 240 pp. (Important, informative monograph, industrial labour force.)

Food supplies/agriculture

Arutyunyan, Yu.V., *Sovetskoe krestyanstvo v gody VOV* (Moscow: Nauka, 1st and 2nd edns 1963 and 1970). (Much debated, much discussed pioneer work on Soviet agriculture/Soviet peasantry in wartime.)

Chernyavskii, U.G., *Voina i prodovol'stvie snabzhenie gorodskovo naseleniya v VOV 1941–1945 gg.* (Moscow: Nauka 1964), 208 pp. (Soviet rationing/food supply, nutrition.)

Zelenin, I.E., *Sovkhozy SSSR (1941–1950)* (Moscow: Nauka 1969). See pt 1 for the *sovkhoz* in wartime, pp. 19–130. (Specialist monograph, using mainly archival material.)

Medical/military medical services

Smirnov, Col.-Gen. (Med.) E.I., *Voina i voennaya meditsina 1939–1945 gody* (Moscow: Meditsina 1979), 528 pp. (See esp. pts 2–3; General Smirnov's study includes his own reports as head of Red Army medical service, with detailed studies of medical organization in the main military operations.)

Also Ivanov, F.I., *Reaktivnye psikhozy v voennoe vremya* (Leningrad: Meditsina 1970). See chs 4–5.

Vishnevskii, Col.-Gen. (Med.) A.A., *Dnevnik khiruga. VOV 1941–1945 gg.* (Moscow: Meditsina, 2nd edn 1970). Foreword by Marshal Zhukov. (Wartime diary, 'diary of a surgeon', also much material on military-medical services.)

Soviet women at war

Murmantseva, Major V., 'Sovetskie zhenshchiny v VOV 1941–1945 godov', *VIZ*, 1968 (2), pp. 47–54. (Soviet women on active service.)

The Moscow meeting (October 1944) pp. 411–422

Bryant, Arthur, *Triumph in the West 1943–1946* (Diaries, autobiographical role of Field-Marshal Viscount Alanbrooke) (London: Collins 1959), pp. 234–45, the Moscow meeting, conference with Antonov (Oct. 14), briefing on situation in Far East, Soviet concentration of 'adequate forces', Stalin's emphasis on the *political aspects*, Stalin explains at next meeting logistics/rail movement problems—Alanbrooke much impressed—Polish political discussions 'hanging fire'. (On Far East discussions, cf. S.M. Shtemenko.)

Churchill, Winston S., *The Second World War*, vol. 6, pp. 179–206, prelude to the Moscow visit (Oct. 44), Stalin's cordial invitation; '90 per cent Soviet predominance in Rumania' (pp. 194–5), Churchill to Roosevelt, Churchill memorandum to Stalin on common policy in Balkans (pp. 198–9), meeting with 'Lublin Poles', planning for Soviet entry against Japan, the Polish question, impression of a successful visit.

Moran, Lord, *Winston Churchill: Struggle for Survival*, pt 3, pp. 215–28, on Moscow visit/conference, PM-Eden discussion (Oct. 9), PM-Mikolajczyk, Churchill on Stalin.

Wheeler-Bennett, John and Nicholls, Anthony, *The Semblance of Peace*. On the Moscow meeting Oct. 1944, see ch. 10, pp. 195–200. (Though brief, this account I found to be the most astute and at the same time very even-handed.)

Woodward, Sir Llewellyn, *British Foreign Policy* (single volume, 1962), pp. 306–11, Moscow conference, Churchill's misgivings over the Balkans, wishes to convince Stalin of genuine British desire for co-operation, first discussions Bulgaria/Rumania, the Polish question, Stalin intent on securing Curzon line.

Woodward, Sir L., *British Foreign Policy*, vol. III, ch. XXXVIII (iv, vi), Eden memorandum 9 Aug. on Soviet policy in Europe, outside Balkans, some risk of Anglo–Soviet conflict over policy to Hungary, danger of rift over Poland . . . , pp. 123–31; Moscow meeting, question of degree of overall Soviet co-operation with Western powers, Churchill's misgivings over the Balkans as imperilling future Anglo–Soviet co-operation, American doubts over Soviet policy (footnote, p. 147), bargaining over 'Balkan percentages', pp. 146–52; also ch. XL(ii), the Polish question at the Moscow meeting, Churchill–Stalin conversations, Eden–Stalin–Molotov (Oct. 15) on draft declaration, Stalin insists on Lvov and deletion of references to 'Prime Minister Mikolajczyk', only Stalin and Molotov in Soviet leadership who wished to deal 'softly' with Mikolajczyk, pp. 224–31.

Diplomatic correspondence/diplomatic documents

Perepiska . . . , vol. 1, No. 326, Churchill to Stalin, mention of Stalin's ill health, possible visit to Moscow, Sept. 27, pp. 305–6; No. 328, Stalin–Churchill, cordial invitation to Moscow, Sept. 30, p. 307; No. 331, Stalin and Churchill to Roosevelt, on programme for Moscow meeting, Harriman to be present, Oct. 4, p. 308; No. 332, Churchill–Stalin, to arrange talks on 'military matters' for Oct. 14, Oct. 12, pp. 310–11; No. 336, Churchill–Stalin, on further conversations with Mikolajczyk who wishes to see Stalin alone, Oct. 17, pp. 312–13.

Perepiska . . . , vol. 2, No. 230, Roosevelt–Stalin, Harriman to attend but *not* to commit US government, Oct. 5, pp. 171–2; No. 231, Stalin–Roosevelt, disclaims knowledge of 'points to be discussed in Moscow', Oct. 8, p. 172; No. 234, Stalin–Roosevelt, results of meeting 'very useful', 'more favourable prospects' for solution over Polish question, possibility of meeting in November (1944), Oct. 19, pp. 173–4.

Sherwood, Robert E., *Roosevelt and Hopkins*, pp. 832–4, President Roosevelt's draft signal (Oct. 3) to Stalin with implication that Churchill might speak for the USA as well as Great Britain, stopped by Hopkins, revised message to Stalin with Moscow meeting merely 'preliminary to a conference of the three of us', Harriman as President's personal observer.

Documents on Polish–Soviet Relations, vol. 2, Doc. No. 237, Moscow Conference/ proceedings—Polish affairs, Moscow, Oct. 13 (5–7.30 pm), stenographic record, pp. 405–15; No. 238, observations, Mikolajczyk–Harriman (sent 18.10.44) dated Moscow Oct. 14, pp. 415–16; No. 239, Mikolajczyk–Churchill, conversation Oct. 14 (11.30 am–2 pm) on the territorial question, reconstruction of the Polish government, pp. 416–21; No. 241, Mikolajczyk–Churchill, on the Curzon line, with members of Polish delegation, Moscow, Oct. 14, pp. 423–4; No. 243, Molotov–Grabski, on leaving Lvov with Poland, Oct. 15, pp. 425–7; No. 246,

Mikolajczyk's farewell visit to Stalin, conversation, conditions of existence of Poland in the future, Stalin's views and stipulations, Oct. 18, pp. 430–33; No. 250, Mikolajczyk–Churchill *et al.*, discussion in London on Polish position in face of Soviet demands, Oct. 26, pp. 439–41.

Soviet materials

IVOVSS, 4, pt 4, ch. 21(2–4), on the EAC, Moscow conference, Dumbarton Oaks (in that order): on the Moscow conference, pp. 665–9, Quebec conference and planning for war in Pacific, American 'official circles' trying to drag USSR 'prematurely' into war with Japan, threat of cancelling Lend-Lease, collapse of Churchill's plans for a 'Balkan strategy', the Polish question and Polish frontiers, general agreement on the Balkans, discussions on the future of Germany.

Israelyan, V.L., *Diplomaticheskaya istoriya VOV*, pp. 248–64, Dumbarton Oaks (pp. 248–53), Moscow conference, discussions on future of Germany, Balkans–Soviet policy based on non-interference in internal affairs of other states, hence rejection of 'spheres of influence' (p. 260), the Polish question, Anglo–Soviet agreement 'in general terms' on future Polish frontiers, military reports on the strategic situation, Moscow meeting affirmed the idea of post-war collaboration among the Great Powers, supported by popular feelings.

Israelyan, V.L., *Antigitlerovskaya koalitsiya 1941–1945*, pt 3, ch. XIX, Dumbarton Oaks, Quebec, Moscow conferences, esp. pp. 462–72 on Moscow conference, with more detailed discussion of the Polish question. See also *Sovetskii Soyuz na mezhdunarodnykh konferentsiyakh . . .* , Tom III, 'Konferentsiya . . . v Dumbarton–Okse'. Sbornik dokumentov (Moscow: Politizdat 1978).

Shtemenko, S.M., *The Soviet General Staff at War 1941–1945*. See here ch. 14, creation in 1942 of post of Deputy Chief/GS, Far East, Lomov and Shevchenko change places, pressure from Western allies to draw USSR into war with Japan, Stalin orders estimates of deployment/logistics requirements *for Far East* (Sept. 44), Stalin uses these estimates at Moscow meeting (cf. FM Alanbrooke), pp. 322–4. (Soviet text, *General'nyi shtab . . .* , vol. 1, 1968, ch. 14, pp. 332–4.)

Baltic operations: Riga–Memel–Courland pp. 422–430

Allen, W.E.D. and Muratoff, Paul, *The Russian Campaigns*, pp. 206–16, autumn operations in the Baltic, border of E Prussia.

Philippi, A. and Heim, F., *Der Feldzug gegen Sowjetrussland*, pt 2, pp. 265–8, Soviet autumn offensive in the Baltic, loss of Estonia, drive on Memel.

Seaton, Albert, *The Russo–German War*, pp. 522–6, on the Soviet offensive into the Baltic States (1st, 2nd and 3rd Baltic Fronts), Soviet change of plan to strike for Memel, Bagramyan's regrouping from right to left flank, fall of Riga, Courland bridgehead, 3rd Belorussian Front thrust into E Prussia. (An extremely valuable review of Soviet and German operations.)

GMD

OKH/Kriegsgesch. Abt. Maps: *1 u 2 Schlacht um Kurland*, Durchbruch auf Memel; *1 Schlacht um Ostpreussen* (Goldap–Gumbinnen), 5.10.44–7.11.44. T-78/R136, 6065208–262. (Very clear and very dramatic maps.)

Soviet materials

IVOVSS, 4, pt 2, pp. 354–63, Soviet offensive operations, Memel–Riga: 2nd and 3rd Baltic Front operations for Riga, Volskii's 5th Guards Tank Army in drive for Memel, Stalin's wish to liquidate Courland group, reinforcement not available due to operations in E Prussia and W Poland, assault on Memel inevitably delayed. (A good chronology of *Stavka* decisions.)

Bagramyan, I.Kh., *Kak my shli k pobede*, pp. 419–80, the shift from the 'Riga axis' to the 'Memel axis', thrust to E Prussia. (Highly detailed but highly informative, with much analysis and evaluation.)

Bor'ba za Sovetskuyu Pribaltiku . . . , vol. 2, pp. 127–33, situation in Sept. 44, drive on Riga, Leningrad Front drive into Estonia, fighting on the 'Sigulda line', 1st and 3rd Baltic Front operations for Memel, fall of Riga. (A terse unadorned operational narrative, using military archives almost exclusively.)

Portnov, S.I. (ed.), *V srazheniyakh za Sovetskuyu Latviyu*, pp. 148–76, operations in central region of Latvia, fall of Riga. (Very detailed operational narrative.)

Shtemenko, S.M., *The Soviet General Staff at War 1941–1945*, pp. 289–93, the Baltic Fronts, decisive operations Sept. 14, regrouping for Memel thrust, Bagramyan's 'highly original generalship', capture of Riga, blockading of German forces/ Courland grouping.

Vasilevskii, A.M., *Delo vsei zhizni*. On the Baltic strategic operation, autumn 1944, pp. 483–7. (Short summary, outlining main operational decisions, including the 'Memel drive'.)

Yeremenko, A.I., *Gody vozmezdiya*, ch. 11, pp. 437–88, the drive on Riga—with rebuttal of the criticisms levelled by *Sandalov* on Yeremenko's performance, missing the opportunity to deal a mortal blow to Army Group North.

The balance sheet, end 1944:
Soviet strategic planning pp. 422–430

Allen, W.E.D. and Muratoff, Paul, *The Russian Campaigns (1944–45)*, pp. 221–9, general situation, eve of last winter campaign (Dec. 44).

Irving, David, *Hitler's War*, pp. 733–6, Hitler's preparations for Ardennes counter-blow, quiet on Eastern Front save for Hungary, Hitler's departure from E Prussia, postponement of Ardennes attack, anticipation of the collapse of the Allied coalition— 'this entire artificially erected common front'.

GMD

FHO (Chef), Reports: *Wichtigste Feindfeststellungen* (Nov.–Dec. 44), Front movements, assessments. T-78/R466, 6445345–407.

FHO (I), Teil A. *Zusammenstellung . . . abgefassten Beurteilungen der Feindlage (1942–1944)*. Intelligence appreciations: see No. 3508/44, 7.10.44, Feindbeurteilung (build-up of Soviet reserves, Stalin's need to destroy Ostheer, to do this quickly to establish Soviet power ahead of Anglo–American advances); No. 3697/44, 19.10.44, situation report on Bulgaria/Bulgarian forces; No. 4012/44, 10.11.44, Beurteilung (assessment of Soviet operational planning and intentions), see also Anlage 1, on operations 3rd Ukrainian Front, 1st and 2nd Belorussian Fronts; No. 4142/44, 11.11.44, Kurze Beurteilung (Army Group South, Hungary); No. 4404/44,

5.12.44, Zusammenfassende Auswertung . . . (evaluation of Soviet planning based on PW interrogation, also 'secret intelligence'; a precise and highly accurate review of Soviet plans and intentions, with detailed observations on Front plans/assignments); No. 4640/44, 22.12.44, adjustments to previous estimate of Soviet operational plans/intentions. (These are quite remarkable assessments, which closely follow the Soviet operational planning process and adjustments to the Soviet master plan.) T-78/R466, 6446197–230.

FHO (IIa). Reports: *Frontaufklärungsmeldungen*. . . . (daily intelligence summaries, tactical-operational intelligence, Nov.–Dec. 44). T-78/R466, 6445718–871.

FHO (IIc). Tables/diagrams: *Gliederung des sow. russ. Feldheeres*, Order-of-battle tables/ Red Army: Front composition, with Tank armies, indep. Tank, Mech., Cav. Corps (for period Oct.–Dec. 44). T-78/R493, 6480686–710.

Soviet materials

IVOVSS, 4, pt 2, pp. 499–504, summary of the results of the Soviet summer-autumn offensive campaign.

Rokossovskii, K.K., *A Soldier's Duty* (Moscow: Progress Pub. translation from *Soldatskii dolg*), see 'Inside Germany', Rokossovskii appointed commander 2nd Belorussian Front by Stalin Nov. 12, took over from G.F. Zakharov, to *Stavka* and personal briefing by Stalin, axis of advance in NW direction but not to be concerned with 'E Prussian grouping' which would be dealt with by 3rd Belorussian Front, emphasis on co-ordination with Zhukov's 1st Belorussian Front, Stalin insisted that 2nd Belorussian Front *not* a secondary sector, 2nd Belorussian Front also assigned 2nd Shock Army, Grishin's 49th Army and Volskii's 5th Guards Tank Army, pp. 265–9.

Shtemenko, S.M., *The Soviet General Staff at War 1941–1945*, pp. 296–306, on Soviet planning, end 1944, estimate of results of summer/autumn offensive, depletion of Soviet forces, review of operational opportunities–heavy enemy defences in Kurland, less favourable for Germans in E Prussia, stiff resistance expected on Warsaw/Poznan/Silesian axes, much greater success for capture of Budapest, approaches to Vienna—necessity for Soviet regrouping, need to choose 'most promising lines of advance', beginning Nov. *Stavka* survey of situation 2nd, 1st Belorussian Fronts and 1st Ukrainian Front, absence of necessary Soviet superiority, decision to turn to defensive (Antonov's insistent point), *Stavka* directive Nov. 4, final Soviet campaign to be carried out in *two* stages, October plan merely an outline, beginning Nov. work on more specific lines, discussion between Antonov, Shtemenko, Gryzlov and Lomov, Soviet design to put pressure on E Prussia and Hungary, this proved by further concentration of German forces (uncovering 'the Berlin sector'), General Staff decision to 'punch through' the weak centre towards Berlin, question of *Front* assignments, no special conference for Front commanders but each Front commander summoned separately early Nov., provisional timing fixed for 20 Jan. 1945, Stalin's decision to appoint Zhukov commander of the armies to take Berlin, co-ordination of all four Fronts committed to 'the Berlin axis' assigned to Stalin by Stalin himself, Vasilevskii thus left in charge of only 1st and 2nd Baltic Fronts, General Staff view of 1st Ukrainian Front operations, to outflank Silesia from NE and N, aim to preserve Silesian industrial resources,

Zhukov in Moscow, Nov. 27, proposed attack towards Lodz and on to Poznan, Stalin's agreement with this revised plan, Koniev given Breslau as his main objective (as opposed to Kalisz), main operational plan outlined by end Nov. finally confirmed end Dec. (See original Soviet text, *General'nyi shtab v gody voiny*, pp. 303–16.)

Zhukov, G.K., *Vospominaniya . . .* , vol. 2, ch. 21, from the Vistula to the Oder, pp. 284–8: statement of German strength, Anglo–American strength in the west, Soviet strength (6 million men, 14,000 tanks/SP guns, 14,500 aircraft), *Stavka* planning with 'Warsaw–Berlin axis' main line of advance, Zhukov's insistence that 'the mission of Soviet troops to capture Berlin' under Allied agreement, denunciation of Churchill's 'secret intentions' which prompted 'certain caution' on the Soviet side (p. 286), Zhukov assigned to work on offensive plans late Oct.–early Nov. to open on the southern front in direction of Vienna, the serious problem of E Prussia (recalls his own plan submitted during summer offensive), Nov. 1–2 with Stalin, plan presented by Antonov but approved by Zhukov, Stalin again refused to reinforce 2nd Belorussian Front to knock out E Prussian concentration, further elaboration of plan, Nov. 15 Zhukov to Lublin, Nov. 16 appointed commander 1st Belorussian Front, assumed command Nov. 18, *Stavka* approved attack plan late Nov., provisional timing 15–20 Jan. 1945.

7 THE ASSAULT ON THE *REICH*: JANUARY–MARCH 1945

Allen, W.E.D. and Muratoff, Paul, *The Russian Campaigns 1944–45*, pp. 230–53, the Budapest operation (Nov. 44–13 Feb. 45).

Irving, David, *Hitler's War*. See Endkampf, 'The Gamble', on Hitler and the Ardennes attack, with the significant note (p. 748) that Guderian waited *until 14 January 1945* to ask Hitler to shift the main effort to the Eastern Front—not Dec. 1944 as Guderian himself has it. In view of Mr Irving's attention to the documentary record, inspection at once scrupulous and rigorous, this revision must stand; see also the Hitler–Guderian exchange, 9 Jan. 1945, with Hitler refusing to countenance a planned withdrawal from the Vistula line on a given signal, also Hitler handing over only two divisions, pp. 752–3.

Seaton, Albert, *The Russo–German War*, ch. 29, Soviet and German operations, Hungary/Budapest, pp. 497–501.

Warlimont, Walter, *Inside Hitler's Headquarters*, pt VI, pp. 495–9, Hitler–Gen. Thomale talk Dec. 29–30, Guderian's attempt to shift emphasis to Eastern Front, Hitler's dismissal of Gehlen's intelligence reports, Jodl retains and reinforces divisions in the West.

KTB/GMD

KTB/OKW. See vol IV (pt 2), 1 Abschnitt, from Lagebuch/WFStab: Lagebuch 1–31.1, Lagebuch 1–28.2. See pp. 976–1134. (Situation reports, all fronts.)

OKH/Kriegsgesch. Abt. Maps: Ungarn I. Teil. 11.1944. (Complete map display, Budapest operation, Hungary to March 1945.) T-78/R136, 6065497–624.

OKH/GenStdH/Op. Abt. See Chefsache Anlagen zum *KTB/Op. Abt.* Hitler's directives/instructions for operations Army Group South, Guderian's corrections/corrected drafts, redeployment *SS* units, also intelligence report, evaluation 18.2.45 with maps ('Gruppierung der Reserven', also 'vermutliche Weiterführung der sowj. russ. Operationen'). T-78/R305, 6255785–8667 (Jan.–Feb.) *Note:* see also H. Guderian, *Panzer Leader* (London: Michael Joseph 1952).

OKH/GenStdH/Op. Abt. KTB Anlagen: Hitler's instructions and directives, operations in Hungary, fall of Budapest; see Op. Abt. Nr 2786/45, 17.2.45, Abschlussmeldung Budapest, also reporting German losses 12/44–2/45—1,111 officers, 32,997 men. T-78/R304, 6255440–612 (for Feb. 45).

NOTE: Behaviour of Red Army/occupied enemy territory: 1944–5. See *FHO* (IIb), collection of materials: captured and translated Soviet orders, interrogation of Soviet PWs, disorder, indiscipline in Soviet rear in occupied areas (Koniev/Krainyukov orders), details of Soviet *strafbats* (penal battalions), military orders for treatment of German civilians/property (June 44–March/April 45). T-78/R488, 6474390–648.

FHO

Gehlen intelligence reports: No. 4404/44 (5.12.44), No. 4640/44 (22.12.44). T-78/R466, 6446222–230 (cf. notes on *GMD*/Chapter 6, above).

Nr 81/45, 'Beurteilung der Feindlage . . .', Stand 5.1.45 (based on data from above reports), also maps, '. . . vermutliche Operationsrichtungen des Gegners 4.1.45', '. . . Meldungen des geheim. Meldedienstes . . .' (2.12.44–2.1.45). T-78/R503, no frame numbers.

Nr 26/45, 'Gedanken zur Feindbeurteilung' (Stand 2.2.45) (3 copies) (also maps). T-78/R496, 6484222–230.

Nr 1161/45, 'Beurteilung . . .' (Stand 25.2.45), based on Jan. data. Also Anlagen (on Soviet decisions/operations). T-78/R501, 6489736–744.

FHO (IIa). *Sowjetruss. Wehrkraft,* dated 1.2.45: total 484 rifle divisions (397 deployed), 38 tank/mech. corps (33 deployed/immediate reserve), 155 indep. tank formations (79 deployed/immediate reserve), 7 cavalry corps. T-78/R489, 6475305.

FHO (I/W). Lageberichte Ost: daily situation reports, Jan–Feb. 45. Lageberichte Januar 45, Februar 45. See T-78/R472, 6453856–6454660 and R473, 6454250–661.

Soviet materials

Biryukov, Lt.-Gen. N., 'Na podstupakh k Budapeshtu', *VIZ,* 1965 (3), pp. 87–94. (20th Guards Rifle Corps operations, Budapest, Dec. 44).

Collective authorship, *Ot Volgi do Pragi* (Moscow: Voenizdat 1966). (Combat record 7th Guards Army.) On Budapest operation (involving 30th Rifle Corps), see pp. 193–214.

Koniev, I.S. (ed.), *Za osvobozhdenie Chekhoslovakii,* pp. 139–76, operations of 4th and 2nd Ukrainian Fronts, western Carpathians Jan–Feb. 45, liberation of central Slovakia (Jan. 45), heavy resistance/heavy losses 53rd Army and 1st Cav.-Mech.

Group (only 14 tanks left late Jan. 45, p. 155), Soviet defenders river Hron mid-Feb. severely pressed (divisions with only half manpower, companies down to 25–30 men, 4th Mech. Corps with only 20 tanks, p. 172). *Note on Soviet losses:* during Jan.–Feb. operations, *4th and 2nd Ukrainian Fronts* in W Carpathians, Soviet forces lost 16,000 killed in action, 50,000 wounded; 1st Czechoslovak Corps 209 men killed, 777 wounded (see pp. 173–4).

Kuznetsov, P.G., *Marshal Tolbukhin*, pp. 207–22, on Budapest operations, Tolbukhin's direction and decisions Dec. 44–Feb. 45.

Malakhov, M.M., *Osvobozhdenie Vengrii . . .*, pp. 91–158, Budapest operations, repulse of German counter-blow (2–7 Jan.), 2nd Ukrainian Front thrust to Komarno (6–10 Jan.), second German attack (7–13 Jan.), repulse of third German counter-blow (18–27 Jan.), elimination of German breakout to Danube (27 Jan.–16 Feb.). (Virtually day-by-day operational narrative.)

Malinovskii, R.Ya. (ed.), *Budapesht Vena Praga,* pp. 97–172, Budapest operation, organization of 'Budapest force', command assigned to Managarov when Afonin wounded (p. 157), final assault opened Feb. 5. (for period Dec. 44–Feb. 45).

Managarov, I.M., *V srazhenii za Khar'kov,* pp. 231–4, Managarov with 53rd Army, Budapest, in command special operational group 21 Jan. 45.

Pushkash, A.I., *Vengrii v VMV.* See ch. 11 on Szeged–Debreczen political assemblies, composition of various party groups, planning for provisional national assembly and provisional government, pp. 476–8; see also M.M. Minasyan, *op cit.,* pp. 370–75.

Minasyan, M.M., *Osvobozhdenie . . . (1967),* ch. 4(5), Budapest operations, Dec. 44–Feb. 45, pp. 343–70; note also reference to Soviet strength Dec. 44 (39 Rifle Divs, 14 Rumanian divs, Soviet divisional strength varied from 3,500 to 4,500, with 11 divisions deploying 5,000–5,500 men, only two divs. having 6,000 men, see p. 345); also *General Staff criticism* of handling of operations in Buda, p. 368.

Samsonov, A.M. (ed.), *Osvobozhdenie Vengrii ot fashizma* (Moscow: Nauka 1965). (Collected memoirs). See Malinovskii, pp. 19–24 (Budapest); M.V. Zakharov on Budapest, pp. 29–39; V.A. Sudets, 17th Air Army operations, pp. 54–90; I.T. Shlemin, 46th Army operations, pp. 102–15; on Red Army truce negotiator Ostapenko, pp. 193–5.

Tarasov, S.P., *Boi u ozera Balaton* (Moscow: Voenizdat 1959).

Tolubko, V.F. and Baryshev, N.I., *Na yuzhnom flange,* pp. 361–76, 4th Guards Mech. Corps operations on right-flank 2nd Ukrainian Front (Dec. 44–Feb. 45)—strength beg. Jan. 45 reduced to 5,200 men, 14 tanks, 96 guns and mortars (p. 368).

Varaki, Colonel P., 'Nekotorye voprosy boevovo primeneniya 6-i gvardeiskoi tankovoi armii v Budapeshtskoi operatsii', *VIZ,* 1973 (12), pp. 64–9. (Analysis of 6th Guards Tank Army operations, Budapest, Dec. 44.)

Vorontsov, T.F. *et al., Ot volzhskikh stepei do avstriiskikh Alp.* (Moscow: Voenizdat 1971). (Combat record 4th Guards Army.) See 4th Guards/Budapest operation, commitment to outer encirclement, pp. 136–82. (Note: G.F. Zakharov, 4th Guards commander.)

Zakharov, M.V. (ed.), *Osvobozhdenie . . . (1970).* See pp. 335–99, Budapest operation Dec. 44–Feb. 45.

Zheltov, Col.–Gen. A., 'Osvobozhdenie Vengrii', *VIZ,* 1974 (10), pp. 43–50. (General survey, Soviet operations, Hungary.)

Zavizion, G.T. and Kornyushin, P.A., *I na Tikhom Okeane . . .* (6th Guards Tank).
    See ch. VI, 6th Guards Tank operations Komarno, 26 Jan. 44 drawn into reserve,
    Feb. 21 tank/SP gun strength built up to 224, pp. 125–50 (cf. *VIZ*, 1973 (12),
    loc. cit.).

Planning/preparation Vistula–Oder operation   pp. 447–455

Diplomatic correspondence

Perepiska . . . , vol. 1. No. 383, Churchill–Stalin, 6 Jan. 45, enquiry about possible
    Soviet offensive in the East, pp. 348–49; No. 384, Stalin–Churchill, Jan. 7, Soviet
    offensive not later than second half of Jan., p. 349; No. 385, Churchill–Stalin,
    Jan. 9, acknowledgement, p. 350.

Soviet materials

IVOVSS, 5, pt 1, pp. 32–6, strategic planning, Soviet intention to attack along entire
    front along four axes (coastal-Baltic, Berlin, Prague, Vienna), Front assignments
    for Jan. 45 offensive (involving 33 rifle armies, 5 tank and 7 air armies, 10 tank/
    mech./cav. corps, also Baltic Fleet units), tank armies to penetrate to depth of
    400–450 kms, Soviet estimates of German strength and deployments, Soviet
    superiority on given sectors, co-ordination of Allied operations, impact of German
    offensive in the Ardennes. *Note, p. 27, on Soviet strength, Jan. 45:* 55 rifle armies,
    6 tank and 13 air armies on Soviet–German front, with about 500 rifle divisions.
    Total manpower: 7,109,000 (577,000 in *Stavka* reserve), 488 divisions (including
    airborne deployed), 34 tank/mech. corps, 155 aviation divisions, 115,100 guns/
    mortars, 15,100 tanks/SP guns, 15,815 aircraft. See also on the *Soviet armed forces
    1945*, pp. 39–46.
IVMV, 10, pt 1, pp. 37–45, Soviet–German strength Jan. 45 (Soviet deployed forces—
    10 Front commands, 2 Fleets, 3 Flotillas, 51 rifle armies, 6 tank, 10 air armies,
    2 Air Defence/PVO Front commands: 473 divisions, 21 tank/12 mech. corps;
    Stavka reserve 2 Front administrations, 4 rifle and 2 air armies, 4 tank/mech.
    corps, 20 rifle divisions, p. 37), 72 per cent of Soviet manpower, 74 per cent
    artillery, 77 per cent tanks/SP guns, 65 per cent air strength deployed on Soviet–
    German front; analysis of German deployment, Allied operations in NW Europe
    and Italy; Soviet operational planning beginning Nov. 44, *Stavka* directives for E
    Prussian and Warsaw–Berlin operations issued 25 Nov.–3 Dec. 44, Soviet intention
    to divert German strength to the flanks with heavy deception measures to conceal
    offensive intentions at the centre of the Front, movement of Soviet reinforcements/
    replacements (483,000 men Nov.–Dec. 44, 6,100 tanks), careful distribution of
    strategic reserves (11 rifle, 4 tank armies).
Blinov, Colonel S.I., *Ot Visly do Odera* (Moscow: Voenizdat 1962), pp. 18–57 (both
    Army operations), operational planning/preparation Army commander Kurochkin's
    assignments to formations, combat deployment, regrouping, logistics planning.
Chuikov, V.I. Marshal Chuikov has produced several very different versions of the
    fortunes of 8th Guards Army 1944–45 and the road to Berlin, making it difficult
    to disentangle fact from contrived opinion. *Konets tret'evo reikha* began life in the
    journal *Oktyabr* (1964), followed by a first published version (1965), anti-Zhukov

in almost all essentials; that first version was produced in English translation, *The End of the Third Reich* (London: MK 1967), followed by a second, less polemical version published in 1973 (Moscow: Sov. Rossiya), also in Belorussian and Ukrainian editions (Kiev: Politvidav Ukraini 1975). Now we have *Ot Stalingrada do Berlina* (1980), with the Zhukov vendetta erased and no denunciation of logistics failures (see note below on Soviet logistics; Antipenko, *Na glavnom napravlenii* had earlier refuted Chuikov's charges). See *Ot Stalingrada . . . *, pp. 502–7, on preparations for Vistula–Oder.

Galitskii, General K.N., *V boyakh za Vostochnuyu Prussiyu* (Moscow: Nauka 1970) (11th Guards Army operations). Ch. 5, *Stavka* concept of E Prussia operation, directive 3 Dec. 44, Chernyakhovskii's operational decision, Front regrouping and deployment (pp. 196–7), 11th Guards Army planning, corps assignments, pp. 197–217. (Galitskii emphasizes that in later stages of the war Stalin allowed Front commanders rather more latitude in developing Front plans/operational decisions.)

Kharitonov, Colonel A.D., *Gumbinnenskii proryv* (Moscow: Voenizdat 1960) (28th Army, Gumbinnen operation). Ch. 2, decisions of 3rd Belorussian Front commander, 28th Army command decisions, corps commanders' decisions, logistics, signals, regrouping, pp. 15–57.

Kir'yan, Colonel M.M., *S Sandomirskovo platsdarma* (Moscow: Voenizdat 1960) (5th Guards Army operations). Ch. 2, Col.-Gen. Zhadov's operational planning/decisions, planned use of armoured forces, logistics, signals, regrouping, pp. 26–94.

Koniev, I.S., *Sorok pyatyi* (Moscow: Voenizdat (VM) 1966, also 1970 edn). See Progress Publishers (Moscow), translation, *Year of Victory* (1969). 'From the Vistula to the Oder', planning, Stalin's inspection Nov. 44 of Koniev's plan, emphasis on preserving Silesian region—'Gold'—Antonov's signals on alteration to timing (9 Jan. 45), camouflage and deception measures, pp. 5–16.

Kuznetsov, P.G., *General Chernyakhovskii*, pp. 208–14. On planning E Prussian operation, General Staff view, Chernyakhovskii's plan (see map, operational concept 3rd Belorussian Front, Tilsit–Insterburg operation, p. 212), assignments to Front armies.

Rokossovskii, K.K., *A Soldier's Duty* (Moscow, 1970), pp. 268–75. On the planning/ preparation 2nd Belorussian Front, assumption of command from G.F. Zakharov, composition Front forces, problem of Front co-ordination (problem also of Rokossovskii's right flank), Front attack plan with left-flank forces, only formations transferred from *Stavka* reserve fully manned, operational assignments to armies, planning of artillery preparation.

Shtemenko, S.M., 'Kak planirovalas poslednyaya kampaniya po razgromu gitlerovskoi Germanii', *VIZ*, 1965 (5), see pp. 56–64, review of Soviet strategic/operational planning for January offensive.

Zhukov, G.K., *Vospominaniya . . . *, vol. 2, ch. 20, pp. 284–92, from the Vistula to the Oder, main strategic plan, the problem of E Prussia, difficulties of adequate tactical intelligence, war-game Jan. 4 to organize closer co-operation between bridgeheads, strategic objectives of 1st Belorussian Front, initially designated the 'Warsaw–Poznan operation', detailed operational plan with main attack from Magnuszew bridgehead.

Note on Soviet logistics, January 1945. In the Magnuszew bridgehead, 10 Jan. 1945, ammunition stocks amounted to 2,479,800 artillery rounds and mines (2,132 railway-truck loads), 1,311,900 artillery rounds/mines in the Pulawy bridgehead; Front held 55,989 tons of fuel (1st Belorussian Front), 1st Ukrainian Front (Koniev) held 114,336 tons of ammunition, 57,215 tons of fuel/lubricants, 47,805 tons of food. See *IVOVSS*, 5, p. 64.

Malopolska, East Prussia, on to the Oder pp. 455–469

Allen, W.E.D. and Muratoff, Paul, *The Russian Campaigns 1944–45*, pp. 253–88, operations in Malopolska, E Prussia.

Philippi, A, and Heim, F., *Der Feldzug gegen Sowjetrussland*, I, 'Feldzug d. Jahres 1945', Soviet winter offensive, Soviet thrust into Silesia, isolation of German forces in E Prussia, pp. 274–7.

Schieder, Theodor (ed.), *Dokumentation der Vertreibung der Deutschen aus Ost–Mitteleuropa*. Band I/2 (Herausg.: Bundesministerium für Vertriebene n.d.).

Seaton, Albert, *The Russo-German War*, pp. 530–39, Vistula to the Oder, German planning, deployments, expectations, Red Army launches 'one of the greatest strategic operations of the war', puzzle of *timing* (Jan. 12–14, p. 534), 1st Ukrainian Front breakthrough, Zhukov attack from Magnuszew bridgehead, Hitler's fury over loss of Warsaw, Soviet drive into E Prussia, fall of Tannenberg, redesignation of German army groups (p. 539), appointment of Himmler to command. See also Dieckert, K., and Grossmann, H., *Der Kampf um Ostpreussen* (Munich: Gräfe u. Unzer 1960); Kissel H., *Der deutsche Volkssturm* (Frankfurt: Mittler 1962).

KTB/GMD

KTB/OKW, IV/2. See 1 Abschnitt, Lagebuch (for January), from 12.1.45, pp. 1008ff; see also WFStab/*KTB*, summary of events, second half of January (Col. Meyer-Detring am 29.1, 19 Uhr), pp. 1052–6. Also Lagebuch, 24.1.45, 'Die neugebildete Heeresgr. Weichsel, zu deren OB der Reichsführer SS ernannt worden ist, übernimmt den Abschnitt von Glogau bis Elbing . . .', p. 1035.

OKH/GenStdH/Op. Abt. KTB Anlagen: signals/instructions on Soviet offensive Vistula–Oder, filling out of fortresses Posen, Glogan, Zhukov Order of the Day (translated text—*Wir werden uns grausam rächen für alles*—6255627 frame). T-78/R304, 6255440ff. Ref. also T-78/R477, documentary material on discipline/behaviour Soviet troops.

Soviet materials

IVOVSS, 5, pt 1, ch. 2(3), Soviet operations in Poland, Jan. 45: narrative 1st Ukrainian Front operations, 1st Belorussian Front operations, liberation of Warsaw, revised *Stavka* directive Jan. 17 (p. 80), 1st Ukrainian Front operations Upper Silesia, drive to the Oder, pp. 69–82; ch. 3(2–3), E Prussia operation, weakness of poor co-ordination of Fronts (p. 99), Front command decisions (3rd and 2nd Belorussian Fronts), problem of reinforcements for Rokossovskii, pp. 97–104; offensive opened Jan. 13–14, German resistance, Jan. 19–26 splitting up of German defenders and isolation of E Prussia, conduct of Soviet troops (p. 113), *Stavka* directive Jan. 21 to 2nd Belorussian Front to strike to Deutsch–Eylau/Marienburg, Dyachenko's thrust to Elbing (p. 115), break to the sea and Vistula, 3rd Belorussian Front destruction of German 'Insterburg group', closing on Königsberg, German counter-blow at 48th Army/2nd Belorussian Front Jan. 27, Soviet lack of supplies, pp. 97–122.

IVMV, 10, pt 1, ch. 2(3), Vistula–Oder operation, operational narrative, German losses put at 35 divisions destroyed, 147,000 prisoners, pp. 70–88; ch. 3(2), E Prussian operations, pp. 99–111. (More terse, restrained account than *IVOVSS*, 5).

'Vislo–Oderskaya operatsiya v tsifrakh', *VIZ*, 1965 (1), pp. 71–81. (Vistula–Oder operation, statistical information/tables, strength/deployments, command (down to corps).)

Babadzhanyan, A.Kh. *et al.*, *Lyuki otkryli v Berline* (1st Guards Tank Army), pp. 231–49, Vistula–Oder operation, drive to Poznan, one brigade assigned to blockading force, drive to the German frontier. (Operational narrative based on Soviet military archives.) See also Marshal (Tank Troops) A. Babadzhanyan, *Dorogi pobedy* (Moscow: Mol. Gvardiya, 2nd edn 1975), pp. 212–36, Vistula–Oder operation. (A racy, highly personalized account with Babadzhanyan as corps commander.)

Blinov, S.I., *Ot Visly do Odera*, p. 58–125, 60th Army operations, drive on Cracow. (Detailed operational narrative.)

Galitskii, K.N., *V boyakh za Vostochnuyu Prussiyu*, pp. 218–25, 11th Guards Army operations, unsuccessful start Jan. 13, operations with 5th Army, assigned to junction 39th and 5th Army, advance on Wehlau, drive on Insterburg. (Extremely detailed operational narrative by 11th Guards commander, frank and full disclosures of shortcomings, useful and illuminating 'cross-checking' with post-war German records, 'captured documents', including Third *Panzer* materials.)

Gladysh, Colonel S., '2-ya udarnaya armiya v Vostochno–Prusskoi operatsii', *VIZ*, 1975 (2), pp. 20–28. (Detailed operational narrative/analysis, 2nd Shock Army/E Prussia, Jan. 45.)

Kharitonov, A.D., *Gumbinnenskii proryv* (28th Army operations), pp. 60–95, Soviet breakthrough, fall of Gumbinnen, beginning of drive westwards.

Kir'yan, M.M., *S Sandomirskovo platsdarma*, pp. 95–158, breakthrough and pursuit, 5th Guards Army, 'Czestochowa axis'. (Extremely detailed narrative.)

Koniev, I.S., *Year of Victory*, pp. 17–45, breakout 1st Ukrainian Front, rapid advance on Cracow, problem of taking Silesian industrial area, wide envelopment with armour, force Germans out of encirclement into open country, success of Rybalko (3rd Guards Tank) and Lelyushenko (4th Tank), Silesian trap closed, link with 1st Belorussian Front, Oder bridgeheads.

Korovnikov, Col.-Gen. I., 'Udar na Krakov', *VIZ*, 1975 (1), pp. 51–6. (59th Army operations, Cracow.)

Matsulenko, V., 'Operativnaya maskirovka voisk v Vislo–Oderskoi operatsii', *VIZ*, 1975 (1), pp. 10–21. (Deception/camouflage, Vistula–Oder operation.)

Platonov, Lt.-Gen. S., 'Kratkii obzor veonnykh deistvii', *VIZ*, 1964 (2), pp. 14–24. (Soviet operations in Poland; see also Maj.-Gen. Pavlenko, on Soviet military art, pp. 25–36.)

Radzievskii, General A., 'Stremitel'nye deistviya tankovykh armii', *VIZ*, 1965 (1), pp. 8–15. (On tank army operations, Vistula–Oder.)

Rokossovskii, K.K., *A Soldier's Duty*. On the first phase of Jan. offensive, weather precludes air support, improvement Jan. 16, breakthrough from Lomza to mouth of Narew, thrust for the Vistula, pp. 276–80. 'On two fronts', Jan. 20 orders to turn N and NE into E Prussia, 'complete surprise' and total change of plans (from directive of Nov. 28/44), many errors of judgement in planning E Prussian campaign, problem of lagging behind Zhukov, rebuke from Zhukov for this, 50th Army failure to detect German withdrawal, fall of Marienburg, Elbing unsuccessfully rushed, German blow Jan. 26, danger to 48th Army, movement of Volskii's tanks, Oslikovskii's cavalry to the rescue, on conduct of Soviet troops, call for 'highest discipline', pp. 281–9.

Rokossovskii, K.K., 'Na berlinskom i vostochno-prusskom napravleniyakh', *VIZ*, 1965 (2), pp. 25–8. (Interview, on E Prussian operation, on the conduct of Soviet troops—'violation of prescribed norms'.)

Vysotskii, F.I., *Gvardeiskaya tankovaya* (2nd Guards Tank Army), pp. 147–56, 2nd Guards Tank, Vistula–Oder operation.

Zhukov, G.K., *Vospominaniya . . .*, vol. 2, pp. 294–8, successful breakthrough, German withdrawal from Warsaw, *Stavka* directive Jan. 17, Zhukov–Stalin discussion Jan. 25 (p. 297), Zhukov request not to stop his offensive, blockade of Poznan, redeployment to face possible threat from E Pomerania.

Polish materials

Dolata, B., *Wyzwolenie Polski 1944–1945*, pt II, pp. 95–233, operations 2nd and 3rd Belorussian Fronts, 1st Belorussian Front, Polish forces, liberation of Warsaw, 1st Ukrainian Front operations/Silesia, pp. 95–233. (Extremely detailed operational narrative, with enormously detailed appendix on the military chronology, communiqués, Soviet–Polish formations/units with commanders.)

Poplawski, General S., '1-ya armiya Voiska Pol'skovo v boyakh za Varshavu', *VIZ*, 1965 (1), pp. 47–53 (1st Polish Army, Warsaw, Jan. 45). See also *Towarzysze frontowych dróg* (Warsaw: MON 1965), ch. XI, liberation of Warsaw, p. 172.

Slawecki, R., *Manewr który ocalil Kraków* (Cracow: Wydaw. Lit., 2nd edn 1971). Collection of materials (including Soviet memoirs), liberation of Cracow, 1st Ukrainian Front (60th Army).

Sobczak, K., *Wyzwolenie pólnocnych i zachodnich ziem polskich w roku 1945* (Poznan: Wydaw. Poznanskie 1971). See chs II–IV, Soviet–Polish operations Jan. 45. (Political and military narrative, using variety of archival materials.)

On 'the Berlin axis' pp. 469–476

Note: With respect to the 'battle of Berlin', I had the opportunity to discuss and explore both the planning and the execution with senior Soviet commanders, as well as having access to the relevant Soviet documentation (*Stavka* directives, operational orders, war diaries, etc.). The conversations and exchanges I duly recorded and preserved in my own 'Moscow notebooks', while the documentation speaks for itself. One example may suffice: it was possible to conduct a lengthy review with Marshal Koniev of his own initial operational plan (submitted to the General Staff, January 28) involving a thrust on to Berlin, the point being the discrepancy between *Stavka* provision that only the right flank of 1st Ukrainian Front would be so involved while Marshal Koniev had the 'main body' of his Front in mind (with orders properly formulated and prescribed). By the 'main body' Marshal Koniev was clearly thinking of his tank armies (3rd and

4th Tank Armies under Rybalko and Lelyushenko), operating under a specific operational design long contemplated and well formulated, hence Marshal Koniev's rebuke to me for suggesting that he 'swung' (the verb was *povernut'*) his armies about. His 'January plan' made full planned provision for such movement, thus diminishing if not actually resolving an apparent contradiction, for Marshal Koniev was steadily shifting his main weight to the right flank, thus making his 'right-flank forces' virtually synonymous with his 'main force'. My own impression was that Marshal Koniev had duly registered Berlin as 'his' target in these late January days and planned accordingly. By the same .oken it was important to have Marshal Rokossovskii's own commentary upon and elucidation of his command decisions and assessments—and so to quite a number of Soviet commanders.

KTB/GMD

OKH/GenStdH/Op. Abt. KTB Anlagen: signals/reports, *Festungen Glogau, Posen* (details of strength, weapons) for February 1945. See under T-78/R304, 6255440–785.

FHO(I). Signals Heeresgruppe Kurland; telegrams Heeresgr. Nord, Festungskommandant Danzig/also Königsberg, Armeeabteilung Samland. T-78/R477, 6459238–837.

Soviet materials

Bagramyan, I.Kh., *Kak shli my k pobede,* pp. 511–17, operation *Zemland* (Samland), blockading of German forces, prospect of further German heavy resistance, Chernyakhovskii reports Stalin's concern that Rendulic (commander Army Group North) might be able to withdraw in good order, hence orders to eliminate German Fourth Army, pen-portrait of commander 11th Guards Army (Galitskii), problem of diminished Soviet strength, lack of tanks, death of Chernyakhovskii.

Chuikov, V.I., *The End of the Third Reich* (translation), ch. VII, on miscalculations, Chuikov's celebrated—or notorious—assertions that an assault on Berlin in February was quite feasible: that the Supreme Command displayed 'excessive caution', especially with respect to the threat from Pomerania; that there were sufficient forces with Zhukov's 1st Belorussian Front to strike on Berlin (five armies, plus 3–4 from 1st Ukrainian Front), while the concern for 1st Belorussian Front right flank was 'groundless' (p. 117); that Zhukov's 'orientation' was, in fact, disorientation (although Chuikov does point in this version to serious logistical shortcomings). In this account also Chuikov recounts a command meeting with Zhukov (Feb. 6), a meeting interrupted by Stalin's telephone call and Zhukov's sudden 'postponement' of the Berlin attack. See also V.I. Chuikov, 'Kapitulyatsiya gitlerovskii Germanii', *Novaya i noveishaya istoriya,* 1965, No. 2, p. 6, where this meeting is dated February 4, but with the same interruption from Stalin. (Zhukov demolished this in devastating fashion.) A completely revised version has now been supplied in Chuikov's *Ot Stalingrada do Berlina,* pp. 563–69, citing Zhukov's order/directive Jan. 26, also the directive of Feb. 4 (with a fresh insertion on Franco–Hoare conversations!). In general, this volume conforms to the general thesis of the threat from Pomerania and the need to redeploy 1st Belorussian Front to meet it.

Galitskii, K.N., *V boyakh za Vostochnuyu Prussiyu,* pp. 306–28, 11th Guards Army, Frisches Haff, German counterblows against left flank 11th Guards, heavy German losses (Third *Panzer*) but 11th Guards badly mauled (12 Feb. divisions down to

3,500–4,500 men, companies reduced to 20–35 men, p. 327), already Feb. 9 Front commander ordered turn to defensive, preparations for a full assault on Königsberg, 11th Guards regroups.

Koniev, I.S., *Year of Victory (Moscow)*, pp. 50–51, from the Oder to the Neisse, planning of Lower Silesian operation late Jan. 45, initial plan submitted Jan. 28—encirclement of Breslau, drive with 'main group' on to Berlin—encirclement of Breslau and Glogau completed, impossible to carry through 'Lower Silesian operation' to its full depth.

Vorob'ev, F.D., Parotkin, I.V. and Shimanskii, A.N.,. *Poslednii shturm (Berlinskaya operatsiya 1945 g.)* (Moscow: Voenizdat, 2nd edn 1975). See pp. 39–42, on *Stavka* strategic design/evaluation, decisions at Front level: analysis at end Jan. 45 led Soviet command to believe in feasibility of rapid thrust on Berlin (p. 40), General Staff operational map duly 'marked up' Jan. 19 with Berlin as objective and to be taken by 1st Belorussian Front, but to avoid blundering the *Stavka* did not take a final decision, asked for news of Front commanders once Soviet troops on Bromberg–Poznan–Breslau line, Zhukov and Koniev submitted operational appreciations (Jan. 26 and Jan. 28 respectively), both received *Stavka* approval Jan. 27 and Jan. 29; beginning Feb. growing concern over threat from E Pomerania, danger to flank and rear of 1st Belorussian Front, 33 German divisions in E Pomerania (13 on 'the Berlin axis'), 1st Belorussian Front forces perforce swung northwards leaving Zhukov with only 3½ armies pointed along the Berlin axis, also heavy losses incurred by 1st Belorussian Front and 1st Ukrainian Front (divisional strength down to 4,000–5,000 men), logistical difficulties and shortages particularly ammunition. (This is certainly the standard Soviet work on the Berlin operation; it is also one which affirms the 'Zhukov line' and is presumably intended to sweep away all traces of Chuikov's assertions about the feasibility of a February thrust on Berlin.)

Zhukov, G.K., *Vospominaniya . . .* , vol. 2, pp. 297–301, Jan. 25 conversation with Stalin–Zhukov proposed continuing drive to Oder, Stalin points to gap with 2nd Belorussian Front (150 km), also need to wait on 1st Ukrainian Front, Zhukov asks permission to continue his drive, particularly to penetrate Miedzyrzecz line, Stalin makes no immediate reply—redeployment of 1st Belorussian Front armies to face north but time enough to reach Oder before Pomerania threat materialized, Jan. 31 signal to Stalin on situation of right flank 1st Belorussian Front and need to urge 70th Army (Rokossovskii's 2nd Belorussian Front) forward (p. 302), attack on and denunciation of Chuikov's previous arguments about 'non-stop' drive for Berlin (pp. 303–4), Jan. 26 submission of provisional attack plan to *Stavka* (similar submission by Koniev), *Stavka* endorsement Jan. 27–29, 1st Belorussian Front 'orientation' (text, pp. 304–5), danger from E Pomerania further refutation of Chuikov that enough force available to strike on Berlin, only 4 under-strength armies actually available (out of 8 rifle and 2 tank armies), 3–4 tank armies (as suggested by Chuikov) simply not available, impact of heavy losses on Soviet divisional strength, tank brigades with only 15–20 tanks (p. 308), logistics problems, need to redeploy aviation, no meeting on Feb. 4 as Chuikov suggested and no call from Stalin (p. 309), Zhukov's instruction to 5th Shock Army.

Note on Soviet logistics: The strain on the supply system, particularly lorried transport, had become almost intolerable; if during the 15 days before the offensive lorries delivered 165,900 tons of supplies, in the next 15 days of active operations they delivered 320,101 tons, but daily runs were now reduced from a planned 200 kms to only 140 kms and reached a low of 100 kms due to poor road conditions. As 1st Belorussian Front raced westwards, a full run from base to the front and back took 10–12 days; the Front command therefore decided to utilize 500 gun-towing tractors to move supplies, but this left the heavy guns marooned. More lorries were needed to move field hospitals forward and captured supplies back to the rear. In moving fuel up to the Front the lorries consumed a great deal themselves—never less than a quarter. Each lorry moved an average of 2 tons per day, but the Front command demanded priority for ammunition and offered cash bonuses to drivers who exceeded their 'ton/kilometre' norms; some drivers received cash payments of more than 500 roubles during the course of the month. See N.A. Antipenko, *Na glavnom napravlenii* (Nauka, 2nd edn 1971), pp. 220–25. General Antipenko was commander/logistics 1st Belorussian Front at this time.

Polish materials

Golczewski, K., *Wyzwolenie Pomorza Zachodniego w roku 1945* (Poznań: Wydaw. Poznanskie 1971). (Operations, western Pomerania.)

Majewski, R. and Sozańska, T., *Bitwa o Wroclaw* (Wroclaw/Warsaw: Ossolineum 1972). (Breslau/Wroclaw; siege, assault.)

Majewski, R. (ed.), *Wroclawska epopeja* (Wroclaw/Warsaw: Ossolineum, 1975). (Wroclaw/Breslau.)

Okęcki, S., *Wyzwolenie Poznania 1945* (Warsaw: MON 1975), pp. 9–82, Poznan operations Jan.–Feb. 45. (Extensive use of Polish and Soviet military archives, captured German documents incl. *Fremde Heere Ost* situation reports.)

Peikert, Paul, *'Festung Breslau' in den Berichten eines Pfarrers,* 22 Januar bis 6 Mai 1945 (Wroclaw/Warsaw: Ossolineum 1966). (Diary, newspaper reports, orders, leaflets—Breslau.)

Stąpor, Z., *Bitwa o Berlin. Dzialania 1 Armii WP kwiecień–maj 1945* (Warsaw: MON 1973), pp. 45–59, deployment, operational role of 1st Polish Army, regrouped right-flank 1st Belorussian Front (29 Jan.–20 Feb. 45). (1st Polish Army operational assignment, changes in Soviet operational plan, redeployments.)

Yalta (Crimean Conference)   pp. 476–489 and pp. 489–507

The circumstances of Yalta (the Crimean Conference) have by now been thoroughly rehearsed both in documents and memoirs, but the dispute over its impact—sometimes seen starkly in terms of Western surrender and Soviet aggrandisement—continues. Among the accounts by participants I have made essential recourse to Arthur Bryant, *Triumph in the West 1943–1946* (ch. 12, Yalta, Brooke on the meetings of the Chiefs of Staff, with his comment on General Antonov); Winston S. Churchill, *The Second World War,* vol. 6: *Triumph and Tragedy,* bk II chs XX–XXIII (preparations for a new conference, Yalta and planning for world peace, the Polish problem and the Soviet promise, Yalta finale); Anthony Eden (Earl of Avon), *The Reckoning* (London, Boston, 1965) and also my own conversations with Sir Anthony Eden on Stalin and Stalin's conduct of affairs; Lord Moran, *Winston Churchill*, pt 3, ch. 24, 'Yalta Diary'; Robert E. Sherwood, *Roosevelt and Hopkins;* and Edward R. Stettinius, *Roosevelt and the Russians: the Yalta Conference* (New York: Doubleday 1949). Not being a diplomatic historian, I remain enormously indebted to studies by Diane Shaver Clemens, *Yalta* (New York: OUP 1970) (an account as comprehensive as it is judicious, especially 'Yalta as History', pp. 274–9, and 'Yalta as a Negotiating Experience', pp. 279ff.); David Dallin, *The Big Three* (London: Allen & Unwin 1946); Herbert Feis, *Churchill, Roosevelt and Stalin*, and *The China Tangle* (Princeton: Princeton UP 1957); William Hardy McNeill, *America, Britain and Russia: Their Co-operation and Conflict, 1941–1946* (New York: OUP (RIIA) 1953); Edward J. Rozek, *Allied Wartime Diplomacy. A Pattern in Poland* (especially ch. 7, Yalta and Stalin's 'tactical handling' of Polish problem, pp. 338–56); John L. Snell (ed.), *The Meaning of Yalta* (Baton Rouge: Louisiana State Univ. Press 1956), Tang Tsou, *America's Failure in China, 1941–1950* (Chicago/London: Chicago Univ. Press 1963) (see especially ch. VII, pp. 237–52, Yalta agreement, American planning and Stalin's 'dual course', effect of secrecy of Yalta agreement—lack of firm evidence of Soviet intentions nurtured Japanese illusion that via Soviet mediation she might obtain peace settlement with the Allies); John W. Wheeler-Bennett and Anthony Nicholls, *The Semblance of Peace* (pt 1, ch. 11 on Yalta conference, pp. 214–50, also ch. 16, on the question of Soviet participation in the Pacific War, pp. 348–52). I should like to note here that I have used the *Soviet* transcript/records of Yalta, all to the end of depicting *Stalin's* behaviour and negotiating mode, not to mention his 'tactical handling'.

Documents

(1) *US Department of State. Foreign Relations of the United States: The Conferences at Malta and Yalta, 1945* (Washington, DC: US Govt, Printing Office 1955). (See a Soviet appraisal, I. Nikolayev, 'Eshchë odna popytka falsifikatsii istorii. K opublikovaniyu Gosdepartamentom SShA 'dokumentov' Krymskoi konferentsii', *Mezhdunarodnaya zhizn*, 1955, No. 5, pp. 35–47.)

(2) *Soviet documents: Yalta (Crimean Conference). Krymskaya konferentsiya rukovoditelei trekh soyuznykh derzhav—SSSR, SShA i Velikobritanii (4–11 fevralya 1945)*. Sbornik dokumentov, vol. IV in series *Sovetskii Soyuz na mezhdunarodnykh konferentsiyakh perioda VOV 1941–1945 gg*. (Moscow: Politizdat 1979), 326 pp.

    Pt 1. Record of conversations: Molotov with Harriman, Molotov with Eden, Feb. 4, pp. 45–8; Stalin–Churchill, Feb. 4, pp. 48–9; Stalin–Roosevelt, Feb. 4, pp. 49–53; conversations, three heads of government, 4–5 Feb., pp. 53–83; Foreign Ministers' meeting, Feb. 6, pp. 84–7; conversations, three heads of government, Feb. 6, pp. 87–103 (appendices: American position on voting, draft proposal on voting in Securtiy Council, pp. 104–7); Foreign Ministers' meeting, Feb. 7, pp. 107–14 (appendices: on special French zone of occupation in Germany, levying of reparations on Germany, pp. 114–15); conversations, three heads of government, Feb. 7, pp. 116–27 (appendices: decisions, Foreign Ministers' meeting on dismemberment of Germany, Roosevelt letter to Stalin—Feb. 6—on Polish question, Soviet draft on Polish frontiers and Polish government, pp. 127–31); meeting, Foreign Ministers, Feb. 8, pp. 131–7; conversation, Stalin–Roosevelt, Feb. 8 (on Soviet entry into war against Japan), pp. 139–43; Memorandum to Stalin, Feb.

7, on making airfield/refuelling facilities near Budapest available to US aircraft, p. 144, also Roosevelt memorandum to Stalin (on bombing survey), p. 145; Memorandum, Roosevelt to Stalin, Feb. 5, on supply line through Pacific to E Siberia, basing of US aircraft in Komsomolsk, p. 145; conversations, three heads of government, Feb. 8, pp. 146–57; Foreign Ministers' report, Feb. 8, inclusion of two (or three) constituent Soviet republics in world organization . . . , pp. 157–8; US delegation draft on the Polish question (received Feb. 8), pp. 158–9; revised formulation/Polish frontiers, Polish government, pp. 159–60; Foreign Ministers' meeting, record of conversations, Feb. 9, pp. 160–67 (appendices: on world security organization, agreement on admission of two Soviet constituent republics, Stettinius proposal on question of Polish government, Feb. 9, on reparations from Germany, on voting procedures/Security Council, draft agreement on Persia, British delegation amendments to Tito–Šubašić agreement, alternative British formulation on question of the Polish government, pp. 166–73); record of conversations, three heads of government, Feb. 9, pp. 173–84 (appendix: report to plenary session on Foreign Ministers' meeting—Polish question, reparations, Dumbarton-Oaks, Iran, Yugoslavia, declaration on liberated Europe, revision to the draft, Churchill to Stalin, Feb. 9, on operations in Germany and on situation in Greece, pp. 184–9); record of conversations, Foreign Ministers' meeting, Feb. 10, pp. 194–7 (appendices: revision to text/Polish question, reparations from Germany, note on Austro–Yugoslav frontier Venezia–Giulia, petroleum installations in Rumania/reparations, Greek claims on Bulgaria, on Allied/Soviet Control Commission in Bulgaria, pp. 198–207); record of conversation, Stalin–Churchill–Eden, Feb. 10, pp. 207–12 (Churchill's question to Stalin on role of German generals captured by the Red Army); record of conversation, three heads of government, Feb. 10, pp. 212–18 (appendices: draft statement on Poland, British draft on Yugoslavia for Soviet and American consideration, British draft declaration on Polish frontiers, pp. 218–20); record of conversations, three heads of government, Feb. 11, pp. 220–23 (appendices: draft press communiqué on results of Crimean conference, on reparations, draft text communiqué (Stettinius draft), pp. 223–38); Foreign Ministers' meeting, record of conversations, 11 Feb., review of proposal communiqué, drafts of Conference decisions, draft telegram from three heads of government to De Gaulle, pp. 238–55; Eden–Molotov letter, Feb. 11, on unfinished business, pp. 255–6 (appendices: Austro–Yugoslav frontier question, British memorandum on organization of relief, Soviet contingent to London for participation in preparatory work on Control Commission for Germany, pp. 256–9); Roosevelt–Stalin letters, Feb. 10–11, on raising US vote to three in World Organization, pp. 259–60.

Pt II. Documents/notes agreement on the Far East, protocol of Conference proceedings, on liberated prisoners of war and displaced citizens, pp. 282–300. (An earlier version of the 'Yalta records' was published in the journal *Mezhdunarodnaya Zhizn* (also in translation, *International Affairs*/Moscow), 1965, Nos. 6–10, under 'Dokumenty: Krymskaya i Potdamskaya konferentsii rukovoditelei trekh velikikh derzhav'. This has now been wholly superseded by the composite volume (with appendices, documents) on the 'Crimean conference', vol. IV, cited above.)

(3) *Polish documents: Yalta*

Documents on Polish–Soviet Relations 1939–1945, vol. 2: *1943–1945*. No. 305, Roosevelt–Stalin, Feb. 6, proposed invitation to Yalta of representatives of Lublin regime and émigrés from London, pp. 517–18. No. 306, Molotov's proposals, Feb. 7, on Polish frontiers and new Polish government, pp. 518–19. No. 307, US memorandum on reorganization of Polish government (dropping Presidential Committee), p. 519. No. 308, resolutions of Crimean Conference, Feb. 11, on Poland, pp. 520–21. No. 309, protest of Polish government in London, Feb. 13, on Crimean Conference resolutions, pp. 521–2. No. 311, Roosevelt–Arciszewski (and reply) on decisions over Poland, Feb. 16/17, pp. 522–3. No. 312, Tarnowski–Sir Owen O'Malley on resolutions on Poland, Feb. 18, pp. 523–7. No. 314, Raczyński–Eden conversation, Feb. 20, on Polish protest at decisions of Crimean Conference and appointment of new Polish government, pp. 528–32. (Eden denial that agreement at Yalta a Soviet success and loss of full independence for Poland.)

Diplomatic/official histories

Woodward, Sir Llewellyn, *British Foreign Policy in the Second World War* (single volume), ch. XXVIII, Yalta conference, pp. 484–501: no preliminary meeting of Foreign Secretaries, US–Soviet dealings over Far East, on the Declaration on Liberated Europe; discussions on dismemberment of Germany, reparations question, Soviet acceptance of compromise on voting for World Council, Anglo–Soviet disagreement over reparations figures, the Polish question at Yalta.

Woodward, Sir L. *British Foreign Policy in the Second World War*, III, ch. XL(V), the Polish question at the Yalta Conference, pp. 252–73. Also vol. V (HMSO 1976), in collaboration with M.E. Lambert, ch. LXV, discussions on World Security Organization and treatment of Germany/Yalta conference; proposals for three-power conference, Soviet–American agreement on the Far East, Declaration on Liberated Europe and discussion thereof; issue of dismemberment of Germany, inclusion of France in occupation of Germany, German reparations; discussions on World organization, voting procedures/Security Council, separate membership for Ukraine and Belorussia, Prime Minister's report (Feb. 19) to War Cabinet on Conference, pp. 261–300.

IVOVSS, 5, pt 1, pp. 124–38, Crimean conference, (account stressing effectiveness of wartime collaboration and positive role of Crimean conference).

IVMV, 10, pt 1, pp. 127–38, pre-conference political and military scene, plans for final defeat of Germany and Japan, policies for the postwar world. (Allied 'goodwill' overcame sharp differences to produce agreement.)

Israelyan, V.L., *Diplomaticheskaya istoriya VOV*, pp. 279–99, Crimean conference.

Israelyan, V.L., *Antigitlerovskaya koalitsiya 1941–1945*, pt 3, pp. 473–512, Crimean conference.

Batowski, Henryk, *Wojna a diplomacja* 1945 (Poznan: Wyd. Poznańskie 1972), ch. 4, 'Konferencja krymska' (Yalta conference), pp. 59–85. (Uses a combination of Western and Soviet sources.)

Balaton operations, the end in Hungary pp. 508–517

Allen, W.E.D. and Muratoff, Paul, *The Russian Campaigns 1944–45*, ch. XII, end of the Danubian–Carpathian campaign, the 'battle of Lake Balaton', Soviet defensive operations and counter-blow, pp. 294–302. (Though placing special emphasis on the terrain factor, this account is far from accurate in dates and Soviet deployments.)

Seaton, Albert, *The Russo–German War*, pp. 554–7, on the German offensive, Balaton, Soviet and German strength, German Army Group 'E' attack across the Drava and Second *Panzer* Army (Angelis) attack south of Balaton, role of Nedelin's artillery reserves (3rd Ukrainian Front), end of German resistance in Hungary, collapse of improvised defence on the line of the river Raab. (Though brief, this is an excellently balanced account.)

Werth, Alexander, *Russia at War*. See pt 8, ch. I, 'Into Germany', on Soviet behaviour in Germany coupled with Soviet propaganda—to call it a 'tricky subject' is a vast understatement; how difficult it was (and is) I discovered for myself in Moscow, though there is much documentary evidence (field tribunal/court-martial reports) that some control was exercised. The Soviet view was that rape on the part of the Germans in Russia was part of planned subjugation, but this was not so with Soviet troops, even if the second echelon behaved badly. In a huge army, such as the Red Army, inevitably 'there were troubles, but we took measures'. (In looking at court-martial records, I noted that for a soldier to plead the loss of his family or destruction of his home was not admitted as mitigation. Example: a senior sergeant got drunk, broke into a flat, found the wardrobe filled with Ukrainian costumes, so that he shot the owner when he returned. The sergeant had lost his father and brother, his two sisters had been deported to Germany; three members of the German family had served in the Ukraine, the dead man had been a Party member. This was not regarded as mitigation, the Soviet sergeant was sentenced—amidst the protests of his men, who saw no reason in the punishment.) Like Alex Werth, I have read the wartime press and the Ehrenburg articles, with the *Krasnaya Zvezda* article of Feb. 9 cautioning against an excess of anti-German feeling and the *Pravda* article (April 14) officially disowning Ehrenburg's 'hate propaganda' and his insinuations about the Allies; see Werth, pp. 963–9. See also under *GMD*.

Note: For Ehrenburg's own version of this affair and the role of G.F. Aleksandrov (*Pravda* article), see his memoirs under 'Lyudi, gody, zhizn', *Novyi Mir*, 1963 (3), pp. 130–31, an exuberantly unrepentant piece. In *The Russians and Berlin 1945* (London: Heinemann 1968) Erich Kuby refers (p. 262) to his own discussion with Ehrenburg, who recognized that Stalin could well have wished to 'steal a march' on the Allies with his elaboration of policy towards Germany and the Germans, hence the abrupt high-level and widely publicized disowning of Ehrenburg; Germany was not 'one vast gang', indeed this contradicted Stalin's maxim (uttered in 1942) that 'Hitlers may come and go, but the German people remain. . . .' Nevertheless, Ehrenburg felt that he had been made a scapegoat unnecessarily so. Aleksandrov did not reply to his letter of explanation; Soviet troops still feted him, bemused as they were by having to regard the butchers let loose in Russia as 'unwitting and enslaved accomplices' of Hitler.

GMD

GenStdH/Abt. FHO. Folder, two sections, 75c, 75d: the first covers material on Nationalkomitee Freies Deutschland (Jan.–Mar. 45); the second, translations of Soviet press, including Ehrenburg material. T-78/R483, 6467342–7674.

Diplomatic correspondence

Perepiska . . . , vol. 2, No. 288, Stalin–Roosevelt, on Gen. Marshall's intelligence on German intentions (Feb.), incorrect information, failure to predict German attack in Balaton area, enclosed copy of General Antonov's letter to General John R. Deane. Antonov–Deane information supplied by General Marshall 'at variance with the actual course of events . . .', 7 April 1945, pp. 223–5.

Soviet materials

IVOVSS, 5, pt 1, pp. 191–210, Balaton defensive operation, strength/deployment 2nd and 3rd Ukrainian Fronts, planning to raise four Hungarian divisions to fight with Red Army, strength of German Army Group South, *Stavka* directive Feb. 17 prescribes March 15 for opening of fresh Soviet drive on Brno–Vienna, Timoshenko *Stavka* 'co-ordinator', German plans for counter-blow Balaton area, 807 German tanks for main assault, mid-Feb. *Stavka* and Soviet Front commands without firm information on German plans, surprise blow against Shumilov's 7th Guards Army (Hron bridgehead), Antonov–Marshall exchange, only after loss of Hron bridgehead Soviet command confirmed German plan to strike 3rd Ukrainian Front, 3rd Ukrainian Front strength 407,000 men, 6,890 guns/mortars, 407 tanks/SP guns, 965 aircraft (p. 195), Tolbukhin's defensive measures, Soviet assistance to 1st Bulgarian Army, Nedelin's use of artillery (3rd Ukrainian Front), AA guns finally brought into action against German tanks, Tolbukhin's reserves near exhaustion but *Stavka* refused to permit commitment of 9th Guards Army since German attack running out of power, *Stavka* directive March 9 redefining assignments 2nd and 3rd Ukrainian Fronts for drive on Vienna, co-ordination with Yugoslav units, Soviet counter-offensive March 16 with 9th and 4th Guards Army against heavy German resistance, 6th Guards Tank Army committed March 19, failure to complete encirclement of Sixth *SS Panzer* Army (lack of ammunition, slow progress of Soviet assault force, shortage of infantry support tanks, delay in committing 6th Guards Tank Army principal Soviet shortcomings here).

IVMV, 10, pt 1, pp. 176–93, *Stavka* directive Feb. 17 for the Bratislava–Brno and the Vienna operation, unreliability of Anglo–American intelligence, German attack Feb. 17 on 7th Guards Army—a mistake, according to *IVMV*, since it cost the Germans the element of surprise and helped to disclose their operational intentions in Hungary, despite other efforts at camouflage and deception (p. 178)—Soviet defensive planning and measures, Tolbukhin's deployment and difficulties with supply of fuel and ammunition, 14 March final German attack with last reserve 6th *Panzer* Division, turn to defensive March 15, superiority of the flexibility and manoeuvrability of Soviet reserves amply demonstrated, extensive use of minefields (German losses here 130 tanks/assault guns), Soviet counter-blow and pursuit, *Stavka* directive March 9, Tolbukhin's assault force consisted of 18 rifle divisions, 3,900 guns, 197 tanks/SP guns, Sixth *SS Panzer* encircled but not annihilated, final clearing of Hungarian territory (Soviet casualties—killed in action—set at more than 140,000 officers and men in the course of Red Army operations in Hungary). (Much less informative version than *IVOVSS*, 5, eschewing both amplification and criticism of Soviet performance, particularly the opening and closing phases of the Balaton operation.)

Ivanov, General S., 'Sryv kontrnastupleniya nemetsko-fashistskikh voisk u ozera Balaton', *VIZ*, 1969 (3), pp. 14–29. Operational narrative-analysis from Gen. Ivanov, then Chief of Staff, 3rd Ukrainian Front: initial disbelief in Soviet General Staff at 3rd Ukrainian Front intelligence that German armour moving to Balaton—why was that armour not defending Berlin?—confirmation of movement of Sixth *Panzer*, *Stavka* directive Feb. 17, 3rd Ukrainian Front strength (incl. 400 tanks), Tolbukhin's decision on defence Feb. 20, assignments to armies, readiness by Mar. 3, Stalin's misgivings and enquiry of Tolbukhin about withdrawal to east bank of Danube, Tokbukhin's proposal to stand fast accepted by Stalin, German offensive and Soviet defensive actions, *Stavka*'s refusal of Tolbukhin's request to bring 19th Guards Army out of reserve, importance of artillery and aviation in repelling German offensive. (*Note:* This highly authoritative account tends to undermine, if not actually contradict, Shtemenko, *General'nyi shtab*, vol. 2.)

Kuznetsov, P.G., *Marshal Tolbukhin*. See 'On the Vienna axis', the Balaton defensive battle, pp. 224–35.

Malakhov, Colonel M.M., *Osvobozhdenie Vengrii i vostochnoi Avstrii*, ch. 2, Balaton defensive operation, 3rd Ukrainian Front action Feb. 20–Mar. 16, pp. 175–218; see also summary of operational characteristics, pp. 225–33; ch. 3, Soviet planning for drive on Vienna, Soviet counter-blow Balaton, pp. 234–62. (Detailed operational narrative, stage-by-stage analysis of Soviet counter-blow.)

Malinovskii, R.Ya. (ed.), *Budapesht Vena Praga*, ch. 4, 'Balatonskaya bitva', Balaton operations, pp. 173–224. (Mixture of analytical and memoir material, also referring to Anglo–American 'underhand' dealings for a German surrender in N Italy in order to beat the Red Army into Austria.)

Minasyan, M.M., *Osvobozhdenie . . . ,* pp. 380–402, Balaton operations (third stage of Soviet operations in Hungary), *Stavka* directive Feb. 17 for 2nd and 3rd Ukrainian Fronts to drive on Vienna, offensive to open March 15, analysis of German decision to move 6 *SS Panzer* to Hungary and strengthen entire southern wing, German attack on Soviet bridgehead on the Hron defended by 7th Guards Army a complete surprise, 7th Guards Army lost 8,800 men Feb. 17–24 and forced to eastern bank of Hron (p. 385), see analysis of causes of Soviet reverse—lack of depth in army/corps deployments, lack of reserves . . . (p. 385), Marshall's signal to Gen. Antonov, Stalin's retort that this possibly a form of disinformation (see *Perepiska*, vol. 2), Soviet preparations for Balaton defensive battle, German operational plan, *Stavka* instructions to Tolbukhin (p. 388), Tolbukhin's deployments, overall weakness in 3rd Ukrainian Front armies (divisional strength in 4th Army down to 5,100, 26th Army 4,250, 27th Army 4,100 men—18th and 23rd Tank Corps, 1st Guards Mech. Corps had only 166 tanks between them, tank/sp-gun regiments reduced to 2–8 tanks or SP guns, see p. 389), German offensive March 6, *Stavka* refuses permission to commit 9th Guards Army to defensive battle—signal March 9 (p. 391), importance of operations of 17th Air Army (6,000 sorties) also Goryunov's 5th Air Army, operations on the river Drava line, Soviet offensive opened March 16 on 'Budapest–Vienna axis', alterations in operational concept embodied in *Stavka* directive March 9, main attack to be mounted by 3rd Ukrainian Front, Tolbukhin's planning for Soviet counter-blow, 6th Guards Tank Army assigned to 3rd Ukrainian Front March 16, 9th Guards

Army well equipped (nine divisions each with 11,000 men, substantial artillery complement) but lacking combat experience, no infantry-support tanks and too many 76mm SP guns (pp. 396–7), heavy German losses between Danube and Balaton March 16–23/25, final clearing of Hungarian territory, *Stavka* directive 1 April for joint operation 2nd and 3rd Ukrainian Fronts aimed at Vienna. (This is a very detailed analysis which must be accounted the best and most reliable Soviet account.)

Sharokhin, Col.-Gen. M.N. and Petrukhin, Colonel V.S., *Put' k Balatonu* (Moscow: Voenizdat 1966), 143 pp. (Combined memoir-operational analysis, Sharokhin commander 57th Army, lake Balaton operations, information on German offensive, p. 90, co-ordination problems, p. 95, also on special artillery deployment, plan Shtorm, pp. 88–9.)

Shtemenko, S.M., *General'nyi shtab v gody voiny*, vol. 2. See pp. 269–76 on Balaton, German blow against Shumilov's 7th Guards Army, Tolbukhin's exchange with Stalin on 9th Guards Army (p. 275) and Stalin's comment on Tolbukhin's suggestion that he might pull his HQ at least over to the eastern side of the Danube—'Comrade Tolbukhin, if you are thinking of dragging on the war for a further five–six months, then by all means pull back beyond the Danube. . . .' (*IVMV*, 10, has relied quite heavily on Shtemenko's text and the interpretation of Soviet knowledge of German plans and intentions; however, M.M. Minasyan furnishes a more reliable and credible analysis.)

Vorontsov, T.F. *et al.*, *Ot volzhskikh stepei do avstriiskikh Alp*, (4th Guards Army). See 'Na Venu', 4th Guards Army, Balaton defensive operation, assault on Szekesfehervar, pp. 186–98.

Zakharov, M.V. (ed.), *Osvobozhdenie . . .* , pp. 409–51, Balaton operations, position of 2nd and 3rd Ukrainian Fronts, General Marshall's signal Feb. 20 on possible German counter-blows (p. 413), unfortunately failed to mention transfer of 6th *SS Panzer* (similar information from the British), German strength and operational plans, unfavourable position of 3rd Ukrainian Front, Tolbukhin's decisions on defensive operations (pp. 419–20), operations Mar. 6, deterioration of situation at centre of 3rd Ukrainian Front, *Stavka* categorically refuses to allow Tolbukhin to use 9th Guards Army in defensive battle (p. 441), concentration of 6th Guards Tank Army SW Budapest, final German push Mar. 14–15, Dulles–Wolff talks in Switzerland (pp. 448–9), final German defeat with loss of 45,000 men, 500 tanks, 280 guns.

Zavizion, G.T. and Kornyushin, P.A., *I na Tikhom Okeane . . .* (6th Guards Tank Army), pp. 152–70, 6th Guards Tank in Balaton operations, German attack on 7th Guards Army (2nd Ukrainian Front) on the Hron, Tolbukhin's defensive measures, 6th Guards Tank Army re-equipping (during winter of 1944–5 663 tanks and SP guns returned to service by field workshops), tank army and 9th Guards Army held in reserve, 6th Guards Tank initially assigned to exploit 46th Army operations on 2nd Ukrainian Front by March 16, assigned to 3rd Ukrainian Front in order to operate with 4th and 9th Guards Army which had only 200 tanks (6th Guards Tank at that time *fielded 406 tanks and SP guns*), redeployment of tank army, assigned by Tolbukhin to attack with 9th Guards Army on morning of March 19, encirclement of German tank forces assigned to 5th Guards Tank

Corps with outer encirclement by 9th Guards Mechanized Corps, drive on the 'Vienna axis'.

The flanks: E Pomerania and Silesia,
Feb.–Mar. 1945   pp. 517–526

Allen, W.E.D. and Muratoff, Paul, *The Russian Campaigns 1944–45*, pp. 306–15, East Prussia, Danzig/Stettin: defensive resources of E Prussia, struggle for Samland, preparation of attack on Königsberg, capture of Heiligenbeil, breakthrough to Pomeranian coast, thrust on Kolberg, approach to Danzig, storming of Gdynia and then Danzig, fighting for Altdamm. (Based on Soviet communiqués.)

Irving, David, *Hitler's War*, pt 6, 'Waiting for a Telegram', pp. 772–6, claim that 6–8,000 Soviet tanks destroyed since mid-January, General Staff conviction that assault on Berlin imminent in spite of danger from Army Group Vistula (Himmler), General von Hauenschildt designated commander of the Berlin district, Zhukov's massive breakthrough in Pomerania Feb. 27, Soviet thrust on Köslin and the Baltic coast, Hiler's promise of immediate reinforcement for Himmler, Danzig corridor to be held at all costs, deception measures to convey impression of formidable defences between Oder and Berlin, inevitable loss of East and West Prussia without success of Himmler's counter-attack, deterioration of situation March 8, Hitler's loss of faith in Himmler, General Raus in Berlin to explain defeat in Pomerania, Manteuffel to replace Raus, Guderian March 8 predicts main Soviet assault on Berlin within one week now that threat to Red Army's northern flank removed.

Note on Stalin's PW son. See David Irving, *Hitler's War*, notes to p. 285 (v. p. 847): Stalin's son, a PW since 1941, *committed suicide in 1943*, after British PWs 'made life unbearable for him' on account of his 'uncouth behaviour'.

Soviet materials

IVOVSS, 5, pt 1, pp. 138–53, East Pomerania and Upper Silesia operations, *Stavka* directive Feb. 8 to 2nd Belorussian Front, originally 1st Belorussian Front not to be wholly involved in E Pomerania operation, Feb. 15 Zhukov authorized to participate with 2nd Belorussian Front, revised dates for offensive—Feb. 24 and March 1—in five days 1st Belorussian Front broke through German defences and split Third *Panzer*, further assignment to clear Baltic coast between the Vistula and the Oder, 1st Guards Tank Army transferred to 2nd Belorussian Front, Himmler removed from command and replaced by Heinrici, Soviet thrust on Danzig and Gdynia, German Second Army finally destroyed, Baltic Fleet able to play only limited role, meanwhile 1st Belorussian Front operations to improve Küstrin position, Koniev's Upper Silesian operation, encirclement of four German divisions SW of Oppeln, important role of Lelyushenko's 4th Tank Army (March 17 awarded Guards designation).

IVMV, 10, pt 1, Ch. 5 (1–2), E Pomerania and Silesia: (1), pp. 139–49, early Feb. *Stavka* decision to continue with preparations for offensive aimed at Berlin and Dresden but to attack E Pomerania group and reach lower Vistula, this the basis of Feb. 8 directive assigning E Pomerania blow to 2nd Belorussian Front, problem of heavy German pressure on Zhukov's right flank, Feb.15 Rokossovskii report proposing reinforcement for his left flank, following day (Feb. 16) Zhukov's plan to use his right-flank forces in E Pomeranian operation, *Stavka* acceptance and plan envisaging 2nd Belorussian Front attacking towards Köslin and 1st Belorussian Front towards Kolberg to split up German forces, on Zhukov's 1st Belorussian Front two tank armies—with 955 tanks/SP guns—assigned to this operation (560 other tanks/SP guns available in tank and mech. corps, or for infantry support), 2nd Belorussian Front offensive renewed Feb. 24, 1st Belorussian Front attack opened March 1 with relatively slow progress by 2nd Guards Tank Army operating in 61st Army area but rapid advance by 1st Guards Tank Army to Baltic coast, encirclement of 10th *SS* Corps also one 'Corps group' (finished off by 1st Polish Army), March 5 Third *Panzer* virtually crippled, German losses 103,000 men, 188 tanks captured, *Stavka* directive Mar. 5 with further assignment for 2nd Belorussian Front and transfer of 1st Guards Tank Army to Rokossovskii, March 13–21 heavy German resistance and slow Soviet progress, fall of Danzig and Gdynia, destruction of German Second Army.

(2), pp. 149–59, results of Lower Silesia operation, *Stavka*'s concern over possible German thrust to recover Silesia and flank blow on 'Ratibor axis', 1st Ukrainian Front plan to *Stavka* Feb. 28 for left-flank operation Upper Silesia, *Stavka* order to 4th Ukrainian Front to attack Mar. 10 towards Olomouc in order to hinder movement of German reserves, Koniev's two assault groups (31 rifle divisions, 5,640 guns, 988 tanks/SP guns) but several rifle divisions down to 3,000 men (p. 155), operation concluded with encirclement of five German divisions—total German losses in Silesia amounted to 28 divisions routed, five destroyed. (This account concentrates particularly on the planning/command decisions aspect. The E Pomerania operation is assessed as gain in that it freed 11 armies (including two tank armies) for operations on the 'Berlin axis'; in conjunction with the Silesian operation, this removed appreciable threats to Soviet flanks, while the Silesian operation itself prevented the movement of German forces into Hungary—or to the north—while actually weakening Army Group Centre in an attempt to head off disaster in Silesia.)

Achkasov, Navy Captain V.I. (ed.), *Krasnoznamennyi Baltiiskii flot 1944–1945 gg.* (Moscow: Nauka 1976). See pp. 165–71, V.I. Achkasov on Baltic Fleet operations against German sea communications, Soviet submarine actions against convoys, Baltic Fleet directives Jan. 7 and 24, sinking of German transport *Goya* by Soviet submarine *L–3* (out of 7,000 aboard, only 195 saved), effectiveness of Soviet submarine operations limited by RAF minelaying operations which impinged on Baltic Fleet operational zones, Soviet MTB operations against German shipping involved using larger groups of boats (6–12 torpedo boats), problem posed by mines and shortage of minesweepers, Baltic Fleet aviation employed torpedo bombers and attack bombers.

Chuikov, V.I., *Ot Stalingrada do Berlina*, pt 3, storming of the Küstrin citadel, pp. 569–75. (See also *The End of the Third Reich*, ch. VIII, fall of Poznan Feb. 23, pp. 123–9 and ch. IX, Küstrin, pp. 130–36.)

Katukov, M.E., *Na ostrie glavnovo udara* (2nd edn), (1st Guards Tank Army), pp. 374–86, E Pomerania operation, westerly thrust halted and swing northwards, briefing from Zhukov (p. 377), rapid drive to the Baltic, 1200 hrs Mar. 8 assigned to 2nd Belorussian Front, Rokossovskii's briefing for drive on Stolp, joint attack with 19th Army on Gdynia.

Koniev, I.S., *Year of Victory* (Moscow), pp. 67–78. See 'The so-called lull', on the Upper Silesian operation, Stalin's warnings about possible German attempts to recover Silesia—'You had better look out . . .' (p. 68)—German reinforcement in Oppeln area, Koniev's encirclement plan with two assault groups (North and South), Gusev's mistake in trying to conserve artillery ammunition, heavy losses to Soviet tank units, Moskalenko's attack on 4th Ukrainian Front, 60th Army captured Rybnik and crossed Oder, fall of Ratibor.

Pyatkov, V.K. *et al., Tret'ya udarnaya* (3rd Shock Army), ch. 4, 3rd Shock operations, E Pomerania, pp. 141–69. (Based largely on military archives, unit actions in detail.)

Rokossovskii, K.K., *A Soldier's Duty* (Moscow), pp. 293–312. See under 'Eastern Pomerania', informed by Vasilevskii of Zhukov's E Pomerania plan, Rokossovskii proposes attack with his left flank, joint strike by two Fronts (1st and 2nd Belorussian), attack timed for Feb. 24 but inevitable delay in acquiring 19th Army and 3rd Tank Corps, fighting actually began Feb. 22, few tanks available to 2nd Belorussian Front, attack on exposed left flank of 19th Army, Stalin query— 'Zhukov is up to something?' (p. 300)—German assault on flanks, capture of Koslin, 3rd Tank Corps reaches Baltic cutting German forces in half, transfer of 1st Guards Tank Army to 2nd Belorussian Front, Zhukov requires return of 1st Tank in 'same state' (p. 305), approach to Danzig, clearing Sopot and Oliwa, fighting for Gdynia, storming of Danzig (Gdansk).

Tributs, Admiral V.F., *Baltiitsy nastupayut* (Kalingrad: Knizh. Izd. 1968), pp. 327–47, Baltic Fleet operations in support of 3rd and 2nd Belorussian Front operations, attack on German communications.

Vasilevskii, A.M., 'Vostochno–Prusskaya operatsiya', *VIZ,* 1969 (3), pp. 34–55. Report to Stalin Feb. 17 on E Prussia situation, rapid conclusion would mean reinforcement for 'Berlin axis' and free troops for transfer to the Far East (where Vasilevskii himself would be going—two armies, 5th and 39th, latterly withdrawn from E Prussian operations for transfer to Far East), request to be relieved from post of Chief of General Staff, news of Chernyakhovskii's death (Feb. 18), immediate conference with Stalin, assigned to command 3rd Belorussian Front, also officially included in membership of the *Stavka* (pp. 43–4)—thus amending GKO ordinance of 10 July 1941, hitherto Zhukov the only Front commander included in the *Stavka*—decision of Feb. 24 to wind up Bagramyan's 1st Baltic Front (converted into the Samland Group), Bagramyan simultaneously into Group commander and deputy commander 3rd Belorussian Front, problem of reducing German 'Heilsberg group', preparations for attack Feb. 22–Mar. 12; March 16 Vasilevskii's submission to Stalin (Königsberg attack plan—document No. 215/k, March 16, signed Vasilevskii, Makarov, Pokrovskii, full text pp. 46–50), accepted March 17, operation to begin not later than March 28, same night (March 17) Vasilevskii requested postponement from Stalin, Stalin agreed. (This is a much more detailed and explicit account than the published memoir, *Delo vsei zhizni,* pp. 496–504. Nevertheless, Marshal Vasilevskii went to considerable pains to refute criticism of the planning and handling of operations in E Prussia—a point aimed at Rokossovskii.)

Vysotskii, F.I. *et al., Gvardeiskaya tankovaya* (2nd Guards Tank Army), pp. 169–81, E Pomeranian operation, failure of attempt to rush Altdam, 2nd Guards Tank regrouped to the south.

Yakubov, Colonel V., 'Vostochno–Pomeranskaya operatsiya', *VIZ*, 1975 (3), pp. 11–18. E Pomerania operation: originally a single Front operation involving only 2nd Belorussian Front, German counterblow Feb. 16 with ten divisions on right flank 1st Belorussian Front, more powerful German blow in the offing, *Stavka* directive Feb. 17 for operations 1st and 2nd Belorussian Front, *Stavka* assignments, concentric attacks by two Fronts, *Stavka* attention to main attack of 2nd Belorussian Front—on Waldenberg–Keslin axis—19th Army drawn from *Stavka* reserve for 2nd Belorussian Front operations, 2nd Belorussian Front operations opened Feb. 24, Kozlov's 19th Army cleared way for 3rd Guards Tank Corps, 1st Belorussian Front attack at 0845 hrs March 1, Zhukov committed tank armies same afternoon, revised *Stavka* instructions March 5, German forces completely split, storming of Gdansk and Gdynia end March.

Zavyalov, A.S. and Kalyadin, T.E., *Vostochno–Pomeranskaya nastupatel'naya operatsiya sovetskikh voisk* (Moscow: Voenizdat 1960). Ch. 1: situation on the right flank of the Front, 10 Feb. 1945, pp. 13–16; ch. 2, *Stavka* and command decisions, pp. 20–44; ch. 3, 2nd Belorussian Front operations, storming of Elbing, right-flank operations 1st Belorussian Front Feb. 10–18, pp. 59–86; ch. 3, splitting German forces, *Stavka* directives to 1st and 2nd Belorussian Fronts, pp. 94–6; Front command decisions, 1st and 2nd Belorussian Fronts, right-flank operations 1st Belorussian Front Feb. 24–March 5, pp. 94–155. (Detailed monograph, planning/execution E Pomerania operation, based largely on Soviet military archives.)

Zhukov, G.K., *Vospominaniya . . .* , 2, pp. 315–17. March 7–8, visit to Stalin in Moscow, Stalin far from well, Zhukov's question about Stalin's son Yakov (PW in Germany), Stalin on the Yalta conference, question of 'control mechanism' in Germany, lack of agreement over Polish government, Zhukov to review calculations for the Berlin operation.

Polish materials

Dolata, B., *Wyzwolenie Polski 1944–1945,* pt II, ch III, operations in Pomerania, (2nd Belorussian Front and 1st Polish Armoured Brigade), Köslin (Koszalin) operation, liberation of Gdynia and Gdansk, Szczezin, also 1st Belorussian Front and 1st Polish Army operations, Stargard, Polish drive to the Baltic, fighting for Kolobrzeg (Kolberg), pp. 246–84; ch. IV, operations in Silesia (Feb.–Mar.), Lower Silesia operations, Upper Silesia, battle for Ratibor, pp. 285–327.

Jadziak, E., *Wyzwolenie Pomorza. Dzialania 1 Armii WP w operacji pomorskiej Armii Radzieckiej* (6 III-7 IV, 1945), 354 pp. (Extremely detailed study under auspices of Polish General Staff Academy, operations 1st Polish Army East Pomerania.)

'Regrettable apprehension and mistrust' pp. 526–529

Churchill, Winston S., *The Second World War,* vol. VI, ch. XXV, on the Polish dispute and the aftermath of the Yalta conference; ch. XXVI, on Soviet suspicions over negotiations for the surrender of Kesselring's forces; ch. XXVII, 'Western strategic divergences', implications and criticism of Eisenhower's cable to Stalin on Allied military intentions.

Deane, John R., *The Strange Alliance*, pp. 157–8, on Eisenhower's cable to Stalin and Stalin's response.

Ehrmann, John, *Grand Strategy*, vol. VI (London: HMSO 1956), p. 132, text of Eisenhower cable to Stalin.

Eisenhower, General Dwight D., *Crusade in Europe* (New York: Doubleday 1948). On the decision to attack towards Dresden rather than Berlin, difficulties (and the proximity of the Red Army) which made a thrust on Berlin 'more than unwise, it was stupid', p. 396.

Diplomatic correspondence

Perepiska . . . , vol. 2. No. 280, Roosevelt–Stalin, March 25, on Molotov's absence at San Francisco Conference, p. 210; No. 281, Roosevelt–Stalin, March 25, on misunderstanding over proposed German surrender in Italy, pp. 211–12; No. 282, Stalin–Roosevelt, March 27, Gromyko to replace Molotov at San Francisco, p. 213; No. 283, Stalin–Roosevelt, March 29, on proposed German surrender in Italy, circumstances 'engender distrust', pp. 213–15; No. 284, Roosevelt–Stalin, April 1, on Yalta agreements and the Polish question, pp. 215–18; No. 285, Roosevelt–Stalin, April 1, 'regrettable apprehension and mistrust' induced over meetings for German surrender in Italy—but *no* negotiations, pp. 218–20; No. 286, Stalin–Roosevelt, April 3, 'negotiations' are taking place over German surrender in Italy, pp. 220–21.

　　Also vol. 1: No. 416, Churchill–Stalin, April 1, 'spirit of Yalta' not maintained in Moscow discussions (over Poland), Churchill's support for Soviet cause, pp. 365–7; No. 417, Churchill–Stalin, April 5, no negotiations over German surrender in Italy, pp. 368–70.

Diplomatic history

Woodward, Sir Llewellyn, *British Foreign Policy in the Second World War*, III. See ch. XLV, pp. 490–519, the Moscow Commission, Molotov's attitude and refusal to accept Anglo–American view of Yalta communiqué, Churchill's proposal for message to Stalin; communications to Molotov, March 19; messages from Churchill and Roosevelt to Stalin, pp. 490–519. Also vol. V, ch. LXVII, (iii), pp. 374–87, German approaches for surrender in Italy, Soviet misunderstandings, Anglo–American exchanges with Stalin.

Soviet materials

Vorob'ev, F.D. *et al.*, *Poslednii shturm*, pp. 43–5, General Staff revisions to Berlin attack plan completed end March, Zhukov March 28 presentation of Plans A and B (Plan A envisaging attack from the Küstrin bridgehead, Plan B to develop operations to seize new bridgehead south of Schwedt, also to expand Frankfurt bridgehead), March 31 General Staff conference with Zhukov and Koniev, problem of boundary between 1st Belorussian Front and 1st Ukrainian Front, April 1 *Stavka* session, Stalin's insistence on capture of Berlin in shortest possible time—offensive to begin April 16, to last 12–15 days.

Zhukov, G.K., *Vospominaniya . . .*, vol. 2, ch. 21, the Berlin operation, pp. 318–25: British harbouring ideas of taking Berlin first (in spite of Yalta decisions on Soviet zone, west of Berlin), Eisenhower on April 7 intimated that capture of Berlin still a possibility after the fall of Leipzig, at the end of March Stalin had received information from Eisenhower on his plan 'to come out to the agreed line on the Berlin axis', Stalin's recognition of Nazi attempts to arrange a separate peace in the west and cease fighting in the west to allow Anglo–American forces into Berlin, Stalin's commendation of Eisenhower and his plan, Zhukov in Moscow March 29 with 1st Belorussian Front operational plan for Berlin, Stalin–Zhukov talk and Stalin's review of German forces on Berlin axis, 1st Belorussian Front able to take offensive in two weeks, 2nd Belorussian Front (Rokossovskii) inevitably delayed in joining 1st Belorussian Front and 1st Ukrainian Front, Stalin's suspicion of Churchill, 'proof' of dealings between Nazis and 'British government circles', Koniev at *Stavka* March 31, Antonov's report on proposed Berlin operation to *Stavka* April 1, Stalin's alteration of boundary line between 1st Belorussian Front and 1st Ukrainian Front—ran only as far as Lübben—decision to open operations on April 16 (2nd Belorussian Front to join offensive April 20).

8 NO TIME TO DIE:
APRIL–MAY 1945

There is now a voluminous literature on the last days of the Third *Reich* and the final, massive assault on Berlin, not to mention the import of the Western decision to halt on the line of the river Elbe—'We're not going to Berlin, Sid' (General Simpson to the commander 2nd US Armoured Division). I must acknowledge at once my extreme indebtedness to these publications, duly listed below, with special reference to my access to the material amassed by the late Cornelius Ryan, while my account of Soviet operations has been largely compiled from my own transcripts of interviews with Red Army officers and men, including several Marshals of the Soviet Union. In addition, I worked on materials from the Soviet military archives, particularly *Stavka* directives (2–23 April 1945) and directives to Fronts and armies; the stipulation was that I might have full and unrestricted use of the papers but not to photocopy them, for which reason I copied them by hand into my 'Moscow notebooks' and translated them at a later date. Thus, it will be seen that there are discrepancies between subsequent 'official translations' of the Chuikov–Krebs conversations, but the version reproduced here was taken from the original diary (and the original diarist). Finally, in delineating Soviet materials relating to the assault on Berlin—*poslednii shturm*—I decided to present this by following the fortunes of each Front (1st Belorussian, 1st Ukrainian, 2nd Belorussian) and the particular formations involved (for example, the four tank armies), and then moving down to units, those involved in the final phases of the fighting in Berlin and the assault on the *Reichstag*.

(i) Gar Alperovitz, *Atomic Diplomacy: Hiroshima and Potsdam* (New York: Vintage Books 1967, esp. ch. II, 'Strategy of a Delayed Showdown'); Lev Bezymenski, *The Death of Adolf Hitler* (unknown documents from Soviet Archives; London:

Michael Joseph 1968; translated from German, original Soviet material); Willi
A. Boelcke (ed.), *Deutschlands Rüstung im Zweiten Weltkrieg* (Hitler–Speer con-
ferences); General Theodor Busse, 'Die letzte Schlacht der 9 Armee', *Wehrwissen-
schaftliche Rundschau*, 1955, No. 4; Marshal SU V.I. Chuikov, *The End of the
Third Reich*, chs. XIII–XVII, assault on Berlin; Winston S. Churchill, *The Second
World War*, vol. VI: *Triumph and Tragedy*, chs. XXVIII–XXXII, Roosevelt's death,
growing friction with Russia, final advance, German surrender; Department of the
Army (US), *German Defense Tactics against Russian Break-Throughs*, Pamphlet
No. 20-233, October 1951 (historical study); Admiral Karl Doenitz, *Memoirs*
(Cleveland: World Pub. Co. 1958); Dieter Dreetz, Hans Höhn, 'Die Zerstörung
Berlins war von der Wehrmachtführung einkalkuliert' (Documents), *Zeitschrift für
Militärgeschichte* (E Berlin, 1965), No. 2 (see pp. 177–94, with map); *Hitler-
Dokumente*: 'Hitlers letzte Lagebesprechung', see *Der Spiegel*, 10 Jan. 1966, pp.
30–46; David Irving, *Hitler's War*, pt 6, '*Endkampf*'; Paul Kecskemeti, *Strategic
Surrender. The Politics of Victory and Defeat* (Stanford UP 1958; see pt 2, ch. 5);
Erich Kuby, *The Russians and Berlin 1945* (trans. Arnold J. Pomerans; London:
Heinemann 1968); Franz Kurowsky, *Armee Wenck. Die 12 Armee zwischen Elbe
und Oder* (Neckargemünd: 1967); Wojtech Mastny, *Russia's Road to the Cold War:
Diplomacy, Warfare and the Politics of Communism 1941–1945* (New York: Columbia
UP 1979; a major work of analysis and comprehensive review of Soviet strategy
and tactics); Field-Marshal Sir Bernard Montgomery, *Normandy to the Baltic* (BAOR
Printing Service 1946; also Hutchinson, London), and *The Memoirs of Field-
Marshal the Viscount Montgomery of Alamein* (London: Collins 1958); Samuel Eliot
Morison, *Strategy and Compromise* (Boston: Little, Brown 1958); P.U. O'Donnell,
Die Katakombe (April 1945) (Stuttgart: DVA 1975); Forrest C. Pogue, see 'Decision
to halt on the Elbe' in *Command Decisions* (ed. Kent R. Greenfield; Washington:
Govt. Printing Office 1960); Edward J. Rozek, *Allied Wartime Diplomacy: A
Pattern in Poland* (ch. 7, 3–4, attempts to implement Yalta decisions, liquidation
of the Polish Government); Cornelius Ryan, *The Last Battle* (London: Collins
1966) (I worked closely with Mr Ryan on this book and had the significant benefit
of inspecting his voluminous holdings on Berlin); Albert Seaton, *The Russo–German
War 1941–45*, ch. 34, the storming of Berlin; V. Sevrule (ed.), *How Wars End.
Eye-Witness Accounts of the Fall of Berlin* (Moscow: Progress Pub. 1969) (Soviet
translation; Marshal Koniev on the Berlin operation, V. Vishnevskii on Berlin
surrender, Roman Karmen 'Doctor Goebbels on the phone'); General S.M. Shtemenko, *The Last Six Months. Russia's Final Battles . . .* (trans. Guy Daniels;
London: Wm. Kimber 1978; a useful translation but with certain imprecisions
which demand care in using this volume); Jean Edward Smith, *The Defense of
Berlin* (Johns Hopkins/OUP 1963; see esp. ch. 3, the military decision to halt
at the Elbe); Albert Speer, *Inside the Third Reich* (New York: Macmillan 1970)
(orig. German, *Erinnerungen*, 1969), ch. 32, 'Annihilation'; General John Strawson,
The Battle for Berlin (New York: Scribners 1974); Hans Georg Studnitz, *Als
Berlin brannte* (Stuttgart, 1963); John Toland, *The Last 100 Days* (New York:
Random House 1966); Nikolai Tolstoy, *Victims of Yalta*, see esp. ch. 4, British
and American agreement at Yalta, agreement on PWs, predominance of British
view (with no provision concerning the return/forced repatriation of unwilling
citizens of the USSR)—see also further on the fate of *Vlasov* and the *Vlasov*

movement (this is a truly appalling story of inertia, incompetence and insensitivity to basic rights, with the burden of responsibility falling in disgraceful fashion on British diplomats and administrators, not excluding some illustrious personages); H.R. Trevor-Roper (Intro.), *Hitler's War Directives 1939–1945* (London: Sidgwick & Jackson 1964), see under *1945;* H.R. Trevor-Roper, *The Last Days of Hitler* (London: Macmillan 1947, and subsequent editions); Walter Warlimont, *Inside Hitler's Headquarters 1939–45,* pt VI, 'Death-throes'; General H. Weidling, 'Der Endkampf in Berlin', *Wehrwissenschaftliche Rundschau,* 1962, nos. 1–3.

(ii) *German war diaries/GMD*

KTB/OKW, IV/ii. 4 Abschnitt (D): 'Dokumente, Befehle, Kapitulationsurkunden usw . . .', pp. 1659–84; Anhänge, 'Aufzeichnungen über Hitler . . .', pp. 1684–1740. See also 1 Abschnitt: under Lagebuch 1–19 April, pp. 1215–51, and V Anhang: 'Die letzten Wehrmachtberichte . . .', pp. 1253–82 (with Abschlussmeldung); also under 3 Abschnitt (B), *KTB,* geführt von Major I.G. Joachim Schultz (= Naumann), 20 April–16 May, pp. 1451–98.

Oberkommando der Kriegsmarine (OKM)/4. Adm. Meisel war diary: command of Northern sector conferred on Dönitz (frames 17–41); *OKM/40:* Letztes Kriegstagebuch O.K.M. Dönitz (frames 42–112), for period 20 April–15 May 1945. T-608/Roll 1.

OKW/OKM. OKW/24 folder: Dönitz files, death of Hitler and succession; *OKW/1898:* Hitler order to Dönitz to defend Northern area (April 20); *OKW/2132:* from Speer's files, telegrams/signals on Dönitz succession, displacing of Göring. . . . T-77/R775, 5500501ff, 5501186ff.

OKW North/Flensburg. OKW/2: Folder, documentation on surrender, Keitel exchanges with Soviet generals Malinin and Serov (May 1945). T-77/R858, 5604775ff.

OKW North/Flensburg. OKW/4.2: collection of material, *Politische Angelegenheiten* (for proposed German 'White Book'), narrative of surrender, Anlagen of related papers, depositions (including an article, 'Sowjetischer Mensch und europäisches Menschentum'). T-77/R859, 5605319–5705.

GenStdH/Org. Abt. Summary of *'Operation ECLIPSE'* plans (dated Jan. 1945), German notations. T-78/R434, 6405864–6085. (See also *OKW/2029* on ECLIPSE: T-77/R873, 5620228ff.)

FHO (I). Situation Reports: *Lageberichte Ost,* March 1945 (daily reports); *Lageberichte Ost,* April 1945 (April 1–25); also *Lagebericht ab 23.4, Lagebericht Ost* Nr 1414 (April 29); *Lageberichte Ost,* 23–28 April 1945. T-78/R473, 6454661–5161.

(Vlasov movement). Folder: translations into German from *Za rodinu* (Feb. 1945), Vlasov's assumption of command/600th and 650th Infantry Divisions, speeches Vlasov and Köstring. T-78/R501, 6489663–730.

(iii) *Soviet materials/documents, interviews, press, collected memoir material*

(a) *Materials from Soviet military archives.* Planning/operational documents, Berlin: *Stavka* directives* (2–23 April), beginning Directive No. 11059 (April 2) to Directive No. 11074 (issued 0045 hrs, April 23); *Front operational directives (operativnaya direktiva)* for 1st Belorussian, 1st Ukrainian, 2nd Belorussian Fronts, beginning operational Directive No. 00211/op, Staff 1st Ukrainian Front, 8 April 1945. . . . Also *operational orders (boevoi prikaz) for corps,* with intelligence/enemy order-of-battle reports *(razvedsvodka); archival records/capitulation proceedings/in- terrogations—Opisanie peregovorov s nachal'nikom Generalnovo shtaba Sukhoputnykh voisk Germanskoi Armii generalom pekhoty Gansom Krebsom i komanduyushchym oborony goroda Berlin generatom artillerii Veidlingom o kapitulyatsii nemelskikh voisk v Berline* (Report, Lt.-Col. Gladkii, Chief of Intelligence, 8th Guards Army). (*Note:* the record of the Chuikov–Krebs exchange I have taken from my own transcript of the original on-the-spot notation, set down *verbatim).* Also: *Protokol,* interrogation of Reichsmarschall Hermann Göring (17 June 1945); *Protokol,* Interrogation of General Weidling by Maj.-Gen. Trusov (May 1945, no exact date recorded).

(b) *Interviews/Red Army officers and men.* These included MSUs Sokolovskii, Koniev, Rokossovskii, Chuikov, through to corps commanders (e.g. Yushchuk, 11th Tank Corps) to Colonel Neustroyev (then a captain) and unit level.

(c) *Press.* Contemporary press reports, plus '20th anniversary' press reporting (1965): *Pravda, Izvestiya, Pravda Vostoka* (Uzbekistan), *Kazakhstanskaya Pravda, Turk- menskaya Iskra, Kommunist Tadzhikistana* and, not least, *Krasnaya Zvezda.*

(d) *Collected memoir/documentary materials.* See V.S. Veselov (General Editor), *Shturm Berlina. Vospominaniya, pisma, dnevniki . . .* (Moscow: Voenizdat 1948), 488 pp. (I found this a useful compilation of raw materials, especially at the level of unit performance.) This has now been superseded (or augmented) by *9 maya 1945 goda,* ed. A.M. Samsonov (Moscow: Nauka 1970), 760 pp.; though some of this memoir material had appeared previously, Professor Samsonov's editorial control has ensured both authenticity and reliability: see under Zhukov, Koniev, Rokos- sovskii, M.Z. Zakharov (to Prague), Yeremenko (Prague), Bagramyan, Moskalenko, Lelyushenko, Pliev, Radzievskii, Sandalov. I have cited this work as *9 maya 1945 goda.*

Note on Soviet strength/Berlin operation

While it has become virtually a Soviet convention to cite the total of 6,250 tanks committed to the Berlin operation, specific order-of-battle and tank strength was 4 tank armies, 2 mechanized corps, 11 tank corps, 29 tank regiments for all three Fronts: *total 3,594 tanks.* Many tank formations had only 50–60 per cent of their full strength, with tank brigades and regiments distributed as infantry support. Strength in self-propelled/assault guns amounted to 3 brigades, 61 regiments and 25 batteries: *total 2,519 SP guns.* See also 'Berlinskaya operatsiya v tsefrakh', *VIZ,* 1965 (4), pp. 79–86 (tables, strengths, deployments, list of Front command staffs).

(iv) *Polish materials*

Duszynski, Z., *Dzialania 1 warszawskiej diwizji piechoty im. T. Kościuszki w Berlinie* (Warsaw: MON 1952).

Gać, S., *Udzial 2 armii Wojska Polskiego w operacji Praskiej* (Warsaw: MON 1962). 2nd Polish Army, Prague.

Krzeminski, G., *Lotnictwo polskie w operacji berlińskiej* (Warsaw: MON 1970). Polish air force, Berlin.

Stąpor, Z., *Bitwa o Berlin, Dzialania 1 Armii WP kwiecień-maj 1945* (Warsaw: MON 1973). 1st Polish Army, Berlin.

Berlin: Soviet planning pp. 531–542

Diplomatic correspondence

Perepiska . . . , see vol. 2: No. 283, Stalin–Roosevelt, March 29, complaint over 'Berne negotiations', pp. 213–15; No. 284, Roosevelt–Stalin, April 1, on the Polish question, pp. 215–18; No. 286, Stalin–Roosevelt, April 3, disputing the President's view of the 'Berne talks', pp. 220–21; No. 287, Roosevelt–Stalin, April 5, on 'vile misrepresentations' of Stalin's informants, pp. 221–2; No. 288, Stalin–Roosevelt, April 7, on German surrenders in the west, fierce resistance in ᵗʰᵉ east for all points as unnecessary as a 'poultice to a dead man', pp. 223–4; No. 289, Stalin–Roosevelt, April 7, on the Polish question, pp. 226–8.

Vol. 1: No. 417, Churchill–Stalin, April 5, on the 'Berne talks', pp. 368–70; No. 418, Stalin–Churchill, April 7, on the Polish question (enclosing Stalin–Roosevelt letter), pp. 370–74; No. 419, Stalin–Churchill, April 7, disclaiming any intention of 'blackening' anyone, pp. 374–5.

Diplomatic history

Woodward, Sir Llewellyn, *British Foreign Policy . . . ,* III, ch. XLV, Great Britain and Soviet–Polish relations, see pp. 500–6, Anglo–American exchanges for approach to Soviet government; pp. 519–23, meeting of Commission, April 2, Stalin's replies to Churchill and Roosevelt (April 10); pp. 540–44, Soviet decision to conclude treaty with Polish Provisional Government, disappearance of 15 Polish leaders after March 27–28 meetings, Churchill's disagreement with the idea of Yugoslavia as a 'model' for Poland. (The contrived numbers game between 'old' and 'new' political representatives in the government of Yugoslavia gave Marshal Tito's adherents 23 seats out of 28 and, of the remaining five, two were assigned to Partisans, thus making Tito's grand total 25, leaving only three seats to the supporters of the Royal Government.)

Documents on Polish–Soviet Relations 1939–1945, vol. 2: *1943–45,* No. 323, invitation for Polish leaders to a conference with 'the Representative of the 1st White Russian Front command . . .', Warsaw, March 11, pp. 543–4; No. 331, Raczynski–Eden, on the arrest of Polish political leaders, April 1, pp. 553–5.

'Jagodzinski mission'

See Edward J. Rozek, *Allied Wartime Diplomacy. A Pattern in Poland,* p. 365, quoting vol. X, p. 17 of the Mikolajczyk Papers. Once again I must express my indebtedness to Professor Rozek for his assistance in treating this aspect.

Soviet materials

(i) *Stavka directives*

No. 11059, dated 2 April, to 1st Belorrussian Front (the discrepancy of 1–2 April in dating may be that Stalin signed on 1 April as frequently stated but the directive became operational as of April 2); No. 11060, dated 3 April, timed 2100 hrs, to 1st Ukrainian Front (Koniev); No. 11062, dated 6 April, to 2nd Belorussian Front (Rokossovskii).

(ii) *IVOVSS,* 5, pt 1, pp. 246–63, preparation and planning of Berlin operation: on Anglo–American planning, Berlin as an objective, Eisenhower's decision and British objections, German preparations to defend Berlin, German strength (1 million men, 10,400 guns, 1,500 tanks, 3 million *Faustpatronen,* 3,300 combat aircraft), Soviet planning conference 1–3 April, *Stavka* plan for three-front operation, also offensive operations on southern flank (4th, 2nd and 3rd Ukrainian Fronts) to deny German command freedom of manoeuvre, Stalin's reply to Eisenhower with statement of Soviet intention to take Berlin with a portion of Red Army forces, summary of Front operational plans/directives, air support planning, assault bridging/combat engineer support, Soviet 'disinformation' (2nd Belorussian Front misleading 'deployment' of 2nd Shock Army along Stettin axis, 1st Belorussian Front efforts to suggest an attack from the flanks, not the centre).

IVMV, 10, pt 1, pp. 310–25, military-political situation in mid-April, planning/ preparation of Berlin attack: German defensive preparations for Berlin, *Stavka* planning for speedy operation, Stalin's reply to Eisenhower (giving general indications of the timing of the Soviet offensive), summary of *Stavka* directives, Front command decisions, Zhukov's plans for use of two tank armies, and attempts to build up powerful 'shock groups' and high tactical densities, heavy artillery concentration (also Zhukov's utilization of searchlights), air support planning, engineering support, problems posed by shortage of time and need to regroup, role of *maskirovka* (deception) with Koniev carefully screening his redeployment to the right flank by installing dummy tanks and continuing normal radio traffic on his left, large-scale distribution of instruction leaflets on assault river crossing and fighting in built-up areas.

(iii) Babadzhanyan, A.Kh. *et al., Lyuki otkryli v Berline* (1st Guards Tank Army). See under 'Last Battles', pp. 289–99, 1st Guards Tank reverts to 1st Belorussian Front, preparations for Berlin operation, formation of 'assault groups'—3 to a mechanized brigade, 2 to a tank brigade—command/staff exercises April 5 in Birnbaum, address by Marshal Zhukov, map exercise with objectives identified by numbers, Malinin (Front Chief of Staff) on German order of battle, features of Berlin fortifications, Zhukov's final briefing on operational assignments, assignment in detail to 1st Guards Tank Army, co-operation with 8th Guards Army, planning for 11th Tank Corps, 11th Guards Tank Corps and 8th Guards Mechanized Corps, reinforcement for 1st Guards Tank Army—290 tanks and SP guns.

Batov, General P.I., *Operatsiya 'Oder'* (Moscow: Voenizdat 1965) (65th Army operations, April–May 1945). See pp. 13–26, on the regrouping of 2nd Belorussian Front, first movements with 49th and 70th Armies followed by 65th Army. (Monograph treatment, using Soviet military archives.)

Katukov, M.E., *Na ostrie glavnovo udara* (2nd edn), pp. 388–92, 1st Guards Tank Army duly returned to 1st Belorussian Front (from 2nd Belorussian Front), reinforcements and replacements (Yushchuk's 11th Tank Corps assigned to 1st

Guards Tank, bringing total tank/SP-gun strength to 854), special maps of Berlin supplied to topographic section of Front staff, Front command/staff exercise April 5, study of German strength/order of battle, Front directive issued to 1st Guards Tank April 12, tank army to be committed behind 8th Guards Army, with subsequent movement to the south-west and outflank city from the south, daily rate of advance fixed at 35–37 kms—was Zhukov's decision to throw two tank armies against an unsuppressed defence correct?

Koniev, I.S., *Year of Victory* (Moscow). See 'The Berlin Operation', pp. 79–91, meeting in *Stavka* April 1, Shtemenko report on plans of US–British command to capture Berlin, main Allied attack to come from north of the Ruhr, Stalin—'Well, then, who is going to take Berlin . . .'—need for Koniev to regroup, report to *Stavka* April 3 on operational plans, Stalin offers 28th and 31st Armies as reinforcement, 1st Ukrainian Front offensive plan (and directive), Stalin pencils in boundary line between 1st Belorussian and 1st Ukrainian Front, the line cut short at Lübben, text of *Stavka* directive April 3, Koniev's Front plan with special instruction to 3rd Guards Tank Army—'. . . to bear in mind the possibility of attacking Berlin from the south with a reinforced tank corps . . .'—planned employment of tank armies, air support and role of air in laying down extensive smokescreens.

Rokossovskii, K.K., *A Soldier's Duty*. See under 'The Oder–Elbe', pp. 314–18, problems of regrouping 2nd Belorussian Front along Stettin–Rostock axis, movement begun April 4–5, march plans, briefing at *Stavka* on role of 2nd Belorussian Front in Berlin operation, four-day delay for Rokossovskii (attack timed for April 20), unfavourable terrain for operations (East and West Oder), troops deploying into position by April 13.

Shtemenko, S.M., 'Na poslednikh rubezhakh v Evrope', *VIZ*, 1971 (4), pp. 63–7. (Emphasizes German attempts to come to a separate understanding with the Anglo–Americans, also Soviet concern at reports of the 'Alpine Redoubt'—the Nazi government literally shifting itself closer to the Anglo–American armies—while these rumours of a separate agreement were also designed to sow dissension; Stalin April 17 instructed Zhukov to ignore Hitler's 'web'—spider's web, *pautina*—spun about Berlin, a web to be cut by Soviet forces taking Berlin. 'We can do it, we must do it.') Shtemenko's argument is that Soviet policy prevented severe inter-allied dissension, while Stalin's solution was the speedy capture of Berlin by the Red Army.

Vorob'ev, F.D. *el al.*, *Poslednii shturm* (1975 edn), ch. 2, on planning meetings, 1–2 April, *Stavka* decisions (and directives 2–3 April), main axes of attack delineated, *Stavka* ruling on artillery densities, reinforcement for 1st Belorussian Front, role of 1st Ukrainian Front and assignment for 2nd Belorussian Front, pp. 44–9; decisions of Front commands and operational assignments to armies, pp. 49–66 (note observation, p. 50, defending Zhukov's decision to use 1st Guards Tank Army in an outflanking move to the south of Berlin rather than operating to the north with 2nd Guards Tank Army, a decision approved by Stalin himself; this account rejects criticism of Zhukov by some Soviet specialists—redeploying 1st Guards Tank did not appreciably weaken the force assigned to the northern outflanking movements, for this force proved to be adequate to its task without 1st Guards Tank). It is worth noting that precisely this observation, even to the same phraseology, is made by Lt.-Gen. V. Poznyak in 'Zavershayushchie udary po vragu', *VIZ*, 1965 (5), p. 29.

Zhukov, G.K., *Vospominaniiya* . . . , vol. 2, pp. 323–30, Berlin operation, Stalin on *vot Cherchill*, *Stavka* directive for 1st Belorussian Front operations, problem with enforced delay in opening 2nd Belorussian Front offensive (leaving Zhukov with bare right flank), 2nd Belorussian Front operations to north would only bear upon the enemy by April 23–24, 1st Belorussian Front staff/command exercises April 5–7, plan to use searchlights, decision to deploy 1st Guards Tank Army 'directly behind' 8th Guards Army, Stalin advised, 'Do as you think fit, you can see better on the spot'.

(iv) *Troop transfers to the Far East*

See *Finale* (Moscow: Progress Pub. 1972—translation of *Final. Istoriko-memuarnyi ocherk* . . . , ed. Marshal M.V. Zakharov, Moscow: Nauka 1969), pp. 69–70, the planning phase, *Stavka* decision March 1945 to supply new T-34 tanks to one tank battalion in each tank brigade in Far East and Transbaikal Military Districts (Fronts), old tanks left as a reserve for brigade commanders, new tanks also supplied to 1st Tank Regiments of 61st and 111th Tank Divisions (Transbaikal)—670 T-34s assigned to Far Eastern theatre, consideration of further troop deployments in order to ensure rapid defeat of the Kwantung Army.

See also S.M. Shtemenko, *The Soviet General Staff at War* (Moscow: Progress Pub. 1970), pp. 324–7, estimates for reinforcement and logistical requirements in Far East completed beginning October 1944, terms of the Yalta agreement on Soviet entry into war against Japan, denunciation of Neutrality Pact 5 April 1945, this 'serious warning went unheeded' by the Japanese, *Stavka* decision not to break up existing command in the Far East, former Karelian Front command to be transferred—assigned to Meretskov, 'the wily man from Yaroslavl' as Stalin called him, recalled experience of Meretskov in fighting through forest and fortified areas.

Further to the Yalta agreement and Soviet participation in the war against Japan, in particular Stalin's views on informing Chiang Kai-shek on this matter, see, under *Diplomatic correspondence/diplomatic history*, 'Hurley–Stalin talk, 15 April 1945' in *Notes to pp. 552–568*, below.

Königsberg–Ostrava–Vienna   pp. 542–552

(i) *Königsberg/'Samland'*

Bagramyan, I.Kh., *Tak shli my k pobede*. See ch. 10, on Operation *Samland*, pp. 509–88. (Detailed memoir/analysis of the organization and execution of the Königsberg assault.)

Bagramyan, I.Kh., 'Shturm Kenigsberg', *VIZ*, 1976 (8), pp. 56–64 and (9), pp. 47–57.

Collective authorship, *Shturm Kenigsberga* (Kaliningrad: Kalingradskoe Izd. 1966), 254 pp. (Collected memoir accounts). See Bagramyan on *Samland*, pp. 65–74; Khryukin, pp. 74–82; also Lyudnikov, pp. 55–65.

Collective authorship, *Shturm Kenigsberga* (Kaliningrad, 1973), 384 pp. See accounts by Vasilevskii, Bagramyan, Khlebnikov (on artillery), pp. 53–116; also Galitskii (11th Guards Army), pp. 121–9.

Galitskii, K.N., *V boyakh za Vostochnuyu Prussiyu* (11th Guards Army), ch. 9, 11th Guards preparation for assault on Köningsberg, army/corps decisions, special operational deployments, pp. 343–66; ch. 11, 11th Guards in storming Königsberg, night April 11, drawn into Front reserve, pp. 385–436; ch. 12, destruction of German Samland group, capture of Pillau, pp. 437–55. (Extremely detailed, day-by-day operational narrative.)

Lyudnikov, Col.-Gen. I.I., *Doroga dlinoyu v zhizn* (Moscow: Voenizdat (VM) 1969). See 'Shturm Kenigsberga', pp. 155–64. (39th Army, Königsberg assault.)

Novikov, Air Chief Marshal A., 'Sovetskaya aviatsiya v boyakh za Kenigsberg', *VIZ*, 1968 (9), pp. 71–81. (Soviet air operations; need to master techniques of saturation bombing of major city.)

Popov, Lt.-Gen. (Artillery) S.E., *Na ognevykh rubezhakh* (Moscow: Voenizdat 1971). (3rd Guards Artillery Breakthrough Division/Supreme Command Reserve.) See under 'Shturm', artillery in the Königsberg assault, pp. 152–67.

Vasilevskii, A.M., *Delo vsei zhizni* (2nd edn). On the Konigsberg assault, offensive against German Samland group, pp. 503–10.

Vasilevskii, A.M., 'Vostochno–Prusskaya operatsiya', *VIZ*, 1969 (3), pp. 46–55. Planning documents for the reduction of Königsberg, German refusal to surrender, final Soviet assault.

(ii) *Ostrava–Prague*

Collective authorship, *V srazheniyakh za Pobedu* (38th Army combat history). See ch. 14, 'Ostrava–Praga', pp. 511–7, little progress with mid-March offensive, planning to outflank M-Ostrava from the north, fresh attack 24 March, 38th Army bridgehead on the Oder, stiffening of German resistance, Yeremenko orders defensive action 5 April in order to prepare fresh offensive.

Grechko, A.A., *Cherez Karpaty*. See pp. 348–68, M-Ostrava operation, failure of February–March offensive operations (divisional strength in 38th Army down to 2,800–3,100 men), slow progress by 1st Guards Army in March offensive, Soviet attacks called off 17 March, *Stavka* criticism of 4th Ukrainian Front command for poor planning and execution of operation, German forces well aware of time and place of Soviet attack, also poor weather conditions, Petrov replaced as Front commander—but Grechko (p. 360) exonerates him from personal blame, pointing to shortages of men and munitions as the true cause of failure in March—progress by 38th Army and 1st Guards Army continued to be slow, revised *Stavka* directive 3 April to 4th Ukrainian Front, movement of 60th Army to 4th Ukrainian Front. (Detailed narrative based largely on Soviet military archives, emphasis on difficulties caused by well-organized German resistance and fighting in built-up areas.)

Koniev, I.S. (ed.), *Za osvobozhdenie Chekhoslovakii*, pp. 185–94, Ostrava operation, advance to Bratislava and Brno (4th and 2nd Ukrainian Fronts): 10 March offensive by 4th Ukrainian Front south of Zorau, impeded by bad weather, main burden borne by infantry, slow pace of advance, operation called off 17 March, *Stavka* criticism of 4th Ukrainian Front command, Petrov removed from command and replaced by Yeremenko (26 March), 60th Army (1st Ukrainian Front) engaged

in battle for Ratibor linking up with 4th Ukrainian Front, 24 March 4th Ukrainian
Front renewed offensive, 5 rifle corps with 38th Army mounting main attack,
Czechoslovak Tank Brigade in action, 1st Guards Army to attack towards Friestadt,
18th Army to break enemy defence in valley of river Vag, Zorau stormed, slow
progress late March towards Oder north-east of M-Ostrava, after 12 days' heavy
fighting still 20 miles from M-Ostrava, heavy German counter-attacks early April,
more success for 2nd Ukrainian Front, fall of Banska Bystrica 25 March, lead
elements only 20 miles from Bratislava end March, 1 April revised instructions
from *Stavka* to 2nd Ukrainian Front, to drive north of Danube and capture
Bratislava no later than 5–6 April, revised directive to 4th Ukrainian Front 3
April (p. 194), Soviet aim to encircle main body of German Army Group Centre
in the Carpathians.

Moskalenko, K.S., *Na yugo-zapadnom napravlenii 1943–45*, bk 2. (This is an important,
detailed and objective account by 38th Army commander of the failure of the
March offensive.) See ch. 17, on M-Ostrava operation, pp. 568–77, heavy German
resistance was coupled with poor Soviet planning, Moskalenko summoned to Front
CP for discussion with Petrov and Lev Mekhlis, an 'unofficial' meeting where
Petrov sought to determine reasons for failure, Moskalenko pointed to unfortunate
choice of axis of main attack, Mekhlis took continuous notes at this 'unofficial'
meeting, sent material as a telegram to Moscow, 16 March Moskalenko summoned
to telephone to talk to Antonov in Moscow, Antonov on Stalin's instructions
enquired about Moskalenko's views on the failure of the offensive, Antonov well
informed about the 'unofficial' meeting with Petrov and Mekhlis, the problem of
fixing favourable line of attack, Petrov telephone call shortly after to Moskalenko
accepting idea of attacking from area of Zorau, further reinforcement for 38th
Army, *text of Stavka signal—17.3.1945, personal to Petrov and Mekhlis*—repri-
manding Petrov and citing Mekhlis's evidence about poor planning (p. 570),
arrival of Yeremenko and acceptance of idea of outflanking M-Ostrava from the
north, improvement in work of Front command/administration, work on fresh
operational plan.

Sandalov, Col.-Gen. L.M., 'Cherez Karpaty v Pragu', in Samsonov (ed.), *9 maya 1945
goda*, pp. 704–17. Summoned from 2nd Baltic Front to Moscow, informed by
Antonov—Chief of the General Staff—that he was now chief of staff to 4th
Ukrainian Front, Yeremenko to be Front commander, Antonov's comments on
failure of 4th Ukrainian Front operations in March, visits to Front armies with
Yeremenko, reports to the General Staff, Svoboda with Czechoslovak Corps appointed
Defence Minister of the Czechoslovak Republic, 60th Army transferred from 1st
Ukrainian Front and finally moved into position with 4th Ukrainian Front.

Yeremenko, A.I., *Gody vozmezdiya*. See pp. 510–36, operations M-Ostrava, failure of
March offensive, slow pace of advance, Yeremenko assumes command 4th Ukrainian
Front, planning for powerful offensive blow, inspection visit to 38th Army (Moskalenko), 27 March inspection visit to 1st Guards Army, visit to 1st Czechoslovak
Corps, Stalin's insistence that M-Ostrava industrial region must be taken without
further delay, Yeremenko's request to delay offensive due to shortage of ammunition
categorically refused.

See also:

Holub, Ota, *Československé tanky a tankisté* (Prague: Naše Vojsko 1980), *passim*. (Czechoslovak tanks and tank troops.)

Tvarůžek, Břetislav, *Operační cíl Ostrava* (Ostrava: Profil 1973), 229 pp. (Ostrava operation, narrative and analysis based on Czechoslovak and Soviet materials.)

(iii) *Vienna–Bratislava*

Ivanov, Army General S., 'Na venskom napravlenii', *VIZ*, 1969 (6), pp. 23–38. Crisp but informative summary of Vienna operation, beginning with general review of situation, Timoshenko (*Stavka* 'co-ordinator') agreement to mount main attack with 3rd Ukrainian Front as opposed to original intention to use 2nd Ukrainian Front, Stalin's agreement, *Stavka* directive 9 March, Tolbukhin's operational planning, breaching of enemy defences and opening of drive on Vienna, request to *Stavka* for transfer of 6th Guards Tank Army to 3rd Ukrainian Front approved by Stalin (6th Guards Tank Army at that time with strength of 286 tanks and SP guns) *Stavka* directive 1 April on capture of Vienna and advance line to be reached by 12–15 April, 2nd Ukrainian Front drive to cut German lines of communication to the north-west, to speed final assault on Vienna staff officers assigned to units and sub-units, important roles in Front operational work by Lt.-Gen. A.P. Tarasov and Maj.-Gen. A.S. Rogov, head of Front intelligence.

Kuznetsov, P.G., *Marshal Tolbukhin*. See 'Na venskom napravlenii', the Vienna operation, pp. 235–49: Tolbukhin's operational plan (using 9th and 4th Guards Army), failure to complete encirclement of Sixth *SS Panzer* cause for concern to *Stavka*, approach to Vienna and flanking movements to cut German escape routes, Tolbukhin's orders for night and day operations, Vienna cleared April 13, further advance in direction of Graz.

Malakhov, M.M., *Osvobozhdenie Vengrii i vostochnoi Avstrii*, pp. 234–80, Soviet planning for Vienna operation, preparations, drive on Vienna by 2nd and 3rd Ukrainian Fronts, assault on Vienna, April 5–13. (Very detailed operational narrative.)

Malinovskii, R.Ya. (ed.), *Budapest Vena Praga*, ch. 5, Vienna operation, pp. 229–88: mid-March 2nd and 3rd Ukrainian Fronts drive in two directions—Vienna and Bratislava—Vienna operation opened in wake of Balaton defensive fighting, preliminary planning for Vienna attack begun with small group of hand-picked officers in mid-February (three days after fall of Budapest), 46th Army heavily reinforced (12 divisions, 165 tanks and SP guns), 7th Guards Army to break defences on the river Hron, followed by thrust on Bratislava with 53rd Army, Tolbukhin's decision to use 9th and 4th Guards Army, detailed planning for artillery support, first stage of operation 16–25 March, second stage lasted 26 March–4 April, sudden transfer of 6th Guards Tank Army to 3rd Ukrainian Front after discussion with Stalin, breaking of German defences between the Danube and lake Balaton, 46th Army (2nd Ukrainian Front) and right wing 3rd Ukrainian Front in pursuit of German forces, left-flank offensive 3rd Ukrainian Front opened 29 March, *Stavka* plan to complete capture Vienna with right flank 3rd Ukrainian Front with 7th Guards Army striking for Brno, fighting at approaches to Vienna 5 April, assault opened at 0700 hours 6 April, street fighting 8 April, meanwhile 46th Army had crossed Danube in area of Bratislava (April 2), Vienna cleared by noon 13 April, 3rd Ukrainian Front opens drive towards Graz, revised *Stavka* directive 13 April to 3rd Ukrainian Front.

Zavizion, G.T. and Kornyushin, P.A., *I na Tikhom Okeane* . . . (6th Guards Tank Army). See ch. 7, Vienna operation, pp. 172–83: *Stavka* instructions, 6th Guards Tank Army regrouped, German resistance with SS divisions at approaches to Austria, 5th Guards Tank Corps driving on Wiener Neustadt, 9th Guards Mech. Corps approaching river Leithe, brigade strength in 6th Guards Tank Army dropping to 7–10 tanks, drive on Vienna, heavy fighting at approaches to Austrian capital, Kravchenko's decision to outflank and attack from west and south-west approved by Timoshenko, low strength in tanks (46th Guards Tank Brigade had only 13 tanks, SP regiment only 4–5 guns), German links to the west and north-west cut, street fighting until 13 April, Vienna cleared at 1400 hours 13 April.

Ot volzhskikh stepei . . . (4th Guards Army). See under 'Na Venu!', the assault on Vienna, pp. 204–22.

Air operations

17-ya vozdushnaya . . . (17th Air Army). Ch. 6, 17th Air Army and Vienna operations, pp. 236–41: 24,100 sorties, 148 air combats, 155 enemy aircraft shot down, 5,023 tons of bombs dropped on rail links, 7,276 rockets fired, 2 million rounds of ammunition for aircraft cannon/machine-guns fired off.

Breaking into Berlin, 16–23 April   pp. 552–568

Churchill, Winston S., *The Second World War*, vol. 6: *Triumph and Tragedy*, bk II, ch. XXX, 'The Final Advance' (especially Churchill–Eden, 19 April, Anglo-American forces 'not immediately in a position' to fight their way into Berlin), *passim*.

Irving, David, *Hitler's War*. See under 'Endkampf. Hitler Goes to Ground', pp. 786–7: Mr Irving emphasizes Hitler's Order of 30 March 1945, on the occasion of his demand for fanatical resistance from Army Group Vistula (and Heinrici himself), ordering also the construction of a main battleline (*Hauptkampflinie: HKL*) 2–4 miles behind the existing front line, with Heinrici falling back on this second line once the Soviet assault opened. See also the important footnote to p. 794, intimating that for all the second *HKL*, Heinrici had decided that in the event of the collapse of the Oder Front, he would abandon Berlin without a fight (having already tried at this juncture to move his HQ behind Berlin, a move frustrated by Hitler himself).

In *Inside the Third Reich*, Speer himself records a conference on 15 April with Reymann and Heinrici; Heinrici did much to countermand orders for the mass demolition of bridges in the city, asserting privately to Speer that 'there will not be any battle for Berlin', Berlin would be taken 'at least without much resistance' (see pt 3, ch. 31, 'The Thirteenth Hour').

Kuby, Erich, *The Russians and Berlin, 1945, passim.*

Ryan, Cornelius, *The Last Battle*, ch. 6, 'The Decision', see p. 261 ('We're not going to Berlin, Sid . . .', General Simpson to Brigadier-General Hinds).

Seaton, Albert, *Stalin as Warlord* (London: Batsford 1976). See ch. 11 on 1945, especially pp. 245–55 on Stalin's handling of the final phase of the war in Europe.

Smith, Jean Edward, *The Defense of Berlin, op. cit.* See ch. 3, 'The Military Decision to Halt at the Elbe', pp. 34–53 (A detailed analysis with detailed supporting evidence).

Trevor-Roper, H.R. (ed.), *Hitler's War Directives 1939–1945,* (London, Sidgwick & Jackson, 1964). (Orig. *Hitlers Weisungen für die Kriegsführung . . .* , ed. W. Hubatsch): under *1945,* Hitler's Order of the Day to Soldiers of the Eastern Front (dated 15 April).

Diplomatic correspondence/diplomatic history

Perepiska . . . , vol. 2. No. 291, Stalin–Truman, 13 April, sympathy on death of President Roosevelt, p. 229; No. 293, Truman (and Churchill)–Stalin, 18 April, on the Polish question and the Warsaw government, pp. 230–32; No. 295, Truman–Stalin, on Allied–Soviet link-up, 21 April, pp. 232–3.

Perepiska . . . , vol. 1. No. 436, Churchill–Stalin, 22 April, on Mikolajczyk statement and acceptance of Curzon line, p. 380; No. 439, Stalin–Churchill, 24 April, Soviet response on Poland to joint Anglo–American message 18 April, pp. 390–92.

Harriman, W. Averell and Abel, Elie, *Special Envoy to Churchill and Stalin 1941–46* (London: Hutchinson 1976), pp. 445–6, April 15 meeting—Stalin, Molotov, Harriman, Hurley—Stalin's accusations of conspiracy with anti-Communist Polish underground, rebuttal of these charges, Stalin's agreement to send Molotov to United States.

Hurley–Stalin talk, 15 April 1945: Yalta agreement and Nationalist China. General Hurley first visited Moscow in November 1942, when he found Stalin both direct in statement and accommodating about information. In August 1944 Hurley was again in Moscow, seeking clarification of the Soviet attitude to China, whereupon Molotov disclaimed any ulterior Soviet interest in the Chinese Communists. On the night of 15 April, in the company of Averell Harriman and Molotov, Hurley talked with Stalin, when Stalin broached the matter of disclosing details of the Yalta agreement to Chiang Kai-shek; Stalin argued that he needed 2–3 months to build up Soviet forces in the Far East, though he would leave the timing of the disclosure in Chungking to Hurley. However, it was agreed that Hurley would wait on Stalin's signal. (Yet with the Soviet termination of the Soviet–Japanese Neutrality Pact, a plain signal had already been sent from Moscow.)

No small amount of controversy has centred on Hurley's interpretation of Stalin's attitude to American policy in China. Hurley himself evidently took Stalin's statements at their face value, emphasizing Stalin's support for the unification of military forces in China and Chiang Kai-shek's leadership of the National Government—precisely the outline of American policy. Others were not so persuaded, including Ambassador Harriman himself.

See Herbert Feis, *The China Tangle* (Princeton UP/New York: Atheneum 1965), ch. 26, 'The Soviet Side', pp. 284–6; Tang Tsou, *America's Failure in China 1941–50,* ch. VII(D), pp. 251–5, the Yalta agreement, Soviet intentions, Hurley's report to the effect that Stalin would co-operate with the United States to obtain military unification in China, 'unqualified' agreement on the part of Stalin with American policy in China, correctness of Hurley's view that Stalin did indeed pursue the military and political unification of China—but failure to realize that Stalin's policy of co-operation with Chiang Kai-shek a tactical device.

For disclaimers of Hurley's views on Soviet policy see George F. Kennan, *Memoirs 1925–1950* (Boston: Little, Brown 1967), pp. 236–9, repercussions of Yalta, Hurley's summary of Molotov's views on China ('the so-called Chinese Communists are not in fact Communists . . .'), Hurley's talk with Stalin, Hurley report could convey 'serious misimpression' about Soviet policy, Kennan–Harriman message on Soviet policy in China (as corrective to Hurley's views, text p. 238).

Soviet materials

Official histories, general compilation, collected memoir material

IVOVSS, 5, pt 1, pp. 255–80, preparation of the Soviet attack on Berlin, breakthrough on the Oder and the Neisse, encirclement of Berlin.

IVMV, 10, pt 1, pp. 314–25, preparations for the Soviet assault on Berlin.

Vorob'ev, F.D. *et al.*, *Poslednii shturm (Berlinskaya operatsiya 1945 g.)* (2nd edn). (This must be accounted the Soviet 'standard work' on the Berlin operation and is extremely detailed.) See ch. 3, the preparation of the operation—artillery, air defence, air, combat engineers, Dnieper flotilla preparations, command/control, logistics/supply, 'political preparation', pp. 67–110; ch. 4, breaking the German defences, 1st Belorussian Front 16–21 April, 1st Ukrainian Front 16–18 April, pp. 127–84; ch. 5, encirclement and splitting of German forces in Berlin, 1st Ukrainian Front operations 19–25 April, the Dresden axis 19–25 April, 1st Belorussian Front operations to encircle the Berlin and Frankfurt–Guben groups 22–25 April, pp. 185–246; ch. 7, destruction of the Frankfurt–Guben group, pp. 271–303; ch. 8, the storming of Berlin, characteristics of the defensive system in Berlin, situation on 26 April, storming the *Reichstag*, fall of Berlin, the destruction of Third *Panzer* Army, pp. 304–89.

Samsonov, A.M. (ed.), *9 maya 1945 goda*. In this major collection of memoir material, see especially G.K. Zhukov (the Berlin operation), pp. 66–121; K.K. Rokossovskii (2nd Belorussian Front operations), pp. 161–82; A.A. Novikov (Soviet aviation in the Königsberg and Berlin operations), pp. 273–325; A.A. Radzievskii (2nd Guards Tank Army operations), pp. 685–702; N.A. Antipenko (Logistics/'Rear Services', Berlin operation), pp. 722–50.

1st Belorussian Front (Zhukov)

Zhukov, G.K., *Vospominaniya . . .* , vol. 2, ch. 21, the Berlin operation, pp. 338–47: Zhukov at Chuikov's HQ (8th Guards), artillery preparation at 0500 hours, 140 searchlights switched on, stiff German resistance Seelow Heights, German defences 'basically intact', 1500 hours call to Stalin who reported Koniev making good progress, further call to Stalin in evening, Stalin's rebuke about Zhukov's commitment of 1st Guards Tank Army on 8th Guards sector, Zhukov promises breaching of Seelow defences by 17 April, Stalin proposes to use Koniev's tank armies to drive on Berlin from the south, *Stavka* directive 18 April to Koniev and Rokossovskii, Zhukov accepts blame for initial failure but also implicates army commanders and their artillery preparation, Zhukov's retrospective views on how the Berlin operation might have been carried through differently (pp. 344–5) but Stalin required attack across a broad front, Koniev encounters heavier resistance at Zossen signals Rybalko (3rd Guards Tank Army) to speed up (text, pp. 345–6), April 21 breakthrough to suburbs of Berlin, 61st Army and 1st Polish Army pushing on to the Elbe, April 23–24 1st Belorussian Front armies pushing into centre of Berlin while 3rd Guards Tank Army (1st Ukrainian Front) fighting in southern suburbs of Berlin.

Note on Zhukov's use of massed searchlights: in 1916 General Kuropatkin, who had scarcely distinguished himself in the Russo–Japanese war, was given command of a Grenadier corps and proposed using searchlights to mount a night attack. The calamitous result was merely to silhouette Russian troops in their own beams, the corps losing 8,000 men in one night.

Note also criticism of Zhukov's decision on employment of 1st Guards Tank Army (a criticism voiced at the time by Stalin): in *IVOVSS*, 5, p. 258, it was argued that Zhukov's decision weakened the northerly attack by 1st Belorussian Front: with reinforcement to the left flank, 1st Belorussian Front might well have taken Berlin singlehanded, but Zhukov counters this by referring to Stalin's decision for 'a blow on a broad front'. Arguably Zhukov had no intention of leaving the 'southern route' open to Koniev, but the gamble did not quite come off. The late Marshal Babadzhanyan in *Dorogi pobedy* (p. 270) indirectly criticizes Zhukov's use of 1st Guards Tank Army, but Katukov in *Na ostrie glavnovo udara* in spite of mild criticism concludes that in the event Zhukov's decision was justified.

1st Guards Tank Army (1st Belorussian Front)

Babadzhanyan, A.Kh. *et al., Lyuki otkryli v Berline* (1st Guards Tank Army). See 'Poslednie srazheniya', pp. 301–17: Berlin operation, 1st Guards Tank with strength of 45,000 men, 709 tanks/SP guns, 700 guns, 44 MRLs, 0300 hours 16 April lead brigades at the Oder, rifle armies on the Seelow Heights unable to develop situation for favourable use of armour, success of Yushchuk's 11th Tank Corps 17 April, capture of Seelow Heights—only 50 km to Berlin—renewed offensive with 8th Guards Army 18 April, revised operational orders for 1st Guards Tank, outflanking of Müncheberg, signal to 1st Guards Tank 2150 hours 20 April (complete text, p. 312) about breaking into Berlin in order to announce this to Stalin and the press, orders to force the Spree, Katukov's orders 24 April, German resistance on the Spree. (Terse operational narrative in war-diary style, using mainly Soviet military archives.)

Katukov, M.E., *Na ostrie glavnovo udara* (2nd edn), ch. 18, Berlin operation, pp. 393–409: 1st Guards Tank with 854 tanks and SP guns (with addition of 11th Tank Corps), operational orders received 12 April, to operate in 8th Guards Army sector, terrain inhibited deployment of main body of armour, 17 April breach of second defensive line, 17–18 April progress not more than 4 *kilometres*, armour acting as infantry support, 20 April Zhukov's signal (text, p. 401) 1st Guards Tank to break into Berlin not later than 0400 hours 21 April 'at any price', two brigades (1st and 44th) selected, 24 April 1st Guards Tank and 8th Guards cross the Spree, beginning of street fighting.

11th Guards Tank Corps/1st Guards Tank Army
(1st Belorussian Front)

Babadzhanyan, A.Kh., *Dorogoi pobedy* (2nd edn), ch. VIII, Berlin operation, pp. 268–73: 1st Guards Tank Corps/1st Guards Tank Army in Berlin assault, suspicious about existence of second German *HKL* (ignored by Front command), confusion on Seelow Heights, blame laid on tank troops at emergency conference with Telegin (political member, Front command), Gusakovskii's 44th Tank Brigade and Fedorovich's 27th Motor-Rifle Brigade reach the Berlin ringroad, 20 April Front signal to 1st Guards Tank Army to break into Berlin by 21 April—note that this text (p. 271) differs from that cited by Katukov in that *it adds* the phrase about the report to Stalin and the press announcement.

Getman, A.L., *Tanki idut na Berlin* (11th Guards Tank Corps/1st Guards Tank Army), ch. 12, Berlin operation, pp. 327–42: corps with strength of 148 tanks and 58 SP guns beginning Berlin operation, fighting on Seelow Heights, morning of 21 April fresh orders from Zhukov—1st Guards Tank Army to be the first to break into Berlin—brigades to be detached from corps to strike into Berlin, 44th Brigade pushed forward, first tanks in Berlin, Red banner hoisted 0800 hours 22 April, main body of 11th Guards Tank Corps by this time in eastern suburbs of Berlin.

11th Tank Corps/1st Guards Tank Army (1st Belorussian Front)

Yushchuk, I.I., *Odinnadtsatyi tankovyi korpus . . .*, pt VI, Berlin operation, pp. 147–62: 11th Tank Corps to have support of 3rd Guards Ground-Attack Air Division, operational orders issued 14 April, lack of success in initial attack by 8th Guards Army and 11th Tank Corps, revised orders 17 April, operations with 35th Guards Rifle Corps, difficulties in attaining freedom of manoeuvre, 21 April two bodies of 11th Tank Corps linked up at Egersdorf and joint drive on Berlin, 22 April on eastern outskirts of Berlin, same day 11th Tank Corps subordinated to Berzarin's 5th Shock Army on Zhukov's orders, heavy street fighting.

2nd Guards Tank Army (1st Belorussian Front)

Vysotskii, F.I. *et al.*, *Gvardeiskaya tankovaya* (2nd Guards Tank Army), ch. 7, Berlin operation, pp. 187–97: opening of Soviet attack, first echelon tank corps (2nd Guards Tank) committed in direction of Bernau, operating with 47th Army and 3rd Shock, assault on second line of defences, Krivoshein's 1st Mech. Corps to force the Alte–Oder 17 April, fighting in third defensive zone, at 2000 hours 21 April 12th Guards Tank Corps fighting in Berlin suburb of Falkenberg, move to outflank left wing of the Berlin garrison.

3rd Shock Army (1st Belorussian Front)

Pyatkov, V.K. *et al.*, *Tret'ya udarnaya* (3rd Shock Army), ch. 5, Berlin operation, pp. 185–205: night 16 April attack with 20 searchlights to blind enemy, 9th Tank Corps committed to exploit success of Perevertkin's 79th Rifle Corps, neighbouring 47th Army also enjoying success, attack renewed 18 April with 9th Tank Corps and elements 1st Mech. Corps (from 2nd Guards Tank Army), storming of Kunersdorf, possibility of breakout and manoeuvre to outflank enemy east of Pretzel, fresh orders from Zhukov evening 18 April, by evening 21 April 3rd Shock fighting in north-east suburbs of Berlin, Zhukov at this point ordered 3rd Shock to change direction of advance and thrust directly to the centre of the city (rather than outflanking to the north), Army commander V.I. Kuznetsov order to set up assault squads for street-fighting, 22–23 April 3rd Shock breached inner defence line of Berlin. (Much detail on performance of units and sub-units, also reference to Soviet military archives.)

8th Guards Army (1st Belorussian Front)

Chuikov, V.I., *Ot Stalingrada do Berlina*, pt 4, storming of Berlin, pp. 576–98: 8th Guards Army and fighting for Seelow Heights, situation more favourable 20 April, 21 April 8th Guards breakthrough to Berlin ring-road, push through eastern suburbs, 1st Guards Tank embroiled in street fighting, forcing the Spree, 24 April 8th Guards linked up in Berlin with 1st Ukrainian Front.

1st Polish Army (1st Belorussian Front)

Stąpor, Z., *Bitwa o Berlin. Dzialania 1 Armii WP kwiecien–maj 1945* (Warsaw: MON 1973). (Detailed operational study, 1st Polish Army, Berlin operation.)

301st Rifle Division/5th Shock Army (1st Belorussian Front)

Antonov, Maj.-Gen. V.S., *Put' k Berlinu* (Moscow: Nauka 1975) (301st Rifle Division/ 5th Shock Army), ch. 5, battle for Berlin, pp. 272–307: assault on the Seelow Heights, heavy fighting 16 April, destruction of 18th *SS* Division, rifle divisions of 5th Shock with 2nd Guards Tank in support breaching third defensive zone, heavy German resistance 20 April, Zhukov changes axis of advance for 5th Shock with 3rd Shock beginning assault on northern suburbs, 8th Guards Army to assault southern reaches of city, 301st Division in Berlin fighting in Karlshorst, preparations for full assault.

1st Ukrainian Front (Koniev)

Koniev, I.S., *Year of Victory*. See 'The Berlin operation', pp. 79–132: meeting with Stalin ('Who is going to take Berlin . . . ?'), problem of boundary line between Fronts, Koniev with Pukhov's 13th Army, German defences on the Neisse, tank armies (3rd and 4th Guards) cross the Neisse, Fourth *Panzer* split and isolated, full depth of German defences penetrated, reaching the river Spree, Rybalko's tanks beyond the Spree, conversation with Stalin (p. 105) when Koniev resists idea of sending Zhukov's troops through gap torn by 1st Ukrainian Front, Koniev's Front directive 17 April (pp. 107–8), operations 18–20 April, dealing with 'Cottbus group', fresh orders to Zhadov's 5th Army, Luchinskii's 28th Army committed 20 April, clearing of the 'Spremberg group' by 5th Guards Army, break into Zossen, importance of operations 22 April, 0600 hours 23 April *Stavka* delineation of fresh demarcation between 1st Belorussian Front and 1st Ukrainian Front.

4th Guards Tank Army (1st Ukrainian Front)

Lelyushenko, D.D., *Moskva–Stalingrad–Berlin–Praga* (4th Guards Tank Army), ch. 8, Berlin operation/1st Ukrainian Front, pp. 311–30: replacements for losses among commanders before April offensive, Koniev's very close attention to operational decisions, close co-operation and long-time friendship with Rybalko (3rd Guards Tank Army), no delay in committing armour into breaches in enemy defences— 'the cardinal point'—problem of lack of infantry-support tanks in 5th Guards

Army, solution to push forward reinforced lead elements of 4th Tank once 60-ton bridges laid over Neisse, Petrov alarmed at this solution which went 'against the book' and proposed holding armour back until both Neisse and Spree forced by 5th Guards infantry, 16 April 1300 hours 60-ton bridges laid over Neisse and two lead brigades (62nd Tank and 29th Motor-Rifle/10th Mech. Corps) across, 18 April forcing of the Spree and break-out, 20 April Koniev's order to 4th and 3rd Tank armies—'to break into Berlin during the night'—Zhukov on 21 April in eastern suburbs of Berlin, 4th Tank in south-western suburbs, morning of 23 April assault crossing of Teltow Canal, on the right 3rd Guards Tank Army fighting in southern suburbs of Berlin.

Lelyushenko, D.D., 'Pered nam Berlin!', *VIZ*, 1970 (6), pp. 65–71. (A 'stripped-down' operational narrative, dates and timings for 4th Tank operations 16–24 April.)

5th Guards Mechanized Corps/4th Guards Tank Army
(1st Ukrainian Front)

Ryazanskii, Maj.-Gen. A.P., *V ogne tankovykh srazhenii* (Moscow: Nauka 1975), ch. 6, Berlin operation, pp. 162–82: 5th Guards Mech. Corps/4th Guards Tank Army, 1st Ukrainian Front, concentrated at 0600 hours 14 April, reinforcements of 1,000 men, 30 T-34s, 11 SU-122 SP guns, 15 SU-76 SP guns, bringing 5th Mech. up to 12,135 men, 64 T-34s, 51 APCs, 35 armoured cars, 22 SU-122s, 30 SU-76s, 32 76mm guns, 27 57mm guns, 51 120mm mortars, 43 heavy MGs, 126 light MGs, 8,765 rifles and machine carbines (p. 165); 5 Mech. Corps in 2nd echelon of 4th Tank Army, use of smokescreens on the Neisse, crossing of Neisse by 5th Mech. at 2000 hours 16 April, both tank armies (3rd and 4th Guards) swinging north-westwards on Stalin's orders, 5th Mech. to force Spree, covering Lelyushenko's left flank also holding off German attempts to break through to Berlin. (A highly detailed day-to-day narrative, certainly one of the best histories of Soviet tank/mechanized formations.)

5th Guards Army (1st Ukrainian Front)

Zhadov, Army General A.S., *Chetyre goda voiny* (Moscow: Voenizdat (VM) 1978), pp. 255–80, 5th Guards Army, 1st Ukrainian Front, operating with first echelon on line of main thrust, 2nd Polish Army on left flank to drive on 'Dresden axis', short time in which to regroup 5th Guards, characteristics of Neisse defensive line, 5th Guards operating with three corps (32nd, 33rd and 34th Corps, each with three divisions) also one tank corps (4th Guards Tank), tank strength/SP guns amounted to 110, planning to force Neisse, Koniev as commander and front-line leader, praise for Petrov (recently displaced as 4th Ukrainian Front commander) as Chief of Staff—Koniev suggested this appointment—successful assault crossing of Neisse by 5th Guards, 17 April to force Spree with Poluboyarov's 4th Tank Corps, Stalin 18 April decision to exploit success of 13th Army but this meant neutralizing German forces at Spremberg, Koniev at 5th Guards 19 April orders all-out attack on Spremberg group, 20–22 April 5th Guards assault on 'Spremberg group', 22 April orders for 5th Guards to strike for the river Elbe on the Torgau sector, lead elements on the Elbe 23 April but reported no American troops in sight. (Although published in the *Voennye Memuary* series, this is a serious, detailed

operational narrative, the only 'personal touch' being the pen-portraits of various
Soviet commanders.)

28th Army (1st Ukrainian Front)

Luchinskii, A., 'Na Berlin!', *VIZ*, 1965 (5), pp. 81–91. (28th Army operations, Berlin.)

2nd Belorussian Front (Rokossovskii)

Rokossovskii, K.K., *A Soldier's Duty*. See 'The Oder–Elbe', pp. 314–31: regrouping
completed by 17 April plus mobile formations and Vershinin's 4th Air Army,
enemy defences on the Oder, positions of Third *Panzer* Army, enemy concentrating
on very sector where Rokossovskii planned to attack, 19 April report to Stalin
that 2nd Belorussian Front ready to attack, April 20 three armies' assault crossing
of West Oder, success on Batov's sector (65th Army), serious concern over 49th
Army operations, problems caused by flooding of river valley, 25 April enemy
defences broken and move to envelop main body of Third *Panzer*.

Rokossovskii, K.K., 'Severnee Berlina', *VIZ*, 1965 (5), pp. 36–41 (2nd Belorussian
Front operations).

65th Army (2nd Belorussian Front)

Batov, P.I., *Operatsiya 'Oder'* (Moscow: Voenizdat 1965), ch. III, pp. 28–78, preparations
for Oder operation, April 1945; ch. IV, pp. 79–104, first stage of operations West
Oder, offensive opened 20 April with 4th Air Army in support, bridgehead on
West Oder, poor reconnaissance by 70th and 49th Army, premature report of
success to *Stavka* (p. 91), 1st Guards (Don) Tank Corps crossed West Oder 23
April at 0430 hours, greater success for 70th Army though 49th Army still stuck,
enemy defensive system breached and movement into 'operational depth', Rokossovskii's orders for rapid offensive action with 65th and 70th Army operating
with locked flanks on axis of Berlin motor highway, timed for 25 April. (Detailed,
day-by-day account, based on Soviet military archives.)

Air operations

Collective authorship, *16-ya vozdushnaya* (16th Air Army), ch. V, Berlin operations,
pp. 321–62: *Stavka* reinforcement for 16th Air, strength 28 aviation divisions and
7 independent air regiments, 3,033 aircraft (repaired/renovated), 2,738 crews with
operational experience—most powerful air formation ever assembled in Great
Patriotic War—Novikov himself co-ordinating operations of 4th Air (2nd Belorussian Front), 2nd Air (1st Ukrainian Front) plus 800 aircraft (Long-Range
Aviation/18th Air Army) and 300 Polish aircraft—7,500 combat aircraft in all—
planning for air support for ground operations, sortie rates during attack on Seelow
Heights, Luftwaffe resistance and sortie rates, 19 April 16th Air flew 4,398 sorties
(236 reconnaissance missions), 20 April 4,054 sorties, 16th Air 22 April assigned
to support left-flank armies and assist encirclement operation Frankfurt am Oder,
ground-attack aviation in small groups supporting fighting inside city. (Detailed
narrative, treating each air division of 16th Air Army.)

Rudenko, S.I., *Kryl'ya pobedy*. See 'Smerch nad logovom', pp. 325–51, air operations/
Berlin: planning of air support, deployment of air/Küstrin, co-ordination of four

air armies, problem of encountering Allied aircraft (long-range radar observation to monitor Allied air), control of radio traffic, organization to control fighter operations, role of Polish air force units, Novikov issues final orders, 0607 hours 16 April 743 Bombers for 42 minutes bombed German positions, 2,192 sorties by 1300 hours, in air combat Soviet losses 87, German losses 165 aircraft, by 2100 hours 16th Air Army 5,424 sorties (8,300 planned), 18th Air 766, 4th Air 440 sorties, 1,500 tons of bombs dropped (p. 342), 18–19 April maximum effort to support ground operations, organization of air support for close-quarter street fighting in Berlin.

Krzemiński, Czeslaw, *Lotnictwo polskie w operacji Berlińskiej* (Warsaw: MON 1970). Polish air force operations, Berlin.

Logistics/'rear services'

Antipenko, N.A., *Na glavnom napravlenii* (2nd edn). See 'Tyl v Berlinskoi operatsii', pp. 220–48: 25 road bridges over Oder (1,671,188 lorry movements, 600,000 people on foot—many Russian and Polish repatriates), rail links for 1st Belorussian Front, enormous demand for artillery ammunition—14,000 guns and mortars on 1st Belorussian Front—plan to expend 1,147,659 artillery rounds on first day of operations, 49,490 multiple-rocket rounds all requiring 2,382 wagon-loads, only 'fills' for fuel and food actually met but this *not* the case with ammunition, 6,000 waggon-loads of ammunition delivered to 1st Belorussian Front and 1st Ukrainian Front after April 16, coping with Soviet losses—300,000 killed and wounded, loss of 21,000 horses, 200,000 tons of ammunition fired off, 150,000 tons of fuel consumed, 300,000 tons of food and fodder, *5th Shock Army and 8th Guards Army lose 25 per cent of their men,* other armies had average of 2–3,000 wounded, quantities of German weapons captured (table, p. 247).

Closing in for the kill   pp. 568–589

Note: In addition to official operational narratives and Soviet memoir material, I have drawn extensively for detail from interviews with Marshal Sokolovskii, Marshal Chuikov, Marshal Koniev, Marshal Rokossovskii, General Yushchuk (11th Tank Corps), Colonel K.Ya. Samsonov (in 1945 Senior Lieutenant, commander 1st Battalion, 380th Rifle Regiment/171st Rifle Division, *Reichstag* fighting with battalions under Neustroyev and Davydov from 150th Rifle Division), also numerous eye-witness' accounts.

'Hitlers letzte Lagebesprechung' (Lagebesprechungen am 23., 25., and 27 April 1945), *Der Spiegel*, 10 Jan. 1966, pp. 32–46.

Irving, David, *Hitler's War*. See under 'Endkampf', pp. 807–8: for admirable explanation and documentation of Hitler's plan to lure Soviet armies into a spectacular trap—Lorenz notes on Hitler conference 3 pm 23 April, Hitler's fury at apparent disappearance of LVI *Panzer* Corps (Weidling), announcement that 'the Führer is in Berlin . . .', plan to use Wenck's Twelfth Army to link up with Busse's Ninth Army (taking German forces away from the Elbe and Muhlde fronts facing the Americans), link up south of Berlin followed by attack northwards to Potsdam and Berlin; Wenck to aim for the autobahn at Ferch (near Potsdam), while XLI *Panzer* Corps (under Holste) would be brought back across the Elbe and attack between Spandau and Oranienburg—*SS* General Steiner to hand over two divisions (25th *Panzer*-Grenadier and 7th *Panzer*) to Holste.

Kuby, Erich, *The Russians and Berlin 1945*. See ch. 9, 'Chronology of the End (20–30 April 1945)', pp. 92–161.

KTB/GMD

KTB/OKW, IV/2. See under 'KTB des Führungsstabs Nord (A) . . . 1. KTB, geführt von Major I.G. Joachim Schultz (20 April bis 16. Mai)'; esp. entry 29 April, 2300 hrs, Jodl–Hitler, 2330 hrs situation of Twelfth Army, impossibility of attack towards Berlin, threat to flanks and rear from US forces, pp. 1465–6.

FHO (I). 'Wesentliche Merkmale des Feinbildes Ostfront 1945' (for April 1945). T-78/R492, 6479415–552.

FHO (I). *Lagebericht Ost:* see No. 1414 (29 April 1945) to No. 1408 (23 April)—reverse order. T-78/R473, 6455134–157.

Soviet materials

Official history/Weidling documentation

Vorob'ev, F.D. *et al.*, *Poslednii shturm* (2nd edn). See ch. 5, encirclement of German forces in Berlin, 19–25 April: 1st Ukrainian Front operations to encircle Berlin forces and 'Frankfurt–Guben group', pp. 185–220; also operations on 'Dresden axis', pp. 221–2; ch. 7, destruction of German 'Frankfurt–Guben group' (26 April–1 May), operations on 'Görlitz axis', pp. 278–302; also ch. 8, storming of Berlin, operational situation 26 April, fighting in central sectors of the city, preparations for storming of *Reichstag*, pp. 318–45.

General Weidling. See 'Agoniya fashistskoi kliki v Berline. (Iz vospominaniya generala Veidlinga)', *VIZ*, 1960 (10), pp. 88–90, also (11), pp. 83–92. (General Weidling on the final stages of the defence of Berlin; see also 'Der Endkampf in Berlin', *Wehrwiss. Rundschau*, 1962, Nos. 1–3, *loc. cit.*)

Operational narratives/memoir material

Antonov, V.S., *Put' k Berlinu* (301st Rifle Division, 5th Shock Army). See 'Shturm zdaniya gestapo', attack on Gestapo HQ, pp. 327–31.

Babadzhanyan, A.Kh. *et al.*, *Lyuki otkryli v Berline* (1st Guards Tank Army). See 'Shturm Berlina', pp. 317–24, situation 24 April, difficulties of tank army operations in street fighting, 'assault groups' (and sub-groups) with rifle and tank companies (4–6 tanks), battery of SP guns (2–4 guns), battery of 76mm guns, MG, engineer and anti-tank sections, 45-minute artillery bombardment 25 April, forcing of Teltow canal, Soviet aviation now unable to carry out massed attacks as operational area shrank, fighting in city centre 28 April, shortage of infantry to complete elimination of small enemy groups in city buildings and apartments, 29 April 1st Guards Tank ordered to co-operate with 8th Guards Army to clear Tiergarten also to link up with 3rd Shock and 2nd Guards Tank Army operating to the north and north-west.

Bokov, Lt.-Gen. F., 'Pyataya udarnaya armiya v boyakh za Berlin', *VIZ*, 1970 (6), pp. 54–64. (Berzarin's 5th Shock Army, Berlin operations).

Bondar, Colonel M., 'K reikhstagu!', *VIZ*, 1966 (1), pp. 57–61. (Bondar adjutant to commander 79th Rifle Corps; preparations to storm the *Reichstag*.)

Koniev, I.S., *Year of Victory*, pp. 132–90, assault crossing of Teltow Canal, Lelyushenko's 4th Guards Tank Army advance on Potsdam outflanking Berlin from south-west, Luchinskii with 28th Army driving on Berlin, need to speed advance on Barut, arrival of three corps on the Elbe, German counter-attack with 'Görlitz group', unfavourable situation on the 'Dresden axis', here heavy pressure on 48th Corps/52nd Army and 2nd Polish Army, German thrust on Spremberg checked, role of V.I. Kostylëv (Chief of Operations Administration, 1st Ukrainian Front), German preparations to attack *from the west* (Wenck's Twelfth Army), need to work out details of link-up on the Elbe with US troops, rather unenthusiastic pen-portrait of Petrov, forcing of Teltow Canal, German counter-attacks on Rybalko (3rd Guards Tank), Wenck's first panzer attacks 24 April, refusal to allow Gluzdovskii active operations against Breslau, Koniev's decision not to storm Breslau, operations in southern sector of Berlin, 25 April 'psychological turning point' for Wenck due to massed Soviet air attacks (*note:* in the Russian edition Koniev described Wenck's attacks with the phrase '*nastupali prosto dlya otvoda glaz*', literally 'making the whole thing a blind' or pulling the wool over someone's eyes), failure of German attempts to cut 1st Ukrainian Front in half, new demarcation line with 1st Belorussian Front and redeployment of Rybalko's corps, 1330 hrs 25 April at Strela on the Elbe contact with 69th US Infantry Division, also contact at Torgau, difficulties of dealing with fortified bunkers in Berlin, 800 Soviet tanks and SP guns lost fighting in city limits (p. 177), Wenck fighting only 'according to protocol' while Busse's Ninth Army 'fought bravely, to the death', telephone call from Stalin/*Stavka*—'*Who, do you think, will be taking Prague*' (p. 187)—Koniev's reply that it would evidently have to be taken by 1st Ukrainian Front, meanwhile new demarcation line between 1st Ukrainian Front and 1st Belorussian Front effective 2400 hrs 28 April (this necessitated further withdrawal by 3rd Guards Tank and 28th Army units), fighting for Wannsee island, 30 April position of German forces in Berlin 'hopeless'.

Lelyushenko, D., 'Pered nam Berlin!', *VIZ*, 1970 (6), pp. 68–72 (4th Guards Tank Army operations). See also *Moskva–Stalingrad–Berlin–Praga*, ch. 8).

Luchinskii, General A., 'Na Berlin!, *VIZ*, 1965 (5), pp. 81–91 (28th Army operations, Luchinskii army commander).

Neustroyev, S.A., 'Shturm Reikhstaga', *VIZ*, 1960 (5), pp. 42–51. (Preparations for storming *Reichstag*, 150th and 171st Rifle Divisions' operations.)

Neustroyev, Lt.-Col. S.A., *Put' k Reikhstagu* (Moscow: Voenizdat (VM) 1961). See under 'Boevoe sorevnovanie', fresh operational orders to 150th Rifle Division, 26 April—to force Verbindungskanal, presentation of Red Banner No. 5 for planting on *Reichstag*, Colonel Zinchenko's decisions, Neustroyev's battalion driving to Moabit prison, orders to advance along line of the Spree, pp. 52–6; see also 'Forsirovanie Shpree', reinforcement by corps commander, 500 men left in Neustroyev's battalion, Neustroyev ordered to force Spree, fighting to enlarge bridgehead, elimination of German resistance in 'Himmler's house', pp. 57–63.

Pyatkov, V.K. *et al.*, *Tret'ya udarnaya* (3rd Shock), ch. 5, under 'Reshayushchii shturm', pp. 212–21, opening of third stage of Berlin operations 26 April, plan to split up Berlin garrison, Soviet offensive renewed with heavy air support, 3rd Shock to drive south-eastwards on to Tiergarten and effect junction with 8th Guards Army, 79th Rifle Corps clearing of Moabit and drive to the Spree, 29 April opening action in battle for the *Reichstag*, capture assigned to 79th Rifle Corps, Samsonov (380th Rifle Regiment/171st Rifle Division) and Neustroyev (1st Battalion/756th Rifle Regiment with 150th Rifle Division) closing on *Reichstag*.

Rokossovskii, K.K., 'Severnee Berlina', *VIZ*, 1965 (5), pp. 36–41. (2nd Belorussian Front operations: successful conclusion to task of isolating Third *Panzer* Army from main body of German forces in Berlin.)

Ryazanskii, A.P., *V ogne tankovykh srazhenii* (5th Guards Mech. Corps), pp. 182–93, estimate of threat from Wenck, German plan to link up with Ninth Army encircled north-east of Barut, Soviet defensive measures, fighting for Treuenbrietzen, three divisions from Wenck's Twelfth Army attack 25 April, fresh German attacks in direction of Beelitz, Lelyushenko's orders to prevent breakout of German Ninth Army to the west.

Shatilov, Col.-Gen. V.M., *Znamya nad Reikhstagom* (Moscow: Voenizdat (VM), 2nd edn 1970). See under 'Shturm reikhstaga', pp. 291–304: Shatilov, commander 150th Rifle Division, capture of 'Himmler's house', crossing of the Spree, Zinchenko's report on Neustroyev's deployment, last reserves committed in fighting for 'Himmler's house', company strength down to 30–40 men, final preparations for storming of *Reichstag*.

Surchenko, Maj.-Gen. A., 'Na poslednem NP marshala K.K. Rokossovskovo', *VIZ*, 1972 (5), pp. 61–5 (2nd Belorussian Front operations—Surchenko deputy chief/ operations, 2nd Belorussian Front).

Zhadov, A.S., *Chetyre goda voiny* (5th Guards Army), pp. 279–93, lead elements on the Elbe, 23 April, contact with Americans 25 April at Strela (north-west of Riesa) 1330 hrs—173rd Guards Rifle Regiment/58th Guards Rifle Division link with recon. group US 69th Infantry Division, one hour later Soviet–American contact at Torgau, formal linking up at 1100 hrs 26 April, this recognized in Stalin's Order of the Day No. 346, Zhadov's exchanges with General Hodges and thanks for US Dodge and Studebaker trucks and US jeeps, Soviet decorations for US officers including Jnr Lt. William Robertson (awarded Order of Alexander Nevskii), pp. 279–93.

Zinchenko, Colonel F., 'Znamya Pobedy nad Reikhstagom', *VIZ*, 1980 (4), pp. 53–9, and (5), pp. 58–64. (Storming of *Reichstag*: 756th Rifle Regiment/150th Rifle Division.)

In at the death: the Berlin capitulation pp. 589–604

The bulk of this section is based on extensive exchanges with Marshal V.I. Chuikov (commander 8th Guards Army in 1945) and Marshal V.D. Sokolovskii (deputy commander, 1st Belorussian Front). Marshal Sokolovskii, in particular, filled in a number of details pertaining to the talks at 8th Guards Army HQ, not least his impressions of Krebs and Weidling. Krebs had been formerly German military attaché in Moscow before the war and had a good command of Russian; according to Marshal Sokolovskii Krebs had begun to drink heavily in 1944 but he was completely sober throughout the talks. Weidling struck Sokolovskii as a reasonable person, convinced that further resistance was senseless but carrying out his orders to fight on.

I have taken the text of the Chuikov–Sokolovskii–Krebs talks from the stenographic record (notebook) made available to me in Moscow; other versions (e.g. Vsevolod Vishnevskii, *Sobranie sochinenii. Dnevniki voennykh let 1943–1945*, Tom 4. Moscow: Khudozh. Lit. 1958, pp. 869–905) are perhaps more elaborate, but using 'raw text' perforce introduces some ungainliness. Finally, I had the benefit of Marshal Chuikov's own comments and commentary on these exchanges, not least his personal impressions and reactions.

Official histories

IVOVSS, 5. See pt 1, ch. 7 (3–4): encirclement and capture of Berlin, pp. 263–90. See also ch. 9 (1) on frustration of German moves for a separate peace, pp. 332ff.

IVMV, 10. See pt 1, ch. 11 (2–3): destruction of the German 'Berlin group', capture of Berlin, pp. 314–47. See also ch. 12 (1), on the frustration of (German) plans for a separate peace, pp. 356–64. In this latter connection see a recent publication by G.L. Rozanov, *Uzhe ne sekretno* (Moscow: Politizdat 1981), 224 pp., which outlines the manoeuvres by the Nazi government in the final stage of the war to split the Allied coalition and the response which these intrigues evoked in 'anti-Soviet, anti-Communist circles' in the West.

Vorob'ev, F.D. *et al.*, *Poslednii shturm* (2nd edn), ch. 8, 'Shturm reikhstaga' (assault on the *Reichstag*), pp. 340–51. See also:

(i) *Fall of Berlin*, pp. 351–71, operations to eliminate German forces, 47th Army operations south-west of Potsdam, 5th Shock Army 29 April pushing to the west, 8th Guards Army across Landwehr canal to south of Tiergarten, German plans for limited break-out, 2nd Guards Tank Army in heavy fighting in western part of Tiergarten, 30 April German forces holding north-eastern sectors of Berlin cut off from units holding Tiergarten, 3rd Guards Tank and 28th Army continued move to the north-west, 10th Guards Tank Corps fighting for Wannsee, 30 April German forces split into four isolated groups, 2330 hrs 30 April von Seifert approach to Soviet lines, Krebs to Chuikov 0330 hrs 1 May, Soviet conditions for capitulation, 0040 hrs 2 May radio signal to 79th Guards Rifle Division from LVI *Panzer* Corps requesting ceasefire and proposing meeting of emissaries 1250 hrs (night) on Potsdam bridge, 1st Belorussian Front command instruction to Weidling to lay down arms from 0700 hrs 2 May, Weidling surrendered personally 0600 hrs 2 May, mass German surrenders (1st Belorussian Front took 100,700 prisoners, 1st Ukrainian Front 34,000), further German attempts to break out of encirclement, checking break-out across Havel lasted until 5 May, column of 30,000 attempted break-out from Spandau.

(ii) *Destruction of 3rd Panzer Army (2nd Belorussian Front operations)*, pp. 379–88, 2nd Shock Army operations aimed at Anklam–Stralsund, 65th Army directed to Pasewalk/Demmin, 70th and 49th Army operating on north-west and westerly axes to reach Wismar, Schwerin—to link up with British Second Army—Third *Panzer* plans to hold Soviet forces as far east as possible, 27 April German defences on western bank of Oder pierced, Soviet breakthrough at Prentzlau threatened rear of Third *Panzer*, Soviet forces engaged in general pursuit after 27 April, 3

May lead elements 70th Army in contact east of Wismar with forward units British Second Army, 4 May main force 70th Army on demarcation line, final operation to take Rugen (108th Rifle Corps).

Documentary publication

'Iz istorii kapitulyatsii vooruzhennykh sil fashistskoi Getmanii', *VIZ*, 1959 (5), pp. 78–95 (documents). (i) Record of conversations between General Krebs and General Weidling on capitulation of German troops in Berlin (signed Lt.-Col. Gladkii, Chief of Intelligence/Staff, 8th Guards Army), pp. 81–9. (ii) Interrogation of General Weidling by Maj.-Gen. Trusov, pp. 89–95.

Note: Though the record of the Krebs–Weidling talks mentions (p. 85) a telephone link with the German lines, Marshal Sokolovskii insisted categorically that *no line* was laid and that here the *VIZ* version is incorrect—'pure invention', to quote the Marshal directly.

Protocol: Interrogation of Reichsmarshal H. Göring, 17 June 1945. ('Question: Is it true that Hitler had doubles *(dvoiniki)*? Answer: 'Well, that's what all the rumours are about. If you want my opinion, I would not be at all surprised if Hitler had a double. It would not be difficult to find a man like him. But if *I* had wanted a double, that would have been much more difficult.')

'Pomoshch Sovetskovo pravitel'stva i komandovaniya sovetskikh voisk nasileniyu Berlina v 1945', *VIZ*, 1959 (8), pp. 76–99 (documents). (Establishment of military administration, Col.-Gen. Berzarin, 5th Shock Army commander, appointed city commandant; Berzarin died shortly after from injuries in a road accident, though rumour had it that he was ambushed by Germans.)

Collected memoir material

Shturm Berlina. Vospominaniya pis'ma, dnevniki uchastnikov boev za Berlin, ed. V.S. Veselov (Moscow: Voenizdat 1948), 488 pp. Assorted materials, eye-witness accounts, extracts from diaries; see especially S. Perevertkin (commander 79th Rifle Corps), on storming of *Reichstag,* pp. 393–7.

Chuikov, V.I., *Ot Stalingrada do Berlina,* pt 4, 'V dui shturma Berlina', Chuikov–Krebs, pp. 631–47; further to Chuikov–Krebs talks, pp. 631–58, with interpretation of the German tactic to split the Allied coalition even at this late stage, all duly frustrated by the unswerving Soviet attitude on unconditional capitulation.

A partial translation of the text of the Chuikov–Krebs talks is presented in *The End of the Third Reich,* ch. XVII, 'Krebs Comes to my Command Post', pp. 213–30.

Krivoshein, S., *Ratnaya byl'* (Moscow: Mol. Gvardiya 1962), pp. 222–35, the *SMERSH* investigation of Krivoshein in Berlin, capture of German photographs showing a Soviet *kombrig* (brigade commander) posing with Guderian in 1939 on the occasion of the Nazi–Soviet link-up in Brest–Litovsk, the Soviet *kombrig* identified as Krivoshein (presently commander 1st Guards Mech. Corps committed in Berlin operations), Krivoshein explains.

Neustroyev, S.A., *Put' k reikhstagu.* See 'Znamya nad reikhstagom', hoisting Red Banner over the *Reichstag,* fighting in the building, pp. 65–74. (Neustroyev's battalion action.)

Sevruk, V. (ed.), *How Wars End. Eye-Witness Accounts of the Fall of Berlin* (Moscow: Progress 1969). See especially Yelena Rzhevskaya, interpreter, her role in the investigation of the death of Hitler and Eva Braun, pp. 195–272. (See also Ye. Rzhevskaya, *Berlin, Mai 1945*, Moscow: Sov. Pisatel 1970, 302 pp.)

Shatilov, V.M., *Znamya nad reikhstagom*. See 'Shturm reikhstaga', pp. 291–341. (Memoir, 150th Rifle Division commander, detail of the assault on the *Reichstag*.)

Zhukov, G.K., *Vospominaniya . . .*, vol. 2. See ch. 21, pp. 357–61, Berlin operation: Order No. 0025/28 April, 79th Rifle Corps operational order for capture of *Reichstag*, 2150 hrs 30 April Red Banner hoisted, 1 May only Tiergarten and area of government buildings still in German hands; ch. 22, 'Unconditional Surrender . . .', pp. 362–8: Krebs at HQ 8th Guards Army 0350 hrs 1 May, 0400 Chuikov to Zhukov with news of Hitler's suicide, Zhukov orders Sokolovskii to 8th Guards HQ and call to Stalin, Stalin wakened with news of Hitler's death (Stalin: *'Doigralsya, podlets!'*—translated in Delacorte Press/Novosti, *Memoirs* as 'So that's the end of the bastard!', p. 622), Stalin's demand for unconditional surrender, Sokolovskii to Zhukov 0500 hrs that Germans simply 'stringing us along', Zhukov requires capitulation by 1000 hrs else massive Soviet blow, 1040 hrs Soviet guns fired off huge salvo at remnants of the special defence sector in the centre, 1800 hrs Sokolovskii reported rejection by Goebbels and Bormann of Soviet condition, 1830 hrs renewed Soviet assault 'with unprecedented force' on *Reichskanzlei*, 20 German tanks reported speeding to north-west, tanks destroyed 2 May but no Nazi leaders found in wreckage, surrender of Weidling, Fritsche's broadcast, interrogated by Zhukov himself then sent on to Moscow for further questioning, search for Hitler's body, discovey of Goebbels' children and corpses of Goebbels and his wife.

Hitler corpse/autopsy

Bezymenski, Lev, *The Death of Adolf Hitler. Unknown Documents from Soviet Archives* (London: Michael Joseph 1968; orig., *Der Tod des Adolf Hitler* (Hamburg: C. Wegner Verlag 1968). See esp. Appendix 'Protocol . . . Discovery of the Goebbels Family', pp. 79–84, also Autopsy Reports (the Goebbels family, General Krebs, 'unknown woman (presumably the wife of Hitler)': also 'Documents No. 12 and No. 13'—forensic examination of a male corpse disfigured by fire (Hitler's body), p. 44–51, with conclusion that death due to poisoning by cyanide compounds. Note, however, that David Irving in *Hitler's War* (note, p. 902), insists that Hitler did shoot himself as well as taking poison. As for the delay in publishing the results of the autopsies and the forensic-medical reports, Lev Bezymenski (p. 66) states that these were 'held in reserve' lest some imposter claimed to be 'the Führer miraculously saved' (shades of the False Dmitrii in Russian history), while there was further investigation to exclude either error or deception. (On the other hand, by early June at the latest, the Soviet leadership and military command had accepted the medical findings, for as I was told—and Lev Bezymenski duly confirms—*all* bodies were taken to a barracks on the outskirts of Berlin, one final process of identification carried out and then the bodies were burned completely, the ashes being scattered at will.) As far as I understood from senior Soviet officers who were present, one of the first bodies to be uncovered was that of Fegelein, followed by the discovery of a Hitler 'double' (of which I have a photograph, with uncanny facial resemblance—though the darned socks ruled him out as *the* Führer). I am still somewhat puzzled by the shunting about of Goebbels' body, though again eye-witnesses explained that on a first entry into the Führerbunker loose wires hanging in the lower levels suggested that the structure was mined (on the pattern of Zossen) and a rapid evacuation took place, followed by some 're-creation' of the original scene. There are also odd points raised in V.S. Antonov's *Put' k Berlinu* (esp. p. 346)—how did Klimenko get through Colonel Shevtsov's guards so magically, how did Shevtsov know that here were the corpses of Goebbels and his wife? As far as I can determine, *SMERSH* had not yet appeared on the scene.

Cf. Erich Kuby, *The Russians and Berlin, 1945*, ch. 10, 'The Death of Hitler', to which Lev Bezymenski refers in some detail: as for 'no one daring to tell Stalin of Hitler's death', Zhukov informed Stalin at once of news of the suicide, with Stalin expressing his chagrin that the Führer had not been taken alive. No credence can be given to the notion of a Hitler corpse sealed in a lead coffin or preserved in spirit—the final, collective cremation early in June 1945 did dispose of Hitler's remains. It is also worth noting some comments by S.M. Shtemenko, *General'nyi shtab v gody voiny*, vol. 2, ch. 12, p. 437–40: first information on Hitler's death 1 May from Chuikov–Krebs talks, but difficulty in believing this since Hitler's remains not found, only on 4 May news that 'something resembling Hitler' had been found, night 4 May telegram from Zhukov and Telegin on the Goebbels's corpses but nothing about Hitler—'Comrade Zhukov also has doubts about Hitler's death. . . . We have to check everything' (Stalin)—NKGB (State Security) to send investigation team to Berlin, two corpses—Hitler and Eva Braun—found, confirmation of death through 'poisoning by virulent cyanide compounds'.

2nd Belorussian Front operations

Batov, P.I., *Operatsiya 'Oder'*, ch. IV, second stage of the operation, pp. 113–29: 26 April 65th Army renews offensive, general pursuit of German forces, crossing of river Randow, breach of second line of German defences and capture of Stettin, Third *Panzer* withdrawing covered by small fighting rearguards—PWs reported complete demoralization—fall of Rostock, 65th Army on Baltic coast, assault on Rügen with limited forces—105th Rifle Corps commander used captured motorized barge to lift small force of volunteers, one salvo from multiple rocket launcher met by white flags and German surrender (2,000 men), no further resistance and 65th Army completed its war role.

Rokossovskii, K.K., *A Soldier's Duty*. See 'The Oder–Elbe', pp. 330–35, 25 April three corps of 65th Army, two corps of 70th Army (with a third in ready reserve) across the Oder, German defence broken and approach to river Randow, operations to envelop main forces of Third *Panzer* Army—to prevent Third *Panzer* assisting Berlin defence and to check any retreat to the west—65th Army (with 1st Guards Tank Corps) to strike north-west to bottle up German forces north-east of Stettin–Neubrandenburg–Rostock, 2nd Shock Army to advance towards Anklam–Stralsund, 70th Army to advance towards Wismar, 26 April Stettin stormed by 65th Army, 2nd Belorussian Front command post moved to Stettin, 27 April general pursuit of German forces, 3 May contact with British Second Army (3rd

Guards Tank Corps in the lead), 4 May 70th and 49th Army on the demarcation line, 19th and 2nd Shock Army 'mopping up' on Usedom and Rügen islands, German forces on Bornholm reject Soviet ultimatum hence assault landing by 19th Army with two divisions, 12,000 Germans taken prisoner.

Kozlov, Colonel L., 'Osvobozhdenie ostrova Bornkholm', *VIZ*, 1975 (5), pp. 126–8 (132nd Rifle Corps/19th Army: Bornholm operation).

The last battles, the final surrender   pp. 604–622

Churchill, Winston S., *The Second World War*, vol. VI: *Triumph and Tragedy*, bk II, ch. XXXII, 'The German Surrender', *passim*.

Osers, Ewald, 'The Liberation of Prague: Fact and Fiction', *Survey*, Summer 1970, pp. 99–111. (With particular reference to Czech, German and Soviet radio broadcasts, duly assembled in BBC Monitoring Service archives.)

Táborský, Eduard, 'Benes and Stalin–Moscow, 1943 and 1945', *Journal of Central European Affairs*, Vol. XIII, July 1953, pp. 154–81. (*Note:* the references to Stalin's 'neo-Slav' speech come from a participant at the dinner and derive from the papers of Dr Benes, utilized here by Dr Táborský, see pp. 178–80.)

Diplomatic correspondence/diplomatic history

Perepiska . . . , vol. 1. No. 444, Stalin–Churchill, on Himmler's offer of surrender on the Western Front, 25 April, p. 396; No. 449, Churchill–Stalin, need for declaration recording defeat and unconditional surrender of Germany, 28 April, p. 400; No. 450, Churchill–Stalin on the Polish question, 28 April, pp. 406–7; No. 452, Stalin–Churchill, in response to No. 449, no objection to publication of declaration on German defeat, 29 April, p. 407; No. 454, Stalin–Churchill, instructions when Soviet troops come into contact with Allied troops, 2 May, p. 409; No. 456, Stalin–Churchill, on the Polish question and the arrest of General Okulicki: failure to consider Polish Provisional Government as basis for future Government of National Unity 'precludes possibility of an agreed decision on the Polish question', 4 May, pp. 410–12; No. 461, Churchill–Stalin, 8 May to be treated as VE Day, 7 May, pp. 414–15; No. 462, Stalin–Churchill, Soviet command wishes to wait until German surrender takes effect before victory announcement, 7 May, p. 415; No. 463, Churchill–Stalin, cannot postpone announcement for 24 hours, need for Parliament to be informed of signing at Reims, 8 May, p. 416.

Woodward, Sir Llewellyn, *British Foreign Policy in the Second World War*. V. See ch. LXVII(V), pp. 390–400, unconditional surrender of Germany, rapidity of final stages of German surrender, Churchill to Stalin on proceedings at Field-Marshal Alexander's HQ, place of signing of Instrument of Surrender, Eisenhower refuses surrender on basis of German forces in the West, Jodl signing of Act of Military Surrender, Soviet approval withdrawn and suggestion of signing ceremony in Berlin, also Soviet requirement to wait until surrender actually effected on Eastern Front before any announcement, hence postponement until 7 pm Moscow time 9 May, Churchill's announcement that he could not wait but not anxious to risk reproach from Stalin.

Official histories

IVOVSS, 5, pt 1, ch. 8(3), establishment of 'National Front' with Czechs and Slovaks, the Prague rising, pp. 309–17; ch. 9(2), signing of the Act of Capitulation, pp. 349–59.

IVMV, 10, pt 1, ch. 11(4), Prague operation, final liberation of Czechoslovakia, pp. 347–55; ch. 12(2), signing of the Act of Unconditional Surrender, pp. 364–8.

Prague operation   pp. 622–640

Grechko, A.A., *Cherez Karpaty*, pp. 391–401, successful conclusion of Bratislava–Brno and Ostrava operations laid basis for thrust on Prague, Army Group Centre with three armies (Fourth and First *Panzer*, 17th Army) resisting 1st and 4th Ukrainian Fronts, impact of the Prague rising 5 May, *Stavka* directive to 1st Ukrainian Front, command decisions of 2nd Ukrainian Front (Malinovskii), 4th Ukrainian Front concentrating forces to reduce Olomouc, mobile group set up in 60th Army (4th Ukrainian Front) and supervised by General G.F. Zakharov (deputy Front commander), mobile group also set up by 38th Army, 1st Guards Army established its own small mobile group (SP-gun regiment, motor-machine-gun battalion, anti-tank regiment), 4th Ukrainian Front snagged in battle for Olomouc, fall of Olomouc 8 May, Soviet advance 80–120km towards Prague 8 May, Soviet demand for surrender of German forces, 1st Ukrainian Front armour in Prague early hours 9 May, link up of 1st and 2nd Ukrainian Fronts in Prague cut German escape routes to west and south-west, 10–11 May disarming and despatching German forces as prisoners. (Operational narrative, based largely on military archives.)

Koniev, I.S. (ed.), *Za osvobozhdenie Chekhoslovakii*, pp. 209–76, destruction of German forces in Czechoslovakia, liberation of Prague: situation of German forces beginning May 1945, secret German instructions to surrender in the west but to fight on in the east, German plans to hold western Czechoslovakia, Eisenhower's signal 30 April about demarcation line, Soviet rejection of idea to adjust demarcation, Antonov's signal 5 May reaffirming Soviet position, urgency of Soviet move into Czechoslovakia and reduction of German forces, preparation of the Prague uprising, first hours of the rising, German response, Czech General Pik at 1500 hrs 6 May requests Soviet help, Soviet operational planning for Prague operation (1st, 4th and 2nd Ukrainian Fronts), this gave a front running from Potsdam to the Danube and involved 18 field armies, 3 tank armies, 3 air armies, 7 mobile/mechanized corps, 3 cavalry corps—153 rifle divisions, 24,500 guns/mortars, 2,100 tanks, 4,000 aircraft—also Czech, Polish and Rumanian units, German strength 62 divisions (16 *Panzer* and motorized divisions), greatest strength deployed against 1st Ukrainian Front, in all some 900,000 men, 2,200 tanks, 1,000 aircraft, 28 April Stalin sounded out Koniev about Prague operation, *Stavka* directive 0130 hrs 1 May to 1st Belorussian Front to take up 1st Ukrainian Front positions south of Berlin no later than 4 May, 1940 hrs 2 May *Stavka* directive to 2nd Ukrainian Front (Malinovskii), Koniev's operational directive issued 0110 hrs 4 May (1st Ukrainian Front) specifying three thrusts, Malinovskii's orders to open offensive 7 May, *Stavka* dissatisfied with planning in 2nd Ukrainian Front which did not ensure high-speed operations hence transfer of 9th Guards Army to 2nd Ukrainian Front (specified in *Stavka* directive 0200 hrs 5 May), regrouping on 1st Ukrainian

Front, news of Prague rising 5 May, opening 1st Ukrainian Front offensive 6 May and Koniev's decision at 1000 hrs to commit main forces of his right flank, capitulation of German garrison at Breslau, 7 May 2nd Ukrainian Front opened offensive driving on Olomouc, German capitulation at 0241 hrs 7 May, Churchill's signal to Eisenhower urging move on Prague, fall of Dresden, German surrender but continued resistance by Schörner's Army Group Centre, 1800 hrs 8 May beginning of German withdrawal from Prague, 10th Guards Tank Corps (4th Guards Tank Army) closing on Prague, 1300 hrs 9 May 62nd Tank Brigade in south-east suburbs, 3rd Guards Tank Army also in Prague early hours 9 May, infantry units from 3rd Guards and 13th Army moving into Prague, link-up 1st and 2nd Ukrainian Fronts, 10 May V.N. Gordov (commander 3rd Guards Army) appointed military commandant of Prague, 10 May *Stavka* set new demarcation lines and assignments to take German forces encircled north-east of Prague prisoner and 2nd Ukrainian Front to continue movement to the west, Soviet forces on the demarcation line with British and US forces, Soviet forces took 859,400 prisoners (60 generals) with 41,000 prisoners in Breslau, Soviet losses in the Prague operation amounted to more than 8,000 killed and 28,000 wounded (for 1st, 2nd and 4th Ukrainian Fronts). (A detailed and authoritative account, extensive use of Soviet military archives.)

Koniev, I.S., *Year of Victory,* pp. 193–231, Nazi belief that Schörner could hold out for three weeks, Dönitz wanted withdrawal to south-west to surrender to Americans, idea of moving 'Dönitz government' to Prague, Eisenhower intimates that Allies ready to advance into Czechoslovakia (4 May), Koniev–Bradley exchange, Koniev requests that US forces do not 'muddle things up', in planning Prague operation need to break through Krusnehory Mountains, assault force—three field armies, two tank armies, two tank corps, five artillery divisions—organized on right flank 1st Ukrainian Front north-west of Dresden, aim to envelop Prague from west and south-west, secondary attack from Görlitz, also reduction of enemy forces at Dresden (assigned to 5th Guards Army), mobile/mechanized units to capture Prague by assault from column of march (ten corps—1,600 tanks committed), one and a half times regular fuel supply distributed, 2nd Air Army committed 1,900 aircraft to main assault and 355 to support secondary assault, 2nd Polish Army also committed to Prague operation, *Stavka* orders to launch operation 6 May (instead of 7 May), Prague rising had broken out 5 May, surrender of Breslau garrison to Gluzdovskii's 6th Army at 1800 hrs 6 May (40,000 men surrendered), Koniev's refusal to see General Nickhoff—did not deserve any special treatment—7 May 2nd Ukrainian and 4th Ukrainian Fronts resumed offensive and began their own advance on Prague, Yermakov's 5th Guards Mech. Corps wiped out the staff of Schörner's Army Group Centre at Zatec, Koniev's call for unconditional surrender at 2000 hrs 8 May but operations to continue if no reply by 2300 hrs, capture of Dresden, Soviet breakthrough into Prague at 0300 hrs 9 May, mobile group from 4th Ukrainian Front also in Prague, capture of Vlasov, Vlasov brought to Koniev's command post in Dresden—Vlasov taken prisoner by Captain M.I. Yakushev, commander of a motor-rifle battalion in 162nd Tank Brigade.

Lelyushenko, D.D., *Moskva–Stalingrad–Berlin–Praga.* See ch. 9, Prague operation, pp. 344–65: 4th Guards Tank Army, 1st Ukrainian Front operational directive 1 May, instruction to take Prague on sixth day of operations, three attacks planned, 4th Guards Tank to operate with 13th Army (3rd Guards Tank with 3rd Guards Army), 2nd Air Army in support, readiness to launch operation on 6 May, strict instructions to advance with all speed especially during first two days of the operation and especially to 10th Guards Mech. Brigade's (5th Guards Mech. Corps) attack on the staff of Army Group Centre trying to break out towards Pilsen, Schörner signal recording surprise at Soviet armoured thrust, approach to south-western suburbs of Prague, 0300 hrs 9 May 4th Guards Tank elements in centre of Prague and fighting in area of General Staff building, 0400 hrs main body of 4th Guards Tank in Prague with ten tank corps occupying the centre, 3rd Guards Tank also moving in from the north with infantry following breach enemy defences in mountainous terrain, also to operate at night and to have reserve fuel to hand, 0830 hrs 6 May offensive opened by lead battalions, 1030 hrs Lelyushenko requested permission from Koniev to commit his main force, news of rising in Prague, 4th Ukrainian Front also attacking from the east with 2nd Ukrainian Front moving up from the south-east, lead elements of 4th Guards Tank already in Czechoslovakia, 7 May 150–160km north-west of Prague with 13th Army following Soviet armour—but first unit to enter Prague was a tank from Fomichev's 63rd Guards Tank Brigade/4th Guards Tank Army.

Lelyushenko, D.D., 'Tanki speshat na pomoshch Prage', *VIZ*, 1965 (5), pp. 92–8. (4th Guards Tank Army operations, Prague.)

Malinovskii, R.Ya. (ed.), *Budapesht Vena Praga*, ch. 6, Prague operation, pp. 356–68: preparation of the Prague rising, first successes of the insurgents 5 May, *Stavka* directive to 2nd Ukrainian Front 2 May, 2nd Ukrainian Front command decision to drive on Prague from south of Brno with 7th Guards Army to link up with 6th Guards Army, transfer of Glagolev's 9th Guards Army from 3rd Ukrainian Front to 2nd Ukrainian Front, 1st Ukrainian Front offensive opened 6 May followed by 2nd Ukrainian Front 7 May, 24th Guards Rifle Corps with 6th Guards Tank Army to reach Prague no later than 10 May (24th Corps assigned 1,200 lorries for high-speed movement), 4th Ukrainian Front capture of Olomouc with 60th Army, 8 May operations across 600km front and outflanking Army Group Centre from north-west and south-east, German withdrawal westwards, 1st Ukrainian Front armour in Prague, lead elements from 6th Guards Tank Army driving from Brno, between 1100 and 1800 hrs 9 May lead elements of 4th Ukrainian Front in eastern sector Prague, morning 10 May 38th Army mobile group in the city.

Moskalenko, K.S., 'Prazhskaya operatsiya', *VIZ*, 1975 (5), pp. 103–10 (operational narrative, Prague operation).

Moskalenko, K.S., *Na yugo-zapadnom napravlenii 1943–1945*, vol. 2. See ch. 18, 38th Army and Prague operation, pp. 591–607: clearing of Ostrava by 1st Guards and 18th Army, 60th and 38th Army moving southwards, threat to encircle First *Panzer* Army, the route to Olomouc and Prague, *Stavka* instruction to provide aid to Prague insurgents, operation to begin 6 May, no parachute troops available on 4th Ukrainian Front but Yeremenko ordered Moskalenko to organize a mobile group from 38th Army to drive on Prague, orders to 101st Rifle Corps, this mobile group detached from operations to capture Olomouc, signal about capitulation document at Reims, text communicated to German forces with instructions on surrender, morning 8 May three Soviet fronts driving on Prague mobile group sent on rapid thrust to Prague, 9 May lead element of 38th Army mobile group closing on Prague, contact with tanks of 4th Guards Tank Army, Army Group Centre encircled.

Nedorezov, A.I., *Natsional'no-osvoboditel'noe dvizhenie v Chekhoslovakii 1938–1945* (Moscow: Sotsekgiz 1961), ch. 5, pp. 307–65, Czechoslovak resistance movement Spring 1945, creation of National Front government and its programme, the Prague rising.

Ryazanskii, A.P., *V ogne tankovykh srazhenii* (5th Guards Mech. Corps), ch. 7, Prague operation, pp. 205–16: German forces with strength of 900,000 men, 2,200 tanks, some 1,000 aircraft, three Soviet fronts with 1 million men, 23,000 guns/mortars, 1,800 tanks/SP guns, 4,000 aircraft; 4th Guards Tank Army to operate in area of 13th Army and on sixth day of operations to strike on Prague from the west and south-west, 3rd Guards Tank Army to operate with 3rd Guards Army and to strike Prague from north and north-east, news of Prague rising 5 May, 0530 hrs 6 May 4th Guards Tank Army opened offensive with lead battalions of 13th Army, capture of the staff of Army Group Centre, Schörner himself escaped, 0230 hrs 9 May lead elements 10th Guards Tank Corps in Prague, main body of 4th Guards Tank Army in the city at 0400 hrs, 3rd Guards Tank, 3rd Guards and 13th Army also closing on Prague, junction of forces from 1st and 2nd Ukrainian Fronts thus completing encirclement of German forces.

Shtemenko, S.M., *General'nyi shtab v gody voiny*, vol. 2. See ch. 12, Prague operation, German capitulation, pp. 413–30: Nazi manoeuvres to preserve their forces from total defeat on the Eastern Front, Nazi 'political nets' cast even wider in April, Hitler's suicide 30 April, Stalin's instruction that now time to strike for Prague, evening 30 April ordered *Stavka* directive to 2nd Ukrainian Front and Marshal Timoshenko (*Stavka* representative), operation to last two weeks in view of strength of Schörner's Army Group Centre, 1 May orders to 1st Ukrainian Front to regroup, 1310 hrs 4 May *Stavka* directive for Prague operation, meeting between Koniev and Bradley, Prague rising at noon 5 May, broadcast appeals for help, Koniev's attack advanced to 6 May on Stalin's specific orders. Negotiations at Reims, pp. 430–34: Jodl only empowered to conclude an armistice, talks to 6 May with Jodl's refusal to surrender German forces in the east, Eisenhower invitation to General Susloparov (chief of Soviet Military Mission), Eisenhower smilingly reports that Jodl offers to surrender to the Anglo-Americans but to carry on fighting in the east—'What, General, do you say to that?'—but Eisenhower's insistence on complete German surrender, text of surrender to be sent to Moscow with cessation of hostilities timed for 0001 hrs (Moscow time) 9 May, Susloparov without instructions and decided to sign instrument of surrender but with amendment that this did not preclude the signing of a further more complete document, document signed 0241 hrs 7 May 1945, Susloparov sent his report to Moscow only to have this cross with his belated instructions from Moscow—'Do not sign *any* documents'. Stalin's reaction, pp. 440–44: agreement at Reims not to be abrogated but must not be recognized, Stalin's requirement that Zhukov find a building in Berlin for signing of unconditional surrender, Reims agreement to be regarded as a 'preliminary surrender', Zhukov to sign for USSR with Vyshinskii as his political deputy, Stalin personally telephoned Zhukov to inform him of this arrangement, directive then sent to all Fronts on surrender procedures (text, pp. 442–3) and signed 2235 hrs 7 May, preparations for Karlshorst surrender, Zhukov opened proceedings, Vyshinskii informed Susloparov that Stalin bore him no ill-will for his action in signing at Reims.

Yeremenko, A.I., *Gody vozmezdiya*, ch. 14, Prague operations, pp. 566–76: German strength in Czechoslovakia (62 divisions), Prague rising, 4th Ukrainian Front driving on Prague from the east, organization of Front mobile group (rifle division with a tank brigade, also a rifle battalion with 10 aircraft), also mobile groups set up in 38th, 60th and 1st Guards Army, Front mobile group concentrated at Opava, first assignment to capture Olomouc, capture of General Trukhin from Vlasov Army, Yeremenko confirms his identity since Trukhin a lecturer with him at General Staff Academy in 1938 (p. 572), signal from Moscow on Reims capitulation, some German commanders reject ultimatum, 60th and 38th Army continue drive to the west, new boundary lines between 1st and 4th Ukrainian Fronts set by *Stavka* during night of 10 May.

Zavizion, G.T. and Kornyushin, P.A., *I na Tikhom Okeane . . .* (6th Guards Tank Army), ch. VII, 'Na Pragu', pp. 185–96: Prague operation, capture of Brno 26 April, at opening of Prague operation 6th Guards Tank had only *151 tanks and SP guns* (9th Guards Mech. Corps had only *21 tanks*), *Stavka* plan to launch two powerful blows on both flanks of Army Group Centre and then close on Prague with concentric attacks to encircle enemy forces east of Prague cutting off German escape routes to the west and south-west, offensive of 2nd and 4th Ukrainian Fronts timed for 7 May, at 0530 hrs 6th Guards Tank committed into breach of enemy defences cleared by 7th Guards Army, 1300 hrs 9 May lead elements 5th Guards Tank Corps in Prague from the south-east and linked up with 3rd Guards Tank Army/1st Ukrainian Front, 9th Guards Mech. Corps also approached from the south, 7th Guards and 53rd Army following in wake of 6th Guards Tank, junction with 3rd and 4th Guards Tank armies completed encirclement of main body of Army Group Centre, escape route to the Americans severed, lead elements of 9th Guards Mech. Corps made contact with American forces 40km south-west of Prague.

Polish materials

Gać, Stanislaw, *Udzial 2 Armii Wojska Polskiego w operacji praskiej* (Warsaw: MON 1962), 176 pp. (2nd Polish Army: Prague operation).

Vlasov/Vlasov movement: KONR

'Die Aktion des Generals Wlassow', see Teil B., 'Die Behandlung des russischen Problems während der Zeit des ns. Regimes in Deutschland.' (Manuscript), ch. OX: 1 ROA Division on the Oder front, Vlasov's plans and intentions, the Schörner–Bunyachenko confrontation, the final days, pp. 278–83.

Steenberg, Sven, *Vlasov*, ch. V, 'Too Little and Too Late': Vlasov on the Oder front 8 April, journey to Prague 16 April Vlasov–Klecanda meeting, Bunyachenko's march south, Schörner–Bunyachenko confrontation, pp. 183–94; ch. VI, 'Marching toward Doom': Vlasov troops and Czech rising in Prague, Vlasov reaches American forward post, Vlasov in Soviet hands, pp. 195–211.

Strik–Strikfeldt, Wilfried, *Against Stalin and Hitler* (trans. David Footman), ch. 19, 'Last Meeting with Vlasov', plans for approach to the Americans (and British), Strik–Strikfeldt to have Vlasovite identity card as 'Colonel Verevkin', pp. 222–30; ch. 20, 'The End': the Mannheim camp, conversation with captured senior German officers on Russia, Russian campaign and the Vlasov movement, arrest of General Vlasov on Czechoslovak soil, pp. 231–45.

Tolstoy, Nikolai, *Victims of Yalta*. See ch. 12, 'The End of General Vlasov', pp. 278–303: the most detailed study of the final circumstances of Vlasov and the *KONR*, the strange affair of the 'handover' and a note on a 1973 article in the USSR on Vlasov's trial.

Bibliog...

NOTE ON SOURCES AND MATERIALS RELA...
TO THE SOVIET–GERMAN WAR (1941–45)

To assemble any account of the Soviet-German war, or the 'Great Patriotic War' in its Soviet guise, involves nothing less than scaling a mighty mountain of material, not least the formidable escarpments of captured German military documents (GMD) and the massive outcrop of Soviet publication amounting to more than 15,000 volumes to date. Such circumstances must perforce make any claim to comprehensive identification and listing pretentious, even absurd, though by the same token some method must be devised and implemented to account for the diversity and internal complexity of these materials. To this end I have divided the material into four sections, beginning with *Soviet sources,* followed by *German Military Documents, East European* items and *non-Soviet works,* all of which is intended to comprehend the bulk of sources and materials utilized in the preparation of the present work as well as its predecessor, *The Road to Stalingrad.*

The ordering and classification of Soviet materials has proved to be no simple undertaking. Sheer bulk apart, the several revisions of the wartime history of the Soviet Union—prompted by political exigency—necessitate some form of differentiation, a matter to which I have attended in the first instance by listing the several Soviet *bibliographies* of publications related to the war (including wartime materials themselves). Wartime censorship and the need for morale-boosting propaganda (designed for internal and external consumption) all too obviously impregnated this wartime output, but in which embattled nation was this not so? Nevertheless, it is quite impossible to discount the wartime issues of the newspaper *Krasnaya Zvezda,* those essential communiqués from the important collection *Soobshcheniya Sovetskogo Informatsionnovo byuro (Sovinformbyuro),* with almost 3,000 pages to it, and also *Soviet War News* (published by the press department of the Soviet Embassy in London); one of the best compilations of the most pertinent wartime military monographs and patriotic brochures—representing names such as Talenskii, Zamyatin, Fokin, Sidorov and Tarle—is to be found in Maj.-Gen. A. Grylev's article, 'Sovetskaya voennaya istoriografiya v gody Velikoi Otechestvennoi voiny i poslevoennyi period' (*Voenno-istoricheskii Zhurnal,* 1968 (1), pp. 90–100). Just what could be accomplished by skilful exploitation of these contemporary sources was shown in that excellent two-volume study, one which even today retains considerable value, *The Russian Campaigns of 1941–1943/1944–1945* by W.E.D. Allen and Paul Muratoff, published by Penguin Books in 1944–6. There is also much to be derived from Marshal Stalin's Orders of the Day (*Prikazy Verkhovnovo Glavnokomanduyushchevo*),

...ught back to sight and sound in the 1975 Soviet

y must have its place and I have combined this with the Soviet
...cial histories' of the war, technically a misnomer but easily recognizable
...hat form, principally the earlier six-volume history and the current publication on
the history of the Second World War, now completed in twelve volumes. Campaign
histories, operational narratives and formation/unit histories are self-explanatory, but
'memoirs' pose something of a problem due to their highly variegated nature: while
Voennye Memuary form a distinct series, I have followed that admirable Soviet handbook
O voine, o tovarishchakh, o sebe (Voenidzat 1977) as to what constitutes 'voenno-
memuarnaya literatura' and which books should be included under the rubric of a
'memoir'. The difficulty is compounded by the expansion of that series 'Vtoraya mirovaya
voina v issledovaniyakh, vospominaniyakh, dokumentakh', supervised and published
by the Academy of Sciences, not least as a corrective to the more exuberant 'subjectivism'
of the authors published in *Voennye Memuary*. Additionally, it is necessary to take
account of yet another category, the 'Istoriko-memuarnyi ocherk', a combination of
documentary research with personal reminiscences and memoir material, hence my
subdivision into memoirs in a personalized form, *Voennye Memuary* (selected for their
historical relevance) and, finally, memoirs in a collective context with collective contributions.

Within all this literature *Voenno-istoricheskii Zhurnal* enjoys a very singular place,
that major journal which resumed publication in 1959 and is now in the twenty-third
year of its resuscitated existence. The memoir material in this journal is of prime
importance, often being a more technical (and reliable) version of what subsequently
appeared in *Voennye Memuary;* the documentary evidence adduced is also of commanding
importance, a significant example being the wide spread of Marshal Vasilevskii's
contributions suffused with command papers, transcripts and signals. Marshal of the
Soviet Union Vasilevskii is a much underestimated soldier, a figure who flits about
Soviet historiography but a commander inured to the battlefield yet deft in his handling
of the whole Soviet war machine. For that reason alone—illuminating the role of
Marshal Vasilevskii—*Voenno-istoricheskii Zhurnal* must command the attention of every
historian, but there is the additional dimension of quite stringent analysis of Soviet
operational decisions, operational performance and command systems—a feature which
became more pronounced in the mid-1970s as the treatment of wartime experience
was integrated more fully into contemporary military research, particularly what is
presently labelled 'command and control'. For that reason, as well as others, the military
statistics provided by this journal also enjoy singular relevance.

Mention of Soviet 'military statistics' brings us to the *massif* of the captured German
Military Documents. I should say at once that in terms of 'raw data' (order of battle,
strengths, dispositions, weapons performance, assessments of intentions) derived from
contemporary sources, the German and Soviet materials do not differ appreciably. What
has been constructed in retrospect is another matter, but I have tried here to assemble
out of the many thousands of pages of German documents a collection which can
represent the 'comparability' of Soviet and German sources—hence (i) the main command
decisions and related papers at Army Group/Army level, the *Chefsachen* and operational
planning papers, (ii) that invaluable agglomeration of intelligence material amassed by

Fremde Heere Ost, perhaps best described as 'assessments and evaluations', and (iii) 'collected papers' comprising the multiple collections of studies, compilations, analyses, statistical data, map folders, interrogations and captured mail—both yielding masses of information—and so into the manic, horrifying records of the *Reich* Ministry for the Occupied Eastern Territories, coupled with the even more chilling files of the *Reichsführer SS* which retail the unrestrained horrors of *Bandenkrieg*, the battle with the Soviet partisans and the sinister business with General Vlasov. These same 'collections' also provide a wealth of information related to technical intelligence, ranging from the study of the logistic support for Soviet tank troops to the narrow but revealing data from *OHK/General der Eisenbahntruppen*, the railway troops (material which can be duly compared with the Soviet analysis of railway operations presented by G.A. Kumanev in *Na sluzhbe fronta i tyla*, Nauka 1976). From this and other material it is possible to assemble what I might best call a 'sub-archive' of original Soviet documents, papers and orders captured by German units—a prime example is furnished by the *FHO*(IIb) file (T-78/R488) on the conduct of Soviet troops on German territory, with original Soviet orders and instructions as well as PW interrogation and details on Soviet procedures, including the organization of Soviet *strafbats*, the punishment battalions.

There is clearly a case for some separate identification of East European (as opposed to Soviet) sources, with some considerable quantity of Polish material worthy of notice. I have prefaced each of these small collections with one main bibliographical reference, such as the Yugoslav volume *Bibliografia o ratu i revoluciji. . .* , intended to cover a much wider spectrum of publications. Recondite though some of this may seem, there are important items to be uncovered, such as the heavy losses sustained by the Rumanian Army in its operations conducted on the side of the Red Army after 1944.

Non-Soviet research and documentary publication on the Soviet-German war is already rich and grows richer with each year, though once again there is much recompense in turning to wartime publications, for example, Alexander Werth's *tour de force*, *The Year of Stalingrad*, or that bitter but shrewd book by Curzio Malaparte, *The Volga Rises in Europe*, which remarks that 'the supreme industrial creation of Soviet Russia is her Army', a thesis advanced with macabre battlefield evidence:

Look closely at these dead, these Tartar dead, these Russian dead. They are new corpses . . . just delivered from the great factory of the *pyatiletka*. See how bright their eyes are. Observe their low foreheads, their thick lips. Peasants, are they? Workers? Yes, they are workers—specialists, *udarniki*. . . . They typify a new race, a tough race, these corpses of workers killed in an industrial accident.

Malaparte also had caustic words for those who expected (as many did) an easy and imminent collapse of the system. Indeed, one of the main Soviet charges is that of collusion on the part of the Western powers in German plans for an attack on the USSR, or at least a passive attitude in the face of these deep-laid German designs, hence the importance of non-Soviet memoirs (and official documents) in delineating the circumstances of the wartime alliance fashioned with the Soviet Union. Non-Soviet sources are also mandatory in dealing with the whole gigantic effort involved in Lend-Lease and Allied aid to wartime Russia.

Of necessity, German memoir material, documentary publication and military analysis must loom large in any listing of essential references. The memoirs of senior German commanders—Guderian, von Manstein and their fellows—are indispensable, while the series *Die Wehrmacht im Kampf* supplies a combination of memoir with military records; formal campaign histories are not lacking, in the style of *Der Feldzug gegen Sowjetrussland* by Alfred Philippi and Ferdinand Heim, as well as the publications in the series *Studien und Dokumente zur Geschichte des Zweiten Weltkrieges*. There is also the 'historical-memoir' on the lines of Heinz Schröter's *Stalingrad* (based on his wartime compilation) and so towards evaluations of tactical aspects, exemplified in General Middeldorf's study, *Taktik im Russlandfeldzug*. Suffice it to say that German historiography is virtually a subject in itself, one which demands its own specialization and particular competences; what I have tried to represent here is demonstrably merely the tip of a vast and impressive iceberg. Perhaps the most pertinent proof of the relevance and the rigour of these publications is the assiduous attention which Soviet military specialists and historians pay to them (and, additionally, the East German military-historical journal, *Militär Geschichte*.)

All this merely reinforces my original submission that any claim to a comprehensive, much less exhaustive, catalogue of sources and materials would merely border on the fatuous. Perhaps the best that can be managed is to register those prime materials which directly illuminate the command decisions, the operational narrative and the war-supporting activities which kept mighty armies in the field for month after agonizing month. Little wonder that such a titanic conflict continues to leave behind it a great trail of records, recollection, analysis, self-justification, vainglorious boast, fruitless railing, memories steeped in pain—and, in some rare instances, even remorse.

Contents of Bibliography

3. Map collections

III. *Eastern European memoirs/monographs*

    (a) Polish

    (b) Czechoslovak

    (c) Rumanian

    (d) Yugoslav

    (e) Albanian

    (f) Hungarian

    (g) Bulgarian

IV. *Non-Soviet materials*

I. SOVIET MATERIALS

1. Bibliographies (arranged chronologically)

Tolstikhinaya, A.I. (ed.), *Velikaya Otechestvennaya voina Sovetskovo naroda* (Moscow: Gos. bibl.-bibliograf. izd. 1942). The first bibliographical compilation.

Kaufman, I.M. *et al.*, *Velikaya Otechestvennaya voina*. Ukazatel. literatury. Vyp. 1–1o. (Moscow: Lenin Library 1943–6).

Kumanev, G.A., *Velikaya Otechestvennaya voina Sovetskovo Soyuza (1941–1945)* (Moscow: Acad. Nauk 1960). Works published 1946–59.

Istoriya Velikoi Otechestvennoi voiny Sovetskovo Soyuza 1941–1945 (Moscow: Voenizdat 1965), vol. 6. See pp. 403–604 for sources/bibliographies, Soviet and non-Soviet.

Velikaya Otechestvennaya voina Sovetskovo Soyuza (1941–1945 gg.) Rekomendatelnyi ukazatel literatury (Moscow: Kniga 1965).

Grylev, A., 'Sovetskaya voennaya istoriografiya v gody Velikoi Otechestvennoi voiny i poslevoennyi period', *Voenno-istoricheskii Zhurnal*, 1968(1), pp. 90–100 and (3), pp. 77–89. (Both parts of this article are important, especially 1968(1), an essential reference for wartime publications.)

Geroi Velikoi Otechestvennoi Voiny. Stranitsy biografii. Rekomendatelnyi ukazatel' . . . (Moscow: Kniga 1970).

(Lenin Library) *Velikii Podvig*. Rekomendatel'nyi ukazatel' . . . (Moscow: Kniga 1970).

Aksenova, N.A. and Vasileva, M.V., *Soldaty Dzerzhinskovo Soyuz beregut. Rekom. ukazatel . . . o chekistakh* (Moscow: Kniga 1972).

Dokuchayev, G.A., *Sibir v Velikoi Otechestvennoi voiny* (Novosibirsk, Akad. Nauk 1972). Books published 1941–71; 600 copies printed of this bibliography, photo-offset.

K 30-letiyu velikoi pobedy. Ukazatel osnovnoi literatory 1973–1975. (Moscow: Akad. Nauk 1975). Entries and index; 1,000 copies of this bibliography printed, photo-offset.

Tula i oblast v Velikoi Otechestvennoi voine. Bibliograficheskii ukazatel . . . (Tula: Tul. obl., k-ka 1975).

(Lenin Library) *Velikaya Pobeda*. Rekomendatelnyi ukazatel' . . . (Moscow: Kniga 1975).

Amurtsy v gody Velikoi Otechestvennoi voiny. Rekomendatelnyi ukazatel . . . (Blagoveshchensk: Amur Oblast Library 1975).

Bashkiriya v gody Velikoi Otechestvennoi voiny (1941–1945 gg.) Bibliograficheskii ukazatel
(Ufa: Bashkir Lib. 1975).

Sibir v gody Velikoi Otechestvennoi voiny (iyun 1941–sentyabr 1945). Bibliograficheskii
ukazatel (Novosibirsk: Akad. Nauk 1976). 800 copies printed of this bibliography,
photo-offset.

Problems of the Contemporary World (38), 'Soviet Studies on the Second World War'
(Moscow: Acad. Sciences 1976). (In English.)

Dyuzhev, Yu.I., *Velikaya Otechestvennaya voina na severe v sovetskoi literature* (Petrozavodsk: Kareliya 1976). Materials published 1941–72.

Goldas, M., *Tarybine Armija-Tarybu lietuvos isvaduotoja* (Vilnius: LTSR Valst.b-ka.
1976).

Puce, O., Smatova, T. and Valdmane, I., *Latviesu tautas cina lielaja tevijas kara
1941–1945* (Riga: State Library 1976).

Collective authorship, *O voine, o tovarishchakh, o sebe.* Annotirovannyi ukazatel' voenno-
memuarnoi literatory (1941–1977 gg.) (Moscow: Voenizdat 1977). This is an
important and immensely useful compilation on memoir material, plus *reviews* of
books and articles. (2nd edn 1982.)

(Lenin Library: Military Section) *Vooruzhennye sily SSSR na strazhe Rodiny* (Moscow:
Kniga 1977). See pp. 45–100.

Collective authorship, *Istoriya SSSR. Ukazatel' Sovetskoi literatury za 1917–1967 gg.*
Tom III, Vypusk 4: *SSSR v gody Velikoi Otechestvennoi voiny (iyun 1941–sentyabr
1945 g.). Ukazatel Sovetskoi literatury za 1941–1967 gg.* (Moscow: Nauka 1977),
with supplement (subject and author index).

With almost 8,000 entries, this bibliography must occupy pride of place as a
guide to Soviet writing on the Great Patriotic War, with its use enhanced by the
author index. The main section on military operations has been arranged under
the accepted periodization of the Great Patriotic War (June 1941–November
1942, November 1942–3 and 1944–May 1945) with a separate compilation for
the Soviet campaign in the Far East (August–September 1945). Two sections of
this Part III cover publications and tactics in the Great Patriotic War (see pp.
318–78, numbered entries 3617–4420).

By way of amplification and verification it is possible to use the booklists supplied
by *Fremde Heere Ost* (IIId):Ic-Unterlagen Ost, which catalogue Soviet military
publications seized by the German army. Quite a large amount of this material
dates back before 1941, but that simply serves the cause of continuity: see *Russisches
Militärschrifttum: Bücherverzeichnis* (by separate number), GMD.

It is worth noting also that Stalin receives two citations in this latest Soviet
bibliography, his *O Velikoi Otechestvennoi voine Sovetskovo Soyuza* in its five editions
(1942, two in 1943, 1944 and 1951) and his wartime correspondence with Allied
leaders. Brezhnev was honoured with no less than *eight* bibliographical entries and
is included in the first section on the Leninist legacy, Party and state documents,
Party and government leaders' pronouncements.

2. 'Official histories', the Party and the government (arranged chronologically)

Stalin, J.V., *O Velikoi Otechestvennoi voine Sovetskovo Soyuza* (Moscow: Gospolitizdat
1942 (51 pp.), 2nd and 3rd edns 1943, 4th edn 1944, 5th edn 1951 (208 pp.)

Golikov, S., *Vydayushchiesya pobedy Sovetskoi Armii v Velikoi Otechestvennoi voine* (Moscow: Gospolitizdat, 2nd edn 1954). An 'official', stylised, Stalinized version of the Great Patriotic War.

Platonov, S.P. (ed.), *Vtoraya mirovaya voina 1939–1945 gg.* (Moscow: Voenizdat 1958). ('Biblioteka Ofitsera' series; map supplement.) A major and useful history, deservedly utilized for many years.

Telpukhovskii, B.S., *Velikaya Otechestvennaya voina Sovetskovo Soyuza 1941–1945*, Kratkii ocherk (Moscow: Gospolitizdat 1959). Tendentious and far from accurate.

Vorob'ev, F.D. and Kravtsov, V.M., *Velikaya Otechestvennaya voina Sovetskovo Soyuza 1941–1945 gg.* (Moscow: Voenizdat 1961). Written for 'generals and officers' of the Soviet Army, this remains a useful and lucid work.

Istoriya Velikoi Otechestvennoi voiny Sovetskovo Soyuza 1941–1945, in six volumes (P.N. Pospelov, Chairman Editorial Commission). Vol. 1 1960, vol. 2 1961, vol. 3 1961, vol. 4 1962, vol. 5 1963, vol. 6 1965. (An enlarged, corrected edition of vol. 1 was issued in 1968 under this reprint label, though this cannot really be described as a second edition; both versions were heavily slanted in the direction of magnifying Khrushchev's wartime role, together with that of his wartime associates. However, the data suffered no manipulation and this historical work still retains a certain value.) Vols. 1–6 (Moscow: Institut Marksizma-Leninizma/ Voenizdat 1960–65; also revised with vol. 1, 1963–).

Velikaya Otechestvennaya voina Sovetskovo Soyuza 1941–1945, Kratkaya istoriya (Editorial Commission Chairman, P.N. Pospelov), (Moscow: Voenizdat 1965). See also 2nd edn (Voenizdat 1970) and English language edition, *Great Patriotic War of the Soviet Union* (Moscow: Progress Publishers; abridged).

Zhilin, P.A. (ed.), *Velikaya Otechestvennaya voina*, Kratkii nauch.-popul. ocherk (Moscow: Politizdat 1970). (Produced under the auspices of the Institute of Military History.)

Velikaya Otechestvennaya Voina 1941–1945, Kratkii nauchno-populyarnyi ocherk, Institut Voennoi Istorii Ministerstva Oborony SSSR (Moscow: Politizdat 1970).

Velikaya Otechestvennaya Voina 1941–1945, Institut Voennoi Istorii Ministerstva Oborony SSSR (Moscow: Politizdat 1973).

Velikaya Pobeda Sovetskogo Naroda 1941–1945, Akademiya Nauk SSSR (Moscow: Nauka 1976).

Istoriya vtoroi mirovoi voiny 1939–1945. In 1973 the first volume of this new twelve-volume history of the Second World War was published, a comprehensive and scientific work obviously intended to replace the earlier six-volume history of the Great Patriotic War which had appeared in the Khrushchev period. Four main institutes are involved, the Institute of Military History, the Institute of Marxism-Leninism, the Institute of General History (Academy of Sciences) and the Academy's Institute of History. Until his death in 1976, Marshal of the Soviet Union A.A. Grechko was named as the head of the Main Editorial Commission; he was followed by Marshal of the Soviet Union D.F. Ustinov, the present Defence Minister. All twelve volumes have now been published, under the imprint of Voenizdat. See vol. 1 1973, vol. 2 1974, vol. 3 1973, vol. 4 1975, vol. 5 1975, vol. 6 1976, vol. 7 1976, vol. 8 1977, vol. 9 1978, vol. 10 1979, vol. 11 1980, vol. 12 1982. The Soviet-German war opens with volume 4.

Samsonov, A.M. (ed.), *Sovetskii Soyuz v gody Velikoi Otechestvennoi voiny 1941–1945*, Institut Istorii, Akad. Nauk SSSR (Moscow: Nauka 1976).

Ideologicheskaya rabota KPSS na fronte (1941–1945 gg.) (Moscow: Voenizdat, 1960).

Kommunisticheskaya Partiya v period Velikoi Otechestvennoi voiny, 1941–1945, Dokumenty i Materialy (Moscow: Gospolitizdat 1961), 704 pp.

Partiino-politicheskaya rabota v Sovetskikh vooruzhennykh silakh v gody Velikoi Otechestvennoi voiny (Moscow: Voenizdat 1963).

Petrov, Yu.P., *Partiinoi stroitel'stvo v Sovetskoi Armii i Flote (1918–1961)* (Moscow: Voenizdat 1964). (See pp. 341–440 on Party/*Komsomol,* WWII.)

Komkov, G.D., *Ideino-politcheskaya rabota KPSS v 1944–1945 gg.* (Moscow: Nauka 1965).

Sbornik Dokumentov i Materialov po istorii SSSR Sovetskogo Perioda (1917–1956gg.) (Moscow: Moscow University 1966).

Partiino-Politicheskaya rabota v Sovetskikh Vooruzhennykh silakh v gody Velikoi Otechestvennoi voiny, 1941–1945, Kratkii Istoricheskii Obzor, Ministerstva Oborony SSSR (Moscow: Voenizdat 1968).

Kommunisticheskaya Partiya v Velikoi Otechestvennoi voine, 1941–1945, Dokumenty i Materialy (Moscow: Voenizdat 1970).

Kirsanov, N.A., *Partiinye mobilizatsii na front v gody Velikoi Otechestvennoi voiny* (Moscow: Moscow University 1972).

SSSR v Velikoi Otechestvennoi voine 1941–1945 (Kratkaya khronika), Akademiya Nauk SSSR, Institut Istorii (Moscow: Voenizdat 1964).

SSSR v Velikoi Otechestvennoi voine 1941–1945gg. Kratkaya khronika (Moscow: Voenizdat 1970; 2nd edn, revised and enlarged).

3. Theatres of War, Campaigns and Operations

Anfilov, V.A., *Nachalo Velikoi Otechestvennoi voiny (22 iyunya- seredina iyulya 1941 goda)* (Moscow: Voenizdat 1962).

Anfilov, V.A., *Bessmertnyi podvig.* Issledovanie kanuna i pervovo etapa VOV (Moscow: Nauka 1971).

Anfilov, V.A., *Proval 'blitskriga'* (Moscow: Nauka 1974). (The above three books by Anfilov are major works on the German surprise attack and the first stage of the war.)

Antosyak, A.V., *V boyakh za svobodu Rumynii* (Moscow: Voenizdat 1974). Soviet operations in Rumania.

Bagramyan, I.Kh., *Gorod-voin na Dnepre* (Moscow: Politizdat 1965). Fall of Kiev/ 1941.

Barbashin, I.P. and Kharitonov, A.D., *Boevye deistviya Sovetskoi Armii pod Tikhvinom v 1941 godu* (Moscow: Voenizdat 1958).

Batov, P.I., *Operatsiya 'Oder'* (Moscow: Voenizdat 1965). 65th Army in the Berlin operation.

Belkin, I.M., *13-ya Armiya v Lutsko-Rovenskoi operatsii 1944 g.* (Moscow: Voenizdat 1960). 13th Army, January–February 1944.

Biryuzov, S.S. (ed.), *Sovetskie vooruzhennye sily v bor'be za osvobozhdenie narodov Yugoslavii* (Moscow: Voenizdat 1960). Soviet operations in Yugoslavia.

Blinov, S.I., *Ot Visly do Odera* (Moscow: Voenizdat 1962). 60th Army Operations, January 1945.

Bor'ba za Sovetskuyu Baltiku v Velikoi Otechestvennoi voine 1941–1945, vols. 1 and 2 (Riga: Liesma 1966–7). (See also vol. 3.)

Chuikov, V.I., *Gvardeitsy Stalingrada idut na zapad*. (Moscow: Sov. Rossiya 1972). (Also as *V boyakh za Ukrainu*, Kiev, 1972.)

Chuikov, V.I., *Konets Tret'evo Reikha* (Moscow: Sov. Rossiya 1973). (Also in Ukrainian: *Kinets Tretovo Reikhu*, Kiev, 1975).

Chuikov, V.I., *Srazhenie veka* (Moscow: Sov. Rossiya 1975). Stalingrad, Soviet drive into Ukraine; Berlin 1945.

Eliseyev, E.P., *Na Belostokskom napravlenii* (Moscow: Nauka 1971). 2nd Belorussian Front, July 1944.

Evstigneyev, V.N. (ed.), *Velikaya bitva pod Moskvoi* (Moscow: Voenizdat 1961). Battle of Moscow.

Galitskii, K.N., *V boyakh za Vostochnuyu Prussiyu* (Moscow: Nauka 1970). 11th Guards Army, 1944–5.

Grechko, A.A., *Bitva za Kavkaz* (Moscow: Voenizdat 1967, 2nd edn 1971).

Grechko, A.A., *Cherez Karpaty* (Moscow: Voenizdat, 2nd edn 1972). Across Carpathians, Soviet operations in Czechoslovakia.

Grylev, A.N., *Za Dneprom* (Moscow: Voenizdat 1963). Ukrainian operations: January–April 1944.

Grylev, A.N., *Dnepr-Karpaty-Krim. Osvobozhdenie Pravoberezhnoi Ukrainy i Kryma v 1944 godu.* (Moscow: Nauka 1970).

Istomin, V.P., *Smolenskaya nastupatel'naya operatsiya (1943 g.)* (Moscow: Voenizdat 1975).

Kharitonov, A.D., *Gumbinnenskii proryv* (Moscow: Voenizdat 1960). 28th Army, Gumbinnen.

Kir'yan, M.M., *S Sandomirskovo platsdarma* (Moscow: Voenizdat 1961). 5th Guards Army, January 1945.

Kiryukhin, S.P., *43 Armiya v Vitebskoi operatsii* (Moscow: Voenizdat 1961).

Klimov, I.D., *Geroicheskaya oborona Tuly* (Moscow: Voenizdat 1961). 50th Army, defence of Tula, October–December 1941.

Koltunov, G.A. and Solov'ev, B.G., *Kurskaya bitva* (Moscow: Voenizdat 1970). The standard Soviet work on Kursk.

Koltunov, G.A. and Solov'ev, B.G., *Ognennaya duga* (Moscow: Voenizdat 1973). Kursk, 1943.

Koniev, I.S. (ed.), *Za osvobozhdenie Chekhoslovakii* (Moscow: Voenizdat 1965). Soviet operations, Czechoslovakia; a major campaign study, with invaluable data and figures.

Korovnikov, I.T., *Novgorodsko-Luzhskaya operatsiya* (Moscow: Voenizdat 1960). 59th Army offensive, January–February 1944.

Lyudnikov, I.I., *Pod Vitebskom* (Moscow: Voenizdat 1962). 39th Army operations, June 1944, Vitebsk.

Malinovskii, R.Ya. (ed.), *Yassko-Kishinevskie kanny* (Moscow: Nauka 1964). Jassy-Kishinev operation.

Markin, I., *Kurskaya bitva* (Moscow: Voenizdat 1958).

Matsulenko, V.A., *Udar s dnestrovskovo platsdarma* (Moscow: Voenizdat 1961). 37th Army operations, August 1944.

Minasyan, M.M., *Osvobozhdenie narodov Yugo-vostochnoi Evropy* (Moscow: Voenizdat 1967). (Map supplement.)

Morozov, V.P., *Zapadnee Voronezha* (Moscow: Voenizdat 1956). Soviet offensive, January–February 1943; one of the very best Soviet military monographs, an invaluable source.

Muriev, D.Z., *Proval Operatsii 'Taifun'* (Moscow: Voenizdat 1972).

Na Severo-zapadnom fronte, 1941–1943 (Moscow: Nauka 1969).

Nekrich, A.M., *1941 22 iyunya* (Moscow: Nauka 1965).

Oreshkin, A.K., *Oboronitel'naya operatsiya 9-i Armii* (Moscow: Voenizdat 1960). 9th Army, October–November 1941, Rostov.

Platonov, S.P. (ed.), *Bitva za Leningrad 1941–1944* (Moscow: Voenizdat 1964). (Map supplement.) The basic work on Soviet operations.

Pokrovskii, S.N., *Kazakhstanskie soyedineniya v bitve na Kurskoi duge* (Alma-Ata: Nauka 1973).

Polushkin, M.A., *Na Sandomirskom napravlenii* (Moscow: Voenizdat 1969). Lvov-Sandomierz, 1944.

Proektor, D.M., *Cherez Duklinskii pereval* (Moscow: Voenizdat 1960).

Rokossovskii, K.K. (ed.), *Velikaya pobeda na Volge* (Moscow: Voenizdat 1965; with map supplement).

Rotmistrov, P.A., *Tankovoe srazhenie pod Prokhorovkoi* (Moscow: Voenizdat 1960).

Rumyantsev, N.M., *Pobeda Sovetskoi Armii v Zapolyar'e* (Moscow: Voenizdat 1955) 1944 operations.

Rumyantsev, N.M., *Razgrom vraga v Zapolyar'e (1941–1944 gg.)* (Moscow: Voenizdat 1963).

Samsonov, A.M., *Stalingradskaya bitva* (Moscow: Akad. Nauk, 1st edn 1960; 2nd edn Moscow: Nauka 1968). The 2nd edn especially must be regarded as the definitive work on Soviet operations at Stalingrad; it utilizes much original material.

Sandalov, L.M., *Pogorelo-Gorodishchenskaya operatsiya* (Moscow: Voenizdat 1960). 20th Army, Western Front, August 1942.

Sharokhin, M.N. and.Petrukhin, V.S., *Put' k Balatonu* (Moscow: Voenizdat 1966). 57th Army operations, Hungary/Balaton, 1944–5.

Shturm Kënigsberga. Sbornik (Kaliningrad: Kn. Izd.-vo., 3rd edn 1973).

Sofronov. G.P., *Vozdushnye desanty vo vtoroi mirovoi voine* (Moscow: Voenizdat 1962). Soviet airborne operations; ch. II, January–February 1942/Kanev September–October 1943.

Sokolovskii, V.D., (ed.), *Razgrom nemetsko-fashistskikh voisk pod Moskvoi* (Moscow: Voenizdat 1964; map supplement).

Solov'ev, V.G., *Vermakht na puti k gibeli* (Moscow: Nauka 1973). Kursk and its aftermath.

Sviridov, V.P. *et al.*, *Bitva za Leningrad 1941–1944* (Leningrad: Lenizdat 1962).

Terekhov, P.V., *Boevye deistviya tankov na severo-zapade v 1944 g.* (Moscow: Voenizdat 1965). Soviet tank operations, Karelia, 1944.

Tolubko, V.F. and Baryshev, N.I., *Ot Vidina do Belgrada* (Moscow: Nauka 1968). Soviet armour, Belgrade operation 1944.

Utkin, G., *Shturm 'Vostochnovo vala'* (Moscow: Voenizdat 1967). Ukraine/Dnieper operations, 1943.

Vaneev, G.I. *et al.*, *Geroicheskaya oborona Sevastopolya 1941–1942* (Moscow: Voenizdat 1969).

Vnotchenko. L.N., *Pobeda na Dal'nem Vostoke*. (Moscow: Voenizdat, 2nd edn 1971). Highly authoritative study of preparation and execution of Soviet operations in the Far East, August–September 1945.

Vorob'ev, D.F. *et al.*, *Poslednii shturm (Berlinskaya operatsiya 1945 g.)* (Moscow: Voenizdat 1970, 2nd edn 1975; map supplements).

Yarkunov, V.M., *Cherez Nevu* (Moscow: Voenizdat 1960). 67th Army, January 1943, Leningrad.

Yeremenko, A.I., *Na zapadnom napravlenii* (Moscow: Voenizdat 1958). Operations of 4th Shock Army, 1941.

Zakharov, M.V. (ed.), *Proval gitlerovskovo nastupleniya na Moskvu* (Moscow: Nauka 1966).

Zakharov, M.V., *Osvobozhdenie yugo-vostochnoi i tsentralnoi Evropy voiskami 2-go i 3-go Ukrainskikh frontov 1944–1945* (Moscow: Nauka 1970).

Zav'yalov, A.S. and Kalyadin, T.E., *Vostochno-pomeranskaya nastupatel'naya operatsiya Sovetskikh voisk.* Voenno-istoricheskii ocherk (Moscow: Voenizdat 1960). East Pomerania, February–March 1945.

4. Formation and unit histories

Altukhov, P.K. *et al.*, *Nezabyvaemye dorogi* (Moscow: Voenizdat 1974). 10th Guards Army.

Babadzhanyan, A.Kh. *et al.*, *Lyuki otkryli v Berline* (Moscow: Voenizdat 1973). War history, 1st Guards Tank Army.

Collective authorship, *V srazheniyakh za Pobedu* (Moscow: Nauka 1974). 38th Army, 1941–5.

Domnikov, V.M., *V nastuplenii Gvardiya* (Moscow: Voenizdat 1971). 2nd Guards Army.

Dragunskii, D.A. (ed.), *Ot Volgi do Pragi* (Moscow: Voenizdat 1966). 7th Guards Army.

Korovnikov, I.T. *et al.*, *Na trëkh frontakh* (Moscow: Voenizdat 1974). 59th Army.

Krylov, N.I. *et al.*, *Navstrechu pobede* (Moscow: Nauka 1970). 5th Army.

Pyatkov, V.K. *et al.*, *Tretya udarnaya* (Moscow: Voenizdat 1976). 3rd Shock Army.

Vorontsov, T.F. *et al.*, *Ot volzhskikh stepei do avstriiskikh Alp.* (Moscow: Voenizdat 1971). 24th Army to 1943, then 4th Guards Army.

Vysotskii, F.I. *et al.*, *Gvardeiskaya tankovaya* (Moscow: Voenizdat 1963). 2nd Guards Tank Army.

Zavizion, G.T. and Kornyushin, P.A., *I na Tikhom okeane . . .* (Moscow: Voenizdat 1967). 6th Guards Tank Army.

Abrosimov, G.N. *et al.*, *Gvardeiskii Nikolaevsko-Budapeshtskii* (Moscow: Voenizdat 1976). 2nd Guards Mechanized Corps. Formed from 22nd/363rd Guards Rifle Division.

Kuzmin, A.V. and Krasnov, I.I., *Kantemirovtsy* (Moscow: Voenizdat 1971). 4th Guards Tank Corps.

Ryazanskii, A.P., *V ogne tankovykh srazhenii* (Moscow: Nauka 1975). 5th Guards Mechanized Corps.

Samsonov, A.M., *Ot Volgi do Baltiki* (Moscow: Nauka 2nd edn 1973). 3rd Guards Mechanized Corps, 1942–5).

Solomatin, M.D., *Krasnogradtsy* (Moscow: Voenizdat 1963). 1st Mechanized Corps.

Tolubko, V.F. and Baryshev, N.I., *Na yuzhnom flange* (Moscow: Nauka 1972). 4th Guards Mechanized Corps, 1942–5.

Yushchuk, I.I., *Odinadtsatyi tankovyi korpus v boyakh za Rodinu* (Moscow: Voenizdat 1962). 11th Tank Corps.

Andreyev, A.A., *Po voennym dorogam* (Moscow: Voenizdat 1971). 69th Rifle Division.

Avramov, I.F., *82-ya Yartsevskaya* (Moscow: Voenizdat 1973). 82nd Rifle Division.

Bezuglyi, I.S. *et al.*, *Dvazhdy Krasnoznammenaya* (Moscow: Mosk. rabochii 1977). 5th Moscow/158th Rifle Division.

Gvardeiskaya Chernigovskaya (Moscow: Voenizdat 1976). 76th Guards Rifle Division.

Krapivin,V.I., *313-ya Petrozavodskaya* (Petrozavodsk: Kareliya 1971). 313th Rifle Division.

Kuznetsov. P.G., *Gvardeitsy-Moskvichi* (Moscow: Voenizdat 1962). Moscow Proletarian Rifle Division; 1st Guards Moscow–Minsk Rifle Division.

Mal'kov, D.K., *Skvoz dym i plamya* (Moscow: Voenizdat 1966). 12th Guards Rifle Division.

Napalkov, F.M. *et al.*, *Ot Tyumen do Kirkenesa* (Sverdlovsk: Sredne-Uralskoe Kh. Izd. 1976). 368th Rifle Division.

Nikolaev, A.N. and Dudnikov, A.G., *139-ya Roslavlskaya Krasnoznammenaya* (Cherbokssary: Khniz. Izd. 1975). 139th Rifle Division.

Ordena Lenina Strelkovaya (Perm: Permskoe Khnizh. Izd. 1967). 359th Rifle Division.

Rizhskie Gvardeiskie. Sbornik voenno-istoricheskikh ocherkov (Riga: Liesma 1972). On Latvian formations: 52nd Guards RD, 30th Guards RD, 85th Guards RD, 43rd Guards RD, 22nd Guards RD, 65th Guards RD, 315th Fighter Aviation Division.

Samchuk, I.A., *Trinadtsataya Gvardeiskaya* (Moscow: Voenizdat 1962). (2nd Edn. 1971). 13th Guards Rifle Division.

Samchuk, I.A., *Gvardeiskaya Poltavskaya* (Moscow: Voenizdat 1965). 97th Guards Rifle Division.

Sazonov, I.F., *Pervaya Gvardeiskaya* (Moscow: Voenizdat 1961). 100th Rifle Division; 1st Guards Rifle Division.

Shevchenko, I.N. and Kalinovskii, P.N., *Devyataya plastunskaya* (Moscow: Voenizdat 1970). 9th Rifle Division (pp. 102–88 for World War II).

Smakotin, M.P., *Ot Dona do Berlina* (Moscow: Voenizdat 1962). 153rd/57th Guards Rifle Division.

123-ya shla vperëd (Leningrad: Lenizdat 1971). 123rd Rifle Division.

Terekhov, A.F. *et al.*, *Gvardeiskaya Tamanskaya* (Moscow: Voenizdat 1972). 127th Rifle Division; Taman Guards Division.

Tuzov, A.V., *V ogne voiny* (Moscow: Voenizdat 1970). 50th Guards Rifle Division.

Vasilev, S.I. and Dikan, A.P., *Gvardeitsyi pyatnatsatoi* (Moscow: Voenizdat 1960). 15th Guards Rifle Division.

Zeinalov, R.E. and Borodetskii, L.S., *416 Taganrogskaya* (Baku: Azerbaidzh. Gos. Izd. 1969).

Dragan, I.G., *Vilenskaya Krasnoznamennaya* (Moscow: Voenizdat 1977). 144th Rifle Division.

Belan, P.S. *et al.*, *Frontovye dorogi*, (Alma-Ata: Kazakhstan 1978). 391st Rifle Division.

Zakurenkov, N.K., *32-ya Gvardeiskaya* (Moscow: Voenizdat 1978). 32nd RD; 32nd Guards Tamam RD.

Collective authorship, *S boyami do El'by* (Moscow: Mosk. rabochii 1979). 1st People's Militia; 60th Rifle Division.

Gurkin, V.V. and Ivashchenko, A.E., *5-ya Gvardeiskaya Kalinkovskaya* (Moscow: Voenizdat 1979). 5th Guards Mortar; MRL Division.

Venkov, B.S. and Dudinov, P.P., *Gvardeiskaya doblest'* (Moscow: Voenizdat 1979). 70th Guards Rifle Division.

Bogatyrev, A.T., *Ognevoi val.* (Kiev: Izd. Pol. Lit. Ukrainy 1977). 5th Artillery Breakthrough Division.

Popov, S.E., *Na ognevykh rubezhakh* (Moscow: Voenizdat 1971). 3rd Guards Artillery Breakthrough Division.

Nersesyan, N.G., *Fastovskaya Gvardeiskaya* (Moscow: Voenizdat 1964). 53rd Guards Tank Brigade.

Vinogradov, I.N., *Oborona-shturm-pobeda* (Moscow: Nauka 1968). 159th Field 'Fortified District'.

Grinko, A.I. (ed.), *Voronezhskii dobrovol'cheskii* (Voronezh: Tsentr.-Chernozem. Knizh.-Izdvo 1972). 4th Guards Voronezh Rifle Regiment.

5. Operational art and tactics

Achkasov, V.I. and Pavlovich, N.B., *Sovetskoe voenno-morskoe iskusstvo v Velikoi Otechestvennoi voine* (Moscow: Voenizdat 1973).

Andronikov, N.G. *et al.*, *Bronetankovye i mekhanizirovannye voiska Sovetskoi Armii* (Moscow: Voenizdat 1958). Tank armies; tank operations.

Batitskii, P.F., (ed.), *Voiska protivovozdushnoi oborony strany*. Istoricheskii ocherk (Moscow: Voenizdat 1968). Air Defence Troops/PVO Strany; see Pt 2, pp. 67–334.

Frunze Academy, *Proryv podgotovlennoi oborony strelkovymi soyedineniyami*. Sbornik statei (Moscow: Voenizdat 1957).

Frunze Academy, *Razvitie taktiki Sovetskoi armii v gody Velikoi Otechestvennoi voiny (1941–1945 gg.)* (Moscow: Voenizdat 1958).

Frunze Academy, *Sbornik materialov Sovetskovo voennovo iskusstva v Velikoi Otechestvennoi voine 1941–1945 gg.* (Vypusk 4) (Moscow: Voenizdat 1956).

Inzhenernye voiska Sovetskoi Armii v vazhneishikh operatsiyakh Velikoi Otechestvennoi voiny (Moscow: Voenizdat 1958). Soviet combat engineers, WWII.

Kurochkin, P.A. (ed.), *Obshchevoiskovaya armiya v nastuplenii* (Moscow: Voenizdat 1966).

Peresypkin, I.T., *Svyaz' v Velikoi Otechestvennoi voine* (Moscow: Nauka 1973). Soviet Signals Troops.

Popel, N.N. *et al.*, *Upravlenie voiskami v gody Velikoi Otechestvennoi voiny* (Moscow: Voenizdat 1974).

Radzievskii, A.I., *Tankovyi udar* (Moscow: Voenizdat 1977). Soviet tank armies in offensive operations.

Sychev, K.V. and Malakhov, M.M. (eds.), *Nastuplenie strelkovo korpusa* (Sbornik takticheskikh primerov . . .) (Moscow: Voenizdat 1958). Map Supplement.

Taktika v boevykh primerakh (Moscow: Voenizdat 1974–6), 5 vols: Division, Regiment, Battalion, Company and Section. See also *Armeiskie operatsii* (Moscow: Voenizdat 1977). Army operations.

Terekhin, K.P. *et al.*, *Voiny stal'nykh magistralei* (Moscow: Voenizdat 1969). Soviet railway troops, WWII.

Timokhovich, I.V., *Operativnoe iskusstvo Sovetskikh VVS v Velikoi Otechestvennoi voine* (Moscow: Voenizdat 1976).

Voroshilov Academy (General Staff Academy), *Sbornik materialov po istorii voennovo iskusstva v Velikoi Otechestvennoi voine* (Moscow: Voenizdat 1955), vols. 1–4 (map supplement).

Zhilin, P.A.. (ed.), *Vazhneishie operatsii Velikoi Otechestvennoi voiny 1941–1945 gg.* (Moscow: Voenizdat 1956).

6. Soviet Navy, Soviet Air Force

Soviet Navy

Achkasov, V.I. (ed.), *Krasnoznammennyi Baltiiskii flot v bitve za Leningrad 1941–1944 gg.* (Moscow: Nauka 1973).

Achkasov, V.I. (ed.), *Krasnoznammennyi Baltiiskii flot 1944–1945 gg.* (Moscow: Nauka 1975).

Collective authorship, *Kursami doblesti i slavy* (Moscow: Voenizdat 1975). Soviet MTB operations.

Dmitriev, V.I., *Atakuyut podvodniki* (Moscow: Voenizdat 1964).

Edlinskii, S.F., *Baltiiskii transportnyi flot v Velikoi Otechestvennoi voine 1941–1945 gg.* (Moscow: Mor. Transport 1957).

Kamalov, Kh.Kh., *Morskaya pekhota v boyakh za Rodinu* (Moscow: Voenizdat 1966). Naval infantry.

Kirin, I.D., *Chernomorskii Flot v bitve za Kavkaz* (Moscow: Voenizdat 1958).

Kozlov, I.A. and Shlomin, V.S., *Krasnoznamennyi Baltiiskii Flot v geroicheskoi oborone Leningrada* (Leningrad: Lenizdat 1976).

Kozlov, I.A. and Shlomin, V.S., *Krasnoznammenyi Severnyi flot* (Moscow: Voenizdat, 2nd edn 1977). Chapters 5–7 for World War II operations.

Loktionov, I.I., *Dunaiskaya Flotiliya v Velikoi Otechestvennoi voine, 1941–1945* (Moscow: Voenizdat 1962).

Mushnikov, A.N., *V boyakh za Vyborg i Petrozavodsk* (Moscow: Voenizdat 1957).

Shashkov, Z.A., *Rechniki v boyakh za Rodinu* (Moscow: Znanie 1975). River flotillas/ river transport, wartime role.

Solov'ev, A.G. (ed.), *V nebe—letchiki Baltiki* (Tallinn: Eesti Raamat 1974). Memoirs/ accounts, Baltic fleet naval air arm.

Tributs, V.F., *Podvodniki Baltiki atakuyut* (Leningrad: Lenizdat 1963).

Tributs, V.F., *Baltiitsy nastupayut* (Kaliningrad: Knizh. Izd. 1968). See also *Baltiitsy vstupayut v boi* (Kaliningrad, 1972), pp. 25–368, for World War II operations.

Vainer, B.A., *Severnyi Flot v Velikoi Otechestvennoi voine* (Moscow: Voenizdat 1974).

V'yunenko. N.P., *Chernomorskii flot v Velikoi Otechestvennoi voine* (Moscow: Voenizdat 1957). Black Sea Fleet.

V'yunenko, N.P. and Mordvinov, R.N., *Voennye flotilii v Velikoi Otechestvennoi voine* (Moscow: Voenizdat 1957). Flotilla operations.

Air Force

Collective authorship, *Sovetskie Voenno-vozdushnye sily v Velikoi Otechestvennoi voine 1941-1945* (Moscow: Voenizdat 1968). A most uninformative 'official history' of the Soviet Air Force.

Collective authorship, *16-ya Vozdushnaya* (Moscow: Voenizdat 1973). 16th Air Army, 1942-5).

Collective authorship, *17-ya Vozdushnaya Armiya v boyakh ot Stalilngrada do Veny* (Moscow: Voenizdat 1977). 17th Air Army combat record.

Fedorov, A.G., *Aviatsiya v bitve pod Moskvoi* (Moscow: Nauka 1971). An important military monograph.

Inozemtsev, I.G., *Pod krylom—Leningrad* (Moscow: Voenizdat 1978). WS/Leningrad Front and 13th Air Army.

Kozhevnikov, M.N., *Komandovanie i shtab VVS Sovetskoi Armii v Velikoi Otechestvennoi voine 1941-1945 gg.* (Moscow: Nauka 1977). An extremely important work on command/staff SAF.

Novikov, A.A., Air Chief Marshal, *V nebe Leningrada. Zapiski Komanduyushchego Aviatsiei* (Moscow: Nauka 1970).

Svetlishin, N.A., *Voiska PVO strany v Velikoi Otechestvennoi voine. Voprosy operativno-strategicheskovo primeneniya* (Moscow: Nauka 1979). An important technical monograph on Soviet air defences, using much archival material.

Timokhovich, I.V., *Operativnoe iskusstvo Sovetskikh VVS Velikoi Otechestvennoi voine* (Moscow: Voenizdat 1976). A major work on Soviet air operations, with much statistical data and operational analysis, sortie rates, missions, army-air co-operation.

7. Memoirs

(a) Personal memoirs

Antipenko, N.A., *Na glavnom napravlenii* (Moscow: Nauka, 2nd edn 1971). 'Rear services' command, operations at Front level.

Antonov, V.S., *Put' k Berlinu* (Moscow: Nauka 1975).

Babadzhanyan, A., *Dorogi pobedy* (Moscow: Mol. Gvard, 2nd edn 1975).

Biryuzov, S.S., *Surovye gody* (Moscow: Nauka 1966). See under *Voennye Memuary*.

Borshchev, S.N., *Ot Nevy do Elby* (Leningrad: Lenizdat, 2nd edn 1973).

Chuyanov, A., *Stalingradskii Dnevnik 1941-1943* (Volgograd: Volgogradskaya Pravda 1968).

Galitskii, K.N., *Gody surovykh ispytanii 1941-1944. Zapiski komandarma* (Moscow: Nauka 1973).

Getman, A.L., *Tanki idut na Berlin (1941-1945)* (Moscow: Nauka 1973).

Grechko, A.A., *Gody voiny 1941-1943* (Moscow: Voenizdat 1976).

Golikov, F.I., *V Moskovskoi bitve. Zapiski komandarma* (Moscow: Nauka 1967).

Kazar'yan, A.V., *Chetvert' veka na tankakh* (Yerevan: Aiastan 1972).

Koniev, I.S., *Zapiski komanduyushchevo frontom 1943-1944* (Moscow: Nauka 1972).

Lyudnikov, I.I., *Skovz' grozy* (Donetsk: Donbas 1973).

Malinovskii, R.Ya. (ed.), *Budapesht-Vena-Praga. Istoriko-memuarnyi trud* (Moscow: Nauka 1965).

Managarov, I.M., *S srazhenii za Kharkov* (Kharkov: Prapor, 2nd edn 1978).

Meretskov, K.A., *Na sluzhbe narodu*. Stranitsy vospominaniya (Moscow: Politizdat, 2nd edn 1970). Though not actually penned in its final literary form by Marshal Meretskov, this memoir has some useful information.

Morozov, I.K., *Ot Stalingrada do Pragi* (Volgograd: Nizh.-Volzh. Knizh. Izd. 1976). Memoirs, commander 422nd/81st Guards Rifle Division.

Moskalenko, K.S., *Na yugo-zapadnom napravlenii. Vospominaniya komandarma* (Moscow: Nauka, 2nd edn 1973), vols. 1–2. Important, beginning in 1941, 1942 Kharkov/ Stalingrad, Kursk, Carpathians and Czechoslovakia.

Paderin, I., *Na glavnom napravlenii. Zapiski ofitsera*. (Novosibirsk: Zap.-Sib. Knizh. Izd. 1970).

Pavlov, D.V., *Leningrad v blokade* (Moscow: Sovetskaya Rossiya 1969).

Peresypkin, I.T., *Svyaz serdets boevykh* (Donetsk: Donbas 1974). Commander, Soviet Signals Troops.

Pern, L. *V vikhre voennykh let*. Vospominaniya (Tallin: Eesti Raamat, 2nd edn 1976). Commander, Estonian Rifle Corps.

Pliev, I.A., *Pod gvardeiskim znamenem* (Ordzhonikidze: Ir 1976).

Popel, N.K., *Geroi Kurskoi bitvy* (Moscow: Prosveshchenie 1971). Popel served with the Military Council, 1st Guards Tank Army.

Pukhov, N.P., *Gody ispytanii* (Moscow: Voenizdat 1959). 13th Army commander.

Telegin, K.F., *Ne otdali Moskvy!* (Moscow: Sov. Rossiya, 2nd edn 1975).

Vasilevskii, A.M., *Delo vsei zhizni* (Moscow: Politizdat 1974; also 2nd edn 1975, with additional material on the General Staff).

Yeremenko, A.I., *Stalingrad. Zapiski komanduyushchevo frontom* (Moscow: Voenizdat 1961, map supplement). Not wholly reliable and also credited Khrushchev with 'thinking up' the Stalingrad counter-offensive.

Yeremenko, A.I., *V nachale voiny* (Moscow: Nauka 1964). Violently criticized by Soviet experts and the explanations offered discredited.

Yeremenko, A.I., *Gody vozmezdiya. 1943–1945* (Moscow: Nauka 1969).

Yeremenko, A.I., *Pomni voinu,* (Donetsk: Donbas 1971). Military career and wartime commands.

Zakharov, M.V. (ed.), *Final. Istoriko-memuarnyi ocherk o razgrome imperialisticheskoi Yaponii v 1945 gody* (Moscow: Nauka, 2nd edn 1969).

Zhukov, G.K., *Vospominaniya i razmyshleniya* (Moscow: Novosti 1970). See also 2-vol. revised and enlarged edition, same title (Novosti 1975).

(b) Voennye Memuary series

Several hundred volumes have now been published in this series, where quality tends to vary very considerably. Largely for this reason I have restricted this present list to substantive (and verifiable) accounts or to those making a specific contribution. Since all volumes have been published in Moscow by *Voenizdat*, it is only necessary to indicate the year of publication.

Agafonov, V.P., *Neman! Neman! Ya-Dunai!* (1967). Signals troops.

Azarov, I.I. *Osazhdennaya Odessa* (2nd edn 1966).

Bagramyan, I.Kh., *Tak nachinalas' voina* (1971). (Note: There is a further edition but published in Kiev, by Dnipro, in 1975.) And, same author, *Tak shli my k pobede* (1977). Two outstandingly important accounts by Marshal Bagramyan, dealing with 1941/SW Front operations and Soviet operations 1943–5, respectively.

Basistyi, N.E., *More i bereg* (1970). Fleet commander, Black Sea.

Batov, P.I., *V pokhodakh i boyakh* (1962, 2nd edn 1966).

Belov, P.A., *Za nami Moskva* (1963). Distinguished cavalry commander, much important information on Soviet operations 1941–2.

Belyavskii, V.A., *Strely skrestilis' na Shpree* (1973).

Biryuzov, S.S., *Kogda gremeli pushki* (1962) and *Sovetskii Soldat na Balkanakh* (1963). These volumes are also combined in a single work, *Surovye gody* (Moscow: Nauka 1966).

Blazhei, A.K., *V armeiskom shtabe* (1967).

Boldin, I.V., *Stranitsy zhizni* (1961). A frank and informative account by 50th Army commander, important for 1941.

Bychevskii, B.V., *Gorod-Front* (1963). Defence of Leningrad.

Chuikov, V.I., *Nachalo puti* (1959). Almost a classic in its own right; Chuikov's account of the defence of Stalingrad is undoubtedly the best version.

Degtyarev, G.E., *Taran i shchit* (1966).

Dragunskii, D.A., *Gody v brone* (1973).

Efimov, A.N., *Nad polem boya* (1976). Air Marshal Efimov, wartime fighter pilot.

Egorov, A.V., *S veroi v pobedu* (1974).

Eroshenko, V.N., *Lider 'Tashkent'* (1966). Soviet flotilla leader *Tashkent*, built in Italy and 'mis-employed as a fast transport' (see J. Meister, *Soviet Warships . . . ,* p. 49).

Federov, V.G., *V poiskakh oruzhiya* (1964).

Fedyuninskii, I.I., *Podnyatye po trevoge* (1964). Shock Army commander.

Galkin, F.I., *Tanki vozvrashchayutsya v boi* (1964). Technical support/tank operations.

Gladkov, V.F., *Desant na El'tigen* (1972).

Golovko, A.G., *Vmeste s flotom* (1960).

Golushko, I.M., *Tanki ozhivali vnov'* (1974). Armament production, Leningrad.

Gorbatov, A.V., *Gody i voiny* (1965). An illuminating and even dispirited account by a senior officer, erstwhile victim of the purges and 'rehabilitated'.

Gorchakov, P.A., *Vremya trevog i pobed* (1977). Party-political work.

Grushevoi, K.S., *Togda, v sorok pervom . . .* (1974).

Gulyaeb, V.T., *Chelovek v brone* (1964). Most informative on armoured operations, armoured support, political work.

Kabanov, P.A., *Stal'nye peregony* (1973). Railway troops.

Kalinin, P.Z., *Partizanskaya Respublika* (1964). An important and reputable account of partisan operations.

Katukov, M.E., *Na ostrie glavnovo udara* (1974, 2nd edn 1976). Marshal Katukov on his command, 1st Guards Tank Army.

Kazakov, M.I., *Nad kartoi bylykh srazhenii* (1965). An important and perceptive account, with much detail on Soviet operational planning and operations 1942–3.

Kazakov, V.I., *Na perelome* (1962). Artillery commander, operations Moscow/Stalingrad.

Kharchenko, V.K., . . . *Spetsial'novo Naznacheniya* (1973).

Khetagurov, G.I., *Ispolnenie dolga* (1977).

Khlebnikov, H.M., *Pod grokhot soten batarei* (1974).

Khudalov, Kh.A., *U kromki kontinenta* (1974).

Kilyshkin, I.A., *V glubinakh polyarnykh morei* (1964). Submarine operations.

Kondratev, Z.I., *Dorogi voiny* (1968). Road/motor transportation.

Koniev, I.S., *Sorok pyatyi* (2nd edn 1970). Marshal Koniev, Berlin-Prague 1945.

Koshevoi, P.K., *V gody voennye* (1978). Marshal Koshevoi, Leningrad/Stalingrad operations.

Kozhevnikov, A.L., *Startuet muzhestvo* (1966).

Krainyukov, K.V., *Ot Dnepra do Visly* (1971) and *Oruzhie osobovo roda* (1977). Member of military soviet, 1st Ukrainian Front.

Krasovskii, S.A., *Zhizn v aviatsii* (2nd edn 1968). SAF command/operations.

Krylov, A.I., *Po prikazu Stavki* (1977).

Krylov, N.I., *Ne pomerknet nikogda* (1969).

Kurochkin, P.M., *Pozyvnye fronta* (1969). Signals troops.

Kuznetsov, N.G., *Nakanune* (1966). Pre-June 1941 situation, pp. 229–343: German attack.

Kuznetsov, P.G., *Dni boevye* (1964).

Lashchenko, P.N., *Iz boya—v boi* (1972).

Lebedenko, P.P., *V izluchine Dona* (1965). 1st Tank Army operations, July–August 1942.

Lobachev, A.A., *Trudnymi dorogami* (1960). One of the best of *VM*, especially for 1941, defence of Moscow.

Lobanov, M.M., *My—voennye inzhenery* (1977). An original and very significant first-hand account of Soviet radar development.

Lyudnikov, I.I., *Doroga dlinoyu v zhizn'* (1969). Army commander, assault/breakthrough operations from Stalingrad to Königsberg.

Nadysev, G.S., *Na sluzhbe shtabnoi* (2nd edn 1976). Role of staff officer, staff work.

Neustroyev, S.A., *Put' k Reikhstagu* (1961). Participant, storming of *Reichstag*.

Panteleev, Yu.A., *Morskoi Front* (1965). Baltic fleet, command and operations.

Panteleev, Yu.A., *Polveka na flote* (1974). Chief of Staff, Baltic Fleet.

Pokryshkin, A.I., *Nebo voiny* (1970).

Popel, N.K., *V tyazhkuyu poru* (1959) and *Tanki povernuli na zapad* (1960). Much criticized in the Soviet press, but valuable for insights into Soviet tank operations, 1943 (at Kursk) and the spring of 1944.

Poplavskii, S.G., *Tovarishchi v bor'be* (2nd edn 1974). Commander of 1st Polish Army.

Rokossovskii, K.K., *Soldatskii dolg* (1972).

Rudenko, S.I., *Krylya pobedy* (1976). Air Marshal Rudenko, Soviet air operations.

Saburov, A.N., *Sily neischislimye* (1967) and *Otvoevannaya vesna* (2 vols, 1968). Partisan operations/planning/command.

Sandalov, L.M., *Trudnye rubezhi* (1965). 2nd Baltic Front operations, 1944.

Sandalov, L.M., *Perezhitoe* (1966). Very important and informative account, Red Army 1936–June 1941, also German attack.

Sevastyanov, P.V., *Neman-Volga-Dunai* (1961). Useful information on the German attack, 1941.

Shatilov, V.M., *Znamya nad Reikhstagom* (2nd edn 1970).

Shchedrin, G.I., *Na bortu 'S-56'* (1963). Submarine operations.

Shepelev, A.L., *V nebe i na zemle* (1974). Technical support for Soviet Air Force.

Shtemenko, S.M., *Generalnyi shtab v gody voiny*, vol. 1 (1st edn 1968, 2nd edn 1975) and vol. 2 (1973). The Soviet General Staff at war; a useful but much overrated account by General Shtemenko.

Solov'ev, V.K., *Pod Naro-Fominskom* (1960).

Starinov, I.G., *Miny zhdut svoevo chasa* (1964). Red Army combat engineers/military engineering.

Strel'bitskii, I.S., *Shturm* (1962).

Stuchenko, A.T., *Zavidnaya nasha sud'ba* (1964).

Travkin, I.V., *Vsem smertyam nazlo* (1964).

Tyulenev, I.V., *Cherez tri Voiny* (1960).

U Chernomorskikh tverdyn'. Otdel'naya Primorskaya Armiya v oborone Odessy i Sevastopolya. Vospominaniya (1967). Defence of Odessa/Sevastopol: Independent Coastal Army operations.

Vershigora, P.P., *Reid na San i Visly* (1960). Deep partisan/Red Army penetration raiding.

Vershinin, K.A., *Chetvertaya vozdushnaya* (1975). Air Chief Marshal Vershinin on 4th Air Army operations.

Voronov, N.N., *Na sluzhbe voennoi* (1963). Arguably the most important book in this series and certainly a major source in view of Chief Artillery Marshal Voronov's command responsibilities—and capabilities.

Vorozheikin, A.V., *Nad Kurskoi dugoi* (1964). Air operations, Kursk 1943.

Yakubovskii, I.I., *Zemlya v ogne* (1975). Combined archival/memoir material used by Marshal Yakubovskii: tank operations.

Zhuravlev, D.A., *Ognevoi shchit Moskvy* (1972). AA defence of Moscow.

(c) Collective memoirs

Berbinskii, M.V. *et al.* (eds.), *God 1941. Yugo-zapadnyi front. Vospominaniya. Ocherki. Dokumenty* (Lvov: Kamenyar, 2nd edn 1975).

Bitva za Stalingrad (Volgograd: Nizh.-Volzh. Knizh. Izd.-vo. 1969).

Boitsov, S.M. and Borshchev, S.N. (eds.), *Operatsiya 'Iskra'* (Leningrad: Lenizdat 1973). Breaking the siege of Leningrad, January 1943.

Danishevskii, I.M. (ed.), *Proval operatsii 'Tsitadel'* (Moscow: Politizdat 1967).

Dorogoi Bor'by i Slavy (Moscow: Gospolitizdat 1961).

Druzhinin, B.V., *Dvesti ognennykh dnei* (Moscow: Voenizdat 1968). Stalingrad.

Gody frontovye (Moscow: DOSAAF 1964).

Grekov, V.A. *et al.* (eds.), *Bug v ogne* (Minsk: Belarus, 3rd edn 1977).

Grishchinskii, K.K., (ed.), *Gangut 1941. Sbornik vospominanii . . .* (Leningrad: Lenizdat 1974). Hangö, 1941.

Lokshin, V.S. (ed.), *V bol'shom nastuplenii. Vospominaniya, ocherkii . . .* (Moscow: Voenizdat 1964). Liberation of Ukraine, 1943–4.

Malan'in, K.A. (ed.), *Polki idut na zapad* (Moscow: Voenizdat 1964). Reminiscences: Soviet offensive, Belorussia 1944.

Moskalenko, K.S. (ed.), *Bitva na Kurskoi duge* (Moscow: Nauka 1975).

Parol—'Pobeda' (Leningrad: Lenizdat 1969). Defence of Leningrad, de-blockading operation, offensive operations.

Parotkin, I.V. (ed.), *Kurskaya bitva* (Moscow: Nauka 1970).

Radi zhizni na Zemle. Ocherki o geroizme nashikh zemlyakov v gody Otechestvennoi voiny (Voronezh: Tsentral'no-Chernozemnoe Kh. Izd. 1970).

Samsonov, A.M. (ed.), *9 Maya 1945 goda* (Moscow: Nauka 1970).

Samsonov, A.M. (ed.), *Osvobozhdenie Belorussii 1944* (Moscow: Nauka 1974). An important collection.

Samsonov, A.M. (ed.), *Stalingradskaya epopeya* (Moscow: Nauka 1968). Senior commanders' accounts, Stalingrad operation.

Samsonov, A.M. (ed.), *Osvobozhdenie Vengrii ot fashizma* (Moscow: Nauka 1965).

Shturm Berlina. Vospominaniya, pisma, dnevnik uchastnikov . . . (Moscow: Voenizdat 1948).

Stalingrad: Uroki istorii. Svidetel'stvyut uchastniki bitvy na Volge (Moscow: Progress 1976).

Tikhvin, god 1941–i (Leningrad: Lenizdat 1974).

Verbinskii, M.V. and Samarin, B.V. (eds.), *Brodovskii kotel'. Vospominaniya, ocherki* . . . (Lvov: Kamenyar 1974). Liberation of the Ukraine.

Za Moskvu, za frontu (Moscow: Mosk. rabochii 1964). Defence of Moscow.

Zhunin, S.G. (ed.), *Ot Dnepra do Buga.* Memuary (Minsk: Belarus 1974).

8. The war economy, 'rear services'

Bazhanova, E.V. (ed.), *Narodnoe khozyaistvo SSSR v gody Velikoi Otechestvennoi voiny (iyun 1941–mai 1945 gg.).* Bibliograficheskii ukazatel'. (Moscow: Nauka 1971). A bibliographical guide to publications on the Soviet economy 1941–5, material published 1941–68. Index of authors, geographical place names. 3,200 copies printed. Invaluable reference guide.

Arutyunyan, Yu.V., *Sovetskoe krest'yanstvo v gody Velikoi Otechestvennoi voiny* (Moscow: Nauka 1963, 2nd edn 1970).

Budanov, F. and Dubrovin, N. *Tyl pravovo flanga* (Murmansk, Mur. Knizh. Izd. 1976). Rear services/logistics, Northern Fleet.

Chadaev, Ya.E., *Ekonomika SSSR v period Velikoi Otechestvennoi voiny (1941–1945)* (Moscow: Voenizdat 1965).

Chernyavskii, U.G., *Voina i prodovol'stvie* (Moscow: Nauka 1964). Soviet urban food supply/rationing, 1941–5).

Dokuchaev, G.A., *Sibirskii tyl v Velikoi Otechestvennoi voine* (Novosibirsk: Nauka 1968). Basic work on the Siberian 'rear'.

Eshelony idut na vostok. Sbornik statei i vospominaniya (Moscow: Nauka 1966). Industrial evacuation, 1941–2.

Gladkov, I.A. (ed.), *Sovetskaya ekonomika v period Velikoi Otechestvennoi voiny 1941–1945* (Moscow: Nauka 1970).

Ivanov, F.I., *Reaktivnye psikhozy v voennoe vremya* (Leningrad: Meditsina 1970). Nervous/mental disorders in wartime.

Kotlyar, E.S., *Gosudarstvennye trudovye rezervy SSSR v gody Velikoi Otechestvennoi voiny* (Moscow: Vysh. Shkola 1975). On technical education/skilled labour.

Kozybaev, M., *Kazakhstan-arsenal fronta* (Alma-Ata: Kazakhstan 1970).

Kravchenko, G.S., *Voennaya ekonomika SSSR 1941–1945* (Moscow: Voenizdat 1963).

Kumanev, G.A., *Sovetskie zheleznodorozhniki v gody Velikoi Otechestvennoi Voiny (1941–1945)* (Moscow: Nauka 1963).

Kumanev, G.A., *Na sluzhbe fronta i tyla* (Moscow: Nauka 1976). Soviet railways, 1938–45.

Kurkotkin, S.K., *Tyl Sovetskikh vooruzhennykh sil v Velikoi Otechestvennoi voine 1941–1945 gg.* (Moscow: Voenizdat 1977). A major and comprehensive study of Soviet 'Rear Services'/logistics.

Kuvshinskii, D.D. and Georgievskii, A.S., *Ocherkii istorii Sovetskoi voennoi meditsiny* (Leningrad: Meditsina 1968).

Kuzmin, M.K., *Mediki-Geroi Sovetskovo Soyuza* (Moscow: Meditsina 1970). Gallantry awards, HSU, medical personnel.

Levshin, B.V., *Akademiya Nauk SSSR v gody Velikoi Otechestvennoi voiny* (Moscow: Nauka 1966).

Malin, V.N. and Korobov, A.V. (eds.), *Direktivy KPSS i Sovetskovo pravitel'stva po khozyaistvennym voprosam*. Sbornik dokumentov (Moscow: Gospolitizdat 1957).

Pospelov, N.P. (ed.), *Sovetskii tyl v Velikoi Otechestvennoi voine* (Moscow: Mysl 1974), 2 vols. This collection of essays and studies is most useful, covering a wide variety of topics; see also vol. 1, pp. 223–94, for a very substantial bibliography.

Shigalin, G.I., *Narodnoe khozyaistvo SSSR v period Velikoi Otechestvennoi voiny* (Moscow: Izd. Sots.-Ekon. Lit. 1960).

Smirnov, V.I., *Podvig Sovetskovo krest'yanstva* (Moscow: Mosk. rabochii 1976). Kalinin *oblast:* peasantry.

Sovetskie profsoyuzy v Velikoi Otechestvennoi voine 1941–1945 (Moscow: Profizdat 1975). Trade-union organization in war.

Sovetskii Tyl v Velikoi Otechestvennoi voine (Moscow: Mysl 1974). Vol. 1: *Obshchie Problemy;* vol. 2: *Trudovoi Podvig Naroda.*

Ugryumov, B.L., *Zapiski infektsionista* (Moscow: Meditsina 1973).

V groznye gody. Trudy nauchnoi konferentsii 'Sibiryaki-frontu' (Omsk: Pedagog. Institut 1973).

Vishnevskii, A.A., *Dnevnik khirurga. Velikaya Otechestvennaya voina 1941–1945 gg.* (Moscow: Meditsina, 2nd edn 1970). Wartime diary of Col.-Gen. (Medical Services) A.A. Vishnevskii.

Volkov, B.N. (ed.) *et al., Sibir' v Velikoi Otechestvennoi voine* (Novosibirsk: Nauka 1977). Conference papers on Siberia at war, Party organization, industrial mobilization, Siberian formations with Red Army.

Voznesenskii, N.A., *Voennaya ekonomika SSSR v period Velikoi Otechestvennoi voiny* (Moscow: Gospolitizdat 1947). One of the earliest works on the Soviet war economy by a leading wartime economic planner—subsequently shot by Stalin.

Zelenin, I.E., *Sovkhozy SSSR (1941–1950)* (Moscow: Nauka 1969).

Soviet Nuclear Development

Astashenkov, P.T., *Akademik I.V. Kurchatov* (Moscow: Voenizdat 1971).

9. Republics, regions and cities

Akulov, M.R. *et al., Podvig zemli bogatyrskoi* (Moscow: Mysl 1970). Siberia at war, 1941–5.

Aleshchenko, N.M. *et al., Moskovskoe opolchenie* (Moscow: Voenizdat 1969). Moscow, militia.

Collective editorship, *Azerbaidzhanskaya SSSR v period Velikoi Otechestvennoi voiny (1941–1945 gg).* Sbornik dokumentov i materialov (Baku: Azerb. Goz. Izd. 1976 (vol. 1) and 1977 (vol. 2)).

Belan, P.S., *Kazakhstantsy v boyakh za Leningrad* (Alma-Ata: Nauka 1973).

Belyaev, S. and Kuznetsov, P., *Narodnoe opolchenie Leningrada* (Leningrad: Lenizdat 1959). Leningrad militia.

Buryatiya v gody Velikoi Otechestvennoi voiny 1941–1945 gg. Sbornik Dokumentov (Ulan-Ude: Buryatskow Kh. Izd. 1975).

Chuvashskaya ASSR v Period Velikoi Otechestvennoi voiny (Iyun' 1941–1945 gg.) Sbornik Dokumentov i Materialov (Cheboksary: Chuvashskoe Kh. Idz. 1975).

Dokycharov, G.A., *Rabochii klass Sibiri i Dal'nevo Vostoka v gody Velikoi Otechestvennoi voiny* (Moscow: Nauka 1973). Very important monograph on Siberia/FE.

Drizul, A.A. *et al., Bor'ba Latyshskovo naroda v gody Velikoi Otechestvennoi voiny 1941–1945* (Riga: Zinatne 1970).

Collective editorship, *Estonskii narod v Velikoi Otechestvennoi voine Sovetskovo Soyuza 1941–1945* (Tallin: Eesti Raamat 1973), 2 vols.

Gor'kovchane v Velikoi Otechestvennoi Voine, 1941–1945 (Gorkii: Voenizdat 1970).

Kaimarazov, G.Sh. *et al., Dagestan v gody Velikoi Otechestvennoi voiny 1941–1945 gg.* (Makhachkala: Dagenstanskow Gos. Kh. Izd. 1963).

Kamalov, Kh.Kh. *et al.* (eds.), *900 geroicheskikh dnei* (Moscow/Leningrad: Nauka 1966).

Karasev, A.V., *Leningradtsy v gody blokady: 1941–1943* (Moscow: Akad. Nauk 1959). One of the earliest major studies of Leningrad but still among the best.

Kareliya v gody Velikoi Otechestvennoi voiny 1941–1945. Dokumenty i Materialy (Petrozavolsk: Kareliya 1975).

Kazakhstan v period Velikoi Otechestvennoi voiny Sovetskovo Soyuza 1941–1945. Sbornik dokumentov i materialov (Alma-Ata: Nauka 1974 (vol. 1) and 1967 (vol. 2)).

Kerch geroicheskaya. Vospominaniya, ocherki, dokumenty (Simferopol: Tavriya 1974).

Khersonskaya Oblast' v gody Velikoi Otechestvennoi voiny (1941–1945 gg.) Sbornik dokumentov i materialov (Odessa: Mayak 1968).

Kolesnik, A.D., *Narodnoe opolchenie gorodov-geroev* (Moscow: Nauka 1974). Militia formations—Leningrad, Moscow, Kiev, Odessa, Sevastopol, Stalingrad.

Kondaurov, I.A., *Ratnyi podvig kommunistov Prikam'ya (1941–1945)* (Perm: Knizh. Izd. 1970). Perm *oblast*, military and economic contributions to war effort.

Koval'chuk, V.M. *Leningrad i Bol'shaya Zemlya* (Leningrad: Nauka 1975). A major and definitive work on the Ladoga 'ice-road', Leningrad blockade 1941–3.

Krym v period Velikoi Otechestvennoi voiny 1941–1945. Sbornik dokumentov . . . (Simferopol: Tavriya 1973).

Kuznetsov, I.I., *Vostochnaya Sibir' v gody Velikoi Otechestvennoi voiny 1941–1945* (Irkutsk: Vostochno-Sibirskoe Kh. Idz. 1974).

Mariiskaya ASSR v gody Velikoi Otechestvennoi voiny. Sbornik i Materialov (Ioshkar-Ola: Mariiskoe Kh. Idz. 1967).

Moldavskaya SSSR v Velikoi Otechestvennoi voine Sovetskogo Soyuza 1941–1945. Vol. 1: *Na Frontakh Voiny i v Sovetskom Tylu* (Kishinev: Shtiintsa 1975); vol. 2: *V Tylu Vraga* (1976).

Narodnoe opolchenie Moskvy (Moscow: Inst. Ist. Partii MK i MGK PKSS 1961). Militia formations, Moscow.

Nikolaevshchina v gody Velikoi Otechestvennoi voiny 1941–1945 gg. Dokumenty i materialy (Odessa: Mayak 1964).

Ocherki istorii Leningrada, vol. 5: *Period Velikoi Otechestvennoi voiny . . .* (Leningrad: Nauka 1967).

Shepelev, S.P. (ed.), *Kostroma-frontu* (Yaroslavl: Verkh.-Volzh. Khn. Izdvo. 1975).

Shumilov, N.D., *V Dni blokady* (Moscow: Mysl, 2nd edn 1977).

Sobolov, T.L., *Uchenye Leningrada v gody Velikoi Otechestvennoi voiny* (Moscow/Leningrad: Nauka 1966). Leningrad scientists, wartime work and role.

Sovetskaya Armeniya v gody Velikoi Otechestvennoi voiny (1941–1945). Sbornik Dokumentov i Materialov (Erevan: Nauka 1975).

Stavropol'e v Velikoi Otechestvennoi voine 1941–1945 gg. Sbornik dokumentov . . . (Stavropol: Kn. Izd.-vo. 1962).

Tskitishvili, K., *Na Frontakh Velikoi Otechestvennoi* (Tbilisi: Sabcgota Sakartvelo 1975).

Tskitishvili, K.V., *Zakavkaz'e v gody Velikoi Otechestvennoi voiny 1941–1945 gg.* (Tbilisi: Izd. Tsk KP Gruzii 1969).

Ukrainskaya SSSR v Velikoi Otechestvennoi voine Sovetskovo Soyuza 1941–1945 gg. (Kiev: Izd. Pol. Lit. Ukr. 1975), 3 vols.

Ul'yanovskaya Oblast' v gody Velikoi Otechestvennoi voiny (1941–1945). Dokumenty i Materialy (Saratov: Privolzhskoe Kh. Izd. 1974).

V gody Velikoi Otechestvennoi. Vospominaniya (Irkutsk: Vostochno-Sibirskoe Kh. Izd. 1975).

Volkov, B.N. (ed.), *Sibir' v Velikoi Otechestvennoi voine.* (Novosibirsk: Nauka 1977). Conference papers: Siberia at war.

Zakharov, M.V. (ed.), *Oborona Leningrada 1941–1944* (Leningrad: Nauka 1968).

10. Partisan warfare, Intelligence operations, Resistance movements

Andrianov, V.N. *et al., Voina v tylu vraga* (Moscow: Politizdat, 1st edn 1974). The beginnings of an 'official history' of the partisan movement.

Asmolov, A.N., *Front v tylu Vermakhta* (Moscow: Politizdat 1977). Partisan operations, NW Russia, SW Ukraine.

Bondarenko, V.P. and Reznova, P.I. (eds.), *Antifashistskoe dvizhenie soprotivleniya v stranakh Evropy v gody vtoroi mirovoi voiny* (Moscow: Izd. Sots-Ekon. Lit. 1962).

Brodskii, E.A., *Vo imya pobedy nad Fashizmom. Antifashistskaya bor'ba Sovetskikh lyudei v Gitlerovskoi Germanii (1941–1945)* (Moscow: Nauka 1970).

Buchkov, L.N., *Partizanskoe dvizhenie v gody Velikoi Otechestvennoi voiny 1941–1945* (Moscow: Mysl 1965).

Dzhuraev, T.D., *Uzbekistantsyi—uchastniki partizanskoi voiny* (Tashkent: Uzbekistan Izd. 1975).

812   Bibliography

Egorov, V., *Zagovor protiv Evriki* (Moscow: Sov. Ross. 1968). Frustration of the German plot against Teheran conference, 1943.

Front bez linii fronta (Moscow: Novosti 1965) and *Front bez linii fronta* (Moscow: Mosk. rabochii 1970). Two works with the same title but differing substantially in scope; both treat Soviet wartime intelligence operations.

Gridnev, V.M., *Bor'ba krestyanstva okkupirovannykh oblastei RSFSR protiv nemetsko-fashistskoi okkupatsionnoi politiki 1941–1944* (Moscow: Nauka 1976).

Grigorovich, D. *et al., Kommunisticheskoe podpol'e na Ukraine v gody Velikoi Otechestvennoi voiny* (Kiev: Politizdat, Ukr. 1976).

Kalinin, P., *Partizanskaya respublika* (Minsk: Belarus 1968).

Iz istorii partizanskovo dvizheniya v Belorussii (1941–1944 gg.) Sbornik vospominanii (Minsk: Gosizdat 1961).

Klyatskin, S.M. (ed.), *V tylu vraga.* Listovki partiinykh organizatsii i partizan . . . (Moscow: Gospolitizdat 1962). Reprints, leaflets, partisan movement.

Kolesnikov, M., *Takim byl Rikhard Zorge* (Moscow: Voenizdat 1965).

Kupriyanov, G.N., *Za liniei Karel'skovo fronta* (Petrozavodsk: Kareliya 1975).

Logunova, T.A., *Partiinoe podpol'e i partizanskoe dvizhenie v tsentral'nykh oblastyakh RSFSR (1941–1943)* (Moscow: Moscow University 1973). Scholarly dissertation using archives.

Makarov, N., *Nepokorennaya zemlya Rossiiskaya* (Moscow: Politizdat 1976). History of partisan movement.

Nedorezov, A.I., *Natsional'no-osnoboditel'noe dvizhenie Chekhoslovakii. 1938–1945* (Moscow: Sots.-Ekon. Lit. 1961).

Nepokorennaya zemlya Pskovskaya 1941–1944. Dokumenty i materialy (Pskov: Pskov Pravda 1964). Materials from the Pskov *oblast* Party archive.

O chem ne govorilos v svodkakh (Moscow: Voenizdat 1962). Soviet PWs in European resistance movements.

Partiya vo glave narodnoi bor'by v Tyle Vraga 1941–1944 (Moscow: Mysl 1976).

Partizanyi Bryanshchiny. Sbornik dok. i mat. (Bryanskii: Izd. Bryanskii Rabochii 1962).

Petrov, Yu.P., *Partizanskoe dvizhenie v Leningradskoi oblasti 1941–1944* (Leningrad: Lenizdat 1973).

Petrova, Z.A. *et al.* (eds.), *Partizany Bryanshchiny* (Ula: Priokskoe Khn.-Izd. 1970).

Podpol'nye Komsomol'skie organy Belorussii v gody Velikoi Otechestvennoi voiny (1941–1944) (Minsk: Belarus 1976).

Podpol'nye Partiinye organy Kompartii Belorussii v gody Velikoi Otechestvennoi voiny (1941–1944) (Minsk: Belarus 1975).

Shmelev, I.I., *Soldaty nevidimykh srazhenii* (Moscow: Voenizdat 1968). Soviet intelligence World War II: see pp. 131–269.

Slinko, I.I., *Pidpilya i partizanskii rakh na Ukraini* (Kiev: Naukova Dumka 1970). (In Ukrainian.)

Sovetskie partizany (Moscow: Gospolitizdat, 2nd edn 1963).

Tskitishvili, K., *Zakavkaz'e v partizanskoi voine 1941–1945 gg.* (Tbilisi: Izd. Isk KP Gruzii 1973).

Vsenarodnoe Partizanskoe dvizhenie v Belorussiya v gody Velikoi Otechestvennoi voiny (Iyun' 1941–iyul' 1944). Dokumenty i Materialy v trekh tomakh (Minsk: Belarus, vol. 1 1967, vol. 2 1973, vol. 3 1982).

Zalesskii, A.I., *V partizanskikh krayakh i zonakh* (Moscow: Sots-Ekon. Lit. 1962).

11. Diplomatic documents/diplomatic history

Perepiska predsedatelya Soveta ministrov SSSR vo vremya Velikoi Otechestvennoi voiny 1941–1945 gg. (Moscow: Gospolitizdat 1958), vols. 1 and 2. See also 2nd edn (Moscow: Politizdat 1976), vols. 1 and 2. For one-volume English translation, see *Stalin's Correspondence with Churchill, Attlee, Roosevelt and Truman 1941–45* (London: Lawrence and Wishart 1958).

Conference documents

(1) See 6-volume series, *Sovetskii Soyuz na mezhdunarodnykh konferentsiyakh perioda Velikoi Otechestvennoi voiny 1941–1945 gg.* (Moscow: Politizdat 1978–80). (Collective editorship: Chief Editor, A.A. Gromyko), publication under the auspices of the Soviet Ministry of Foreign Affairs. Vol. I, Foreign Ministers' conference, Moscow, 19–30 October 1943 (1978); Vol. II Teheran conference, 28 November–1 December 1943 (1978); Vol. III Dumbarton Oaks conference, 21 August–28 September 1944 (1978); Vol. IV Crimea (Yalta) conference, 4–11 February 1945 (1979); Vol. V United Nations conference, San Francisco, 25 April–26 June 1945 (1980); Vol. VI Berlin (Potsdam) conference, 17 July–2 August 1945 (In two parts: published 1980).

Tegeran-Yalta-Potsdam. Sbornik dokumentov (Moscow: Mezh. Otnosh. 1967). Soviet records, Teheran-Yalta.

'Tegeranskaya konferentsiya rukovoditelei trekh velikikh derzhav (1943 g.)', *Mezhdunarodnaya zhizn'*, 1961(7), pp. 176–90 and (8), pp. 144–58. Soviet record, Teheran conference.

'Krymskaya i Potsdamskaya konferentsii trekh rukovoditelei trekh velikikh derzhav', *Mezhdunarodnaya zhizn'*, 1965(6), pp. 142–60; (7), pp. 153–60; (8), pp. 153–60; (9), pp. 185–92; (10), pp. 151–60; (12), pp. 139–51; 1966(1), pp. 153–60; (3), pp. 150–60; (5), pp. 152–60; (6), pp. 155–60; (7), pp. 140–57; (8), pp. 154–60; (9), pp. 177–92. Soviet record, Yalta conference.

Sovetsko-frantsuzskie otnosheniya vo vremya Velikoi Otechestvennoi voiny 1941–1945 gg. Dokumenty i Materialy (Moscow: Gospolitizdat 1959).

SSSR v bor'be za mir nakanune Vtoroi Mirovoi voiny (Sentyabr 1938–Avgust 1939) (Moscow: Politizdat 1971).

SSSR v bor'be protiv Fashistskoi agressii 1933–1945 (Moscow: Nauka 1976).

Berezhkov, V., *S diplomaticheskoi missiei v Berlin 1940–1941* (Moscow: Novosti 1966).

Israelyan, V.L., *Diplomaticheskaya istoriya Velikoi Otechestvennoi Voiny, 1941–1945* (Moscow: IMO 1959).

Israelyan, V.L., *Antigitlerovskaya Koalitsiya* (Diplomatichestoe Sotrudinchestvo SSSR, SSHA i Anglii v gody Vtoroi Mirovoi voiny) (Moscow: IMO 1964).

Israelyan, V.L. and Kutakov, L.N., *Diplomatiya Agressorov* (Moscow: Nauka 1967).

Koval, V.S., *SSHA vo vtoroi mirovoi voine: nekotorye problemy vneshnei politiki* (Kiev: Naukova Dumka 1976). US foreign policy, World War II.

Kundyuba, I.D., *Sovetsko-polskie otnosheniya (1939–1945 gg.),* (Kiev: Kiev University 1963).

Kutakov, L.N., *Istoriya Sovetsko-Yaponskikh diplomaticheskikh otnoshenii*, (Moscow: Izd. IMO 1962).

Maiskii, I.M., *Vospominaniya Sovetskovo posla* (Moscow: Nauka 1964), 2 vols.

Nekrich, A.M., *Vneshnyaya politika Anglii v gody Vtoroi Mirovoi voine* (Moscow: Akad. Nauk 1963).

Noskov, A.M., *Skandinavskii platsdarm vo Vtoroi Mirovoi voine* (Moscow: Nauka 1977).

Trukhanovskii, V.G., *Uinston Cherchill'* (Moscow: Mysl 1968). 'Political biography' of Winston Churchill.

12. The USSR, the Allies and the Enemy

Collective authors, *Protiv falsifikatsii istorii* (Moscow: Sots-Ekon. Lit. 1959).

Dashichev, V.I., *Bankrotstvo Strategii Germanskovo Fashizma*, Istoricheskie Ocherki, Dokumenty i Materialy. Vol. 1: *Podgotovka i razvertyvanie natsistskoi Agressii v Evrope 1933–1941* (Moscow: Nauka 1973); vol. 2: *Agressiya Protiv SSSR. Padenie 'Tret'ei Imperii' 1941–1945 gg.*

Dashichev, V.I. (ed.), *Sovershenno Sekretno! Tol'ko dlya komandovaniya!*, Strategiya fashistskoi Germanii v voine protiv SSSR (Moscow: Nauka 1967).

Deborin, G.A. and Telpukhovskii, B.S., *Itogi i uroki Velikoi Otechestvennoi voiny* (Moscow: Mysl, 2nd edn 1975).

Derevyanko, P.M. and Gurov, A.A., *Protiv falsifikatorov istorii Vtoroi Mirovoi voiny* (Moscow: Voenizdat 1959).

Grechko, A.A. (ed.), *Osvoboditel'naya missiya Sovetskikh vooruzhennykh sil vo Vtoroi Mirovoi voine* (Moscow: Politizdat 1971).

Kir'yakidis, G.D., *Gretsiya v vtoroi mirovoi voine* (Moscow: Nauka 1967). Greece, World War II.

Klyuev, S.V., *Mify i Pravda*. Kritika burzhuaznykh izmyshlenii o prichinakh ekonomicheskoi pobedy SSSR v Velikoi Otechestvennoi voine. (Leningrad: Lenizdat 1969).

Kulish, V.M., *Istoriya vtorovo fronta* (Moscow: Nauka 1971). Survey of the 'Second Front', political and military aspects.

Kulish, V.M., *Vtoroi front* (Moscow: Voenizdat 1960). Map supplement.

Kulish, V.M., *Raskrytaya taina*. Predystoriya vtorovo fronta v Evrope (Moscow: Nauka 1965).

Nekrich, A.M., *Protiv falsifikatsii istorii Vtoroi Mirovoi voiny* (Moscow: Nauka 1964).

Nekrich, A.M., *1941 22 iyunya* (Moscow: Nauka 1965).

Proektor, D.M., *Agressiya i Katastrofa*. Vysshee voennoe rukovodstvo fashistskoi Germanii vo vtoroi mirovoi voine 1939–1945 (Moscow: Nauka 1968).

Reutov, G.N., *Pravda i vymysel o Vtoroi Mirovoi voine* (Moscow: Mezh. otnosheniya, 2nd edn 1970).

Sapozhnikov, V.G., *Kitaiskii front vo Vtoroi Mirovoi voine* (Moscow: Nauka 1971).

Sekistov, V.A., *Voina i politika* (Moscow: Voenizdat 1970). Operations in Western Europe/Mediterranean 1939–45.

Sekistov, V.A. (ed.), *Bol'shaya lozh' o voine* (Moscow: Voenizdat 1971).

Sevostyanov, G.N., *Podgotovka voiny na Tikhom Okeane 1939–1941* (Moscow: Akad. Nauk 1962).

Bibliography 815

Strel'nikov, V.S. and Cherepanov, N.M., *Voina bez riska* (Moscow: Voenizdat 1965). The Italian campaign.

Strokov, A.A., *Uroki istorii neoproverzhimy* (Moscow: Voenizdat 1964). On World War II, Soviet role in defeat of Germany.

Zhilin, P.A. (chief ed.), *Vtoraya mirovaya voina i sovremennost'* (Moscow: Nauka 1972). Collected essays on World War II.

13. Select articles

VI	*Voprosy Istorii*
Ist. SSSR	*Istoriya SSSR*
Ist. Arkhiv	*Istoricheskii Arkhiv*
VIZ	*Voenno-istoricheskii Zhurnal*
VVI	*Vestnik voennoi istorii*

Antosyak, A., 'Rumyniya vo vtoroi mirovoi voine', *VVI*, 1971 (2), pp. 154–76.

Baranov, S.V., 'Rost tekhnicheskoi osnashchennosti Sovetskikh vooruzhennykh sil v gody Velikoi Otechestvennoi voiny', *VI*, 1975 (5), pp. 22–35.

'42-ya Armiya v boyakh za Leningrad', *Ist. Arkhiv*, 1959(2), pp. 68–88. War diary, 42nd Army.

Erenburg, I., 'Lyudi, gody, zhizn', *Novyi Mir*, 1963 (1)–(3).

'K 20-letiyu bitvy na Volge. Postanovleniya Gorodskovo komiteta oborony. Okt. 1941–iyul. 1942 gg.', *Ist. Arkhiv*, 1962 (3), pp. 3–56. Documents, Stalingrad Defence Committee.

Kalyagin, A.Ya., 'Sredstva inzhenernovo vooruzheniya v Velikoi Otechestvennoi voine', *VI*, 1976 (7), pp. 101–12. Military engineering work/equipment and supplies.

Komarov, N.Ya. and Orlov, A.S., ' "Sekretnoe oruzhie" Fyurera i protivovozdushnaya oborona gorodov SSSR v 1944–1945 godakh', *Ist. SSSR*, 1975 (1), pp. 121–8. Defensive measures against German V-1/V-2 'secret weapons'.

Kukin, D.M., 'Partiinoe i gosudarstvennoe rukovodstvo ekonomikii v gody Velikoi Otechestvennoi voiny', *VI*, 1971 (8), pp. 27–42.

Morozov, V.P., 'Nekotorye voprosy organizatsii strategicheskovo rukovodstva v Velikoi Otechestvennoi voine', *Ist. SSSR*, 1975 (3), pp. 12–29. High command organization/command role.

Petrov, Yu.P., 'Sostoyanie i zadachi razrabotki istorii partizanskovo dvizhenie v gody Velikoi Otechestvennoi voiny.' *VI*, 1971 (5), pp. 11–33.

Shakurin, A.I., 'Aviatsionnaya promyshlennost'v gody Velikoi Otechestvennoi voiny', *VI*, 1975 (3), pp. 134–54 and (4), pp. 91–105. Memoir by commissar for aircraft production.

Shinkarev, I., 'Bolgariya vo vtoroi mirovoi voine', *VVI*, 1970 (1), pp. 200–22.

Solov'ev, B., 'Faktor strategicheskoi vnezapnosti v bitve pod Kurskom', *VVI*, 1970 (1), pp. 144–63.

Vannikov, B.L., 'Oboronnaya promyshlennost' SSSR nakanune voiny', *VI*, 1969 (1), pp. 122–35.

Vasilevskii, A.M., 'K voprosy o rukovodstve vooruzhennoi bor'boi v Velikoi Otechestvennoi voine', *VI*, 1970 (5), pp. 49–71. Strategic command/control.

Vasilevskii, A.M., 'Osvobozhdenie Donbassa levoberezhnoi Ukrainy. Bor'ba za Dnepr', *Ist. SSSR*, 1970 (3), pp. 3–45. Important article by Marshal Vasilevskii.

Volkotrubenko, I.I., 'Boepripasy i artsnabzhenie v Velikoi Otechestvennoi voiny', *VI*, 1972 (11), pp. 82–91. Ammunition production.

Articles in VIZ 1959–80 (in chronological order)

'Iz istorii kapitulyatsii vooruzhennykh sil fashistskoi Germanii', Documents, 1959(5), pp. 79–95. Interrogation of General Weidling.

Krasil'nikov, S., 'O strategicheskom rukovodstve v Velikoi Otechestvennoi voine', 1960(6), pp. 3–13.

Sokolovskii, V., 'O sovetskom voennom iskusstve v bitve pod Moskvoi', 1961(11), pp. 15–28.

Zakharov, M.V.., 'Umanskaya nastupatel'naya operatsiya 2-vo Ukrainskovo fronta', 1962(4), pp. 12–32.

Anan'ev, I., 'Tankovye armii v nastupatel'nykh operatsiyakh Velikoi Otechestvennoi voine', 1962(5), pp. 10–24.

Lobanov, M., 'K voprosy vozniknoveniya i razvitiya otechestvennoi radiolokatsii', 1962(8), pp. 13–29. Soviet radar programme.

Utenkov, F., 'Nekotorye voprosy oboronitel'novo srazheniya na dal'nykh podstupakh k Stalingradu', 1962(9), pp. 34–48.

Bagramyan, I., 'Shaulyaisko-Mitavskaya operatsiya voisk 1-vo Pribaltiiskovo fronta', 1962(10), pp. 3–23.

Nikitin, A., 'Perestroika raboty voennoi promyshlennosti SSSR v pervoi periode Velikoi Otechestvennoi voiny', 1963(2), pp. 11–20. War industry.

Morozov, V., 'Pochemu ne zavershilos nastuplenie v Donbasse vesnoi 1943 goda', 1963(3), pp. 14—34. Important analysis of Soviet operations, 1943.

Kravchenko, I., 'Vstrechnye boi tankovykh i mekhanizirovannykh korpusov v Velikoi Otechestvennoi voine', 1963(5), pp. 24–35.

Zakharov, M.V., 'O sovetskom voennom iskusstve v bitve pod Kurskom', 1963(6), pp. 15–25 and (7), pp. 11–20.

Koniev, I.S., 'Na kharkovskom napravlenii', 1963(8), pp. 49–61. Memoir.

Sandalov, L., 'Bryanskii front v Orlovskaya operatsiya', 1963(8), pp. 62–72. Memoir.

Shekhovtsov, N., 'Razvitie strategicheskovo nastupleniya letom i osenyu 1943 goda', 1963(9), pp. 12–29. Strategic planning, 1943.

Kazakov, M., 'Velikaya pobeda pod Leningradom', 1964(1), pp. 3–15.

Platonov, S. and Pavlenko, N., 'Strategicheskoe nastuplenie Sovetskoi armii na territorii Polshi', 1964(2), pp. 14–36.

Dorofeev, M., 'O nekotorykh prichinakh neudachnyk deistvii mekhanizirovannykh korpusov v nachalnom periode Velikoi Otechestvennoi voiny', 1964(3), pp. 32–44. Important analysis.

'Velikaya pobeda v Belorussi', 1964(6), pp. 3–51, 74–86. Belorussian offensive, 1944: memoirs, statistical material Soviet strength/deployment.

Zakharov, M.V., 'Molnienosnaya operatsiya', 1964(8), pp. 15–28. Jassy-Kishinev, 1944.

'Pravda o gibeli generala M.P. Kirponosa', 1964(9), pp. 61–9. Report on death of General Kirponos, 1941.

Kazakov, M., 'Na voronezhskom napravlenii letom 1942 goda', 1964(10), pp. 27–44. Memoir/analysis.

Al'shits, A., 'Dostizhenie vnezapnosti v nastupatel'nykh operatsiyakh Velikoi Otechest-vennoi voiny', 1964(11), pp. 10–21. Surprise in Soviet operations.

Zhelanov, V., 'Iz opyta pervoi operatsii na okruzhenie', 1964(12), pp. 20–34. Extremely important analysis, Soviet operations winter 1941–2.

Meretskov, K., 'Na volkhovskikh rubezhakh', 1965(1), pp. 54–70. Volkhov, Vlasov and 2nd Shock Army, 1942.

'Vislo-Oderskaya operatsiya v tsifrakh', 1965(1), pp. 71–81. Vistula/Oder 1945, statistical data.

'Vostochno-Prusskaya operatsiya v tsifrakh', 1965(2), pp. 80–90. East Prussia, statistical data Soviet forces.

Kravchenko, G., 'Ekonomicheskaya pobeda sovetskovo naroda v Velikoi Otechestvennoi voine', 1965(4), pp. 37–47. War economy.

Zhukov, G., 'Na berlinskom napravlenii', 1965(6), pp. 12–22. Memoir.

Achkasov, V., 'Voenno-Morskoi Flot v khode Velikoi Otechestvennoi voiny', 1965(7), pp. 24–34. General survey, Soviet navy.

Vasilevskii, A., 'Nekotorye voprosy rukovodstva vooruzhennoi bor'boi letom 1942 goda', 1965(8), pp. 3–10. Important evidence, Soviet operations 1942.

Vasilevskii, A., 'Nezabyvaemye dni', 1965(10), pp. 13–25. Essential evidence, Stalingrad 1942.

Korkodinov, P., 'Fakty i mysli o nachal'nom periode Velikoi Otechestvennoi voiny', 1965(10), pp. 26–34. Beginning of war.

Shesterin, F., 'Bor'ba za gospodstvo v vozdukhe', 1965(11), pp. 15–27. Battle for air supremacy.

Lototskii, S., 'Iz opyta vedeniya armeiskikh nastupatel'nykh operatsii', 1965(12), pp. 3–14. Offensive operations.

Vasilevskii, A., 'Nezabyvaemye dni', 1966(1), pp. 13–25. Stalingrad 1942.

Khozin, M., 'Ob odnoi maloissledovannoi operatsii', 1966(2), pp. 35–46. Leningrad/Volkhov Fronts, 1941–2.

Shtemenko, S., 'Pered udarom v Belorussii', 1966(2), pp. 58–77. Table of work of *Stavka* représentatives.

Pavlenko, N., 'Kharakternye cherty strategicheskovo nastupleniya Sovetskikh vooru-zhennykh sil v Velikoi Otechestvennoi voine', 1966(3), pp. 9–23. Soviet offensive operations.

Vasilevskii, A., 'Nezabyvaemye dni', 1966(3), pp. 24–44 (cont'd.).

Absalyamov, M. and Andrianov, V., 'Organizatsiya partizanskikh sil i formy rukovodstva ikh boevoi deyatelnostyu v Otechestvennoi voine', 1966(9), pp. 18–26. Soviet partisan warfare.

Domorad, K., 'Tak li dolzhny pisatsya voennye memuary?', 1966(11), pp. 82–92. Critique of military memoirs.

'Moskovskaya bitva v tsifrakh', 1967(1), pp. 89–101. Military statistics/data, Moscow counter-offensive. See also 1967(2), pp. 69–79 (defensive phase).

Koltunov, G., 'Udar voisk 1-vo Ukrainskovo fronta na zhitomirskom napravlenii zimoi 1943/44 goda', 1967(2), pp. 12–23. Important analysis.

Slyunin, N. and Badanin, B., 'Razvitie voenno-inzhenernovo iskusstva', 1967(6), pp. 16–28. Military engineers/engineering.

Malanin, K., 'Razvitie organizatsionnykh form sukhoputnykh voisk v Velikoi Ote-chestvennoi voine', 1967(8), pp. 28–39. Red Army organization/structure, 1941–5.

818   Bibliography

Matsulenko, V., 'Razvitie operativnovo iskusstva v nastupatelnykh operatsiyakh', 1967(10), pp. 39–53. Operational art and offensive operations.

Absalyamov, M. and Andrianov, V., 'Taktika sovetskikh partizan', 1968(1), pp. 42–55. Partisan tactics.

Murmantseva, V., 'Sovetskie zhenshchiny v Velikoi Otechestvennoi voine . . .', 1968(2), pp. 47–54. Soviet women at war.

Gurkin, V., 'Kontranastuplenie pod Stalingradom v tsifrakh', 1968(3), pp. 64–76. Stalingrad counter-offensive, statistical data.

Filatov, G., 'Razgrom ital'yanskoi ekspeditsionnoi armii na sovetsko-germanskom fronte', 1968(4), pp. 44–54. Destruction of Italian forces in Russia.

Koltunov, G., 'Kurskaya bitva v tsifrakh', 1968(6), pp. 58–68 and (7), pp. 77–92. Statistics, Kursk 1943.

Shekhovtsov, N., 'Nastuplenie voisk Stepnovo fronta na krivorozhskom napravlenii v oktyabre 1943 goda', 1968(10), pp. 28–43.

Okhotnikov, N., 'Strelkovoe vooruzhenie Sovetskoi Armii v Velikoi Otechestvennoi voine', 1969(1), pp. 29–38. Soviet small arms.

Svetlishin, N., 'O nekotorykh osobennostyakh zimnei kampanii 1944 goda', 1969(2), pp. 15–30. Important analysis.

Ivanov, S., 'Sryv kontrnastupleniya nemetsko-fashistskikh voisk u ozera Balaton', 1969(3), pp. 14–29. Balaton, 1945.

Vasilevskii, A., 'Vostochno-Prusskaya operatsiya', 1969(3), pp. 35–45. Important memoir, East Prussian operations.

Tereshchenko, N., 'Korsun-Shevchenkovskaya operatsiya v tsifrakh', 1969(7), pp. 45–52. Korsun-Shevchenkovskii operations, 1944: statistics.

Polushkin, M., 'Lvovsko-Sandomirskaya nastupatelnaya operatsiya 1-vo Ukrainskovo fronta v tsifrakh', 1969(8), pp. 54–67. Lvov-Sandomierz, figures/statistics.

Vasilevskii, A., 'Belorusskaya strategicheskaya operatsiya', 1969(9), pp. 47–58 and (10), pp. 63–76. Belorussian offensive, 1944.

Kozhevnikov, M., 'Razvitie operativnovo iskusstva VVS', 1969(11), pp. 15–25. Soviet Air Force, operational art.

Chepelyuk, S., 'Razvitie taktiki shturmovoi aviatsii v Velikoi Otechestvennoi voina', 1970(1), pp. 23–33. Ground-attack aviation.

Shekhovstov, N., 'Kharakternye cherty kampanii 1945 goda v Evrope', 1970(2), pp. 15–26. Important analysis, final campaign.

Zakharov, M.V., 'Strategicheskoe rukovodstvo vooruzhennymi silami', 1970(5), pp, 23–34. Strategic command/control.

'Voenachal'niki vspominayut . . .'. Zhukov, Vasilevskii, Koniev, Novikov, Kuznetsov, Maryakhim, Krainyukov, 1970(5), pp. 52–101. General memoirs.

Shimanskii, A., 'Narashchivanie usilii v khode strategicheskovo nastupleniya', 1970(7), pp. 14–22. Echelons and reinforcements.

Kazakov, K., 'Sovershenstvovanie artilleriiskovo nastupleniya', 1970(11), pp. 33–9. Artillery offensive.

Vasilevskii, A., 'Osvobozhdenie Pravoberezhnoi Ukrainy', 1971(1), pp. 59–73 and (2), pp. 62–77. Important memoir plus documents.

Peresypkin, I., 'Svyaz General'novo shtaba', 1971(4), pp. 19–25. General Staff signals nets.

Vasilevskii, A., 'Osvobozhdenie Kryma ot nemetsko-fashistskikh zakhvatchikov v 1944 godu', 1971(5), pp. 71–85 and (6), pp. 57–72. Important memoir plus documents.

Kozhevnikov, M., 'Sovershenstvovanie aviatsionnovo nastupleniya', 1971(5), pp. 14–21. Soviet air offensive.

Saltykov, N., 'Predstaviteli General'novo shtaba . . .', 1971(9), pp. 54–9. Important on General Staff functions.

Zemskov, V., 'Nekotorye voprosy sozdaniya i ispolzovaniya strategicheskikh rezervov', 1971(10), pp. 12–19. On strategic reserves.

Timokhovich, I., 'Nekotorye voprosy operativnovo iskusstva VVS', 1971(11), pp. 12–21. Important for Soviet Air Force operations.

Maslov, P., 'Formirovanie i podgotovka tankovykh rezervov', 1972(1), pp. 21–7. Tank reserves.

Novikov, A. and Kozhevnikov, M., 'Bor'ba za strategicheskoe gospodstvo v vozdukhe', 1972(3), pp. 22–31. Air supremacy.

Krainyukov, K. and Kuznetsov, Ya., 'Deyatel'nost voennykh sovetov v operatsiyakh Sovetskoi Armii za rubezhom', 1972(4), pp. 31–9. Military councils.

Kazakov, M., 'Ispol'zovanie strategicheskikh rezervov', 1972(5), pp. 28–35. Important, strategic reserves.

Povalii, M., 'Upravlenie voiskami vo frontovykh nastupatel'nykh operatsiyakh', 1972(7), pp. 34–42. Command and control/offensive.

Tsvetkov, A., 'Boevye deistviya vozdushnykh i morskikh desantov v tylu protivnika', 1972(8), pp. 20–25. Airborne/amphibious operations.

Babadzhanyan, A. and Kravchenko, I., '1-ya tankovaya armiya v Zhitomirsko-Berdichevskoi operatsii', 1972(9), pp. 21–31.

Ananev, I., 'Sozdanie tankovykh armii i sovershenstvovanie ikh organizatsionnoi struktury', 1972(10), pp. 38–47. Soviet tank armies.

'K 30-letiyu Stalingradskoi bitvy', 1972(11), pp. 20–77. On Stalingrad. See also 1973(2), pp. 34–66.

Smirnov, V., 'Vstrechnye srazheniya', 1973(4), pp. 20–28. Meeting engagements.

Maramzin, V., 'O metodakh raboty komanduyushchevo armiei po prinyatiyu resheniya na nastupatel'nuyu operatsiyu', 1973(5), pp. 10–16. Command/staff work.

Myagkov, V., 'Razvitie taktiki istrebitel'noi aviatsii', 1973(6), pp. 23–31. Soviet fighter tactics.

'K 30-letiyu Kurskoi bitvy', 1973(7), pp. 9–76 and (8), pp. 11–72. On Kursk, 1943.

'K 30-letiyu bitvy za Dnepr', 1973(9), pp. 10–53. Dnieper operations, 1943, also statistical data.

Pokrovskii, A. and Istomin, V., 'Smolenskaya nastupatel'naya operatsiya 1943 goda', 1973(10), pp. 11–23.

Kir'yan, M., 'Razvitie sposoba planirovaniya armeiskikh nastupatel'nykh operatsii', 1973(11), pp. 12–19. Soviet offensive operations/planning organization.

Kuznetsov, K., 'O strategicheskikh peregruppirovakh', 1973(12), pp. 12–19. Important, on strategic regrouping.

'Direktivnoe pismo Stavki Verkhovnovo Glavnokomandovaniya ot 10 yanvarya 1942 goda', 1974(1), pp. 70–74. Instruction on tactics.

Kozhevnikov, M., 'Koordinatsiya deistvii VVS predstavitelyami Stavki VGK po aviatsii', 1974(2), pp. 31–8. Control of air operations.

Myagkov, V., 'Razvitie taktiki bombardirovochnoi aviatsii', 1974(3), pp. 35–44. Bomber tactics.

Radzievskii, A., 'Dostizhenie vnezapnosti v nastupatel'nykh operatsiyakh', 1974(4), pp. 12–21. On attaining surprise.

'Navstrechu 30-letiyu Pobedy', 1974(5), pp. 10–34; (6), pp. 10–35; (7), pp. 10–37. Operational art.

Koltunov, G. and Isaev, S., 'Krymskaya operatsiya v tsifrakh', 1974(5), pp. 35–42. Crimean operations/data.

Chernyaev, V., 'Operativnaya maskirovka v Belorusskoi operatsii', 1974(8), pp. 11–21. Camouflage/deception, Belorussian offensive 1944.

Medvedev, N., 'Osvobozhdenie Pribaltiki', 1974(9), pp. 11–22.

Skomorokhov, N., 'Operativnoe iskusstvo VVS v nastupatel'nykh operatsiyakh tret'evo perioda Velikoi Otechestvennoi voiny', 1974(9), pp. 32–42. Air operational art.

'Prikaz NKO No. 306 ot 8 oktyabr 1942', 1974(9), pp. 62–6. Document.

'Prikaz NKO No. 525 ot 16 oktyabr 1942 g', 1974(10), pp. 68–73. Document.

Biryukov, G. and Totrov, S., 'Nekotorye voprosy primeneniya artillerii vo frontovykh operatsiyakh', 1974(11), pp. 11–17. Artillery.

Vyazankin, I., 'Forsirovanie rek s khody', 1975(2), pp. 10–19. Assault river crossings.

'Polozhenie i instruktsiya po rabote korpusa ofitserov-predstavitelei General'novo shtaba Krasnoi Armii', 1975(2), pp. 62–6. General Staff work: document.

'Ukazaniya po podgotovke artillerii 2-vo Belorusskovo fronta k Vostochno-Prusskoi operatsii', 1975(3), pp. 52–6. Artillery planning: document.

'30-letie Velikoi Pobedy', 1975(5), pp. 3–80. Memoirs/analysis, wartime period.

Kulikov, V., 'Strategicheskoe rukovodstvo vooruzhennymi silami', 1975(6), pp. 12–24. Important, on 'high command', strategic direction.

Andrianov, V., 'Partizanskaya voina i voennaya strategiya', 1975(7), pp. 29–38. Partisan war and strategy.

'O zadachakh partizanskovo dvizheniya': Prikaz NKO 5 sentyabrya 1942, 1975(8), pp. 61–5. Instruction to partisan movement.

Yakovlev, N., 'Operativnye peregruppirovki voisk pri podgotovke Belorusskoi operatsii', 1975(9), pp. 91–7.

'Instruktsiya po organizatsii i provedeniya dvoinovo ognevovo vala', 1975(11), pp. 52–9. Artillery instruction,' 1944: document.

Tsykin, A., 'Taktika aviatsii dal'nevo deistviya vo vtorom periode voiny', 1976(1), pp. 19–25. Long-range aviation tactics.

Radzievskii, A., 'Vvod tankovykh armii v proryv', 1976(2), pp. 19–26. Important study, employment of tank armies.

Radzievskii, A., 'Podderzhanie i vosstanovlenie boesposobnosti tankovykh armii v nastupatel'nykh operatsiyakh', 1976(3), pp. 13–21. Important study, sustained combat capability of tank armies.

'Prikazy NKO SSSR o primenenii shturmovoi i istrebitel'noi aviatsii na pole v kachestve dnevnykh bombardirovshchikov', 1976(3), pp. 73–4. Document, June 1942.

Silant'ev, A., 'Upravlenie aviatsiei v nastupatel'nykh deistviyakh voisk', 1976(4), pp. 29–38. Air support in offensive operations.

Chernyaev, V., 'Razvitie taktiki oboronitel'novo boya', 1976(6), pp. 20–36. Soviet defensive tactics.

Mikoyan, A., 'Ob obrazovanii Rezervnovo fronta v 1943 godu', 1976(6), pp. 61–9. Memoir.

Tovstukha, P. and Savelev, V., 'Nekotorye voprosy upravleniya voiskami v nastupatel'nom boyu', 1976(7), pp. 11–19.

Koniev, I.S., 'Operatsii na okruzhenie', 1976(7), pp. 70–80. Unpublished memoir by Marshal Koniev on encirclement operations.

Utenkov, F., 'Dokumenty sovetskovo komandovaniya po bor'be s tankami protivnika', 1976(8), pp. 65–8. Instructions on anti-tank defence.

Kulikov, I., 'Ofitsery-predstaviteli General'novo shtaba v oboronitel'nom srazhenii pod Kurskom', 1976(8), pp. 79–84. General Staff officers, Kursk 1943.

'Prikazy i direktivy NKO i Stavki VGK o sovetskoi gvardii i upravlenii voiskami', 1976(9), pp. 58–60. Guards designations, troop control: documents.

Kozhevnikov, M., 'Sozdanie i ispol'zovanie aviatsionnykh rezervov Stavki VGK', 1976(10), pp. 28–35. Air reserves.

Direktivy Stavki VGK o sovershenstvovanii operativnovo rukovodstva flotami i flotiliyami', 1976(11), pp. 66–9. Command and control, naval forces: documents.

Semenov, G., 'Iz opyta organizatsii i vedeniya nastupatel'noi operatsii 3-i udarnoi armiei zimoi 1942 goda', 1977(1), pp. 85–92. 3rd Shock Army operations.

Popov, N., 'Razvitie samokhodnoi artillerii', 1977(1), pp. 27–31. SP guns.

Golubovich, V., 'Sozdanie strategicheskikh rezervov', 1977(4), pp. 12–19. Important data on strategic reserves.

Palii, A., 'Radioelektronnaya bor'ba v khode voiny', 1977(5), pp. 10–19. Rare discussion of Soviet SIGINT.

Malakhov, M., 'Iz opyta sozdaniya i ispolzovaniya operativnykh grupp v khode voiny', 1977(6), pp. 23–9. Operational/battle groups.

Kazarnovskii, Yu., 'Sozdanie i ispolzovanie udarnykh armii', 1977(8), pp. 86–91. On shock armies.

Frolov, B., 'Vstrechnye srazheniya tankovykh armii v nastupatel'nykh operatsiyakh', 1977(9), pp. 24–33. Important study, tank meeting engagements.

Vorob'ev, V., 'Korablestroenie v gody voiny', 1977(12), pp. 35–42. Wartime naval shipbuilding.

Mikhailovskii, G. and Vyrodov, I., 'Vysshie organy rukovodstva voiny', 1978(4), pp. 16–26. Organization of High Command.

Ryabyshev, D., 'Ob uchastii 8-vo mekhanizirovannovo korpusa v kontrudare Yugo-zapadnovo fronta (1 yun 1941 g.)', 1978(6), pp. 67–74. Very rare account, tank operations, June 1941.

Kolokol'tsev, S., 'Operativnoe primenenie tankovykh voisk Vermakhta', 1978(7), pp. 80–86. *Wehrmacht*'s use of armour.

Syropyatov, V., 'Razvitie tankotekhnicheskovo obespecheniya v gody voiny', 1978(9), pp. 39–47. Technical maintenance, tank forces.

Kudryashov, O., 'O povyshenii i podderzhanii boesposobnosti voisk', 1978(11), pp. 26–31. Sustaining wartime combat capability of troops.

'Prikaz Stavki VGK ot 28 noyabrya 1941 goda', 1978(12), pp. 39–40. Document, engineering support.

Bokov, F., 'Soveshchanie v Stavke o reorganizatsii tankovoi armii', 1979(3), pp. 38–41. *Stavka* discussions on reorganization of Soviet tank armies.

Lukin, M. 'V Smolenskom srazhenii', 1979(7), pp. 42–54. Important and unusual memoir by 16th Army commander at Smolensk (1941) who was taken prisoner at Vyazma when commanding 20th Army; foreword by Marshal Vasilevskii. The full text of General Lukin's memoirs is being prepared for publication.

Ramanichev, N.M., 'Iz opyta peregruppirovki armii pri podgotovke Berlinskoi operatsii', 1979(8), pp. 9–16. Regrouping for Berlin operation.

Krupchenko, I., 'Kharakternye cherty razvitiya i primeneniya tankovykh voisk', 1979(9), pp. 25–32. Employment of Soviet armoured forces.

Pervov, A., 'O faktorakh, vliyayushchikh na manevr aviasoedineniyami RVGK', 1979(9), pp. 39–44. Deployment of High Command aviation reserves.

Samoilenko, Ya., 'Iz opyta upravleniya vozdushnymi desantami v gody voiny', 1979(12), pp. 15–21. Useful and rather singular article on planning and command and control, Soviet airborne operations.

Pervov, A., 'Podgotovka i vospolnenie poter aviatsionnykh korpusov RVGK', 1980(2), pp. 10–15. Formation/loss replacement in High Command aviation corps.

Alferov, A., 'Peregruppirovka 3-i gvardeiskoi tankovoi armii v bitve za Dnepr (oktyabr 1943 g.)', 1980(3), pp. 16–24. 3rd Guards Tank Army, Dnieper 1943.

14. Wartime press, reportage, literature

Newspapers, war communiqués, war reports

Krasnaya Zvezda (wartime issues), January–October 1941; February 1942; January–December 1943 (Hoover Institution holdings).

Soobshcheniya Sovetskovo Informbyuro, summaries of operations, campaigns, illustrations, 22 June 1941–15 May 1945, vols. 1–8 (Hoover Institution holdings).

Soviet War News, published by press department, Soviet Embassy, London, 1941–5.

Stalingrad (Moscow: FLPH 1943). Communiqués, press reports.

Series: Vsesoyuznaya Khnizhnaya Palata, (Moscow): Wartime publications.

Petrukhin, I.S. (ed.), Marksizm-Leninizm o voinakh i zashchite sotsialisticheskovo otechestva. Ukazatel' lit. (Moscow, 1942).

Primakovskii, A.P. (ed.), Osobennosti i kharakter Velikoi Otechestvennoi voiny. Ukazatel' lit, (Moscow, 1942).

Smirnova, B.A. (ed.), Geroicheskii Leningrad. Kratkii annot. spisok lit. (Moscow: Lenin Library 1943).

Timofeyev, A.S. (ed.), Voenno-morskoi flot. Ukazatel' lit. (Moscow, 1943).

Timofeyev, A.S. (ed.), Voiska svyazi. Ukazatel' lit. (Moscow, 1943).

Tolkachev, N.T. (ed.), Izuchai vraga. Ukazatel' lit. (Moscow, 1942).

Tolkachev, N.T. (ed.), Voennoe iskusstvo. Ukazatel' lit. (Moscow, 1943).

Tolkachev, N.T. (ed.), Voenno-inzhenernoe delo. Ukazatel' lit. (Moscow, 1943).

Tolkachev, N.T. (ed.), Pekhota. Istoriya organizatsiya, vooruzhenie i taktika. Ukazatel' lit. (Moscow, 1942).

Geroi i podvigi. Sovetskie listovki Velikoi Otechestvennoi voiny 1941–1945 gg. (Moscow: Gospolitizdat 1958). Reprints, Soviet wartime pamphlets.

Voennaya publitsistika i frontovye ocherki (Moscow: Khudozhestvennaya Lit. 1966).

Voina. Narod. Pobeda 1941–1945. Stati, ocherki, vospominaniya (Moscow: Politizdat 1976), vols 1 and 2. Reprints of articles, memoirs.

Kim, M.P. *et al.* (eds.), *Sovetskaya kultura v gody Velikoi Otechestvennoi voiny* (Moscow: Nauka 1976).

Zhukov, S.I., *Frontovaya pechat' v gody Velikoi Otechestvennoi voiny* (Moscow: Moscow University 1968).

Frontovye ocherki o Velikoi Otechestvennoi voine (Moscow: Voenizdat 1958), 3 vols.

Pavlovskii, A., *Russkaya sovetskaya poeziya v gody Velikoi Otechestvennoi voiny* (Leningrad: Nauka 1967).

Velikaya Otechestvennaya, Vol. 1: *Stikhotvoreniya i Poemy*, Izd. Vtoroe, dopolnennoe (Moscow: Khudozh. Lit. 1975); vol. 2: *Stikhotvoreniya i Poemy*, Izd. Vtoroe, dopolnennoe (Moscow: Khudozh. Lit. 1975).

Collective authors, *Vo imya otchizny*. Kazanskii universitet v gody Velikoi Otechestvennoi voiny (Kazan: Izd. Kazan. universiteta 1975). Contribution of university, staff and students to war effort.

Denisov, N.N., *1418 dnei frontovo korrespondenta* (Moscow: Voenizdat 1969). Wartime special correspondent for *Krasnaya Zvezda*.

Kondrat'ev, V.A. and Politov, Z.N., *Govoryat pogibshie geroi* (Moscow: Politizdat, 5th edn 1973). Wartime letters.

Mozhukhovskaya, E.V., *Na ognevykh rubezhakh*. Moskovskie khudozhniki frontovoi pechati 1941–1945 (Leningrad: Khudozhnik RSFSR 1972). Posters, graphic art.

Ovechkin, V., *S frontovym privetom*. Povest', ocherki i frontovye gazetnye publikatsii (Moscow: Voenizdat 1973).

Selishchev, I.P. and Shukanov, V.F., *O voine, o tovarishchakh, o sebe* (Moscow: Politizdat 1969). Reprints, letters, wartime notes.

Vorob'ev, E., *Tovarishchi s Zapadnovo fronta* (Moscow: Voenizdat 1972). War correspondent for *Krasnoarmeiskaya Pravda*: notes, wartime reports.

Reportazh s frontov voiny (Moscow: Politizdat 1970). Reprints, Soviet wartime press reports.

War novels

Baklanov, G., *Iyul' 41 goda*. Roman (Moscow: Sov. pisatel 1965).

Baklanov, G., *Voennye povesti* (Moscow: Sov. pisatel 1967).

Bek, A., *Volokolamskoe shosse* (Moscow: Voenizdat 1959).

Grossman, V., *Za pravoe delo* (series: 'Sovetskii voennyi roman') (Moscow: Voenizdat 1959).

Melezh, I., *Minskoe napravlenie*. Roman (Minsk: Gos. Izd. BSSR 1956).

Simonov, K., *Dni i Nochi* (Moscow: Voenizdat 1955).

Simonov, K., *Front*. Ocherki i rasskazy 1941–1945 (Moscow: Voenizdat 1960).

Simonov, K., *Zhivye i Mertvye* (series: 'Sovetskii voennyi roman') (Moscow: Voenizdat 1961).

Vishnevskii, Vs., *Dnevniki voennykh let (1943, 1945)* (Moscow: Sov. Rossiya 1974).

Zhukov, Yu., *Lyudi 40-kh godov*. Zapiski voennovo korrespondenta (Moscow: Sov. Rossiya 1969).

Zhukov, Yu., *Lyudi sorokovykh godov 1941–1945*. Zapiski voennovo korrespondenta (Moscow: Sov. Rossiya 1975).

15. Translations

Chuikov, V.I., *The Beginning of the Road* (London: MacGibbon and Kee 1973).

Chuikov, V.I., *The End of the Third Reich* (London: MacGibbon and Kee 1967).

Deborin, G., *Thirty Years of Victory* (Moscow: Progress Pub. 1975).

Dërr, G., *Pokhod na Stalingrad* (Operativnyi Obzor) (Moscow: Voenizdat 1957).

Galder, F., *Voennyi Dnevnik,* vols 1, 2, 3 (parts 1 and 2) (Moscow: Voenizdat 1968–71). (F. Halder: *Kriegstagebuch*.)

Got, G., *Tankovye operatsii* (Moscow: Voenizdat 1961); translation: Hoth, *Panzer Operationen*.

Grechko, A., *Battle for the Caucasus* (Moscow: Progress Pub. 1971).

How Wars End. Eye-witness accounts of the fall of Berlin compiled by Sevruk, V. (Moscow: Progress Pub. 1969).

Kaval'evo, U., *Zapiski o Voine.* Dnevnik Nachal'nika Ital'yanskogo General'novo Shtaba. (Moscow: Voenizdat 1968).

Khattori, T., *Yaponiya v voine 1941–1945* (Moscow: Voenizdat 1973). (Trans: T. Khattori, Japanese orig.)

Krylov, N., *Glory Eternal: Defence of Odessa 1941* (Moscow: Progress Pub. 1972).

Kolyshkin, I., *Submarines in Arctic Waters* (Moscow: Progress Pub. 1966).

Koniev, I.S., *Year of Victory* (Moscow: Progress Pub. 1969).

Koniev, I.S. *et al., The Great March of Liberation* (Moscow: Progress Pub. 1972).

Mansergh, Sir Aubrey (ed.), *With the Red Fleet: The War Memoirs of the late Admiral A.G. Golovko* (London: Putnam 1965).

Melentin, F., *Tankovye srazheniya 1939–1945 gg.* (Moscow: Inostr. Lit. 1957).

Minz, I., *The Army of the Soviet Union* (Moscow: FLPH 1942).

Rokossovskii, K.K., *A Soldier's Duty* (Moscow: Progress Pub. 1970).

Shtemenko, S.M., *The Soviet General Staff at War 1941–1945* (Moscow: Progress Pub. 1970).

Shtemenko, S.M., *The Last Six Months* (London: Wm Kimber 1978).

Soviet Peace Efforts on the Eve of World War II (Moscow: Progress Pub. 1973).

Stalin, J.V., *On the Great Patriotic War of the Soviet Union* (Moscow, 1944 and Hutchinson, London, 1945). (English translation: J.V. Stalin.)

Strategy and Tactics of the Soviet-German War, by officers of the Red Army (London, n.d.—pub. with *Soviet War News*).

The Battle of Kursk (Moscow: Progress Pub. 1974).

Two Hundred Days of Fire. Accounts by participants and witnesses of the battle of Stalingrad (Moscow: Progress Pub. 1970).

Zhilin, P., *They Sealed their own Doom* (Moscow: Progress Pub. 1970).

The Memoirs of Marshal Zhukov (London: Jonathan Cape 1971).

16. Interviews

Marshal of the Soviet Union V.D. Sokolovskii

Marshal of the Soviet Union K.K. Rokossovskii

Marshal of the Soviet Union V.I. Chuikov

Marshal of the Soviet Union I.S. Koniev

Additional interview material from: Marshal of the Soviet Union A.I. Yeremenko; Chief Marshal (Artillery) N. Voronov; General S.P. Platonov; General N.G. Pavlenko;

General P.I. Batov; General A.E. Boltin; General I.I. Yushchuk; General B.S. Tel'pukhovskii; Colonel B. Polevoi; Colonel K. Ya. Samsonov; Lt.-Col. S.A. Neustroyev; Irena Nikolaevna Levchenko.

I have retained complete transcripts of these exchanges and I have drawn upon them extensively for this present volume. In addition, I was able to make considerable use of the original *Stavka* directives and associated operational orders. To supplement this invaluable material I also turned to personal diaries and personal archives made available to me, so that there may be some discrepancies between what is recorded in official accounts and what I have uncovered from contemporary, personal records—in which event I have relied almost exclusively on the contemporary record, as opposed to any retrospective construction and interpretation.

II. GERMAN MILITARY DOCUMENTS (GMD)

For this Bibliography, the German materials have been grouped as follows:
1. General/*Chefsachen*/War diaries *(KTB)*
   (a) Army Groups
   (b) Armies/Corps
2. Intelligence reports/assessments of Soviet forces (organization, command, weapons, tactics)
3. Map collections

This compilation cannot pretend in the least to be comprehensive; it is intended merely to identify types of material utilized throughout the present work, such as *Chefsachen*, or army/corps records where relevant. Under (2) I have attempted to assemble a profile of significant intelligence reports and assessments.

1. General/*Chefsachen*/War diaries *(KTB)*

'Aufmarsch Barbarossa 1941' (Chefsachen). See: *Aufmarschanweisung 'Barbarossa'* (Chefsachen), January 1941, April–September 1941, OKH/GenStdH/Op. Abt. T-78/R335, 6291208–1819. *'Barbarossa Bd. 3'*, Op. Abt. III (Chefsachen), September 1941–February 1942. T-78/R335, 6291819–958.

' . . . *über dem Umbau des Heeres nach Abschluss Barbarossa'* (Chefsache), July 1941 (Vortragsnotiz, prepared by Op. Abt.). T-78/R338, 6292343–433.

'Barbarossa Bd. 4', Op. Abt. III (Chefsachen), Operation 'Blau': operational material March–July 1942. T-78/R336, 6291960–2175.

'Barbarossa Bd. 5', Op. Abt. III (Chefsachen), Continuation Bd. 4, to June–October 1942. T-78/R336, 6292175–334.

'Kaukasus': Planning papers for 'Unternehmen Kaukasus', Op. Abt. II, 1940–42. T-78/R336, 6292583–726.

Plans/dispositions campaign in Russia 1942. GenStdH/Org. Abt. Evaluations Soviet strength, German dispositions (1942). See esp. 'Weisung für die Aufgaben des Ostheeres im Winter 1941/42' (6402283–) and 'Auffrischung und Umbildung des Ostheeres im Frühjahr 1942' (6402374–). T-78/R430, 6402397–2694.

War Diary: OKH/GenStdH/Op. Abt. Ia: KTB (1945). For period 2–24 April 1945; includes Feindlage, operational material. T-78/R304, 6254545–5440. (See also

KTB Anlagen, capture of Budapest, Soviet January 1945 offensive, *Festungen* . . . for period 1–28 February 1945; 6255440–785.)

War Diary: Chefsachen Anlagen zum KTB/OKH/GenStdH/Op. Abt. Ia. Hitler's directives, Guderian papers, regrouping on Eastern Front (January–March 1945). T-78/R305, 6255787–6059.

Chefsachen ab 1.1.45. FHO (Chef): OKH/GenSt/Op. Abt. Operational orders, period 11 January–13 April 1945. T-78/R496, 6484110–286. (See maps 'Vermutliche Weiterführung der sowj. russ. Operationen': Stand 2.2.45.) (Important collection.)

After-action reports/survivors/units disbanded or disabled: Eastern Front 1944–5. *OKH/ Allgemeines Heeresamt/Abwicklungsstab:*

    Reports, survivors units mauled on Ostfront: Jan.–March 1945

    Reports, survivors units, Crimea, April–May 1944

    Reports, survivors, Rumania, August 1944

    9th *Luftwaffe-Felddivision,* Oranienburg pocket, February 1944

    Fate of units, Army Group Centre, destroyed by Soviet offensive, June–July/ September 1944

    Destruction, units of 4th Army, June–July 1944

    Additional files, German units/Army Group Centre, destroyed June–July 1944. T-78/R139, 6067660–6069008.

Rumania: *Deutsche Heeresmission in Rumänien*. Folder: June–July 1941, papers, reports, Rumanian-Soviet situation. T-501/R280, 1093–1190. Folder: *Deutsche Mission* . . . Conferences, Antonescu and military questions, military operations in areas AGps A and B (1942). T-501/R281, 619–1175.

Sonderakte Verhalten der Rumänen, FHO(II). Collapse of 3rd Rumanian Army, Rumanian resistançe nw Stalingrad, November 1942–March 1943. T-78/R459, 6437425–501.

Ungarn-Chefs. v 29.3–2.4.44. OKH (GenStdH). Defence of Hungarian territory, mobilization of Hungarian forces. T-78/R333, 6291114–122.

Ungarn, Bd. III, v. 5.3.–21.3.44 (Chefsachen). OKH/GenStdH/Op. Abt. II. Operations in Hungary, performance Hungarian troops (papers for Feb. 1942–March 1944). T-78/R333, 6290687–844.

Bulgarien vom 4.2.43–16.5.44 (Chefs.). OKH/GenStdH/Op. Abt. II. Operations in Bulgaria, plans, possible Turkish policies. T-78/R333, 6290413–482.

(a) Army Groups

Heeresgruppe Nord (AGp North). Tactical groupings for 'Barbarossa', battle reports 16A and 18A, 3rd and 4th *Panzergruppen,* opening/siege of Leningrad, Leningrad-Volkhov operations: March 1941–Jan. 1942. T-311/R51, 7063699–7066741.

War Diary (KTB): Volkhov-Neva-Ilmen-Tikhvin (November 1941); Staraya Russa/Kholm (January 1942); Volkhov-Finnish front (April 1942). T-311/R54, 7066372–7067843.

War Diary (KTB): Volkhov pocket, AGp North sector (June 1942); Volkhov operations (July 1942); Soviet/German operations, Volkhov/Staraya Russa. T-311/R55, 7067846–8670.

Spanische Division/Spanische Legion. Spanish Legion, operations near Leningrad, replacement by German units (October 1941–August 1942). T-311/R72, 7093678–920.

Operation 'Nordlicht' (capture of Leningrad). Operational directives, maps, signals (August–October 1942). T-311/R75, 7098019–8290.

Heeresgruppe Nord. OKH/GenStdH/Op. Abt. IN. Operation *Nordlicht* (capture of Leningrad), plans, operational orders, June–September 1942. T-78/R337, 6293179–336.

Cancellation of *'Nordlicht'*, operational plans AGp North for winter 1942–3. T-78/R337, 6293336–587.

Chefsachen/*Heeresgruppe Nord/AOK 11 and 16*. Operational papers, October 1942–December 1943. T-78/R337, 6293587–885.

Signals troops/signals traffic, signals intelligence. Daily reports, preparation 'Barbarossa' (1941–3): signals intelligence of Soviet operations. T-311/R82, 7106792–7108200.

Feindbeurteilung. Evaluations of Soviet situation, capabilities, units, operations, partisan operations (1943). T-311/R98, 7128953–7130455.

Der Feldzug gegen die Sowjet-Union, Kriegsjahr 1941; *Der Feldzug gegen die Sowjet-Union*, Kriegsjahr 1942; *Der Feldzug gegen die Sowjet-Union*, Kriegsjahr 1943. (Bound volumes, prepared by Führungsabteilung, Heeresgruppe Nord; extensive operational maps, aerial photographs. T-311/R136, 7181449–2041.

Heeresgruppe Mitte (?) (AGp Centre). Papers: 'Sommerschlacht um den Orelbogen vom 5 Juli bis 18 August 1943'. Maps of Soviet deployment, Soviet offensive, German withdrawal. T-78/R352, 6312119–134.

Heeresgruppe Weichsel (AGp Vistula). (Operational as from 24 January 1945 under Himmler, charged with defence of Danzig/Posen/E Prussia; General Heinrici assumed command March 1945.) T-311/R167–171 *passim*.

War Diary (KTB/Anlagen). Hitler-Himmler exchanges, organization of Army Group, situation reports (January 1945). T-311/R167, 7218514–805.

War Diary (KTB/Anlagen). German operations, Poland/E Prussia, *Volkssturm*, Himmler-Fegelein exchanges (to 14 March 1945). T-311/R169, 7220309–879.

War Diary (KTB/Anlagen). Operations Pomerania/Brandenburg, material on 9th Army and Third *Panzer* (to 19 April 1945). T-311/R169, 7221389–2005.

War Diary (KTB/Anlagen). Operations, Berlin area, signals, messages, Heinrici's orders, problem of civilians (20–29 April 1945). T-311/R170, 7222005–519.

Telegrams: Unterrichtungen/*Tagesmeldungen Heeresgruppe Kurland* (21 March–9 April 1945). *Heeresgruppe Nord*, Festungskommandant (Danzig, Königsberg), AOK 2, AOK 4, Armeeabteilung Samland: end of resistance, Danzig, Königsberg. T-78/R477, 6459238–837.

Telegrams: *Tagesmeldungen Heeresgruppe Mitte/Kurland*, situation reports 15–30 April 1945. T-78/R477, 6459837–950.

(b) Armies/Corps

AOK 4 (4th Army) (Microcopy T-312)

R145 Ia(Ops). Anlagen zum KTB Nv. 9. (Operations, operational orders) September–October 1941.

R150 Ia(Ops). Operationsbefehle. Anlagen zum KTB. September–December 1941 (Operations in central Russia—Moscow).

R159 Ia(Ops). Anlagen zum KTB Nv. 8. (Operations, operational orders) June–July 1941.

R178 Ia(Ops). KREML und WIRBELWIND (Operations). May–July 1942.

R189 Ia(Ops). Anlagen zum KTB Nr 14. Operations, operational orders; Soviet attack methods, heavy German tank losses, Rzhev. September 1942.

AOK 6 (6th Army) (Microcopy T-312)

R1426 Ia(Ops). Erkundungen der Luftwaffe. Air reconnaissance of USSR, October 1940–January 1941.

R1408 Ic(Int.). Tagesmeldungen (Soviet OB). August 1941.

R1409 Ic(Int.). Tagesmeldungen Kiev-Romny.

R1413 Ic Tagesmeldungen: Voroshilovgrad-Taganrog-Simferopol. October 1941.

R1416 Ic Tagesmeldungen: Soviet units facing First *Panzer* Army. 3–12 December 1941.

R1424 Ic. 'Unterlagen zum Feindnachrichten-Blatt; Feindnachrichtenblätter fremder Kdo.-Stellen.' (Intelligence data and reports) October–November 1941.

R1452. 'Anlage zum KTB Armee/Abt. Hollidt Befehle u. sonst. Anlagen' (3rd Rumanian Army), north-east Rostov November–December 1942; also Tägliche Meldungen. See also A/Abt. Hollidt. Skizzen, front situation SE Boguchar November 1942; and Anlage zum KTB A/Abt. Hollidt Don-Chir Front: Lagekarten. December 1942.

R1467. 'Die Juli Abwehrschlacht der 6 Armee am Mius.' July–August 1943.

R1469. 'Die Winterschlachten der 6 Armee im grossen Dnjepr-Bogen . . . ' January–February 1944. See also: 'Die zweite Winterschlacht der 6 Armee Zwischen Dnjepr, Ingulez und Bug'. 3–23 March 1944.

AOK 9 (9th Army) (Microcopy T-312)

R273. Anlagen zum KTB. Vorbereitung der Operation BARBAROSSA. (Reports, directives, conference minutes) April–June 1941.

R320 Ia(Ops). Anlage zum KTB Nr 8. *Chefsache* orders/reports: *Zitadelle*, March–August 1943.

R320 Ia(Ops). Anlage zum KTB Nr 8. Kluge letter on collaboration with Vlasov, 'Plan für die Einsetzung eines National-Komitees im Bereich der Heeresgruppe Mitte', March–August 1943.

R320. Anlage zum KTB Nr 7. 'Büffel' Sonderanlage 1–3, January–March 1943.

R320. Operationskarten. Anlage zum KTB Nr 8, March–August 1943.

R350 Ia(Ops). Die Kessel-schlacht sw. Rschew; Die Winter-Schlacht von Rschew. January–February 1942.

AOK 16 (16th Army) (Microcopy T-312)

R558. Aufmarschanweisung: BARBAROSSA (Studie); Chefsache: BARBAROSSA, May–June 1941.

R542 Ia(Ops). Anlage zum KTB Nr 5. (Plan for operations if Russia rejects 'New Order'.) Dresden conference on operations in Baltic region, February 1941.

R543. Aufmarschanweisung BARBAROSSA (Studie). February–April/May–July 1941.

R583 Ia(Ops). Anlagenband O zum KTB Nr 5. Maps/Operations: Pusta und Silberstreifen Ilmen. October–November 1942.

R584 Ia(Ops). Anlagenband WII zum KTB Nr 5. Soviet partisans/organization/ deployment September 1942–March 1943.

R584. Anlagenband WIII zum KTB Nr 5. Partisanen Sonderakten, October 1942–March 1943.

R585 Ia(Ops). Anlagenband WXIV zum KTB Nr 5. Soviet partisans/German interrogations, June–November 1942.

AOK 17 (17th Army) (Microcopy T-312)

R674. Anlagen zum KTB Nr 1, July–September 1941. (Anlage 9: 'Lagekarten und Sondervorgänge zum Dnjepr.'-Übergang u. zur Brückenkopfbildung', August–September 1941.)

R713. Anlage 2 zum KTB Nr 5. Recapture Goten bridgehead/Tuapse, December 1942–January 1943.

R732. Beilage 1 zum KTB Nr 7: Anlage Ic/Lagekarten. July 1943. Tätigkeitsberichte (Anlage), Lagekarten/Hochaufklärung, July–October 1943.

R733. Führungsabteilung Ic. Beilage 1 zum KTB Nr 7. Tätigkeitsberichte, July–October 1943.

I Armeekorps (Microcopy T-314)

R52. Wolchow-Kessel: Anlagen zum KTB, April–September 1942.

R57. Denkschrift des I AK in der Schlacht am Wolchow, January–June 1942.

R56 Ic(Int.). Tätigkeitsbericht zum KTB. Mgafront: attempted Soviet breakthrough, October–December 1942.

II Armeekorps (Microcopy T-314)

R108. Tactical preparations for BARBAROSSA. (Map exercises, simulating Soviet defence of border-Vistula) June 1941.

R117. Handakte zur Studie BARBAROSSA. (German bridgehead near Kaunas, divisional assemblies) April–June 1941.

R125. Unterlagen Ostfeldzug. Bd. 24, Meldungen, January 1942; Rzhev, Bd. 38, March–April 1942.

R140. Feindnachrichten (Soviet organization, tactics), February–March 1942.

R233 Ia(Ops). KTB 1/Bd. 1. Preparations/march from Rostov to Tormossin, 23–31 December 1942.

R197 Ia(Ops). Anlagen zum KTB VIII. Kharkov-Belgorod area: plan for operation *Shark*, April–June 1943.

R197. KTB Bd. IX. Directive No. 1 for *Zitadelle,* June–July 1943.

R237 Ia(Ops). Anlagenband 3 zum KTB 13. Situation maps Rakotino area, Stalingrad, November 1942–January 1943.

R124. Sonderakte Studie F. Withdrawal of German troops into areas west of Lovat, January–February 1943.

R200. Korpsintendant: difficulties in corps withdrawal from Terek to the Don, critical supply situation, January–July 1943.

III Panzerkorps (Microcopy T-314)

R182. Generalstabs-Ausbildung Studie. (Anlage zum KTB Nr 5 III Panzer Korps.) Plans for Eastern attack, January 1941.

R182 Ia(Ops). Anlagen. Führungsabt: documents/organization/charts, May–June 1941.

R183 Ia(Ops). Anlage B (KTB), Lagenkarten: Kiev sector, June–July 1941.

R183. Rowno-Klewan fighting, 1–12 July 1941.

R194 Ia(Ops). Anlagen zum KTB. Operations for 1942: Donets battles, Terek, retreat to Malkakiva.

R194 Ia(Ops). Textheft für das KTB 3 Bd. 1. Malka-Pyatigorsk-Cherkassk operations, January–April 1943.

2. Intelligence reports/assessments

Die Rote Armee und Marine und sonstige geheime russische Angelegenheiten. Geheim-Akten. OKW/Abteilung Inland Intelligence on USSR, to 1939: on Red Army/Navy. T-77/R794, 5523278–4035.

Feindbeurteilung. Stand: 20.5.41. FHO. Estimate of Soviet order of battle, intentions, May 1941. T-78/R479, 6462469–76.

Operationskalender. Operational record/German-Soviet operations, June 1941–August 1943; brief summary of operations, Army Groups. T-78/R477, 6460261–291.

An die Front zugeführte, neu russ, Verbände (January–July 1942). Soviet formations introduced before each German Army Group. T-78/R486, 6470347–363.

Russischer Kräfteeinsatz Stand 25.2.42. FHO. Soviet OB/reinforcement, January 1942. T-78/R486, 6470366–371.

Angriff-Charkow Chi-Abwehrmeldung. FHO(II). German intelligence/acquisition of sources/analysis Soviet intentions, April–May 1942. T-78/R496, 6483905–4110.

Beurteilung der Feindlage vor deutscher Ostfront . . . Anlagenband (April 1942–December 1944). FHO. Intelligence reports/Soviet intentions, OB. T-78/R498, 6485725–856.

Teil A. Zusammenstellung der in der Zeit vom April 1942—Dezember 1944 in der Abt. FHO abgefassten Beurteilung der feindlage vor deutscher Ostfront im grossen. (Anlagenband/Kartenband). FHO. Important; Soviet OB/intentions, maps, intelligence evaluations (to January 1945). T-78/R466, 6445876–6236.

Kurze Beurteilungen der Feindlage. FHO. Daily reports, Soviet deployments April–September 1942. T-78/R467, 6446516–7108.

Kurze Feindbeurteilung der Feindlage vom 26.8.1942–31.12.42. FHO (I). Daily reports, Soviet deployments, intelligence data, development of situation at Stalingrad (failure to uncover Soviet counter-offensive); a very important collection. T-78/R467, 6447108–653.

Einzelnachrichten des Ic-Dienstes Ost. Nr 5 'Erfahrungen bei dem russischen Angriff im Donbogen und südlich Stalingrad'. Analysis, Soviet operational performance, 26 December 1942. T-78/R491, 6478308–315.

Kurze Beurteilung der Feindlage vom 26.8.1942–31.12.1942. FHO. Important intelligence assessments/evaluations, daily FHO reports, maps. T-78/R467, 6447108–655.

Interrogation of Major-General Privalov (commander 15th Rifle Corps). 22 December 1942 (*Reichsführer SS* files). T-175/R66, 2582895–948.

Feindkräfteberechnungen/Unterlagen. FHO(IIc). Soviet forces, deployed, in reserve, strategic reserves: March 1942–April 1945. T-78/R462, 6441660–1880.

Zahlenmässige Zusammenstellung der bekannten Verbände . . . Stand 11.7.43. FHO(I). Soviet strength/Kursk. T-78/R483, 6468341–343. See also: *Kräftegegenüber-*

stellung: Stand 20.7.43 (GenStdH/Org. Abt.). Soviet-German strength (table). T-78/R343, 6406539–540.

Soviet forces in the Far East. FHO(IIa) (1 April 1943). Also Red Army units transferred to Europe since June 1941. T-78/R486, 6470809–842.

Beurteilung der Feindabsichten vor der deutschen Ostfront im grossen . . . (February 1943). FHO (IIa). Intelligence data/analysis, Soviet intentions. T-78/R488, 6474351–365.

Gesamtbeurteilungen bis 3.6.43. FHO(I). Intelligence analysis/reports/29 August 1942–8 May 1943; Soviet reserves, Stalingrad Feb. 1943, maps AGp Centre. T-78/R466, 6446239–340.

Unterlagen für grosse Kräftegegenüberstellg. FHO (IIc). Comparison of Soviet-German forces (July 1943–October 1944): manpower, tanks, artillery. (Important data.) T-78/R463, 6441974–2027.

Beurteilung der Feindlage vor deutscher Ostfront. Stand: 7.10.44. FHO(Ia). T-78/R497, 6485604–611.

Wichtigste Feindfeststellungen 30.7.44–19.2.45. FHO (Chef). Daily appreciations/ evaluations, Soviet intentions against all German Army Group fronts. T-78/R466, 6445290–509.

Beurteilung im Grossen 30.3.1944. FHO (Chef). Analysis with grave view of developments on Eastern front; data on Soviet OB/deployments/reserves/intentions/maps and graphs. T-78/R497, 6485491–602.

Beurteilung der Feindlage vor deutscher Ostfront. FHO(I). 7 October 1944. T-78/R497, 6485605–610.

Vertragsnotizen. FHO(I). Soviet intentions, OB, important map Agp N Ukraine, March–September 1944. T-78/R466, 6446341–423.

Vertragsnotizen Gruppe I . . . FHO. Soviet strengths/intentions, beginning summer offensive 1944, important comparisons Soviet-German strength/tank strength (1944–5). T-78/R466, 6446425–514.

Feindkräfteberechnungen. FHO(IIc). Tables, daily estimates, Soviet forces deployed, in reserve, Far East, unknown locations: January–August 1944. T-78/R483, 6468345–589. See also: T-78/R484, 6468589–9842: same daily estimates for August 1944–January 1945; June–December 1943; July 1942–May 1943; July 1941–June 1942.

Personelle Ersatzzuführung vor Heeresgruppe Weichsel (February 1945). FHO (IIa). Soviet reinforcement, facing AGp Vistula; noted for 'Führer-Lagevortrag v. 27.2.45'. T-78/R479, 6463292–98.

Feindkräfteberechnungen. FHO(IIc). Daily issues, identifications Soviet forces, 19 February–15 April 1945. T-78/R496, 6484286–349.

Beurteilung . . . FHO. Dated 19 February 1945. Appreciation of situation, Soviet intentions, Soviet manpower/armour/reserves. T-78/R494, 6480847–861.

Ersatzeinheiten und Offiziersschulen der R.A. FHO(IIc). February 1945. Attached list of Soviet tank divisions destroyed/disbanded, 1941. T-78/R494, 6481666–688.

Anzeichen für sowjetrussische Durchbruchsangriffe . . . 25.2.45. FHO. Indicators of Soviet breakthrough attack; diagram of method. T-78/R501, 6489647–658.

Gliederung des sow. russ. Feldheeres. Stand 25.2.45. Detailed tables, with annotations: infantry, tank brigades, 'Operative Panzertruppe u. Kavallerie'. T-78/R479, 6462166–176.

Gliederung des sow. russ. Feldheeres. Stand: 25.3.45. FHO(IIc). Order-of-battle tables; important data. T-78/R486, 6470721–768.

Anti-Wlassow Propaganda Nr 8. FHO. Soviet propaganda leaflets, anti-Vlasov, plans to kill/capture Vlasov, April–October 1943. T-78/R491, 6477761–889.

Führerstellenbesetzung der Roten Armee (August 1943–December 1944). FHO(IIc). T-78/R463, 6442178–3155. (Alphabetic listing, biog. data, Red Army senior commanders: bi-monthly, monthly bulletins.)

Truppen-Übersicht und Kriegsgliederungen der Roten Armee (Stand August 1944). FHO(IIc). T-78/R459, 6437543–end. (Booklet, organization/deployment, Red Army divisions and regiments, org. charts; previous issue December 1943.)

Grosses Orientierungsheft, Russland. 1 February and 1 March 1939: 'Gliederung, Dislokation und Stärke der Roten Armee'. Handbook (FHO?): Red Army organization. T-78/R496, 6483772–903 (also T-77/R794).

Der sowjetische Soldat. Pamphlet: *Reichsführer SS.* T-78/R498, 6486044–095.

Rangliste des Oberkommandos der Roten Armee . . . (20 May 1940). Gen. Köstring's report, German Embassy, Moscow. T-78/R464, 6443403–443.

Die Wehrwirtschaft der UdSSR: Teil II (Stand March 1941). (OKW printing) Soviet war industry; OKW study. T-78/R479, 6462177–292.

Orientierungsheft über die Deutscher Wehrmacht. FHO(IIIc). Partial translation, Soviet intelligence document/assessment of *Wehrmacht*, 1943. T-78/R479, 6462892–3024.

Red Army weapons/equipment. Folder/no title: diagrams, silhouettes. T-78/R502, 6490073–260.

Die politische Erziehung in der Roten Armee. Booklet: *Reichsführer SS.* No date. On Red Army political education/administration. T-78/R493, 6479967–80042.

Gutachten russ. Kriegsgefangenen: Luftgaukommando II. Interrogation/psychological examination, Soviet Air Force personnel, November–December 1941. T-78/R489, 6474650–665.

Russisches Militärschrifttum. Bücherverzeichnis Nr 2/4: 1942–4. FHO(IIId). Lists of captured Soviet books, manuals, publications; invaluable bibliography. T-78/R479, 6463098–256.

Gefangene-erbeutete u. vernichtete Panzer-Geschütze-Waffen (January 1942–March 1945). FHO(IId). Tables of PWs, Soviet losses weapons/equipment. T-78/R481, 6464699–953. Also: *Beute und Verluste . . .* Daily reports, PWs, Soviet losses in weapons, June 1941, 1942, June 1944. T-78/R489, 6474667–5088.

Kommandobehörden der Roten Armee (Feldheer). October 1944. FHO(I/Bd). Handbook: Soviet OB, first appearances, present deployment of Front/Army/Corps; organization charts. T-78/R493, 6480508–667.

Soviet tank maintenance/replacement/Red Army logistics (November 1941–April 1945). FHO(IId). Folder: intelligence reports, assessments of Soviet logistics, original Soviet orders. T-78/R481, 6465470–6023.

Soviet tanks/SP guns. Folder: OKW/Feldwirtschaftsamt. Soviet tank production/development, maps, tables, photos, November 1943–April 1945. T-78/R477, 6460740–1092.

Soviet tanks/SP guns. Technical drawings, technical evaluation, photos, March 1942–April 1945. Folder: reports to Chef der Heeresrüstung. FHO (IId). T-78/R478, 6461092–1520.

Materialsammlung Gliederungen Bd. 1. FHO. Folder: PW interrogations, translation Soviet orders, on organization/equipment Soviet units, August 1943–March 1945. T-78/R460, 6438302–637.

Forschungsdienst Ost. Bulletins (October 1944–January 1945). Political/military intelligence, on *SMERSH/NKGB,* also Red Army political administration. T-78/R493, 6480045–396.

Übersicht über höhere Führer der Roten Armee, Stand August 1944 . . . FHO(IIc). Lists of senior commanders, command appointments, photographs, biographies. T-78/R490, 6476395–557.

Truppen-Übersicht und Kriegsgliederungen der Roten Armee. Stand: August 1944. FHO(?). Lists of Soviet units, identification, previous history. T-78/R496, 6483278–560.

Kriegsgliederungen der Roten Armee (Stand: 1944). FHO(IIc). Organization/war strength Red Army formations/units. T-78/R496, 6483560–608.

Soviet tanks/SP guns. Folder: 331116 Band 4. 16 May–31 October 1944. FHO(IId). Field intelligence reports/Soviet production tanks, SP guns, factories and plants. T-78/R495, 6482278–546.

Soviet armaments industry: '33 III d Band 1: 1.1.42–30.11.44' (Folder title). FHO. Soviet armaments industry, location/types of factories, artillery production (figures for 1929–44): 1942–4. T-78/R491, 6477156–334.

Generalleutnante (1942). FHO(II). Soviet commanders, promotions, biog. data. T-78/R464, 6443157–444.

Sonderinformationen. FHO(II). Folder, PW interrogations on Red Army special units (penal battalions, sabotage units . . .). T-78/R463, 6442029–086.

Gliederung von Stäben. FHO(II). Organization army/corps/division staffs, Leningrad MD (1942, also 1944). T-78/R483, 6468025–104.

Gefechtsvorschrift für die Infanteria der Roten Armee (Trans. of *Soviet FRS*/1942): Teil I/II. T-78/R498, 6485856–6042 and 6486530–730.

Kriegsgliederungen der Roten Armee (Materialsammlung) (November 1942–March 1945). Organization/war strength Red Army units, also specialist troops (chemical, *NKVD*). T-78/R461, 6439568–40167; also 6440169–0637.

Meldungen über die sowjetische Rüstungsindustrie. FHO. Reports on Soviet war industry, 1944, tank/weapons' production. T-78/R479, 6462341–450.

Vertragsnotiz über Instandsetzung abgeschossener Panzerkampfwagen . . . (1.10.43). FHO(IId). Soviet tank losses/replacements: Panzerverluste Ost/1943, German-Soviet. T-78/R478, 6461202–220.

Feldpostbriefe Presseauszüge (OKW/Feldwirtschaftsamt). Extracts from captured mail, various areas USSR: food, food rationing, morale. T-78/R477, 6460649–738.

General der Eisenbahntruppen files. (OKH). Soviet railway construction, attempts to supply Leningrad. T-78/R119, 6044128–636. Also: *3 K 10: fremdländische Eisenbahnen, Russland* (1943–44). Soviet railway operations, WWII: captured Soviet documents, PW interrogations. T-78/R119, 6042527–998.

Führungsstäbe der Roten Armee. FHO(III/II). October 1944. Booklet. Text/diagrams, field administration/Front, Army, Corps. T-78/R463, 6442161–176.

. . . *Handbuch der Partisanen* (July 1944). FHO(Bd). Translation, Soviet manual for partisans. T-78/R479, 6463026–096.

Bandenlage im Osten/Anlagen. FHO(I Bd). Partisan warfare/anti-partisan operations. T-78/R489, 6475170–228 (with translated section from Partisan Handbook).

Nachrichten über Bandenkrieg. FHO(I Bd). Partisan/anti-partisan operations: bulletins May 1943–June 1944. T-78/R493, 6480398–508.

Politische Angelegenheiten (German 'White Book' on the war: 1945). Details of captured Allied orders, *'Eclipse'*. T-77/R859, 5605315–705.

3. Map collections

Map collections (1): *Übersichtskarten* . . . T-78/R500–501, 6488356– . Showing Soviet order of battle, 1941–2, also 'Operationskarten Osten' 1941–2.

Map collections (2): *1944 operations* (E Prussia/Vienna 1945) T-78/R136, 6065135–5626.

Encirclement AGp North	July/Aug. 1944
Tukum/west of Riga	Aug. 1944
Estonia/AGp North	Sept. 1944
Courland, breakthrough to Memel: E Prussia	Oct./Nov. 1944–March 1945
Breakthrough AGp S Ukraine	Aug. 1944
I Pz. Army breakout to Hungary	March/April 1944
Bug and Dniester	March/April 1944
Collapse of Rumania	Aug./Sept. 1944
Breakthrough AGp Centre	June/Aug. 1944
Warsaw, Narev, Bug	Aug./Sept. 1944
Crimean operations	April/May 1944
Budapest-Vienna (pts I and II)	Oct./Nov. 1944–April 1945

III. EASTERN EUROPEAN MEMOIRS/MONOGRAPHS

(a) Polish

Polski czyn zbrojny w II wojnie światowej. Bibliografia wojny wyzwolenczej narodu polskiego 1939–1945 (Warsaw: MON 1973).

Blagowieszczański, I., *Dzieje 1 Armii Polskiej W ZSRR Maj-Lipiec 1944 R.* (Warsaw: MON 1972).

Dolata, B., *Wyzwolenie Polski 1944–1945* (Warsaw: MON 1974). Soviet-Polish operations.

Gać, S., *7 Dywizja Piechoty* (Warsaw: MON 1971).

Gać, S., *Udzial 2 armii Wojska Polskiege w operacji Praskiej* (Warsaw: MON 1962). 2nd Polish Army, Prague operation.

Golczewski, K., *Wyzwolenie Pomorza zachodniego w roku 1945* (Poznan: Wyd. Poznanskie 1971).

Jurgielewicz, W., *Organizacja Ludowego Wojska Polskiego (22.7.1944–9.5.1945)* (Warsaw: MON 1968).

Karpiński, A., *Pod Dęblinem, Pulawami i Warka* (Warsaw: MON 1967).

Karpiński, A., *Dowodzenie w Armii Radzieckiej podczas II Wojny Światowej* (Warsaw: MON 1973). Tactical direction/command in the Red Army in World War II.

Krzeminski, G., *Lotnictwo polskie w operacji berlińskiej* (Warsaw: MON 1970). Polish air force, Berlin 1945.

Majewski, R. and Sozańska, T., *Bitwa o Wrocław, Styczen-maj 1945g.* (Wroclaw: Zaklad Narodowy im. Ossolinskich 1975).

Margules, J., *Boje 1 Armii WP w obszarze Warszawy (Sierpien-Wrzesien 1944)* (Warsaw: MON 1967).

Okęcki, S., *Wyzwolenie Poznania 1945* (Warsaw: MON 1975).

Poplawski, S., *Towarzysze frontowych dróg* (Warsaw: MON 1965).

Przygoński, A., *Udzial PPR i AL w powstaniu Warszawskim* (Warsaw: Ksiazka i Wiedza 1970).

Rawski, T. *et al.*, *Wojna wyzwoleńcza narodu polskiego w latach 1939–1945* (Warsaw: MON 1966).

Rzepski, S., *8 Dywizja Piechoty* (Warsaw: MON 1970).

Sek-Malecki, J., *Armia Ludowa w powstaniu warszawskim. Wspomnienia* (Warsaw: Wyd. Iskry 1962).

Slawecki, R., *Manewr który ocalil Kraków* (Cracow: Wyd. Lit., 2nd edn 1971). Liberation of Cracow.

Stąpor, Z., *Bitwa o Berlin* (Warsaw: MON 1973).

Warszawa-Lewa Podmiejska 1942–1945 (Warsaw: MON 1971).

Zhilin, P.A. (ed.), *Boevoe sodruzhestvo Sovetskovo i Pol'skovo narodov* (Moscow: Mysl 1973). Though in Russian, this is a joint Soviet-Polish research publication with informative articles.

(b) Czechoslovak

Druhá světova válka. Výběrová bibliografie české a slovenské knižní a časopisecké literatury (1958–1963). Historie a vojenstvi, 1963, No. 4.

Svoboda, L., *Z Buzuluke do Prahy* (Prague: Naše Vojsko 1967).

Dukla v dokumentech (Prague: Naše Vojsko 1970). Photostat collection: operational documents Dukla operation.

Tvarůžek, B., *Operační cíl Ostrava* (Ostrava: Profil 1973).

(c) Rumanian

Collective authorship, *Contributia Rominiel la rázboiul antihitlerist* (Bucharest, 1958). Soviet version: *Vklad Rumynii v razgrom fashistskoi Germanii* (Moscow: Voenizdat 1959).

Ilie, Lt.-Col. P. and Stoen, Lt.-Col. G., *Romania in razboiul antihitlerist*. Contributii bibliografice (Bucharest: Editura Militara 1971).

Romanescu, F. and Loghin, L., *Cronica participárii armatei Române la rázboiul antihitlerist* (Bucharest: Editura Militara 1971). A detailed and informative compilation.

(d) Yugoslav

Beogradska operacija 20 oktobar 1944 (Belgrade: Vojnoist. Institut. 1964). Joint Soviet-Yugoslav work on the Belgrade operation.

Čulinović, F., *Slom stare Jugoslavije* (Zagreb: Škol. knjiga 1958).

Donlagić, A. *et al.*, *Yugoslavia in the Second World War* (Belgrade: Interpress 1967).

Kljakić, D., *Ustaško Domobranska Legija pod Staljingradom* (Biblioteka vreme plov). (Zagreb: August Cesarec 1979). Destruction of the *Ustaša Legion* at Stalingrad.

Oslobodilački rat naroda Jugoslavije 1941–1945 (Belgrade: Vojni Istoriski Institut 1958), vol. 2: *Od drugog zasedanja AVNOJ-a do konačne pobede*.

Pajović, B. and Radević, M., *Bibliografija o ratu i revoluciji u Jugoslaviji. Posebna izdanja 1945-1965* (Belgrade: Savezni odbor subnor Jug. 1969).

(e) Albanian

Conférence Nationale des Etudes sur la Lutte AntiFasciste de Libération Nationale du Peuple Albanais (Tirana: 8 Nëntori 1975).

(f) Hungarian

Magyarország felszabadítása (Budapest: Koss. Konyvkiado 1975). Soviet operations in Hungary 1944-5.

Miklos, H., *A 2. magyar hadsereg megsemmisülése a Donnál* (Budapest: 1958). Destruction of 2nd Hungarian Army on the Don.

Ölvedi, I., *A budai vár és a debreceni csata. Horthyék katasztrófapolitikája 1944 öszén.* (Budapest: Zrinyi Katonai Kiado, 2nd edn 1974). Collapse of Horthy regime in autumn 1944.

Ránki, G., *A második világháború története* (Budapest: Gondolat. 1976).

(g) Bulgarian

Gornenski, N., *V'or'zhenata borna 1941-1944* (Sofia: Izd. B'lgar. Kom. partiya 1971).

Spasitelniyat B'lgariya Otechestven Front. Sbornik (Sofia: Izd. na Otech. Front 1975).

Trunski, S., *From the Tactics of Partisan Warfare in Bulgaria* (Sofia: Sofia Press 1970). Official English translation.

Voini antifashist (Sofia: D'rzhav. voenno izd. 1974).

IV. NON-SOVIET MATERIALS

Ainsztein, R., *Jewish Resistance in Nazi-occupied Eastern Europe* (London: Paul Elek 1974) See pt 5: 'Jewish Partisans'.

Ainsztein, R., 'The Soviet Russian War Novel since Stalin's Death', *Twentieth Century,* April 1960, pp. 328-38. A perceptive and informative analysis.

Alexander, J., *Russian Aircraft since 1940* (London: Putnam 1975).

Allen, W.E.D. and Muratoff, P., *The Russian Campaigns of 1941-1943* and *The Russian Campaigns of 1944-1945* (Harmondsworth: Penguin Books 1944 and 1946). These two books remain a remarkable achievement even at this distance, particularly the second volume, and can be read with profit, not least for the elucidation of terrain factors.

Armstrong, J.A., *Ukrainian Nationalism 1939-1945* (New York: Columbia U.P. 1955).

Armstrong, J.A., *Soviet Partisans in World War II* (Madison: University Wisconsin Press 1964). This is an outstandingly important work on Soviet partisan organization and operations; comprehensive use of German military records.

Armstrong, J.A., 'Recent Soviet Publications on World War II', *Slavic Review,* XXI(3), September 1962, pp. 508-19.

Berman, H.J. and Kerner, M., *Soviet Military Law and Administration* (Cambridge, Mass.: Harvard U.P. 1955). An important study, including Kerner's own account of wartime experience with the Red Army.

Bialer, S., *Stalin and his Generals. Soviet Military Memoirs of World War II.* (New York: Pegasus 1969).

Bór-Komorowski, T., *The Secret Army* (London: Gollancz 1950).

Carell, P., *Hitler's War on Russia* (vol. 1) and *Scorched Earth* (vol. 2) (London: Harrap 1964 and 1970).

Churchill, W.S., *The Second World War*, vols 1–6 (London: Cassell 1948–54).

Clark, A. *Barbarossa. The Russo-German Conflict 1941–1945* (London: Hutchinson 1965).

Clemens, D.A., *Yalta* (New York: Oxford U.P. 1970).

Cookridge, E.H., *Gehlen: Spy of the Century* (London: Hodder & Stoughton 1971). See chapters 4–8 on Gehlen and *FHO.*)

Craig, W., *Enemy at the Gates. The Battle for Stalingrad* (New York: Reader's Digest Press 1973).

van Crefeld, M., 'The German attack on the USSR: the Destruction of a Legend', *European Studies Review*, vol. 2 (1), January 1972, pp. 69–86.

Dallin, A., *German Rule in Russia 1941–1945* (London: Macmillan 1957; 2nd edn 1981 and Boulder, Colorado: Westview Press 1981).

Deane, J.R., *The Strange Alliance* (London: John Murray 1947).

Dedijer, V., *Tito Speaks* (London: Weidenfeld & Nicolson 1953).

Djilas, M. *Conversations with Stalin* (London: Rupert Hart-Davis 1962).

Documents on Polish-Soviet Relations 1939–1945. General Sikorski Historical Institute. Vol. I: 1939–43, vol. II: 1943–5. (London: Heinemann 1961 and 1967).

Douglas, J., 'Stalin in the Second World War', *Survey*, 17, 1971(4), pp. 179–87.

Eden, A. (Lord Avon), *The Reckoning* (London: Cassell 1965).

Feis, H., *Churchill, Roosevelt, Stalin, The War They Waged and the Peace They Sought* (Princeton: Princeton U.P. 1957).

Fischer, G., *Soviet Opposition to Stalin.* A case study in World War II (Cambridge, Mass., 1952).

Foote, A., *Handbook for Spies* (London: Museum Press 1956). Foote worked as an operator for Soviet intelligence.

Gallagher, Matthew P., *The Soviet History of World War II. Myths, Memories and Realities* (New York/London: Praeger 1963). An important, original and penetrating study of the politics of Soviet historiography of the war.

Garlinski, J., *Poland, SOE and the Allies* (London: Allen & Unwin 1969).

Gouré, L., *The Siege of Leningrad* (Stanford: Stanford U.P. 1962). This is a major work, excellently researched,

Green, W. and Swanborough, G., *Soviet Air Force Fighters*, parts 1 and 2 (London: Macdonald and Janes 1977–8).

Hagen, L., *The Secret War for Europe, a Dossier of Espionage* (London: Macdonald 1968).

Harriman, A.W., and Abel, E., *Special Envoy to Churchill and Stalin 1941–1946* (London: Hutchinson 1976).

Higgins, T., *Hitler and Russia. The Third Reich in a Two-Front War (1937–1943)* (New York: Collier-Macmillan 1966).

Admiral Horthy's Papers. The confidential papers of Admiral Horthy (Budapest: University Printing House 1965).

Howell, E.M., *The Soviet Partisan Movement 1941–1944* (US Department of Army, Pamphlet No. 20-244, August 1956).

Irving, D., *Hitler's War* (London: Hodder & Stoughton 1977).

Jacobsen, H.A. and Rohwer, J. (eds.), *Decisive Battles of World War II; the German View* (London: Deutsch 1965).

Jukes, G., *Kursk: the Clash of Armour* (London: Macdonald and Janes 1969).

Kuby, E., *The Russians and Berlin, 1945* (trans. A.J. Pomerans) (London: Heinemann 1968).

Leach, B.A., *German Strategy against Russia 1939–1941* (Oxford: Clarendon Press 1973).

Lukas, R.C., *Eagles East. The Army Air Forces and the Soviet Union: 1941–1945* (Tallahassee: Florida State U.P. 1970).

Malaparte, C., *The Volga Rises in Europe* (trans. from Italian), (London: Alvin Redman 1957).

Manstein, E. von, *Lost Victories* (orig., *Verlorene Siege*) (Chicago: Regnery 1958).

Meister, J., *Soviet Warships of the Second World War* (London: Macdonald and Janes 1977).

Milson, J., *Russian Tanks 1900–1970* (London: Arms & Armour Press 1970).

Moran, Lord, *Winston Churchill: The Struggle for Survival 1940–1965* (London: Constable 1966).

Nazi-Soviet Relations 1939–1941 (German Foreign Office documents) (Washington: Department of State 1948).

Perrault, G., *The Red Orchestra* (orig., *L'Orchestre Rouge*) (London: Arthur Barker 1968).

Rozek, E.J., *Allied Wartime Diplomacy. A Pattern in Poland* (New York: John Wiley 1958).

Ryan, C., *The Last Battle* (London: Collins 1966).

Sajer, G., *The Forgotten Soldier* (trans. from French; orig., *Le Soldat Oublié* (London: 1971).

Salisbury, H.E., *The Siege of Leningrad* (London: Secker & Warburg 1969).

Schröter, H., *Stalingrad* (trans. Constantine Fitzgibbon) (London: Michael Joseph 1958).

Schofield, B.B., *The Russian Convoys* (London: Batsford 1964).

Seaton, A., *The Russo-German War 1941–1945* (London: Arthur Barker 1971).

Seaton, A., *Stalin as Warlord* (London: Batsford 1976).

Sella, A., ' "Barbarossa": Surprise Attack and Communication', *Journal of Contemporary History*, 13 (1978), pp. 555–83.

Seton-Watson, H., *The East European Revolution* (London: Methuen 1950). See pt 2, 'War'.

Sherwood, R.E., *Roosevelt and Hopkins. An Intimate History* (New York: Grosset & Dunlop 1950).

Steenberg, S., *Vlasov* (New York: Knopf 1970).

Strik-Strikfeldt, W., *Against Stalin and Hitler, 1941–1945* (London: Macmillan 1970).

Tolstoy, N., *Victims of Yalta* (London: Hodder & Stoughton 1977). A thorough and shattering account of the forced repatriation of Russians, including Vlasov men; much of the material is new and drawn from documents 1945–6.

Turney, A., *Disaster at Moscow: Von Bock's Campaigns, 1941–1942* (London: Cassell 1971).

Wagner, R. (ed.), *The Soviet Air Force in World War II*. The official history, originally published by the Ministry of Defense of the USSR, translated by Leland Fetzer.

Werth, A., *The Year of Stalingrad* (London: Hamish Hamilton 1946). A major chronicle of Russia at war, utilizing much important Russian material.

Werth, A., *Russia at War 1941–1945* (London: Barrie & Rockliff).

Whaley, B., *Codeword BARBAROSSA* (Cambridge, Mass.: MIT Press 1973). An original and important study.

Who's Who of Prominent Germans in the USSR (Official handbook) (London(?): September 1944).

Woodward, Sir L., *British Foreign Policy in the Second World War* (London: HMSO 1962, one-volume publication). Also vol. I (London: HMSO 1970); vol. II (London: HMSO 1971); and vol. III (London: HMSO 1971).

Zhukov, G.K., (ed. H.E. Salisbury), *Marshal Zhukov's Greatest Battles* (London: Macdonald 1969).

Ziemke, E., *Stalingrad to Berlin. The German Campaign in Russia, 1942–1945* (Washington DC: 1968).

Non-Soviet: German

Kriegstagebuch des Oberkommandos der Wehrmacht 1940–1945 (ed. P.E. Schramm), vols 1–4 (Frankfurt: Bernard & Graefe Verlag 1961–4).

Halder, F., *Kriegstagebuch* (ed. H.-A. Jacobsen), vols 2 and 3 (Stuttgart: Kohlhammer 1963 and 1964).

Der deutsche Imperialismus und der zweite Weltkrieg. Vol. 1: *Hauptreferate und Dokumente der Konferenz* (Berlin: Rutten & Loening 1959).

Adam, W., *Der schwere Entschluss* (Berlin: Verlag der Nation 1965). Former 1st Adjutant, German Sixth Army, Stalingrad.

Bekker, C., *Angriffshöne 4000* (Hamburg: G. Stalling Verlag 1964). English translation, *The Luftwaffe War Diaries* (London: 1966).

Doerr, H., *Der Feldzug Nach Stalingrad. Versuch eines operativen Uberblickes* (Darmstadt: E.S. Mittler 1955).

Fabry, P.W., *Der Hitler-Stalin Pakt* (Darmstadt: Fundus Verlag 1962).

Fischer, A., *Sowjetische Deutschlandpolitik im Zweiten Weltkrieg 1941–1945* (Stuttgart: DVA 1975).

Förster, J., *Stalingrad. Risse im Bündnis 1942–1943* (Freiburg i Br.: Verlag Rombach 1975).

Gosztony, P., *Hitlers Fremde Heere. Das Schicksal der nichtdeutschen Armeen im Ostfeldzug* (Düsseldorf-Vienna: Econ. Verlag 1976).

Heidkämper, O., *Vitebsk, Kampf und Untergang der 3. Panzerarmee* (Heidelberg: Vowinckel 1954).

Helmdach, E., *Überfall? Der sowjetisch-deutsche Aufmarsch 1941* (Neckargemund: Vowinckel, 3rd edn 1976).

Hesse, E., *Der sowjetrussische Partisanenkrieg 1941–1944* (Göttingen: Musterschmidt-Verlag 1969).

Hossbach, F., *Infanterie im Ostfeldzug 1941–1942* (Osterode: Giebel/Oehlschlägel 1951).

Kehrig, M., *Stalingrad. Analyse und Dokumentation einer Schlacht* (Stuttgart: DVA 1974). Virtually unrivalled source material/documentation plus eye-witness evidence establishes this massive volume as the most comprehensive and penetrating account of German operations at Stalingrad and as a definitive analysis of the complex offensive and defensive phases of the battle.

Kleist, P., *Zwischen Hitler und Stalin 1939–1945* (Bonn: Athenaum-Verlag 1950). Important work, essential material on Vlasov movement; see *Dokumente Anhang.*

Klink, E., *Das Gesetz des Handelns: die operation Zitadelle* (Stuttgart: Deut. Verlag 1966).

Mader, J. *et al.*, *Dr Sorge Funkt aus Tokyo* (Berlin: Deutscher Militärverlag 1966).

Middeldorf, E., *Taktik im Russlandfeldzug. Erfahrungen und Folgerungen* (Darmstadt: E.S. Mittler 1956).

Philippi, A. and Heim, F., *Der Feldzug gegen Sowjetrussland 1941 bis 1945. Ein operativer Überblick* (Stuttgart: Kohlhammer 1962).

Stenzel, E., 'Die Entwicklung der sowjetischen Artillerie bis zum Ende des zweiten Weltkrieges', *Militärgeschichte,* 1977 (4), pp. 475–90.

Trepper, L., *Die Wahrheit. Ich war der Chef der Rote Kapelle* (Kindler: 1975). Personal account by chief of Rote Kapelle ('Red Orchestra').

Warlimont, W., *Im Hauptquartier der deutschen Wehrmacht 1939–1945* (Frankfurt: Bernard & Graefe Verlag 1962).

Wilhelm, H-H., *Die Prognosen der Abteilung Fremde Heere Ost 1942–1945* (Stuttgart: DVA 1974).

French
Desroches, A., *La Campagne de Russie d'Adolf Hitler (Juin 1941–Mai 1945)* (Paris: G.P. Maisonneuve and Larose 1964).

Guillaume, A., *La guerre germano-soviétique (1941–1945)* (Paris: Payot 1949).

Italian
La campagna di Rossia (2 vols), Grafica nazionale editrice (Rome: 1950–51).

Spanish
Arbiol, G.A., and Sánchez, C.G., *De Leningrado a Odesa* (Barcelona: Editorial AHR 1958).

Addendum to Bibliography

Mastny, V., *Russia's Road to the Cold War: Diplomacy, Warfare and the Politics of Communism 1941–45* (New York: Columbia U.P. 1979).

Millar, J.R., 'Financing the Soviet effort in World War II', *Soviet Studies* (Univ. Glasgow), XXXII(1), January 1980, pp. 106–23. A most important analysis of the Soviet war economy.

Soviet materials
Collective authorship, *Istoriografiya Velikoi Otechestvennoi voiny* Sbornik statei (Moscow: Nauka 1980).

Kim, Academician M.P. (chief ed.), *Istoriografiya Velikoi Otechestvennoi voiny*. Sbornik statei (Moscow: Nauka 1980). Historiographical essays: role of the Party, military operations, 'the rear'.

Klemin, Lt.-Gen. A.S. (ed.), *Eshelon za eshelonom* (Moscow: Voenizdat 1981). Detailed study of operations of VOSO *(Voennye soobshchenie):* military traffic/traffic control and organization, railway troops, also river/coastal waterways movement.

Kovalev, I.V., *Transport v Velikoi Otechestvennoi voine (1941–1945 gg.)* (Moscow: Nauka 1981).

Kumanev, G.A. (chief ed.), *Narodnyi podvig v bitve za Kavkaz*. Sbornik statei (Moscow: Nauka 1981).

Losik, Marshal of Tank Troops O.A. (ed.), *Stroitel'stvo i boevoe primenenie Sovetskikh tankovykh voisk v gody Velikoi Otechestvennoi voiny* (Moscow: Voenizdat 1979).

Peredel'skii, Marshal (Artillery) G.Ye. *et al., Artilleriya v boyu i operatsii* (Moscow: Voenizdat 1980). Soviet artillery; wartime employment; statistical material, tabulations, deployment maps.

Popov, N.P. and Gorokhov, N.A., *Sovetskaya voennaya pechat' v gody Velikoi Otechestvennoi voiny 1941–1945* (Moscow: Voenizdat 1981). Monograph on wartime Soviet military press.

Radzievskii, A.I., *Proryv (Po opytu Velikoi Otechestvennoi voiny 1941–1945 gg.)* (Moscow: Voenizdat 1979).

Samsonov, A.M. (editor in chief), *Krasnoznamennyi Flot v Velikoi Otechestvennoi voine 1941–1945*. Stat'i i ocherki (Moscow: Nauka 1981). Baltic Fleet, section on technical problems—anti-mine warfare, ship construction, modernization.

Samsonov, A.M., *Krakh fashistskoi agressii 1939–1945*. Istoricheskii ocherk (Moscow: Nauka, 2nd edn 1980).

Shtemenko, Army General S.M., *General'nyi shtab v gody voiny* (Moscow: Voenizdat (VM) 1981), vols 1–2. (Two-volume *Voennye Memuary* reprint of previous separate volumes.)

Shushkin, N.N. and Ulitin, S.D., *Soyuz rabochikh i krest'yan v Velikoi Otechestvennoi voine* (Leningrad: Izd. Leningrad Universiteta 1977). Party-political work, north-western regions of USSR.

Smirnov, E.I., *Voina i voennaya meditsina 1939–1945 gody* (Moscow: Meditsina, 2nd edn 1979).

Svetlishin, V.A., *Voiska PVO Strany v Velikoi Otechestvennoi voine. Voprosy operativno-strategicheskovo primeneniya* (Moscow: Nauka 1979).

Tkachenko, B.A., *Istoriya razmagnichivaniya korablei Sovetskovo Voenno-morskovo flota* (Leningrad: Nauka 1981). History of Soviet degaussing, magnetic mine counter-measures.

Zvartsev, Col.-Gen. A.M. (ed.), *3-ya gvardeiskaya tankovaya. Boevoi put' 3-i gvardeiskoi tankovoi armii* (Moscow: Voenizdat 1982). 3rd Guards Tank Army, wartime history.

Vasil'ev, A.F., *Promyshlennost' Urals v gody, VOV 1941–1945* (Moscow: Nauka 1982). The Urals war-production region.

Babin, A.I. (ed.), *Na volkhovskom fronte 1941–1944 gg.* (Moscow: Nauka 1982). Volkhov Front operations.

The reader's attention is also drawn to *Records of the Joint Chiefs of Staff* (microfilm, University Publications of America), pt I: *1942–1945 (The Soviet Union)*. I have read this unique material but have not incorporated it directly in this present work. In particular, reel 2 of this collection includes the Bradley Mission/Bombers for the Far East (1943), Red Army action to facilitate *Overlord* (3 April 1944), US-Soviet-British military co-ordination (1944), liaison of theatre commanders and 'the Russian armies' (1944), Russian strength winter 1942–3, US aid to Russia (1943), and Russian food situation (1942).

Index